302074

Microsoft®

Windows® Internals,
Fifth Edition

Mark E. Russinovich
David A. Solomon
with Alex Ionescu

PUBLISHED BY
Microsoft Press
A Division of Microsoft Corporation
One Microsoft Way
Redmond, Washington 98052-6399

Library of Congress Control Number: 2009927697

Printed and bound in the United States of America.

1 2 3 4 5 6 7 8 9 QWT 4 3 2 1 0 9

Distributed in Canada by H.B. Fenn and Company Ltd.

A CIP catalogue record for this book is available from the British Library.

Microsoft Press books are available through booksellers and distributors worldwide. For further information about international editions, contact your local Microsoft Corporation office or contact Microsoft Press International directly at fax (425) 936-7329. Visit our Web site at www.microsoft.com/mspress. Send comments to mspinput@microsoft.com.

Acquisitions Editor: Ben Ryan
Developmental Editor: Devon Musgrave
Project Editor: John Pierce
Editorial Production: Curtis Philips, Publishing.com
Cover: Tom Draper Design

Body Part No. X14-95072

To Jim Allchin, our OS and rock star

Table of Contents

What do you think of this book? We want to hear from you!

Microsoft is interested in hearing your feedback so we can continually improve our books and learning resources for you. To participate in a brief online survey, please visit:

www.microsoft.com/learning/booksurvey/

What do you think of this book? We want to hear from you!

Microsoft is interested in hearing your feedback so we can continually improve our books and learning resources for you. To participate in a brief online survey, please visit:

www.microsoft.com/learning/booksurvey/

Foreword

It's both a pleasure and an honor for me to write the foreword for this latest edition of *Windows Internals*. Many significant changes have occurred in Windows since the last edition of the book, and David, Mark, and Alex have done an excellent job of updating the book to address them. Whether you are new to Windows internals or an old hand at kernel development, you will find lots of detailed analysis and examples to help improve your understanding of the core mechanisms of Windows as well as the general principles of operating system design.

Today, Windows enjoys unprecedented breadth and depth in the computing world. Variants of the original Windows NT design run on everything from Xbox game consoles to desktop and laptop computers to clusters of servers with dozens of processors and petabytes of storage. Advances such as hypervisors, 64-bit computing, multicore and many-core processor designs, flash-based storage, and wireless and peer-to-peer networking continue to provide plenty of interesting and innovative areas for operating system design.

One such area of innovation is security. Over the past decade, the entire computing industry—and Microsoft in particular—has been confronted with huge new threats, and security has become the top issue facing many of our customers. Attacks such as Blaster and Sasser threatened to bring the entire Internet to its knees, and Windows was at the eye of the hurricane. It was obvious to us that we could no longer afford to do business as usual, as many of the usability and simplicity features designed into Windows were being used to attack it for nefarious reasons. At first the hackers were teenagers trying to gain notoriety by breaking into systems or adding graffiti to a corporate Web site, but pretty soon the attacks intensified and went underground. The hackers became more sophisticated and evaded inspection. You rarely see headlines about viruses and worms these days, but make no mistake—botnets and identity theft are big business today, as are industrial and government espionage through targeted attacks.

In January 2002, Bill Gates sent his now-famous "Trustworthy Computing" memorandum to all Microsoft employees. It was a call to action that resonated well and charted the course for how we would build software and conduct business over the coming years. Nearly the entire Windows engineering team was diverted to work on Windows XP SP2, a service pack dedicated almost entirely to improving the security of the operating system. The Security Development Lifecycle (SDL) was developed and applied to all Microsoft products, with particular emphasis on Windows Vista as the first version of the operating system designed from the ground up to be secure. SDL specifies strict guidelines and processes for secure software development. Sophisticated tools have been developed to scan everything from source code to system binaries to network protocols for common security vulnerabilities. Every time a new security vulnerability is discovered, it is analyzed, and mitigations are developed to address that potential attack vector. Windows Vista has now been in the market for

two years, and it is by far the most secure version of Windows. Some industry analysts have pointed out that it is, in fact, the most secure general purpose operating system shipping today.

The Windows team has continued to innovate over the past few years. Windows XP, Windows Server 2003, Windows Server 2003 R2, Windows XP SP2, Windows Vista, Windows Server 2008, and Hyper-V are all major accomplishments and great successes—as well as great additions to the Windows family of products.

Frankly, I can't think of a more exciting and challenging topic. Nor can I think of a more authoritative and well-written book. David, Mark, and Alex have done a thorough job of dissecting the Windows architecture and providing diagnostic tools for hands-on learning. I hope you enjoy reading and learning about Windows as much as we all enjoy working on it.

Ben Fathi
Corporate Vice President, Windows Core Development
Microsoft Corporation

Acknowledgments

We dedicate this edition to **Jim Allchin**, our executive sponsor and champion before he retired from Microsoft. Jim supported our book work on this and earlier editions and was instrumental in bringing Mark Russinovich to Microsoft. In addition to shepherding Windows Vista out the door, Jim also oversaw the delivery of Windows 2000, Windows XP, and Windows Server 2003.

Each edition of this book has to acknowledge **Dave Cutler**, Senior Technical Fellow and the original architect of Windows NT. Dave originally approved David Solomon's source code access and has been supportive of his work to explain the internals of Windows through his training business as well as during the writing of the editions of this book.

We also thank three developers at Microsoft for contributing content that was incorporated into this edition:

- **Christian Allred,** who wrote detailed descriptions on transactional NTFS (TxF) internals, data structures, and behaviors

- **Stone Cong,** who wrote content and created diagrams about the Common Log File System (CLFS)

- **Adrian Marinescu,** who updated his heap manager section in the memory management chapter

This book wouldn't contain the depth of technical detail or the level of accuracy it has without the input, and support of key members of the Windows development team. We want to thank the following people, who provided technical review and input to the book:

Dmitry Anipko	Kwan Hyun	Ravi Mumulla	Jon Schwartz
Eugene Bak	Mehmet Iyigun	Adi Oltean	Valerie See
Karlito Bonnevie	Philippe Joubert	Vince Orgovan	Matt Setzer
Jon Cargille	Kwan Hyun Kim	Bernard Ourghanlian	Andrey Shedel
Dean DeWhitt	Kinshuman Kinshumann	Alexey Pakhunov	Neeraj Singh
Apurva Doshi	Alex Kirshenbaum	Milos Petrbok	Vikram Singh
Joseph East	Norbert Kusters	Daniel Pravat	Paul Sliwowicz
Tahsin Erdogan	Jeff Lambert	Ravi Pudipeddi	John Stephens
Cenk Ergan	Paul Leach	Melur Raghuraman	Deepu Thomas
Osman Ertugay	Scott Lee	Ramu Ramanathan	J. R. Tipton
Tom Fout	Mark Lloyd	Vlad Sadovsky	Davis Walker
Nar Ganapathy	Karan Mehra	Dragos Sambotin	Brad Waters
Robin Giese	Derek Moore	Jamie Schwartz	Bruce Worthington

Thanks also to Daniel Pearson (who teaches Windows internals for Dave Solomon) for his review and input.

Others might have contributed by answering questions in the hallway or cafeteria or by providing technical material—if we missed you, please forgive us!

The authors would like to thank Ilfak Guilfanov of Hex-Rays (*www.hex-rays.com*) for the IDA Pro Advanced and Hex-Rays licenses for Alex Ionescu for his use in speeding his reverse engineering of the Windows kernel. Alex chose not to have Windows source code access (as did Mark Russinovich before he joined Microsoft) to research the information for his work on this book, and these tools greatly facilitated his work. IDA's features turn reverse engineering into a powerful tool for understanding Windows internals. Combined with the Hex-Rays Decompiler, this analysis becomes even faster and more refined, as C code is directly presented instead of assembler, including all the right types.

Thanks also to Matt Ginzton of VMware, who arranged for Alex and David to receive VMware Workstation to use in their research for the book. VMware Workstation was used instead of Microsoft Virtual PC because of its support for 64-bit guests and multiple snapshots with nonpersisent disks. (These features are now supported by Hyper-V, Microsoft's new server virtualization offering, but at the time of writing, this support was not available).

Thanks to Mike Vance of AMD for providing Dave Solomon's AMD64 laptop for use in his book research and live classes.

Finally, we want to thank the team at Microsoft Press who helped turn this book from idea into reality:

- Ben Ryan (acquisitions editor at Microsoft Press) for shepherding another edition of this great book
- Kathleen Atkins (project editor) and Devon Musgrave (developmental editor) for launching and overseeing the project
- Andrea Fox (proofreader), Curtis Philips (project and production manager), and John Pierce (project editor and copyeditor) for laboriously going through all our chapters to tighten up text, find inconsistencies, and keep the manuscript to the high standards of Microsoft Press

Alex Ionescu, Mark Russinovich, and David Solomon
May 2009

Introduction

Windows Internals, Fifth Edition is intended for advanced computer professionals (both developers and system administrators) who want to understand how the core components of the Windows Vista and Windows Server 2008 operating systems work internally. With this knowledge, developers can better comprehend the rationale behind design choices when building applications specific to the Windows platform. Such knowledge can also help developers debug complex problems. System administrators can benefit from this information as well, because understanding how the operating system works "under the covers" facilitates understanding the performance behavior of the system and makes troubleshooting system problems much easier when things go wrong. After reading this book, you should have a better understanding of how Windows works and why it behaves as it does.

Structure of the Book

The first two chapters ("Concepts and Tools" and "System Architecture") lay the foundation with definitions and explanations of terms and concepts used throughout the rest of the book. The next two chapters—"System Mechanisms" and "Management Mechanisms"—describe key underlying mechanisms in the system. The next eight chapters explain the core components of the operating system: processes, threads, and jobs; security; the I/O system; storage management; memory management; the cache manager; file systems; and networking. The last two chapters cover startup and shutdown process and crash dump analysis.

History of the Book

This is the fifth edition of a book that was originally called *Inside Windows NT* (Microsoft Press, 1992), written by Helen Custer (prior to the initial release of Microsoft Windows NT 3.1). *Inside Windows NT* was the first book ever published about Windows NT and provided key insights into the architecture and design of the system. *Inside Windows NT, Second Edition* (Microsoft Press, 1998) was written by David Solomon. It updated the original book to cover Windows NT 4.0 and had a greatly increased level of technical depth. *Inside Windows 2000, Third Edition* (Microsoft Press, 2000) was authored by David Solomon and Mark Russinovich. It added many new topics, such as startup and shutdown, service internals, registry internals, file system drivers, and networking. It also covered kernel changes in Windows 2000, such as the Windows Driver Model (WDM), Plug and Play, power management, Windows Management Instrumentation (WMI), encryption, the job object, and Terminal Services. *Windows Internals, Fourth Edition* was the Windows XP and Windows Server 2003 update

and added more content focused on helping IT professionals make use of their knowledge of Windows internals, such as using key tools from Windows Sysinternals (*www.microsoft.com/technet/sysinternals*) and analyzing crash dumps.

Fifth Edition Changes

This latest edition has been updated to cover the kernel changes made in Windows Vista and Windows Server 2008. Hands-on experiments have been updated to reflect changes in tools, and newly added experiments use tools not available when the fourth edition was written. Additionally, content has been added to cover mechanisms that were not previously described, such as the image loader and user-mode debugging facility, and information about previously covered subjects has been expanded as well.

Hands-On Experiments

Even without access to the Windows source code, you can glean much about Windows internals from tools such as the kernel debugger and tools from Sysinternals and Winsider Seminars & Solutions (*www.winsiderss.com*). When a tool can be used to expose or demonstrate some aspect of the internal behavior of Windows, the steps for trying the tool yourself are listed in "Experiment" boxes. These appear throughout the book, and we encourage you to try these as you're reading—seeing visible proof of how Windows works internally will make much more of an impression on you than just reading about it will.

Topics Not Covered

Windows is a large and complex operating system. This book doesn't cover everything relevant to Windows internals but instead focuses on the base system components. For example, this book doesn't describe COM+, the Windows distributed object-oriented programming infrastructure, or the .NET Framework, the foundation of managed code applications.

Because this is an internals book and not a user, programming, or system administration book, it doesn't describe how to use, program, or configure Windows.

A Warning and a Caveat

Because this book describes undocumented behavior of the internal architecture and operation of the Windows operating system (such as internal kernel structures and functions), this

content is subject to change between releases. (External interfaces, such as the Windows API, are not subject to incompatible changes.)

By "subject to change," we don't necessarily mean that details described in this book *will* change between releases, but you can't count on them not changing. Any software that uses these undocumented interfaces might not work on future releases of Windows. Even worse, software that runs in kernel mode (such as device drivers) and uses these undocumented interfaces might experience a system crash when running on a newer release of Windows.

Find Additional Content Online

As new or updated material becomes available that complements this book, it will be posted online on the Microsoft Press Online Developer Tools Web site. The type of material you might find includes updates to book content, articles, links to companion content, errata, sample chapters, and more. This Web content is available at *www.microsoft.com/learning/ books/online/developer* and is updated periodically.

Support

Every effort has been made to ensure the accuracy of this book. Should you run into any problems or issues, please refer to the sources listed below.

From the Authors

This book isn't perfect. No doubt it contains some inaccuracies, or possibly we've omitted some topics we should have covered. If you find anything you think is incorrect, or if you believe we should have included material that isn't here, please feel free to send e-mail to *wininit@solsem.com*. Updates and corrections will be posted on the Web site *http://technet. microsoft.com/en-us/sysinternals/bb963901.aspx*.

From Microsoft Press

Microsoft Press provides corrections for books through the World Wide Web at the following address:

www.microsoft.com/mspress/support

Questions and Comments

In addition to sending feedback directly to the authors, if you have comments, questions, or ideas regarding the presentation or use of this book, you can send them to Microsoft using either of the following methods:

Postal mail:

Microsoft Press
Attn: Windows Internals Editor
One Microsoft Way
Redmond, WA 98052-6399

E-mail:

mspinput@microsoft.com

Please note that product support isn't offered through these mail addresses. For support information, visit Microsoft's Web site at *http://support.microsoft.com/.*

Chapter 1
Concepts and Tools

In this chapter, we'll introduce the key Microsoft Windows operating system concepts and terms we'll be using throughout this book, such as the Windows API, processes, threads, virtual memory, kernel mode and user mode, objects, handles, security, and the registry. We'll also introduce the tools that you can use to explore Windows internals, such as the kernel debugger, the Reliability and Performance Monitor, and key tools from Windows Sysinternals (*www.microsoft.com/technet/sysinternals*). In addition, we'll explain how you can use the Windows Driver Kit (WDK) and the Windows Software Development Kit (SDK) as resources for finding further information on Windows internals.

Be sure that you understand everything in this chapter—the remainder of the book is written assuming that you do.

Windows Operating System Versions

This book covers the two most recent versions of the Microsoft Windows operating system based on the Windows NT code base: Windows Vista (32-bit and 64-bit versions) and Windows Server 2008 (32-bit and 64-bit versions). Unless specifically stated, the text applies to all versions. As background information, Table 1-1 lists the releases of the Windows NT code base, their internal version number, and the external product name.

TABLE 1-1 Windows Operating System Releases

Product Name	Internal Version Number	Release Date
Windows NT 3.1	3.1	July 1993
Windows NT 3.5	3.5	September 1994
Windows NT 3.51	3.51	May 1995
Windows NT 4.0	4.0	July 1996
Windows 2000	5.0	December 1999
Windows XP	5.1	August 2001
Windows Server 2003	5.2	March 2003
Windows Vista	6.0 (Build 6000)	January 2007
Windows Server 2008	6.0 (Build 6001)	March 2008

Foundation Concepts and Terms

In the course of this book, we'll be referring to some structures and concepts that might be unfamiliar to some readers. In this section, we'll define the terms we'll be using throughout. You should become familiar with them before proceeding to subsequent chapters.

Windows API

The Windows application programming interface (API) is the system programming interface to the Windows operating system family. Prior to the introduction of 64-bit versions of Windows XP and Windows Server 2003, the programming interface to the 32-bit versions of the Windows operating systems was called the Win32 API, to distinguish it from the original 16-bit Windows API, which was the programming interface to the original 16-bit versions of Windows. In this book, the term *Windows API* refers to both the 32-bit and 64-bit programming interfaces to Windows Vista and Windows Server 2008.

> **Note** The Windows API is described in the Windows Software Development Kit (SDK) documentation. (See the section "Windows Software Development Kit" later in this chapter.) This documentation is available for free viewing online at *www.msdn.microsoft.com*. It is also included with all subscription levels to the Microsoft Developer Network (MSDN), Microsoft's support program for developers. For more information, see *www.msdn.microsoft.com*. An excellent description of how to program the Windows base API is the book *Windows via C/C++*, Fifth Edition by Jeffrey Richter and Christophe Nasarre (Microsoft Press, 2007).

The Windows API consists of thousands of callable functions, which are divided into the following major categories:

- Base Services
- Component Services
- User Interface Services
- Graphics and Multimedia Services
- Messaging and Collaboration
- Networking
- Web Services

This book focuses on the internals of the key base services, such as processes and threads, memory management, I/O, and security.

What About .NET?

The .NET Framework consists of a library of classes called the Framework Class Library (FCL) and a Common Language Runtime (CLR) that provides a managed code execution environment with features such as just-in-time compilation, type verification, garbage collection, and code access security. By offering these features, the CLR provides a development environment that improves programmer productivity and reduces common programming errors. For an excellent description of the .NET Framework and its core architecture, see *CLR via C#*, Second Edition by Jeffrey Richter (Microsoft Press, 2006).

The CLR is implemented as a classic COM server whose code resides in a standard user-mode Windows DLL. In fact, all components of the .NET Framework are implemented as standard user-mode Windows DLLs layered over unmanaged Windows API functions. (None of the .NET Framework runs in kernel mode.) Figure 1-1 illustrates the relationship between these components:

FIGURE 1-1 Relationship between .NET Framework components

History of the Win32 API

Interestingly, Win32 wasn't slated to be the original programming interface to Microsoft Windows NT. Because the Windows NT project started as a replacement for OS/2 version 2, the primary programming interface was the 32-bit OS/2 Presentation Manager API. A year into the project, however, Microsoft Windows 3.0 hit the market and took off. As a result, Microsoft changed direction and made Windows NT the future replacement for the Windows family of products as opposed to the replacement for OS/2. It was at this juncture that the need to specify the Windows API arose— before this, the Windows API existed only as a 16-bit interface.

Although the Windows API would introduce many new functions that hadn't been available on Windows 3.1, Microsoft decided to make the new API compatible with the 16-bit Windows API function names, semantics, and use of data types whenever possible to ease the burden of porting existing 16-bit Windows applications to Windows NT. So those of you who are looking at the Windows API for the first time and wondering why many function names and interfaces seem inconsistent should keep in mind that one reason for the inconsistency was to ensure that the Windows API is compatible with the old 16-bit Windows API.

Services, Functions, and Routines

Several terms in the Windows user and programming documentation have different meanings in different contexts. For example, the word *service* can refer to a callable routine in the operating system, a device driver, or a server process. The following list describes what certain terms mean in this book:

- **Windows API functions** Documented, callable subroutines in the Windows API. Examples include *CreateProcess*, *CreateFile*, and *GetMessage*.

- **Native system services (or executive system services)** The undocumented, underlying services in the operating system that are callable from user mode. For example, *NtCreateProcessEx* is the internal system service the Windows *CreateProcess* function calls to create a new process. (For a definition of native functions, see the section "System Service Dispatching" in Chapter 3.)

- **Kernel support functions (or routines)** Subroutines inside the Windows operating system that can be called only from kernel mode (defined later in this chapter). For example, *ExAllocatePoolWithTag* is the routine that device drivers call to allocate memory from the Windows system heaps (called *pools*).

- **Windows services** Processes started by the Windows service control manager. (Although the registry defines Windows device drivers as "services," we don't refer to them as such in this book.) For example, the Task Scheduler service runs in a user-mode process that supports the *at* command (which is similar to the UNIX commands *at* or *cron*).

- **DLLs (dynamic-link libraries)** A set of callable subroutines linked together as a binary file that can be dynamically loaded by applications that use the subroutines. Examples include Msvcrt.dll (the C run-time library) and Kernel32.dll (one of the Windows API subsystem libraries). Windows user-mode components and applications use DLLs extensively. The advantage DLLs provide over static libraries is that applications can share DLLs, and Windows ensures that there is only one in-memory copy of a DLL's code among the applications that are referencing it.

Processes, Threads, and Jobs

Although programs and processes appear similar on the surface, they are fundamentally different. A *program* is a static sequence of instructions, whereas a *process* is a container for a set of resources used when executing the instance of the program. At the highest level of abstraction, a Windows process comprises the following:

- A *private virtual address space*, which is a set of virtual memory addresses that the process can use

- An executable program, which defines initial code and data and is mapped into the process's virtual address space

- A list of open handles to various system resources, such as semaphores, communication ports, and files, that are accessible to all threads in the process

- A security context called an *access token* that identifies the user, security groups, privileges, User Access Control (UAC) virtualization state, session, and limited user account state associated with the process

- A unique identifier called a *process ID* (internally part of an identifier called a *client ID*)

- At least one thread of execution (although an "empty" process is possible, it is not useful)

Each process also points to its parent or creator process. However, if the parent exits, this information is not updated. Therefore, it is possible for a process to point to a nonexistent parent. This is not a problem, as nothing relies on this information being present. The following experiment illustrates this case.

EXPERIMENT: Viewing the Process Tree

One unique attribute about a process that most tools don't display is the parent or creator process ID. You can retrieve this value with the Performance Monitor (or programmatically) by querying the Creating Process ID. The Tlist.exe tool (in the Debugging Tools for Windows) can show the process tree by using the /t switch. Here's an example of output from *tlist /t*:

```
C:\>tlist /t
System Process (0)
System (4)
  smss.exe (480)
csrss.exe (548)
wininit.exe (612)
     services.exe (656)
        svchost.exe (848)
        svchost.exe (880)
        svchost.exe (924)
        svchost.exe (980)
          audiodg.exe (1040)
```

```
        svchost.exe (1108)
          dwm.exe (123)
        svchost.exe (96)
          taskeng.exe (604)
          tasking.exe (1532)
        SLsvc.exe (1814)
          svchost.exe (2988)
      lsass.exe (672)
      lsm.exe (680)
  csrss.exe (624)
  winlogon.exe (824)
  explorer.exe (724) Program Manager
    WINWORD.EXE (3512) WinInt5E_Chapter01.doc [Compatibility Mode] - Microsoft Word
    cmd.exe (3936) Command Prompt - tlist /t
      tlist.exe (1344)
```

The list indents each process to show its parent/child relationship. Processes whose parents aren't alive are left-justified (as is Explorer.exe in the preceding example) because even if a grandparent process exists, there's no way to find that relationship. Windows maintains only the creator process ID, not a link back to the creator of the creator, and so forth.

To demonstrate the fact that Windows doesn't keep track of more than just the parent process ID, follow these steps:

1. Open a Command Prompt window.

2. Type **start cmd** (which starts a second command prompt).

3. Bring up Task Manager.

4. Switch to the second command prompt.

5. Type **mspaint** (which runs Microsoft Paint).

6. Click the intermediate (second) Command Prompt window.

7. Type **exit**. (Notice that Paint remains.)

8. Switch to Task Manager.

9. Click the Applications tab.

10. Right-click on the Command Prompt task, and select Go To Process.

11. Click on the Cmd.exe process highlighted in blue.

12. Right-click on this process, and select End Process Tree.

13. Click Yes in the Task Manager Warning message box.

The first Command Prompt window will disappear, but you should still see the Paint window because it was the grandchild of the command prompt process you terminated; and because the intermediate process (the parent of Paint) was terminated, there was no link between the parent and the grandchild.

A number of tools for viewing (and modifying) processes and process information are available. The following experiments illustrate the various views of process information you can obtain with some of these tools. These tools are included within Windows itself and within the Debugging Tools for Windows, the Windows SDK, and from Sysinternals. Many of these tools show overlapping subsets of the core process and thread information, sometimes identified by different names.

Probably the most widely used tool to examine process activity is Task Manager. (Interestingly, there is no such thing as a "task" in the Windows kernel, so Task Manager is really a tool to manage processes.) The following experiment shows the difference between what Task Manager lists as applications and processes.

EXPERIMENT: Viewing Process Information with Task Manager

The built-in Windows Task Manager provides a quick list of the processes running on the system. You can start Task Manager in one of three ways: (1) press Ctrl+Shift+Esc, (2) right-click on the taskbar and select Task Manager, or (3) press Ctrl+Alt+Delete and click the Task Manager button. Once Task Manager has started, click the Processes tab to see the list of running processes. Notice that processes are identified by the name of the image of which they are an instance. Unlike some objects in Windows, processes can't be given global names. To display additional details, choose Select Columns from the View menu and select additional columns to be added, as shown here:

Although what you see in the Task Manager Processes tab is clearly a list of processes, what the Applications tab displays isn't as obvious. The Applications tab lists the top-level visible windows on all the desktops in the interactive window station. (By default, there are two desktop objects—you can create more by using the Windows *CreateDesktop* function.) The Status column indicates whether or not the thread that

owns the window is in a Windows message wait state. "Running" means the thread is waiting for windowing input; "Not Responding" means the thread isn't waiting for windowing input (for example, the thread might be running or waiting for I/O or some Windows synchronization object).

From the Applications tab, you can match a task to the process that owns the thread that owns the task window by right-clicking on the task name and choosing Go To Process.

Process Explorer, from Sysinternals, shows more details about processes and threads than any other available tool, which is why you will see it used in a number of experiments throughout the book. The following are some of the unique things that Process Explorer shows or enables:

- Full path name for the image being executed
- Process security token (list of groups and privileges, virtualization state, and session)
- Highlighting to show changes in the process and thread list
- List of services inside service-hosting processes, including display name and description
- Processes that are part of a job and job details

- Processes running .NET applications and .NET-specific details (such as the list of app-domains and CLR performance counters)

- Start time for processes and threads

- Complete list of memory-mapped files (not just DLLs)

- Ability to suspend a process

- Ability to kill an individual thread

- Easy identification of which processes were consuming the most CPU time over a period of time (The Reliability and Performance Monitor can display process CPU utilization for a given set of processes, but it won't automatically show processes created after the performance monitoring session has started—only a manual trace in binary output format can do that.)

Process Explorer also provides easy access to information in one place, such as:

- Process tree (with ability to collapse parts of the tree)

- Open handles in a process (including unnamed handles) without prior setup (The Microsoft tools to show open handles require the setting of a systemwide flag and a reboot before they can be used.)

- List of DLLs (and memory-mapped files) in a process

- Thread activity within a process

- User-mode thread stacks (including mapping of addresses to names using the debugging tools' symbol engine)

- Kernel-mode thread stacks for system threads (including mapping of addresses to names using the debugging tools' symbol engine)

- Context switch delta (a better representation of CPU activity, as explained in Chapter 5)

- Time stamp counter (an even better representation of precise CPU activity, as explained in Chapter 5)

- 64-bit vs. 32-bit image type

- Integrity level

- Virtualization state

- Kernel memory (paged and nonpaged pool) limits (other tools show only current size)

An introductory experiment using Process Explorer follows.

EXPERIMENT: Viewing Process Details with Process Explorer

Download the latest version of Process Explorer from Sysinternals and run it. The first time you run it, you will receive a message that symbols are not currently configured. If properly configured, Process Explorer can access symbol information to display the symbolic name of the thread start function and functions on its call stack (available by double-clicking on a process and clicking on the Threads tab). This is useful for identifying what threads are doing within a process. To access symbols, you must have the Debugging Tools for Windows installed (described later in this chapter). Then click on Options, choose Configure Symbols, and fill in the appropriate symbols path. For example:

In the preceding example, the on-demand symbol server is being used to access symbols and a copy of the symbol files is being stored on the local machine in the c:\symbols folder. For more information on configuring use of the symbol server, see *www.microsoft.com/whdc/devtools/debugging/debugstart.mspx*.

When Process Explorer starts, it shows by default the process list on the top half and the open handles for the currently selected process on the bottom half. It also shows tooltips for four kinds of hosting processes:

- The running services inside a service-hosting process (Svchost.exe) if you hover your mouse over the name
- The running COM object tasks part of a Taskeng.exe process
- The target of a Rundll32.exe process (used for things such as Control Panel items)
- The COM object being hosted inside a Dllhost.exe process

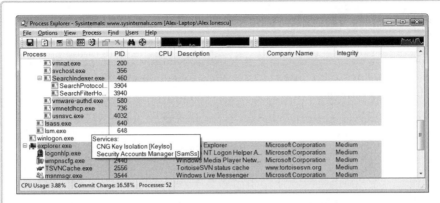

Here are a few steps to walk you through some basic capabilities of Process Explorer:

1. Turn off the lower pane by deselecting View, Show Lower Pane. (The lower pane can show open handles or mapped DLLs and memory-mapped files—these are explored in Chapters 3 and 9.)

2. Notice that processes hosting services are highlighted by default in pink. Your own processes are highlighted in blue. (These colors can be configured.)

3. Hover your mouse pointer over the image name for processes, and notice the full path displayed by the tooltip.

4. Click on View, Select Columns, and add the image path.

5. Sort on the process column, and notice the tree view disappears. (You can either display tree view or sort by any of the columns shown.) Click again to sort from Z to A. Then click again, and the display returns to tree view.

6. Deselect View, Show Processes From All Users to show only your processes.

7. Go to Options, Difference Highlight Duration, and change the value to 5 seconds. Then launch a new process (anything), and notice the new process highlighted in green for 5 seconds. Exit this new process, and notice the process is highlighted in red for 5 seconds before disappearing from the display. This can be useful to see processes being created and exiting on your system.

8. Finally, double-click on a process and explore the various tabs available from the process properties display. (These will be referenced in various experiments throughout the book where the information being shown is being explained.)

A *thread* is the entity within a process that Windows schedules for execution. Without it, the process's program can't run. A thread includes the following essential components:

- The contents of a set of CPU registers representing the state of the processor.

- Two stacks, one for the thread to use while executing in kernel mode and one for executing in user mode.

- A private storage area called thread-local storage (TLS) for use by subsystems, run-time libraries, and DLLs.

- A unique identifier called a *thread ID* (also internally called a *client ID*—process IDs and thread IDs are generated out of the same namespace, so they never overlap).

- Threads sometimes have their own security context that is often used by multithreaded server applications that impersonate the security context of the clients that they serve.

The volatile registers, stacks, and private storage area are called the thread's *context*. Because this information is different for each machine architecture that Windows runs on, this structure, by necessity, is architecture-specific. The Windows *GetThreadContext* function provides access to this architecture-specific information (called the CONTEXT block).

Fibers vs. Threads

Fibers allow an application to schedule its own "threads" of execution rather than rely on the priority-based scheduling mechanism built into Windows. Fibers are often called "lightweight" threads, and in terms of scheduling, they're invisible to the kernel because they're implemented in user mode in Kernel32.dll. To use fibers, a call is first made to the Windows *ConvertThreadToFiber* function. This function converts the thread to a running fiber. Afterward, the newly converted fiber can create additional fibers with the *CreateFiber* function. (Each fiber can have its own set of fibers.) Unlike a thread, however, a fiber doesn't begin execution until it's manually selected through a call to the *SwitchToFiber* function. The new fiber runs until it exits or until it calls *SwitchToFiber*, again selecting another fiber to run. For more information, see the Windows SDK documentation on fiber functions.

Although threads have their own execution context, every thread within a process shares the process's virtual address space (in addition to the rest of the resources belonging to the process), meaning that all the threads in a process can write to and read from each other's memory. Threads cannot accidentally reference the address space of another process, however, unless the other process makes available part of its private address space as a *shared memory section* (called a *file mapping object* in the Windows API) or unless one process has the right to open another process to use cross-process memory functions such as *ReadProcessMemory* and *WriteProcessMemory*.

In addition to a private address space and one or more threads, each process has a security identification and a list of open handles to objects such as files, shared memory sections, or one of the synchronization objects such as mutexes, events, or semaphores, as illustrated in Figure 1-2.

FIGURE 1-2 A process and its resources

Every process has a security context that is stored in an object called an *access token*. The process access token contains the security identification and credentials for the process. By default, threads don't have their own access token, but they can obtain one, thus allowing individual threads to impersonate the security context of another process—including processes running on a remote Windows system—without affecting other threads in the process. (See Chapter 6 for more details on process and thread security.)

The *virtual address descriptors* (VADs) are data structures that the memory manager uses to keep track of the virtual addresses the process is using. These data structures are described in more depth in Chapter 9.

Windows provides an extension to the process model called a *job*. A job object's main function is to allow groups of processes to be managed and manipulated as a unit. A job object allows control of certain attributes and provides limits for the process or processes associated with the job. It also records basic accounting information for all processes associated with the job and for all processes that were associated with the job but have since terminated. In some ways, the job object compensates for the lack of a structured process tree in Windows—yet in many ways it is more powerful than a UNIX-style process tree.

You'll find out much more about the internal structure of jobs, processes and threads, the mechanics of process and thread creation, and the thread-scheduling algorithms in Chapter 5.

Virtual Memory

Windows implements a virtual memory system based on a flat (linear) address space that provides each process with the illusion of having its own large, private address space. Virtual memory provides a logical view of memory that might not correspond to its physical layout. At run time, the memory manager, with assistance from hardware, translates, or *maps*, the virtual addresses into physical addresses, where the data is actually stored. By controlling the protection and mapping, the operating system can ensure that individual processes don't bump into one another or overwrite operating system data. Figure 1-3 illustrates three virtually contiguous pages mapped to three discontiguous pages in physical memory.

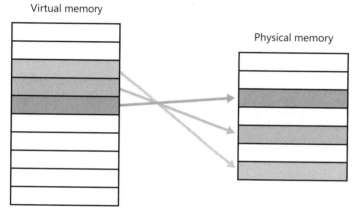

FIGURE 1-3 Mapping virtual memory to physical memory

Because most systems have much less physical memory than the total virtual memory in use by the running processes, the memory manager transfers, or *pages*, some of the memory contents to disk. Paging data to disk frees physical memory so that it can be used for other processes or for the operating system itself. When a thread accesses a virtual address that has been paged to disk, the virtual memory manager loads the information back into memory from disk. Applications don't have to be altered in any way to take advantage of paging because hardware support enables the memory manager to page without the knowledge or assistance of processes or threads.

The size of the virtual address space varies for each hardware platform. On 32-bit x86 systems, the total virtual address space has a theoretical maximum of 4 GB. By default, Windows allocates half this address space (the lower half of the 4-GB virtual address space, from x00000000 through x7FFFFFFF) to processes for their unique private storage and uses the other half (the upper half, addresses x80000000 through xFFFFFFFF) for its own protected operating system memory utilization. The mappings of the lower half change to reflect the virtual address space of the currently executing process, but the mappings of the upper half always consist of the operating system's virtual memory. Windows Vista and Windows Server 2008 support boot-time options (the *increaseuserva* qualifier in the Boot Configuration Database (BCD), described in Chapter 13) that give processes running specially marked programs

(the large address space aware flag must be set in the header of the executable image) the ability to use up to 3 GB of private address space (leaving 1 GB for the operating system). This option allows applications such as database servers to keep larger portions of a database in the process address space, thus reducing the need to map subset views of the database. Figure 1-4 shows the two virtual address space layouts supported by 32-bit Windows.

FIGURE 1-4 Address space layouts for 32-bit Windows

Although 3 GB is better than 2 GB, it's still not enough virtual address space to map very large (multigigabyte) databases. To address this need on 32-bit systems, Windows provides a mechanism called *Address Windowing Extension* (AWE), which allows a 32-bit application to allocate up to 64 GB of physical memory and then map views, or windows, into its 2-GB virtual address space. Although using AWE puts the burden of managing mappings of virtual to physical memory on the programmer, it does address the need of being able to directly access more physical memory than can be mapped at any one time in a 32-bit process address space.

64-bit Windows provides a much larger address space for processes: 7152 GB on IA-64 systems and 8192 GB on x64 systems. Figure 1-5 shows a simplified view of the 64-bit system address space layouts. (For a detailed description, see Chapter 9.) Note that these sizes do not represent the architectural limits for these platforms. Sixty-four bits of address space is over 17 billion GB, but current 64-bit hardware limits this to smaller values. And Windows implementation limits in the current versions of 64-bit Windows reduce this to 8192 GB (8 TB).

FIGURE 1-5 Address space layouts for 64-bit Windows

Details of the implementation of the memory manager, including how address translation works and how Windows manages physical memory, are described in Chapter 9.

Kernel Mode vs. User Mode

To protect user applications from accessing and/or modifying critical operating system data, Windows uses two processor access modes (even if the processor on which Windows is running supports more than two): *user mode* and *kernel mode*. User application code runs in user mode, whereas operating system code (such as system services and device drivers) runs in kernel mode. Kernel mode refers to a mode of execution in a processor that grants access to all system memory and all CPU instructions. By providing the operating system software with a higher privilege level than the application software has, the processor provides a necessary foundation for operating system designers to ensure that a misbehaving application can't disrupt the stability of the system as a whole.

> **Note** The architecture of the x86 and x64 processor defines four privilege levels, or rings, to protect system code and data from being overwritten either inadvertently or maliciously by code of lesser privilege. Windows uses privilege level 0 (or ring 0) for kernel mode and privilege level 3 (or ring 3) for user mode. The reason Windows uses only two levels is that some hardware architectures that were supported in the past (such as Compaq Alpha and Silicon Graphics MIPS) implemented only two privilege levels.

Although each Windows process has its own private memory space, the kernel-mode operating system and device driver code share a single virtual address space. Each page in virtual memory is tagged as to what access mode the processor must be in to read and/or write the page. Pages in system space can be accessed only from kernel mode, whereas all pages in the user address space are accessible from user mode. Read-only pages (such as those that contain static data) are not writable from any mode. Additionally, on processors that support no-execute memory protection, Windows marks pages containing data as nonexecutable, thus preventing inadvertent code execution in data areas.

Thirty-two-bit Windows doesn't provide any protection to private read/write system memory being used by components running in kernel mode. In other words, once in kernel mode, operating system and device driver code has complete access to system space memory and can bypass Windows security to access objects. Because the bulk of the Windows operating system code runs in kernel mode, it is vital that components that run in kernel mode be carefully designed and tested to ensure that they don't violate system security and cause system instability.

This lack of protection also emphasizes the need to take care when loading a third-party device driver, because once in kernel mode the software has complete access to all operating system data. This vulnerability was one of the reasons behind the driver-signing mechanism introduced in Windows, which warns the user if an attempt is made to add an unauthorized (unsigned) driver. (See Chapter 7 for more information on driver signing.) Also, a mechanism called Driver Verifier helps device driver writers to find bugs (such as buffer overruns or memory leaks) that can cause security or reliability issues. Driver Verifier is explained in Chapter 9.

Additionally, also on 64-bit versions of Windows, the kernel mode code signing (KMCS) policy dictates that 64-bit device drivers must be signed with a cryptographic key assigned by one of the major code certification authorities. Unlike 32-bit versions of Windows, the user cannot explicitly force the installation of an unsigned driver, even as an administrator (unless this restriction is disabled manually at boot time by pressing F8 and choosing the advanced boot option Disable Driver Signature Enforcement).

As you'll see in Chapter 2, user applications switch from user mode to kernel mode when they make a system service call. For example, a Windows *ReadFile* function eventually needs to call the internal Windows routine that actually handles reading data from a file. That routine, because it accesses internal system data structures, must run in kernel mode. The transition from user mode to kernel mode is accomplished by the use of a special processor instruction that causes the processor to switch to kernel mode. The operating system traps this instruction, notices that a system service is being requested, validates the arguments the thread passed to the system function, and then executes the internal function. Before returning control to the user thread, the processor mode is switched back to user mode. In this way, the operating system protects itself and its data from perusal and modification by user processes.

Note A transition from user mode to kernel mode (and back) does *not* affect thread scheduling per se—a mode transition is *not* a context switch. Further details on system service dispatching are included in Chapter 3.

Thus, it's normal for a user thread to spend part of its time executing in user mode and part in kernel mode. In fact, because the bulk of the graphics and windowing system also runs in kernel mode, graphics-intensive applications spend more of their time in kernel mode than in user mode. An easy way to test this is to run a graphics-intensive application such as Microsoft Paint or Microsoft Chess Titans and watch the time split between user mode and kernel mode using one of the performance counters listed in Table 1-2.

TABLE 1-2 Mode-Related Performance Counters

Object: Counter	Function
Processor: % Privileged Time	Percentage of time that an individual CPU (or all CPUs) has run in kernel mode during a specified interval
Processor: % User Time	Percentage of time that an individual CPU (or all CPUs) has run in user mode during a specified interval
Process: % Privileged Time	Percentage of time that the threads in a process have run in kernel mode during a specified interval
Process: % User Time	Percentage of time that the threads in a process have run in user mode during a specified interval
Thread: % Privileged Time	Percentage of time that a thread has run in kernel mode during a specified interval
Thread: % User Time	Percentage of time that a thread has run in user mode during a specified interval

EXPERIMENT: Kernel Mode vs. User Mode

You can use the Reliability and Performance Monitor to see how much time your system spends executing in kernel mode vs. in user mode. Follow these steps:

1. Run the Reliability and Performance Monitor by opening the Start menu and selecting Programs/Administrative Tools/Reliability and Performance Monitor. Choose the Performance Monitor view.

2. Click the Add button (+) on the toolbar.

3. With the Processor performance object selected, click the % Privileged Time counter and, while holding down the Ctrl key, click the % User Time counter.

4. Click Add, and then click Close.

5. Move the mouse rapidly back and forth. You should notice, similar to the illustration below, the % Privileged Time line going up when you move the mouse around, reflecting the time spent servicing the mouse interrupts and the time spent in the graphics part of the windowing system (which, as explained in Chapter 2, runs primarily as a device driver in kernel mode).

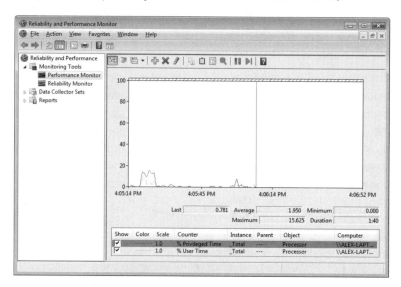

6. When you're finished, just close the tool.

You can also quickly see this activity by using Task Manager. Just click the Performance tab, and then select Show Kernel Times from the View menu. The CPU usage bar will show total CPU usage in green and kernel-mode time in red.

To see how the Reliability and Performance Monitor itself uses kernel time and user time, run it again, but add the individual Process counters % User Time and % Privileged Time for every process in the system:

1. If it's not already running, run the Reliability and Performance Monitor again. (If it is already running, start with a blank display by clicking the New Counter Set button on the toolbar.)

2. Click the Add button (+) on the toolbar.

3. Change the performance object to Process.

4. Select the % Privileged Time and % User Time counters.

5. Select all processes in the Instance box (except the _Total process).

6. Click Add, and then click Close.

7. Move the mouse rapidly back and forth.

8. Press Ctrl+H to turn on highlighting mode. This highlights the currently selected counter in black.

9. Scroll through the counters at the bottom of the display to identify the processes whose threads were running when you moved the mouse, and note whether they were running in user mode or kernel mode.

You should see the Reliability and Performance Monitor process (by looking in the Instance column for the mmc process) kernel-mode *and* user-mode time go up when you move the mouse because it is executing application code in user mode and calling Windows functions that run in kernel mode. You'll also notice kernel-mode thread activity in a process named csrss when you move the mouse. This activity occurs because the Windows subsystem's kernel-mode raw input thread, which handles keyboard and mouse input, is attached to this process. (See Chapter 2 for more information about system threads.) Finally, the process named Idle that you see spending nearly 100 percent of its time in kernel mode isn't really a process—it's a fake process used to account for idle CPU cycles. As you can observe from the mode in which the threads in the Idle process run, when Windows has nothing to do, it does it in kernel mode.

Terminal Services and Multiple Sessions

Terminal Services refers to the support in Windows for multiple interactive user sessions on a single system. With Windows Terminal Services, a remote user can establish a session on another machine, log in, and run applications on the server. The server transmits the

graphical user interface to the client, and the client transmits the user's input back to the server. (Similar to the X Window System, Windows Vista and Windows Server 2008 permit running individual applications on a server system with the display remoted to the client instead of remoting the entire desktop.)

The first session is considered the services session, or session zero, and contains system service–hosting processes (explained in further detail in Chapter 4). The first login session at the physical console of the machine is session one, and additional sessions can be created through the use of the remote desktop connection program (Mstsc.exe) or through the use of fast user switching (described later).

Windows Vista permits a single remote user to connect to the machine, but if someone is logged in at the console, the workstation is locked (that is, someone can be using the system either locally or remotely, but not at the same time). Windows Vista Home Premium and Ultimate editions allow one interactive session and up to four Media Center Extender sessions.

Windows Server 2008 supports two simultaneous remote connections. (This is to facilitate remote management—for example, use of management tools that require being logged in to the machine being managed.) Windows Server 2008 Standard and Datacenter editions can support more than two sessions if appropriately licensed and configured as a terminal server.

Although Windows Vista editions other than Media Center do not support multiple remote desktop connections, they do support multiple sessions created locally through a feature called fast user switching. When a user chooses to disconnect their session instead of log off (for example, by clicking Start, clicking Log Off, and choosing Switch User or by holding down the Windows key and pressing L), the current session (that is, the processes running in that session and all the session-wide data structures that describe the session) remains in the system and the system returns to the main logon screen. If a new user logs in, a new session is created.

For applications that want to be aware of running in a terminal server session, there are a set of Windows APIs for programmatically detecting that as well as for controlling various aspects of Terminal Services. (See the Windows SDK for details.)

Chapter 2 describes briefly how sessions are created and has some experiments showing how to view session information with various tools, including the kernel debugger. The "Object Manager" section in Chapter 3 describes how the system namespace for objects is instantiated on a per-session basis and how applications that need to be aware of other instances of themselves on the same system can accomplish that. Finally, Chapter 9 covers how the memory manager sets up and manages session-wide data.

Objects and Handles

In the Windows operating system, an *object* is a single, run-time instance of a statically defined object type. An *object type* comprises a system-defined data type, functions that operate on instances of the data type, and a set of object attributes. If you write Windows applications, you might encounter process, thread, file, and event objects, to name just a few examples. These objects are based on lower-level objects that Windows creates and manages. In Windows, a process is an instance of the process object type, a file is an instance of the file object type, and so on.

An *object attribute* is a field of data in an object that partially defines the object's state. An object of type *process*, for example, would have attributes that include the process ID, a base scheduling priority, and a pointer to an access token object. *Object methods*, the means for manipulating objects, usually read or change the object attributes. For example, the *open* method for a process would accept a process identifier as input and return a pointer to the object as output.

> **Note** Although there is a parameter named *ObjectAttributes* that a caller supplies when creating an object using either the Windows API or native object services, that parameter shouldn't be confused with the more general meaning of the term as used in this book.

The most fundamental difference between an object and an ordinary data structure is that the internal structure of an object is opaque. You must call an object service to get data out of an object or to put data into it. You can't directly read or change data inside an object. This difference separates the underlying implementation of the object from code that merely uses it, a technique that allows object implementations to be changed easily over time.

Objects, through the help of a kernel component called the *object manager*, provide a convenient means for accomplishing the following four important operating system tasks:

- Providing human-readable names for system resources
- Sharing resources and data among processes
- Protecting resources from unauthorized access
- Reference tracking, which allows the system to know when an object is no longer in use so that it can be automatically deallocated

Not all data structures in the Windows operating system are objects. Only data that needs to be shared, protected, named, or made visible to user-mode programs (via system services) is placed in objects. Structures used by only one component of the operating system to implement internal functions are not objects. Objects and handles (references to an instance of an object) are discussed in more detail in Chapter 3.

Security

Windows was designed from the start to be secure and to meet the requirements of various formal government and industry security ratings, such as the Common Criteria for Information Technology Security Evaluation (CCITSE) specification. Achieving a government-approved security rating allows an operating system to compete in that arena. Of course, many of these required capabilities are advantageous features for any multiuser system.

The core security capabilities of Windows include discretionary (need-to-know) and mandatory integrity protection for all shareable system objects (such as files, directories, processes, threads, and so forth), security auditing (for accountability of subjects, or users and the actions they initiate), user authentication at logon, and the prevention of one user from accessing uninitialized resources (such as free memory or disk space) that another user has deallocated.

Windows has three forms of access control over objects. The first form—discretionary access control—is the protection mechanism that most people think of when they think of operating system security. It's the method by which owners of objects (such as files or printers) grant or deny access to others. When users log in, they are given a set of security credentials, or a security context. When they attempt to access objects, their security context is compared to the access control list on the object they are trying to access to determine whether they have permission to perform the requested operation.

Privileged access control is necessary for those times when discretionary access control isn't enough. It's a method of ensuring that someone can get to protected objects if the owner isn't available. For example, if an employee leaves a company, the administrator needs a way to gain access to files that might have been accessible only to that employee. In that case, under Windows, the administrator can take ownership of the file so that you can manage its rights as necessary.

Finally, mandatory integrity control is required when an additional level of security control is required to protect objects that are being accessed from within the same user account. It's used both to isolate Protected Mode Internet Explorer from a user's configuration and to protect objects created by an elevated administrator account from access by a nonelevated administrator account. (See Chapter 6 for more information on User Account Control—UAC.)

Security pervades the interface of the Windows API. The Windows subsystem implements object-based security in the same way the operating system does; the Windows subsystem protects shared Windows objects from unauthorized access by placing Windows security descriptors on them. The first time an application tries to access a shared object, the Windows subsystem verifies the application's right to do so. If the security check succeeds, the Windows subsystem allows the application to proceed.

The Windows subsystem implements object security on a number of shared objects, some of which were built on top of native Windows objects. The Windows objects include desktop objects, window objects, menu objects, files, processes, threads, and several synchronization objects.

For a comprehensive description of Windows security, see Chapter 6.

Registry

If you've worked at all with Windows operating systems, you've probably heard about or looked at the registry. You can't talk much about Windows internals without referring to the registry because it's the system database that contains the information required to boot and configure the system, systemwide software settings that control the operation of Windows, the security database, and per-user configuration settings (such as which screen saver to use).

In addition, the registry is a window into in-memory volatile data, such as the current hardware state of the system (what device drivers are loaded, the resources they are using, and so on) as well as the Windows performance counters. The performance counters, which aren't actually "in" the registry, are accessed through the registry functions. See Chapter 4 for more on how performance counter information is accessed from the registry.

Although many Windows users and administrators will never need to look directly into the registry (because you can view or change most configuration settings with standard administrative utilities), it is still a useful source of Windows internals information because it contains many settings that affect system performance and behavior. (If you decide to directly change registry settings, you must exercise extreme caution; any changes might adversely affect system performance or, worse, cause the system to fail to boot successfully.) You'll find references to individual registry keys throughout this book as they pertain to the component being described. Most registry keys referred to in this book are under HKEY_LOCAL_MACHINE, which we'll abbreviate throughout as HKLM.

For further information on the registry and its internal structure, see Chapter 4.

Unicode

Windows differs from most other operating systems in that most internal text strings are stored and processed as 16-bit-wide Unicode characters. Unicode is an international character set standard that defines unique 16-bit values for most of the world's known character sets. (For more information about Unicode, see *www.unicode.org* as well as the programming documentation in the MSDN Library.)

Because many applications deal with 8-bit (single-byte) ANSI character strings, Windows functions that accept string parameters have two entry points: a Unicode (wide, 16-bit) and

an ANSI (narrow, 8-bit) version. The Windows 95, Windows 98, and Windows Millennium Edition implementations of Windows don't implement all the Unicode interfaces to all the Windows functions, so applications designed to run on one of these operating systems as well as Windows Vista and Windows Server 2008 typically use the narrow versions. If you call the narrow version of a Windows function, input string parameters are converted to Unicode before being processed by the system and output parameters are converted from Unicode to ANSI before being returned to the application. Thus, if you have an older service or piece of code that you need to run on Windows but this code is written using ANSI character text strings, Windows will convert the ANSI characters into Unicode for its own use. However, Windows never converts the *data* inside files—it's up to the application to decide whether to store data as Unicode or as ANSI.

Regardless of language, all versions of Windows contain the same functions. Instead of having separate language versions, Windows has a single worldwide binary so that a single installation can support multiple languages (by adding various language packs). Applications can also take advantage of Windows functions that allow single worldwide application binaries that can support multiple languages.

Digging into Windows Internals

Although much of the information in this book is based on reading the Windows source code and talking to the developers, you don't have to take *everything* on faith. Many details about the internals of Windows can be exposed and demonstrated by using a variety of available tools, such as those that come with Windows and the Windows debugging tools. These tool packages are briefly described later in this section.

To encourage your exploration of Windows internals, we've included "Experiment" sidebars throughout the book that describe steps you can take to examine a particular aspect of Windows internal behavior. (You already saw a few of these sections earlier in this chapter.) We encourage you to try these experiments so that you can see in action many of the internals topics described in this book.

Table 1-3 shows a list of the principal tools used in this book and where they come from.

TABLE 1-3 Tools for Viewing Windows Internals

Tool	Image Name	Origin
Startup Programs Viewer	AUTORUNS	Sysinternals
Access Check	ACCESSCHK	Sysinternals
Dependency Walker	DEPENDS	Windows SDK or www.dependencywalker.com
DLL List	LISTDLLS	Sysinternals
Global Flags	GFLAGS	Debugging tools

Tool	Image Name	Origin
Handle Viewer	HANDLE	Sysinternals
Kernel debuggers	WINDBG, KD	Debugging tools, Windows SDK
Logon Sessions	LOGONSESSIONS	Sysinternals
Object Viewer	WINOBJ	Sysinternals
Reliability and Performance Monitor	PERFMON.MSC	Windows built-in tool
Pool Monitor	POOLMON	Windows Driver Kit
Process Explorer	PROCEXP	Sysinternals
Get SID tool	PSGETSID	Sysinternals
Process Monitor	REGMON	Sysinternals
Service Control	SC	Windows built-in tool
Task (Process) List	TLIST	Debugging tools
Task Manager	TASKMGR	Windows built-in tool

Reliability and Performance Monitor

We'll refer to the Reliability and Performance Monitor found in the Administrative Tools folder on the Start menu (or via Control Panel) throughout this book; specifically, we'll focus on the Performance Monitor and Resource Monitor. The Performance Monitor has three functions: system monitoring, viewing performance counter logs, and setting alerts (by using data collector sets, which also contain performance counter logs and trace and configuration data). For simplicity, when we refer to the Performance Monitor, we are referring to the System Monitor function within the tool.

The Performance Monitor can provide more information about how your system is operating than any other single utility. It includes hundreds of counters for various objects. For each major topic described in this book, a table of the relevant Windows performance counters is included.

The Performance Monitor contains a brief description for each counter. To see the descriptions, select a counter in the Add Counters window and select the Show Description check box.

Although all the low-level system monitoring we'll do in this book can be done with the Performance Monitor, Windows Vista also includes a Resource Monitor utility that shows four primary system resources: CPU, Disk, Network, and Memory. In their basic states, these resources are displayed with the same level of information that you would find in Task Manager. However, they also provide columns that can be expanded for more information.

When expanded, the CPU column displays information about per-process CPU usage, just like Task Manager. However, it adds a column for average CPU usage, which can give you a better idea of which processes are most active. The Disk column, on the other hand, displays per-file

information for I/Os in a way that makes it easy to identify the most accessed, written to, or read from files on the system.

The Networking column displays the active network connections and which processes own them, as well as how much data is going through them. This information makes it possible to see background network activity that might be hard to detect otherwise. Finally, the Memory column displays much of the same information that one can obtain with Task Manager, but it is organized for the entire system.

Note that all the Windows performance counters are accessible programmatically. The section "HKEY_PERFORMANCE_DATA" in Chapter 4 has a brief description of the components involved in retrieving performance counters through the Windows API.

Kernel Debugging

Kernel debugging means examining internal kernel data structures and/or stepping through functions in the kernel. It is a useful way to investigate Windows internals because you can display internal system information not available through any other tools and get a clearer idea of code flows within the kernel.

Kernel debugging can be performed with a variety of tools: the Debugging Tools for Windows from Microsoft, LiveKD from Sysinternals, or Syser Debugger from *www.syser-soft.com*. However, we'll focus on the Windows debugging tools because they are the only supported way to perform kernel debugging on Windows. Before describing these tools, let's examine a set of files that you'll need in order to perform any type of kernel debugging.

Symbols for Kernel Debugging

Symbol files contain the names of functions and variables. They are generated by the linker and used by debuggers to reference and display these names during a debug session. This information is not usually stored in the binary image because it is not needed to execute the code. This means that binaries are smaller and faster. However, this means that when debugging, you must make sure that the debugger can access the symbol files that are associated with the images you are referencing during a debugging session.

To use any of the kernel debugging tools to examine internal Windows kernel data structures (such as the process list, thread blocks, loaded driver list, memory usage information, and so on), you must have the correct symbol files for at least the kernel image, Ntoskrnl.exe. (The section "Architecture Overview" in Chapter 2 explains more about this file.) Symbol table files must match the version of the image they were taken from. For example, if you install a Windows Service Pack or hot fix that updates the kernel, you must obtain the matching, updated symbol files for at least the kernel image; otherwise, you'll get a symbol error when you try to start the kernel debugger.

While it is possible to download and install symbols for various versions of Windows, updated symbols for hot fixes are not always available. The easiest solution to obtain the correct version of symbols for debugging is to use the Microsoft on-demand symbol server by using a special syntax for the symbol path that you specify in the debugger. For example, the following symbol path causes the debugging tools to load required symbols from the Internet symbol server and keep a local copy in the c:\symbols folder:

```
srv*c:\symbols*http://msdl.microsoft.com/download/symbols
```

For detailed instructions on how to use the symbol server, see the debugging tools help file or the Web page *www.microsoft.com/whdc/devtools/debugging/debugstart.mspx*.

Debugging Tools for Windows

The Debugging Tools for Windows package contains advanced debugging tools used in this book to explore Windows internals. You can find the latest 32-bit version at *www.microsoft.com/whdc/devtools/debugging/installx86.mspx* and the latest 64-bit version at *www.microsoft.com/whdc/devtools/debugging/install64bit.mspx*. These tools can be used to debug user-mode processes as well as the kernel. (See the following sidebar.)

Note The Debugging Tools for Windows are updated frequently and released independently of Windows operating system versions, so check often for new versions.

User-Mode Debugging

The debugging tools can also be used to attach to a user-mode process and examine and/or change process memory. There are two options when attaching to a process:

- **Invasive** Unless specified otherwise, when you attach to a running process, the *DebugActiveProcess* Windows function is used to establish a connection between the debugger and the debugee. This permits examining and/or changing process memory, setting breakpoints, and performing other debugging functions. Windows allows you to stop debugging without killing the target process, as long as the debugger is detached, not killed.

- **Noninvasive** With this option, the debugger simply opens the process with the *OpenProcess* function. It does not attach to the process as a debugger. This allows you to examine and/or change memory in the target process, but you cannot set breakpoints.

You can also open user-mode process dump files with the debugging tools. User-mode dump files are explained in Chapter 3 in the section on exception dispatching.

There are two primary variants of the Microsoft debuggers that can be used for kernel debugging: a command-line version (Kd.exe) and a graphical user interface (GUI) version (Windbg.exe). Both provide the same set of commands, so which you choose is a matter of personal preference. You can perform three types of kernel debugging with these tools:

- Open a crash dump file created as a result of a Windows system crash. (See Chapter 14 for more information on crash dumps.)

- Connect to a live, running system and examine the system state (or set breakpoints if you're debugging device driver code). This operation requires two computers—a target and a host. The target is the system being debugged, and the host is the system running the debugger. The target system can be either local (connected to the host via a null modem cable, an IEEE 1394 cable, or a USB 2.0 cable) or remote (connected to the host via a modem). The target system must be booted in debugging mode (either by pressing F8 during the boot process and selecting Debugging Mode or by adding the option with the BCDEdit tool). You can also connect through a named pipe, which is useful when debugging through a virtual machine product such as Virtual PC or VMWare, by exposing the guest operating system's serial port as a named pipe device.

- Windows systems also allow you to connect to the local system and examine the system state. This is called *local kernel debugging*. To initiate local kernel debugging with WinDbg, open the File menu, choose Kernel Debug, click on the Local tab, and then click OK. The target system must be booted in debugging mode, a side effect of which is that the Windows decoders for protected content, such as MPEG2 DVD movies, will intentionally fault to prevent access to content decryption keys. An example output screen is shown in Figure 1-6. Some kernel debugger commands do not work when used in local kernel debugging mode (such as creating a memory dump with the .dump command—however, this can be done with LiveKD, described later in this section).

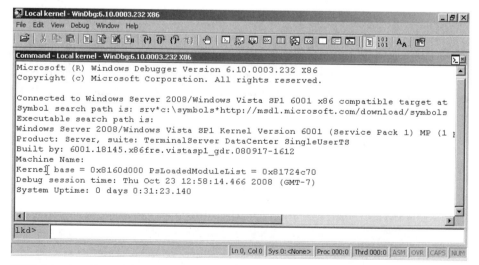

FIGURE 1-6 Local kernel debugging

Once connected in kernel debugging mode, you can use one of the many *debugger extension commands* (commands that begin with "!") to display the contents of internal data structures such as threads, processes, I/O request packets, and memory management information. Throughout this book, the relevant kernel debugger commands and output are included as they apply to each topic being discussed. An excellent companion reference is the Debugger.chm help file, contained in the WinDbg installation folder, which documents all the kernel debugger functionality and extensions. In addition, the *dt* (display type) command can format over 1,000 kernel structures because the kernel symbol files for Windows contain type information that the debugger can use to format structures.

EXPERIMENT: Displaying Type Information for Kernel Structures

To display the list of kernel structures whose type information is included in the kernel symbols, type **dt nt!_*** in the kernel debugger. A sample partial output is shown below:

```
lkd> dt nt!_*
         nt!_LIST_ENTRY
         nt!_LIST_ENTRY
         nt!_IMAGE_NT_HEADERS
         nt!_IMAGE_FILE_HEADER
         nt!_IMAGE_OPTIONAL_HEADER
         nt!_IMAGE_NT_HEADERS
         nt!_LARGE_INTEGER
```

You can also use the *dt* command to search for specific structures by using its wildcard lookup capability. For example, if you were looking for the structure name for an interrupt object, type **dt nt!_*interrupt***:

```
lkd> dt nt!_*interrupt*
         nt!_KINTERRUPT
         nt!_KINTERRUPT_MODE
         nt!_KINTERRUPT_POLARITY
         nt!_PCI_HOTPLUG_SLOT_INTERRUPT
```

Then, you can use *dt* to format a specific structure as shown below:

```
lkd> dt nt!_kinterrupt
nt!_KINTERRUPT
   +0x002 Size              : Int2B
   +0x004 InterruptListEntry : _LIST_ENTRY
   +0x00c ServiceRoutine    : Ptr32       unsigned char
   +0x010 MessageServiceRoutine : Ptr32       unsigned char
   +0x014 MessageIndex      : Uint4B
   +0x018 ServiceContext    : Ptr32 Void
   +0x01c SpinLock          : Uint4B
   +0x020 TickCount         : Uint4B
   +0x024 ActualLock        : Ptr32 Uint4B
   +0x028 DispatchAddress   : Ptr32       void
   +0x02c Vector            : Uint4B
   +0x030 Irql              : UChar
   +0x031 SynchronizeIrql   : UChar
   +0x032 FloatingSave      : UChar
```

```
+0x033 Connected          : UChar
+0x034 Number             : Char
+0x035 ShareVector        : UChar
+0x038 Mode               : _KINTERRUPT_MODE
+0x03c Polarity           : _KINTERRUPT_POLARITY
+0x040 ServiceCount       : Uint4B
+0x044 DispatchCount      : Uint4B
+0x048 Rsvd1              : Uint8B
+0x050 DispatchCode       : [135] Uint4B
```

Note that *dt* does not show substructures (structures within structures) by default. To recurse through substructures, use the *−r* switch. For example, using this switch to display the kernel interrupt object shows the format of the _LIST_ENTRY structure stored at the InterruptListEntry field:

```
lkd> dt nt!_kinterrupt -r
nt!_KINTERRUPT
   +0x000 Type              : Int2B
   +0x002 Size              : Int2B
   +0x004 InterruptListEntry : _LIST_ENTRY
      +0x000 Flink               : Ptr32 _LIST_ENTRY
         +0x000 Flink                : Ptr32 _LIST_ENTRY
         +0x004 Blink                : Ptr32 _LIST_ENTRY
      +0x004 Blink               : Ptr32 _LIST_ENTRY
         +0x000 Flink                : Ptr32 _LIST_ENTRY
         +0x004 Blink                : Ptr32 _LIST_ENTRY
```

The Debugging Tools for Windows help file also explains how to set up and use the kernel debuggers. Additional details on using the kernel debuggers that are aimed primarily at device driver writers can be found in the Windows Driver Kit documentation. There are also several useful Knowledge Base articles on the kernel debugger. Search for "debugref" in the Windows Knowledge Base (an online database of technical articles) on *support.microsoft.com*.

LiveKd Tool

LiveKd is a free tool from Sysinternals that allows you to use the standard Microsoft kernel debuggers just described to examine the running system without booting the system in debugging mode. This approach might be useful when kernel-level troubleshooting is required on a machine that wasn't booted in debugging mode—certain issues may be hard to reproduce reliably, so a reboot with the *debug* option enabled may not reexhibit the error.

You run LiveKd just as you would WinDbg or Kd. LiveKd passes any command-line options you specify to the debugger you select. By default, LiveKd runs the new command-line kernel debugger (Kd). To run WinDbg, specify the *−w* switch. To see the help files for LiveKd switches, specify the *−?* switch.

LiveKd presents a simulated crash dump file to the debugger, so you can perform any operations in LiveKd that are supported on a crash dump. Because LiveKd is relying on physical memory to back the simulated dump, the kernel debugger might run into situations in which data structures are in the middle of being changed by the system and are inconsistent. Each time the debugger is launched, it starts with a fresh view of the system state. If you want to refresh the snapshot, quit the debugger (with the *q* command), and LiveKd will ask you whether you want to start it again. If the debugger enters a loop in printing output, press Ctrl+C to interrupt the output, quit, and rerun it. If it hangs, press Ctrl+Break, which will terminate the debugger process and ask you whether you want to run the debugger again.

Windows Software Development Kit

The Windows Software Development Kit (SDK) is available as part of the MSDN subscription program or can be downloaded for free from *www.msdn.microsoft.com*. It contains the documentation, C header files, and libraries necessary to compile and link Windows applications. (Although Microsoft Visual C++ comes with a copy of these header files, the versions contained in the Windows SDK always match the latest version of the Windows operating systems, whereas the version that comes with Visual C++ might be an older version that was current when Visual C++ was released.) From an internals perspective, items of interest in the Windows SDK include the Windows API header files (\Program Files\Microsoft SDK\Include) as well as some utilities (such as Pstat.exe and Vadump.exe). A few of these tools are also shipped as sample source code in both the Windows SDK and the MSDN Library.

Windows Driver Kit

The Windows Driver Kit (WDK) is also available through the MSDN subscription program, and just like the Windows SDK, it is available for free download. The Windows Driver Kit documentation is included in the MSDN Library.

Although the WDK is aimed at device driver developers, it is an abundant source of Windows internals information. For example, while Chapter 7 describes the I/O system architecture, driver model, and basic device driver data structures, it does not describe the individual kernel support functions in detail. The WDK documentation contains a comprehensive description of all the Windows kernel support functions and mechanisms used by device drivers in both a tutorial and reference form.

Besides including the documentation, the WDK contains header files (in particular, ntddk.h, ntifs.h, and wdm.h) that define key internal data structures and constants as well as interfaces to many internal system routines. These files are useful when exploring Windows internal data structures with the kernel debugger because although the general layout and content of these structures are shown in this book, detailed field-level descriptions (such as size and data types) are not. A number of these data structures (such as object dispatcher

headers, wait blocks, events, mutants, semaphores, and so on) are, however, fully described in the WDK.

So if you want to dig into the I/O system and driver model beyond what is presented in this book, read the WDK documentation (especially the Kernel-Mode Driver Architecture Design Guide and Reference manuals). Another excellent source is *Programming the Microsoft Windows Driver Model, Second Edition* by Walter Oney (Microsoft Press, 2002).

Sysinternals Tools

Many experiments in this book use freeware tools that you can download from Sysinternals. Mark Russinovich, coauthor of this book, wrote most of these tools. The most popular tools include Process Explorer and Process Monitor. Note that many of these utilities involve the installation and execution of kernel-mode device drivers and thus require administrator privileges.

Conclusion

In this chapter, you've been introduced to the key Windows technical concepts and terms that will be used throughout the book. You've also had a glimpse of the many useful tools available for digging into Windows internals. Now we're ready to begin our exploration of the internal design of the system, beginning with an overall view of the system architecture and its key components.

Chapter 2
System Architecture

Now that we've covered the terms, concepts, and tools you need to be familiar with, we're ready to start our exploration of the internal design goals and structure of the Microsoft Windows operating system. This chapter explains the overall architecture of the system—the key components, how they interact with each other, and the context in which they run. To provide a framework for understanding the internals of Windows, let's first review the requirements and goals that shaped the original design and specification of the system.

Requirements and Design Goals

The following requirements drove the specification of Windows NT back in 1989:

- Provide a true 32-bit, preemptive, reentrant, virtual memory operating system

- Run on multiple hardware architectures and platforms

- Run and scale well on symmetric multiprocessing systems

- Be a great distributed computing platform, both as a network client and as a server

- Run most existing 16-bit MS-DOS and Microsoft Windows 3.1 applications

- Meet government requirements for POSIX 1003.1 compliance

- Meet government and industry requirements for operating system security

- Be easily adaptable to the global market by supporting Unicode

To guide the thousands of decisions that had to be made to create a system that met these requirements, the Windows NT design team adopted the following design goals at the beginning of the project:

- **Extensibility** The code must be written to comfortably grow and change as market requirements change.

- **Portability** The system must be able to run on multiple hardware architectures and must be able to move with relative ease to new ones as market demands dictate.

- **Reliability and robustness** The system should protect itself from both internal malfunction and external tampering. Applications should not be able to harm the operating system or other applications.

- **Compatibility** Although Windows NT should extend existing technology, its user interface and APIs should be compatible with older versions of Windows and with

MS-DOS. It should also interoperate well with other systems, such as UNIX, OS/2, and NetWare.

■ **Performance** Within the constraints of the other design goals, the system should be as fast and responsive as possible on each hardware platform.

As we explore the details of the internal structure and operation of Windows, you'll see how these original design goals and market requirements were woven successfully into the construction of the system. But before we start that exploration, let's examine the overall design model for Windows and compare it with other modern operating systems.

Operating System Model

In most multiuser operating systems, applications are separated from the operating system itself—the operating system kernel code runs in a privileged processor mode (referred to as *kernel mode* in this book), with access to system data and to the hardware; application code runs in a nonprivileged processor mode (called *user mode*), with a limited set of interfaces available, limited access to system data, and no direct access to hardware. When a user-mode program calls a system service, the processor traps the call and then switches the calling thread to kernel mode. When the system service completes, the operating system switches the thread context back to user mode and allows the caller to continue.

Windows is similar to most UNIX systems in that it's a monolithic operating system in the sense that the bulk of the operating system and device driver code shares the same kernel-mode protected memory space. This means that any operating system component or device driver can potentially corrupt data being used by other operating system components.

Is Windows a Microkernel-Based System?

Although some claim it as such, Windows isn't a microkernel-based operating system in the classic definition of microkernels, where the principal operating system components (such as the memory manager, process manager, and I/O manager) run as separate processes in their own private address spaces, layered on a primitive set of services the microkernel provides. For example, the Carnegie Mellon University Mach operating system, a contemporary example of a microkernel architecture, implements a minimal kernel that comprises thread scheduling, message passing, virtual memory, and device drivers. Everything else, including various APIs, file systems, and networking, runs in user mode. However, commercial implementations of the Mach microkernel operating system typically run at least all file system, networking, and memory management code in kernel mode. The reason is simple: the pure microkernel design is commercially impractical because it's too inefficient.

Does the fact that so much of Windows runs in kernel mode mean that it's more susceptible to crashes than a true microkernel operating system? Not at all. Consider the following scenario. Suppose the file system code of an operating system has a bug that causes it to crash from time to time. In a traditional operating system, a bug in kernel-mode code such as the memory manager or the file system would likely crash the entire operating system. In a pure microkernel operating system, such components run in user mode, so theoretically a bug would simply mean that the component's process exits. But in practical terms, the system would crash because recovering from the failure of such a critical process would likely be impossible.

All these operating system components are, of course, fully protected from errant applications because applications don't have direct access to the code and data of the privileged part of the operating system (although they can quickly call other kernel services). This protection is one of the reasons that Windows has the reputation for being both robust and stable as an application server and as a workstation platform yet fast and nimble from the perspective of core operating system services, such as virtual memory management, file I/O, networking, and file and print sharing.

The kernel-mode components of Windows also embody basic object-oriented design principles. For example, they don't in general reach into one another's data structures to access information maintained by individual components. Instead, they use formal interfaces to pass parameters and access and/or modify data structures.

Despite its pervasive use of objects to represent shared system resources, Windows is not an object-oriented system in the strict sense. Most of the operating system code is written in C for portability and because C development tools are widely available. C doesn't directly support object-oriented constructs such as dynamic binding of data types, polymorphic functions, or class inheritance. Therefore, the C-based implementation of objects in Windows borrows from, but doesn't depend on, features of particular object-oriented languages.

Architecture Overview

With this brief overview of the design goals and packaging of Windows, let's take a look at the key system components that make up its architecture. A simplified version of this architecture is shown in Figure 2-1. Keep in mind that this diagram is basic—it doesn't show everything. (For example, the networking components and the various types of device driver layering are not shown.)

FIGURE 2-1 Simplified Windows architecture

In Figure 2-1, first notice the line dividing the user-mode and kernel-mode parts of the Windows operating system. The boxes above the line represent user-mode processes, and the components below the line are kernel-mode operating system services. As mentioned in Chapter 1, user-mode threads execute in a protected process address space (although while they are executing in kernel mode, they have access to system space). Thus, system support processes, service processes, user applications, and environment subsystems each have their own private process address space.

The four basic types of user-mode processes are described as follows:

- Fixed (or hardwired) *system support processes*, such as the logon process and the Session Manager, that are not Windows services. (That is, they are not started by the service control manager. Chapter 4 describes services in detail.)

- *Service processes* that host Windows services, such as the Task Scheduler and Print Spooler services. Services generally have the requirement that they run independently of user logons. Many Windows server applications, such as Microsoft SQL Server and Microsoft Exchange Server, also include components that run as services.

- *User applications*, which can be one of five types: Windows 32-bit, Windows 64-bit, Windows 3.1 16-bit, MS-DOS 16-bit, or POSIX 32-bit.

- *Environment subsystem server processes*, which implement part of the support for the operating system *environment*, or personality presented to the user and programmer. Windows NT originally shipped with three environment subsystems: Windows, POSIX, and OS/2. However, OS/2 last shipped with Windows 2000. Windows Vista Ultimate and Enterprise include support for an enhanced POSIX subsystem called Subsystem for Unix-based Applications (SUA).

In Figure 2-1, notice the "Subsystem DLLs" box below the "Service processes" and "User applications" boxes. Under Windows, user applications don't call the native Windows

operating system services directly; rather, they go through one or more *subsystem dynamic-link libraries* (DLLs). The role of the subsystem DLLs is to translate a documented function into the appropriate internal (and generally undocumented) native system service calls. This translation might or might not involve sending a message to the environment subsystem process that is serving the user application.

The kernel-mode components of Windows include the following:

- The Windows *executive* contains the base operating system services, such as memory management, process and thread management, security, I/O, networking, and inter-process communication.

- The Windows *kernel* consists of low-level operating system functions, such as thread scheduling, interrupt and exception dispatching, and multiprocessor synchronization. It also provides a set of routines and basic objects that the rest of the executive uses to implement higher-level constructs.

- *Device drivers* include both hardware device drivers, which translate user I/O function calls into specific hardware device I/O requests, as well as file system and network drivers.

- The *hardware abstraction layer* (HAL) is a layer of code that isolates the kernel, device drivers, and the rest of the Windows executive from platform-specific hardware differences (such as differences between motherboards).

- The *windowing and graphics system* implements the graphical user interface (GUI) functions (better known as the Windows USER and GDI functions), such as dealing with windows, user interface controls, and drawing.

Table 2-1 lists the file names of the core Windows operating system components. (You'll need to know these file names because we'll be referring to some system files by name.) Each of these components is covered in greater detail both later in this chapter and in the chapters that follow.

TABLE 2-1 Core Windows System Files

File Name	Components
Ntoskrnl.exe	Executive and kernel
Ntkrnlpa.exe (32-bit systems only)	Executive and kernel with support for Physical Address Extension (PAE), which allows addressing of up to 64 GB of physical memory
Hal.dll	Hardware abstraction layer
Win32k.sys	Kernel-mode part of the Windows subsystem
Ntdll.dll	Internal support functions and system service dispatch stubs to executive functions
Kernel32.dll, Advapi32.dll, User32.dll, Gdi32.dll	Core Windows subsystem DLLs

Before we dig into the details of these system components, though, let's examine how Windows achieves portability across multiple hardware architectures.

Portability

Windows was designed to run on a variety of hardware architectures, including Intel-based CISC systems as well as RISC systems. The initial release of Windows NT supported the x86 and MIPS architectures. Support for the Digital Equipment Corporation (which was bought by Compaq, which later merged with Hewlett-Packard) Alpha AXP was added shortly thereafter. (Although Alpha AXP was a 64-bit processor, Windows NT ran in 32-bit mode. During the development of Windows 2000, a native 64-bit version was running on Alpha AXP, but this never was released.) Support for a fourth processor architecture, the Motorola PowerPC, was added in Windows NT 3.51. Because of changing market demands, however, support for the MIPS and PowerPC architectures was dropped before development began on Windows 2000. Later, Compaq withdrew support for the Alpha AXP architecture, resulting in Windows 2000 being supported only on the x86 architecture. Windows XP and Windows Server 2003 added support for three 64-bit processor families: the Intel Itanium IA-64 family, the AMD64 family, and the Intel 64-bit Extension Technology (EM64T) for x86 (which is compatible with the AMD64 architecture, although there are slight differences in instructions supported). The latter two processor families are called *64-bit extended systems* and in this book are referred to as *x64*. (How Windows runs 32-bit applications on 64-bit Windows is explained in Chapter 3.)

Windows achieves portability across hardware architectures and platforms in two primary ways:

- Windows has a layered design, with low-level portions of the system that are processor-architecture-specific or platform-specific isolated into separate modules so that upper layers of the system can be shielded from the differences between architectures and among hardware platforms. The two key components that provide operating system portability are the kernel (contained in Ntoskrnl.exe) and the hardware abstraction layer (or HAL, contained in Hal.dll). Both these components are described in more detail later in this chapter. Functions that are architecture-specific (such as thread context switching and trap dispatching) are implemented in the kernel. Functions that can differ among systems within the same architecture (for example, different motherboards) are implemented in the HAL. The only other component with a significant amount of architecture-specific code is the memory manager, but even that is a small amount compared to the system as a whole.

- The vast majority of Windows is written in C, with some portions in C++. Assembly language is used only for those parts of the operating system that need to communicate directly with system hardware (such as the interrupt trap handler) or that are extremely performance-sensitive (such as context switching). Assembly language code exists not only in the kernel and the HAL but also in a few other places within the core operating system (such as the routines that implement interlocked instructions as well as one

module in the local procedure call facility), in the kernel-mode part of the Windows subsystem, and even in some user-mode libraries, such as the process startup code in Ntdll.dll (a system library explained later in this chapter).

Symmetric Multiprocessing

Multitasking is the operating system technique for sharing a single processor among multiple threads of execution. When a computer has more than one processor, however, it can execute multiple threads simultaneously. Thus, whereas a multitasking operating system only appears to execute multiple threads at the same time, a multiprocessing operating system actually does it, executing one thread on each of its processors.

As mentioned at the beginning of this chapter, one of the key design goals for Windows was that it had to run well on multiprocessor computer systems. Windows is a *symmetric multiprocessing* (SMP) operating system. There is no master processor—the operating system as well as user threads can be scheduled to run on any processor. Also, all the processors share just one memory space. This model contrasts with *asymmetric multiprocessing* (ASMP), in which the operating system typically selects one processor to execute operating system kernel code while other processors run only user code. The differences in the two multiprocessing models are illustrated in Figure 2-2.

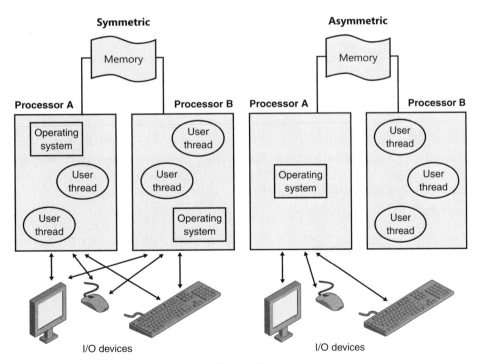

FIGURE 2-2 Symmetric vs. asymmetric multiprocessing

Windows Vista and Windows Server 2008 also support two modern types of multiprocessor systems: hyperthreading and NUMA (non-uniform memory architecture). These are briefly mentioned in the following paragraphs. (For a complete, detailed description of the scheduling support for these systems, see the thread scheduling section in Chapter 5.)

Naturally, Windows also natively supports multicore systems—because these systems have real physical cores (simply on the same package), the original SMP code in Windows treats them as discrete processors, except for certain accounting and identification tasks (such as licensing, described shortly) that distinguish between cores on the same processor and cores on different sockets.

Hyperthreading is a technology introduced by Intel that provides many logical processors on one physical processor. Each logical processor has its CPU state, but the execution engine and onboard cache are shared. This permits one logical CPU to make progress while the other logical CPUs are busy (such as performing interrupt processing work, which prevents threads from running on that logical processor). The scheduling algorithms are enhanced to make optimal use of multiprocessor hyperthreaded machines, such as by scheduling threads on an idle physical processor versus choosing an idle logical processor on a physical processor whose other logical processors are busy.

In NUMA systems, processors are grouped in smaller units called *nodes*. Each node has its own processors and memory and is connected to the larger system through a cache-coherent interconnect bus. Windows on a NUMA system still runs as an SMP system, in that all processors have access to all memory—it's just that node-local memory is faster to reference than memory attached to other nodes. The system attempts to improve performance by scheduling threads on processors that are in the same node as the memory being used. It attempts to satisfy memory-allocation requests from within the node, but will allocate memory from other nodes if necessary.

Although Windows was originally designed to support up to 32 processors, nothing inherent in the multiprocessor design limits the number of processors to 32—that number is simply an obvious and convenient limit because 32 processors can easily be represented as a bit mask using a native 32-bit data type. In fact, the 64-bit versions of Windows support up to 64 processors, because the native size of a word on a 64-bit machine is 64 bits.

The actual number of supported processors depends on the edition of Windows being used. (See Table 2-3.) This number is stored in the system license policy file (\Windows\ServiceProfiles\NetworkService\AppData\Roaming\Microsoft\SoftwareLicensing\tokens.dat) as a policy value called "Kernel-MaximumProcessors." (Keep in mind that tampering with that data is a violation of the software license and modifying licensing policies to allow the use of more processors involves more than just changing this value.)

As of Windows Vista and Windows Server 2008, there is a unified kernel regardless of whether the system is a uniprocessor or multiprocessor machine. This change, compared to earlier versions of Windows, which had separate kernels for each machine type, was made both because the majority of systems currently sold include at least two cores and because the few uniprocessor-only optimizations result in negligible performance improvement. However, 32-bit versions of Windows still come in two flavors of the kernel, depending on whether PAE is enabled and supported. Because no-execute memory support (known as NX on AMD processors and XD on Intel processors) in today's processors makes use of PAE structures, most 32-bit systems use the PAE kernel. On 64-bit Windows systems there is no PAE kernel (there isn't a need for it), so there is only a single kernel image.

At installation time, the appropriate files are selected and copied to the local %SystemRoot% directory. Table 2-2 shows the correspondence of installed file names to their original names on the installation media.

TABLE 2-2 Internal System File Names

Type of File	Name of PAE Version on Distribution Media	Name of Non-PAE Version on Distribution Media
Kernel	Ntkrpamp.exe	Ntkrnlmp.exe
HAL	Depends on system type (See the list of HALs in Table 2-5.)	Depends on system type (See the list of HALs in Table 2-5.)

The rest of the system files that make up Windows (including all utilities, libraries, and device drivers) have the same version on all types of systems (that is, they handle multiprocessor synchronization and PAE issues correctly). You should use this approach on any software you build, whether it is a Windows application or a device driver—keep multiprocessor synchronization issues in mind when you design your software, and test the software on both uniprocessor and multiprocessor systems. For legacy applications, Windows implements a number of flags to provide backward compatibility. For example, applications need to be specifically made "large address aware" for PAE support, and they can also set a "uniprocessor only" field in their image if they break on SMP systems.

EXPERIMENT: Checking Which Ntoskrnl Version You're Running

Windows has no utility to show which version of Ntoskrnl you are running. However, an Event Log entry is written each time the system boots that does record the type of kernel image that loaded (multiprocessor and free vs. checked), as shown in the following screen shot. (From the Start menu, select Programs/Administrative Tools/Event Viewer, select Windows Logs/System, and then double-click an Event Log entry with an Event ID of 6009, indicating the entry was written at the system start.)

This Event Log entry doesn't indicate whether you booted the PAE version of the kernel image that supports more than 4 GB of physical memory (Ntkrnlpa.exe). However, you can tell if you booted the PAE kernel by looking at the registry value HKLM\SYSTEM\CurrentControlSet\Control\Session Manager\Memory Management\ PhysicalAddressExtension. You can also determine which version of the kernel you're running by using WinDbg and opening a local kernel debugging session. Be sure you have the symbols loaded (enter the .reload command), and then type the "list module" command to list details for the kernel image (nt): **lm mv nt**. The output below shows a PAE multiprocessor kernel, as you can tell by the name.

```
lkd> lm vm nt
start    end       module name
82000000 823a1000  nt          (pdb symbols)
    c:\programming\symbols\ntkrpamp.pdb\7018E534B06E4A5BB6C63F6F2AA802072\ntkrpamp.pdb
    Loaded symbol image file: ntkrpamp.exe
    Image path: ntkrpamp.exe
    Image name: ntkrpamp.exe
    Timestamp:        Tue Oct 09 21:46:20 2007 (470C2EEC)
    CheckSum:         00366023
    ImageSize:        003A1000
    File version:     6.0.6000.20697
    Product version:  6.0.6000.20697
    File flags:       0 (Mask 3F)
    File OS:          40004 NT Win32
    File type:        1.0 App
    File date:        00000000.00000000
    Translations:     0409.04b0
    CompanyName:      Microsoft Corporation
```

```
ProductName:      Microsoft® Windows® Operating System
InternalName:     ntkrpamp.exe
OriginalFilename: ntkrpamp.exe
ProductVersion:   6.0.6000.20697
FileVersion:      6.0.6000.20697 (vista_ldr.071009-1543)
FileDescription:  NT Kernel & System
LegalCopyright:   © Microsoft Corporation. All rights reserved.
```

Scalability

One of the key issues with multiprocessor systems is *scalability*. To run correctly on an SMP system, operating system code must adhere to strict guidelines and rules. Resource contention and other performance issues are more complicated in multiprocessing systems than in uniprocessor systems and must be accounted for in the system's design. Windows incorporates several features that are crucial to its success as a multiprocessor operating system:

- The ability to run operating system code on any available processor and on multiple processors at the same time

- Multiple threads of execution within a single process, each of which can execute simultaneously on different processors

- Fine-grained synchronization within the kernel (such as spinlocks, queued spinlocks, and pushlocks, described in Chapter 3) as well as within device drivers and server processes, which allows more components to run concurrently on multiple processors

- Programming mechanisms such as I/O completion ports (described in Chapter 7) that facilitate the efficient implementation of multithreaded server processes that can scale well on multiprocessor systems

The scalability of the Windows kernel has evolved over time. For example, Windows Server 2003 has per-CPU scheduling queues, which permit thread scheduling decisions to occur in parallel on multiple processors. Multiprocessor thread scheduling details are covered in Chapter 5. Further details on multiprocessor synchronization can be found in Chapter 3.

Differences Between Client and Server Versions

Windows ships in both client and server retail packages. There are six client versions of Windows Vista: Windows Vista Home Basic, Windows Vista Home Premium, Windows Vista Business, Windows Vista Ultimate, Windows Vista Enterprise, and Windows Vista Starter.

There are five main variants of Windows Server 2008: Windows Web Server 2008, Windows Server 2008 Standard, Windows Server 2008 Enterprise, Windows Server 2008 Datacenter, and Windows Server 2008 for Itanium-Based Systems.

Additionally, there are "N" versions of the client that do not include Windows Media Player. Finally, the Standard, Enterprise, and Datacenter editions of Windows Server 2008 also include "without Hyper-V" editions, which do not include Hyper-V. (Hyper-V virtualization is discussed in Chapter 3).

These versions differ by:

- The number of processors supported (in terms of physical packages, not cores)

- The amount of physical memory supported

- The number of concurrent network connections supported (For example, a maximum of 10 concurrent connections are allowed to the file and print services in the client version.)

- Support for Tablet PC and/or Media Center Edition

- Support for features such as BitLocker, DVD burning, Windows Fax and Scan, Backup, and more than 100 other configurable licensing policy values

- Layered services that come with Windows Server editions that don't come with the client editions (for example, directory services and clustering)

Table 2-3 lists the differences in memory and processor support for Windows Vista and Windows Server 2008. For a detailed comparison chart of the different editions of Windows Server 2008, see *www.microsoft.com/windowsserver2008/en/us/compare-specs.aspx*.

TABLE 2-3 Differences Between Windows Vista and Windows Server 2008

	Number of Processors Supported (32-Bit Edition)	Physical Memory Supported (32-Bit Edition)	Number of Processors Supported (64-Bit Edition)	Physical Memory Supported (Itanium Editions)	Physical Memory Supported (x64 Editions)
Windows Vista Starter Edition	1	4 GB	Not available	Not available	Not available
Windows Vista Home Basic Edition	1	4 GB	1	Not available	8 GB
Windows Vista Home Premium	1	4 GB	1	Not available	16 GB
Windows Vista Business	2	4 GB	2	Not available	128 GB
Windows Vista Enterprise	2	4 GB	2	Not available	128 GB
Windows Vista Ultimate	2	4 GB	2	Not available	128 GB
Windows Web Server 2008	2	4 GB	2	Not available	32 GB

	Number of Processors Supported (32-Bit Edition)	Physical Memory Supported (32-Bit Edition)	Number of Processors Supported (64-Bit Edition)	Physical Memory Supported (Itanium Editions)	Physical Memory Supported (x64 Editions)
Windows Server 2008 Standard Edition	4	4 GB	4	Not available	32 GB
Windows Server 2008 Enterprise Edition	8	32 GB	8	Not available	2048 GB
Windows Server 2008 Datacenter Edition	32	64 GB	64	2048 GB	2048 GB
Windows Server 2008 for Itanium-Based Systems	Not available	Not available	64	2048 GB	Not available

Although there are several client and server retail packages of the Windows operating system, they share a common set of core system files, including the kernel image, Ntoskrnl.exe (and the PAE version, Ntkrnlpa.exe); the HAL libraries; the device drivers; and the base system utilities and DLLs. Starting with Windows Vista SP1, these files are identical for all editions of Windows.

> **Note** Because Windows Vista shipped about a year before Windows Server 2008, there was a short period during which the two operating systems had different kernels (development on Windows Server 2008 was continuing on an updated version of the Vista kernel). As Windows Vista SP1 was being developed, the kernels for the two editions were synced up, and both Windows Vista SP1 and Windows Server 2008 launched together, unifying the kernels for the first time since Windows 2000.

With so many different versions of Windows, but with each having the same kernel image, how does the system know which edition is booted? By querying the registry values ProductType and ProductSuite under the HKLM\SYSTEM\CurrentControlSet\Control\ProductOptions key. ProductType is used to distinguish whether the system is a client system or a server system (of any flavor). The valid values are listed in Table 2-4. The result is stored in the system global variable *MmProductType*, which can be queried from a device driver using the kernel-mode support function *MmIsThisAnNtAsSystem*, documented in the Windows Driver Kit (WDK). These values are loaded into the registry based on the licensing policy file described earlier.

TABLE 2-4 ProductType Registry Values

Edition of Windows	Value of ProductType
Windows Vista	WinNT
Windows Server 2008 (domain controller)	LanmanNT
Windows Server 2008 (server only)	ServerNT

A different registry value, ProductPolicy, contains a cached copy of the data inside the tokens.dat file, which differentiates between the editions of Windows and the features that they enable.

If user programs need to determine which edition of Windows is running, they can call the Windows *VerifyVersionInfo* function, documented in the Windows Software Development Kit (SDK). Device drivers can call the kernel-mode function *RtlGetVersion*, documented in the WDK.

So if the core files are essentially the same for the client and server versions, how do the systems differ in operation? In short, server systems are by default optimized for system throughput as high-performance application servers, whereas the client version, although it has server capabilities, is optimized for response time for interactive desktop use. For example, based on the product type, several resource allocation decisions are made differently at system boot time, such as the size and number of operating system heaps (or pools), the number of internal system worker threads, and the size of the system data cache. Also, run-time policy decisions, such as the way the memory manager trades off system and process memory demands, differ between the server and client editions. Even some thread scheduling details have different default behavior in the two families (the default length of the time slice, or thread *quantum*—see Chapter 5 for details). Where there are significant operational differences in the two products, these are highlighted in the pertinent chapters throughout the rest of this book. Unless otherwise noted, everything in this book applies to both the client and server versions.

EXPERIMENT: Determining Features Enabled by Licensing Policy

As mentioned earlier, Windows supports more than 100 different features that can be enabled through the software licensing mechanism. These policy settings determine the various differences not only between a client Windows installation (such as Windows Vista) and a server installation (such as Windows Server 2008) but also between each edition (or SKU) of the operating system, such as enabling BitLocker support on Ultimate and Enterprise editions of Vista. You can use the SlPolicy tool available from Winsider Seminars & Solutions (*www.winsiderss.com/tools/slpolicy.htm*) to display these policy values on your machine.

Policy settings are organized by a *facility*, which represents the owner module for which the policy applies. You can display a list of all facilities on your system by running Slpolicy.exe with the –f switch:

```
SlPolicy v1.01 - Show Software Licensing Policies
Copyright (C) 2008 Alex Ionescu
www.alex-ionescu.com

Software Licensing Facilities:

Kernel
Licensing and Activation
Core
```

You can then add the name of any facility after the switch to display the policy value for that facility. For example, to look at the limitations on CPUs and available memory, use the Kernel facility. Here's the expected output on a machine running Windows Vista Ultimate:

```
C:\>SlPolicy.exe -f Kernel

Slpolicy v1.01 - Show Software Licensing Policies
Copyright (C) 2008 Alex Ionescu
www.alex-ionescu.com

Kernel
------
Processor Limit: 2
Maximum Memory Allowed (x86): 4096 MB
Maximum Memory Allowed (x64): 131072 MB
Maximum Memory Allowed (IA64): 131072 MB
Maximum Physical Page: 4096
```

Checked Build

There is a special debug version of Windows called the *checked build* (available only with an MSDN Professional or higher subscription). It is a recompilation of the Windows source code with a compile-time flag defined called "DBG" (to cause compile time conditional debugging and tracing code to be included). Also, to make it easier to understand the machine code, the post-processing of the Windows binaries to optimize code layout for faster execution is not performed. (See the section "Performance-Optimized Code" in the Debugging Tools for Windows help file.)

The checked build is provided primarily to aid device driver developers because it performs more stringent error checking on kernel-mode functions called by device drivers or other system code. For example, if a driver (or some other piece of kernel-mode code) makes an invalid call to a system function that is checking parameters (such as acquiring a spinlock

at the wrong interrupt level), the system will stop execution when the problem is detected rather than allow some data structure to be corrupted and the system to possibly crash at a later time.

EXPERIMENT: Determining If You Are Running the Checked Build

There is no built-in tool to display whether you are running the checked build or the retail build (called the *free build*). However, this information is available through the "Debug" property of the Windows Management Instrumentation (WMI) Win32_ OperatingSystem class. The following sample Visual Basic script displays this property:

```
strComputer = "."
Set objWMIService = GetObject("winmgmts:" _
 & "{impersonationLevel=impersonate}!\\" & strComputer & "\root\cimv2")
Set colOperatingSystems = objWMIService.ExecQuery _
 ("SELECT * FROM Win32_OperatingSystem")
For Each objOperatingSystem in colOperatingSystems
 Wscript.Echo "Caption: " & objOperatingSystem.Caption
 Wscript.Echo "Debug: " & objOperatingSystem.Debug
 Wscript.Echo "Version: " & objOperatingSystem.Version
Next
```

To try this, type in the preceding script and save it as file. The following is the output from running the script:

```
C:\>cscript osversion.vbs
Microsoft (R) Windows Script Host Version 5.7
Copyright (C) Microsoft Corporation. All rights reserved.

Caption: Microsoft Windows Vista
Debug: False
Version: 6.0.6000
```

This system is not running the checked build, as the Debug flag shown here says False.

Much of the additional code in the checked-build binaries is a result of using the ASSERT macro, which is defined in the WDK header file Ntddk.h and documented in the WDK documentation. This macro tests a condition (such as the validity of a data structure or parameter), and if the expression evaluates to FALSE, the macro calls the kernel-mode function *RtlAssert*, which calls *DbgPrintEx* to send the text of the debug message to a debug message buffer. If a kernel debugger is attached, this message is displayed automatically followed by a prompt asking the user what to do about the assertion failure (breakpoint, ignore, terminate process, or terminate thread). If the system wasn't booted with the kernel debugger (using the *debug* option in the Boot Configuration Database—BCD) and no kernel debugger is currently attached, failure of an ASSERT test will bugcheck the system. For a list of ASSERT checks made by some of the kernel support routines, see the section "Checked Build ASSERTs" in the WDK documentation.

The checked build is also useful for system administrators because of the additional detailed informational tracing that can be enabled for certain components. (For detailed instructions, see the Microsoft Knowledge Base Article number 314743, titled *HOWTO: Enable Verbose Debug Tracing in Various Drivers and Subsystems*.) This information output is sent to an internal debug message buffer using the *DbgPrintEx* function referred to earlier. To view the debug messages, you can either attach a kernel debugger to the target system (which requires booting the target system in debugging mode), use the *!dbgprint* command while performing local kernel debugging, or use the Dbgview.exe tool from Windows Sysinternals (*www.microsoft.com/technet/sysinternals*).

You don't have to install the entire checked build to take advantage of the debug version of the operating system. You can just copy the checked version of the kernel image (Ntoskrnl.exe) and the appropriate HAL (Hal.dll) to a normal retail installation. The advantage of this approach is that device drivers and other kernel code get the rigorous checking of the checked build without having to run the slower debug versions of all components in the system. For detailed instructions on how to do this, see the section "Installing Just the Checked Operating System and HAL" in the WDK documentation.

Finally, the checked build can also be useful for testing user-mode code only because the timing of the system is different. (This is because of the additional checking taking place within the kernel and the fact that the components are compiled without optimizations.) Often, multithreaded synchronization bugs are related to specific timing conditions. By running your tests on a system running the checked build (or at least the checked kernel and HAL), the fact that the timing of the whole system is different might cause latent timing bugs to surface that do not occur on a normal retail system.

Key System Components

Now that we've looked at the high-level architecture of Windows, let's delve deeper into the internal structure and the role each key operating system component plays. Figure 2-3 is a more detailed and complete diagram of the core Windows system architecture and components than was shown earlier in the chapter (in Figure 2-1). Note that it still does not show all components (networking in particular, which is explained in Chapter 12).

The following sections elaborate on each major element of this diagram. Chapter 3 explains the primary control mechanisms the system uses (such as the object manager, interrupts, and so forth). Chapter 13 describes the process of starting and shutting down Windows, and Chapter 4 details management mechanisms such as the registry, service processes, and Windows Management Instrumentation. Then the remaining chapters explore in even more detail the internal structure and operation of key areas such as processes and threads, memory management, security, the I/O manager, storage management, the cache manager, the Windows file system (NTFS), and networking.

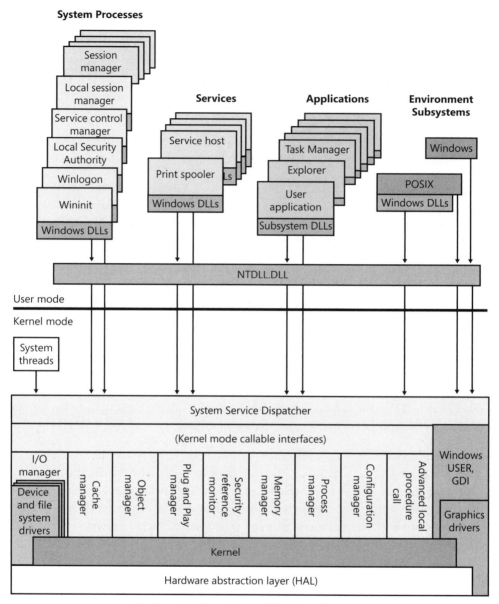

FIGURE 2-3 Windows architecture

Environment Subsystems and Subsystem DLLs

Although the basic POSIX subsystem that originally shipped with Windows no longer ships with the system, a greatly enhanced version is available on Windows Vista Ultimate and

Enterprise editions, called Subsystem for Unix-based Applications (SUA [POSIX]), shown in Figure 2-3.

As we'll explain shortly, the Windows subsystem is special in that Windows can't run without it. (It owns the keyboard, mouse, and display, and it is required to be present even on server systems with no interactive users logged in.) In fact, the other two subsystems are configured to start on demand, whereas the Windows subsystem must always be running.

The subsystem startup information is stored under the registry key HKLM\SYSTEM\ CurrentControlSet\Control\Session Manager\SubSystems. Figure 2-4 shows the values under this key.

FIGURE 2-4 Registry Editor showing Windows startup information

The Required value lists the subsystems that load when the system boots. The value has two strings: Windows and Debug. The Windows value contains the file specification of the Windows subsystem, Csrss.exe, which stands for Client/Server Run-Time Subsystem. (See the Note later in this section.) Debug is blank (because it's used for internal testing) and there-fore does nothing. The Optional value indicates that the POSIX subsystem will be started on demand. The registry value Kmode contains the file name of the kernel-mode portion of the Windows subsystem, Win32k.sys (explained later in this chapter).

The role of an environment subsystem is to expose some subset of the base Windows execu-tive system services to application programs. Each subsystem can provide access to different subsets of the native services in Windows. That means that some things can be done from an application built on one subsystem that can't be done by an application built on another sub-system. For example, a Windows application can't use the POSIX *fork* function.

Each executable image (.exe) is bound to one and only one subsystem. When an image is run, the process creation code examines the subsystem type code in the image header so that it can notify the proper subsystem of the new process. This type code is specified with the /SUBSYSTEM qualifier of the *link* command in Microsoft Visual C++.

Note As a historical note, the reason the Windows subsystem process is called Csrss.exe is that in the original design of Windows NT, all the subsystems were going to execute as threads inside a single systemwide environment subsystem process. When the POSIX and OS/2 subsystems were removed and put in their own processes, the file name for the Windows subsystem process wasn't changed.

As mentioned earlier, user applications don't call Windows system services directly. Instead, they go through one or more subsystem DLLs. These libraries export the documented interface that the programs linked to that subsystem can call. For example, the Windows subsystem DLLs (such as Kernel32.dll, Advapi32.dll, User32.dll, and Gdi32.dll) implement the Windows API functions. The POSIX subsystem DLL (Psxdll.dll) implements the POSIX API functions.

EXPERIMENT: Viewing the Image Subsystem Type

You can see the image subsystem type by using the Dependency Walker tool (Depends.exe) in the Windows SDK. For example, notice the image types for two different Windows images, Notepad.exe (the simple text editor) and Cmd.exe (the Windows command prompt):

This shows that Notepad is a GUI program, while Cmd is a console, or character-based, program. And although this implies there are two different subsystems for GUI and character-based programs, there is just one Windows subsystem, and GUI programs can have consoles, just like console programs can display GUIs.

When an application calls a function in a subsystem DLL, one of three things can occur:

- The function is entirely implemented in user mode inside the subsystem DLL. In other words, no message is sent to the environment subsystem process, and no Windows executive system services are called. The function is performed in user mode, and the results are returned to the caller. Examples of such functions include *GetCurrentProcess* (which always returns –1, a value that is defined to refer to the current process in all process-related functions) and *GetCurrentProcessId*. (The process ID doesn't change for a running process, so this ID is retrieved from a cached location, thus avoiding the need to call into the kernel.)

- The function requires one or more calls to the Windows executive. For example, the Windows *ReadFile* and *WriteFile* functions involve calling the underlying internal (and undocumented) Windows I/O system services *NtReadFile* and *NtWriteFile*, respectively.

- The function requires some work to be done in the environment subsystem process. (The environment subsystem processes, running in user mode, are responsible for maintaining the state of the client applications running under their control.) In this case, a client/server request is made to the environment subsystem via a message sent to the subsystem to perform some operation. The subsystem DLL then waits for a reply before returning to the caller.

Some functions can be a combination of the second and third items just listed, such as the Windows *CreateProcess* and *CreateThread* functions.

Although Windows was designed to support multiple, independent environment subsystems, from a practical perspective, having each subsystem implement all the code to handle windowing and display I/O would result in a large amount of duplication of system functions that, ultimately, would have negatively affected both system size and performance. Because Windows was the primary subsystem, the Windows designers decided to locate these basic functions there and have the other subsystems call on the Windows subsystem to perform display I/O. Thus, the POSIX subsystem calls services in the Windows subsystem to perform display I/O. (In fact, if you examine the subsystem type for these images, you'll see that they are Windows executables.)

Let's take a closer look at each of the environment subsystems.

Windows Subsystem

The Windows subsystem consists of the following major components:

- The environment subsystem process (Csrss.exe) loads three DLLs (Basesrv.dll, Winsrv.dll, and Csrsrv.dll) that contain support for:

 - ❏ Console (text) windows

 - ❏ Creating and deleting processes and threads

 - ❏ Portions of the support for 16-bit virtual DOS machine (VDM) processes

 - ❏ Side-by-Side (SxS)/Fusion and manifest support

 - ❏ Other miscellaneous functions, such as *GetTempFile*, *DefineDosDevice*, *ExitWindowsEx*, and several natural language support functions

- The kernel-mode device driver (Win32k.sys) contains:

 - ❏ The window manager, which controls window displays; manages screen output; collects input from keyboard, mouse, and other devices; and passes user messages to applications.

 - ❏ The Graphics Device Interface (GDI), which is a library of functions for graphics output devices. It includes functions for line, text, and figure drawing and for graphics manipulation.

 - ❏ Wrappers for DirectX support that is implemented in another kernel driver (Dxgkrnl.sys).

- Subsystem DLLs (such as Kernel32.dll, Advapi32.dll, User32.dll, and Gdi32.dll) translate documented Windows API functions into the appropriate and mostly undocumented kernel-mode system service calls to Ntoskrnl.exe and Win32k.sys.

- Graphics device drivers are hardware-dependent graphics display drivers, printer drivers, and video miniport drivers.

Applications call the standard USER functions to create user interface controls, such as windows and buttons, on the display. The window manager communicates these requests to the GDI, which passes them to the graphics device drivers, where they are formatted for the display device. A display driver is paired with a video miniport driver to complete video display support.

The GDI provides a set of standard two-dimensional functions that let applications communicate with graphics devices without knowing anything about the devices. GDI functions mediate between applications and graphics devices such as display drivers and printer drivers. The GDI interprets application requests for graphic output and sends the requests to graphics display drivers. It also provides a standard interface for applications to use varying graphics output devices. This interface enables application code to be independent of the hardware

devices and their drivers. The GDI tailors its messages to the capabilities of the device, often dividing the request into manageable parts. For example, some devices can understand directions to draw an ellipse; others require the GDI to interpret the command as a series of pixels placed at certain coordinates. For more information about the graphics and video driver architecture, see the "Design Guide" section of the "Display (Adapters and Monitors)" chapter in the Windows Driver Kit.

Prior to Windows NT 4, the window manager and graphics services were part of the user-mode Windows subsystem process. In Windows NT 4, the bulk of the windowing and graphics code was moved from running in the context of the Windows subsystem process to a set of callable services running in kernel mode (in the file Win32k.sys). The primary reason for this shift was to improve overall system performance. Having a separate server process that contains the Windows graphics subsystem required multiple thread and process context switches, which consumed considerable CPU cycles and memory resources even though the original design was highly optimized.

For example, for each thread on the client side there was a dedicated, paired server thread in the Windows subsystem process waiting on the client thread for requests. A special inter-process communication facility called *fast LPC* was used to send messages between these threads. Unlike normal thread context switches, transitions between paired threads via fast LPC don't cause a rescheduling event in the kernel, thereby enabling the server thread to run for the remaining time slice of the client thread before having to take its turn in the kernel's preemptive thread scheduler. Moreover, shared memory buffers were used to allow fast passing of large data structures, such as bitmaps, and clients had direct but read-only access to key server data structures to minimize the need for thread/process transitions between clients and the Windows server. Also, GDI operations were (and still are) batched. *Batching* means that a series of graphics calls by a Windows application aren't "pushed" over to the server and drawn on the output device until a GDI batching queue is filled. You can set the size of the queue by using the Windows *GdiSetBatchLimit* function, and you can flush the queue at any time with *GdiFlush*. Conversely, read-only properties and data structures of GDI, once they were obtained from the Windows subsystem process, were cached on the client side for fast subsequent access.

Despite these optimizations, however, the overall system performance was still not adequate for graphics-intensive applications. The obvious solution was to eliminate the need for the additional threads and resulting context switches by moving the windowing and graphics system into kernel mode. Also, once applications have called into the window manager and the GDI, those subsystems can access other Windows executive components directly without the cost of user-mode or kernel-mode transitions. This direct access is especially important in the case of the GDI calling through video drivers, a process that involves interaction with video hardware at high frequencies and high bandwidths.

So, what remains in the user-mode process part of the Windows subsystem? All the drawing and updating for console or text windows are handled by it because console applications have no notion of repainting a window. It's easy to see this activity—simply open a command prompt and drag another window over it, and you'll see the Windows subsystem consuming CPU time as it repaints the console window. But other than console window support, only a few Windows functions result in sending a message to the Windows subsystem process anymore: process and thread creation and termination, network drive letter mapping, and creation of temporary files. In general, a running Windows application won't be causing many, if any, context switches to the Windows subsystem process.

POSIX Subsystem

POSIX, an acronym loosely defined as "a portable operating system interface based on UNIX," refers to a collection of international standards for UNIX-style operating system interfaces. The POSIX standards encourage vendors implementing UNIX-style interfaces to make them compatible so that programmers can move their applications easily from one system to another.

Windows initially implemented only one of the many POSIX standards, POSIX.1, formally known as ISO/IEC 9945-1:1990 or IEEE POSIX standard 1003.1-1990. This standard was included primarily to meet U.S. government procurement requirements set in the mid-to-late 1980s that mandated POSIX.1 compliance as specified in Federal Information Processing Standard (FIPS) 151-2, developed by the National Institute of Standards and Technology. Windows NT 3.5, 3.51, and 4 were formally tested and certified according to FIPS 151-2.

Because POSIX.1 compliance was a mandatory goal for Windows, the operating system was designed to ensure that the required base system support was present to allow for the implementation of a POSIX.1 subsystem (such as the *fork* function, which is implemented in the Windows executive, and the support for hard file links in the Windows file system).

Windows Vista and Windows Server 2008 provide the Windows Subsystem for Unix-based Applications (SUA), which includes an enhanced POSIX subsystem environment that provides nearly 2,000 UNIX functions and 300 UNIX-like tools and utilities. (See *http://technet.micro-soft.com/en-us/library/cc779522.aspx* for more information on SUA.) SUA can be enabled on any Windows Server 2008 machine, as well as Windows Vista Ultimate and Enterprise editions.

This enhanced POSIX subsystem assists in porting UNIX applications to Windows because it also supports the POSIX.2 standard, which adds many APIs (such as the pthread API) and libraries to the bare set that POSIX.1 defined. Additionally, it also adds support for 64-bit binaries and, most importantly, mixed-mode support, meaning that for the first time UNIX-based applications can call Windows APIs alongside POSIX APIs, greatly alleviating the task of porting the application.

EXPERIMENT: Watching the POSIX Subsystem Start

The POSIX subsystem is configured by default to start the first time a POSIX executable is run, so you can watch it start by running a POSIX program, such as one of the POSIX utilities that comes with SUA. Follow these steps to watch the POSIX subsystem start:

1. Start a command prompt.

2. Run Process Explorer and check that the POSIX subsystem isn't already running (that is, that there's no Psxss.exe process on the system). Make sure Process Explorer is displaying the process list in tree view (by pressing Ctrl+T).

3. Run a POSIX program, such as the C Shell or Korn Shell included with the SUA.

4. Go back to Process Explorer and notice the new Psxss.exe process that is a child of Smss.exe (which, depending on your different highlight duration, might still be highlighted as a new process on the display).

To compile and link a POSIX application in Windows requires the POSIX headers and libraries from the Windows SDK. POSIX executables are linked against the POSIX subsystem library, Psxdll.dll. Because by default Windows is configured to start the POSIX subsystem on demand, the first time you run a POSIX application, the POSIX subsystem process (Psxss.exe) must be started. It remains running until the system reboots. (If you kill the POSIX subsystem process, you won't be able to run more POSIX applications until you reboot.) The POSIX image itself isn't run directly—instead, a special support image called Posix.exe is launched, which in turn creates a child process to run the POSIX application.

For more information on how Windows handles running POSIX applications, see the section "Flow of *CreateProcess*" in Chapter 5.

Ntdll.dll

Ntdll.dll is a special system support library primarily for the use of subsystem DLLs. It contains two types of functions:

- System service dispatch stubs to Windows executive system services

- Internal support functions used by subsystems, subsystem DLLs, and other native images

The first group of functions provides the interface to the Windows executive system services that can be called from user mode. There are more than 400 such functions, such as *NtCreateFile*, *NtSetEvent*, and so on. As noted earlier, most of the capabilities of these functions are accessible through the Windows API. (A number are not, however, and are for use within the operating system.)

For each of these functions, Ntdll contains an entry point with the same name. The code inside the function contains the architecture-specific instruction that causes a transition into kernel mode to invoke the system service dispatcher (explained in more detail in Chapter 3), which, after verifying some parameters, calls the actual kernel-mode system service that contains the real code inside Ntoskrnl.exe.

Ntdll also contains many support functions, such as the image loader (functions that start with *Ldr*), the heap manager, and Windows subsystem process communication functions (functions that start with *Csr*). Ntdll also contains general run-time library routines (functions that start with *Rtl*), support for user-mode debugging (functions that start with *DbgUi*) and Event Tracing for Windows (functions starting in *Etw),* and the user-mode asynchronous procedure call (APC) dispatcher and exception dispatcher. (APCs and exceptions are explained in Chapter 3.) Finally, you'll find a small subset of the C Run-Time (CRT) routines, limited to those routines that are part of the string and standard libraries (such as *memcpy, strcpy, itoa,* and so on).

Executive

The Windows executive is the upper layer of Ntoskrnl.exe. (The kernel is the lower layer.) The executive includes the following types of functions:

- Functions that are exported and callable from user mode. These functions are called *system services* and are exported via Ntdll. Most of the services are accessible through the Windows API or the APIs of another environment subsystem. A few services, however, aren't available through any documented subsystem function. (Examples include LPCs and various query functions such as *NtQueryInformationProcess*, specialized functions such as *NtCreatePagingFile*, and so on.)

- Device driver functions that are called through the use of the *DeviceIoControl* function. This provides a general interface from user mode to kernel mode to call functions in device drivers that are not associated with a read or write.

- Functions that can be called only from kernel mode that are exported and are documented in the WDK.

- Functions that are exported and callable from kernel mode but are not documented in the WDK (such as the functions called by the boot video driver, which start with *Inbv*).

- Functions that are defined as global symbols but are not exported. These include internal support functions called within Ntoskrnl, such as those that start with *Iop* (internal I/O manager support functions) or *Mi* (internal memory management support functions).

- Functions that are internal to a module that are not defined as global symbols.

The executive contains the following major components, each of which is covered in detail in a subsequent chapter of this book:

- The *configuration manager* (explained in Chapter 4) is responsible for implementing and managing the system registry.

- The *process and thread manager* (explained in Chapter 5) creates and terminates processes and threads. The underlying support for processes and threads is implemented in the Windows kernel; the executive adds additional semantics and functions to these lower-level objects.

- The *security reference monitor* (or SRM, described in Chapter 6) enforces security policies on the local computer. It guards operating system resources, performing run-time object protection and auditing.

- The *I/O manager* (explained in Chapter 7) implements device-independent I/O and is responsible for dispatching to the appropriate device drivers for further processing.

- The *Plug and Play (PnP) manager* (explained in Chapter 7) determines which drivers are required to support a particular device and loads those drivers. It retrieves the hardware resource requirements for each device during enumeration. Based on the resource requirements of each device, the PnP manager assigns the appropriate hardware resources such as I/O ports, IRQs, DMA channels, and memory locations. It is also responsible for sending proper event notification for device changes (addition or removal of a device) on the system.

- The *power manager* (explained in Chapter 7) coordinates power events and generates power management I/O notifications to device drivers. When the system is idle, the power manager can be configured to reduce power consumption by putting the CPU to sleep. Changes in power consumption by individual devices are handled by device drivers but are coordinated by the power manager.

- The *Windows Driver Model Windows Management Instrumentation routines* (explained in Chapter 4) enable device drivers to publish performance and configuration information and receive commands from the user-mode WMI service. Consumers of WMI information can be on the local machine or remote across the network.

- The *cache manager* (explained in Chapter 10) improves the performance of file-based I/O by causing recently referenced disk data to reside in main memory for quick access (and by deferring disk writes by holding the updates in memory for a short time before sending them to the disk). As you'll see, it does this by using the memory manager's support for mapped files.

- The *memory manager* (explained in Chapter 9) implements *virtual memory*, a memory management scheme that provides a large, private address space for each process that can exceed available physical memory. The memory manager also provides the underlying support for the cache manager.

- The *logical prefetcher* and *Superfetch* (explained in Chapter 9) accelerate system and process startup by optimizing the loading of data referenced during the startup of the system or a process.

In addition, the executive contains four main groups of support functions that are used by the executive components just listed. About a third of these support functions are documented in the WDK because device drivers also use them. These are the four categories of support functions:

- The *object manager*, which creates, manages, and deletes Windows executive objects and abstract data types that are used to represent operating system resources such as processes, threads, and the various synchronization objects. The object manager is explained in Chapter 3.

- The *Advanced LPC facility* (ALPC, explained in Chapter 3) passes messages between a client process and a server process on the same computer. Among other things, ALPC is used as a local transport for *remote procedure call* (RPC), an industry-standard communication facility for client and server processes across a network.

- A broad set of common *run-time library* functions, such as string processing, arithmetic operations, data type conversion, and security structure processing.

- Executive support routines, such as system memory allocation (paged and nonpaged pool), interlocked memory access, as well as three special types of synchronization objects: resources, fast mutexes, and pushlocks.

The executive also contains a variety of other infrastructure routines, some of which we will only mention briefly throughout the book:

- The *kernel debugger* library, which allows debugging of the kernel from a debugger supporting KD, a portable protocol supported over a variety of transports (such as USB and IEEE 1394) and implemented by WinDbg and the Kd.exe utilities.

- The *user-mode debugging framework*, which is responsible for sending events to the user-mode debugging API and allowing breakpoints and stepping through code to work, as well as for changing contexts of running threads.

- The *kernel transaction manager*, which provides a common, two-phase commit mechanism to resource managers, such as the transactional registry (TxR) and transactional NTFS (TxF).

- The *hypervisor library*, part of the Hyper-V stack in Windows Server 2008, provides kernel support for the virtual machine environment and optimizes certain parts of the code when the system knows it's running in a client partition (virtual environment).

- The *errata manager* provides workarounds for nonstandard or noncompliant hardware devices.

- The *Driver Verifier* implements optional integrity checks of kernel-mode drivers and code.

- *Event Tracing for Windows* provides helper routines for systemwide event tracing for kernel-mode and user-mode components.

- The *Windows diagnostic infrastructure* enables intelligent tracing of system activity based on diagnostic scenarios.

- The *Windows hardware error architecture* support routines provide a common framework for reporting hardware errors.

- The *file-system runtime library* provides common support routines for file system drivers.

Kernel

The kernel consists of a set of functions in Ntoskrnl.exe that provide fundamental mechanisms (such as thread scheduling and synchronization services) used by the executive components, as well as low-level hardware architecture–dependent support (such as interrupt and exception dispatching), that is different on each processor architecture. The kernel code is written primarily in C, with assembly code reserved for those tasks that require access to specialized processor instructions and registers not easily accessible from C.

Like the various executive support functions mentioned in the preceding section, a number of functions in the kernel are documented in the WDK (and can be found by searching for functions beginning with *Ke*) because they are needed to implement device drivers.

Kernel Objects

The kernel provides a low-level base of well-defined, predictable operating system primitives and mechanisms that allow higher-level components of the executive to do what they need to do. The kernel separates itself from the rest of the executive by implementing operating system mechanisms and avoiding policy making. It leaves nearly all policy decisions to the executive, with the exception of thread scheduling and dispatching, which the kernel implements.

Outside the kernel, the executive represents threads and other shareable resources as objects. These objects require some policy overhead, such as object handles to manipulate them, security checks to protect them, and resource quotas to be deducted when they are created. This overhead is eliminated in the kernel, which implements a set of simpler objects, called *kernel objects*, that help the kernel control central processing and support the creation of executive objects. Most executive-level objects encapsulate one or more kernel objects, incorporating their kernel-defined attributes.

One set of kernel objects, called *control objects*, establishes semantics for controlling various operating system functions. This set includes the APC object, the *deferred procedure call* (DPC) object, and several objects the I/O manager uses, such as the interrupt object.

Another set of kernel objects, known as *dispatcher objects*, incorporates synchronization capabilities that alter or affect thread scheduling. The dispatcher objects include the kernel thread, mutex (called *mutant* internally), event, kernel event pair, semaphore, timer, and waitable timer. The executive uses kernel functions to create instances of kernel objects, to manipulate them, and to construct the more complex objects it provides to user mode. Objects are explained in more detail in Chapter 3, and processes and threads are described in Chapter 5.

Kernel Processor Control Region and Control Block (KPCR and KPRCB)

The kernel uses a data structure called the *processor control region,* or KPCR, to store processor-specific data. The KPCR contains basic information such as the processor's interrupt table (IDT), task-state segment (TSS), and global descriptor table (GDT). It also includes the interrupt controller state, which it shares with other modules, such as the ACPI driver and the HAL. To provide easy access to the KPCR, the kernel stores a pointer to it in the *fs* register on 32-bit Windows and in the *gs* register on an x64 Windows system. On IA64 systems, the KPCR is always located at 0xe0000000ffff0000.

The KPCR also contains an embedded data structure called the *kernel processor control block* (KPRCB). Unlike the KPCR, which is documented for third-party drivers and other internal Windows kernel components, the KPRCB is a private structure used only by the kernel code in Ntoskrnl.exe. It contains scheduling information such as the current, next, and idle threads scheduled for execution on the processor, the dispatcher database for the processor (which includes the ready queues for each priority level), the DPC queue, CPU vendor and identifier information (model, stepping, speed, feature bits), CPU and NUMA topology (node information, cores per package, logical processors per core, and so on), cache sizes, time accounting information (such as the DPC and interrupt time), and more. The KPRCB also contains all the statistics for the processor, such as I/O statistics, cache manager statistics (see Chapter 10 for a description of these), DPC statistics, and memory manager statistics (see Chapter 9 for more information). Finally, the KPRCB is sometimes used to store cache-aligned, per-processor structures to optimize memory access, especially on NUMA systems. For example, the non-paged and paged-pool system lookaside lists are stored in the KPRCB.

EXPERIMENT: Viewing the KPCR and KPRCB

You can view the contents of the KPCR and KPRCB by using the *!pcr* and *!prcb* kernel debugger commands. If you don't include flags, the debugger will display information for CPU 0 by default; otherwise, you can specify a CPU by adding its number after the command (for example, *!pcr 2*). The following example shows what the output of the *!pcr* and *!prcb* commands looks like. If the system had pending DPCs, those would also be shown.

```
lkd> !pcr
KPCR for Processor 0 at 81d09800:
    Major 1 Minor 1
      NtTib.ExceptionList: 9b31ca3c
        NtTib.StackBase: 00000000
       NtTib.StackLimit: 00000000
     NtTib.SubSystemTib: 80150000
          NtTib.Version: 1c47209e
      NtTib.UserPointer: 00000001
        NtTib.SelfTib: 7ffde000

                SelfPcr: 81d09800
                   Prcb: 81d09920
                   Irql: 00000002
                    IRR: 00000000
                    IDR: ffffffff
          InterruptMode: 00000000
                    IDT: 82fb8400
                    GDT: 82fb8000
                    TSS: 80150000

          CurrentThread: 86d317e8
             NextThread: 00000000
             IdleThread: 81d0d640

               DpcQueue:

lkd> !prcb
PRCB for Processor 0 at 81d09920:
Current IRQL -- 0
Threads--  Current 86d317e8 Next 00000000 Idle 81d0d640
Number 0 SetMember 1
Interrupt Count -- 294ccce0
Times -- Dpc    0002a87f Interrupt 00010b87
         Kernel 026270a1 User       00140e5e
```

You can use the *dt* command to directly dump the _KPCR and _KPRCB data structures because both debugger commands give you the address of the structure (shown in bold for clarity in the previous output). For example, if you wanted to determine the speed of the processor, you could look at the MHz field with the following command.

```
lkd> dt _KPRCB 81d09920 MHz
nt!_KPRCB
    +0x3c4 MHz : 0xbb4
lkd> ? bb4
Evaluate expression: 2996 = 00000bb4
```

On this machine, the processor was running at about 3GHz.

Hardware Support

The other major job of the kernel is to abstract or isolate the executive and device drivers from variations between the hardware architectures supported by Windows. This job includes handling variations in functions such as interrupt handling, exception dispatching, and multi-processor synchronization.

Even for these hardware-related functions, the design of the kernel attempts to maximize the amount of common code. The kernel supports a set of interfaces that are portable and semantically identical across architectures. Most of the code that implements these portable interfaces is also identical across architectures.

Some of these interfaces are implemented differently on different architectures, however, or some of the interfaces are partially implemented with architecture-specific code. These architecturally independent interfaces can be called on any machine, and the semantics of the interface will be the same whether or not the code varies by architecture. Some kernel interfaces (such as spinlock routines, which are described in Chapter 3) are actually implemented in the HAL (described in the next section) because their implementation can vary for systems within the same architecture family.

The kernel also contains a small amount of code with x86-specific interfaces needed to support old MS-DOS programs. These x86 interfaces aren't portable in the sense that they can't be called on a machine based on any other architecture; they won't be present. This x86-specific code, for example, supports calls to manipulate global descriptor tables (GDTs) and local descriptor tables (LDTs), hardware features of the x86.

Other examples of architecture-specific code in the kernel include the interfaces to provide translation buffer and CPU cache support. This support requires different code for the different architectures because of the way caches are implemented.

Another example is context switching. Although at a high level the same algorithm is used for thread selection and context switching (the context of the previous thread is saved,

the context of the new thread is loaded, and the new thread is started), there are architectural differences among the implementations on different processors. Because the context is described by the processor state (registers and so on), what is saved and loaded varies depending on the architecture.

Hardware Abstraction Layer

As mentioned at the beginning of this chapter, one of the crucial elements of the Windows design is its portability across a variety of hardware platforms. The hardware abstraction layer (HAL) is a key part of making this portability possible. The HAL is a loadable kernel-mode module (Hal.dll) that provides the low-level interface to the hardware platform on which Windows is running. It hides hardware-dependent details such as I/O interfaces, interrupt controllers, and multiprocessor communication mechanisms—any functions that are both architecture-specific and machine-dependent.

So rather than access hardware directly, Windows internal components as well as user-written device drivers maintain portability by calling the HAL routines when they need platform-dependent information. For this reason, the HAL routines are documented in the WDK. To find out more about the HAL and its use by device drivers, refer to the WDK.

Although several HALs are included with Windows (as shown in Table 2-5), Windows Vista and Windows Server 2008 have the ability to detect at boot-up time which HAL should be used, eliminating the problem that existed on earlier versions of Windows when attempting to boot a Windows installation on a different kind of system.

TABLE 2-5 List of x86 HALs

HAL File Name	Systems Supported
Halacpi.dll	Advanced Configuration and Power Interface (ACPI) PCs. Implies uniprocessor-only machine, without APIC support (the presence of either one would make the system use the HAL below instead).
Halmacpi.dll	Advanced Programmable Interrupt Controller (APIC) PCs with an ACPI. The existence of an APIC implies SMP support.

Note On x64 machines, there is only one HAL image, called Hal.dll. This results from all x64 machines having the same motherboard configuration, since the processors require ACPI and APIC support. Therefore, there is no need to support machines without ACPI or with a standard PIC.

EXPERIMENT: Determining Which HAL You're Running

You can determine which version of the HAL you're running by using WinDbg and opening a local kernel debugging session. Be sure you have the symbols loaded (write .reload) and then type **lm mv hal**. For example, the following output is from a system running the ACPI HAL:

```
lkd> lm vm hal
start    end              module name
823a1000 823d5000    hal            (pdb symbols)
    c:\programming\symbols\halmacpi.pdb\0D335CFD77384CE695E1748F3249184B1\halmacpi.pdb
    Loaded symbol image file: halmacpi.dll
    Image path: halmacpi.dll
    Image name: halmacpi.dll
    Timestamp:        Sat Dec 23 23:05:34 2006 (458DFC8E)
    CheckSum:         00035DC3
    ImageSize:        00034000
    File version:     6.0.6000.16407
    Product version:  6.0.6000.16407
    File flags:       0 (Mask 3F)
    File OS:          40004 NT Win32
    File type:        2.0 Dll
    File date:        00000000.00000000
    Translations:     0409.04b0
    CompanyName:      Microsoft Corporation
    ProductName:      Microsoft® Windows® Operating System
    InternalName:     halmacpi.dll
    OriginalFilename: halmacpi.dll
    ProductVersion:   6.0.6000.16407
    FileVersion:      6.0.6000.16407 (vista_gdr.061223-1640)
    FileDescription:  Hardware Abstraction Layer DLL
    LegalCopyright:   © Microsoft Corporation. All rights reserved.
```

EXPERIMENT: Viewing NTOSKRNL and HAL Image Dependencies

You can view the relationship of the kernel and HAL images by examining their export and import tables using the Dependency Walker tool (Depends.exe), which is contained in the Windows SDK. To examine an image in the Dependency Walker, select Open from the File menu to open the desired image file.

Here is a sample of output you can see by viewing the dependencies of Ntoskrnl using this tool:

Notice that Ntoskrnl is linked against the HAL, which is in turn linked against Ntoskrnl. (They both use functions in each other.) Ntoskrnl is also linked to the following binaries:

- Pshed.dll, the Platform-Specific Hardware Error Driver. The PSHED provides an abstraction of the hardware error reporting facilities of the underlying platform by hiding the details of a platform's error handling mechanisms from the operating system and exposing a consistent interface to the Windows operating system.

- Bootvid.dll, the Boot Video Driver. Bootvid provides support for the VGA commands required to display boot text and the boot logo during startup. On x64 kernels, this library is built into the kernel to avoid conflicts with Kernel Patch Protection (KPP). (See Chapter 3 for more information on KPP and PatchGuard.)

- Kdcom.dll, the Kernel Debugger Protocol (KD) Communications Library, described earlier.

- Ci.dll, the code integrity library, described earlier.

- Clfs.sys, the common logging file system driver, used, among other things, by the Kernel Transaction Manager (KTM). (See Chapter 3 for more information on the KTM.)

For a detailed description of the information displayed by this tool, see the Dependency Walker help file (Depends.hlp).

Device Drivers

Although device drivers are explained in detail in Chapter 7, this section provides a brief overview of the types of drivers and explains how to list the drivers installed and loaded on your system.

Device drivers are loadable kernel-mode modules (typically ending in .sys) that interface between the I/O manager and the relevant hardware. They run in kernel mode in one of three contexts:

- In the context of the user thread that initiated an I/O function
- In the context of a kernel-mode system thread
- As a result of an interrupt (and therefore not in the context of any particular process or thread—whichever process or thread was current when the interrupt occurred)

As stated in the preceding section, device drivers in Windows don't manipulate hardware directly, but rather they call functions in the HAL to interface with the hardware. Drivers are typically written in C (sometimes C++) and therefore, with proper use of HAL routines, can be source code portable across the CPU architectures supported by Windows and binary portable within an architecture family.

There are several types of device drivers:

- *Hardware device drivers* manipulate hardware (using the HAL) to write output to or retrieve input from a physical device or network. There are many types of hardware device drivers, such as bus drivers, human interface drivers, mass storage drivers, and so on.
- *File system drivers* are Windows drivers that accept file-oriented I/O requests and translate them into I/O requests bound for a particular device.
- *File system filter drivers*, such as those that perform disk mirroring and encryption, intercept I/Os and perform some added-value processing before passing the I/O to the next layer.
- *Network redirectors and servers* are file system drivers that transmit file system I/O requests to a machine on the network and receive such requests, respectively.
- *Protocol drivers* implement a networking protocol such as TCP/IP, NetBEUI, and IPX/SPX.
- *Kernel streaming filter drivers* are chained together to perform signal processing on data streams, such as recording or displaying audio and video.

Because installing a device driver is the only way to add user-written kernel-mode code to the system, some programmers have written device drivers simply as a way to access internal operating system functions or data structures that are not accessible from user mode (but that are documented and supported in the DDK). For example, many of the utilities from Sysinternals combine a Windows GUI application and a device driver that is used to gather internal system state and call kernel-mode-only accessible functions not accessible from the user-mode Windows API.

Windows Driver Model (WDM)

Windows 2000 added support for Plug and Play, Power Options, and an extension to the Windows NT driver model called the Windows Driver Model (WDM). Windows 2000 and later can run legacy Windows NT 4 drivers, but because these don't support Plug and Play and Power Options, systems running these drivers will have reduced capabilities in these two areas.

From the WDM perspective, there are three kinds of drivers:

- A *bus driver* services a bus controller, adapter, bridge, or any device that has child devices. Bus drivers are required drivers, and Microsoft generally provides them; each type of bus (such as PCI, PCMCIA, and USB) on a system has one bus driver. Third parties can write bus drivers to provide support for new buses, such as VMEbus, Multibus, and Futurebus.

- A *function driver* is the main device driver and provides the operational interface for its device. It is a required driver unless the device is used raw (an implementation in which I/O is done by the bus driver and any bus filter drivers, such as SCSI PassThru). A function driver is by definition the driver that knows the most about a particular device, and it is usually the only driver that accesses device-specific registers.

- A *filter driver* is used to add functionality to a device (or existing driver) or to modify I/O requests or responses from other drivers (and is often used to fix hardware that provides incorrect information about its hardware resource requirements). Filter drivers are optional and can exist in any number, placed above or below a function driver and above a bus driver. Usually, system original equipment manufacturers (OEMs) or independent hardware vendors (IHVs) supply filter drivers.

In the WDM driver environment, no single driver controls all aspects of a device: a bus driver is concerned with reporting the devices on its bus to the PnP manager, while a function driver manipulates the device.

In most cases, lower-level filter drivers modify the behavior of device hardware. For example, if a device reports to its bus driver that it requires 4 I/O ports when it actually requires 16 I/O ports, a lower-level, device-specific function filter driver could intercept the list of hardware resources reported by the bus driver to the PnP manager and update the count of I/O ports.

Upper-level filter drivers usually provide added-value features for a device. For example, an upper-level device filter driver for a keyboard can enforce additional security checks.

Interrupt processing is explained in Chapter 3. Further details about the I/O manager, WDM, Plug and Play, and Power Options are included in Chapter 7.

Windows Driver Foundation

The Windows Driver Foundation (WDF) simplifies Windows driver development by providing two frameworks: the Kernel-Mode Driver Framework (KMDF) and the User-Mode Driver Framework (UMDF). Developers can use KMDF to write drivers for Windows 2000 SP4 and later, while UMDF supports Windows XP and later.

KMDF provides a simple interface to WDM and hides its complexity from the driver writer without modifying the underlying bus/function/filter model. KMDF drivers respond to events that they can register and call into the KMDF library to perform work that isn't specific to the hardware they are managing, such as generic power management or synchronization. (Previously, each driver had to implement this on its own.) In some cases, more than 200 lines of WDM code can be replaced by a single KMDF function call.

UMDF enables certain classes of drivers (mostly USB-based or other high-latency protocol buses), such as those for video cameras, MP3 players, cell phones, PDAs, and printers, to be implemented as user-mode drivers. UMDF runs each user-mode driver in what is essentially a user-mode service, and it uses ALPC to communicate to a kernel-mode wrapper driver that provides actual access to hardware. If a UMDF driver crashes, the process dies and usually restarts, so the system doesn't become unstable—the device simply becomes unavailable while the service hosting the driver restarts. Finally, UMDF drivers are written in C++ using COM-like classes and semantics, further lowering the bar for programmers to write device drivers.

EXPERIMENT: Viewing the Installed Device Drivers

You can list the installed drivers by running Msinfo32. (Click Start, Run, and then type **Msinfo32**.) Under System Summary, expand Software Environment and open System Drivers. Here's an example output of the list of installed drivers:

This window displays the list of device drivers defined in the registry, their type, and their state (Running or Stopped). Device drivers and Windows service processes are both defined in the same place: HKLM\SYSTEM\CurrentControlSet\Services. However, they are distinguished by a type code—for example, type 1 is a kernel-mode device driver. (For a complete list of the information stored in the registry for device drivers, see Table 4-7.)

Alternatively, you can list the currently loaded device drivers by selecting the System process in Process Explorer and opening the DLL view.

Peering into Undocumented Interfaces

Examining the names of the exported or global symbols in key system images (such as Ntoskrnl.exe, Hal.dll, or Ntdll.dll) can be enlightening—you can get an idea of the kinds of things Windows can do versus what happens to be documented and supported today. Of course, just because you know the names of these functions doesn't mean that you can or should call them—the interfaces are undocumented and are subject to change. We suggest that you look at these functions purely to gain more insight into the kinds of internal functions Windows performs, not to bypass supported interfaces.

For example, looking at the list of functions in Ntdll.dll gives you the list of all the system services that Windows provides to user-mode subsystem DLLs versus the subset that each subsystem exposes. Although many of these functions map clearly to documented and supported Windows functions, several are not exposed via the Windows API. (See the article "Inside the Native API" from Sysinternals.)

Conversely, it's also interesting to examine the imports of Windows subsystem DLLs (such as Kernel32.dll or Advapi32.dll) and which functions they call in Ntdll.

Another interesting image to dump is Ntoskrnl.exe—although many of the exported routines that kernel-mode device drivers use are documented in the Windows Driver Kit, quite a few are not. You might also find it interesting to take a look at the import table for Ntoskrnl and the HAL; this table shows the list of functions in the HAL that Ntoskrnl uses and vice versa.

Table 2-6 lists most of the commonly used function name prefixes for the executive components. Each of these major executive components also uses a variation of the prefix to denote internal functions—either the first letter of the prefix followed by an *i* (for *internal*) or the full prefix followed by a *p* (for *private*). For example, *Ki* represents internal kernel functions, and *Psp* refers to internal process support functions.

TABLE 2-6 Commonly Used Prefixes

Prefix	Component
Alpc	Advanced Local Inter-Process Communication
Cc	Common Cache
Cm	Configuration manager
Dbgk	Debugging Framework for User-Mode
Em	Errata Manager
Etw	Event Tracing for Windows
Ex	Executive support routines

Prefix	Component
FsRtl	File system driver run-time library
Hal	Hardware abstraction layer
Hvl	Hypervisor Library
Io	I/O manager
Kd	Kernel Debugger
Ke	Kernel
Lsa	Local Security Authority
Mm	Memory manager
Nt	NT system services (most of which are exported as Windows functions)
Ob	Object manager
Pf	Prefetcher
Po	Power manager
Pp	PnP manager
Ps	Process support
Rtl	Run-time library
Se	Security
Tm	Transaction Manager
Vf	Verifier
Whea	Windows Hardware Error Architecture
Wmi	Windows Management Instrumentation
Wdi	Windows Diagnostic Infrastructure
Zw	Mirror entry point for system services (beginning with Nt) that sets previous access mode to kernel, which eliminates parameter validation, because Nt system services validate parameters only if previous access mode is user

You can decipher the names of these exported functions more easily if you understand the naming convention for Windows system routines. The general format is:

<Prefix><Operation><Object>

In this format, *Prefix* is the internal component that exports the routine, *Operation* tells what is being done to the object or resource, and *Object* identifies what is being operated on.

For example, *ExAllocatePoolWithTag* is the executive support routine to allocate from a paged or nonpaged pool. *KeInitializeThread* is the routine that allocates and sets up a kernel thread object.

System Processes

The following system processes appear on every Windows system. (Two of these—Idle and System—are not full processes, as they are not running a user-mode executable.)

- Idle process (contains one thread per CPU to account for idle CPU time)

- System process (contains the majority of the kernel-mode system threads)

- Session manager (Smss.exe)

- Local session manager (Lsm.exe)

- Windows subsystem (Csrss.exe)

- Session 0 initialization (Wininit.exe)

- Logon process (Winlogon.exe)

- Service control manager (Services.exe) and the child service processes it creates (such as the system-supplied generic service-host process, Svchost.exe)

- Local security authentication server (Lsass.exe)

To understand the relationship of these processes, it is helpful to view the process "tree"—that is, the parent/child relationship between processes. Seeing which process created each process helps to understand where each process comes from. Figure 2-5 is a screen snapshot of the process tree viewed after taking a Process Monitor boot trace. Using Process Monitor is the only way to see the real process tree because, as we'll see later, the session manager will spawn copies of itself for each session being created and then terminate them.

FIGURE 2-5 Initial system process tree

The next sections explain the key system processes shown in Figure 2-5. Although these sections briefly indicate the order of process startup, Chapter 13 contains a detailed description of the steps involved in booting and starting Windows.

Idle Process

The first process listed in Figure 2-5 is the system idle process. As we'll explain in Chapter 5, processes are identified by their image name. However, this process (as well as the process named System) isn't running a real user-mode image (in that there is no "System Idle Process.exe" in the \Windows directory). In addition, the name shown for this process differs from utility to utility (because of implementation details). Table 2-7 lists several of the names given to the Idle process (process ID 0). The Idle process is explained in detail in Chapter 5.

TABLE 2-7 Names for Process ID 0 in Various Utilities

Utility	Name for Process ID 0
Task Manager	System Idle Process
Process Status (Pstat.exe)	Idle Process
Process Explorer (Procexp.exe)	System Idle Process
Task List (Tasklist.exe)	System Idle Process

Now let's look at system threads and the purpose of each of the system processes that are running real images.

Interrupts and DPCs

The two lines labeled Interrupts and DPCs represent time spent servicing interrupts and deferred procedure calls. These mechanisms are explained in Chapter 3. Note that while Process Explorer displays these as entries in the process list, they are not processes. They are shown because they account for CPU time not charged to any process. (For example, a system with heavy interrupt activity will not appear as a process consuming CPU time.) Note that Task Manager includes interrupt and DPC time in the system idle time. Thus a system with heavy interrupt activity will appear to be idle when using Task Manager.

System Process and System Threads

The System process (process ID 4) is the home for a special kind of thread that runs only in kernel mode: a *kernel-mode system thread*. System threads have all the attributes and contexts of regular user-mode threads (such as a hardware context, priority, and so on) but are different in that they run only in kernel-mode executing code loaded in system space, whether that is in Ntoskrnl.exe or in any other loaded device driver. In addition, system threads don't have a user process address space and hence must allocate any dynamic storage from operating system memory heaps, such as a paged or nonpaged pool.

System threads are created by the *PsCreateSystemThread* function (documented in the WDK), which can be called only from kernel mode. Windows as well as various device drivers create system threads during system initialization to perform operations that require thread context, such as issuing and waiting for I/Os or other objects or polling a device. For example, the memory manager uses system threads to implement such functions as writing dirty pages to the page file or mapped files, swapping processes in and out of memory, and so forth. The kernel creates a system thread called the *balance set manager* that wakes up once per second to possibly initiate various scheduling and memory management–related events. The cache manager also uses system threads to implement both read-ahead and write-behind I/Os. The file server device driver (Srv2.sys) uses system threads to respond to network I/O requests for file data on disk partitions shared to the network. Even the floppy driver has a system thread to poll the floppy device. (Polling is more efficient in this case because an interrupt-driven floppy driver consumes a large amount of system resources.) Further information on specific system threads is included in the chapters in which the component is described.

By default, system threads are owned by the System process, but a device driver can create a system thread in any process. For example, the Windows subsystem device driver (Win32k.sys) creates a system thread inside the Canonical Display Driver (Cdd.dll) part of the Windows subsystem process (Csrss.exe) so that it can easily access data in the user-mode address space of that process.

When you're troubleshooting or going through a system analysis, it's useful to be able to map the execution of individual system threads back to the driver or even to the subroutine that contains the code. For example, on a heavily loaded file server, the System process will likely be consuming considerable CPU time. But the knowledge that when the System process is running that "some system thread" is running isn't enough to determine which device driver or operating system component is running.

So if threads in the System process are running, first determine which ones are running (for example, with the Performance tool). Once you find the thread (or threads) that is running, look up in which driver the system thread began execution (which at least tells you which driver likely created the thread) or examine the call stack (or at least the current address) of the thread in question, which would indicate where the thread is currently executing.

Both of these techniques are illustrated in the following experiments.

EXPERIMENT: Mapping a System Thread to a Device Driver

In this experiment, we'll see how to map CPU activity in the System process to the responsible system thread (and the driver it falls in) generating the activity. This is important because when the System process is running, you must go to the thread granularity to really understand what's going on. For this experiment, we will generate system thread activity by generating file server activity on your machine. (The file server driver, Srv2.sys, creates system threads to handle inbound requests for file I/O. See Chapter 12 for more information on this component.)

1. Open a command prompt.

2. Do a directory listing of your entire C drive using a network path to access your C drive. For example, if your computer name is COMPUTER1, type **dir \\computer1\c$ /s**. (The /s switch lists all subdirectories.)

3. Run Process Explorer, and double-click on the System process.

4. Click on the Threads tab.

5. Sort by the CSwitch Delta (context switch delta) column. You should see one or more threads in Srv2.sys running, such as the following:

If you see a system thread running and you are not sure what the driver is, click the Module button, which will bring up the file properties. Clicking the Module button while highlighting the thread in Srv2.sys previously shown results in the following display.

Session Manager (Smss)

The session manager (%SystemRoot%\Smss.exe) is the first user-mode process created in the system. The kernel-mode system thread that performs the final phase of the initialization of the executive and kernel creates the actual Smss process.

The session manager is responsible for a number of important steps in starting Windows, such as opening additional page files, performing delayed file rename and delete operations, and creating system environment variables. It also launches the subsystem processes (normally just Csrss.exe) and either the Wininit or Winlogon processes, the former of which in turn creates the rest of the system processes.

Much of the configuration information in the registry that drives the initialization steps of Smss can be found under HKLM\SYSTEM\CurrentControlSet\Control\Session Manager. Some of these are explained in Chapter 13 in the section on Smss.

Smss also creates user sessions. When Smss creates the first interactive user session (the console session) or when a request to create a session is received, it creates a copy of itself inside that session. The copy calls *NtSetSystemInformation* with a request to set up kernel-mode session data structures. This in turn calls the internal memory manager function *MmSessionCreate*, which sets up the session virtual address space that will contain the session

paged pool and the per-session data structures allocated by the kernel-mode part of the Windows subsystem (Win32k.sys) and other session-space device drivers. (See Chapter 9 for more details.) Smss then creates an instance of Winlogon and Csrss for the session. For session 0, Smss creates Wininit instead.

By having parallel copies of itself during boot-up and Terminal Services session creation, Smss can create multiple sessions at the same time (at minimum four concurrent sessions, plus one more for each extra CPU beyond one). This ability enhances logon performance on Terminal Server systems where multiple users connect at the same time. Once a session finishes initializing, the copy of Smss terminates. As a result, only the initial Smss.exe process remains active.

The main thread in Smss waits forever on the process handles to Csrss and Winlogon. If either of these processes terminates unexpectedly, Smss crashes the system (using the crash code STATUS_SYSTEM_PROCESS_TERMINATED, or 0xC000021A), because Windows relies on their existence. Meanwhile, Smss waits for requests to load subsystems, debug events, and requests to create new Terminal Server sessions. (For a description of Terminal Services, see the section "Terminal Services and Multiple Sessions" in Chapter 1.)

Winlogon, LogonUI, LSASS, and Userinit

The Windows logon process (%SystemRoot%\Winlogon.exe) handles interactive user logons and logoffs. Winlogon is notified of a user logon request when the *secure attention sequence* (SAS) keystroke combination is entered. The default SAS on Windows is the combination Ctrl+Alt+Delete. The reason for the SAS is to protect users from password-capture programs that simulate the logon process, because this keyboard sequence cannot be intercepted by a user-mode application.

The identification and authentication aspects of the logon process are implemented through DLLs called *credential providers*. The standard Windows credential providers implement the default Windows authentication interfaces: password and smartcard. However, developers can provide their own credential providers to implement other identification and authentication mechanisms in place of the standard Windows username/password method (such as one based on a voice print or a biometric device such as a fingerprint reader). Because Winlogon is a critical system process on which the system depends, credential providers and the UI to display the logon dialog box run inside a child process of Winlogon called LogonUI. When Winlogon detects the SAS, it launches this process, which initializes the credential providers. Once the user enters her credentials or dismisses the logon interface, the LogonUI process terminates.

In addition, Winlogon can load additional network provider DLLs that need to perform secondary authentication. This capability allows multiple network providers to gather identification and authentication information all at one time during normal logon.

Once the username and password have been captured, they are sent to the local security authentication server process (%SystemRoot%\Lsass.exe, described in Chapter 6) to be authenticated. LSASS calls the appropriate authentication package (implemented as a DLL) to perform the actual verification, such as checking whether a password matches what is stored in the Active Directory or the SAM (the part of the registry that contains the definition of the users and groups).

Upon a successful authentication, LSASS calls a function in the security reference monitor (for example, *NtCreateToken*) to generate an access token object that contains the user's security profile. If User Account Control (UAC) is used and the user logging on is a member of the administrators group or has administrator privileges, LSASS will create a second, *restricted* version of the token. This access token is then used by Winlogon to create the initial process(es) in the user's session. The initial process(es) are stored in the registry value *Userinit* under the registry key HKLM\SOFTWARE\Microsoft\Windows NT\CurrentVersion\Winlogon. (The default is Userinit.exe, but there can be more than one image in the list.)

Userinit performs some initialization of the user environment (such as running the login script and applying group policies) and then looks in the registry at the *Shell* value (under the same Winlogon key referred to previously) and creates a process to run the system-defined shell (by default, Explorer.exe). Then Userinit exits. This is the reason Explorer.exe is shown with no parent—its parent has exited, and as explained in Chapter 1, tlist left-justifies processes whose parent isn't running. (Another way of looking at it is that Explorer is the grandchild of Winlogon.)

Winlogon is active not only during user logon and logoff but also whenever it intercepts the SAS from the keyboard. For example, when you press Ctrl+Alt+Delete while logged on, the Windows Security dialog box comes up, providing the options to log off, start the Task Manager, lock the workstation, shut down the system, and so forth. Winlogon is the process that handles this interaction.

For a complete description of the steps involved in the logon process, see the section "Smss, Csrss, and Wininit" in Chapter 13. For more details on security authentication, see Chapter 6. For details on the callable functions that interface with LSASS (the functions that start with *Lsa*), see the documentation in the Windows SDK.

Service Control Manager (SCM)

Recall from earlier in the chapter that "services" on Windows can refer either to a server process or to a device driver. This section deals with services that are user-mode processes. Services are like UNIX "daemon processes" or VMS "detached processes" in that they can be configured to start automatically at system boot time without requiring an interactive logon. They can also be started manually (such as by running the Services administrative tool or by calling the Windows *StartService* function). Typically, services do not interact with the logged-on user, although there are special conditions when this is possible. (See Chapter 4.)

The service control manager is a special system process running the image %SystemRoot%\ Services.exe that is responsible for starting, stopping, and interacting with service processes. Service programs are really just Windows images that call special Windows functions to interact with the service control manager to perform such actions as registering the service's successful startup, responding to status requests, or pausing or shutting down the service. Services are defined in the registry under HKLM\SYSTEM\CurrentControlSet\Services.

Keep in mind that services have three names: the process name you see running on the system, the internal name in the registry, and the display name shown in the Services administrative tool. (Not all services have a display name—if a service doesn't have a display name, the internal name is shown.) With Windows, services can also have a description field that further details what the service does.

To map a service process to the services contained in that process, use the *tlist /s* or *tasklist /svc* command. Note that there isn't always one-to-one mapping between service process and running services, however, because some services share a process with other services. In the registry, the type code indicates whether the service runs in its own process or shares a process with other services in the image.

A number of Windows components are implemented as services, such as the Print Spooler, Event Log, Task Scheduler, and various networking components.

EXPERIMENT: Listing Installed Services

To list the installed services, select Administrative Tools from Control Panel, and then select Services. You should see output like this:

To see the detailed properties about a service, right-click on a service and select Properties. For example, here are the properties for the Print Spooler service (high-lighted in the previous screen shot):

Notice that the Path To Executable field identifies the program that contains this service. Remember that some services share a process with other services—mapping isn't always one to one.

EXPERIMENT: Viewing Service Details Inside Service Processes

Process Explorer highlights processes hosting one service or more. (You can configure this by selecting the Configure Highlighting entry in the Options menu.) If you double-click on a service-hosting process, you will see a Services tab that lists the services inside the process, the name of the registry key that defines the service, the display name seen by the administrator, the description text for that service (if present), and for Svchost services, the path to the DLL that implements the service. For example, listing the services in a Svchost.exe process on Windows Vista running under the System account looks like the following.

For more details on services, see Chapter 4.

Conclusion

In this chapter, we've taken a broad look at the overall system architecture of Windows. We've examined the key components of Windows and seen how they interrelate. In the next chapter, we'll look in more detail at the core system mechanisms that these components are built on, such as the object manager and synchronization.

Chapter 3
System Mechanisms

The Windows operating system provides several base mechanisms that kernel-mode components such as the executive, the kernel, and device drivers use. This chapter explains the following system mechanisms and describes how they are used:

- Trap dispatching, including interrupts, deferred procedure calls (DPCs), asynchronous procedure calls (APCs), exception dispatching, and system service dispatching

- The executive object manager

- Synchronization, including spinlocks, kernel dispatcher objects, how waits are implemented, as well as user-mode-specific synchronization primitives that avoid trips to kernel mode (unlike typical dispatcher objects)

- System worker threads

- Miscellaneous mechanisms such as Windows global flags

- Advanced local procedure calls (ALPCs)

- Kernel Event Tracing

- Wow64

- User-mode debugging

- The image loader

- Hypervisor (Hyper-V)

- Kernel Transaction Manager (KTM)

- Kernel Patch Protection (KPP)

- Code integrity

Trap Dispatching

Interrupts and exceptions are operating system conditions that divert the processor to code outside the normal flow of control. Either hardware or software can detect them. The term *trap* refers to a processor's mechanism for capturing an executing thread when an exception or an interrupt occurs and transferring control to a fixed location in the operating system. In Windows, the processor transfers control to a *trap handler*, a function specific to a particular interrupt or exception. Figure 3-1 illustrates some of the conditions that activate trap handlers.

The kernel distinguishes between interrupts and exceptions in the following way. An *interrupt* is an asynchronous event (one that can occur at any time) that is unrelated to what the processor is executing. Interrupts are generated primarily by I/O devices, processor clocks, or timers, and they can be enabled (turned on) or disabled (turned off). An *exception*, in contrast, is a synchronous condition that results from the execution of a particular instruction. Running a program a second time with the same data under the same conditions can reproduce exceptions. Examples of exceptions include memory access violations, certain debugger instructions, and divide-by-zero errors. The kernel also regards system service calls as exceptions (although technically they're system traps).

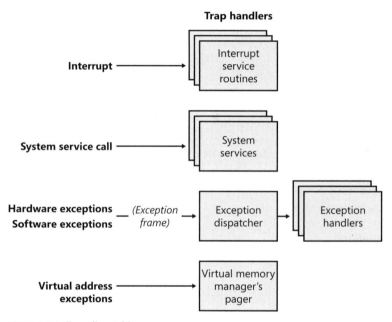

FIGURE 3-1 Trap dispatching

Either hardware or software can generate exceptions and interrupts. For example, a bus error exception is caused by a hardware problem, whereas a divide-by-zero exception is the result of a software bug. Likewise, an I/O device can generate an interrupt, or the kernel itself can issue a software interrupt (such as an APC or DPC, described later in this chapter).

When a hardware exception or interrupt is generated, the processor records enough machine state on the kernel stack of the thread that's interrupted so that it can return to that point in the control flow and continue execution as if nothing had happened. If the thread was executing in user mode, Windows switches to the thread's kernel-mode stack. Windows then creates a *trap frame* on the kernel stack of the interrupted thread into which it stores the execution state of the thread. The trap frame is a subset of a thread's complete context, and you can view its definition by typing **dt nt!_ktrap_frame** in the kernel debugger. (Thread context is described in Chapter 5.) The kernel handles software interrupts either as part of hardware

interrupt handling or synchronously when a thread invokes kernel functions related to the software interrupt.

In most cases, the kernel installs front-end trap handling functions that perform general trap handling tasks before and after transferring control to other functions that field the trap. For example, if the condition was a device interrupt, a kernel hardware interrupt trap handler transfers control to the *interrupt service routine* (ISR) that the device driver provided for the interrupting device. If the condition was caused by a call to a system service, the general system service trap handler transfers control to the specified system service function in the executive. The kernel also installs trap handlers for traps that it doesn't expect to see or doesn't handle. These trap handlers typically execute the system function *KeBugCheckEx*, which halts the computer when the kernel detects problematic or incorrect behavior that, if left unchecked, could result in data corruption. (For more information on bug checks, see Chapter 14.) The following sections describe interrupt, exception, and system service dispatching in greater detail.

Interrupt Dispatching

Hardware-generated interrupts typically originate from I/O devices that must notify the processor when they need service. Interrupt-driven devices allow the operating system to get the maximum use out of the processor by overlapping central processing with I/O operations. A thread starts an I/O transfer to or from a device and then can execute other useful work while the device completes the transfer. When the device is finished, it interrupts the processor for service. Pointing devices, printers, keyboards, disk drives, and network cards are generally interrupt driven.

System software can also generate interrupts. For example, the kernel can issue a software interrupt to initiate thread dispatching and to asynchronously break into the execution of a thread. The kernel can also disable interrupts so that the processor isn't interrupted, but it does so only infrequently—at critical moments while it's processing an interrupt or dispatching an exception, for example.

The kernel installs interrupt trap handlers to respond to device interrupts. Interrupt trap handlers transfer control either to an external routine (the ISR) that handles the interrupt or to an internal kernel routine that responds to the interrupt. Device drivers supply ISRs to service device interrupts, and the kernel provides interrupt handling routines for other types of interrupts.

In the following subsections, you'll find out how the hardware notifies the processor of device interrupts, the types of interrupts the kernel supports, the way device drivers interact with the kernel (as a part of interrupt processing), and the software interrupts the kernel recognizes (plus the kernel objects that are used to implement them).

Hardware Interrupt Processing

On the hardware platforms supported by Windows, external I/O interrupts come into one of the lines on an interrupt controller. The controller in turn interrupts the processor on a single line. Once the processor is interrupted, it queries the controller to get the *interrupt request* (IRQ). The interrupt controller translates the IRQ to an interrupt number, uses this number as an index into a structure called the *interrupt dispatch table* (IDT), and transfers control to the appropriate interrupt dispatch routine. At system boot time, Windows fills in the IDT with pointers to the kernel routines that handle each interrupt and exception.

EXPERIMENT: Viewing the IDT

You can view the contents of the IDT, including information on what trap handlers Windows has assigned to interrupts (including exceptions and IRQs), using the *!idt* kernel debugger command. The *!idt* command with no flags shows vectors that map to addresses in modules other than Ntoskrnl.exe.

The following example shows what the output of the *!idt* command looks like:

```
1kd> !idt

Dumping IDT:

37:   823b50e8 hal!PicSpuriousService37
51:   89714cd0 dxgkrnl!DpiFdoLineInterruptRoutine (KINTERRUPT 89714c80)
52:   887f52d0 USBPORT!USBPORT_InterruptService (KINTERRUPT 887f5280)
62:   887f5a50 USBPORT!USBPORT_InterruptService (KINTERRUPT 887f5a00)
               USBPORT!USBPORT_InterruptService (KINTERRUPT 887f5000)
72:   861137d0 ataport!IdePortInterrupt (KINTERRUPT 86113780)
81:   89237050 i8042prt!I8042KeyboardInterruptService (KINTERRUPT 89237000)
82:   86113a50 ataport!IdePortInterrupt (KINTERRUPT 86113a00)
91:   892372d0 i8042prt!I8042MouseInterruptService (KINTERRUPT 89237280)
a2:   89237cd0 sdbus!SdbusInterrupt (KINTERRUPT 89237c80)
               rimmptsk+0x682E (KINTERRUPT 89237a00)
               rimsptsk+0x6780 (KINTERRUPT 89237780)
               rixdptsk+0x6820 (KINTERRUPT 89237500)
a3:   887f57d0 USBPORT!USBPORT_InterruptService (KINTERRUPT 887f5780)
               HDAudBus!HdaController::Isr (KINTERRUPT 86113280)
a8:   86113050 ndis!ndisMiniportMessageIsr (KINTERRUPT 86113000)
a9:   87d35cd0 ndis!ndisMiniportMessageIsr (KINTERRUPT 87d35c80)
aa:   87d35a50 ndis!ndisMiniportMessageIsr (KINTERRUPT 87d35a00)
ab:   87d357d0 ndis!ndisMiniportMessageIsr (KINTERRUPT 87d35780)
ac:   87d35550 ndis!ndisMiniportMessageIsr (KINTERRUPT 87d35500)
ad:   87d352d0 ndis!ndisMiniportMessageIsr (KINTERRUPT 87d35280)
ae:   87d35050 ndis!ndisMiniportMessageIsr (KINTERRUPT 87d35000)
af:   887f5cd0 ndis!ndisMiniportMessageIsr (KINTERRUPT 887f5c80)
b0:   86113550 ndis!ndisMiniportMessageIsr (KINTERRUPT 86113500)
b1:   86113cd0 acpi!ACPIInterruptServiceRoutine (KINTERRUPT 86113c80)
b3:   887f5550 USBPORT!USBPORT_InterruptService (KINTERRUPT 887f5500)
c1:   823b53d8 hal!HalpBroadcastCallService
d1:   823a3c64 hal!HalpHpetClockInterrupt
```

```
d2:  823a3f08 hal!HalpHpetRolloverInterrupt
df:  823b51c0 hal!HalpApicRebootService
e1:  823b5934 hal!HalpIpiHandler
e3:  823b56d4 hal!HalpLocalApicErrorService
fd:  823b5edc hal!HalpProfileInterrupt
```

On the system used to provide the output for this experiment, the keyboard device driver's (I8042prt.sys) keyboard ISR is at interrupt number 0x91.

Windows maps hardware IRQs to interrupt numbers in the IDT, and the system also uses the IDT to configure trap handlers for exceptions. For example, the x86 and x64 exception number for a page fault (an exception that occurs when a thread attempts to access a page of virtual memory that isn't defined or present) is 0xe. Thus, entry 0xe in the IDT points to the system's page fault handler. Although the architectures supported by Windows allow up to 256 IDT entries, the number of IRQs a particular machine can support is determined by the design of the interrupt controller the machine uses.

Each processor has a separate IDT so that different processors can run different ISRs, if appropriate. For example, in a multiprocessor system, each processor receives the clock interrupt, but only one processor updates the system clock in response to this interrupt. All the processors, however, use the interrupt to measure thread quantum and to initiate rescheduling when a thread's quantum ends. Similarly, some system configurations might require that a particular processor handle certain device interrupts.

x86 Interrupt Controllers

Most x86 systems rely on either the i8259A Programmable Interrupt Controller (PIC) or a variant of the i82489 Advanced Programmable Interrupt Controller (APIC); the majority of new computers include an APIC. The PIC standard originates with the original IBM PC. The i8259A PIC works only with uniprocessor systems and only has 8 interrupt lines. However, the IBM PC architecture defined the addition of a second PIC, called the *slave*, whose interrupts are multiplexed into one of the master PIC's interrupt lines. This provides 15 total interrupts (7 on the master and 8 on the slave, multiplexed through the master's eighth interrupt line). APICs and Streamlined Advanced Programmable Interrupt Controllers (SAPICs, discussed shortly) work with multiprocessor systems and have 256 interrupt lines. Intel and other companies have defined the Multiprocessor Specification (MP Specification), a design standard for x86 multiprocessor systems that centers on the use of APIC. To provide compatibility with uniprocessor operating systems and boot code that starts a multiprocessor system in uniprocessor mode, APICs support a PIC compatibility mode with 15 interrupts and delivery of interrupts to only the primary processor. Figure 3-2 depicts the APIC architecture. The APIC actually consists of several components: an I/O APIC that receives interrupts from devices, local APICs that receive interrupts from the I/O APIC on the bus and that interrupt the CPU they are associated with, and an i8259A-compatible interrupt controller that translates APIC input into

PIC-equivalent signals. Because there can be multiple I/O APICs on the system, motherboards typically have a piece of core logic that sits between them and the processors. This logic is responsible for implementing interrupt routing algorithms that both balance the device interrupt load across processors and attempt to take advantage of locality, delivering device interrupts to the same processor that has just fielded a previous interrupt of the same type. Software programs can reprogram the I/O APICs with a fixed routing algorithm that bypasses this piece of chipset logic. Windows does this by programming the APICs in "interrupt one processor in the following set" routing mode.

FIGURE 3-2 x86 APIC architecture

x64 Interrupt Controllers

Because the x64 architecture is compatible with x86 operating systems, x64 systems must provide the same interrupt controllers as does the x86. A significant difference, however, is that the x64 versions of Windows will not run on systems that do not have an APIC as they use the APIC for interrupt control.

IA64 Interrupt Controllers

The IA64 architecture relies on the Streamlined Advanced Programmable Interrupt Controller (SAPIC), which is an evolution of the APIC. Even if load balancing and routing are present in the firmware, Windows does not take advantage of it; instead, it statically assigns interrupts to processors in a round-robin manner.

EXPERIMENT: Viewing the PIC and APIC

You can view the configuration of the PIC on a uniprocessor and the APIC on a multi-processor by using the *!pic* and *!apic* kernel debugger commands, respectively. Here's the output of the *!pic* command on a uniprocessor. (Note that the *!pic* command doesn't work if your system is using an APIC HAL.)

```
lkd> !pic
----- IRQ Number ----- 00 01 02 03 04 05 06 07 08 09 0A 0B 0C 0D 0E 0F
Physically in service:  .  .  .  .  .  .  .  .  .  .  .  .  .  .  .  .
Physically masked:      .  .  .  Y  .  .  Y  Y  .  .  Y  .  .  Y  .  .
Physically requested:   .  .  .  .  .  .  .  .  .  .  .  .  .  .  .  .
Level Triggered:        .  .  .  .  .  Y  .  .  .  Y  .  Y  .  .  .  .
```

Here's the output of the *!apic* command on a system running with the MPS HAL:

```
lkd> !apic
Apic @ fffe0000  ID:0 (40010)  LogDesc:01000000  DestFmt:ffffffff  TPR 20
TimeCnt: 0bebc200clk  SpurVec:3f  FaultVec:e3  error:0
Ipi Cmd: 0004001f  Vec:1F  FixedDel    Dest=Self      edg  high
Timer..: 000300fd  Vec:FD  FixedDel    Dest=Self      edg  high       masked
Linti0.: 0001003f  Vec:3F  FixedDel    Dest=Self      edg  high       masked
Linti1.: 000184ff  Vec:FF  NMI         Dest=Self      lvl  high       masked
TMR: 61, 82, 91-92, B1
IRR:
ISR:
```

The following output is for the *!ioapic* command, which displays the configuration of the I/O APICs, the interrupt controller components connected to devices:

```
0: kd> !ioapic
IoApic @ ffd02000  ID:8 (11)  Arb:0
Inti00.: 000100ff  Vec:FF  FixedDel    PhysDest:00  edg  masked
Inti01.: 00000962  Vec:62  LowestDl    Lg:03000000  edg
Inti02.: 000100ff  Vec:FF  FixedDel    PhysDest:00  edg  masked
Inti03.: 00000971  Vec:71  LowestDl    Lg:03000000  edg
Inti04.: 000100ff  Vec:FF  FixedDel    PhysDest:00  edg  masked
Inti05.: 00000961  Vec:61  LowestDl    Lg:03000000  edg
Inti06.: 00010982  Vec:82  LowestDl    Lg:02000000  edg  masked
Inti07.: 000100ff  Vec:FF  FixedDel    PhysDest:00  edg  masked
Inti08.: 000008d1  Vec:D1  FixedDel    Lg:01000000  edg
Inti09.: 000100ff  Vec:FF  FixedDel    PhysDest:00  edg  masked
Inti0A.: 000100ff  Vec:FF  FixedDel    PhysDest:00  edg  masked
Inti0B.: 000100ff  Vec:FF  FixedDel    PhysDest:00  edg  masked
Inti0C.: 00000972  Vec:72  LowestDl    Lg:03000000  edg
Inti0D.: 000100ff  Vec:FF  FixedDel    PhysDest:00  edg  masked
Inti0E.: 00000992  Vec:92  LowestDl    Lg:03000000  edg
Inti0F.: 000100ff  Vec:FF  FixedDel    PhysDest:00  edg  masked
Inti10.: 000100ff  Vec:FF  FixedDel    PhysDest:00  edg  masked
Inti11.: 000100ff  Vec:FF  FixedDel    PhysDest:00  edg  masked
```

```
Inti12.: 000100ff  Vec:FF  FixedDel  PhysDest:00  edg  masked
Inti13.: 000100ff  Vec:FF  FixedDel  PhysDest:00  edg  masked
Inti14.: 0000a9a3  Vec:A3  LowestD1  Lg:03000000  lvl
Inti15.: 0000a993  Vec:93  LowestD1  Lg:03000000  lvl
Inti16.: 000100ff  Vec:FF  FixedDel  PhysDest:00  edg  masked
Inti17.: 000100ff  Vec:FF  FixedDel  PhysDest:00  edg  masked
```

Software Interrupt Request Levels (IRQLs)

Although interrupt controllers perform a level of interrupt prioritization, Windows imposes its own interrupt priority scheme known as *interrupt request levels* (IRQLs). The kernel represents IRQLs internally as a number from 0 through 31 on x86 and from 0 to 15 on x64 and IA64, with higher numbers representing higher-priority interrupts. Although the kernel defines the standard set of IRQLs for software interrupts, the HAL maps hardware-interrupt numbers to the IRQLs. Figure 3-3 shows IRQLs defined for the x86 architecture, and Figure 3-4 shows IRQLs for the x64 and IA64 architectures.

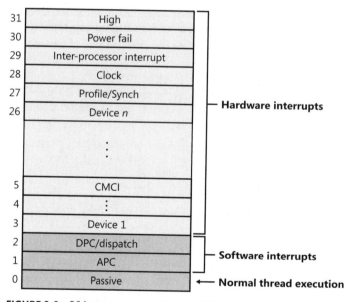

FIGURE 3-3 x86 interrupt request levels (IRQLs)

Interrupts are serviced in priority order, and a higher-priority interrupt preempts the servicing of a lower-priority interrupt. When a high-priority interrupt occurs, the processor saves the interrupted thread's state and invokes the trap dispatchers associated with the interrupt. The trap dispatcher raises the IRQL and calls the interrupt's service routine. After the service routine executes, the interrupt dispatcher lowers the processor's IRQL to where it was before the interrupt occurred and then loads the saved machine state. The interrupted thread resumes executing where it left off. When the kernel lowers the IRQL, lower-priority

interrupts that were masked might materialize. If this happens, the kernel repeats the process to handle the new interrupts.

	x64	IA64
15	High/Profile	High/Profile/Power
14	Inter-processor interrupt/Power	Inter-processor interrupt
13	Clock	Clock
12	Synch	Synch
11	Device *n*	Device *n*
		⋮
4	⋮	Device 1
3	Device 1	Correctable Machine Check
2	Dispatch/DPC	Dispatch/DPC & Synch
1	APC	APC
0	Passive/Low	Passive/Low

FIGURE 3-4 x64 and IA64 interrupt request levels (IRQLs)

IRQL priority levels have a completely different meaning than thread-scheduling priorities (which are described in Chapter 5). A scheduling priority is an attribute of a thread, whereas an IRQL is an attribute of an interrupt source, such as a keyboard or a mouse. In addition, each processor has an IRQL setting that changes as operating system code executes.

Each processor's IRQL setting determines which interrupts that processor can receive. IRQLs are also used to synchronize access to kernel-mode data structures. (You'll find out more about synchronization later in this chapter.) As a kernel-mode thread runs, it raises or lowers the processor's IRQL either directly by calling *KeRaiseIrql* and *KeLowerIrql* or, more commonly, indirectly via calls to functions that acquire kernel synchronization objects. As Figure 3-5 illustrates, interrupts from a source with an IRQL above the current level interrupt the processor, whereas interrupts from sources with IRQLs equal to or below the current level are *masked* until an executing thread lowers the IRQL.

Because accessing a PIC is a relatively slow operation, HALs that require accessing the I/O bus to change IRQLs, such as for PIC and 32-bit Advanced Configuration and Power Interface (ACPI) systems, implement a performance optimization, called *lazy IRQL*, that avoids PIC accesses. When the IRQL is raised, the HAL notes the new IRQL internally instead of changing the interrupt mask. If a lower-priority interrupt subsequently occurs, the HAL sets the interrupt mask to the settings appropriate for the first interrupt and postpones the lower-priority interrupt until the IRQL is lowered. Thus, if no lower-priority interrupts occur while the IRQL is raised, the HAL doesn't need to modify the PIC.

FIGURE 3-5 Masking interrupts

A kernel-mode thread raises and lowers the IRQL of the processor on which it's running, depending on what it's trying to do. For example, when an interrupt occurs, the trap handler (or perhaps the processor) raises the processor's IRQL to the assigned IRQL of the interrupt source. This elevation masks all interrupts at and below that IRQL (on that processor only), which ensures that the processor servicing the interrupt isn't waylaid by an interrupt at the same or a lower level. The masked interrupts are either handled by another processor or held back until the IRQL drops. Therefore, all components of the system, including the kernel and device drivers, attempt to keep the IRQL at passive level (sometimes called low level). They do this because device drivers can respond to hardware interrupts in a timelier manner if the IRQL isn't kept unnecessarily elevated for long periods.

Note An exception to the rule that raising the IRQL blocks interrupts of that level and lower relates to APC-level interrupts. If a thread raises the IRQL to APC level and then is rescheduled because of a dispatch/DPC-level interrupt, the system might deliver an APC level interrupt to the newly scheduled thread. Thus, APC level can be considered a thread-local rather than processor-wide IRQL.

EXPERIMENT: Viewing the IRQL

You can view a processor's saved IRQL with the *!irql* debugger command. The saved IRQL represents the IRQL at the time just before the break-in to the debugger, which raises the IRQL to a static, meaningless value:

```
kd> !irql
Debugger saved IRQL for processor 0x0 -- 0 (LOW_LEVEL)
```

Note that the IRQL value is saved in two locations. The first, which represents the current IRQL, is the processor control region (PCR), while its extension, the processor control block (PRCB), contains the saved IRQL in the DebuggerSaveIrql field. The PCR and PRCB contain information about the state of each processor in the system, such as the current IRQL, a pointer to the hardware IDT, the currently running thread, and the next thread selected to run. The kernel and the HAL use this information to perform architecture-specific and machine-specific actions. Portions of the PCR and PRCB structures are defined publicly in the Windows Driver Kit (WDK) header file Ntddk.h, so examine that file if you want a complete definition of these structures.

You can view the contents of the PCR with the kernel debugger by using the *!pcr* command:

```
lkd> !pcr
KPCR for Processor 0 at 820f4700:
    Major 1 Minor 1
      NtTib.ExceptionList: 9cee5cc8
        NtTib.StackBase: 00000000
       NtTib.StackLimit: 00000000
     NtTib.SubSystemTib: 801ca000
           NtTib.Version: 294308d9
       NtTib.UserPointer: 00000001
         NtTib.SelfTib: 7ffdf000

                SelfPcr: 820f4700
                   Prcb: 820f4820
                   Irql: 00000004
                    IRR: 00000000
                    IDR: ffffffff
          InterruptMode: 00000000
                    IDT: 81d7f400
                    GDT: 81d7f000
                    TSS: 801ca000

          CurrentThread: 8952d030
             NextThread: 00000000
             IdleThread: 820f8300

               DpcQueue:
```

Because changing a processor's IRQL has such a significant effect on system operation, the change can be made only in kernel mode—user-mode threads can't change the processor's IRQL. This means that a processor's IRQL is always at passive level when it's executing user-mode code. Only when the processor is executing kernel-mode code can the IRQL be higher.

Each interrupt level has a specific purpose. For example, the kernel issues an *interprocessor interrupt* (IPI) to request that another processor perform an action, such as dispatching a particular thread for execution or updating its translation look-aside buffer (TLB) cache. The system clock generates an interrupt at regular intervals, and the kernel responds by updating the clock and measuring thread execution time. If a hardware platform supports two clocks, the kernel adds another clock interrupt level to measure performance. The HAL provides a number of interrupt levels for use by interrupt-driven devices; the exact number varies with the processor and system configuration. The kernel uses software interrupts (described later in this chapter) to initiate thread scheduling and to asynchronously break into a thread's execution.

Mapping Interrupts to IRQLs IRQL levels aren't the same as the interrupt requests (IRQs) defined by interrupt controllers—the architectures on which Windows runs don't implement the concept of IRQLs in hardware. So how does Windows determine what IRQL to assign to an interrupt? The answer lies in the HAL. In Windows, a type of device driver called a *bus driver* determines the presence of devices on its bus (PCI, USB, and so on) and what interrupts can be assigned to a device. The bus driver reports this information to the Plug and Play manager, which decides, after taking into account the acceptable interrupt assignments for all other devices, which interrupt will be assigned to each device. Then it calls a Plug and Play interrupt arbiter, which maps interrupts to IRQLs.

The algorithm for assignment differs for the various HALs that Windows includes. On ACPI systems (including x86, x64, and IA64), the HAL computes the IRQL for a given interrupt by dividing the interrupt vector assigned to the IRQ by 16. As for selecting an interrupt vector for the IRQ, this depends on the type of interrupt controller present on the system. On today's APIC systems, this number is generated in a round-robin fashion, so there is no computable way to figure out the IRQ based on the interrupt vector or the IRQL.

Predefined IRQLs Let's take a closer look at the use of the predefined IRQLs, starting from the highest level shown in Figure 3-4:

- The kernel uses *high* level only when it's halting the system in *KeBugCheckEx* and masking out all interrupts.

- *Power fail level* originated in the original Windows NT design documents, which specified the behavior of system power failure code, but this IRQL has never been used.

- *Inter-processor interrupt* level is used to request another processor to perform an action, such as updating the processor's TLB cache, system shutdown, or system crash.

- *Clock* level is used for the system's clock, which the kernel uses to track the time of day as well as to measure and allot CPU time to threads.

- The system's real-time clock (or another source, such as the local APIC timer) uses *profile* level when kernel profiling, a performance measurement mechanism, is enabled. When kernel profiling is active, the kernel's profiling trap handler records the address of the code that was executing when the interrupt occurred. A table of address samples is constructed over time that tools can extract and analyze. You can obtain Kernrate, a kernel profiling tool that you can use to configure and view profiling-generated statistics, from the Windows Driver Kit (WDK). See the Kernrate experiment for more information on using this tool.

- The *device* IRQLs are used to prioritize device interrupts. (See the previous section for how hardware interrupt levels are mapped to IRQLs.)

- The *correctible machine check interrupt* level is used after a serious but correctible (by the operating system) hardware condition or error was reported by the CPU or firmware.

- *DPC/dispatch*-level and *APC*-level interrupts are software interrupts that the kernel and device drivers generate. (DPCs and APCs are explained in more detail later in this chapter.)

- The lowest IRQL, *passive* level, isn't really an interrupt level at all; it's the setting at which normal thread execution takes place and all interrupts are allowed to occur.

EXPERIMENT: Using Kernel Profiler (Kernrate) to Profile Execution

You can use the Kernel Profiler tool (Kernrate) to enable the system profiling timer, collect samples of the code that is executing when the timer fires, and display a summary showing the frequency distribution across image files and functions. It can be used to track CPU usage consumed by individual processes and/or time spent in kernel mode independent of processes (for example, interrupt service routines). Kernel profiling is useful when you want to obtain a breakdown of where the system is spending time.

In its simplest form, Kernrate samples where time has been spent in each kernel module (for example, Ntoskrnl, drivers, and so on). For example, after installing the Windows Driver Kit, try performing the following steps:

1. Open a command prompt.
2. Type **cd c:\winddk\6001\tools\other**.
3. Type **dir**. (You will see directories for each platform.)
4. Run the image that matches your platform (with no arguments or switches). For example, i386\kernrate.exe is the image for an x86 system.

5. While Kernrate is running, go perform some other activity on the system. For example, run Windows Media Player and play some music, run a graphics-intensive game, or perform network activity such as doing a directory of a remote network share.

6. Press Ctrl+C to stop Kernrate. This causes Kernrate to display the statistics from the sampling period.

In the sample output from Kernrate, Windows Media Player was running, playing a recorded movie from disk.

```
C:\Windows\system32>c:\Programming\ddk\tools\other\i386\kernrate.exe
 /===============================\
 <           KERNRATE LOG          >
 \===============================/
Date: 2008/03/09   Time: 16:44:24
Machine Name: ALEX-LAPTOP
Number of Processors: 2
PROCESSOR_ARCHITECTURE: x86
PROCESSOR_LEVEL: 6
PROCESSOR_REVISION: 0f06
Physical Memory: 3310 MB
Pagefile Total: 7285 MB
Virtual Total: 2047 MB
PageFile1: \??\C:\pagefile.sys, 4100MB
OS Version: 6.0 Build 6000 Service-Pack: 0.0
WinDir: C:\Windows

Kernrate Executable Location: C:\PROGRAMMING\DDK\TOOLS\OTHER\I386

Kernrate User-Specified Command Line:
c:\Programming\ddk\tools\other\i386\kernrate.exe

Kernel Profile (PID = 0): Source= Time,
Using Kernrate Default Rate of 25000 events/hit
Starting to collect profile data

***> Press ctrl-c to finish collecting profile data
===> Finished Collecting Data, Starting to Process Results

-----------Overall Summary:--------------

P0    K 0:00:00.000 ( 0.0%)  U 0:00:00.234 ( 4.7%)  I 0:00:04.789 (95.3%)
DPC 0:00:00.000 ( 0.0%)  Interrupt 0:00:00.000 ( 0.0%)
      Interrupts= 9254, Interrupt Rate= 1842/sec.

P1    K 0:00:00.031 ( 0.6%)  U 0:00:00.140 ( 2.8%)  I 0:00:04.851 (96.6%)
DPC 0:00:00.000 ( 0.0%)  Interrupt 0:00:00.000 ( 0.0%)
      Interrupts= 7051, Interrupt Rate= 1404/sec.

TOTAL K 0:00:00.031 ( 0.3%)  U 0:00:00.374 ( 3.7%)  I 0:00:09.640 (96.0%)
DPC 0:00:00.000 ( 0.0%)  Interrupt 0:00:00.000 ( 0.0%)
      Total Interrupts= 16305, Total Interrupt Rate= 3246/sec.
```

```
Total Profile Time = 5023 msec

                                       BytesStart         BytesStop        BytesDiff.
        Available Physical Memory  ,   1716359168,       1716195328,       -163840
        Available Pagefile(s)      ,   5973733376,       5972783104,       -950272
        Available Virtual          ,   2122145792,       2122145792,             0
        Available Extended Virtual ,            0,                0,             0
        Committed Memory Bytes     ,   1665404928,       1666355200,        950272
        Non Paged Pool Usage Bytes ,     66211840,         66211840,             0
        Paged Pool Usage Bytes     ,    189083648,        189087744,          4096
        Paged Pool Available Bytes ,    150593536,        150593536,             0
        Free System PTEs           ,        37322,            37322,             0

                                   Total       Avg. Rate
        Context Switches     ,     30152,      6003/sec.
        System Calls         ,    110807,      22059/sec.
        Page Faults          ,       226,      45/sec.
        I/O Read Operations  ,       730,      145/sec.
        I/O Write Operations ,      1038,      207/sec.
        I/O Other Operations ,       858,      171/sec.
        I/O Read Bytes       ,   2013850,      2759/ I/O
        I/O Write Bytes      ,     28212,      27/ I/O
        I/O Other Bytes      ,     19902,      23/ I/O

    ----------------------------

Results for Kernel Mode:
----------------------------

OutputResults: KernelModuleCount = 167
Percentage in the following table is based on the Total Hits for the Kernel

Time    3814 hits, 25000 events per hit --------
Module                          Hits      msec    %Total   Events/Sec
NTKRNLPA                        3768      5036     98 %     18705321
NVLDDMKM                          12      5036      0 %        59571
HAL                               12      5036      0 %        59571
WIN32K                            10      5037      0 %        49632
DXGKRNL                            9      5036      0 %        44678
NETW4V32                           2      5036      0 %         9928
FLTMGR                             1      5036      0 %         4964

=============================== END OF RUN ===================================
=========================== NORMAL END OF RUN ================================
```

The overall summary shows that the system spent 0.3 percent of the time in kernel mode, 3.7 percent in user mode, 96.0 percent idle, 0.0 percent at DPC level, and 0.0 percent at interrupt level. The module with the highest hit rate was Ntkrnlpa.exe, the kernel for machines with Physical Address Extension (PAE) or NX support. The module with the second highest hit rate was nvlddmkm.sys, the driver for the video card on the machine used for the test. This makes sense because the major activity going on in the system was Windows Media Player sending video I/O to the video driver.

If you have symbols available, you can zoom in on individual modules and see the time spent by function name. For example, profiling the system while rapidly dragging a window around the screen resulted in the following (partial) output:

```
C:\Windows\system32>c:\Programming\ddk\tools\other\i386\kernrate.exe -z ntkrnlpa -z
win32k
   /===============================\
  <          KERNRATE LOG          >
   \===============================/
Date: 2008/03/09    Time: 16:49:56

Time    4191 hits, 25000 events per hit --------
Module                        Hits       msec   %Total   Events/Sec
NTKRNLPA                      3623       5695   86 %      15904302
WIN32K                         303       5696    7 %       1329880
INTELPPM                       141       5696    3 %        618855
HAL                             61       5695    1 %        267778
CDD                             30       5696    0 %        131671
NVLDDMKM                        13       5696    0 %         57057

----- Zoomed module WIN32K.SYS (Bucket size = 16 bytes, Rounding Down) --------
Module                        Hits       msec   %Total   Events/Sec
BltLnkReadPat                   34       5696   10 %        149227
memmove                         21       5696    6 %         92169
vSrcTranCopyS8D32               17       5696    5 %         74613
memcpy                          12       5696    3 %         52668
RGNOBJ::bMerge                  10       5696    3 %         43890
HANDLELOCK::vLockHandle          8       5696    2 %         35112

----- Zoomed module NTKRNLPA.EXE (Bucket size = 16 bytes, Rounding Down) --------
Module                        Hits       msec   %Total   Events/Sec
KiIdleLoop                    3288       5695   87 %      14433713
READ_REGISTER_USHORT            95       5695    2 %        417032
READ_REGISTER_ULONG             93       5695    2 %        408252
RtlFillMemoryUlong              31       5695    0 %        136084
KiFastCallEntry                 18       5695    0 %         79016
```

The module with the second hit rate was Win32k.sys, the windowing system driver. Also high on the list were the video driver and Cdd.dll, a global video driver used for the 3D-accelerated Aero desktop theme. These results make sense because the main activity in the system was drawing on the screen. Note that in the zoomed display for Win32k.sys, the functions with the highest hits are related to merging, copying, and moving bits, the main GDI operations for painting a window dragged on the screen.

One important restriction on code running at DPC/dispatch level or above is that it can't wait for an object if doing so would necessitate the scheduler to select another thread to execute, which is an illegal operation because the scheduler synchronizes its data structures at DPC/dispatch level and cannot therefore be invoked to perform a reschedule. Another restriction is that only nonpaged memory can be accessed at IRQL DPC/dispatch level or higher.

This rule is actually a side-effect of the first restriction because attempting to access memory that isn't resident results in a page fault. When a page fault occurs, the memory manager initiates a disk I/O and then needs to wait for the file system driver to read the page in from disk. This wait would in turn require the scheduler to perform a context switch (perhaps to the idle thread if no user thread is waiting to run), thus violating the rule that the scheduler can't be invoked (because the IRQL is still DPC/dispatch level or higher at the time of the disk read).

If either of these two restrictions is violated, the system crashes with an IRQL_NOT_LESS_OR_EQUAL or a DRIVER_IRQL_NOT_LESS_OR_EQUAL crash code. (See Chapter 14 for a thorough discussion of system crashes.) Violating these restrictions is a common bug in device drivers. The Windows Driver Verifier, explained in the section "Driver Verifier" in Chapter 9, has an option you can set to assist in finding this particular type of bug.

Interrupt Objects The kernel provides a portable mechanism—a kernel control object called an *interrupt object*—that allows device drivers to register ISRs for their devices. An interrupt object contains all the information the kernel needs to associate a device ISR with a particular level of interrupt, including the address of the ISR, the IRQL at which the device interrupts, and the entry in the kernel's IDT with which the ISR should be associated. When an interrupt object is initialized, a few instructions of assembly language code, called the *dispatch code*, are copied from an interrupt handling template, *KiInterruptTemplate*, and stored in the object. When an interrupt occurs, this code is executed.

This interrupt-object resident code calls the real interrupt dispatcher, which is typically either the kernel's *KiInterruptDispatch* or *KiChainedDispatch* routine, passing it a pointer to the interrupt object. *KiInterruptDispatch* is the routine used for interrupt vectors for which only one interrupt object is registered, and *KiChainedDispatch* is for vectors shared among multiple interrupt objects. The interrupt object contains information this second dispatcher routine needs to locate and properly call the ISR the device driver provides.

The interrupt object also stores the IRQL associated with the interrupt so that *KiInterruptDispatch* or *KiChainedDispatch* can raise the IRQL to the correct level before calling the ISR and then lower the IRQL after the ISR has returned. This two-step process is required because there's no way to pass a pointer to the interrupt object (or any other argument for that matter) on the initial dispatch because the initial dispatch is done by hardware. On a multiprocessor system, the kernel allocates and initializes an interrupt object for each CPU, enabling the local APIC on that CPU to accept the particular interrupt.

Another kernel interrupt handler is *KiFloatingDispatch,* which is used for interrupts that require saving the floating-point state. Unlike kernel-mode code, which typically is not allowed to use floating-point (MMX, SSE, 3DNow!) operations because these registers won't be saved across context switches, ISRs might need to use these registers (such as the video card ISR performing a quick drawing operation). When connecting an interrupt, drivers can set the *FloatingSave* argument to TRUE, requesting that the kernel use the floating-point

dispatch routine, which will save the floating registers. (However, this will greatly increase interrupt latency.) Note that this is supported only on 32-bit systems.

Figure 3-6 shows typical interrupt control flow for interrupts associated with interrupt objects.

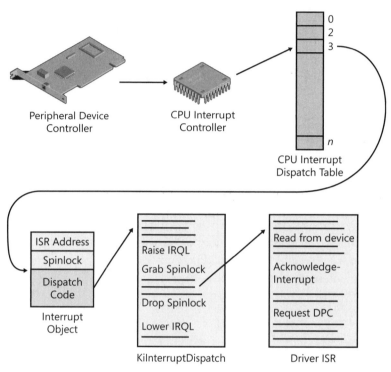

FIGURE 3-6 Typical interrupt control flow

EXPERIMENT: Examining Interrupt Internals

Using the kernel debugger, you can view details of an interrupt object, including its IRQL, ISR address, and custom interrupt dispatching code. First, execute the *!idt* command and locate the entry that includes a reference to *I8042KeyboardInterruptService*, the ISR routine for the PS2 keyboard device:

```
81:  89237050 i8042prt!I8042KeyboardInterruptService (KINTERRUPT 89237000)
```

To view the contents of the interrupt object associated with the interrupt, execute *dt nt!_kinterrupt* with the address following KINTERRUPT:

```
lkd> dt nt!_KINTERRUPT 89237000
   +0x000 Type             : 22
   +0x002 Size             : 624
   +0x004 InterruptListEntry : _LIST_ENTRY [ 0x89237004 - 0x89237004 ]
```

```
+0x00c ServiceRoutine        : 0x8f60e15c      unsigned char
                                               i8042prt!I8042KeyboardInterruptService+0
+0x010 MessageServiceRoutine : (null)
+0x014 MessageIndex          : 0
+0x018 ServiceContext        : 0x87c707a0
+0x01c SpinLock              : 0
+0x020 TickCount             : 0xffffffff
+0x024 ActualLock            : 0x87c70860   -> 0
+0x028 DispatchAddress       : 0x82090b40      void  nt!KiInterruptDispatch+0
+0x02c Vector                : 0x81
+0x030 Irql                  : 0x7 ''
+0x031 SynchronizeIrql       : 0x8 ''
+0x032 FloatingSave          : 0 ''
+0x033 Connected             : 0x1 ''
+0x034 Number                : 0 ''
+0x035 ShareVector           : 0 ''
+0x038 Mode                  : 1 ( Latched )
+0x03c Polarity              : 0 ( InterruptPolarityUnknown )
+0x040 ServiceCount          : 0
+0x044 DispatchCount         : 0xffffffff
+0x048 Rsvd1                 : 0
+0x050 DispatchCode          : [135] 0x56535554
```

In this example, the IRQL that Windows assigned to the interrupt is 7. Because this output is from an APIC system, the only way to verify the IRQ is to open the Device Manager (on the Hardware tab in the System item in Control Panel), locate the PS/2 keyboard device, and view its resource assignments, as shown in the following screen shot:

On an x64 or IA64 system you will see that the IRQ is the interrupt vector number (0x81—129 decimal—in this example) divided by 16 minus 1.

The ISR's address for the interrupt object is stored in the ServiceRoutine field (which is what *!idt* displays in its output), and the interrupt code that actually executes when an interrupt occurs is stored in the *DispatchCode* array at the end of the interrupt object. The interrupt code stored there is programmed to build the trap frame on the stack and then call the function stored in the DispatchAddress field (*KiInterruptDispatch* in the example), passing it a pointer to the interrupt object.

Windows and Real-Time Processing

Deadline requirements, either hard or soft, characterize real-time environments. Hard real-time systems (for example, a nuclear power plant control system) have deadlines that the system must meet to avoid catastrophic failures such as loss of equipment or life. Soft real-time systems (for example, a car's fuel-economy optimization system) have deadlines that the system can miss, but timeliness is still a desirable trait. In real-time systems, computers have sensor input devices and control output devices. The designer of a real-time computer system must know worst-case delays between the time an input device generates an interrupt and the time the device's driver can control the output device to respond. This worst-case analysis must take into account the delays the operating system introduces as well as the delays the application and device drivers impose.

Because Windows doesn't prioritize device IRQs in any controllable way and user-level applications execute only when a processor's IRQL is at passive level, Windows isn't always suitable as a real-time operating system. The system's devices and device drivers—not Windows—ultimately determine the worst-case delay. This factor becomes a problem when the real-time system's designer uses off-the-shelf hardware. The designer can have difficulty determining how long every off-the-shelf device's ISR or DPC might take in the worst case. Even after testing, the designer can't guarantee that a special case in a live system won't cause the system to miss an important deadline. Furthermore, the sum of all the delays a system's DPCs and ISRs can introduce usually far exceeds the tolerance of a time-sensitive system.

Although many types of embedded systems (for example, printers and automotive computers) have real-time requirements, Windows Embedded Standard doesn't have real-time characteristics. It is simply a version of Windows XP that makes it possible, using system-designer technology that Microsoft licensed from VenturCom (formerly Ardence and now part of IntervalZero), to produce small-footprint versions of Windows XP suitable for running on devices with limited resources. For example, a device that has no networking capability would omit all the Windows XP components related to

networking, including network management tools and adapter and protocol stack device drivers.

Still, there are third-party vendors that supply real-time kernels for Windows. The approach these vendors take is to embed their real-time kernel in a custom HAL and to have Windows run as a task in the real-time operating system. The task running Windows serves as the user interface to the system and has a lower priority than the tasks responsible for managing the device. See IntervalZero's Web site, *www.inter-valzero.com*, for an example of a third-party real-time kernel extension for Windows.

Associating an ISR with a particular level of interrupt is called *connecting an interrupt object*, and dissociating an ISR from an IDT entry is called *disconnecting an interrupt object*. These operations, accomplished by calling the kernel functions *IoConnectInterrupt* and *IoDisconnectInterrupt*, allow a device driver to "turn on" an ISR when the driver is loaded into the system and to "turn off" the ISR if the driver is unloaded.

Using the interrupt object to register an ISR prevents device drivers from fiddling directly with interrupt hardware (which differs among processor architectures) and from needing to know any details about the IDT. This kernel feature aids in creating portable device drivers because it eliminates the need to code in assembly language or to reflect processor differences in device drivers.

Interrupt objects provide other benefits as well. By using the interrupt object, the kernel can synchronize the execution of the ISR with other parts of a device driver that might share data with the ISR. (See Chapter 7 for more information about how device drivers respond to interrupts.)

Furthermore, interrupt objects allow the kernel to easily call more than one ISR for any interrupt level. If multiple device drivers create interrupt objects and connect them to the same IDT entry, the interrupt dispatcher calls each routine when an interrupt occurs at the specified interrupt line. This capability allows the kernel to easily support "daisy-chain" configurations, in which several devices share the same interrupt line. The chain breaks when one of the ISRs claims ownership for the interrupt by returning a status to the interrupt dispatcher.

If multiple devices sharing the same interrupt require service at the same time, devices not acknowledged by their ISRs will interrupt the system again once the interrupt dispatcher has lowered the IRQL. Chaining is permitted only if all the device drivers wanting to use the same interrupt indicate to the kernel that they can share the interrupt; if they can't, the Plug and Play manager reorganizes their interrupt assignments to ensure that it honors the sharing requirements of each. If the interrupt vector is shared, the interrupt object invokes *KiChainedDispatch*, which will invoke the ISRs of each registered interrupt object in turn until one of them claims the interrupt or all have been executed. In the earlier sample *!idt* output, vector 0xa2 is connected to several chained interrupt objects.

Even though connecting and disconnecting interrupts in previous versions of Windows was a portable operation that abstracted much of the internal system functionality from the developer, it still required a great deal of information from the device driver developer, which could result in anything from subtle bugs to hardware damage should these parameters be input improperly. As part of the many enhancements to the interrupt mechanisms in the kernel and HAL, Windows Vista introduced a new API, *IoConnectInterruptEx*, that added support for more advanced types of interrupts (called *message-based interrupts*) and enhanced the current support for standard interrupts (also called *line-based interrupts*). The new *IoConnectInterruptEx* API also takes fewer parameters than its predecessor. Notably missing are the vector (interrupt number), IRQL, affinity, and edge versus level-trigged parameters.

Software Interrupts

Although hardware generates most interrupts, the Windows kernel also generates software interrupts for a variety of tasks, including these:

- Initiating thread dispatching
- Non-time-critical interrupt processing
- Handling timer expiration
- Asynchronously executing a procedure in the context of a particular thread
- Supporting asynchronous I/O operations

These tasks are described in the following subsections.

Dispatch or Deferred Procedure Call (DPC) Interrupts When a thread can no longer continue executing, perhaps because it has terminated or because it voluntarily enters a wait state, the kernel calls the dispatcher directly to effect an immediate context switch. Sometimes, however, the kernel detects that rescheduling should occur when it is deep within many layers of code. In this situation, the kernel requests dispatching but defers its occurrence until it completes its current activity. Using a DPC software interrupt is a convenient way to achieve this delay.

The kernel always raises the processor's IRQL to DPC/dispatch level or above when it needs to synchronize access to shared kernel structures. This disables additional software interrupts and thread dispatching. When the kernel detects that dispatching should occur, it requests a DPC/dispatch-level interrupt; but because the IRQL is at or above that level, the processor holds the interrupt in check. When the kernel completes its current activity, it sees that it's going to lower the IRQL below DPC/dispatch level and checks to see whether any dispatch interrupts are pending. If there are, the IRQL drops to DPC/dispatch level and the dispatch interrupts are processed. Activating the thread dispatcher by using a software interrupt is a way to defer dispatching until conditions are right. However, Windows uses software interrupts to defer other types of processing as well.

In addition to thread dispatching, the kernel also processes deferred procedure calls (DPCs) at this IRQL. A DPC is a function that performs a system task—a task that is less time-critical than the current one. The functions are called *deferred* because they might not execute immediately.

DPCs provide the operating system with the capability to generate an interrupt and execute a system function in kernel mode. The kernel uses DPCs to process timer expiration (and release threads waiting for the timers) and to reschedule the processor after a thread's quantum expires. Device drivers use DPCs to complete I/O requests. To provide timely service for hardware interrupts, Windows—with the cooperation of device drivers—attempts to keep the IRQL below device IRQL levels. One way that this goal is achieved is for device driver ISRs to perform the minimal work necessary to acknowledge their device, save volatile interrupt state, and defer data transfer or other less time-critical interrupt processing activity for execution in a DPC at DPC/dispatch IRQL. (See Chapter 7 for more information on DPCs and the I/O system.)

A DPC is represented by a *DPC object*, a kernel control object that is not visible to user-mode programs but is visible to device drivers and other system code. The most important piece of information the DPC object contains is the address of the system function that the kernel will call when it processes the DPC interrupt. DPC routines that are waiting to execute are stored in kernel-managed queues, one per processor, called *DPC queues*. To request a DPC, system code calls the kernel to initialize a DPC object and then places it in a DPC queue.

By default, the kernel places DPC objects at the end of the DPC queue of the processor on which the DPC was requested (typically the processor on which the ISR executed). A device driver can override this behavior, however, by specifying a DPC priority (low, medium, or high, where medium is the default) and by targeting the DPC at a particular processor. A DPC aimed at a specific CPU is known as a *targeted DPC*. If the DPC has a low or medium priority, the kernel places the DPC object at the end of the queue; if the DPC has a high priority, the kernel inserts the DPC object at the front of the queue.

When the processor's IRQL is about to drop from an IRQL of DPC/dispatch level or higher to a lower IRQL (APC or passive level), the kernel processes DPCs. Windows ensures that the IRQL remains at DPC/dispatch level and pulls DPC objects off the current processor's queue until the queue is empty (that is, the kernel "drains" the queue), calling each DPC function in turn. Only when the queue is empty will the kernel let the IRQL drop below DPC/dispatch level and let regular thread execution continue. DPC processing is depicted in Figure 3-7.

DPC priorities can affect system behavior another way. The kernel usually initiates DPC queue draining with a DPC/dispatch-level interrupt. The kernel generates such an interrupt only if the DPC is directed at the processor the ISR is requested on and the DPC has a high or medium priority. If the DPC has a low priority, the kernel requests the interrupt only if the number of outstanding DPC requests for the processor rises above a threshold or if the number of DPCs requested on the processor within a time window is low.

FIGURE 3-7 Delivering a DPC

If a DPC is targeted at a CPU different from the one on which the ISR is running and the DPC's priority is high, the kernel immediately signals the target CPU (by sending it a dispatch IPI) to drain its DPC queue. If the priority is medium or low, the number of DPCs queued on the target processor must exceed a threshold for the kernel to trigger a DPC/dispatch interrupt. The system idle thread also drains the DPC queue for the processor it runs on. Although DPC targeting and priority levels are flexible, device drivers rarely need to change the default behavior of their DPC objects. Table 3-1 summarizes the situations that initiate DPC queue draining.

TABLE 3-1 DPC Interrupt Generation Rules

DPC Priority	DPC Targeted at ISR's Processor	DPC Targeted at Another Processor
Low	DPC queue length exceeds maximum DPC queue length or DPC request rate is less than minimum DPC request rate	DPC queue length exceeds maximum DPC queue length or system is idle
Medium	Always	DPC queue length exceeds maximum DPC queue length or system is idle
High	Always	Always

Because user-mode threads execute at low IRQL, the chances are good that a DPC will interrupt the execution of an ordinary user's thread. DPC routines execute without regard to what thread is running, meaning that when a DPC routine runs, it can't assume what process address space is currently mapped. DPC routines can call kernel functions, but they can't call system services, generate page faults, or create or wait for dispatcher objects (explained later in this chapter). They can, however, access nonpaged system memory addresses, because system address space is always mapped regardless of what the current process is.

DPCs are provided primarily for device drivers, but the kernel uses them too. The kernel most frequently uses a DPC to handle quantum expiration. At every tick of the system clock, an interrupt occurs at clock IRQL. The *clock interrupt handler* (running at clock IRQL) updates the system time and then decrements a counter that tracks how long the current thread has run. When the counter reaches 0, the thread's time quantum has expired and the kernel might need to reschedule the processor, a lower-priority task that should be done at DPC/dispatch IRQL. The clock interrupt handler queues a DPC to initiate thread dispatching and then finishes its work and lowers the processor's IRQL. Because the DPC interrupt has a lower priority than do device interrupts, any pending device interrupts that surface before the clock interrupt completes are handled before the DPC interrupt occurs.

EXPERIMENT: Listing System Timers

You can use the kernel debugger to dump all the current registered timers on the system, as well as information on the DPC associated with each timer (if any). See the output below for a sample:

```
lkd> !timer
Dump system timers

Interrupt time: 437df8b4 00000330 [ 5/19/2008 15:56:27.044]

List Timer       Interrupt Low/High      Fire Time              DPC/thread
  1 886dd6f0     45b1ecca 00000330 [ 5/19/2008 15:56:30.739]  srv+1005
  7 884966a8     0ebf5dcb 00001387 [ 6/08/2008 10:58:03.373]  thread 88496620
 11 8553b8f8     4f4db783 00000330 [ 5/19/2008 15:56:46.860]  thread 8553b870
    85404be0     4f4db783 00000330 [ 5/19/2008 15:56:46.860]  thread 85404b58
 16 89a1c0a8     a62084ac 00000331 [ 5/19/2008 16:06:22.022]  thread 89a1c020
 18 8ab02198     ec7a2c4c 00000330 [ 5/19/2008 16:01:10.554]  thread 8ab02110
 19 8564aa20     45dae868 00000330 [ 5/19/2008 15:56:31.008]  thread 8564a998
 20 86314738     4a9ffc6a 00000330 [ 5/19/2008 15:56:39.010]  thread 863146b0
    88c21320     4aa0719b 00000330 [ 5/19/2008 15:56:39.013]  thread 88c21298
 21 88985e00     4f655e8c 00000330 [ 5/19/2008 15:56:47.015]  thread 88985d78
 22 88d00748     542b35e0 00000330 [ 5/19/2008 15:56:55.022]  thread 88d006c0
    899764c0     542b35e0 00000330 [ 5/19/2008 15:56:55.022]  thread 89976438
    861f8b70     542b35e0 00000330 [ 5/19/2008 15:56:55.022]  thread 861f8ae8
    861e71d8     542b5cf0 00000330 [ 5/19/2008 15:56:55.023]  thread 861e7150
 26 8870ee00     45ec1074 00000330 [ 5/19/2008 15:56:31.120]  thread 8870ed78
 29 8846e348     4f7a35a4 00000330 [ 5/19/2008 15:56:47.152]  thread 8846e2c0
    86b8f110     543d1b8c 00000330 [ 5/19/2008 15:56:55.140]  ndis!NdisCancelTimer-
                                                                Object+aa
 38 88a56610     460a2035 00000330 [ 5/19/2008 15:56:31.317]  afd!AfdTimeoutPoll
```

In this example, there are three driver-associated timers, due to expire shortly, associated with the Srv.sys, Ndis.sys, and Afd.sys drivers (all related to networking). Additionally, there are a dozen or so timers that don't have any DPC associated with them—this likely indicates user-mode or kernel-mode timers that are used for wait dispatching. You can use *!thread* on the thread pointers to verify this.

Because DPCs execute regardless of whichever thread is currently running on the system (much like interrupts), they are a primary cause for perceived system unresponsiveness of client systems or workstation workloads because even the highest-priority thread will be interrupted by a pending DPC. Some DPCs run long enough that users may perceive video or sound lagging, and even abnormal mouse or keyboard latencies, so for the benefit of drivers with long-running DPCs, Windows supports *threaded DPCs*.

Threaded DPCs, as their name implies, function by executing the DPC routine at passive level on a real-time priority (priority 31) thread. This allows the DPC to preempt most user-mode threads (because most application threads don't run at real-time priority ranges), but allows other interrupts, non-threaded DPCs, APCs, and higher-priority threads to preempt the routine.

The threaded DPC mechanism is enabled by default, but you can disable it by editing the HKEY_LOCAL_MACHINE\System\CurrentControlSet\Control\SessionManager\Kernel\ ThreadDpcEnable value and setting it to 0. Because threaded DPCs can be disabled, driver developers who make use of threaded DPCs must write their routines following the same rules as for non-threaded DPC routines and cannot access paged memory, perform dispatcher waits, or make assumptions about the IRQL level at which they are executing. In addition, they must not use the *KeAcquire/ReleaseSpinLockAtDpcLevel* APIs because the functions assume the CPU is at dispatch level. Instead, threaded DPCs must use *KeAcquire/ReleaseSpinLockForDpc*, which performs the appropriate action after checking the current IRQL.

EXPERIMENT: Monitoring Interrupt and DPC Activity

You can use Process Explorer to monitor interrupt and DPC activity by adding the Context Switch Delta column and watching the Interrupt and DPC processes. (See the following screen shot.) These are not real processes, but they are shown as processes for convenience and therefore do not incur context switches. Process Explorer's context switch count for these pseudo processes reflects the number of occurrences of each within the previous refresh interval. You can stimulate interrupt and DPC activity by moving the mouse quickly around the screen.

You can also trace the execution of specific interrupt service routines and deferred pro-cedure calls with the built-in event tracing support (described later in this chapter).

1. Start capturing events by typing the following command:

 tracelog –start –f kernel.etl –dpcisr –UsePerfCounter –b 64

2. Stop capturing events by typing:

tracelog –stop

3. Generate reports for the event capture by typing:

tracerpt kernel.etl –report report.html –f html

This will generate a Web page called report.html

4. Open report.html and expand the DPC/ISR subsection. Expand the DPC/ISR Breakdown area, and you will see summaries of the time spent in ISRs and DPCs by each driver. For example:

Running an *ln* command in the kernel debugger on the address of each event record shows the name of the function that executed the DPC or ISR:

```
1kd> ln 0x806321C7
(806321c7)   ndis!ndisInterruptDpc

1kd> ln 0x820AED3F
(820aed3f)   nt!IopTimerDispatch

1kd> ln 0x82051312
(82051312)   nt!PpmPerfIdleDpc
```

The first is a DPC queued by a network card NDIS miniport driver. The second is a DPC for a generic I/O timer expiration. The third address is the address of a DPC for an idle performance operation. For more information, see *www.microsoft.com/whdc/driver/perform/mmdrv.mspx*.

Asynchronous Procedure Call (APC) Interrupts Asynchronous procedure calls (APCs) provide a way for user programs and system code to execute in the context of a particular user thread (and hence a particular process address space). Because APCs are queued to execute in the context of a particular thread and run at an IRQL less than DPC/dispatch level, they don't operate under the same restrictions as a DPC. An APC routine can acquire resources (objects), wait for object handles, incur page faults, and call system services.

APCs are described by a kernel control object, called an *APC object*. APCs waiting to execute reside in a kernel-managed *APC queue*. Unlike the DPC queue, which is systemwide, the APC queue is thread-specific—each thread has its own APC queue. When asked to queue an APC, the kernel inserts it into the queue belonging to the thread that will execute the APC routine. The kernel, in turn, requests a software interrupt at APC level, and when the thread eventually begins running, it executes the APC.

There are two kinds of APCs: kernel mode and user mode. Kernel-mode APCs don't require "permission" from a target thread to run in that thread's context, while user-mode APCs do. Kernel-mode APCs interrupt a thread and execute a procedure without the thread's intervention or consent. There are also two types of kernel-mode APCs: normal and special. Special APCs execute at APC level and allow the APC routine to modify some of the APC parameters. Normal APCs execute at passive level and receive the modified parameters from the special APC routine (or the original parameters if they weren't modified).

Both normal and special APCs can be disabled by raising the IRQL to APC level or by calling *KeEnterGuardedRegion*. *KeEnterGuardedRegion* disables APC delivery by setting the SpecialApcDisable field in the calling thread's KTHREAD structure (described further in Chapter 5). A thread can disable normal APCs only by calling *KeEnterCriticalRegion*, which sets the KernelApcDisable field in the thread's KTHREAD structure. Table 3-2 summarizes APC insertion and delivery behavior for each type of APC.

The executive uses kernel-mode APCs to perform operating system work that must be completed within the address space (in the context) of a particular thread. It can use special kernel-mode APCs to direct a thread to stop executing an interruptible system service, for example, or to record the results of an asynchronous I/O operation in a thread's address space. Environment subsystems use special kernel-mode APCs to make a thread suspend or terminate itself or to get or set its user-mode execution context. The POSIX subsystem uses kernel-mode APCs to emulate the delivery of POSIX signals to POSIX processes.

Another important use of kernel-mode APCs is related to thread suspension and termination. Because these operations can be initiated from arbitrary threads and be directed to other arbitrary threads, the kernel uses an APC to query the thread context as well as to terminate the thread. Device drivers will often block APCs or enter a critical or guarded region to prevent these operations from occurring while they are holding a lock; otherwise, the lock may never be released, and the system would hang.

TABLE 3-2 APC Insertion and Delivery

APC Type	Insertion Behavior	Delivery Behavior
Special (kernel)	Inserted at the tail of the kernel-mode APC list.	Delivered at APC level as soon as IRQL drops and the thread is not in a guarded region. Given pointers to arguments specified when inserting the APC.
Normal (kernel)	Inserted right after the last special APC (at the head of all other normal APCs).	Delivered at PASSIVE_LEVEL after the associated special APC was executed. Given arguments returned by the associated special APC (may be the original arguments used during insertion or new ones).
Normal (user)	Inserted at the tail of the user-mode APC list.	Delivered at PASSIVE_LEVEL as soon as IRQL drops, the thread is not in a critical (or guarded) region, and the thread is in an alerted state. Given arguments returned by the associated special APC (may be the original arguments used during insertion or new ones).
Normal (user) Thread Exit (*PsExitSpecialApc*)	Inserted at the head of the user-mode APC list.	Delivered at PASSIVE_LEVEL on return to user mode, if the thread is doing an alerted user-mode wait. Given arguments returned by the thread termination special APC.

Device drivers also use kernel-mode APCs. For example, if an I/O operation is initiated and a thread goes into a wait state, another thread in another process can be scheduled to run. When the device finishes transferring data, the I/O system must somehow get back into the context of the thread that initiated the I/O so that it can copy the results of the I/O operation to the buffer in the address space of the process containing that thread. The I/O system uses a special kernel-mode APC to perform this action, unless the application used the *SetFileIoOverlappedRange* API or I/O completion ports, in which case the buffer will either be global in memory or only copied after the thread pulls a completion item from the port. (The use of APCs in the I/O system is discussed in more detail in Chapter 7.)

Several Windows APIs, such as *ReadFileEx*, *WriteFileEx*, and *QueueUserAPC*, use user-mode APCs. For example, the *ReadFileEx* and *WriteFileEx* functions allow the caller to specify a completion routine to be called when the I/O operation finishes. The I/O completion is implemented by queuing an APC to the thread that issued the I/O. However, the callback to the completion routine doesn't necessarily take place when the APC is queued because user-mode APCs are delivered to a thread only when it's in an *alertable wait state*. A thread can enter a wait state either by waiting for an object handle and specifying that its wait is alertable (with the Windows *WaitForMultipleObjectsEx* function) or by testing directly whether it has a pending APC (using *SleepEx*). In both cases, if a user-mode APC is pending, the kernel interrupts (alerts) the thread, transfers control to the APC routine, and resumes the thread's execution when the APC routine completes. Unlike kernel-mode APCs, which can execute at APC level, user-mode APCs execute at passive level.

APC delivery can reorder the wait queues—the lists of which threads are waiting for what, and in what order they are waiting. (Wait resolution is described in the section "Low-IRQL Synchronization" later in this chapter.) If the thread is in a wait state when an APC is delivered, after the APC routine completes, the wait is reissued or reexecuted. If the wait still isn't resolved, the thread returns to the wait state, but now it will be at the end of the list of objects it's waiting for. For example, because APCs are used to suspend a thread from execution, if the thread is waiting for any objects, its wait will be removed until the thread is resumed, after which that thread will be at the end of the list of threads waiting to access the objects it was waiting for. A thread performing an alertable kernel-mode wait will also be woken up during thread termination, allowing such a thread to check whether it woke up as a result of termination or a different reason.

Exception Dispatching

In contrast to interrupts, which can occur at any time, exceptions are conditions that result directly from the execution of the program that is running. Windows uses a facility known as *structured exception handling*, which allows applications to gain control when exceptions occur. The application can then fix the condition and return to the place the exception occurred, unwind the stack (thus terminating execution of the subroutine that raised the exception), or declare back to the system that the exception isn't recognized and the system should continue searching for an exception handler that might process the exception. This section assumes you're familiar with the basic concepts behind Windows structured exception handling—if you're not, you should read the overview in the Windows API reference documentation in the Windows SDK or Chapters 23 through 25 in Jeffrey Richter's book *Windows via C/C++* (Microsoft Press, 2007) before proceeding. Keep in mind that although exception handling is made accessible through language extensions (for example, the __try construct in Microsoft Visual C++), it is a system mechanism and hence isn't language-specific. Other examples of consumers of Windows exception handling include C++ and Java exceptions.

On the x86 and x64 processors, all exceptions have predefined interrupt numbers that directly correspond to the entry in the IDT that points to the trap handler for a particular exception. Table 3-3 shows x86-defined exceptions and their assigned interrupt numbers. Because the first entries of the IDT are used for exceptions, hardware interrupts are assigned entries later in the table, as mentioned earlier.

All exceptions, except those simple enough to be resolved by the trap handler, are serviced by a kernel module called the *exception dispatcher*. The exception dispatcher's job is to find an exception handler that can "dispose of" the exception. Examples of architecture-independent exceptions that the kernel defines include memory access violations, integer divide-by-zero, integer overflow, floating-point exceptions, and debugger breakpoints. For a complete list of architecture-independent exceptions, consult the Windows SDK reference documentation.

TABLE 3-3 x86 Exceptions and Their Interrupt Numbers

Interrupt Number	Exception
0	Divide Error
1	Debug (Single Step)
2	Non-Maskable Interrupt (NMI)
3	Breakpoint
4	Overflow
5	Bounds Check
6	Invalid Opcode
7	NPX Not Available
8	Double Fault
9	NPX Segment Overrun
10	Invalid Task State Segment (TSS)
11	Segment Not Present
12	Stack Fault
13	General Protection
14	Page Fault
15	Intel Reserved
16	Floating Point
17	Alignment Check
18	Machine Check
19	SIMD Floating Point

The kernel traps and handles some of these exceptions transparently to user programs. For example, encountering a breakpoint while executing a program being debugged generates an exception, which the kernel handles by calling the debugger. The kernel handles certain other exceptions by returning an unsuccessful status code to the caller.

A few exceptions are allowed to filter back, untouched, to user mode. For example, certain types of memory access violations or an arithmetic overflow generate an exception that the operating system doesn't handle. 32-bit applications can establish *frame-based exception handlers* to deal with these exceptions. The term *frame-based* refers to an exception handler's association with a particular procedure activation. When a procedure is invoked, a *stack frame* representing that activation of the procedure is pushed onto the stack. A stack frame can have one or more exception handlers associated with it, each of which protects a particular block of code in the source program. When an exception occurs, the kernel searches for an exception handler associated with the current stack frame. If none exists, the kernel searches for an exception handler associated with the previous stack frame, and so on, until it finds a frame-based exception handler. If no exception handler is found, the kernel calls its own default exception handlers.

For 64-bit applications, structured exception handling does not use frame-based handlers. Instead, a table of handlers for each function is built into the image during compilation. The kernel looks for handlers associated with each function and generally follows the same algorithm we've described for 32-bit code.

Structured exception handling is heavily used within the kernel itself so that it can safely verify whether pointers from user mode can be safely accessed for read or write access. Drivers can make use of this same technique when dealing with pointers sent during I/O control codes (IOCTLs). Another mechanism of exception handling is called *vectored exception handling*. This method can only be used by user-mode applications. You can find more information about it in the Windows SDK or the MSDN Library.

When an exception occurs, whether it is explicitly raised by software or implicitly raised by hardware, a chain of events begins in the kernel. The CPU hardware transfers control to the kernel trap handler, which creates a trap frame (as it does when an interrupt occurs). The trap frame allows the system to resume where it left off if the exception is resolved. The trap handler also creates an exception record that contains the reason for the exception and other pertinent information.

If the exception occurred in kernel mode, the exception dispatcher simply calls a routine to locate a frame-based exception handler that will handle the exception. Because unhandled kernel-mode exceptions are considered fatal operating system errors, you can assume that the dispatcher always finds an exception handler. Some traps, however, do not lead into an exception handler because the kernel always assumes such errors to be fatal—these are errors that could have been caused only by severe bugs in the internal kernel code or by major inconsistencies in driver code (that could have only occurred through deliberate low-level system modifications that drivers should not be responsible for). Such fatal errors will result in a bug check with the UNEXPECTED_KERNEL_MODE_TRAP code.

If the exception occurred in user mode, the exception dispatcher does something more elaborate. As you'll see in Chapter 5, the Windows subsystem has a debugger port (this is actually a debugger object, which will be discussed later) and an exception port to receive notification of user-mode exceptions in Windows processes. (In this case, by "port" we mean an LPC port object, which will be discussed later in this chapter.) The kernel uses these ports in its default exception handling, as illustrated in Figure 3-8.

Debugger breakpoints are common sources of exceptions. Therefore, the first action the exception dispatcher takes is to see whether the process that incurred the exception has an associated debugger process. If it does, the exception dispatcher sends a debugger object message to the *debug object* associated with the process (which internally the system refers to as a port for compatibility with programs that might rely on behavior in Windows 2000, which used an LPC port instead of a debug object).

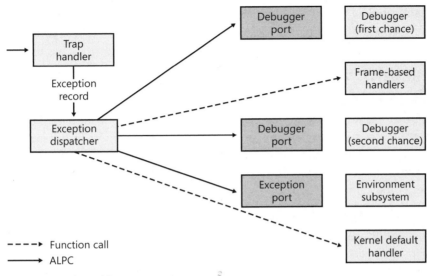

- - - - → Function call

——→ ALPC

FIGURE 3-8 Dispatching an exception

If the process has no debugger process attached, or if the debugger doesn't handle the exception, the exception dispatcher switches into user mode, copies the trap frame to the user stack formatted as a CONTEXT data structure (documented in the Windows SDK), and calls a routine to find a structured or vectored exception handler. If none is found, or if none handles the exception, the exception dispatcher switches back into kernel mode and calls the debugger again to allow the user to do more debugging. (This is called the second-chance notification.)

If the debugger isn't running and no user-mode exception handlers are found, the kernel sends a message to the exception port associated with the thread's process. This exception port, if one exists, was registered by the environment subsystem that controls this thread. The exception port gives the environment subsystem, which presumably is listening at the port, the opportunity to translate the exception into an environment-specific signal or exception. Csrss (Client/Server Run-Time Subsystem) uses this signal for Windows Error Reporting (WER)—which will be discussed shortly—and when POSIX gets a message from the kernel that one of its threads generated an exception, the POSIX subsystem sends a POSIX-style signal to the thread that caused the exception. However, if the kernel progresses this far in processing the exception and the subsystem doesn't handle the exception, the kernel executes a default exception handler that simply terminates the process whose thread caused the exception.

Unhandled Exceptions

All Windows threads have an exception handler that processes unhandled exceptions. This exception handler is declared in the internal Windows *start-of-thread* function. The start-of-thread function runs when a user creates a process or any additional threads. It calls the

environment-supplied thread start routine specified in the initial thread context structure, which in turn calls the user-supplied thread start routine specified in the *CreateThread* call.

EXPERIMENT: Viewing the Real User Start Address for Windows Threads

The fact that each Windows thread begins execution in a system-supplied function (and not the user-supplied function) explains why the start address for thread 0 is the same for every Windows process in the system (and why the start addresses for secondary threads are also the same). To see the user-supplied function address, use Process Explorer or the kernel debugger.

Because most threads in Windows processes start at one of the system-supplied wrapper functions, Process Explorer, when displaying the start address of threads in a process, skips the initial call frame that represents the wrapper function and instead shows the second frame on the stack. For example, notice the thread start address of a process running Notepad.exe:

Process Explorer does display the complete call hierarchy when it displays the call stack. Notice the following results when the Stack button is clicked:

Line 18 in the preceding screen shot is the first frame on the stack—the start of the internal thread wrapper. The second frame (line 17) is the environment subsystem's thread wrapper, in this case kernel32, because we are dealing with a Windows subsystem application. The third frame (line 16) is the main entry point into Notepad.exe.

The generic code for the internal thread start functions is shown here:

```
VOID RtlUserThreadStart(VOID){

    LPVOID lpStartAddr = (R/E)AX; // Located in the initial thread context structure
    LPVOID lpvThreadParm = (R/E)BX; // Located in the initial thread context structure
    LPVOID lpWin32StartAddr;

    lpWin32StartAddr = Kernel32ThreadInitThunkFunction ? Kernel32ThreadInitThunkFunction :
lpStartAddr;
    __try {

        DWORD dwThreadExitCode = lpWin32StartAddr(lpvThreadParm);
        RtlExitUserThread(dwThreadExitCode);

    } __except(RtlUnhandledExceptionFilter(
            GetExceptionInformation())) {

        RtlExitUserProcess(GetExceptionCode());
    }
}
void Win32StartOfProcess(
    LPTHREAD_START_ROUTINE lpStartAddr,
    LPVOID lpvThreadParm){

    lpStartAddr(lpvThreadParm);
}
```

Notice that the Windows unhandled exception filter is called if the thread has an exception that it doesn't handle. The purpose of this function is to provide the system-defined behavior for what to do when an exception is not handled, which is based on the contents of the HKLM\SOFTWARE\Microsoft\Windows NT\CurrentVersion\AeDebug registry key and on whether the process is on the exclusion list. There are two important values: Auto and Debugger. Auto tells the unhandled exception filter whether to automatically run the debugger or ask the user what to do. Installing development tools, such as Microsoft Visual Studio, will change this value to 0. The Debugger value is a string that points to the path of the debugger executable to run in the case of an unhandled exception.

Windows Error Reporting

Windows Error Reporting (WER) is a sophisticated mechanism that automates the submission of both user-mode process crashes as well as kernel-mode system crashes. (For a description of how this applies to system crashes, see Chapter 14.)

Windows Error Reporting can be configured by going to Control Panel, choosing Problem Reports And Solutions, and then Change Settings. (See Figure 3-9.) Alternatively, you can launch the Wercon.exe application from a command prompt or by using Start, Run.

FIGURE 3-9 Problem Reports And Solutions configuration dialog box

When an unhandled exception is caught by the unhandled exception filter (described in the previous section), it builds context information (such as the current value of the registers and stack) and opens an LPC port connection to the WER service. This service will begin to analyze the crashed program's state and perform the appropriate actions to notify the user. In most cases, this means launching the WerFault.exe program, which executes with the current user's credentials and displays a message box informing the user of the crash, as shown in Figure 3-10. (The figure shows the Accvio.exe program, downloadable from the book home page on Windows Sysinternals, *www.microsoft.com/technet/sysinternals*.) On systems where a debugger is installed, an additional option to debug the process will be shown. When you click the Debug button, the debugger (registered in the Debugger string described earlier in the AeDebug key) will be launched so it can attach to the crashing process.

FIGURE 3-10 Windows Error Reporting dialog box

On default configured systems, an error report (a minidump and an XML file with various details, such as the DLL version numbers loaded in the process) is sent to Microsoft's online crash analysis server. Eventually, as the service is notified of a solution for a problem, it will display a tooltip to the user informing her of steps that should be taken to solve the problem. An entry will also be displayed in the Problem Reports And Solutions configuration dialog box. By clicking on the tooltip, or the link under the configuration dialog box, WER displays a solution pane, as shown in Figure 3-11.

In environments where systems are not connected to the Internet or where the administrator wants to control which error reports are submitted to Microsoft, the destination for the error report can be configured to be an internal file server. Microsoft provides to qualified customers a tool set, called Microsoft Systems Center 2007, that understands the directory structure created by Windows Error Reporting and provides the administrator with the option to take selective error reports and submit them to Microsoft.

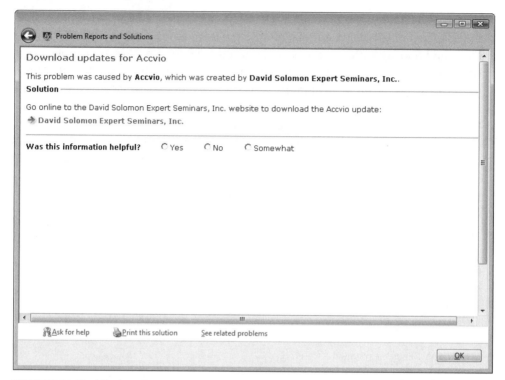

FIGURE 3-11 The Windows Error Reporting solution pane

Until Windows Vista, all the operations we've described had to occur within the crashing thread's context; that is to say, as part of the unhandled exception filter that was initially set up. In certain types of crashes, these complex operations became impossible for a badly damaged thread to perform, so the unhandled exception filter itself crashed. This "silent process death" was not logged anywhere, which made it hard to debug and also resulted in invisible crashes in cases where no user was present on the machine. (This also meant that services or applications could crash on servers without any trace.) Windows Vista and later versions improved the WER mechanism by performing this work externally from the crashed thread, if the unhandled exception filter itself crashes.

WER contains many customizable settings that can be configured by the user through the Group Policy editor or by manually making changes to the registry. Table 3-4 lists the WER registry configuration options, their use, and possible values. These values are located under the HKLM\SOFTWARE\Microsoft\Windows\Windows Error Reporting subkey for computer configuration and in the equivalent path under HKEY_CURRENT_USER for per-user configuration.

TABLE 3-4 WER Registry Settings

Setting	Meaning	Values
ConfigureArchive	Contents of archived data	1 for parameters, 2 for all data
Consent\DefaultConsent	What kind of data should require consent	1 for any data, 2 for parameters only, 3 for parameters and safe data, 4 for all data.
Consent\ DefaultOverrideBehavior	Whether the DefaultConsent overrides WER plug-in consent values	1 to enable override
Consent*PluginName*	Consent value for a specific WER plug-in	Same as DefaultConsent
CorporateWERDirectory	Directory for a corporate WER store	String containing the path
CorporateWERPort-Number	Port to use for a corporate WER store	Port number
CorporateWERServer	Name to use for a corporate WER store	String containing the name
CorporateWERUse-Authentication	Use Windows Integrated Authentication for corporate WER store	1 to enable built-in authentication
CorporateWERUseSSL	Use SSL for corporate WER store	1 to enable SSL
DebugApplications\ *ExeName*	List of applications that require the user to choose between Debug and Continue	String containing the application list
DisableArchive	Whether the archive is enabled	1 to disable archive
Disabled	Whether WER is disabled	1 to disable WER
DisableQueue	Determines whether reports are to be queued	1 to disable queue
DontShowUI	Disables or enables the WER UI	1 to disable UI
DontSendAdditionalData	Prevents additional crash data from being sent	1 not to send
ExcludedApplications\ *AppName*	List of applications excluded from WER	String containing the application list
ForceQueue	Whether reports should be sent to the user queue	1 to send reports to the queue
LocalDumps\Dump-Folder	Path at which to store the dump files	String containing the path
LocalDumps\DumpCount	Maximum number of dump files in the path	Count
LocalDumps\DumpType	Type of dump to generate during a crash	0 for a custom dump, 1 for a minidump, 2 for a full dump

Setting	Meaning	Values
LocalDumps\ CustomDumpFlags	For custom dumps, specifies custom options	Values defined in MINIDUMP_ TYPE (see Chapter 13 for more information)
LoggingDisabled	Enables or disables logging	1 to disable logging
MaxArchiveCount	Maximum size of the archive (in files)	Value between 1–5000
MaxQueueCount	Maximum size of the queue	Value between 1–500
QueuePesterInterval	Days between requests to have the user check for solutions	Number of days

Note The values listed under LocalDumps can also be configured per application by adding the application name in the subkey path between LocalDumps and the relevant value. However, they cannot be configured per user; they exist only in the HKLM path.

As discussed, the WER service uses an ALPC port for communicating with crashed processes. This mechanism has been extended to function as well over the standard exception port mechanism that has always been present in the Windows exception dispatching design. As a result, all Windows processes now have an error port that is actually an ALPC port object registered by the WER service. The kernel, which is first notified of an exception, will use this port to send a message to the WER service, which will then analyze the crashing process. This means that even in severe cases of thread state damage, WER will still be able to receive notifications and launch WerFault.exe to display a user interface instead of having to do this work within the crashing thread itself. Additionally, WER will be able to generate a crash dump for the process, and a message will be written to the Event Log. This solves all the problems of silent process death: users are notified, debugging can occur, and service administrators can see the crash event. The next experiment will demonstrate this improved behavior.

EXPERIMENT: Silent Process Exception Termination

One typical crash that the error reporting mechanism prior to Windows Vista could not handle was stack trashing. This means that the stack of the crashed thread was damaged, perhaps even deallocated, so that even calling a new function (which puts the return address as well as arguments on the stack) would generate another, subsequent crash, prompting the kernel to terminate the process. You can see this behavior on a system running Windows Vista or later by temporarily turning off the WER service and then enabling it again. Follow these steps:

1. Open the Services.msc Microsoft Management Console (MMC) snap-in.

2. Double-click on Windows Error Reporting, and then click the Stop button under the Service status label.

3. Launch the Stacktrash.exe application (downloadable from the book home page on Sysinternals).

4. Click the Trash Stack button. You should see the process disappear without a trace.

5. Now click the Start button in the Windows Error Reporting service configuration dialog box again, and then launch Stacktrash.exe one more time. You should see the WER dialog box displayed along with a pop-up balloon near the system tray notifying you that the application encountered an error.

System Service Dispatching

As Figure 3-1 illustrated, the kernel's trap handlers dispatch interrupts, exceptions, and system service calls. In the preceding sections, you've seen how interrupt and exception handling work; in this section, you'll learn about system services. A system service dispatch is triggered as a result of executing an instruction assigned to system service dispatching. The instruction that Windows uses for system service dispatching depends on the processor on which it's executing.

32-Bit System Service Dispatching

On x86 processors prior to the Pentium II, Windows uses the *int 0x2e* instruction (46 decimal), which results in a trap. Windows fills in entry 46 in the IDT to point to the system service dispatcher. (Refer to Table 3-1.) The trap causes the executing thread to transition into kernel mode and enter the system service dispatcher. A numeric argument passed in the EAX processor register indicates the system service number being requested. The EDX register points to the list of parameters the caller passes to the system service. To return to user mode, the system service dispatcher uses the *iretd* (interrupt return instruction).

On x86 Pentium II processors and higher, Windows uses the special *sysenter* instruction, which Intel defined specifically for fast system service dispatches. To support the instruction, Windows stores at boot time the address of the kernel's system service dispatcher routine in a *machine specific register* (MSR) associated with the instruction. The execution of the instruction causes the change to kernel mode and execution of the system service dispatcher. The system service number is passed in the EAX processor register and the EDX register points to the list of caller arguments. To return to user mode, the system service dispatcher usually executes the *sysexit* instruction. (In some cases, like when the single-step flag is enabled on the processor, the system service dispatcher uses the *iretd* instead because stepping over a *sysexit* instruction with the kernel debugger would result in an undefined system state leading to a crash.)

> **Note** Because certain older applications may have been hardcoded to use the *int 0x2e* instruction to manually perform a system call (an unsupported operation), Windows keeps this mechanism usable even on systems that support the *sysenter* instruction by still having the handler registered.

EXPERIMENT: Locating the System Service Dispatcher

As mentioned, system calls occur through an interrupt, which means that the handler needs to be registered in the IDT or through a special *sysenter* instruction that uses an MSR to store the handler address at boot time. Here's how you can locate the appropriate routine for either method:

1. To see the handler for the interrupt 2E version of the system call dispatcher, type **!idt 2e** in the kernel debugger:

```
lkd> !idt 2e

Dumping IDT:

2e:     8208c8ee nt!KiSystemService
```

2. To see the handler for the *sysenter* version, use the *rdmsr* debugger command to read from the MSR register 0x176, which stores the handler:

```
lkd> rdmsr 176
msr[176] = 00000000`8208c9c0
lkd> ln 00000000`8208c9c0
(8208c9c0)   nt!KiFastCallEntry
```

3. You can disassemble the *KiSystemService* routine with the *u* command. You'll eventually notice the following instructions:

```
nt!KiSystemService+0x7b:
8208c969 897d04             mov       dword ptr [ebp+4],edi
8208c96c fb                 sti
8208c96d e9dd000000         jmp       nt!KiFastCallEntry+0x8f (8208ca4f)
```

Because the actual system call dispatching operations are common regardless of the mechanism used to reach the handler, the older interrupt-based handler simply calls into the middle of the newer *sysenter*-based handler to perform the same generic tasks. The only parts of the handlers that are different are related to the generation of the trap frame and the setup of certain registers.

On K6 and higher 32-bit AMD processors, Windows uses the special *syscall* instruction, which functions similarly to the x86 *sysenter* instruction, with Windows configuring a *syscall*-associated processor register with the address of the kernel's system service dispatcher. The system call number is passed in the EAX register, and the stack stores the caller arguments. After completing the dispatch, the kernel executes the *sysret* instruction.

At boot time, Windows detects the type of processor on which it's executing and sets up the appropriate system call code to use by storing a pointer to the correct code in the SharedUserData structure. The system service code for *NtReadFile* in user mode looks like this:

```
0:000> u NtReadFile
ntdll!ZwReadFile:
77020074 b802010000      mov     eax,102h
77020079 ba0003fe7f      mov     edx,offset SharedUserData!SystemCallStub (7ffe0300)
7702007e ff12            call    dword ptr [edx]
77020080 c22400          ret     24h
77020083 90              nop
```

The system service number is 0x102 (258 in decimal) and the *call* instruction executes the system service dispatch code set up by the kernel, whose pointer is at address 0x7ffe0300. (This corresponds to the *SystemCallStub* member of the KUSER_SHARED_DATA structure, which starts at 0x7FFE0000.) Because the following output was taken from an Intel Core 2 Duo, it contains a pointer to *sysenter*:

```
0:000> dd SharedUserData!SystemCallStub l 1
7ffe0300  77020f30
0:000> u 77020f30
ntdll!KiFastSystemCall:
77020f30 8bd4            mov     edx,esp
77020f32 0f34            sysenter
```

64-Bit System Service Dispatching

On the x64 architecture, Windows uses the *syscall* instruction, which functions like the AMD K6's *syscall* instruction, for system service dispatching, passing the system call number in the EAX register, the first four parameters in registers, and any parameters beyond those four on the stack:

```
ntdll!NtReadFile:
00000000`77f9fc60 4c8bd1          mov     r10,rcx
00000000`77f9fc63 b810200000      mov     eax,0x102
00000000`77f9fc68 0f05            syscall
00000000`77f9fc6a c3              ret
```

On the IA64 architecture, Windows uses the *epc* (Enter Privileged Mode) instruction. The first eight system call arguments are passed in registers, and the rest are passed on the stack.

Kernel-Mode System Service Dispatching

As Figure 3-12 illustrates, the kernel uses the system call number to locate the system service information in the *system service dispatch table*. This table is similar to the interrupt dispatch table described earlier in the chapter except that each entry contains a pointer to a system service rather than to an interrupt handling routine.

Note System service numbers can change between service packs—Microsoft occasionally adds or removes system services, and the system service numbers are generated automatically as part of a kernel compile.

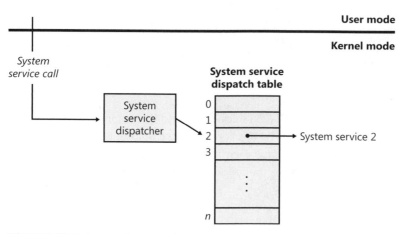

FIGURE 3-12 System service exceptions

The system service dispatcher, *KiSystemService*, copies the caller's arguments from the thread's user-mode stack to its kernel-mode stack (so that the user can't change the arguments as the kernel is accessing them), and then executes the system service. If the arguments passed to a system service point to buffers in user space, these buffers must be probed for accessibility before kernel-mode code can copy data to or from them. This probing is performed only if the *previous mode* of the thread is set to user mode. The *previous mode* is a value (kernel or user) that the kernel saves in the thread whenever it executes a trap handler and identifies the privilege level of the incoming exception, trap, or system call. As an optimization, if a system call comes from a driver or the kernel itself, the probing and capturing of parameters is skipped, and all parameters are assumed to be pointing to valid kernel-mode buffers (also, access to kernel-mode data is allowed).

Because kernel-mode code can also make system calls, let's look at the way these are done. Because the code for each system call is in kernel mode, and the caller is already in kernel mode, you can see that there shouldn't be a need for an interrupt or *sysenter* operation: the CPU is already at the right privilege level, and drivers, as well as the kernel, should only be able to directly call the function required. In the executive's case, this is actually what happens: the kernel has access to all its own routines and can simply call them just like standard routines. Externally, however, drivers can only access these system calls if they have been exported just like other standard kernel-mode APIs. In fact, quite a few of the system calls

are exported. Drivers, however, are not supposed to access system calls this way. Instead, drivers must use the *Zw* versions of these call—that is, instead of *NtCreateFile*, they must use *ZwCreateFile*. These *Zw* versions must also be manually exported by the kernel, and only a handful are, but they are fully documented and supported.

The *Zw* versions are officially available only for drivers because of the *previous mode* concept discussed earlier. Because this value is only updated each time the kernel builds a trap frame, its value won't actually change across a simple API call—no trap frame is being generated. By calling a function such as *NtCreateFile* directly, the kernel preserves the *previous mode* value that indicates that it is user-mode, detects that the address passed is a kernel-mode address, and fails the call, correctly asserting that user-mode applications should not pass kernel-mode pointers. However, this is not actually what happens, so how can the kernel be aware of the correct *previous mode*? The answer lies in the *Zw* calls.

These exported APIs are not actually simple aliases or wrappers around the *Nt* versions. Instead, they are "trampolines" to the appropriate *Nt* system call, which use the same system call dispatching mechanism. Instead of generating an interrupt or a *sysenter*, which would be slow and/or unsupported, they build a fake interrupt stack (the stack that the CPU would generate after an interrupt) and call the *KiSystemService* routine directly, essentially emulating the CPU interrupt. The handler will execute the same operations as if this call came from user mode, except it will detect the actual privilege level this call came from and set the *previous mode* to kernel. Now *NtCreateEvent* sees that the call came from the kernel and does not fail anymore. Here's what the kernel-mode trampolines look like:

```
lkd> u nt!ZwReadFile
nt!ZwReadFile:
8207f118 b802010000      mov      eax,102h
8207f11d 8d542404        lea      edx,[esp+4]
8207f121 9c              pushfd
8207f122 6a08            push     8
8207f124 e8c5d70000      call     nt!KiSystemService (8208c8ee)
8207f129 c22400          ret      24h
```

As you'll see in Chapter 5, each thread has a pointer to its system service table (on 32-bit and IA64 versions of Windows only; otherwise, the table address is hard-coded). Windows has two built-in system service tables, and third-party drivers cannot extend the tables to add their own service calls. The system service dispatcher determines which table contains the requested service by interpreting a 2-bit field in the 32-bit system service number as a table index. The low 12 bits of the system service number serve as the index into the table specified by the table index. The fields are shown in Figure 3-13.

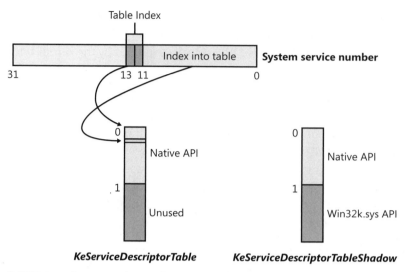

FIGURE 3-13 System service number to system service translation

Service Descriptor Tables

A primary default array table, *KeServiceDescriptorTable*, defines the core executive system services implemented in Ntosrknl.exe. The other table array, *KeServiceDescriptorTableShadow*, includes the Windows USER and GDI services implemented in the kernel-mode part of the Windows subsystem, Win32k.sys. The first time a Windows thread calls a Windows USER or GDI service, the address of the thread's system service table is changed to point to a table that includes the Windows USER and GDI services. The *KeAddSystemServiceTable* function allows Win32k.sys to add a system service table.

The system service dispatch instructions for Windows executive services exist in the system library Ntdll.dll. Subsystem DLLs call functions in Ntdll to implement their documented functions. The exception is Windows USER and GDI functions, in which the system service dispatch instructions are implemented directly in User32.dll and Gdi32.dll—there is no Ntdll.dll involved. These two cases are shown in Figure 3-14.

As shown in Figure 3-14, the Windows *WriteFile* function in Kernel32.dll calls the *NtWriteFile* function in Ntdll.dll, which in turn executes the appropriate instruction to cause a system service trap, passing the system service number representing *NtWriteFile*. The system service dispatcher (function *KiSystemService* in Ntoskrnl.exe) then calls the real *NtWriteFile* to process the I/O request. For Windows USER and GDI functions, the system service dispatch calls functions in the loadable kernel-mode part of the Windows subsystem, Win32k.sys.

FIGURE 3-14 System service dispatching

EXPERIMENT: Mapping System Call Numbers to Functions

You can duplicate the same lookup performed by the kernel when dealing with a system call ID to figure out which function is responsible for handling it.

1. The *KeServiceDescriptorTable* and *KeServiceDescriptorTableShadow* tables both point to the same array of pointers for kernel system calls, called *KiServiceTable*. You can use the kernel debugger command *dds* to dump the data along with symbolic information. The debugger will attempt to match each pointer with a symbol. Here's a partial output:

```
lkd> dds KiServiceTable
820807d0  821be2e5 nt!NtAcceptConnectPort
820807d4  820659a6 nt!NtAccessCheck
820807d8  8224a953 nt!NtAccessCheckAndAuditAlarm
```

```
820807dc  820659dd  nt!NtAccessCheckByType
820807e0  8224a992  nt!NtAccessCheckByTypeAndAuditAlarm
820807e4  82065a18  nt!NtAccessCheckByTypeResultList
820807e8  8224a9db  nt!NtAccessCheckByTypeResultListAndAuditAlarm
820807ec  8224aa24  nt!NtAccessCheckByTypeResultListAndAuditAlarmByHandle
820807f0  822892af  nt!NtAddAtom
```

2. Instead of dumping the entire table, you can also look up a specific number. Because each system call number is an index into the table, and because each element is 4 bytes, you can use the following calculation: *Handler = KiServiceTable + Number * 4*. Let's use the number 0x102, obtained during our description of the *NtReadFile* stub code in Ntdll.dll.

```
lkd> ln poi(KiServiceTable + 102 * 4)
(82193023)   nt!NtReadFile
```

3. Because drivers, including kernel-mode rootkits, are able to patch this table on 32-bit versions of Windows, which is something the operating system does not support, you can use *dds* to dump the entire table and look for any values outside the range of valid kernel addresses (*dds* will also make this clear by not being able to look up a symbol for the function). Sixty-four bit Windows organizes the system call table differently and uses relative pointers (an offset) to system calls instead of the absolute addresses used by 32-bit Windows. Because code on 64-bit Windows is guaranteed to be aligned on a 16-byte boundary, only the top 28 bits are used to describe the offset, since the bottom 4 bits are always 0. Windows takes advantage of this fact by using the bottom 4 bits to pack information on the number of arguments that each system call takes (based on the data stored in *KiArgumentTable*). The base of the pointer is the *KiServiceTable* itself, so you'll have to dump the data in its raw format with the *dd* command. Here's an example of output from a 64-bit system:

```
lkd> dd KiServiceTable
fffff800`0105efc0  003021e0 0021efc0 fffc7b80 00202755
```

Each offset can be mapped to each function with the *ln* command, by stripping off the bottom 4 bits (used as described above) and adding the remaining value to the base of *KiServiceTable* itself, as shown here:

```
lkd> ln KiServiceTable+(003021e0 & -16)
(fffff800`013611a0)   nt!NtMapUserPhysicalPagesScatter
```

EXPERIMENT: Viewing System Service Activity

You can monitor system service activity by watching the System Calls/Sec performance counter in the System object. Run the Reliability and Performance Monitor, and in chart view, click the Add button to add a counter to the chart. Select the System object, select the System Calls/Sec counter, and then click the Add button to add the counter to the chart.

Object Manager

As mentioned in Chapter 2, Windows implements an object model to provide consistent and secure access to the various internal services implemented in the executive. This section describes the Windows *object manager*, the executive component responsible for creating, deleting, protecting, and tracking objects. The object manager centralizes resource control operations that otherwise would be scattered throughout the operating system. It was designed to meet the goals listed on the next page.

EXPERIMENT: Exploring the Object Manager

Throughout this section, you'll find experiments that show you how to peer into the object manager database. These experiments use the following tools, which you should become familiar with if you aren't already:

- WinObj (available from Sysinternals) displays the internal object manager's namespace and information about objects (such as the reference count, the number of open handles, security descriptors, and so forth).

- Process Explorer and Handle from Sysinternals (introduced in Chapter 1) display the open handles for a process.

- The *Openfiles /query* command displays the open file handles for a process, but it requires a global flag to be set in order to operate.

- The kernel debugger *!handle* command displays the open handles for a process.

WinObj from Sysinternals provides a way to traverse the namespace that the object manager maintains. (As we'll explain later, not all objects have names.) Run WinObj and examine the layout, shown next.

As noted previously, the Windows *Openfiles /query* command requires that a Windows global flag called *maintain objects list* be enabled. (See the "Windows Global Flags" section later in this chapter for more details about global flags.) If you type **Openfiles /Local**, it will tell you whether the flag is enabled. You can enable it with the *Openfiles /Local ON* command. In either case, you must reboot the system for the setting to take effect. Neither Process Explorer nor Handle from Sysinternals require object tracking to be turned on because they use a device driver to obtain the information.

The object manager was designed to meet the following goals:

- Provide a common, uniform mechanism for using system resources

- Isolate object protection to one location in the operating system so that C2 security compliance can be achieved

- Provide a mechanism to charge processes for their use of objects so that limits can be placed on the usage of system resources

- Establish an object-naming scheme that can readily incorporate existing objects, such as the devices, files, and directories of a file system, or other independent collections of objects

- Support the requirements of various operating system environments, such as the ability of a process to inherit resources from a parent process (needed by Windows and POSIX) and the ability to create case-sensitive file names (needed by POSIX)

- Establish uniform rules for object retention (that is, for keeping an object available until all processes have finished using it)

- Provide the ability to isolate objects for a specific session to allow for both *local* and *global* objects in the namespace

Internally, Windows has three kinds of objects: *executive objects*, *kernel objects*, and *GDI/User objects*. Executive objects are objects implemented by various components of the executive (such as the process manager, memory manager, I/O subsystem, and so on). Kernel objects are a more primitive set of objects implemented by the Windows kernel. These objects are not visible to user-mode code but are created and used only within the executive. Kernel objects provide fundamental capabilities, such as synchronization, on which executive objects are built. Thus, many executive objects contain (encapsulate) one or more kernel objects, as shown in Figure 3-15.

Owned by the object manager
Name
HandleCount
ReferenceCount
Type

Owned by the kernel
Kernel object

Owned by the executive
Executive object

FIGURE 3-15 Executive objects that contain kernel objects

Note: GDI/User objects, on the other hand, belong to the Windows subsystem (Win32k.sys) and do not interact with the kernel. For this reason, they are outside the scope of this book, but you can get more information on them from the Windows SDK, the MSDN Library, or from the book *Windows Graphics Programming: Win32 GDI and DirectDraw*, by Feng Yuan (Prentice Hall, 2000).

Details about the structure of kernel objects and how they are used to implement synchronization are given later in this chapter. In the remainder of this section, we'll focus on how the object manager works and on the structure of executive objects, handles, and handle tables. Here we'll just briefly describe how objects are involved in implementing Windows security access checking; we'll cover this topic thoroughly in Chapter 6.

Executive Objects

Each Windows environment subsystem projects to its applications a different image of the operating system. The executive objects and object services are primitives that the environment subsystems use to construct their own versions of objects and other resources.

Executive objects are typically created either by an environment subsystem on behalf of a user application or by various components of the operating system as part of their normal operation. For example, to create a file, a Windows application calls the Windows *CreateFile* function, implemented in the Windows subsystem DLL Kernel32.dll. After some validation and initialization, *CreateFile* in turn calls the native Windows service *NtCreateFile* to create an executive file object.

The set of objects an environment subsystem supplies to its applications might be larger or smaller than the set the executive provides. The Windows subsystem uses executive objects to export its own set of objects, many of which correspond directly to executive objects. For example, the Windows mutexes and semaphores are directly based on executive objects (which are in turn based on corresponding kernel objects). In addition, the Windows subsystem supplies named pipes and mailslots, resources that are based on executive file objects. Some subsystems, such as POSIX, don't support objects as objects at all. The POSIX subsystem uses executive objects and services as the basis for presenting POSIX-style processes, pipes, and other resources to its applications.

Table 3-5 lists the primary objects the executive provides and briefly describes what they represent. You can find further details on executive objects in the chapters that describe the related executive components (or in the case of executive objects directly exported to Windows, in the Windows API reference documentation).

Note The executive implements a total of 37 object types. Many of these objects are for use only by the executive component that defines them and are not directly accessible by Windows APIs. Examples of these objects include *Driver*, *Device*, and *EventPair*.

TABLE 3-5 Executive Objects Exposed to the Windows API

Object Type	Represents
Process	The virtual address space and control information necessary for the execution of a set of thread objects.
Thread	An executable entity within a process.
Job	A collection of processes manageable as a single entity through the job.
Section	A region of shared memory (known as a file mapping object in Windows).
File	An instance of an opened file or an I/O device.

Object Type	Represents
Token	The security profile (security ID, user rights, and so on) of a process or a thread.
Event	An object with a persistent state (signaled or not signaled) that can be used for synchronization or notification.
Semaphore	A counter that provides a resource gate by allowing some maximum number of threads to access the resources protected by the semaphore.
Mutex	A synchronization mechanism used to serialize access to a resource.
Timer	A mechanism to notify a thread when a fixed period of time elapses.
IoCompletion	A method for threads to enqueue and dequeue notifications of the completion of I/O operations (known as an I/O completion port in the Windows API).
Key	A mechanism to refer to data in the registry. Although keys appear in the object manager namespace, they are managed by the configuration manager, in a way similar to that in which file objects are managed by file system drivers. Zero or more key values are associated with a key object; key values contain data about the key.
Directory	A virtual directory in the object manager's namespace responsible for containing other objects or object directories.
TpWorkerFactory	A collection of threads assigned to perform a specific set of tasks. The kernel can manage the number of work items that will be performed on the queue, how many threads should be responsible for the work, and dynamic creation and termination of worker threads, respecting certain limits the caller can set. Windows Vista and later expose the worker factory object through *thread pools*.
TmRm (Resource Manager), TmTx (Transaction), TmTm (Transaction Manager), TmEn (Enlistment)	Objects used by the Kernel Transaction Manager (KTM) for various *transactions* and/or *enlistments* as part of a *resource manager* or *transaction manager*. Objects can be created through the new *CreateTransactionManager, CreateResourceManager, CreateTransaction,* and *CreateEnlistment* APIs.
WindowStation	An object that contains a clipboard, a set of global atoms, and a group of Desktop objects.
Desktop	An object contained within a window station. A desktop has a logical display surface and contains windows, menus, and hooks.

 Note As Windows NT was originally supposed to support the OS/2 operating system, the mutex had to be compatible with the existing design of OS/2 mutual-exclusion objects, a design that required that a thread be able to abandon the object, leaving it inaccessible. Because this behavior was considered unusual for such an object, another kernel object—the *mutant*—was created. Eventually, OS/2 support was dropped, and the object became used by the Windows 32 subsystem under the name *mutex* (but it is still called *mutant* internally).

Object Structure

As shown in Figure 3-16, each object has an object header and an object body. The object manager controls the object headers, and the owning executive components control the object bodies of the object types they create. Each object header also points to a special object, called the *type object,* that contains information common to each instance of the object. Additionally, up to four optional subheaders exist: the name information header, the quota information header, the handle information header, and the creator information header.

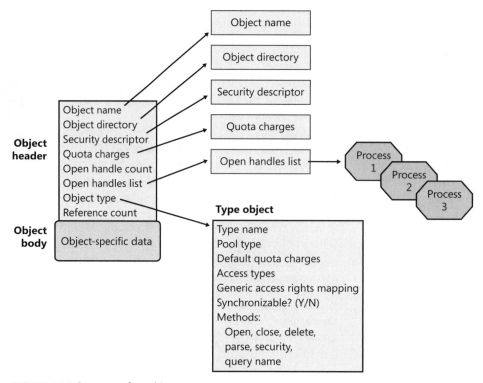

FIGURE 3-16 Structure of an object

Object Headers and Bodies

The object manager uses the data stored in an object's header to manage objects without regard to their type. Table 3-6 briefly describes the object header fields, and Table 3-7 describes the fields found in the optional object subheaders.

TABLE 3-6 Object Header Fields

Field	Purpose
Handle count	Maintains a count of the number of currently opened handles to the object.
Pointer count	Maintains a count of the number of references to the object (including one reference for each handle). Kernel-mode components can reference an object *by pointer* without using a handle.
Security descriptor	Determines who can use the object and what they can do with it. Note that unnamed objects by definition cannot have security.
Object type	Points to a type object that contains attributes common to objects of this type.
Subheader offsets	Negative offsets to the optional subheader structures described in Table 3-7, except for the creator information subheader, which, if present, always precedes the object header.
Flags	Characteristics and object attributes for the object. See Table 3-9 for a list of all the object flags.

In addition to the object header, which contains information that applies to any kind of object, the subheaders contain optional information regarding specific aspects of the object. Note that these structures are located at a variable offset from the top of the object header, the value of which is stored in the object header itself (except, as mentioned above, for creator information). If any of these offsets is 0, the object manager assumes that no subheader is associated with that offset. In the case of creator information, a value in the object header flags determines whether the subheader is present. (See Table 3-9 for information about these flags.)

TABLE 3-7 Optional Object Subheaders

Name	Purpose	Location
Name information	Contains the object name, responsible for making an object visible to other processes for sharing, and a pointer to the object directory, which provides the hierarchical structure in which the object names are stored	Object header— NameInfoOffset
Quota information	Lists the resource charges levied against a process when it opens a handle to the object	Object header— QuotaInfoOffset
Handle information	Contains a database of entries (or just a single entry) for a process that has an open handle to the object (along with a per-process handle count)	Object header— HandleInfoOffset
Creator information	Links the object into a list for all the objects of the same type, and records the process that created the object, along with a back trace	Object header— size of creator information structure

> **Note** The quota information subheader might also contain a pointer to the *exclusive process* that allows access to this object if the object was created with the *exclusive object* flag. Also, this subheader does not necessarily contain information on quotas being levied against the process. More information on exclusive objects follows later in the chapter.

Each of these subheaders is optional and is present only under certain conditions, either during system boot up or at object creation time. Table 3-8 describes each of these conditions.

TABLE 3-8 Conditions Required for Presence of Object Subheaders

Name	Condition
Name information	The object must have been created with a name.
Quota information	The object must have different memory usage values than the default values configured during the creation of the object type (more on object types later), or must have a security descriptor larger than 2 KB and not be the initial system process, or must have been created with the *exclusive object* flag. (See Table 3-9 for object flags.)
Handle information	The object type must have enabled the *maintain handle count* flag. File objects, WindowStation objects, and Desktop objects have this flag set in their object type structure.
Creator information	The object type must have enabled the *maintain type list* flag. LPC port objects and Driver objects (only if Driver Verifier is enabled) have this flag set. However, enabling the *maintain object type list* global flag (discussed earlier) will enable this for all objects. *Type* objects also have the flag set, for a reason we'll describe shortly.

Finally, a number of attributes and/or flags determine the behavior of the object during creation time or during certain operations. These flags are received by the object manager whenever any new object is being created, in a structure called the *object attributes*. This structure defines the object name, the root object directory where it should be inserted, the security descriptor for the object, and the *object attribute flags*. Table 3-9 lists the various flags that can be associated with an object.

> **Note** When an object is being created through an API in the Windows subsystem (such as *CreateEvent* or *CreateFile),* the caller does not specify any object attributes—the subsystem DLL will perform the work behind the scenes. For this reason, all named objects created through Win32 will go in the BaseNamedObjects directory because this is the root object directory that Kernel32.dll specifies as part of the object attributes structure. More information on BaseNamedObjects and how it relates to the per-session namespace will follow later in this chapter.

TABLE 3-9 Object Flags

Attributes Flag	Header Flag	Purpose
OBJ_INHERIT	Saved in the handle table entry	Determines whether the handle to the object will be inherited by child processes, and whether a process can use *DuplicateHandle* to make a copy
OBJ_PERMANENT	OB_FLAG_PERMANENT_OBJECT	Defines object retention behavior related to reference counts, described later
OBJ_EXCLUSIVE	OB_FLAG_EXCLUSIVE_OBJECT	Specifies that the object can only be used by the process that created it
OBJ_CASE_INSENSITIVE	Stored in the handle table entry	Specifies that lookups for this object in the namespace should be case insensitive. May be overridden by the *case insensitive* flag in the object type
OBJ_OPENIF	Not stored, used at run time	Specifies that a create operation for this object name should result in an open, if the object exists, instead of a failure
OBJ_OPENLINK	Not stored, used at run time	Specifies that the object manager should open a handle to the symbolic link, not the target
OBJ_KERNEL_HANDLE	OB_FLAG_KERNEL_OBJECT	Specifies that the handle to this object should be a *kernel handle* (more on this later)
OBJ_FORCE_ACCESS_CHECK	Not stored, used at run time	Specifies that even if the object is being opened from kernel mode, full access checks should be performed
OBJ_KERNEL_EXCLUSIVE	Stored in the object name subheader as *QueryReferences*	Disables any user-mode process from opening a handle to the object; used to protect the */Device/PhysicalMemory* section object
N/A	OB_FLAG_CREATOR_INFO	Specifies that there is an object creator information subheader on top of the object header
N/A	OF_FLAG_DEFAULT_SECURITY_ QUOTA	Specifies that the object's security descriptor is using the default 2-KB quota

Attributes Flag	Header Flag	Purpose
N/A	OB_FLAG_SINGLE_HANDLE_ ENTRY	Specifies that the handle information subheader contains only a single entry and not a database
N/A	OB_FLAG_NEW_OBJECT	Specifies that the object has been created but not yet inserted into the object namespace yet
N/A	OB_FLAG_DEFER_DELETE	Specifies that the object is being deleted through the *deferred deletion worker thread*

In addition to an object header, each object has an object body whose format and contents are unique to its object type; all objects of the same type share the same object body format. By creating an object type and supplying services for it, an executive component can control the manipulation of data in all object bodies of that type. Because the object header has a static and well-known size, the object manager can easily look up the object header for an object simply by subtracting the size of the header from the pointer of the object. As explained earlier, to access the subheaders, the object manager subtracts yet another value from the pointer of the object header.

Because of the standardized object header and subheader structures, the object manager is able to provide a small set of generic services that can operate on the attributes stored in any object header and can be used on objects of any type (although some generic services don't make sense for certain objects). These generic services, some of which the Windows subsystem makes available to Windows applications, are listed in Table 3-10.

Although these generic object services are supported for all object types, each object has its own create, open, and query services. For example, the I/O system implements a create file service for its file objects, and the process manager implements a create process service for its process objects.

Although a single create object service could have been implemented, such a routine would have been quite complicated, because the set of parameters required to initialize a file object, for example, differs markedly from that required to initialize a process object. Also, the object manager would have incurred additional processing overhead each time a thread called an object service to determine the type of object the handle referred to and to call the appropriate version of the service.

TABLE 3-10 Generic Object Services

Service	Purpose
Close	Closes a handle to an object
Duplicate	Shares an object by duplicating a handle and giving it to another process
Query object	Gets information about an object's standard attributes

Service	Purpose
Query security	Gets an object's security descriptor
Set security	Changes the protection on an object
Wait for a single object	Synchronizes a thread's execution with one object
Wait for multiple objects	Synchronizes a thread's execution with multiple objects

Type Objects

Object headers contain data that is common to all objects but that can take on different values for each instance of an object. For example, each object has a unique name and can have a unique security descriptor. However, objects also contain some data that remains constant for all objects of a particular type. For example, you can select from a set of access rights specific to a type of object when you open a handle to objects of that type. The executive supplies terminate and suspend access (among others) for thread objects and read, write, append, and delete access (among others) for file objects. Another example of an object-type-specific attribute is synchronization, which is described shortly.

To conserve memory, the object manager stores these static, object-type-specific attributes once when creating a new object type. It uses an object of its own, a type object, to record this data. As Figure 3-17 illustrates, if the object-tracking debug flag (described in the "Windows Global Flags" section later in this chapter) is set, a type object also links together all objects of the same type (in this case the process type), allowing the object manager to find and enumerate them, if necessary. This functionality takes advantage of the creator information subheader discussed previously.

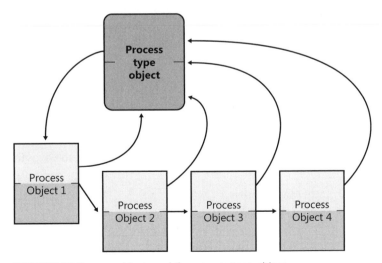

FIGURE 3-17 Process objects and the process type object

EXPERIMENT: Viewing Object Headers and Type Objects

You can see the list of type objects declared to the object manager with the WinObj tool from Sysinternals. After running WinObj, open the \ObjectTypes directory, as shown here:

You can look at the process object type data structure in the kernel debugger by first identifying a process object with the *!process* command:

```
lkd> !process 0 0
**** NT ACTIVE PROCESS DUMP ****
PROCESS 860f1ab0  SessionId: none  Cid: 0004    Peb: 00000000  ParentCid: 0000
    DirBase: 00122000  ObjectTable: 83000118  HandleCount: 484.
    Image: System
```

Then execute the *!object* command with the process object address as the argument:

```
lkd> !object 860f1ab0
Object: 860f1ab0  Type: (860f1ed0) Process
    ObjectHeader: 860f1a98 (old version)
    HandleCount: 4  PointerCount: 139
```

Notice that the object header starts 0x18 (24 decimal) bytes prior to the start of the object body—the size of the object header itself. You can view the object header with this command:

```
lkd> dt nt!_OBJECT_HEADER 860f1a98
   +0x000 PointerCount     : 139
   +0x004 HandleCount      : 4
   +0x004 NextToFree       : 0x00000004
   +0x008 Type             : 0x860f1ed0 _OBJECT_TYPE
   +0x00c NameInfoOffset   : 0 ''
   +0x00d HandleInfoOffset : 0 ''
   +0x00e QuotaInfoOffset  : 0 ''
   +0x00f Flags            : 0x22 '"'
   +0x010 ObjectCreateInfo : 0x82109380 _OBJECT_CREATE_INFORMATION
   +0x010 QuotaBlockCharged : 0x82109380
   +0x014 SecurityDescriptor : 0x83003482
   +0x018 Body             : _QUAD
```

Now look at the object type data structure by obtaining its address from the Type field
of the object header data structure:

```
lkd> dt nt!_OBJECT_TYPE 0x860f1ed0
   +0x000 Mutex            : _ERESOURCE
   +0x038 TypeList         : _LIST_ENTRY [ 0x860f1f08 - 0x860f1f08 ]
   +0x040 Name             : _UNICODE_STRING "Process"
   +0x048 DefaultObject    : (null)
   +0x04c Index            : 6
   +0x050 TotalNumberOfObjects : 0x4f
   +0x054 TotalNumberOfHandles : 0x12d
   +0x058 HighWaterNumberOfObjects : 0x52
   +0x05c HighWaterNumberOfHandles : 0x141
   +0x060 TypeInfo         : _OBJECT_TYPE_INITIALIZER
   +0x0ac Key              : 0x636f7250
   +0x0b0 ObjectLocks      : [32] _EX_PUSH_LOCK
```

The output shows that the object type structure includes the name of the object type,
tracks the total number of active objects of that type, and tracks the peak number
of handles and objects of that type. The TypeInfo field stores the pointer to the data
structure that stores attributes common to all objects of the object type as well as
pointers to the object type's methods:

```
lkd> dt nt!_OBJECT_TYPE_INITIALIZER 0x860f1ed0+60
   +0x000 Length           : 0x4c
   +0x002 ObjectTypeFlags  : 0xa ''
   +0x002 CaseInsensitive  : 0y0
   +0x002 UnnamedObjectsOnly : 0y1
   +0x002 UseDefaultObject : 0y0
   +0x002 SecurityRequired : 0y1
   +0x002 MaintainHandleCount : 0y0
   +0x002 MaintainTypeList : 0y0
   +0x004 ObjectTypeCode   : 0
   +0x008 InvalidAttributes : 0
   +0x00c GenericMapping   : _GENERIC_MAPPING
   +0x01c ValidAccessMask  : 0x1fffff
   +0x020 PoolType         : 0 ( NonPagedPool )
   +0x024 DefaultPagedPoolCharge : 0x1000
   +0x028 DefaultNonPagedPoolCharge : 0x2a0
```

```
+0x02c DumpProcedure      : (null)
+0x030 OpenProcedure      : 0x822137d3    long  nt!PspProcessOpen+0
+0x034 CloseProcedure     : 0x8221c3d4    void  nt!PspProcessClose+0
+0x038 DeleteProcedure    : 0x8221c1e2    void  nt!PspProcessDelete+0
+0x03c ParseProcedure     : (null)
+0x040 SecurityProcedure  : 0x822502bb    long  nt!SeDefaultObjectMethod+0
+0x044 QueryNameProcedure : (null)
+0x048 OkayToCloseProcedure : (null)
```

Type objects can't be manipulated from user mode because the object manager supplies no services for them. However, some of the attributes they define are visible through certain native services and through Windows API routines. The information stored in the type initializers is described in Table 3-11.

TABLE 3-11 Type Initializer Fields

Attribute	Purpose
Type name	The name for objects of this type ("process," "event," "port," and so on).
Pool type	Indicates whether objects of this type should be allocated from paged or nonpaged memory.
Default quota charges	Default paged and nonpaged pool values to charge to process quotas.
Valid access mask	The types of access a thread can request when opening a handle to an object of this type ("read," "write," "terminate," "suspend," and so on).
Generic access rights mapping	A mapping between the four generic access rights (read, write, execute, and all) to the type-specific access rights.
Flags	Indicate whether objects must never have names (such as process objects), whether they require a security descriptor, and whether a handle database (handle information subheader) and/or a type-list linkage (creator information subheader) should be maintained. The *use default object* flag also defines the behavior for the *default object* field below.
Invalid attributes	Specifies object attribute flags (shown earlier in Table 3-9) that are invalid for this object type.
Default object	Specifies the internal object manager event that should be used during waits for this object, if the object type creator requested one. Note that for File objects, the object manager hardcodes the default object to an internal member inside the FILE_OBJECT structure called Event.
Methods	One or more routines that the object manager calls automatically at certain points in an object's lifetime.

Synchronization, one of the attributes visible to Windows applications, refers to a thread's ability to synchronize its execution by waiting for an object to change from one state to another. A thread can synchronize with executive job, process, thread, file, event, semaphore,

mutex, and timer objects. Other executive objects don't support synchronization. An object's ability to support synchronization is based on three possibilities:

- The executive object contains an embedded dispatcher object, a kernel object that is covered in the section "Low-IRQL Synchronization" later in this chapter.

- The creator of the object type requested a *default object*, and the object manager provided one.

- The object type is a file and the object manager manually hardcoded a value inside the object body (described in Table 3-11).

Object Methods

The last attribute in Table 3-11, methods, comprises a set of internal routines that are similar to C++ constructors and destructors—that is, routines that are automatically called when an object is created or destroyed. The object manager extends this idea by calling an object method in other situations as well, such as when someone opens or closes a handle to an object or when someone attempts to change the protection on an object. Some object types specify methods, whereas others don't, depending on how the object type is to be used.

When an executive component creates a new object type, it can register one or more methods with the object manager. Thereafter, the object manager calls the methods at well-defined points in the lifetime of objects of that type, usually when an object is created, deleted, or modified in some way. The methods that the object manager supports are listed in Table 3-12.

The reason for these object methods is to address the fact that, as we've seen, certain object operations are generic (close, duplicate, security, and so on). Fully generalizing these generic routines would have required the designers of the object manager to anticipate all object types. However, the routines to create an object type are exported by the kernel, enabling third-party components to create their own object types. Although this functionality is not documented for driver developers, it is internally used by Win32k.sys to define WindowStation and Desktop objects. Through object method extensibility, Win32k.sys defines its routines for handling operations such as create and query.

One exception to this rule is the *security* routine, which does, unless otherwise instructed, default to *SeDefaultObjectMethod*. This routine does not need to know the internal structure of the object because it only deals with the security descriptor for the object, and we've seen that the pointer to the security descriptor is stored in the generic object header, not inside the object body. However, if an object does require its own additional security checks, it can define a custom security routine. The other reason for having a generic security method is to avoid complexity, because most objects rely on the security reference monitor to manage their security.

TABLE 3-12 Object Methods

Method	When Method Is Called
Open	When an object handle is opened
Close	When an object handle is closed
Delete	Before the object manager deletes an object
Query name	When a thread requests the name of an object, such as a file, that exists in a secondary object namespace
Parse	When the object manager is searching for an object name that exists in a secondary object namespace
Dump	Not used
Okay to close	When the object manager is instructed to close a handle
Security	When a process reads or changes the protection of an object, such as a file, that exists in a secondary object namespace

The object manager calls the open method whenever it creates a handle to an object, which it does when an object is created or opened. The WindowStation and Desktop objects provide an open method; for example, the WindowStation object type requires an open method so that Win32k.sys can share a piece of memory with the process that serves as a desktop-related memory pool.

An example of the use of a close method occurs in the I/O system. The I/O manager registers a close method for the file object type, and the object manager calls the close method each time it closes a file object handle. This close method checks whether the process that is closing the file handle owns any outstanding locks on the file and, if so, removes them. Checking for file locks isn't something the object manager itself could or should do.

The object manager calls a delete method, if one is registered, before it deletes a temporary object from memory. The memory manager, for example, registers a delete method for the section object type that frees the physical pages being used by the section. It also verifies that any internal data structures the memory manager has allocated for a section are deleted before the section object is deleted. Once again, the object manager can't do this work because it knows nothing about the internal workings of the memory manager. Delete methods for other types of objects perform similar functions.

The parse method (and similarly, the query name method) allows the object manager to relinquish control of finding an object to a secondary object manager if it finds an object that exists outside the object manager namespace. When the object manager looks up an object name, it suspends its search when it encounters an object in the path that has an associated parse method. The object manager calls the parse method, passing to it the remainder of the object name it is looking for. There are two namespaces in Windows in addition to the object manager's: the registry namespace, which the configuration manager implements, and the file system namespace, which the I/O manager implements with the aid of file system drivers.

(See Chapter 4 for more information on the configuration manager and Chapter 7 for more about the I/O manager and file system drivers.)

For example, when a process opens a handle to the object named \Device\Floppy0\docs\ resume.doc, the object manager traverses its name tree until it reaches the device object named Floppy0. It sees that a parse method is associated with this object, and it calls the method, passing to it the rest of the object name it was searching for—in this case, the string \docs\resume.doc. The parse method for device objects is an I/O routine because the I/O manager defines the device object type and registers a parse method for it. The I/O manager's parse routine takes the name string and passes it to the appropriate file system, which finds the file on the disk and opens it.

The security method, which the I/O system also uses, is similar to the parse method. It is called whenever a thread tries to query or change the security information protecting a file. This information is different for files than for other objects because security information is stored in the file itself rather than in memory. The I/O system, therefore, must be called to find the security information and read or change it.

Finally, the okay-to-close method is used as an additional layer of protection around the malicious—or incorrect—closing of handles being used for system purposes. For example, each process has a handle to the Desktop object(s) on which its thread or threads have windows visible. Under the standard security model, it would be possible for those threads to close their handles to their desktops because the process has full control of its own objects. In this scenario, the threads would end up without a desktop associated with them—a violation of the windowing model. Win32k.sys registers an okay-to-close routine for the Desktop and WindowStation objects to prevent this behavior.

Object Handles and the Process Handle Table

When a process creates or opens an object by name, it receives a *handle* that represents its access to the object. Referring to an object by its handle is faster than using its name because the object manager can skip the name lookup and find the object directly. Processes can also acquire handles to objects by inheriting handles at process creation time (if the creator specifies the inherit handle flag on the *CreateProcess* call and the handle was marked as inheritable, either at the time it was created or afterward by using the Windows *SetHandleInformation* function) or by receiving a duplicated handle from another process. (See the Windows *DuplicateHandle* function.)

All user-mode processes must own a handle to an object before their threads can use the object. Using handles to manipulate system resources isn't a new idea. C and Pascal (an older programming language similar to Delphi) run-time libraries, for example, return handles to opened files. Handles serve as indirect pointers to system resources; this indirection keeps application programs from fiddling directly with system data structures.

> **Note** Executive components and device drivers can access objects directly because they are running in kernel mode and therefore have access to the object structures in system memory. However, they must declare their usage of the object by incrementing the reference count so that the object won't be deallocated while it's still being used. (See the section "Object Retention" later in this chapter for more details.) To successfully make use of this object, however, device drivers need to know the internal structure definition of the object, and this is not provided for most objects. Instead, device drivers are encouraged to use the appropriate kernel APIs to modify or read information from the object. For example, although device drivers can get a pointer to the Process object (EPROCESS), the structure is opaque, and *Ps** APIs must be used. For other objects, the type itself is opaque (such as most executive objects that wrap a dispatcher object—for example, events or mutexes). For these objects, drivers must use the same system calls that user-mode applications end up calling (such as *ZwCreateEvent)* and use handles instead of object pointers.

Object handles provide additional benefits. First, except for what they refer to, there is no difference between a file handle, an event handle, and a process handle. This similarity provides a consistent interface to reference objects, regardless of their type. Second, the object manager has the exclusive right to create handles and to locate an object that a handle refers to. This means that the object manager can scrutinize every user-mode action that affects an object to see whether the security profile of the caller allows the operation requested on the object in question.

EXPERIMENT: Viewing Open Handles

Run Process Explorer, and make sure the lower pane is enabled and configured to show open handles. (Click on View, Lower Pane View, and then Handles). Then open a command prompt and view the handle table for the new Cmd.exe process. You should see an open file handle to the current directory. For example, assuming the current directory is C:\, Process Explorer shows the following:

If you then change the current directory with the *cd* command, you will see in Process Explorer that the handle to the previous current directory is closed and a new handle is opened to the new current directory. The previous handle is highlighted briefly in red, and the new handle is highlighted in green. The duration of the highlight can be adjusted by clicking Options and then Difference Highlight Duration.

Process Explorer's differences highlighting feature makes it easy to see changes in the handle table. For example, if a process is leaking handles, viewing the handle table with Process Explorer can quickly show what handle or handles are being opened but not closed. This information can help the programmer find the handle leak.

You can also display the open handle table by using the command-line Handle tool from Sysinternals. For example, note the following partial output of Handle examining the file object handles located in the handle table for a Cmd.exe process before and after changing the directory. By default, Handle will filter out nonfile handles unless the *–a* switch is used, which displays all the handles in the process, similar to Process Explorer.

```
C:\>handle -p cmd.exe

Handle v3.3
Copyright (C) 1997-2007 Mark Russinovich
Sysinternals - www.sysinternals.com

------------------------------------------------------------------------
cmd.exe pid: 5124 Alex-Laptop\Alex Ionescu
   3C: File  (R-D)   C:\Windows\System32\en-US\cmd.exe.mui
   44: File  (RW-)   C:\

C:\>cd windows

C:\Windows>handle -p cmd.exe

Handle v3.3
Copyright (C) 1997-2007 Mark Russinovich
Sysinternals - www.sysinternals.com

------------------------------------------------------------------------
cmd.exe pid: 5124 Alex-Laptop\Alex Ionescu
   3C: File  (R-D)   C:\Windows\System32\en-US\cmd.exe.mui
   40: File  (RW-)   C:\Windows
```

An *object handle* is an index into a process-specific *handle table*, pointed to by the executive process (EPROCESS) block (described in Chapter 5). The first handle index is 4, the second 8, and so on. A process's handle table contains pointers to all the objects that the process has opened a handle to. Handle tables are implemented as a three-level scheme, similar to the way that the x86 memory management unit implements virtual-to-physical address

translation, giving a maximum of more than 16,000,000 handles per process. (See Chapter 9 for details about memory management in x86 systems.)

Only the lowest-level handle table is allocated on process creation—the other levels are created as needed. The subhandle table consists of as many entries as will fit in a page minus one entry that is used for handle auditing. For example, for x86 systems a page is 4096 bytes, divided by the size of a handle table entry (8 bytes), which is 512, minus 1, which is a total of 511 entries in the lowest-level handle table. The mid-level handle table contains a full page of pointers to subhandle tables, so the number of subhandle tables depends on the size of the page and the size of a pointer for the platform. Figure 3-18 describes the handle table layout on Windows.

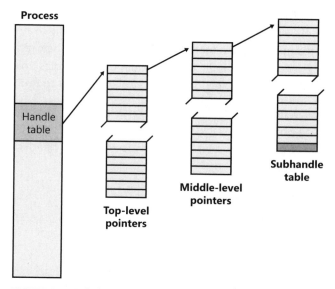

FIGURE 3-18 Windows process handle table architecture

EXPERIMENT: Creating the Maximum Number of Handles

The test program Testlimit from Sysinternals has an option to open handles to an object until it cannot open any more handles. You can use this to see how many handles can be created in a single process on your system. Because handle tables are allocated from paged pool, you might run out of paged pool before you hit the maximum number of handles that can be created in a single process. To see how many handles you can create on your system, follow these steps:

1. Download the Testlimit .zip file from *www.microsoft.com/technet/sysinternals*, and unzip it into a directory.

2. Run Process Explorer, and then click View and then System Information. Notice the current and maximum size of paged pool. (To display the maximum pool size values, Process Explorer must be configured properly to access the symbols for the kernel image, Ntoskrnl.exe.) Leave this system information display running so that you can see pool utilization when you run the Testlimit program.

3. Open a command prompt.

4. Run the Testlimit program with the -*h* switch (do this by typing **testlimit –h**). When Testlimit fails to open a new handle, it will display the total number of handles it was able to create. If the number is less than approximately 16 million, you are probably running out of paged pool before hitting the theoretical per-process handle limit.

5. Close the Command Prompt window; doing this will kill the Testlimit process, thus closing all the open handles.

As shown in Figure 3-19, on x86 systems, each handle entry consists of a structure with two 32-bit members: a pointer to the object (with flags), and the granted access mask. On 64-bit systems, a handle table entry is 12 bytes long: a 64-bit pointer to the object header and a 32-bit access mask. (Access masks are described in Chapter 6.)

FIGURE 3-19 Structure of a handle table entry

The first flag is a lock bit, indicating whether the entry is currently in use. The second flag is the inheritance designation—that is, it indicates whether processes created by this process will get a copy of this handle in their handle tables. As already noted, handle inheritance can be specified on handle creation or later with the *SetHandleInformation* function. (This flag can also be specified with the Windows *SetHandleInformation* function.) The third flag indicates whether closing the object should generate an audit message. (This flag isn't exposed to Windows—the object manager uses it internally.) Finally, the protect from close bit, stored in an unused portion of the access mask, indicates whether the caller is allowed to close this handle. (This flag can be set with the *NtSetInformationObject* system call.)

System components and device drivers often need to open handles to objects that user-mode applications shouldn't have access to. This is done by creating handles in the *kernel handle table* (referenced internally with the name *ObpKernelHandleTable*). The handles in this table are accessible only from kernel mode and in any process context. This means that a kernel-mode function can reference the handle in any process context with no performance impact. The object manager recognizes references to handles from the kernel handle table when the high bit of the handle is set—that is, when references to kernel-handle-table handles have values greater than 0x80000000. The kernel handle table also serves as the handle table for the System process.

EXPERIMENT: Viewing the Handle Table with the Kernel Debugger

The *!handle* command in the kernel debugger takes three arguments:

```
!handle <handle index> <flags> <processid>
```

The handle index identifies the handle entry in the handle table. (Zero means display all handles.) The first handle is index 4, the second 8, and so on. For example, typing **!handle 4** will show the first handle for the current process.

The flags you can specify are a bitmask, where bit 0 means display only the information in the handle entry, bit 1 means display free handles (not just used handles), and bit 2 means display information about the object that the handle refers to. The following command displays full details about the handle table for process ID 0x408:

```
lkd> !handle 0 7 acc
processor number 0, process 00000acc
Searching for Process with Cid == acc
PROCESS 89e1ead8  SessionId: 1  Cid: 0acc    Peb: 7ffd3000  ParentCid: 0a28
    DirBase: b25c8740  ObjectTable: f1a76c78  HandleCount: 246.
    Image: windbg.exe

Handle table at f0aaa000 with 246 Entries in use
0000: free handle, Entry address f0aaa000, Next Entry fffffffe
0004: Object: 95d02d70  GrantedAccess: 00000003 Entry: f0aaa008
Object: 95d02d70  Type: (860f5d60) Directory
    ObjectHeader: 95d02d58 (old version)
        HandleCount: 74  PointerCount: 103
        Directory Object: 83007470  Name: KnownDlls

0008: Object: 89e1a468  GrantedAccess: 00100020 Entry: f0aaa010
Object: 89e1a468  Type: (8613f040) File
    ObjectHeader: 89e1a450 (old version)
        HandleCount: 1 PointerCount: 1
        Directory Object: 00000000  Name: \Program Files\Debugging Tools for Windows
{HarddiskVolume3}
```

EXPERIMENT: Searching for Open Files with the Kernel Debugger

Although you can use Process Explorer as well as the OpenFiles.exe utility to search for open file handles, these tools are not available when looking at a crash dump or analyzing a system remotely. You can instead use the *!devhandles* command to search for handles opened to files on a specific volume. (See Chapter 7 for more information on devices, files, and volumes.)

1. First you need to pick the drive letter you are interested in and obtain the pointer to its *Device object*. You can use the *!object* command as shown here:

```
lkd> !object \GLOBAL??\C:
Object: 8d274e68  Type: (84d10bc0) SymbolicLink
    ObjectHeader: 8d274e50 (old version)
    HandleCount: 0  PointerCount: 1
    Directory Object: 8b6053b8  Name: C:
    Target String is '\Device\HarddiskVolume3'
    Drive Letter Index is 3 (C:)
```

2. Next use the *!devobj* command to get the Device object of the target volume name:

```
lkd> !devobj \Device\HarddiskVolume3
Device object (86623e10) is for:
```

3. Now you can use the pointer of the Device object with the *!devhandles* command. Each object shown points to a file:

```
lkd> !devhandles 86623e10

Checking handle table for process 0x84d0da90
Handle table at 890d6000 with 545 Entries in use
PROCESS 84d0da90  SessionId: none  Cid: 0004    Peb: 00000000  ParentCid: 0000
    DirBase: 00122000  ObjectTable: 8b602008  HandleCount: 545.
    Image: System

0084: Object: 8684c4b8  GrantedAccess: 0012019f

PROCESS 84d0da90  SessionId: none  Cid: 0004    Peb: 00000000  ParentCid: 0000
    DirBase: 00122000  ObjectTable: 8b602008  HandleCount: 545.
    Image: System

0088: Object: 8684c348  GrantedAccess: 0012019f

PROCESS 84d0da90  SessionId: none  Cid: 0004    Peb: 00000000  ParentCid: 0000
    DirBase: 00122000  ObjectTable: 8b602008  HandleCount: 545.
    Image: System
```

4. Finally, you can repeat the *!object* command on these objects to figure out to which file they refer:

```
lkd> !object 8684c4b8
Object: 8684c4b8  Type: (84d5a040) File
    ObjectHeader: 8684c4a0 (old version)
    HandleCount: 1  PointerCount: 2
    Directory Object: 00000000  Name:
\$Extend\$RmMetadata\$TxfLog\$TxfLogContainer00000000000000000004
{HarddiskVolume3}
```

Because handle leaks can be dangerous to the system by leaking kernel pool memory and eventually causing systemwide memory starvation—and can also break applications in subtle ways—Windows includes a couple of debugging mechanisms that can be enabled to monitor, analyze, and debug issues with handles. Additionally, the Debugging Tools for Windows come with two extensions that tap into these mechanisms and provide easy graphical analysis. Table 3-13 illustrates them:

TABLE 3-13 Debugging Mechanisms for Object Handles

Mechanism	Enabled By	Kernel Debugger Extension
Handle Tracing Database	Kernel Stack Trace systemwide and/or per-process with the User Stack Trace option checked with Gflags.exe.	*!htrace <handle value> <process ID>*
Object Reference Tracing	Per-process-name(s), or per-object-type-pool-tag(s), with Gflags.exe, under Object Reference Tracing.	*!obtrace <object pointer>*

Enabling the handle tracing database is useful when attempting to understand the use of each handle within an application or the system context. The *!htrace* debugger extension can display the stack trace captured at the time a specified handle was opened. After you discover a handle leak, the stack trace can pinpoint the code that is creating the handle, and it can be analyzed for a missing call to a function such as *CloseHandle*.

The object reference tracing *!obtrace* extension monitors even more by showing the stack trace for each new handle created as well as each time a handle is referenced by the kernel (and also opened, duplicated, or inherited) and dereferenced. By analyzing these patterns, misuse of an object at the system level can be more easily debugged. Additionally, these reference traces provide a way to understand the behavior of the system when dealing with certain objects. Tracing processes, for example, will display references from all the drivers on the system that have registered callback notifications (such as Process Monitor) and helps detect rogue or buggy third-party drivers that may be referencing handles in kernel mode but never dereferencing them.

Note When enabling object reference tracing for a specific object type, you can obtain the name of its pool tag by looking at the *key* member of the OBJECT_TYPE structure when using the *dt* command. Each object type on the system has a global variable that references this structure—for example, *PsProcessType*. Alternatively, you can use the *!object* command, which displays the pointer to this structure.

Object Security

When you open a file, you must specify whether you intend to read or to write. If you try to write to a file that is opened for read access, you get an error. Likewise, in the executive, when a process creates an object or opens a handle to an existing object, the process must specify a set of *desired access rights*—that is, what it wants to do with the object. It can request either a set of standard access rights (such as read, write, and execute) that apply to all object types or specific access rights that vary depending on the object type. For example, the process can request delete access or append access to a file object. Similarly, it might require the ability to suspend or terminate a thread object.

When a process opens a handle to an object, the object manager calls the *security reference monitor*, the kernel-mode portion of the security system, sending it the process's set of desired access rights. The security reference monitor checks whether the object's security descriptor permits the type of access the process is requesting. If it does, the reference monitor returns a set of *granted access rights* that the process is allowed, and the object manager stores them in the object handle it creates. How the security system determines who gets access to which objects is explored in Chapter 6.

Thereafter, whenever the process's threads use the handle, the object manager can quickly check whether the set of granted access rights stored in the handle corresponds to the usage implied by the object service the threads have called. For example, if the caller asked for read access to a section object but then calls a service to write to it, the service fails.

EXPERIMENT: Looking at Object Security

You can look at the various permissions on an object by using either Process Explorer, WinObj, or AccessCheck, all tools from Sysinternals. Let's look at different ways you can display the access control list (ACL) for an object.

1. You can use WinObj to navigate to any object on the system, including object directories, right-click on the object, and select Properties. For example, select the BaseNamedObjects directory, select Properties, and click on the Security tab. You should see a dialog box similar to the one shown next.

By examining the settings in the dialog box, you can see that the Everyone group doesn't have *delete* access to the directory, for example, but the SYSTEM account does (because this is where session 0 services with SYSTEM privileges will store their objects). Note that even though Everyone has the Add Object permission, a special privilege is required to be able to insert objects in this directory when running in another session.

2. Instead of using WinObj, you can view the handle table of a process using Process Explorer, as shown in the experiment "Viewing Open Handles" earlier in the chapter. Look at the handle table for the Explorer.exe process. You should notice a Directory object handle to the \Sessions\n\BaseNamedObjects directory. (We'll describe the per-session namespace shortly.) You can double-click on the object handle and then click on the Security tab and see a similar dialog box (with more users and rights granted). Unfortunately, Process Explorer cannot decode the specific object directory access rights, so all you'll see are generic rights.

3. Finally, you can use AccessCheck to query the security information of any object by using the –o switch as shown in the following output. Note that using AccessCheck will also show you the *integrity level* of the object. (See Chapter 6 for more information on integrity levels and the security reference monitor.)

```
C:\Windows>accesschk -o \Sessions\1\BaseNamedObjects

AccessChk v4.02 - Check access of files, keys, objects, processes or services
Copyright (C) 2006-2007 Mark Russinovich
Sysinternals - www.sysinternals.com
```

```
\Sessions\1\BaseNamedObjects
  Type: Directory
  Low Mandatory Level [No-Write-Up]
  RW NT AUTHORITY\SYSTEM
  RW Alex-Laptop\Alex Ionescu
  RW BUILTIN\Administrators
  R  Everyone
     NT AUTHORITY\RESTRICTED
```

Windows also supports *Ex* (Extended) versions of the APIs—*CreateEventEx, CreateMutexEx, CreateSemaphoreEx*—that add another argument for specifying the access mask. This makes it possible for applications to properly use discretionary access control lists (DACLs) to secure their objects without breaking their ability to use the create object APIs to open a handle to them. You might be wondering why a client application would not simply use *OpenEvent*, which does support a desired access argument. Using the open object APIs leads to an inherent race condition when dealing with a failure in the open call—that is to say, when the client application has attempted to open the event before it has been created. In most applications of this kind, the open API would be followed by a create API in the failure case. Unfortunately, there is no guaranteed way to make this create operation *atomic*—in other words, to only occur once. Indeed, it would be possible for multiple threads and/or processes to have executed the create API concurrently and all attempt to create the event at the same time. This race condition and the extra complexity required to try and handle it makes using the open object APIs an inappropriate solution to the problem, which is why the *Ex* APIs should be used instead.

Object Retention

There are two types of objects: temporary and permanent. Most objects are temporary—that is, they remain while they are in use and are freed when they are no longer needed. Permanent objects remain until they are explicitly freed. Because most objects are temporary, the rest of this section describes how the object manager implements *object retention*—that is, retaining temporary objects only as long as they are in use and then deleting them. Because all user-mode processes that access an object must first open a handle to it, the object manager can easily track how many of these processes, and even which ones, are using an object. Tracking these handles represents one part in implementing retention. The object manager implements object retention in two phases. The first phase is called *name retention*, and it is controlled by the number of open handles to an object that exist. Every time a process opens a handle to an object, the object manager increments the open handle counter in the object's header. As processes finish using the object and close their handles to it, the object manager decrements the open handle counter. When the counter drops to 0, the object manager deletes the object's name from its global namespace. This deletion prevents new processes from opening a handle to the object.

The second phase of object retention is to stop retaining the objects themselves (that is, to delete them) when they are no longer in use. Because operating system code usually accesses objects by using pointers instead of handles, the object manager must also record how many object pointers it has dispensed to operating system processes. It increments a *reference count* for an object each time it gives out a pointer to the object; when kernel-mode components finish using the pointer, they call the object manager to decrement the object's reference count. The system also increments the reference count when it increments the handle count, and likewise decrements the reference count when the handle count decrements, because a handle is also a reference to the object that must be tracked. (For further details on object retention, see the WDK documentation on the functions *ObReferenceObjectByPointer* and *ObDereferenceObject*.)

Figure 3-20 illustrates two event objects that are in use. Process A has the first event open. Process B has both events open. In addition, the first event is being referenced by some kernel-mode structure; thus, the reference count is 3. So even if Processes A and B closed their handles to the first event object, it would continue to exist because its reference count is 1. However, when Process B closes its handle to the second event object, the object would be deallocated.

So even after an object's open handle counter reaches 0, the object's reference count might remain positive, indicating that the operating system is still using the object. Ultimately, when the reference count drops to 0, the object manager deletes the object from memory. This deletion has to respect certain rules and also requires cooperation from the caller in certain cases. For example, because objects can be present both in paged or nonpaged pool memory (depending on the settings located in their object type), if a dereference occurs at an IRQL level of dispatch or higher, and this dereference causes the pointer count to drop to 0, the system would crash if it attempted to immediately free the memory of a paged-pool object. (Recall that such access is illegal because the page fault will never be serviced.) In this scenario, the object manager will perform a *deferred delete* operation, queuing the operation on a worker thread running at passive level (IRQL 0). We'll describe more about system worker threads later in this chapter.

Another scenario that requires deferred deletion is when dealing with Kernel Transaction Manager (KTM) objects. In some scenarios, certain drivers may hold a lock related to this object, and attempting to delete the object will result in the system attempting to acquire this lock. However, the driver may never get the chance to release its lock, causing a deadlock. When dealing with KTM objects, driver developers must use *ObDereferenceObjectDeferDelete* to force deferred deletion regardless of IRQL level. Finally, the I/O manager will also use this mechanism as an optimization so that certain I/Os can complete more quickly, instead of waiting for the object manager to delete the object.

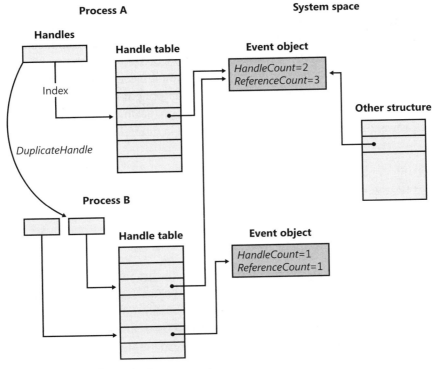

FIGURE 3-20 Handles and reference counts

Because of the way object retention works, an application can ensure that an object and its name remain in memory simply by keeping a handle open to the object. Programmers who write applications that contain two or more cooperating processes need not be concerned that one process might delete an object before the other process has finished using it. In addition, closing an application's object handles won't cause an object to be deleted if the operating system is still using it. For example, one process might create a second process to execute a program in the background; it then immediately closes its handle to the process. Because the operating system needs the second process to run the program, it maintains a reference to its process object. Only when the background program finishes executing does the object manager decrement the second process's reference count and then delete it.

Resource Accounting

Resource accounting, like object retention, is closely related to the use of object handles. A positive open handle count indicates that some process is using that resource. It also indicates that some process is being charged for the memory the object occupies. When an object's handle count and reference count drop to 0, the process that was using the object should no longer be charged for it.

Many operating systems use a quota system to limit processes' access to system resources. However, the types of quotas imposed on processes are sometimes diverse and complicated, and the code to track the quotas is spread throughout the operating system. For example, in some operating systems, an I/O component might record and limit the number of files a process can open, whereas a memory component might impose a limit on the amount of memory a process's threads can allocate. A process component might limit users to some maximum number of new processes they can create or a maximum number of threads within a process. Each of these limits is tracked and enforced in different parts of the operating system.

In contrast, the Windows object manager provides a central facility for resource accounting. Each object header contains an attribute called *quota charges* that records how much the object manager subtracts from a process's allotted paged and/or nonpaged pool quota when a thread in the process opens a handle to the object.

Each process on Windows points to a quota structure that records the limits and current values for nonpaged pool, paged pool, and page file usage. These quotas default to 0 (no limit) but can be specified by modifying registry values. (See *NonPagedPoolQuota*, *PagedPoolQuota*, and *PagingFileQuota* under HKLM\SYSTEM\CurrentControlSet\Session Manager\Memory Management.) Note that all the processes in an interactive session share the same quota block (and there's no documented way to create processes with their own quota blocks).

Object Names

An important consideration in creating a multitude of objects is the need to devise a successful system for keeping track of them. The object manager requires the following information to help you do so:

- A way to distinguish one object from another
- A method for finding and retrieving a particular object

The first requirement is served by allowing names to be assigned to objects. This is an extension of what most operating systems provide—the ability to name selected resources, files, pipes, or a block of shared memory, for example. The executive, in contrast, allows any resource represented by an object to have a name. The second requirement, finding and retrieving an object, is also satisfied by object names. If the object manager stores objects by name, it can find an object by looking up its name.

Object names also satisfy a third requirement, which is to allow processes to share objects. The executive's object namespace is a global one, visible to all processes in the system. One process can create an object and place its name in the global namespace, and a second process can open a handle to the object by specifying the object's name. If an object isn't meant to be shared in this way, its creator doesn't need to give it a name.

To increase efficiency, the object manager doesn't look up an object's name each time someone uses the object. Instead, it looks up a name under only two circumstances. The first is when a process creates a named object: the object manager looks up the name to verify that it doesn't already exist before storing the new name in the global namespace. The second is when a process opens a handle to a named object: the object manager looks up the name, finds the object, and then returns an object handle to the caller; thereafter, the caller uses the handle to refer to the object. When looking up a name, the object manager allows the caller to select either a case-sensitive or a case-insensitive search, a feature that supports POSIX and other environments that use case-sensitive file names.

Where the names of objects are stored depends on the object type. Table 3-14 lists the standard object directories found on all Windows systems and what types of objects have their names stored there. Of the directories listed, only \BaseNamedObjects and \Global?? are visible to user programs (see the "Session Namespace" section later in this chapter for more information).

TABLE 3-14 Standard Object Directories

Directory	Types of Object Names Stored
\GLOBAL??	MS-DOS device names (The \Sessions\0\DosDevices\<LUID>\ Global directories are symbolic links to this directory.)
\ArcNames	Symbolic links mapping ARC-style paths to NT-style paths.
\BaseNamedObjects	Mutexes, events, semaphores, waitable timers, and section objects for Session 0 (services).
\Callback	Callback objects
\Device	Device objects
\Driver	Driver objects
\FileSystem	File system driver objects and file system recognizer device objects
\KnownDlls	Section names and path for known DLLs (DLLs mapped by the system at startup time)
\Nls	Section names for mapped national language support tables
\ObjectTypes	ames of types of objects
\RPC Control	Port objects used by remote procedure calls (RPCs)
\Security	ALPC ports used by names of objects specific to the security subsystem
\Sessions	Per-session namespace directory (see the next subsection)
\UMDFCommunicationPorts	ALPC ports used by the User-Mode Driver Framework (UMDF)
\Windows	Windows subsystem ports and window stations

Because the base kernel objects such as mutexes, events, semaphores, waitable timers, and sections have their names stored in a single object directory, no two of these objects can have the same name, even if they are of a different type. This restriction emphasizes the need

to choose names carefully so that they don't collide with other names. For example, prefix names with a GUID and/or combine the name with the user's security identifier (SID).

Object names are global to a single computer (or to all processors on a multiprocessor computer), but they're not visible across a network. However, the object manager's parse method makes it possible to access named objects that exist on other computers. For example, the I/O manager, which supplies file object services, extends the functions of the object manager to remote files. When asked to open a remote file object, the object manager calls a parse method, which allows the I/O manager to intercept the request and deliver it to a network redirector, a driver that accesses files across the network. Server code on the remote Windows system calls the object manager and the I/O manager on that system to find the file object and return the information back across the network.

Object Directories The object directory object is the object manager's means for supporting this hierarchical naming structure. This object is analogous to a file system directory and contains the names of other objects, possibly even other object directories. The object directory object maintains enough information to translate these object names into pointers to the objects themselves. The object manager uses the pointers to construct the object handles that it returns to user-mode callers. Both kernel-mode code (including executive components and device drivers) and user-mode code (such as subsystems) can create object directories in which to store objects. For example, the I/O manager creates an object directory named \Device, which contains the names of objects representing I/O devices.

One security consideration to keep in mind when dealing with named objects is the possibility of *object name squatting*. Although object names in different sessions are protected from each other, there's no standard protection inside the current session namespace that can be set with the standard Windows API. This makes it possible for an unprivileged application running in the same session as a privileged application to access its objects, as described earlier in the object security subsection. Unfortunately, even if the object creator used a proper DACL to secure the object, this doesn't help against the *squatting* attack, in which the unprivileged application creates the object *before* the privileged application, thus denying access to the legitimate application.

The concept of a *private namespace* was introduced in Windows Vista to alleviate this issue. It allows user-mode applications to create object directories through the *CreatePrivate-Namespace* API and associate these directories with *boundary descriptors*, which are special data structures protecting the directories. These descriptors contain SIDs describing which security principals are allowed access to the object directory. In this manner, a privileged application can be sure that unprivileged applications will not be able to conduct a denial of service attack against its objects (this doesn't stop a privileged application from doing the same, however, but this point is moot).

EXPERIMENT: Looking at the Base Named Objects

You can see the list of base objects that have names with the WinObj tool from Sysinternals. Run Winobj.exe. and click on \BaseNamedObjects, as shown here:

The named objects are shown on the right. The icons indicate the object type.

- Mutexes are indicated with a stop sign.

- Sections (Windows file mapping objects) are shown as memory chips.

- Events are shown as exclamation points.

- Semaphores are indicated with an icon that resembles a traffic signal.

- Symbolic links have icons that are curved arrows.

- Folders indicate object directories.

- Gears indicate other objects, such as ALPC ports.

EXPERIMENT: Tampering with Single Instancing

Applications such as Windows Media Player and those in Microsoft Office are common examples of single instancing enforcement through named objects. Notice that when launching the Wmplayer.exe executable, Windows Media Player appears only once—every other launch simply results in the window coming back into focus. We can tamper with the handle list by using Process Explorer to turn the computer into a media mixer! Here's how:

1. Launch Windows Media Player and Process Explorer, and then view the handle table (by clicking View, Lower Pane View, and then Handles). You should see a handle containing CheckForOtherInstanceMutex.

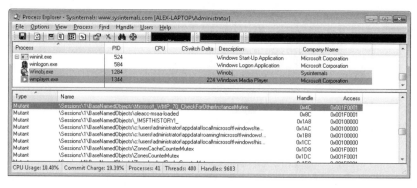

2. Right-click on the handle, and select Close Handle. Confirm the action when asked.

3. Now run Windows Media Player again. Notice that this time a second process is created.

4. Go ahead and play a different song in each instance. You can also use the Sound Mixer in the system tray (click on the Volume icon) to select which of the two processes will have greater volume, effectively creating a mixing environment.

Instead of closing a handle to a named object, an application could have run on its own before Windows Media Player and created an object with the same name. In this scenario, Windows Media Player would never run, fooled into believing it was already running on the system.

Symbolic Links In certain file systems (on NTFS and some UNIX systems, for example), a symbolic link lets a user create a file name or a directory name that, when used, is translated by the operating system into a different file or directory name. Using a symbolic link is a simple method for allowing users to indirectly share a file or the contents of a directory, creating a cross-link between different directories in the ordinarily hierarchical directory structure.

The object manager implements an object called a *symbolic link object*, which performs a similar function for object names in its object namespace. A symbolic link can occur anywhere within an object name string. When a caller refers to a symbolic link object's name, the object manager traverses its object namespace until it reaches the symbolic link object. It looks inside the symbolic link and finds a string that it substitutes for the symbolic link name. It then restarts its name lookup.

One place in which the executive uses symbolic link objects is in translating MS-DOS-style device names into Windows internal device names. In Windows, a user refers to hard disk drives using the names C:, D:, and so on and serial ports as COM1, COM2, and so on. The Windows subsystem makes these symbolic link objects protected, global data by placing them in the object manager namespace under the \Global?? directory.

Session Namespace

Services have access to the *global* namespace, a namespace that serves as the first instance of the namespace. Additional sessions (including a console user) are given a session-private view of the namespace known as a *local* namespace. The parts of the namespace that are localized for each session include \DosDevices, \Windows, and \BaseNamedObjects. Making separate copies of the same parts of the namespace is known as *instancing* the namespace. Instancing \DosDevices makes it possible for each user to have different network drive letters and Windows objects such as serial ports. On Windows, the global \DosDevices directory is named \Global?? and is the directory to which \DosDevices points, and local \DosDevices directories are identified by the logon session ID.

The \Windows directory is where Win32k.sys creates the interactive window station, \WinSta0. A Terminal Services environment can support multiple interactive users, but each user needs an individual version of WinSta0 to preserve the illusion that he or she is accessing the predefined interactive window station in Windows. Finally, applications and the system create shared objects in \BaseNamedObjects, including events, mutexes, and memory sections. If two users are running an application that creates a named object, each user session must have a private version of the object so that the two instances of the application don't interfere with one another by accessing the same object.

The object manager implements a local namespace by creating the private versions of the three directories mentioned under a directory associated with the user's session under \Sessions\n (where *n* is the session identifier). When a Windows application in remote session two creates a named event, for example, the object manager transparently redirects the object's name from \BaseNamedObjects to \Sessions\2\BaseNamedObjects.

All object manager functions related to namespace management are aware of the instanced directories and participate in providing the illusion that nonconsole sessions use the same namespace as the console session. Windows subsystem DLLs prefix names passed by Windows applications that reference objects in \DosDevices with \?? (for example, C:\Windows becomes \??\C:\Windows). When the object manager sees the special \?? prefix, the steps it takes depends on the version of Windows, but it always relies on a field named DeviceMap in the executive process object (EPROCESS, which is described further in Chapter 5) that points to a data structure shared by other processes in the same session.

The DosDevicesDirectory field of the DeviceMap structure points at the object manager directory that represents the process's local \DosDevices. When the object manager sees a reference to \??, it locates the process's local \DosDevices by using the DosDevicesDirectory field of the DeviceMap. If the object manager doesn't find the object in that directory, it checks the DeviceMap field of the directory object, and if it's valid it looks for the object in the directory pointed to by the GlobalDosDevicesDirectory field of the DeviceMap structure, which is always \Global??.

Under certain circumstances, applications that are Terminal Services–aware need to access objects in the console session even if the application is running in a remote session. The application might want to do this to synchronize with instances of itself running in other remote sessions or with the console session. For these cases, the object manager provides the special override "\Global" that an application can prefix to any object name to access the global namespace. For example, an application in session two opening an object named \Global\ApplicationInitialized is directed to \BaseNamedObjects\ApplicationInitialized instead of \Sessions\2\BaseNamedObjects\ApplicationInitialized.

An application that wants to access an object in the global \DosDevices directory does not need to use the \Global prefix as long as the object doesn't exist in its local \DosDevices directory. This is because the object manager will automatically look in the global directory for the object if it doesn't find it in the local directory. Session directories are isolated from each other, and administrative privileges are required to create a global object (except for section objects). A special privilege named *create global object* is verified before allowing such operations.

EXPERIMENT: Viewing Namespace Instancing

You can see the separation between the session 0 namespace and other session namespaces as soon as you log in. The reason you can is that the first console user is logged in to session 1 (while services run in session 0). Run Winobj.exe, and click on the \Sessions directory. You'll see a subdirectory with a numeric name for each active session. If you open one of these directories, you'll see subdirectories named \DosDevices, \Windows, and \BaseNamedObjects, which are the local namespace subdirectories of the session. The following screen shot shows a local namespace:

Next run Process Explorer and select a process in your session (such as Explorer.exe), and then view the handle table (by clicking View, Lower Pane View, and then Handles). You should see a handle to \Windows\WindowStations\WinSta0 underneath \Sessions*n*, where *n* is the session ID.

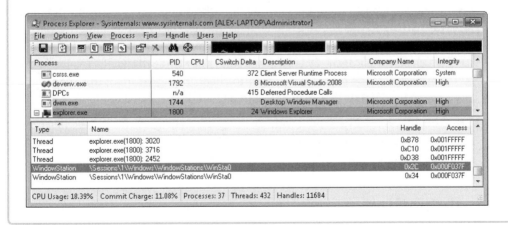

Object Filtering

Windows includes a filtering model in the object manager, similar to the file system mini-filter model described in Chapter 7. One of the primary benefits of this filtering model is the ability to use the *altitude* concept that these existing filtering technologies use, which means that multiple drivers can filter object manager events at appropriate locations in the filtering stack. Additionally, drivers are permitted to intercept calls such as *NtOpenThread* and *NtOpenProcess* and even to modify the access masks being requested from the process manager. This allows protection against certain operations on an open handle—however, an open operation cannot be entirely blocked because doing so would too closely resemble a malicious operation (processes that could never be managed).

Furthermore, drivers are able to take advantage of both *pre* and *post* callbacks, allowing them to prepare for a certain operation before it occurs, as well as to react or finalize information after the operation has occurred. These callbacks can be specified for each operation (currently, only open, create, and duplicate are supported) and be specific for each object type (currently, only process and thread objects are supported). For each callback, drivers can specify their own internal context value, which can be returned across all calls to the driver or across a pre/post pair. These callbacks can be registered with the *ObRegisterCallback* API and unregistered with the *ObUnregisterCallback* API—it is the responsibility of the driver to ensure deregistration happens.

Use of the APIs is restricted to images that have certain characteristics:

- The image must be signed, even on 32-bit computers, according to the same rules set forth in the Kernel Mode Code Signing (KMCS) policy. (Code integrity will be discussed later in this chapter.) The image must be compiled with the /integritycheck linker flag, which sets the IMAGE_DLLCHARACTERISTICS_FORCE_INTEGRITY value in the PE header. This instructs the memory manager to check the signature of the image regardless of any other defaults that may not normally result in a check.

- The image must be signed with a catalog containing cryptographic per-page hashes of the executable code. This allows the system to detect changes to the image after it has been loaded in memory.

Synchronization

The concept of *mutual exclusion* is a crucial one in operating systems development. It refers to the guarantee that one, and only one, thread can access a particular resource at a time. Mutual exclusion is necessary when a resource doesn't lend itself to shared access or when sharing would result in an unpredictable outcome. For example, if two threads copy a file to a printer port at the same time, their output could be interspersed. Similarly, if one thread reads a memory location while another one writes to it, the first thread will receive unpredictable data. In general, writable resources can't be shared without restrictions, whereas

resources that aren't subject to modification can be shared. Figure 3-21 illustrates what happens when two threads running on different processors both write data to a circular queue.

Time

Processor A

Get queue tail
Insert data at current location

⋮

Increment tail pointer

⋮

Processor B

⋮

Get queue tail

⋮

Insert data at current location /*ERROR*/
Increment tail pointer

⋮

FIGURE 3-21 Incorrect sharing of memory

Because the second thread obtained the value of the queue tail pointer before the first thread had finished updating it, the second thread inserted its data into the same location that the first thread had used, overwriting data and leaving one queue location empty. Even though Figure 3-21 illustrates what could happen on a multiprocessor system, the same error could occur on a single-processor system if the operating system were to perform a context switch to the second thread before the first thread updated the queue tail pointer.

Sections of code that access a nonshareable resource are called *critical* sections. To ensure correct code, only one thread at a time can execute in a critical section. While one thread is writing to a file, updating a database, or modifying a shared variable, no other thread can be allowed to access the same resource. The pseudocode shown in Figure 3-21 is a critical section that incorrectly accesses a shared data structure without mutual exclusion.

The issue of mutual exclusion, although important for all operating systems, is especially important (and intricate) for a *tightly coupled, symmetric multiprocessing* (SMP) operating system such as Windows, in which the same system code runs simultaneously on more than one processor, sharing certain data structures stored in global memory. In Windows, it is the kernel's job to provide mechanisms that system code can use to prevent two threads from modifying the same structure at the same time. The kernel provides mutual-exclusion primitives that it and the rest of the executive use to synchronize their access to global data structures.

Because the scheduler synchronizes access to its data structures at DPC/dispatch level IRQL, the kernel and executive cannot rely on synchronization mechanisms that would result in a page fault or reschedule operation to synchronize access to data structures when the IRQL is DPC/dispatch level or higher (levels known as an *elevated* or *high* IRQL). In the following sections, you'll find out how the kernel and executive use mutual exclusion to protect their

global data structures when the IRQL is high and what mutual-exclusion and synchronization mechanisms the kernel and executive use when the IRQL is *low* (below DPC/dispatch level).

High-IRQL Synchronization

At various stages during its execution, the kernel must guarantee that one, and only one, processor at a time is executing within a critical section. Kernel critical sections are the code segments that modify a global data structure such as the kernel's dispatcher database or its DPC queue. The operating system can't function correctly unless the kernel can guarantee that threads access these data structures in a mutually exclusive manner.

The biggest area of concern is interrupts. For example, the kernel might be updating a global data structure when an interrupt occurs whose interrupt-handling routine also modifies the structure. Simple single-processor operating systems sometimes prevent such a scenario by disabling all interrupts each time they access global data, but the Windows kernel has a more sophisticated solution. Before using a global resource, the kernel temporarily masks those interrupts whose interrupt handlers also use the resource. It does so by raising the processor's IRQL to the highest level used by any potential interrupt source that accesses the global data. For example, an interrupt at DPC/dispatch level causes the dispatcher, which uses the dispatcher database, to run. Therefore, any other part of the kernel that uses the dispatcher database raises the IRQL to DPC/dispatch level, masking DPC/dispatch-level interrupts before using the dispatcher database.

This strategy is fine for a single-processor system, but it's inadequate for a multiprocessor configuration. Raising the IRQL on one processor doesn't prevent an interrupt from occurring on another processor. The kernel also needs to guarantee mutually exclusive access across several processors.

Interlocked Operations

The simplest form of synchronization mechanisms rely on hardware support for multiprocessor-safe manipulation of integer values and for performing comparisons. They include functions such as *InterlockedIncrement*, *InterlockedDecrement*, *InterlockedExchange*, and *InterlockedCompareExchange*. The *InterlockedDecrement* function, for example, uses the x86 *lock* instruction prefix (for example, *lock xadd*) to lock the multiprocessor bus during the subtraction operation so that another processor that's also modifying the memory location being decremented won't be able to modify it between the decrementing processor's read of the original value and its write of the decremented value. This form of basic synchronization is used by the kernel and drivers. In today's Microsoft compiler suite, these functions are called *intrinsic* because the code for them is generated in inline assembler, directly during the compilation phase, instead of going through a function call. (It's likely that pushing

the parameters onto the stack, calling the function, copying the parameters into registers, and then popping the parameters off the stack and returning to the caller would be a more expensive operation than the actual work the function is supposed to do in the first place.)

Spinlocks

The mechanism the kernel uses to achieve multiprocessor mutual exclusion is called a *spin-lock*. A spinlock is a locking primitive associated with a global data structure such as the DPC queue shown in Figure 3-22.

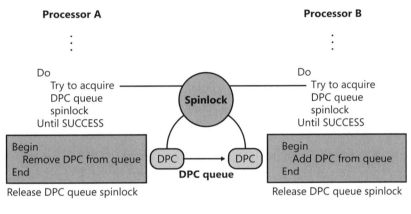

FIGURE 3-22 Using a spinlock

Before entering either critical section shown in Figure 3-22, the kernel must acquire the spinlock associated with the protected DPC queue. If the spinlock isn't free, the kernel keeps trying to acquire the lock until it succeeds. The spinlock gets its name from the fact that the kernel (and thus, the processor) waits, "spinning," until it gets the lock.

Spinlocks, like the data structures they protect, reside in nonpaged memory mapped into the system address space. The code to acquire and release a spinlock is written in assembly language for speed and to exploit whatever locking mechanism the underlying processor architecture provides. On many architectures, spinlocks are implemented with a hardware-supported test-and-set operation, which tests the value of a lock variable and acquires the lock in one atomic instruction. Testing and acquiring the lock in one instruction prevents a second thread from grabbing the lock between the time the first thread tests the variable and the time it acquires the lock. Additionally, the *lock* instruction mentioned earlier can also be used on the test-and-set operation, resulting in the combined *lock bts* assembly operation, which also locks the multiprocessor bus; otherwise, it would be possible for more than one processor to atomically perform the operation (without the *lock*, the operation is only guaranteed to be atomic on the current processor).

All kernel-mode spinlocks in Windows have an associated IRQL that is always DPC/dispatch level or higher. Thus, when a thread is trying to acquire a spinlock, all other activity at the spinlock's IRQL or lower ceases on that processor. Because thread dispatching happens at DPC/dispatch level, a thread that holds a spinlock is never preempted because the IRQL masks the dispatching mechanisms. This masking allows code executing in a critical section protected by a spinlock to continue executing so that it will release the lock quickly. The kernel uses spinlocks with great care, minimizing the number of instructions it executes while it holds a spinlock. Any processor that attempts to acquire the spinlock will essentially be busy, waiting indefinitely, consuming power (a busy wait results in 100% CPU usage) and performing no actual work.

On newer (Pentium 4 and later) processors, a special *pause* assembly instruction can be inserted in busy wait loops. This instruction offers a *hint* to the processor that the loop instructions it is processing are part of a spinlock (or a similar construct) acquisition loop. The instruction provides three benefits:

- It significantly reduces power usage by delaying the core ever so slightly instead of continuously looping.

- On HyperThreaded cores, it allows the CPU to realize that the "work" being done by the spinning logical core is not terribly important and awards more CPU time to the second logical core instead.

- Because a busy wait loop results in a storm of read requests coming to the bus from the waiting thread (which may be generated out-of-order), the CPU will attempt to correct for violations of memory order as soon as it detects a write (that is, when the owning thread releases the lock). Thus, as soon as the spinlock is released, the CPU will reorder any pending memory read operations to ensure proper ordering. This reordering results in a large penalty in system performance and can be avoided with the *pause* instruction.

The kernel makes spinlocks available to other parts of the executive through a set of kernel functions, including *KeAcquireSpinLock* and *KeReleaseSpinLock*. Device drivers, for example, require spinlocks to guarantee that device registers and other global data structures are accessed by only one part of a device driver (and from only one processor) at a time. Spinlocks are not for use by user programs—user programs should use the objects described in the next section. Device drivers also need to protect access to their own data structures from interrupts associated with themselves. Because the spinlock APIs typically only raise the IRQL to DPC/dispatch level, this isn't enough to protect against interrupts. For this reason, the kernel also exports the *KeAcquireInterruptSpinLock* and *KeReleaseInterruptSpinLock* APIs that take as a parameter the KINTERRUPT object discussed at the beginning of this chapter. The

system will look inside the interrupt object for the associated DIRQL with the interrupt and raise the IRQL to the appropriate level to ensure correct access to structures shared with the ISR. Devices can use the *KeSynchronizeExecution* API to synchronize an entire function with an ISR, instead of just a critical section. In all cases, the code protected by an interrupt spinlock must execute extremely quickly—any delay causes higher than normal interrupt latency and will have significant negative performance effects.

Kernel spinlocks carry with them restrictions for code that uses them. Because spinlocks always have an IRQL of DPC/dispatch level or higher, as explained earlier, code holding a spinlock will crash the system if it attempts to make the scheduler perform a dispatch operation or if it causes a page fault.

Queued Spinlocks

To increase the scalability of spinlocks, a special type of spinlock, called a *queued spinlock*, is used in most circumstances instead of a standard spinlock. A queued spinlock works like this: When a processor wants to acquire a queued spinlock that is currently held, it places its identifier in a queue associated with the spinlock. When the processor that's holding the spinlock releases it, it hands the lock over to the first processor identified in the queue. In the meantime, a processor waiting for a busy spinlock checks the status not of the spinlock itself but of a per-processor flag that the processor ahead of it in the queue sets to indicate that the waiting processor's turn has arrived.

The fact that queued spinlocks result in spinning on per-processor flags rather than global spinlocks has two effects. The first is that the multiprocessor's bus isn't as heavily trafficked by interprocessor synchronization. The second is that instead of a random processor in a waiting group acquiring a spinlock, the queued spinlock enforces first-in, first-out (FIFO) ordering to the lock. FIFO ordering means more consistent performance across processors accessing the same locks.

Windows defines a number of global queued spinlocks by storing pointers to them in an array contained in each processor's *processor region control block* (PRCB). A global spinlock can be acquired by calling *KeAcquireQueuedSpinLock* with the index into the PRCB array at which the pointer to the spinlock is stored. The number of global spinlocks has grown in each release of the operating system, and the table of index definitions for them is published in the WDK header file Ntddk.h. Note, however, that acquiring one of these queued spinlocks from a device driver is an unsupported and heavily frowned upon operation. These locks are reserved for the kernel's own internal use.

EXPERIMENT: Viewing Global Queued Spinlocks

You can view the state of the global queued spinlocks (the ones pointed to by the queued spinlock array in each processor's PCR) by using the *!qlocks* kernel debugger command. In the following example, the page frame number (PFN) database queued spinlock is held by processor 1, and the other queued spinlocks are not acquired. (The PFN database is described in Chapter 9.)

```
lkd> !qlocks
Key: O = Owner, 1-n = Wait order, blank = not owned/waiting, C = Corrupt

                        Processor Number
        Lock Name       0  1

KE      - Dispatcher
MM      - Expansion
MM      - PFN                   O
MM      - System Space
CC      - Vacb
CC      - Master
```

Instack Queued Spinlocks

Driver developers who recognized the significant improvement in the queued spin-lock mechanism (over standard spinlocks) might have been disappointed to know that these locks were not available to third-party developers. Device drivers can now use dynamically allocated queued spinlocks with the *KeAcquireInStackQueuedSpinLock* and *KeReleaseInStackQueuedSpinLock* functions. Several components—including the cache manager, executive pool manager, and NTFS—take advantage of these types of locks (when a global static queued spinlock would simply be too wasteful), and the functions are documented in the WDK for use by third-party driver writers.

KeAcquireInStackQueuedSpinLock takes a pointer to a spinlock data structure and a spinlock queue handle. The spinlock handle is actually a data structure in which the kernel stores information about the lock's status, including the lock's ownership and the queue of processors that might be waiting for the lock to become available. For this reason, the handle shouldn't be a global variable. It is usually a stack variable, guaranteeing *locality* to the caller thread, and is responsible for the *InStack* part of the spinlock and API name.

Executive Interlocked Operations

The kernel supplies a number of simple synchronization functions constructed on spinlocks for more advanced operations, such as adding and removing entries from singly and doubly linked lists. Examples include *ExInterlockedPopEntryList* and *ExInterlockedPushEntryList* for singly linked lists, and *ExInterlockedInsertHeadList* and *ExInterlockedRemoveHeadList* for

doubly linked lists. All these functions require a standard spinlock as a parameter and are used throughout the kernel and device drivers.

Instead of relying on the standard APIs to acquire and release the spinlock parameter, these functions place the code required inline and also use a different ordering scheme. Whereas the *Ke* spinlock APIs will first test and set the bit to see whether the lock is released and then atomically do a locked test-and-set operation to actually make the acquisition, these routines will disable interrupts on the processor and immediately attempt an atomic test-and-set. If the initial attempt fails, interrupts are enabled again, and the standard busy waiting algorithm continues until the test-and-set operation returns 0—in which case the whole function is restarted again. Because of these subtle differences, a spinlock used for the executive interlocked functions must not be used with the standard kernel APIs discussed previously. Naturally, noninterlocked list operations must not be mixed with interlocked operations.

> **Note** Certain of the executive interlocked operations actually silently ignore the spinlock when possible. For example, the *ExInterlockedIncrementLong* or *ExInterlockedCompareExchange* APIs actually use the same *lock* prefix used by the standard interlocked functions and the intrinsic functions. These functions were useful on older systems (or non-x86 systems) where the *lock* operation was not suitable or available. For this reason, these calls are now deprecated in favor of the intrinsic functions.

Low-IRQL Synchronization

Executive software outside the kernel also needs to synchronize access to global data structures in a multiprocessor environment. For example, the memory manager has only one page frame database, which it accesses as a global data structure, and device drivers need to ensure that they can gain exclusive access to their devices. By calling kernel functions, the executive can create a spinlock, acquire it, and release it.

Spinlocks only partially fill the executive's needs for synchronization mechanisms, however. Because waiting for a spinlock literally stalls a processor, spinlocks can be used only under the following strictly limited circumstances:

- The protected resource must be accessed quickly and without complicated interactions with other code.

- The critical section code can't be paged out of memory, can't make references to pageable data, can't call external procedures (including system services), and can't generate interrupts or exceptions.

These restrictions are confining and can't be met under all circumstances. Furthermore, the executive needs to perform other types of synchronization in addition to mutual exclusion, and it must also provide synchronization mechanisms to user mode.

There are several additional synchronization mechanisms for use when spinlocks are not suitable:

- Kernel dispatcher objects
- Fast mutexes and guarded mutexes
- Executive resources
- Pushlocks

Additionally, user-mode code, which also executes at low IRQL, must be able to have its own locking primitives. Windows supports various user-mode specific primitives:

- Condition variables (CondVars)
- Slim reader-writer locks (SRWs)
- Run once initialization (InitOnce)
- Critical sections

We'll take a look at the user-mode primitives and their underlying kernel-mode support later; for now we'll focus on kernel-mode objects. Table 3-15 serves as a reference that compares and contrasts the capabilities of these mechanisms and their interaction with kernel-mode APC delivery.

TABLE 3-15 Kernel Synchronization Mechanisms

	Exposed for Use by Device Drivers	Disables Normal Kernel-Mode APCs	Disables Special Kernel-Mode APCs	Supports Recursive Acquisition	Supports Shared and Exclusive Acquisition
Kernel dispatcher mutexes	Yes	Yes	No	Yes	No
Kernel dispatcher semaphores or events	Yes	No	No	No	No
Fast mutexes	Yes	Yes	Yes	No	No
Guarded mutexes	Yes	Yes	Yes	No	No
Pushlocks	No	No	No	No	Yes
Executive resources	Yes	No	No	Yes	Yes

Kernel Dispatcher Objects

The kernel furnishes additional synchronization mechanisms to the executive in the form of kernel objects, known collectively as *dispatcher objects*. The user-visible synchronization objects acquire their synchronization capabilities from these kernel dispatcher objects. Each user-visible object that supports synchronization encapsulates at least one kernel dispatcher

object. The executive's synchronization semantics are visible to Windows programmers through the *WaitForSingleObject* and *WaitForMultipleObjects* functions, which the Windows subsystem implements by calling analogous system services that the object manager supplies. A thread in a Windows application can synchronize with a Windows process, thread, event, semaphore, mutex, waitable timer, I/O completion port, or file object.

One other type of executive synchronization object worth noting is called an *executive resource*. Executive resources provide exclusive access (like a mutex) as well as shared read access (multiple readers sharing read-only access to a structure). However, they're available only to kernel-mode code and thus are not accessible from the Windows API. Executive resources are not dispatcher objects but data structures, allocated directly from nonpaged pool, that have their own specialized services to initialize, lock, release, query, and wait for them. The remaining subsections describe the implementation details of waiting for dispatcher objects.

Waiting for Dispatcher Objects A thread can synchronize with a dispatcher object by waiting for the object's handle. Doing so causes the kernel to put the thread in a wait state.

At any given moment, a synchronization object is in one of two states: *signaled state* or *nonsignaled state*. A thread can't resume its execution until its wait is satisfied. This change occurs when the dispatcher object whose handle the thread is waiting for also undergoes a state change, from the nonsignaled state to the signaled state (when a thread sets an event object, for example). To synchronize with an object, a thread calls one of the wait system services that the object manager supplies, passing a handle to the object it wants to synchronize with. The thread can wait for one or several objects and can also specify that its wait should be canceled if it hasn't ended within a certain amount of time. Whenever the kernel sets an object to the signaled state, the kernel's *KiWaitTest* function (or sometimes, specialized inline code) checks to see whether any threads are waiting for the object and not also waiting for other objects to become signaled. If there are, the kernel releases one or more of the threads from their waiting state so that they can continue executing.

The following example of setting an event illustrates how synchronization interacts with thread dispatching:

- A user-mode thread waits for an event object's handle.

- The kernel changes the thread's scheduling state to waiting and then adds the thread to a list of threads waiting for the event.

- Another thread sets the event.

- The kernel marches down the list of threads waiting for the event. If a thread's conditions for waiting are satisfied (see the following note), the kernel takes the thread out of the waiting state. If it is a variable-priority thread, the kernel might also boost its execution priority. (For details on thread scheduling, see Chapter 5.)

> **Note** Some threads might be waiting for more than one object, so they continue waiting, unless they specified a *WaitAny* wait, which will wake them up as soon as one object (instead of all) is signaled.

What Signals an Object? The signaled state is defined differently for different objects. A thread object is in the nonsignaled state during its lifetime and is set to the signaled state by the kernel when the thread terminates. Similarly, the kernel sets a process object to the signaled state when the process's last thread terminates. In contrast, the timer object, like an alarm, is set to "go off" at a certain time. When its time expires, the kernel sets the timer object to the signaled state.

When choosing a synchronization mechanism, a program must take into account the rules governing the behavior of different synchronization objects. Whether a thread's wait ends when an object is set to the signaled state varies with the type of object the thread is waiting for, as Table 3-16 illustrates.

TABLE 3-16 Definitions of the Signaled State

Object Type	Set to Signaled State When	Effect on Waiting Threads
Process	Last thread terminates	All released
Thread	Thread terminates	All released
File	I/O operation completes	All released
Debug object	Debug message is queued to the object	All released
Event (notification type)	Thread sets the event	All released
Event (synchronization type)	Thread sets the event	One thread released; event object reset
Gate	Thread signals the gate	First waiting thread released
Keyed event	Thread sets event with a key	Thread waiting for key and which is of same process as signaler is released
Semaphore	Semaphore count drops by 1	One thread released
Timer (notification type)	Set time arrives or time interval expires	All released
Timer (synchronization type)	Set time arrives or time interval expires	One thread released
Mutex	Thread releases the mutex	One thread released
Queue	Item is placed on queue	One thread released

When an object is set to the signaled state, waiting threads are generally released from their wait states immediately. Some of the kernel dispatcher objects and the system events that induce their state changes are shown in Figure 3-23.

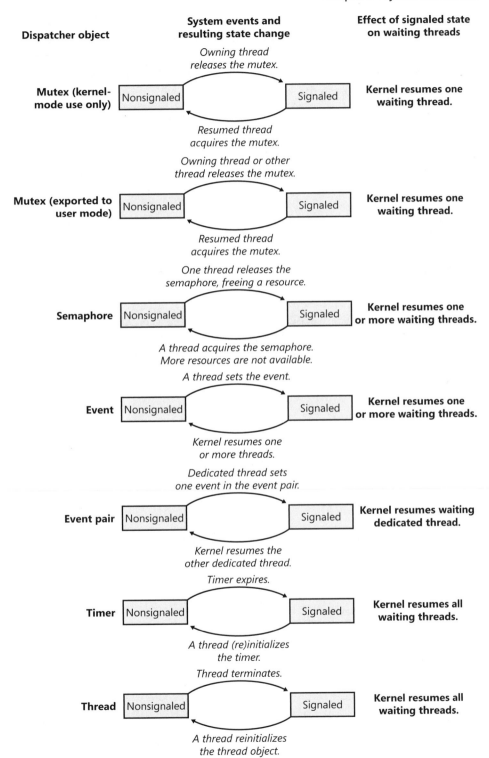

FIGURE 3-23 Selected kernel dispatcher objects

For example, a notification event object (called a *manual reset event* in the Windows API) is used to announce the occurrence of some event. When the event object is set to the signaled state, all threads waiting for the event are released. The exception is any thread that is waiting for more than one object at a time; such a thread might be required to continue waiting until additional objects reach the signaled state.

In contrast to an event object, a mutex object has ownership associated with it (unless it was acquired during a DPC). It is used to gain mutually exclusive access to a resource, and only one thread at a time can hold the mutex. When the mutex object becomes free, the kernel sets it to the signaled state and then selects one waiting thread to execute. The thread selected by the kernel acquires the mutex object, and all other threads continue waiting.

This brief discussion wasn't meant to enumerate all the reasons and applications for using the various executive objects but rather to list their basic functionality and synchronization behavior. For information on how to put these objects to use in Windows programs, see the Windows reference documentation on synchronization objects or Jeffrey Richter's book *Windows via C/C++*.

Data Structures Two data structures are key to tracking who is waiting for what: *dispatcher headers* and *wait blocks*. Both these structures are publicly defined in the WDK include file Ntddk.h. The definitions are reproduced here for convenience:

```
typedef struct _DISPATCHER_HEADER {
    union {
        struct {
            UCHAR Type;
            union {
                UCHAR Abandoned;
                UCHAR Absolute;
                UCHAR NpxIrql;
                BOOLEAN Signalling;
            } DUMMYUNIONNAME;

            union {
                UCHAR Size;
                UCHAR Hand;
            } DUMMYUNIONNAME2;

            union {
                UCHAR Inserted;
                BOOLEAN DebugActive;
                BOOLEAN DpcActive;
            } DUMMYUNIONNAME3;
        } DUMMYSTRUCTNAME;

        volatile LONG Lock;
    } DUMMYUNIONNAME;

    LONG SignalState;
    LIST_ENTRY WaitListHead;
} DISPATCHER_HEADER;
```

Chapter 3 System Mechanisms **183**

```
typedef struct _KWAIT_BLOCK {
    LIST_ENTRY WaitListEntry;
    struct _KTHREAD *Thread;
    PVOID Object;
    struct _KWAIT_BLOCK *NextWaitBlock;
    USHORT WaitKey;
    UCHAR WaitType;
    UCHAR SpareByte;
#if defined(_AMD64_)
    LONG SpareLong;
#endif
} KWAIT_BLOCK, *PKWAIT_BLOCK, *PRKWAIT_BLOCK;
```

The dispatcher header is a packed structure because it needs to hold lots of information in a fixed-size structure. One of the main tricks is to define mutually exclusive flags at the same memory location (offset) in the structure. By using the *Type* field, the kernel knows which of these fields actually applies. For example, a mutex can be abandoned, but a timer can be absolute or relative. Similarly, a timer can be inserted into the timer list, but the *debug active* field only makes sense for processes. On the other hand, the dispatcher header does contain information generic for any dispatcher object: the object type, signaled state, and a list of the threads waiting for that object.

> **Note** The *debug active* flag used to determine whether a process is currently being debugged is actually a bit mask that specifies which debug registers on the CPU are in use. Because the valid debug registers are DR0–3, DR6, and DR7, the bit positions for DR4 and 5 are overloaded with other meanings. For example, the kernel uses the fifth bit (0x20—DR4) to disable CPU cycle time accounting for the process. (CPU cycle time accounting is described in Chapter 5.)

The wait block represents a thread waiting for an object. Each thread that is in a wait state has a list of the wait blocks that represent the objects the thread is waiting for. Each dispatcher object has a list of the wait blocks that represent which threads are waiting for the object. This list is kept so that when a dispatcher object is signaled, the kernel can quickly determine who is waiting for that object. The wait block has a pointer to the object being waited for, a pointer to the thread waiting for the object, and a pointer to the next wait block (if the thread is waiting for more than one object). It also records the type of wait (any or all) as well as the position of that entry in the array of handles passed by the thread on the *WaitForMultipleObjects* call (position 0 if the thread was waiting for only one object).

Figure 3-24 shows the relationship of dispatcher objects to wait blocks to threads. In this example, thread 1 is waiting for object B, and thread 2 is waiting for objects A and B. If object A is signaled, the kernel will see that because thread 2 is also waiting for another object, thread 2 can't be readied for execution. On the other hand, if object B is signaled, the kernel can ready thread 1 for execution right away because it isn't waiting for any other objects.

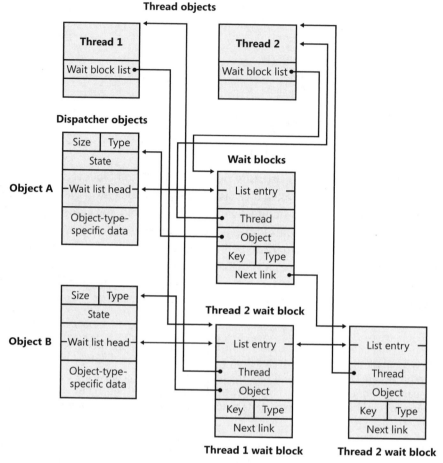

FIGURE 3-24 Wait data structures

EXPERIMENT: Looking at Wait Queues

You can see the list of objects a thread is waiting for with the kernel debugger's *!thread* command. For example, the following excerpt from the output of a *!process* command shows that the thread is waiting for an event object:

```
kd> !process
§
        THREAD 8952d030  Cid 0acc.050c  Teb: 7ffdf000 Win32Thread: fe82c4c0 WAIT:
(WrUserRequest) UserMode Non-Alertable
        89dd01c8  SynchronizationEvent
```

You can use the *dt* command to interpret the dispatcher header of the object like this:

```
lkd> dt nt!_DISPATCHER_HEADER 89dd01c8
   +0x000 Type        : 0x1 ''
   +0x001 Abandoned   : 0 ''
```

```
   +0x001 Absolute          : 0 ''
   +0x001 NpxIrql           : 0 ''
   +0x001 Signalling        : 0 ''
   +0x002 Size              : 0x4 ''
   +0x002 Hand              : 0x4 ''
   +0x003 Inserted          : 0x89 ''
   +0x003 DebugActive       : 0x89 ''
   +0x003 DpcActive         : 0x89 ''
   +0x000 Lock              : -1996226559
   +0x004 SignalState       : 0
   +0x008 WaitListHead      : _LIST_ENTRY [ 0x89dd01d0 - 0x89dd01d0 ]
```

Note that you should ignore the 0x89 value: none of the Inserted, DebugActive, or DpcActive fields apply to event objects, so the kernel has simply not bothered to initialize those fields to 0 as an optimization. As a result, they contain whatever value was previously stored. (We can assume a pointer was there previously because 0x89 seems to be the beginning of the address of the dispatcher header.) Table 3-17 lists the dispatcher header flags and the objects to which they apply.

TABLE 3-17 Usage and Meaning of the Dispatcher Header Flags

Flag	Applies To	Meaning
Abandoned	Mutexes	The thread holding the mutex was terminated
Absolute	Timers	The expiration time is absolute, not relative
NpxIrql	Threads	The IRQL at which the FPU registers were saved
Signaling	Gates	A priority boost should be applied to the woken thread when the gate is signaled
Size	All objects	Size of the object divided by 4
Hand	Timers	Index into the timer handle table
Inserted	Timers	Set if the timer was inserted into the timer handle table
DebugActive	Processes	Specifies if the process is being debugged
DpcActive	Mutexes	The mutex was acquired during a DPC
Lock	Gates and Queues	Used for locking an object without acquiring the dispatcher lock; actually corresponds to bit 7 (0x80) of the Type field

Apart from these flags, the Type field contains the identifier for the object. This identifier corresponds to a number in the KOBJECTS enumeration, which you can dump with the debugger:

```
lkd> dt nt!_KOBJECTS
   EventNotificationObject = 0
   EventSynchronizationObject = 1
   MutantObject = 2
   ProcessObject = 3
   QueueObject = 4
   SemaphoreObject = 5
```

```
    ThreadObject = 6
    GateObject = 7
    TimerNotificationObject = 8
    TimerSynchronizationObject = 9
    Spare2Object = 10
    Spare3Object = 11
    Spare4Object = 12
    Spare5Object = 13
    Spare6Object = 14
    Spare7Object = 15
    Spare8Object = 16
    Spare9Object = 17
    ApcObject = 18
    DpcObject = 19
    DeviceQueueObject = 20
    EventPairObject = 21
    InterruptObject = 22
    ProfileObject = 23
    ThreadedDpcObject = 24
    MaximumKernelObject = 25
```

The wait list head pointers are identical, so there are no waiting threads waiting on this object. Dumping a wait block for an object that is part of a multiple wait from a thread, or that multiple threads are waiting on, could yield the following:

```
lkd> dt nt!_KWAIT_BLOCK 0x879796c8
    +0x000 WaitListEntry    : _LIST_ENTRY [ 0x89d65d80 - 0x89d65d80 ]
    +0x008 Thread           : 0x87979610 _KTHREAD
    +0x00c Object           : 0x89d65d78
    +0x010 NextWaitBlock    : 0x879796e0 _KWAIT_BLOCK
    +0x014 WaitKey          : 0
    +0x016 WaitType         : 0x1 ''
    +0x017 SpareByte        : 0x1 ''
```

If the wait list had more than one entry, you could execute the same command on the second pointer value in the WaitListEntry field of each wait block (by executing !thread on the thread pointer in the wait block) to traverse the list and see what other threads are waiting for the object. This would indicate more than one thread waiting on this object. On the other hand, when dealing with an object that's part of a collection of objects being waited on by a single thread, you will have to parse the NextWaitBlock field instead.

Keyed Events

A synchronization object called a *keyed event* bears special mention because of the role it plays in user-mode-exclusive synchronization primitives. Keyed events were originally implemented to help processes deal with low-memory situations when using critical sections, a user-mode synchronization object we'll see more about shortly. A keyed event, which is not

documented, allows a thread to specify a "key" for which it waits, where the thread wakes when another thread of the same process signals the event with the same key.

If there is contention, *EnterCriticalSection* dynamically allocates an event object, and the thread wanting to acquire the critical section waits for the thread that owns the critical section to signal it in *LeaveCriticalSection*. Unfortunately, this introduces a new problem. Before keyed events were implemented, it was possible for the system to be critically out of memory and for critical section acquisition to fail because the system was unable to allocate the event object required. The low-memory condition itself may have been caused by the application trying to acquire the critical section, so the system would deadlock in this situation. Low memory isn't the only scenario that could have caused this to fail: a less likely scenario is handle exhaustion. If the process had reached its 16 million handle limit, the new handle for the event object could fail.

The failure caused by low-memory conditions would typically be an exception from the code responsible for acquiring the critical section. Unfortunately, the result would also be a damaged critical section, which made the situation hard to debug, and the object useless for a reacquisition attempt. Attempting a *LeaveCriticalSection* would attempt another event object allocation, further generating exceptions and corrupting the structure. An initial "solution" to the problem was introduced through a magic value to the *InitializeCriticalSectionAndSpinCount* API. By making the spin count have its high bit set (ORing with the 0x80000000 value), this preallocated the event, which avoided the issue but reverted back to the scalability problems of Windows NT 4.

Having allocated a global standard event object would not have fixed the issue, because standard event primitives can only be used for a single object. Each critical section in the process would still require its own event object, so the same problem would resurface. The implementation of keyed events allows multiple critical sections (waiters) to use the same global (per-process) keyed event handle. This allows the critical section functions to operate properly even when memory is temporarily low.

When a thread signals a keyed event or performs a wait on it, it uses a unique identifier called a *key*, which identifies the instance of the keyed event (an association of the keyed event to a single critical section). When the owner thread releases the keyed event by signaling it, only a single thread waiting on the key is woken up (the same behavior as *synchronization events* in contrast to *notification events*). Additionally, only the waiters in the current process are awakened, so the key is even isolated across processes, meaning that there is actually only a single keyed event object for the entire system. When a critical section uses the keyed event, *EnterCriticalSection* sets the key as the address of the critical section and performs a wait.

Returning to critical sections, the use of keyed events was improved even further with the release of Windows Vista. When *EnterCriticalSection* calls *NtWaitForKeyedEvent* to perform a wait on the keyed event, it can now specify a handle of NULL for the keyed event, telling the kernel that it was unable to create a keyed event. The kernel recognizes this behavior and

uses a global keyed event named *ExpCritSecOutOfMemoryEvent*. The primary benefit is that processes don't need to waste a handle for a named keyed event anymore because the kernel keeps track of the object and its references.

However, keyed events are more than just fallback objects for low-memory conditions. When multiple waiters are waiting on the same key and need to be woken up, the key is actually signaled multiple times, which requires the object to keep a list of all the waiters so that it can perform a "wake" operation on each of them (recall that waking a keyed event is the same as waking a synchronization event). However, it's possible for a thread to signal a keyed event without any threads on the waiter list. In this scenario, the setting thread will actually perform a wait of its own! Without this fallback, it would be possible for a setter thread to signal the keyed event during the time that the user-mode code saw the keyed event as unsignaled and attempt a wait. The wait might have come *after* the setting thread signaled the keyed event, resulting in a missed pulse, so the waiting thread would deadlock. By forcing the setting thread to wait in this scenario, it will only actually signal the keyed event when someone is looking (waiting).

 Note When the keyed event wait code itself needs to perform a wait, it uses a built-in semaphore located in the kernel-mode thread object (ETHREAD) called *KeyedWaitSemaphore*. (This semaphore actually shares its location with the ALPC wait semaphore.) See Chapter 5 for more information on thread objects.

Keyed events, however, do not replace standard event objects in the critical section implementation. The initial reason, during the Windows XP timeframe, was that keyed events do not offer scalable performance in heavy-usage scenarios. Recall that all the algorithms described were only meant to be used in critical, low-memory scenarios, when performance and scalability aren't all that important. To replace the standard event object would place strain on keyed events that they weren't implemented to handle. The primary performance bottleneck was that keyed events maintained the list of waiters described in a doubly linked list. This kind of list has poor *traversal speed*, meaning the time required to loop through the list. In this case, this time depended on the number of waiter threads. Because the object is global, it would be possible for dozens of threads to be on the list, requiring long traversal times every single time a key was set or waited on.

 Note The head of the list is kept in the keyed event object, while the threads are actually linked through the KeyedWaitChain field (which is actually shared with the thread's exit time, stored as a LARGE_INTEGER, the same size as a doubly linked list) in the kernel-mode thread object (ETHREAD). See Chapter 5 for more information on this object.

Windows improves keyed event performance by using a hash table instead of a linked list to hold the waiter threads. This optimization allows Windows to include three new lightweight user-mode synchronization primitives (to be discussed shortly) that all depend on the keyed event. Critical sections, however, still continue to use event objects, primarily for application compatibility and debugging, because the event object and internals are well-known and documented, while keyed events are opaque and not exposed to the Win32 API.

Fast Mutexes and Guarded Mutexes

Fast mutexes, which are also known as *executive mutexes*, usually offer better performance than mutex objects because, although they are built on dispatcher event objects, they perform a wait through the dispatcher only if the fast mutex is contended, unlike a standard mutex, which will always attempt the acquisition through the dispatcher. This gives the fast mutex especially good performance in a multiprocessor environment. Fast mutexes are used widely in device drivers.

However, fast mutexes are suitable only when normal kernel-mode APC (described earlier in this chapter) delivery can be disabled. The executive defines two functions for acquiring them: *ExAcquireFastMutex* and *ExAcquireFastMutexUnsafe*. The former function blocks all APC delivery by raising the IRQL of the processor to APC level. The latter expects to be called with normal kernel-mode APC delivery disabled, which can be done by raising the IRQL to APC level. Another limitation of fast mutexes is that they can't be acquired recursively, like mutex objects can.

Guarded mutexes are essentially the same as fast mutexes (although they use a different synchronization object, the KGATE, internally). They are acquired with the *KeAcquireGuardedMutex* and *KeAcquireGuardedMutexUnsafe* functions, but instead of disabling APCs by raising the IRQL to APC level, they disable all kernel-mode APC delivery by calling *KeEnterGuardedRegion*. Recall that a guarded region, unlike a critical region, disables both special and normal kernel-mode APCs, hence allowing the guarded mutex to avoid raising the IRQL.

Three implementation changes made the guarded mutex faster than a fast mutex:

- By avoiding raising the IRQL, the kernel can avoid talking to the local APIC of every processor on the bus, which is a significant operation on heavy SMP systems. On uniprocessor systems this isn't a problem because of lazy IRQL evaluation, but lowering the IRQL may still require accessing the PIC.

- The gate primitive is an optimized version of the event. By not having both synchronization and notification versions, and by being the exclusive object that a thread can wait on, the code for acquiring and releasing a gate is heavily optimized. Gates even have their own dispatcher lock instead of acquiring the entire dispatcher database.

- In the noncontended case, acquisition and release of a guarded mutex works on a single bit, with an atomic bit test-and-reset operation instead of the more complex integer operations fast mutexes perform.

> **Note** The code for a fast mutex is also optimized to account for almost all these optimizations—it uses the same *atomic lock* operation, and the event object is actually a gate object (although by dumping the type in the kernel debugger, you would still see an event object structure; this is actually a compatibility lie). However, fast mutexes still raise the IRQL instead of using guarded regions.

Because the flag responsible for special kernel APC delivery disabling (and the guarded region functionality) was not added until Windows Server 2003, most drivers do not yet take advantage of guarded mutexes. Doing so would raise compatibility issues with earlier versions of Windows, which require a recompiled driver making use only of fast mutexes. Internally, however, the Windows kernel has replaced almost all uses of fast mutexes with guarded mutexes, as the two have identical semantics and can be easily interchanged.

Another problem related to the guarded mutex was the kernel function *KeAreApcsDisabled*. Prior to Windows Server 2003, this function indicated whether normal APCs were disabled by checking if the code was running inside a critical section. In Windows Server 2003, this function was changed to indicate whether the code was in a critical, or guarded, region, changing the functionality to also return TRUE if special kernel APCs are also disabled.

Because there are certain operations that drivers should not perform when special kernel APCs are disabled, it makes sense to call *KeGetCurrentIrql* to check whether the IRQL is APC level or not, which is the only way special kernel APCs could have been disabled. However, because the memory manager makes use of guarded mutexes instead, this check fails because guarded mutexes do not raise IRQL. Drivers should therefore call *KeAreAllApcsDisabled* for this purpose. This function checks whether special kernel APCs are disabled and/or whether the IRQL is APC level—the sure-fire way to detect both guarded mutexes and fast mutexes.

Executive Resources

Executive resources are a synchronization mechanism that supports shared and exclusive access, and, like fast mutexes, they require that normal kernel-mode APC delivery be disabled before they are acquired. They are also built on dispatcher objects that are only used when there is contention. Executive resources are used throughout the system, especially in file-system drivers.

Threads waiting to acquire a resource for shared access wait for a semaphore associated with the resource, and threads waiting to acquire a resource for exclusive access wait for an event. A semaphore with unlimited count is used for shared waiters because they can all be woken and granted access to the resource when an exclusive holder releases the resource simply by signaling the semaphore. When a thread waits for exclusive access of a resource that is currently owned, it waits on a synchronization event object because only one of the waiters will wake when the event is signaled.

Because of the flexibility that shared and exclusive access offers, there are a number of functions for acquiring resources: *ExAcquireResourceSharedLite*, *ExAcquireResource-ExclusiveLite*, *ExAcquireSharedStarveExclusive*, *ExAcquireWaitForExclusive*, and *ExTryToAcquireResourceExclusiveLite*. These functions are documented in the WDK.

EXPERIMENT: Listing Acquired Executive Resources

The kernel debugger *!locks* command searches paged pool for executive resource objects and dumps their state. By default, the command lists only executive resources that are currently owned, but the *−d* option will list all executive resources. Here is partial output of the command:

```
lkd> !locks
**** DUMP OF ALL RESOURCE OBJECTS ****
KD: Scanning for held locks.

Resource @ 0x89929320    Exclusively owned
    Contention Count = 3911396
     Threads: 8952d030-01<*>

KD: Scanning for held locks...................................

Resource @ 0x89da1a68    Shared 1 owning threads
     Threads: 8a4cb533-01<*> *** Actual Thread 8a4cb530
```

Note that the contention count, which is extracted from the resource structure, records the number of times threads have tried to acquire the resource and had to wait because it was already owned.

You can examine the details of a specific resource object, including the thread that owns the resource and any threads that are waiting for the resource, by specifying the *−v* switch and the address of the resource:

```
lkd> !locks -v 0x89929320

Resource @ 0x89929320    Exclusively owned
    Contention Count = 3913573
     Threads: 8952d030-01<*>
```

```
      THREAD 8952d030  Cid 0acc.050c  Teb: 7ffdf000 Win32Thread: fe82c4c0 RUNNING on
processor 0
      Not impersonating
      DeviceMap              9aa0bdb8
      Owning Process         89e1ead8       Image:          windbg.exe
      Wait Start TickCount   24620588       Ticks: 12 (0:00:00:00.187)
      Context Switch Count   772193
      UserTime               00:00:02.293
      KernelTime             00:00:09.828
      Win32 Start Address windbg (0x006e63b8)
      Stack Init a7eba000 Current a7eb9c10 Base a7eba000 Limit a7eb7000 Call 0
      Priority 10 BasePriority 8 PriorityDecrement 0 IoPriority 2 PagePriority 5
Unable to get context for thread running on processor 1, HRESULT 0x80004001
1 total locks, 1 locks currently held
```

Pushlocks

Pushlocks are another optimized synchronization mechanism built on gate objects, and, like guarded mutexes, they wait for a gate object only when there's contention on the lock. They offer advantages over the guarded mutex in that they can be acquired in shared or exclusive mode. However, their main advantage is their size: a resource object is 56 bytes, but a push-lock is pointer-size. Unfortunately, they are not documented in the WDK and are therefore reserved for use by the operating system (although the APIs are exported, so internal drivers do use them).

There are two types of pushlocks: normal and cache-aware. Normal pushlocks require only the size of a pointer in storage (4 bytes on 32-bit systems, and 8 bytes on 64-bit systems). When a thread acquires a normal pushlock, the pushlock code marks the pushlock as owned if it is not currently owned. If the pushlock is owned exclusively or the thread wants to acquire the thread exclusively and the pushlock is owned on a shared basis, the thread allocates a wait block on the thread's stack, initializes a gate object in the wait block, and adds the wait block to the wait list associated with the pushlock. When a thread releases a push-lock, the thread wakes a waiter, if any are present, by signaling the event in the waiter's wait block.

Because a pushlock is only pointer-sized, it actually contains a variety of bits to describe its state. The meaning of those bits changes as the pushlock changes from being contended to noncontended. In its initial state, the pushlock contains the following structure:

- 1 lock bit, set to 1 if the lock is acquired

- 1 waiting bit, set to 1 if the lock is contended and someone is waiting on it

- 1 waking bit, set to 1 if the lock is being granted to a thread and the waiter's list needs to be optimized

- 1 multiple shared bit, set to 1 if the pushlock is shared and currently acquired by more than one thread

- 28 share count bits, containing the number of threads that have acquired the pushlock

As discussed previously, when a thread acquires a pushlock exclusively while the pushlock is already acquired by either multiple readers or a writer, the kernel will allocate a pushlock wait block. The structure of the pushlock value itself changes. The 28 share count bits now become the pointer to the wait block. Because this wait block is allocated on the stack and the header files contain a special alignment directive to force it to be 16-byte aligned, the bottom 4 bits of any pushlock wait-block structure will be all zeros. Therefore, those bits are ignored for the purposes of pointer dereferencing, and instead, the 4 bits shown earlier are combined with the pointer value. Because this alignment removes the share count bits, the share count is now stored in the wait block instead.

A cache-aware pushlock adds layers to the normal (basic) pushlock by allocating a pushlock for each processor in the system and associating it with the cache-aware pushlock. When a thread wants to acquire a cache-aware pushlock for shared access, it simply acquires the pushlock allocated for its current processor in shared mode; to acquire a cache-aware push-lock exclusively, the thread acquires the pushlock for each processor in exclusive mode.

Other than a much smaller memory footprint, one of the large advantages that pushlocks have over executive resources is that in the noncontended case they do not require lengthy accounting and integer operations to perform acquisition or release. By being as small as a pointer, the kernel can use atomic CPU instructions to perform these tasks (*lock cmpxchg* is used, which atomically compares and exchanges the old lock with a new lock). If the atomic compare and exchange fails, the lock contains values the caller did not expect (callers usu-ally expect the lock to be unused or acquired as shared), and a call is then made to the more complex contended version. To push performance even further, the kernel exposes the push-lock functionality as inline functions, meaning that no function calls are ever generated dur-ing noncontended acquisition—the assembly code is directly in each function. This increases code size slightly, but it avoids the slowness of a function call. Finally, pushlocks use several algorithmic tricks to avoid lock convoys (a situation that can occur when multiple threads of the same priority are all waiting on a lock and no actual work gets done), and they are also self-optimizing: the list of threads waiting on a pushlock will be periodically rearranged to provide fairer behavior when the pushlock is released.

Areas in which pushlocks are used include the object manager, where they protect global object manager data structures and object security descriptors, and the memory manager, where they protect Address Windowing Extension (AWE) data structures.

Deadlock Detection with Driver Verifier

A deadlock is a synchronization issue resulting from two threads or processors holding resources that the other wants and neither yielding what it has. This situation might result in system or process hangs. Driver Verifier, described in Chapter 7 and Chapter 9, has an option to check for deadlocks involving spinlocks, fast mutexes, and mutexes. For information on when to enable Driver Verifier to help resolve system hangs, see Chapter 14.

Critical Sections

Critical sections are one of the main synchronization primitives that Windows provides to user-mode applications on top of the kernel-based synchronization primitives. Critical sections and the other user-mode primitives we'll see later have one major advantage over their kernel counterparts, which is saving a round-trip to kernel mode in cases in which the lock is noncontended (which is typically 99% of the time or more). Contended cases will still require calling the kernel, however, because it is the only piece of the system that is able to perform the complex waking and dispatching logic required to make these objects work.

Critical sections are able to remain in user mode by using a local bit to provide the main exclusive locking logic, much like a spinlock. If the bit is 0, the critical section can be acquired, and the owner sets the bit to 1. This operation doesn't require calling the kernel but uses the interlocked CPU operations discussed earlier. Releasing the critical section behaves similarly, with bit state changing from 1 to 0 with an interlocked operation. On the other hand, as you can probably guess, when the bit is already 1 and another caller attempts to acquire the critical section, the kernel must be called to put the thread in a wait state.

Critical sections also provide more fine-grained locking mechanisms than kernel primitives. A critical section can be acquired for shared or for exclusive mode, allowing it to function as a multiple-reader (shared), single-writer (exclusive) lock for data structures such as databases. When a critical section is acquired in shared mode and other threads attempt to acquire the same critical section, no trip to the kernel is required because none of the threads will be waiting. Only when a thread attempts to acquire the critical section for exclusive access, or the critical section is already locked by an exclusive owner, will this be required.

To make use of the same dispatching and synchronization mechanism we've seen in the kernel, critical sections actually make use of existing kernel primitives. A critical section data structure actually contains a kernel mutex as well as a kernel semaphore object. When the critical section is acquired exclusively by more than one thread, the mutex is used because it permits only one owner. When the critical section is acquired in shared mode by more than one thread, a semaphore is used because it allows multiple owner counts. This level of detail

is typically hidden from the programmer, and these internal objects should never be used directly.

Finally, because critical sections are actually not full-blown kernel objects, they do have certain limitations. The primary one is that you cannot obtain a kernel handle to a critical section, and as such, no security, naming, or other object manager functionality can be applied to a critical section. Two processes cannot use the same critical section to coordinate their operations, nor can duplication or inheritance be used.

Condition Variables

Condition variables provide a Windows native implementation for synchronizing a set of threads that are waiting on a specific result to a conditional test. While this operation was possible with other user-mode synchronization methods, there was no *atomic* mechanism to check the result of the conditional test and to begin waiting on a change in the result. This required that additional synchronization be used around such pieces of code.

A user-mode thread initializes a condition variable by calling *InitializeConditionVariable* to set up the initial state. When it wants to initiate a wait on the variable, it can call *SleepConditionVariableCS*, which uses a critical section (that the thread must have initialized) to wait for changes to the variable. The setting thread must use *WakeConditionVariable* (or *WakeAllConditionVariable*) after it has modified the variable (there is no automatic detection mechanism). This call will release the critical section of either one or all waiting threads, depending on which function was used.

Before condition variables, it was common to use either a *notification event* or a *synchronization event* (recall that these are referred to as *auto-reset* or *manual-reset* in the Windows API) to signal the change to a variable such as the state of a worker queue. Waiting for a change required a critical section to be acquired and then released, followed by a wait on an event. After the wait, the critical section would have to be re-acquired. During this series of acquisitions and releases, the thread may have switched contexts, causing problems if one of the threads called *PulseEvent* (a similar problem to the one that keyed events solve by forcing a wait for the setting thread if there is no waiter). With condition variables, acquisition of the critical section can be maintained by the application while *SleepConditionVariableCS* is called and be released only after the actual work is done. This makes writing work-queue code (and similar implementations) much simpler and predictable.

Internally, conditional variables can be thought of as a port of the existing pushlock algorithms present in kernel mode, with the additional complexity of acquiring and releasing critical sections in the *SleepConditionVariableCS* API. Conditional variables are pointer-size (just like pushlocks), avoid using the dispatcher (which requires a ring transition to kernel mode in this scenario, making the advantage even more noticeable), automatically optimize the wait list during wait operations, and protect against lock convoys. Additionally, condition variables

make full use of keyed events instead of the regular event object that developers would have used on their own, which makes even contended cases more optimized.

Slim Reader Writer Locks

Although condition variables are a synchronization mechanism, they are not fully primitive locking objects. As we've seen, they still depend on the critical section lock, whose acquisition and release uses standard dispatcher event objects, so trips through kernel mode can still happen and callers still require the initialization of the large critical section object. If condition variables share a lot of similarities with pushlocks, slim reader writer (SRW) locks are nearly identical. They are also pointer-size, use atomic operations for acquisition and release, rearrange their waiter lists, protect against lock convoys, and can be acquired both in shared and exclusive mode. Some differences from pushlocks, however, include the fact that SRW locks cannot be "upgraded" or converted from shared to exclusive or vice versa. Additionally, they cannot be recursively acquired. Finally, SRW locks are exclusive to user-mode code, while pushlocks are exclusive to kernel-mode code, and the two cannot be shared or exposed from one layer to the other.

Not only can SRW locks entirely replace critical sections in application code, but they also offer multiple-reader, single-writer functionality. SRW locks must first be initialized with *InitializeSRWLock*, after which they can be acquired or released in either exclusive or shared mode with the appropriate APIs: *AcquireSRWLockExclusive, ReleaseSRWLockExclusive, AcquireSRWLockShared,* and *ReleaseSRWLockShared.*

> **Note** Unlike most other Windows APIs, the SRW locking functions do not return with a value—instead they generate exceptions if the lock could not be acquired. This makes it obvious that an acquisition has failed so that code that assumes success will terminate instead of potentially proceeding to corrupt user data.

The Windows SRW locks do not prefer readers or writers, meaning that the performance for either case should be the same. This makes them great replacements for critical sections, which are writer-only or *exclusive* synchronization mechanisms. If SRW locks were optimized for readers, they would be poor exclusive-only locks, but this isn't the case. As a result, the design of the condition variable mechanism introduced earlier also allows for the use of SRW locks instead of critical sections, through the *SleepConditionVariableSRW* API. Finally, SRW locks also use keyed events instead of standard event objects, so the combination of condition variables and SRW locks results in scalable, pointer-size synchronization mechanisms with very few trips to kernel mode—except in contended cases, which are optimized to take less time and memory to wake and set because of the use of keyed events.

Run Once Initialization

The ability to guarantee the *atomic* execution of a piece of code responsible for performing some sort of initialization task—such as allocating memory, initializing certain variables, or even creating objects on demand—is a typical problem in multithreaded programming. In a piece of code that can be called simultaneously by multiple threads (a good example is the *DllMain* routine, which initializes DLLs) there are several ways of attempting to ensure the correct, atomic, and unique execution of initialization tasks.

In this scenario, Windows implements *init once*, or *one-time initialization* (also called *run once initialization* internally). This mechanism allows for both synchronous (meaning that the other threads must wait for initialization to complete) execution of a certain piece of code, as well as asynchronous (meaning that the other threads can attempt to do their own initialization and race) execution. We'll look at the logic behind asynchronous execution later after explaining the synchronous mechanism.

In the synchronous case, the developer writes the piece of code that would normally have executed after double-checking the global variable in a dedicated function. Any information that this routine needs can be passed through the *parameter* variable that the init-once routine accepts. Any output information is returned through the *context* variable (the status of the initialization itself is returned as a Boolean). All the developer has to do to ensure proper execution is call *InitOnceExecuteOnce* with the *parameter*, *context*, and run-once function pointer after initializing an InitOnce object with *InitOnceInitialize* API. The system will take care of the rest.

For applications that want to use the asynchronous model instead, the threads call *InitOnceBeginInitialize* and receive a *pending status* and the *context* described earlier. If the *pending status* is FALSE, initialization has already taken place, and the thread uses the context value for the result. (It's also possible for the function itself to return FALSE, meaning that initialization failed.) However, if the pending status comes back as TRUE, the thread should now *race* to be the first to create the object. The code that will follow will perform whatever initialization tasks are required, such as creating some sort of object or allocating memory. When this work is done, the thread calls *InitOnceComplete* with the result of the work as the context and receives a *status*. If the status is TRUE, the thread won the race, and the object it created or allocated should be the global object. The thread can now save this object or return it to a caller, depending on the usage.

In a more complex scenario when the status is FALSE, this means that the thread lost the race. The thread must now undo all the work it did, such as deleting the object or freeing the memory, and then call *InitOnceBeginInitialize* again. However, instead of requesting to start a race as it did initially, it uses the INIT_ONCE_CHECK_ONLY flag, knowing that it has lost, and requests the winner's context instead (for example, the object or memory that had to be created or allocated). This returns another *status*, which can be TRUE, meaning that the context is valid and should be used or returned to the caller, or FALSE, meaning that initialization

failed and nobody has actually been able to perform the work (such as in the case of a low-memory condition, perhaps).

In both cases, the mechanism for run once initialization is similar to the mechanism for condition variables and slim reader writer locks. The *init once* structure is pointer-size, and inline assembly versions of the SRW acquisition/release code are used for the noncontended case, while keyed events are used when contention has occurred (which happens when the mechanism is used in synchronous mode) and the other threads must wait for initialization. In the asynchronous case, the locks are used in shared mode, so multiple threads can perform initialization at the same time.

System Worker Threads

During system initialization, Windows creates several threads in the System process, called *system worker threads*, which exist solely to perform work on behalf of other threads. In many cases, threads executing at DPC/dispatch level need to execute functions that can be performed only at a lower IRQL. For example, a DPC routine, which executes in an arbitrary thread context (because DPC execution can usurp any thread in the system) at DPC/dispatch level IRQL, might need to access paged pool or wait for a dispatcher object used to synchronize execution with an application thread. Because a DPC routine can't lower the IRQL, it must pass such processing to a thread that executes at an IRQL below DPC/dispatch level.

Some device drivers and executive components create their own threads dedicated to processing work at passive level; however, most use system worker threads instead, which avoids the unnecessary scheduling and memory overhead associated with having additional threads in the system. An executive component requests a system worker thread's services by calling the executive functions *ExQueueWorkItem* or *IoQueueWorkItem*. Device drivers should only use the latter (because this associates the work item with a Device object, allowing for greater accountability and the handling of scenarios in which a driver unloads while its work item is active). These functions place a *work item* on a queue dispatcher object where the threads look for work. (Queue dispatcher objects are described in more detail in the section "I/O Completion Ports" in Chapter 7.)

The *IoQueueWorkItemEx, IoSizeofWorkItem, IoInitializeWorkItem,* and *IoUninitializeWorkItem* APIs act similarly, but they create an association with a driver's Driver object or one of its Device objects.

Work items include a pointer to a routine and a parameter that the thread passes to the routine when it processes the work item. The device driver or executive component that requires passive-level execution implements the routine. For example, a DPC routine that must wait for a dispatcher object can initialize a work item that points to the routine in the driver that

waits for the dispatcher object, and perhaps points to a pointer to the object. At some stage, a system worker thread will remove the work item from its queue and execute the driver's routine. When the driver's routine finishes, the system worker thread checks to see whether there are more work items to process. If there aren't any more, the system worker thread blocks until a work item is placed on the queue. The DPC routine might or might not have finished executing when the system worker thread processes its work item.

There are three types of system worker threads:

- *Delayed worker threads* execute at priority 12, process work items that aren't considered time-critical, and can have their stack paged out to a paging file while they wait for work items. The object manager uses a delayed work item to perform deferred object deletion, which deletes kernel objects after they have been scheduled for freeing.

- *Critical worker threads* execute at priority 13, process time-critical work items, and on Windows Server systems have their stacks present in physical memory at all times.

- A single *hypercritical worker thread* executes at priority 15 and also keeps its stack in memory. The process manager uses the hypercritical work item to execute the thread "reaper" function that frees terminated threads.

The number of delayed and critical worker threads created by the executive's *ExpWorker-Initialization* function, which is called early in the boot process, depends on the amount of memory present on the system and whether the system is a server. Table 3-18 shows the initial number of threads created on default configurations. You can specify that *ExpInitializeWorker* create up to 16 additional delayed and 16 additional critical worker threads with the AdditionalDelayedWorkerThreads and AdditionalCriticalWorkerThreads values under the registry key HKLM\SYSTEM\CurrentControlSet\Control\Session Manager\ Executive.

TABLE 3-18 Initial Number of System Worker Threads

Work Queue Type	Default Number of Threads
Delayed	7
Critical	5
Hypercritical	1

The executive tries to match the number of critical worker threads with changing workloads as the system executes. Once every second, the executive function *ExpWorkerThreadBalance-Manager* determines whether it should create a new critical worker thread. The critical worker threads that are created by *ExpWorkerThreadBalanceManager* are called *dynamic worker threads*, and all the following conditions must be satisfied before such a thread is created:

- Work items exist in the critical work queue.

■ The number of inactive critical worker threads (ones that are either blocked waiting for work items or that have blocked on dispatcher objects while executing a work routine) must be less than the number of processors on the system.

■ There are fewer than 16 dynamic worker threads.

Dynamic worker threads exit after 10 minutes of inactivity. Thus, when the workload dictates, the executive can create up to 16 dynamic worker threads.

EXPERIMENT: Listing System Worker Threads

You can use the *!exqueue* kernel debugger command to see a listing of system worker threads classified by their type:

```
1kd> !exqueue
Dumping ExWorkerQueue: 820FDE40

**** Critical WorkQueue( current = 0 maximum = 2 )
THREAD 861160b8  Cid 0004.001c  Teb: 00000000 Win32Thread: 00000000 WAIT
THREAD 8613b020  Cid 0004.0020  Teb: 00000000 Win32Thread: 00000000 WAIT
THREAD 8613bd78  Cid 0004.0024  Teb: 00000000 Win32Thread: 00000000 WAIT
THREAD 8613bad0  Cid 0004.0028  Teb: 00000000 Win32Thread: 00000000 WAIT
THREAD 8613b828  Cid 0004.002c  Teb: 00000000 Win32Thread: 00000000 WAIT

**** Delayed WorkQueue( current = 0 maximum = 2 )
THREAD 8613b580  Cid 0004.0030  Teb: 00000000 Win32Thread: 00000000 WAIT
THREAD 8613b2d8  Cid 0004.0034  Teb: 00000000 Win32Thread: 00000000 WAIT
THREAD 8613c020  Cid 0004.0038  Teb: 00000000 Win32Thread: 00000000 WAIT
THREAD 8613cd78  Cid 0004.003c  Teb: 00000000 Win32Thread: 00000000 WAIT
THREAD 8613cad0  Cid 0004.0040  Teb: 00000000 Win32Thread: 00000000 WAIT
THREAD 8613c828  Cid 0004.0044  Teb: 00000000 Win32Thread: 00000000 WAIT
THREAD 8613c580  Cid 0004.0048  Teb: 00000000 Win32Thread: 00000000 WAIT

**** HyperCritical WorkQueue( current = 0 maximum = 2 )
THREAD 8613c2d8  Cid 0004.004c  Teb: 00000000 Win32Thread: 00000000 WAIT
```

Windows Global Flags

Windows has a set of flags stored in a systemwide global variable named *NtGlobalFlag* that enable various internal debugging, tracing, and validation support in the operating system. The system variable *NtGlobalFlag* is initialized from the registry key HKLM\SYSTEM\CurrentControlSet\Control\Session Manager in the value GlobalFlag at system boot time. By default, this registry value is 0, so it's likely that on your systems, you're not using any global flags. In addition, each image has a set of global flags that also turn on internal tracing and validation code (although the bit layout of these flags is entirely different from the system-wide global flags).

Fortunately, the Windows SDK and the debugging tools contain a utility named Gflags.exe that allows you to view and change the system global flags (either in the registry or in the running system) as well as image global flags. Gflags has both a command-line and a GUI interface. To see the command-line flags, type **gflags /?**. If you run the utility without any switches, the dialog box shown in Figure 3-25 is displayed.

FIGURE 3-25 Setting system debugging options with Gflags

You can configure a variable's settings in the registry on the System Registry page or the current value of a variable in system memory on the Kernel Flags page. You must click the Apply button to make the changes. (You'll exit if you click the OK button.)

The Image File page requires you to fill in the file name of an executable image. Use this option to change a set of global flags that apply to an individual image (rather than to the whole system). In Figure 3-26, notice that the flags are different from the operating system ones shown in Figure 3-25.

FIGURE 3-26 Setting image global flags with Gflags

EXPERIMENT: Viewing and Setting *NtGlobalFlag*

You can use the *!gflag* kernel debugger command to view and set the state of the *NtGlobalFlag* kernel variable. The *!gflag* command lists all the flags that are enabled. You can use *!gflag -?* to get the entire list of supported global flags.

```
lkd> !gflag
Current NtGlobalFlag contents: 0x00004400
    ptg - Enable pool tagging
    otl - Maintain a list of objects for each type
```

Advanced Local Procedure Calls (ALPCs)

An advanced local procedure call (ALPC) is an interprocess communication facility for high-speed message passing. It is not directly available through the Windows API; it is an internal mechanism available only to Windows operating system components. Here are some examples of where ALPCs are used:

- Windows applications that use remote procedure calls (RPCs), a documented API, indirectly use ALPCs when they specify local-RPC, a form of RPC used to communicate between processes on the same system.

- A few Windows APIs result in sending messages to the Windows subsystem process.

- Winlogon uses ALPCs to communicate with the local security authentication server process, LSASS.

- The security reference monitor (an executive component explained in Chapter 6) uses ALPCs to communicate with the LSASS process.

Note Before ALPCs were introduced in Windows Vista, the kernel supported an IPC mechanism called simply LPC (local procedure call). LPC's scalability limitations and inherent deadlock scenarios made them a poor choice for the implementation of the User-Mode Driver Framework (UMDF), which requires high-speed, scalable communication with UMDF components in the executive to perform hardware operations. Supporting UMDF was one of the many reasons the ALPC mechanism was written to supplant LPC. (For more information on UMDF, see Chapter 7.)

EXPERIMENT: Viewing ALPC Port Objects

You can see named ALPC port objects with the WinObj tool from Sysinternals. Run Winobj.exe and select the root directory. A gear icon identifies the port objects, as shown here:

To see the ALPC port objects used by RPC, select the \RPC Control directory, as shown here:

```
WinObj - Sysinternals: www.sysinternals.com
File  View  Help

\                               Name               Type        SymLink
    ArcName                     actkernel          ALPC Port
    BaseNamedObjects            AudioClientRpc     ALPC Port
    Callback                    AudioDeviceGraph   ALPC Port
    Device                      Audiosrv           ALPC Port
    Driver                      audit              ALPC Port
    FileSystem                  dhcpcsvc           ALPC Port
    GLOBAL??                    dhcpcsvc6          ALPC Port
    KernelObjects               DSEC20c            Section
    KnownDlls                   DSEC248            Section
    NLS                         DSEC26c            Section
    ObjectTypes                 DSEC278            Section
    RPC Control                 DSEC280            Section
    Security                    DSEC2c8            Section
    Sessions                    DSEC2e4            Section
    UMDFCommunicationPorts      DSEC30c            Section
    Windows                     DSEC344            Section
                                DSEC370            Section
                                DSEC3c0            Section
                                DSEC3e4            Section
                                DSEC410            Section
                                DSEC4c8            Section

\RPC Control\DSEC20c
```

Typically, ALPCs are used between a server process and one or more client processes of that server. An ALPC connection can be established between two user-mode processes or between a kernel-mode component and a user-mode process. For example, as noted in Chapter 2, Windows processes send occasional messages to the Windows subsystem by using ALPCs. Also, some system processes use ALPCs to communicate, such as Winlogon and Lsass. An example of a kernel-mode component using an ALPC to talk to a user process is the communication between the security reference monitor and the Lsass process.

ALPCs support the following three methods of exchanging messages:

- A message that is shorter than 256 bytes can be sent by calling the ALPC with a buffer containing the message. This message is then copied from the address space of the sending process into system address space, and from there to the address space of the receiving process.

- If a client and a server want to exchange more than 256 bytes of data, they can choose to use a shared section to which both are mapped. The sender places message data

in the shared section and then sends a small message to the receiver with pointers to where the data is to be found in the shared section.

- When a server wants to read or write larger amounts of data than will fit in a shared section, data can be directly read from or written to a client's address space.

An ALPC exports a single executive object called the *port object* to maintain the state needed for communication. Although an ALPC uses a single ALPC port object, it has several kinds of ports:

- **Server connection port** A named port that is a server connection request point. Clients can connect to the server by connecting to this port.

- **Server communication port** An unnamed port a server uses to communicate with a particular client. The server has one such port per active client.

- **Client communication port** An unnamed port a particular client thread uses to communicate with a particular server.

ALPCs are typically used as follows: A server creates a named server connection port object. A client makes a connect request to this port. If the request is granted, two new unnamed ports, a client communication port and a server communication port, are created. The client gets a handle to the client communication port, and the server gets a handle to the server communication port. The client and the server will then use these new ports for their communication.

ALPC supports several features and behaviors that offer communication abilities for processes. For example, applications can create their own sections to associate with an ALPC port and manage (create and delete) views of the section. As mentioned earlier, when a server wants to read or write larger amounts of data than will fit in a shared section, data can be directly read from or written to a client's address space. The ALPC component supplies two functions that a server can use to accomplish this. A message sent by the first function is used to synchronize the message passing. Another option is to create a message zone, a locked-down buffer in system memory that will never be paged out and allows messages to be copied back and forth without attaching to the correct process, which is useful when using the I/O completion port feature described later. Yet a third capability in terms of memory requirements is to request the kernel to reserve ALPC resources so that messages can still be delivered during low-memory situations (such messages may be critical to solving or notifying the kernel about the situation in the first place).

From a throughput and performance point of view, ALPC ports can be configured to perform work over an I/O completion port instead of the typical request/reply synchronous wait mechanism that LPCs use. This allows for large-scale communication to occur, and the ALPC port object will automatically balance the number of messages and threads for high-speed communication. Additionally, ALPC messages can be batched together so that multiple replies and requests can be sent, minimizing trips from user to kernel mode and vice versa.

Finally, apart from limits on message data and header size, applications can also set bandwidth limits and maximum section, view, and pool usage.

The ALPC mechanism is also secured. ALPC objects are managed by the same object manager interfaces that manage object security, and secure ports can be created, allowing only a specific SID to use them. Applications can also easily get a handle to the sender thread (and process) of an ALPC message to perform actions such as impersonation. Furthermore, applications have fine control over the security context associated with an ALPC port—for example, they can set and query per-message SID information, as well as test for changes in the security context of a token associated with the ALPC message.

ALPC messages can be fully logged and traced to any thread participating in ALPC communications. Additionally, new Event Tracing for Windows (ETW) messages and logging can be enabled for IT administrators and troubleshooters to monitor ALPC messages.

A completed connection between a client and a server is shown in Figure 3-27.

FIGURE 3-27 Use of ALPC ports

Kernel Event Tracing

Various components of the Windows kernel and several core device drivers are instrumented to record trace data of their operations for use in system troubleshooting. They rely on a common infrastructure in the kernel that provides trace data to the user-mode Event Tracing for Windows (ETW) facility. An application that uses ETW falls into one or more of three categories:

- **Controller** A controller starts and stops logging sessions and manages buffer pools.

- **Provider** A provider defines GUIDs (globally unique identifiers) for the event classes it can produce traces for and registers them with ETW. The provider accepts commands from a controller for starting and stopping traces of the event classes for which it's responsible.

- **Consumer** A consumer selects one or more trace sessions for which it wants to read trace data. They can receive the events in buffers in real-time or in log files.

Windows Server systems include several built-in providers in user mode, including ones for Active Directory, Kerberos, and Netlogon. ETW defines a logging session with the name NT Kernel Logger (also known as the kernel logger) for use by the kernel and core drivers. The provider for the NT Kernel Logger is implemented by the ETW code in Ntoskrnl.exe and by the core drivers sending traces.

When a controller in user mode enables the kernel logger, the ETW library, which is implemented in \Windows\System32\Ntdll.dll, calls the *NtTraceControl* system call, telling the ETW code in the kernel which event classes the controller wants to start tracing. If file logging is configured (as opposed to in-memory logging to a buffer), the kernel creates a system thread in the system process that creates a log file. When the kernel receives trace events from the enabled trace sources, it records them to a buffer. If it was started, the file logging thread wakes up once per second to dump the contents of the buffers to the log file.

Trace records generated for the kernel logger have a standard ETW trace event header, which records time stamp, process, and thread IDs, as well as information on what class of event the record corresponds to. Event classes can provide additional data specific to their events. For example, disk event class trace records indicate the operation type (read or write), disk number at which the operation is directed, and sector offset and length of the operation.

The trace classes that can be enabled for the kernel logger and the component that generates each class include:

- **Disk I/O** Disk class driver
- **File I/O** File system drivers
- **File I/O Completion** File system drivers

- **Hardware Configuration** Plug and Play manager (See Chapter 7 for information on the Plug and Play manager.)

- **Image Load/Unload** The system image loader in the kernel

- **Page Faults** Memory manager (See Chapter 9 for more information on page faults.)

- **Hard Page Faults** Memory manager

- **Process Create/Delete** Process manager (See Chapter 5 for more information on the process manager.)

- **Thread Create/Delete** Process manager

- **Registry Activity** Configuration manager (See "The Registry" section in Chapter 4 for more information on the configuration manager.)

- **Network TCP/IP** TCP/IP driver

- **Process Counters** Process manager

- **Context Switches** Kernel dispatcher

- **Deferred Procedure Calls** Kernel dispatcher

- **Interrupts** Kernel dispatcher

- **System Calls** Kernel dispatcher

- **Sample Based Profiling** Kernel dispatcher and HAL

- **Driver Delays** I/O manager

- **ALPC** Advanced local procedure call

You can find more information on ETW and the kernel logger, including sample code for controllers and consumers, in the Windows SDK.

EXPERIMENT: Tracing TCP/IP Activity with the Kernel Logger

To enable the kernel logger and have it generate a log file of TCP/IP activity, follow these steps:

1. Run the Reliability and Performance Monitor, and click on Data Collector Sets, User Defined.

2. Right-click on User Defined, choose New, and select Data Collector Set.

3. When prompted, enter a name for the data collector set (for example, **experiment**), and choose Create Manually (Advanced).

4. In the dialog box that opens, select Create Data Logs, check Event Trace Data, and then click Next. In the Providers area, click Add, and locate Windows Kernel Trace. In the Properties list, select Keywords(Any), and then click Edit.

5. From this list, check only Net for Network TCP/IP, and then click OK.

6. Select a location to save the files. By default, this location is C:\Perflogs\experiment\, if this is how you named the data collector set. Click Next, and in the Run As edit box, enter the Administrator account name and set the password to match it. Click Finish. You should now see a window similar to the one shown here:

7. Right-click on "experiment" (or whatever name you gave your data collector set), and then click Start. Now generate some network activity by opening a browser and visiting a Web site.

8. Right-click on the data collector set node again, and then click Stop.

9. Open a command prompt, and change to the C:\Perflogs\experiment\00001 directory (or the directory into which you specified that the trace log file be stored).

10. Run tracerpt and pass it the name of the trace log file:

 tracerpt DataCollector01.etl –o dumpfile.csv –of CSV

11. Open dumpfile.csv in Microsoft Excel or in a text editor. You should see TCP and/or UDP trace records like the following:

Tcpip	SendIPV4	0xFFFFFFFF	1.28663E+17	0	0	1992	1388	157.54.86.28	172.31.234.35	80	49414	646659	646661
Udpip	RecvIPV4	0xFFFFFFFF	1.28663E+17	0	0	4	50	172.31.239.255	172.31.233.110	137	137	0	0x0
Udpip	RecvIPV4	0xFFFFFFFF	1.28663E+17	0	0	4	50	172.31.239.255	172.31.234.162	137	137	0	0x0
Tcpip	RecvIPV4	0xFFFFFFFF	1.28663E+17	0	0	1992	1425	157.54.86.28	172.31.234.35	80	49414	0	0x0
Tcpip	RecvIPV4	0xFFFFFFFF	1.28663E+17	0	0	1992	1380	157.54.86.28	172.31.234.35	80	49414	0	0x0
Tcpip	RecvIPV4	0xFFFFFFFF	1.28663E+17	0	0	1992	45	157.54.86.28	172.31.234.35	80	49414	0	0x0
Tcpip	RecvIPV4	0xFFFFFFFF	1.28663E+17	0	0	1992	1415	157.54.86.28	172.31.234.35	80	49414	0	0x0
Tcpip	RecvIPV4	0xFFFFFFFF	1.28663E+17	0	0	1992	740	157.54.86.28	172.31.234.35	80	49414	0	0x0

Wow64

Wow64 (Win32 emulation on 64-bit Windows) refers to the software that permits the execution of 32-bit x86 applications on 64-bit Windows. It is implemented as a set of user-mode DLLs:

- Wow64.dll: Manages process and thread creation, and hooks exception dispatching and base system calls exported by Ntoskrnl.exe. It also implements file system redirection and registry redirection and reflection.

- Wow64Cpu.dll: Manages the 32-bit CPU context of each running thread inside Wow64 and provides processor architecture-specific support for switching CPU mode from 32-bit to 64-bit and vice versa.

- Wow64Win.dll: Intercepts the GUI system calls exported by Win32k.sys.

- IA32Exec.bin and Wowia32x.dll on IA64 systems: Contain the IA-32 software emulator and its interface library. Because Itanium processors cannot natively execute x86 32-bit instructions, software emulation is required through the use of these two additional components.

The relationship of these DLLs is shown in Figure 3-28.

FIGURE 3-28 Wow64 architecture

Wow64 Process Address Space Layout

Wow64 processes may run with 2 GB or 4 GB of virtual space. If the image header has the large address aware flag set, then the memory manager will reserve the user-mode address space above the 4 GB boundary through the end of the user-mode boundary. If the image is not marked large address space aware, the memory manager will reserve the user-mode address space above 2 GB. (For more information on large address space support, see the section "x86 User Address Space Layouts" in Chapter 9.)

System Calls

Wow64 hooks all the code paths where 32-bit code would transition to the native 64-bit system or when the native system needs to call into 32-bit user-mode code. During process creation, the process manager maps into the process address space the native 64-bit Ntdll.dll, as well as the 32-bit Ntdll.dll for Wow64 processes. When the loader initialization is called, it calls the Wow64 initialization code inside Wow64.dll. Wow64 then sets up the startup context inside Ntdll, switches the CPU mode to 32-bits, and starts executing the 32-bit loader. From this point onward, execution continues as if the process is running on a native 32-bit system.

Special 32-bit versions of Ntdll.dll, User32.dll, and Gdi32.dll are located in the \Windows\Syswow64 folder. These call into Wow64 rather than issuing the native 32-bit system call instruction. Wow64 transitions to native 64-bit mode, captures the parameters associated with the system call (converting 32-bit pointers to 64-bit pointers), and issues the corresponding native 64-bit system call. When the native system call returns, Wow64 converts any output parameters if necessary from 64-bit to 32-bit formats before returning to 32-bit mode.

Exception Dispatching

Wow64 hooks exception dispatching through Ntdll's KiUserExceptionDispatcher. Whenever the 64-bit kernel is about to dispatch an exception to a Wow64 process, Wow64 captures the native exception and context record in user mode and then prepares a 32-bit exception and context record and dispatches it the same way the native 32-bit kernel would do.

User Callbacks

Wow64 intercepts all callbacks from the kernel into user mode. Wow64 treats such calls as system calls; however, the data conversion is done in the reverse order: input parameters are converted from 64 bits to 32 bits and output parameters are converted when the callback returns from 32 bits to 64 bits.

File System Redirection

To maintain application compatibility and to reduce the effort of porting applications from Win32 to 64-bit Windows, system directory names were kept the same. Therefore, the \Windows\System32 folder contains native 64-bit images. Wow64, as it hooks all the system calls, translates all the path-related APIs and replaces the path name of the \Windows\System32 folder with \Windows\Syswow64. Wow64 also redirects \Windows\LastGood to \Windows\LastGood\syswow64 and \Windows\Regedit.exe to \Windows\syswow64\Regedit.exe. Through the use of system environment variables, the %PROGRAMFILES% variable is also set to \Program Files (x86) for 32-bit applications, while it is set to the normal \Program Files folder for 64-bit applications.

> **Note** Because certain 32-bit applications may indeed be aware and able to deal with 64-bit images, a virtual directory, \Windows\Sysnative, allows any I/Os originating from a 32-bit application to this directory to be exempted from file redirection. This directory doesn't actually exist—it is a virtual path that allows access to the real System32 directory, even from an application running under Wow64.

There are a few subdirectories of \Windows\System32 that, for compatibility reasons, are exempted from being redirected such that accesses to them made by 32-bit applications actually access the real one. These directories include:

- %windir%\system32\drivers\etc
- %windir%\system32\spool
- %windir%\system32\catroot and %windir%\system32\catroot2
- %windir%\system32\logfiles

Finally, Wow64 provides a mechanism to control the file system redirection built into Wow64 on a per-thread basis through the *Wow64DisableWow64FsRedirection* and *Wow64RevertWow64FsRedirection* functions.

Registry Redirection and Reflection

Applications and components store their configuration data in the registry. Components usually write their configuration data in the registry when they are registered during installation. If the same component is installed and registered both as a 32-bit binary and a 64-bit binary, then the last component being registered will override the registration of the previous component as they both write to the same location in the registry.

To help solve this problem transparently without introducing any code changes to 32-bit components, the registry is split into two portions: Native and Wow64. By default, 32-bit components access the 32-bit view, and 64-bit components access the 64-bit view. This provides a safe execution environment for 32-bit and 64-bit components and separates the 32-bit application state from the 64-bit one if it exists.

To implement this, Wow64 intercepts all the system calls that open registry keys and retranslates the key path to point it to the Wow64 view of the registry. Wow64 splits the registry at these points:

- HKLM\SOFTWARE
- HKEY_CLASSES_ROOT

Under each of these keys, Wow64 creates a key called Wow6432Node. Under this key is stored 32-bit configuration information. All other portions of the registry are shared between 32-bit and 64-bit applications (for example, HKLM\SYSTEM).

For applications that need to explicitly specify a registry key for a certain view, the following flags on the *RegOpenKeyEx*, *RegCreateKeyEx*, and *RegDeleteKeyEx* functions permit this:

- KEY_WOW64_64KEY – explicitly opens a 64-bit key from either a 32-bit or 64-bit application
- KEY_WOW64_32KEY – explicitly opens a 32-bit key from either a 32-bit or 64-bit application

To enable interoperability through 32-bit and 64-bit COM components, Wow64 mirrors certain portions of the registry when updated in one view to the other. It does this by intercepting updates to any of the reflected keys and mirroring the changes intelligently to the other view of the registry. The list of reflected keys is:

- HKEY_LOCAL_MACHINE\SOFTWARE\Classes (except the Installer subkey)
- HKEY_LOCAL_MACHINE\SOFTWARE\Ole
- HKEY_LOCAL_MACHINE\SOFTWARE\Rpc
- HKEY_LOCAL_MACHINE\SOFTWARE\COM3
- HKEY_LOCAL_MACHINE\SOFTWARE\EventSystem

Reflection of HKLM\SOFTWARE\Classes\CLSID is intelligent; only LocalServer32 CLSIDs are reflected because they run out of process, thus they can be COM-activated by 32-bit or 64-bit applications. However, InProcServer32 CLSIDs are not reflected because 32-bit COM DLLs can't be loaded in a 64-bit process, and likewise 64-bit COM DLLs can't be loaded in a 32-bit process.

When reflecting a key/value, the registry reflector marks the key so that it understands that it has been created by the reflector. This is to help the deletion case when deleting a key that has been reflected; thus the reflector will be able to tell if it needs to delete the reflected key if it has been written by the reflector.

I/O Control Requests

Besides normal read and write operations, applications can communicate with some device drivers through device I/O control functions using the Windows *DeviceIoControlFile* API. The application may specify an input and/or output buffer along with the call. If the buffer contains pointer-dependent data, and the process sending the control request is a Wow64 process, then the view of the input and/or output structure is different between the 32-bit application and the 64-bit driver, since pointers are 4 bytes for 32-bit applications and 8

bytes for 64-bit applications. In this case, the kernel driver is expected to convert the associated pointer-dependent structures. Drivers can call the *IoIs32bitProcess* function to detect if an I/O request originated from a Wow64 process or not.

16-Bit Installer Applications

Wow64 doesn't support running 16-bit applications. However, since many application installers are 16-bit programs, Wow64 has special case code to make references to certain well-known 16-bit installers work. These installers include:

- Microsoft ACME Setup version: 2.6, 3.0, 3.01, and 3.1.

- InstallShield version 5.x (where x is any minor version number).

Whenever a 16-bit process is about to be created using the *CreateProcess()* API, Ntvdm64.dll is loaded and control is transferred to it to inspect whether the 16-bit executable is one of the supported installers. If it is, another *CreateProcess* is issued to launch a 32-bit version of the installer with the same command-line arguments.

Printing

32-bit printer drivers cannot be used on 64-bit Windows. Print drivers must be ported to native 64-bit versions. However, since printer drivers run in the user-mode address space of the requesting process, and since only native 64-bit printer drivers are supported on 64-bit Windows, a special mechanism is needed to support printing from 32-bit processes. This is done by redirecting all printing functions to Splwow64.exe, the Wow64 RPC print server. Since Splwow64 is a 64-bit process, it can load 64-bit printer drivers.

Restrictions

Wow64 does not support the execution of 16-bit applications (this is supported on 32-bit versions of Windows) or the loading of 32-bit kernel-mode device drivers (they must be ported to native 64-bits). Wow64 processes can only load 32-bit DLLs and can't load native 64-bit DLLs. Likewise, native 64-bit processes can't load 32-bit DLLs. The one exception is the ability to load *resource-only DLLs* cross-architecture, which is allowed because those DLLs only contain resource data, not code.

In addition to the above, due to page size differences, Wow64 on IA64 systems does not support the *ReadFileScatter*, *WriteFileGather*, *GetWriteWatch*, or AWE functions. Also, hardware acceleration through DirectX is not available (software emulation is provided for Wow64 processes).

User-Mode Debugging

Support for user-mode debugging is split into three different modules. The first one is located in the executive itself and has the prefix *dbgk*, which stands for *debugging framework*. It provides the necessary internal functions for registering and listening for debug events, managing the debug object, and packaging the information for consumption by its user-mode counterpart. The user-mode component that talks directly to *dbgk* is located in the native system library, Ntdll.dll, under a set of APIs that begin with the prefix *DbgUi*. These APIs are responsible for wrapping the underlying debug object implementation (which is opaque) and allow all subsystem applications to use debugging by wrapping their own APIs around the *DbgUi* implementation. Finally, the third component in user-mode debugging belongs to the subsystem DLLs. It is the exposed, documented API (located in Kernel32.dll for the Windows subsystem) that each subsystem supports for performing debugging of other applications.

Kernel Support

The kernel supports user-mode debugging through an object mentioned earlier, the *debug object*. It provides a series of system calls, most of which map directly to the Windows debugging API, typically accessed through the *DbgUi* layer first. The debug object itself is a simple construct, composed of a series of flags that determine state, an event to notify any waiters that debugger events are present, a doubly linked list of debug events waiting to be processed, and a fast mutex used for locking the object. This is all the information that the kernel requires for successfully receiving and sending debugger events, and each debugged process has a *debug port* member in its structure pointing to this debug object.

Once a process has an associated debug port, a couple of different events can cause a debug event to be inserted into the list of events. Table 3-19 describes these events.

TABLE 3-19 **Kernel Mode Debugging Events**

Event Identifier	Meaning	Triggered By
DbgKmExceptionApi	An exception has occurred	*KiDispatchException* during an exception that occurred in user mode
DbgKmCreateThreadApi	A new thread has been created	Startup of a user-mode thread
DbgKmCreateProcessApi	A new process has been created	Startup of a user-mode thread that is the first thread in the process
DbgKmExitThreadApi	A thread has exited	Death of a user-mode thread
DbgKmExitProcessApi	A process has exited	Death of a user-mode thread that was the last thread in the process
DbgKmLoadDllApi	A DLL was loaded	*NtMapViewOfSection* when the section is an image file (could be an EXE as well)

Event Identifier	Meaning	Triggered By
DbgKmUnloadDllApi	A DLL was unloaded	*NtUnmapViewOfSection* when the section is an image file (could be an EXE as well)
DbgKmErrorReportApi	An exception needs to be forwarded to Windows Error Reporting (WER)	*KiDispatchException* during an exception that occurred in user mode, after the debugger was unable to handle it

Apart from the causes mentioned in the table, there are a couple of special triggering cases outside the regular scenarios that occur at the time a debugger object first becomes associated with a process. The first *create process* and *create thread* messages will be manually sent when the debugger is attached, first for the process itself and its main thread, followed by create thread messages for all the other threads in the process. Finally, *load dll* events for the executable being debugged (Ntdll.dll) and then all the current DLLs loaded in the debugged process will be sent.

Once a debugger object has been associated with a process, all the threads in the process are suspended. At this point, it is the debugger's responsibility to start requesting that debug events be sent through. Debuggers request that debug events be sent back to user mode by performing a *wait* on the debug object. This call will loop the list of debug events. As each request is removed from the list, its contents are converted from the internal *dbgk* structure to the *native* structure that the next layer up understands. As we'll see, this structure is different from the Win32 structure as well, and another layer of conversion has to occur. Even after all pending debug messages have been processed by the debugger, the kernel will not automatically resume the process. It is the debugger's responsibility to call the *ContinueDebugEvent* function to resume execution.

Apart from some more complex handling of certain multithreading issues, the basic model for the framework is a simple matter of *producers*—code in the kernel that generates the debug events in the previous table—and *consumers*—the debugger waiting on these events and acknowledging their receipt.

Native Support

Although the basic protocol for user-mode debugging is quite simple, it's not directly usable by Windows applications—instead, it's wrapped by the *DbgUi* functions in Ntdll.dll. This abstraction is required to allow native applications, as well as different subsystems, to use these routines (because code inside Ntdll.dll has no dependencies). The functions that this component provides are mostly analogous to the Windows API functions and related system calls. Internally the code also provides the functionality required to create a debug object associated with the thread. The handle to a debug object that is created is never exposed. It is saved instead in the thread environment block (TEB) of the debugger's thread that is

performing the attachment. (For more information on the TEB, see Chapter 5.) This value is saved in *DbgSsReserved[1]*.

When a debugger attaches to a process, it expects the process to be *broken into*—that is to say, an *int 3 (*breakpoint) operation should have happened, generated by a thread injected into the process; otherwise, the debugger would never actually be able to take control of the process and would merely see debug events flying by. Ntdll.dll is responsible for creating and injecting that thread into the target process.

Finally, Ntdll.dll also provides APIs to convert the native structure for debug events into the structure that the Windows API understands.

EXPERIMENT: Viewing Debugger Objects

Although we've been using WinDbg to do kernel-mode debugging, you can also use it to debug user-mode programs. Go ahead and try starting Notepad.exe with the debugger attached using these steps:

1. Run WinDbg, and then click File, Open Executable.

2. Navigate to the \Windows\System32\ directory, and choose Notepad.exe.

3. We're not going to do any debugging, so simply ignore whatever might come up. You can type **g** in the command window to instruct WinDbg to continue executing Notepad.

Now run Process Explorer, and be sure the lower pane is enabled and configured to show open handles. (Click on View, Lower Pane View, and then Handles.) We also want to look at unnamed handles, so click on View, Show Unnamed Handles And Mappings.

Now click on the Windbg.exe process, and look at its handle table. You should see an open, unnamed handle to a debug object. (You can organize the table by Type to find this entry more readily.) You should see information something like the following:

You can try right-clicking on the handle and closing it. Notepad should disappear, and the following message should appear in WinDbg:

```
ERROR: WaitForEvent failed, NTSTATUS 0xC0000354
This usually indicates that the debuggee has been
killed out from underneath the debugger.
You can use .tlist to see if the debuggee still exists.
WaitForEvent failed
```

In fact, if you look at the description for the NTSTATUS code given, you will find the text: "An attempt to do an operation on a debug port failed because the port is in the process of being deleted," which is exactly what we've done by closing the handle.

As you can see, the native *DbgUi* interface doesn't do much work to support the framework except for this abstraction. In fact, the most complicated task it does is the conversion between native and Win32 debugger structures. This involves several additional changes to the structures.

Windows Subsystem Support

The final component responsible for allowing debuggers such as Microsoft Visual Studio or WinDbg to debug user-mode applications is in Kernel32.dll. It provides the documented Windows APIs enumerated at the beginning of our discussion. Apart from this trivial conversion of one function name to another, there is one important management job that this side of the debugging infrastructure is responsible for: managing the duplicated file and thread handles.

Recall that each time a *load DLL* event is sent, a handle to the image file is duplicated by the kernel and handed off in the event structure, as is the case with the handle to the process executable during the *create process* event. During each *wait* call, Kernel32.dll checks whether this is an event that results in new duplicated process and/or thread handles from the kernel (the two *create* events). If so, it allocates a structure in which it stores the process ID, thread ID, and the thread and/or process handle associated with the event. This structure is linked into the first *DbgSsReserved* array index in the TEB, where we mentioned the debug object handle is stored. Likewise, Kernel32.dll will also check for *exit* events. When it detects such an event, it will "mark" the handles in the data structure.

Once the debugger is finished using the handles and performs the *continue* call, Kernel32.dll will parse these structures, look for any handles whose threads have exited, and close the handles for the debugger. Otherwise, those threads and processes would actually never exit, because there would always be open handles to them as long as the debugger was running.

Image Loader

When a process is started on the system, the kernel creates a *process object* to represent it (see Chapter 5 for more information on processes) and performs various kernel-related initialization tasks. However, these tasks do not result in the execution of the application but merely in the preparation of its context and environment. In fact, unlike drivers, which are kernel-mode code, applications execute in user mode, so most of the actual initialization work is done outside the kernel. This work is performed by the *image loader*, also internally referred as *Ldr*.

The image loader lives in the user-mode system DLL *Ntdll.dll* and not in the kernel library. Therefore, it behaves just like standard code that is part of a DLL, and it is subject to the same restrictions in terms of memory access and security rights. What makes this code special is the guaranty that it will always be present in the running process (Ntdll.dll is always loaded) and that it is the first piece of code to run in user mode as part of a new application. (When the system builds the initial context, the program counter, or instruction pointer, is set to an initialization function inside Ntdll.dll. See Chapter 5 for more information.)

Because the loader runs before the actual application code, it is usually invisible to users and developers. Additionally, although the loader's initialization tasks are hidden, a program typically does interact with its interfaces during the run time of a program—for example, whenever loading or unloading a DLL or querying the base address of one. Some of the main tasks the loader is responsible for include:

- Initializing the user-mode state for the application, such as creating the initial heap and setting up the thread local storage (TLS) and fiber local storage (FLS) slots

- Parsing the import table (IAT) of the application to look for all DLLs that it requires (and then recursively parsing the IAT of each DLL), followed by parsing the export table of the DLLs to make sure the function is actually present (Special *forwarder entries* can also redirect an export to yet another DLL.)

- Loading and unloading DLLs at run time, as well as on demand, and maintaining a list of all loaded modules (the module database)

- Allowing for run-time patching (called *hotpatching*) support, explained later in the chapter

- Handling manifest files

- Reading the application compatibility database for any shims, and loading the shim engine DLL if required

As you can see, most of these tasks are critical to enabling an application to actually run its code; otherwise, everything from calling external functions to using the heap would immediately fail. After the process has been created, the loader will call a special native API to continue execution based on a context frame located on the stack. This context frame, built

by the kernel, will contain the actual entry point of the application. Therefore, because the loader doesn't use a standard call or jump into the running application, you will never see the loader initialization functions as part of the call tree in a stack trace for a thread.

EXPERIMENT: Watching the Image Loader

In this experiment, we're going to use global flags to enable a debugging feature called *loader snaps*. This will allow us to see debug output from the image loader while debugging application startup.

1. From the directory where you've installed WinDbg, launch the Gflags.exe application, and then click on the Image File tab.

2. In the Image field, type Notepad.exe, and then press the Tab key. This should enable the check boxes. Check the Show Loader Snaps option, and then click OK to dismiss the dialog box.

3. Now follow the steps in the experiment "Viewing Debugger Options" to start debugging the Notepad.exe application.

4. You should now see a couple of screens of debug information similar to that shown here:

```
0924:0248 @ 116983652 - LdrpInitializeProcess - INFO: Initializing process 0x924
0924:0248 @ 116983652 - LdrpInitializeProcess - INFO: Beginning execution of
        notepad.exe (C:\Windows\notepad.exe)
0924:0248 @ 116983652 - LdrpLoadDll - INFO: Loading DLL "kernel32.dll" from path
        "C:\Windows;C:\Windows\system32;C:\Windows\system;C:\Windows;
0924:0248 @ 116983652 - LdrpMapDll - INFO: Mapped DLL "kernel32.dll" at address
        76BD000
0924:0248 @ 116983652 - LdrGetProcedureAddressEx - INFO: Locating procedure
        "BaseThreadInitThunk" by name
0924:0248 @ 116983652 - LdrpRunInitializeRoutines - INFO: Calling init routine
        76C14592 for DLL "C:\Windows\system32\kernel32.dll"
0924:0248 @ 116983652 - LdrGetProcedureAddressEx - INFO: Locating procedure
        "BaseQueryModuleData" by name
```

5. Eventually, the debugger will break somewhere inside the loader code, at a special place where the image loader checks whether a debugger is attached and fires a breakpoint. If you press the G key to continue execution, you will see even more messages from the loader, and Notepad will appear.

6. Try interacting with Notepad and see how certain operations will invoke the loader. A good experiment is to try opening the Save/Open dialog. This will demonstrate that the loader not only runs at startup, but continuously responds to user requests that can cause *delayed loads* of other modules (which can then be unloaded after use).

Early Process Initialization

Because the loader is present in Ntdll.dll, which is a native DLL that's not attached to any sub-system, all applications on a Windows machine will be subject to the same loader behavior (with some minor differences). In Chapter 5, we'll look in detail at the steps that lead to the creation of a process in kernel mode, as well as some of the work performed by the Windows function *CreateProcess*. Here, however, we will cover the work that takes place in user mode, independent of any subsystem, as soon as the first user-mode instruction starts execution. Here are some of the main steps performed by the loader when a process starts up. The loader will:

1. Build the image path name for the application and query the Image File Execution Options key for the application.

2. Look inside the executable's header to see whether it is a .NET application (specified by the presence of a .NET-specific image directory).

3. Initialize the National Language Support (NLS for internationalization) tables for the process.

4. Load any configuration options specified in the configuration directory of the image executable's header. This image directory contains settings for the behavior of the executable, which a developer can define when compiling the application.

5. Set the affinity mask if one was specified in the image header.

6. Set up support for fiber local storage (FLS) and thread local storage (TLS).

7. Initialize the heap manager for the current process and create the first process heap.

8. Allocate an SxS (Side-by-Side Assembly)/Fusion activation context for the process. This allows the system to use the appropriate DLL version file, instead of defaulting to the DLL that shipped with the operating system. (See Chapter 5 for more information.)

9. Open the \KnownDlls object directory and build the known DLL path.

10. Figure out the current directory and the default path (used when loading images).

11. Build the first loader data table entries for the application executable and Ntdll.dll, and insert them into the module database.

At this point, the image loader is ready to start parsing the import table of the executable belonging to the application and start loading any DLLs that were dynamically linked during the compilation of the application. Because each imported DLL can also have its own import table, this operation will continue recursively until all DLLs have been satisfied and all functions to be imported have been found. As each DLL is loaded, the loader will keep state information for it and build the module database.

Loaded Module Database

Just as the kernel maintains a list of all kernel-mode drivers that have been loaded, the loader also maintains a list of all modules (DLLs as well as the primary executable) that have been loaded by a process. This information is stored in a per-process structure called the Process Environment Block, or PEB (see Chapter 5 for a full description of the PEB), namely in a sub-structure identified by *Ldr* and called PEB_LDR_DATA. In the structure, the loader maintains three doubly linked lists, all containing the same information but ordered differently (either by load order, memory location, or initialization order). These lists contain structures called *loader data table entries* (LDR_DATA_TABLE_ENTRY) that store information about each module. Table 3-20 lists the various pieces of information the loader maintains in an entry.

TABLE 3-20 Fields in a Loader Data Table Entry

Field	Meaning
BaseDllName	Name of the module itself, without the full path
DllBase	Holds the base address at which the module was loaded
EntryPoint	Contains the initial routine of the module (such as DllMain)
EntryPointActivationContext	Contains the SxS/Fusion activation context when calling initializers
Flags	Loader state flags for this module (see Table 3-21 for a description of the flags)
ForwarderLinks	Linked list of modules that were loaded as a result of export table forwarders from the module
FullDllName	Fully qualified path name of the module
HashLinks	Linked list used during process startup and shutdown for quicker lookups
List Entry Links	Links this entry into each of the three ordered lists part of the loader database
LoadCount	Reference count for the module (that is, how many times it has been loaded)
PatchInformation	Information relevant during a hotpatch operation on this module
ServiceTagLinks	Linked list of services (see Chapter 4 for more information) referencing this module
SizeOfImage	Size of the module in memory
StaticLinks	Linked list of modules loaded as a result of static references from this one
TimeDateStamp	Time stamp written by the linker when the module was linked, which the loader obtains from the module's image PE header
TlsIndex	Thread local storage slot associated with this module

One way to look at a process's loader database is to use WinDbg and its formatted output of the PEB. The next experiment shows you how to do this and how to look at the LDR_DATA_TABLE_ENTRY structures on your own.

EXPERIMENT: Dumping the Loaded Modules Database

Before starting the experiment, perform the same steps as in the previous two experiments to launch Notepad.exe with WinDbg as the debugger. When you get to the first prompt (where you've been instructed to type **g** until now), follow these instructions:

1. You can look at the PEB of the current process with the *!peb* command. For now, we're only interested in the *Ldr* data that will be displayed. (See Chapter 5 for details about other information stored in the PEB.)

```
0:001> !peb
PEB at 7ffde000
    InheritedAddressSpace:    No
    ReadImageFileExecOptions: No
    BeingDebugged:            Yes
    ImageBaseAddress:         00d80000
    Ldr                       76fd4cc0
    Ldr.Initialized:          Yes
    Ldr.InInitializationOrderModuleList: 001c1d78 . 001d9830
    Ldr.InLoadOrderModuleList:           001c1cf8 . 001d9820
    Ldr.InMemoryOrderModuleList:         001c1d00 . 001d9828
        Base TimeStamp                     Module
          d80000 47918ea2 Jan 19 00:46:10 2008 C:\Windows\notepad.exe
        76f10000 4791a7a6 Jan 19 02:32:54 2008 C:\Windows\system32\ntdll.dll
        76bd0000 4791a76d Jan 19 02:31:57 2008 C:\Windows\system32\kernel32.dll
        76b00000 4791a64b Jan 19 02:27:07 2008 C:\Windows\system32\ADVAPI32.dll
        75950000 4791a751 Jan 19 02:31:29 2008 C:\Windows\system32\RPCRT4.dll
```

2. The address shown on the Ldr line is a pointer to the PEB_LDR_DATA structure described earlier. Notice that WinDbg shows you the address of the three lists and dumps the initialization order list for you, displaying the full path, time stamp, and base address of each module.

3. You can also analyze each module entry on its own by going through the module list and then dumping the data at each address, formatted as a LDR_DATA_TABLE_ENTRY structure. Instead of doing this for each entry, however, WinDbg can do most of the work by using the *!list* extension and the following syntax:

 !list –t ntdll!_LIST_ENTRY.Flink –x "dt ntdll!_LDR_DATA_TABLE_ENTRY @$extret\" 001c1cf8

 Note that the last number is variable: it depends on whatever is shown on your machine under Ldr.InLoadOrderModuleList.

4. You should then see the actual entries for each module:

```
0:001> !list -t ntdll!_LIST_ENTRY.Flink -x "dt ntdll!_LDR_DATA_TABLE_ENTRY
@$extret\" 001c1cf8
    +0x000 InLoadOrderLinks : _LIST_ENTRY [ 0x1c1d68 - 0x76fd4ccc ]
    +0x008 InMemoryOrderLinks : _LIST_ENTRY [ 0x1c1d70 - 0x76fd4cd4 ]
    +0x010 InInitializationOrderLinks : _LIST_ENTRY [ 0x0 - 0x0 ]
    +0x018 DllBase          : 0x00d80000
    +0x01c EntryPoint       : 0x00d831ed
    +0x020 SizeOfImage      : 0x28000
    +0x024 FullDllName      : _UNICODE_STRING "C:\Windows\notepad.exe"
    +0x02c BaseDllName      : _UNICODE_STRING "notepad.exe"
    +0x034 Flags            : 0x4010
```

Looking at the list in this raw format gives you some extra insight into the loader's internals, such as the flags field, which contains state information that *!peb* on its own would not show you. See Table 3-21 for their meaning.

TABLE 3-21 Loader Data Table Entry Flags

Flag	Meaning
LDRP_STATIC_LINK (0x2)	This module is referenced by an import table and is required
LDRP_IMAGE_DLL (0x4)	The module is an image DLL (and not a data DLL or executable)
LDRP_LOAD_IN_PROGRESS (0x1000)	This module is currently being loaded
LDRP_UNLOAD_IN_PROGRESS (0x2000)	This module is currently being unloaded
LDRP_ENTRY_PROCESSED (0x4000)	The loader has finished processing this module
LDRP_DONT_CALL_FOR_THREADS (0x40000)	Do not send DLL_THREAD_ATTACH/DETACH notifications to this DLL
LDRP_PROCESS_ATTACH_CALLED (0x80000)	This DLL has been sent the DLL_PROCESS_ATTACH notification
LDRP_IMAGE_NOT_AT_BASE (0x200000)	This image was relocated from its original base address
LDRP_COR_IMAGE (0x400000)	This module is a .NET application
LDRP_COR_OWNS_UNMAP (0x800000)	This module should be unmapped by the .NET runtime
LDRP_REDIRECTED (0x10000000)	The manifest file specified a redirected file for this DLL
LDRP_COMPAT_DATABASE_PROCESSED (0x80000000)	The shim engine has processed this DLL

Import Parsing

Now that we've explained the way the loader keeps track of all the modules loaded for a process, we can continue analyzing the startup initialization tasks performed by the loader. During this step, the loader will:

1. Load each DLL referenced in the import table of the process's executable image.

2. Check whether the DLL has already been loaded by checking the module database. If it doesn't find it in the list, the loader will open the DLL and map it into memory.

3. During the mapping operation, the loader will first look at the various paths where it should attempt to find this DLL, as well as whether this DLL is a "known DLL," meaning that the system has already loaded it at startup and provided a global memory mapped file for accessing it. Certain deviations from the standard lookup algorithm can also occur, either through the use of a .local file (which forces the loader to use DLLs in the local path) or through a manifest file, which can specify a redirected DLL to use to guarantee a specific version.

4. After the DLL has been found on disk and mapped, the loader checks whether the kernel has loaded it somewhere else—this is called *relocation*. If the loader detects relocation, it will parse the relocation information in the DLL and perform the operations required. If no relocation information is present, DLL loading will fail.

5. The loader will then create a loader data table entry for this DLL and insert it into the database.

6. After a DLL has been mapped, the process is repeated for this DLL to parse its import table and all its dependencies.

7. After each DLL is loaded, the loader parses the IAT to look for specific functions that are being imported. Usually this is done by name, but it can also be done by ordinal (an index number). For each name, the loader parses the *export table* of the imported DLL and tries to locate a match. If no match is found, the operation is aborted.

8. The import table of an image can also be *bound*. This means that at link time, the developers already assigned static addresses pointing to imported functions in external DLLs. This removes the need to do the lookup for each name, but it assumes that the DLLs the application will use will always be located at the same address. Because Windows uses address space randomization (see Chapter 9 for more information on Address Space Load Randomization, or ASLR), this is usually not the case for system applications and libraries.

9. The export table of an imported DLL can use a *forwarder entry*, meaning that the actual function is implemented in another DLL. Essentially this must be treated like an import or dependency, so after parsing the export table, each DLL referenced by a forwarder is also loaded and goes back to step 1.

After all imported DLLs (and their own dependencies, or imports) have been loaded, all the required imported functions have been looked up and found, and all forwarders also loaded and processed, the step is complete: all dependencies that were defined at compile time by the application and its various DLLs have now been fulfilled. During execution, delayed dependencies (called *delay load*), as well as run-time operations (such as calling *LoadLibrary*) can call into the loader and essentially repeat the same tasks. Note, however, that a failure in these steps will result in an error launching the application if they are done during process startup. For example, attempting to run an application that requires a function that isn't present in the current version of the operating system can result in a message similar to the one in Figure 3-29.

FIGURE 3-29 Dialog box shown when a required (imported) function is not present in a DLL

Post Import Process Initialization

After the required dependencies have been loaded, there are several initialization tasks that must be performed to fully finalize launching the application. In this step, the loader will:

1. Check if the application itself requires relocation and process the relocation entries for the application. If the application cannot be relocated, or does not have relocation information, the loading will fail.

2. Check if the application makes use of TLS and look in the application executable for the TLS entries it needs to allocate and configure.

3. At this point, the initial debugger breakpoint will be hit when using a debugger such as WinDbg. This is where you had to type "go" to continue execution in the earlier experiments.

4. Make sure that the application will be able to run properly if the system is a multiprocessor system.

5. Set up the default data execution prevention (DEP) options. (See Chapter 9 for more information on DEP.)

6. Check whether this application requires any application compatibility work, and load the shim engine if required.

7. Detect if this application is protected by SecuROM, SafeDisc, and other kinds of wrapper or protection utilities that could have issues with DEP (and reconfigure DEP settings in those cases).

8. Run the initializers for all the loaded modules.

Running the initializers is the last main step in the loader's work. This is the step that will call the *DllMain* routine for each DLL (allowing each DLL to perform its own initialization work, which may even include loading new DLLs at run time) as well as process the TLS initializers of each DLL. This is one of the last steps in which loading an application can fail. If all the loaded DLLs do not return a successful return code after finishing their *DllMain* routines, the loader will abort starting the application. As a very last step, the loader will call the TLS initializer of the actual application.

As you can see, before a single line of code from the application's main entry point executes, there are possibly thousands of lines of code being executed by the loader, followed by every single DLL that has been imported. The Windows kernel has been improved to decrease startup time, most recently with the introduction of SuperFetch, which directly affects the time it takes to load all the DLLs during startup. (For more information on SuperFetch, see Chapter 9.)

Hypervisor (Hyper-V)

One of the key technologies in the software industry, used by system administrators, developers, and testers alike, is called *virtualization*, and it refers to the ability to run multiple operating systems simultaneously. One operating system, in which the virtualization software is executing, is called the *host*, while the other operating systems are running as *guests* inside the virtualization software. The usage scenarios for this model cover everything from being able to test an application on different platforms to having fully virtual servers all actually running as part of the same machine and managed through one central point.

Until recently, all the virtualization was done by the software itself, sometimes assisted by hardware-level virtualization technology (called *host-based virtualization*). Thanks to hardware virtualization, the CPU can do most of the notifications required for trapping instructions and virtualizing access to memory. These notifications, as well as the various configuration steps required for allowing guest operating systems to run concurrently, must be handled by a piece of infrastructure compatible with the CPU's virtualization support. Instead of relying on a piece of separate software running inside a host operating system to perform these tasks, a thin piece of low-level system software, which uses strictly hardware-assisted virtualization support, can be used—a *hypervisor*. Figure 3-30 shows a simple architectural overview of these two kinds of systems.

FIGURE 3-30 Two architectures for virtualization

With Hyper-V, Windows Server 2008 computers can install support for hypervisor-based virtualization as a special role (as long as an edition with Hyper-V support is licensed). Because the hypervisor is part of the operating system, managing the guests inside it, as well as interacting with them, is fully integrated in the operating system through standard management mechanisms such as WMI and services (see Chapter 4 for more information on these topics), and there are no complex third-party tools involved that require training or servicing.

Finally, apart from having a hypervisor that allows running other guests managed by a Windows Server host, both client and server editions of Windows also ship with *enlightenments*, which are special optimizations in the kernel and possibly device drivers that detect that the code is being run as a guest under a hypervisor and perform certain tasks differently, or more efficiently, considering this environment. We will look at some of these improvements later; for now, we'll take a look at the basic architecture of the Windows virtualization stack, shown in Figure 3-31.

FIGURE 3-31 Windows Hyper-V architectural stack

Partitions

One of the key architectural components behind the Windows hypervisor is the concept of a *partition*. A partition essentially references an instance of an operating system installation, which could refer either to what's traditionally called the host or to the guest. Under the Windows hypervisor model, these two terms are not used; instead, we talk of either a *root partition* or a *child partition*, respectively. Consequently, at a minimum, a Hyper-V system will have a root partition, which is recommended to contain a Windows Server Core installation, as well as the virtualization stack and its associated components. Although this installation type is recommended because it allows minimizing patches and reducing security surface area, resulting in increased availability of the server, a full installation is also supported. Each operating system running within the virtualized environment will represent a child partition, which may contain certain additional tools that optimize access to the hardware or allow management of the operating system.

Root Partition

One of the main goals behind the design of the Windows hypervisor was to have it as small and modular as possible, much like a microkernel, instead of providing a full, monolithic module. This means that most of the virtualization work is actually done by a separate virtualization stack and that there are also no *hypervisor drivers*. In lieu of these, the hypervisor uses the existing Windows driver architecture and talks to actual Windows device drivers. This architecture results in several components that provide and manage this behavior, which are collectively called the *hypervisor stack*.

Logically, it is the root partition that is responsible for providing the hypervisor, as well as the entire hypervisor stack. Because these are Microsoft components, only a Windows machine can be a root partition, naturally. A root partition should have almost no resource usage for itself because its role is to run other operating systems. The main components that the root partition provides are shown in Figure 3-32.

FIGURE 3-32 Components of a root partition

Root Partition Operating System

The Windows installation (typically the minimal footprint server installation, called Windows Server Core, to minimize resource usage) is responsible for providing the hypervisor and the device drivers for the hardware on the system (which the hypervisor will need to access), as well as for running the hypervisor stack. It is also the management point for all the child partitions.

VM Service and Worker Processes

The virtual machine service is responsible for providing the WMI interface to the hypervisor, which allows managing the child partitions through a Microsoft Management Console (MMC) plug-in. It is also responsible for communicating requests to applications that need to communicate to the hypervisor or to child partitions. It controls settings such as which devices are visible to child partitions, how the memory and processor allocation for each partition is defined, and more.

The worker processes, on the other hand, perform various virtualization work that a typical monolithic hypervisor would perform (similar as well to the work of a software-based virtualization solution). This means managing the state machine for a given child partition (to allow support for features such as snapshots and state transitions), responding to various notifications coming in from the hypervisor, performing the emulation of certain devices exposed to child partitions, and collaborating with the VM service and configuration component.

On a system with child partitions performing lots of I/O or privileged operations, you would expect most of the CPU usage to be visible in the root partition: you can identify them by the name Vmwp.exe (one for each child partition). The worker process also includes components responsible for remote management of the virtualization stack, as well as an RDP component that allows using the remote desktop client to connect to any child partition and remotely view its user interface and interact with it.

Virtualization Service Providers

Virtualization service providers (VSPs) are responsible for the high-speed emulation of certain devices visible to child partitions (the exact difference between VSP-emulated devices and user-mode–process-emulated devices will be explained later), and unlike the VM service and processes, VSPs can also run in kernel mode as drivers. More detail on VSPs will follow in the section that describes device architecture in the virtualization stack.

VM Infrastructure Driver and Hypervisor API Library

Because the hypervisor cannot be directly accessed by user-mode applications, such as the VM service that is responsible for management, the virtualization stack must actually talk to a driver in kernel mode that is responsible for relaying the requests to the hypervisor. This is the job of the VM infrastructure driver (VID). The VID also provides support for certain low-memory memory devices, such as MMIO and ROM emulation.

A library located in kernel mode provides the actual interface to the hypervisor (called *hypercalls*). Messages can also come from child partitions (which will perform their own hypercalls), because there is only one hypervisor for the whole system and it can listen to messages coming from any partition. You can find this functionality in the Winhv.sys device driver.

Hypervisor

At the bottom of the architecture is the hypervisor itself, which registers itself with the processor at system boot-up time and provides its services for the stack to use (through the use of the hypercall interface). This early initialization is performed by the hvboot.sys driver, which is configured to start early on during a system boot. Because Intel and AMD processors have slightly differing implementations of hardware-assisted virtualization, there are actually two different hypervisors—the correct one is selected at boot-up time by querying the processor through CPUID instructions. On Intel systems, the Hvix64.exe binary is loaded, while on AMD systems, the Hvax64.exe image is used.

Child Partitions

The child partition, as discussed earlier, is an instance of any operating system running parallel to the root partition. (Because you can save or pause the state of any child, it might not

necessarily be running, but there will be a worker process for it.) Unlike the root partition, which has full access to the APIC, I/O ports, and physical memory, child partitions are limited for security and management reasons to their own view of address space (the Guest Virtual Address Space, or GVA, which is managed by the hypervisor), and have no direct access to hardware. In terms of hypervisor access, it is also limited mainly to notifications and state changes. For example, a child partition doesn't have control over other partitions (and can't create new ones).

Child partitions have many fewer virtualization components than a root partition, because they are not responsible for running the virtualization stack—only for communicating with it. Also, these components can also be considered optional because they enhance performance of the environment but are not critical to its use. Figure 3-33 shows the components present in a typical Windows child partition.

FIGURE 3-33 Components in a child partition

Virtualization Service Clients

Virtualization service clients (VSCs) are the child partition analogues of VSPs. Like VSPs, VSCs are used for device emulation, which is a topic of later discussion.

Enlightenments

Enlightenments are one of the key performance optimizations that Windows virtualization takes advantage of. They are direct modifications to the standard Windows kernel code that can detect that this operating system is running in a child partition and perform work differently. Usually, these optimizations are highly hardware-specific and result in a hypercall to notify the hypervisor. An example is notifying the hypervisor of a long busy-wait spin loop. The hypervisor can keep some state stale in this scenario instead of keeping track of the state

at every single loop instruction. Entering and exiting an interrupt state can also be coordinated with the hypervisor, as well as access to the APIC, which can be enlightened to avoid trapping the real access and then virtualizing it.

Another example has to do with memory management, specifically TLB flushing and changing address space. (See Chapter 9 for more information on these concepts.) Usually, the operating system will execute a CPU instruction to flush this information, which affects the entire processor. However, because a child partition could be sharing a CPU with many other child partitions, such an operation would also flush this information for those operating systems, resulting in noticeable performance degradation. If Windows is running under a hypervisor, it will instead issue a hypercall to have the hypervisor flush only the specific information belonging to the child partition.

Hardware Emulation and Support

A virtualization solution must also provide optimized access to devices. Unfortunately, most devices aren't made to accept multiple requests coming in from different operating systems. The hypervisor steps in by providing the same level of synchronization where possible and by emulating certain devices when real access to hardware cannot be permitted. In addition to devices, memory and processors must also be virtualized. Table 3-22 describes the three types of hardware that the hypervisor must manage.

TABLE 3-22 Virtualized Hardware

Component	Managed By	Usage
Processor	Hypervisor built-in scheduler and related microkernel components.	Manage usage of hardware's processing power, share multiple processors across multiple child partitions, manage and switch processor states (such as registers).
Memory	Hypervisor built-in memory manager and related microkernel components.	Manage usage of hardware's RAM usage and availability. Protect memory from child partitions and root partition. Provide a contiguous view of physical memory starting at address 0.
Devices	VM worker processes—hypervisor only responsible for interception and notification.	Provide hardware multiplexing so that multiple child partitions can access the same device on the physical machine. Optimize access to physical devices to be as fast as possible.

Instead of exposing actual hardware to child partitions, the hypervisor exposes virtual devices (called *VDevs*). VDevs are packaged as COM components that run inside a VM worker process, and they are the central manageable object behind the device. (Usually, VDevs expose a WMI interface.) The Windows virtualization stack provides support for two kinds of virtual devices: *emulated devices* and *synthetic devices* (also called *enlightened I/O*). The former provide support for various devices that the operating systems on the child partition would expect to find, while the latter requires specific support from the guest operating system. On

the other hand, synthetic devices provide a significant performance benefit by reducing CPU overhead.

Emulated Devices

Emulated devices work by presenting the child partition with a set of I/O ports, memory ranges, and interrupts that are being controlled and monitored by the hypervisor. When access to these resources is detected, the VM worker process eventually gets notified through the virtualization stack (shown earlier in Figure 3-31). The process will then emulate whatever action is expected from the device and complete the request, going back through the hypervisor and then to the child partition. From this topological view alone, one can see that there is a definite loss in performance, without even considering that the software emulation of a hardware device is usually slow.

The need for emulated devices comes from the fact that the hypervisor needs to support nonhypervisor-aware operating systems, as well as the early installation steps of even Windows itself. During the boot process, the installer can't simply load all the child partition's required components (such as VSCs) to use synthetic devices, so a Windows installation will always use emulated devices (which is why installation will seem very slow, but once installed the operating system will run quite close to native speed). Emulated devices are also used for hardware that doesn't require high-speed emulation and for which software emulation may even be faster. This includes items such as COM (serial) ports, parallel ports, or the motherboard itself.

> **Note** Hyper-V emulates an Intel i440BX motherboard, an S3 Trio video card, and an Intel 21140 NIC.

Synthetic Devices

Although emulated devices work adequately for 10-Mbit network connections, low-resolution VGA displays, and 16-bit sound cards, the operating systems and hardware that child partitions will usually require in today's usage scenarios require a lot more processing power, such as support for 1000-Mbit GbE connections; full-color, high-resolution 3D support; and high-speed access to storage devices. To support this kind of virtualized hardware access at an acceptable CPU usage level and virtualized throughput, the virtualization stack uses a variety of components to optimize device I/Os to their fullest (similar to kernel enlightenments). Three components are part of this support, and they all belong to what's presented to the user as *integration components* or ICs. They include:

- Virtualization service providers
- Virtualization service clients/consumers
- VMBus

Figure 3-34 shows a diagram of how an enlightened, or synthetic storage I/O, is handled by the virtualization stack.

FIGURE 3-34 I/O handling paths in Hyper-V

As shown in Figure 3-32, VSPs run in the root partition, where they are associated with a specific device that they are responsible for *enlightening*. (We'll use that as a term instead of *emulating* when referring to synthetic devices.) VSCs reside in the child partition and are also associated with a specific device. Note, however, that the term *provider* can refer to multiple components spread across the device stack. For example, a VSP can either be:

- A user-mode service
- A user-mode COM component
- A kernel-mode driver

In all three cases, the VSP will be associated with the actual virtual device inside the VM worker process. VSCs, on the other hand, are almost always designed to be drivers sitting at the lowest level of the device stack (see Chapter 7 for more information on device stacks)

and intercept I/Os to a device and redirect them through a more optimized path. The main optimization that is performed by this model is to avoid actual hardware access and use VMBus instead. Under this model, the hypervisor is unaware of the I/O, and the VSP redirects it directly to the root partition's kernel storage stack, avoiding a trip to user mode as well. Other VSPs can perform work directly on the device, by talking to the actual hardware and bypassing any driver that may have been loaded on the root partition. Another option is to have a user-mode VSP, which can make sense when dealing with lower-bandwidth devices.

As described earlier, VMBus is the name of the bus transport used to optimize device access by implementing a communications protocol using hypervisor services. VMBus is a bus driver present on both the root partition and the child partitions responsible for the Plug and Play enumeration of synthetic devices in a child. It also contains the optimized cross-partition messaging protocol that uses a transport method that is appropriate for the data size. One of these methods is to provide a shared ring buffer between each partition—essentially an area of memory on which a certain amount of data is loaded on one side and unloaded on the other side. No memory needs to be allocated or freed because the buffer is continuously reused and simply "rotated." Eventually, it may become full with requests, which would mean that newer I/Os would overwrite older I/Os. In this uncommon scenario, VMBus will simply delay newer requests until older ones complete. The other messaging transport is direct child memory mapping to the parent address space for large enough transfers.

Virtual Processors

Just as the hypervisor doesn't allow direct access to hardware (or to memory, as we'll see later, child partitions don't really see the actual processors on the machine but have a virtualized view of CPUs as well. On the root machine, the administrator and the operating system deal with *logical processors,* which are the actual processors on which threads can run (for example, a dual quad-core machine has eight logical processors), and assign these processors to various child partitions. For example, one child partition could be assigned logical processors 1, 2, 3, and 4, while the second child partition might be assigned processors 4, 6, 7, and 8. Note that the second child partition will never have access to processor 5 and that processor 4 will be shared across multiple partitions. These operations are all made possible through the use of *virtual processors,* or VPs.

Because processors can be shared across multiple child partitions, the hypervisor includes its own scheduler that distributes the workload of the various partitions across each processor. Additionally, the hypervisor maintains the register state for each virtual processor and to an appropriate "processor switch" when the same logical processor is now being used by another child partition. The root partition has the ability to access all these contexts and modify them as required, an essential part of the virtualization stack that must respond to certain instructions and perform actions.

The hypervisor is also directly responsible for virtualizing processor APICs and providing a simpler, less featured virtual APIC, including support for the timer that's found on most APICs (however, at a slower rate). Because not all operating systems support APICs, the hypervisor also allows for the injection of interrupts through a hypercall, which permits the virtualization stack to emulate a standard i8059 PIC.

Finally, because Windows supports dynamic processor addition, it's possible for an administrator to add new processors to a child partition at run time to increase the responsiveness of the guest operating systems if it's under heavy load.

Memory Virtualization

The final piece of hardware that must be abstracted away from child partitions is memory, not only for the normal behavior of the guest operating systems, but also for security and stability. Improperly managing the child partitions' access to memory could result in privacy disclosures and data corruption, as well as possible malicious attacks by "escaping" the child partition and attacking the root (which would then allow attacks on the other children). Apart from this aspect, there is also the matter of the guest operating system's view of physical address space. Almost all operating systems expect memory to begin at address 0 and be somewhat contiguous, so simply assigning chunks of physical memory to each child partition wouldn't work even if enough memory was available on the system.

To solve this problem, the hypervisor implements an address space called the *guest physical address space* (GPA space). The GPA starts at address 0, which satisfies the needs of operating systems inside child partitions. However, the GPA is not a simple mapping to a chunk of physical memory because of the second problem (the lack of contiguous memory). As such, GPAs can point to any location in the machine's physical memory (which is called the *system physical address space*, or SPA space), and there must be a translation system to go from one address type to another. This translation system is maintained by the hypervisor and is nearly identical to the way virtual memory is mapped to physical memory on x86 and x86-64 processors. (See Chapter 9 for more information on the memory manager and address translation.)

As for actual virtual addresses in the child partition (which are called *guest virtual address space*—GVA space), these continue to be managed by the operating system without any change in behavior. What the operating system believes are real physical addresses in its own page tables will actually be SPAs. Figure 3-35 shows an overview of the mapping between each level.

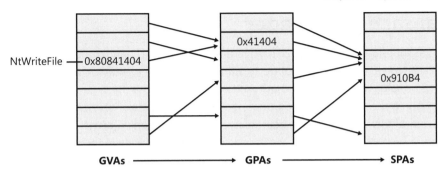

FIGURE 3-35 Guest virtual and physical address translation

This means that when a guest operating system boots up and creates the page tables to map virtual to physical memory, the hypervisor intercepts SPAs and keeps its own copy of the page tables. Conceptually, whenever a piece of code accesses a virtual address inside a guest operating system, the hypervisor does the initial page table translation to go from the guest virtual address to the GPA and then maps that GPA to the respective SPA. In reality, this operation is optimized through the use of *shadow page tables* (SPTs), which the hypervisor maintains to have direct GVA to SPA translations and simply loads when appropriate so that the guest accesses the SPA directly.

Intercepts

We've talked about the various ways in which access to hardware, processors, and memory is virtualized by the hypervisor and sometimes handed off to a VM worker process, but we haven't yet talked about the mechanism that allows this to happen—*intercepts*. Intercepts are configurable "hooks" that a root partition can install and configure in order to respond to. These can include:

- I/O intercepts, useful for device emulation
- MSR intercepts, useful for APIC emulation and profiling
- Access to GPAs, useful for device emulation, monitoring, and profiling (Additionally, the intercept can be fine-tuned to a specific access, such as read, write, or execute.)
- Exception intercepts such as page faults, useful for maintaining machine state and memory emulation (for example, maintaining copy-on-write)

Once the hypervisor detects an event for which an intercept has been registered, it sends an intercept message through the virtualization stack and puts the VP in a suspended state. The virtualization stack (usually the worker process) must then handle the event and resume the VP (typically with a modified register state that reflects the work performed to handle the intercept).

Kernel Transaction Manager

One of the more tedious aspects of software development is handling error conditions. This is especially true if, in the course of performing a high-level operation, an application has completed one or more subtasks that result in changes to the file system or registry. For example, an application's software updating service might make several registry updates, replace one of the application's executables, and then be denied access when it attempts to update a second executable. If the service doesn't want to leave the application in the resulting inconsistent state, it must track all the changes it makes and be prepared to undo them. Testing the error-recovery code is difficult, and consequently often skipped, so errors in the recovery code can negate the effort.

Applications can, with very little effort, gain automatic error-recovery capabilities by using a kernel mechanism called the *Kernel Transaction Manager* (KMT), which provides the facilities required to perform such transactions and enables services such as the *distributed transaction coordinator* (DTC) in user mode to take advantage of them. Any developer who uses the appropriate APIs can take advantage of these services as well.

KTM does more than solve large-scale issues such as the one presented. Even on single-user home computers, installing a service patch or performing a system restore are large operations that involve both files and registry keys. Unplug an older Windows computer during such an operation, and the chances for a successful boot are very slim. Even though the NT File System (NTFS) has always had a log file permitting the file system to guarantee atomic operations (see Chapter 11 for more information on NTFS), this only means that whichever file was being written to during the process will get fully written or fully deleted—it does not guarantee the entire update or restore operation. Likewise, the registry has had numerous improvements over the years to deal with corruption (see Chapter 4 for more information on the registry), but the fixes apply only at the key/value level.

As the heart of transaction support, KTM allows transactional resource managers such as NTFS and the registry to coordinate their updates for a specific set of changes made by an application. NTFS uses an extension to support transactions, called TxF. The registry uses a similar extension, called TxR. These kernel-mode resource managers work with KTM to coordinate the transaction state, just as user-mode resource managers use DTC to coordinate transaction state across multiple user-mode resource managers. Third parties can also use KTM to implement their own resource managers.

TxF and TxR both define a new set of file system and registry APIs that are similar to existing ones, except that they include a transaction parameter. If an application wants to create a file within a transaction, it first uses KTM to create the transaction, and then it passes the resulting transaction handle to the new file creation API. Although we'll look at the registry and NTFS implementations of KTM later, these are not its only possible uses. In fact, it provides three system objects that allow a variety of different operations to be supported. These are listed in Table 3-23.

TABLE 3-23 **KTM Objects**

Object	Meaning	Usage
Transaction	Collection of data operations to be performed. Provides *atomic*, *consistent*, *isolated*, and *durable* operations.	Can be associated to registry and file I/O in order to make those operations part of the same larger operation.
Enlistment	Association between a resource manager and a transaction.	Register with a transaction in order to receive notifications on it. The enlistment can specify which notifications should be generated.
Resource Manager (RM)	Container for the transactions and the data on which they operate.	Provides an interface for clients to read and write the data, typically on a database.
Transaction Manager (TM)	Container of all transactions that are part of the associated resource managers. An instance of a log, it knows about all transaction states but not their data.	Provides an infrastructure through which clients and resource managers can communicate, and provides and coordinates recovery operations after a crash. Clients use the TM for transactions, RMs use the TM for enlistments.

EXPERIMENT: Listing Transaction Managers

Windows ships with a built-in tool called Ktmutil.exe that allows you to see ongoing transactions as well as registered transaction managers on the system (and force the outcome of ongoing transactions). In this experiment, we will use it to display the transaction managers typically seen on a Windows machine.

Start an elevated command prompt and type:

Ktmutil.exe list tms

Here's an example of output on a typical Windows Vista system:

```
C:\Windows\system32>ktmutil list tms
TmGuid                                  TmLogPath
--------------------------------------- ----------------------------------------------
{0f69445a-6a70-11db-8eb3-806e6f6e6963}  \SystemRoot\System32\Config\TxR\{250834B7-750C-
                                        494d-BDC3-DA86B6E2101B}.TM
{0f694463-6a70-11db-8eb3-985e31beb686}  \Device\HarddiskVolume3\Windows\
                                        ServiceProfiles\NetworkService\ntuser.dat
                                        {0f694461-6a70-11db-8eb3-985e31beb686}.TM
{0f694467-6a70-11db-8eb3-985e31beb686}  \Device\HarddiskVolume3\Windows\ServiceProfiles\
                                        LocalService\ntuser.dat{0f694465-6a70-11db-8eb3-
                                        985e31beb686}.TM
{7697f183-6b73-11dc-9bbd-00197edc55d8}  \Device\HarddiskVolume3\Users\Bob\ntuser.dat
                                        {0f69446d-6a70-11db-8eb3-985e31beb686}.TM
{7697f187-6b73-11dc-9bbd-00197edc55d8}  \Device\HarddiskVolume3\Users\Bob\AppData\Local\
                                        Microsoft\Windows\UsrClass.dat{7697f185-6b73-
                                        11dc-9bbd-00197edc55d8}.TM
```

```
{cf7234df-39e3-11dc-bdce-00188bdd5f49} \Device\HarddiskVolume2\$Extend\$RmMetadata\
                                        $TxfLog\$TxfLog::KtmLog
{cf7234e6-39e3-11dc-bdce-00188bdd5f49} \Device\HarddiskVolume3\$Extend\$RmMetadata\
                                        $TxfLog\$TxfLog::KtmLog
```

Hotpatch Support

Rebooting a machine to apply the latest patches can mean significant downtime for a server, which is why Windows supports a run-time method of patching, called a *hot patch* (or simply *hotpatch*), in contrast to a *cold patch,* which requires a reboot. Hotpatching doesn't simply allow files to be overwritten during execution; instead it includes a complex series of operations that can be requested (and combined). These operations are listed in Table 3-24.

TABLE 3-24 Hotpatch Operations

Operation	Meaning	Usage
Rename Image	Replacing a DLL that is on the disk, and currently used by other applications, or replacing a driver that is on the disk and is currently loaded by the kernel	When an entire library in user mode needs to be replaced, the kernel can detect which processes and services are referencing it, unload them, and then update the DLL and restart the programs and services (this is done through the *restart manager*). When an entire driver needs to be replaced, the kernel can unload the driver (the driver requires an unload routine), update it, and then reload it.
Object Swap	Atomically renaming an object in the object directory namespace	When a file (typically a *known DLL*) needs to be renamed atomically and behind the back of any applications that may be using it (so that they can start using the new file immediately, using the old handle).
Patch Function Code	Replacing the code of one or more functions inside an image file with another version	If a DLL or driver can't be replaced or renamed during run time, functions in the image can be directly patched. A hotpatch DLL that contains the newer code is jumped to whenever an older function is called.
Refresh System DLL	Reload the memory mapped section object for Ntdll.dll	The system native library, Ntdll.dll, is only loaded once during boot-up and then simply duplicated into the address space of every new process. If it has been hotpatched, the system must refresh this section to load the newer version.

Although hotpatches utilize internal kernel mechanisms, their actual implementation is no different from coldpatches. The patch is delivered through Windows Update, typically as an executable file containing a program called Update.exe that will perform the extraction of the patch and the update process. For hotpatches, however, an additional hotpatch file, containing the *.hp* extension, will be present. This file contains a special PE header called *.HOT1*. This header will contain a data structure describing the various *patch descriptors* present inside the file. Each of these descriptors identifies the offset in the original file that needs to be patched, a validation mechanism (which can include a simple comparison of the old data, a checksum, or a hash), and the new data to be patched. The kernel will parse these descriptors and apply the appropriate modifications. In the case of a *protected process* (see Chapter 5 for more information on processes) and other digitally signed images, the hotpatch must also be digitally signed, in order to prevent "fake" patches from being performed to sensitive files or processes.

> **Note** Because the hotpatch file also includes the original data, the hotpatching mechanism can also be used to uninstall a patch at run time.

Compile-time hotpatching support works by adding 7 dummy bytes to the beginning of each function—4 are considered part of the end of the previous function, and 2 are part of the *function prolog;* that is, the function's beginning. Here's an example of a function that was built with hotpatching information:

```
lkd> u NtCreateFile - 5
nt!FsRtlTeardownPerFileContexts+0x169:
82227ea5 90                 nop
82227ea6 90                 nop
82227ea7 90                 nop
82227ea8 90                 nop
82227ea9 90                 nop
nt!NtCreateFile:
82227eaa 8bff               mov       edi,edi
```

Notice that the five *nop* instructions don't actually do anything, while the *mov edi, edi* at the beginning of the *NtCreateFile* function are also essentially meaningless—no actual state-changing operation takes place. Because 7 bytes are available, the *NtCreateFile* prologue can be transformed into a *short jump* to the buffer of five instructions available, which are then converted to a *near jump* instruction to the patched routine. Here's *NtCreateFile* after having been hotpatched:

```
lkd> u NtCreateFile - 5
nt!FsRtlTeardownPerFileContexts+0x169:
82227ea5 e93d020010         jmp       nt_patch!NtCreateFile (922280e7)
nt!NtCreateFile:
82227ea5 ebfc               jmp       nt!FsRtlTeardownPerFileContexts+0x169 (82227ea5)
```

This method allows only the addition of 2 bytes to each function by jumping into the previous function's alignment padding that it would most likely have at its end anyway.

There are some limitations to the hotpatching functionality:

- Patches that third-party applications such as security software might block or that might be incompatible with the operation of third-party applications
- Patches that modify a file's export table or import table
- Patches that change data structures, fix infinite loops, or contain inline assembly code

Kernel Patch Protection

Some 32-bit device drivers modify the behavior of Windows in unsupported ways. For example, they patch the system call table to intercept system calls or patch the kernel image in memory to add functionality to specific internal functions.

To prevent these kinds of changes, Windows implements Kernel Patch Protection (KPP), also referred to as PatchGuard. KPP's job on the system is similar to what its name implies—it attempts to deter common techniques for patching the system, or hooking it. Table 3-25 lists which components or structures are protected and for what purpose.

TABLE 3-25 Components Protected by KPP

Component	Legitimate Usage	Potential Malicious Usage
Ntoskrnl.exe, Hal.dll, Ci.dll, Kdcom.dll, Pshed.dll, Clfs.sys, Ndis.sys, Tcpip.sys	Kernel, HAL, and their dependencies. Lower layer of network stack.	Patching code in the kernel and/or HAL to subvert normal operation and behavior. Patching Ndis.sys to silently add backdoors on open ports.
Global Descriptor Table (GDT)	CPU hardware protection for the implementation of ring privilege levels (Ring 0 vs. Ring 3).	Ability to set up a "callgate," a CPU mechanism through which user (Ring 3) code could perform operations with kernel privileges (Ring 0).
Interrupt Descriptor Table (IDT)	Table read by the CPU to deliver interrupt vectors to the correct handling routine.	Malicious drivers could intercept file I/Os directly at the interrupt level, or hook page faults to hide contents of memory. Rootkits could hook the INT2E handler to hook all system calls from a single point.
System Service Descriptor Table (SSDT)	Table containing the array of pointers for each system call handler.	Rootkits could modify the output or input of calls from user mode and hide processes, files, or registry keys.
Processor Machine State Registers (MSRs)	LSTAR MSR is used to set the handler of the SYSENTER and/or SYSCALL instructions used for system calls.	LSTAR could be overwritten by a malicious driver to provide a single hook for all system calls performed on the system.

Component	Legitimate Usage	Potential Malicious Usage
KdpStub, KiDebugRoutine, KdpTrap function pointers	Used for run-time configuration of where exceptions should be delivered, based on whether a kernel debugger is remotely connected to the machine.	Value of the pointers could be overwritten by a malicious rootkit to take control of the system at predetermined times and perform invisible background tasks.
PsInvertedFunctionTable	Cache of exception directories used on x64, allowing quick mapping between code where an exception happened and its handler.	Could be used to take control of the system during the exception handling of unrelated system code, including KPP's own exception code responsible for detecting modifications in the first place.
Kernel stacks	Store function arguments, the call stack (where a function should return), and variables.	A driver could allocate memory on the side, set it as a kernel stack for a thread, and then manipulate its contents to redirect calls and parameters.
Object types	Definitions for the various objects (such as processes and files) that the system supports through the object manager.	Could be used as part of a technique called DKOM (Direct Kernel Object Modification) to modify system behavior, for example by hooking the object callbacks that each object type has registered.
Other	Code related to bug-checking the system during a KPP violation, executing the DPCs and timers associated with KPP, and more.	By modifying certain parts of the system used by KPP, malicious drivers could attempt to silence, ignore, or otherwise cripple KPP.

Note Because certain 64-bit Intel processors implement a slightly different feature set of the x64 architecture, the kernel needs to perform run-time code patching to work around the lack of a *prefetch* instruction. KPP can deter kernel patching even on these processors, by exempting those specific patches from detection. Additionally, because of hypervisor (Hyper-V) enlighten-ments (more information on the hypervisor is provided earlier in this chapter), certain functions in the kernel are patched at boot time, such as the *swap context* routine. These patches are also allowed by very explicit checks to make sure they are known patches to the hypervisor-enlightened versions.

When KPP detects a change in any of the structures mentioned (as well as some other internal consistency checks), it crashes the system with code 0x109—CRITICAL_STRUCTURE_CORRUPTION.

For third-party developers who used techniques that KPP deters, the following supported techniques can be used:

- File system minifilters (see Chapter 7 for more information on these) to hook all file operations, including loading image files and DLLs, that can be intercepted to purge malicious code on-the-fly or block reading of known bad executables.

- Registry filter notifications (see Chapter 4 for more information on these notifications) to hook all registry operations. Security software can block modification of critical parts of the registry, as well as heuristically determine malicious software by registry access patterns or known bad registry keys.

- Process notifications (see Chapter 5 for more information on these notifications). Security software can monitor the execution and termination of all processes and threads on the system, as well as DLLs being loaded or unloaded. With the enhanced notifications added in Windows Vista SP1 and Windows Server 2008, they also have the ability to block process launch.

- Object manager filtering (explained in the object manager section earlier). Security software can remove certain access rights being granted to processes and/or threads to defend their own utilities against certain operations.

Code Integrity

Code integrity is a Windows mechanism that authenticates the integrity and source of executable images (such as applications, DLLs, or drivers) by validating a digital certificate contained within the image's resources. This mechanism works in conjunction with system policies, defining how signing should be enforced. One of these policies is the *Kernel Mode Code Signing* (KMCS) policy, which requires that kernel-mode code be signed with a valid Authenticode certificate rooted by one of several recognized code signing authorities, such as Verisign or Thawte.

To address backward compatibility concerns, the KMCS policy is only fully enforced on 64-bit machines, as those drivers have to be recompiled recently in order to run on that Windows architecture. This in turn implies that a company or individual is still responsible for maintaining the driver and is able to sign it. On 32-bit machines, however, many older devices ship with outdated drivers, possibly from out-of-business companies, so signing those drivers would sometimes be unfeasible. Figure 3-36 shows the warning displayed on 64-bit Windows machines that attempt to load an unsigned driver.

Note Windows also has a second driver signing policy, part of the Plug and Play manager. This policy is applied solely to Plug and Play drivers, and unlike the kernel-mode code signing policy, it can be configured to allow unsigned Plug and Play drivers (but not on 64-bit systems, where the KMCS policy takes precedence). See Chapter 7 for more information on the Plug and Play manager.

FIGURE 3-36 Warning when attempting to install an unsigned 64-bit driver

Note that even on 32-bit machines, code integrity will generate a warning when such a driver is loaded, which can be viewed in the Event Log.

Note Protected Media Path applications can also query the kernel for its *integrity state*, which includes information on whether or not unsigned 32-bit drivers are loaded on the system. In such scenarios, they are allowed to disable protected, high-definition media playback as a method to ensure the security and reliability of the encrypted stream.

The code integrity mechanism doesn't stop at driver load time, however. Stronger measures also exist to authenticate per-page image contents for executable pages. This requires using a special flag while signing the driver binary and will generate a catalog with the crypto-graphic hash of every executable page on which the driver will reside. (Pages are a unit of protection on the CPU; for more information, see Chapter 9.) This method allows for detection of modification of an existing driver, which may either happen at run time by another driver or through a page file or hibernation file attack (in which the contents of memory are edited on the disk and then reloaded into memory). Generating such per-page hashes is also a requirement for the new filtering model, as well as Protected Media Path components.

Conclusion

In this chapter, we've examined the key base system mechanisms on which the Windows executive is built. In the next chapter, we'll look at three important mechanisms involved with the management infrastructure of Windows: the registry, services, and Windows Management Instrumentation (WMI).

Chapter 4
Management Mechanisms

This chapter describes four fundamental mechanisms in the Windows operating system that are critical to its management and configuration:

- The registry
- Services
- Windows Management Instrumentation
- Windows Diagnostics Infrastructure

The Registry

The registry plays a key role in the configuration and control of Windows systems. It is the repository for both systemwide and per-user settings. Although most people think of the registry as static data stored on the hard disk, as you'll see in this section, the registry is also a window into various in-memory structures maintained by the Windows executive and kernel.

We'll start by providing you with an overview of the registry structure, a discussion of the data types it supports, and a brief tour of the key information Windows maintains in the registry. Then we'll look inside the internals of the *configuration manager*, the executive component responsible for implementing the registry database. Among the topics we'll cover are the internal on-disk structure of the registry, how Windows retrieves configuration information when an application requests it, and what measures are employed to protect this critical system database.

Viewing and Changing the Registry

In general, you should never have to edit the registry directly: application and system settings stored in the registry that might require manual changes should have a corresponding user interface to control their modification. However, as you've already seen a number of times in this book, some advanced and debug settings have no editing user interface. Therefore, both graphical user interface (GUI) and command-line tools are included with Windows to enable you to view and modify the registry.

Windows comes with one main GUI tool for editing the registry—Regedit.exe—and a number of command-line registry tools. Reg.exe, for instance, has the ability to import, export, back up, and restore keys, as well as to compare, modify, and delete keys and values.

Regini.exe, on the other hand, allows you to import registry data based on text files that contain ASCII or Unicode configuration data.

Registry Usage

There are four principal times that configuration data is read:

- During the initial boot process, the boot loader reads the list of boot device drivers to load into memory before initializing the kernel.

- During the kernel boot process, the kernel reads settings that specify which device drivers to load and how various subsystems—such as the memory manager and process manager—configure themselves and tune system behavior.

- During logon, Explorer and other Windows components read per-user preferences from the registry, including network drive-letter mappings, desktop wallpaper, screen saver, menu behavior, and icon placement.

- During their startup, applications read systemwide settings, such as a list of optionally installed components and licensing data, as well as per-user settings that might include menu and toolbar placement and a list of most-recently accessed documents.

However, the registry can be read at other times as well, such as in response to a modification of a registry value or key. Some applications monitor their configuration settings in the registry and read updated settings when they see a change. In general, however, on an idle system there should be no registry activity.

The registry is commonly modified in the following cases:

- Although not a modification, the registry's initial structure and many default settings are defined by a prototype version of the registry that ships on the Windows setup media that is copied onto a new installation.

- Application setup utilities create default application settings and settings that reflect installation configuration choices.

- During the installation of a device driver, the Plug and Play system creates settings in the registry that tell the I/O manager how to start the driver and creates other settings that configure the driver's operation. (See Chapter 7 for more information on how device drivers are installed.)

- When you change application or system settings through user interfaces, the changes are often stored in the registry.

> **Note** Sadly, some applications poll the registry looking for changes when they should be using the registry's *RegNotifyChangeKey* function, which puts a thread to sleep until a change occurs to the area of the registry in which they're interested.

Registry Data Types

The registry is a database whose structure is similar to that of a disk volume. The registry contains *keys*, which are similar to a disk's directories, and *values*, which are comparable to files on a disk. A key is a container that can consist of other keys (*subkeys*) or values. Values, on the other hand, store data. Top-level keys are *root keys*. Throughout this section, we'll use the words *subkey* and *key* interchangeably.

Both keys and values borrow their naming convention from the file system. Thus, you can uniquely identify a value with the name mark, which is stored in a key called trade, with the name trade\mark. One exception to this naming scheme is each key's unnamed value. Regedit displays the unnamed value as (Default).

Values store different kinds of data and can be one of the 14 types listed in Table 4-1. The majority of registry values are REG_DWORD, REG_BINARY, or REG_SZ. Values of type REG_DWORD can store numbers or Booleans (on/off values); REG_BINARY values can store numbers larger than 32 bits or raw data such as encrypted passwords; REG_SZ values store strings (Unicode, of course) that can represent elements such as names, file names, paths, and types.

TABLE 4-1 Registry Value Types

Value Type	Description
REG_NONE	No value type.
REG_SZ	Fixed-length Unicode string.
REG_EXPAND_SZ	Variable-length Unicode string that can have embedded environment variables.
REG_BINARY	Arbitrary-length binary data.
REG_DWORD	32-bit number.
REG_DWORD_LITTLE_ENDIAN	32-bit number, with low byte first. This is equivalent to REG_DWORD.
REG_DWORD_BIG_ENDIAN	32-bit number, with high byte first.
REG_LINK	Unicode symbolic link.
REG_MULTI_SZ	Array of Unicode NULL-terminated strings.
REG_RESOURCE_LIST	Hardware resource description.
REG_FULL_RESOURCE_DESCRIPTOR	Hardware resource description.
REG_RESOURCE_REQUIREMENTS_LIST	Resource requirements.
REG_QWORD	64-bit number.
REG_QWORD_LITTLE_ENDIAN	64-bit number, with low byte first. This is equivalent to REG_QWORD.

The REG_LINK type is particularly interesting because it lets a key transparently point to another key or value. When you traverse the registry through a link, the path searching continues at the target of the link. For example, if \Root1\Link has a REG_LINK value of \Root2\RegKey, and RegKey contains the value RegValue, two paths identify RegValue: \Root1\Link\RegValue

and \Root2\RegKey\RegValue. As explained in the next section, Windows prominently uses registry links: three of the six registry root keys are links to subkeys within the three nonlink root keys.

Registry Logical Structure

You can chart the organization of the registry via the data stored within it. There are six root keys (and you can't add new root keys or delete existing ones) that store information, as shown in Table 4-2.

TABLE 4-2 The Six Root Keys

Root Key	Description
HKEY_CURRENT_USER	Stores data associated with the currently logged-on user
HKEY_USERS	Stores information about all the accounts on the machine
HKEY_CLASSES_ROOT	Stores file association and Component Object Model (COM) object registration information
HKEY_LOCAL_MACHINE	Stores system-related information
HKEY_PERFORMANCE_DATA	Stores performance information
HKEY_CURRENT_CONFIG	Stores some information about the current hardware profile

Why do root-key names begin with an H? Because the root-key names represent Windows handles (H) to keys (KEY). As mentioned in Chapter 1, HKLM is an abbreviation used for HKEY_LOCAL_MACHINE. Table 4-3 lists all the root keys and their abbreviations. The following sections explain in detail the contents and purpose of each of these six root keys.

TABLE 4-3 Registry Root Keys

Root Key	Abbreviation	Description	Link
HKEY_CURRENT_USER	HKCU	Points to the user profile of the currently logged-on user	Subkey under HKEY_USERS corresponding to currently logged-on user
HKEY_USERS	HKU	Contains subkeys for all loaded user profiles	Not a link
HKEY_CLASSES_ROOT	HKCR	Contains file association and COM registration information	Not a direct link; rather, a merged view of HKLM\ SOFTWARE\Classes and HKEY_USERS\<SID>\Classes
HKEY_LOCAL_MACHINE	HKLM	Placeholder—contains other keys	Not a link
HKEY_CURRENT_CONFIG	HKCC	Current hardware profile	HKLM\SYSTEM\ CurrentControlSet\ Hardware Profiles\Current
HKEY_PERFORMANCE_ DATA	HKPD	Performance counters	Not a link

HKEY_CURRENT_USER

The HKCU root key contains data regarding the preferences and software configuration of the locally logged-on user. It points to the currently logged-on user's user profile, located on the hard disk at \Users\<username>\Ntuser.dat. (See the section "Registry Internals" later in this chapter to find out how root keys are mapped to files on the hard disk.) Whenever a user profile is loaded (such as at logon time or when a service process runs under the context of a specific user name), HKCU is created to map to the user's key under HKEY_USERS. Table 4-4 lists some of the subkeys under HKCU.

TABLE 4-4 HKEY_CURRENT_USER Subkeys

Subkey	Description
AppEvents	Sound/event associations
Console	Command window settings (for example, width, height, and colors)
Control Panel	Screen saver, desktop scheme, keyboard, and mouse settings, as well as accessibility and regional settings
Environment	Environment variable definitions
EUDC	Information on end-user defined characters
Identities	Windows Mail account information
Keyboard Layout	Keyboard layout setting (for example, U.S. or U.K.)
Network	Network drive mappings and settings
Printers	Printer connection settings
Session Information	Number of taskbar-visible programs running in the current session
Software	User-specific software preferences
UNICODE Program Groups	User-specific Start menu group definitions
Volatile Environment	Volatile environment variable definitions

HKEY_USERS

HKU contains a subkey for each loaded user profile and user class registration database on the system. It also contains a subkey named HKU\.DEFAULT that is linked to the profile for the system (which is used by processes running under the local system account and is described in more detail in the section "Services" later in this chapter). This is the profile used by Winlogon, for example, so that changes to the desktop background settings in that profile will be implemented on the logon screen. When a user logs on to a system for the first time and her account does not depend on a roaming domain profile (that is, the user's profile is obtained from a central network location at the direction of a domain controller), the system creates a profile for her account that's based on the profile stored in %SystemDrive%\Users\Default.

The location under which the system stores profiles is defined by the registry value HKLM\
Software\Microsoft\Windows NT\CurrentVersion\ProfileList\ProfilesDirectory, which is by
default set to %SystemDrive%\Users. The ProfileList key also stores the list of profiles present
on a system. Information for each profile resides under a subkey that has a name reflecting
the security identifier (SID) of the account to which the profile corresponds. (See Chapter 6
for more information on SIDs.) Data stored in a profile's key includes the time of the last load
of the profile in the *ProfileLoadTimeLow* and *ProfileLoadTimeHigh* values, the binary repre-
sentation of the account SID in the *Sid* value, and the path to the profile's on-disk hive (which
is described later in this chapter in the "Hives" section) in the ProfileImagePath directory.
Windows shows the list of profiles stored on a system in the User Profiles management dialog
box, shown in Figure 4-1, which you access by clicking Settings in the User Profiles section of
the Advanced Tab in the System Control Panel applet.

FIGURE 4-1 The User Profiles management dialog box

EXPERIMENT: Watching Profile Loading and Unloading

You can see a profile load into the registry and then unload by using the Runas com-
mand to launch a process in an account that's not currently logged on to the machine.
While the new process is running, run Regedit and note the loaded profile key under
HKEY_USERS. After terminating the process, perform a refresh in Regedit by pressing
the F5 key and the profile should no longer be present.

HKEY_CLASSES_ROOT

HKCR consists of three types of information: file extension associations, COM class registrations, and the virtualized registry root for User Account Control (UAC). (See Chapter 6 for more information on UAC.) A key exists for every registered file name extension. Most keys contain a REG_SZ value that points to another key in HKCR containing the association information for the class of files that extension represents.

For example, HKCR\.xls would point to information on Microsoft Office Excel files in a key such as HKCU\Excel.Sheet.8. Other keys contain configuration details for COM objects registered on the system. The UAC virtualized registry is located in the VirtualStore key, which is not related to the other kinds of data stored in HKCR.

The data under HKEY_CLASSES_ROOT comes from two sources:

- The per-user class registration data in HKCU\SOFTWARE\Classes (mapped to the file on hard disk \Users\<username>\AppData\Local\Microsoft\Windows\Usrclass.dat)

- Systemwide class registration data in HKLM\SOFTWARE\Classes

The reason that there is a separation of per-user registration data from systemwide registration data is so that roaming profiles can contain these customizations. It also closes a security hole: a nonprivileged user cannot change or delete keys in the systemwide version HKEY_CLASSES_ROOT, and thus cannot affect the operation of applications on the system. Nonprivileged users and applications can read systemwide data and can add new keys and values to systemwide data (which are mirrored in their per-user data), but they can modify existing keys and values in their private data only.

HKEY_LOCAL_MACHINE

HKLM is the root key that contains all the systemwide configuration subkeys: BCD, COMPONENTS, HARDWARE, SAM, SECURITY, SOFTWARE, and SYSTEM.

The HKLM\BCD subkey contains the Boot Configuration Database (BCD) information loaded as a registry hive. This database replaces the Boot.ini file that was used before Windows Vista and adds greater flexibility and isolation of per-installation boot configuration data. (For more information on the BCD, see Chapter 13.)

Each entry in the BCD, such as a Windows installation or the command-line settings for the installation, is stored in the Objects subkey, either as an object referenced by a GUID (in the case of a boot entry) or as a numeric subkey called an *element*. Most of these raw elements are documented in the BCD reference in the MSDN Library and define various command-line settings or boot parameters. The value associated with each element subkey corresponds to the value for its respective command-line flag or boot parameter.

The BCDEdit command-line utility allows you to modify the BCD using symbolic names for the elements and objects. It also provides extensive help for all the boot options available; unfortunately, it only works locally. Because the registry can be opened remotely as well as imported from a hive file, you can modify or read the BCD of a remote computer by using the Registry Editor. The following experiment shows you how to enable kernel debugging by using the Registry Editor.

EXPERIMENT: Offline or Remote BCD Editing

In this experiment, you will enable debugging through editing the BCD inside the registry. For the purposes of this example, you'll be editing the local copy of the BCD, but the point of this technique is that it can be used on any BCD hive. Follow these steps to add the /DEBUG command-line flag:

1. Open the Registry Editor, and then navigate to the HKLM\BCD00000000 key. Expand every subkey so that the numerical identifiers of each "Elements" key are fully visible.

2. Identify the boot entry for your Windows installation by locating Description elements, which have an ID of 0x12000004. In the Element value of those subkeys, you should find one called Windows Vista or Windows Server 2008. If you have more than one Windows installation on your machine, you need to check the 0x22000002 subkey, which contains the path, such as \Windows.

3. Now that you've found the correct GUID for your Windows installation, create a new subkey under the Elements subkey for that GUID and call it 0x260000a0. If this subkey already exists, simply navigate to it.

4. If you had to create the subkey, now create a binary value called Element inside it.

5. Edit the value and set it to 01. This will enable kernel-mode debugging. Here's what these changes should look like:

Note The 0x12000004 ID corresponds to BcdLibraryString_ApplicationPath, while the 0x22000002 ID corresponds to BcdOSLoaderString_SystemRoot. Finally, the ID we added, 0x260000a0, corresponds to BcdOSLoaderBoolean_KernelDebuggerEnabled. These values are documented in the BCD reference in MSDN Library.

The HKLM\COMPONENTS subkey contains information pertinent to the Component Based Servicing (CBS) stack. This stack contains various files and resources that are part of a Windows installation image (used by the Automated Installation Kit or the OEM Preinstallation Kit) or an active installation. The CBS APIs that exist for servicing purposes

use the information located in this key to identify installed components and their configuration information. This information is used whenever components are installed, updated, or removed either individually (called units) or in groups (called packages).

The HKLM\HARDWARE subkey maintains descriptions of the system's hardware and all hardware device-to-driver mappings. The Device Manager tool (which is available by running System from Control Panel and then clicking Device Manager) lets you view registry hardware information that it obtains by simply reading values out of the HARDWARE key.

EXPERIMENT: Fun with the Hardware Key

You can fool your coworkers or friends into thinking that you have the latest and greatest processor by modifying the value of the *ProcessorNameString* value under HKLM\HARDWARE\DESCRIPTION\System\CentralProcessor\0. The System item in Control Panel displays the *ProcessorNameString* value on the main page. Changes you make to other values in that key, such as the ~MHz value, do not have any effect on what the System item displays, however, because the system caches many of the values for use by functions that applications use to query the system's processor capabilities.

HKLM\SAM holds local account and group information, such as user passwords, group definitions, and domain associations. Windows Server systems that are operating as domain controllers store domain accounts and groups in Active Directory, a database that stores domainwide settings and information. (Active Directory isn't described in this book.) By default, the security descriptor on the SAM key is configured so that even the administrator account doesn't have access.

HKLM\SECURITY stores systemwide security policies and user-rights assignments. HKLM\SAM is linked into the SECURITY subkey under HKLM\SECURITY\SAM. By default, you can't view the contents of HKLM\SECURITY or HKLM\SAM\SAM because the security settings of those keys allow access only by the System account. (System accounts are discussed in greater detail later in this chapter.) You can change the security descriptor to allow read access to administrators, or you can use PsExec to run Regedit in the local system account if you want to peer inside. However, that glimpse won't be very revealing because the data is undocumented and the passwords are encrypted with one-way mapping—that is, you can't determine a password from its encrypted form.

HKLM\SOFTWARE is where Windows stores systemwide configuration information not needed to boot the system. Also, third-party applications store their systemwide settings here, such as paths to application files and directories and licensing and expiration date information.

HKLM\SYSTEM contains the systemwide configuration information needed to boot the system, such as which device drivers to load and which services to start. Because this information is critical to starting the system, Windows also maintains a copy of part of this information, called the *last known good control set*, under this key. The maintenance of a copy allows an administrator to select a previously working control set in the case that configuration changes made to the current control set prevent the system from booting. For details on when Windows declares the current control set "good," see the section "Accepting the Boot and Last Known Good" later in this chapter.

HKEY_CURRENT_CONFIG

HKEY_CURRENT_CONFIG is just a link to the current hardware profile, stored under HKLM\SYSTEM\CurrentControlSet\Hardware Profiles\Current. Hardware profiles allow an administrator to configure variations to the base system driver settings. Although the underlying profile might change from boot to boot, applications can always reference the currently active profile through this key. Hardware profile management is managed through the Hardware Profiles dialog box that you access by clicking Settings in the Hardware Profiles section on the Hardware page of the Control Panel's System item. During the boot process, Winload will prompt you to specify which profile it should use if there is more than one.

HKEY_PERFORMANCE_DATA

The registry is the mechanism to access performance counter values on Windows, whether those are from operating system components or server applications. One of the side benefits of providing access to the performance counters via the registry is that remote performance monitoring works "for free" because the registry is easily accessible remotely through the normal registry APIs.

You can access the registry performance counter information directly by opening a special key named HKEY_PERFORMANCE_DATA and querying values beneath it. You won't find this key by looking in the Registry Editor; this key is available only programmatically through the Windows registry functions, such as *RegQueryValueEx*. Performance information isn't actually stored in the registry; the registry functions use this key to locate the information from performance data providers.

You can also access performance counter information by using the Performance Data Helper (PDH) functions available through the Performance Data Helper API (Pdh.dll). Figure 4-2 shows the components involved in accessing performance counter information.

FIGURE 4-2 Registry performance counter architecture

Transactional Registry (TxR)

Before Windows Vista, there was no easy, guaranteed way to perform transactional operations on the registry, and it was even harder to link those operations with other, nonregistry operations, such as file operations. Thanks to the Kernel Transaction Manager (KTM; for more information see the section about the KTM in Chapter 3), developers now have access to a straightforward API that allows them to implement robust error-recovery capabilities when performing registry operations.

Three APIs support transactional modification of the registry: *RegCreateKeyTransacted,* *RegOpenKeyTransacted,* and *RegDeleteKeyTransacted*. These new routines take the same parameters as their nontransacted analogues, except that a new transaction handle parameter is added. A developer supplies this handle after calling the KTM function *CreateTransaction*.

After a transacted create or open operation, all subsequent registry operations, such as creating, deleting, or modifying values inside the key, will also be transacted. However, operations on the subkeys of a transacted key will not be automatically transacted, which is why the third API, *RegDeleteKeyTransacted* exists. It allows the transacted deletion of subkeys, which *RegDeleteKeyEx* would not normally do.

Data for these transacted operations is written to log files using the common logging file system (CLFS) services, similar to other KTM operations. Until the transaction itself is committed or rolled back (both of which might happen programmatically or as a result of a power failure or system crash, depending on the state of the transaction), the keys, values, and other

registry modifications performed with the transaction handle will not be visible to external applications through the nontransacted APIs. Also, transactions are isolated from each other; modifications made inside one transaction will not be visible from inside other transactions or outside the transaction until the transaction is committed.

Note A nontransactional writer will abort a transaction in case of conflict—for example, if a value was created inside a transaction and later, while the transaction is still active, a nontransactional writer tries to create a value under the same key. The nontransactional operation will succeed and all operations in the conflicting transaction will be aborted.

The isolation level (the "I" in ACID) implemented by TxR resource managers is read-commit, which means that changes become available to other readers (transacted or not) immediately after being committed. This mechanism is important for people who are familiar with transactions in databases, where the isolation level is predictable-reads (or cursor-stability, as it is called in database literature). With a predictable-reads isolation level, after you read a value inside a transaction, subsequent reads will give you back the same data. Read-commit does not make this guarantee. One of the consequences is that registry transactions can't be used for "atomic" increment/decrement operations on a registry value.

To make permanent changes to the registry, the application that has been using the transaction handle must call the KTM function *CommitTransaction*. (If the application decides to undo the changes, such as during a failure path, it can call the *RollbackTransaction* API.) The changes will then be visible through the regular registry APIs as well.

Note If a transaction handle created with *CreateTransaction* is closed before the transaction is committed (and there are no other handles open to that transaction), the system will roll back that transaction.

Apart from using the CLFS support provided by the KTM, TxR also stores its own internal log files in the %SystemRoot%\System32\Config\Txr folder on the system volume; these files have a .regtrans-ms extension and are hidden by default. Even if there are no third-party applications installed, it is likely that your system will contain files in this directory because Windows Update and Component Based Servicing take advantage of TxR to atomically write data to the registry to avoid system failure or inconsistent component data in the case of an incomplete update. In fact, if you take a look at some of the transaction files, you should be able to see the key names on which the transaction was being performed.

There is a global registry resource manager (RM) that services all the hives that are mounted at boot time. For every hive that is mounted explicitly, an RM is created. For applications that use registry transactions, the creation of an RM is transparent because KTM ensures that all RMs taking part in the same transaction are coordinated in the two-phase commit/abort protocol. For the global registry RM, the CLFS log files are stored, as mentioned earlier, inside

System32\Config\Txr. For other hives, they are stored alongside the hive (in same directory). They are hidden and follow the same naming convention, ending in .regtrans-ms. The log file names are prefixed with the name of the hive to which they correspond.

Monitoring Registry Activity

Because the system and applications depend so heavily on configuration settings to guide their behavior, system and application failures can result from changing registry data or security. When the system or an application fails to read settings that it assumes it will always be able to access, it may not function properly, display error messages that hide the root cause, or even crash. It's virtually impossible to know what registry keys or values are mis-configured without understanding how the system or the application that's failing is access-ing the registry. In such situations, the Process Monitor utility from Windows Sysinternals (*www.microsoft.com/technet/sysinternals*) might provide the answer.

Process Monitor lets you monitor registry activity as it occurs. For each registry access, Process Monitor shows you the process that performed the access; the time, type, and result of the access; and the stack of the thread at the moment of the access. This information is useful for seeing how applications and the system rely on the registry, discovering where applications and the system store configuration settings, and troubleshooting problems related to applications having missing registry keys or values. Process Monitor includes advanced filtering and highlighting so that you can zoom in on activity related to specific keys or values or to the activity of particular processes.

Process Monitor Internals

Process Monitor relies on a device driver that it extracts from its executable image at run time and then starts. Its first execution requires that the account running it have the Load Driver privilege as well as the Debug privilege; subsequent executions in the same boot ses-sion require only the Debug privilege because once loaded, the driver remains resident.

EXPERIMENT: Viewing Registry Activity on an Idle System

Because the registry implements the *RegNotifyChangeKey* function that applications can use to request notification of registry changes without polling for them, when you launch Process Monitor on a system that's idle you should not see repetitive accesses to the same registry keys or values. Any such activity identifies a poorly written application that unnecessarily negatively affects a system's overall performance.

Run Process Monitor, and after several seconds examine the output log to see whether you can spot polling behavior. Right-click on an output line associated with polling, and then choose Process Properties from the context menu to view details about the pro-cess performing the activity.

EXPERIMENT: Using Process Monitor to Locate Application Registry Settings

In some troubleshooting scenarios, you might need to determine where in the registry the system or an application stores particular settings. This experiment has you use Process Monitor to discover the location of Notepad's settings. Notepad, like most Windows applications, saves user preferences—such as word-wrap mode, font and font size, and window position—across executions. By having Process Monitor watching when Notepad reads or writes its settings, you can identify the registry key in which the settings are stored. Here are the steps for doing this:

1. Have Notepad save a setting that you can easily search for in a Process Monitor trace. You can do this by running Notepad, setting the font to Times New Roman, and then exiting Notepad.

2. Run Process Monitor. Open the filter dialog box, and the Process Name filter, and enter **notepad.exe** as the string to match. This step specifies that Process Monitor will log only activity by the notepad.exe process.

3. Run Notepad again, and after it has launched stop Process Monitor's event capture by toggling Capture Events on the Process Monitor File menu.

4. Scroll to the top line of the resultant log and select it.

5. Press Ctrl+F to open a Find dialog box, and search for **times new**. Process Monitor should highlight a line like the one shown in the following screen that represents Notepad reading the font value from the registry. Other operations in the immediate vicinity should relate to other Notepad settings.

6. Finally, double-click the highlighted line. Process Monitor will execute Regedit (if it's not already running) and cause it to navigate to and select the Notepad-referenced registry value.

Process Monitor Troubleshooting Techniques

Two basic Process Monitor troubleshooting techniques are effective for discovering the cause of registry-related application or system problems:

- Look at the last thing in the Process Monitor trace that the application did before it failed. This action might point to the problem.

- Compare a Process Monitor trace of the failing application with a trace from a working system.

To follow the first approach, run Process Monitor and then run the application. At the point the failure occurs, go back to Process Monitor and stop the logging (by pressing Ctrl+E). Then go to the end of the log and find the last operations performed by the application before it failed (or crashed, hung, or whatever). Starting with the last line, work your way backward, examining the files, registry keys, or both that were referenced—often this will help pinpoint the problem.

Use the second approach when the application fails on one system but works on another. Capture a Process Monitor trace of the application on the working and failing systems, and save the output to a log file. Then open the good and bad log files with Microsoft Excel (accepting the defaults in the Import wizard), and delete the first three columns. (If you don't delete the first three columns, the comparison will show every line as different because the first three columns contain information that is different from run to run, such as the time and the process ID.) Finally, compare the resulting log files. (You can do this by using WinDiff, which is included in the Windows SDK).

Entries in a Process Monitor trace that have values of NAME NOT FOUND or ACCESS DENIED in the Result column are ones that you should investigate. NAME NOT FOUND is reported when an application attempts to read from a registry key or value that doesn't exist. In many cases, a missing key or value is innocuous because a process that fails to read a setting from the registry simply falls back on default values. In some cases, however, applications expect to find values for which there is no default and will fail if they are missing.

Access-denied errors are a common source of registry-related application failures and occur when an application doesn't have permission to access a key the way that it wants. Applications that do not validate registry operation results or perform proper error recovery will fail.

A common result string that might appear suspicious is BUFFER OVERFLOW. It does not indicate a buffer-overflow exploit in the application that receives it. Instead, it's used by the configuration manager to inform an application that the buffer it specified to store a registry value is too small to hold the value. Application developers often take advantage of this behavior to determine how large a buffer to allocate to store a value. They first perform a registry query with a 0-length buffer that returns a buffer-overflow error and the length of

the data it attempted to read. The application then allocates a buffer of the indicated size and rereads the value. You should therefore see operations that return BUFFER OVERFLOW repeat with a successful result.

In one example of Process Monitor being used to troubleshoot a real problem, it saved a user from doing a complete reinstall of his Windows system. The symptom was that Internet Explorer would hang on startup if the user did not first manually dial the Internet connection. This Internet connection was set as the default connection for the system, so starting Internet Explorer should have caused an automatic dial-up to the Internet (because Internet Explorer was set to display a default home page upon startup).

An examination of a Process Monitor log of Internet Explorer startup activity, going backward from the point in the log where Internet Explorer hung, showed a query to a key under HKCU\Software\Microsoft\RAS Phonebook. The user reported that he had previously uninstalled the dialer program associated with the key and manually created the dial-up connection. Because the dial-up connection name did not match that of the uninstalled dialer program, it appeared that the key had not been deleted by the dialer's uninstall program and that it was causing Internet Explorer to hang. After the key was deleted, Internet Explorer functioned as expected.

Logging Activity in Unprivileged Accounts or During Logon/Logoff

A common application-failure scenario is that an application works when run in an account that has Administrative group membership but not when run in the account of an unprivileged user. As described earlier, executing Process Monitor requires security privileges that are not normally assigned to standard user accounts, but you can capture a trace of applications executing in the logon session of an unprivileged user by using the Runas command to execute Process Monitor in an administrative account.

If a registry problem relates to account logon or logoff, you'll also have to take special steps to be able to use Process Monitor to capture a trace of those phases of a logon session. Applications that are run in the local system account are not terminated when a user logs off, and you can take advantage of that fact to have Process Monitor run through a logoff and subsequent logon. You can launch Process Monitor in the local system account either by using the *At* command that's built into Windows and specifying the */interactive* flag, or by using the Sysinternals PsExec utility, like this:

psexec –i 0 –s –d c:\procmon.exe

The *–i* switch directs PsExec to have Process Monitor's window appear on the interactive console, the *–s* switch has PsExec run Process Monitor in the local system account, and the *–d* switch has PsExec launch Process Monitor and exit without waiting for Process Monitor to terminate. When you execute this command, the instance of Process Monitor that executes

will survive logoff and reappear on the desktop when you log back on, having captured the registry activity of both actions.

Another way to monitor registry activity during the logon, logoff, boot, or shutdown process is to use the Process Monitor log boot feature, which you can enable by selecting Log Boot on the Options menu. The next time you boot the system, the Process Monitor device driver logs registry activity from early in the boot to %SystemRoot%\Procmon.pml. It will continue logging to that file until disk space runs out, the system shuts down, or you run Process Monitor. A log file storing a registry trace of startup, logon, logoff, and shutdown on a Windows system will typically be between 50 and 150 MB in size.

Registry Internals

In this section, you'll find out how the configuration manager—the executive subsystem that implements the registry—organizes the registry's on-disk files. We'll examine how the configuration manager manages the registry as applications and other operating system components read and change registry keys and values. We'll also discuss the mechanisms by which the configuration manager tries to ensure that the registry is always in a recoverable state, even if the system crashes while the registry is being modified.

Hives

On disk, the registry isn't simply one large file but rather a set of discrete files called *hives*. Each hive contains a registry tree, which has a key that serves as the root or starting point of the tree. Subkeys and their values reside beneath the root. You might think that the root keys displayed by the Registry Editor correlate to the root keys in the hives, but such is not the case. Table 4-5 lists registry hives and their on-disk file names. The path names of all hives except for user profiles are coded into the configuration manager. As the configuration manager loads hives, including system profiles, it notes each hive's path in the values under the HKLM\SYSTEM\CurrentControlSet\Control\Hivelist subkey, removing the path if the hive is unloaded. It creates the root keys, linking these hives together to build the registry structure you're familiar with and that the Registry Editor displays.

You'll notice that some of the hives listed in Table 4-5 are volatile and don't have associated files. The system creates and manages these hives entirely in memory; the hives are therefore temporary. The system creates volatile hives every time it boots. An example of a volatile hive is the HKLM\HARDWARE hive, which stores information about physical devices and the devices' assigned resources. Resource assignment and hardware detection occur every time the system boots, so not storing this data on disk is logical.

TABLE 4-5 **On-Disk Files Corresponding to Paths in the Registry**

Hive Registry Path	Hive File Path
HKEY_LOCAL_MACHINE\BCD00000000	\Boot\BCD
HKEY_LOCAL_MACHINE\COMPONENTS	%SystemRoot%\System32\Config\Components
HKEY_LOCAL_MACHINE\SYSTEM	%SystemRoot%\System32\Config\System
HKEY_LOCAL_MACHINE\SAM	%SystemRoot%\System32\Config\Sam
HKEY_LOCAL_MACHINE\SECURITY	%SystemRoot%\System32\Config\Security
HKEY_LOCAL_MACHINE\SOFTWARE	%SystemRoot%\System32\Config\Software
HKEY_LOCAL_MACHINE\HARDWARE	Volatile hive
HKEY_USERS\<SID of local service account>	%SystemRoot%\ServiceProfiles\LocalService\Ntuser.dat
HKEY_USERS\<SID of network service account>	%SystemRoot%\ServiceProfiles\NetworkService\NtUser.dat
HKEY_USERS\<SID of username>	\Users\<username>\Ntuser.dat
HKEY_USERS\<SID of username>_Classes	\Users\<username>\AppData\Local\Microsoft\Windows\Usrclass.dat
HKEY_USERS\.DEFAULT	%SystemRoot%\System32\Config\Default

EXPERIMENT: Manually Loading and Unloading Hives

Regedit has the ability to load hives that you can access through its File menu. This capability can be useful in troubleshooting scenarios where you want to view or edit a hive from an unbootable system or a backup medium. In this experiment, you'll use Regedit to load a version of the HKLM\SYSTEM hive that Windows Setup creates during the install process.

1. Hives can be loaded only underneath HKLM or HKU, so open Regedit, select HKLM, and choose Load Hive from the Regedit File menu.

2. Navigate to the %SystemRoot%\System32\Config directory in the Load Hive dialog box, select System.sav, and open it. When prompted, enter **Test** as the name of the key under which it will load.

3. Open the newly created HKLM\Test key, and explore the contents of the hive.

4. Open HKLM\SYSTEM\CurrentControlSet\Control\Hivelist, and locate the entry \Registry\Machine\Test, which demonstrates how the configuration manager lists loaded hives in the Hivelist key.

5. Select HKLM\Test, and then choose Unload Hive from the Regedit File menu to unload the hive.

Hive Size Limits

In some cases, hive sizes are limited. For example, Windows places a limit on the size of the HKLM\SYSTEM hive. It does so because Winload reads the entire HKLM\SYSTEM hive into physical memory near the start of the boot process when virtual memory paging is not enabled. Winload also loads Ntoskrnl and boot device drivers into physical memory, so it must constrain the amount of physical memory assigned to HKLM\SYSTEM. (See Chapter 13 for more information on the role Winload plays during the startup process.) On 32-bit systems, Winload allows the hive to be as large as 400 MB or one-half the amount of physical memory on the system, whichever is lower. On x64 systems, the lower bound is 1.5 GB. On Itanium systems, it is 32 MB.

To avoid using too much virtual memory for registry hives at one time, especially in the case of a Terminal Server, which must have the per-user registry settings of dozens of users available for reading and writing, the configuration manager on 32-bit versions of Windows does not use paged pool and instead relies on the memory manager's memory-mapping functions to map into system memory only the portions of registry hives that it's accessing at any given point in time. This allows the total size of loaded hives not to constrain the scalability of Terminal Services. Because 64-bit systems have ample virtual address space, and because of the additional bookkeeping that memory-mapping requires, 64-bit Windows uses paged pool instead.

A special type of key known as a *symbolic link* makes it possible for the configuration manager to link keys to organize the registry. A symbolic link is a key that redirects the configuration manager to another key. Thus, the key HKLM\SAM is a symbolic link to the key at the root of the SAM hive. Symbolic links are created by specifying the REG_CREATE_LINK parameter to *RegCreateKey* or *RegCreateKeyEx*. Internally, the configuration manager will create a REG_LINK value called SymbolicLinkValue, which will contain the path to the target key. Because this value is a REG_LINK instead of a REG_SZ, it will not be visible with Regedit—it is, however, part of the on-disk registry hive.

EXPERIMENT: Looking at Hive Handles

The configuration manager opens hives by using the kernel handle table (described in Chapter 3) so that it can access hives from any process context. Using the kernel handle table is an efficient alternative to approaches that involve using drivers or executive components to access from the System process only handles that must be protected from user processes. You can use Process Explorer to see the hive handles, which will be displayed as being opened in the System process. Select the System process, and then select Handles from the Lower Pane View menu entry on the View menu. Sort by handle type, and scroll until you see the hive files, as shown in the following screen.

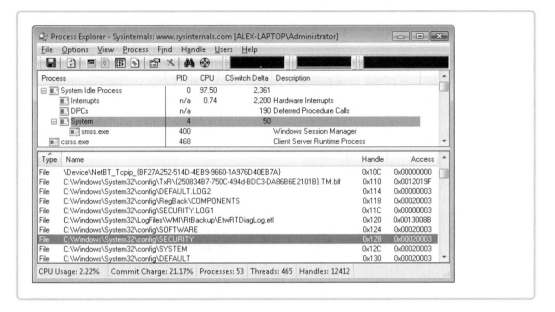

Hive Structure

The configuration manager logically divides a hive into allocation units called *blocks* in much the same way that a file system divides a disk into clusters. By definition, the registry block size is 4096 bytes (4 KB). When new data expands a hive, the hive always expands in block-granular increments. The first block of a hive is the *base block*.

The base block includes global information about the hive, including a signature—*regf*—that identifies the file as a hive, updated sequence numbers, a time stamp that shows the last time a write operation was initiated on the hive, information on registry repair or recovery performed by Winload, the hive format version number, a checksum, and the hive file's internal file name (for example, \Device\HarddiskVolume1\WINDOWS\SYSTEM32\CONFIG\SAM). We'll clarify the significance of the updated sequence numbers and time stamp when we describe how data is written to a hive file.

The hive format version number specifies the data format within the hive. The configuration manager uses hive format version 1.3 (this version improved searching by caching the first four characters of the name inside the cell index structure for quick lookups) for all hives except for System and Software for roaming profile compatibility with Windows 2000. For System and Software hives, it uses version 1.5 because of the later format's optimizations for large values (values larger than 1 MB are supported) and searching (instead of caching the first four characters of a name, a hash of the entire name is used to reduce collisions).

Windows organizes the registry data that a hive stores in containers called *cells*. A cell can hold a key, a value, a security descriptor, a list of subkeys, or a list of key values. A field at the

beginning of a cell's data describes the data's type. Table 4-6 describes each cell data type in detail. A cell's header is a field that specifies the cell's size. When a cell joins a hive and the hive must expand to contain the cell, the system creates an allocation unit called a *bin*.

A bin is the size of the new cell rounded up to the next block or page boundary, whichever is higher. The system considers any space between the end of the cell and the end of the bin to be free space that it can allocate to other cells. Bins also have headers that contain a signature, *hbin*, and a field that records the offset into the hive file of the bin and the bin's size.

TABLE 4-6 Cell Data Types

Data Type	Description
Key cell	A cell that contains a registry key, also called a *key node*. A key cell contains a signature (*kn* for a key, *kl* for a link node), the time stamp of the most recent update to the key, the cell index of the key's parent key cell, the cell index of the subkey-list cell that identifies the key's subkeys, a cell index for the key's security descriptor cell, a cell index for a string key that specifies the class name of the key, and the name of the key (for example, CurrentControlSet). It also saves cached information such as the number of subkeys under the key, as well as the size of the largest key name, value name, value data, and class name of the subkeys under this key.
Value cell	A cell that contains information about a key's value. This cell includes a signature (*kv*), the value's type (for example, REG_ DWORD or REG_ BINARY), and the value's name (for example, Boot-Execute). A value cell also contains the cell index of the cell that contains the value's data.
Subkey-list cell	A cell composed of a list of cell indexes for key cells that are all subkeys of a common parent key.
Value-list cell	A cell composed of a list of cell indexes for value cells that are all values of a common parent key.
Security-descriptor cell	A cell that contains a security descriptor. Security-descriptor cells include a signature (*ks*) at the head of the cell and a reference count that records the number of key nodes that share the security descriptor. Multiple key cells can share security-descriptor cells.

By using bins, instead of cells, to track active parts of the registry, Windows minimizes some management chores. For example, the system usually allocates and deallocates bins less frequently than it does cells, which lets the configuration manager manage memory more efficiently. When the configuration manager reads a registry hive into memory, it reads the whole hive, including empty bins, but it can choose to discard them later. When the system adds and deletes cells in a hive, the hive can contain empty bins interspersed with active bins. This situation is similar to disk fragmentation, which occurs when the system creates and deletes files on the disk. When a bin becomes empty, the configuration manager joins to the empty bin any adjacent empty bins to form as large a contiguous empty bin as possible. The configuration manager also joins adjacent deleted cells to form larger free cells. (The configuration manager shrinks a hive only when bins at the end of the hive become free. You can

compact the registry by backing it up and restoring it using the Windows *RegSaveKey* and *RegReplaceKey* functions, which are used by the Windows Backup utility.)

The links that create the structure of a hive are called *cell indexes*. A cell index is the offset of a cell into the hive file minus the size of the base block. Thus, a cell index is like a pointer from one cell to another cell that the configuration manager interprets relative to the start of a hive. For example, as you saw in Table 4-6, a cell that describes a key contains a field specifying the cell index of its parent key; a cell index for a subkey specifies the cell that describes the subkeys that are subordinate to the specified subkey. A subkey-list cell contains a list of cell indexes that refer to the subkey's key cells. Therefore, if you want to locate, for example, the key cell of subkey A, whose parent is key B, you must first locate the cell containing key B's subkey list using the subkey-list cell index in key B's cell. Then you locate each of key B's subkey cells by using the list of cell indexes in the subkey-list cell. For each subkey cell, you check to see whether the subkey's name, which a key cell stores, matches the one you want to locate, in this case, subkey A.

The distinction between cells, bins, and blocks can be confusing, so let's look at an example of a simple registry hive layout to help clarify the differences. The sample registry hive file in Figure 4-3 contains a base block and two bins. The first bin is empty, and the second bin contains several cells. Logically, the hive has only two keys: the root key Root, and a subkey of Root, Sub Key. Root has two values, *Val 1* and *Val 2*. A subkey-list cell locates the root key's subkey, and a value-list cell locates the root key's values. The free spaces in the second bin are empty cells. Figure 4-3 doesn't show the security cells for the two keys, which would be present in a hive.

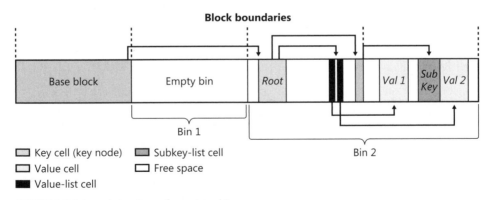

FIGURE 4-3 Internal structure of a registry hive

Figure 4-4 shows an example of the Disk Probe utility (Dskprobe.exe) examining the first bin in a SYSTEM hive. Notice the bin's signature, *hbin*, at the top right side of the image. Look beneath the bin signature and you'll see the signature *nk*. This signature is the signature of a key cell (*kn*). The signature displays backward because of the way x86 computers store data. The cell is the SYSTEM hive's root cell, which the configuration manager has named internally CMI-CreateHive{C619BFE8-791A-4B77-922B-F114AB570920}, as specified by the name that follows the *nk* signature.

FIGURE 4-4 Binary contents of first bin in the SYSTEM hive

To optimize searches for both values and subkeys, the configuration manager sorts subkey-list cells alphabetically. The configuration manager can then perform a binary search when it looks for a subkey within a list of subkeys. The configuration manager examines the subkey in the middle of the list, and if the name of the subkey the configuration manager is looking for is alphabetically before the name of the middle subkey, the configuration manager knows that the subkey is in the first half of the subkey list; otherwise, the subkey is in the second half of the subkey list. This splitting process continues until the configuration manager locates the subkey or finds no match. Value-list cells aren't sorted, however, so new values are always added to the end of the list.

Cell Maps

The configuration manager doesn't access a hive's image on disk every time a registry access occurs. Instead, the configuration manager maps portions of a hive into memory as it needs to access them. It uses the cache manager's file mapping functions to map 16-KB views into the hive files. (See Chapter 10 for more information on the cache manager.) To prevent hive mapping from consuming all the cache manager's address range, the configuration manager tries to keep no more than 256 views of a hive mapped at any given point in time by unmapping least-recently-used (LRU) views when it reaches that limit. The configuration manager still uses the paged pool to store various data structures (including the LRU list of views).

Note The configuration manager will store a block in the paged pool instead of mapping it if the block exceeds 256 KB in size.

If hives never grew, the configuration manager could perform all its registry management on the in-memory version of a hive as if the hive were a file. Given a cell index, the configuration manager could calculate the location in memory of a cell simply by adding the cell index, which is a hive file offset, to the base of the in-memory hive image. Early in the system boot, this process is exactly what Winload does with the SYSTEM hive: Winload reads the entire SYSTEM hive into memory as a read-only hive and adds the cell indexes to the base of the in-memory hive image to locate cells. Unfortunately, hives grow as they take on new keys and values, which means the system must allocate paged pool memory to store the new bins that contain added keys and values. Thus, the paged pool that keeps the registry data in memory isn't necessarily contiguous.

EXPERIMENT: Viewing Hive Paged Pool Usage

There are no administrative-level tools that show you the amount of paged pool that registry hives, including user profiles, are consuming on Windows. However, the *!reg dumppool* kernel debugger command shows you not only how many pages of the paged pool each loaded hive consumes but also how many of the pages store volatile and nonvolatile data. The command prints the total hive memory usage at the end of the output. (The command shows only the last 32 characters of a hive's name.)

```
kd> !reg dumppool

dumping hive at e20d66a8 (a\Microsoft\Windows\UsrClass.dat)
  Stable Length = 1000
  1/1 pages present
  Volatile Length = 0

dumping hive at e215ee88 (ettings\Administrator\ntuser.dat)
  Stable Length = f2000
  242/242 pages present
  Volatile Length = 2000
  2/2 pages present

dumping hive at e13fa188 (\SystemRoot\System32\Config\SAM)
  Stable Length = 5000
  5/5 pages present
  Volatile Length = 0

...
```

EXPERIMENT: Viewing Hive Memory Usage

You can view statistics on hive memory usage, including its stable (on-disk) size and nonvolatile size, the number of active views, and the number of views that are locked into memory, using the *!reg hivelist* command (note that the line output wraps):

```
---------------------------------------------------------------------------------------
-----------------------
| HiveAddr |Stable Length|Stable Map|Volatile Length|Volatile Map|MappedViews|PinnedVi
ews|U(Cnt)| BaseBlock | FileName
---------------------------------------------------------------------------------------
-----------------------
| 9b106a30 |      24000  | 9b106aa8 |             0  | 00000000  |       10  |
0  |     0| 9b19d000 | files\NetworkService\ntuser.dat
| 9b1d3008 |      23000  | 9b1d3080 |             0  | 00000000  |        9  |
0  |     0| 9b1d2000 | rofiles\LocalService\ntuser.dat
| 9c1a8008 |     374000  | 9c0b3000 |          2000  | 9c1a81bc  |      174  |
0  |     0| 9c080000 | :\Users\Abby\ntuser.dat
| 9cfdba30 |     219000  | 9ce77000 |          1000  | 9cfdbbe4  |      103  |
0  |     0| 9c0f8000 | \Microsoft\Windows\UsrClass.dat
...
```

In the preceding output, the Abby account's profile hive (the full path of which, \Users\Abby\ntuser.dat, is truncated in the output) has 174 mapped views and is approximately 3.45 MB in size (0x374000 in decimal). The *!reg viewlist* command will dump the mapped views of the hive you specify. Here's the output of that command when executed for the UsrClass.dat hive that was printed as the last hive of the *!reg hivelist* command's output:

```
lkd> !reg viewlist 9cfdba30

   0  Pinned Views ; PinViewListHead = 9cfdbd5c 9cfdbd5c

 103  Mapped Views ; LRUViewListHead = 91d3e058 91d3bd60
---------------------------------------------------------------------------------------
-----------------------
| ViewAddr |FileOffset|  Size  |ViewAddress|   Bcb    |    LRUViewList      |
PinViewList   | UseCount |
---------------------------------------------------------------------------------------
-----------------------
| 91d3e058 |     1000 |   3000 | 9de81000  | 8611dd11 | 975c6870  9cfdbd54  |
91d3e060  91d3e060 |    0  |

| 975c6870 |   138000 |   4000 | 9dfb8000  | 8611dd91 | 96756278  91d3e058  |
975c6878  975c6878 |    0  |
```

The output shows the addresses of the two views that the *hivelist* command reported for the hive in the ViewAddress column. Using the debugger's *db* command to dump the contents of memory at the address of the first view reveals that it maps a base block of the hive, recognizable with its *hbin* signature.

```
lkd> db 9de81000
9de81000  68 62 69 6e 00 00 00 00-00 10 00 00 00 00 00 00   hbin............
9de81010  00 00 00 00 56 b1 b8 fe-2b 61 c8 01 00 00 00 00   ....V...+a......
9de81020  78 ff ff ff 6e 6b 2c 00-10 63 0b c6 89 58 c8 01   x...nk,..c...X..
9de81030  00 00 00 00 e0 06 00 00-56 00 00 00 00 00 00 00   ........V.......
9de81040  a0 af 01 00 ff ff ff ff-00 00 00 00 ff ff ff ff   ................
9de81050  28 01 00 00 ff ff ff ff-4c 00 00 00 00 00 00 00   (.......L.......
9de81060  00 00 00 00 00 00 00 00-00 00 00 00 36 00 00 00   ............6...
9de81070  53 2d 31 2d 35 2d 32 31-2d 34 30 34 37 36 30 39   S-1-5-21-4047609
```

To deal with noncontiguous memory addresses referencing hive data in memory, the configuration manager adopts a strategy similar to what the Windows memory manager uses to map virtual memory addresses to physical memory addresses. The configuration manager employs a two-level scheme, which Figure 4-5 illustrates, that takes as input a cell index (that is, a hive file offset) and returns as output both the address in memory of the block the cell index resides in and the address in memory of the block the cell resides in. Remember that a bin can contain one or more blocks and that hives grow in bins, so Windows always represents a bin with a contiguous region of memory. Therefore, all blocks within a bin occur within the same cache manager view.

FIGURE 4-5 Structure of a cell index

To implement the mapping, the configuration manager divides a cell index logically into fields, in the same way that the memory manager divides a virtual address into fields. Windows interprets a cell index's first field as an index into a hive's cell map directory. The cell map directory contains 1024 entries, each of which refers to a cell map table that contains 512 map entries. An entry in this cell map table is specified by the second field in the

cell index. That entry locates the bin and block memory addresses of the cell. Not all bins are necessarily mapped into memory, and if a cell lookup yields an address of 0, the configuration manager maps the bin into memory, unmapping another on the mapping LRU list it maintains, if necessary.

In the final step of the translation process, the configuration manager interprets the last field of the cell index as an offset into the identified block to precisely locate a cell in memory. When a hive initializes, the configuration manager dynamically creates the mapping tables, designating a map entry for each block in the hive, and it adds and deletes tables from the cell directory as the changing size of the hive requires.

The Registry Namespace and Operation

The configuration manager defines a *key object* object type to integrate the registry's namespace with the kernel's general namespace. The configuration manager inserts a key object named *Registry* into the root of the Windows namespace, which serves as the entry point to the registry. Regedit shows key names in the form HKEY_LOCAL_MACHINE\SYSTEM\CurrentControlSet, but the Windows subsystem translates such names into their object namespace form (for example, \Registry\Machine\System\CurrentControlSet). When the Windows object manager parses this name, it encounters the key object by the name of Registry first and hands the rest of the name to the configuration manager. The configuration manager takes over the name parsing, looking through its internal hive tree to find the desired key or value. Before we describe the flow of control for a typical registry operation, we need to discuss key objects and *key control blocks*. Whenever an application opens or creates a registry key, the object manager gives a handle with which to reference the key to the application. The handle corresponds to a key object that the configuration manager allocates with the help of the object manager. By using the object manager's object support, the configuration manager takes advantage of the security and reference-counting functionality that the object manager provides.

For each open registry key, the configuration manager also allocates a key control block. A key control block stores the name of the key, includes the cell index of the key node that the control block refers to, and contains a flag that notes whether the configuration manager needs to delete the key cell that the key control block refers to when the last handle for the key closes. Windows places all key control blocks into a hash table to enable quick searches for existing key control blocks by name. A key object points to its corresponding key control block, so if two applications open the same registry key, each will receive a key object, and both key objects will point to a common key control block.

When an application opens an existing registry key, the flow of control starts with the application specifying the name of the key in a registry API that invokes the object manager's name-parsing routine. The object manager, upon encountering the configuration manager's registry key object in the namespace, hands the path name to the configuration manager. The configuration manager performs a lookup on the key control block hash table. If the related key control block is found there, there's no need for any further work; otherwise, the lookup provides the configuration manager with the closest key control block to the searched key, and the lookup continues by using the in-memory hive data structures to search through keys and subkeys to find the specified key. If the configuration manager finds the key cell, the configuration manager searches the key control block tree to determine whether the key is open (by the same or another application). The search routine is optimized to always start from the closest ancestor with a key control block already opened. For example, if an application opens \Registry\Machine\Key1\Subkey2, and \Registry\Machine is already opened, the parse routine uses the key control block of \Registry\Machine as a starting point. If the key is open, the configuration manager increments the existing key control block's reference count. If the key isn't open, the configuration manager allocates a new key control block and inserts it into the tree. Then the configuration manager allocates a key object, points the key object at the key control block, and returns control to the object manager, which returns a handle to the application.

When an application creates a new registry key, the configuration manager first finds the key cell for the new key's parent. The configuration manager then searches the list of free cells for the hive in which the new key will reside to determine whether cells exist that are large enough to hold the new key cell. If there aren't any free cells large enough, the configuration manager allocates a new bin and uses it for the cell, placing any space at the end of the bin on the free cell list. The new key cell fills with pertinent information—including the key's name—and the configuration manager adds the key cell to the subkey list of the parent key's subkey-list cell. Finally, the system stores the cell index of the parent cell in the new subkey's key cell.

The configuration manager uses a key control block's reference count to determine when to delete the key control block. When all the handles that refer to a key in a key control block close, the reference count becomes 0, which denotes that the key control block is no longer necessary. If an application that calls an API to delete the key sets the delete flag, the configuration manager can delete the associated key from the key's hive because it knows that no application is keeping the key open.

EXPERIMENT: Viewing Key Control Blocks

You can use the kernel debugger to list all the key control blocks allocated on a system with the command *!reg openkeys*. Alternatively, if you want to view the key control block for a particular open key, use *!reg findkcb*:

```
kd> !reg findkcb \registry\machine\software\microsoft

Found KCB = e1034d40 :: \REGISTRY\MACHINE\SOFTWARE\MICROSOFT
```

You can then examine a reported key control block with the *!reg kcb* command:

```
kd> !reg kcb e1034d40

Key                : \REGISTRY\MACHINE\SOFTWARE\MICROSOFT
RefCount           : 1f
Flags              : CompressedName, Stable
ExtFlags           :
Parent             : 0xe1997368
KeyHive            : 0xe1c8a768
KeyCell            : 0x64e598 [cell index]
TotalLevels        : 4
DelayedCloseIndex: 2048
MaxNameLen         : 0x3c
MaxValueNameLen   : 0x0
MaxValueDataLen   : 0x0
LastWriteTime     : 0x 1c42501:0x7eb6d470
KeyBodyListHead   : 0xe1034d70 0xe1034d70
SubKeyCount       : 137
ValueCache.Count  : 0
KCBLock            : 0xe1034d40
KeyLock            : 0xe1034d40
```

The Flags field indicates that the name is stored in compressed form, and the SubKeyCount field shows that the key has 137 subkeys.

Stable Storage

To make sure that a nonvolatile registry hive (one with an on-disk file) is always in a recoverable state, the configuration manager uses *log hives*. Each nonvolatile hive has an associated log hive, which is a hidden file with the same base name as the hive and a *logN* extension. To ensure forward progress, the configuration manger uses a dual-logging scheme. There are potentially two log files: *.log1* and *.log2*. If, for any reason, *.log1* was written but a failure occurred while writing dirty data to the primary log file, the next time a flush happens, a switch to *.log2* will occur with the cumulative dirty data. If that fails as well, the cumulative dirty data (the data in *.log1* and the data that was dirtied in between) is saved in *.log2*. As a consequence, *.log1* will be used again next time around, until a successful write operation is done to the primary log file. If no failure occurs, only *.log1* is used.

For example, if you look in your %SystemRoot%\System32\Config directory (and you have the Show Hidden Files And Folders folder option selected), you'll see System.log1, Sam.log1, and other .log1 and .log2 files. When a hive initializes, the configuration manager allocates a bit array in which each bit represents a 512-byte portion, or *sector*, of the hive. This array is called the *dirty sector array* because an *on* bit in the array means that the system has modified the corresponding sector in the hive in memory and must write the sector back to the hive file. (An *off* bit means that the corresponding sector is up to date with the in-memory hive's contents.)

When the creation of a new key or value or the modification of an existing key or value takes place, the configuration manager notes the sectors of the hive that change in the hive's dirty sector array. Then the configuration manager schedules a lazy write operation, or a *hive sync*. The hive lazy writer system thread wakes up 5 seconds after the request to synchronize the hive and writes dirty hive sectors for all hives from memory to the hive files on disk. Thus, the system flushes, at the same time, all the registry modifications that take place between the time a hive sync is requested and the time the hive sync occurs. When a hive sync takes place, the next hive sync will occur no sooner than 5 seconds later.

> **Note** The *RegFlushKey* API's name implies that the function only flushes modified data for a specified key to disk, but it actually triggers a full registry flush, which has a major performance impact on the system. For that reason and the fact that the registry automatically makes sure that modified data is in stable storage within seconds, application programmers should avoid using it.

If the lazy writer simply wrote all a hive's dirty sectors to the hive file and the system crashed in mid-operation, the hive file would be in an inconsistent (corrupted) and unrecoverable state. To prevent such an occurrence, the lazy writer first dumps the hive's dirty sector array and all the dirty sectors to the hive's log file, increasing the log file's size if necessary. The lazy writer then updates a sequence number in the hive's base block and writes the dirty sectors to the hive. When the lazy writer is finished, it updates a second sequence number in the base block. Thus, if the system crashes during the write operations to the hive, at the next reboot the configuration manager will notice that the two sequence numbers in the hive's base block don't match. The configuration manager can update the hive with the dirty sectors in the hive's log file to roll the hive forward. The hive is then up to date and consistent.

The Windows Boot Loader also contains some code related to registry reliability. For example, it can parse the System.log file before the kernel is loaded and do repairs to fix consistency. Additionally, in certain cases of hive corruption (such as if a base block, bin, or cell contains data that fails consistency checks) the configuration manager can reinitialize corrupted data structures, possibly deleting subkeys in the process, and continue normal operation. If it has to resort to self-healing operation, it pops up a system error dialog box notifying the user.

 Note When you look at the hidden files on %SystemRoot%\System32\Config, you'll also see a file named System.sav. System.sav is the version of the SYSTEM hive that served as the initial copy of the System hive and is what Windows Setup copied from the install media.

Registry Filtering

The configuration manager in the Windows kernel implements a powerful model of registry filtering, which allows for monitoring of registry activity by tools such as Process Monitor. When a driver uses the callback mechanism, it registers a callback function with the configuration manager. The configuration manager executes the driver's callback function before and after the execution of registry system services so that the driver has full visibility and control over registry accesses. Antivirus products that scan registry data for viruses or prevent unauthorized processes from modifying the registry are other users of the callback mechanism.

Registry callbacks are also associated with the concept of *altitudes*. Altitudes are a way for different vendors to register a "height" on the registry filtering stack so that the order in which the system calls each callback routine can be deterministic and correct. This avoids a scenario in which an antivirus product would be scanning encrypted keys before an encryption product would run its own callback to decrypt them. With the Windows registry callback model, both types of tools are assigned a base altitude corresponding to the type of filtering they are doing—in this case, encryption versus scanning. Secondly, companies that create these types of tools must register with Microsoft so that within their own group, they will not collide with similar and/or competing products. The most up-to-date version of this list can be downloaded from *http://download.microsoft.com/download/9/c/5/9c5b2167-8017-4bae-9fde-d599bac8184a/Alloc-Alt.xls*.

The filtering model also includes the ability to either completely take over the processing of the registry operation (bypassing the configuration manager and preventing it from handling the request) or redirect the operation to a different operation (such as Wow64's registry redirection). Additionally, it is also possible to modify the output parameters as well as the return value of a registry operation.

Finally, drivers can assign and tag per-key or per-operation driver-defined information for their own purposes. A driver can create and assign this context data during a create or open operation, which the configuration manager will remember and return during each subsequent operation on the key.

Registry Optimizations

The configuration manager makes a few noteworthy performance optimizations. First, virtually every registry key has a security descriptor that protects access to the key. Storing a

unique security-descriptor copy for every key in a hive would be highly inefficient, however, because the same security settings often apply to entire subtrees of the registry. When the system applies security to a key, the configuration manager checks a pool of the unique security descriptors used within the same hive as the key to which new security is being applied, and it shares any existing descriptor for the key, ensuring that there is at most one copy of every unique security descriptor in a hive.

The configuration manager also optimizes the way it stores key and value names in a hive. Although the registry is fully Unicode-capable and specifies all names using the Unicode convention, if a name contains only ASCII characters, the configuration manager stores the name in ASCII form in the hive. When the configuration manager reads the name (such as when performing name lookups), it converts the name into Unicode form in memory. Storing the name in ASCII form can significantly reduce the size of a hive.

To minimize memory usage, key control blocks don't store full key registry path names. Instead, they reference only a key's name. For example, a key control block that refers to \Registry\System\Control would refer to the name *Control* rather than to the full path. A further memory optimization is that the configuration manager uses key name control blocks to store key names, and all key control blocks for keys with the same name share the same key name control block. To optimize performance, the configuration manager stores the key control block names in a hash table for quick lookups.

To provide fast access to key control blocks, the configuration manager stores frequently accessed key control blocks in the cache table, which is configured as a hash table. When the configuration manager needs to look up a key control block, it first checks the cache table. Finally, the configuration manager has another cache, the delayed close table, that stores key control blocks that applications close so that an application can quickly reopen a key it has recently closed. The configuration manager removes the oldest key control blocks from the delayed close table as it adds the most recently closed blocks to the table.

Services

Almost every operating system has a mechanism to start processes at system startup time that provide services not tied to an interactive user. In Windows, such processes are called *services* or *Windows services*, because they rely on the Windows API to interact with the system. Services are similar to UNIX daemon processes and often implement the server side of client/server applications. An example of a Windows service might be a Web server, because it must be running regardless of whether anyone is logged on to the computer and it must start running when the system starts so that an administrator doesn't have to remember, or even be present, to start it.

Windows services consist of three components: a service application, a service control program (SCP), and the service control manager (SCM). First, we'll describe service applications, service accounts, and the operations of the SCM. Then we'll explain how auto-start services are started during the system boot. We'll also cover the steps the SCM takes when a service fails during its startup and the way the SCM shuts down services.

Service Applications

Service applications, such as Web servers, consist of at least one executable that runs as a Windows service. A user wanting to start, stop, or configure a service uses an SCP. Although Windows supplies built-in SCPs that provide general start, stop, pause, and continue functionality, some service applications include their own SCP that allows administrators to specify configuration settings particular to the service they manage.

Service applications are simply Windows executables (GUI or console) with additional code to receive commands from the SCM as well as to communicate the application's status back to the SCM. Because most services don't have a user interface, they are built as console programs.

When you install an application that includes a service, the application's setup program must register the service with the system. To register the service, the setup program calls the Windows *CreateService* function, a services-related function implemented in Advapi32.dll (%SystemRoot%\System32\Advapi32.dll). Advapi32, the "Advanced API" DLL, implements all the client-side SCM APIs.

When a setup program registers a service by calling *CreateService*, a message is sent to the SCM on the machine where the service will reside. The SCM then creates a registry key for the service under HKLM\SYSTEM\CurrentControlSet\Services. The Services key is the non-volatile representation of the SCM's database. The individual keys for each service define the path of the executable image that contains the service as well as parameters and configuration options.

After creating a service, an installation or management application can start the service via the *StartService* function. Because some service-based applications also must initialize during the boot process to function, it's not unusual for a setup program to register a service as an auto-start service, ask the user to reboot the system to complete an installation, and let the SCM start the service as the system boots.

When a program calls *CreateService*, it must specify a number of parameters describing the service's characteristics. The characteristics include the service's type (whether it's a service that runs in its own process rather than a service that shares a process with other services), the location of the service's executable image file, an optional display name, an optional

account name and password used to start the service in a particular account's security context, a start type that indicates whether the service starts automatically when the system boots or manually under the direction of an SCP, an error code that indicates how the system should react if the service detects an error when starting, and, if the service starts automatically, optional information that specifies when the service starts relative to other services.

The SCM stores each characteristic as a value in the service's registry key. Figure 4-6 shows an example of a service registry key.

FIGURE 4-6 Example of a service registry key

Table 4-7 lists all the service characteristics, many of which also apply to device drivers. (Not every characteristic applies to every type of service or device driver.) If a service needs to store configuration information that is private to the service, the convention is to create a subkey named Parameters under its service key and then store the configuration information in values under that subkey. The service then can retrieve the values by using standard registry functions.

Note The SCM does not access a service's Parameters subkey until the service is deleted, at which time the SCM deletes the service's entire key, including subkeys like Parameters.

TABLE 4-7 **Service and Driver Registry Parameters**

Value Setting	Value Name	Value Setting Description
Start	SERVICE_BOOT_START (0)	Winload preloads the driver so that it is in memory during the boot. These drivers are initialized just prior to SERVICE_ SYSTEM_START drivers.
	SERVICE_SYSTEM_START (1)	The driver loads and initializes during kernel initialization after SERVICE_ BOOT_START drivers have initialized.
	SERVICE_AUTO_START (2)	The SCM starts the driver or service after the SCM process, Services.exe, starts.
	SERVICE_DEMAND_START (3)	The SCM starts the driver or service on demand.
	SERVICE_DISABLED (4)	The driver or service doesn't load or initialize.
ErrorControl	SERVICE_ERROR_IGNORE (0)	Any error the driver or service returns is ignored and no warning is logged or displayed.
	SERVICE_ERROR_NORMAL (1)	If the driver or service reports an error, an event log message is written.
	SERVICE_ERROR_SEVERE (2)	If the driver or service returns an error and last known good isn't being used, reboot into last known good; otherwise, continue the boot.
	SERVICE_ERROR_CRITICAL (3)	If the driver or service returns an error and last known good isn't being used, reboot into last known good; otherwise, stop the boot with a blue screen crash.
Type	SERVICE_KERNEL_DRIVER (1)	Device driver.
	SERVICE_FILE_SYSTEM_DRIVER (2)	Kernel-mode file system driver.
	SERVICE_ADAPTER (4)	Obsolete.
	SERVICE_RECOGNIZER_DRIVER (8)	File system recognizer driver.
	SERVICE_WIN32_OWN_PROCESS (16)	The service runs in a process that hosts only one service.
	SERVICE_WIN32_SHARE_PROCESS (32)	The service runs in a process that hosts multiple services.

Value Setting	Value Name	Value Setting Description
	SERVICE_INTERACTIVE_PROCESS (256)	The service is allowed to display windows on the console and receive user input, but only on the console session (0) to prevent interacting with user/console applications on other sessions.
Group	Group name	The driver or service initializes when its group is initialized.
Tag	Tag number	The specified location in a group initialization order. This parameter doesn't apply to services.
ImagePath	Path to service or driver executable file	If *ImagePath* isn't specified, the I/O manager looks for drivers in %SystemRoot%\System32\Drivers. Required for Windows services.
DependOnGroup	Group name	The driver or service won't load unless a driver or service from the specified group loads.
DependOnService	Service name	The service won't load until after the specified service loads. This parameter doesn't apply to device drivers other than those with a start type of SERVICE_AUTO_START or SERVICE_DEMAND_START.
ObjectName	Usually LocalSystem, but can be an account name, such as .\Administrator	Specifies the account in which the service will run. If ObjectName isn't specified, LocalSystem is the account used. This parameter doesn't apply to device drivers.
DisplayName	Name of service	The service application shows services by this name. If no name is specified, the name of the service's registry key becomes its name.
Description	Description of service	Up to 32767-byte description of the service.
FailureActions	Description of actions the SCM should take when service process exits unexpectedly	Failure actions include restarting the service process, rebooting the system, and running a specified program. This value doesn't apply to drivers.
FailureCommand	Program command line	The SCM reads this value only if FailureActions specifies that a program should execute upon service failure. This value doesn't apply to drivers.

Value Setting	Value Name	Value Setting Description
DelayedAutoStart	0 or 1 (TRUE or FALSE)	Tells the SCM to start this service after a certain delay has passed since the SCM was starting. This reduces the number of services starting simultaneously during startup.
PreshutdownTimeout	Timeout in milliseconds	This value allows services to override the default preshutdown notification timeout of 180 seconds. After this timeout, the SCM will perform shutdown actions on the service.
ServiceSidType	SERVICE_SID_TYPE_NONE (0)	Backward compatibility setting.
	SERVICE_SID_TYPE_UNRESTRICTED (1)	The SCM will add the service SID as a group owner to the service process's token when it is created.
	SERVICE_SID_TYPE_RESTRICTED (3)	Same as above, but the SCM will also add the service SID to the restricted SID list of the service process, along with the world, logon, and write-restricted SIDs.
RequiredPrivileges	List of privileges	This value contains the list of privileges that the service requires to function. The SCM will compute their union when creating the token for the shared process related to this service, if any.
Security	Security descriptor	This value contains the optional security descriptor that defines who has what access to the service object created internally by the SCM. If this value is omitted, the SCM applies a default security descriptor.

Notice that Type values include three that apply to device drivers: device driver, file system driver, and file system recognizer. These are used by Windows device drivers, which also store their parameters as registry data in the Services registry key. The SCM is responsible for starting drivers with a Start value of SERVICE_AUTO_START or SERVICE_DEMAND_START, so it's natural for the SCM database to include drivers. Services use the other types, SERVICE_WIN32_OWN_PROCESS and SERVICE_WIN32_SHARE_PROCESS, which are mutually exclusive.

An executable that hosts more than one service specifies the SERVICE_WIN32_SHARE_ PROCESS type.

An advantage to having a process run more than one service is that the system resources that would otherwise be required to run them in distinct processes are saved. A potential disadvantage is that if one of the services of a collection running in the same process causes an error that terminates the process, all the services of that process terminate. Also, another limitation is that all the services must run under the same account (however, if a service takes advantage of service security hardening mechanisms added in Windows Vista and Windows Server 2008, it can limit some of its exposure to malicious attacks).

When the SCM starts a service process, the process immediately invokes the *StartService-CtrlDispatcher* function. *StartServiceCtrlDispatcher* accepts a list of entry points into services, one entry point for each service in the process. Each entry point is identified by the name of the service the entry point corresponds to. After making a named pipe communications con-nection to the SCM, *StartServiceCtrlDispatcher* sits in a loop (or for better performance, regis-ters a notification) waiting for commands to come through the pipe from the SCM. The SCM sends a service-start command each time it starts a service the process owns. For each start command it receives, the *StartServiceCtrlDispatcher* function creates a thread, called a service thread, to invoke the starting service's entry point and implement the command loop for the service. *StartServiceCtrlDispatcher* waits indefinitely for commands from the SCM and returns control to the process's main function only when all the process's services have stopped, allowing the service process to clean up resources before exiting.

A service entry point's first action is to call the *RegisterServiceCtrlHandler* function. This func-tion receives and stores a pointer to a function, called the *control handler*, which the service implements to handle various commands it receives from the SCM. *RegisterServiceCtrlHandler* doesn't communicate with the SCM, but it stores the function in local process memory for the *StartServiceCtrlDispatcher* function. The service entry point continues initializing the ser-vice, which can include allocating memory, creating communications end points, and reading private configuration data from the registry. A convention most services follow is to store their parameters under a subkey of their service registry key, named Parameters.

While the entry point is initializing the service, it might periodically send status messages, using the *SetServiceStatus* function, to the SCM indicating how the service's startup is pro-gressing. After the entry point finishes initialization, a service thread usually sits in a loop waiting for requests from client applications. For example, a Web server would initialize a TCP listen socket and wait for inbound HTTP connection requests.

A service process's main thread, which executes in the *StartServiceCtrlDispatcher* function, receives SCM commands directed at services in the process and invokes the target service's control handler function (stored by *RegisterServiceCtrlHandler*). SCM commands include stop,

pause, resume, interrogate, and shutdown or application-defined commands. Figure 4-7 shows the internal organization of a service process. Pictured are the two threads that make up a process hosting one service: the main thread and the service thread.

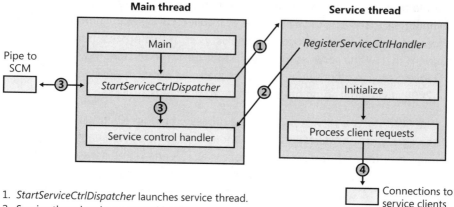

1. *StartServiceCtrlDispatcher* launches service thread.
2. Service thread registers control handler.
3. *StartServiceCtrlDispatcher* calls handlers in response to SCM commands.
4. Service thread processes client requests.

FIGURE 4-7 Inside a service process

Service Accounts

The security context of a service is an important consideration for service developers as well as for system administrators because it dictates what resources the process can access. Unless a service installation program or administrator specifies otherwise, most services run in the security context of the *local system account* (displayed sometimes as SYSTEM and other times as LocalSystem). Two other built-in accounts are the *network service* and *local service* accounts. These accounts have fewer capabilities than the local system account from a security standpoint, and any built-in Windows service that does not require the power of the local system account runs in the appropriate alternate service account. The following subsections describe the special characteristics of these accounts.

The Local System Account

The local system account is the same account in which core Windows user-mode operating system components run, including the Session Manager (%SystemRoot%\System32\Smss.exe), the Windows subsystem process (Csrss.exe), the Local Security Authority process (%SystemRoot%\System32\Lsass.exe), and the Logon process (%SystemRoot%\System32\Winlogon.exe). For more information on these latter two processes, see Chapter 6.

From a security perspective, the local system account is extremely powerful—more powerful than any local or domain account when it comes to security ability on a local system. This account has the following characteristics:

- It is a member of the local administrators group. Table 4-8 shows the groups to which the local system account belongs. (See Chapter 6 for information on how group membership is used in object access checks.)

- It has the right to enable virtually every privilege (even privileges not normally granted to the local administrator account, such as creating security tokens). See Table 4-9 for the list of privileges assigned to the local system account. (Chapter 6 describes the use of each privilege.)

- Most files and registry keys grant full access to the local system account. (Even if they don't grant full access, a process running under the local system account can exercise the take-ownership privilege to gain access.)

- Processes running under the local system account run with the default user profile (HKU\.DEFAULT). Therefore, they can't access configuration information stored in the user profiles of other accounts.

- When a system is a member of a Windows domain, the local system account includes the machine security identifier (SID) for the computer on which a service process is running. Therefore, a service running in the local system account will be automatically authenticated on other machines in the same forest by using its computer account. (A *forest* is a grouping of domains.)

- Unless the machine account is specifically granted access to resources (such as network shares, named pipes, and so on), a process can access network resources that allow null sessions—that is, connections that require no credentials. You can specify the shares and pipes on a particular computer that permit null sessions in the NullSessionPipes and NullSessionShares registry values under HKLM\SYSTEM\CurrentControlSet\ Services\lanmanserver\parameters.

TABLE 4-8 Service Account Group Membership

Local System	Network Service	Local Service
Everyone	Everyone	Everyone
Authenticated Users	Authenticated Users	Authenticated Users
Administrators	Users	Users
	Local	Local
	Network Service	Local Service
	Service	Service

TABLE 4-9 Service Account Privileges

Local System	Network Service	Local Service
SeAssignPrimaryToken Privilege	SeAssignPrimaryToken Privilege	SeAssignPrimaryTokenPrivilege
SeAuditPrivilege	SeAuditPrivilege	SeAuditPrivilege
SeBackupPrivilege	SeChangeNotifyPrivilege	SeChangeNotifyPrivilege
SeChangeNotifyPrivilege	SeCreateGlobalPrivilege	SeCreateGlobalPrivilege
SeCreateGlobalPrivilege	SeImpersonatePrivilege	SeImpersonatePrivilege
SeCreatePagefilePrivilege	SeIncreaseQuotaPrivilege	SeIncreaseQuotaPrivilege
SeCreatePermanentPrivilege	SeShutdownPrivilege	SeShutdownPrivilege
SeCreateTokenPrivilege	SeUndockPrivilege (client only)	SeUndockPrivilege (client only)
SeDebugPrivilege	Privileges assigned to the Everyone, Authenticated Users, and Users groups	Privileges assigned to the Everyone, Authenticated Users, and Users groups
SeImpersonatePrivilege		
SeIncreaseBasePriorityPrivilege		
SeIncreaseQuotaPrivilege		
SeLoadDriverPrivilege		
SeLockMemoryPrivilege		
SeManageVolumePrivilege		
SeProfileSingleProcessPrivilege		
SeRestorePrivilege		
SeSecurityPrivilege		
SeShutdownPrivilege		
SeSystemEnvironmentPrivilege		
SeSystemTimePrivilege		
SeTakeOwnershipPrivilege		
SeTcbPrivilege		
SeUndockPrivilege (client only)		

The Network Service Account

The network service account is intended for use by services that want to authenticate to other machines on the network using the computer account, as does the local system account, but do not have the need for membership in the Administrators group or the use of many of the privileges assigned to the local system account. Because the network service account does not belong to the Administrators group, services running in the network service account by default have access to far fewer registry keys and file system folders and files than the services running in the local system account. Further, the assignment of few privileges limits the scope of a compromised network service process. For example, a process running in the network service account cannot load a device driver or open arbitrary processes.

Another difference between the network service and local system accounts is that processes running in the network service account use the network service account's profile. The registry component of the network service profile loads under HKU\S-1-5-20, and the files and directories that make up the component reside in %SystemRoot%\ServiceProfiles\NetworkService.

A service that runs in the network service account is the DNS client, which is responsible for resolving DNS names and for locating domain controllers.

The Local Service Account

The local service account is virtually identical to the network service account with the important difference that it can access only network resources that allow anonymous access. Table 4-9 shows that the network service account has the same privileges as the local service account, and Table 4-8 shows that it belongs to the same groups with the exception that it belongs to the Network Service group instead of the Local Service group. The profile used by processes running in the local service loads into HKU\S-1-5-19 and is stored in %SystemRoot%\ServiceProfiles\LocalService.

Examples of services that run in the local service account include the Remote Registry Service, which allows remote access to the local system's registry, and the LmHosts service, which performs NetBIOS name resolution.

Running Services in Alternate Accounts

Because of the restrictions just outlined, some services need to run with the security credentials of a user account. You can configure a service to run in an alternate account when the service is created or by specifying an account and password that the service should run under with the Windows Services MMC snap-in. In the Services snap-in, right-click on a service and select Properties, click the Log On tab, and select the This Account option, as shown in Figure 4-8.

Running with Least Privilege

Prior to Windows Vista and Windows Server 2008, services were subject to an all-or-nothing model, meaning that all privileges available to the account the service process was running under would be available to a service running in the process that might require only a subset of those privileges. To better conform to the principle of least privilege, in which Windows assigns services only the privileges they require, in Windows Vista and Windows Server 2008 developers can specify the privileges their service requires, and the SCM creates a security token that contains only those privileges.

FIGURE 4-8 Service account settings

> **Note** The privileges a service specifies must be a subset of those that are available to the service account in which it runs

Service developers use the *ChangeServiceConfig2* API to indicate the list of privileges they desire. The API saves that information in the registry under the Parameters key for the service. When the service starts, the SCM reads the key and adds those privileges to the token of the process in which the service is running.

If there is a RequiredPrivileges value and the service is stand-alone (running as a dedicated process), the SCM will create a token containing only the privileges that the service needs. For services running as part of a multiservice service process (as are most services that are part of Windows) and specifying required privileges, the SCM will compute the union of those privileges and combine them for the service-hosting process's token. In other words, only the privileges not specified by any of the services that are part of that service group will be removed. In the case in which the registry value does not exist, the SCM has no choice but to assume that the service is either incompatible with least privileges or requires all privileges in order to function. In this case, the full token is created, containing all privileges, and no additional security is offered by this model. To strip almost all privileges, services can specify only the "Change Notify" privilege.

EXPERIMENT: Viewing Privileges Required by Services

You can look at the privileges a service requires with the Service Control utility, Sc.exe, and the qprivs option. Additionally, Process Explorer can show you information about the security token of any service process on the system, so you can compare the information returned by Sc.exe with the privileges part of the token. The following steps show you how to do this for some of the best locked-down services on the system.

1. Use Sc.exe to take a look at the required privileges specified by Dhcp by typing into a command prompt:

 sc qprivs dhcp

 You should see two privileges being requested: the SeCreateGlobalPrivilege and the SeChangeNotifyPrivilege.

2. Run Process Explorer and take a look at the process list.

 You should see a couple of Svchost.exe processes that are hosting the services on your machine. Process Explorer highlights these in pink.

3. Now locate the service hosting process in which the Dhcp service is running. It should be running alongside other services that are part of the LocalServiceNetworkRestricted service group, such as the Audiosrv service and Eventlog service. You can do this by hovering the mouse over each Svchost process and reading the tooltip, which contains the names of the services running inside the service host.

4. Once you've found the process, double-click to open the Properties dialog box and select the Security tab.

Note that although the service is running as part of the local service account, the list of privileges Windows assigned to it is much shorter than the list available to the local service account shown in Table 4-9.

Because for a service-hosting process, the privileges part of the token is the union of the privileges requested by all the services running inside it, this must mean that services such as Audiosrv and Eventlog have not requested privileges other than the ones shown by Process Explorer. You can verify this by running the Sc.exe tool on those other services as well.

Service Isolation

Although restricting the privileges that a service has access to helps lessen the ability of a compromised service process to compromise other processes, it does nothing to isolate the service from resources that the account in which it is running has access to under normal conditions. As mentioned earlier, the local system account has complete access to critical system files, registry keys, and other securable objects on the system because the access control lists (ACLs) grant permissions to that account.

At times, access to some of these resources is indeed critical to a service's operation, while other objects should be secured from the service. Previously, to avoid running in the local system account to obtain access to required resources, a service would be run under a standard user account and ACLs would be added on the system objects, which greatly increased the risk of malicious code attacking the system. Another solution was to create dedicated

service accounts and set specific ACLs for each account (associated to a service), but this approach easily became an administrative hassle.

Windows now combines these two approaches into a much more manageable solution: it allows services to run in a nonprivileged account but still have access to specific privileged resources without lowering the security of those objects. In a manner similar to the second pre–Windows Vista solution, the ACLs on an object can now set permissions directly for a service, but not by requiring a dedicated account. Instead, the SCM generates a service SID to represent a service, and this SID can be used to set permissions on resources such as registry keys and files. Service SIDs are implemented in the group SIDs part of the token for any process hosting a service. They are generated by the SCM during system startup for each service that has requested one via the *ChangeServiceConfig2* API. In the case of service-hosting processes (a process that contains more than one service), the process's token will contain the service SIDs of all services that are part of the service group associated with the process, including services that are not started because there is no way to add new SIDs after a token has been created.

The usefulness of having a SID for each service extends beyond the mere ability to add ACL entries and permissions for various objects on the system as a way to have fine-grained control over their access. Our discussion initially covered the case in which certain objects on the system, accessible by a given account, must be protected from a service running within that same account. As we've described to this point, service SIDs only prevent that problem by requiring that Deny entries associated with the service SID be placed on every object that needs to be secured, a clearly unmanageable approach.

To avoid requiring Deny access control entries (ACEs) as a way to prevent services from having access to resources that the user account in which they run does have access, there are two types of service SIDs: the restricted service SID (SERVICE_SID_TYPE_RESTRICTED) and the unrestricted service SID (SERVICE_SID_TYPE_UNRESTRICTED), the latter being the default and the case we've looked at until now.

Unrestricted service SIDs are created as enabled-by-default, group owner SIDs, and the process token is also given a new ACE providing full permission to the service logon SID, which allows the service to continue communicating with the SCM. (A primary use of this would be to enable or disable service SIDs inside the process during service startup or shutdown.)

A restricted service SID, on the other hand, turns the service-hosting process's token into a write-restricted token (see Chapter 6 for more information on tokens), which means that only objects granting explicit write access to the service SID will be writable by the service, regardless of the account it's running as. Because of this, all services running inside that process (part of the same service group) must have the restricted SID type; otherwise, services with the restricted SID type will fail to start. Once the token becomes write-restricted, three more SIDs are added for compatibility reasons:

- The world SID is added to allow write access to objects that are normally accessible by anyone anyway, most importantly certain DLLs in the load path.

- The service logon SID is added to allow the service to communicate with the SCM.

- The write-restricted SID is added to allow objects to explicitly allow any write-restricted service write access to them. For example, Event Tracing for Windows (ETW) uses this SID on its objects to allow any write-restricted service to generate events.

Figure 4-9 shows an example of a service-hosting process containing services that have been marked as having restricted service SIDs. For example, the Base Filtering Engine (BFE), which is responsible for applying Windows Firewall filtering rules, is part of this service because these rules are stored in registry keys that must be protected from malicious write access should a service be compromised (this could allow a service exploit to disable the outgoing traffic firewall rules, enabling bidirectional communication with an attacker, for example).

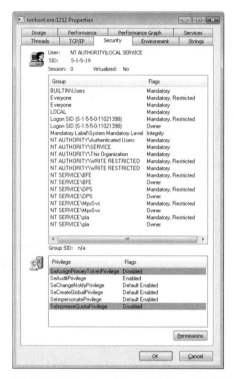

FIGURE 4-9 Service with restricted service SIDs

By blocking write access to objects that would otherwise be writable by the service (through inheriting the permissions of the account it is running as), restricted service SIDs solve the other side of the problem we initially presented because users do not need to do anything to prevent a service running in a privileged account from having write access to critical system files, registry keys, or other objects, limiting the attack exposure of any such service that may have been compromised.

Windows also allows for firewall rules that reference service SIDs linked to one of the three behaviors described in Table 4-10.

TABLE 4-10 Network Restriction Rules

Scenario	Example	Restrictions
Network access blocked	The shell hardware detection service (ShellHWDetection).	All network communications are blocked (both incoming and outgoing).
Network access statically port-restricted	The RPC service (Rpcss) operates on port 135 (TCP and UDP).	Network communications are restricted to specific TCP or UDP ports.
Network access dynamically port-restricted	The DNS service (Dns) listens on variable ports (UDP).	Network communications are restricted to configurable TCP or UDP ports.

Interactive Services and Session 0 Isolation

One restriction for services running under the local system, local service, and network service accounts that has always been present in Windows is that these services could not (without using a special flag on the *MessageBox* function, discussed in a moment) display dialog boxes or windows on the interactive user's desktop. This limitation wasn't the direct result of running under these accounts but rather a consequence of the way the Windows subsystem assigns service processes to window stations. In Windows Vista, this restriction has been further enhanced by the use of sessions, in a model called Session 0 Isolation, a result of which is that services can no longer directly interact with a user's desktop.

The Windows subsystem associates every Windows process with a *window station*. A window station contains desktops, and desktops contain windows. Only one window station can be visible on a console and receive user mouse and keyboard input. In a Terminal Services environment, one window station per session is visible, but services all run as part of the console session. Windows names the visible window station WinSta0, and all interactive processes access WinSta0.

Unless otherwise directed, the Windows subsystem associates services running in the local system account with a nonvisible window station named Service-0x0-3e7$ that all noninteractive services share. The number in the name, *3e7*, represents the logon session identifier that the Local Security Authority process (LSASS) assigns to the logon session the SCM uses for noninteractive services running in the local system account.

Services configured to run under a user account (that is, not the local system account) are run in a different nonvisible window station named with the LSASS logon identifier assigned for the service's logon session. Figure 4-10 shows a sample display from the Sysinternals WinObj tool, viewing the object manager directory in which Windows places window station objects. Visible are the interactive window station (WinSta0) and the noninteractive system service window station (Service-0x0-3e7$).

FIGURE 4-10 List of window stations

Regardless of whether services are running in a user account, the local system account, or the local or network service accounts, services that aren't running on the visible window station can't receive input from a user or display windows on the console. In fact, if a service were to pop up a normal dialog box on the window station, the service would appear hung because no user would be able to see the dialog box, which of course would prevent the user from providing keyboard or mouse input to dismiss it and allow the service to continue executing.

> **Note** In the past, it was possible to use the special MB_SERVICE_NOTIFICATION or MB_DEFAULT_DESKTOP_ONLY flags with the *MessageBox* API to display messages on the interactive window station even if the service was marked as noninteractive. As of Windows Vista and Windows Server 2008, any service using this flag will receive an immediate IDOK return value, and the message box will never be displayed.

In rare cases, a service can have a valid reason to interact with the user via dialog boxes or windows. To configure a service with the right to interact with the user, the SERVICE_INTERACTIVE_PROCESS modifier must be present in the service's registry key's Type parameter. (Note that services configured to run under a user account can't be marked as interactive.) When the SCM starts a service marked as interactive, it launches the service's process in the local system account's security context but connects the service with WinSta0 instead of the noninteractive service window station.

On versions of Windows prior to Windows Vista, this connection to WinSta0 allowed the service to display dialog boxes and windows on the console and allowed those windows to respond to user input because the processes used by the console user run in session 0 and therefore share the window station with the interactive services. However, in Windows Vista and Windows Server 2008, only processes owned by the system and Windows services run in session 0; all other logon sessions, including those of console users, run in different sessions. Any window displayed by processes in session 0 is therefore not visible to the user.

This change was made to prevent "shatter attacks," whereby a less privileged application sends window messages to a window visible on the same window station to exploit a bug in a more privileged process that owns the window, which permits it to execute code in the more privileged process.

To remain compatible with services that depend on user input, Windows includes a service that notifies users when a service has displayed a window. The Interactive Services Detection (UI0Detect) service looks for visible windows on the main desktop of the WinSta0 window station of session 0 and displays a notification dialog box on the console user's desktop, allowing the user to switch to session 0 and view the service's UI (this is akin to connecting to a local Terminal Services session or switching users).

> **Note** The Interactive Services Detection mechanism is purely for application compatibility, and developers are strongly recommended to move away from interactive services and use a secondary, nonprivileged helper application to communicate visually with the user. Local RPC or COM can be used between this helper application and the service for configuration purposes after UI input has been received.

The dialog box, an example of which is shown in Figure 4-11, includes the process name, the time when the UI message was displayed, and the title of the window being displayed. Once the user connects to session 0, a similar dialog box provides a portal back to the user's session. In the figure, the service displaying a window is Microsoft Paint, which was explicitly started by the Sysinternals PsExec utility with options that caused PsExec to run Paint in session 0. You can try this yourself with the following command:

```
psexec –s –i 0 –d mspaint.exe
```

This tells PsExec to run Microsoft Paint as a system process (–s) running on session 0 (–i 0), and to return immediately instead of waiting for the process to finish (–d).

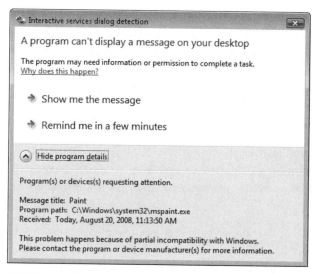

FIGURE 4-11 The Interactive Services Detection service at work

If you click Show Me The Message, you can switch to the console for session 0 (and switch back again with a similar window on the console).

The Service Control Manager

The SCM's executable file is %SystemRoot%\System32\Services.exe, and like most service processes, it runs as a Windows console program. The Wininit process starts the SCM early during the system boot. (Refer to Chapter 13 for details on the boot process.) The SCM's startup function, *SvcCtrlMain*, orchestrates the launching of services that are configured for automatic startup.

SvcCtrlMain first creates a synchronization event named SvcctrlStartEvent_A3752DX that it initializes as nonsignaled. Only after the SCM completes steps necessary to prepare it to receive commands from SCPs does the SCM set the event to a signaled state. The function that an SCP uses to establish a dialog with the SCM is *OpenSCManager*. *OpenSCManager* prevents an SCP from trying to contact the SCM before the SCM has initialized by waiting for SvcctrlStartEvent_A3752DX to become signaled.

Next, *SvcCtrlMain* gets down to business and calls *ScGenerateServiceDB*, the function that builds the SCM's internal service database. *ScGenerateServiceDB* reads and stores the contents of HKLM\SYSTEM\CurrentControlSet\Control\ServiceGroupOrder\List, a REG_MULTI_SZ value that lists the names and order of the defined service groups. A service's registry key contains an optional Group value if that service or device driver needs to control its startup ordering with respect to services from other groups. For example, the Windows networking stack is built from the bottom up, so networking services must specify Group values that

place them later in the startup sequence than networking device drivers. The SCM internally creates a group list that preserves the ordering of the groups it reads from the registry. Groups include (but are not limited to) NDIS, TDI, Primary Disk, Keyboard Port, and Keyboard Class. Add-on and third-party applications can even define their own groups and add them to the list. Microsoft Transaction Server, for example, adds a group named MS Transactions.

ScGenerateServiceDB then scans the contents of HKLM\SYSTEM\CurrentControlSet\Services, creating an entry in the service database for each key it encounters. A database entry includes all the service-related parameters defined for a service as well as fields that track the service's status. The SCM adds entries for device drivers as well as for services because the SCM starts services and drivers marked as auto-start and detects startup failures for drivers marked boot-start and system-start. It also provides a means for applications to query the status of drivers. The I/O manager loads drivers marked boot-start and system-start before any user-mode processes execute, and therefore any drivers having these start types load before the SCM starts.

ScGenerateServiceDB reads a service's Group value to determine its membership in a group and associates this value with the group's entry in the group list created earlier. The function also reads and records in the database the service's group and service dependencies by querying its DependOnGroup and DependOnService registry values. Figure 4-12 shows how the SCM organizes the service entry and group order lists. Notice that the service list is alphabetically sorted. The reason this list is sorted alphabetically is that the SCM creates the list from the Services registry key, and Windows stores registry keys alphabetically.

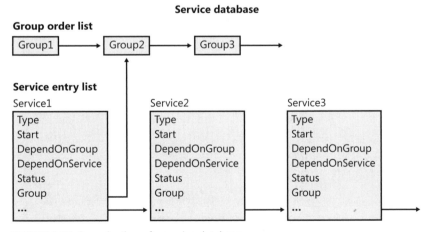

FIGURE 4-12 Organization of a service database

During service startup, the SCM will call on LSASS (for example, to log on a service in a non-local system account), so the SCM waits for LSASS to signal the LSA_RPC_SERVER_ACTIVE synchronization event, which it does when it finishes initializing. Wininit also starts the

LSASS process, so the initialization of LSASS is concurrent with that of the SCM, and the order in which LSASS and the SCM complete initialization can vary. Then *SvcCtrlMain* calls *ScGetBootAndSystemDriverState* to scan the service database looking for boot-start and system-start device driver entries.

ScGetBootAndSystemDriverState determines whether or not a driver successfully started by looking up its name in the object manager namespace directory named \Driver. When a device driver successfully loads, the I/O manager inserts the driver's object in the namespace under this directory, so if its name isn't present, it hasn't loaded. Figure 4-13 shows WinObj displaying the contents of the Driver directory. *SvcCtrlMain* notes the names of drivers that haven't started and that are part of the current profile in a list named ScFailedDrivers.

Before starting the auto-start services, the SCM performs a few more steps. It creates its remote procedure call (RPC) named pipe, which is named \Pipe\Ntsvcs, and then RPC launches a thread to listen on the pipe for incoming messages from SCPs. The SCM then signals its initialization-complete event, SvcctrlStartEvent_A3752DX. Registering a console application shutdown event handler and registering with the Windows subsystem process via *RegisterServiceProcess* prepares the SCM for system shutdown.

FIGURE 4-13 List of driver objects

Network Drive Letters

In addition to its role as an interface to services, the SCM has another totally unrelated responsibility: it notifies GUI applications in a system whenever the system creates or deletes a network drive-letter connection. The SCM waits for the Multiple Provider Router (MPR) to signal a named event, \BaseNamedObjects\ScNetDrvMsg, which MPR signals whenever an application assigns a drive letter to a remote network share or deletes a remote-share drive-letter assignment. (See Chapter 12 for more information on MPR.) When MPR signals the event, the SCM calls the *GetDriveType* Windows function to query the list of connected network drive letters. If the list changes across the event signal, the SCM sends a Windows broadcast message of type WM_DEVICECHANGE. The SCM uses either DBT_ DEVICEREMOVECOMPLETE or DBT_DEVICEARRIVAL as the message's subtype. This message is primarily intended for Windows Explorer so that it can update any open Computer windows to show the presence or absence of a network drive letter.

Service Startup

SvcCtrlMain invokes the SCM function *ScAutoStartServices* to start all services that have a Start value designating auto-start (except delayed auto-start services). *ScAutoStartServices* also starts auto-start device drivers. To avoid confusion, you should assume that the term *services* means services and drivers unless indicated otherwise. The algorithm in *ScAutoStartServices* for starting services in the correct order proceeds in phases, whereby a phase corresponds to a group and phases proceed in the sequence defined by the group ordering stored in the HKLM\SYSTEM\CurrentControlSet\Control\ServiceGroupOrder\List registry value. The List value, shown in Figure 4-14, includes the names of groups in the order that the SCM should start them. Thus, assigning a service to a group has no effect other than to fine-tune its startup with respect to other services belonging to different groups.

FIGURE 4-14 ServiceGroupOrder registry key

When a phase starts, *ScAutoStartServices* marks all the service entries belonging to the phase's group for startup. Then *ScAutoStartServices* loops through the marked services seeing whether it can start each one. Part of this check includes seeing whether the service is marked as delayed auto-start, which causes the SCM to start it at a later stage. (Delayed auto-start services must also be ungrouped.) Another part of the check it makes consists of determining whether the service has a dependency on another group, as specified by the existence of the DependOnGroup value in the service's registry key. If a dependency exists, the group on which the service is dependent must have already initialized, and at least one service of that group must have successfully started. If the service depends on a group that starts later than the service's group in the group startup sequence, the SCM notes a "circular dependency" error for the service. If *ScAutoStartServices* is considering a Windows service or an auto-start device driver, it next checks to see whether the service depends on one or more other services, and if so, if those services have already started. Service dependencies are indicated with the DependOnService registry value in a service's registry key. If a service depends on other services that belong to groups that come later in the ServiceGroupOrder\ List, the SCM also generates a "circular dependency" error and doesn't start the service. If the service depends on any services from the same group that haven't yet started, the service is skipped.

When the dependencies of a service have been satisfied, *ScAutoStartServices* makes a final check to see whether the service is part of the current boot configuration before starting the service. When the system is booted in safe mode, the SCM ensures that the service is either identified by name or by group in the appropriate safe boot registry key. There are two safe boot keys, Minimal and Network, under HKLM\SYSTEM\CurrentControlSet\Control\SafeBoot, and the one that the SCM checks depends on what safe mode the user booted. If the user chose Safe Mode or Safe Mode With Command Prompt at the special boot menu (which you can access by pressing F8 when prompted in the boot process), the SCM references the Minimal key; if the user chose Safe Mode With Networking, the SCM refers to Network. The existence of a string value named Option under the SafeBoot key indicates not only that the system booted in safe mode but also the type of safe mode the user selected. For more information about safe boots, see the section "Safe Mode" in Chapter 13.

Once the SCM decides to start a service, it calls *ScStartService*, which takes different steps for services than for device drivers. When *ScStartService* starts a Windows service, it first determines the name of the file that runs the service's process by reading the ImagePath value from the service's registry key. It then examines the service's Type value, and if that value is SERVICE_WINDOWS_SHARE_PROCESS (0x20), the SCM ensures that the process the service runs in, if already started, is logged on using the same account as specified for the service being started (this is to ensure that the service is not configured with the wrong account, such as a LocalService account, but with an image path pointing to a running Svchost, such as netsvcs, which runs as LocalSystem). A service's ObjectName registry value stores the user account in which the service should run. A service with no ObjectName or an ObjectName of LocalSystem runs in the local system account.

The SCM verifies that the service's process hasn't already been started in a different account by checking to see whether the service's ImagePath value has an entry in an internal SCM database called the *image database*. If the image database doesn't have an entry for the ImagePath value, the SCM creates one. When the SCM creates a new entry, it stores the logon account name used for the service and the data from the service's ImagePath value. The SCM requires services to have an ImagePath value. If a service doesn't have an ImagePath value, the SCM reports an error stating that it couldn't find the service's path and isn't able to start the service. If the SCM locates an existing image database entry with matching ImagePath data, the SCM ensures that the user account information for the service it's starting is the same as the information stored in the database entry—a process can be logged on as only one account, so the SCM reports an error when a service specifies a different account name than another service that has already started in the same process.

The SCM calls *ScLogonAndStartImage* to log on a service if the service's configuration specifies and to start the service's process. The SCM logs on services that don't run in the System account by calling the LSASS function *LogonUserEx*. *LogonUserEx* normally requires a password, but the SCM indicates to LSASS that the password is stored as a service's LSASS "secret" under the key HKLM\SECURITY\Policy\Secrets in the registry. (Keep in mind that the contents of SECURITY aren't typically visible because its default security settings permit access only from the System account.) When the SCM calls *LogonUserEx*, it specifies a service logon as the logon type, so LSASS looks up the password in the Secrets subkey that has a name in the form _SC_<service name>.

The SCM directs LSASS to store a logon password as a secret using the *LsaStorePrivateData* function when an SCP configures a service's logon information. When a logon is successful, *LogonUserEx* returns a handle to an access token to the caller. Windows uses access tokens to represent a user's security context, and the SCM later associates the access token with the process that implements the service.

After a successful logon, the SCM loads the account's profile information, if it's not already loaded, by calling the UserEnv DLL's (%SystemRoot%\System32\Userenv.dll) *LoadUserProfile* function. The value HKLM\SOFTWARE\Microsoft\Windows NT\CurrentVersion\Profile-List\<user profile key>\ProfileImagePath contains the location on disk of a registry hive that *LoadUserProfile* loads into the registry, making the information in the hive the HKEY_CURRENT_USER key for the service.

An interactive service must open the WinSta0 window station, but before *ScLogonAndStart-Image* allows an interactive service to access WinSta0 it checks to see whether the value HKLM\SYSTEM\CurrentControlSet\Control\Windows\NoInteractiveServices is set. Administrators set this value to prevent services marked as interactive from displaying windows on the console. This option is desirable in unattended server environments in which no user is present to respond to the Session 0 UI Discovery notification from interactive services.

As its next step, *ScLogonAndStartImage* proceeds to launch the service's process, if the process hasn't already been started (for another service, for example). The SCM starts the process in a suspended state with the *CreateProcessAsUser* Windows function. The SCM next creates a named pipe through which it communicates with the service process, and it assigns the pipe the name \Pipe\Net\NtControlPipeX, where *X* is a number that increments each time the SCM creates a pipe. The SCM resumes the service process via the *ResumeThread* function and waits for the service to connect to its SCM pipe. If it exists, the registry value HKLM\ SYSTEM\CurrentControlSet\Control\ServicesPipeTimeout determines the length of time that the SCM waits for a service to call *StartServiceCtrlDispatcher* and connect before it gives up, terminates the process, and concludes that the service failed to start. If ServicesPipeTimeout doesn't exist, the SCM uses a default timeout of 30 seconds. The SCM uses the same timeout value for all its service communications.

When a service connects to the SCM through the pipe, the SCM sends the service a start command. If the service fails to respond positively to the start command within the timeout period, the SCM gives up and moves on to start the next service. When a service doesn't respond to a start request, the SCM doesn't terminate the process, as it does when a service doesn't call *StartServiceCtrlDispatcher* within the timeout; instead, it notes an error in the system Event Log that indicates the service failed to start in a timely manner.

If the service the SCM starts with a call to *ScStartService* has a Type registry value of SERVICE_ KERNEL_DRIVER or SERVICE_FILE_SYSTEM_DRIVER, the service is really a device driver, and so *ScStartService* calls *ScLoadDeviceDriver* to load the driver. *ScLoadDeviceDriver* enables the load driver security privilege for the SCM process and then invokes the kernel service *NtLoadDriver*, passing in the data in the ImagePath value of the driver's registry key. Unlike services, drivers don't need to specify an ImagePath value, and if the value is absent, the SCM builds an image path by appending the driver's name to the string %SystemRoot%\ System32\Drivers\.

ScAutoStartServices continues looping through the services belonging to a group until all the services have either started or generated dependency errors. This looping is the SCM's way of automatically ordering services within a group according to their DependOnService dependencies. The SCM will start the services that other services depend on in earlier loops, skipping the dependent services until subsequent loops. Note that the SCM ignores Tag values for Windows services, which you might come across in subkeys under the HKLM\SYSTEM\ CurrentControlSet\Services key; the I/O manager honors Tag values to order device driver startup within a group for boot-start and system-start drivers. Once the SCM completes phases for all the groups listed in the ServiceGroupOrder\List value, it performs a phase for services belonging to groups not listed in the value and then executes a final phase for services without a group.

After handling auto-start services, the SCM calls *ScInitDelayStart*, which queues a delayed work item associated with a worker thread responsible for processing all the services that

ScAutoStartServices skipped because they were marked delayed auto-start. This worker thread will execute after the delay. The default delay is 120 seconds, but it can be overridden by the AutoStartDelay value in HKLM\SYSTEM\CurrentControlSet\Control. The SCM performs the same actions as those used during startup of nondelayed auto-start services.

Delayed Auto-Start Services

Delayed auto-start services were added in Windows Vista and Windows Server 2008 to cope with the growing number of services that are being started when a user logs on, bogging down the boot-up process and increasing the time before a user is able to get responsiveness from the desktop. The design of auto-start services was primarily intended for services required early in the boot process because other services depend on them, a good example being the RPC service, on which all other services depend. The other use was to allow unattended startup of a service, such as the Windows Update service. Because many auto-start services fall in this second category, marking them as delayed auto-start allows critical services to start faster and for the user's desktop to be ready sooner when a user logs on immediately after booting. Configuring a service for delayed auto-start requires calling the *ChangeServiceConfig2* API. You can check the state of the flag for a service by using the qc bits option instead.

 Note If a nondelayed auto-start service has a delayed auto-start service as one of its dependencies, the delayed auto-start flag will be ignored and the service will be started immediately in order to satisfy the dependency.

When it's finished starting all auto-start services and drivers, as well as setting up the delayed auto-start work item, the SCM signals the event \BaseNamedObjects\SC_AutoStartComplete. This event is used by the Windows Setup program to gauge startup progress during installation.

Startup Errors

If a driver or a service reports an error in response to the SCM's startup command, the ErrorControl value of the service's registry key determines how the SCM reacts. If the ErrorControl value is SERVICE_ERROR_IGNORE (0) or the ErrorControl value isn't specified, the SCM simply ignores the error and continues processing service startups. If the ErrorControl value is SERVICE_ERROR_NORMAL (1), the SCM writes an event to the system Event Log that says, "The <service name> service failed to start due to the following error:". The SCM includes the textual representation of the Windows error code that the service returned to the SCM as the reason for the startup failure in the Event Log record. Figure 4-15 shows the Event Log entry that reports a service startup error.

FIGURE 4-15 Service startup failure Event Log entry

If a service with an ErrorControl value of SERVICE_ERROR_SEVERE (2) or SERVICE_ERROR_CRITICAL (3) reports a startup error, the SCM logs a record to the Event Log and then calls the internal function *ScRevertToLastKnownGood*. This function switches the system's registry configuration to a version, named last known good, with which the system last booted successfully. Then it restarts the system using the *NtShutdownSystem* system service, which is implemented in the executive. If the system is already booting with the last known good configuration, the system just reboots.

Accepting the Boot and Last Known Good

Besides starting services, the system charges the SCM with determining when the system's registry configuration, HKLM\SYSTEM\CurrentControlSet, should be saved as the last known good control set. The CurrentControlSet key contains the Services key as a subkey, so CurrentControlSet includes the registry representation of the SCM database. It also contains the Control key, which stores many kernel-mode and user-mode subsystem configuration settings. By default, a successful boot consists of a successful startup of auto-start services and a successful user logon. A boot fails if the system halts because a device driver crashes the system during the boot or if an auto-start service with an ErrorControl value of SERVICE_ERROR_SEVERE or SERVICE_ERROR_CRITICAL reports a startup error.

The SCM obviously knows when it has completed a successful startup of the auto-start services, but Winlogon (%SystemRoot%\System32\Winlogon.exe) must notify it when there is

a successful logon. Winlogon invokes the *NotifyBootConfigStatus* function when a user logs on, and *NotifyBootConfigStatus* sends a message to the SCM. Following the successful start of the auto-start services or the receipt of the message from *NotifyBootConfigStatus* (whichever comes last), the SCM calls the system function *NtInitializeRegistry* to save the current registry startup configuration.

Third-party software developers can supersede Winlogon's definition of a successful logon with their own definition. For example, a system running Microsoft SQL Server might not consider a boot successful until after SQL Server is able to accept and process transactions. Developers impose their definition of a successful boot by writing a boot-verification program and installing the program by pointing to its location on disk with the value stored in the registry key HKLM\SYSTEM\CurrentControlSet\Control\BootVerificationProgram. In addition, a boot-verification program's installation must disable Winlogon's call to *NotifyBootConfigStatus* by setting HKLM\SOFTWARE\Microsoft\Windows NT\CurrentVersion\ Winlogon\ReportBootOk to 0. When a boot-verification program is installed, the SCM launches it after finishing auto-start services and waits for the program's call to *NotifyBootConfigStatus* before saving the last known good control set.

Windows maintains several copies of CurrentControlSet, and CurrentControlSet is really a symbolic registry link that points to one of the copies. The control sets have names in the form HKLM\SYSTEM\ControlSet*nnn*, where *nnn* is a number such as 001 or 002. The HKLM\ SYSTEM\Select key contains values that identify the role of each control set. For example, if CurrentControlSet points to ControlSet001, the Current value under Select has a value of 1. The LastKnownGood value under Select contains the number of the last known good control set, which is the control set last used to boot successfully. Another value that might be on your system under the Select key is Failed, which points to the last control set for which the boot was deemed unsuccessful and aborted in favor of an attempt at booting with the last known good control set. Figure 4-16 displays a system's control sets and Select values.

NtInitializeRegistry takes the contents of the last known good control set and synchronizes it with that of the CurrentControlSet key's tree. If this was the system's first successful boot, the last known good won't exist and the system will create a new control set for it. If the last known good tree exists, the system simply updates it with differences between it and CurrentControlSet.

Last known good is helpful in situations in which a change to CurrentControlSet, such as the modification of a system performance-tuning value under HKLM\SYSTEM\Control or the addition of a service or device driver, causes the subsequent boot to fail. Users can press F8 early in the boot process to bring up a menu that lets them direct the boot to use the last known good control set, rolling the system's registry configuration back to the way it was the last time the system booted successfully. Chapter 13 describes in more detail the use of last known good and other recovery mechanisms for troubleshooting system startup problems.

FIGURE 4-16 Control set selection key

Service Failures

A service can have optional FailureActions and FailureCommand values in its registry key that the SCM records during the service's startup. The SCM registers with the system so that the system signals the SCM when a service process exits. When a service process terminates unexpectedly, the SCM determines which services ran in the process and takes the recovery steps specified by their failure-related registry values.

Additionally, as of Windows Vista and Windows Server 2008, services are no longer limited to requesting failure actions during crashes or unexpected service termination, since other problems, such as a memory leak, could also result in service failure.

If a service enters the SERVICE_STOPPED state and the error code returned to the SCM is not ERROR_SUCCESS, the SCM will check whether the service has the FailureActionsOn-NonCrashFailures flag set and perform the same recovery as if the service had crashed. To use this functionality, the service must be configured via the *ChangeServiceConfig2* API or the system administrator can use the Sc.exe utility with the Failureflag parameter to set FailureActionsOnNonCrashFailures to 1. The default value being 0, the SCM will continue to honor the same behavior as on earlier versions of Windows for all other services.

Actions that a service can configure for the SCM include restarting the service, running a program, and rebooting the computer. Furthermore, a service can specify the failure actions

that take place the first time the service process fails, the second time, and subsequent times, and it can indicate a delay period that the SCM waits before restarting the service if the service asks to be restarted. The service failure action of the IIS Admin Service results in the SCM running the IISReset application, which performs cleanup work and then restarts the service. You can easily manage the recovery actions for a service with the Recovery tab of the service's Properties dialog box in the Services MMC snap-in, as shown in Figure 4-17.

FIGURE 4-17 Service recovery options

Service Shutdown

When Winlogon calls the Windows *ExitWindowsEx* function, *ExitWindowsEx* sends a message to Csrss, the Windows subsystem process, to invoke Csrss's shutdown routine. Csrss loops through the active processes and notifies them that the system is shutting down. For every system process except the SCM, Csrss waits up to the number of seconds specified by HKU\.DEFAULT\Control Panel\Desktop\WaitToKillAppTimeout (which defaults to 20 seconds) for the process to exit before moving on to the next process. When Csrss encounters the SCM process, it also notifies it that the system is shutting down but employs a timeout specific to the SCM. Csrss recognizes the SCM using the process ID Csrss saved when the SCM registered with Csrss using the *RegisterServicesProcess* function during system initialization. The SCM's timeout differs from that of other processes because Csrss knows that the SCM communicates with services that need to perform cleanup when they shut down, and so an administrator might need to tune only the SCM's timeout. The SCM's timeout value resides in the HKLM\SYSTEM\CurrentControlSet\Control\WaitToKillServiceTimeout registry value, and it defaults to 20 seconds.

The SCM's shutdown handler is responsible for sending shutdown notifications to all the services that requested shutdown notification when they initialized with the SCM. The SCM function *ScShutdownAllServices* loops through the SCM services database searching for services desiring shutdown notification and sends each one a shutdown command. For each service to which it sends a shutdown command, the SCM records the value of the service's *wait hint*, a value that a service also specifies when it registers with the SCM. The SCM keeps track of the largest wait hint it receives. After sending the shutdown messages, the SCM waits either until one of the services it notified of shutdown exits or until the time specified by the largest wait hint passes.

If the wait hint expires without a service exiting, the SCM determines whether one or more of the services it was waiting on to exit have sent a message to the SCM telling the SCM that the service is progressing in its shutdown process. If at least one service made progress, the SCM waits again for the duration of the wait hint. The SCM continues executing this wait loop until either all the services have exited or none of the services upon which it's waiting has notified it of progress within the wait hint timeout period.

While the SCM is busy telling services to shut down and waiting for them to exit, Csrss waits for the SCM to exit. On versions of Windows prior to Windows Vista, if Csrss's wait ended without the SCM having exited (the WaitToKillServiceTimeout time expired), Csrss would kill the SCM and continue the shutdown process. Thus, services that failed to shut down in a timely manner were killed. This logic let the system shut down in the face of services that would never complete a shutdown as a result of flawed design, but it meant that services that required more than 20 seconds would not complete their shutdown operations.

Additionally, because the shutdown order is not deterministic, services that might have depended on other services to shut down first (called *shutdown dependencies*) had no way to report this to the SCM and may have never had the chance to clean up either.

To address these needs, Windows now implements preshutdown notifications and shutdown ordering to combat the problems caused by these two scenarios. Preshutdown notifications are sent, using the same mechanism as shutdown notifications, to services that have requested preshutdown notification via the *SetServiceStatus* API, and the SCM will wait for them to be acknowledged.

The idea behind these notifications is to flag services that may take a long time to clean up (such as database server services) and give them more time to complete their work. The SCM will send a progress query request and wait 3 minutes for a service to respond to this notification. If the service does not respond within this time, it will be killed during the shutdown procedure; otherwise, it can keep running as long as it needs as long as it continues to respond to the SCM.

Services that participate in the preshutdown can also specify a shutdown order with respect to other preshutdown services. Services that depend on other services to shut down first (for example, the Group Policy service needs to wait for Windows Update to finish) can specify their shutdown dependencies in the HKLM\SYSTEM\CurrentControlSet\Control\ PreshutdownOrder registry value.

Shared Service Processes

Running every service in its own process instead of having services share a process whenever possible wastes system resources. However, sharing processes means that if any of the services in the process has a bug that causes the process to exit, all the services in that process terminate.

Of the Windows built-in services, some run in their own process and some share a process with other services. For example, the LSASS process contains security-related services—such as the Security Accounts Manager (SamSs) service, the Net Logon (Netlogon) service, and the Crypto Next Generation (CNG) Key Isolation (KeyIso) service.

There is also a "generic" process named Service Host (SvcHost—%SystemRoot%\System32\ Svchost.exe) to contain multiple services. Multiple instances of SvcHost can be running in different processes. Services that run in SvcHost processes include Telephony (TapiSrv), Remote Procedure Call (RpcSs), and Remote Access Connection Manager (RasMan). Windows implements services that run in SvcHost as DLLs and includes an ImagePath definition of the form "%SystemRoot%\System32\svchost.exe –k netsvcs" in the service's registry key. The service's registry key must also have a registry value named ServiceDll under a Parameters subkey that points to the service's DLL file.

All services that share a common SvcHost process specify the same parameter ("–k netsvcs" in the example in the preceding paragraph) so that they have a single entry in the SCM's image database. When the SCM encounters the first service that has a SvcHost ImagePath with a particular parameter during service startup, it creates a new image database entry and launches a SvcHost process with the parameter. The new SvcHost process takes the parameter and looks for a value having the same name as the parameter under HKLM\SOFTWARE\ Microsoft\Windows NT\CurrentVersion\Svchost. SvcHost reads the contents of the value, interpreting it as a list of service names, and notifies the SCM that it's hosting those services when SvcHost registers with the SCM.

When the SCM encounters a SvcHost service (by checking the service type value) during service startup with an ImagePath matching an entry it already has in the image database, it doesn't launch a second process but instead just sends a start command for the service to the SvcHost it already started for that ImagePath value. The existing SvcHost process reads the ServiceDll parameter in the service's registry key and loads the DLL into its process to start the service.

Table 4-11 lists all the default service groupings on Windows Vista and Windows Server 2008 and some of the services that are registered for each of them.

TABLE 4-11 Major Service Groupings

Service Group	Services	Notes
LocalService	Windows Time, COM+ Event System, Remote Registry, UPnP and SSDP, Workstation, WebClient	Services that run in the local service account and make use of the network on various ports or have no network usage at all (and hence no restrictions).
LocalServiceRestricted	Remote API Manager, Windows CE Communications Service (ActiveSync)	Services that run in the local service account and make use of the network on a fixed set of ports. Services run with a write-restricted token.
LocalServiceNetworkRestricted	DHCP, Event Logger, Windows Audio, Peer to Peer Services	Services that run in the local service account and make use of the network on a fixed set of ports.
LocalServiceNoNetwork	Media Center Edition Service, Base Filtering Engine, Performance Logging and Alerts	Services that run in the local service account but make no use of the network at all. Services run with a write-restricted token.
LocalSystemNetworkRestricted	HID Access, User-Mode Driver Framework Service, Superfetch, Program Compatibility Service, WDI System Host Service	Services that run in the local system account and make use of the network on a fixed set of ports.
NetworkService	Cryptographic Services, Terminal Services, KTM over DTC, DNS Client, Telephony	Services that run in the network service account and make use of the network on various ports (or have no enforced network restrictions).
NetworkServiceRestricted	None by default	Services that run in the network service account and make use of the network on a fixed set of ports. Services run with a write-restricted token.
NetworkServiceNetworkRestricted	IPSec Policy Agent	Services that run in the network service account and make use of the network on a fixed set of ports.

EXPERIMENT: Viewing Services Running Inside Processes

The Process Explorer utility shows detailed information about the services running within processes. Run Process Explorer and view the Services tab in the Process Properties dialog box for the following processes: Services.exe, Lsass.exe, and Svchost.exe. Several instances of SvcHost will be running on your system, and you can see the account in which each is running by adding the Username column to the Process Explorer display or by looking at the Username field on the Image tab of a process's Process Properties dialog box. The following screen shows the list of services running within a SvcHost executing in the local service account:

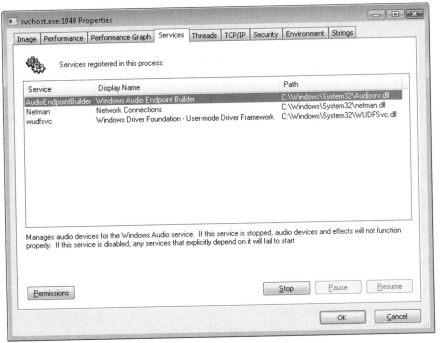

The information displayed includes the service's name, display name, and description, if it has one, which Process Explorer shows beneath the service list when you select a service. Additionally, the path of the DLL containing the service is shown. This information is useful for mapping thread start addresses (shown on the Threads tab) to their respective services, which may help in cases of service-related problems such as troubleshooting high CPU usage.

You can also use the tlist.exe tool from the Debugging Tools for Windows or Tasklist, which ships with Windows, to view the list of services running within processes from a command prompt. The syntax to see services with Tlist is:

```
tlist /s
```

The syntax for tasklist is:

```
tasklist /svc
```

Note that these utilities do not show service display names or descriptions, only service names.

Service Tags

One of the disadvantages of using service-hosting processes is that accounting for CPU time and usage, as well as for the usage of resources, by a specific service is much harder because each service is sharing the memory address space, handle table, and per-process CPU accounting numbers with the other services that are part of the same service group. Although there is always a thread inside the service-hosting process that belongs to a certain service, this association may not always be easy to make. For example, the service may be using worker threads to perform its operation, or perhaps the start address and stack of the thread do not reveal the service's DLL name, making it hard to figure out what kind of work a thread may exactly be doing and to which service it may belong.

Windows Vista and Windows Server 2008 introduce a service attribute called the *service tag*, which the SCM generates by calling *ScGenerateServiceTag* when a service is created or when the service database is generated during system boot. The attribute is simply an index identifying the service. The service tag is stored in the SubProcessTag field of the thread environment block (TEB) of each thread (see Chapter 5 for more information on the TEB) and is propagated across all threads that a main service thread creates (except threads created indirectly by thread pool APIs).

Although the service tag is kept internal to the SCM, several Windows utilities, like Netstat.exe (a utility that you can use for displaying which programs have opened which ports on the network), use undocumented APIs to query service tags and map them to service names. Because the TCP/IP stack saves the service tag of the threads that create TCP/IP end points, when you run Netstat with the –b parameter, Netstat can report the service name for end points created by services. Another tool you can use to look at service tags is ScTagQuery from Winsider Seminars & Solutions Inc. (*www.winsiderss.com/tools/sctag-query.html*). It can query the SCM for the mappings of every service tag and display them either systemwide or per-process. It can also show you to which services all the threads inside a service-hosting process belong (this is conditional on those threads having a proper service tag associated with them). This way, if you have a runaway service consuming lots of CPU time, you can identify the culprit service in case the thread start address or stack does not have an obvious service DLL associated with it.

Service Control Programs

Service control programs are standard Windows applications that use SCM service management functions, including *CreateService*, *OpenService*, *StartService*, *ControlService*, *QueryServiceStatus*, and *DeleteService*. To use the SCM functions, an SCP must first open a communications channel to the SCM by calling the *OpenSCManager* function. At the time of the open call, the SCP must specify what types of actions it wants to perform. For example, if an SCP simply wants to enumerate and display the services present in the SCM's database, it requests enumerate-service access in its call to *OpenSCManager*. During its initialization, the SCM creates an internal object that represents the SCM database and uses the Windows security functions to protect the object with a security descriptor that specifies what accounts can open the object with what access permissions. For example, the security descriptor indicates that the Authenticated Users group can open the SCM object with enumerate-service access. However, only administrators can open the object with the access required to create or delete a service.

As it does for the SCM database, the SCM implements security for services themselves. When an SCP creates a service by using the *CreateService* function, it specifies a security descriptor that the SCM associates internally with the service's entry in the service database. The SCM stores the security descriptor in the service's registry key as the Security value, and it reads that value when it scans the registry's Services key during initialization so that the security settings persist across reboots. In the same way that an SCP must specify what types of access it wants to the SCM database in its call to *OpenSCManager*, an SCP must tell the SCM what access it wants to a service in a call to *OpenService*. Accesses that an SCP can request include the ability to query a service's status and to configure, stop, and start a service.

The SCP you're probably most familiar with is the Services MMC snap-in that's included in Windows, which resides in %SystemRoot%\System32\Filemgmt.dll. Windows also includes Sc.exe (Service Controller tool), a command-line service control program that we've mentioned multiple times.

SCPs sometimes layer service policy on top of what the SCM implements. A good example is the timeout that the Services MMC snap-in implements when a service is started manually. The snap-in presents a progress bar that represents the progress of a service's startup. Services indirectly interact with SCPs by setting their configuration status to reflect their progress as they respond to SCM commands such as the start command. SCPs query the status with the *QueryServiceStatus* function. They can tell when a service actively updates the status versus when a service appears to be hung, and the SCM can take appropriate actions in notifying a user about what the service is doing.

Windows Management Instrumentation

Windows Management Instrumentation (WMI) is an implementation of Web-Based Enterprise Management (WBEM), a standard that the Distributed Management Task Force (DMTF—an industry consortium) defines. The WBEM standard encompasses the design of an extensible enterprise data-collection and data-management facility that has the flexibility and extensibility required to manage local and remote systems that comprise arbitrary components.

WMI Architecture

WMI consists of four main components, as shown in Figure 4-18: management applications, WMI infrastructure, providers, and managed objects. Management applications are Windows applications that access and display or process data that the applications obtain about managed objects. A simple example of a management application is a performance tool replacement that relies on WMI rather than the Performance API to obtain performance information. A more complex example is an enterprise-management tool that lets administrators perform automated inventories of the software and hardware configuration of every computer in their enterprise.

FIGURE 4-18 WMI architecture

Developers typically must target management applications to collect data from and manage specific objects. An object might represent one component, such as a network adapter

device, or a collection of components, such as a computer (the computer object might contain the network adapter object). Providers need to define and export the representation of the objects that management applications are interested in. For example, the vendor of a network adapter might want to add adapter-specific properties to the network adapter WMI support that Windows includes, querying and setting the adapter's state and behavior as the management applications direct. In some cases (for example, for device drivers), Microsoft supplies a provider that has its own API to help developers leverage the provider's implementation for their own managed objects with minimal coding effort.

The WMI infrastructure, the heart of which is the Common Information Model (CIM) Object Manager (CIMOM), is the glue that binds management applications and providers. (CIM is described later in this chapter.) The infrastructure also serves as the object-class store and, in many cases, as the storage manager for persistent object properties. WMI implements the store, or repository, as an on-disk database named the CIMOM Object Repository. As part of its infrastructure, WMI supports several APIs through which management applications access object data and providers supply data and class definitions.

Windows programs use the WMI COM API, the primary management API, to directly interact with WMI. Other APIs layer on top of the COM API and include an Open Database Connectivity (ODBC) adapter for the Microsoft Access database application. A database developer uses the WMI ODBC adapter to embed references to object data in the developer's database. Then the developer can easily generate reports with database queries that contain WMI-based data. WMI ActiveX controls support another layered API. Web developers use the ActiveX controls to construct Web-based interfaces to WMI data. Another management API is the WMI scripting API, for use in script-based applications and Microsoft Visual Basic programs. WMI scripting support exists for all Microsoft programming language technologies.

As they are for management applications, WMI COM interfaces constitute the primary API for providers. However, unlike management applications, which are COM clients, providers are COM or Distributed COM (DCOM) servers (that is, the providers implement COM objects that WMI interacts with). Possible embodiments of a WMI provider include DLLs that load into WMI's manager process or stand-alone Windows applications or Windows services. Microsoft includes a number of built-in providers that present data from well-known sources, such as the Performance API, the registry, the Event Manager, Active Directory, SNMP, and Windows Driver Model (WDM) device drivers. The WMI SDK lets developers develop third-party WMI providers.

Providers

At the core of WBEM is the DMTF-designed CIM specification. The CIM specifies how management systems represent, from a systems management perspective, anything from a computer to an application or device on a computer. Provider developers use the CIM to

represent the components that make up the parts of an application for which the developers want to enable management. Developers use the Managed Object Format (MOF) language to implement a CIM representation.

In addition to defining classes that represent objects, a provider must interface WMI to the objects. WMI classifies providers according to the interface features the providers supply. Table 4-12 lists WMI provider classifications. Note that a provider can implement one or more features; therefore, a provider can be, for example, both a class and an event provider. To clarify the feature definitions in Table 4-12, let's look at a provider that implements several of those features. The Event Log provider supports several objects, including an Event Log Computer, an Event Log Record, and an Event Log File. The Event Log is an Instance provider because it can define multiple instances for several of its classes. One class for which the Event Log provider defines multiple instances is the Event Log File class (Win32_NTEventlogFile); the Event Log provider defines an instance of this class for each of the system's event logs (that is, System Event Log, Application Event Log, and Security Event Log).

TABLE 4-12 Provider Classifications

Classification	Description
Class	Can supply, modify, delete, and enumerate a provider-specific class. Can also support query processing. Active Directory is a rare example of a service that is a class provider.
Instance	Can supply, modify, delete, and enumerate instances of system and provider-specific classes. An instance represents a managed object. Can also support query processing.
Property	Can supply and modify individual object property values.
Method	Supplies methods for a provider-specific class.
Event	Generates event notifications.
Event consumer	Maps a physical consumer to a logical consumer to support event notification.

The Event Log provider defines the instance data and lets management applications enumerate the records. To let management applications use WMI to back up and restore the Event Log files, the Event Log provider implements backup and restore methods for Event Log File objects. Doing so makes the Event Log provider a Method provider. Finally, a management application can register to receive notification whenever a new record writes to one of the Event Logs. Thus, the Event Log provider serves as an Event provider when it uses WMI event notification to tell WMI that Event Log records have arrived.

The Common Information Model and the Managed Object Format Language

The CIM follows in the steps of object-oriented languages such as C++ and Java, in which a modeler designs representations as classes. Working with classes lets developers use the

powerful modeling techniques of inheritance and composition. Subclasses can inherit the attributes of a parent class, and they can add their own characteristics and override the characteristics they inherit from the parent class. A class that inherits properties from another class *derives* from that class. Classes also *compose*: a developer can build a class that includes other classes.

The DMTF provides multiple classes as part of the WBEM standard. These classes are CIM's basic language and represent objects that apply to all areas of management. The classes are part of the CIM *core model*. An example of a core class is CIM_ManagedSystemElement. This class contains a few basic properties that identify physical components such as hardware devices and logical components such as processes and files. The properties include a caption, description, installation date, and status. Thus, the CIM_LogicalElement and CIM_PhysicalElement classes inherit the attributes of the CIM_ManagedSystemElement class. These two classes are also part of the CIM core model. The WBEM standard calls these classes *abstract* classes because they exist solely as classes that other classes inherit (that is, no object instances of an abstract class exist). You can therefore think of abstract classes as templates that define properties for use in other classes.

A second category of classes represents objects that are specific to management areas but independent of a particular implementation. These classes constitute the *common model* and are considered an extension of the core model. An example of a common-model class is the CIM_FileSystem class, which inherits the attributes of CIM_LogicalElement. Because virtually every operating system—including Windows, Linux, and other varieties of UNIX—rely on file-system-based structured storage, the CIM_FileSystem class is an appropriate constituent of the common model.

The final class category, the *extended model*, comprises technology-specific additions to the common model. Windows defines a large set of these classes to represent objects specific to the Windows environment. Because all operating systems store data in files, the CIM common model includes the CIM_LogicalFile class. The CIM_DataFile class inherits the CIM_LogicalFile class, and Windows adds the Win32_PageFile and Win32_ShortcutFile file classes for those Windows file types.

The Event Log provider makes extensive use of inheritance. Figure 4-19 shows a view of the WMI CIM Studio, a class browser that ships with the WMI Administrative Tools that you can obtain from the Microsoft download center at the Microsoft Web site. You can see where the Event Log provider relies on inheritance in the provider's Win32_NTEventlogFile class, which derives from CIM_DataFile. Event Log files are data files that have additional Event Log–specific attributes such as a log file name (LogfileName) and a count of the number of records that the file contains (NumberOfRecords). The tree that the class browser shows reveals that Win32_NTEventlogFile is based on several levels of inheritance, in which CIM_DataFile derives from CIM_LogicalFile, which derives from CIM_LogicalElement, and CIM_LogicalElement derives from CIM_ManagedSystemElement.

FIGURE 4-19 WMI CIM Studio

As stated earlier, WMI provider developers write their classes in the MOF language. The following output shows the definition of the Event Log provider's Win32_NTEventlogFile, which is selected in Figure 4-19. Notice the correlation between the properties that the right panel in Figure 4-19 lists and those properties' definitions in the MOF file below. CIM Studio uses yellow arrows to tag those properties that a class inherits. Thus, you don't see those properties specified in Win32_NTEventlogFile's definition.

```
dynamic: ToInstance, provider("MS_NT_EVENTLOG_PROVIDER"), Locale(1033), UUID("{8502C57B-
5FBB-11D2-AAC1-006008C78BC7}")]
class Win32_NTEventlogFile : CIM_DataFile
{
[read] string LogfileName;
```

```
[read, write] uint32 MaxFileSize;
[read] uint32 NumberOfRecords;
[read, volatile, ValueMap{"0", "1..365", "4294967295"}] string OverWritePolicy;
[read, write, Units("Days"), Range("0-365 | 4294967295")] uint32 OverwriteOutDated;
[read] string Sources[];
[implemented, Privileges{"SeSecurityPrivilege",
"SeBackupPrivilege"}] uint32 ClearEventlog([in] string ArchiveFileName);
[implemented, Privileges{"SeSecurityPrivilege",
"SeBackupPrivilege"}] uint32 BackupEventlog([in] string ArchiveFileName);
};
```

One term worth reviewing is *dynamic*, which is a descriptive designator for the Win32_
NTEventlogFile class that the MOF file in the preceding output shows. *Dynamic* means that
the WMI infrastructure asks the WMI provider for the values of properties associated with
an object of that class whenever a management application queries the object's properties.
A *static* class is one in the WMI repository; the WMI infrastructure refers to the repository to
obtain the values instead of asking a provider for the values. Because updating the repository
is a relatively expensive operation, dynamic providers are more efficient for objects that have
properties that change frequently.

EXPERIMENT: Viewing the MOF Definitions of WMI Classes

You can view the MOF definition for any WMI class by using the WbemTest tool that
comes with Windows. In this experiment, we'll look at the MOF definition for the
Win32_NTEventLogFile class:

1. Run Wbemtest from the Start menu's Run dialog box.

2. Click the Connect button, change the Namespace to root\cimv2, and connect.

3. Select Enum Classes, select the Recursive option button, and then click OK.

4. Find Win32_NTEventLogFile in the list of classes, and then double-click it to see
 its class properties.

5. Click the Show MOF button to open a window that displays the MOF text.

After constructing classes in MOF, WMI developers can supply the class definitions to WMI
in several ways. WDM provider developers compile a MOF file into a binary MOF (BMF)
file—a more compact binary representation than a MOF file—and give the BMF files to the
WDM infrastructure. Another way is for the provider to compile the MOF and use WMI COM
APIs to give the definitions to the WMI infrastructure. Finally, a provider can use the MOF
Compiler (Mofcomp.exe) tool to give the WMI infrastructure a classes-compiled representa-
tion directly.

The WMI Namespace

Classes define the properties of objects, and objects are class instances on a system. WMI uses a namespace that contains several subnamespaces that WMI arranges hierarchically to organize objects. A management application must connect to a namespace before the application can access objects within the namespace.

WMI names the namespace root directory *root*. All WMI installations have four predefined namespaces that reside beneath root: CIMV2, Default, Security, and WMI. Some of these namespaces have other namespaces within them. For example, CIMV2 includes the Applications and ms_409 namespaces as subnamespaces. Providers sometimes define their own namespaces; you can see the WMI namespace (which the Windows device driver WMI provider defines) beneath root in Windows.

EXPERIMENT: Viewing WMI Namespaces

You can see what namespaces are defined on a system with WMI CIM Studio. WMI CIM Studio presents a connection dialog box when you run it that includes a namespace browsing button to the right of the namespace edit box. Opening the browser and selecting a namespace has WMI CIM Studio connect to that namespace. Windows Vista defines over a dozen namespaces beneath root, some of which are visible here:

Unlike a file system namespace, which comprises a hierarchy of directories and files, a WMI namespace is only one level deep. Instead of using names as a file system does, WMI uses object properties that it defines as *keys* to identify the objects. Management applications specify class names with key names to locate specific objects within a namespace. Thus, each instance of a class must be uniquely identifiable by its key values. For example, the Event Log provider uses the Win32_NTLogEvent class to represent records in an Event Log. This class has two keys: Logfile, a string; and RecordNumber, an unsigned integer. A management application that queries WMI for instances of Event Log records obtains them from the

provider key pairs that identify records. The application refers to a record using the syntax that you see in this sample object path name:

```
\\DARYL\root\CIMV2:Win32_NTLogEvent.Logfile="Application",
                                   RecordNumber="1"
```

The first component in the name (\\DARYL) identifies the computer on which the object is located, and the second component (\root\CIMV2) is the namespace in which the object resides. The class name follows the colon, and key names and their associated values follow the period. A comma separates the key values.

WMI provides interfaces that let applications enumerate all the objects in a particular class or to make queries that return instances of a class that match a query criterion.

Class Association

Many object types are related to one another in some way. For example, a computer object has a processor, software, an operating system, active processes, and so on. WMI lets providers construct an *association class* to represent a logical connection between two different classes. Association classes associate one class with another, so the classes have only two properties: a class name and the *Ref* modifier. The following output shows an association in which the Event Log provider's MOF file associates the Win32_NTLogEvent class with the Win32_ComputerSystem class. Given an object, a management application can query associated objects. In this way, a provider defines a hierarchy of objects.

```
[dynamic: ToInstance, provider("MS_NT_EVENTLOG_PROVIDER"): ToInstance, EnumPrivileges{"Se
SecurityPrivilege"}: ToSubClass, Locale(1033): ToInstance, UUID("{8502C57F-5FBB-11D2-AAC1-
006008C78BC7}"): ToInstance, Association: DisableOverride ToInstance ToSubClass]
class Win32_NTLogEventComputer
{
    [key, read: ToSubClass] Win32_ComputerSystem ref Computer;
    [key, read: ToSubClass] Win32_NTLogEvent ref Record;
};
```

Figure 4-20 shows the WMI Object Browser (another tool that the WMI Administrative Tools includes) displaying the contents of the CIMV2 namespace. Windows system components typically place their objects within the CIMV2 namespace. The Object Browser first locates the Win32_ComputerSystem object instance ALEX-LAPTOP, which is the object that represents the computer. Then the Object Browser obtains the objects associated with Win32_ComputerSystem and displays them beneath ALEX-LAPTOP. The Object Browser user interface displays association objects with a double-arrow folder icon. The associated class type's objects display beneath the folder.

You can see in the Object Browser that the Event Log provider's association class Win32_NTLogEventComputer is beneath ALEX-LAPTOP and that numerous instances of the

Win32_NTLogEvent class exist. Refer to the preceding output to verify that the MOF file defines the Win32_NTLogEventComputer class to associate the Win32_ComputerSystem class with the Win32_NTLogEvent class. Selecting an instance of Win32_NTLogEvent in the Object Browser reveals that class's properties under the Properties tab in the right-hand pane. Microsoft intended the Object Browser to help WMI developers examine their objects, but a management application would perform the same operations and display properties or collected information more intelligibly.

FIGURE 4-20 WMI Object Browser

EXPERIMENT: Using WMI Scripts to Manage Systems

A powerful aspect of WMI is its support for scripting languages. Microsoft has generated hundreds of scripts that perform common administrative tasks for managing user accounts, files, the registry, processes, and hardware devices. The Microsoft TechNet Scripting Center Web site serves as the central location for Microsoft scripts. Using a script from the scripting center is as easy as copying its text from your Internet browser, storing it in a file with a .vbs extension, and running it with the command cscript *script*.vbs, where "script" is the name you gave the script. Cscript is the command-line interface to Windows Script Host (WSH).

Here's a sample TechNet script that registers to receive events when Win32_Process object instances are created, which occurs whenever a process starts, and prints a line with the name of the process that the object represents:

```
strComputer = "."
Set objWMIService = GetObject("winmgmts:" _
    & "{impersonationLevel=impersonate}!\\" & strComputer & "\root\cimv2")
Set colMonitoredProcesses = objWMIService. _
    ExecNotificationQuery("select * from __instancecreationevent " _
        & " within 1 where TargetInstance isa 'Win32_Process'")
i = 0
Do While i = 0
    Set objLatestProcess = colMonitoredProcesses.NextEvent
    Wscript.Echo objLatestProcess.TargetInstance.Name
Loop
```

The line that invokes *ExecNotificationQuery* does so with a parameter that includes a "select" statement, which highlights WMI's support for a read-only subset of the ANSI standard Structured Query Language (SQL), known as WQL, to provide a flexible way for WMI consumers to specify the information that they want to extract from WMI providers. Running the sample script with Cscript and then starting Notepad results in the following output:

```
C:\>cscript monproc.vbs
Microsoft (R) Windows Script Host Version 5.7
Copyright (C) Microsoft Corporation. All rights reserved.

NOTEPAD.EXE
```

WMI Implementation

The WMI service runs in a shared Svchost process that executes in the local system account. It loads providers into the Wmiprvse.exe provider-hosting process, which launches as a child of the RPC service process. WMI executes Wmiprvse in the local system, local service, or network service accounts, depending on the value of the *HostingModel* property of the WMI Win32Provider object instance that represents the provider implementation. A Wmiprvse process exits after the provider is removed from the cache, one minute following the last provider request it receives.

EXPERIMENT: Viewing Wmiprvse Creation

You can see Wmiprvse being created by running Process Explorer and executing Wmic. A Wmiprvse process will appear beneath the Svchost process that hosts the RPC service. If Process Explorer job highlighting is enabled, it will appear with the job highlight color because, to prevent a runaway provider from consuming all virtual memory resources on a system, Wmiprvse executes in a job object that limits the number of child processes it can create and the amount of virtual memory each process and all the processes of the job can allocate. (See Chapter 5 for more information on job objects.)

Most WMI components reside by default in %SystemRoot%\System32 and %SystemRoot%\ System32\Wbem, including Windows MOF files, built-in provider DLLs, and management application WMI DLLs. Look in the %SystemRoot%\System32\Wbem directory, and you'll find Ntevt.mof, the Event Log provider MOF file. You'll also find Ntevt.dll, the Event Log provider's DLL, which the WMI service uses.

Directories beneath %SystemRoot%\System32\Wbem store the repository, log files, and third-party MOF files. WMI implements the repository—named the CIMOM repository— using a proprietary version of the Microsoft JET database engine. The database file, by default, resides in %SystemRoot%\System32\Wbem\Repository\.

WMI honors numerous registry settings that the service's HKLM\SOFTWARE\Microsoft\ WBEM\CIMOM registry key stores, such as thresholds and maximum values for certain parameters.

Device drivers use special interfaces to provide data to and accept commands—called the WMI System Control commands—from WMI. These interfaces are part of the WDM, which is explained in Chapter 7. Because the interfaces are cross-platform, they fall under the \root\ WMI namespace.

WMIC

Windows also includes Wmic.exe, a utility that allows you to interact with WMI from a WMI-aware command-line shell. All WMI objects and their properties, including their methods, are accessible through the shell, which makes WMIC an advanced systems management console.

WMI Security

WMI implements security at the namespace level. If a management application success-
fully connects to a namespace, the application can view and access the properties of all the
objects in that namespace. An administrator can use the WMI Control application to control
which users can access a namespace. To start the WMI Control application, from the Start
menu, select Control Panel. From there, select System And Maintenance, Administrative
Tools, Computer Management. Next, open the Services And Applications branch. Right-click
WMI Control, and select Properties to launch the WMI Control Properties dialog box, which
Figure 4-21 shows. To configure security for namespaces, click the Security tab, select the
namespace, and click Security. The other tabs in the WMI Control Properties dialog box let
you modify the performance and backup settings that the registry stores.

FIGURE 4-21 WMI security properties

Windows Diagnostic Infrastructure

The *Windows Diagnostic Infrastructure* (WDI) helps to detect, diagnose, and resolve common
problem scenarios with minimal user intervention. Windows components implement triggers
that cause WDI to launch scenario-specific troubleshooting modules to detect the occurrence
of a problem scenario. A trigger can indicate that the system is approaching or has reached a
problematic state. Once a troubleshooting module has identified a root cause, it can invoke
a problem resolver to address it. A resolution may be as simple as changing a registry setting
or interacting with the user to perform recovery steps or configuration changes. Ultimately,

WDI's main role is to provide a unified framework for Windows components to perform the tasks involved in automated problem detection, diagnosis, and resolution.

WDI Instrumentation

Windows or application components must add instrumentation to notify WDI when a problem scenario is occurring. Components can wait for the results of diagnosis synchronously or can continue operating and let diagnosis proceed asynchronously. WDI implements two different types of instrumentation APIs to support these models.

- Event-based diagnosis, which can be used for minimally invasive diagnostics instrumentation, can be added to a component without requiring any changes to its implementation. WDI supports two kinds of event-based diagnosis: simple scenarios and start-stop scenarios. In a simple scenario, a single point in code is responsible for the failure and an event is raised to trigger diagnostics. In a start-stop scenario, an entire code path is deemed risky and is instrumented for diagnosis. One event is raised at the beginning of the scenario to a real-time Event Tracing for Windows (ETW) session named the DiagLog. At the same time, a kernel facility called the Scenario Event Mapper (SEM) enables a collection of additional ETW traces to the WDI context loggers. A second event is raised to signal the end of the diagnostic scenario, at which time the SEM disables the verbose tracing. This "just-in-time tracing" mechanism keeps the performance overhead of detailed tracing low while maintaining enough contextual information for WDI to find the root cause without a reproduction of the problem, if a failure should occur.

- On-demand diagnosis, which allows applications to request diagnosis on their own, interact with the diagnostic, receive notifications when the diagnostic has completed, and modify its behavior based on the results of the diagnosis. On-demand instrumentation is particularly useful when diagnosis needs to be performed in a privileged security context. WDI facilitates the transfer of context across trust and process boundaries and also supports impersonation of the caller when necessary.

Diagnostic Policy Service

The Diagnostic Policy Service (DPS, %SystemRoot%\System32\Dps.dll) implements most of the WDI scenario back end. DPS is a multithreaded service (running in a Svchost) that accepts on-demand scenario requests and also monitors and watches for diagnostic events delivered via DiagLog. (See Figure 4-22, which shows the relationship of DPS to the other key WDI components.) In response to these requests, DPS launches the appropriate troubleshooting module, which encodes domain-specific knowledge, such as how to find the root cause of a network problem. In addition, DPS makes all the contextual information related to the

scenario available to the modules in the form of captured traces. Troubleshooting modules perform automated analysis of the data and can request DPS to launch a secondary module called a resolver, which is responsible for fixing the problem, silently if possible.

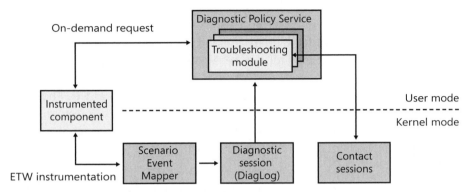

FIGURE 4-22 Windows Diagnostic Infrastructure architecture

DPS controls and enforces Group Policy settings for diagnostic scenarios. You can use the Group Policy Editor (%SystemRoot%\System32\Gpedit.msc) to configure the settings for the diagnostics and automatic recovery options. You can access these settings from Computer Configuration, Administrative Templates, System, Troubleshooting And Diagnostics, shown in Figure 4-23.

FIGURE 4-23 Configuring Diagnostic Policy Service settings

Diagnostic Functionality

Windows implements several built-in diagnostic scenarios and utilities. Some examples include:

- Disk diagnostics, which include the presence of Self-Monitoring Analysis and Reporting Technology (SMART) code inside the storage class driver (%SystemRoot%\System32\ Driver\Classspnp.sys) to monitor disk health. WDI notifies and guides the user through data backup after an impending disk failure is detected. In addition, Windows monitors application crashes caused by disk corruptions in critical system files. The diagnostic utilizes the Windows File Protection mechanism to automatically restore such damaged system files from a backup cache when possible. For more information on Windows storage management, see Chapter 8.

- Network diagnostics and troubleshooting extends WDI to handle different classes of networking related problems, such as file sharing, Internet access, wireless networks, third-party firewalls, and general network connectivity. For more information on net-working, see Chapter 12.

- Resource exhaustion prevention, which includes Windows memory leak diagnosis and Windows resource exhaustion detection and resolution. These diagnostics can detect when the commit limit is approaching its maximum and alert the user of the situation, including the top memory and resource consumers. The user can then choose to termi-nate these applications to attempt to free some resources. For more information on the commit limit and virtual memory, see Chapter 9.

- Windows memory diagnostic tool, which can be manually executed by the user from the Boot Manager on startup or automatically recommended by Windows Error Reporting (WER) after a system crash that was analyzed as potentially the result of faulty RAM. For more information on the boot process, see Chapter 13.

- Windows startup repair tool, which attempts to automatically fix certain classes of errors commonly responsible for users being unable to boot the system, such as incor-rect BCD settings, damaged disk structures such as the MBR or boot sector, and faulty drivers. When system boot is unsuccessful, the Boot Manager automatically launches the startup repair tool, if it is installed, which also includes manual recovery options and access to a command prompt. For more information on the startup repair tool, see Chapter 13.

- Windows performance diagnostics, which include Windows boot performance diag-nostics, Windows shutdown performance diagnostics, Windows standby/resume per-formance diagnostics, and Windows system responsiveness performance diagnostics. Based on certain timing thresholds and internal behavioral expectations of these mechanisms, Windows can detect problems caused by slow performance and log them to the Event Log, which in turn is used by WDI to provide resolutions and walkthroughs for the user to attempt to fix the problem.

■ Program Compatibility Assistant (PCA), which enables legacy applications to execute on Windows Vista despite compatibility problems. PCA detects application installation failures caused by a mismatch during version checks and run-time failures caused by deprecated binaries and User Account Control (UAC) settings. PCA attempts to recover from these failures by applying the appropriate compatibility setting for the application, which takes effect during the next run. In addition, PCA maintains a database of programs with known compatibility issues and informs the users about potential problems at program startup.

Conclusion

So far, we've examined the overall structure of Windows, the core system mechanisms on which the structure is built, and core management mechanisms. With this foundation laid, we're ready to explore the individual executive components in more detail, starting with processes and threads.

Chapter 5
Processes, Threads, and Jobs

In this chapter, we'll explain the data structures and algorithms that deal with processes, threads, and jobs in the Windows operating system. The first section focuses on the internal structures that make up a process. The second section outlines the steps involved in creating a process (and its initial thread). The internals of threads and thread scheduling are then described. The chapter concludes with a description of the job object.

Where relevant performance counters or kernel variables exist, they are mentioned. Although this book isn't a Windows programming book, the pertinent process, thread, and job Windows functions are listed so that you can pursue additional information on their use.

Because processes and threads touch so many components in Windows, a number of terms and data structures (such as working sets, objects and handles, system memory heaps, and so on) are referred to in this chapter but are explained in detail elsewhere in the book. To fully understand this chapter, you need to be familiar with the terms and concepts explained in Chapters 1 and 2, such as the difference between a process and a thread, the Windows virtual address space layout, and the difference between user mode and kernel mode.

Process Internals

This section describes the key Windows process data structures. Also listed are key kernel variables, performance counters, and functions and tools that relate to processes.

Data Structures

Each Windows process is represented by an executive process (EPROCESS) block. Besides containing many attributes relating to a process, an EPROCESS block contains and points to a number of other related data structures. For example, each process has one or more threads represented by executive thread (ETHREAD) blocks. (Thread data structures are explained in the section "Thread Internals" later in this chapter.) The EPROCESS block and its related data structures exist in system address space, with the exception of the process environment block (PEB), which exists in the process address space (because it contains information that needs to be accessed by user-mode code).

In addition to the EPROCESS block and the PEB, the Windows subsystem process (Csrss) maintains a parallel structure for each process that is executing a Windows program. Finally,

the kernel-mode part of the Windows subsystem (Win32k.sys) will also maintain a per-process data structure that is created the first time a thread calls a Windows USER or GDI function that is implemented in kernel mode.

Figure 5-1 is a simplified diagram of the process and thread data structures. Each data structure shown in the figure is described in detail in this chapter.

FIGURE 5-1 Data structures associated with processes and threads

First let's focus on the process block. (We'll get to the thread block in the section "Thread Internals" later in the chapter.) Figure 5-2 shows the key fields in an EPROCESS block.

PsActiveProcessHead →

FIGURE 5-2 Structure of an executive process block

EXPERIMENT: Displaying the Format of an EPROCESS Block

For a list of the fields that make up an EPROCESS block and their offsets in hexadecimal, type **dt _eprocess** in the kernel debugger. (See Chapter 1 for more information on the kernel debugger and how to perform kernel debugging on the local system.) The output (truncated for the sake of space) on a 32-bit system looks like this:

```
lkd> dt _eprocess
nt!_EPROCESS
    +0x000 Pcb               : _KPROCESS
    +0x080 ProcessLock       : _EX_PUSH_LOCK
    +0x088 CreateTime        : _LARGE_INTEGER
    +0x090 ExitTime          : _LARGE_INTEGER
    +0x098 RundownProtect    : _EX_RUNDOWN_REF
    +0x09c UniqueProcessId   : Ptr32 Void
    +0x0a0 ActiveProcessLinks : _LIST_ENTRY
    +0x0a8 QuotaUsage        : [3] Uint4B
    +0x0b4 QuotaPeak         : [3] Uint4B
    +0x0c0 CommitCharge      : Uint4B
    +0x0c4 PeakVirtualSize   : Uint4B
    +0x0c8 VirtualSize       : Uint4B
    +0x0cc SessionProcessLinks : _LIST_ENTRY
    +0x0d4 DebugPort         : Ptr32 Void
    +0x0d8 ExceptionPortData : Ptr32 Void
```

```
    +0x0d8 ExceptionPortValue : Uint4B
    +0x0d8 ExceptionPortState : Pos 0, 3 Bits
    +0x0dc ObjectTable        : Ptr32 _HANDLE_TABLE
    +0x0e0 Token              : _EX_FAST_REF
    +0x0e4 WorkingSetPage     : Uint4B
    +0x0e8 AddressCreationLock : _EX_PUSH_LOCK
    +0x0ec RotateInProgress   : Ptr32 _ETHREAD
    +0x0f0 ForkInProgress     : Ptr32 _ETHREAD
    +0x0f4 HardwareTrigger    : Uint4B
    +0x0f8 PhysicalVadRoot    : Ptr32 _MM_AVL_TABLE
    +0x0fc CloneRoot          : Ptr32 Void
    +0x100 NumberOfPrivatePages : Uint4B
    +0x104 NumberOfLockedPages : Uint4B
    +0x108 Win32Process       : Ptr32 Void
    +0x10c Job                : Ptr32 _EJOB
    +0x110 SectionObject      : Ptr32 Void
    +0x114 SectionBaseAddress : Ptr32 Void
    +0x118 QuotaBlock         : Ptr32 _EPROCESS_QUOTA_BLOCK
```

Note that the first field (Pcb) is actually a substructure, the kernel process block
(KPROCESS), which is where scheduling-related information is stored. To display the for-
mat of the kernel process block, type **dt _kprocess**:

```
lkd> dt _kprocess
nt!_KPROCESS
    +0x000 Header             : _DISPATCHER_HEADER
    +0x010 ProfileListHead    : _LIST_ENTRY
    +0x018 DirectoryTableBase : Uint4B
    +0x01c Unused0            : Uint4B
    +0x020 LdtDescriptor      : _KGDTENTRY
    +0x028 Int21Descriptor    : _KIDTENTRY
    +0x030 IopmOffset         : Uint2B
    +0x032 Iopl               : UChar
    +0x033 Unused             : UChar
    +0x034 ActiveProcessors   : Uint4B
    +0x038 KernelTime         : Uint4B
    +0x03c UserTime           : Uint4B
    +0x040 ReadyListHead      : _LIST_ENTRY
    +0x048 SwapListEntry      : _SINGLE_LIST_ENTRY
    +0x04c VdmTrapcHandler    : Ptr32 Void
    +0x050 ThreadListHead     : _LIST_ENTRY
    +0x058 ProcessLock        : Uint4B
    +0x05c Affinity           : Uint4B
    +0x060 AutoAlignment      : Pos 0, 1 Bit
    +0x060 DisableBoost       : Pos 1, 1 Bit
    +0x060 DisableQuantum     : Pos 2, 1 Bit
    +0x060 ReservedFlags      : Pos 3, 29 Bits
    +0x060 ProcessFlags       : Int4B
    +0x064 BasePriority       : Char
    +0x065 QuantumReset       : Char
    +0x066 State              : UChar
    +0x067 ThreadSeed         : UChar
    +0x068 PowerState         : UChar
    +0x069 IdealNode          : UChar
```

```
+0x06a Visited         : UChar
+0x06b Flags           : _KEXECUTE_OPTIONS
+0x06b ExecuteOptions  : UChar
+0x06c StackCount      : Uint4B
+0x070 ProcessListEntry : _LIST_ENTRY
+0x078 CycleTime       : Uint8B
```

An alternative way to see the KPROCESS (and other substructures in the EPROCESS) is to use the recursion (–r) switch of the *dt* command. For example, typing **dt _eprocess –r1** will recurse and display all substructures one level deep.

The *dt* command shows the format of a process block, not its contents. To show an instance of an actual process, you can specify the address of an EPROCESS structure as an argument to the *dt* command. You can get the address of all the EPROCESS blocks in the system by using the *!process 0 0* command. An annotated example of the output from this command is included later in this chapter.

Table 5-1 explains some of the fields in the preceding experiment in more detail and includes references to other places in the book where you can find more information about them. As we've said before and will no doubt say again, processes and threads are such integral parts of Windows that it's impossible to talk about them without referring to many other parts of the system. To keep the length of this chapter manageable, however, we've covered those related subjects (such as memory management, security, objects, and handles) elsewhere.

TABLE 5-1 Contents of the EPROCESS Block

Element	Purpose	Additional Reference
Kernel process (KPROCESS) block	Common dispatcher object header, pointer to the process page directory, list of kernel thread (KTHREAD) blocks belonging to the process, default base priority, affinity mask, and total kernel and user time and CPU clock cycles for the threads in the process.	Thread scheduling (Chapter 5)
Process identification	Unique process ID, creating process ID, name of image being run, window station process is running on.	
Quota block	Limits on processor usage, nonpaged pool, paged pool, and page file usage plus current and peak process nonpaged and paged pool usage. (Note: Several processes can share this structure: all the system processes in session 0 point to a single systemwide quota block; all other processes in interactive sessions share a single quota block.)	

Element	Purpose	Additional Reference
Virtual address descriptors (VADs)	Series of data structures that describes the status of the portions of the address space that exist in the process.	Virtual address descriptors (Chapter 9)
Working set information	Pointer to working set list (MMWSL structure); current, peak, minimum, and maximum working set size; last trim time; page fault count; memory priority; outswap flags; page fault history.	Working sets (Chapter 9)
Virtual memory information	Current and peak virtual size, page file usage, hardware page table entry for process page directory.	Chapter 9
Exception legacy local procedure call (LPC) port	Interprocess communication channel to which the process manager sends a message when one of the process's threads causes an exception.	Exception dispatching (Chapter 3)
Debugging object	Executive object through which the user-mode debugging infrastructure sends notifications when one of the process's threads causes a debug event.	User-mode debugging (Chapter 3)
Access token (TOKEN)	Executive object describing the security profile of this process.	Chapter 6
Handle table	Address of per-process handle table.	Object handles and the process handle table (Chapter 3)
Device map	Address of object directory to resolve device name references in (supports multiple users).	Object names (Chapter 3)
Process environment block (PEB)	Image information (base address, version numbers, module list), process heap information, and thread-local storage utilization. (Note: The pointers to the process heaps start at the first byte after the PEB.)	Chapter 5
Windows subsystem process block (W32PROCESS)	Process details needed by the kernel-mode component of the Windows subsystem.	

The kernel process (KPROCESS) block, which is part of the EPROCESS block, and the process environment block (PEB), which is pointed to by the EPROCESS block, contain additional details about the process object. The KPROCESS block (which is sometimes called the PCB or process control block) is illustrated in Figure 5-3. It contains the basic information that the Windows kernel needs to schedule the threads inside a process. (Page directories are covered in Chapter 9, and kernel thread blocks are described in more detail later in this chapter.)

The PEB, which lives in the user process address space, contains information needed by the image loader, the heap manager, and other Windows system DLLs that need to access it from user mode. (The EPROCESS and KPROCESS blocks are accessible only from kernel mode.) The basic structure of the PEB is illustrated in Figure 5-4 and is explained in more detail later in this chapter.

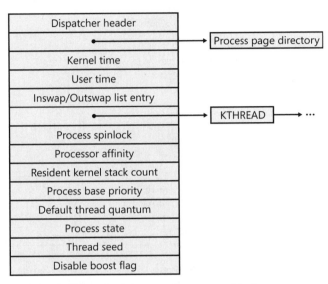

FIGURE 5-3 Structure of the executive process block

FIGURE 5-4 Fields of the process environment block

EXPERIMENT: Examining the PEB

You can dump the PEB structure with the *!peb* command in the kernel debugger. To get the address of the PEB, use the *!process* command as follows:

```
lkd> !process
PROCESS 8575f030  SessionId: 1  Cid: 08d0    Peb: 7ffd9000  ParentCid: 0360
    DirBase: 1a81b000  ObjectTable: e12bd418  HandleCount:  66.
    Image: windbg.exe
```

Then specify that address to the *!peb* command as follows:

```
lkd> !peb 7ffd9000
PEB at 7ffd9000
    InheritedAddressSpace:    No
    ReadImageFileExecOptions: No
    BeingDebugged:            No
    ImageBaseAddress:         002a0000
    Ldr                       77895d00
    Ldr.Initialized:          Yes
    Ldr.InInitializationOrderModuleList: 00151c38 . 00191558
    Ldr.InLoadOrderModuleList:           00151bb8 . 00191548
    Ldr.InMemoryOrderModuleList:         00151bc0 . 00191550
            Base TimeStamp                     Module
          2a0000 4678a41e Jun 19 23:50:54 2007 C:\Program Files\Debugging Tools for
              Windows\windbg.exe
         777d0000 4549bdc9 Nov 02 05:43:37 2006 C:\Windows\system32\Ntdll.dll
         764c0000 4549bd80 Nov 02 05:42:24 2006 C:\Windows\system32\kernel32.dll
    SubSystemData:     00000000
    ProcessHeap:       00150000
    ProcessParameters: 001512e0
    WindowTitle:  'C:\Users\Alex Ionescu\Desktop\WinDbg.lnk'
    ImageFile:    'C:\Program Files\Debugging Tools for Windows\windbg.exe'
    CommandLine:  '"C:\Program Files\Debugging Tools for Windows\windbg.exe" '
    DllPath:      'C:\Program Files\Debugging Tools for Windows;C:\Windows\
        system32;C:\Windows\system;C:\Windows;.;C:\Windows\system32;C:\Windows;
        C:\Windows\System32\Wbem;C:\Program Files\Common Files\Roxio Shared\
        DLLShared\;C:\Program Files\Common Files\Roxio Shared\DLLShared\;C:\Program
        Files\Common Files\Roxio Shared\9.0\DLLShared\;c:\sysint;C:\Program Files\
        QuickTime\QTSystem\'
    Environment:  001850a8
        ALLUSERSPROFILE=C:\ProgramData
        APPDATA=C:\Users\Alex Ionescu\AppData\Roaming
        .
        .
        .
```

Kernel Variables

A few key kernel global variables that relate to processes are listed in Table 5-2. These variables are referred to later in the chapter, when the steps in creating a process are described.

TABLE 5-2 Process-Related Kernel Variables

Element	Purpose	Additional Reference
PsActiveProcessHead	Doubly linked list	List head of process blocks
PsIdleProcess	Pointer to EPROCESS	Idle process block
PsInitialSystemProcess	Pointer to EPROCESS	Pointer to the process block of the initial system process that contains the system threads
PspCreateProcessNotifyRoutine	Array of executive call-back objects	Array of callback objects describing the routines to be called on process creation and deletion (maximum of eight)
PspCreateProcessNotifyRoutineCount	32-bit integer	Count of registered process notification routines
PspCreateProcessNotifyRoutineCountEx	32-bit integer	Count of registered extended process notification routines
PspLoadImageNotifyRoutine	Array of executive call-back objects	Array of callback objects describing the routines to be called on image load (maximum of eight)
PspLoadImageNotifyRoutineCount	32-bit integer	Count of registered image-load notification routines
PspNotifyEnableMask	32-bit integer	Mask for quickly checking whether any extended or standard notification routines are enabled
PspCidTable	Pointer to HANDLE_TABLE	Handle table for process and thread client IDs

Performance Counters

Windows maintains a number of counters with which you can track the processes running on your system; you can retrieve these counters programmatically or view them with the Performance tool. Table 5-3 lists the performance counters relevant to processes.

TABLE 5-3 Process-Related Performance Counters

Object: Counter	Function
Process: % Privileged Time	Describes the percentage of time that the threads in the process have run in kernel mode during a specified interval.
Process: % Processor Time	Describes the percentage of CPU time that the threads in the process have used during a specified interval. This count is the sum of % Privileged Time and % User Time.

Object: Counter	Function
Process: % User Time	Describes the percentage of time that the threads in the process have run in user mode during a specified interval.
Process: Elapsed Time	Describes the total elapsed time in seconds since this process was created.
Process: ID Process	Returns the process ID. This ID applies only while the process exists because process IDs are reused.
Process: Creating Process ID	Returns the process ID of the creating process. This value isn't updated if the creating process exits.
Process: Thread Count	Returns the number of threads in the process.
Process: Handle Count	Returns the number of handles open in the process.

Relevant Functions

For reference purposes, some of the Windows functions that apply to processes are described in Table 5-4. For further information, consult the Windows API documentation in the MSDN Library.

TABLE 5-4 Process-Related Functions

Function	Description
CreateProcess	Creates a new process and thread using the caller's security identification
CreateProcessAsUser	Creates a new process and thread with the specified alternate security token
CreateProcessWithLogonW	Creates a new process and thread to run under the credentials of the specified username and password
CreateProcessWithTokenW	Creates a new process and thread with the specified alternate security token, with additional options such as allowing the user profile to be loaded
OpenProcess	Returns a handle to the specified process object
ExitProcess	Ends a process, and notifies all attached DLLs
TerminateProcess	Ends a process without notifying the DLLs
FlushInstructionCache	Empties the specified process's instruction cache
FlushProcessWriteBuffers	Empties the specified process's write queue
GetProcessTimes	Obtains a process's timing information, describing how much time the threads inside the process spent in user and kernel mode
QueryProcessCycleTimeCounter	Obtains a process's CPU timing information, describing how many clock cycles the threads inside the process have spent in total
Query/ SetProcessAffinityUpdateMode	Defines whether the process's affinity is automatically updated if new processors are added to the running system

Function	Description
Get/SetProcessDEPPolicy	Returns or sets the DEP (Data Execution Protection) policy for the process
GetExitCodeProcess	Returns the exit code for a process, indicating how and why the process shut down
GetCommandLine	Returns a pointer to the command-line string passed to the current process
QueryFullProcessImageName	Returns the full name of the executable image associated with the process
GetCurrentProcess	Returns a pseudo handle for the current process
GetCurrentProcessId	Returns the ID of the current process
GetProcessVersion	Returns the major and minor versions of the Windows version on which the specified process expects to run
GetStartupInfo	Returns the contents of the STARTUPINFO structure specified during *CreateProcess*
GetEnvironmentStrings	Returns the address of the environment block
Get/SetEnvironmentVariable	Returns or sets a specific environment variable
Get/ SetProcessShutdownParameters	Defines the shutdown priority and number of retries for the current process
SetProcessDPIAware	Specifies whether the process is aware of dots per inch (DPI) settings
GetGuiResources	Returns a count of User and GDI handles

EXPERIMENT: Using the Kernel Debugger *!process* Command

The kernel debugger *!process* command displays a subset of the information in an EPROCESS block. This output is arranged in two parts for each process. First you see the information about the process, as shown here (when you don't specify a process address or ID, *!process* lists information for the active process on the current CPU):

```
lkd> !process
PROCESS 85857160  SessionId: 1  Cid: 0bcc    Peb: 7ffd9000  ParentCid: 090c
    DirBase: b45b0820  ObjectTable: b94ffda0  HandleCount:  99.
    Image: windbg.exe
    VadRoot 85a1c8e8 Vads 97 Clone 0 Private 5919. Modified 153. Locked 1.
    DeviceMap 9d32ee50
    Token                             ebaa1938
    ElapsedTime                       00:48:44.125
    UserTime                          00:00:00.000
    KernelTime                        00:00:00.000
    QuotaPoolUsage[PagedPool]         166784
    QuotaPoolUsage[NonPagedPool]      4776
    Working Set Sizes (now,min,max)   (8938, 50, 345) (35752KB, 200KB, 1380KB)
    PeakWorkingSetSize                8938
    VirtualSize                       106 Mb
    PeakVirtualSize                   108 Mb
```

```
PageFaultCount          37066
MemoryPriority          BACKGROUND
BasePriority            8
CommitCharge            6242
```

After the basic process output comes a list of the threads in the process. That output is explained in the "Experiment: Using the Kernel Debugger *!thread* Command" section later in the chapter. Other commands that display process information include *!handle*, which dumps the process handle table (which is described in more detail in the section "Object Handles and the Process Handle Table" in Chapter 3). Process and thread security structures are described in Chapter 6.

Protected Processes

In the Windows security model, any process running with a token containing the debug privilege (such as an administrator's account) can request any access right that it desires to any other process running on the machine—for example, it can read and write arbitrary process memory, inject code, suspend and resume threads, and query information on other processes. Tools like Process Explorer and Task Manager need and request these access rights to provide their functionality to users.

This logical behavior (which helps ensure that administrators will always have full control of the running code on the system) clashes with the system behavior for digital rights management requirements imposed by the media industry on computer operating systems that need to support playback of advanced, high-quality digital content such as BluRay and HD-DVD media. To support reliable and protected playback of such content, Windows uses *protected processes*. These processes exist alongside normal Windows processes, but they add significant constraints to the access rights that other processes on the system (even when running with administrative privileges) can request.

Protected processes can be created by any application; however, the operating system will only allow a process to be protected if the image file has been digitally signed with a special Windows Media Certificate. The Protected Media Path (PMP) in Windows Vista makes use of protected processes to provide protection for high-value media, and developers of applications such as DVD players can make use of protected processes by using the Media Foundation API.

The Audio Device Graph process (Audiodg.exe) is a protected process, since protected music content may be decoded through it. Similarly, the Windows Error Reporting (WER;

see Chapter 3 for more information) client process (Werfault.exe) can also run protected because it needs to have access to protected processes in case one of them crashes. Finally, the System process itself is protected because some of the decryption information is generated by the Ksecdd.sys driver and stored in its user-mode memory. The System process is also protected to protect the integrity of all kernel handles (since the System process's handle table contains all the kernel handles on the system).

At the kernel level, support for protected processes is twofold: first, the bulk of process creation occurs in kernel mode to avoid injection attacks. (The flow for both protected and standard process creation is described in detail in the next section.) Second, protected processes have a special bit set in their EPROCESS structure that modifies the behavior of security-related routines in the process manager to deny certain access rights that would normally be granted to administrators. Table 5-5 indicates access rights that are limited or denied.

TABLE 5-5 Process Access Rights Denied for Protected Processes

Object: Access Mask	Function
Standard: READ_CONTROL	Prevents the protected process's access control list (ACL) from being read.
Standard: WRITE_DAC, WRITE_OWNER	Prevents access to the protected process's access control list or modifying its owner (which would grant the former).
Process: PROCESS_ALL_ACCESS	Prevents full access to the protected process.
Process: PROCESS_CREATE_PROCESS	Prevents creation of a child process of a protected process.
Process: PROCESS_CREATE_THREAD	Prevents creation of a thread inside a protected process.
Process: PROCESS_DUP_HANDLE	Prevents duplication of a handle owned by the protected process.
Process: PROCESS_QUERY_INFORMATION	Prevents querying all information on a protected process. However, a new access right was added, PROCESS_QUERY_LIMITED_INFORMATION, that grants limited access to information on the process.
Process: PROCESS_SET_QUOTA	Prevents setting memory or processor-usage limits on a protected process.
Process: PROCESS_SET_INFORMATION	Prevents modification of process settings for a protected process.
Process: PROCESS_VM_OPERATION, PROCESS_VM_READ, PROCESS_VM_WRITE	Prevents accessing the memory of a protected process.

Certain access rights are also disabled for threads running inside protected processes; we will look at those access rights later in this chapter in the section "Thread Internals."

Because Process Explorer uses standard user-mode Windows APIs to query information on process internals, it is unable to perform certain operations on such processes. On the other

hand, a tool like WinDbg in kernel debugging mode, which uses kernel-mode infrastructure to obtain this information, will be able to display complete information. See the experiment in the thread internals section on how Process Explorer behaves when confronted with a protected process such as Audiodg.exe.

> **Note** As mentioned in Chapter 1, to perform local kernel debugging you must boot in debugging mode (enabled by using "bcdedit /debug on" or by using the Msconfig advanced boot options). This protects against debugger-based attacks on protected processes and the Protected Media Path (PMP). When booted in debugging mode, high-definition content playback will not work; for example, attempting to play MPEG2 media such as a DVD will result in an access violation inside the media player (this is by design).

Limiting these access rights reliably allows the kernel to sandbox a protected process from user-mode access. On the other hand, because a protected process is indicated by a flag in the EPROCESS block, an administrator can still load a kernel-mode driver that disables this bit. However, this would be a violation of the PMP model and considered malicious, and such a driver would likely eventually be blocked from loading on a 64-bit system because the kernel-mode code-signing policy prohibits the digital signing of malicious code. Even on 32-bit systems, the driver has to be recognized by PMP policy or else the playback will be halted. This policy is implemented by Microsoft and not by any kernel detection. This block would require manual action from Microsoft to identify the signature as malicious and update the kernel.

Flow of *CreateProcess*

So far in this chapter, you've seen the structures that are part of a process and the API functions with which you (and the operating system) can manipulate processes. You've also found out how you can use tools to view how processes interact with your system. But how did those processes come into being, and how do they exit once they've fulfilled their purpose? In the following sections, you'll discover how a Windows process comes to life.

A Windows subsystem process is created when an application calls one of the process creation functions, such as *CreateProcess*, *CreateProcessAsUser*, *CreateProcessWithTokenW*, or *CreateProcessWithLogonW*. Creating a Windows process consists of several stages carried out in three parts of the operating system: the Windows client-side library Kernel32.dll (in the case of the *CreateProcessAsUser*, *CreateProcessWithTokenW*, and *CreateProcessWithLogonW* routines, part of the work is first done in Advapi32.dll), the Windows executive, and the Windows subsystem process (Csrss).

Because of the multiple environment subsystem architecture of Windows, creating an executive process object (which other subsystems can use) is separated from the work involved in creating a Windows subsystem process. So, although the following description of the flow of the Windows *CreateProcess* function is complicated, keep in mind that part of the work is specific to the semantics added by the Windows subsystem as opposed to the core work needed to create an executive process object.

The following list summarizes the main stages of creating a process with the Windows *CreateProcess* function. The operations performed in each stage are described in detail in the subsequent sections. Some of these operations may be performed by *CreateProcess* itself (or other helper routines in user mode), while others will be performed by *NtCreateUserProcess* or one of its helper routines in kernel mode. In our detailed analysis to follow, we will differentiate between the two at each step required.

 Note Many steps of *CreateProcess* are related to the setup of the process virtual address space and therefore refer to many memory management terms and structures that are defined in Chapter 9.

1. Validate parameters; convert Windows subsystem flags and options to their native counterparts; parse, validate, and convert the attribute list to its native counterpart.

2. Open the image file (.exe) to be executed inside the process.

3. Create the Windows executive process object.

4. Create the initial thread (stack, context, and Windows executive thread object).

5. Perform post-creation, Windows-subsystem-specific process initialization.

6. Start execution of the initial thread (unless the CREATE_ SUSPENDED flag was specified).

7. In the context of the new process and thread, complete the initialization of the address space (such as load required DLLs) and begin execution of the program.

Figure 5-5 shows an overview of the stages Windows follows to create a process.

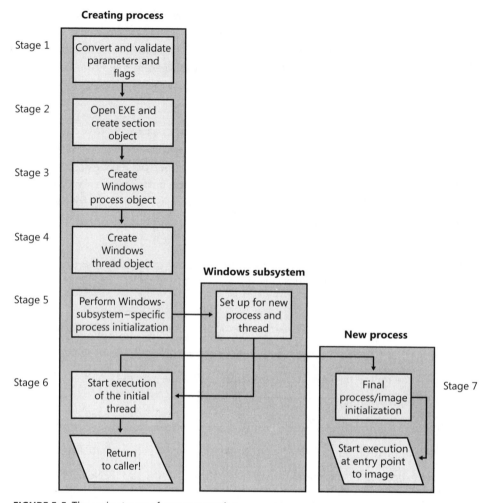

FIGURE 5-5 The main stages of process creation

Stage 1: Converting and Validating Parameters and Flags

Before opening the executable image to run, *CreateProcess* performs the following steps:

- In *CreateProcess*, the priority class for the new process is specified as independent bits in the *CreationFlags* parameter. Thus, you can specify more than one priority class for a single *CreateProcess* call. Windows resolves the question of which priority class to assign to the process by choosing the lowest-priority class set.

- If no priority class is specified for the new process, the priority class defaults to Normal unless the priority class of the process that created it is Idle or Below Normal, in which case the priority class of the new process will have the same priority as the creating class.

- If a Real-time priority class is specified for the new process and the process's caller doesn't have the Increase Scheduling Priority privilege, the High priority class is used instead. In other words, *CreateProcess* doesn't fail just because the caller has insufficient privileges to create the process in the Real-time priority class; the new process just won't have as high a priority as Real-time.

- All windows are associated with desktops, the graphical representation of a workspace. If no desktop is specified in *CreateProcess*, the process is associated with the caller's current desktop.

- If the process is part of a job object, but the creation flags requested a separate virtual DOS machine (VDM), the flag is ignored.

- If the caller is sending a handle to a monitor as an output handle instead of a console handle, standard handle flags are ignored.

- If the creation flags specify that the process will be debugged, Kernel32 initiates a connection to the native debugging code in Ntdll.dll by calling *DbgUiConnectToDbg* and gets a handle to the debug object from the thread environment block (TEB) once the function returns.

- Kernel32.dll sets the default hard error mode if the creation flags specified one.

- The user-specified attribute list is converted from Windows subsystem format to native format, and internal attributes are added to it.

> **Note** The attribute list passed on a *CreateProcess* call permits passing back to the caller information beyond a simple status code, such as the TEB address of the initial thread or information on the image section. This is necessary for protected processes since the parent cannot query this information after the child is created.

Once these steps are completed, *CreateProcess* will perform the initial call to *NtCreateUserProcess* to attempt creation of the process. Because Kernel32.dll has no idea at this point whether the application image name is a real Windows application, or if it might be a POSIX, 16-bit, or DOS application, the call may fail, at which point *CreateProcess* will look at the error reason and attempt to correct the situation.

Stage 2: Opening the Image to Be Executed

As illustrated in Figure 5-6, the first stage in *NtCreateUserProcess* is to find the appropriate Windows image that will run the executable file specified by the caller and to create a section object to later map it into the address space of the new process. If the call failed for any reason, it will return to *CreateProcess* with a failure state (see Table 5-6) that will cause *CreateProcess* to attempt execution again.

If the executable file specified is a Windows .exe, *NtCreateUserProcess* will try to open the file and create a section object for it. The object isn't mapped into memory yet, but it is opened.

Just because a section object has been successfully created doesn't mean that the file is a valid Windows image, however; it could be a DLL or a POSIX executable. If the file is a POSIX executable, the image to be run changes to Posix.exe, and *CreateProcess* restarts from the beginning of Stage 1. If the file is a DLL, *CreateProcess* fails.

Now that *NtCreateUserProcess* has found a valid Windows executable image, as part of the process creation code described in Stage 3 it looks in the registry under HKLM\SOFTWARE\ Microsoft\Windows NT\CurrentVersion\Image File Execution Options to see whether a sub-key with the file name and extension of the executable image (but without the directory and path information—for example, Image.exe) exists there. If it does, *PspAllocateProcess* looks for a value named Debugger for that key. If this value is present, the image to be run becomes the string in that value and *CreateProcess* restarts at Stage 1.

> **Tip** You can take advantage of this process creation behavior and debug the startup code of Windows services processes before they start rather than attach the debugger after starting a service, which doesn't allow you to debug the startup code.

On the other hand, if the image is not a Windows .exe (for example, if it's an MS-DOS, Win16, or a POSIX application), *CreateProcess* goes through a series of steps to find a Windows *support image* to run it. This process is necessary because non-Windows applications aren't run directly—Windows instead uses one of a few special support images that in turn are responsible for actually running the non-Windows program. For example, if you attempt to run a POSIX application, *CreateProcess* identifies it as such and changes the image to be run to the Windows executable file Posix.exe. If you attempt to run an MS-DOS or a Win16 executable, the image to be run becomes the Windows executable Ntvdm.exe. In short, you can't directly create a process that is *not* a Windows process. If Windows can't find a way to resolve the activated image as a Windows process (as shown in Table 5-6), *CreateProcess* fails.

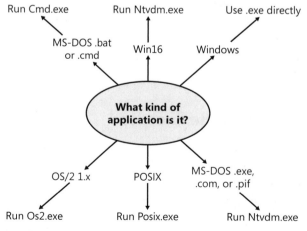

FIGURE 5-6 Choosing a Windows image to activate

TABLE 5-6 Decision Tree for Stage 1 of *CreateProcess*

If the Image . . .	Create State Code	This Image Will Run and This Will Happen
Is a POSIX executable file	*PsCreateSuccess*	Posix.exe	*CreateProcess* restarts Stage 1.
Is an MS-DOS application with an .exe, a .com, or a .pif extension	*PsCreateFailOnSectionCreate*	Ntvdm.exe	*CreateProcess* restarts Stage 1.
Is a Win16 application	*PsCreateFailOnSectionCreate*	Ntvdm.exe	*CreateProcess* restarts Stage 1.
Is a Win64 application on a 32-bit system (or a PPC, MIPS, or Alpha Binary)	*PsCreateFailMachineMismatch*	N/A	*CreateProcess* will fail.
Has a Debugger key with another image name	*PsCreateFailExeName*	Name specified in the Debugger key	*CreateProcess* restarts Stage 1.
Is an invalid or damaged Windows EXE	*PsCreateFailExeFormat*	N/A	*CreateProcess* will fail.
Cannot be opened	*PsCreateFailOnFileOpen*	N/A	*CreateProcess* will fail.
Is a command procedure (application with a .bat or a .cmd extension)	*PsCreateFailOnSectionCreate*	Cmd.exe	*CreateProcess* restarts Stage 1.

Specifically, the decision tree that *CreateProcess* goes through to run an image is as follows:

- If the image is an MS-DOS application with an .exe, a .com, or a .pif extension, a message is sent to the Windows subsystem to check whether an MS-DOS support process (Ntvdm.exe, specified in the registry value HKLM\SYSTEM\CurrentControlSet\Control\WOW\cmdline) has already been created for this session. If a support process has been created, it is used to run the MS-DOS application. (The Windows subsystem sends the message to the VDM [Virtual DOS Machine] process to run the new image.) Then *CreateProcess* returns. If a support process hasn't been created, the image to be run changes to Ntvdm.exe and *CreateProcess* restarts at Stage 1.

- If the file to run has a .bat or a .cmd extension, the image to be run becomes Cmd.exe, the Windows command prompt, and *CreateProcess* restarts at Stage 1. (The name of the batch file is passed as the first parameter to Cmd.exe.)

- If the image is a Win16 (Windows 3.1) executable, *CreateProcess* must decide whether a new VDM process must be created to run it or whether it should use the default sessionwide shared VDM process (which might not yet have been created). The *CreateProcess* flags CREATE_SEPARATE_WOW_VDM and CREATE_SHARED_WOW_VDM control this decision. If these flags aren't specified, the registry value HKLM\SYSTEM\CurrentControlSet\Control\WOW\DefaultSeparateVDM dictates the default behavior.

If the application is to be run in a separate VDM, the image to be run changes to the value of HKLM\SYSTEM\CurrentControlSet\Control\WOW\wowcmdline and *CreateProcess* restarts at Stage 1. Otherwise, the Windows subsystem sends a message to see whether the shared VDM process exists and can be used. (If the VDM process is running on a different desktop or isn't running under the same security as the caller, it can't be used and a new VDM process must be created.) If a shared VDM process can be used, the Windows subsystem sends a message to it to run the new image and *CreateProcess* returns. If the VDM process hasn't yet been created (or if it exists but can't be used), the image to be run changes to the VDM support image and *CreateProcess* restarts at Stage 1.

Stage 3: Creating the Windows Executive Process Object (*PspAllocateProcess*)

At this point, *NtCreateUserProcess* has opened a valid Windows executable file and created a section object to map it into the new process address space. Next it creates a Windows executive process object to run the image by calling the internal system function *PspAllocateProcess*. Creating the executive process object (which is done by the creating thread) involves the following substages:

- Setting up the EPROCESS block

- Creating the initial process address space

- Initializing the kernel process block (KPROCESS)

- Setting up the PEB

- Concluding the setup of the process address space (which includes initializing the working set list and virtual address space descriptors and mapping the image into address space)

 Note The only time there won't be a parent process is during system initialization. After that point, a parent process is always required to provide a security context for the new process.

Stage 3A: Setting Up the EPROCESS Block

This substage involves the following steps:

1. Allocate and initialize the Windows EPROCESS block.

2. Inherit the Windows device namespace (including the definition of drive letters, COM ports, and so on).

3. Inherit the process affinity mask and page priority from the parent process. If there is no parent process, the default page priority (5) is used, and an affinity mask of all processors (*KeActiveProcessors*) is used.

4. Set the new process's quota block to the address of its parent process's quota block, and increment the reference count for the parent's quota block. If the process was created through *CreateProcessAsUser*, this step won't occur.

5. The process minimum and maximum working set size are set to the values of *PspMinimumWorkingSet* and *PspMaximumWorkingSet*, respectively. These values can be overridden if performance options were specified in the PerfOptions key part of Image File Execution Options, in which case the maximum working set is taken from there.

6. Store the parent process's process ID in the *InheritedFromUniqueProcessId* field in the new process object.

7. Attach the process to the session of the parent process.

8. Initialize the KPROCESS part of the process object. (See Stage 3C.)

9. Create the process's primary access token (a duplicate of its parent's primary token). New processes inherit the security profile of their parents. If the *CreateProcessAsUser* function is being used to specify a different access token for the new process, the token is then changed appropriately.

10. The process handle table is initialized. If the inherit handles flag is set for the parent process, any inheritable handles are copied from the parent's object handle table into the new process. (For more information about object handle tables, see Chapter 3.) A process attribute can also be used to specify only a subset of handles, which is useful when you are using *CreateProcessAsUser* to restrict which objects should be inherited by the child process.

11. If performance options were specified through the PerfOptions key, these are now applied. The PerfOptions key includes overrides for the working set limit, I/O priority, page priority, and CPU priority class of the process.

12. The process priority class and quantum are computed and set.

13. Set the new process's exit status to STATUS_PENDING.

Stage 3B: Creating the Initial Process Address Space

The initial process address space consists of the following pages:

- Page directory (and it's possible there'll be more than one for systems with page tables more than two levels, such as x86 systems in PAE mode or 64-bit systems)

- Hyperspace page

- Working set list

To create these three pages, the following steps are taken:

1. Page table entries are created in the appropriate page tables to map the initial pages.

2. The number of pages is deducted from the kernel variable *MmTotalCommittedPages* and added to *MmProcessCommit*.

3. The systemwide default process minimum working set size (*PsMinimumWorkingSet*) is deducted from *MmResidentAvailablePages*.

4. The page table pages for the nonpaged portion of system space and the system cache are mapped into the process.

Stage 3C: Creating the Kernel Process Block

The next stage of *PspAllocateProcess* is the initialization of the KPROCESS block. This work is performed by *KeInitializeProcess*, which contains:

- A pointer to a list of kernel threads. (The kernel has no knowledge of handles, so it bypasses the object table.)

- A pointer to the process's page table directory (which is used to keep track of the process's virtual address space).

- The total time the process's threads have executed.

- The number of clock cycles the process's threads have consumed.

- The process's default base-scheduling priority (which starts as Normal, or 8, unless the parent process was set to Idle or Below Normal, in which case the setting is inherited).

- The default processor affinity for the threads in the process.

- The process swapping state (resident, out-swapped, or in transition).

- The NUMA ideal node (initially set to 0).

- The thread seed, based on the ideal processor that the kernel has chosen for this process (which is based on the previously created process's ideal processor, effectively randomizing this in a round-robin manner). Creating a new process will update the seed in *KeNodeBlock* (the initial NUMA node block) so that the next new process will get a different ideal processor seed.

- The initial value (or reset value) of the process default quantum (which is described in more detail in the "Thread Scheduling" section later in the chapter), which is hard-coded to 6 until it is initialized later (by *PspComputeQuantumAndPriority*).

Note The default initial quantum differs between Windows client and server systems. For more information on thread quantums, turn to their discussion in the section "Thread Scheduling."

Stage 3D: Concluding the Setup of the Process Address Space

Setting up the address space for a new process is somewhat complicated, so let's look at what's involved one step at a time. To get the most out of this section, you should have some familiarity with the internals of the Windows memory manager, which are described in Chapter 9.

- The virtual memory manager sets the value of the process's last trim time to the current time. The working set manager (which runs in the context of the balance set manager system thread) uses this value to determine when to initiate working set trimming.

- The memory manager initializes the process's working set list—page faults can now be taken.

- The section (created when the image file was opened) is now mapped into the new process's address space, and the process section base address is set to the base address of the image.

- Ntdll.dll is mapped into the process.

> **Note** POSIX processes clone the address space of their parents, so they don't have to go through these steps to create a new address space. In the case of POSIX applications, the new process's section base address is set to that of its parent process and the parent's PEB is cloned for the new process.

Stage 3E: Setting Up the PEB

NtCreateUserProcess calls *MmCreatePeb,* which first maps the systemwide national language support (NLS) tables into the process's address space. It next calls *MiCreatePebOrTeb* to allocate a page for the PEB and then initializes a number of fields, which are described in Table 5-7.

TABLE 5-7 Initial Values of the Fields of the PEB

Field	Initial Value
ImageBaseAddress	Base address of section
NumberOfProcessors	*KeNumberProcessors* kernel variable
NtGlobalFlag	*NtGlobalFlag* kernel variable
CriticalSectionTimeout	*MmCriticalSectionTimeout* kernel variable
HeapSegmentReserve	*MmHeapSegmentReserve* kernel variable
HeapSegmentCommit	*MmHeapSegmentCommit* kernel variable
HeapDeCommitTotalFreeThreshold	*MmHeapDeCommitTotalFreeThreshold* kernel variable
HeapDeCommitFreeBlockThreshold	*MmHeapDeCommitFreeBlockThreshold* kernel variable
NumberOfHeaps	0

Field	Initial Value
MaximumNumberOfHeaps	(Size of a page – size of a PEB) / 4
ProcessHeaps	First byte after PEB
MinimumStackCommit	*MmMinimumStackCommitInBytes* kernel variable
ImageProcessAffinityMask	*KeActiveProcessors* or 1 << *MmRotatingUniprocessorNumber* kernel variable (for uniprocessor-only images)
SessionId	Result of *MmGetSessionId*
ImageSubSystem	OptionalHeader.Subsystem
ImageSubSystemMajorVersion	OptionalHeader.MajorSubsystemVersion
ImageSubSystemMinorVersion	OptionalHeader.MinorSubsystemVersion
OSMajorVersion	*NtMajorVersion* kernel variable
OSMinorVersion	*NtMinorVersion* kernel variable
OSBuildNumber	*NtBuildNumber* kernel variable & 0x3FFF, combined with *CmNtCSDVersion* for service packs
OSPlatformId	2

However, if the image file specifies explicit Windows version or affinity values, this information replaces the initial values shown in Table 5-7. The mapping from image information fields to PEB fields is described in Table 5-8.

TABLE 5-8 Windows Replacements for Initial PEB Values

Field Name	Value Taken from Image Header
OSMajorVersion	OptionalHeader.Win32VersionValue & 0xFF
OSMinorVersion	(OptionalHeader.Win32VersionValue >> 8) & 0xFF
OSBuildNumber	(OptionalHeader.Win32VersionValue >> 16) & 0x3FFF, combined with ImageLoadConfigDirectory.CSDVersion
OSPlatformId	(OptionalHeader.Win32VersionValue >> 30) ^ 0x2
ImageProcessAffinityMask	ImageLoadConfigDirectory.ProcessAffinityMask

If the image header characteristics IMAGE_FILE_UP_SYSTEM_ONLY flag is set (indicating that the image can run only on a uniprocessor system), a single CPU is chosen for all the threads in this new process to run on. The selection process is performed by simply cycling through the available processors—each time this type of image is run, the next processor is used. In this way, these types of images are spread evenly across the processors.

If the image specifies an explicit processor affinity mask (for example, a field in the configuration header), this value is copied to the PEB and later set as the default process affinity mask.

Stage 3F: Completing the Setup of the Executive Process Object (*PspInsertProcess*)

Before the handle to the new process can be returned, a few final setup steps must be completed, which are performed by *PspInsertProcess* and its helper functions:

1. If systemwide auditing of processes is enabled (either as a result of local policy settings or group policy settings from a domain controller), the process's creation is written to the Security event log.

2. If the parent process was contained in a job, the job is recovered from the job level set of the parent and then bound to the session of the newly created process. Finally, the new process is added to the job.

3. *PspInsertProcess* inserts the new process block at the end of the Windows list of active processes (*PsActiveProcessHead*).

4. The process debug port of the parent process is copied to the new child process, unless the NoDebugInherit flag is set (which can be requested when creating the process). If a debug port was specified, it is attached to the new process at this time.

5. Finally, *PspInsertProcess* notifies any registered callback routines, creates a handle for the new process by calling *ObOpenObjectByPointer,* and then returns this handle to the caller.

Stage 4: Creating the Initial Thread and Its Stack and Context

At this point, the Windows executive process object is completely set up. It still has no thread, however, so it can't do anything yet. It's now time to start that work. Normally, the *PspCreateThread* routine is responsible for all aspects of thread creation and is called by *NtCreateThread* when a new thread is being created. However, because the initial thread is created internally by the kernel without user-mode input, the two helper routines that *PspCreateThread* relies on are used instead: *PspAllocateThread* and *PspInsertThread*.

PspAllocateThread handles the actual creation and initialization of the executive thread object itself, while *PspInsertThread* handles the creation of the thread handle and security attributes and the call to *KeStartThread* to turn the executive object into a schedulable thread on the system. However, the thread won't do anything yet—it is created in a suspended state and isn't resumed until the process is completely initialized (as described in Stage 5).

Note The thread parameter (which can't be specified in *CreateProcess* but can be specified in *CreateThread*) is the address of the PEB. This parameter will be used by the initialization code that runs in the context of this new thread (as described in Stage 6).

PspAllocateThread performs the following steps:

1. An executive thread block (ETHREAD) is created and initialized.

2. Before the thread can execute, it needs a stack and a context in which to run, so these are set up. The stack size for the initial thread is taken from the image—there's no way to specify another size.

3. The thread environment block (TEB) is allocated for the new thread.

4. The user-mode thread start address is stored in the ETHREAD. This is the system-supplied thread startup function in Ntdll.dll (*RtlUserThreadStart*). The user's specified Windows start address is stored in the ETHREAD block in a different location so that debugging tools such as Process Explorer can query the information.

5. *KeInitThread* is called to set up the KTHREAD block. The thread's initial and current base priorities are set to the process's base priority, and its affinity and quantum are set to that of the process. This function also sets the initial thread ideal processor. (See the section "Ideal and Last Processor" for a description of how this is chosen.) *KeInitThread* next allocates a kernel stack for the thread and initializes the machine-dependent hardware context for the thread, including the context, trap, and exception frames. The thread's context is set up so that the thread will start in kernel mode in *KiThreadStartup*. Finally, *KeInitThread* sets the thread's state to Initialized and returns to *PspAllocateThread*.

Once that work is finished, *NtCreateUserProcess* will call *PspInsertThread* to perform the following steps:

1. A thread ID is generated for the new thread.

2. The thread count in the process object is incremented, and the thread is added into the process thread list.

3. The thread is put into a suspended state.

4. The object is inserted and any registered thread callbacks are called.

5. The handle is created with *ObOpenObjectByName*.

6. The thread is readied for execution by calling *KeStartThread*.

Stage 5: Performing Windows Subsystem–Specific Post-Initialization

Once *NtCreateUserProcess* returns with a success code, all the necessary executive process and thread objects have been created. Kernel32.dll will now perform various operations related to Windows subsystem–specific operations to finish initializing the process.

First of all, various checks are made for whether Windows should allow the executable to run. These checks includes validating the image version in the header and checking whether Windows application certification has blocked the process (through a group policy). On specialized editions of Windows Server 2008, such as Windows Web Server 2008 and Windows HPC Server 2008, additional checks are made to see if the application imports any disallowed APIs.

If software restriction policies dictate, a restricted token is created for the new process. Afterward, the application compatibility database is queried to see if an entry exists in either the registry or system application database for the process. Compatibility shims will not be applied at this point—the information will be stored in the PEB once the initial thread starts executing (Stage 6).

At this point, Kernel32.dll sends a message to the Windows subsystem so that it can set up SxS information (see the end of this section for more information on side-by-side assemblies) such as manifest files, DLL redirection paths, and out-of-process execution for the new process. It also initializes the Windows subsystem structures for the process and initial thread. The message includes the following information:

- Process and thread handles
- Entries in the creation flags
- ID of the process's creator
- Flag indicating whether the process belongs to a Windows application (so that Csrss can determine whether or not to show the startup cursor)
- UI language Information
- DLL redirection and .local flags
- Manifest file information

The Windows subsystem performs the following steps when it receives this message:

1. *CsrCreateProcess* duplicates a handle for the process and thread. In this step, the usage count of the process and the thread is incremented from 1 (which was set at creation time) to 2.

2. If a process priority class isn't specified, *CsrCreateProcess* sets it according to the algorithm described earlier in this section.

3. The Csrss process block is allocated.

4. The new process's exception port is set to be the general function port for the Windows subsystem so that the Windows subsystem will receive a message when a second chance exception occurs in the process. (For further information on exception handling, see Chapter 3.)

5. The Csrss thread block is allocated and initialized.

6. *CsrCreateThread* inserts the thread in the list of threads for the process.

7. The count of processes in this session is incremented.

8. The process shutdown level is set to 0x280 (the default process shutdown level— see *SetProcessShutdownParameters* in the MSDN Library documentation for more information).

9. The new process block is inserted into the list of Windows subsystem-wide processes.

10. The per-process data structure used by the kernel-mode part of the Windows subsystem (W32PROCESS structure) is allocated and initialized.

11. The application start cursor is displayed. This cursor is the familiar rolling doughnut shape—the way that Windows says to the user, "I'm starting something, but you can use the cursor in the meantime." If the process doesn't make a GUI call after 2 seconds, the cursor reverts to the standard pointer. If the process does make a GUI call in the allotted time, *CsrCreateProcess* waits 5 seconds for the application to show a window. After that time, *CsrCreateProcess* will reset the cursor again.

After Csrss has performed these steps, *CreateProcess* checks whether the process was run elevated (which means it was executed through *ShellExecute* and elevated by the AppInfo service after the consent dialog box was shown to the user). This includes checking whether the process was a setup program. If it was, the process's token is opened, and the virtualization flag is turned on so that the application is virtualized. (See the information on UAC and virtualization in Chapter 6.) If the application contained elevation shims or had a requested elevation level in its manifest, the process is destroyed and an elevation request is sent to the AppInfo service. (See Chapter 6 for more information on elevation.)

Note that most of these checks are not performed for protected processes; because these processes must have been designed for Windows Vista or later, there's no reason why they should require elevation, virtualization, or application compatibility checks and processing. Additionally, allowing mechanisms such as the shim engine to use its usual hooking and memory patching techniques on a protected process would result in a security hole if someone could figure how to insert arbitrary shims that modify the behavior of the protected process.

Stage 6: Starting Execution of the Initial Thread

At this point, the process environment has been determined, resources for its threads to use have been allocated, the process has a thread, and the Windows subsystem knows about the new process. Unless the caller specified the CREATE_SUSPENDED flag, the initial thread is now resumed so that it can start running and perform the remainder of the process initialization work that occurs in the context of the new process (Stage 7).

Stage 7: Performing Process Initialization in the Context of the New Process

The new thread begins life running the kernel-mode thread startup routine *KiThreadStartup*. *KiThreadStartup* lowers the thread's IRQL level from DPC/dispatch level to APC level and then calls the system initial thread routine, *PspUserThreadStartup*. The user-specified thread start address is passed as a parameter to this routine.

First, this function sets the Locale ID and the ideal processor in the TEB, based on the information present in kernel-mode data structures, and then it checks if thread creation actually failed. Next it calls *DbgkCreateThread,* which checks if image notifications were sent for the new process. If they weren't, and notifications are enabled, an image notification is sent first for the process and then for the image load of Ntdll.dll. Note that this is done in this stage rather than when the images were first mapped, because the process ID (which is required for the callouts) is not yet allocated at that time.

Once those checks are completed, another check is performed to see whether the process is a debuggee. If it is, then *PspUserThreadStartup* checks if the debugger notifications have already been sent for this process. If not, then a create process message is sent through the debug object (if one is present) so that the process startup debug event (CREATE_PROCESS_ DEBUG_INFO) can be sent to the appropriate debugger process. This is followed by a similar thread startup debug event and by another debug event for the image load of Ntdll.dll. *DbgkCreateThread* then waits for the Windows subsystem to get the reply from the debugger (via the *ContinueDebugEvent* function).

Now that the debugger has been notified, *PspUserThreadStartup* looks at the result of the initial check on the thread's life. If it was killed on startup, the thread is terminated. This check is done after the debugger and image notifications to be sure that the kernel-mode and user-mode debuggers don't miss information on the thread, even if the thread never got a chance to run.

Otherwise, the routine checks whether application prefetching is enabled on the system and, if so, calls the prefetcher (and Superfetch) to process the prefetch instruction file (if it exists) and prefetch pages referenced during the first 10 seconds the last time the process ran. (For details on the prefetcher and Superfetch, see Chapter 9.)

PspUserThreadStartup then checks if the systemwide cookie in the SharedUserData structure has been set up yet. If it hasn't, it generates it based on a hash of system information such as the number of interrupts processed, DPC deliveries, and page faults. This systemwide cookie is used in the internal decoding and encoding of pointers, such as in the heap manager (for more information on heap manager security, see Chapter 9), to protect against certain classes of exploitation.

Finally, *PspUserThreadStartup* sets up the initial thunk context to run the image loader initial-ization routine (*LdrInitializeThunk* in Ntdll.dll), as well as the systemwide thread startup stub (*RtlUserThreadStart* in Ntdll.dll). These steps are done by editing the context of the thread in place and then issuing an *exit from system service* operation, which will load the specially crafted user context. The *LdrInitializeThunk* routine initializes the loader, heap manager, NLS tables, thread-local storage (TLS) and fiber-local storage (FLS) array, and critical section struc-tures. It then loads any required DLLs and calls the DLL entry points with the DLL_PROCESS_ ATTACH function code. (See the sidebar "Side-by-Side Assemblies" for a description of a mechanism Windows uses to address DLL versioning problems.)

Once the function returns, *NtContinue* will restore the new user context and return back to user mode—thread execution now truly starts.

RtlUserThreadStart will use the address of the actual image entry point and the start param-eter and call the application. These two parameters have also already been pushed onto the stack by the kernel. This complicated series of events has two purposes. First of all, it allows the image loader inside Ntdll.dll to set up the process internally and behind the scenes so that other user-mode code can run properly (otherwise, it would have no heap, no thread local storage, and so on).

Second, having all threads begin in a common routine allows them to be wrapped in excep-tion handling, so that when they crash, Ntdll.dll is aware of that and can call the unhandled exception filter inside Kernel32.dll. It is also able to coordinate thread exit on return from the thread's start routine and to perform various cleanup work. Application developers can also call *SetUnhandledExceptionFilter* to add their own unhandled exception handling code.

Side-by-Side Assemblies

In order to isolate DLLs distributed with applications from DLLs that ship with the oper-ating system, Windows allows applications to use private copies of these core DLLs. To use a private copy of a DLL instead of the one in the system directory, an application's installation must include a file named *Application*.exe.local (where *Application* is the name of the application's executable), which directs the loader to first look for DLLs in that directory. Note that any DLLs that are loaded from the list of KnownDLLs (DLLs that are permanently mapped into memory) or that are loaded by those DLLs cannot be redirected using this mechanism.

To further address application and DLL compatibility while allowing sharing, Windows implements the concept of *shared assemblies*. An *assembly* consists of a group of resources, including DLLs, and an XML manifest file that describes the assembly and its contents. An application references an assembly through the existence of its own XML manifest. The manifest can be a file in the application's installation directory that has

the same name as the application with ".manifest" appended (for example, application.exe.manifest), or it can be linked into the application as a resource. The manifest describes the application and its dependence on assemblies.

There are two types of assemblies: private and shared. The difference between the two is that shared assemblies are digitally signed so that corruption or modification of their contents can be detected. In addition, shared assemblies are stored under the \Windows\Winsxs directory, whereas private assemblies are stored in an application's installation directory. Thus, shared assemblies also have an associated catalog file (.cat) that contains its digital signature information. Shared assemblies can be "side-by-side" assemblies because multiple versions of a DLL can reside on a system simultaneously, with applications dependent on a particular version of a DLL always using that particular version.

An assembly's manifest file typically has a name that includes the name of the assembly, version information, some text that represents a unique signature, and the extension ".manifest". The manifests are stored in \Windows\Winsxs\Manifests, and the rest of the assembly's resources are stored in subdirectories of \Windows\Winsxs that have the same name as the corresponding manifest files, with the exception of the trailing .manifest extension.

An example of a shared assembly is version 6 of the Windows common controls DLL, comctl32.dll. Its manifest file is named \Windows\Winsxs\Manifests\x86_Microsoft.Windows.Common-Controls_6595b64144ccf1df_6.0.0.0_x-ww_1382d70a.manifest. It has an associated catalog file (which is the same name with the .cat extension) and a subdirectory of Winsxs that includes comctl32.dll.

Version 6 of Comctl32.dll added integration with Windows themes, and because applications not written with theme support in mind might not appear correctly with the new DLL, it's available only to applications that explicitly reference the shared assembly containing it—the version of Comctl32.dll installed in \Windows\System32 is an instance of version 5.x, which is not theme aware. When an application loads, the loader looks for the application's manifest, and if one exists, loads the DLLs from the assemblies specified. DLLs not included in assemblies referenced in the manifest are loaded in the traditional way. Legacy applications, therefore, link against the version in \Windows\System32, whereas theme-aware applications can specify the new version in their manifest.

A final advantage that shared assemblies have is that a publisher can issue a publisher configuration, which can redirect all applications that use a particular assembly to use an updated version. Publishers would do this if they were preserving backward compatibility while addressing bugs. Ultimately, however, because of the flexibility inherent in the assembly model, an application could decide to override the new setting and continue to use an older version.

EXPERIMENT: Tracing Process Startup

Now that we've looked in detail at how a process starts up and the different operations required to begin executing an application, we're going to use Process Monitor to take a look at some of the file I/O and registry keys that are accessed during this process.

Although this experiment will not provide a complete picture of all the internal steps we've described, you'll be able to see several parts of the system in action, notably Prefetch and Superfetch, image file execution options and other compatibility checks, and the image loader's DLL mapping.

We're going to be looking at a very simple executable—Notepad.exe—and we will be launching it from a Command Prompt window (Cmd.exe). It's important that we look both at the operations inside Cmd.exe and those inside Notepad.exe. Recall that a lot of the user-mode work is performed by *CreateProcess*, which is called by the parent process before the kernel has created a new process object.

To set things up correctly, add two filters to Process Monitor: one for Cmd.exe, and one for Notepad.exe—these are the only two processes we want to include. It will be helpful to be sure that you don't have any currently running instances of these two processes so that you know you're looking at the right events. The filter window should look like this:

Next, make sure that event logging is currently disabled (clear File, Capture Events), and then start up the command prompt. Enable event logging (using the File menu again, or simply press CTRL+E or click the magnifying glass icon on the toolbar) and then enter **Notepad.exe** and press Enter. On a typical Windows Vista system, you should see anywhere between 500 and 1500 events appear. Go ahead and hide the Sequence and Time Of Day columns so that we can focus our attention on the columns of interest. Your window should look similar to the one shown next.

Just as described in Stage 1 of the *CreateProcess* flow, one of the first things to notice is that just before the process is started and the first thread is created, Cmd.exe does a registry read at HKLM\SOFTWARE\Microsoft\Windows NT\CurrentVersion\Image File Execution Options. Because there were no image execution options associated with Notepad.exe, the process was created as is.

As with this and any other event in Process Monitor's log, you have the ability to see whether each part of the process creation flow was performed in user mode or kernel mode, and by which routines, by looking at the stack of the event. To do this, double-click on the RegOpenKey event mentioned and switch to the Stack tab. The following screen shows the standard stack on a 32-bit Windows Vista machine.

This stack shows that we have already reached the part of process creation performed in kernel mode (through *NtCreateUserProcess*) and that the helper routine *PspAllocateProcess* is responsible for this check.

Going down the list of events after the thread and process have been created, you will notice three groups of events. The first is a simple check for application compatibility flags, which will let the user-mode process creation code know if checks inside the application compatibility database are required through the shim engine.

This check is followed by multiple reads to Side-By-Side, Manifest, and MUI/Language keys, which are part of the assembly framework mentioned earlier. Finally, you may see file I/O to one or more .sdb files, which are the application compatibility databases on the system. This I/O is where additional checks are done to see if the shim engine needs to be invoked for this application. Since Notepad is a well behaved Microsoft program, it doesn't require any shims.

The following screen shows the next series of events, which happen inside the Notepad process itself. These are actions initiated by the user-mode thread startup wrapper in kernel mode, which performs the actions described earlier. The first two are the Notepad.exe and Ntdll.dll image load debug notification messages, which can only be generated now that code is running inside Notepad's process context and not the context for the command prompt.

Next, the prefetcher kicks in, looking for a prefetch database file that has already been generated for Notepad. (For more information on the prefetcher, see Chapter 9). On a system where Notepad has already been run at least once, this database will exist, and the prefetcher will begin executing the commands specified inside it. If this is the case, scrolling down you will see multiple DLLs being read and queried. Unlike typical DLL loading, which is done by the user-mode image loader by looking at the import tables or when an application manually loads a DLL, these events are being generated by the prefetcher, which is already aware of the libraries that Notepad will require. Typical image loading of the DLLs required happens next, and you will see events similar to the ones shown here.

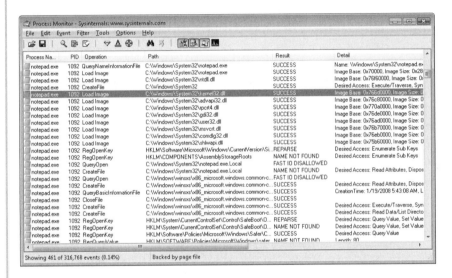

These events are now being generated from code running inside user mode, which was called once the kernel-mode wrapper function finished its work. Therefore, these are the first events coming from *LdrpInitializeProcess*, which we mentioned is the internal system wrapper function for any new process, before the start address wrapper is called. You can confirm this on your own by looking at the stack of these events; for example, the kernel32.dll image load event, which is shown in the next screen.

Further events are generated by this routine and its associated helper functions until you finally reach events generated by the *WinMain* function inside Notepad, which is where code under the developer's control is now being executed. Describing in detail all the events and user-mode components that come into play during process execution would fill up this entire chapter, so exploration of any further events is left as an exercise for the reader.

Thread Internals

Now that we've dissected processes, let's turn our attention to the structure of a thread. Unless explicitly stated otherwise, you can assume that anything in this section applies to both user-mode threads and kernel-mode system threads (which are described in Chapter 2).

Data Structures

At the operating-system level, a Windows thread is represented by an executive thread (ETHREAD) block, which is illustrated in Figure 5-7. The ETHREAD block and the structures it points to exist in the system address space, with the exception of the thread environment block (TEB), which exists in the process address space (again, because user-mode components need to have access to it).

In addition, the Windows subsystem process (Csrss) also maintains a parallel structure for each thread created in a Windows subsystem application. Also, for threads that have called a Windows subsystem USER or GDI function, the kernel-mode portion of the Windows subsystem (Win32k.sys) maintains a per-thread data structure (called the W32THREAD structure) that the ETHREAD block points to.

FIGURE 5-7 Structure of the executive thread block

Most of the fields illustrated in Figure 5-7 are self-explanatory. The first field is the kernel thread (KTHREAD) block. Following that are the thread identification information, the process identification information (including a pointer to the owning process so that its environment information can be accessed), security information in the form of a pointer to the access token and impersonation information, and finally, fields relating to ALPC messages and pending I/O requests. As you can see in Table 5-9, some of these key fields are covered in more detail elsewhere in this book. For more details on the internal structure of an ETHREAD block, you can use the kernel debugger *dt* command to display the format of the structure.

TABLE 5-9 Key Contents of the Executive Thread Block

Field Name	Value Taken from Image Header	Additional Information
KTHREAD	See Table 5-10.	
Thread time	Thread create and exit time information.	
Process identification	Process ID and pointer to EPROCESS block of the process that the thread belongs to.	
Start address	Address of thread start routine.	
Impersonation information	Access token and impersonation level (if the thread is impersonating a client).	Chapter 6
ALPC information	Message ID that the thread is waiting for and address of message.	Advanced local procedure calls (ALPC) (Chapter 3)
I/O information	List of pending I/O request packets (IRPs).	I/O system (Chapter 7)

Let's take a closer look at two of the key thread data structures referred to in the preceding text: the KTHREAD block and the TEB. The KTHREAD block (also called the TCB, or thread control block) contains the information that the Windows kernel needs to access to perform thread scheduling and synchronization on behalf of running threads. Its layout is illustrated in Figure 5-8.

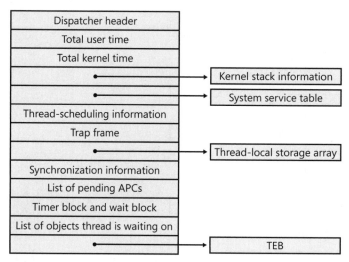

FIGURE 5-8 Structure of the kernel thread block

The key fields of the KTHREAD block are described briefly in Table 5-10.

TABLE 5-10 Key Contents of the KTHREAD Block

Element	Description	Additional Reference
Dispatcher header	Because the thread is an object that can be waited on, it starts with a standard kernel dispatcher object header.	Kernel dispatcher objects (Chapter 3)
Execution time	Total user and kernel CPU time.	
Cycle time	Total CPU cycle time.	Thread scheduling
Pointer to kernel stack information	Base and upper address of the kernel stack.	Memory management (Chapter 9)
Pointer to system service table	Each thread starts out with this field service table pointing to the main system service table (*KeServiceDescriptorTable*). When a thread first calls a Windows GUI service, its system service table is changed to one that includes the GDI and USER services in Win32k.sys.	System service dispatching (Chapter 3)

Element	Description	Additional Reference
Scheduling information	Base and current priority, quantum target, quantum reset, affinity mask, ideal processor, deferred processor, next processor, scheduling state, freeze count, suspend count, adjust increment and adjust reason.	Thread scheduling
Wait blocks	The thread block contains four built-in wait blocks so that wait blocks don't have to be allocated and initialized each time the thread waits for something. (One wait block is dedicated to timers.)	Synchronization (Chapter 3)
Wait information	List of objects the thread is waiting for, wait reason, IRQL at the time of wait, result of the wait, and time at which the thread entered the wait state.	Synchronization (Chapter 3)
Mutant list	List of mutant objects the thread owns.	Synchronization (Chapter 3)
APC queues	List of pending user-mode and kernel-mode APCs, alerted flag, and flags to disable APCs.	Asynchronous procedure call (APC) interrupts (Chapter 3)
Timer block	Built-in timer block (also a corresponding wait block).	
Suspend APC and semaphore	Built-in APC and semaphore used when suspending and resuming a thread.	Synchronization (Chapter 3)
Queue	Pointer to queue object that the thread is associated with.	Synchronization (Chapter 3)
Gate	Pointer to gate object that the thread is waiting on.	Synchronization (Chapter 3)
Pointer to TEB	Thread ID, TLS and FLS information, PEB pointer, and Winsock, RPC, GDI, OpenGL, and other user-mode information.	

EXPERIMENT: Displaying ETHREAD and KTHREAD Structures

The ETHREAD and KTHREAD structures can be displayed with the *dt* command in the kernel debugger. The following output shows the format of an ETHREAD on a 32-bit system:

```
lkd> dt nt!_ethread
nt!_ETHREAD
   +0x000 Tcb                : _KTHREAD
   +0x1e0 CreateTime         : _LARGE_INTEGER
   +0x1e8 ExitTime           : _LARGE_INTEGER
   +0x1e8 KeyedWaitChain     : _LIST_ENTRY
   +0x1f0 ExitStatus         : Int4B
   +0x1f0 OfsChain           : Ptr32 Void
   +0x1f4 PostBlockList      : _LIST_ENTRY
   +0x1f4 ForwardLinkShadow  : Ptr32 Void
   +0x1f8 StartAddress       : Ptr32 Void
   +0x1fc TerminationPort    : Ptr32 _TERMINATION_PORT
   +0x1fc ReaperLink         : Ptr32 _ETHREAD
   +0x1fc KeyedWaitValue     : Ptr32 Void
   +0x1fc Win32StartParameter : Ptr32 Void
   +0x200 ActiveTimerListLock : Uint4B
   +0x204 ActiveTimerListHead : _LIST_ENTRY
   +0x20c Cid                : _CLIENT_ID
   +0x214 KeyedWaitSemaphore : _KSEMAPHORE
   +0x214 AlpcWaitSemaphore  : _KSEMAPHORE
   +0x228 ClientSecurity     : _PS_CLIENT_SECURITY_CONTEXT
   +0x22c IrpList            : _LIST_ENTRY
   +0x234 TopLevelIrp        : Uint4B
   +0x238 DeviceToVerify     : Ptr32 _DEVICE_OBJECT
   +0x23c RateControlApc     : Ptr32 _PSP_RATE_APC
   +0x240 Win32StartAddress  : Ptr32 Void
   +0x244 SparePtr0          : Ptr32 Void
   +0x248 ThreadListEntry    : _LIST_ENTRY
   +0x250 RundownProtect     : _EX_RUNDOWN_REF
   +0x254 ThreadLock         : _EX_PUSH_LOCK
   +0x258 ReadClusterSize    : Uint4B
   +0x25c MmLockOrdering     : Int4B
   +0x260 CrossThreadFlags   : Uint4B
   +0x260 Terminated         : Pos 0, 1 Bit
   +0x260 ThreadInserted     : Pos 1, 1 Bit
   +0x260 HideFromDebugger   : Pos 2, 1 Bit
   +0x260 ActiveImpersonationInfo : Pos 3, 1 Bit
   +0x260 SystemThread       : Pos 4, 1 Bit
   +0x260 HardErrorsAreDisabled : Pos 5, 1 Bit
   +0x260 BreakOnTermination : Pos 6, 1 Bit
   +0x260 SkipCreationMsg    : Pos 7, 1 Bit
   +0x260 SkipTerminationMsg : Pos 8, 1 Bit
   +0x260 CopyTokenOnOpen    : Pos 9, 1 Bit
   +0x260 ThreadIoPriority   : Pos 10, 3 Bits
   +0x260 ThreadPagePriority : Pos 13, 3 Bits
   +0x260 RundownFail        : Pos 16, 1 Bit
   +0x264 SameThreadPassiveFlags : Uint4B
   +0x264 ActiveExWorker     : Pos 0, 1 Bit
   +0x264 ExWorkerCanWaitUser : Pos 1, 1 Bit
```

```
+0x264 MemoryMaker      : Pos 2, 1 Bit
+0x264 ClonedThread     : Pos 3, 1 Bit
+0x264 KeyedEventInUse  : Pos 4, 1 Bit
+0x264 RateApcState     : Pos 5, 2 Bits
+0x264 SelfTerminate    : Pos 7, 1 Bit
+0x268 SameThreadApcFlags : Uint4B
+0x268 Spare            : Pos 0, 1 Bit
+0x268 StartAddressInvalid : Pos 1, 1 Bit
+0x268 EtwPageFaultCalloutActive : Pos 2, 1 Bit
+0x268 OwnsProcessWorkingSetExclusive : Pos 3, 1 Bit
+0x268 OwnsProcessWorkingSetShared : Pos 4, 1 Bit
+0x268 OwnsSystemWorkingSetExclusive : Pos 5, 1 Bit
+0x268 OwnsSystemWorkingSetShared : Pos 6, 1 Bit
+0x268 OwnsSessionWorkingSetExclusive : Pos 7, 1 Bit
+0x269 OwnsSessionWorkingSetShared : Pos 0, 1 Bit
+0x269 OwnsProcessAddressSpaceExclusive : Pos 1, 1 Bit
+0x269 OwnsProcessAddressSpaceShared : Pos 2, 1 Bit
+0x269 SuppressSymbolLoad : Pos 3, 1 Bit
+0x269 Prefetching      : Pos 4, 1 Bit
+0x269 OwnsDynamicMemoryShared : Pos 5, 1 Bit
+0x269 OwnsChangeControlAreaExclusive : Pos 6, 1 Bit
+0x269 OwnsChangeControlAreaShared : Pos 7, 1 Bit
+0x26a PriorityRegionActive : Pos 0, 4 Bits
+0x26c CacheManagerActive : UChar
+0x26d DisablePageFaultClustering : UChar
+0x26e ActiveFaultCount : UChar
+0x270 AlpcMessageId    : Uint4B
+0x274 AlpcMessage      : Ptr32 Void
+0x274 AlpcReceiveAttributeSet : Uint4B
+0x278 AlpcWaitListEntry : _LIST_ENTRY
+0x280 CacheManagerCount : Uint4B
```

The KTHREAD can be displayed with a similar command:

```
lkd> dt nt!_kthread
nt!_KTHREAD
   +0x000 Header           : _DISPATCHER_HEADER
   +0x010 CycleTime        : Uint8B
   +0x018 HighCycleTime    : Uint4B
   +0x020 QuantumTarget    : Uint8B
   +0x028 InitialStack     : Ptr32 Void
   +0x02c StackLimit       : Ptr32 Void
   +0x030 KernelStack      : Ptr32 Void
   +0x034 ThreadLock       : Uint4B
   +0x038 ApcState         : _KAPC_STATE
   +0x038 ApcStateFill     : [23] UChar
   +0x04f Priority         : Char
   +0x050 NextProcessor    : Uint2B
   +0x052 DeferredProcessor : Uint2B
   +0x054 ApcQueueLock     : Uint4B
   +0x058 ContextSwitches  : Uint4B
   +0x05c State            : UChar
   +0x05d NpxState         : UChar
   +0x05e WaitIrql         : UChar
   +0x05f WaitMode         : Char
   +0x060 WaitStatus       : Int4B
```

EXPERIMENT: Using the Kernel Debugger *!thread* Command

The kernel debugger *!thread* command dumps a subset of the information in the thread data structures. Some key elements of the information the kernel debugger displays can't be displayed by any utility: internal structure addresses; priority details; stack information; the pending I/O request list; and, for threads in a wait state, the list of objects the thread is waiting for.

To display thread information, use either the *!process* command (which displays all the thread blocks after displaying the process block) or the *!thread* command to dump a specific thread. The output of the thread information, along with some annotations of key fields, is shown here:

Stack dump

EXPERIMENT: Viewing Thread Information

The following output is the detailed display of a process produced by using the Tlist utility in the Debugging Tools for Windows. Notice that the thread list shows the "Win32StartAddr." This is the address passed to the *CreateThread* function by the application. All the other utilities, except Process Explorer, that show the thread start address show the actual start address (a function in Ntdll.dll), not the application-specified start address.

```
C:\> tlist winword
2400 WINWORD.EXE        WinInt5E_Chapter06.doc [Compatibility Mode] - Microsoft Word
   CWD:     C:\Users\Alex Ionescu\Documents\
   CmdLine: "C:\Program Files\Microsoft Office\Office12\WINWORD.EXE" /n /dde
   VirtualSize:    310656 KB  PeakVirtualSize:    343552 KB
   WorkingSetSize: 91548 KB   PeakWorkingSetSize:100788 KB
   NumberOfThreads: 6
   2456 Win32StartAddr:0x2f7f10cc LastErr:0x00000000 State:Waiting
   1452 Win32StartAddr:0x6882f519 LastErr:0x00000000 State:Waiting
   2464 Win32StartAddr:0x6b603850 LastErr:0x00000000 State:Waiting
   3036 Win32StartAddr:0x690dc17f LastErr:0x00000002 State:Waiting
   3932 Win32StartAddr:0x775cac65 LastErr:0x00000102 State:Waiting
   3140 Win32StartAddr:0x687d6ffd LastErr:0x000003f0 State:Waiting
  12.0.4518.1014 shp  0x2F7F0000  C:\Program Files\Microsoft Office\Office12\
     WINWORD.EXE
   6.0.6000.16386 shp  0x777D0000  C:\Windows\system32\Ntdll.dll
   6.0.6000.16386 shp  0x764C0000  C:\Windows\system32\kernel32.dll
          §           list of DLLs loaded in process
```

The TEB, illustrated in Figure 5-9, is the only data structure explained in this section that exists in the process address space (as opposed to the system space).

The TEB stores context information for the image loader and various Windows DLLs. Because these components run in user mode, they need a data structure writable from user mode. That's why this structure exists in the process address space instead of in the system space, where it would be writable only from kernel mode. You can find the address of the TEB with the kernel debugger *!thread* command.

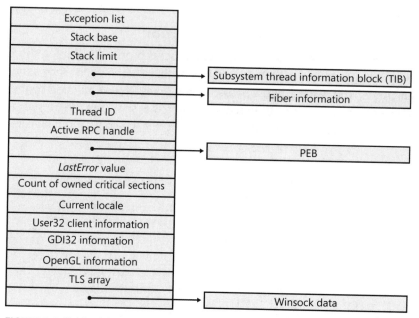

FIGURE 5-9 Fields of the thread environment block

EXPERIMENT: Examining the TEB

You can dump the TEB structure with the *!teb* command in the kernel debugger. The output looks like this:

```
kd> !teb
TEB at 7ffde000
    ExceptionList:        019e8e44
    StackBase:            019f0000
    StackLimit:           019db000
    SubSystemTib:         00000000
    FiberData:            00001e00
    ArbitraryUserPointer: 00000000
    Self:                 7ffde000
    EnvironmentPointer:   00000000
    ClientId:             00000bcc . 00000864
    RpcHandle:            00000000
    Tls Storage:          7ffde02c
    PEB Address:          7ffd9000
    LastErrorValue:       0
    LastStatusValue:      c0000139
    Count Owned Locks:    0
    HardErrorMode:        0
```

Kernel Variables

As with processes, a number of Windows kernel variables control how threads run. Table 5-11 shows the kernel-mode kernel variables that relate to threads.

TABLE 5-11 **Thread-Related Kernel Variables**

Variable	Type	Description
PspCreateThreadNotifyRoutine	Array of executive callback objects	Array of callback objects describing the routines to be called on thread creation and deletion (maximum of 64)
PspCreateThreadNotifyRoutineCount	32-bit integer	Count of registered thread-notification routines

Performance Counters

Most of the key information in the thread data structures is exported as performance counters, which are listed in Table 5-12. You can extract much information about the internals of a thread just by using the Reliability and Performance Monitor in Windows.

TABLE 5-12 **Thread-Related Performance Counters**

Object: Counter	Function
Process: Priority Base	Returns the current base priority of the process. This is the starting priority for threads created within this process.
Thread: % Privileged Time	Describes the percentage of time that the thread has run in kernel mode during a specified interval.
Thread: % Processor Time	Describes the percentage of CPU time that the thread has used during a specified interval. This count is the sum of % Privileged Time and % User Time.
Thread: % User Time	Describes the percentage of time that the thread has run in user mode during a specified interval.
Thread: Context Switches/Sec	Returns the number of context switches per second that the system is executing.
Thread: Elapsed Time	Returns the amount of CPU time (in seconds) that the thread has consumed.
Thread: ID Process	Returns the process ID of the thread's process.
Thread: ID Thread	Returns the thread's thread ID. This ID is valid only during the thread's lifetime because thread IDs are reused.
Thread: Priority Base	Returns the thread's current base priority. This number might be different from the thread's starting base priority.
Thread: Priority Current	Returns the thread's current dynamic priority.
Thread: Start Address	Returns the thread's starting virtual address (*Note*: This address will be the same for most threads.)

Object: Counter	Function
Thread: Thread State	Returns a value from 0 through 7 relating to the current state of the thread.
Thread: Thread Wait Reason	Returns a value from 0 through 19 relating to the reason why the thread is in a wait state.

Relevant Functions

Table 5-13 shows the Windows functions for creating and manipulating threads. This table doesn't include functions that have to do with thread scheduling and priorities—those are included in the section "Thread Scheduling" later in this chapter.

TABLE 5-13 Windows Thread Functions

Function	Description
CreateThread	Creates a new thread
CreateRemoteThread	Creates a thread in another process
OpenThread	Opens an existing thread
ExitThread	Ends execution of a thread normally
TerminateThread	Terminates a thread
IsThreadAFiber	Returns whether the current thread is a fiber
GetExitCodeThread	Gets another thread's exit code
GetThreadTimes	Returns timing information for a thread
QueryThreadCycleTime	Returns CPU clock cycle information for a thread
GetCurrentThread	Returns a pseudo handle for the current thread
GetCurrentProcessId	Returns the thread ID of the current thread
GetThreadId	Returns the thread ID of the specified thread
Get/SetThreadContext	Returns or changes a thread's CPU registers
GetThreadSelectorEntry	Returns another thread's descriptor table entry (applies only to x86 systems)

Birth of a Thread

A thread's life cycle starts when a program creates a new thread. The request filters down to the Windows executive, where the process manager allocates space for a thread object and calls the kernel to initialize the kernel thread block. The steps in the following list are taken inside the Windows *CreateThread* function in Kernel32.dll to create a Windows thread.

1. *CreateThread* converts the Windows API parameters to native flags and builds a native structure describing object parameters (OBJECT_ATTRIBUTES). See Chapter 3 for more information.

2. *CreateThread* builds an attribute list with two entries: client ID and TEB address. This allows *CreateThread* to receive those values once the thread has been created. (For more information on attribute lists, see the section "Flow of *CreateProcess*" earlier in this chapter.)

3. *NtCreateThreadEx* is called to create the user-mode context and probe and capture the attribute list. It then calls *PspCreateThread* to create a suspended executive thread object. For a description of the steps performed by this function, see the descriptions of Stage 3 and Stage 5 in the section "Flow of *CreateProcess*."

4. *CreateThread* allocates an activation stack for the thread used by side-by-side assembly support. It then queries the activation stack to see if it requires activation, and does so if needed. The activation stack pointer is saved in the new thread's TEB.

5. *CreateThread* notifies the Windows subsystem about the new thread, and the subsystem does some setup work for the new thread.

6. The thread handle and the thread ID (generated during step 3) are returned to the caller.

7. Unless the caller created the thread with the CREATE_SUSPENDED flag set, the thread is now resumed so that it can be scheduled for execution. When the thread starts running, it executes the steps described in the earlier section "Stage 7: Performing Process Initialization in the Context of the New Process" before calling the actual user's specified start address.

Examining Thread Activity

Examining thread activity is especially important if you are trying to determine why a process that is hosting multiple services is running (such as Svchost.exe, Dllhost.exe, or Lsass.exe) or why a process is hung.

There are several tools that expose various elements of the state of Windows threads: WinDbg (in user-process attach and kernel debugging mode), the Reliability and Performance Monitor, and Process Explorer. (The tools that show thread-scheduling information are listed in the section "Thread Scheduling.")

To view the threads in a process with Process Explorer, select a process and open the process properties (double-click on the process or click on the Process, Properties menu item). Then click on the Threads tab. This tab shows a list of the threads in the process and three columns of information. For each thread it shows the percentage of CPU consumed (based on the refresh interval configured), the number of context switches to the thread, and the thread start address. You can sort by any of these three columns.

New threads that are created are highlighted in green, and threads that exit are highlighted in red. (The highlight duration can be configured with the Options, Configure Highlighting menu item.) This might be helpful to discover unnecessary thread creation occurring in a process. (In general, threads should be created at process startup, not every time a request is processed inside a process.)

As you select each thread in the list, Process Explorer displays the thread ID, start time, state, CPU time counters, number of context switches, and the base and current priority. There is a Kill button, which will terminate an individual thread, but this should be used with extreme care.

The best way to measure actual CPU activity with Process Explorer is to add the clock cycle delta column, which uses the clock cycle counter designed for thread run-time account-ing (as described later in this chapter). Because many threads run for such a short amount of time that they are seldom (if ever) the currently running thread when the clock interval timer interrupt occurs, they are not charged for much of their CPU time. The total number of clock cycles represents the actual number of processor cycles that each thread in the process accrued. It is independent of the clock interval timer's resolution because the count is main-tained internally by the processor at each cycle and updated by Windows at each interrupt entry (a final accumulation is done before a context switch).

The thread start address is displayed in the form *"module!function"*, where *module* is the name of the .exe or .dll. The function name relies on access to symbol files for the module. (See "Experiment: Viewing Process Details with Process Explorer" in Chapter 1.) If you are unsure what the module is, click the Module button. This opens an Explorer file properties window for the module containing the thread's start address (for example, the .exe or .dll).

> **Note** For threads created by the Windows *CreateThread* function, Process Explorer displays the function passed to *CreateThread*, not the actual thread start function. That is because all Windows threads start at a common thread startup wrapper function (*RtlUserThreadStart* in Ntdll.dll). If Process Explorer showed the actual start address, most threads in processes would appear to have started at the same address, which would not be helpful in trying to understand what code the thread was executing. However, if Process Explorer can't query the user-defined startup address (such as in the case of a protected process), it will show the wrapper function, so you will see all threads starting at *RtlUserThreadStart*.

However, the thread start address displayed might not be enough information to pinpoint what the thread is doing and which component within the process is responsible for the CPU consumed by the thread. This is especially true if the thread start address is a generic startup function (for example, if the function name does not indicate what the thread is actually doing). In this case, examining the thread stack might answer the question. To view the stack for a thread, double-click on the thread of interest (or select it and click the Stack button).

Process Explorer displays the thread's stack (both user and kernel, if the thread was in kernel mode).

> **Note** While the user-mode debuggers (WinDbg, Ntsd, and Cdb) permit you to attach to a process and display the user stack for a thread, Process Explorer shows both the user and kernel stack in one easy click of a button. You can also examine user and kernel thread stacks using WinDbg in local kernel debugging mode.

Viewing the thread stack can also help you determine why a process is hung. As an example, on one system, Microsoft Office PowerPoint was hanging for one minute on startup. To determine why it was hung, after starting PowerPoint, Process Explorer was used to examine the thread stack of the one thread in the process. The result is shown in Figure 5-10.

FIGURE 5-10 Hung thread stack in PowerPoint

This thread stack shows that PowerPoint (line 10) called a function in Mso.dll (the central Microsoft Office DLL), which called the *OpenPrinterW* function in Winspool.drv (a DLL used to connect to printers). Winspool.drv then dispatched to a function *OpenPrinterRPC*, which then called a function in the RPC runtime DLL, indicating it was sending the request to a remote printer. So, without having to understand the internals of PowerPoint, the module and function names displayed on the thread stack indicate that the thread was waiting to connect to a network printer. On this particular system, there was a network printer that was not responding, which explained the delay starting PowerPoint. (Microsoft Office applications connect to all configured printers at process startup.) The connection to that printer was deleted from the user's system, and the problem went away.

Finally, when looking at 32-bit applications running on 64-bit systems as a Wow64 process (see Chapter 3 for more information on Wow64), Process Explorer shows both the 32-bit and 64-bit stack for threads. Because at the time of the system call proper, the thread has been switched to a 64-bit stack and context, simply looking at the thread's 64-bit stack would reveal only half the story—the 64-bit part of the thread, with Wow64's thunking code. So, when examining Wow64 processes, be sure to take into account both the 32-bit and 64-bit stacks. An example of a Wow64 thread inside Microsoft Office Word 2007 is shown in Figure 5-11. The stack frames highlighted in the box are the 32-bit stack frames from the 32-bit stack.

FIGURE 5-11 Example Wow64 stack

Limitations on Protected Process Threads

As we discussed in the process internals section, protected processes have several limitations in terms of which access rights will be granted, even to the users with the highest privileges on the system. These limitations also apply to threads inside such a process. This ensures that the actual code running inside the protected process cannot be hijacked or otherwise affected through standard Windows functions, which require the access rights in Table 5-14.

TABLE 5-14 Thread Access Rights Denied for Threads Inside a Protected Process

Object: Access Mask	Function
Thread: THREAD_ALL_ACCESS	Disables full access to a thread inside a protected process.
Thread: THREAD_DIRECT_IMPERSONATION	Disables impersonating a thread inside a protected process.
Thread: THREAD_GET_CONTEXT, THREAD_SET_CONTEXT	Disables accessing and/or modifying the CPU context (registers and stack) of a thread inside a protected process.
Thread: THREAD_QUERY_INFORMATION	Disables querying all information on a thread inside a protected process. However, a new access right was added, THREAD_QUERY_LIMITED_INFORMATION, that grants limited access to information on the thread.

Object: Access Mask	Function
Thread: THREAD_SET_INFORMATION	Disables setting all information on a thread inside a protected process. However, a new access right was added, THREAD_SET_LIMITED_INFORMATION, that grants limited access to modifying information on the thread.
Thread: THREAD_SET_THREAD_TOKEN	Disables setting an impersonation token for a thread inside a protected process.
Thread: THREAD_TERMINATE	Disables terminating a thread inside a protected process. Note that terminating all threads atomically through process termination is allowed.

EXPERIMENT: Viewing Protected Process Thread Information

In the previous section, we took a look at how Process Explorer can be helpful in examining thread activity to determine the cause of potential system or application issues. This time, we'll use Process Explorer to look at a protected process and see how the different access rights being denied affect its ability and usefulness on such a process.

Find the Audiodg.exe service inside the process list. This is a process responsible for much of the core work behind the user-mode audio stack in Windows Vista, and it requires protection to ensure that high-definition decrypted audio content does not leak out to untrusted sources. Bring up the process properties view and take a look at the Image tab. Notice how the numbers for WS Private, WS Shareable, and WS Shared are 0, although the total Working Set is still displayed. This is an example of the THREAD_QUERY_INFORMATION versus THREAD_QUERY_LIMITED_INFORMATION rights.

More importantly, take a look at the Threads tab. As you can see here, Process Explorer is unable to show the Win32 thread start address and instead displays the standard thread start wrapper inside Ntdll.dll. If you try clicking on the Stack button, you'll get an error, because Process Explorer needs to read the virtual memory inside the protected process, which it can't do.

Finally, note that although the Base and Dynamic priorities are shown, the I/O and Memory priorities are not, another example of the limited versus full query information access right. As you try to kill a thread inside Audiodg.exe, notice yet another access denied error: recall the lack of THREAD_TERMINATE access shown earlier in Table 5-14.

Worker Factories (Thread Pools)

Worker factories refer to the internal mechanism used to implement user-mode thread pools. Prior to Windows Vista, the thread pool routines were completely implemented in user mode inside the Ntdll.dll library, and the Windows API provided various routines to call into the relevant routines, which provided waitable timers, wait callbacks, and automatic thread creation and deletion depending on the amount of work being done.

Note Information on the new thread pool API is available on MSDN at *http://msdn2.micro-soft.com/en-us/library/ms686760.aspx*. It includes information on the APIs introduced and the APIs retired, as well as important differences in certain details of the way the two APIs are implemented.

In Windows Vista, the thread pool implementation in user mode was completely re-archi-tected, and part of the management functionality has been moved to kernel mode in order to improve efficiency and performance and minimize complexity. The original thread pool implementation required the user-mode code inside Ntdll.dll to remain aware of how many threads were currently active as worker threads, and to enlarge this number in periods of high demand.

Because querying the information necessary to make this decision, as well as the work to cre-ate the threads, took place in user mode, several system calls were required that could have been avoided if these operations were performed in kernel mode. Moving this code into kernel mode means fewer transitions between user and kernel mode, and it allows Ntdll.dll to manage the thread pool itself and not the system mechanisms behind it. It also provides other benefits, such as the ability to remotely create a thread pool in a process other than the calling process (although possible in user mode, it would be very complex given the necessity of using APIs to access the remote process's address space).

The functionality in Windows Vista is introduced by a new object manager type called *TpWorkerFactory*, as well as four new native system calls for managing the factory and its workers—*NtCreateWorkerFactory, NtWorkerFactoryWorkerReady, NtReleaseWorker-FactoryWorker, NtShutdownWorkerFactory*—two new query/set native calls (*NtQuery-InformationWorkerFactory* and *NtSetInformationWorkerFactory*), and a new wait call, *NtWaitForWorkViaWorkerFactory*.

Just like other native system calls, these calls provide user mode with a handle to the *TpWorkerFactory* object, which contains information such as the name and object attributes, the desired access mask, and a security descriptor. Unlike other system calls wrapped by the Windows API, however, thread pool management is handled by Ntdll.dll's native code, which means that developers work with an opaque descriptor (a TP_WORK pointer) owned by Ntdll.dll, in which the actual handle is stored.

As its name suggests, the worker factory implementation is responsible for allocating worker threads (and calling the given user-mode worker thread entry point), maintaining a minimum and maximum thread count (allowing for either permanent worker pools or totally dynamic pools), as well as other accounting information. This enables operations such as shutting down the thread pool to be performed with a single call to the kernel, because the kernel has been the only component responsible for thread creation and termination.

Because the kernel dynamically creates new threads as requested, this also increases the scal-ability of applications using the new thread pool implementation. Developers have always been able to take advantage of as many threads as possible (based on the number of proces-sors on the system) through the old implementation, but through support for dynamic pro-cessors in Windows Vista (see the section on this topic later in this chapter), it's now possible for applications using thread pools to automatically take advantage of new processors added at run time.

It's important to note that the new worker factory support is merely a wrapper to manage mundane tasks that would otherwise have to be performed in user mode (at a loss of performance). Many of the improvements in the new thread pool code are the result of changes in the Ntdll.dll side of this architecture. Also, it is not the worker factory code that provides the scalability, wait internals, and efficiency of work processing. Instead, it is a much older component of Windows that we have already discussed—I/O completion ports, or more correctly, kernel queues (KQUEUE; see Chapter 7 for more information).

In fact, when creating a worker factory, an I/O completion port must have already been created by user mode, and the handle needs to be passed on. It is through this I/O completion port that the user-mode implementation will queue work and also wait for work—but by calling the worker factory system calls instead of the I/O completion port APIs. Internally, however, the "release" worker factory call (which queues work) is a wrapper around *IoSetIoCompletion,* which increases pending work, while the "wait" call is a wrapper around *IoRemoveIoCompletion.* Both these routines call into the kernel queue implementation.

Therefore, the job of the worker factory code is to manage either a persistent, static, or dynamic thread pool; wrap the I/O completion port model into interfaces that try to prevent stalled worker queues by automatically creating dynamic threads; and to simplify global cleanup and termination operations during a factory shutdown request (as well as to easily block new requests against the factory in such a scenario).

Unfortunately, the data structures used by the worker factory implementation are not in the public symbols, but it is still possible to look at some worker pools, as we'll show in the next experiment.

EXPERIMENT: Looking at Thread Pools

Because of the more efficient and simpler thread pool implementation in Windows Vista, many core system components and applications were updated to make use of it. One of the ways to identify which processes are using a worker factory is to look at the handle list in Process Explorer. Follow these steps to look at some details behind them:

1. Run Process Explorer and select Show Unnamed Handles And Mappings from the View menu. Unfortunately, worker factories aren't named by Ntdll.dll, so you need to take this step in order to see the handles.

2. Select Lsm.exe from the list of processes, and look at the handle table. Make sure that the lower pane is shown (View, Show Lower Pane) and is displaying handle table mode (View, Lower Pane View, Handles).

3. Right-click on the lower pane columns, and then click on Select Columns. Make sure that the Type column is selected to be shown.

4. Now scroll down the handles, looking at the Type column, until you find a handle of type *TpWorkerFactory*. You should see something like this:

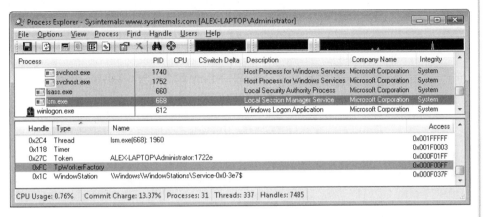

Notice how the *TpWorkerFactory* handle is immediately preceded by an *IoCompletion* handle. As was described previously, this occurs because before creating a worker factory, a handle to an I/O completion port on which work will be sent must be created.

5. Now double-click Lsm.exe in the list of processes, and go to the Threads tab. You should see something similar to the image here:

On this system (with two processors), the worker factory has created six worker threads at the request of Lsm.exe (processes can define a minimum and maximum number of threads) and based on its usage and the count of processors on the machine. These threads are identified as *TppWorkerThread*, which is Ntdll.dll's worker entry point when calling the worker factory system calls.

6. Ntdll.dll is responsible for its own internal accounting inside the worker thread wrapper (*TppWorkerThread*) before calling the worker callback that the application has registered. By looking at the Wait reason in the State information for each thread, you can get a rough idea of what each worker thread may be doing. Double-click on one of the threads inside an LPC wait to look at its stack. Here's an example:

```
Stack for thread 912

 0   ntkrnlpa.exe!KiSwapContext+0x26
 1   ntkrnlpa.exe!KiSwapThread+0x44f
 2   ntkrnlpa.exe!KeWaitForSingleObject+0x492
 3   ntkrnlpa.exe!KiSuspendThread+0x18
 4   ntkrnlpa.exe!KiDeliverApc+0x138
 5   ntkrnlpa.exe!KiSwapThread+0x472
 6   ntkrnlpa.exe!KeWaitForSingleObject+0x492
 7   ntkrnlpa.exe!AlpcpReceiveMessagePort+0x221
 8   ntkrnlpa.exe!AlpcpReceiveLegacyMessage+0x197
 9   ntkrnlpa.exe!NtReplyWaitReceivePortEx+0x100
10   ntkrnlpa.exe!NtReplyWaitReceivePort+0x18
11   ntkrnlpa.exe!KiFastCallEntry+0x12a
12   ntdll.dll!KiFastSystemCallRet
13   ntdll.dll!ZwReplyWaitReceivePort+0xc
14   lsm.exe!CCsrMgr::LpcWorker+0x44
15   lsm.exe!CCsrMgr::staticLpcWorker+0xd
16   ntdll.dll!RtlpTpWorkCallback+0xbf
17   ntdll.dll!TppWorkerThread+0x545
18   kernel32.dll!BaseThreadInitThunk+0xe
19   ntdll.dll!__RtlUserThreadStart+0x23
20   ntdll.dll!_RtlUserThreadStart+0x1b

     Copy                              OK
```

This specific worker thread is being used by Lsm.exe for LPC communication. Because the local session manager needs to communicate with other components such as Smss and Csrss through LPC, it makes sense that it would want a number of its threads to be busy replying and waiting for LPC messages (the more threads doing this, the less stalling on the LPC pipeline).

If you look at other worker threads, you'll see some are waiting for objects such as events. A process can have multiple thread pools, and each thread pool can have a variety of threads doing completely unrelated tasks. It's up to the developer to assign work and to call the thread pool APIs to register this work through Ntdll.dll.

Thread Scheduling

This section describes the Windows scheduling policies and algorithms. The first subsection provides a condensed description of how scheduling works on Windows and a definition of key terms. Then Windows priority levels are described from both the Windows API and the Windows kernel points of view. After a review of the relevant Windows functions and Windows utilities and tools that relate to scheduling, the detailed data structures and algorithms that make up the Windows scheduling system are presented, with uniprocessor systems examined first and then multiprocessor systems.

Overview of Windows Scheduling

Windows implements a priority-driven, preemptive scheduling system—the highest-priority runnable (*ready*) thread always runs, with the caveat that the thread chosen to run might be limited by the processors on which the thread is allowed to run, a phenomenon called *processor affinity*. By default, threads can run on any available processor, but you can alter processor affinity by using one of the Windows scheduling functions listed in Table 5-15 (shown later in the chapter) or by setting an affinity mask in the image header.

EXPERIMENT: Viewing Ready Threads

You can view the list of ready threads with the kernel debugger *!ready* command. This command displays the thread or list of threads that are ready to run at each priority level. In the following example, generated on a 32-bit machine with a dual-core processor, five threads are ready to run at priority 8 on the first processor, and three threads at priority 10, two threads at priority 9, and six threads at priority 8 are ready to run on the second processor. Determining which of these threads get to run on their respective processor is a complex result at the end of several algorithms that the scheduler uses. We will cover this topic later in this section.

```
kd> !ready
Processor 0: Ready Threads at priority 8
    THREAD 857d9030  Cid 0ec8.0e30  Teb: 7ffdd000 Win32Thread: 00000000 READY
    THREAD 855c8300  Cid 0ec8.0eb0  Teb: 7ff9c000 Win32Thread: 00000000 READY
    THREAD 8576c030  Cid 0ec8.0c9c  Teb: 7ffa8000 Win32Thread: 00000000 READY
    THREAD 85a8a7f0  Cid 0ec8.0d3c  Teb: 7ff97000 Win32Thread: 00000000 READY
    THREAD 87d34488  Cid 0c48.04a0  Teb: 7ffde000 Win32Thread: 00000000 READY
Processor 1: Ready Threads at priority 10
    THREAD 857c0030  Cid 04c8.0378  Teb: 7ffdf000 Win32Thread: fef7f8c0 READY
    THREAD 856cc8e8  Cid 0e84.0a70  Teb: 7ffdb000 Win32Thread: f98fb4c0 READY
    THREAD 85c41c68  Cid 0e84.00ac  Teb: 7ffde000 Win32Thread: ff460668 READY
Processor 1: Ready Threads at priority 9
    THREAD 87fc86f0  Cid 0ec8.04c0  Teb: 7ffd3000 Win32Thread: 00000000 READY
    THREAD 88696700  Cid 0ec8.0ce8  Teb: 7ffa0000 Win32Thread: 00000000 READY
```

```
Processor 1: Ready Threads at priority 8
    THREAD 856e5520  Cid 0ec8.0228  Teb: 7ff98000 Win32Thread: 00000000 READY
    THREAD 85609d78  Cid 0ec8.09b0  Teb: 7ffd9000 Win32Thread: 00000000 READY
    THREAD 85fdeb78  Cid 0ec8.0218  Teb: 7ff72000 Win32Thread: 00000000 READY
    THREAD 86086278  Cid 0ec8.0cc8  Teb: 7ff8d000 Win32Thread: 00000000 READY
    THREAD 8816f7f0  Cid 0ec8.0b60  Teb: 7ffd5000 Win32Thread: 00000000 READY
    THREAD 87710d78  Cid 0004.01b4  Teb: 00000000 Win32Thread: 00000000 READY
```

When a thread is selected to run, it runs for an amount of time called a *quantum*. A quantum is the length of time a thread is allowed to run before another thread at the same priority level (or higher, which can occur on a multiprocessor system) is given a turn to run. Quantum values can vary from system to system and process to process for any of three reasons: system configuration settings (long or short quantums), foreground/background status of the process, or use of the job object to alter the quantum. (Quantums are described in more detail in the "Quantum" section later in the chapter.) A thread might not get to complete its quantum, however. Because Windows implements a preemptive scheduler, if another thread with a higher priority becomes ready to run, the currently running thread might be preempted before finishing its time slice. In fact, a thread can be selected to run next and be preempted before even beginning its quantum!

The Windows scheduling code is implemented in the kernel. There's no single "scheduler" module or routine, however—the code is spread throughout the kernel in which scheduling-related events occur. The routines that perform these duties are collectively called the kernel's *dispatcher*. The following events might require thread dispatching:

- A thread becomes ready to execute—for example, a thread has been newly created or has just been released from the wait state.

- A thread leaves the running state because its time quantum ends, it terminates, it yields execution, or it enters a wait state.

- A thread's priority changes, either because of a system service call or because Windows itself changes the priority value.

- A thread's processor affinity changes so that it will no longer run on the processor on which it was running.

At each of these junctions, Windows must determine which thread should run next. When Windows selects a new thread to run, it performs a *context switch* to it. A context switch is the procedure of saving the volatile machine state associated with a running thread, loading another thread's volatile state, and starting the new thread's execution.

As already noted, Windows schedules at the thread granularity. This approach makes sense when you consider that processes don't run but only provide resources and a context in

which their threads run. Because scheduling decisions are made strictly on a thread basis, no consideration is given to what process the thread belongs to. For example, if process *A* has 10 runnable threads, process *B* has 2 runnable threads, and all 12 threads are at the same priority, each thread would theoretically receive one-twelfth of the CPU time—Windows wouldn't give 50 percent of the CPU to process *A* and 50 percent to process *B*.

Priority Levels

To understand the thread-scheduling algorithms, you must first understand the priority levels that Windows uses. As illustrated in Figure 5-12, internally Windows uses 32 priority levels, ranging from 0 through 31. These values divide up as follows:

- Sixteen real-time levels (16 through 31)

- Fifteen variable levels (1 through 15)

- One system level (0), reserved for the zero page thread

FIGURE 5-12 Thread priority levels

Thread priority levels are assigned from two different perspectives: those of the Windows API and those of the Windows kernel. The Windows API first organizes processes by the priority class to which they are assigned at creation (Real-time, High, Above Normal, Normal, Below Normal, and Idle) and then by the relative priority of the individual threads within those processes (Time-critical, Highest, Above-normal, Normal, Below-normal, Lowest, and Idle).

In the Windows API, each thread has a base priority that is a function of its process priority class and its relative thread priority. The mapping from Windows priority to internal Windows numeric priority is shown in Figure 5-13.

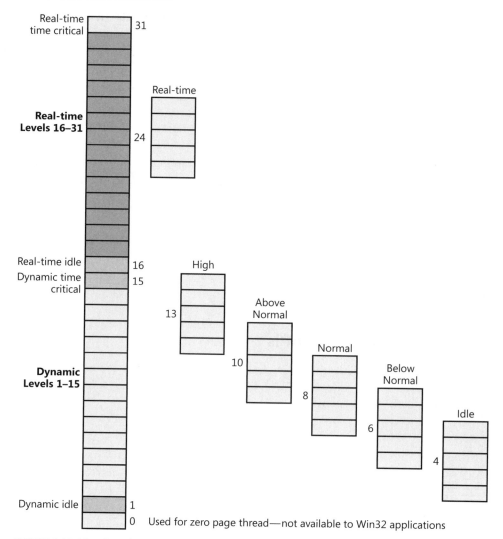

FIGURE 5-13 Mapping of Windows kernel priorities to the Windows API

Whereas a process has only a single base priority value, each thread has two priority values: current and base. Scheduling decisions are made based on the current priority. As explained in the following section on priority boosting, the system under certain circumstances increases the priority of threads in the dynamic range (1 through 15) for brief periods. Windows never adjusts the priority of threads in the real-time range (16 through 31), so they always have the same base and current priority.

A thread's initial base priority is inherited from the process base priority. A process, by default, inherits its base priority from the process that created it. This behavior can be over-ridden on the *CreateProcess* function or by using the command-line *start* command. A process priority can also be changed after being created by using the *SetPriorityClass* function or

various tools that expose that function, such as Task Manager and Process Explorer (by right-clicking on the process and choosing a new priority class). For example, you can lower the priority of a CPU-intensive process so that it does not interfere with normal system activities. Changing the priority of a process changes the thread priorities up or down, but their relative settings remain the same. It usually doesn't make sense, however, to change individual thread priorities within a process, because unless you wrote the program or have the source code, you don't really know what the individual threads are doing, and changing their relative importance might cause the program not to behave in the intended fashion.

Normally, the process base priority (and therefore the starting thread base priority) will default to the value at the middle of each process priority range (24, 13, 10, 8, 6, or 4). However, some Windows system processes (such as the Session Manager, service controller, and local security authentication server) have a base process priority slightly higher than the default for the Normal class (8). This higher default value ensures that the threads in these processes will all start at a higher priority than the default value of 8. These system processes use an internal system call (*NtSetInformationProcess*) to set their process base priority to a numeric value other than the normal default starting base priority.

Windows Scheduling APIs

The Windows API functions that relate to thread scheduling are listed in Table 5-15. (For more information, see the Windows API reference documentation.)

TABLE 5-15 Scheduling-Related APIs and Their Functions

API	Function
Suspend/ResumeThread	Suspends or resumes a paused thread from execution.
Get/SetPriorityClass	Returns or sets a process's priority class (base priority).
Get/SetThreadPriority	Returns or sets a thread's priority (relative to its process base priority).
Get/SetProcessAffinityMask	Returns or sets a process's affinity mask.
SetThreadAffinityMask	Sets a thread's affinity mask (must be a subset of the process's affinity mask) for a particular set of processors, restricting it to running on those processors.
SetInformationJobObject	Sets attributes for a job; some of the attributes affect scheduling, such as affinity and priority. (See the "Job Objects" section later in the chapter for a description of the job object.)
GetLogicalProcessorInformation	Returns details about processor hardware configuration (for hyperthreaded and NUMA systems).
Get/SetThreadPriorityBoost	Returns or sets the ability for Windows to boost the priority of a thread temporarily. (This ability applies only to threads in the dynamic range.)
SetThreadIdealProcessor	Establishes a preferred processor for a particular thread, but doesn't restrict the thread to that processor.

API	Function
Get/SetProcessPriorityBoost	Returns or sets the default priority boost control state of the current process. (This function is used to set the thread priority boost control state when a thread is created.)
WaitForSingle/MultipleObject(s)	Puts the current thread into a wait state until the specified object(s) is/are satisfied, or until the specified time interval (figured in milliseconds [msec]) expires, if given.
SwitchToThread	Yields execution to another thread (at priority 1 or higher) that is ready to run on the current processor.
Sleep	Puts the current thread into a wait state for a specified time interval (figured in milliseconds [msec]). A zero value relinquishes the rest of the thread's quantum.
SleepEx	Causes the current thread to go into a wait state until either an I/O completion callback is completed, an APC is queued to the thread, or the specified time interval ends.

Relevant Tools

You can change (and view) the base process priority with Task Manager and Process Explorer. You can kill individual threads in a process with Process Explorer (which should be done, of course, with extreme care).

You can view individual thread priorities with the Reliability and Performance Monitor, Process Explorer, or WinDbg. While it might be useful to increase or lower the priority of a process, it typically does not make sense to adjust individual thread priorities within a process because only a person who thoroughly understands the program (in other words, typically only the developer himself) would understand the relative importance of the threads within the process.

The only way to specify a starting priority class for a process is with the *start* command in the Windows command prompt. If you want to have a program start every time with a specific priority, you can define a shortcut to use the *start* command by beginning the command with **cmd /c**. This runs the command prompt, executes the command on the command line, and terminates the command prompt. For example, to run Notepad in the low-process priority, the shortcut would be **cmd /c start /low Notepad.exe**.

EXPERIMENT: Examining and Specifying Process and Thread Priorities

Try the following experiment:

1. From an elevated command prompt, type **start /realtime notepad**. Notepad should open.

2. Run Process Explorer and select Notepad.exe from the list of processes. Double-click on Notepad.exe to show the process properties window, and then click on the Threads tab, as shown here. Notice that the dynamic priority of the thread in Notepad is 24. This matches the real-time value shown in this image:

3. Task Manager can show you similar information. Press Ctrl+Shift+Esc to start Task Manager, and go to the Processes tab. Right-click on the Notepad.exe process, and select the Set Priority option. You can see that Notepad's process priority class is Realtime, as shown in the following dialog box.

Windows System Resource Manager

Windows Server 2008 Enterprise Edition and Windows Server 2008 Datacenter Edition include an optionally installable component called Windows System Resource Manager (WSRM). It permits the administrator to configure policies that specify CPU utilization, affinity settings, and memory limits (both physical and virtual) for processes. In addition, WSRM can generate resource utilization reports that can be used for accounting and verification of service-level agreements with users.

Policies can be applied for specific applications (by matching the name of the image with or without specific command-line arguments), users, or groups. The policies can be scheduled to take effect at certain periods or can be enabled all the time.

After you have set a resource-allocation policy to manage specific processes, the WSRM service monitors CPU consumption of managed processes and adjusts process base priorities when those processes do not meet their target CPU allocations.

The physical memory limitation uses the function *SetProcessWorkingSetSizeEx* to set a hard-working set maximum. The virtual memory limit is implemented by the service checking the private virtual memory consumed by the processes. (See Chapter 9 for an explanation of these memory limits.) If this limit is exceeded, WSRM can be configured to either kill the processes or write an entry to the Event Log. This behavior could be used to detect a process with a memory leak before it consumes all the available committed virtual memory on the system. Note that WSRM memory limits do not apply to Address Windowing Extensions (AWE) memory, large page memory, or kernel memory (nonpaged or paged pool).

Real-Time Priorities

You can raise or lower thread priorities within the dynamic range in any application; however, you must have the *increase scheduling priority* privilege to enter the real-time range. Be aware that many important Windows kernel-mode system threads run in the real-time priority range, so if threads spend excessive time running in this range, they might block critical system functions (such as in the memory manager, cache manager, or other device drivers).

Note As illustrated in the following figure showing the x86 interrupt request levels (IRQLs), although Windows has a set of priorities called *real-time*, they are not real-time in the common definition of the term. This is because Windows doesn't provide true real-time operating system facilities, such as guaranteed interrupt latency or a way for threads to obtain a guaranteed execution time. For more information, see the sidebar "Windows and Real-Time Processing" in Chapter 3 as well as the MSDN Library article "Real-Time Systems and Microsoft Windows NT."

Interrupt Levels vs. Priority Levels

As illustrated in the following figure of the interrupt request levels (IRQLs) for a 32-bit system, threads normally run at IRQL 0 or 1. (For a description of how Windows uses interrupt levels, see Chapter 3.) User-mode code always runs at IRQL 0. Because of this, no user-mode thread, regardless of its priority, blocks hardware interrupts (although high-priority real-time threads can block the execution of important system threads). Only kernel-mode APCs execute at IRQL 1 because they interrupt the execution of a thread. (For more information on APCs, see Chapter 3.) Threads running in kernel mode can raise IRQL to higher levels, though—for example, while executing a system call that involves thread dispatching.

Thread States

Before you can comprehend the thread-scheduling algorithms, you need to understand the various execution states that a thread can be in. Figure 5-14 illustrates the state transitions for threads. (The numeric values shown represent the value of the thread state performance counter.) More details on what happens at each transition are included later in this section.

The thread states are as follows:

- **Ready** A thread in the ready state is waiting to execute. When looking for a thread to execute, the dispatcher considers only the pool of threads in the ready state.

- **Deferred ready** This state is used for threads that have been selected to run on a specific processor but have not yet been scheduled. This state exists so that the kernel can minimize the amount of time the systemwide lock on the scheduling database is held.

- **Standby** A thread in the standby state has been selected to run next on a particular processor. When the correct conditions exist, the dispatcher performs a context switch to this thread. Only one thread can be in the standby state for each processor on the system. Note that a thread can be preempted out of the standby state before it ever executes (if, for example, a higher priority thread becomes runnable before the standby thread begins execution).

- **Running** Once the dispatcher performs a context switch to a thread, the thread enters the running state and executes. The thread's execution continues until its quantum ends (and another thread at the same priority is ready to run), it is preempted by a higher priority thread, it terminates, it yields execution, or it voluntarily enters the wait state.

- **Waiting** A thread can enter the wait state in several ways: a thread can voluntarily wait for an object to synchronize its execution, the operating system can wait on the thread's behalf (such as to resolve a paging I/O), or an environment subsystem can direct the thread to suspend itself. When the thread's wait ends, depending on the priority, the thread either begins running immediately or is moved back to the ready state.

- **Gate Waiting** When a thread does a wait on a gate dispatcher object (see Chapter 3 for more information on gates), it enters the gate waiting state instead of the waiting state. This difference is important when breaking a thread's wait as the result of an APC. Because gates don't use the dispatcher lock, but a per-object lock, the kernel needs to perform some unique locking operations when breaking the wait of a thread waiting on a gate and a way to differentiate this from a normal wait.

- **Transition** A thread enters the transition state if it is ready for execution but its kernel stack is paged out of memory. Once its kernel stack is brought back into memory, the thread enters the ready state.

- **Terminated** When a thread finishes executing, it enters the terminated state. Once the thread is terminated, the executive thread block (the data structure in nonpaged pool that describes the thread) might or might not be deallocated. (The object manager sets policy regarding when to delete the object.)

- **Initialized** This state is used internally while a thread is being created.

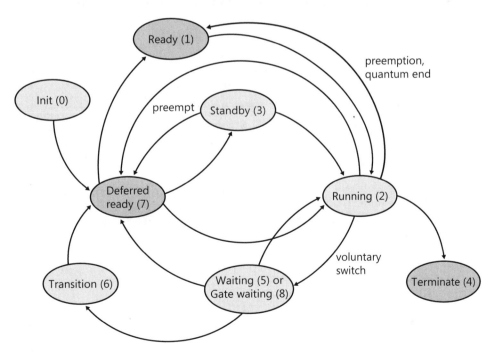

FIGURE 5-14 Thread states and transitions

EXPERIMENT: Thread-Scheduling State Changes

You can watch thread-scheduling state changes with the Performance tool in Windows. This utility can be useful when you're debugging a multithreaded application and you're unsure about the state of the threads running in the process. To watch thread-scheduling state changes by using the Performance tool, follow these steps:

1. Run Notepad (Notepad.exe).

2. Start the Performance tool by selecting Programs from the Start menu and then selecting Reliability and Performance Monitor from the Administrative Tools menu. Click on the Performance Monitor entry under Monitoring Tools.

3. Select chart view if you're in some other view.

4. Right-click on the graph, and choose Properties.

5. Click the Graph tab, and change the chart vertical scale maximum to 7. (As you'll see from the explanation text for the performance counter, thread states are numbered from 0 through 7.) Click OK.

6. Click the Add button on the toolbar to bring up the Add Counters dialog box.

7. Select the Thread performance object, and then select the Thread State counter. Select the Show Description check box to see the definition of the values:

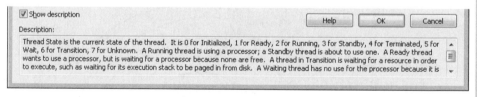

8. In the Instances box, select <All instances> and click Search. Scroll down until you see the Notepad process (notepad/0); select it, and click the Add button.

9. Scroll back up in the Instances box to the Mmc process (the Microsoft Management Console process running the System Monitor), select all the threads (mmc/0, mmc/1, and so on), and add them to the chart by clicking the Add button. Before you click Add, you should see something like the following dialog box.

10. Now close the Add Counters dialog box by clicking OK

11. You should see the state of the Notepad thread (the very top line in the following figure) as a 5, which, as shown in the explanation text you saw under step 7, represents the waiting state (because the thread is waiting for GUI input):

12. Notice that one thread in the Mmc process (running the Performance tool snap-in) is in the running state (number 2). This is the thread that's querying the thread states, so it's always displayed in the running state.

13. You'll never see Notepad in the running state (unless you're on a multiprocessor system) because Mmc is always in the running state when it gathers the state of the threads you're monitoring.

Dispatcher Database

To make thread-scheduling decisions, the kernel maintains a set of data structures known collectively as the *dispatcher database*, illustrated in Figure 5-15. The dispatcher database keeps track of which threads are waiting to execute and which processors are executing which threads.

To improve scalability, including thread-dispatching concurrency, Windows multiprocessor systems have per-processor dispatcher ready queues, as illustrated in Figure 5-15. In this way each CPU can check its own ready queues for the next thread to run without having to lock the systemwide ready queues. (Versions of Windows before Windows Server 2003 used a global database).

The per-processor ready queues, as well as the per-processor ready summary, are part of the processor control block (PRCB) structure. (To see the fields in the PRCB, type **dt nt!_prcb** in the kernel debugger.) The names of each component that we will talk about (in italics) are field members of the PRCB structure.

The dispatcher *ready queues (DispatcherReadyListHead)* contain the threads that are in the ready state, waiting to be scheduled for execution. There is one queue for each of the 32 priority levels. To speed up the selection of which thread to run or preempt, Windows maintains a 32-bit bit mask called the *ready summary (ReadySummary)*. Each bit set indicates one or more threads in the ready queue for that priority level. (Bit 0 represents priority 0, and so on.)

Instead of scanning each ready list to see whether it is empty or not (which would make scheduling decisions dependent on the number of different priority threads), a single bit scan is performed as a native processor command to find the highest bit set. Regardless of the number of threads in the ready queue, this operation takes a constant amount of time, which is why you may sometimes see the Windows scheduling algorithm referred to as an O(1), or constant time, algorithm.

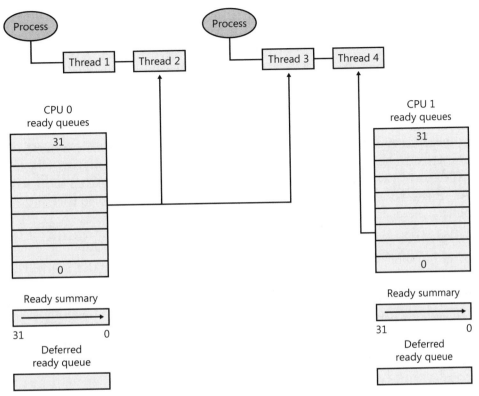

FIGURE 5-15 Windows multiprocessor dispatcher database

Table 5-16 lists the KPRCB fields involved in thread scheduling.

TABLE 5-16 Thread-Scheduling KPRCB Fields

KPRCB Field	Type	Description
ReadySummary	Bitmask (32 bits)	Bitmask of priority levels that have one or more ready threads
DeferredReadyListHead	Singly linked list	Single list head for the deferred ready queue
DispatcherReadyListHead	Array of 32 list entries	List heads for the 32 ready queues

The dispatcher database is synchronized by raising IRQL to SYNCH_LEVEL (which is defined as level 2). (For an explanation of interrupt priority levels, see the "Trap Dispatching" section in Chapter 3.) Raising IRQL in this way prevents other threads from interrupting thread dispatching on the processor because threads normally run at IRQL 0 or 1. However, on a multiprocessor system, more is required than just raising IRQL because other processors can simultaneously raise to the same IRQL and attempt to operate on the dispatcher database. How Windows synchronizes access to the dispatcher database is explained in the "Multiprocessor Systems" section later in the chapter.

Quantum

As mentioned earlier in the chapter, a quantum is the amount of time a thread gets to run before Windows checks to see whether another thread at the same priority is waiting to run. If a thread completes its quantum and there are no other threads at its priority, Windows permits the thread to run for another quantum.

On Windows Vista, threads run by default for 2 clock intervals; on Windows Server systems, by default, a thread runs for 12 clock intervals. (We'll explain how you can change these values later.) The rationale for the longer default value on server systems is to minimize context switching. By having a longer quantum, server applications that wake up as the result of a client request have a better chance of completing the request and going back into a wait state before their quantum ends.

The length of the clock interval varies according to the hardware platform. The frequency of the clock interrupts is up to the HAL, not the kernel. For example, the clock interval for most x86 uniprocessors is about 10 milliseconds, and for most x86 and x64 multiprocessors it is about 15 milliseconds. This clock interval is stored in the kernel variable *KeMaximumIncrement* as hundreds of nanoseconds.

Because of changes in thread run-time accounting in Windows Vista (briefly mentioned earlier in the thread activity experiment), although threads still run in units of clock intervals, the system does not use the count of clock ticks as the deciding factor for how long a thread has run and whether its quantum has expired. Instead, when the system starts up, a calculation is made whose result is the number of clock cycles that each quantum is equivalent to (this value is stored in the kernel variable *KiCyclesPerClockQuantum*). This calculation is made by multiplying the processor speed in Hz (CPU clock cycles per second) with the number of seconds it takes for one clock tick to fire (based on the *KeMaximumIncrement* value described above).

The end result of this new accounting method is that, as of Windows Vista, threads do not actually run for a quantum number based on clock ticks; they instead run for a *quantum target*, which represents an estimate of what the number of CPU clock cycles the thread has consumed should be when its turn would be given up. This target should be equal to an equivalent number of clock interval timer ticks because, as we've just seen, the calculation of clock cycles per quantum is based on the clock interval timer frequency, which you can check using the following experiment. On the other hand, because interrupt cycles are not charged to the thread, the actual clock time may be longer.

EXPERIMENT: Determining the Clock Interval Frequency

The Windows *GetSystemTimeAdjustment* function returns the clock interval. To determine the clock interval, download and run the Clockres program from Windows Sysinternals (*www.microsoft.com/technet/sysinternals*). Here's the output from a dual-core 32-bit Windows Vista system:

```
C:\>clockres

ClockRes - View the system clock resolution
By Mark Russinovich
SysInternals - www.sysinternals.com

The system clock interval is 15.600100 ms
```

Quantum Accounting

Each process has a quantum reset value in the kernel process block. This value is used when creating new threads inside the process and is duplicated in the kernel thread block, which is then used when giving a thread a new quantum target. The quantum reset value is stored in terms of actual quantum units (we'll discuss what these mean soon), which are then multiplied by the number of clock cycles per quantum, resulting in the quantum target.

As a thread runs, CPU clock cycles are charged at different events (context switches, interrupts, and certain scheduling decisions). If at a clock interval timer interrupt, the number of CPU clock cycles charged has reached (or passed) the quantum target, then quantum end processing is triggered. If there is another thread at the same priority waiting to run, a context switch occurs to the next thread in the ready queue.

Internally, a quantum unit is represented as one third of a clock tick (so one clock tick equals three quantums). This means that on Windows Vista systems, threads, by default, have a quantum reset value of 6 (2 * 3), and that Windows Server 2008 systems have a quantum reset value of 36 (12 * 3). For this reason, the *KiCyclesPerClockQuantum* value is divided by three at the end of the calculation previously described, since the original value would describe only CPU clock cycles per clock interval timer tick.

The reason a quantum was stored internally as a fraction of a clock tick rather than as an entire tick was to allow for partial quantum decay on wait completion on versions of Windows prior to Windows Vista. Prior versions used the clock interval timer for quantum expiration. If this adjustment were not made, it would have been possible for threads never to have their quantums reduced. For example, if a thread ran, entered a wait state, ran again, and entered another wait state but was never the currently running thread when the clock interval timer fired, it would never have its quantum charged for the time it was running. Because threads now have CPU clock cycles charged instead of quantums, and because this no longer depends on the clock interval timer, these adjustments are not required.

EXPERIMENT: Determining the Clock Cycles per Quantum

Windows doesn't expose the number of clock cycles per quantum through any function, but with the calculation and description we've given, you should be able to determine this on your own using the following steps and a kernel debugger such as WinDbg in local debugging mode.

1. Obtain your processor frequency as Windows has detected it. You can use the value stored in the PRCB's MHz field, which can be displayed with the !cpuinfo command. Here is a sample output of a dual-core Intel system running at 2829 MHz.

```
1kd> !cpuinfo
CP  F/M/S Manufacturer  MHz PRCB Signature   MSR 8B Signature Features
 0  6,15,6 GenuineIntel 2829 000000c700000000 >000000c700000000<a00f3fff
 1  6,15,6 GenuineIntel 2829 000000c700000000                  a00f3fff
                   Cached Update Signature 000000c700000000
                   Initial Update Signature 000000c700000000
```

2. Convert the number to Hertz (Hz). This is the number of CPU clock cycles that occur each second on your system. In this case, 2,829,000,000 cycles per second.

3. Obtain the clock interval on your system by using *clockres*. This measures how long it takes before the clock fires. On the sample system used here, this interval was 15.600100 ms.

4. Convert this number to the number of times the clock interval timer fires each second. One second is 1000 ms, so divide the number derived in step 3 by 1000. In this case, the timer fires every 0.0156001 second.

5. Multiply this count by the number of cycles each second that you obtained in step 2. In our case, 44,132,682.9 cycles have elapsed after each clock interval.

6. Remember that each quantum unit is one-third of a clock interval, so divide the number of cycles by three. In our example, this gives us 14,710,894, or 0xE0786E in hexidecimal. This is the number of clock cycles each quantum unit should take on a system running at 2829 MHz with a clock interval of around 15 ms.

7. To verify your calculation, dump the value of *KiCyclesPerClockQuantum* on your system—it should match.

```
1kd> dd nt!KiCyclesPerClockQuantum 11
81d31ae8  00e0786e
```

Controlling the Quantum

You can change the thread quantum for all processes, but you can choose only one of two settings: short (2 clock ticks, the default for client machines) or long (12 clock ticks, the default for server systems).

> **Note** By using the job object on a system running with long quantums, you can select other quantum values for the processes in the job. For more information on the job object, see the "Job Objects" section later in the chapter.

To change this setting, right-click on your computer name's icon on the desktop, choose Properties, click the Advanced System Settings label, select the Advanced tab, click the Settings button in the Performance section, and finally click the Advanced tab. The dialog box displayed is shown in Figure 5-16.

FIGURE 5-16 Quantum configuration in the Performance Options dialog box

The Programs setting designates the use of short, variable quantums—the default for Windows Vista. If you install Terminal Services on Windows Server 2008 systems and configure the server as an application server, this setting is selected so that the users on the terminal server will have the same quantum settings that would normally be set on a desktop or client system. You might also select this manually if you were running Windows Server as your desktop operating system.

The Background Services option designates the use of long, fixed quantums—the default for Windows Server 2008 systems. The only reason you might select this option on a workstation system is if you were using the workstation as a server system.

One additional difference between the Programs and Background Services settings is the effect they have on the quantum of the threads in the foreground process. This is explained in the next section.

Quantum Boosting

When a window is brought into the foreground on a client system, all the threads in the process containing the thread that owns the foreground window have their quantums tripled. Thus, threads in the foreground process run with a quantum of 6 clock ticks, whereas threads in other processes have the default client quantum of 2 clock ticks. In this way, when you switch away from a CPU-intensive process, the new foreground process will get proportionally more of the CPU, because when its threads run they will have a longer turn than background threads (again, assuming the thread priorities are the same in both the foreground and background processes).

Note that this adjustment of quantums applies only to processes with a priority higher than Idle on systems configured to Programs in the Performance Options settings described in the previous section. Thread quantums are not changed for the foreground process on systems configured to Background Services (the default on Windows Server 2008 systems).

Quantum Settings Registry Value

The user interface to control quantum settings described earlier modifies the registry value HKLM\SYSTEM\CurrentControlSet\Control\PriorityControl\Win32PrioritySeparation. In addition to specifying the relative length of thread quantums (short or long), this registry value also defines whether or not threads in the foreground process should have their quantums boosted (and if so, the amount of the boost). This value consists of 6 bits divided into the three 2-bit fields shown in Figure 5-17.

FIGURE 5-17 Fields of the Win32PrioritySeparation registry value

The fields shown in Figure 5-17 can be defined as follows:

- **Short vs. Long** A setting of 1 specifies long, and 2 specifies short. A setting of 0 or 3 indicates that the default will be used (short for Windows Vista, long for Windows Server 2008 systems).

- **Variable vs. Fixed** A setting of 1 means to vary the quantum for the foreground process, and 2 means that quantum values don't change for foreground processes. A setting of 0 or 3 means that the default (which is variable for Windows Vista and fixed for Windows Server 2008 systems) will be used.

- **Foreground Quantum Boost** This field (stored in the kernel variable *PsPrioritySeperation*) must have a value of 0, 1, or 2. (A setting of 3 is invalid and treated as 2.) It is used as an index into a three-element byte array named *PspForegroundQuantum* to obtain the quantum for the threads in the foreground process. The quantum for threads in background processes is taken from the first entry in this quantum table. Table 5-17 shows the possible settings for *PspForegroundQuantum*.

TABLE 5-17 Quantum Values

	Short			Long		
Variable	6	12	18	12	24	36
Fixed	18	18	18	36	36	36

Note that when you're using the Performance Options dialog box described earlier, you can choose from only two combinations: short quantums with foreground quantums tripled, or long quantums with no quantum changes for foreground threads. However, you can select other combinations by modifying the Win32PrioritySeparation registry value directly.

EXPERIMENT: Effects of Changing the Quantum Configuration

Using a local debugger (Kd or WinDbg), you can see how the two quantum configuration settings, Programs and Background Services, affect the *PsPrioritySeperation* and *PspForegroundQuantum* tables, as well as modify the *QuantumReset* value of threads on the system. Take the following steps:

1. Open the System utility in Control Panel (or right-click on your computer name's icon on the desktop, and choose Properties). Click the Advanced System Settings label, select the Advanced tab, click the Settings button in the Performance section, and finally click the Advanced tab. Select the Programs option and click Apply. Keep this window open for the duration of the experiment.

2. Dump the values of *PsPrioritySeperation* (this is a deliberate misspelling inside the Windows kernel, not an error in this book) and *PspForegroundQuantum,* as shown here. The values shown are what you should see on a Windows Vista system after making the change in step 1. Notice how the variable, short quantum table is being used, and that a priority boost of 2 will apply to foreground applications.

```
lkd> dd PsPrioritySeperation l1
81d3101c  00000002
lkd> db PspForegroundQuantum l3
81d0946c  06 0c 12                              . . .
```

3. Now take a look at the *QuantumReset* value of any process on the system. As described earlier, this is the default, full quantum of each thread on the system when it is replenished. This value is cached into each thread of the process, but the KPROCESS structure is easier to look at. Notice in this case it is 6, since WinDbg, like most other applications, gets the quantum set in the first entry of the *PspForegroundQuantum* table.

```
lkd> .process
Implicit process is now 85b32d90
lkd> dt _KPROCESS 85b32d90
nt!_KPROCESS
   +0x000 Header            : _DISPATCHER_HEADER
   +0x010 ProfileListHead   : _LIST_ENTRY [ 0x85b32da0 - 0x85b32da0 ]
   +0x018 DirectoryTableBase : 0xb45b0880
   +0x01c Unused0           : 0
   +0x020 LdtDescriptor     : _KGDTENTRY
   +0x028 Int21Descriptor   : _KIDTENTRY
   +0x030 IopmOffset        : 0x20ac
   +0x032 Iopl              : 0 ''
   +0x033 Unused            : 0 ''
   +0x034 ActiveProcessors  : 1
   +0x038 KernelTime        : 0
   +0x03c UserTime          : 0
   +0x040 ReadyListHead     : _LIST_ENTRY [ 0x85b32dd0 - 0x85b32dd0 ]
   +0x048 SwapListEntry     : _SINGLE_LIST_ENTRY
   +0x04c VdmTrapcHandler   : (null)
   +0x050 ThreadListHead    : _LIST_ENTRY [ 0x861e7e0c - 0x8620637c ]
   +0x058 ProcessLock       : 0
   +0x05c Affinity          : 3
   +0x060 AutoAlignment     : 0y0
   +0x060 DisableBoost      : 0y0
   +0x060 DisableQuantum    : 0y0
   +0x060 ReservedFlags     : 0y00000000000000000000000000000000 (0)
   +0x060 ProcessFlags      : 0
   +0x064 BasePriority      : 8 ''
   +0x065 QuantumReset      : 6 ''
```

4. Now change the Performance option to Background Services in the dialog box you opened in step 1.

5. Repeat the commands shown in steps 2 and 3. You should see the values change in a manner consistent with our discussion in this section:

```
lkd> dd PsPrioritySeperation L1
81d3101c  00000000
lkd> db PspForegroundQuantum 1 3
81d0946c  24 24 24                                          $$$
lkd> dt _KPROCESS 85b32d90
nt!_KPROCESS
   +0x000 Header            : _DISPATCHER_HEADER
   +0x010 ProfileListHead   : _LIST_ENTRY [ 0x85b32da0 - 0x85b32da0 ]
   +0x018 DirectoryTableBase : 0xb45b0880
   +0x01c Unused0           : 0
```

```
+0x020 LdtDescriptor     : _KGDTENTRY
+0x028 Int21Descriptor   : _KIDTENTRY
+0x030 IopmOffset        : 0x20ac
+0x032 Iopl              : 0 ''
+0x033 Unused            : 0 ''
+0x034 ActiveProcessors  : 1
+0x038 KernelTime        : 0
+0x03c UserTime          : 0
+0x040 ReadyListHead     : _LIST_ENTRY [ 0x85b32dd0 - 0x85b32dd0 ]
+0x048 SwapListEntry     : _SINGLE_LIST_ENTRY
+0x04c VdmTrapHandler    : (null)
+0x050 ThreadListHead    : _LIST_ENTRY [ 0x861e7e0c - 0x860c14f4 ]
+0x058 ProcessLock       : 0
+0x05c Affinity          : 3
+0x060 AutoAlignment     : 0y0
+0x060 DisableBoost      : 0y0
+0x060 DisableQuantum    : 0y0
+0x060 ReservedFlags     : 0y00000000000000000000000000000000 (0)
+0x060 ProcessFlags      : 0
+0x064 BasePriority      : 8 ''
+0x065 QuantumReset      : 36 '$'
```

Scheduling Scenarios

Windows bases the question of "Who gets the CPU?" on thread priority; but how does this approach work in practice? The following sections illustrate just how priority-driven preemptive multitasking works on the thread level.

Voluntary Switch

First a thread might voluntarily relinquish use of the processor by entering a wait state on some object (such as an event, a mutex, a semaphore, an I/O completion port, a process, a thread, a window message, and so on) by calling one of the Windows wait functions (such as *WaitForSingleObject* or *WaitForMultipleObjects*). Waiting for objects is described in more detail in Chapter 3.

Figure 5-18 illustrates a thread entering a wait state and Windows selecting a new thread to run.

In Figure 5-18, the top block (thread) is voluntarily relinquishing the processor so that the next thread in the ready queue can run (as represented by the halo it has when in the Running column). Although it might appear from this figure that the relinquishing thread's priority is being reduced, it's not—it's just being moved to the wait queue of the objects the thread is waiting for.

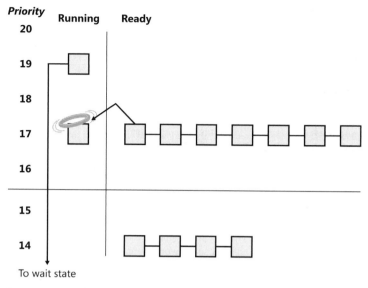

FIGURE 5-18 Voluntary switching

Preemption

In this scheduling scenario, a lower-priority thread is preempted when a higher-priority thread becomes ready to run. This situation might occur for a couple of reasons:

- A higher-priority thread's wait completes. (The event that the other thread was waiting for has occurred.)
- A thread priority is increased or decreased.

In either of these cases, Windows must determine whether the currently running thread should still continue to run or whether it should be preempted to allow a higher-priority thread to run.

 Note Threads running in user mode can preempt threads running in kernel mode—the mode in which the thread is running doesn't matter. The thread priority is the determining factor.

When a thread is preempted, it is put at the head of the ready queue for the priority it was running at. Figure 5-19 illustrates this situation.

In Figure 5-19, a thread with priority 18 emerges from a wait state and repossesses the CPU, causing the thread that had been running (at priority 16) to be bumped to the head of the ready queue. Notice that the bumped thread isn't going to the end of the queue but to the beginning; when the preempting thread has finished running, the bumped thread can complete its quantum.

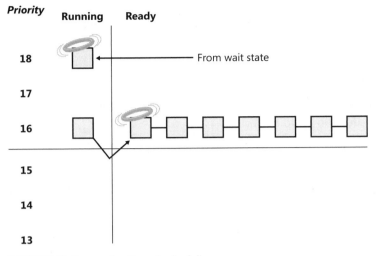

FIGURE 5-19 Preemptive thread scheduling

Quantum End

When the running thread exhausts its CPU quantum, Windows must determine whether the thread's priority should be decremented and then whether another thread should be scheduled on the processor.

If the thread priority is reduced, Windows looks for a more appropriate thread to schedule. (For example, a more appropriate thread would be a thread in a ready queue with a higher priority than the new priority for the currently running thread.) If the thread priority isn't reduced and there are other threads in the ready queue at the same priority level, Windows selects the next thread in the ready queue at that same priority level and moves the previously running thread to the tail of that queue (giving it a new quantum value and changing its state from running to ready). This case is illustrated in Figure 5-20. If no other thread of the same priority is ready to run, the thread gets to run for another quantum.

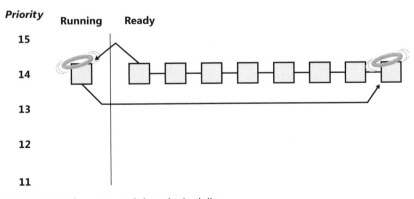

FIGURE 5-20 Quantum end thread scheduling

As we've seen, instead of simply relying on a clock interval timer–based quantum to schedule threads, Windows uses an accurate CPU clock cycle count to maintain quantum targets. One factor we haven't yet mentioned is that Windows also uses this count to determine whether quantum end is currently appropriate for the thread—something that may have happened previously and is important to discuss.

Under the scheduling model prior to Windows Vista, which relied only on the clock interval timer, the following situation could occur:

- Threads A and B become ready to run during the middle of an interval (scheduling code runs not just at each clock interval, so this is often the case).

- Thread A starts running but is interrupted for a while. The time spent handling the interrupt is charged to the thread.

- Interrupt processing finishes, thread A starts running again, but it quickly hits the next clock interval. The scheduler can only assume that thread A had been running all this time and now switches to thread B.

- Thread B starts running and has a chance to run for a full clock interval (barring preemption or interrupt handling).

In this scenario, thread A was unfairly penalized in two different ways. First of all, the time that it had to spend handling a device interrupt was accounted to its own CPU time, even though the thread had probably nothing to do with the interrupt. (Recall that interrupts are handled in the context of whichever thread had been running at the time.) It was also unfairly penalized for the time the system was idling inside that clock interval before it was scheduled.

Figure 5-21 represents this scenario.

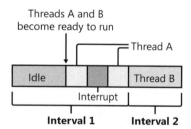

FIGURE 5-21 Unfair time slicing in previous versions of Windows

Because Windows keeps an accurate count of the exact number of CPU clock cycles spent doing work that the thread was scheduled to do (which means excluding interrupts), and because it keeps a quantum target of clock cycles that should have been spent by the thread at the end of its quantum, both of the unfair decisions that would have been made against thread A will not happen in Windows.

Instead, the following situation will occur:

- Threads *A* and *B* become ready to run during the middle of an interval.

- Thread *A* starts running but is interrupted for a while. The CPU clock cycles spent handling the interrupt are not charged to the thread.

- Interrupt processing finishes, thread *A* starts running again, but it quickly hits the next clock interval. The scheduler looks at the number of CPU clock cycles that have been charged to the thread and compares them to the expected CPU clock cycles that should have been charged at quantum end.

- Because the former number is much smaller than it should be, the scheduler assumes that thread *A* started running in the middle of a clock interval and may have additionally been interrupted.

- Thread *A* gets its quantum increased by another clock interval, and the quantum target is recalculated. Thread *A* now has its chance to run for a full clock interval.

- At the next clock interval, thread *A* has finished its quantum, and thread *B* now gets a chance to run.

Figure 5-22 represents this scenario.

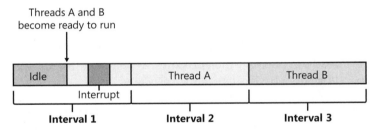

FIGURE 5-22 Fair time slicing in current versions of Windows

Termination

When a thread finishes running (either because it returned from its main routine, called *ExitThread*, or was killed with *TerminateThread*), it moves from the running state to the terminated state. If there are no handles open on the thread object, the thread is removed from the process thread list and the associated data structures are deallocated and released.

Context Switching

A thread's context and the procedure for context switching vary depending on the processor's architecture. A typical context switch requires saving and reloading the following data:

- Instruction pointer
- Kernel stack pointer
- A pointer to the address space in which the thread runs (the process's page table directory)

The kernel saves this information from the old thread by pushing it onto the current (old thread's) kernel-mode stack, updating the stack pointer, and saving the stack pointer in the old thread's KTHREAD block. The kernel stack pointer is then set to the new thread's kernel stack, and the new thread's context is loaded. If the new thread is in a different process, it loads the address of its page table directory into a special processor register so that its address space is available. (See the description of address translation in Chapter 9.) If a kernel APC that needs to be delivered is pending, an interrupt at IRQL 1 is requested. Otherwise, control passes to the new thread's restored instruction pointer and the new thread resumes execution.

Idle Thread

When no runnable thread exists on a CPU, Windows dispatches the per-CPU idle thread. Each CPU is allotted one idle thread because on a multiprocessor system one CPU can be executing a thread while other CPUs might have no threads to execute.

Various Windows process viewer utilities report the idle process using different names. Task Manager and Process Explorer call it "System Idle Process," while Tlist calls it "System Process." If you look at the EPROCESS structure's *ImageFileName* member, you'll see the internal name for the process is "Idle." Windows reports the priority of the idle thread as 0 (15 on x64 systems). In reality, however, the idle threads don't have a priority level because they run only when there are no real threads to run—they are not scheduled and never part of any ready queues. (Remember, only one thread per Windows system is actually running at priority 0—the zero page thread, explained in Chapter 9.)

Apart from priority, there are many other fields in the idle process or its threads that may be reported as 0. This occurs because the idle process is not an actual full-blown object manager process object, and neither are its idle threads. Instead, the initial idle thread and idle process objects are statically allocated and used to bootstrap the system before the process manager initializes. Subsequent idle thread structures are allocated dynamically as additional processors are brought online. Once process management initializes, it uses the special variable *PsIdleProcess* to refer to the idle process.

Apart from some critical fields provided so that these threads and their process can have a PID and name, everything else is ignored, which means that query APIs may simply return zeroed data.

The idle loop runs at DPC/dispatch level, polling for work to do, such as delivering deferred procedure calls (DPCs) or looking for threads to dispatch to. Although some details of the flow vary between architectures, the basic flow of control of the idle thread is as follows:

1. Enables and disables interrupts (allowing any pending interrupts to be delivered).

2. Checks whether any DPCs (described in Chapter 3) are pending on the processor. If DPCs are pending, clears the pending software interrupt and delivers them. (This will also perform timer expiration, as well as deferred ready processing. The latter is explained in the upcoming multiprocessor scheduling section.)

3. Checks whether a thread has been selected to run next on the processor, and if so, dispatches that thread.

4. Calls the registered power management processor idle routine (in case any power management functions need to be performed), which is either in the processor power driver (such as intelppm.sys) or in the HAL if such a driver is unavailable.

5. On debug systems, checks if there is a kernel debugger trying to break into the system and gives it access.

6. If requested, checks for threads waiting to run on other processors and schedules them locally. (This operation is also explained in the upcoming multiprocessor scheduling section.)

Priority Boosts

In six cases, the Windows scheduler can boost (increase) the current priority value of threads:

- On completion of I/O operations

- After waiting for executive events or semaphores

- When a thread has been waiting on an executive resource for too long

- After threads in the foreground process complete a wait operation

- When GUI threads wake up because of windowing activity

- When a thread that's ready to run hasn't been running for some time (CPU starvation)

The intent of these adjustments is to improve overall system throughput and responsiveness as well as resolve potentially unfair scheduling scenarios. Like any scheduling algorithms, however, these adjustments aren't perfect, and they might not benefit all applications.

> **Note** Windows never boosts the priority of threads in the real-time range (16 through 31). Therefore, scheduling is always predictable with respect to other threads in the real-time range. Windows assumes that if you're using the real-time thread priorities, you know what you're doing.

Windows Vista adds one more scenario in which a priority boost can occur, multimedia playback. Unlike the other priority boosts, which are applied directly by kernel code, multimedia playback boosts are managed by a user-mode service called the MultiMedia Class Scheduler Service (MMCSS). (Although the boosts are still done *in* kernel mode, the request to boost the threads is managed by this user-mode service.) We'll first cover the typical kernel-managed priority boosts and then talk about MMCSS and the kind of boosting it performs.

Priority Boosting after I/O Completion

Windows gives temporary priority boosts upon completion of certain I/O operations so that threads that were waiting for an I/O will have more of a chance to run right away and process whatever was being waited for. Recall that 1 quantum unit is deducted from the thread's remaining quantum when it wakes up so that I/O bound threads aren't unfairly favored. Although you'll find recommended boost values in the Windows Driver Kit (WDK) header files (by searching for "#define IO" in Wdm.h or Ntddk.h), the actual value for the boost is up to the device driver. (These values are listed in Table 5-18.) It is the device driver that specifies the boost when it completes an I/O request on its call to the kernel function *IoCompleteRequest*. In Table 5-18, notice that I/O requests to devices that warrant better responsiveness have higher boost values.

TABLE 5-18 Recommended Boost Values

Device	Boost
Disk, CD-ROM, parallel, video	1
Network, mailslot, named pipe, serial	2
Keyboard, mouse	6
Sound	8

The boost is always applied to a thread's current priority, not its base priority. As illustrated in Figure 5-23, after the boost is applied, the thread gets to run for one quantum at the elevated priority level. After the thread has completed its quantum, it decays one priority level and then runs another quantum. This cycle continues until the thread's priority level has decayed back to its base priority. A thread with a higher priority can still preempt the boosted thread, but the interrupted thread gets to finish its time slice at the boosted priority level before it decays to the next lower priority.

FIGURE 5-23 Priority boosting and decay

As noted earlier, these boosts apply only to threads in the dynamic priority range (0 through 15). No matter how large the boost is, the thread will never be boosted beyond level 15 into the real-time priority range. In other words, a priority 14 thread that receives a boost of 5 will go up to priority 15. A priority 15 thread that receives a boost will remain at priority 15.

Boosts After Waiting for Events and Semaphores

When a thread that was waiting for an executive event or a semaphore object has its wait satisfied (because of a call to the function *SetEvent*, *PulseEvent*, or *ReleaseSemaphore*), it receives a boost of 1. (See the value for EVENT_ INCREMENT and SEMAPHORE_INCREMENT in the WDK header files.) Threads that wait for events and semaphores warrant a boost for the same reason that threads that wait for I/O operations do—threads that block on events are requesting CPU cycles less frequently than CPU-bound threads. This adjustment helps balance the scales.

This boost operates the same as the boost that occurs after I/O completion, as described in the previous section:

- The boost is always applied to the base priority (not the current priority).

- The priority will never be boosted above 15.

- The thread gets to run at the elevated priority for its remaining quantum (as described earlier, quantums are reduced by 1 when threads exit a wait) before decaying one priority level at a time until it reaches its original base priority.

A special boost is applied to threads that are awoken as a result of setting an event with the special functions *NtSetEventBoostPriority* (used in Ntdll.dll for critical sections) and *KeSetEventBoostPriority* (used for executive resources) or if a signaling gate is used (such as with pushlocks). If a thread waiting for an event is woken up as a result of the special event

boost function and its priority is 13 or below, it will have its priority boosted to be the setting thread's priority plus one. If its quantum is less than 4 quantum units, it is set to 4 quantum units. This boost is removed at quantum end.

Boosts During Waiting on Executive Resources

When a thread attempts to acquire an executive resource (ERESOURCE; see Chapter 3 for more information on kernel synchronization objects) that is already owned exclusively by another thread, it must enter a wait state until the other thread has released the resource. To avoid deadlocks, the executive performs this wait in intervals of five seconds instead of doing an infinite wait on the resource.

At the end of these five seconds, if the resource is still owned, the executive will attempt to prevent CPU starvation by acquiring the dispatcher lock, boosting the owning thread or threads, and performing another wait. Because the dispatcher lock is held and the thread's *WaitNext* flag is set to TRUE, this ensures a consistent state during the boosting process until the next wait is done.

This boost operates in the following manner:

- The boost is always applied to the base priority (not the current priority) of the owner thread.

- The boost raises priority to 14.

- The boost is only applied if the owner thread has a lower priority than the waiting thread, and only if the owner thread's priority isn't already 14.

- The quantum of the thread is reset so that the thread gets to run at the elevated priority for a full quantum, instead of only the quantum it had left. Just like other boosts, at each quantum end, the priority boost will slowly decrease by one level.

Because executive resources can be either shared or exclusive, the kernel will first boost the exclusive owner and then check for shared owners and boost all of them. When the waiting thread enters the wait state again, the hope is that the scheduler will schedule one of the owner threads, which will have enough time to complete its work and release the resource. It's important to note that this boosting mechanism is used only if the resource doesn't have the Disable Boost flag set, which developers can choose to set if the priority inversion mechanism described here works well with their usage of the resource.

Additionally, this mechanism isn't perfect. For example, if the resource has multiple shared owners, the executive will boost all those threads to priority 14, resulting in a sudden surge of high-priority threads on the system, all with full quantums. Although the exclusive thread will run first (since it was the first to be boosted and therefore first on the ready list), the other shared owners will run next, since the waiting thread's priority was not boosted. Only until after all the shared owners have gotten a chance to run and their priority decreased

below the waiting thread will the waiting thread finally get its chance to acquire the resource. Because shared owners can promote or convert their ownership from shared to exclusive as soon as the exclusive owner releases the resource, it's possible for this mechanism not to work as intended.

Priority Boosts for Foreground Threads After Waits

Whenever a thread in the foreground process completes a wait operation on a kernel object, the kernel function *KiUnwaitThread* boosts its current (not base) priority by the current value of *PsPrioritySeparation*. (The windowing system is responsible for determining which process is considered to be in the foreground.) As described in the section on quantum controls, *PsPrioritySeperation* reflects the quantum-table index used to select quantums for the threads of foreground applications. However, in this case, it is being used as a priority boost value.

The reason for this boost is to improve the responsiveness of interactive applications—by giving the foreground application a small boost when it completes a wait, it has a better chance of running right away, especially when other processes at the same base priority might be running in the background.

Unlike other types of boosting, this boost applies to all Windows systems, and you *can't* disable this boost, even if you've disabled priority boosting using the Windows *SetThreadPriorityBoost* function.

EXPERIMENT: Watching Foreground Priority Boosts and Decays

Using the CPU Stress tool, you can watch priority boosts in action. Take the following steps:

1. Open the System utility in Control Panel (or right-click on your computer name's icon on the desktop, and choose Properties). Click the Advanced System Settings label, select the Advanced tab, click the Settings button in the Performance section, and finally click the Advanced tab. Select the Programs option. This causes *PsPrioritySeperation* to get a value of 2.

2. Run Cpustres.exe, and change the activity of thread 1 from Low to Busy.

3. Start the Performance tool by selecting Programs from the Start menu and then selecting Reliability And Performance Monitor from the Administrative Tools menu. Click on the Performance Monitor entry under Monitoring Tools.

4. Click the Add Counter toolbar button (or press Ctrl+I) to bring up the Add Counters dialog box.

5. Select the Thread object, and then select the % Processor Time counter.

6. In the Instances box, select <All instances> and click Search. Scroll down until you see the CPUSTRES process. Select the second thread (thread 1). (The first thread is the GUI thread.) You should see something like this:

7. Click the Add button, and then click OK.

8. Select Properties from the Action menu. Change the Vertical Scale Maximum to 16 and set the interval to Sample Every *N* Seconds in the Graph Elements area.

9. Now bring the CPUSTRES process to the foreground. You should see the priority of the CPUSTRES thread being boosted by 2 and then decaying back to the base priority as follows:

10. The reason CPUSTRES receives a boost of 2 periodically is because the thread you're monitoring is sleeping about 25 percent of the time and then waking up (this is the Busy Activity level). The boost is applied when the thread wakes up. If you set the Activity level to Maximum, you won't see any boosts because Maximum in CPUSTRES puts the thread into an infinite loop. Therefore, the thread doesn't invoke any wait functions and as a result doesn't receive any boosts.

11. When you've finished, exit Reliability and Performance Monitor and CPU Stress.

Priority Boosts After GUI Threads Wake Up

Threads that own windows receive an additional boost of 2 when they wake up because of windowing activity such as the arrival of window messages. The windowing system (Win32k.sys) applies this boost when it calls *KeSetEvent* to set an event used to wake up a GUI thread. The reason for this boost is similar to the previous one—to favor interactive applications.

EXPERIMENT: Watching Priority Boosts on GUI Threads

You can also see the windowing system apply its boost of 2 for GUI threads that wake up to process window messages by monitoring the current priority of a GUI application and moving the mouse across the window. Just follow these steps:

1. Open the System utility in Control Panel (or right-click on your computer name's icon on the desktop, and choose Properties). Click the Advanced System Settings label, select the Advanced tab, click the Settings button in the Performance section, and finally click the Advanced tab. Be sure that the Programs option is selected. This causes *PsPrioritySeperation* to get a value of 2.

2. Run Notepad from the Start menu by selecting Programs/Accessories/Notepad.

3. Start the Performance tool by selecting Programs from the Start menu and then selecting Reliability And Performance Monitor from the Administrative Tools menu. Click on the Performance Monitor entry under Monitoring Tools.

4. Click the Add Counter toolbar button (or press Ctrl+I) to bring up the Add Counters dialog box.

5. Select the Thread object, and then select the % Processor Time counter.

6. In the Instances box, select <All instances>, and then click Search. Scroll down until you see Notepad thread 0. Click it, click the Add button, and then click OK.

7. As in the previous experiment, select Properties from the Action menu. Change the Vertical Scale Maximum to 16, set the interval to Sample Every *N* Seconds in the Graph Elements area, and click OK.

8. You should see the priority of thread 0 in Notepad at 8, 9, or 10. Because Notepad entered a wait state shortly after it received the boost of 2 that threads in the foreground process receive, it might not yet have decayed from 10 to 9 and then to 8.

9. With Reliability and Performance Monitor in the foreground, move the mouse across the Notepad window. (Make both windows visible on the desktop.) You'll see that the priority sometimes remains at 10 and sometimes at 9, for the reasons just explained. (The reason you won't likely catch Notepad at 8 is that it runs so little after receiving the GUI thread boost of 2 that it never experiences more than one priority level of decay before waking up again because of additional windowing activity and receiving the boost of 2 again.)

10. Now bring Notepad to the foreground. You should see the priority rise to 12 and remain there (or drop to 11, because it might experience the normal priority decay that occurs for boosted threads on the quantum end) because the thread is receiving two boosts: the boost of 2 applied to GUI threads when they wake up

to process windowing input and an additional boost of 2 because Notepad is in the foreground.

11. If you then move the mouse over Notepad (while it's still in the foreground), you might see the priority drop to 11 (or maybe even 10) as it experiences the priority decay that normally occurs on boosted threads as they complete their turn. However, the boost of 2 that is applied because it's the foreground process remains as long as Notepad remains in the foreground.

12. When you've finished, exit Reliability and Performance Monitor and Notepad.

Priority Boosts for CPU Starvation

Imagine the following situation: you have a priority 7 thread that's running, preventing a priority 4 thread from ever receiving CPU time; however, a priority 11 thread is waiting for some resource that the priority 4 thread has locked. But because the priority 7 thread in the middle is eating up all the CPU time, the priority 4 thread will never run long enough to finish whatever it's doing and release the resource blocking the priority 11 thread. What does Windows do to address this situation?

We have previously seen how the executive code responsible for executive resources manages this scenario by boosting the owner threads so that they can have a chance to run and release the resource. However, executive resources are only one of the many synchronization constructs available to developers, and the boosting technique will not apply to any other primitive. Therefore, Windows also includes a generic CPU starvation relief mechanism as part of a thread called the *balance set manager* (a system thread that exists primarily to perform memory management functions and is described in more detail in Chapter 9).

Once per second, this thread scans the ready queues for any threads that have been in the ready state (that is, haven't run) for approximately 4 seconds. If it finds such a thread, the balance set manager boosts the thread's priority to 15 and sets the quantum target to an equivalent CPU clock cycle count of 4 quantum units. Once the quantum is expired, the thread's priority decays immediately to its original base priority. If the thread wasn't finished and a higher priority thread is ready to run, the decayed thread will return to the ready queue, where it again becomes eligible for another boost if it remains there for another 4 seconds.

The balance set manager doesn't actually scan all ready threads every time it runs. To minimize the CPU time it uses, it scans only 16 ready threads; if there are more threads at that priority level, it remembers where it left off and picks up again on the next pass. Also, it will boost only 10 threads per pass—if it finds 10 threads meriting this particular boost (which would indicate an unusually busy system), it stops the scan at that point and picks up again on the next pass.

Note We mentioned earlier that scheduling decisions in Windows are not affected by the number of threads, and that they are made in *constant time*, or O(1). Because the balance set manager does need to scan ready queues manually, this operation does depend on the number of threads on the system, and more threads will require more scanning time. However, the balance set manager is not considered part of the scheduler or its algorithms and is simply an extended mechanism to increase reliability. Additionally, because of the cap on threads and queues to scan, the performance impact is minimized and predictable in a worst-case scenario.

Will this algorithm always solve the priority inversion issue? No—it's not perfect by any means. But over time, CPU-starved threads should get enough CPU time to finish whatever processing they were doing and reenter a wait state.

EXPERIMENT: Watching Priority Boosts for CPU Starvation

Using the CPU Stress tool, you can watch priority boosts in action. In this experiment, we'll see CPU usage change when a thread's priority is boosted. Take the following steps:

1. Run Cpustres.exe. Change the activity level of the active thread (by default, Thread 1) from Low to Maximum. Change the thread priority from Normal to Below Normal. The screen should look like this:

2. Start the Performance tool by selecting Programs from the Start menu and then selecting Reliability And Performance Monitor from the Administrative Tools menu. Click on the Performance Monitor entry under Monitoring Tools.

3. Click the Add Counter toolbar button (or press Ctrl+I) to bring up the Add Counters dialog box.

4. Select the Thread object, and then select the % Processor Time counter.

5. In the Instances box, select <All instances>, and then click Search. Scroll down until you see the CPUSTRES process. Select the second thread (thread 1). (The first thread is the GUI thread.) You should see something like this:

6. Click the Add button, and then click OK.

7. Raise the priority of Performance Monitor to real time by running Task Manager, clicking the Processes tab, and selecting the Mmc.exe process. Right-click the process, select Set Priority, and then select Realtime. (If you receive a Task Manager Warning message box warning you of system instability, click the Yes button.) If you have a multiprocessor system, you will also need to change the affinity of the process: right-click and select Set Affinity. Then clear all other CPUs except for CPU 0.

8. Run another copy of CPU Stress. In this copy, change the activity level of Thread 1 from Low to Maximum.

9. Now switch back to Performance Monitor. You should see CPU activity every 6 or so seconds because the thread is boosted to priority 15. You can force updates to occur more frequently than every second by pausing the display with Ctrl+F, and then pressing Ctrl+U, which forces a manual update of the counters. Keep Ctrl+U pressed for continual refreshes.

When you've finished, exit Performance Monitor and the two copies of CPU Stress.

EXPERIMENT: "Listening" to Priority Boosting

To "hear" the effect of priority boosting for CPU starvation, perform the following steps on a system with a sound card:

1. Because of MMCSS's priority boosts (which we will describe in the next subsection), you will need to stop the MultiMedia Class Scheduler Service by opening the Services management interface (Start, Programs, Administrative Tools, Services).

2. Run Windows Media Player (or some other audio playback program), and begin playing some audio content.

3. Run Cpustres, and set the activity level of Thread 1 to Maximum.

4. Raise the priority of Thread 1 from Normal to Time Critical.

5. You should hear the music playback stop as the compute-bound thread begins consuming all available CPU time.

6. Every so often, you should hear bits of sound as the starved thread in the audio playback process gets boosted to 15 and runs enough to send more data to the sound card.

7. Stop Cpustres and Windows Media Player, and start the MMCSS service again.

Priority Boosts for MultiMedia Applications and Games (MMCSS)

As we've just seen in the last experiment, although Windows's CPU starvation priority boosts may be enough to get a thread out of an abnormally long wait state or potential deadlock, they simply cannot deal with the resource requirements imposed by a CPU-intensive application such as Windows Media Player or a 3D computer game.

Skipping and other audio glitches have been a common source of irritation among Windows users in the past, and the user-mode audio stack in Windows Vista would have only made the situation worse since it offers even more chances for preemption. To address this, Windows Vista incorporates a new service (called MMCSS, described earlier in this chapter) whose purpose is to ensure "glitch-free" multimedia playback for applications that register with it.

MMCSS works by defining several tasks, including:

- Audio
- Capture
- Distribution
- Games

- Playback

- Pro Audio

- Window Manager

> **Note** You can find the settings for MMCSS, including a lists of tasks (which can be modi-
> fied by OEMs to include other specific tasks as appropriate) in the registry keys under HKLM\
> SOFTWARE\Microsoft\Windows NT\CurrentVersion\Multimedia\SystemProfile. Additionally, the
> SystemResponsiveness value allows you to fine-tune how much CPU usage MMCSS guarantees to
> low-priority threads.

In turn, each of these tasks includes information about the various properties that differenti-
ate them. The most important one for scheduling is called the Scheduling Category, which
is the primary factor determining the priority of threads registered with MMCSS. Table 5-19
shows the various scheduling categories.

TABLE 5-19 Scheduling Categories

Category	Priority	Description
High	23-26	Pro Audio threads running at a higher priority than any other thread on the system except for critical system threads.
Medium	16-22	Threads part of a foreground application such as Windows Media Player.
Low	8-15	All other threads not part of the previous categories.
Exhausted	1-7	Threads that have exhausted their share of the CPU and will only continue running if no other higher priority threads are ready to run.

The main mechanism behind MMCSS boosts the priority of threads inside a registered pro-
cess to the priority level matching their scheduling category and relative priority within this
category for a guaranteed period of time. It then lowers those threads to the Exhausted cat-
egory so that other, nonmultimedia threads on the system can also get a chance to execute.

By default, multimedia threads will get 80 percent of the CPU time available, while other
threads will receive 20 percent (based on a sample of 10 ms; in other words, 8 ms and 2 ms).
MMCSS itself runs at priority 27, since it needs to preempt any Pro Audio threads in order to
lower their priority to the Exhausted category.

It is important to emphasize that the kernel still does the actual boosting of the values inside
the KTHREAD (MMCSS simply makes the same kind of system call any other application
would do), and the scheduler is still in control of these threads. It is simply their high prior-
ity that makes them run almost uninterrupted on a machine, since they are in the real-time
range and well above threads that most user applications would be running in.

As was discussed earlier, changing the relative thread priorities within a process does not
usually make sense, and no tool allows this because only developers understand the impor-
tance of the various threads in their programs.

On the other hand, because applications must manually register with MMCSS and provide it with information about what kind of thread this is, MMCSS does have the necessary data to change these relative thread priorities (and developers are well aware that this will be happening).

EXPERIMENT: "Listening" to MMCSS Priority Boosting

We are now going to perform the same experiment as the prior one but without disabling the MMCSS service. In addition, we'll take a look at the Performance tool to check the priority of the Windows Media Player threads.

1. Run Windows Media Player (other playback programs may not yet take advantage of the API calls required to register with MMCSS) and begin playing some audio content.

2. If you have a multiprocessor machine, be sure to set the affinity of the Wmplayer.exe process so that it only runs on one CPU (since we'll be using only one CPUSTRES worker thread).

3. Start the Performance tool by selecting Programs from the Start menu and then selecting Reliability And Performance Monitor from the Administrative Tools menu. Click on the Performance Monitor entry under Monitoring Tools.

4. Click the Add Counter toolbar button (or press Ctrl+I) to bring up the Add Counters dialog box.

5. Select the Thread object, and then select the % Processor Time counter.

6. In the Instances box, select <All instances>, and then click Search. Scroll down until you see Wmplayer, and then select all its threads. Click the Add button, and then click OK.

7. As in the previous experiment, select Properties from the Action menu. Change the Vertical Scale Maximum to 31, set the interval to Sample Every *N* Seconds in the Graph Elements area, and click OK.

 You should see one or more priority 21 threads inside Wmplayer, which will be constantly running unless there is a higher-priority thread requiring the CPU after they are dropped to the Exhausted category.

8. Run Cpustres, and set the activity level of Thread 1 to Maximum.

9. Raise the priority of Thread 1 from Normal to Time Critical.

10. You should notice the system slowing down considerably, but the music playback will continue. Every so often, you'll be able to get back some responsiveness from the rest of the system. Use this time to stop Cpustres.

11. If the Performance tool was unable to capture data during the time Cpustres ran, run it again, but use Highest instead of Time Critical. This change will slow down the system less, but it still requires boosting from MMCSS, and, because once the multimedia thread is put in the Exhausted category, there will always be a higher priority thread requesting the CPU (CPUSTRES), you should notice Wmplayer's priority 21 thread drop every so often, as shown here.

MMCSS's functionality does not stop at simple priority boosting, however. Because of the nature of network drivers on Windows and the NDIS stack, DPCs are quite common mechanisms for delaying work after an interrupt has been received from the network card. Because DPCs run at an IRQL level higher than user-mode code (see Chapter 3 for more information on DPCs and IRQLs), long-running network card driver code could still interrupt media playback during network transfers, or when playing a game for example.

Therefore, MMCSS also sends a special command to the network stack, telling it to throttle network packets during the duration of the media playback. This throttling is designed to maximize playback performance, at the cost of some small loss in network throughput (which would not be noticeable for network operations usually performed during playback, such as playing an online game). The exact mechanisms behind it do not belong to any area of the scheduler, so we will leave them out of this description.

> **Note** The original implementation of the network throttling code had some design issues caus-
> ing significant network throughput loss on machines with 1000 Mbit network adapters, especially
> if multiple adapters were present on the system (a common feature of midrange motherboards).
> This issue was analyzed by the MMCSS and networking teams at Microsoft and later fixed.

Multiprocessor Systems

On a uniprocessor system, scheduling is relatively simple: the highest-priority thread that
wants to run is always running. On a multiprocessor system, it is more complex, as Windows
attempts to schedule threads on the most optimal processor for the thread, taking into
account the thread's preferred and previous processors, as well as the configuration of the
multiprocessor system. Therefore, while Windows attempts to schedule the highest-priority
runnable threads on all available CPUs, it only guarantees to be running the (single) highest-
priority thread somewhere.

Before we describe the specific algorithms used to choose which threads run where and
when, let's examine the additional information Windows maintains to track thread and pro-
cessor state on multiprocessor systems and the two different types of multiprocessor systems
supported by Windows (hyperthreaded, multicore, and NUMA).

Multiprocessor Considerations in the Dispatcher Database

In addition to the ready queues and the ready summary, Windows maintains two bit-
masks that track the state of the processors on the system. (How these bitmasks are used
is explained in the upcoming section "Multiprocessor Thread-Scheduling Algorithms".)
Following are the two bitmasks that Windows maintains:

- The *active processor mask (KeActiveProcessors)*, which has a bit set for each usable pro-
 cessor on the system (This might be less than the number of actual processors if the
 licensing limits of the version of Windows running supports less than the number of
 available physical processors.)

- The *idle summary (KildleSummary)*, in which each set bit represents an idle processor

Whereas on uniprocessor systems, the dispatcher database is locked by raising IRQL to both
DPC/dispatch level and Synch level, on multiprocessor systems more is required, because
each processor could, at the same time, raise IRQL and attempt to operate on the dispatcher
database. (This is true for any systemwide structure accessed from high IRQL.) (See Chapter 3
for a general description of kernel synchronization and spinlocks.)

Because on a multiprocessor system one processor might need to modify another proces-
sor's per-CPU scheduling data structures (such as inserting a thread that would like to run
on a certain processor), these structures are synchronized by using a new per-PRCB queued

spinlock, which is held at IRQL SYNCH_LEVEL. (See Table 5-20 for the various values of SYNCH_LEVEL.) Thus, thread selection can occur while locking only an individual processor's PRCB, in contrast to doing this on Windows XP, where the systemwide dispatcher spinlock had to be held.

TABLE 5-20 IRQL SYNCH_LEVEL on Multiprocessor Systems

CPU Type	IRQL
Systems running on x86	27
Systems running on x64	12
Systems running on IA64	12

There is also a per-CPU list of threads in the deferred ready state. These represent threads that are ready to run but have not yet been readied for execution; the actual ready operation has been deferred to a more appropriate time. Because each processor manipulates only its own per-processor deferred ready list, this list is not synchronized by the PRCB spinlock. The deferred ready thread list is processed before exiting the thread dispatcher, before performing a context switch, and after processing a DPC. Threads on the deferred ready list are either dispatched immediately or are moved to the per-processor ready queue for their priority level.

Note that the systemwide dispatcher spinlock still exists and is used, but it is held only for the time needed to modify systemwide state that might affect which thread runs next. For example, changes to synchronization objects (mutexes, events, and semaphores) and their wait queues require holding the dispatcher lock to prevent more than one processor from changing the state of such objects (and the consequential action of possibly readying threads for execution). Other examples include changing the priority of a thread, timer expiration, and swapping of thread kernel stacks.

Thread context switching is also synchronized by using a finer-grained per-thread spinlock, whereas in Windows XP context switching was synchronized by holding a systemwide context swap spinlock.

Hyperthreaded and Multicore Systems

As described in the "Symmetric Multiprocessing" section in Chapter 2, Windows supports hyperthreaded and multicore multiprocessor systems in two primary ways:

1. Logical processors as well as per-package cores do not count against physical processor licensing limits. For example, Windows Vista Home Basic, which has a licensed processor limit of 1, will use all four cores on a single processor system.

2. When choosing a processor for a thread, if there is a physical processor with all logical processors idle, a logical processor from that physical processor will be selected, as opposed to choosing an idle logical processor on a physical processor that has another logical processor running a thread.

EXPERIMENT: Viewing Hyperthreading Information

You can examine the information Windows maintains for hyperthreaded processors using the *!smt* command in the kernel debugger. The following output is from a dual-processor hyperthreaded Xeon system (four logical processors):

```
lkd> !smt
SMT Summary:
------------

    KeActiveProcessors: ****--------------------------- (0000000f)
          KiIdleSummary: -***--------------------------- (0000000e)
No PRCB      Set Master SMT Set                                    #LP IAID
 0 ffdff120 Master      *-*---------------------------- (00000005)  2  00
 1 f771f120 Master      -*-*--------------------------- (0000000a)  2  06
 2 f7727120 ffdff120    *-*---------------------------- (00000005)  2  01
 3 f772f120 f771f120    -*-*--------------------------- (0000000a)  2  07

   Number of licensed physical processors: 2
```

Logical processors 0 and 1 are on separate physical processors (as indicated by the term "Master").

NUMA Systems

Another type of multiprocessor system supported by Windows is one with a nonuniform memory access (NUMA) architecture. In a NUMA system, processors are grouped together in smaller units called nodes. Each node has its own processors and memory and is connected to the larger system through a cache-coherent interconnect bus. These systems are called "nonuniform" because each node has its own local high-speed memory. While any processor in any node can access all of memory, node-local memory is much faster to access.

The kernel maintains information about each node in a NUMA system in a data structure called KNODE. The kernel variable *KeNodeBlock* is an array of pointers to the KNODE structures for each node. The format of the KNODE structure can be shown using the *dt* command in the kernel debugger, as shown here:

```
lkd> dt nt!_knode
nt!_KNODE
   +0x000 PagedPoolSListHead : _SLIST_HEADER
   +0x008 NonPagedPoolSListHead : [3] _SLIST_HEADER
   +0x020 PfnDereferenceSListHead : _SLIST_HEADER
   +0x028 ProcessorMask     : Uint4B
   +0x02c Color             : UChar
   +0x02d Seed              : UChar
   +0x02e NodeNumber        : UChar
   +0x02f Flags             : _flags
   +0x030 MmShiftedColor    : Uint4B
   +0x034 FreeCount         : [2] Uint4B
   +0x03c PfnDeferredList   : Ptr32 _SINGLE_LIST_ENTRY
   +0x040 CachedKernelStacks : _CACHED_KSTACK_LIST
```



```
NODE 1 (E0000145FF992200):
    ProcessorMask    : ----****----------------------------------------------------
    Color            : 0x00000001
    MmShiftedColor   : 0x00000040
    Seed             : 0x00000007
    Zeroed Page Count: 0x00000000003ED59A
    Free Page Count  : 0x0000000000000000
```

Applications that want to gain the most performance out of NUMA systems can set the affinity mask to restrict a process to the processors in a specific node. This information can be obtained using the functions listed in Table 5-21. Functions that can alter thread affinity are listed in Table 5-13.

TABLE 5-21 NUMA-Related Functions

Function	Description
GetNumaHighestNodeNumber	Retrieves the node that currently has the highest number.
GetNumaNodeProcessorMask	Retrieves the processor mask for the specified node.
GetNumaProximityNode	Returns the NUMA node number for the given proximity ID.
GetNumaProcessorNode	Retrieves the node number for the specified processor.

How the scheduling algorithms take into account NUMA systems will be covered in the upcoming section "Multiprocessor Thread-Scheduling Algorithms" (and the optimizations in the memory manager to take advantage of node-local memory are covered in Chapter 9).

Affinity

Each thread has an *affinity mask* that specifies the processors on which the thread is allowed to run. The thread affinity mask is inherited from the process affinity mask. By default, all processes (and therefore all threads) begin with an affinity mask that is equal to the set of active processors on the system—in other words, the system is free to schedule all threads on any available processor.

However, to optimize throughput and/or partition workloads to a specific set of processors, applications can choose to change the affinity mask for a thread. This can be done at several levels:

- Calling the *SetThreadAffinityMask* function to set the affinity for an individual thread

- Calling the *SetProcessAffinityMask* function to set the affinity for all the threads in a process. Task Manager and Process Explorer provide a GUI to this function if you right-click a process and choose Set Affinity. The Psexec tool (from Sysinternals) provides a command-line interface to this function. (See the *–a* switch.)

- By making a process a member of a job that has a jobwide affinity mask set using the *SetInformationJobObject* function (Jobs are described in the upcoming "Job Objects" section.)

- By specifying an affinity mask in the image header when compiling the application (For more information on the detailed format of Windows images, search for "Portable Executable and Common Object File Format Specification" on *www.microsoft.com*.)

You can also set the "uniprocessor" flag for an image (at compile time). If this flag is set, the system chooses a single processor at process creation time and assigns that as the process affinity mask, starting with the first processor and then going round-robin across all the processors. For example, on a dual-processor system, the first time you run an image marked as uniprocessor, it is assigned to CPU 0; the second time, CPU 1; the third time, CPU 0; the fourth time, CPU 1; and so on. This flag can be useful as a temporary workaround for programs that have multithreaded synchronization bugs that, as a result of race conditions, surface on multiprocessor systems but that don't occur on uniprocessor systems. (This has actually saved the authors of this book on two different occasions.)

EXPERIMENT: Viewing and Changing Process Affinity

In this experiment, you will modify the affinity settings for a process and see that process affinity is inherited by new processes:

1. Run the command prompt (Cmd.exe).

2. Run Task Manager or Process Explorer, and find the Cmd.exe process in the process list.

3. Right-click the process, and select Affinity. A list of processors should be displayed. For example, on a dual-processor system you will see this:

4. Select a subset of the available processors on the system, and click OK. The process's threads are now restricted to run on the processors you just selected.

5. Now run Notepad.exe from the command prompt (by typing **Notepad.exe**).

6. Go back to Task Manager or Process Explorer and find the new Notepad process. Right-click it, and choose Affinity. You should see the same list of processors you chose for the command prompt process. This is because processes inherit their affinity settings from their parent.

Windows won't move a running thread that could run on a different processor from one CPU to a second processor to permit a thread with an affinity for the first processor to run on the first processor. For example, consider this scenario: CPU 0 is running a priority 8 thread that can run on any processor, and CPU 1 is running a priority 4 thread that can run on any processor. A priority 6 thread that can run on only CPU 0 becomes ready. What happens? Windows won't move the priority 8 thread from CPU 0 to CPU 1 (preempting the priority 4 thread) so that the priority 6 thread can run; the priority 6 thread has to wait.

Therefore, changing the affinity mask for a process or a thread can result in threads getting less CPU time than they normally would, as Windows is restricted from running the thread on certain processors. Therefore, setting affinity should be done with extreme care—in most cases, it is optimal to let Windows decide which threads run where.

Ideal and Last Processor

Each thread has two CPU numbers stored in the kernel thread block:

- *Ideal processor,* or the preferred processor that this thread should run on
- *Last processor,* or the processor on which the thread last ran

The ideal processor for a thread is chosen when a thread is created using a seed in the process block. The seed is incremented each time a thread is created so that the ideal processor for each new thread in the process will rotate through the available processors on the system. For example, the first thread in the first process on the system is assigned an ideal processor of 0. The second thread in that process is assigned an ideal processor of 1. However, the next process in the system has its first thread's ideal processor set to 1, the second to 2, and so on. In that way, the threads within each process are spread evenly across the processors.

Note that this assumes the threads within a process are doing an equal amount of work. This is typically not the case in a multithreaded process, which normally has one or more house-keeping threads and then a number of worker threads. Therefore, a multithreaded application that wants to take full advantage of the platform might find it advantageous to specify the ideal processor numbers for its threads by using the *SetThreadIdealProcessor* function.

On hyperthreaded systems, the next ideal processor is the first logical processor on the next physical processor. For example, on a dual-processor hyperthreaded system with four logical processors, if the ideal processor for the first thread is assigned to logical processor 0, the second thread would be assigned to logical processor 2, the third thread to logical processor 1, the fourth thread to logical process 3, and so forth. In this way, the threads are spread evenly across the physical processors.

On NUMA systems, when a process is created, an ideal node for the process is selected. The first process is assigned to node 0, the second process to node 1, and so on. Then, the ideal processors for the threads in the process are chosen from the process's ideal node. The ideal

processor for the first thread in a process is assigned to the first processor in the node. As additional threads are created in processes with the same ideal node, the next processor is used for the next thread's ideal processor, and so on.

Dynamic Processor Addition and Replacement

As we've seen, developers can fine-tune which threads are allowed to (and in the case of the ideal processor, *should*) run on which processor. This works fine on systems that have a constant number of processors during their run time (for example, desktop machines require shutting down the computer to make any sort of hardware changes to the processor or their count).

Today's server systems, however, cannot afford the downtime that CPU replacement or addition normally requires. In fact, one of the times when adding a CPU is required for a server is at times of high load that is above what the machine can support at its current level of performance. Having to shut down the server during a period of peak usage would defeat the purpose. To meet this requirement, the latest generation of server motherboards and systems support the addition of processors (as well as their replacement) while the machine is still running. The ACPI BIOS and related hardware on the machine have been specifically built to allow and be aware of this need, but operating system participation is required for full support.

Dynamic processor support is provided through the HAL, which will notify the kernel of a new processor on the system through the function *KeStartDynamicProcessor*. This routine does similar work to that performed when the system detects more than one processor at startup and needs to initialize the structures related to them. When a dynamic processor is added, a variety of system components perform some additional work. For example, the memory manager allocates new pages and memory structures optimized for the CPU. It also initializes a new DPC kernel stack while the kernel initializes the Global Descriptor Table (GDT), the Interrupt Descriptor Table (IDT), the processor control region (PCR), the processor control block (PRCB), and other related structures for the processor.

Other executive parts of the kernel are also called, mostly to initialize the per-processor lookaside lists for the processor that was added. For example, the I/O manager, the executive lookaside list code, the cache manager, and the object manager all use per-processor lookaside lists for their frequently allocated structures.

Finally, the kernel initializes threaded DPC support for the processor and adjusts exported kernel variables to report the new processor. Different memory manager masks and process seeds based on processor counts are also updated, and processor features need to be updated for the new processor to match the rest of the system (for example, enabling virtualization support on the newly added processor). The initialization sequence completes with the notification to the Windows Hardware Error Architecture (WHEA) component that a new processor is online.

The HAL is also involved in this process. It is called once to start the dynamic processor after the kernel is aware of it, and it is called again after the kernel has finished initialization of the processor. However, these notifications and callbacks only make the kernel aware and respond to processor changes. Although an additional processor increases the throughput of the kernel, it does nothing to help drivers.

To handle drivers, the system has a new default executive callback, the processor add callback, that drivers can register with for notifications. Similar to the callbacks that notify drivers of power state or system time changes, this callback allows driver code to, for example, create a new worker thread if desirable so that it can handle more work at the same time.

Once drivers are notified, the final kernel component called is the Plug and Play manager, which adds the processor to the system's device node and rebalances interrupts so that the new processor can handle interrupts that were already registered for other processors. Unfortunately, until now, CPU-hungry applications have still been left out of this process, but Windows Server 2008 and Windows Vista Service Pack 1 have improved the process to allow applications to be able to take advantage of newer processors as well.

However, a sudden change of affinity can have potentially breaking changes for a running application (especially when going from a single-processor to a multiprocessor environment) through the appearance of potential race conditions or simply misdistribution of work (since the process might have calculated the perfect ratios at startup, based on the number of CPUs it was aware of). As a result, applications do not take advantage of a dynamically added processor by default—they must request it.

The Windows APIs *SetProcessAffinityUpdateMode* and *QueryProcessAffinityMode* (which use the undocumented *NtSet/QueryInformationProcess* system call) tell the process manager that these applications should have their affinity updated (by setting the AffinityUpdateEnable flag in EPROCESS), or that they do not want to deal with affinity updates (by setting the AffinityPermanent flag in EPROCESS). Once an application has told the system that its affinity is permanent, it cannot later change its mind and request affinity updates, so this is a one-time change.

As part of *KeStartDynamicProcessor*, a new step has been added after interrupts are rebalanced, which is to call the process manager to perform affinity updates through *PsUpdateActiveProcessAffinity*. Some Windows core processes and services already have affinity updates enabled, while third-party software will need to be recompiled to take advantage of the new API call. The System process, Svchost processes, and Smss are all compatible with dynamic processor addition.

Multiprocessor Thread-Scheduling Algorithms

Now that we've described the types of multiprocessor systems supported by Windows as well as the thread affinity and ideal processor settings, we're ready to examine how this

information is used to determine which threads run where. There are two basic decisions to describe:

- Choosing a processor for a thread that wants to run
- Choosing a thread on a processor that needs something to do

Choosing a Processor for a Thread When There Are Idle Processors

When a thread becomes ready to run, Windows first tries to schedule the thread to run on an idle processor. If there is a choice of idle processors, preference is given first to the thread's ideal processor, then to the thread's previous processor, and then to the currently executing processor (that is, the CPU on which the scheduling code is running).

To select the best idle processor, Windows starts with the set of idle processors that the thread's affinity mask permits it to run on. If the system is NUMA and there are idle CPUs in the node containing the thread's ideal processor, the list of idle processors is reduced to that set. If this eliminates all idle processors, the reduction is not done. Next, if the system is running hyperthreaded processors and there is a physical processor with all logical processors idle, the list of idle processors is reduced to that set. If that results in an empty set of processors, the reduction is not done.

If the current processor (the processor trying to determine what to do with the thread that wants to run) is in the remaining idle processor set, the thread is scheduled on it. If the current processor is not in the remaining set of idle processors, it is a hyperthreaded system, and there is an idle logical processor on the physical processor containing the ideal processor for the thread, the idle processors are reduced to that set. If not, the system checks whether there are any idle logical processors on the physical processor containing the thread's previous processor. If that set is nonzero, the idle processors are reduced to that list. Finally, the lowest numbered CPU in the remaining set is selected as the processor to run the thread on.

Once a processor has been selected for the thread to run on, that thread is put in the standby state and the idle processor's PRCB is updated to point to this thread. When the idle loop on that processor runs, it will see that a thread has been selected to run and will dispatch that thread.

Choosing a Processor for a Thread When There Are No Idle Processors

If there are no idle processors when a thread wants to run, Windows compares the priority of the thread running (or the one in the standby state) on the thread's ideal processor to determine whether it should preempt that thread.

If the thread's ideal processor already has a thread selected to run next (waiting in the standby state to be scheduled) and that thread's priority is less than the priority of the thread being readied for execution, the new thread preempts that first thread out of the standby

state and becomes the next thread for that CPU. If there is already a thread running on that CPU, Windows checks whether the priority of the currently running thread is less than the thread being readied for execution. If so, the currently running thread is marked to be pre-empted and Windows queues an interprocessor interrupt to the target processor to preempt the currently running thread in favor of this new thread.

Note Windows doesn't look at the priority of the current and next threads on all the CPUs—just on the one CPU selected as just described. If no thread can be preempted on that one CPU, the new thread is put in the ready queue for its priority level, where it awaits its turn to get scheduled. Therefore, Windows does not guarantee to be running all the highest-priority threads, but it will always run the highest-priority thread.

If the ready thread cannot be run right away, it is moved into the ready state where it awaits its turn to run. Note that threads are always put on their ideal processor's per-processor ready queues.

Selecting a Thread to Run on a Specific CPU

Because each processor has its own list of threads waiting to run on that processor, when a thread finishes running, the processor can simply check its per-processor ready queue for the next thread to run. If the per-processor ready queues are empty, the idle thread for that processor is scheduled. The idle thread then begins scanning other processor's ready queues for threads it can run. Note that on NUMA systems, the idle thread first looks at processors on its node before looking at other nodes' processors.

CPU Rate Limits

As part of the new hard quota management system added in Windows Vista (which builds on previous quota support present since the first version of Windows NT, but adds hard limits instead of soft hints), support for limiting CPU usage was added to the system in three different ways: per-session, per-user, or per-system. Unfortunately, information on enabling these new limits has not yet been documented, and no tool that is part of the operating system allows you to set these limits: you must modify the registry settings manually. Because all the quotas—save one—are memory quotas, we will cover those in Chapter 9, which deals with the memory manager, and focus our attention on the CPU rate limit.

The new quota system can be accessed through the registry key HKLM\SYSTEM\Current-ControlSet\Control\Session Manager\QuotaSystem, as well as through the standard *NtSet-InformationProcess* system call. CPU rate limits can therefore be set in one of three ways:

■ By creating a new value called CpuRateLimit and entering the rate information.

- By creating a new key with the security ID (SID) of the account you want to limit, and creating a CpuRateLimit value inside that key.

- By calling *NtSetInformationProcess* and giving it the process handle of the process to limit and the CPU rate limiting information.

In all three cases, the CPU rate limit data is not a straightforward value; it is based on a compressed bitfield, documented in the WDK as part of the RATE_QUOTA_LIMIT structure. The bottom four bits define the *rate phase*, which can be expressed either as one, two, or three seconds—this value defines how often the rate limiting should be applied and is called the PS_RATE_PHASE. The rest of the bits are used for the actual rate, as a value representing a percentage of maximum CPU usage. Because any number from 0 to 100 can be represented with only 7 bits, the rest of the bits are unused. Therefore, a rate limit of 40 percent every 2 seconds would be defined by the value 0x282, or 101000 0010 in binary.

The process manager, which is responsible for enforcing the CPU rate limit, uses a variety of system mechanisms to do its job. First of all, rate limiting is able to reliably work because of the CPU cycle count improvements discussed earlier, which allow the process manager to accurately determine how much CPU time a process has taken and know whether the limit should be enforced. It then uses a combination of DPC and APC routines to throttle down DPC and APC CPU usage, which are outside the direct control of user-mode developers but still result in CPU usage in the system (in the case of a systemwide CPU rate limit).

Finally, the main mechanism through which rate limiting works is by creating an artificial wait on a kernel gate object (making the thread uniquely bound to this object and putting it in a wait state, which does not consume CPU cycles). This mechanism operates through the normal routine of an APC object queued to the thread or threads inside the process currently responsible for the work. The gate is signaled by an internal worker thread inside the process manager responsible for replenishment of the CPU usage, which is queued by a DPC responsible for replenishing systemwide CPU usage requests.

Job Objects

A *job object* is a nameable, securable, shareable kernel object that allows control of one or more processes as a group. A job object's basic function is to allow groups of processes to be managed and manipulated as a unit. A process can be a member of only one job object. By default, its association with the job object can't be broken and all processes created by the process and its descendents are associated with the same job object as well. The job object also records basic accounting information for all processes associated with the job and for all processes that were associated with the job but have since terminated. Table 5-22 lists the Windows functions to create and manipulate job objects.

TABLE 5-22 Windows API Functions for Jobs

Function	Description
CreateJobObject	Creates a job object (with an optional name)
OpenJobObject	Opens an existing job object by name
AssignProcessToJobObject	Adds a process to a job
TerminateJobObject	Terminates all processes in a job
SetInformationJobObject	Sets limits
QueryInformationJobObject	Retrieves information about the job, such as CPU time, page fault count, number of processes, list of process IDs, quotas or limits, and security limits

The following are some of the CPU-related and memory-related limits you can specify for a job:

- **Maximum number of active processes** Limits the number of concurrently existing processes in the job.

- **Jobwide user-mode CPU time limit** Limits the maximum amount of user-mode CPU time that the processes in the job can consume (including processes that have run and exited). Once this limit is reached, by default all the processes in the job will be terminated with an error code and no new processes can be created in the job (unless the limit is reset). The job object is signaled, so any threads waiting for the job will be released. You can change this default behavior with a call to *EndOfJobTimeAction*.

- **Per-process user-mode CPU time limit** Allows each process in the job to accumulate only a fixed maximum amount of user-mode CPU time. When the maximum is reached, the process terminates (with no chance to clean up).

- **Job scheduling class** Sets the length of the time slice (or quantum) for threads in processes in the job. This setting applies only to systems running with long, fixed quantums (the default for Windows Server systems). The value of the job-scheduling class determines the quantum as shown here:

Scheduling Class	Quantum Units
0	6
1	12
2	18
3	24
4	30
5	36
6	42
7	48
8	54
9	Infinite if real-time; 60 otherwise

- **Job processor affinity** Sets the processor affinity mask for each process in the job. (Individual threads can alter their affinity to any subset of the job affinity, but processes can't alter their process affinity setting.)

- **Job process priority class** Sets the priority class for each process in the job. Threads can't increase their priority relative to the class (as they normally can). Attempts to increase thread priority are ignored. (No error is returned on calls to *SetThreadPriority*, but the increase doesn't occur.)

- **Default working set minimum and maximum** Defines the specified working set minimum and maximum for each process in the job. (This setting isn't jobwide—each process has its own working set with the same minimum and maximum values.)

- **Process and job committed virtual memory limit** Defines the maximum amount of virtual address space that can be committed by either a single process or the entire job.

Jobs can also be set to queue an entry to an I/O completion port object, which other threads might be waiting for, with the Windows *GetQueuedCompletionStatus* function.

You can also place security limits on processes in a job. You can set a job so that each process runs under the same jobwide access token. You can then create a job to restrict processes from impersonating or creating processes that have access tokens that contain the local administrator's group. In addition, you can apply security filters so that when threads in processes contained in a job impersonate client threads, certain privileges and security IDs (SIDs) can be eliminated from the impersonation token.

Finally, you can also place user-interface limits on processes in a job. Such limits include being able to restrict processes from opening handles to windows owned by threads outside the job, reading and/or writing to the clipboard, and changing the many user-interface system parameters via the Windows *SystemParametersInfo* function.

EXPERIMENT: Viewing the Job Object

You can view named job objects with the Performance tool. (See the Job Object and Job Object Details performance objects.) You can view unnamed jobs with the kernel debugger *!job* or *dt nt!_ejob* commands.

To see whether a process is associated with a job, you can use the kernel debugger *!process* command or Process Explorer. Follow these steps to create and view an unnamed job object:

1. From the command prompt, use the *runas* command to create a process running the command prompt (Cmd.exe). For example, type **runas /user:<domain>\ < username> cmd**. You'll be prompted for your password. Enter your password, and a Command Prompt window will appear. The Windows service that executes runas commands creates an unnamed job to contain all processes (so that it can terminate these processes at logoff time).

2. From the command prompt, run Notepad.exe.

3. Then run Process Explorer and notice that the Cmd.exe and Notepad.exe processes are highlighted as part of a job. (You can configure the colors used to highlight processes that are members of a job by clicking Options, Configure Highlighting.) Here is a screen shot showing these two processes:

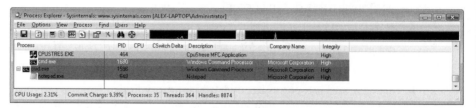

4. Double-click either the Cmd.exe or Notepad.exe process to bring up the process properties. You will see a Job tab in the process properties dialog box.

5. Click the Job tab to view the details about the job. In this case, there are no quotas associated with the job, but there are two member processes:

6. Now run the kernel debugger on the live system, display the process list with
!process, and find the recently created process running Cmd.exe. Then display the
process block by using *!process <process ID>*, find the address of the job object,
and finally display the job object with the *!job* command. Here's some partial
debugger output of these commands on a live system:

```
lkd> !process 0 0
**** NT ACTIVE PROCESS DUMP ****
    .
    .
    .
PROCESS 8567b758  SessionId: 0  Cid: 0fc4    Peb: 7ffdf000  ParentCid: 00b0
    DirBase: 1b3fb000  ObjectTable: e18dd7d0  HandleCount:  19.
    Image: Cmd.exe

PROCESS 856561a0  SessionId: 0  Cid: 0d70    Peb: 7ffdf000  ParentCid: 0fc4
    DirBase: 2e341000  ObjectTable: e19437c8  HandleCount:  16.
    Image: Notepad.exe

lkd> !process 0fc4
Searching for Process with Cid == fc4
PROCESS 8567b758  SessionId: 0  Cid: 0fc4    Peb: 7ffdf000  ParentCid: 00b0
    DirBase: 1b3fb000  ObjectTable: e18dd7d0  HandleCount:  19.
    Image: Cmd.exe
    BasePriority                        8
    .
    .
    Job                                 85557988

lkd> !job 85557988
Job at 85557988
  TotalPageFaultCount      0
  TotalProcesses           2
  ActiveProcesses          2
  TotalTerminatedProcesses 0
  LimitFlags               0
  MinimumWorkingSetSize    0
  MaximumWorkingSetSize    0
  ActiveProcessLimit       0
  PriorityClass            0
  UIRestrictionsClass      0
  SecurityLimitFlags       0
  Token                    00000000
```

7. Finally, use the *dt* command to display the job object and notice the additional
fields shown about the job:

```
lkd> dt nt!_ejob 85557988
nt!_EJOB
    +0x000 Event           : _KEVENT
    +0x010 JobLinks        : _LIST_ENTRY [ 0x81d09478 - 0x87f55030 ]
    +0x018 ProcessListHead : _LIST_ENTRY [ 0x87a08dd4 - 0x8679284c ]
    +0x020 JobLock         : _ERESOURCE
    +0x058 TotalUserTime   : _LARGE_INTEGER 0x0
```

```
+0x060 TotalKernelTime   : _LARGE_INTEGER 0x0
+0x068 ThisPeriodTotalUserTime : _LARGE_INTEGER 0x0
+0x070 ThisPeriodTotalKernelTime : _LARGE_INTEGER 0x0
+0x078 TotalPageFaultCount : 0
+0x07c TotalProcesses    : 2
+0x080 ActiveProcesses   : 2
+0x084 TotalTerminatedProcesses : 0
+0x088 PerProcessUserTimeLimit : _LARGE_INTEGER 0x0
+0x090 PerJobUserTimeLimit : _LARGE_INTEGER 0x0
+0x098 LimitFlags        : 0
+0x09c MinimumWorkingSetSize : 0
+0x0a0 MaximumWorkingSetSize : 0
+0x0a4 ActiveProcessLimit : 0
+0x0a8 Affinity          : 0
+0x0ac PriorityClass     : 0 ''
+0x0b0 AccessState       : (null)
+0x0b4 UIRestrictionsClass : 0
+0x0b8 EndOfJobTimeAction : 0
+0x0bc CompletionPort    : 0x87e3d2e8
+0x0c0 CompletionKey     : 0x07a89508
+0x0c4 SessionId         : 1
+0x0c8 SchedulingClass   : 5
+0x0d0 ReadOperationCount : 0
+0x0d8 WriteOperationCount : 0
+0x0e0 OtherOperationCount : 0
+0x0e8 ReadTransferCount : 0
+0x0f0 WriteTransferCount : 0
+0x0f8 OtherTransferCount : 0
+0x100 ProcessMemoryLimit : 0
+0x104 JobMemoryLimit    : 0
+0x108 PeakProcessMemoryUsed : 0x19e
+0x10c PeakJobMemoryUsed : 0x2ed
+0x110 CurrentJobMemoryUsed : 0x2ed
+0x114 MemoryLimitsLock  : _EX_PUSH_LOCK
+0x118 JobSetLinks       : _LIST_ENTRY [ 0x8575cff0 - 0x8575cff0 ]
+0x120 MemberLevel       : 0
+0x124 JobFlags          : 0
```

Conclusion

In this chapter, we've examined the structure of processes and threads and jobs, seen how they are created, and looked at how Windows decides which threads should run and for how long.

In the next chapter we'll look at a part of the system that's received more attention in the last few years than ever before, Windows security.

Chapter 6
Security

Preventing unauthorized access to sensitive data is essential in any environment in which multiple users have access to the same physical or network resources. An operating system, as well as individual users, must be able to protect files, memory, and configuration settings from unwanted viewing and modification. Operating system security includes obvious mechanisms such as accounts, passwords, and file protection. It also includes less obvious mechanisms, such as protecting the operating system from corruption, preventing less privileged users from performing actions (rebooting the computer, for example), and not allowing user programs to adversely affect the programs of other users or the operating system.

In this chapter, we explain how every aspect of the design and implementation of Windows was influenced in some way by the stringent requirements of providing robust security.

Security Ratings

Having software, including operating systems, rated against well-defined standards helps the government, corporations, and home users protect proprietary and personal data stored in computer systems. The current security rating standard used by the United States and many other countries is the Common Criteria (CC). To understand the security capabilities designed into Windows, however, it's useful to know the history of the security ratings system that influenced the design of Windows, the Trusted Computer System Evaluation Criteria (TCSEC).

Trusted Computer System Evaluation Criteria

The National Computer Security Center (NCSC, at *www.radium.ncsc.mil/tpep/*) was established in 1981 as part of the U.S. Department of Defense's (DoD) National Security Agency (NSA). One goal of the NCSC was to create a range of security ratings, listed in Table 6-1, to be used to indicate the degree of protection commercial operating systems, network components, and trusted applications offer. These security ratings, which can be found at *www.radium.ncsc.mil/tpep/library/rainbow/5200.28-STD.html*, were defined in 1983 and are commonly referred to as "the Orange Book."

The TCSEC standard consists of "levels of trust" ratings, where higher levels build on lower levels by adding more rigorous protection and validation requirements. No operating system meets the A1, or "Verified Design," rating. Although a few operating systems have earned one of the B-level ratings, C2 is considered sufficient and the highest rating practical for a general-purpose operating system.

TABLE 6-1 **TCSEC Rating Levels**

Rating	Description
A1	Verified Design
B3	Security Domains
B2	Structured Protection
B1	Labeled Security Protection
C2	Controlled Access Protection
C1	Discretionary Access Protection (obsolete)
D	Minimal Protection

In July 1995, Windows NT 3.5 (Workstation and Server) with Service Pack 3 was the first version of Windows NT to earn the C2 rating. In March 1999, Windows NT 4 with Service Pack 3 achieved an E3 rating from the U.K. government's Information Technology Security (ITSEC) organization, a rating equivalent to a U.S. C2 rating. In November 1999, Windows NT 4 with Service Pack 6a earned a C2 rating in both stand-alone and networked configurations.

The following were the key requirements for a C2 security rating, and they are still considered the core requirements for any secure operating system:

- A *secure logon facility*, which requires that users can be uniquely identified and that they must be granted access to the computer only after they have been authenticated in some way.

- *Discretionary access control*, which allows the owner of a resource to determine who can access the resource and what they can do with it. The owner grants rights that permit various kinds of access to a user or to a group of users.

- *Security auditing*, which affords the ability to detect and record security-related events or any attempts to create, access, or delete system resources. Logon identifiers record the identities of all users, making it easy to trace anyone who performs an unauthorized action.

- *Object reuse protection*, which prevents users from seeing data that another user has deleted or from accessing memory that another user previously used and then released. For example, in some operating systems, it's possible to create a new file of a certain length and then examine the contents of the file to see data that happens to have occupied the location on the disk where the file is allocated. This data might be sensitive information that was stored in another user's file but had been deleted. Object reuse protection prevents this potential security hole by initializing all objects, including files and memory, before they are allocated to a user.

Windows also meets two requirements of B-level security:

- *Trusted path functionality*, which prevents Trojan horse programs from being able to intercept users' names and passwords as they try to log on. The trusted path functionality in Windows comes in the form of its Ctrl+Alt+Delete logon-attention sequence, which cannot be intercepted by nonprivileged applications. This sequence of key-strokes, which is also known as the *secure attention sequence* (SAS), always pops up a logon dialog box, so would-be Trojan horses can easily be recognized. A Trojan horse presenting a fake logon dialog box will be bypassed when the SAS is entered.

- *Trusted facility management*, which requires support for separate account roles for administrative functions. For example, separate accounts are provided for administration (Administrators), user accounts charged with backing up the computer, and standard users.

Windows meets all of these requirements through its security subsystem and related components.

The Common Criteria

In January 1996, the United States, United Kingdom, Germany, France, Canada, and the Netherlands released the jointly developed Common Criteria for Information Technology Security Evaluation (CCITSE) security evaluation specification. CCITSE, which is usually referred to as the Common Criteria (CC), is the recognized multinational standard for product security evaluation. The CC home page is at *www.niap-ccevs.org/cc-scheme/*.

The CC is more flexible than the TCSEC trust ratings and has a structure closer to the ITSEC standard than to the TCSEC standard. The CC includes the concept of a *Protection Profile* (PP), used to collect security requirements into easily specified and compared sets, and the concept of a *Security Target* (ST), which contains a set of security requirements that can be made by reference to a PP.

Windows Server 2003 SP1 was evaluated as meeting the requirements of the Controlled Access PP, which is the equivalent of TCSEC C2 rating, and additional CC functional and assurance requirements in September of 2006. Details of its conformance can be found at *www.niap-ccevs.org/cc-scheme/vpl*; specifically, the additional requirements satisfied by Windows Server 2003 SP1 can be found in the certified Windows Server 2003/XP Common Criteria Security Target at *www.niap-ccevs.org/cc-scheme/st/st_vid10151-st.pdf*.

Security System Components

These are the core components and databases that implement Windows security:

- **Security reference monitor (SRM)** A component in the Windows executive (%SystemRoot%\System32\Ntoskrnl.exe) that is responsible for defining the access token data structure to represent a security context, performing security access checks on objects, manipulating privileges (user rights), and generating any resulting security audit messages.

- **Local Security Authority subsystem (Lsass)** A user-mode process running the image %SystemRoot%\System32\Lsass.exe that is responsible for the local system security policy (such as which users are allowed to log on to the machine, password policies, privileges granted to users and groups, and the system security auditing settings), user authentication, and sending security audit messages to the Event Log. The Local Security Authority service (Lsasrv—%SystemRoot%\System32\Lsasrv.dll), a library that Lsass loads, implements most of this functionality.

- **Lsass policy database** A database that contains the local system security policy settings. This database is stored in the registry under HKLM\SECURITY. It includes such information as what domains are entrusted to authenticate logon attempts, who has permission to access the system and how (interactive, network, and service logons), who is assigned which privileges, and what kind of security auditing is to be performed. The Lsass policy database also stores "secrets" that include logon information used for cached domain logons and Windows service user-account logons. (See Chapter 4 for more information on Windows services.)

- **Security Accounts Manager (SAM) service** A set of subroutines responsible for managing the database that contains the user names and groups defined on the local machine. The SAM service, which is implemented as %SystemRoot%\System32\Samsrv.dll, runs in the Lsass process.

- **SAM database** A database that on systems not functioning as domain controllers contains the defined local users and groups, along with their passwords and other attributes. On domain controllers, the SAM stores the system's administrator recovery account definition and password. This database is stored in the registry under HKLM\SAM.

- **Active Directory** A directory service that contains a database that stores information about objects in a domain. A *domain* is a collection of computers and their associated security groups that are managed as a single entity. Active Directory stores information

about the objects in the domain, including users, groups, and computers. Password information and privileges for domain users and groups are stored in Active Directory, which is replicated across the computers that are designated as *domain controllers* of the domain. The Active Directory server, implemented as %SystemRoot%\System32\ Ntdsa.dll, runs in the Lsass process. For more information on Active Directory, see Chapter 12.

- **Authentication packages** These include dynamic-link libraries (DLLs) that run both in the context of the Lsass process and client processes and that implement Windows authentication policy. An authentication DLL is responsible for checking whether a given user name and password match, and if so, returning to the Lsass information detailing the user's security identity, which Lsass uses to generate a token.

- **Interactive logon manager (Winlogon)** A user-mode process running %System-Root%\System32\Winlogon.exe that is responsible for responding to the SAS and for managing interactive logon sessions. Winlogon creates a user's first process when the user logs on, for example.

- **Logon user interface (LogonUI)** A user-mode process that presents users with the user interface they can use to authenticate themselves on the system. Uses credential providers to query user credentials through various methods.

- **Credential providers (CPs)** In-process COM objects that run in the LogonUI process (started on demand by Winlogon when the SAS is performed) and used to obtain a user's name and password, smartcard PIN, or biometric data (such as a fingerprint). The standard CPs are %SystemRoot%\System32\authui.dll and %SystemRoot%\System32\ SmartcardCredentialProvider.dll

- **Network logon service (Netlogon)** A Windows service (%SystemRoot%\System32\ Netlogon.dll) that sets up the secure channel to a domain controller, over which security requests—such as an interactive logon (if the domain controller is running Windows NT 4) or LAN Manager and NT LAN Manager (v1 and v2) authentication validation—are sent.

- **Kernel Security Device Driver (KSecDD)** A kernel-mode library of functions that implement the local procedure call (LPC) interfaces that other kernel-mode security components, including the Encrypting File System (EFS), use to communicate with Lsass in user mode. KSecDD is located in %SystemRoot%\System32\Drivers\Ksecdd.sys.

Figure 6-1 shows the relationships among some of these components and the databases they manage.

FIGURE 6-1 Windows security components

EXPERIMENT: Looking Inside HKLM\SAM and HKLM\Security

The security descriptors associated with the SAM and Security keys in the registry prevent access by any account other than the local system account. One way to gain access to these keys for exploration is to reset their security, but that can weaken the system's security. Another way is to execute Regedit.exe while running as the local system account, and PsExec from Windows Sysinternals (*www.microsoft.com/technet/sysinternals*) supports an option that enables you to launch processes in the local system account. Run Regedit using the *PsExec* command, shown below, to gain access to the SAM and Security databases without disturbing their security settings:

```
C:\>psexec -s -i -d c:\windows\regedit.exe
```

The SRM, which runs in kernel mode, and Lsass, which runs in user mode, communicate using the ALPC facility described in Chapter 3. During system initialization, the SRM creates a port, named SeRmCommandPort, to which Lsass connects. When the Lsass process starts, it creates an ALPC port named SeLsaCommandPort. The SRM connects to this port, resulting in the creation of private communication ports. The SRM creates a shared memory section for messages longer than 256 bytes, passing a handle in the connect call. Once the SRM and Lsass connect to each other during system initialization, they no longer listen on their respective connect ports. Therefore, a later user process has no way to connect successfully to either of these ports for malicious purposes—the connect request will never complete.

Figure 6-2 shows the communication paths as they exist after system initialization.

Set audit event
Create logon session
Delete logon session

Write audit message
Delete logon session

FIGURE 6-2 Communication between the SRM and Lsass

Protecting Objects

Object protection and access logging is the essence of discretionary access control and auditing. The objects that can be protected on Windows include files, devices, mailslots, pipes (named and anonymous), jobs, processes, threads, events, keyed events, event pairs, mutexes, semaphores, shared memory sections, I/O completion ports, LPC ports, waitable timers, access tokens, volumes, window stations, desktops, network shares, services, registry keys, printers, and Active Directory objects.

Because system resources that are exported to user mode (and hence require security valida-tion) are implemented as objects in kernel mode, the Windows object manager plays a key role in enforcing object security. (For more information on the object manager, see Chapter 3.) To control who can manipulate an object, the security system must first be sure of each user's identity. This need to guarantee the user's identity is the reason that Windows requires authenticated logon before accessing any system resources. When a process requests a han-dle to an object, the object manager and the security system use the caller's security identi-fication to determine whether the caller should be assigned a handle that grants the process access to the object it desires.

As discussed later in this chapter, a thread can assume a different security context than that of its process. This mechanism is called *impersonation*, and when a thread is impersonat-ing, security validation mechanisms use the thread's security context instead of that of the thread's process. When a thread isn't impersonating, security validation falls back on using the security context of the thread's owning process. It's important to keep in mind that all the threads in a process share the same handle table, so when a thread opens an object—even if it's impersonating—all the threads of the process have access to the object.

Sometimes, validating the identity of a user isn't enough for the system to grant access to a resource that should be accessible by the account. Logically, one can think of a clear distinction between a service running the Alice account, and an unknown application that Alice downloaded while browsing the Internet. Windows achieves this kind of intrauser isolation with the Windows integrity mechanism, which implements *integrity levels*. The Windows integrity mechanism is used by User Account Control (UAC) elevations, Protected Mode Internet Explorer (PMIE), and User Interface Privilege Isolation (UIPI).

Access Checks

The Windows security model requires that a thread specify up front, at the time that it opens an object, what types of actions it wants to perform on the object. The object manager calls the SRM to perform access checks based on a thread's desired access, and if the access is granted, a handle is assigned to the thread's process with which the thread (or other threads in the process) can perform further operations on the object. As explained in Chapter 3, the object manager records the access permissions granted for a handle in the process's handle table.

One event that causes the object manager to perform security access validation is when a process opens an existing object using a name. When an object is opened by name, the object manager performs a lookup of the specified object in the object manager namespace. If the object isn't located in a secondary namespace, such as the configuration manager's registry namespace or a file system driver's file system namespace, the object manager calls the internal function *ObpCreateHandle* once it locates the object. As its name implies, *ObpCreateHandle* creates an entry in the process's handle table that becomes associated with the object. *ObpCreateHandle* first calls *ObpIncrementHandleCount* to see if the thread has permission to access the object, and if the thread does, *ObpCreateHandle* calls the executive function *ExCreateHandle* to create the entry in the process handle table. *ObpIncrementHandleCount* calls *ObCheckObjectAccess* to carry out the security access check.

ObpIncrementHandleCount passes *ObCheckObjectAccess* the security credentials of the thread opening the object, the types of access to the object that the thread is requesting (read, write, delete, and so forth), and a pointer to the object. *ObCheckObjectAccess* first locks the object's security descriptor and the security context of the thread. The object security lock prevents another thread in the system from changing the object's security while the access check is in progress. The lock on the thread's security context prevents another thread of that process or a different process from altering the security identity of the thread while security validation is in progress. *ObCheckObjectAccess* then calls the object's security method to obtain the security settings of the object. (See Chapter 3 for a description of object methods.) The call to the security method might invoke a function in a different executive component. However, many executive objects rely on the system's default security management support.

When an executive component defining an object doesn't want to override the SRM's default security policy, it marks the object type as having default security. Whenever the SRM calls an object's security method, it first checks to see whether the object has default security. An object with default security stores its security information in its header, and its security method is *SeDefaultObjectMethod*. An object that doesn't rely on default security must manage its own security information and supply a specific security method. Objects that rely on default security include mutexes, events, and semaphores. A file object is an example of an object that overrides default security. The I/O manager, which defines the file object type, has the file system driver on which a file resides manage (or choose not to implement) the security for its files. Thus, when the system queries the security on a file object that represents a file on an NTFS volume, the I/O manager file object security method retrieves the file's security using the NTFS file system driver. Note, however, that *ObCheckObjectAccess* isn't executed when files are opened, because they reside in secondary namespaces; the system invokes a file object's security method only when a thread explicitly queries or sets the security on a file (with the Windows *SetFileSecurity* or *GetFileSecurity* functions, for example).

After obtaining an object's security information, *ObCheckObjectAccess* invokes the SRM function *SeAccessCheck*. *SeAccessCheck* is one of the functions at the heart of the Windows security model. Among the input parameters *SeAccessCheck* accepts are the object's security information, the security identity of the thread as captured by *ObCheckObjectAccess*, and the access that the thread is requesting. *SeAccessCheck* returns True or False, depending on whether the thread is granted the access it requested to the object.

Another event that causes the object manager to execute access validation is when a process references an object using an existing handle. Such references often occur indirectly, as when a process calls on a Windows API to manipulate an object and passes an object handle. For example, a thread opening a file can request read permission to a file. If the thread has permission to access the object in this way, as dictated by its security context and the security settings of the file, the object manager creates a handle—representing the file—in the handle table of the thread's process. The accesses the process is granted through the handle are stored with the handle by the object manager.

Subsequently, the thread could attempt to write to the file using the *WriteFile* Windows function, passing the file's handle as a parameter. The system service *NtWriteFile*, which *WriteFile* calls via Ntdll.dll, uses the object manager function *ObReferenceObjectByHandle* to obtain a pointer to the file object from the handle. *ObReferenceObjectByHandle* accepts the access that the caller wants from the object as a parameter. After finding the handle entry in the process's handle table, *ObReferenceObjectByHandle* compares the access being requested with the access granted at the time the file was opened. In this example, *ObReferenceObjectByHandle* will indicate that the write operation should fail because the caller didn't obtain write access when the file was opened.

The Windows security functions also enable Windows applications to define their own private objects and to call on the services of the SRM to enforce the Windows security model on those objects. Many kernel-mode functions that the object manager and other executive components use to protect their own objects are exported as Windows user-mode APIs. The user-mode equivalent of *SeAccessCheck* is *AccessCheck*, for example. Windows applications can therefore leverage the flexibility of the security model and transparently integrate with the authentication and administrative interfaces that are present in Windows.

The essence of the SRM's security model is an equation that takes three inputs: the security identity of a thread, the access that the thread wants to an object, and the security settings of the object. The output is either "yes" or "no" and indicates whether or not the security model grants the thread the access it desires. The following sections describe the inputs in more detail and then document the model's access validation algorithm.

Security Identifiers (SIDs)

Instead of using names (which might or might not be unique) to identify entities that perform actions in a system, Windows uses *security identifiers* (SIDs). Users have SIDs, and so do local and domain groups, local computers, domains, and domain members. A SID is a variable-length numeric value that consists of a SID structure revision number, a 48-bit identifier authority value, and a variable number of 32-bit subauthority or *relative identifier* (RID) values. The authority value identifies the agent that issued the SID, and this agent is typically a Windows local system or a domain. Subauthority values identify trustees relative to the issuing authority, and RIDs are simply a way for Windows to create unique SIDs based on a common-base SID. Because SIDs are long and Windows takes care to generate truly random values within each SID, it is virtually impossible for Windows to issue the same SID twice on machines or domains anywhere in the world.

When displayed textually, each SID carries an *S* prefix, and its various components are separated with hyphens:

S-1-5-21-1463437245-1224812800-863842198-1128

In this SID, the revision number is 1, the identifier authority value is 5 (the Windows security authority), and four subauthority values plus one RID (1128) make up the remainder of the SID. This SID is a domain SID, but a local computer on the domain would have a SID with the same revision number, identifier authority value, and number of subauthority values.

When you install Windows, the Windows Setup program issues the computer a SID. Windows assigns SIDs to local accounts on the computer. Each local-account SID is based on the source computer's SID and has a RID at the end. RIDs for user accounts and groups start at 1000 and increase in increments of 1 for each new user or group. Similarly, Dcpromo.exe, the utility used to create a new Windows domain, reuses the computer SID of the computer being promoted to domain controller as the domain SID, and it re-creates a new SID for the computer

if it is ever demoted. Windows issues to new domain accounts SIDS that are based on the domain SID and have an appended RID (again starting at 1000 and increasing in increments of 1 for each new user or group). A RID of 1028 indicates that the SID is the twenty-ninth SID the domain issued.

Windows issues SIDS that consist of a computer or domain SID with a predefined RID to many predefined accounts and groups. For example, the RID for the administrator account is 500, and the RID for the guest account is 501. A computer's local administrator account, for example, has the computer SID as its base with the RID of 500 appended to it:

S-1-5-21-13124455-12541255-61235125-500

Windows also defines a number of built-in local and domain SIDs to represent groups. For example, a SID that identifies any and every account (except anonymous users) is the Everyone SID: S-1-1-0. Another example of a group that a SID can represent is the network group, which is the group that represents users who have logged on to a machine from the network. The network-group SID is S-1-5-2. Table 6-2, reproduced here from the Windows SDK documentation, shows some basic well-known SIDs, their numeric values, and their use.

Finally, Winlogon creates a unique logon SID for each interactive logon session. A typical use of a logon SID is in an access control entry (ACE) that allows access for the duration of a client's logon session. For example, a Windows service can use the *LogonUser* function to start a new logon session. The *LogonUser* function returns an access token from which the service can extract the logon SID. The service can then use the SID in an ACE that allows the client's logon session to access the interactive window station and desktop. The SID for a logon session is S-1-5-5-0, and the RID is randomly generated.

TABLE 6-2 Well-Known SIDs

SID	Group	Use
S-1-0-0	Nobody	Used when the SID is unknown.
S-1-1-0	Everyone	A group that includes all users except anonymous users.
S-1-2-0	Local	Users who log on to terminals locally (physically) connected to the system.
S-1-3-0	Creator Owner ID	A security identifier to be replaced by the security identifier of the user who created a new object. This SID is used in inheritable ACEs.
S-1-3-1	Creator Group ID	Identifies a security identifier to be replaced by the primary-group SID of the user who created a new object. Use this SID in inheritable ACEs.
S-1-9-0	Resource Manager	Used by third-party applications performing their own security on internal data (such as Microsoft Exchange).

EXPERIMENT: Using PsGetSid and Process Explorer to View SIDs

You can easily see the SID representation for any account you're using by running the PsGetSid utility from Sysinternals.

PsGetSid's options allow you to translate machine and user account names to their corresponding SIDs and vice versa.

If you run PsGetSid with no options, it prints the SID assigned to the local computer. By using the fact that the Administrator's account always has a RID of 500, you can determine the name assigned to the account (in cases where a system administrator has renamed the account for security reasons) simply by passing the machine SID appended with -500 as PsGetSid's command-line argument.

To obtain the SID of a domain account, enter the user name with the domain as a prefix:

```
c:\>psgetsid redmond\daryl
```

You can determine the SID of a domain by specifying the domain's name as the argument to PsGetSid:

```
c:\>psgetsid Redmond
```

Finally, by examining the RID of your own account, you know at least a number of security accounts, equal to the number resulting from subtracting 999 from your RID, have been created in your domain or on your local machine (depending on whether you are using a domain or local machine account). You can determine what accounts have been assigned RIDs by passing a SID with the RID you want to query to PsGetSid. If PsGetSid reports that no mapping between the SID and an account name was possible and the RID is lower than that of your account, you know that the account assigned the RID has been deleted.

For example, to find out the name of the account assigned the twenty-eighth RID, pass the domain SID appended with -1027 to PsGetSid:

```
c:\>psgetsid S-1-5-21-1787744166-3910675280-2727264193-1027
Account for S-1-5-21-1787744166-3910675280-2727264193-1027:
User: redmond\daryl
```

Process Explorer can also show you information on account and group SIDs on your system through its Security tab. This tab shows you information such as who owns this process and which groups the account is a member of. To view this information, simply double-click on any process (for example, Explorer.exe) in the Process list, and then click on the Security tab. You should see something similar to the following.

The information displayed in the User field contains the friendly name of the account owning this process, while the SID field contains the actual SID value. The Group list includes information on all the groups that this account is a member of. (Groups are described later in this chapter.)

Integrity Levels

As mentioned earlier, integrity levels can override discretionary access to differentiate a process and objects running as and owned by the same user, offering the ability to isolate code and data within a user account. The mechanism of mandatory integrity control allows the SRM to have more detailed information about the nature of the caller by associating it with an integrity level. It also provides information on the trust required to access the object by defining an integrity level for it. These integrity levels are specified by a SID, as described in Table 6-3.

TABLE 6-3 Integrity Level SIDs

SID	Name (Level)	Use
S-1-16-0x0	Untrusted (0)	Used by processes started by the Anonymous group. Blocks most write access.
S-1-16-0x1000	Low (1)	Used by Protected Mode Internet Explorer; blocks write access to most objects (such as files and registry keys) on the system.
S-1-16-0x2000	Medium (2)	Used by normal applications being launched while UAC is enabled.

SID	Name (Level)	Use
S-1-16-0x3000	High (3)	Used by administrative applications launched through elevation when UAC is enabled, or normal applications if UAC is disabled and the user is an administrator
S-1-16-0x4000	System (4)	Used by services and other system-level applications (such as Wininit, Winlogon, Smss, etc.)

EXPERIMENT: Looking at the Integrity Level of Processes

You can use Process Explorer from Sysinternals to quickly display the integrity level for the processes on your system. The following steps demonstrate this functionality.

1. Launch Internet Explorer in Protected Mode.

2. Open an elevated Command Prompt window.

3. Open Microsoft Paint normally (without elevating it).

4. Now open Process Explorer, right-click on any of the columns in the Process list, and then click Select Columns. You should see a dialog box similar to the one shown here.

5. Select the Integrity Level check box and close the dialog box.

6. Process Explorer will now show you the integrity level of the processes on your system. You should see the Protected Mode Internet Explorer process at Low, Microsoft Paint at Medium, and the elevated command prompt at High. Also

note that the services and system processes are running at an even higher integrity level, System.

Every process has an integrity level that is represented in the process's token and propagated according to the following rules:

- A process inherits the integrity level of its parent (which means an elevated command prompt will spawn other elevated processes).

- If the file object for the executable image to which the child process belongs has an integrity level and the parent process's integrity level is medium or higher, the child process will inherit the lower of the two.

- A parent process can also create a child process with an explicit integrity level (for example, when launching Protected Mode Internet Explorer from an elevated command prompt).

EXPERIMENT: Understanding Protected Mode Internet Explorer

As mentioned earlier, one of the users of the Windows integrity mechanism is Internet Explorer's Protected Mode, also called Protected Mode Internet Explorer (PMIE). This feature was added in Internet Explorer 7 to take advantage of the Windows integrity levels. This experiment will show you how PMIE utilizes integrity levels to provide a safer Internet experience. To do this, we'll use Process Monitor to trace Internet Explorer's behavior.

1. Make sure that you haven't disabled UAC and PMIE on your systems (they are both on by default), and close any running instances of Internet Explorer.

2. Run Process Monitor, and select Filter, Filter to display the filtering dialog box. Add an include filter for the process name Iexplore.exe, as shown next:

3. Run Process Explorer, and repeat the previous experiment to display the Integrity Level column.

4. Now launch Internet Explorer. You should see a flurry of events appear in the Process Monitor window and a quick succession of events in Process Explorer, showing some processes starting and some exiting.

5. Once Internet Explorer is running, Process Explorer will show you two new processes: Iexplore.exe, running at low integrity level, and Ieuser.exe, running at medium integrity level. Part of the added protection offered by PMIE is that Iexplore.exe runs at low integrity, so this confirms the behavior.

6. You can get more information about the behavior that just occurred by looking at the processes that started and exited based on the Iexplore.exe filter you set up. Reduce the number of Process Monitor events displayed by excluding registry and file events (click the respective icons in the toolbar). You can reduce the number of events even more by right-clicking on the operations Thread Start and Load Image and then selecting Exclude from the pop-up menu that appears. You should be left with the events shown next.

7. Notice what actually occurred: a first instance of Iexplore.exe (PID 748) was
 started, which created the Ieuser.exe process and a second Iexplore.exe process
 (PID 1492). Then, the first Iexplore.exe instance exited, leaving the child process
 behind. You can use the Process Tree functionality in Process Monitor to see these
 events in a more obvious manner. Click on Tools, and then click Process Tree and
 scroll down to the first Iexplore.exe entry. You should see a tree similar to the
 following:

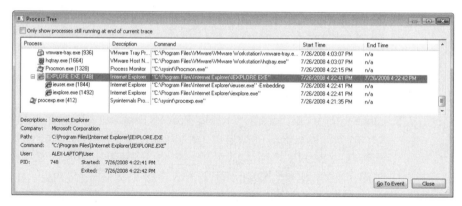

8. You can get more information on the behavior that just occurred by double-
 clicking on the first and second Iexplore.exe Process Start events. Shown next is
 the information for the first process:

9. Note that the integrity level for this process is actually medium, not low, as we would expect. However, if you repeat step 8 on the second instance of Internet Explorer, you'll notice that the integrity level is indeed low. Finally, if you check the Ieuser.exe process, you'll also notice a medium integrity level. This explains why the initial process is actually running at medium. A low integrity level process cannot create a medium integrity level process, so for Ieuser.exe to run at medium, it must be launched from a medium or higher process.

10. Now let's examine Ieuser.exe. Double-click on the Process Create event responsible for creating the process, and take a look at the stack by clicking on the Stack tab. You should see a trace similar to the one shown next.

Note the functions named *LaunchLoRIEModelE* and *CreateBrokerProcess*. The second function is actually responsible for creating the Ieuser.exe process, which is indeed called the IE broker process. This process is used to allow operations such as user-initiated file downloads to be saved to any directory the user has access to. As we'll see, because a process at low integrity level cannot write to files and directories with a higher integrity level, it would not be possible for users to save their downloads if there weren't a broker process at medium integrity level (or higher) to handle this operation.

11. Finally, you can take a look at the stack trace behind the creation of the second Iexplore.exe instance running at low integrity level. You'll see the same function, *LaunchLoRIEModelE,* involved in the operation, which calls *CreateIEInProtected-Mode* and *CreateMICIEProcess* (where MIC stands for Mandatory Integrity Control). The function *LaunchProtectedModeIEWithToken* calls the Windows API function *CreateProcessAsUser* to perform the creation at low integrity level. The following screen shows this sequence of events in the stack trace of the Process Create event:

Table 6-3 lists the integrity level associated with processes, but how about objects? Objects also have an integrity level stored as part of their security descriptor, in a structure that is called the *mandatory label*.

To support migrating from previous versions of Windows (whose registry keys and files would not include integrity level information), as well as to make it simpler for application developers, all objects have an *implicit integrity level* in order to avoid having to manually specify one. This implicit integrity level is the medium level, meaning that the mandatory policy (described shortly) on the object will be performed on tokens accessing this object with an integrity level lower than medium.

When a process creates an object without specifying an integrity level, the system checks the integrity level in the token. For tokens with a level medium or higher, the implicit integrity level of the object remains medium. However, when a token contains an integrity level lower than medium, the object is created with an *explicit integrity level* that matches the level in the token.

The reason that objects that are created by high or system integrity level processes have a medium integrity level themselves is so that users can disable and enable UAC: if object

integrity levels always inherited their creator's integrity level, the applications of an administrator who disables UAC and subsequently reenables it would potentially fail because they would not be able to modify any registry settings or files that they created when running at the high integrity level. Objects can also have an explicit integrity level that is set by the system or by the creator of the object. For example, the following objects are given an explicit integrity level by the kernel when it creates them:

- Processes
- Threads
- Tokens
- Jobs

The reason for assigning an integrity level to these objects is to prevent a process for the same user, but one running at a lower integrity level, from accessing these objects and modifying their content or behavior (for example, DLL injection or code modification).

EXPERIMENT: Looking at the Integrity Level of Objects

You can use the Accesschk tool from Sysinternals to display the integrity level of objects on the system, such as files, processes, and registry keys. Here's an experiment showing the purpose of the LocalLow directory in Windows.

1. Browse to C:\Users*UserName*\ in a command prompt.

2. Try running Accesschk on the AppData folder.

3. Note the differences between Local and LocalLow in your output, similar to the one shown here:

```
C:\Users\Abby\AppData\Local
  Medium Mandatory Level (Default) [No-Write-Up]
  RW Local Abby-PC\Abby
  RW NT AUTHORITY\SYSTEM
  RW BUILTIN\Administrators
C:\Users\Abby\AppData\LocalLow
  Low Mandatory Level [No-Write-Up]
  RW Local Abby-PC\Abby
  RW NT AUTHORITY\SYSTEM
  RW BUILTIN\Administrators
C:\Users\Abby\AppData\Roaming
  Medium Mandatory Level (Default) [No-Write-Up]
  RW Local Abby-PC\Abby
  RW NT AUTHORITY\SYSTEM
  RW BUILTIN\Administrators
```

4. Notice that the LocalLow directory has an integrity level that is set to Low, while the Local and Roaming directories have an integrity level of Medium (Default). The default means the system is using an implicit integrity level.

5. You can pass the –e flag to Accesschk so that it only displays explicit integrity levels. If you run the tool on the AppData folder again, you'll notice only the LocalLow information is displayed.

The –o (Object), –k (Key), and –p (Process) flags allow you to specify something other than a file or directory.

Apart from an integrity level, objects also have a *mandatory policy,* which defines the actual level of protection that's applied based on the integrity level check. Three types are possible, shown in Table 6-4. The integrity level and the mandatory policy are stored together in the same ACE.

TABLE 6-4 Object Mandatory Policies

Policy	Present on, by Default	Description
No-Write-Up	Implicit on all objects	Used to restrict write access coming from a lower integrity level process to the object.
No-Read-Up	Only on process objects	Used to restrict read access coming from a lower integrity level process to the object. Specific use on process objects protects against information leakage by blocking address space reads from an external process.
No-Execute-Up	Only on binaries implementing COM classes	Used to restrict execute access coming from a lower integrity level process to the object. Specific use on COM classes is to restrict launch activation permissions on a COM class.

Tokens

The SRM uses an object called a *token* (or *access token*) to identify the security context of a process or thread. A security context consists of information that describes the privileges, accounts, and groups associated with the process or thread. Tokens also include information such as the session ID, the integrity level, and UAC virtualization state. (We'll describe UAC's virtualization mechanism later in this chapter.)

During the logon process (described at the end of this chapter), Lsass creates an initial token to represent the user logging on. It then determines whether the user logging on is a member of a powerful group or possesses a powerful privilege. Windows Vista considers a user an administrator if the user is a member of any of the administrator-type groups listed here:

- Built-In Administrators
- Certificate Administrators
- Domain Administrators

- Enterprise Administrators
- Policy Administrators
- Schema Administrators
- Domain Controllers
- Enterprise Read-Only Domain Controllers
- Read-Only Domain Controllers
- Account Operators
- Backup Operators
- Cryptographic Operators
- Network Configuration Operators
- Print Operators
- System Operators
- RAS Servers
- Power Users
- Pre-Windows 2000 Compatible Access

Many of the groups listed are used only on domain-joined systems and don't give users local administrative rights directly. Instead they allow users to modify domainwide settings. If one or more of these groups are present, Lsass creates a restricted token for the user (called the *filtered admin token*), and creates a logon session for both. The standard user token is attached to the initial process(es) that Winlogon starts (by default, Userinit.exe).

> **Note** If UAC has been disabled, administrators run with a token that includes their administrator group memberships and privileges.

Because child processes by default inherit a copy of the token of their creators, all processes in the user's session run under the same token. You can also generate a token by using the Windows *LogonUser* function. You can then use this token to create a process that runs within the security context of the user logged on through the *LogonUser* function by passing the token to the Windows *CreateProcessAsUser* function. The *CreateProcessWithLogon* function also creates a token by creating a new logon session with an initial process, which is how the *Runas* command launches processes under alternative tokens.

Tokens vary in size because different user accounts have different sets of privileges and associated group accounts. However, all tokens contain the same information, shown in Figure 6-3.

Token source
Impersonation type
Token ID
Authentication ID
Modified ID
Expiration time
Session ID
Flags
Logon session
Mandatory policy
Default primary group
Default DACL
User account SID
Group 1 SID
Group *n* SID
Restricted SID 1
Restricted SID *n*
Privilege 1
Privilege *n*

FIGURE 6-3 Access tokens

The security mechanisms in Windows use two components to determine what objects can be accessed and what secure operations can be performed. One component comprises the token's user account SID and group SID fields. The SRM uses SIDs to determine whether a process or thread can obtain requested access to a securable object, such as an NTFS file.

The group SIDs in a token indicate which groups a user's account is a member of. For example, a server application can disable specific groups to restrict a token's credentials when the server application is performing actions a client requests. Disabling a group produces nearly the same effect as if the group wasn't present in the token (it results in a deny-only group, described later). (Disabled SIDs are used as part of security access checks, described later in the chapter.) Group SIDs can also include a special SID that contains the integrity level of the

process or thread. The SRM uses another field in the token, which describes the *mandatory integrity policy,* to perform the *mandatory integrity check* described later in the chapter.

The second component in a token that determines what the token's thread or process can do is the privilege array. A token's privilege array is a list of rights associated with the token. An example privilege is the right for the process or thread associated with the token to shut down the computer. Privileges are described in more detail later in this chapter.

A token's default primary group field and default discretionary access control list (DACL) field are security attributes that Windows applies to objects that a process or thread creates when it uses the token. By including security information in tokens, Windows makes it convenient for a process or thread to create objects with standard security attributes, because the process or thread doesn't need to request discrete security information for every object it creates.

Each token's type distinguishes a primary token (a token that identifies the security context of a process) from an impersonation token (a type of token that threads use to temporarily adopt a different security context, usually of another user). Impersonation tokens carry an impersonation level that signifies what type of impersonation is active in the token. (Impersonation is described later in this chapter.)

A token also includes the *mandatory policy* for the process or thread, which defines how MIC will behave when processing this token. There are two policies:

- TOKEN_MANDATORY_NO_WRITE_UP, which is enabled by default, sets the No-Write-Up policy on this token, specifying that the process or thread will not be able to access objects with a higher integrity level for write access.

- TOKEN_MANDATORY_NEW_PROCESS_MIN, which is also enabled by default, specifies that the SRM should look at the integrity level of the executable image when launching a child process and compute the minimum integrity level of the parent process and the file object's integrity level as the child's integrity level.

Token flags include parameters that determine the behavior of certain UAC and UIPI mechanisms, such as virtualization and user interface access, that will be described later in this chapter.

The remainder of the fields in a token serve informational purposes. The token source field contains a short textual description of the entity that created the token. Programs that want to know where a token originated use the token source to distinguish among sources such as the Windows Session Manager, a network file server, or the remote procedure call (RPC) server. The token identifier is a locally unique identifier (LUID) that the SRM assigns to the token when it creates the token. The Windows executive maintains the executive LUID, a counter it uses to assign a unique numeric identifier to each token.

The token authentication ID is another kind of LUID. A token's creator assigns the token's authentication ID when calling the *LsaLogonUser* function. If the creator doesn't specify a LUID, Lsass obtains the LUID from the executive LUID. Lsass copies the authentication ID for all tokens descended from an initial logon token. A program can obtain a token's authentication ID to see whether the token belongs to the same logon session as other tokens the program has examined.

The executive LUID refreshes the modified ID every time a token's characteristics are modified. An application can test the modified ID to discover changes in a security context since the context's last use.

Tokens contain an expiration time field that can be used by applications performing their own security to reject a token after a specified amount of time. However, Windows does not make use of this field internally.

Note To guarantee system security, the fields in a token are immutable (because they are located in kernel memory). Except for fields that can be modified through a specific system call designed to modify certain token attributes (assuming the caller has the appropriate access rights to the token object), data such as the privileges and SIDs in a token can never be modified.

EXPERIMENT: Viewing Access Tokens

The kernel debugger *dt _TOKEN* command displays the format of an internal token object. Although this structure differs from the user-mode token structure returned by Windows API security functions, the fields are similar. For further information on tokens, see the description in the Windows SDK documentation.

The following output is from the kernel debugger's *dt nt!_TOKEN* command:

```
kd> dt nt!_TOKEN
    +0x000 TokenSource      : _TOKEN_SOURCE
    +0x010 TokenId          : _LUID
    +0x018 AuthenticationId : _LUID
    +0x020 ParentTokenId    : _LUID
    +0x028 ExpirationTime   : _LARGE_INTEGER
    +0x030 TokenLock        : Ptr32 _ERESOURCE
    +0x034 ModifiedId       : _LUID
    +0x040 Privileges       : _SEP_TOKEN_PRIVILEGES
    +0x058 AuditPolicy      : _SEP_AUDIT_POLICY
    +0x074 SessionId        : Uint4B
    +0x078 UserAndGroupCount : Uint4B
    +0x07c RestrictedSidCount : Uint4B
    +0x080 VariableLength   : Uint4B
    +0x084 DynamicCharged   : Uint4B
    +0x088 DynamicAvailable : Uint4B
    +0x08c DefaultOwnerIndex : Uint4B
    +0x090 UserAndGroups    : Ptr32 _SID_AND_ATTRIBUTES
```

```
+0x094 RestrictedSids       : Ptr32 _SID_AND_ATTRIBUTES
+0x098 PrimaryGroup         : Ptr32 Void
+0x09c DynamicPart          : Ptr32 Uint4B
+0x0a0 DefaultDacl          : Ptr32 _ACL
+0x0a4 TokenType            : _TOKEN_TYPE
+0x0a8 ImpersonationLevel   : _SECURITY_IMPERSONATION_LEVEL
+0x0ac TokenFlags           : Uint4B
+0x0b0 TokenInUse           : UChar
+0x0b4 IntegrityLevelIndex  : Uint4B
+0x0b8 MandatoryPolicy      : Uint4B
+0x0bc ProxyData            : Ptr32 _SECURITY_TOKEN_PROXY_DATA
+0x0c0 AuditData            : Ptr32 _SECURITY_TOKEN_AUDIT_DATA
+0x0c4 LogonSession         : Ptr32 _SEP_LOGON_SESSION_REFERENCES
+0x0c8 OriginatingLogonSession : _LUID
+0x0d0 SidHash              : _SID_AND_ATTRIBUTES_HASH
+0x158 RestrictedSidHash    : _SID_AND_ATTRIBUTES_HASH
+0x1e0 VariablePart         : Uint4B
```

You can examine the token for a process with the *!token* command. You'll find the address of the token in the output of the *!process* command, as shown here:

```
lkd> !process d6c 1
Searching for Process with Cid == d6c
PROCESS 85450508  SessionId: 1  Cid: 0d6c    Peb: 7ffda000  ParentCid: 0ecc
    DirBase: cc9525e0  ObjectTable: afd75518  HandleCount:   18.
    Image: cmd.exe
    VadRoot 85328e78 Vads 24 Clone 0 Private 148. Modified 0. Locked 0.
    DeviceMap a0688138
    Token                             afd48470
    ElapsedTime                       01:10:14.379
    UserTime                          00:00:00.000
    KernelTime                        00:00:00.000
    QuotaPoolUsage[PagedPool]         42864
    QuotaPoolUsage[NonPagedPool]      1152
    Working Set Sizes (now,min,max)   (566, 50, 345) (2264KB, 200KB, 1380KB)
    PeakWorkingSetSize                582
    VirtualSize                       22 Mb
    PeakVirtualSize                   25 Mb
    PageFaultCount                    680
    MemoryPriority                    BACKGROUND
    BasePriority                      8
    CommitCharge                      437

lkd> !token afd48470
_TOKEN afd48470
TS Session ID: 0x1
User: S-1-5-21-2778343003-3541292008-524615573-500 (User: ALEX-LAPTOP\Administrator)
Groups:
 00 S-1-5-21-2778343003-3541292008-524615573-513 (Group: ALEX-LAPTOP\None)
    Attributes - Mandatory Default Enabled
 01 S-1-1-0 (Well Known Group: localhost\Everyone)
    Attributes - Mandatory Default Enabled
 02 S-1-5-21-2778343003-3541292008-524615573-1000 (Alias: ALEX-LAPTOP\Debugger Users)
    Attributes - Mandatory Default Enabled
```

```
03 S-1-5-32-544 (Alias: BUILTIN\Administrators)
   Attributes - Mandatory Default Enabled Owner
04 S-1-5-32-545 (Alias: BUILTIN\Users)
   Attributes - Mandatory Default Enabled
05 S-1-5-4 (Well Known Group: NT AUTHORITY\INTERACTIVE)
   Attributes - Mandatory Default Enabled
06 S-1-5-11 (Well Known Group: NT AUTHORITY\Authenticated Users)
   Attributes - Mandatory Default Enabled
07 S-1-5-15 (Well Known Group: NT AUTHORITY\This Organization)
   Attributes - Mandatory Default Enabled
08 S-1-5-5-0-89263 (no name mapped)
   Attributes - Mandatory Default Enabled LogonId
09 S-1-2-0 (Well Known Group: localhost\LOCAL)
   Attributes - Mandatory Default Enabled
10 S-1-5-64-10 (Well Known Group: NT AUTHORITY\NTLM Authentication)
   Attributes - Mandatory Default Enabled
11 S-1-16-12288 Unrecognized SID
   Attributes - GroupIntegrity GroupIntegrityEnabled
Primary Group: S-1-5-21-2778343003-3541292008-524615573-513 (Group: ALEX-LAPTOP\None)
Privs:
05 0x000000005 SeIncreaseQuotaPrivilege          Attributes -
08 0x000000008 SeSecurityPrivilege               Attributes -
09 0x000000009 SeTakeOwnershipPrivilege          Attributes -
10 0x00000000a SeLoadDriverPrivilege             Attributes -
11 0x00000000b SeSystemProfilePrivilege          Attributes -
12 0x00000000c SeSystemtimePrivilege             Attributes -
13 0x00000000d SeProfileSingleProcessPrivilege   Attributes -
14 0x00000000e SeIncreaseBasePriorityPrivilege   Attributes -
15 0x00000000f SeCreatePagefilePrivilege         Attributes -
17 0x000000011 SeBackupPrivilege                 Attributes -
18 0x000000012 SeRestorePrivilege                Attributes -
19 0x000000013 SeShutdownPrivilege               Attributes -
20 0x000000014 SeDebugPrivilege                  Attributes -
22 0x000000016 SeSystemEnvironmentPrivilege      Attributes -
23 0x000000017 SeChangeNotifyPrivilege           Attributes - Enabled Default
24 0x000000018 SeRemoteShutdownPrivilege         Attributes -
25 0x000000019 SeUndockPrivilege                 Attributes -
28 0x00000001c SeManageVolumePrivilege           Attributes -
29 0x00000001d SeImpersonatePrivilege            Attributes - Enabled Default
30 0x00000001e SeCreateGlobalPrivilege           Attributes - Enabled Default
33 0x000000021 SeIncreaseWorkingSetPrivilege     Attributes -
34 0x000000022 SeTimeZonePrivilege               Attributes -
35 0x000000023 SeCreateSymbolicLinkPrivilege     Attributes -
Authentication ID:        (0,be1a2)
Impersonation Level:      Identification
TokenType:                Primary
Source: User32            TokenFlags: 0x0 ( Token in use )
Token ID: 711076          ParentToken ID: 0
Modified ID:              (0, 711081)
RestrictedSidCount: 0     RestrictedSids: 00000000
OriginatingLogonSession: 3e7
```

You can indirectly view token contents with Process Explorer's Security tab in its process Properties dialog box. The dialog box shows the groups and privileges included in the token of the process you examine.

EXPERIMENT: Launching a Program at Low Integrity Level

When you elevate a program, either by using the Run As Administrator option or because the program is requesting it, the program is explicitly launched at high integrity level; however, it is also possible to launch a program (other than PMIE) at low integrity level by using Psexec from Sysinternals.

1. Launch Notepad at low integrity level by using the following command:

   ```
   c:\psexec -l notepad.exe
   ```

2. Try opening a file in the %SystemRoot%\System32 directory. Notice that you can browse the directory and open any file contained within it.

3. Now create a new file, write some text, and try saving it in the %SystemRoot%\System32 directory. Notepad should present a message box indicating a lack of permissions and recommend saving the file in the Documents folder.

4. Accept Notepad's suggestion. You will get the same message box again, and repeatedly for each attempt.

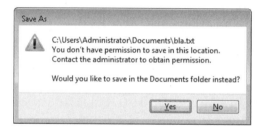

5. Now try saving the file in the LocalLow directory of your user profile, shown in the previous experiment.

In the previous experiment, saving a file in the LocalLow directory worked because Notepad was running with low integrity level, and only the LocalLow directory also had low integrity level. All the other locations where you tried to write the file had an implicit medium integrity level. (You can verify this with Accesschk.) However, reading from the %SystemRoot%\System32 directory, as well as opening files within it, did work, even though the directory and its file also have an implicit medium integrity level.

Impersonation

Impersonation is a powerful feature Windows uses frequently in its security model. Windows also uses impersonation in its client/server programming model. For example, a server application can export resources such as files, printers, or databases. Clients wanting to access a resource send a request to the server. When the server receives the request, it must ensure

that the client has permission to perform the desired operations on the resource. For example, if a user on a remote machine tries to delete a file on an NTFS share, the server exporting the share must determine whether the user is allowed to delete the file. The obvious way to determine whether a user has permission is for the server to query the user's account and group SIDs and scan the security attributes on the file. This approach is tedious to program, prone to errors, and wouldn't permit new security features to be supported transparently. Thus, Windows provides impersonation services to simplify the server's job.

Impersonation lets a server notify the SRM that the server is temporarily adopting the security profile of a client making a resource request. The server can then access resources on behalf of the client, and the SRM carries out the access validations. Usually, a server has access to more resources than a client does and loses some of its security credentials during impersonation. However, the reverse can be true: the server can gain security credentials during impersonation.

A server impersonates a client only within the thread that makes the impersonation request. Thread-control data structures contain an optional entry for an impersonation token. However, a thread's primary token, which represents the thread's real security credentials, is always accessible in the process's control structure.

Windows makes impersonation available through several mechanisms. If a server communicates with a client through a named pipe, the server can use the *ImpersonateNamed-PipeClient* Windows API function to tell the SRM that it wants to impersonate the user on the other end of the pipe. If the server is communicating with the client through Dynamic Data Exchange (DDE) or an RPC, it can make similar impersonation requests using *DdeImpersonateClient* and *RpcImpersonateClient*. A thread can create an impersonation token that's simply a copy of its process token with the *ImpersonateSelf* function. The thread can then alter its impersonation token, to disable SIDs or privileges, for example. Finally, a Security Support Provider Interface (SSPI) package can impersonate its clients with *ImpersonateSecurityContext*. SSPIs implement a network authentication protocol such as LAN Manager version 2 or Kerberos.

After the server thread finishes its task, it reverts to its primary security context. These forms of impersonation are convenient for carrying out specific actions at the request of a client and for ensuring that object accesses are audited correctly. (For example, the audit that is generated gives the identity of the impersonated client rather than that of the server process.) The disadvantage to these forms of impersonation is that they can't execute an entire program in the context of a client. In addition, an impersonation token can't access files or printers on network shares unless it is a delegation-level impersonation (described shortly) and has sufficient credentials to authenticate to the remote machine, or the file or printer share supports null sessions. (A null session is one that results from an anonymous logon.)

If an entire application must execute in a client's security context or must access network resources without using impersonation, the client must be logged on to the system. The

LogonUser Windows API function enables this action. *LogonUser* takes an account name, a password, a domain or computer name, a logon type (such as interactive, batch, or service), and a logon provider as input, and it returns a primary token. A server thread can adopt the token as an impersonation token, or the server can start a program that has the client's credentials as its primary token. From a security standpoint, a process created using the token returned from an interactive logon via *LogonUser*, such as with the *CreateProcessAsUser* API, looks like a program a user starts by logging on to the machine interactively. The disadvantage to this approach is that a server must obtain the user's account name and password. If the server transmits this information across the network, the server must encrypt it securely so that a malicious user snooping network traffic can't capture it.

To prevent the misuse of impersonation, Windows doesn't let servers perform impersonation without a client's consent. A client process can limit the level of impersonation that a server process can perform by specifying a *security quality of service* (SQOS) when connecting to the server. A process can specify SECURITY_ANONYMOUS, SECURITY_IDENTIFICATION, SECURITY_IMPERSONATION, and SECURITY_DELEGATION as flags for the Windows *CreateFile* function. Each level lets a server perform different types of operations with respect to the client's security context:

- *SecurityAnonymous* is the most restrictive level of impersonation—the server can't impersonate or identify the client.

- *SecurityIdentification* level lets the server obtain the identity (the SIDs) of the client and the client's privileges, but the server can't impersonate the client.

- *SecurityImpersonation* level lets the server identify and impersonate the client on the local system.

- *SecurityDelegation* is the most permissive level of impersonation. It lets the server impersonate the client on local and remote systems.

If the client doesn't set an impersonation level, Windows chooses the SecurityImpersonation level by default. The *CreateFile* function also accepts SECURITY_EFFECTIVE_ONLY and SECURITY_CONTEXT_TRACKING as modifiers for the impersonation setting:

- SECURITY_EFFECTIVE_ONLY prevents a server from enabling or disabling a client's privileges or groups while the server is impersonating.

- SECURITY_CONTEXT_TRACKING specifies that any changes a client makes to its security context are reflected in a server that is impersonating it. If this option isn't specified, the server adopts the context of the client at the time of the impersonation and doesn't receive any changes. This option is honored only when the client and server processes are on the same system.

To prevent spoofing scenarios in which a low integrity process could create a user interface that captured user credentials and then used *LogonUser* to obtain that user's token, a special integrity policy applies to impersonation scenarios: a thread cannot impersonate a token of

higher integrity than its own. For example, a low integrity application cannot spoof a dialog box that queries administrative credentials and then attempt to launch a process at a higher privilege level. The integrity mechanism policy for impersonation access tokens is that the integrity level of the access token that is returned by *LsaLogonUser* must be no higher than the integrity level of the calling process.

Restricted Tokens

A *restricted token* is created from a primary or impersonation token using the *CreateRestrictedToken* function. The restricted token is a copy of the token it's derived from, with the following possible modifications:

- Privileges can be removed from the token's privilege array.

- SIDs in the token can be marked as *deny-only*. These SIDs remove access to any resources for which the SID's access is denied by using a matching access-denied ACE that would otherwise be overridden by an ACE granting access to a group containing the SID earlier in the security descriptor.

- SIDs in the token can be marked as *restricted*. These SIDs are subject to a second pass of the access check algorithm, which will parse only the restricted SIDs in the token. The results of both the first pass and the second pass must grant access to the resource or no access is granted to the object.

Restricted tokens are useful when an application wants to impersonate a client at a reduced security level, primarily for safety reasons when running untrusted code. For example, the restricted token can have the shutdown-system privilege removed from it to prevent code executed in the restricted token's security context from rebooting the system.

Filtered Admin Token

As we saw earlier, restricted tokens are also used by UAC to create the filtered admin token that all user applications will inherit. A filtered admin token has the following characteristics:

- The integrity level is set to medium.

- The administrator and administrator-like SIDs mentioned previously are marked as *deny-only* to prevent a security hole if the group was removed altogether. For example, if a file had an access control list (ACL) that denied the Administrators group all access but granted some access to another group the user belongs to, the user would be granted access if the Administrators group was absent from the token, which would give the standard user version of the user's identity more access than the user's administrator identity.

- All privileges are stripped except Change Notify, Shutdown, Undock, Increase Working Set, and Time Zone.

EXPERIMENT: Looking at Filtered Admin Tokens

You can make Explorer launch a process with either the standard user token or the administrator token by following these steps on a Windows machine with UAC enabled:

1. Log on to an account that's a member of the Administrators group.

2. Click Start, Programs, Accessories, Command Prompt, right-click on the shortcut, and then select Run As Administrator. You will see a command prompt with the word Administrator in the title bar.

3. Now repeat the process, but simply click on the shortcut—this will launch a second command prompt without administrative privileges.

4. Run Process Explorer, and view the Security tab in the Properties dialog boxes for the two command prompt processes you launched. Note that the standard user token contains a deny-only SID and a Medium Mandatory Label, and that it has only a couple of privileges. The properties on the right in the following screen shot are from a command prompt running with an administrator token, and the properties on the left are from one running with the filtered administrative token:

Security Descriptors and Access Control

Tokens, which identify a user's credentials, are only part of the object security equation. Another part of the equation is the security information associated with an object, which

specifies who can perform what actions on the object. The data structure for this information is called a *security descriptor*. A security descriptor consists of the following attributes:

- **Revision number** The version of the SRM security model used to create the descriptor.

- **Flags** Optional modifiers that define the behavior or characteristics of the descriptor. These flags are listed in Table 6-5.

- **Owner SID** The owner's security ID.

- **Group SID** The security ID of the primary group for the object (used only by POSIX).

- **Discretionary access control list (DACL)** Specifies who has what access to the object.

- **System access control list (SACL)** Specifies which operations by which users should be logged in the security audit log and the explicit integrity level of an object.

TABLE 6-5 Security Descriptor Flags

Flag	Meaning
SE_OWNER_DEFAULTED	Indicates a security descriptor with a default owner security identifier (SID). Use this bit to find all the objects that have default owner permissions set.
SE_GROUP_DEFAULTED	Indicates a security descriptor with a default group SID. Use this bit to find all the objects that have default group permissions set.
SE_DACL_PRESENT	Indicates a security descriptor that has a DACL. If this flag is not set, or if this flag is set and the DACL is NULL, the security descriptor allows full access to everyone.
SE_DACL_DEFAULTED	Indicates a security descriptor with a default DACL. For example, if an object creator does not specify a DACL, the object receives the default DACL from the access token of the creator. This flag can affect how the system treats the DACL, with respect to access control entry (ACE) inheritance. The system ignores this flag if the SE_DACL_PRESENT flag is not set.
SE_SACL_PRESENT	Indicates a security descriptor that has a system access control list (SACL).
SE_SACL_DEFAULTED	Indicates a security descriptor with a default SACL. For example, if an object creator does not specify an SACL, the object receives the default SACL from the access token of the creator. This flag can affect how the system treats the SACL with respect to ACE inheritance. The system ignores this flag if the SE_SACL_PRESENT flag is not set.
SE_DACL_UNTRUSTED	Indicates that the ACL pointed to by the DACL of the security descriptor was provided by an untrusted source. If this flag is set and a compound ACE is encountered, the system will substitute known valid SIDs for the server SIDs in the ACEs.

Flag	Meaning
SE_SERVER_SECURITY	Requests that the provider for the object protected by the security descriptor should be a server ACL based on the input ACL, regardless of its source (explicit or defaulting). This is done by replacing all the GRANT ACEs with compound ACEs granting the current server access. This flag is only meaningful if the subject is impersonating.
SE_DACL_AUTO_INHERIT_REQ	Requests that the provider for the object protected by the security descriptor automatically propagate the DACL to existing child objects. If the provider supports automatic inheritance, the DACL is propagated to any existing child objects, and the SE_DACL_AUTO_INHERITED bit in the security descriptor of the parent and child objects is set.
SE_SACL_AUTO_INHERIT_REQ	Requests that the provider for the object protected by the security descriptor automatically propagate the SACL to existing child objects. If the provider supports automatic inheritance, the SACL is propagated to any existing child objects, and the SE_SACL_AUTO_INHERITED bit in the security descriptors of the parent object and child objects is set.
SE_DACL_AUTO_INHERITED	Indicates a security descriptor in which the DACL is set up to support automatic propagation of inheritable ACEs to existing child objects. The system sets this bit when it performs the automatic inheritance algorithm for the object and its existing child objects.
SE_SACL_AUTO_INHERITED	Indicates a security descriptor in which the SACL is set up to support automatic propagation of inheritable ACEs to existing child objects. The system sets this bit when it performs the automatic inheritance algorithm for the object and its existing child objects.
SE_DACL_PROTECTED	Prevents the DACL of a security descriptor from being modified by inheritable ACEs.
SE_SACL_PROTECTED	Prevents the SACL of a security descriptor from being modified by inheritable ACEs.
SE_RM_CONTROL_VALID	Indicates that the resource control manager bits in the security descriptor are valid. The resource control manager bits are 8 bits in the security descriptor structure that contains information specific to the resource manager accessing the structure.
SE_SELF_RELATIVE	Indicates a security descriptor in self-relative format, with all the security information in a contiguous block of memory. If this flag is not set, the security descriptor is in absolute format.

An *access control list* (ACL) is made up of a header and zero or more *access control entry* (ACE) structures. There are two types of ACLs: DACLs and SACLs. In a DACL, each ACE contains a SID and an access mask (and a set of flags, explained shortly). Eight types of ACEs can appear in a DACL: access allowed, access denied, allowed-object, denied-object, allowed-callback, denied-callback, allowed-object-callback, and denied-object-callback. As you would expect, the access-allowed ACE grants access to a user, and the access-denied ACE denies the

access rights specified in the access mask. The callback ACEs are used by applications that make use of the AuthZ API (described later) to register a callback that AuthZ will call when it performs an access check involving this ACE.

The difference between allowed-object and access allowed, and between denied-object and access denied, is that the object types are used only within Active Directory. ACEs of these types have a GUID (globally unique identifier) field that indicates that the ACE applies only to particular objects or subobjects (those that have GUID identifiers). In addition, another optional GUID indicates what type of child object will inherit the ACE when a child is created within an Active Directory container that has the ACE applied to it. (A GUID is a 128-bit identifier guaranteed to be universally unique.)

The accumulation of access rights granted by individual ACEs forms the set of access rights granted by an ACL. If no DACL is present (a *null* DACL) in a security descriptor, everyone has full access to the object. If the DACL is empty (that is, it has 0 ACEs), no user has access to the object.

The ACEs used in DACLs also have a set of flags that control and specify characteristics of the ACE related to inheritance. Some object namespaces have *containers* and *objects*. A container can hold other container objects and leaf objects, which are its *child objects*. Examples of containers are directories in the file system namespace and keys in the registry namespace. Certain flags in an ACE control how the ACE propagates to child objects of the container associated with the ACE. Table 6-6, reproduced in part from the Windows SDK, lists the inheritance rules for ACE flags.

TABLE 6-6 **Inheritance Rules for ACE Flags**

Flag	Inheritance Rule
CONTAINER_INHERIT_ACE	Child objects that are containers, such as directories, inherit the ACE as an effective ACE. The inherited ACE is inheritable unless the NO_PROPAGATE_INHERIT_ACE bit flag is also set.
INHERIT_ONLY_ACE	This flag indicates an inherit-only ACE that doesn't control access to the object it's attached to. If this flag is not set, the ACE controls access to the object to which it is attached.
INHERITED_ACE	This flag indicates that the ACE was inherited. The system sets this bit when it propagates an inheritable ACE to a child object.
NO_PROPAGATE_INHERIT_ACE	If the ACE is inherited by a child object, the system clears the OBJECT_INHERIT_ACE and CONTAINER_INHERIT_ACE flags in the inherited ACE. This action prevents the ACE from being inherited by subsequent generations of objects.
OBJECT_INHERIT_ACE	Noncontainer child objects inherit the ACE as an effective ACE. For child objects that are containers, the ACE is inherited as an inherit-only ACE unless the NO_PROPAGATE_INHERIT_ACE bit flag is also set.

A SACL contains two types of ACEs, *system audit* ACEs and *system audit-object* ACEs. These ACEs specify which operations performed on the object by specific users or groups should be audited. Audit information is stored in the system Audit Log. Both successful and unsuccessful attempts can be audited. Like their DACL object-specific ACE cousins, system audit-object ACEs specify a GUID indicating the types of objects or subobjects that the ACE applies to and an optional GUID that controls propagation of the ACE to particular child object types. If a SACL is null, no auditing takes place on the object. (Security auditing is described later in this chapter.) The inheritance flags that apply to DACL ACEs also apply to system audit and system audit-object ACEs.

Figure 6-4 is a simplified picture of a file object and its DACL.

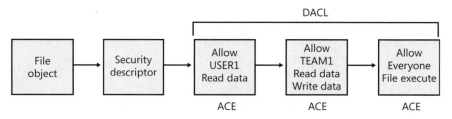

FIGURE 6-4 Discretionary access control list (DACL)

As shown in Figure 6-4, the first ACE allows USER1 to query the file. The second ACE allows members of the group TEAM1 to have read and write access to the file, and the third ACE grants all other users (Everyone) execute access.

EXPERIMENT: Viewing a Security Descriptor

Most executive subsystems rely on the object manager's default security functionality to manage security descriptors for their objects. The object manager's default security functions use the security descriptor pointer to store security descriptors for such objects. For example, the process manager uses default security, so the object manager stores process and thread security descriptors in the object headers of process and thread objects, respectively. The security descriptor pointer of events, mutexes, and semaphores also store their security descriptors. You can use live kernel debugging to view the security descriptors of these objects once you locate their object header, as outlined in the following steps. (Note that both Process Explorer and Accesschk can also show security descriptors for processes.)

1. Start the kernel debugger.

2. Type **!process 0 0 explorer.exe** to obtain process information about Explorer:

```
lkd> !process 0 0 explorer.exe
PROCESS 84fce020  SessionId: 1  Cid: 0804    Peb: 7ffd3000  ParentCid: 05ec
    DirBase: 1f14f420  ObjectTable: 90369388  HandleCount: 428.
    Image: explorer.exe
```

3. Type **!object** with the address following the word PROCESS in the output of the previous command as the argument to show the object data structure:

```
lkd> !object 84fce020
Object: 84fce020  Type: (83dd3bc0) Process
    ObjectHeader: 84fce008 (old version)
    HandleCount: 5  PointerCount: 185
```

4. Type **dt _OBJECT_HEADER** and the address of the object header field from the previous command's output to show the object header data structure, including the security descriptor pointer value:

```
lkd> dt _object_header 84fce008
nt!_OBJECT_HEADER
    +0x000 PointerCount     : 187
    +0x004 HandleCount      : 5
    +0x004 NextToFree       : 0x00000005
    +0x008 Type             : 0x83dd3bc0 _OBJECT_TYPE
    +0x00c NameInfoOffset   : 0 ''
    +0x00d HandleInfoOffset : 0 ''
    +0x00e QuotaInfoOffset  : 0 ''
    +0x00f Flags            : 0x20 ' '
    +0x010 ObjectCreateInfo : 0x84c91b78 _OBJECT_CREATE_INFORMATION
    +0x010 QuotaBlockCharged : 0x84c91b78
    +0x014 SecurityDescriptor : 0x9036770a
    +0x018 Body             : _QUAD
```

5. Security descriptor pointers in the object header use the low three bits as flags, so type the following command to dump the security descriptor by entering the address displayed in the object header structure, but with the low three bits removed:

```
lkd> !sd 0x9036770a  & -8
->Revision: 0x1
->Sbz1    : 0x0
->Control : 0x8814
            SE_DACL_PRESENT
            SE_SACL_PRESENT
            SE_SACL_AUTO_INHERITED
            SE_SELF_RELATIVE
->Owner   : S-1-5-32-544
->Group   : S-1-5-21-529698691-1302229678-416145009-513
->Dacl    :
->Dacl    : ->AclRevision: 0x2
->Dacl    : ->Sbz1        : 0x0
->Dacl    : ->AclSize     : 0x50
->Dacl    : ->AceCount    : 0x3
->Dacl    : ->Sbz2        : 0x0
->Dacl    : ->Ace[0]: ->AceType: ACCESS_ALLOWED_ACE_TYPE
->Dacl    : ->Ace[0]: ->AceFlags: 0x0
->Dacl    : ->Ace[0]: ->AceSize: 0x18
->Dacl    : ->Ace[0]: ->Mask : 0x001fffff
->Dacl    : ->Ace[0]: ->SID: S-1-5-32-544
```

```
->Dacl     : ->Ace[1]: ->AceType: ACCESS_ALLOWED_ACE_TYPE
->Dacl     : ->Ace[1]: ->AceFlags: 0x0
->Dacl     : ->Ace[1]: ->AceSize: 0x14
->Dacl     : ->Ace[1]: ->Mask : 0x001fffff
->Dacl     : ->Ace[1]: ->SID: S-1-5-18

->Dacl     : ->Ace[2]: ->AceType: ACCESS_ALLOWED_ACE_TYPE
->Dacl     : ->Ace[2]: ->AceFlags: 0x0
->Dacl     : ->Ace[2]: ->AceSize: 0x1c
->Dacl     : ->Ace[2]: ->Mask : 0x00121411
->Dacl     : ->Ace[2]: ->SID: S-1-5-5-0-97946

->Sacl     :
->Sacl     : ->AclRevision: 0x2
->Sacl     : ->Sbz1        : 0x0
->Sacl     : ->AclSize     : 0x1c
->Sacl     : ->AceCount    : 0x1
->Sacl     : ->Sbz2        : 0x0
->Sacl     : ->Ace[0]: ->AceType: SYSTEM_MANDATORY_LABEL_ACE_TYPE
->Sacl     : ->Ace[0]: ->AceFlags: 0x0
->Sacl     : ->Ace[0]: ->AceSize: 0x14
->Sacl     : ->Ace[0]: ->Mask : 0x00000003
->Sacl     : ->Ace[0]: ->SID: S-1-16-12288
```

The security descriptor contains three access-allowed ACEs: one for the Administrators group (S-1-5-32-544), one for the System account (S-1-5-18), and the last for the Logon SID (S-1-5-5-0-97946). The system access control list has one entry (S-1-16-12288) labeling the process as high integrity level. (This example output was taken from a Windows Server 2008 system logged on to the Administrator account, which is why Explorer is running at high instead of medium.)

ACL Assignment

To determine which DACL to assign to a new object, the security system uses the first applicable rule of the following four assignment rules:

1. If a caller explicitly provides a security descriptor when creating the object, the security system applies it to the object. If the object has a name and resides in a container object (for example, a named event object in the \BaseNamedObjects object manager namespace directory), the system merges any inheritable ACEs (ACEs that might propagate from the object's container) into the DACL unless the security descriptor has the SE_DACL_PROTECTED flag set, which prevents inheritance.

2. If a caller doesn't supply a security descriptor and the object has a name, the security system looks at the security descriptor in the container in which the new object name is stored. Some of the object directory's ACEs might be marked as inheritable, meaning that they should be applied to new objects created in the object directory. If any of

these inheritable ACEs are present, the security system forms them into an ACL, which it attaches to the new object. (Separate flags indicate ACEs that should be inherited only by container objects rather than by objects that aren't containers.)

3. If no security descriptor is specified and the object doesn't inherit any ACEs, the security system retrieves the default DACL from the caller's access token and applies it to the new object. Several subsystems on Windows have hard-coded DACLs that they assign on object creation (for example, services, LSA, and SAM objects).

4. If there is no specified descriptor, no inherited ACEs, and no default DACL, the system creates the object with no DACL, which allows everyone (all users and groups) full access to the object. This rule is the same as the third rule in which a token contains a null default DACL.

The rules the system uses when assigning a SACL to a new object are similar to those used for DACL assignment, with some exceptions. The first is that inherited system audit ACEs don't propagate to objects with security descriptors marked with the SE_SACL_PROTECTED flag (similar to the SE_DACL_PROTECTED flag, which protects DACLs). Second, if there are no specified security audit ACEs and there is no inherited SACL, no SACL is applied to the object. This behavior is different from that used to apply default DACLs because tokens don't have a default SACL.

When a new security descriptor containing inheritable ACEs is applied to a container, the system automatically propagates the inheritable ACEs to the security descriptors of child objects. (Note that a security descriptor's DACL doesn't accept inherited DACL ACEs if its SE_DACL_PROTECTED flag is enabled, and its SACL doesn't inherit SACL ACEs if the descriptor has the SE_SACL_PROTECTED flag set.) The order in which inheritable ACEs are merged with an existing child object's security descriptor is such that any ACEs that were explicitly applied to the ACL are kept ahead of ACEs that the object inherits. The system uses the following rules for propagating inheritable ACEs:

- If a child object with no DACL inherits an ACE, the result is a child object with a DACL containing only the inherited ACE.

- If a child object with an empty DACL inherits an ACE, the result is a child object with a DACL containing only the inherited ACE.

- For objects in Active Directory only, if an inheritable ACE is removed from a parent object, automatic inheritance removes any copies of the ACE inherited by child objects.

- For objects in Active Directory only, if automatic inheritance results in the removal of all ACEs from a child object's DACL, the child object has an empty DACL rather than no DACL.

As you'll soon discover, the order of ACEs in an ACL is an important aspect of the Windows security model.

> **Note** Inheritance is generally not directly supported by the object stores such as file systems, the registry, or Active Directory. Windows APIs that support inheritance, including *SetSecurityInfo* and *SetNamedSecurityInfo*, do so by invoking appropriate functions within the security inheritance support DLL (%SystemRoot%\System32\Ntmarta.dll) that know how to traverse those object stores.

Determining Access

Two methods are used for determining access to an object:

- The *mandatory integrity check*, which determines whether the integrity level of the caller is high enough to access the resource, based on the resource's own integrity level and its mandatory policy.

- The *discretionary access check*, which determines the access that a specific user account has to an object.

When a process tries to open an object, the integrity check takes place before the standard Windows DACL check in the kernel's *SeAccessCheck* function because it is faster to execute and can quickly eliminate the need to perform the full discretionary access check. Given the default integrity policies, a process can only open an object for write access if its integrity level is equal to or higher than the object's integrity level and the DACL also grants the process the accesses it desires. For example, a low integrity level process cannot open a medium integrity level process for write access, even if the DACL grants the process write access.

With the default integrity policy, processes can open any object—with the exception of process, thread, and token objects—for read access as long as the object's DACL grants them read access. That means a process running at low integrity level can open any files accessible to the user account in which it's running. Protected Mode Internet Explorer uses integrity levels to help prevent malware that infects it from modifying user account settings, but it does not stop malware from reading the user's documents.

Recall that process and thread objects are exceptions because their integrity policy also includes No-Read-Up. That means a process's integrity level must be equal to or higher than the integrity level of the process or thread it wants to open, and the DACL must grant it the accesses it wants for an open to succeed. Assuming the DACLs allow the desired access, Figure 6-5 shows the types of access that the processes running at medium or low have to other processes and objects.

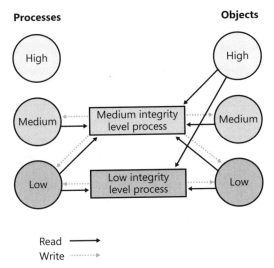

Read ⟶
Write ┄┄┄►

FIGURE 6-5 Access to processes versus objects for medium and low integrity level processes

User Interface Privilege Isolation (UIPI)

The Windows messaging subsystem also honors integrity levels to implement UIPI. The subsystem does this by preventing a process from sending window messages to the windows owned by a process having a higher integrity level, with the following informational messages being exceptions:

- WM_NULL
- WM_MOVE
- WM_SIZE
- WM_GETTEXT
- WM_GETTEXTLENGTH
- WM_GETHOTKEY
- WM_GETICON
- WM_RENDERFORMAT
- WM_DRAWCLIPBOARD
- WM_CHANGECBCHAIN
- WM_THEMECHANGED

This use of integrity levels prevents standard user processes from driving input into the windows of elevated processes or from performing a *shatter attack* (such as sending the process malformed messages that trigger internal buffer overflows, which can lead to the execution of code at the elevated process's privileges). UIPI also blocks window hooks from affecting the windows of higher integrity level processes so that a standard user process can't log the keystrokes the user types into an administrative application, for example. Journal hooks are also blocked in the same way to prevent lower integrity level processes from monitoring the behavior of higher integrity level processes.

Processes can choose to allow additional messages to pass the guard by calling the *ChangeWindowMessageFilter* API. This function is typically used to add messages required by custom controls to communicate outside native common controls in Windows. Because this function is per-process, however, and not per-thread, it is possible for two custom controls inside the same process to be using the same internal window messages, which could lead to one control's potentially malicious window message to be allowed through, simply because it happens to be a query-only message for the other custom control.

Because accessibility applications such as the On-Screen Keyboard (Osk.exe) are subject to UIPI's restrictions (which would require the accessibility application to be executed for each kind of visible integrity level process on the desktop), these processes can enable UI Access. This flag can be present in the manifest file of the image and will run the process at a slightly higher integrity level than medium (between 0x2000 and 0x3000) if launched from a standard user account, or at high integrity level if launched from an administrator account. Note that in the second case, an elevation request won't actually be displayed. For a process to set this flag, its image must also be signed and in one of several secure locations, including %SystemRoot% and %ProgramFiles%.

 Note Threads created by Csrss (which is responsible for console windows and, by extension, all command-line applications) always run with a UIPI integrity level of medium, regardless of how the actual command-line process was started. This means that it is possible to drive input to these kinds of applications from a low integrity level regardless of UIPI.

After the integrity check is complete, and assuming the mandatory policy allows access to the object based on the caller's integrity, one of two algorithms is used for the discretionary check to an object, which will determine the final outcome of the access check:

- One to determine the maximum access allowed to the object, a form of which is exported to user mode with the Windows *GetEffectiveRightsFromAcl* function. This is also used when a program specifies a desired access of MAXIMUM_ALLOWED, which is what the legacy APIs that don't have a desired access parameter use.

- One to determine whether a specific desired access is allowed, which can be done with the Windows *AccessCheck* function or the *AccessCheckByType* function.

The first algorithm examines the entries in the DACL as follows:

1. If the object has no DACL (a null DACL), the object has no protection and the security system grants all access.

2. If the caller has the take-ownership privilege, the security system grants write-owner access before examining the DACL. (Take-ownership privilege and write-owner access are explained in a moment.)

3. If the caller is the owner of the object, the system looks for an OWNER_RIGHTS SID and uses that SID as the SID for the next steps. Otherwise, read-control and write-DACL access rights are granted.

4. For each access-denied ACE that contains a SID that matches one in the caller's access token, the ACE's access mask is removed from the granted-access mask.

5. For each access-allowed ACE that contains a SID that matches one in the caller's access token, the ACE's access mask is added to the granted-access mask being computed, unless that access has already been denied.

When all the entries in the DACL have been examined, the computed granted-access mask is returned to the caller as the maximum allowed access to the object. This mask represents the total set of access types that the caller will be able to successfully request when opening the object.

The preceding description applies only to the kernel-mode form of the algorithm. The Windows version implemented by *GetEffectiveRightsFromAcl* differs in that it doesn't perform step 2, and it considers a single user or group SID rather than an access token.

Owner Rights

Because owners of an object can normally override the security of an object by always being granted read-control and write-DACL rights, a specialized method of controlling this behavior is exposed by Windows: the Owner Rights SID.

The Owner Rights SID exists for two main reasons: improving service hardening in the operating system, and allowing more flexibility for specific usage scenarios. For example, suppose an administrator wants to allow users to create files and folders but not to modify the ACLs on those objects. (Users could inadvertently or maliciously grant access to those files or folders to unwanted accounts.) By using an inheritable Owner Rights SID, the users can be prevented from editing or even viewing the ACL on the objects they create. A second usage scenario relates to group changes. Suppose an

employee has been part of some confidential or sensitive group, has created several files while a member of that group, and has now been removed from the group for business reasons. Since that employee is still a user, he could continue accessing the sensitive files.

As mentioned, Windows also uses the Owner Rights SID to improve service hardening. Whenever a service creates an object at run time, the Owner SID associated with that object is the account the service is running in (such as local system or local service) and not the actual service SID. This means that any other service in the same account would have access to the object by being an owner. The Owner Rights SID prevents that unwanted behavior.

The second algorithm is used to determine whether a specific access request can be granted, based on the caller's access token. Each open function in the Windows API that deals with securable objects has a parameter that specifies the desired access mask, which is the last component of the security equation. To determine whether the caller has access, the following steps are performed:

1. If the object has no DACL (a null DACL), the object has no protection and the security system grants the desired access.

2. If the caller has the take-ownership privilege, the security system grants write-owner access if requested and then examines the DACL. However, if write-owner access was the only access requested by a caller with take-ownership privilege, the security system grants that access and never examines the DACL.

3. If the caller is the owner of the object, the system looks for an OWNER_RIGHTS SID and uses that SID as the SID for the next steps. Otherwise, read-control and write-DACL access rights are granted. If these rights were the only access rights that the caller requested, access is granted without examining the DACL

4. Each ACE in the DACL is examined from first to last. An ACE is processed if one of the following conditions is satisfied:

 a. The ACE is an access-deny ACE, and the SID in the ACE matches an *enabled* SID (SIDs can be enabled or disabled) or a deny-only SID in the caller's access token.

 b. The ACE is an access-allowed ACE, and the SID in the ACE matches an enabled SID in the caller's token that isn't of type deny-only.

 c. It is the second pass through the descriptor for restricted-SID checks, and the SID in the ACE matches a restricted SID in the caller's access token.

 d. The ACE isn't marked as *inherit-only*.

5. If it is an access-allowed ACE, the rights in the access mask in the ACE that were requested are granted; if all the requested access rights have been granted, the access check succeeds. If it is an access-denied ACE and any of the requested access rights are in the denied-access rights, access is denied to the object.

6. If the end of the DACL is reached and some of the requested access rights still haven't been granted, access is denied.

7. If all accesses are granted but the caller's access token has at least one restricted SID, the system rescans the DACL's ACEs looking for ACEs with access-mask matches for the accesses the user is requesting and a match of the ACE's SID with any of the caller's restricted SIDs. Only if both scans of the DACL grant the requested access rights is the user granted access to the object.

The behavior of both access-validation algorithms depends on the relative ordering of allow and deny ACEs. Consider an object with only two ACEs, where one ACE specifies that a certain user is allowed full access to an object and the other ACE denies the user access. If the allow ACE precedes the deny ACE, the user can obtain full access to the object, but if the order is reversed, the user cannot gain any access to the object.

Several Windows functions, such as *SetSecurityInfo* and *SetNamedSecurityInfo*, apply ACEs in the preferred order of explicit deny ACEs preceding explicit allow ACEs. Note that the security editor dialog boxes with which you edit permissions on NTFS files and registry keys, for example, use these functions. *SetSecurityInfo* and *SetNamedSecurityInfo* also apply ACE inheritance rules to the security descriptor on which they are applied.

Figure 6-6 shows an example access validation demonstrating the importance of ACE ordering. In the example, access is denied a user wanting to open a file even though an ACE in the object's DACL grants the access because the ACE denying the user access (by virtue of the user's membership in the Writers group) precedes the ACE granting access.

As we stated earlier, because it wouldn't be efficient for the security system to process the DACL every time a process uses a handle, the SRM makes this access check only when a handle is opened, not each time the handle is used. Thus, once a process successfully opens a handle, the security system can't revoke the access rights that have been granted, even if the object's DACL changes. Also keep in mind that because kernel-mode code uses pointers rather than handles to access objects, the access check isn't performed when the operating system uses objects. In other words, the Windows executive "trusts" itself in a security sense.

The fact that an object's owner is always granted write-DACL access to an object means that users can never be prevented from accessing the objects they own. If, for some reason, an object had an empty DACL (no access), the owner would still be able to open the object with write-DACL access and then apply a new DACL with the desired access permissions.

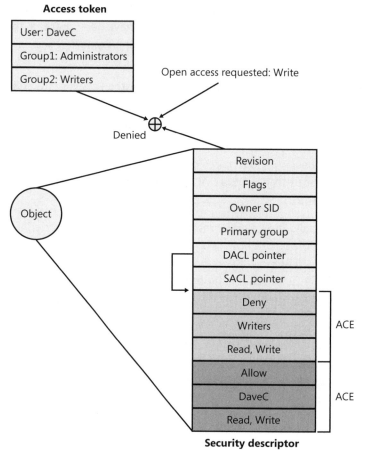

FIGURE 6-6 Access validation example

A Warning Regarding the GUI Security Editors

When you use the GUI permissions editors to modify security settings on a file, a registry, or an Active Directory object, or on another securable object, the main security dialog box shows you a potentially misleading view of the security that's applied to the object. If you allow Full Control to the Everyone group and deny the Administrator group Full Control, the list might lead you to believe that the Everyone group access-allowed ACE precedes the Administrator deny ACE because that's the order in which they appear. However, as we've said, the editors place deny ACEs before allow ACEs when they apply the ACL to the object.

The Permissions tab of the Advanced Security Settings dialog box shows the order of ACEs in the DACL. However, even this dialog box can be confusing because a complex DACL can have deny ACEs for various accesses followed by allow ACEs for other access types.

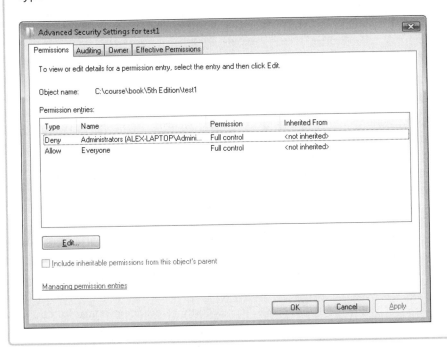

The only definitive way to know what accesses a particular user or group will have to an object (other than having that user or a member of the group try to access the object) is to use the Effective Permissions tab of the dialog box that is displayed when you click the Advanced button in the Properties dialog box. Enter the name of the user or group you want to check, and the dialog box shows you what permissions they are allowed for the object.

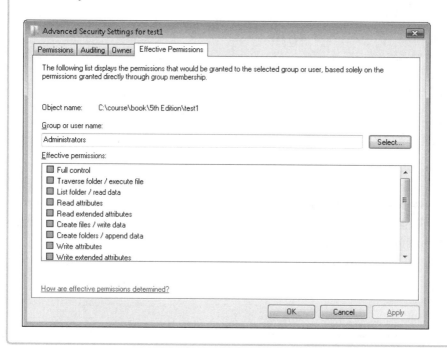

The AuthZ API

The AuthZ Windows API implements the same security model as the security reference monitor, but it implements the model totally in user mode in the %SystemRoot%\System32\Authz.dll library. This gives applications that want to protect their own private objects, such as database tables, the ability to leverage the Windows security model without incurring the cost of user-mode to kernel-mode transitions that they would make if they relied on the security reference monitor.

The AuthZ API uses standard security descriptor data structures, SIDs, and privileges. Instead of using tokens to represent clients, AuthZ uses the AUTHZ_CLIENT_CONTEXT. AuthZ includes user-mode equivalents of all access-check and Windows security functions—for example, *AuthzAccessCheck* is the AuthZ version of the *AccessCheck* Windows API that uses the *SeAccessCheck* security reference monitor function.

Another advantage available to applications that use AuthZ is that they can direct AuthZ to cache the results of security checks to improve subsequent checks that use the same client context and security descriptor.

AuthZ is fully documented in the Windows SDK.

Account Rights and Privileges

Many operations performed by processes as they execute cannot be authorized through object access protection because they do not involve interaction with a particular object. For example, the ability to bypass security checks when opening files for backup is an attribute of an account, not of a particular object. Windows uses both privileges and account rights to allow a system administrator to control what accounts can perform security-related operations.

A privilege is the right of an account to perform a particular system-related operation, such as shutting down the computer or changing the system time. An account right grants or denies the account to which it's assigned the ability to perform a particular type of logon, such as a local logon or interactive logon, to a computer.

A system administrator assigns privileges to groups and accounts using tools such as the Active Directory Users and Groups MMC snap-in for domain accounts or the Local Security Policy Editor. You access the Local Security Policy Editor in the Administrative Tools folder of the Control Panel or the Start menu (if you've configured your Start menu to contain an Administrative Tools link). Figure 6-7 shows User Rights Assignment configuration in the Local Security Policy Editor, which displays the complete list of privileges and account rights available on Windows. Note that the tool makes no distinction between privileges and account rights. However, you can differentiate between them because any user right that contains the words *log on* is an account privilege.

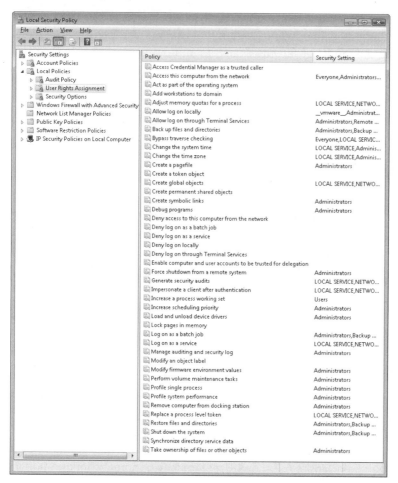

FIGURE 6-7 Local Security Policy Editor user rights assignment

Account Rights

Account rights are not enforced by the security reference monitor, nor are they stored in tokens. The function responsible for logon is *LsaLogonUser*. Winlogon, for example, calls the *LogonUser* API when a user logs on interactively to a computer, and *LogonUser* calls *LsaLogonUser*. The function takes a parameter that indicates the type of logon being performed, which includes interactive, network, batch, service, Terminal Server client, and unlock.

In response to logon requests, the Local Security Authority (LSA) retrieves account rights assigned to a user from the LSA policy database at the time that a user attempts to log on to the system. LSA checks the logon type against the account rights assigned to the user

account logging on and denies the logon if the account does not have the right that permits the logon type or it has the right that denies the logon type. Table 6-7 lists the user rights defined by Windows.

Windows applications can add and remove user rights from an account by using the *LsaAddAccountRights* and *LsaRemoveAccountRights* functions, and they can determine what rights are assigned to an account with *LsaEnumerateAccountRights*.

TABLE 6-7 Account Rights

User Right	Role
Deny logon locally, Allow logon locally	Used for interactive logons that originate on the local machine
Deny logon over the network, Allow logon over the network	Used for logons that originate from a remote machine
Deny logon through Terminal Services, Allow logon through Terminal Services	Used for logons through a Terminal Server client
Deny logon as a service, Allow logon as a service	Used by the service control manager when starting a service in a particular user account
Deny logon as a batch job, Allow logon as a batch job	Used when performing a logon of type *batch*

Privileges

The number of privileges defined by the operating system has grown over time. Unlike user rights, which are enforced in one place by the LSA, different privileges are defined by different components and enforced by those components. For example, the debug privilege, which allows a process to bypass security checks when opening a handle to another process with the *OpenProcess* Windows API, is checked for by the process manager. Table 6-8 is a full list of privileges, and it describes how and when system components check for them.

When a component wants to check a token to see whether a privilege is present, it uses the *PrivilegeCheck* or *LsaEnumerateAccountRights* APIs if running in user mode and *SeSinglePrivilegeCheck* or *SePrivilegeCheck* if running in kernel mode. The privilege-related APIs are not account-right aware, but the account-right APIs are privilege-aware.

Unlike account rights, privileges can be enabled and disabled. For a privilege check to succeed, the privilege must be in the specified token and it must be enabled. The idea behind this scheme is that privileges should be enabled only when their use is required so that a process cannot inadvertently perform a privileged security operation.

EXPERIMENT: Seeing a Privilege Get Enabled

By following these steps, you can see that the Date and Time Control Panel applet enables the SeTimeZonePrivilege privilege in response to you using its interface to change the time zone of the computer.

1. Run Process Explorer, and set the refresh rate to Paused.

2. Open the Date and Time item by right-clicking on the clock in the system tray region of the taskbar, and then select Adjust Date/Time. A new Rundll32 process will appear with a green highlight.

3. Hover the mouse over the Rundll32 process and verify that the target contains the text "Time Date Control Panel Applet" as well as a path to Timedate.cpl. The presence of this argument tells Rundll32, which is a Control Panel DLL hosting process, to load the DLL that implements the user interface that enables you to change the time and date.

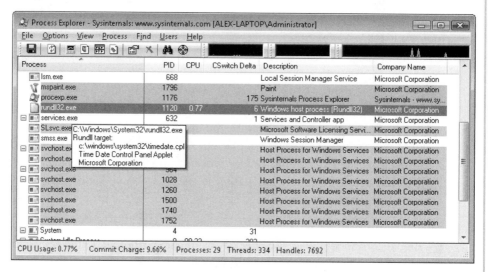

4. View the Security tab of the process Properties dialog box for your Rundll32 process. You should see that the SeTimeZonePrivilege privilege is disabled, which is indicated by its flag and the fact that it's shown in gray.

5. Now click the Change Time Zone button in the Control Panel item, close the process Properties dialog box, and then open it again. On the Security tab, you should now see that the SeTimeZonePrivilege privilege is enabled.

TABLE 6-8 Privileges

Privilege	User Right	Privilege Usage
SeAssignPrimaryTokenPrivilege	Replace a process-level token	Checked for by various components, such as *NtSetInformationJob*, that set a process's token.
SeAuditPrivilege	Generate security audits	Required to generate events for the Security event log with the *ReportEvent* API.
SeBackupPrivilege	Backup files and directories	Causes NTFS to grant the following access to any file or directory, regardless of the security descriptor that's present: READ_CONTROL ACCESS_SYSTEM_SECURITY FILE_GENERIC_READ FILE_TRAVERSE Note that when opening a file for backup, the caller must specify the FILE_FLAG_BACKUP_SEMANTICS flag. Also allows corresponding access to registry keys when using *RegSaveKey*.

Privilege	User Right	Privilege Usage
SeChangeNotifyPrivilege	Bypass traverse checking	Used by NTFS to avoid checking permissions on intermediate directories of a multilevel directory lookup. Also used by file systems when applications register for notification of changes to the file system structure.
SeCreateGlobalPrivilege	Create global objects	Required for a process to create section and symbolic link objects in the directories of the object manager namespace that are assigned to a different session than the caller.
SeCreatePagefilePrivilege	Create a pagefile	Checked for by *NtCreatePagingFile*, which is the function used to create a new paging file.
SeCreatePermanentPrivilege	Create permanent shared objects	Checked for by the object manager when creating a permanent object (one that doesn't get deallocated when there are no more references to it).
SeCreateSymbolicLinkPrivilege	Create symbolic links	Checked for by NTFS when creating symbolic links on the file system with the *CreateSymbolicLink* API.
SeCreateTokenPrivilege	Create a token object	*NtCreateToken*, the function that creates a token object, checks for this privilege.
SeDebugPrivilege	Debug programs	If the caller has this privilege enabled, the process manager allows access to any process or thread using *NtOpenProcess* or *NtOpenThread*, regardless of the process' or thread's security descriptor (except for protected processes).
SeEnableDelegationPrivilege	Enable computer and user accounts to be trusted for delegation	Used by Active Directory services to delegate authenticated credentials.
SeImpersonatePrivilege	Impersonate a client after authentication	The process manager checks for this when a thread wants to use a token for impersonation and the token represents a different user than that of the thread's process token.
SeIncreaseBasePriorityPrivilege	Increase scheduling priority	Checked for by the process manager and is required to raise the priority of a process.
SeIncreaseQuotaPrivilege	Adjust memory quotas for a process	Enforced when changing a process's working set thresholds, a process' paged and nonpaged pool quotas, and a process's CPU rate quota.

Privilege	User Right	Privilege Usage
SeIncreaseWorkingSetPrivilege	Increase a process working set	Required to call *SetProcessWorkingSetSize* to increase the minimum working set. This indirectly allows the process to lock up to the minimum working set of memory using *VirtualLock*.
SeLoadDriverPrivilege	Load and unload device drivers	Checked for by the *NtLoadDriver* and *NtUnloadDriver* driver functions.
SeLockMemoryPrivilege	Lock pages in memory	Checked for by *NtLockVirtualMemory*, the kernel implementation of VirtualLock.
SeMachineAccountPrivilege	Add workstations to the domain	Checked for by the Security Accounts Manager on a domain controller when creating a machine account in a domain.
SeManageVolumePrivilege	Perform volume maintenance tasks	Enforced by file system drivers during a volume open operation, which is required to perform disk checking and defragmenting activities.
SeProfileSingleProcessPrivilege	Profile single process	Checked by Superfetch and the prefetcher when requesting information for an individual process through the *NtQuerySystemInformation* API.
SeRelabelPrivilege	Modify an object label	Checked for by the SRM when raising the integrity level of an object owned by another user, or when attempting to raise the integrity level of an object higher than that of the caller's token.
SeRemoteShutdownPrivilege	Force shutdown from a remote system	Winlogon checks that remote callers of the *InitiateSystemShutdown* function have this privilege.
SeRestorePrivilege	Restore files and directories	This privilege causes NTFS to grant the following access to any file or directory, regardless of the security descriptor that's present: WRITE_DAC WRITE_OWNER ACCESS_SYSTEM_SECURITY FILE_GENERIC_WRITE FILE_ADD_FILE FILE_ADD_SUBDIRECTORY DELETE Note that when opening a file for restore, the caller must specify the FILE_FLAG_BACKUP_SEMANTICS flag. Allows corresponding access to registry keys when using *RegSaveKey*.
SeSecurityPrivilege	Manage auditing and security log	Required to access the SACL of a security descriptor, read and clear the security event log.

Privilege	User Right	Privilege Usage
SeShutdownPrivilege	Shut down the system	This privilege is checked for by *NtShutdownSystem* and *NtRaiseHardError*, which presents a system error dialog box on the interactive console.
SeSyncAgentPrivilege	Synchronize directory service data	Required to use the LDAP directory synchronization services and allows the holder to read all objects and properties in the directory, regardless of the protection on the objects and properties.
SeSystemEnvironmentPrivilege	Modify firmware environment variables	Required by *NtSetSystemEnvironmentValue* and *NtQuerySystemEnvironmentValue* to modify and read firmware environment variables using the HAL.
SeSystemProfilePrivilege	Profile system performance	Checked for by *NtCreateProfile*, the function used to perform profiling of the system. This is used by the Kernprof tool, for example.
SeSystemtimePrivilege	Change the system time	Required to change the time or date.
SeTakeOwnership	Take ownership of files and other objects	Required to take ownership of an object without being granted discretionary access.
SeTcbPrivilege	Act as part of the operating system	Checked for by the security reference monitor when the session ID is set in a token, by the Plug and Play manager for Plug and Play event creation and management, BroadcastSystemMessageEx when called with BSM_ALLDESKTOPS, *LsaRegisterLogonProcess*, and when specifying an application as a VDM with *NtSetInformationProcess*.
SeTimeZonePrivilege	Change the time zone	Required to change the time zone.
SeTrustedCredManAccessPrivilege	Access credential manager as a trusted caller	Checked by the credential manager to verify that it should trust the caller with credential information that can be queried in plain text. Is only granted to Winlogon by default.
SeUndockPrivilege	Remove computer from a docking station	Checked for by the user-mode Plug and Play manager when either a computer undock is initiated or a device eject request is made.
SeUnsolicitedInputPrivilege	Receive unsolicited data from a terminal device	This privilege isn't currently used by Windows.

EXPERIMENT: The Bypass Traverse Checking Privilege

If you are a systems administrator, you must be aware of the Bypass Traverse Checking privilege (internally called SeNotifyPrivilege) and its implications. This experiment demonstrates that not understanding its behavior can lead to improperly applied security.

1. Create a folder and, within that folder, a new text file with some sample text.

2. Navigate in Explorer to the new file, and go to the Security tab of its Properties dialog box. Click the Advanced button, and clear the check box that controls inheritance. Select Copy when you are prompted as to whether you want to remove or copy inherited permissions.

3. Next, modify the security of the new folder so that your account does not have any access to the folder. Do this by selecting your account and selecting all the Deny boxes in the permissions list.

4. Run Notepad, and browse using the File, Open dialog box to the new directory. You should be denied access to the directory.

5. In the File Name field of the Open dialog box, type the full path of the new file. The file should open.

If your account does not have the Bypass Traverse Checking privilege, NTFS performs an access check on each directory of the path to a file when you try to open a file, which results in you being denied access to the file in this example.

Super Privileges

Several privileges are so powerful that a user to which they are assigned is effectively a "super user" who has full control over a computer. These privileges can be used in an infinite number of ways to gain unauthorized access to otherwise off-limit resources and to perform unauthorized operations. However, we'll focus on using the privilege to execute code that grants the user privileges not assigned to the user, with the knowledge that this capability can be leveraged to perform any operation on the local machine that the user desires. This section lists the privileges and discusses the ways that they can be exploited. Other privileges, such as Lock Pages In Physical Memory, can be exploited for denial of service attacks on a system, but these are not discussed. Note that on systems with UAC enabled, these privileges will only be granted to applications running at high integrity level or higher, even if the account possesses them.

- **Debug programs** A user with this privilege can open any process on the system without regard to the security descriptor present on the process. The user could implement a program that opens the Lsass process, for example, copy executable code into its

address space, and then inject a thread with the *CreateRemoteThread* Windows API to execute the injected code in a more-privileged security context. The code could grant the user additional privileges and group memberships.

- **Take ownership** This privilege allows a holder to take ownership of any securable object by writing his own SID into the owner field of the object's security descriptor. Recall that an owner is always granted permission to read and modify the DACL of the security descriptor, so a process with this privilege could modify the DACL to grant itself full access to the object and then close and reopen the object with full access. This would allow the owner to see sensitive data and to even replace system files that execute as part of normal system operation, such as Lsass, with his own programs that grant a user elevated privileges.

- **Restore files and directories** A user assigned this privilege can replace any file on the system with her own. She could exploit this power by replacing system files as described in the preceding paragraph.

- **Load and unload device drivers** A malicious user could use this privilege to load a device driver into the system. Device drivers are considered trusted parts of the operating system that can execute within it with System account credentials, so a driver could launch privileged programs that assign the user other rights.

- **Create a token object** This privilege can be used in the obvious way to generate tokens that represent arbitrary user accounts with arbitrary group membership and privilege assignment.

- **Act as part of operating system** *LsaRegisterLogonProcess*, the function a process calls to establish a trusted connection to Lsass, checks for this privilege. A malicious user with this privilege can establish a trusted-Lsass connection and then execute *LsaLogonUser*, a function used to create new logon sessions. *LsaLogonUser* requires a valid user name and password and accepts an optional list of SIDs that it adds to the initial token created for a new logon session. The user could therefore use her own user name and password to create a new logon session that includes the SIDs of more privileged groups or users in the resulting token.

Note that the use of elevated privilege does not extend past the machine boundary to the network, because any interaction with another computer requires authentication with a domain controller and validation of domain passwords. Domain passwords are not stored on a computer either in plain text or encrypted form, so they are not accessible to malicious code.

Security Auditing

The object manager can generate audit events as a result of an access check, and Windows functions available to user applications can generate them directly. Kernel-mode code is always allowed to generate an audit event. Two privileges, SeSecurityPrivilege and SeAuditPrivilege, relate to auditing. A process must have the SeSecurityPrivilege privilege to manage the security Event Log and to view or set an object's SACL. Processes that call audit system services, however, must have the SeAuditPrivilege privilege to successfully generate an audit record.

The audit policy of the local system controls the decision to audit a particular type of security event. The audit policy, also called the *local security policy,* is one part of the security policy Lsass maintains on the local system, and it is configured with the Local Security Policy Editor shown in Figure 6-8.

FIGURE 6-8 Local Security Policy Editor audit policy configuration

Lsass sends messages to the SRM to inform it of the auditing policy at system initialization time and when the policy changes. Lsass is responsible for receiving audit records generated based on the audit events from the SRM, editing the records, and sending them to the Event Logger. Lsass (instead of the SRM) sends these records because it adds pertinent details, such as the information needed to more completely identify the process that is being audited.

The SRM sends audit records via its ALPC connection to Lsass. The Event Logger then writes the audit record to the security Event Log. In addition to audit records the SRM passes, both Lsass and the SAM generate audit records that Lsass sends directly to the Event Logger, and the AuthZ API allows for applications to generate application-defined audits. Figure 6-9 depicts this overall flow.

FIGURE 6-9 Flow of security audit records

Audit records are put on a queue to be sent to the LSA as they are received—they are not submitted in batches. The audit records are moved from the SRM to the security subsystem in one of two ways. If the audit record is small (less than the maximum ALPC message size), it is sent as an ALPC message. The audit records are copied from the address space of the SRM to the address space of the Lsass process. If the audit record is large, the SRM uses shared memory to make the message available to Lsass and simply passes a pointer in an ALPC message.

Figure 6-10 brings together the concepts covered so far in this chapter by illustrating the basic process and thread security structures. In the figure, notice that the process object and the thread objects have ACLs, as do the access-token objects themselves. Also in this figure, thread 2 and thread 3 each have an impersonation token, whereas thread 1 defaults to the process access token.

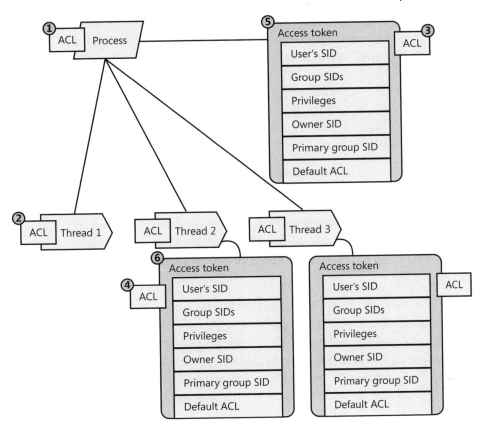

FIGURE 6-10 Process and thread security structures

Logon

Interactive logon (as opposed to network logon) occurs through the interaction of the logon process (Winlogon), the logon user interface process (LogonUI) and its credential providers, Lsass, one or more authentication packages, and the SAM or Active Directory. *Authentication packages* are DLLs that perform authentication checks. Kerberos is the Windows authentication package for interactive logon to a domain, and MSV1_0 is the Windows authentication package for interactive logon to a local computer, for domain logons to trusted pre–Windows 2000 domains, and for times when no domain controller is accessible.

Winlogon is a trusted process responsible for managing security-related user interactions. It coordinates logon, starts the user's first process at logon, handles logoff, and manages various other operations relevant to security, including launching LogonUI for entering passwords at logon, changing passwords, and locking and unlocking the workstation. The Winlogon process must ensure that operations relevant to security aren't visible to any other active processes. For example, Winlogon guarantees that an untrusted process can't get control of the desktop during one of these operations and thus gain access to the password.

Winlogon relies on the credential providers installed on the system to obtain a user's account name or password. Credential providers are COM objects located inside DLLs. The default providers are %SystemRoot%\System32\authui.dll and %SystemRoot%\System32\SmartcardCredentialProvider.dll, which support both password and smartcard PIN authentication. Allowing other credential providers to be installed allows Windows to use different user-identification mechanisms. For example, a third party might supply a credential provider that uses a thumbprint recognition device to identify users and extract their passwords from an encrypted database.

To protect Winlogon's address space from bugs in credential providers that might cause the Winlogon process to crash (which, in turn, will result in a system crash, as Winlogon is considered a critical system process), a separate process, LogonUI.exe, is used to actually load the credential providers and display the Windows logon interface to users. This process is started on demand whenever Winlogon needs to present a user interface to the user, and it exits after the action has finished. It also allows Winlogon to simply restart a new LogonUI process should it crash for any reason.

Winlogon is the only process that intercepts logon requests from the keyboard, which are sent through an RPC message from Win32k.sys. Winlogon immediately launches the LogonUI application to display the user interface for logon. After obtaining a user name and password from credential providers, Winlogon calls Lsass to authenticate the user attempting to log on. If the user is authenticated, the logon process activates a logon shell on behalf of that user. The interaction between the components involved in logon is illustrated in Figure 6-11.

FIGURE 6-11 Components involved in logon

In addition to supporting alternative credential providers, LogonUI can load additional network provider DLLs that need to perform secondary authentication. This capability allows multiple network providers to gather identification and authentication information all at one time during normal logon. A user logging on to a Windows system might simultaneously be authenticated on a UNIX server. That user would then be able to access resources of the UNIX server from the Windows machine without requiring additional authentication. Such a capability is known as one form of *single sign-on*.

Winlogon Initialization

During system initialization, before any user applications are active, Winlogon performs the following steps to ensure that it controls the workstation once the system is ready for user interaction:

1. Creates and opens an interactive window station (for example, \Sessions\1\Windows\ WindowStations\WinSta0 in the object manager namespace) to represent the keyboard, mouse, and monitor. Winlogon creates a security descriptor for the station that has one and only one ACE containing only the System SID. This unique security descriptor ensures that no other process can access the workstation unless explicitly allowed by Winlogon.

2. Creates and opens two desktops: an application desktop (\Sessions\1\Windows\ WinSta0\Default, also known as the interactive desktop) and a Winlogon desktop (\Sessions\1\Windows\WinSta0\Winlogon, also known as the secure desktop). The security on the Winlogon desktop is created so that only Winlogon can access that desktop. The other desktop allows both Winlogon and users to access it. This arrangement means that any time the Winlogon desktop is active, no other process has access to any active code or data associated with the desktop. Windows uses this feature to protect the secure operations that involve passwords and locking and unlocking the desktop.

3. Before anyone logs on to a computer, the visible desktop is Winlogon's. After a user logs on, pressing Ctrl+Alt+Delete switches the desktop from Default to Winlogon and launches LogonUI. (This explains why all the windows on your interactive desktop seem to disappear when you press Ctrl+Alt+Delete and then return when you dismiss the Windows Security dialog box.) Thus, the SAS always brings up a secure desktop controlled by Winlogon.

4. Establishes an ALPC connection with Lsass's *LsaAuthenticationPort*. This connection will be used for exchanging information during logon, logoff, and password operations and is made by calling *LsaRegisterLogonProcess*.

5. It initializes and registers a window class data structure that associates a Winlogon procedure with the window it subsequently creates.

6. It registers the Winlogon RPC message server, which listens for SAS notifications from Win32k. This measure prevents Trojan horse programs from gaining control of the screen when the SAS is entered.

7. It registers the window so that the procedure associated with this window gets called if a user logs off or if the screen saver times out. The Windows subsystem checks to verify that the process requesting notification is the Winlogon process.

> **Note** The Wininit process performs steps similar to steps 1 and 2 to allow legacy interactive services running on session 0 to display windows, but it does not perform any other steps since session 0 is not available for user logon. (See Chapter 3 for more information on Wininit and session isolation.)

How SAS Is Implemented

The SAS is secure because no application can intercept the Ctrl+Alt+Delete keystroke combination or prevent Winlogon from receiving it. Win32k.sys reserves the Ctrl+Alt+Delete key combination so that whenever the Windows input system (implemented in the *raw input thread* in Win32k) sees the combination, it sends an RPC message to Winlogon's message server, which listens for such notifications. The keystrokes that map to a registered hot key are otherwise not sent to any process other than the one that registered it, and only the thread that registered a hot key can unregister it, so a Trojan horse application cannot deregister Winlogon's ownership of the SAS.

A Windows function, *SetWindowsHook*, enables an application to install a hook procedure that's invoked every time a keystroke is pressed, even before hot keys are processed, and it allows the hook to squash keystrokes. However, the Windows hot key processing code contains a special case for Ctrl+Alt+Delete that disables hooks so that the keystroke sequence can't be intercepted. In addition, if the interactive desktop is locked, only hot keys owned by Winlogon are processed.

Once the Winlogon desktop is created during initialization, it becomes the active desktop. When the Winlogon desktop is active, it is always locked. Winlogon unlocks its desktop only to switch to the application desktop or the screen-saver desktop. (Only the Winlogon process can lock or unlock a desktop.)

User Logon Steps

Logon begins when a user presses the SAS (Ctrl+Alt+Delete). After the SAS is pressed, Winlogon starts LogonUI, which calls the credential providers to obtain a user name and password. Winlogon also creates a unique local logon SID for this user that it assigns to this instance of the desktop (keyboard, screen, and mouse). Winlogon passes this SID to Lsass as part of the *LsaLogonUser* call. If the user is successfully logged on, this SID will be included in the logon process token—a step that protects access to the desktop. For example, another

logon to the same account but on a different system will be unable to write to the first machine's desktop because this second logon won't be in the first logon's desktop token.

When the user name and password have been entered, Winlogon retrieves a handle to a package by calling the Lsass function *LsaLookupAuthenticationPackage*. Authentication packages are listed in the registry under HKLM\SYSTEM\CurrentControlSet\Control\Lsa. Winlogon passes logon information to the authentication package via *LsaLogonUser*. Once a package authenticates a user, Winlogon continues the logon process for that user. If none of the authentication packages indicates a successful logon, the logon process is aborted.

Windows uses two standard authentication packages for interactive logons: Kerberos and MSV1_0. The default authentication package on a stand-alone Windows system is MSV1_0 (%SystemRoot%\System32\Msv1_0.dll), an authentication package that implements LAN Manager 2 protocol. Lsass also uses MSV1_0 on domain-member computers to authenticate to pre–Windows 2000 domains and computers that can't locate a domain controller for authentication. (Laptop computers that are disconnected from the network fall into this latter category.) The Kerberos authentication package, %SystemRoot%\System32\Kerberos.dll, is used on computers that are members of Windows domains. The Windows Kerberos package, with the cooperation of Kerberos services running on a domain controller, supports the Kerberos protocol. This protocol is based on Internet RFC 1510. (Visit the Internet Engineering Task Force [IETF] Web site, *www.ietf.org*, for detailed information on the Kerberos standard.)

The MSV1_0 authentication package takes the user name and a hashed version of the password and sends a request to the local SAM to retrieve the account information, which includes the password, the groups to which the user belongs, and any account restrictions. MSV1_0 first checks the account restrictions, such as hours or type of accesses allowed. If the user can't log on because of the restrictions in the SAM database, the logon call fails and MSV1_0 returns a failure status to the LSA.

MSV1_0 then compares the hashed password and user name to that stored by the SAM. In the case of a cached domain logon, MSV1_0 accesses the cached information by using Lsass functions that store and retrieve "secrets" from the LSA database (the SECURITY hive of the registry). If the information matches, MSV1_0 generates an LUID for the logon session and creates the logon session by calling Lsass, associating this unique identifier with the session and passing the information needed to ultimately create an access token for the user. (Recall that an access token includes the user's SID, group SIDs, and assigned privileges.)

Note MSV1_0 does not cache a user's entire password hash in the registry because that would enable someone with physical access to the system to easily compromise a user's domain account and gain access to encrypted files and to network resources the user is authorized to access. Instead, it caches half of the hash. The cached half-hash is sufficient to verify that a user's password is correct, but it isn't sufficient to gain access to EFS keys and to authenticate as the user on a domain because these actions require the full hash.

If MSV1_0 needs to authenticate using a remote system, as when a user logs on to a trusted pre–Windows 2000 domain, MSV1_0 uses the Netlogon service to communicate with an instance of Netlogon on the remote system. Netlogon on the remote system interacts with the MSV1_0 authentication package on that system, passing back authentication results to the system on which the logon is being performed.

The basic control flow for Kerberos authentication is the same as the flow for MSV1_0. However, in most cases, domain logons are performed from member workstations or servers (rather than on a domain controller), so the authentication package must communicate across the network as part of the authentication process. The package does so by communicating via the Kerberos TCP/IP port (port 88) with the Kerberos service on a domain controller. The Kerberos Key Distribution Center service (%SystemRoot%\System32\Kdcsvc.dll), which implements the Kerberos authentication protocol, runs in the Lsass process on domain controllers.

After validating hashed user name and password information with Active Directory's user account objects (using the Active Directory server %SystemRoot%\System32\Ntdsa.dll), Kdcsvc returns domain credentials to Lsass, which returns the result of the authentication and the user's domain logon credentials (if the logon was successful) across the network to the system where the logon is taking place.

> **Note** This description of Kerberos authentication is highly simplified, but it highlights the roles of the various components involved. Although the Kerberos authentication protocol plays a key role in distributed domain security in Windows, its details are outside the scope of this book.

After a logon has been authenticated, Lsass looks in the local policy database for the user's allowed access, including interactive, network, batch, or service process. If the requested logon doesn't match the allowed access, the logon attempt will be terminated. Lsass deletes the newly created logon session by cleaning up any of its data structures and then returns failure to Winlogon, which in turn displays an appropriate message to the user. If the requested access is allowed, Lsass adds the appropriate additional security IDs (such as Everyone, Interactive, and the like). It then checks its policy database for any granted privileges for all the IDs for this user and adds these privileges to the user's access token.

When Lsass has accumulated all the necessary information, it calls the executive to create the access token. The executive creates a primary access token for an interactive or service logon and an impersonation token for a network logon. After the access token is successfully created, Lsass duplicates the token, creating a handle that can be passed to Winlogon, and closes its own handle. If necessary, the logon operation is audited. At this point, Lsass returns success to Winlogon along with a handle to the access token, the LUID for the logon session, and the profile information, if any, that the authentication package returned.

EXPERIMENT: Listing Active Logon Sessions

As long as at least one token exists with a given logon session LUID, Windows considers the logon session to be active. You can use the LogonSessions tool from Sysinternals, which uses the *LsaEnumerateLogonSessions* function (documented in the Windows SDK) to list the active logon sessions:

```
C:\>logonsessions
Logonsesions v1.1
Copyright (C) 2004 Bryce Cogswell and Mark Russinovich
Sysinternals - www.sysinternals.com

[0] Logon session 00000000:000003e7:
    User name:    WORKGROUP\ALEX-LAPTOP$
    Auth package: NTLM
    Logon type:   (none)
    Session:      0
    Sid:          S-1-5-18
    Logon time:   7/19/2008 10:26:56 PM
    Logon server:
    DNS Domain:
    UPN:

[1] Logon session 00000000:0000dcbd:
    User name:
    Auth package: NTLM
    Logon type:   (none)
    Session:      0
    Sid:          (none)
    Logon time:   7/19/2008 10:26:57 PM
    Logon server:
    DNS Domain:
    UPN:

[2] Logon session 00000000:000003e5:
    User name:    NT AUTHORITY\LOCAL SERVICE
    Auth package: Negotiate
    Logon type:   Service
    Session:      0
    Sid:          S-1-5-19
    Logon time:   7/19/2008 10:27:01 PM
    Logon server:
    DNS Domain:
    UPN:

[3] Logon session 00000000:00015cd5:
    User name:    ALEX-LAPTOP\Administrator
    Auth package: NTLM
    Logon type:   Interactive
    Session:      1
    Sid:          S-1-5-21-2778343003-3541292008-524615573-500
    Logon time:   7/19/2008 10:27:05 PM
    Logon server: ALEX-LAPTOP
```

```
    DNS Domain:
    UPN:
```

Information reported for a session includes the SID and name of the user associated with the session, as well as the session's authentication package and logon time. Note that the Negotiate authentication package, seen in logon session 2 in the preceding output, will attempt to authenticate via Kerberos or NTLM, depending on which is most appropriate for the authentication request.

The LUID for a session is displayed on the "Logon Session" line of each session block, and using the Handle utility also from Sysinternals, you can find the tokens that represent a particular logon session. For example, to find the tokens for logon session 3 in the example output just shown, you could enter this command:

```
C:\>handle -a 3bc39
   winlogon.exe       pid: 580      1FC: \BaseNamedObjects\0000000000015cd5_
WlballoonKerberosNotificationEventName
winlogon.exe       pid: 580      22C: ALEX-LAPTOP\Administrator:15cd5
lsass.exe          pid: 628      6A0: ALEX-LAPTOP\Administrator:15cd5
lsm.exe            pid: 636      288: ALEX-LAPTOP\Administrator:15cd5
```

Winlogon then looks in the registry at the value HKLM\SOFTWARE\Microsoft\Windows NT\Current Version\Winlogon\Userinit and creates a process to run whatever the value of that string is. (This value can be several .exes separated by commas). The default value is Userinit.exe, which loads the user profile and then creates a process to run whatever the value of HKCU\SOFTWARE\Microsoft\Windows NT\Current Version\Winlogon\Shell is, if that value exists. That value does not exist by default. If it doesn't exist, Userinit.exe does the same for HKLM\SOFTWARE\Microsoft\Windows NT\Current Version\Winlogon\Shell, which defaults to Explorer.exe. Userinit then exits (which is why Explorer.exe shows up as having no parent when examined in Process Explorer). For more information on the steps followed during the user logon process, see Chapter 13.

User Account Control

UAC is meant to enable users to run with standard user rights, as opposed to administrative rights. Without administrative rights, users cannot accidentally (or deliberately) modify system settings, malware can't normally alter system security settings or disable antivirus software, and users can't compromise the sensitive information of other users on shared computers. Running with standard user rights can thus mitigate the impact of malware and protect sensitive data on shared computers.

UAC had to address several problems to make it practical for a user to run with a standard user account. First, because the Windows usage model has been one of assumed

administrative rights, software developers assumed their programs could access and modify any file, registry key, or operating system setting. The second problem UAC had to address was that users sometimes need administrative rights to perform such operations as installing software, changing the system time, and opening ports in the firewall.

The UAC solution to these problems is to run most applications with standard user rights, obviate the need for administrative rights all the time, and encourage software developers to create applications that run with standard user rights. UAC accomplishes these aims by requiring administrative rights less frequently, enabling legacy applications to run with standard user rights, making it convenient for standard users to access administrative rights when they need them, and enabling even administrative users to run as if they were standard users.

UAC also allows certain tasks that were previously considered reserved for administrators to be performed by standard users, enhancing the usability of the standard user account. For example, changing the time zone (used only for displaying the time to users) is considered a different action than changing the system's actual time (used for security, such as on Kerberos authentication). While the privilege to change the system time is assigned only to the Administrators group, the privilege to change the time zone is also assigned to the Users group. Standard users can also configure WEP settings when they connect to wireless networks, create VPN connections, change power management settings, and install critical Windows updates. In addition, Group Policy settings exist that can enable standard users to install printer and other device drivers approved by IT administrators and to install ActiveX controls from administrator-approved sites.

Virtualization

While some software legitimately requires administrative rights, many programs needlessly store user data in system-global locations. When an application executes, it can be running in different user accounts, and it should therefore store user-specific data in the per-user %AppData% directory and save per-user settings in the user's registry profile under HKEY_CURRENT_USER\ Software. Standard user accounts don't have write access to the %ProgramFiles% directory or HKEY_LOCAL_MACHINE\Software, but because most Windows systems are single-user and most users have been administrators until UAC was implemented, applications that incorrectly saved user data and settings to these locations worked anyway.

Windows enables these legacy applications to run in standard user accounts through the help of file system and registry namespace virtualization. When an application modifies a system-global location in the file system or registry and that operation fails because access is denied, Windows redirects the operation to a per-user area; when the application reads from a system-global location, Windows first checks for data in the per-user area and, if none is found, permits the read attempt from the global location.

Windows will always enable this type of virtualization unless:

- The application is 64-bit. As virtualization is purely an application-compatibility technology meant to help legacy applications, it is enabled only for 32-bit applications. The world of 64-bit applications is relatively new and should follow the development guidelines for creating standard user compatible applications.

- The application is already running with administrative rights. In this case, there is no need for any virtualization.

- The operation came from a kernel-mode caller.

- The operation is being performed while the caller is impersonating. For example, any operations not originating from a process classified as legacy according to this definition, including network file sharing accesses, are not virtualized.

- The executable image for the process has a UAC-compatible manifest (specifying a *requestedExecutionLevel* setting).

- The administrator does not have write access to the file or registry key. This exception exists to enforce backward compatibility, as the legacy application would have failed before UAC was implemented even if the application was run with administrative rights.

You can see the virtualization status (as discussed previously, the process's virtualization status is stored as a flag in its token) of a process by adding the Virtualization column to Task Manager's Processes page, as shown in Figure 6-12. Most Windows components, including the Desktop Window Manager (Dwm.exe), the Client Server Run-Time Subsystem (Csrss.exe), and Explorer, have virtualization disabled because they have a UAC-compatible manifest or are running with administrative rights and so do not allow virtualization. Internet Explorer (Iexplore.exe) has virtualization enabled because it can host multiple ActiveX controls and scripts and must assume that they were not written to operate correctly with standard user rights.

In addition to file system and registry virtualization, some applications require additional help to run correctly with standard user rights. For example, an application that tests the account in which it's running for membership in the Administrators group might otherwise work, but it won't run if it's not in that group. Windows defines a number of application-compatibility shims to enable such applications to work anyway. The shims most commonly applied to legacy applications for operation with standard user rights are shown in Table 6-9. Note that, if required, virtualization can be completely disabled for a system using a local security policy setting.

FIGURE 6-12 Using Task Manager to view virtualization status

TABLE 6-9 UAC Virtualization Shims

Flag	Meaning
ElevateCreateProcess	Changes *CreateProcess* to handle ERROR_ELEVATION_REQUIRED errors by calling the application information service to prompt for elevation.
ForceAdminAccess	Spoofs queries of Administrator group membership.
VirtualizeDeleteFile	Spoofs successful deletion of global files and directories.
LocalMappedObject	Forces global section objects into the user's namespace.
VirtualizeHKCRLite, VirtualizeRegisterTypeLib	Redirects global registration of COM objects to a per-user location.

File Virtualization

The file system locations that are virtualized for legacy processes are %ProgramFiles%, %ProgramData%, and %SystemRoot%, excluding some specific subdirectories. However, any file with an executable extension, including .exe, .bat, .scr, .vbs, and others, is excluded from virtualization. This means that programs that update themselves from a standard user account fail instead of creating private versions of their executables that aren't visible to an administrator running a global updater.

> **Note** To add additional extensions to the exception list, enter them in the HKEY_LOCAL_
> MACHINE\System\CurrentControlSet\Services\Luafv\Parameters\ExcludedExtensionsAdd registry
> key and reboot. Use a multi-string type to delimit multiple extensions, and do not include a lead-
> ing dot in the extension name.

Modifications to virtualized directories by legacy processes are redirected to the user's virtual
root directory, %LocalAppData%\VirtualStore. The Local component of the path highlights
the fact that virtualized files don't roam with the rest of the profile when the account has a
roaming profile. If you navigate in Explorer to a directory containing virtualized files, Explorer
displays a button labeled Compatibility Files in its toolbar, as shown in Figure 6-13. Clicking
the button takes you to the corresponding VirtualStore subdirectory to show you the virtual-
ized files.

FIGURE 6-13 Virtualized files are displayed here.

The UAC File Virtualization Filter Driver (%SystemRoot%\System32\Drivers\Luafv.sys) imple-
ments file system virtualization. Because this is a file system filter driver, it sees all file system
operations, but it only implements functionality for operations from legacy processes. As
shown in Figure 6-14, the filter driver changes the target file path for a legacy process that
creates a file in a system-global location but does not for a nonvirtualized process with stan-
dard user rights. Default permissions on the \Windows directory deny access to the applica-
tion written with UAC support, but the legacy process acts as though the operation succeeds,
when it really created the file in a location fully accessible by the user.

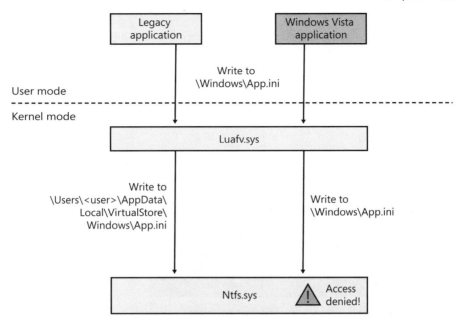

FIGURE 6-14 UAC File Virtualization Filter Driver operation

EXPERIMENT: File Virtualization Behavior

In this experiment, we will enable and disable virtualization on the command prompt and see several behaviors to demonstrate UAC file virtualization.

1. Open a nonelevated command prompt (you must have UAC enabled for this to work), and enable virtualization for it. You can change the virtualization status of a process by selecting Virtualization from the shortcut menu that appears when you right-click the process in Task Manager.

2. Navigate to the C:\Windows directory, and use the following command to write a file:

 echo hello-1 > test.txt

3. Now list the contents of the directory:

 dir test.txt

 You'll see that the file appears.

4. Now disable virtualization by using Task Manager, and then list the directory as in step 3. Notice that the file is gone. However, a directory listing of the VirtualStore directory will reveal the file:

 dir %LOCALAPPDATA%\VirtualStore\Windows\test.txt

5. To take a look at a more complex scenario, create a new Command Prompt window, but elevate it this time, and then repeat steps 2 and 3 using the string "hello-2".

6. Take a look at the text inside these files by using the following command in both command prompts:

 echo test.txt

 The following two screenshots show the expected output.

7. Finally, from your elevated command prompt, delete the test.txt file:

 del test.txt

8. Repeat step 6 of the experiment. Notice that the elevated command prompt cannot find the file anymore, while the standard user command prompt shows the old contents of the file again. This demonstrates the failover mechanism described earlier—read operations will look in the per-user virtual store location first, but if the file doesn't exist, read access to the system location will be granted.

Registry Virtualization

Registry virtualization is implemented slightly differently from file system virtualization. Virtualized registry keys include most of the HKEY_LOCAL_MACHINE\Software branch, but there are numerous exceptions, such as the following:

■ HKLM\Software\Microsoft\Windows

- HKLM\Software\Microsoft\Windows NT

- HKLM\Software\Classes

Only keys that are commonly modified by legacy applications, but which don't introduce compatibility or interoperability problems, are virtualized. Windows redirects modifications of virtualized keys by a legacy application to a user's registry virtual root at HKEY_CURRENT_USER\Software\Classes\VirtualStore. The key is located in the user's Classes hive, %LocalAppData%\Microsoft\Windows\UsrClass.dat, which, like any other virtualized file data, does not roam with a roaming user profile. Instead of maintaining a fixed list of virtualized locations as Windows does for the file system, the virtualization status of a key is stored as a combination of flags, shown in Table 6-10.

TABLE 6-10 Registry Virtualization Flags

Flag	Meaning
REG_KEY_DONT_VIRTUALIZE	Specifies whether virtualization is enabled for this key. If the flag is set, virtualization is disabled.
REG_KEY_DONT_SILENT_FAIL	If the REG_KEY_DONT_VIRTUALIZE flag is set (virtualization is disabled), this key specifies that a legacy application that would be denied access performing an operation on the key is instead granted MAXIMUM_ALLOWED rights to the key (any access the account is granted), instead of the rights the application requested. If this flag is set, it implicitly disables virtualization as well.
REG_KEY_RECURSE_FLAG	Determines whether the virtualization flags will propagate to the child keys (subkeys) of this key.

You can use the Reg.exe utility included in Windows, with the flags option, to display the current virtualization state for a key or to set it. In Figure 6-15, note that the HKLM\Software key is fully virtualized, but the Windows subkey (and all its children) have only silent failure enabled.

FIGURE 6-15 UAC registry virtualization flags on the Software and Windows keys

Unlike file virtualization, which uses a filter driver, registry virtualization is implemented in the configuration manager. (See Chapter 4 for more information on the registry and the configuration manager.) As with file system virtualization, a legacy process creating a subkey of a virtualized key is redirected to the user's registry virtual root, but a UAC-compatible process is denied access by default permissions. This is shown in Figure 6-16.

FIGURE 6-16 UAC registry virtualization operation

Elevation

Even if users run only programs that are compatible with standard user rights, some operations still require administrative rights. The vast majority of software installations require administrative rights to create directories and registry keys in system-global locations or to install services or device drivers. Modifying system-global Windows and application settings also requires administrative rights, as does the Windows Vista parental controls feature. It would be possible to perform most of these operations by switching to a dedicated administrator account, but the inconvenience of doing so would likely result in most users remaining in the administrator account to perform their daily tasks.

It's important to be aware that UAC elevations are conveniences and not security boundaries. A security boundary requires that security policy dictate what can pass through the boundary. User accounts are an example of a security boundary in Windows, because one user can't access the data belonging to another user without having that user's permission.

Because elevations aren't security boundaries, there's no guarantee that malware running on a system with standard user rights can't compromise an elevated process to gain administrative rights. For example, elevation dialog boxes only identify the executable that will be elevated; they say nothing about what it will do when it executes.

Running with Administrator Rights

Windows includes enhanced "run as" functionality so that standard users can conveniently launch processes with administrative rights. This functionality required giving applications a way to identify operations for which the system can obtain administrative rights on behalf of the application, as necessary. (More on this topic shortly.)

To enable users acting as system administrators to run with standard user rights but not have to enter user names and passwords every time they want to access administrative rights, Windows makes use of a mechanism called Admin Approval Mode (AAM). This feature creates two identities for the user at logon: one with standard user rights and another with administrative rights. Since every user on a Windows system is either a standard user or acting for the most part as a standard user in AAM, developers must assume that all Windows users are standard users, which will result in more programs working with standard user rights without virtualization or shims.

Granting administrative rights to a process is called *elevation*. When elevation is performed by a standard user account (or by a user who is part of an administrative group but not the actual Administrators group), it's referred to as an *over-the-shoulder* (OTS) elevation because it requires the entry of credentials for an account that's a member of the Administrators group, something that's usually completed by a user typing over the shoulder of a standard user. An elevation performed by an AAM user is called a *consent* elevation because the user simply has to approve the assignment of his administrative rights.

Stand-alone systems, which are typically home computers, and domain-joined systems treat AAM access by remote users differently because domain-connected computers can use domain administrative groups in their resource permissions. When a user accesses a stand-alone computer's file share, Windows requests the remote user's standard user identity, but on domain-joined systems, Windows honors all the user's domain group memberships by requesting the user's administrative identity.

Executing an image that requests administrative rights causes the application information service (AIS, contained in %SystemRoot%\System32\Appinfo.dll), which runs inside a service host process (%SystemRoot%\System32\Svchost.exe), to launch Consent.exe (%SystemRoot%\System32\Consent.exe). Consent captures a bitmap of the screen, applies a fade effect to it, switches to a desktop that's only accessible to the local system account, paints the bitmap as the background, and displays an elevation dialog box that contains information about the executable. Displaying this dialog box on a separate desktop prevents any application present in the user's account from modifying the appearance of the dialog box.

If an image is a Windows component digitally signed by Microsoft and the image is in the Windows system directory, the dialog box displays a blue stripe across the top, as shown at the top of Figure 6-17. The gray stripe (the dialog box in the middle of the figure) is for images that are digitally signed by someone other than Microsoft, and the orange stripe

(bottom dialog box) is for unsigned images. The elevation dialog box shows the image's icon, description, and publisher for digitally signed images, but it shows only a generic icon, the file name, and Unidentified Publisher for unsigned images. This difference makes it harder for malware to mimic the appearance of legitimate software. The Details button at the bottom of the dialog box expands it to show the command line that will be passed to the executable if it launches.

FIGURE 6-17 UAC elevation dialog boxes based on image signature

The AAM consent dialog box, shown in Figure 6-18, is similar, but instead of prompting for administrator credentials, this dialog box provides Continue and Cancel buttons.

FIGURE 6-18 AAM consent dialog box

If a user declines an elevation, Windows returns an access-denied error to the process that initiated the launch. When a user agrees to an elevation by either entering administrator credentials or clicking Continue, AIS calls *CreateProcessAsUser* to launch the process with the appropriate administrative identity. Although AIS is technically the parent of the elevated process, AIS uses new support in the *CreateProcessAsUser* API that sets the process's parent process ID to that of the process that originally launched it. (See Chapter 5 for more information on processes and this mechanism.) That's why elevated processes don't appear as children of the AIS service-hosting process in tools such as Process Explorer that show process trees. Figure 6-19 shows the operations involved in launching an elevated process from a standard user account.

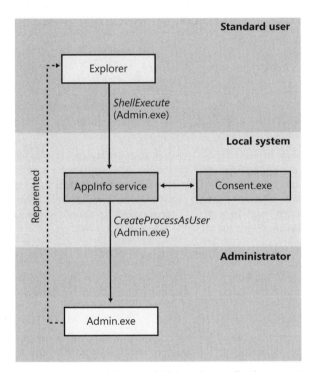

FIGURE 6-19 Launching an administrative application as a standard user

Requesting Administrative Rights

There are a number of ways the system and applications identify a need for administrative rights. One that shows up in the Explorer user interface is the Run As Administrator context menu command and shortcut option. These items also include a colored shield icon that should be placed on any button or menu item that will result in an elevation of rights when it is selected. Choosing the Run As Administrator command causes Explorer to call the *ShellExecute* API with the "runas" verb.

The vast majority of installation programs require administrative rights, so the image loader, which initiates the launch of an executable, includes installer detection code to identify likely legacy installers. Some of the heuristics it uses are as simple as detecting internal version information or whether the image has the words *setup*, *install*, or *update* in its file name. More sophisticated means of detection involve scanning for byte sequences in the executable that are common to third-party installation wrapper utilities. The image loader also calls the application compatibility library to see if the target executable requires administrator rights. The library looks in the application compatibility database to see whether the executable has the *RequireAdministrator* or *RunAsInvoker* compatibility flags associated with it.

The most common way for an executable to request administrative rights is for it to include a *requestedElevationLevel* tag in its application manifest file. The element's *level* attribute can have one of the three values shown in Table 6-11.

TABLE 6-11 Requested Elevation Levels

Elevation Level	Meaning	Usage
As Invoker	No need for administrative rights; never ask for elevation.	Typical user applications that don't need administrative privileges, for example Notepad.
Highest Available	Request approval for highest rights available. If the user is logged on as a standard user, the process will be launched *as invoker;* otherwise, an AAM elevation prompt will appear, and the process will run with full administrative rights.	Applications that can function without full administrative rights but expect users to want full access if it's easily accessible. For example, the Registry Editor, Microsoft Management Console, and the Event Viewer use this level,
Require Administrator	Always request administrative rights—an OTS elevation dialog box prompt will be shown for standard users; otherwise, AAM.	Applications that require administrative rights to work, such as the Firewall Settings editor, which affects systemwide security.

The presence of the *trustInfo* element in a manifest (which you can see in the excerpted string dump of FirewallSettings.exe below), denotes an executable that was written with support for UAC and the *requestedElevationLevel* element nests within it. The *uiAccess* attribute is where accessibility applications can use the UIPI bypass functionality mentioned earlier.

```
C:\>strings c:\Windows\System32\FirewallSettings.exe
...
<trustInfo
 xmlns="urn:schema-microsoft-com:asm.v3">
 <security>
  <requestedPrivileges>
   <requestedExecutionLevel
    Level="requireAdministrator"
    uiAccess="false"/>
  </requestedPrivileges>
 </security>
</trustInfo>
```

An easier way to determine the values specified by an executable is to view its manifest with the Sysinternals Sigcheck utility, like this:

```
sigcheck –m <executable>
```

> **EXPERIMENT: Using Application Compatibility Flags**
>
> In this experiment, we will use an application compatibility flag to run the Registry Editor as a standard user process. This will bypass the *RequireAdministrator* manifest flag and force virtualization on Regedit.exe, allowing you to make changes to the virtualized registry directly.
>
> 1. Navigate to your %SystemRoot%\System32 directory, and copy the Regedt32.exe file to another path on your system (such as C:\ or your Desktop folder).
>
> 2. Go to the HKLM\Software\Microsoft\Windows NT\CurrentVersion\ AppCompatFlags\Layers registry key, and create a new string value whose name is the path where you copied Regedt32.exe, such as c:\regedt32.exe
>
> 3. Set the value of this key to RUNASINVOKER.
>
> 4. Now start Regedt32.exe from its location (be sure to close any running copies of the Registry Editor first). You will not see the typical AAM dialog box, and Regedit.exe will now run with standard user rights. You will also be subject to the virtualized view of the registry, meaning you can now see what legacy applications see when accessing the registry.

Software Restriction Policies

Windows also contains a user-mode mechanism called Software Restriction Policies that enables administrators to control what images and scripts execute on their systems. The Software Restriction Policies node of the Local Security Policy Editor, shown in Figure 6-20, serves as the management interface for a machine's code execution policies, although per-user policies are also possible using domain group policies.

Several global policy settings appear beneath the Software Restriction Policies node.

- The *Enforcement* policy configures whether restriction policies apply to libraries, such as DLLs, and whether policies apply to users only or to administrators as well.

- The *Designated File Types* policy records the extensions for files that are considered executable code.

- *Trusted Publishers* control who can select which certificate publishers are trusted.

FIGURE 6-20 Software Restriction Policy configuration

When configuring a policy for a particular script or image, an administrator can direct the system to recognize it using its path, its hash, its Internet Zone (as defined by Internet Explorer), or its cryptographic certificate, and she can specify whether it is associated with the *Disallowed* or *Unrestricted* security policy.

Enforcement of Software Restriction Policies takes place within various components where files are treated as containing executable code. Some of these components are listed here:

- The user-mode Windows *CreateProcess* function in %SystemRoot%\System32\ Kernel32.dll enforces it for executable images.

- The DLL loading code of Ntdll (%SystemRoot%\System32\Ntdll.dll) enforces it for DLLs.

- The Windows command prompt (%SystemRoot%\System32\Cmd.exe) enforces it for batch file execution.

- Windows Scripting Host components that start scripts—%SystemRoot%\System32\ Cscript.exe (for command-line scripts), %SystemRoot%\System32\Wscript.exe (for UI scripts), and %SystemRoot%\System32\Scrobj.dll (for script objects)—enforce it for script execution.

Each of these components determines whether the restriction policies are enabled by reading the registry value HKEY_LOCAL_MACHINE\Software\Microsoft\Policies\Windows\Safer\ CodeIdentifiers\TransparentEnabled, which if set to 1 indicates that policies are in effect. Then it determines whether the code it's about to execute matches one of the rules specified in a subkey of the CodeIdentifiers key and, if so, whether or not the execution should be allowed. If there is no match, the default policy, as specified in the *DefaultLevel* value of the CodeIdentifiers key, determines whether the execution is allowed.

Software Restriction Policies are a powerful tool for preventing the unauthorized access of code and scripts, but only if properly applied. Unless the default policy is set to disallow

execution, a user can make minor changes to an image that's been marked as disallowed so that he can bypass the rule and execute it. For example, a user can change an innocuous byte of a process image so that a hash rule fails to recognize it, or copy a file to a different location to avoid a path-based rule.

EXPERIMENT: Watching Software Restriction Policy Enforcement

You can indirectly see Software Restriction Policies being enforced by watching accesses to the registry when you attempt to execute an image that you've disallowed.

1. Run secpol.msc to open the Local Security Policy Editor, and navigate to the Software Restriction Policies node.

2. Choose Create New Policies from the context menu if no policies are defined.

3. Create a path-based disallow restriction policy for %SystemRoot%\System32\Notepad.exe.

4. Run Process Monitor, and set an include filter for Safer. (See Chapter 4 for a description of Process Monitor.)

5. Open a command prompt, and run Notepad from the prompt.

Your attempt to run Notepad should result in a message telling you that you cannot execute the specified program, and Process Monitor should show the command prompt (cmd.exe) querying the local machine restriction policies.

Conclusion

Windows provides an extensive array of security functions that meet the key requirements of both government agencies and commercial installations. In this chapter, we've taken a brief tour of the internal components that are the basis of these security features. In the next chapter, we'll look at the I/O system.

Chapter 7

I/O System

The Windows I/O system consists of several executive components that together manage hardware devices and provide interfaces to hardware devices for applications and the system. In this chapter, we'll first list the design goals of the I/O system, which have influenced its implementation. We'll then cover the components that make up the I/O system, including the I/O manager, Plug and Play (PnP) manager, and power manager. Then we'll examine the structure and components of the I/O system and the various types of device drivers. We'll look at the key data structures that describe devices, device drivers, and I/O requests, after which we'll describe the steps necessary to complete I/O requests as they move through the system. Finally, we'll present the way device detection, driver installation, and power management work.

I/O System Components

The design goals for the Windows I/O system are to provide an abstraction of devices, both hardware (physical) and software (virtual or logical), to applications with the following features:

- Uniform security and naming across devices to protect shareable resources. (See Chapter 6 for a description of the Windows security model.)

- High-performance asynchronous packet-based I/O to allow for the implementation of scalable applications.

- Services that allow drivers to be written in a high-level language and easily ported between different machine architectures.

- Layering and extensibility to allow for the addition of drivers that transparently modify the behavior of other drivers or devices, without requiring any changes to the driver whose behavior or device is modified.

- Dynamic loading and unloading of device drivers so that drivers can be loaded on-demand and not consume system resources when unneeded.

- Support for Plug and Play, where the system locates and installs drivers for newly detected hardware, assigns them hardware resources they require, and also allows applications to discover and activate device interfaces.

- Support for power management so that the system or individual devices can enter low power states.

- Support for multiple installable file systems, including FAT, the CD-ROM file system (CDFS), the Universal Disk Format (UDF) file system, and the Windows file system (NTFS). (See Chapter 11 for more specific information on file system types and architecture.)

- Windows Management Instrumentation (WMI) support and diagnosability so that drivers can be managed and monitored through WMI applications and scripts. (WMI is described in Chapter 4.)

To implement these features the Windows I/O system consists of several executive components as well as device drivers, which are shown in Figure 7-1.

- The I/O manager is the heart of the I/O system. It connects applications and system components to virtual, logical, and physical devices, and it defines the infrastructure that supports device drivers.

- A device driver typically provides an I/O interface for a particular type of device. Device drivers receive commands routed to them by the I/O manager that are directed at devices they manage, and they inform the I/O manager when those commands complete. Device drivers often use the I/O manager to forward I/O commands to other device drivers that share in the implementation of a device's interface or control.

- The PnP manager works closely with the I/O manager and a type of device driver called a *bus driver* to guide the allocation of hardware resources as well as to detect and respond to the arrival and removal of hardware devices. The PnP manager and bus drivers are responsible for loading a device's driver when the device is detected. When a device is added to a system that doesn't have an appropriate device driver, the executive Plug and Play component calls on the device installation services of a user-mode PnP manager.

- The power manager also works closely with the I/O manager to guide the system, as well as individual device drivers, through power-state transitions.

- Windows Management Instrumentation support routines, called the Windows Driver Model (WDM) WMI provider, allow device drivers to indirectly act as providers, using the WDM WMI provider as an intermediary to communicate with the WMI service in user mode. (For more information on WMI, see the section "Windows Management Instrumentation" in Chapter 4.)

- The registry serves as a database that stores a description of basic hardware devices attached to the system as well as driver initialization and configuration settings. (See the section "The Registry" in Chapter 4 for more information.)

- INF files, which are designated by the .inf extension, are driver installation files. INF files are the link between a particular hardware device and the driver that assumes primary control of the device. They are made up of scriptlike instructions describing the device they correspond to, the source and target locations of driver files, required driver-

installation registry modifications, and driver dependency information. Digital signatures that Windows uses to verify that a driver file has passed testing by the Microsoft Windows Hardware Quality Labs (WHQL) are stored in .cat files.

■ The hardware abstraction layer (HAL) insulates drivers from the specifics of the processor and interrupt controller by providing APIs that hide differences between platforms. In essence, the HAL is the bus driver for all the devices on the computer's motherboard that aren't controlled by other drivers.

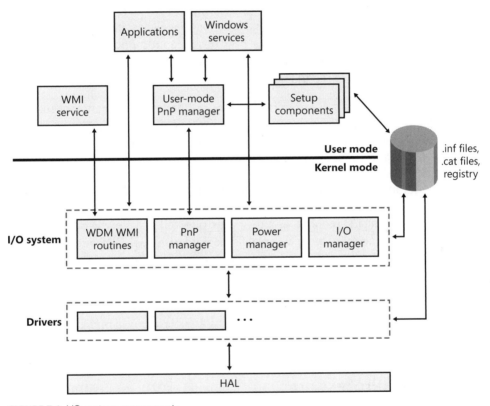

FIGURE 7-1 I/O system components

The I/O Manager

The *I/O manager* is the core of the I/O system because it defines the orderly framework, or model, within which I/O requests are delivered to device drivers. The I/O system is *packet driven*. Most I/O requests are represented by an *I/O request packet* (IRP), which travels from one I/O system component to another. (As you'll discover in the section "Fast I/O," fast I/O is the exception; it doesn't use IRPs.) The design allows an individual application thread to manage multiple I/O requests concurrently. An IRP is a data structure that contains information completely describing an I/O request. (You'll find more information about IRPs in the section "I/O Request Packets.")

The I/O manager creates an IRP that represents an I/O operation, passing a pointer to the IRP to the correct driver and disposing of the packet when the I/O operation is complete. In contrast, a driver receives an IRP, performs the operation the IRP specifies, and passes the IRP back to the I/O manager, either for completion or to be passed on to another driver for further processing.

In addition to creating and disposing of IRPs, the I/O manager supplies code that is common to different drivers and that the drivers call to carry out their I/O processing. By consolidating common tasks in the I/O manager, individual drivers become simpler and more compact. For example, the I/O manager provides a function that allows one driver to call other drivers. It also manages buffers for I/O requests, provides timeout support for drivers, and records which installable file systems are loaded into the operating system. There are close to a hundred different routines in the I/O manager that can be called by device drivers.

The I/O manager also provides flexible I/O services that allow environment subsystems, such as Windows and POSIX, to implement their respective I/O functions. These services include sophisticated services for asynchronous I/O that allow developers to build scalable high-performance server applications.

The uniform, modular interface that drivers present allows the I/O manager to call any driver without requiring any special knowledge of its structure or internal details. The operating system treats all I/O requests as if they were directed at a file; the driver converts the requests from requests made to a virtual file to hardware-specific requests. Drivers can also call each other (using the I/O manager) to achieve layered, independent processing of an I/O request.

Besides providing the normal open, close, read, and write functions, the Windows I/O system provides several advanced features, such as asynchronous, direct, buffered, and scatter/gather I/O, which are described in the "Types of I/O" section later in this chapter.

Typical I/O Processing

Most I/O operations don't involve all the components of the I/O system. A typical I/O request starts with an application executing an I/O-related function (for example, reading data from a device) that is processed by the I/O manager, one or more device drivers, and the HAL.

As just mentioned, in Windows, threads perform I/O on virtual files. The operating system abstracts all I/O requests as operations on a virtual file, hiding the fact that the target of an I/O operation might not be a file-structured device. This abstraction generalizes an application's interface to devices. A virtual file refers to any source or destination for I/O that is treated as if it were a file (such as files, directories, pipes, and mailslots). All data that is read or written is regarded as a simple stream of bytes directed to these virtual files. User-mode applications (whether Windows or POSIX) call documented functions, which in turn call internal I/O system functions to read from a file, write to a file, and perform other operations. The

I/O manager dynamically directs these virtual file requests to the appropriate device driver. Figure 7-2 illustrates the basic structure of a typical I/O request flow.

FIGURE 7-2 The flow of a typical I/O request

In the following sections, we'll be looking at these components more closely, covering the various types of device drivers, how they are structured, how they load and initialize, and how they process I/O requests. Then we'll cover the operation and roles of the PnP manager and the power manager.

Device Drivers

To integrate with the I/O manager and other I/O system components, a device driver must conform to implementation guidelines specific to the type of device it manages and the role it plays in managing the device. In this section, we'll look at the types of device drivers Windows supports as well as the internal structure of a device driver.

Types of Device Drivers

Windows supports a wide range of device driver types and programming environments. Even within a type of device driver, programming environments can differ, depending on the specific type of device for which a driver is intended. The broadest classification of a driver

is whether it is a user-mode or kernel-mode driver. Windows supports several types of user-mode drivers:

- *Virtual device drivers* (VDDs) are used to emulate 16-bit MS-DOS applications. They trap what an MS-DOS application thinks are references to I/O ports and translate them into native Windows I/O functions, which are then passed to the actual device driver. Because Windows is a fully protected operating system, user-mode MS-DOS applications can't access hardware directly and thus must go through a real kernel-mode device driver. Because 64-bit editions of Windows do not support 16-bit applications anymore, these types of drivers are not present on that architecture.

- Windows subsystem *printer drivers* translate device-independent graphics requests to printer-specific commands. These commands are then typically forwarded to a kernel-mode port driver such as the parallel port driver (Parport.sys) or the universal serial bus (USB) printer port driver (Usbprint.sys).

- User-Mode Driver Framework (UMDF) drivers are hardware device drivers that run in user mode. They communicate to the kernel-mode UMDF support library through ALPC. See the "User-Mode Driver Framework (UMDF)" section later in this chapter for more information.

In this chapter, the focus is on kernel-mode device drivers. There are many types of kernel-mode drivers, which can be divided into the following basic categories:

- *File system drivers* accept I/O requests to files and satisfy the requests by issuing their own, more explicit, requests to mass storage or network device drivers.

- *Plug and Play drivers* work with hardware and integrate with the Windows power manager and PnP manager. They include drivers for mass storage devices, video adapters, input devices, and network adapters.

- *Non–Plug and Play drivers*, which also include *kernel extensions*, are drivers or modules that extend the functionality of the system. They do not integrate with the PnP or power managers because they typically do not manage an actual piece of hardware. Examples include network API and protocol drivers. Process Monitor's driver, described in Chapter 4, is also an example.

Within the category of kernel-mode drivers are further classifications based on the driver model that the driver adheres to and its role in servicing device requests.

WDM Drivers

WDM drivers are device drivers that adhere to the Windows Driver Model (WDM). WDM includes support for Windows power management, Plug and Play, and WMI, and most Plug and Play drivers adhere to WDM. There are three types of WDM drivers:

- *Bus drivers* manage a logical or physical bus. Examples of buses include PCMCIA, PCI, USB, IEEE 1394, and ISA. A bus driver is responsible for detecting and informing the PnP

manager of devices attached to the bus it controls as well as managing the power setting of the bus.

- *Function drivers* manage a particular type of device. Bus drivers present devices to function drivers via the PnP manager. The function driver is the driver that exports the operational interface of the device to the operating system. In general, it's the driver with the most knowledge about the operation of the device.

- *Filter drivers* logically layer above or below function drivers, augmenting or changing the behavior of a device or another driver. For example, a keyboard capture utility could be implemented with a keyboard filter driver that layers above the keyboard function driver.

In WDM, no one driver is responsible for controlling all aspects of a particular device. The bus driver is responsible for detecting bus membership changes (device addition or removal), assisting the PnP manager in enumerating the devices on the bus, accessing bus-specific configuration registers, and, in some cases, controlling power to devices on the bus. The function driver is generally the only driver that accesses the device's hardware.

Layered Drivers

Support for an individual piece of hardware is often divided among several drivers, each providing a part of the functionality required to make the device work properly. In addition to WDM bus drivers, function drivers, and filter drivers, hardware support might be split between the following components:

- *Class drivers* implement the I/O processing for a particular class of devices, such as disk, tape, or CD-ROM, where the hardware interfaces have been standardized, so one driver can serve devices from a wide variety of manufacturers.

- *Port drivers* implement the processing of an I/O request specific to a type of I/O port, such as SCSI, and are implemented as kernel-mode libraries of functions rather than actual device drivers. Port drivers are always written by Microsoft because the interfaces to write for are not documented.

- *Miniport drivers* map a generic I/O request to a type of port into an adapter type, such as a specific SCSI adapter. Miniport drivers are actual device drivers that import the functions supplied by a port driver. Miniport drivers are written by third parties, and they provide the interface for the port driver.

An example will help demonstrate how device drivers work. A file system driver accepts a request to write data to a certain location within a particular file. It translates the request into a request to write a certain number of bytes to the disk at a particular "logical" location. It then passes this request (via the I/O manager) to a simple disk driver. The disk driver, in turn, translates the request into a physical location on the disk and communicates with the disk to write the data. This layering is illustrated in Figure 7-3.

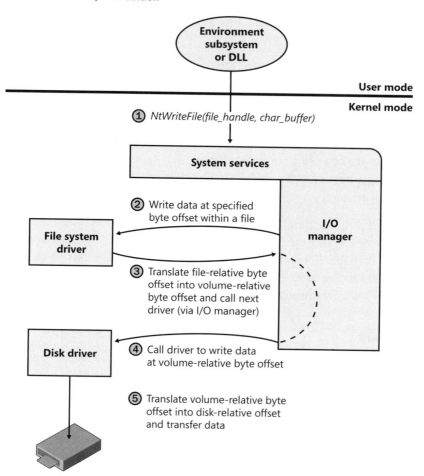

FIGURE 7-3 Layering of a file system driver and a disk driver

This figure illustrates the division of labor between two layered drivers. The I/O manager receives a write request that is relative to the beginning of a particular file. The I/O manager passes the request to the file system driver, which translates the write operation from a file-relative operation to a starting location (a sector boundary on the disk) and a number of bytes to read. The file system driver calls the I/O manager to pass the request to the disk driver, which translates the request to a physical disk location and transfers the data.

Because all drivers—both device drivers and file system drivers—present the same framework to the operating system, another driver can easily be inserted into the hierarchy without altering the existing drivers or the I/O system. For example, several disks can be made to seem like a very large single disk by adding a driver. This logical, volume manager driver is located between the file system and the disk drivers, as shown in Figure 7-4. Volume manager drivers are described in more detail in Chapter 8.

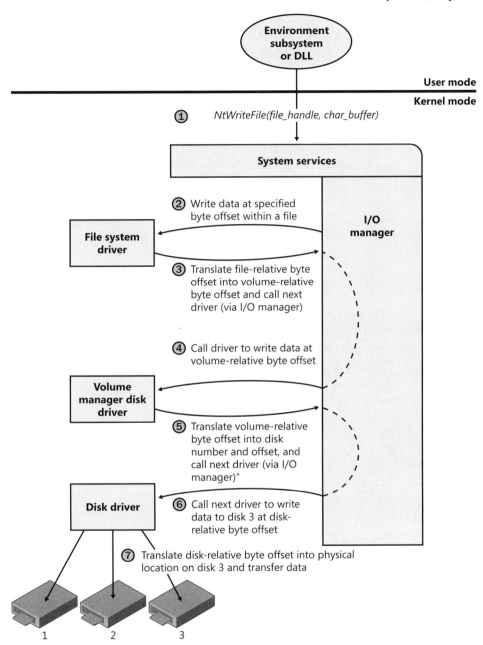

FIGURE 7-4 Adding a layered driver

EXPERIMENT: Viewing the Loaded Driver List

You can see a list of registered drivers by executing the Msinfo32.exe utility from the Run dialog box of the Start menu. Select the System Drivers entry under Software Environment to see the list of drivers configured on the system. Those that are loaded have the text "Yes" in the Started column, as shown here:

You can also view the list of loaded kernel-mode drivers with Process Explorer from Windows Sysinternals (*www.microsoft.com/technet/sysinternals*.) Run Process Explorer, select the System process, and select DLLs from the Lower Pane menu entry in the View menu. Process Explorer lists the loaded drivers, their names, version information (including company and description), and load address (assuming you have configured Process Explorer to display the corresponding columns):

Finally, if you're looking at a crash dump (or live system) with the kernel debugger, you can get a similar display with the kernel debugger *lm kv* command:

```
lkd> lm kv
start    end        module name
82007000 823c0000   nt          (pdb symbols)
c:\programming\symbols\ntkrpamp.pdb\37D328E3BAE5460F8E662756ED80951D2\ntkrpamp.pdb
    Loaded symbol image file: ntkrpamp.exe
    Image path: ntkrpamp.exe
    Image name: ntkrpamp.exe
    Timestamp:        Fri Jan 18 21:30:58 2008 (47918B12)
    CheckSum:         00372038
    ImageSize:        003B9000
    File version:     6.0.6001.18000
    Product version:  6.0.6001.18000
    File flags:       0 (Mask 3F)
    File OS:          40004 NT Win32
    File type:        1.0 App
    File date:        00000000.00000000
    Translations:     0409.04b0
    CompanyName:      Microsoft Corporation
    ProductName:      Microsoft® Windows® Operating System
    InternalName:     ntkrpamp.exe
    OriginalFilename: ntkrpamp.exe
    ProductVersion:   6.0.6001.18000
    FileVersion:      6.0.6001.18000 (longhorn_rtm.080118-1840)
    FileDescription:  NT Kernel & System
    LegalCopyright:   © Microsoft Corporation. All rights reserved.
823c0000 823f3000   hal         (deferred)
    Image path: halmacpi.dll
    Image name: halmacpi.dll
    Timestamp:        Fri Jan 18 21:27:20 2008 (47918A38)
    CheckSum:         0003859F
    ImageSize:        00033000
    Translations:     0000.04b0 0000.04e0 0409.04b0 0409.04e0
82600000 82671000   ksecdd      (deferred)
    Image path: \SystemRoot\System32\Drivers\ksecdd.sys
    Image name: ksecdd.sys
    Timestamp:        Fri Jan 18 21:41:20 2008 (47918D80)
    CheckSum:         0006E742
    ImageSize:        00071000
    Translations:     0000.04b0 0000.04e0 0409.04b0 0409.04e0
```

Structure of a Driver

The I/O system drives the execution of device drivers. Device drivers consist of a set of routines that are called to process the various stages of an I/O request. Figure 7-5 illustrates the key driver-function routines.

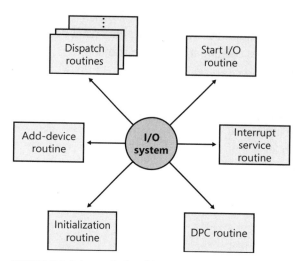

FIGURE 7-5 Primary device driver routines

- **An initialization routine** The I/O manager executes a driver's *initialization routine*, which is typically named *DriverEntry*, when it loads the driver into the operating system. The routine fills in system data structures to register the rest of the driver's routines with the I/O manager and performs any global driver initialization that's necessary.

- **An add-device routine** A driver that supports Plug and Play implements an add-device routine. The PnP manager sends a driver notification via this routine whenever a device for which the driver is responsible is detected. In this routine, a driver typically allocates a device object (described later in this chapter) to represent the device.

- **A set of dispatch routines** *Dispatch routines* are the main functions that a device driver provides. Some examples are open, close, read, and write and any other capabilities the device, file system, or network supports. When called on to perform an I/O operation, the I/O manager generates an IRP and calls a driver through one of the driver's dispatch routines.

- **A start I/O routine** A driver can use a start I/O routine to initiate a data transfer to or from a device. This routine is defined only in drivers that rely on the I/O manager to queue their incoming I/O requests. The I/O manager serializes IRPs for a driver by ensuring that the driver processes only one IRP at a time. Most drivers process multiple IRPs concurrently, but serialization makes sense for some drivers, such as a keyboard driver.

- **An interrupt service routine (ISR)** When a device interrupts, the kernel's interrupt dispatcher transfers control to this routine. In the Windows I/O model, ISRs run at device interrupt request level (DIRQL), so they perform as little work as possible to

avoid blocking lower-level interrupts unnecessarily. (See Chapter 3 for more informa-
tion on IRQLs.) An ISR usually queues a deferred procedure call (DPC), which runs at
a lower IRQL (DPC/dispatch level), to execute the remainder of interrupt processing.
(Only drivers for interrupt-driven devices have ISRs; a file system driver, for example,
doesn't have one.)

- **An interrupt-servicing DPC routine** A DPC routine performs most of the work
 involved in handling a device interrupt after the ISR executes. The DPC routine executes
 at a lower IRQL (DPC/dispatch level) than that of the ISR, which runs at device level, to
 avoid blocking other interrupts unnecessarily. A DPC routine initiates I/O completion
 and starts the next queued I/O operation on a device.

Although the following routines aren't shown in Figure 7-5, they're found in many types of
device drivers:

- **One or more I/O completion routines** A layered driver might have I/O comple-
 tion routines that will notify it when a lower-level driver finishes processing an IRP. For
 example, the I/O manager calls a file system driver's I/O completion routine after a
 device driver finishes transferring data to or from a file. The completion routine notifies
 the file system driver about the operation's success, failure, or cancellation, and it allows
 the file system driver to perform cleanup operations.

- **A cancel I/O routine** If an I/O operation can be canceled, a driver can define one or
 more cancel I/O routines. When the driver receives an IRP for an I/O request that can
 be canceled, it assigns a cancel routine to the IRP. If a thread that issues an I/O request
 exits before the request is completed or cancels the operation (with the *CancelIo*
 Windows function, for example), the I/O manager executes the IRP's cancel routine if
 one is assigned to it. A cancel routine is responsible for performing whatever steps are
 necessary to release any resources acquired during the processing that has already
 taken place for the IRP as well as completing the IRP with a canceled status.

- **Fast dispatch routines** Drivers that make use of the cache manager in Windows (see
 Chapter 10 for more information on the cache manager), such as file system drivers,
 typically provide these routines to allow the kernel to bypass typical I/O processing
 when accessing the driver. For example, operations such as reading or writing can be
 quickly performed by accessing the cached data directly, instead of taking the I/O
 manager's usual path that generates discrete I/O operations. Fast dispatch routines are
 also used as a mechanism for callbacks from the memory manager and cache manager
 to file system drivers. For instance, when creating a section, the memory manager calls
 back into the file system driver to acquire the file exclusively.

- **An unload routine** An unload routine releases any system resources a driver is using
 so that the I/O manager can remove them from memory. Any resources acquired in the
 initialization routine are usually released in the unload routine. A driver can be loaded

and unloaded while the system is running if the driver supports it, but the unload routine will be called only after all file handles to the device are closed.

- **A system shutdown notification routine** This routine allows driver cleanup on system shutdown.

- **Error-logging routines** When unexpected errors occur (for example, when a disk block goes bad), a driver's error-logging routines note the occurrence and notify the I/O manager. The I/O manager writes this information to an error log file.

 Note Most kernel-mode device drivers are written in C. Some drivers are written in C++, but there's no specific support for C++ in the Windows Driver Kit (WDK). Use of assembly language is highly discouraged because of the complexity it introduces and its effect of making a driver difficult to port between hardware architectures such as the x86, x64, and IA64.

Driver Objects and Device Objects

When a thread opens a handle to a file object (described in the "I/O Processing" section later in this chapter), the I/O manager must determine from the file object's name which driver (or drivers) it should call to process the request. Furthermore, the I/O manager must be able to locate this information the next time a thread uses the same file handle. The following system objects fill this need:

- A *driver object* represents an individual driver in the system. The I/O manager obtains the address of each of the driver's dispatch routines (entry points) from the driver object.

- A *device object* represents a physical or logical device on the system and describes its characteristics, such as the alignment it requires for buffers and the location of its device queue to hold incoming IRPs.

The I/O manager creates a driver object when a driver is loaded into the system, and it then calls the driver's initialization routine (for example, *DriverEntry*), which fills in the object attributes with the driver's entry points.

After loading, a driver can create device objects to represent devices, or even an interface to the driver, at any time by calling *IoCreateDevice* or *IoCreateDeviceSecure*. However, most Plug and Play drivers create devices with their add-device routine when the PnP manager informs them of the presence of a device for them to manage. Non–Plug and Play drivers, on the other hand, usually create device objects when the I/O manager invokes their initialization routine. The I/O manager unloads a driver when its last device object has been deleted and no references to the driver remain.

When a driver creates a device object, the driver can optionally assign the device a name. A name places the device object in the object manager namespace, and a driver can either explicitly define a name or let the I/O manager autogenerate one. (The object manager namespace is described in Chapter 3.) By convention, device objects are placed in the \Device directory in the namespace, which is inaccessible by applications using the Windows API.

> **Note** Some drivers place device objects in directories other than \Device. For example, the IDE driver creates the device objects that represent IDE ports and channels in the \Device\Ide directory. See Chapter 8 for a description of storage architecture, including the way storage drivers use device objects.

If a driver needs to make it possible for applications to open the device object, it must create a symbolic link in the \Global?? directory to the device object's name in the \Device directory. (See Chapter 3 for more information on \??.) Non–Plug and Play and file system drivers typically create a symbolic link with a well-known name (for example, \Device\Hardware2). Because well-known names don't work well in an environment in which hardware appears and disappears dynamically, PnP drivers expose one or more interfaces by calling the *IoRegisterDeviceInterface* function, specifying a GUID (globally unique identifier) that represents the type of functionality exposed. GUIDs are 128-bit values that you can generate by using a tool called Guidgen that is included with the WDK and the Windows SDK. Given the range of values that 128 bits represents, it's statistically almost certain that each GUID that Guidgen creates will be forever and globally unique.

IoRegisterDeviceInterface determines the symbolic link that is associated with a device instance; however, a driver must call *IoSetDeviceInterfaceState* to enable the interface to the device before the I/O manager actually creates the link. Drivers usually do this when the PnP manager starts the device by sending the driver a *start-device* command.

An application wanting to open a device object represented with a GUID can call Plug and Play setup functions in user space, such as *SetupDiEnumDeviceInterfaces*, to enumerate the interfaces present for a particular GUID and to obtain the names of the symbolic links it can use to open the device objects. For each device reported by *SetupDiEnumDeviceInterfaces*, an application executes *SetupDiGetDeviceInterfaceDetail* to obtain additional information about the device, such as its autogenerated name. After obtaining a device's name from *SetupDiGetDeviceInterfaceDetail*, the application can execute the Windows function *CreateFile* to open the device and obtain a handle.

EXPERIMENT: Looking at the \Device Directory

You can use the WinObj tool from Sysinternals or the *!object* kernel debugger command to view the device names under \Device in the object manager namespace. The following screen shot shows an I/O manager–assigned symbolic link that points to a device object in \Device with an autogenerated name:

When you run the *!object* kernel debugger command and specify the \Device directory, you should see output similar to the following:

```
lkd> !object \Device
Object: 8b611b88  Type: (84d10d40) Directory
    ObjectHeader: 8b611b70 (old version)
    HandleCount: 0  PointerCount: 365
    Directory Object: 8b602470  Name: Device

    Hash Address  Type          Name
    ---- -------  ----          ----
    00   85557a00 Device        KsecDD
         855589d8 Device        Ndis
         8b6151b0 SymbolicLink  {941D252A-0BDA-4772-B3CB-30697579BD4A}
         86859030 Device        0000009b
         88c92da8 Device        SrvNet
         886723f0 Device        Beep
         8b71fb90 SymbolicLink  ScsiPort2
         84d17a98 Device        00000032
         84d15f00 Device        00000025
         84d13030 Device        00000019
    01   86d44030 Device        NDMP10
         8d291eb0 SymbolicLink  {E85EEE75-32E3-4A94-8905-52709C2C9BCC}
         886da3c8 Device        Netbios
         86862030 Device        0000009c
         84d177c8 Device        00000033
         84d15c70 Device        00000026
    02   86de9030 Device        NDMP11
         84d19320 Device        00000040
```

```
       88633ca0 Device        NetBT_Tcpip_{033C65A4-C1D6-4824-B420-DDAEADFF873E}
       8b7dcdd0 SymbolicLink  Ip
       84d17500 Device        00000034
       84d159a8 Device        00000027
    03 86df3380 Device        NDMP12
       8515ede0 Device        WMIAdminDevice
       84d1a030 Device        00000041
       8862e040 Device        Video0
       86eaec28 Device        KeyboardClass0
       84d03b00 Device        KMDF0
       84d17230 Device        00000035
       84d156e0 Device        00000028
    04 86e0d030 Device        NDMP13
       86e65030 Device        NDMP20
       85541030 Device        VolMgrControl
       86e6c358 Device        Tun0
       84d1ad68 Device        00000042
       8862ec48 Device        Video1
       88e15158 Device        0000009f
       9badd848 SymbolicLink  MailslotRedirector
       86e1d488 Device        KeyboardClass1
    §
```

When you execute *!object* and specify an object manager directory object, the kernel debugger dumps the contents of the directory according to the way the object manager organizes it internally. For fast lookups, a directory stores objects in a hash table based on a hash of the object names, so the output shows the objects stored in each bucket of the directory's hash table.

As Figure 7-6 illustrates, a device object points back to its driver object, which is how the I/O manager knows which driver routine to call when it receives an I/O request. It uses the device object to find the driver object representing the driver that services the device. It then indexes into the driver object by using the function code supplied in the original request; each function code corresponds to a driver entry point. (The function codes shown in Figure 7-6 are described in the section "IRP Stack Locations" later in this chapter.)

A driver object often has multiple device objects associated with it. The list of device objects represents the physical and logical devices that the driver controls. For example, each partition of a hard disk has a separate device object that contains partition-specific information. However, the same hard disk driver is used to access all partitions. When a driver is unloaded from the system, the I/O manager uses the queue of device objects to determine which devices will be affected by the removal of the driver.

Driver object

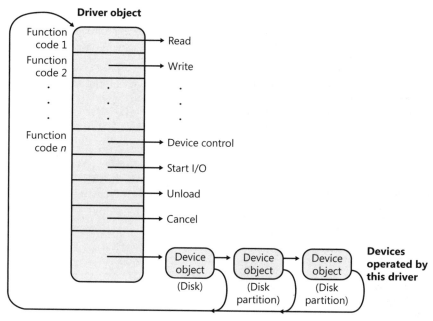

FIGURE 7-6 The driver object

EXPERIMENT: Displaying Driver and Device Objects

You can display driver and device objects with the kernel debugger *!drvobj* and *!devobj* commands, respectively. In the following example, the driver object for the keyboard class driver is examined, and its lone device object viewed:

```
1kd> !drvobj kbdclass
Driver object (86e379a0) is for:
 \Driver\kbdclass
Driver Extension List: (id , addr)

Device Object list:
86e1d488   86eaec28

1kd> !devobj 86eaec28
Device object (86eaec28) is for:
 KeyboardClass0 \Driver\kbdclass DriverObject 86e379a0
Current Irp 00000000 RefCount 0 Type 0000000b Flags 00002044
DevExt 86eaece0 DevObjExt 86eaedc0
ExtensionFlags (0x00000800)
                        Unknown flags 0x00000800
AttachedDevice (Upper) 86e15a40 \Driver\ctrl2cap
AttachedTo (Lower) 86e15020 \Driver\i8042prt
Device queue is not busy
```

Notice that the *!devobj* command also shows you the addresses and names of any device objects that the object you're viewing is layered over (the *AttachedTo* line) as well as the device objects layered on top of the object specified (the *AttachedDevice* line).

Using objects to record information about drivers means that the I/O manager doesn't need to know details about individual drivers. The I/O manager merely follows a pointer to locate a driver, thereby providing a layer of portability and allowing new drivers to be loaded easily. Representing devices and drivers with different objects also makes it easy for the I/O system to assign drivers to control additional or different devices if the system configuration changes.

Opening Devices

File objects are the kernel-mode constructs for handles to files or devices. File objects clearly fit the criteria for objects in Windows: they are system resources that two or more user-mode processes can share, they can have names, they are protected by object-based security, and they support synchronization. Although most shared resources in Windows are memory-based resources, most of those that the I/O system manages are located on physical devices or represent actual physical devices. Despite this difference, shared resources in the I/O system, like those in other components of the Windows executive, are manipulated as objects. (See Chapter 3 for a description of the object manager and Chapter 6 for information on object security.)

File objects provide a memory-based representation of resources that conform to an I/O-centric interface, in which they can be read from or written to. Table 7-1 lists some of the file object's attributes. For specific field declarations and sizes, see the structure definition for FILE_OBJECT in Ntddk.h.

TABLE 7-1 File Object Attributes

Attribute	Purpose
File name	Identifies the physical file that the file object refers to
Current byte offset	Identifies the current location in the file (valid only for synchronous I/O)
Share modes	Indicate whether other callers can open the file for read, write, or delete operations while the current caller is using it
Open mode flags	Indicate whether I/O will be synchronous or asynchronous, cached or noncached, sequential or random, and so on
Pointer to device object	Indicates the type of device the file resides on
Pointer to the volume parameter block (VPB)	Indicates the volume, or partition, that the file resides on
Pointer to section object pointers	Indicates a root structure that describes a mapped/cached file. This structure also contains the shared cache map, which identifies which parts of the file are cached (or rather mapped) by the cache manager and where they reside in the cache
Pointer to private cache map	Used to store per-handle caching information, such as the read patterns for this handle or the page priority for the process.

Attribute	Purpose
List of I/O request packets (IRPs)	If thread-agnostic I/O is used (to be described later) and the file object is associated with a completion port (also described later), this is a list of all the I/O operations that are associated with this file object
I/O completion context	Context information for the current I/O completion port, if one is active
File object extension	Stores the I/O priority for the file and whether share-access checks should be performed on the file object, and contains optional file object extensions that store context-specific information

In order to maintain some level of opacity toward non-kernel code that uses the file object, as well as to enable extending the file object functionality without enlarging the structure, the file object also contains an extension field, which allows for up to six different kinds of additional parameters. These are described in Table 7-2.

TABLE 7-2 File Object Extensions

Extension	Purpose
Transaction parameters	Contains the transaction parameter block, which contains information about a transacted file operation. Returned by *IoGetTransactionParameterBlock*.
Device object hint	Identifies the device object of the filter driver with which this file should be associated. Set with *IoCreateFileEx* or *IoCreateFileSpecifyDeviceObjectHint*.
I/O status block range	Allows applications to lock a user-mode buffer into kernel-mode memory to optimize asynchronous I/Os. See the section on I/O completion port optimizations later in this chapter. Set with *SetFileIoOverlappedRange*.
Generic	Contains filter-driver-specific information, as well as extended create parameters (ECP) that were added by the caller. Set with *IoCreateFileEx*.
Scheduled file I/O	Stores a file's bandwidth reservation information, which is used by the storage system to optimize and guarantee throughput for multimedia applications. See the section on bandwidth reservation later in this chapter. Set with *SetFileBandwidthReservation*.
Symbolic link	Added to the file object upon creation, when a mount point or directory junction is traversed (or a filter explicitly reparses the path). It stores the caller-supplied path, including information about any intermediate junctions, so that if a relative symbolic link is hit, it can walk back through the junctions. See Chapter 11 for more information on NTFS symbolic links, mount points, and directory junctions.

EXPERIMENT: Viewing the File Object Data Structure

You can view the contents of the kernel-mode file object data structure with the kernel debugger's *dt* command:

```
lkd> dt nt!_FILE_OBJECT
   +0x000 Type              : Int2B
   +0x002 Size              : Int2B
   +0x004 DeviceObject      : Ptr32 _DEVICE_OBJECT
   +0x008 Vpb               : Ptr32 _VPB
   +0x00c FsContext         : Ptr32 Void
   +0x010 FsContext2        : Ptr32 Void
   +0x014 SectionObjectPointer : Ptr32 _SECTION_OBJECT_POINTERS
   +0x018 PrivateCacheMap   : Ptr32 Void
   +0x01c FinalStatus       : Int4B
   +0x020 RelatedFileObject : Ptr32 _FILE_OBJECT
   +0x024 LockOperation     : UChar
   +0x025 DeletePending     : UChar
   +0x026 ReadAccess        : UChar
   +0x027 WriteAccess       : UChar
   +0x028 DeleteAccess      : UChar
   +0x029 SharedRead        : UChar
   +0x02a SharedWrite       : UChar
   +0x02b SharedDelete      : UChar
   +0x02c Flags             : Uint4B
   +0x030 FileName          : _UNICODE_STRING
   +0x038 CurrentByteOffset : _LARGE_INTEGER
   +0x040 Waiters           : Uint4B
   +0x044 Busy              : Uint4B
   +0x048 LastLock          : Ptr32 Void
   +0x04c Lock              : _KEVENT
   +0x05c Event             : _KEVENT
   +0x06c CompletionContext : Ptr32 _IO_COMPLETION_CONTEXT
   +0x070 IrpListLock       : Uint4B
   +0x074 IrpList           : _LIST_ENTRY
   +0x07c FileObjectExtension : Ptr32 Void
```

When a caller opens a file or a simple device, the I/O manager returns a handle to a file object. Figure 7-7 illustrates what occurs when a file is opened.

In this example, (1) a C program calls the run-time library function *fopen*, which in turn (2) calls the Windows *CreateFile* function. The Windows subsystem DLL (in this case, Kernel32.dll) then (3) calls the native *NtCreateFile* function in Ntdll.dll. The routine in Ntdll.dll contains the appropriate instruction to cause a transition into kernel mode to the system service dispatcher, which then (4) calls the real *NtCreateFile* routine in Ntoskrnl.exe. (See Chapter 3 for more information about system service dispatching.) Finally, this routine wraps the parameters and flags in such a way that the I/O manager function *IoCreateFile* can actually perform the operation.

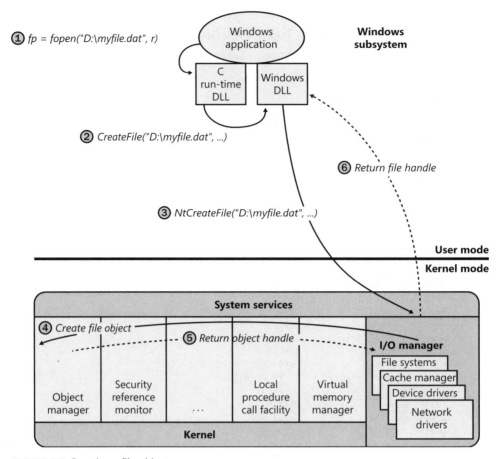

① *fp = fopen("D:\myfile.dat", r)*

② *CreateFile("D:\myfile.dat", ...)*

③ *NtCreateFile("D:\myfile.dat", ...)*

⑥ *Return file handle*

④ *Create file object*

⑤ *Return object handle*

FIGURE 7-7 Opening a file object

Note File objects represent open instances of files, not files themselves. Unlike UNIX systems, which use *vnodes*, Windows does not define the representation of a file; Windows system drivers define their own representations.

Like other executive objects, files are protected by a security descriptor that contains an access-control list (ACL). The I/O manager consults the security subsystem to determine whether a file's ACL allows the process to access the file in the way its thread is requesting. If it does, (5, 6) the object manager grants the access and associates the granted access rights with the file handle that it returns. If this thread or another thread in the process needs to perform additional operations not specified in the original request, the thread must open the same file again with a different request to get another handle, which prompts another security check. (See Chapter 6 for more information about object protection.)

EXPERIMENT: Viewing Device Handles

Any process that has an open handle to a device will have a file object in its handle table corresponding to the open instance. You can view these handles with Process Explorer by selecting a process, checking Show Lower Pane in the View menu and Handles in the Lower Pane View submenu of the View menu. Sort by the Type column and scroll to where you see the handles that represent file objects, which are labeled as File:

In this example the Csrss process has a handle open to a device created by the kernel security device driver (Ksecdd.sys). You can look at the specific file object in the kernel debugger by first identifying the address of the object. The following command reports information on the highlighted handle (handle value 0xF8) in the preceding screen shot, which is in the Csrss.exe process that has a process ID of 504 (0x1f8):

```
lkd> !handle f8 f 1f8
processor number 0, process 000001f8
Searching for Process with Cid == 1f8
PROCESS 88a4a4f0  SessionId: 0  Cid: 01f8    Peb: 7ffdf000  ParentCid: 01ec
    DirBase: cc530060  ObjectTable: 915f8418  HandleCount: 403.
    Image: csrss.exe

Handle table at 98177000 with 403 Entries in use
00f8: Object: 88b99930  GrantedAccess: 193b0022 (Protected) Entry: 915fd1f0
```

```
Object: 88b99930  Type: (8515a040) File
    ObjectHeader: 88b99918 (old version)
    HandleCount: 1  PointerCount: 1
```

Because the object is a file object, you can get information about it with the *!fileobj* command:

```
lkd> !fileobj 88b99930

Device Object: 0x85557a00   \Driver\KSecDD
Vpb is NULL
Event signalled

Flags:  0x40002
    Synchronous IO
    Handle Created

CurrentByteOffset: 0
```

Because a file object is a memory-based representation of a shareable resource and not the resource itself, it's different from other executive objects. A file object contains only data that is unique to an object handle, whereas the file itself contains the data or text to be shared. Each time a thread opens a file, a new file object is created with a new set of handle-specific attributes. For example, the current byte offset attribute refers to the location in the file at which the next read or write operation using that handle will occur. Each handle to a file has a private byte offset even though the underlying file is shared. A file object is also unique to a process, except when a process duplicates a file handle to another process (by using the Windows *DuplicateHandle* function) or when a child process inherits a file handle from a parent process. In these situations, the two processes have separate handles that refer to the same file object.

Although a file handle might be unique to a process, the underlying physical resource is not. Therefore, as with any shared resource, threads must synchronize their access to shareable files, file directories, and devices. If a thread is writing to a file, for example, it should specify exclusive write access when opening the file to prevent other threads from writing to the file at the same time. Alternatively, by using the Windows *LockFile* function, the thread could lock a portion of the file while writing to it.

When a file is opened, the file name includes the name of the device object on which the file resides. For example, the name \Device\HarddiskVolume1\Myfile.dat refers to the file Myfile.dat on the C: volume. The substring \Device\HarddiskVolume1 is the name of the internal Windows device object representing that volume. When opening Myfile.dat, the I/O manager creates a file object and stores a pointer to the Floppy0 device object in the file object and then returns a file handle to the caller. Thereafter, when the caller uses the file handle, the I/O manager can find the HarddiskVolume1 device object directly. Keep in mind that internal Windows device names can't be used in Windows applications—instead, the device name must appear in a special directory in the object manager's namespace, which is \Global??. This directory contains symbolic links to the real, internal Windows device names. Device drivers are responsible for creating links in this directory so that their devices will be accessible to Windows applications. You can examine or even change these links programmatically with the Windows *QueryDosDevice* and *DefineDosDevice* functions.

EXPERIMENT: Viewing Windows Device Name to Windows Device Name Mappings

You can examine the symbolic links that define the Windows device namespace with the WinObj utility from Sysinternals. Run WinObj, and click on the \Global?? directory, as shown here:

Notice the symbolic links on the right. Try double-clicking on the device C:. You should see something like this:

C: is a symbolic link to the internal device named \Device\HarddiskVolume3, or the first volume on the first hard drive in the system. The COM1 entry in WinObj is a symbolic link to \Device\Serial0, and so forth. Try creating your own links with the *subst* command at a command prompt.

I/O Processing

Now that we've covered the structure and types of drivers and the data structures that support them, let's look at how I/O requests flow through the system. I/O requests pass through several predictable stages of processing. The stages vary depending on whether the request is destined for a device operated by a single-layered driver or for a device reached through a multilayered driver. Processing varies further depending on whether the caller specified synchronous or asynchronous I/O, so we'll begin our discussion of I/O types with these two and then move on to others.

Types of I/O

Applications have several options for the I/O requests they issue. For example, they can specify synchronous or asynchronous I/O, I/O that maps a device's data into the application's address space for access via application virtual memory rather than I/O APIs, and I/O that transfers data between a device and noncontiguous application buffers in a single request. Furthermore, the I/O manager gives the drivers the choice of implementing a shortcut I/O interface that can often mitigate IRP allocation for I/O processing. In this section, we'll explain each of these I/O variations.

Synchronous and Asynchronous I/O

Most I/O operations that applications issue are *synchronous*; that is, the application thread waits while the device performs the data transfer and returns a status code when the I/O is complete. The program can then continue and access the transferred data immediately. When used in their simplest form, the Windows *ReadFile* and *WriteFile* functions are executed synchronously. They complete an I/O operation before returning control to the caller.

Asynchronous I/O allows an application to issue an I/O request and then continue executing while the device transfers the data. This type of I/O can improve an application's throughput because it allows the application thread to continue with other work while an I/O operation is in progress. To use asynchronous I/O, you must specify the FILE_FLAG_OVERLAPPED flag when you call the Windows *CreateFile* function. Of course, after issuing an asynchronous I/O operation, the thread must be careful not to access any data from the I/O operation until the device driver has finished the data transfer. The thread must synchronize its execution with the completion of the I/O request by monitoring a handle of a synchronization object (whether that's an event object, an I/O completion port, or the file object itself) that will be signaled when the I/O is complete.

Regardless of the type of I/O request, internally I/O operations issued to a driver on behalf of the application are performed asynchronously; that is, once an I/O request has been initiated, the device driver returns to the I/O system. Whether or not the I/O system returns immediately to the caller depends on whether the file was opened for synchronous or asynchronous I/O. Figure 7-8 illustrates the flow of control when a read operation is initiated. Notice that if a wait is done, which depends on the overlapped flag in the file object, it is done in kernel mode by the *NtReadFile* function.

You can test the status of a pending asynchronous I/O with the Windows *HasOverlappedIo-Completed* function. If you're using I/O completion ports (described in the "I/O Completion Ports" section later in this chapter), you can use the *GetQueuedCompletionStatus* function.

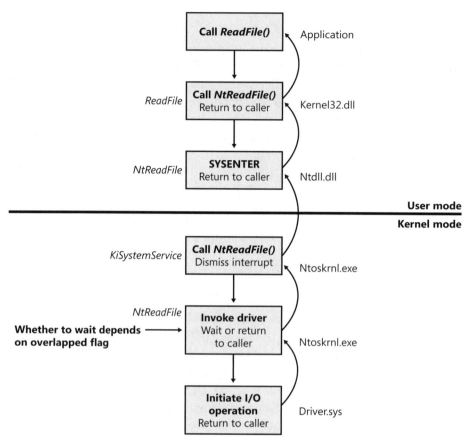

FIGURE 7-8 Control flow for an I/O operation

Fast I/O

Fast I/O is a special mechanism that allows the I/O system to bypass generating an IRP and instead go directly to the file system driver stack to complete an I/O request. (Fast I/O is described in detail in Chapters 10 and 11.) A driver registers its fast I/O entry points by entering them in a structure pointed to by the PFAST_IO_DISPATCH pointer in its driver object.

EXPERIMENT: Looking at a Driver's Registered Fast I/O Routines

The *!drvobj* kernel debugger command can list the fast I/O routines that a driver registers in its driver object. However, typically only file system drivers have any use for fast I/O routines. The following output shows the fast I/O table for the NTFS file system driver object:

```
lkd> !drvobj \FileSystem\Ntfs 2
Driver object (849f27c0) is for:
 \FileSystem\Ntfs
DriverEntry:   82af3b75     Ntfs!GsDriverEntry
DriverStartIo: 00000000
DriverUnload:  00000000
AddDevice:     00000000

Dispatch routines:
[00] IRP_MJ_CREATE                      82a9200a     Ntfs!NtfsFsdCreate

Fast I/O routines:
FastIoCheckIfPossible               82a7f87b     Ntfs!NtfsFastIoCheckIfPossible
FastIoRead                          82a7ec38     Ntfs!NtfsCopyReadA
FastIoWrite                         82a7ff53     Ntfs!NtfsCopyWriteA
FastIoQueryBasicInfo                82a86c3a     Ntfs!NtfsFastQueryBasicInfo
FastIoQueryStandardInfo             82a86aa6     Ntfs!NtfsFastQueryStdInfo
FastIoLock                          82a79f41     Ntfs!NtfsFastLock
FastIoUnlockSingle                  82a79d75     Ntfs!NtfsFastUnlockSingle
FastIoUnlockAll                     82acb7b3     Ntfs!NtfsFastUnlockAll
FastIoUnlockAllByKey                82acb958     Ntfs!NtfsFastUnlockAllByKey
ReleaseFileForNtCreateSection       82a1c904     Ntfs!NtfsReleaseForCreateSection
FastIoQueryNetworkOpenInfo          82a78d84     Ntfs!NtfsFastQueryNetworkOpenInfo
AcquireForModWrite                  82a0a892     Ntfs!NtfsAcquireFileForModWrite
MdlRead                             82acb0d8     Ntfs!NtfsMdlReadA
MdlReadComplete                     81c5aad6     nt!FsRtlMdlReadCompleteDev
PrepareMdlWrite                     82acb31f     Ntfs!NtfsPrepareMdlWriteA
MdlWriteComplete                    81dffa72     nt!FsRtlMdlWriteCompleteDev
FastIoQueryOpen                     82a72d03     Ntfs!NtfsNetworkOpenCreate
AcquireForCcFlush                   82a18b35     Ntfs!NtfsAcquireFileForCcFlush
ReleaseForCcFlush                   82a18a9c     Ntfs!NtfsReleaseFileForCcFlush
```

The output shows that NTFS has registered its *NtfsCopyReadA* routine as the fast I/O table's *FastIoRead* entry. As the name of this fast I/O entry implies, the I/O manager calls this function when issuing a read I/O request if the file is cached. If the call doesn't succeed, the standard IRP path is selected.

Mapped File I/O and File Caching

Mapped file I/O is an important feature of the I/O system, one that the I/O system and the memory manager produce jointly. (See Chapter 9 for details on how mapped files are implemented.) *Mapped file I/O* refers to the ability to view a file residing on disk as part of

a process's virtual memory. A program can access the file as a large array without buffering data or performing disk I/O. The program accesses memory, and the memory manager uses its paging mechanism to load the correct page from the disk file. If the application writes to its virtual address space, the memory manager writes the changes back to the file as part of normal paging.

Mapped file I/O is available in user mode through the Windows *CreateFileMapping* and *MapViewOfFile* functions. Within the operating system, mapped file I/O is used for important operations such as file caching and image activation (loading and running executable programs). The other major consumer of mapped file I/O is the cache manager. File systems use the cache manager to map file data in virtual memory to provide better response time for I/O-bound programs. As the caller uses the file, the memory manager brings accessed pages into memory. Whereas most caching systems allocate a fixed number of bytes for caching files in memory, the Windows cache grows or shrinks depending on how much memory is available. This size variability is possible because the cache manager relies on the memory manager to automatically expand (or shrink) the size of the cache, using the normal working set mechanisms explained in Chapter 9. By taking advantage of the memory manager's paging system, the cache manager avoids duplicating the work that the memory manager already performs. (The workings of the cache manager are explained in detail in Chapter 10.)

Scatter/Gather I/O

Windows also supports a special kind of high-performance I/O that is called *scatter/gather*, available via the Windows *ReadFileScatter* and *WriteFileGather* functions. These functions allow an application to issue a single read or write from more than one buffer in virtual memory to a contiguous area of a file on disk instead of issuing a separate I/O request for each buffer. To use scatter/gather I/O, the file must be opened for noncached I/O, the user buffers being used have to be page-aligned, and the I/Os must be asynchronous (overlapped). Furthermore, if the I/O is directed at a mass storage device, the I/O must be aligned on a device sector boundary and have a length that is a multiple of the sector size.

I/O Request Packets

The I/O request packet (IRP) is where the I/O system stores information it needs to process an I/O request. When a thread calls an I/O service, the I/O manager constructs an IRP to represent the operation as it progresses through the I/O system. If possible, the I/O manager allocates IRPs from one of two per-processor IRP nonpaged look-aside lists: the small-IRP look-aside list stores IRPs with one stack location (IRP stack locations are described shortly), and the large-IRP look-aside list contains IRPs with multiple stack locations. These lists are backed by global look-aside lists as well, allowing efficient cross-CPU IRP flow. By default, the system stores IRPs with 10 stack locations on the large-IRP look-aside list, but once per minute the system adjusts the number of stack locations allocated between the default and a maximum of 20, based on how many stack locations have been required. If an IRP requires

more stack locations than are contained in the IRPs on the large-IRP look-aside list, the I/O manager allocates IRPs from nonpaged pool. After allocating and initializing an IRP, the I/O manager stores a pointer to the caller's file object in the IRP.

> **Note** If defined, the DWORD registry value HKLM\System\CurrentControlSet\Session Manager\
> I/O System\LargIrpStackLocations specifies how many stack locations are contained in IRPs
> stored on the large-IRP look-aside list.

Figure 7-9 shows a sample I/O request that demonstrates the relationship between an IRP and the file, device, and driver objects described in the preceding sections. Although this example shows an I/O request to a single-layered device driver, most I/O operations aren't this direct; they involve one or more layered drivers. (This case will be shown later in this section.)

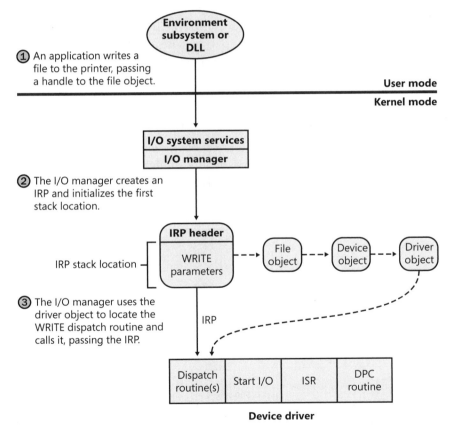

FIGURE 7-9 Data structures involved in a single-layered driver I/O request

IRP Stack Locations

An IRP consists of two parts: a fixed header (often referred to as the IRP's *body*) and one or more stack locations. The fixed portion contains information such as the type and size of the request, whether the request is synchronous or asynchronous, a pointer to a buffer for buffered I/O, and state information that changes as the request progresses. An IRP stack location contains a function code (consisting of a major code and a minor code), function-specific parameters, and a pointer to the caller's file object. The *major function code* identifies which of a driver's dispatch routines the I/O manager invokes when passing an IRP to a driver. An optional *minor function code* sometimes serves as a modifier of the major function code. Power and Plug and Play commands always have minor function codes.

Most drivers specify dispatch routines to handle only a subset of possible major function codes, including create (open), read, write, device I/O control, power, Plug and Play, System (for WMI commands), and close. (See the following experiment for a complete listing of major function codes.) File system drivers are an example of a driver type that often fills in most or all of its dispatch entry points with functions. The I/O manager sets any dispatch entry points that a driver doesn't fill to point to its own *IopInvalidDeviceRequest*, which returns an error code to the caller indicating that the function specified for the device is invalid.

EXPERIMENT: Looking at Driver Dispatch Routines

You can obtain a listing of the functions a driver has defined for its dispatch routines by entering a **7** after the driver object's name (or address) in the *!drvobj* kernel debugger command. The following output shows that drivers support 28 IRP types.

```
lkd> !drvobj Kbdclass 7
Driver object (84b706b8) is for:
 \Driver\kbdclass
Driver Extension List: (id , addr)

Device Object list:
84abfd68  84baf030  84b84880

DriverEntry:   8ed1c802     kbdclass!GsDriverEntry
DriverStartIo: 00000000
DriverUnload:  00000000
AddDevice:     8ed1b7a0     kbdclass!KeyboardAddDevice

Dispatch routines:
[00] IRP_MJ_CREATE                8ed168f4     kbdclass!KeyboardClassCreate
[01] IRP_MJ_CREATE_NAMED_PIPE     81c63fef     nt!IopInvalidDeviceRequest
[02] IRP_MJ_CLOSE                 8ed16b00     kbdclass!KeyboardClassClose
[03] IRP_MJ_READ                  8ed175bc     kbdclass!KeyboardClassRead
[04] IRP_MJ_WRITE                 81c63fef     nt!IopInvalidDeviceRequest
[05] IRP_MJ_QUERY_INFORMATION     81c63fef     nt!IopInvalidDeviceRequest
[06] IRP_MJ_SET_INFORMATION       81c63fef     nt!IopInvalidDeviceRequest
[07] IRP_MJ_QUERY_EA              81c63fef     nt!IopInvalidDeviceRequest
[08] IRP_MJ_SET_EA                81c63fef     nt!IopInvalidDeviceRequest
```

```
[09] IRP_MJ_FLUSH_BUFFERS                    8ed1689a      kbdclass!KeyboardClassFlush
[0a] IRP_MJ_QUERY_VOLUME_INFORMATION         81c63fef      nt!IopInvalidDeviceRequest
[0b] IRP_MJ_SET_VOLUME_INFORMATION           81c63fef      nt!IopInvalidDeviceRequest
[0c] IRP_MJ_DIRECTORY_CONTROL                81c63fef      nt!IopInvalidDeviceRequest
[0d] IRP_MJ_FILE_SYSTEM_CONTROL              81c63fef      nt!IopInvalidDeviceRequest
[0e] IRP_MJ_DEVICE_CONTROL                   8ed1a7f8      kbdclass!KeyboardClassDeviceControl
[0f] IRP_MJ_INTERNAL_DEVICE_CONTROL          8ed1a006      kbdclass!KeyboardClassPassThrough
[10] IRP_MJ_SHUTDOWN                         81c63fef      nt!IopInvalidDeviceRequest
[11] IRP_MJ_LOCK_CONTROL                     81c63fef      nt!IopInvalidDeviceRequest
[12] IRP_MJ_CLEANUP                          8ed16162      kbdclass!KeyboardClassCleanup
[13] IRP_MJ_CREATE_MAILSLOT                  81c63fef      nt!IopInvalidDeviceRequest
[14] IRP_MJ_QUERY_SECURITY                   81c63fef      nt!IopInvalidDeviceRequest
[15] IRP_MJ_SET_SECURITY                     81c63fef      nt!IopInvalidDeviceRequest
[16] IRP_MJ_POWER                            8ed1aeac      kbdclass!KeyboardClassPower
[17] IRP_MJ_SYSTEM_CONTROL                   8ed1a688      kbdclass!KeyboardClassSystemControl
[18] IRP_MJ_DEVICE_CHANGE                    81c63fef      nt!IopInvalidDeviceRequest
[19] IRP_MJ_QUERY_QUOTA                      81c63fef      nt!IopInvalidDeviceRequest
[1a] IRP_MJ_SET_QUOTA                        81c63fef      nt!IopInvalidDeviceRequest
[1b] IRP_MJ_PNP                              8ed1710e      kbdclass!KeyboardPnP
```

While active, each IRP is usually stored in an IRP list associated with the thread that requested the I/O. This arrangement allows the I/O system to find and cancel any outstanding IRPs if a thread terminates or is terminated with outstanding I/O requests.

EXPERIMENT: Looking at a Thread's Outstanding IRPs

When you use the *!thread* command, it prints any IRPs associated with the thread. Run the kernel debugger with live debugging, and locate the service control manager process (Services.exe) in the output generated by the *!process* command:

```
lkd> !process 0 0
**** NT ACTIVE PROCESS DUMP ****
...
PROCESS 8623b840  SessionId: 0  Cid: 0270    Peb: 7ffd6000  ParentCid: 0210
    DirBase: ce21e080  ObjectTable: 964c06a0  HandleCount: 198.
    Image: services.exe
...
```

Then dump the threads for the process by executing the *!process* command on the process object. You should see many threads, with most of them having IRPs reported in the IRP List area of the thread information (note that the debugger will show only the first 17 IRPs for a thread that has more than 17 outstanding I/O requests):

```
lkd> !process 8623b840
PROCESS 8623b840  SessionId: 0  Cid: 0270    Peb: 7ffd6000  ParentCid: 0210
    DirBase: ce21e080  ObjectTable: 964c06a0  HandleCount: 198.
    Image: services.exe
    VadRoot 862b1358 Vads 71 Clone 0 Private 466. Modified 14. Locked 2.
    DeviceMap 8b0087d8
```

```
    ...
        THREAD 86a1d248  Cid 0270.053c  Teb: 7ffdc000 Win32Thread: 00000000 WAIT:
(UserRequest) UserMode Alertable
            86a40ca0  NotificationEvent
            86a40490  NotificationEvent
        IRP List:
            86a81190: (0006,0094) Flags: 00060900  Mdl: 00000000
    ...
```

Choose an IRP, and examine it with the *!irp* command:

```
lkd> !irp 86a81190
Irp is active with 1 stacks 1 is current (= 0x86a81200)
 No Mdl: No System Buffer: Thread 86a1d248:  Irp stack trace.
     cmd  flg cl Device   File      Completion-Context
>[  3, 0]   0  1 86156328 86a4e7a0 00000000-00000000    pending
            \FileSystem\Npfs
            Args: 00000800 00000000 00000000 00000000
```

This IRP has a major function of 3, which corresponds to IRP_MJ_READ. It has one stack
location and is targeted at a device owned by the Npfs driver (the Named Pipe File
System driver). (Npfs is described in Chapter 12.)

IRP Buffer Management

When an application or a device driver indirectly creates an IRP by using the *NtReadFile*,
NtWriteFile, or *NtDeviceIoControlFile* system services (or the Windows API functions corre-
sponding to these services, which are *ReadFile*, *WriteFile*, and *DeviceIoControl*), the I/O man-
ager determines whether it needs to participate in the management of the caller's input or
output buffers. The I/O manager performs three types of buffer management:

- **Buffered I/O** The I/O manager allocates a buffer in nonpaged pool of equal size to
 the caller's buffer. For write operations, the I/O manager copies the caller's buffer data
 into the allocated buffer when creating the IRP. For read operations, the I/O manager
 copies data from the allocated buffer to the user's buffer when the IRP completes and
 then frees the allocated buffer.

- **Direct I/O** When the I/O manager creates the IRP, it locks the user's buffer into mem-
 ory (makes it nonpaged). When the I/O manager has finished using the IRP, it unlocks
 the buffer. The I/O manager stores a description of the memory in the form of a *mem-
 ory descriptor list* (MDL). An MDL specifies the physical memory occupied by a buffer.
 (See the WDK for more information on MDLs.) Devices that perform direct memory
 access (DMA) require only physical descriptions of buffers, so an MDL is sufficient
 for the operation of such devices. (Devices that support DMA transfer data directly
 between the device and the computer's memory, without using the CPU.) If a driver

must access the contents of a buffer, however, it can map the buffer into the system's address space.

- **Neither I/O** The I/O manager doesn't perform any buffer management. Instead, buffer management is left to the discretion of the device driver, which can choose to manually perform the steps the I/O manager performs with the other buffer management types.

For each type of buffer management, the I/O manager places applicable references in the IRP to the locations of the input and output buffers. The type of buffer management the I/O manager performs depends on the type of buffer management a driver requests for each type of operation. A driver registers the type of buffer management it desires for read and write operations in the device object that represents the device. Device I/O control operations (those performed by *NtDeviceIoControlFile*) are specified with driver-defined I/O control codes, and a control code includes a description of the buffer management the I/O manager should use when issuing IRPs that contain that code.

Drivers commonly use buffered I/O when callers transfer requests smaller than one page (4 KB on x86 processors) and use direct I/O for larger requests. A page is approximately the buffer size at which the trade-off between the copy operation of buffered I/O matches the overhead of the memory lock performed by direct I/O. File system drivers commonly use neither I/O because no buffer management overhead is incurred when data can be copied from the file system cache into the caller's original buffer. The reason that most drivers don't use neither I/O is that a pointer to a caller's buffer is valid only while a thread of the caller's process is executing. If a driver must transfer data from or to a device in an ISR or a DPC routine, it must ensure that the caller's data is accessible from any process context, which means that the buffer must have a system virtual address.

Drivers that use neither I/O to access buffers that might be located in user space must take special care to ensure that buffer addresses are both valid and do not reference kernel-mode memory. Failure to do so could result in crashes or in security vulnerabilities, where applications have access to kernel-mode memory or can inject code into the kernel. The *ProbeForRead* and *ProbeForWrite* functions that the kernel makes available to drivers verify that a buffer resides entirely in the user-mode portion of the address space. To avoid a crash from referencing an invalid user-mode address, drivers can access user-mode buffers from within exception-handling code (called try/except blocks) that catch any invalid memory faults and translate them into error codes to return to the application. Additionally, drivers should also capture all input data into a kernel buffer instead of relying on user-mode addresses, since the caller could always modify the data behind the driver's back, even if the memory address itself is still valid.

I/O Request to a Single-Layered Driver

This section traces a synchronous I/O request to a single-layered kernel-mode device driver. Handling a synchronous I/O to a single-layered driver consists of seven steps:

1. The I/O request passes through a subsystem DLL.

2. The subsystem DLL calls the I/O manager's *NtWriteFile* service.

3. The I/O manager allocates an IRP describing the request and sends it to the driver (a device driver in this case) by calling its own *IoCallDriver* function.

4. The driver transfers the data in the IRP to the device and starts the I/O operation.

5. The device signals I/O completion by interrupting the CPU.

6. The device driver services the interrupt.

7. The driver calls the I/O manager's *IoCompleteRequest* function to inform it that it has finished processing the IRP's request, and the I/O manager completes the I/O request.

These seven steps are illustrated in Figure 7-10.

FIGURE 7-10 Issuing and completing a synchronous I/O request

Now that we've seen how an I/O is initiated, let's take a closer look at interrupt processing and I/O completion.

Servicing an Interrupt

After an I/O device completes a data transfer, it interrupts for service and the Windows kernel, I/O manager, and device driver are called into action. Figure 7-11 illustrates the first phase of the process. (Chapter 3 describes the interrupt dispatching mechanism, including DPCs. We've included a brief recap here because DPCs are key to I/O processing.)

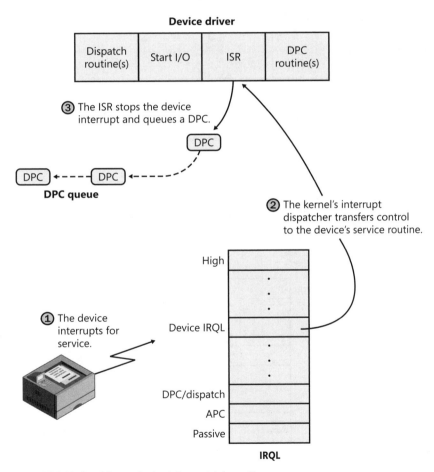

FIGURE 7-11 Servicing a device interrupt (phase 1)

When a device interrupt occurs, the processor transfers control to the kernel trap handler, which indexes into its interrupt dispatch table to locate the ISR for the device. ISRs in Windows typically handle device interrupts in two steps. When an ISR is first invoked, it usually remains at device IRQL only long enough to capture the device status and then stop the device's interrupt. It then queues a DPC and exits, dismissing the interrupt. Later, when the

DPC routine is called, the device finishes processing the interrupt. When that's done, the device calls the I/O manager to complete the I/O and dispose of the IRP. It might also start the next I/O request that is waiting in the device queue.

The advantage of using a DPC to perform most of the device servicing is that any blocked interrupt whose priority lies between the device IRQL and the DPC/dispatch IRQL is allowed to occur before the lower-priority DPC processing occurs. Intermediate-level interrupts are thus serviced more promptly than they otherwise would be. This second phase of an I/O (the DPC processing) is illustrated in Figure 7-12.

FIGURE 7-12 Servicing a device interrupt (phase 2)

Completing an I/O Request

After a device driver's DPC routine has executed, some work still remains before the I/O request can be considered finished. This third stage of I/O processing is called *I/O completion* and is initiated when a driver calls *IoCompleteRequest* to inform the I/O manager that it has completed processing the request specified in the IRP (and the stack location that it owns). The steps I/O completion entails vary with different I/O operations. For example, all the I/O services record the outcome of the operation in an *I/O status block*, a data structure the caller supplies. Similarly, some services that perform buffered I/O require the I/O system to return data to the calling thread.

In both cases, the I/O system must copy some data that is stored in system memory into the caller's virtual address space. If the IRP completed synchronously, the caller's address space is current and directly accessible, but if the IRP completed asynchronously, the I/O manager must delay IRP completion until it can access the caller's address space. To gain access to the caller's virtual address space, the I/O manager must transfer the data "in the context of the caller's thread"—that is, while the caller's thread is executing (which means that caller's process is the current process and has its address space active on the processor). It does so by queuing a kernel-mode asynchronous procedure call (APC) to the thread. This process is illustrated in Figure 7-13.

FIGURE 7-13 Completing an I/O request (phase 1)

As explained in Chapter 3, APCs execute in the context of a particular thread, whereas a DPC executes in arbitrary thread context, meaning that the DPC routine can't touch the user-mode process address space. Remember too that DPCs have a higher software interrupt priority than APCs.

The next time that thread begins to execute at low IRQL (below DISPATCH_LEVEL), the pending APC is delivered. The kernel transfers control to the I/O manager's APC routine, which copies the data (if any) and the return status into the original caller's address space, frees the IRP representing the I/O operation, and either sets the caller's file handle (and any caller-supplied event) to the signaled state for synchronous I/O, or queues an entry to the caller's I/O completion port. The I/O is now considered complete. The original caller or any other threads that are waiting on the file (or other object) handle are released from their waiting state and readied for execution. Figure 7-14 illustrates the second stage of I/O completion.

FIGURE 7-14 Completing an I/O request (phase 2)

A final note about I/O completion: the asynchronous I/O functions *ReadFileEx* and *WriteFileEx* allow a caller to supply a user-mode APC as a parameter. If the caller does so, the I/O manager queues this APC to the caller's thread APC queue as the last step of I/O completion. This feature allows a caller to specify a subroutine to be called when an I/O request is completed or canceled. User-mode APC completion routines execute in the context of the requesting thread and are delivered only when the thread enters an alertable wait state (such as calling the Windows *SleepEx*, *WaitForSingleObjectEx*, or *WaitForMultipleObjectsEx* function).

Synchronization

Drivers must synchronize their access to global driver data and hardware registers for two reasons:

- The execution of a driver can be preempted by higher-priority threads and time-slice (or quantum) expiration or can be interrupted by interrupts.

- On multiprocessor systems, Windows can run driver code simultaneously on more than one processor.

Without synchronization, corruption could occur—for example, because device driver code running at a passive IRQL when a caller initiates an I/O operation can be interrupted by a device interrupt, causing the device driver's ISR to execute while its own device driver is already running. If the device driver was modifying data that its ISR also modifies, such as device registers, heap storage, or static data, the data can become corrupted when the ISR executes. Figure 7-15 illustrates this problem.

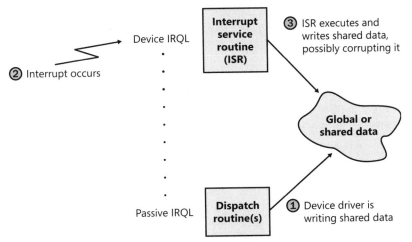

FIGURE 7-15 Concurrent access to shared data by a device driver dispatch routine and ISR

To avoid this situation, a device driver written for Windows must synchronize its access to any data that the device driver shares with its ISR. Before attempting to update shared data, the device driver must lock out all other threads (or CPUs, in the case of a multiprocessor system) to prevent them from updating the same data structure.

The Windows kernel provides a special synchronization routine called *KeSynchronize- Execution* that device drivers call when they access data that their ISRs also access. This kernel synchronization routine keeps the ISR from executing while the shared data is being accessed. A driver can also use *KeAcquireInterruptSpinLock* to access an interrupt object's spinlock directly, although it's generally faster to rely on *KeSynchronizeExecution* for synchronization with an ISR.

By now, you should realize that although ISRs require special attention, any data that a device driver uses is subject to being accessed by the same device driver running on another processor. Therefore, it's critical for device driver code to synchronize its use of any global or shared data (or any accesses to the physical device itself). If the ISR uses that data, the device driver must use *KeSynchronizeExecution*; otherwise, the device driver can use standard kernel spinlocks.

I/O Requests to Layered Drivers

The preceding section showed how an I/O request to a simple device controlled by a single device driver is handled. I/O processing for file-based devices or for requests to other layered drivers happens in much the same way. The major difference is, obviously, that one or more additional layers of processing are added to the model.

Figure 7-16 shows how an asynchronous I/O request travels through layered drivers. It uses as an example a disk controlled by a file system.

Once again, the I/O manager receives the request and creates an I/O request packet to represent it. This time, however, it delivers the packet to a file system driver. The file system driver exercises great control over the I/O operation at that point. Depending on the type of request the caller made, the file system can send the same IRP to the disk driver or it can generate additional IRPs and send them separately to the disk driver.

EXPERIMENT: Viewing a Device Stack

The kernel debugger command *!devstack* shows you the device stack of layered device objects associated with a specified device object. This example shows the device stack associated with a device object, \device\keyboardclass0, which is owned by the keyboard class driver:

```
lkd> !devstack keyboardclass0
  !DevObj           !DrvObj              !DevExt           ObjectName
  fffffa800a5e2040  \Driver\Ctrl2cap     fffffa800a5e2190
> fffffa800a612ce0  \Driver\kbdclass     fffffa800a612e30  KeyboardClass0
  fffffa800a612040  \Driver\i8042prt     fffffa800a612190
  fffffa80076e0a00  \Driver\ACPI         fffffa80076f3a90  0000005c
!DevNode fffffa800770f750 :
  DeviceInst is "ACPI\PNP0303\4&b0a2531&0"
  ServiceName is "i8042prt"
```

The output highlights the entry associated with KeyboardClass0 with the ">" prefix. The entries above that line are drivers layered above the keyboard class driver, and those below are layered beneath it. In general, IRPs flow from the top of the stack to the bottom.

The file system is most likely to reuse an IRP if the request it receives translates into a single straightforward request to a device. For example, if an application issues a read request for the first 512 bytes in a file stored on a volume, the NTFS file system would simply call the volume manager driver, asking it to read one sector from the volume, beginning at the file's starting location.

To accommodate its reuse by multiple drivers in a request to layered drivers, an IRP contains a series of *IRP stack locations* (not to be confused with the stack used by threads to store function parameters and return addresses). These data areas, one for every driver that will be called, contain the information that each driver needs to execute its part of the request—for example, function code, parameters, and driver context information. As Figure 7-16 illustrates, additional stack locations are filled in as the IRP passes from one driver to the next. You can think of an IRP as being similar to a stack in the way data is added to it and removed from it during its lifetime. However, an IRP isn't associated with any particular process, and its allocated size doesn't grow or shrink. The I/O manager allocates an IRP from one of its IRP look-aside lists or nonpaged system memory at the beginning of the I/O operation.

FIGURE 7-16 Queuing an asynchronous request to layered drivers

EXPERIMENT: Examining IRPs

In this experiment, you'll find an uncompleted IRP on the system, and you'll determine the IRP type, the device at which it's directed, the driver that manages the device, the thread that issued the IRP, and what process the thread belongs to.

At any point in time, there are at least a few uncompleted IRPs on a system. This is because there are many devices to which applications can issue IRPs that a driver will only complete when a particular event occurs, such as data becoming available. One example is a blocking read from a network endpoint. You can see the outstanding IRPs on a system with the *!irpfind* kernel debugger command:

```
lkd> !irpfind

Scanning large pool allocation table for Tag: Irp? (86c16000 : 86d16000)
Searching NonPaged pool (80000000 : ffc00000) for Tag: Irp?

  Irp      [ Thread ] irpStack: (Mj,Mn)   DevObj  [Driver]          MDL Process
862d2380 [8666dc68] irpStack: ( c, 2)   84a6f020 [ \FileSystem\Ntfs]
862d2bb0 [864e3d78] irpStack: ( e,20)   86171348 [ \Driver\AFD] 0x864dbd90
862d4518 [865f7600] irpStack: ( d, 0)   86156328 [ \FileSystem\Npfs]
862d4688 [867133f0] irpStack: ( 3, 0)   86156328 [ \FileSystem\Npfs]
862dd008 [00000000] Irp is complete (CurrentLocation 4 > StackCount 3) 0x00420000
862dee28 [864fc030] irpStack: ( 3, 0)   84baf030 [ \Driver\kbdclass]
```

The entry in bold in the output describes an IRP that is directed at the Kbdclass driver, so it is likely that the IRP was issued by the Windows subsystem raw input thread that reads keyboard input. Examining the IRP with the *!irp* command reveals the following:

```
lkd> !irp 862dee28
Irp is active with 3 stacks 3 is current (= 0x862deee0)
 No Mdl: System buffer=864f5108: Thread 864fc030:  Irp stack trace.
    cmd  flg cl Device   File     Completion-Context
 [  0, 0]   0  0 00000000 00000000 00000000-00000000

          Args: 00000000 00000000 00000000 00000000
 [  0, 0]   0  0 00000000 00000000 00000000-00000000

          Args: 00000000 00000000 00000000 00000000
>[  3, 0]   0  1 84baf030 864f52f8 00000000-00000000    pending
          \Driver\kbdclass
          Args: 00000078 00000000 00000000 00000000
```

The active stack location is at the bottom. (The debugger shows the active location with a ">" prefix.) It has a major function of 3, which corresponds to IRP_MJ_READ.

The next step is to see what device object the IRP is targeting by executing the *!devobj* command on the device object address in the active stack location.

```
1kd> !devobj 84baf030
Device object (84baf030) is for:
 KeyboardClass1 \Driver\kbdclass DriverObject 84b706b8
Current Irp 00000000 RefCount 0 Type 0000000b Flags 00002044
Dacl 8b0538b8 DevExt 84baf0e8 DevObjExt 84baf1c8
ExtensionFlags (0x00000800)
                               Unknown flags 0x00000800
AttachedTo (Lower) 84badaa0 \Driver\TermDD
Device queue is not busy.
```

The device at which the IRP is targeted is KeyboardClass1. The presence of a device object owned by the Termdd driver attached beneath it reveals that it is the device that represents keyboard input from a Terminal Server client, not the physical keyboard.

We can see details about the thread and process that issued the IRP by using the *!thread* and *!process* commands:

```
1kd> !thread 864fc030
THREAD 864fc030  Cid 01d4.0234  Teb: 7ffd9000 Win32Thread: ffac4008 WAIT:
(WrUserRequest) KernelMode Alertable
    8623c620  SynchronizationEvent
    864fc3a8  NotificationTimer
    864fc378  SynchronizationTimer
    864fc360  SynchronizationEvent
IRP List:
    86af0e28: (0006,01d8) Flags: 00060970  Mdl: 00000000
    86503958: (0006,0268) Flags: 00060970  Mdl: 00000000
    862dee28: (0006,01d8) Flags: 00060970  Mdl: 00000000
Not impersonating
DeviceMap               8b0087d8
Owning Process          0       Image:          <Unknown>
Attached Process        864d2d90    Image:        csrss.exe
Wait Start TickCount    171909      Ticks: 29 (0:00:00:00.452)
Context Switch Count    121222
UserTime                00:00:00.000
KernelTime              00:00:00.717
Win32 Start Address 0x764d9a30
Stack Init 96f46000 Current 96f45c28 Base 96f46000 Limit 96f43000 Call 0
Priority 15 BasePriority 13 PriorityDecrement 0 IoPriority 2 PagePriority 5

1kd> !process 864d2d90
PROCESS 864d2d90  SessionId: 1 Cid: 0208    Peb: 7ffdf000  ParentCid: 0200
    DirBase: ce21e0a0  ObjectTable: 964a6e68  HandleCount: 284.
    Image: csrss.exe
```

Locating the thread in Process Explorer by opening the Properties dialog box for Csrss.exe and going to the Threads tab confirms, through the names of the functions on its stack, the role of the thread as a raw input thread for the Windows subsystem:

After the disk driver finishes a data transfer, the disk interrupts and the I/O completes, as shown in Figure 7-17.

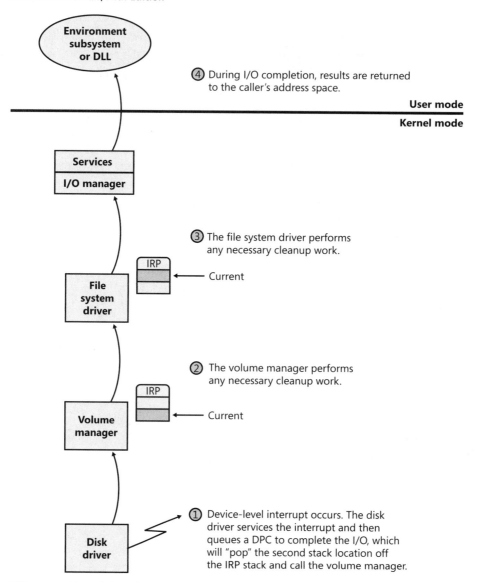

FIGURE 7-17 Completing a layered I/O request

As an alternative to reusing a single IRP, a file system can establish a group of *associated* IRPs that work in parallel on a single I/O request. For example, if the data to be read from a file is dispersed across the disk, the file system driver might create several IRPs, each of which reads some portion of the request from a different sector. This queuing is illustrated in Figure 7-18.

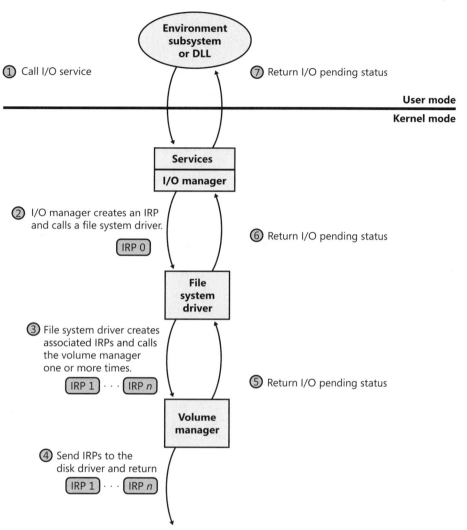

FIGURE 7-18 Queuing associated IRPs

The file system driver delivers the associated IRPs to the volume manager, which in turn sends them to the disk device driver, which queues them to the disk device. They are processed one at a time, and the file system driver keeps track of the returned data. When all the associated IRPs complete, the I/O system completes the original IRP and returns to the caller, as shown in Figure 7-19.

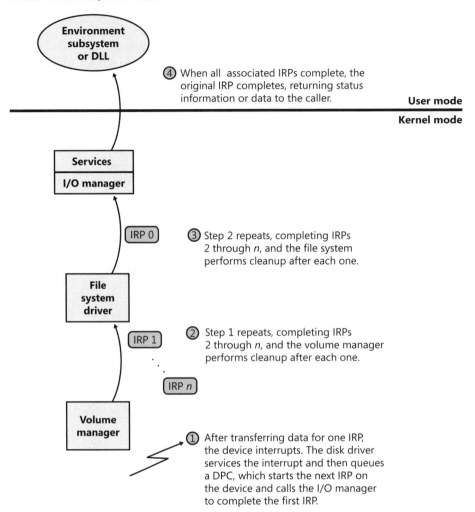

FIGURE 7-19 Completing associated IRPs

Note All Windows file system drivers that manage disk-based file systems are part of a stack of drivers that is at least three layers deep: the file system driver sits at the top, a volume manager in the middle, and a disk driver at the bottom. In addition, any number of filter drivers can be interspersed above and below these drivers. For clarity, the preceding example of layered I/O requests includes only a file system driver and the volume manager driver. See Chapter 8, on storage management, for more information.

Thread Agnostic I/O

In the I/O models described thus far, IRPs are queued to the thread that initiated the I/O and are completed by the I/O manager issuing an APC to that thread so that process or thread-specific context is accessible by completion processing. Thread-specific I/O processing is usually sufficient for the performance and scalability needs of most applications, but Windows also includes support for *thread agnostic I/O* via two mechanisms:

- I/O completion ports, which are described at length later in this chapter
- Locking the user buffer into memory and mapping it into the system address space

With I/O completion ports, the application decides when it wants to check for the completion of I/O, so the thread that happens to have issued an I/O request is not necessarily relevant because any other thread can perform the completion request. As such, instead of completing the IRP inside the specific thread's context, it can be completed in the context of any thread that has access to the completion port.

Likewise, with a locked and kernel-mapped version of the user buffer, there's no need to be in the same memory address space as the issuing thread because the kernel can access the memory from arbitrary contexts. Applications can enable this mechanism by using *SetFileIoOverlappedRange*.

With both completion port I/O and I/O on file buffers set by *SetFileIoOverlappedRange*, the I/O manager associates the IRPs with the file object to which they have been issued instead of the issuing thread. The *!fileobj* extension in WinDbg will show an IRP list for file objects that are used with these mechanisms.

In the next sections, we'll see how thread agnostic I/O increases the reliability and performance of applications on Windows.

I/O Cancellation

While there are many ways in which IRP processing occurs and various methods to complete an I/O request, a great many I/O processing operations actually end in cancellation rather than completion. For example, a device may require removal while IRPs are still active, or the user might cancel a long-running operation to a device, for example a network operation. Another situation requiring I/O cancellation support is thread and process termination. When a thread exits, the I/Os associated with the thread must be cancelled, since the I/O operation is no longer relevant.

The Windows I/O manager, working with drivers, must deal with these requests efficiently and reliably in order to provide a smooth user experience. Drivers manage this need by registering a *cancel routine* for their cancellable I/O operations, which is invoked by the I/O manager to cancel an I/O operation. When drivers fail to play their role in these scenarios,

users may experience unkillable processes, which have disappeared visually but linger and still appear in Task Manager or Process Explorer. (See Chapter 5 for more information on processes and threads.)

User-Initiated I/O Cancellation

Most software uses one thread to handle user interface (UI) input and one or more threads to perform work, including I/O. In some cases, when a user wants to abort an operation he initiated in the UI, an application might need to cancel outstanding I/O operations. Operations that complete quickly might not require cancellation, but for operations that take arbitrary amounts of time—like large data transfers or network operations— Windows provides support for cancelling both synchronous operations and asynchronous operations. A thread can cancel its own outstanding asynchronous I/Os by calling *CancelIo*. It can cancel all asynchronous I/Os issued to a specific file handle, regardless of by which thread, with *CancelIoEx*. *CancelIoEx* also works on operations associated with I/O completion ports through the thread-agnostic support in Windows that was mentioned earlier because the I/O system keeps track of a completion port's outstanding I/Os by linking them with the completion port.

For cancelling synchronous I/Os, a thread can call *CancelSynchronousIo*. *CancelSynchronousIo* enables even create (open) operations to be cancelled when supported by a device driver, and several drivers in Windows support this functionality, including the drivers that manage network file systems (for example, MUP, DFS, and SMB), which can cancel open operations to network paths. Figures 7-20 and 7-21 show synchronous and asynchronous I/O cancellation.

Synchronous I/O Cancellation

FIGURE 7-20 Synchronous I/O cancellation

Asynchronous I/O Cancellation

FIGURE 7-21 Asynchronous I/O cancellation

I/O Cancellation for Thread Termination

The other scenario in which I/Os must be cancelled is when a thread exits, either directly or
as the result of its process terminating (which causes the threads of the process to terminate).
Because every thread has a list of IRPs associated with it, the I/O manager can enumerate this
list, look for cancellable IRPs, and cancel them. Unlike *CancelIoEx*, which does not wait for
an IRP to be cancelled before returning, the process manager will not allow thread termina-
tion to proceed until all I/Os have been cancelled. As a result, if a driver fails to cancel an IRP,
the process and thread object will remain allocated until the system shuts down. Figure 7-22
illustrates the process termination scenario.

Process Termination Example

FIGURE 7-22 Cancellation during process termination

Note Only IRPs for which a driver sets a cancel routine are cancellable. The process manager waits until all I/Os associated with a thread are either cancelled or completed before deleting the thread.

EXPERIMENT: Debugging an Unkillable Process

In this experiment, we'll use Notmyfault from Sysinternals (we'll cover Notmyfault heavily in the "Crash Dump Analysis" section in Chapter 14) to force the unkillable process problem to exhibit itself by causing the Myfault.sys driver (which Notmyfault.exe uses) to indefinitely hold an IRP without having registered a cancel routine for it.

To start, run Notmyfault.exe, select Hang IRP from the list of options, and then click Do Bug. The dialog box should look like the following when properly configured:

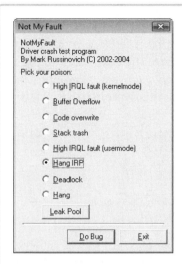

You shouldn't see anything happen, and you should be able to click the Exit button to quit the application. However, you should still see the Notmyfault process in Task Manager or Process Explorer. Attempts to terminate the process will fail because Windows will wait forever for the IRP to complete given that Myfault doesn't register a cancel routine.

To debug an issue such as this, you can use WinDbg to look at what the thread is currently doing (or you could use Process Explorer's Stack view on the Threads tab). Open a local kernel debugger session, and start by listing the information about the Notmyfault.exe process with the *!process* command:

```
lkd> !process 0 7 notmyfault.exe
PROCESS 86843ab0  SessionId: 1  Cid: 0594    Peb: 7ffd8000  ParentCid: 05c8
    DirBase: ce21f380  ObjectTable: 9cfb5070  HandleCount:  33.
    Image: NotMyfault.exe
    VadRoot 86658138 Vads 44 Clone 0 Private 210. Modified 5. Locked 0.
    DeviceMap 987545a8
...
    THREAD 868139b8  Cid 0594.0230  Teb: 7ffde000 Win32Thread: 00000000 WAIT:
(Executive) KernelMode Non-Alertable
        86797c64  NotificationEvent
    IRP List:
        86a51228: (0006,0094) Flags: 00060000  Mdl: 00000000
    ChildEBP RetAddr  Args to Child
    88ae4b78 81cf23bf 868139b8 86813a40 00000000 nt!KiSwapContext+0x26
    88ae4bbc 81c8fcf8 868139b8 86797c08 86797c64 nt!KiSwapThread+0x44f
    88ae4c14 81e8a356 86797c64 00000000 00000000 nt!KeWaitForSingleObject+0x492
    88ae4c40 81e875a3 86a51228 86797c08 86a51228 nt!IopCancelAlertedRequest+0x6d
    88ae4c64 81e87cba 00000103 86797c08 00000000 nt!IopSynchronousServiceTail+0x267
    88ae4d00 81e7198e 86727920 86a51228 00000000 nt!IopXxxControlFile+0x6b7
    88ae4d34 81c92a7a 0000007c 00000000 00000000 nt!NtDeviceIoControlFile+0x2a
    88ae4d34 77139a94 0000007c 00000000 00000000 nt!KiFastCallEntry+0x12a
    01d5fecc 00000000 00000000 00000000 00000000 ntdll!KiFastSystemCallRet
...
```

From the stack trace, you can see that the thread that initiated the I/O realized that the IRP had been cancelled (*IopSynchronousServiceTail* called *IopCancelAlertedRequest*) and is now waiting for the cancellation or completion. The next step is to use the same debugger extension used in the previous experiments, *!irp*, and attempt to analyze the problem. Copy the IRP pointer, and examine it with the *!irp* command:

```
lkd> !irp 86a51228
Irp is active with 1 stacks 1 is current (= 0x86a51298)
 No Mdl: No System Buffer: Thread 868139b8:  Irp stack trace.
     cmd  flg cl Device   File     Completion-Context
>[ e, 0]   5  0 86727920 86797c08 00000000-00000000
           \Driver\MYFAULT
           Args: 00000000 00000000 83360020 00000000
```

From this output, it is obvious who the culprit driver is: *\Driver\MYFAULT*, or Myfault.sys. The name of the driver emphasizes that the only way this situation can happen is through a driver problem and not a buggy application. Unfortunately, now that you know which driver caused this issue, there isn't much you can do—a system reboot is necessary because Windows can never safely assume it is okay to ignore the fact that cancellation hasn't occurred yet. The IRP could return at any time and cause corruption of system memory. If you encounter this situation in practice, you should check for a newer version of the driver, which might include a fix for the bug.

I/O Completion Ports

Writing a high-performance server application requires implementing an efficient threading model. Having either too few or too many server threads to process client requests can lead to performance problems. For example, if a server creates a single thread to handle all requests, clients can become starved because the server will be tied up processing one request at a time. A single thread could simultaneously process multiple requests, switching from one to another as I/O operations are started, but this architecture introduces significant complexity and can't take advantage of multiprocessor systems. At the other extreme, a server could create a big pool of threads so that virtually every client request is processed by a dedicated thread. This scenario usually leads to thread-thrashing, in which lots of threads wake up, perform some CPU processing, block while waiting for I/O, and then, after request processing is completed, block again waiting for a new request. If nothing else, having too many threads results in excessive context switching, caused by the scheduler having to divide processor time among multiple active threads.

The goal of a server is to incur as few context switches as possible by having its threads avoid unnecessary blocking, while at the same time maximizing parallelism by using multiple threads. The ideal is for there to be a thread actively servicing a client request on every processor and for those threads not to block when they complete a request if additional

requests are waiting. For this optimal process to work correctly, however, the application must have a way to activate another thread when a thread processing a client request blocks on I/O (such as when it reads from a file as part of the processing).

The *IoCompletion* Object

Applications use the *IoCompletion* executive object, which is exported to Windows as a *completion port*, as the focal point for the completion of I/O associated with multiple file handles. Once a file is associated with a completion port, any asynchronous I/O operations that complete on the file result in a completion packet being queued to the completion port. A thread can wait for any outstanding I/Os to complete on multiple files simply by waiting for a completion packet to be queued to the completion port. The Windows API provides similar functionality with the *WaitForMultipleObjects* API function, but the advantage that completion ports have is that *concurrency*, or the number of threads that an application has actively servicing client requests, is controlled with the aid of the system.

When an application creates a completion port, it specifies a concurrency value. This value indicates the maximum number of threads associated with the port that should be running at any given time. As stated earlier, the ideal is to have one thread active at any given time for every processor in the system. Windows uses the concurrency value associated with a port to control how many threads an application has active. If the number of active threads associated with a port equals the concurrency value, a thread that is waiting on the completion port won't be allowed to run. Instead, it is expected that one of the active threads will finish processing its current request and check to see whether another packet is waiting at the port. If one is, the thread simply grabs the packet and goes off to process it. When this happens, there is no context switch, and the CPUs are utilized nearly to their full capacity.

Using Completion Ports

Figure 7-23 shows a high-level illustration of completion port operation. A completion port is created with a call to the Windows API function *CreateIoCompletionPort*. Threads that block on a completion port become associated with the port and are awakened in last in, first out (LIFO) order so that the thread that blocked most recently is the one that is given the next packet. Threads that block for long periods of time can have their stacks swapped out to disk, so if there are more threads associated with a port than there is work to process, the in-memory footprints of threads blocked the longest are minimized.

Incoming client request

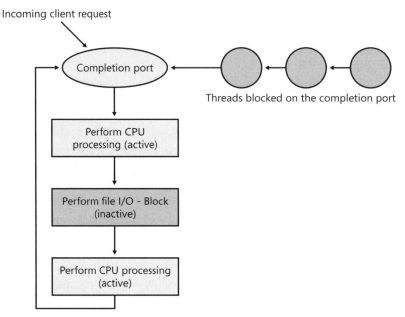

FIGURE 7-23 I/O completion port operation

A server application will usually receive client requests via network endpoints that are represented as file handles. Examples include Windows Sockets 2 (Winsock2) sockets or named pipes. As the server creates its communications endpoints, it associates them with a completion port and its threads wait for incoming requests by calling *GetQueuedCompletionStatus* on the port. When a thread is given a packet from the completion port, it will go off and start processing the request, becoming an active thread. A thread will block many times during its processing, such as when it needs to read or write data to a file on disk or when it synchronizes with other threads. Windows detects this activity and recognizes that the completion port has one less active thread. Therefore, when a thread becomes inactive because it blocks, a thread waiting on the completion port will be awakened if there is a packet in the queue.

An important mechanism that affects performance is called *lock contention*, which is the amount of time a thread spends waiting for a lock instead of doing real work. One of the most critical locks in the Windows kernel is the *dispatcher lock* (see Chapter 5 for more information on the dispatching mechanisms), and any time thread state is modified, especially in situations related to waiting and waking, the dispatcher lock is usually acquired, blocking other processors from doing similar actions.

The I/O completion port mechanism minimizes contention on the dispatcher lock by avoiding its acquisition when possible. For example, this mechanism does not acquire the lock when a completion is queued to a port and no threads are waiting on that port, when a thread calls *GetQueuedCompletionStatus* and there are items in the queue, or when a thread calls *GetQueuedCompletionStatus* with a zero timeout. In all three of these cases, no thread wait or wake-up is necessary, and hence none acquire the dispatcher lock.

Microsoft's guidelines are to set the concurrency value roughly equal to the number of processors in a system. Keep in mind that it's possible for the number of active threads for a completion port to exceed the concurrency limit. Consider a case in which the limit is specified as 1. A client request comes in, and a thread is dispatched to process the request, becoming active. A second request arrives, but a second thread waiting on the port isn't allowed to proceed because the concurrency limit has been reached. Then the first thread blocks waiting for a file I/O, so it becomes inactive. The second thread is then released, and while it's still active, the first thread's file I/O is completed, making it active again. At that point—and until one of the threads blocks—the concurrency value is 2, which is higher than the limit of 1. Most of the time, the active count will remain at or just above the concurrency limit.

The completion port API also makes it possible for a server application to queue privately defined completion packets to a completion port by using the *PostQueuedCompletionStatus* function. A server typically uses this function to inform its threads of external events, such as the need to shut down gracefully.

Applications can use thread agnostic I/O, described earlier, with I/O completion ports to avoid associating threads with their own I/Os and associating them with a completion port object instead. In addition to the other scalability benefits of I/O completion ports, their use can minimize context switches. Standard I/O completions must be executed by the thread that initiated the I/O, but when an I/O associated with an I/O completion port completes, the I/O manager uses any waiting thread to perform the completion operation.

I/O Completion Port Operation

Windows applications create completion ports by calling the Windows API *CreateIoCompletionPort* and specifying a NULL completion port handle. This results in the execution of the *NtCreateIoCompletion* system service. The executive's *IoCompletion* object is based on the kernel synchronization object called a *queue*. Thus, the system service creates a completion port object and initializes a queue object in the port's allocated memory. (A pointer to the port also points to the queue object because the queue is at the start of the port memory.) A queue object has a concurrency value that is specified when a thread initializes it, and in this case the value that is used is the one that was passed to *CreateIoCompletionPort*. *KeInitializeQueue* is the function that *NtCreateIoCompletion* calls to initialize a port's queue object.

When an application calls *CreateIoCompletionPort* to associate a file handle with a port, the *NtSetInformationFile* system service is executed with the file handle as the primary parameter. The information class that is set is *FileCompletionInformation*, and the completion port's handle and the *CompletionKey* parameter from *CreateIoCompletionPort* are the data values. *NtSetInformationFile* dereferences the file handle to obtain the file object and allocates a completion context data structure.

Finally, *NtSetInformationFile* sets the *CompletionContext* field in the file object to point at the context structure. When an asynchronous I/O operation completes on a file object, the I/O manager checks to see whether the *CompletionContext* field in the file object is non-NULL. If it is, the I/O manager allocates a completion packet and queues it to the completion port by calling *KeInsertQueue* with the port as the queue on which to insert the packet. (Remember that the completion port object and queue object have the same address.)

When a server thread invokes *GetQueuedCompletionStatus*, the system service *NtRemoveIo-Completion* is executed. After validating parameters and translating the completion port handle to a pointer to the port, *NtRemoveIoCompletion* calls *IoRemoveIoCompletion*, which eventually calls *KeRemoveQueueEx*. For high-performance scenarios, it's possible that multiple I/Os may have been completed, and although the thread will not block, it will still call into the kernel each time to get one item. The *GetQueuedCompletionStatus* or *GetQueuedCompletionStatusEx* API allows applications to retrieve more than one I/O completion status at the same time, reducing the number of user-to-kernel roundtrips and maintaining peak efficiency. Internally, this is implemented through the *NtRemoveIoCompletionEx* function, which calls *IoRemoveIoCompletion* with a count of queued items, which is passed on to *KeRemoveQueueEx*.

As you can see, *KeRemoveQueueEx* and *KeInsertQueue* are the engines behind completion ports. They are the functions that determine whether a thread waiting for an I/O completion packet should be activated. Internally, a queue object maintains a count of the current number of active threads and the maximum number of active threads. If the current number equals or exceeds the maximum when a thread calls *KeRemoveQueueEx*, the thread will be put (in LIFO order) onto a list of threads waiting for a turn to process a completion packet. The list of threads hangs off the queue object. A thread's control block data structure has a pointer in it that references the queue object of a queue that it's associated with; if the pointer is NULL, the thread isn't associated with a queue.

An improvement to the mechanism, which also improves the performance of other internal mechanisms that use I/O completion ports (such as the worker thread pool mechanism, described in Chapter 3), is the optimization of the KQUEUE dispatcher object, which we've mentioned in Chapter 3. Although we described how all dispatcher objects rely on the dispatcher lock during wait and unwait operations (or, in the case of kernel queues, remove and insert operations), the dispatcher header structure has a Lock member that can be used for an object-specific lock.

The KQUEUE implementation makes use of this member and implements a local, per-object spinlock instead of using the global dispatcher lock whenever possible. Therefore, the *KeInsertQueue* and *KeRemoveQueueEx* APIs actually first call the *KiAttemptFastQueueInsert* and *KiAttemptFastQueueRemove* internal functions and fall back to the dispatcher-lock-based code if the fast operations cannot be used or fail. Because the fast routines don't use

the global lock, the overall throughput of the system is improved—other dispatcher and scheduler operations can happen while I/O completion ports are being used by applications.

Windows keeps track of threads that become inactive because they block on something other than the completion port by relying on the queue pointer in a thread's control block. The scheduler routines that possibly result in a thread blocking (such as *KeWaitForSingleObject*, *KeDelayExecutionThread*, and so on) check the thread's queue pointer. If the pointer isn't NULL, the functions call *KiActivateWaiterQueue*, a queue-related function that decrements the count of active threads associated with the queue. If the resultant number is less than the maximum and at least one completion packet is in the queue, the thread at the front of the queue's thread list is awakened and given the oldest packet. Conversely, whenever a thread that is associated with a queue wakes up after blocking, the scheduler executes the function *KiUnwaitThread*, which increments the queue's active count.

Finally, the *PostQueuedCompletionStatus* Windows API function results in the execution of the *NtSetIoCompletion* system service. This function simply inserts the specified packet onto the completion port's queue by using *KeInsertQueue*.

Figure 7-24 shows an example of a completion port object in operation. Even though two threads are ready to process completion packets, the concurrency value of 1 allows only one thread associated with the completion port to be active, and so the two threads are blocked on the completion port.

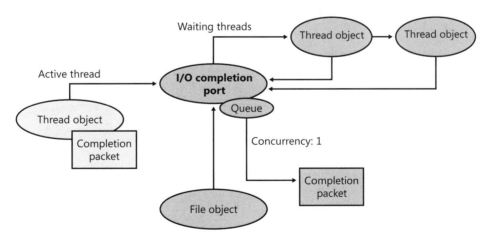

FIGURE 7-24 I/O completion port operation

Finally, the exact notification model of the I/O completion port can be fine-tuned through the *SetFileCompletionNotificationModes* API, which allows application developers to take advantage of additional, specific improvements that usually require code changes but can offer even more throughput. Three notification mode optimizations are supported, which are listed in Table 7-3. Note that these modes are per file handle and permanent.

TABLE 7-3 I/O Completion Port Notification Modes

Notification Mode	Meaning
Skip completion port on success	If the following three conditions are true, the I/O manager does not queue a completion entry to the port when it would ordinarily do so. First, a completion port must be associated with the file handle; second, the file must be opened for asynchronous I/O; third, the request must return success immediately without returning ERROR_PENDING.
Skip set event on handle	The I/O manager does not set the event for the file object if a request returns with a success code or the error returned is ERROR_PENDING and the function that is called is not a synchronous function. If an explicit event is provided for the request, it is still signaled.
Skip set user event on fast I/O	The I/O manager does not set the explicit event provided for the request if a request takes the fast I/O path and returns with a success code or the error returned is ERROR_PENDING and the function that is called is not a synchronous function.

I/O Prioritization

Without I/O priority, background activities like search indexing, virus scanning, and disk defragmenting can severely impact the responsiveness of foreground operations. A user launching an application or opening a document while another process is performing disk I/O, for example, experiences delays as the foreground task waits for disk access. The same interference also affects the streaming playback of multimedia content like music from a hard disk.

Windows includes two types of I/O prioritization to help foreground I/O operations get preference: priority on individual I/O operations and I/O bandwidth reservations.

I/O Priorities

The Windows I/O manager internally includes support for five I/O priorities, as shown in Table 7-4, but only three of the priorities are used. (Future versions of Windows may support High and Low.)

TABLE 7-4 I/O Priorities

I/O Priority	Usage
Critical	Memory manager
High	Not used
Normal	Normal application I/O
Low	Not used
Very Low	Scheduled tasks, Superfetch, defragmenting, content indexing, background activities

I/O has a default priority of Normal and the memory manager uses Critical when it wants to write dirty memory data out to disk under low-memory situations to make room in RAM for other data and code. The Windows Task Scheduler sets the I/O priority for tasks that have the default task priority to Very Low. The priority specified by applications written for Windows Vista that perform background processing is Very Low. All of the Windows Vista background operations, including Windows Defender scanning and desktop search indexing, use Very Low I/O priority.

Internally, these five I/O priorities are divided into two I/O prioritization modes, called *strategies*. These are the *hierarchy prioritization* and the *idle prioritization* strategies. Hierarchy prioritization deals with all the I/O priorities except Very Low. It implements the following strategy:

- All critical-priority I/O must be processed before any high-priority I/O.

- All high-priority I/O must be processed before any normal-priority I/O.

- All normal-priority I/O must be processed before any low-priority I/O.

- All low-priority I/O is processed after all higher priority I/O.

As each application generates I/Os, IRPs are put on different I/O queues based on their priority, and the hierarchy strategy decides the ordering of the operations.

The idle prioritization strategy, on the other hand, uses a separate queue for Very Low priority I/O. Because the system processes all hierarchy prioritized I/O before idle I/O, it's possible for the I/Os in this queue to be starved, as long as there's even a single Very Low priority I/O on the system in the hierarchy priority strategy queue.

To avoid this situation, as well as to control backoff (the sending rate of I/O transfers), the idle strategy uses a timer to monitor the queue and guarantee that at least one I/O is processed per unit of time (typically half a second). Data written using Very Low I/O also causes the cache manager to write modifications to disk immediately instead of doing it later and to bypass its read-ahead logic for read operations that would otherwise preemptively read from the file being accessed. The prioritization strategy also waits for 50 milliseconds after the completion of the last non-idle I/O in order to issue the next idle I/O. Otherwise, idle I/Os would occur in the middle of nonidle streams, causing costly seeks.

Combining these strategies into a virtual global I/O queue for demonstration purposes, a snapshot of this queue might look similar to Figure 7-25. Note that within each queue, the ordering is first-in, first-out (FIFO). The order in the figure is shown only as an example.

I/O Queue

FIGURE 7-25 Sample entries in a global I/O queue

User-mode applications can set I/O priority on three different objects. *SetPriorityClass* and *SetThreadPriority* set the priority for all the I/Os that either the entire process or specific threads will generate (the priority is stored in the IRP of each request). *SetFileInformationByHandle* can set the priority for a specific file object (the priority is stored in the file object). Drivers can also set I/O priority directly on an IRP by using the *IoSetIoPriorityHint* API.

> **Note** The I/O priority field in the IRP and/or file object is a *hint*. There is no guarantee that the I/O priority will be respected or even supported by the different drivers that are part of the storage stack.

The two prioritization strategies are implemented by two different types of drivers. The hierarchy strategy is implemented by the storage *port* drivers, which are responsible for all I/Os on a specific port, such as ATA, SCSI, or USB. As of Windows Vista and Windows Server 2008, only the ATA port driver (%SystemRoot%\System32\Ataport.sys) and USB port driver (%SystemRoot%\System32\Usbstor.sys) implement this strategy, while the SCSI and storage port drivers (%SystemRoot%\System32\Scsiport.sys and %SystemRoot%\System32\Storport.sys) do not.

> **Note** All port drivers check specifically for Critical priority I/Os and move them ahead of their queues, even if they do not support the full hierarchy mechanism. This mechanism is in place to support critical memory manager paging I/Os to ensure system reliability.

This means that consumer mass storage devices such as IDE or SATA hard drives and USB flash disks will take advantage of I/O prioritization, while devices based on SCSI, Fibre Channel, and iSCSI will not.

On the other hand, it is the system storage class device driver (%SystemRoot%\System32\Classpnp.sys) that enforces the idle strategy, so it automatically applies to I/Os directed at all storage devices, including SCSI drives. This separation ensures that idle I/Os will be subject to back-off algorithms to ensure a reliable system during operation under high idle I/O usage and so that applications that use them can make forward progress. Placing support for this

strategy in the Microsoft-provided class driver avoids performance problems that would have been caused by lack of support for it in legacy third-party port drivers.

Figure 7-26 displays a simplified view of the storage stack and where each strategy is implemented. See Chapter 8 for more information on the storage stack.

FIGURE 7-26 Implementation of I/O prioritization across the storage stack

The following experiment will show you an example of Very Low I/O priority and how you can use Process Monitor to look at I/O priorities on different requests.

EXPERIMENT: Very Low vs. Normal I/O Throughput

You can use the IO Priority sample application (included in the book's utilities) to look at the throughput difference between two threads with different I/O priorities. Launch IoPriority.exe, make sure Thread 1 is checked to use Low priority, and then click the Start IO button. You should notice a significant difference in speed between the two threads, as shown in the following screen.

You should also notice that Thread 1's throughput remains fairly constant, around 2 KB/s. This can easily be explained by the fact that IO Priority performs its I/Os at 2 KB/s, which means that the idle prioritization strategy is kicking in and guaranteeing at least one I/O each half-second. Otherwise, Thread 2 would starve any I/O that Thread 1 is attempting to make.

Note that if both threads run at low priority and the system is relatively idle, their throughput will be roughly equal to the throughput of a single normal I/O priority in the example. This is because low priority I/Os are not artificially throttled or otherwise hindered if there isn't any competition from higher priority I/O.

You can also use Process Monitor to trace IO Priority's I/Os and look at their I/O priority hint. Launch Process Monitor, configure a filter for IoPriority.exe, and repeat the experiment. In this application, Thread 1 writes to File_1, and Thread 2 writes to File_2. Scroll down until you see a write to File_1, and you should see output similar to that shown here.

You can see that I/Os directed at File_1 have a priority of Very Low. By looking at the Time Of Day column, you'll also notice that the I/Os are spaced 0.5 second from each other—another sign of the idle strategy in action.

Finally, by using Process Explorer, you can identify Thread 1 in the IoPriority process by looking at the I/O priority for each of its threads on the Threads tab of its process Properties dialog box. You can also see that the priority for the thread is lower than the default of 8 (normal), which indicates that the thread is probably running in *background priority* mode. The following screen shows what you should expect to see.

Note that if IO Priority sets the priority on File_1 instead of on the issuing thread, both threads would look the same. Only Process Monitor could show you the difference in I/O priorities.

Bandwidth Reservation (Scheduled File I/O)

Windows bandwidth reservation support is useful for applications that desire consistent I/O throughput. Using the *SetFileIoBandwidthReservation* call, a media player application asks the I/O system to guarantee it the ability to read data from a device at a specified rate. If the device can deliver data at the requested rate and existing reservations allow it, the I/O system gives the application guidance as to how fast it should issue I/Os and how large the I/Os should be.

The I/O system won't service other I/Os unless it can satisfy the requirements of applications that have made reservations on the target storage device. Figure 7-27 shows a conceptual timeline of I/Os issued on the same file. The shaded regions are the only ones that will be available to other applications. If I/O bandwidth is already taken, new I/Os will have to wait until the next cycle.

FIGURE 7-27 Effect of I/O requests during bandwidth reservation

Like the hierarchy prioritization strategy, bandwidth reservation is implemented at the port driver level, which means it is available only for IDE, SATA, or USB-based mass-storage devices.

Driver Verifier

Driver Verifier is a mechanism that can be used to help find and isolate commonly found bugs in device drivers or other kernel-mode system code. Microsoft uses Driver Verifier to check its own device drivers as well as all device drivers that vendors submit for Hardware Compatibility List (HCL) testing. Doing so ensures that the drivers on the HCL are compatible with Windows and free from common driver errors. (Although not described in this book, there is also a corresponding Application Verifier tool that has resulted in quality improvements for user-mode code in Windows.)

Also, although Driver Verifier serves primarily as a tool to help device driver developers discover bugs in their code, it is also a powerful tool for systems administrators experiencing crashes. Chapter 14 describes its role in crash analysis troubleshooting.

Driver Verifier consists of support in several system components: the memory manager, I/O manager, and the HAL all have driver verification options that can be enabled. These options are configured using the Driver Verifier Manager (%SystemRoot%\Verifier.exe). When you run Driver Verifier with no command-line arguments, it presents a wizard-style interface, as shown in Figure 7-28.

You can also enable and disable Driver Verifier, as well as display current settings, by using its command-line interface. From a command prompt, type **verifier /?** to see the switches.

Even when you don't select any options, Driver Verifier monitors drivers selected for verification, looking for a number of illegal operations, including calling kernel-memory pool functions at invalid IRQL, double-freeing memory, and requesting a zero-size memory allocation.

What follows is a description of the I/O-related verification options (shown in Figure 7-29). The options related to memory management are described in Chapter 9, along with how the memory manager redirects a driver's operating system calls to special verifier versions.

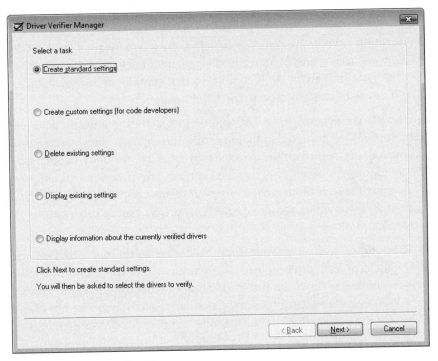

FIGURE 7-28 Driver Verifier Manager

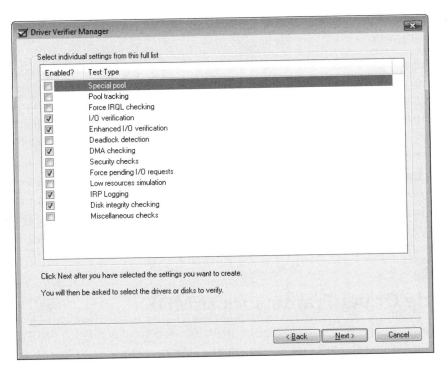

FIGURE 7-29 Driver Verifier I/O-related options

These options have the following effects:

■ **I/O Verification** When this option is selected, the I/O manager allocates IRPs for verified drivers from a special pool and their usage is tracked. In addition, the Verifier crashes the system when an IRP is completed that contains an invalid status and when an invalid device object is passed to the I/O manager.

■ **Enhanced I/O Verification** This option monitors all IRPs to ensure that drivers mark them correctly when completing them asynchronously, that they manage device stack locations correctly, and that they delete device objects only once. In addition, the Verifier randomly stresses drivers by sending them fake power management and WMI IRPs, changing the order that devices are enumerated, and adjusting the status of PnP and power IRPs when they complete to test for drivers that return incorrect status from their dispatch routines.

■ **DMA Checking** This is a hardware-supported mechanism that allows devices to transfer data to or from physical memory without involving the CPU. The I/O manager provides a number of functions that drivers use to schedule and control direct memory access (DMA) operations, and this option enables checks for correct use of the functions and for the buffers that the I/O manager supplies for DMA operations.

■ **Force Pending I/O Requests** For many devices, asynchronous I/Os complete immediately, so drivers may not be coded to properly handle the occasional asynchronous I/O. When this option is enabled, the I/O manager will randomly return STATUS_PENDING in response to a driver's calls to *IoCallDriver*, which simulates the asynchronous completion of an I/O.

■ **IRP Logging** This option monitors a driver's use of IRPs and makes a record of IRP usage, which is stored as WMI information. You can then use the Dc2wmiparser.exe utility in the WDK to convert these WMI records to a text file. Note that only 20 IRPs for each device will be recorded—each subsequent IRP will overwrite the least recently added entry. After a reboot, this information is discarded, so Dc2wmiparser.exe should be run if the contents of the trace are to be analyzed later.

■ **Disk Integrity Checking** When you enable this option, the Verifier monitors disk read and write operations and checksums the associated data. When disk reads complete, it checks to see whether it has a previously stored checksum and crashes the system if the new and old checksum don't match, because that would indicate corruption of the disk at the hardware level.

Kernel-Mode Driver Framework (KMDF)

We've already discussed some details about the Windows Driver Foundation (WDF) in Chapter 2. In this section, we'll take a deeper look at the components and functionality provided by the kernel-mode part of the framework, KMDF. Note that this section will only

briefly touch on some of the core architecture of KMDF. For a much more complete overview on the subject, please refer to *Developing Drivers with Windows Driver Foundation* by Penny Orwick and Guy Smith (Microsoft Press, 2007).

Structure and Operation of a KMDF Driver

First, let's take a look at which kinds of drivers or devices are supported by KMDF. In general, any WDM-conformant driver should be supported by KMDF, as long as it performs standard I/O processing and IRP manipulation. KMDF is not suitable for drivers that don't use the Windows kernel API directly but instead perform library calls into existing port and class drivers. These types of drivers cannot use KMDF because they only provide callbacks for the actual WDM drivers that do the I/O processing. Additionally, if a driver provides its own dispatch functions instead of relying on a port or class driver, IEEE 1394 and ISA, PCI, PCMCIA, and SD Client (for Secure Digital storage devices) drivers can also make use of KMDF.

Although KMDF is a different driver model than WDM, the basic driver structure shown earlier also generally applies to KMDF drivers. At their core, KMDF drivers must have the following functions:

- **An initialization routine** Just like any other driver, a KMDF driver has a *DriverEntry* function that initializes the driver. KMDF drivers will initiate the framework at this point and perform any configuration and initialization steps that are part of the driver or part of describing the driver to the framework. For non–Plug and Play drivers, this is where the first device object should be created.

- **An *add-device* routine** KMDF driver operation is based on events and callbacks (described shortly), and the *EvtDriverDeviceAdd* callback is the single most important one for PnP devices because it receives notifications that the PnP manager in the kernel has enumerated one of the driver's devices.

- **One or more *EvtIo** routines** Just like a WDM driver's dispatch routines, these callback routines handle specific types of I/O requests from a particular device queue. A driver typically creates one or more queues in which KMDF places I/O requests for the driver's devices. These queues can be configured by request type and dispatching type.

The simplest KMDF driver might need to have only an initialization and add-device routine because the framework will provide the default, generic functionality that's required for most types of I/O processing, including power and Plug and Play events. In the KMDF model, *events* refer to run-time states to which a driver can respond or during which a driver can participate. These events are not related to the synchronization primitives (synchronization is discussed in Chapter 3), but are internal to the framework.

For events that are critical to a driver's operation, or which need specialized processing, the driver registers a given callback routine to handle this event. In other cases, a driver can

allow KMDF to perform a default, generic action instead. For example, during an eject event (*EvtDeviceEject*), a driver can choose to support ejection and supply a callback or to fall back to the default KMDF code that will tell the user that the device is not ejectable. Not all events have a default behavior, however, and callbacks must be provided by the driver. One notable example is the *EvtDriverDeviceAdd* event that is at the core of any Plug and Play driver.

EXPERIMENT: Displaying KMDF Drivers

The Wdfkd.dll extension that ships with the Debugging Tools for Windows package provides many commands that can be used to debug and analyze KMDF drivers and devices (instead of using the built-in WDM-style debugging extension that may not offer the same kind of WDF-specific information). You can display installed KMDF drivers with the *!wdfkd.wdfldr* debugger command. In the following example, the output from a Windows Vista SP1 computer is shown, displaying the built-in drivers that are typically installed.

```
lkd> !wdfkd.wdfldr
 LoadedModuleList        0x805ce18c
-----------------------------------
LIBRARY_MODULE  8472f448
  Version        v1.7 build(6001)
  Service        \Registry\Machine\System\CurrentControlSet\Services\Wdf01000
  ImageName      Wdf01000.sys
  ImageAddress   0x80778000
  ImageSize      0x7c000
  Associated Clients: 6

  ImageName      Version     WdfGlobals FxGlobals   ImageAddress ImageSize
  peauth.sys     v0.0(0000) 0x867c00c0 0x867c0008 0x9b0d1000   0x000de000
  monitor.sys    v0.0(0000) 0x8656d9d8 0x8656d920 0x8f527000   0x0000f000
  umbus.sys      v0.0(0000) 0x84bfd4d0 0x84bfd418 0x829d9000   0x0000d000
  HDAudBus.sys   v0.0(0000) 0x84b5d918 0x84b5d860 0x82be2000   0x00012000
  intelppm.sys   v0.0(0000) 0x84ac9ee8 0x84ac9e30 0x82bc6000   0x0000f000
  msisadrv.sys   v0.0(0000) 0x848da858 0x848da7a0 0x82253000   0x00008000
-----------------------------------
Total: 1 library loaded
```

KMDF Data Model

The KMDF data model is object-based, much like the model for the kernel, but it does not make use of the object manager. Instead, KMDF manages its own objects internally, exposing them as handles to drivers and keeping the actual data structures opaque. For each object type, the framework provides routines to perform operations on the object, such as *WdfDeviceCreate*, which creates a device. Additionally, objects can have specific data fields or members that can be accessed by *Get/Set* (used for modifications

that should never fail) or *Assign/Retrieve* APIs (used for modifications that can fail). For example, the *WdfInterruptGetInfo* function returns information on a given interrupt object (WDFINTERRUPT).

Also unlike the implementation of kernel objects, which all refer to distinct and isolated object types, KMDF objects are all part of a hierarchy—most object types are bound to a parent. The root object is the WDFDRIVER structure, which describes the actual driver. The structure and meaning is analogous to the DRIVER_OBJECT structure provided by the I/O manager and all other KMDF structures are children of it. The next most important object is WDFDEVICE, which refers to a given instance of a detected device on the system, which must have been created with *WdfDeviceCreate*. Again, this is analogous to the DEVICE_OBJECT structure that's used in the WDM model and by the I/O manager. Table 7-5 lists the object types supported by KMDF

TABLE 7-5 KMDF Object Types

Object	Type	Description
Child List	WDFCHILDLIST	List of child WDFDEVICE objects associated with the device.
Collection	WDFCOLLECTION	List of objects of a similar type, such as a group of WDFDEVICE objects being filtered.
Device	WDFDEVICE	Instance of a device.
DMA Common Buffer	WDFCOMMONBUFFER	Piece of memory that a device and driver can access for direct memory access (DMA).
DMA Enabler	WDFDMAENABLER	Enables DMA on a given channel for a driver.
DMA Transaction	WDFDMATRANSACTION	Instance of a DMA transaction.
Deferred Procedure Call	WDFDPC	Instance of a DPC object (see Chapter 3 for more information on DPCs).
Driver	WDFDRIVER	Root object for the driver; represents the driver, its parameters, and its callbacks, among other items.
File	WDFFILEOBJECT	Instance of a file object that can be used as a channel for communication between an application and the driver.
Generic Object	WDFOBJECT	Allows driver-defined custom data to be wrapped inside the framework's object data model as an object.
I/O Queue	WDFQUEUE	Represents a given I/O queue.
I/O Request	WDFREQUEST	Represents a given request on a WDFQUEUE.
I/O Target	WDFIOTARGET	Represents the device stack being targeted by a given WDFREQUEST.

Object	Type	Description
Interrupt	WDFINTERRUPT	Instance of an interrupt that the driver must handle.
Look-Aside List	WDFLOOKASIDE	Describes an executive look-aside list.
Memory	WDFMEMORY	Describes a piece of paged or nonpaged pool.
Registry Key	WDFKEY	Describes a registry key.
Resource List	WDFCMRESLIST	Identifies the resources assigned to a WDFDEVICE.
Resource Range List	WDFIORESLIST	Identifies a given possible resource range for a WDFDEVICE.
Resource Requirements List	WDFIORESREQLIST	Contains an array of WDFIORESLIST objects describing all possible resource ranges for a WDFDEVICE.
String	WDFSTRING	Describes a Unicode string structure.
Spinlock	WDFSPINLOCK	Describe a spinlock (see Chapter 3 for more information).
Timer	WDFTIMER	Describes an executive timer (see Chapter 3 for more information).
USB Device	WDFUSBDEVICE	Identifies the one instance of a USB device.
USB Interface	WDFUSBINTERFACE	Identifies one interface on the given WDFUSBDEVICE.
USB Pipe	WDFUSBPIPE	Identifies a bulk or interrupt pipe for a given WDFUSBINTERFACE.
Wait Lock	WDFWAITLOCK	Represents a kernel dispatcher event object.
WMI Instance	WDFWMIINSTANCE	Represents a WMI data block for a given WDFWMIPROVIDER.
WMI Provider	WDFWMIPROVIDER	Describes the WMI schema for all the WDFWMIINSTANCE objects supported by the driver.
Work Item	WDFWORKITEM	Describes an executive work item.

For each of these objects, other KMDF objects can be attached as children—some objects have only one or two valid parents, while other objects can be attached to any parent. For example, a WDFINTERRUPT object must be associated with a given WDFDEVICE, but a WDFSPINLOCK or WDFSTRING can have any object as a parent, allowing fine-grained control over their validity and usage and reducing global state variables. Figure 7-30 shows the entire KMDF object hierarchy.

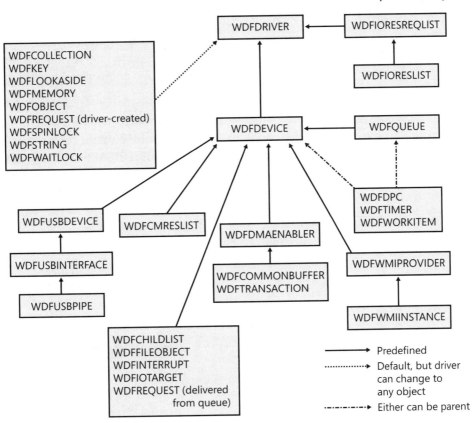

FIGURE 7-30 KMDF object hierarchy

Note that the associations mentioned earlier and shown in the figure are not necessarily immediate. The parent must simply be on the *hierarchy chain,* meaning one of the ancestor nodes must be of this type. This relationship is useful to realize because object hierarchies not only affect the objects' locality but also their lifetime. Each time a child object is created, a reference count is added to it by its link to its parent. Therefore, when a parent object is destroyed, all the child objects are also destroyed, which is why associating objects such as WDFSTRING or WDFMEMORY with a given object, instead of the default WDFDRIVER object, can automatically free up memory and state information when the parent object is destroyed.

Closely related to the concept hierarchy is KMDF's notion of *object context.* Because KMDF objects are opaque, as discussed, and are associated with a parent object for locality, it becomes important to allow drivers to attach their own data to an object in order to track certain specific information outside the framework's capabilities or support.

Object contexts allow all KMDF objects to contain such information, and they additionally allow multiple *object context areas,* which permit multiple layers of code inside the same driver to interact with the same object in different ways. In the WDM model, the *device*

extension data structure allows such information to be associated with a given device, but with KMDF even a spinlock or string can contain context areas. This extensibility allows each library or layer of code responsible for processing an I/O to interact independently of other code, based on the context area that it works with, and allows a mechanism similar to inheritance.

Finally, KMDF objects are also associated with a set of attributes that are shown in Table 7-6. These attributes are usually configured to their defaults, but the values can be overridden by the driver when creating the object by specifying a WDF_OBJECT_ATTRIBUTES structure (similar to the object manager's OBJECT_ATTRIBUTES structure when creating a kernel object).

TABLE 7-6 KMDF Object Attributes

Attribute	Description
ContextSizeOverride	Size of the object context area.
ContextTypeInfo	Type of the object context area.
EvtCleanupCallback	Callback to notify the driver of the object's cleanup before deletion (references may still exist).
EvtDestroyCallback	Callback to notify the driver of the object's imminent deletion (references will be 0).
ExecutionLevel	Describes the maximum IRQL at which the callbacks may be invoked by KMDF.
ParentObject	Identifies the parent of this object.
Size	Size of the object.
SynchronizationScope	Specifies whether callbacks should be synchronized with the parent, a queue or device, or nothing.

KMDF I/O Model

The KMDF I/O model follows the WDM mechanisms discussed earlier in the chapter. In fact, one can even think of the framework itself as a WDM driver, since it uses kernel APIs and WDM behavior to abstract KMDF and make it functional. Under KMDF, the framework driver sets its own WDM-style IRP dispatch routines and takes control over all IRPs sent to the driver. After being handled by one of three KMDF I/O handlers (which we'll describe shortly), it then packages these requests in the appropriate KMDF objects, inserts them in the appropriate queues if required, and performs driver callback if the driver is interested in those events. Figure 7-31 describes the flow of I/O in the framework.

Based on the IRP processing discussed for WDM drivers earlier, KMDF performs one of the following three actions:

- Sends the IRP to the I/O handler, which processes standard device operations

- Sends the IRP to the PnP and power handler that processes these kinds of events and notifies other drivers if the state has changed

- Sends the IRP to the WMI handler, which handles tracing and logging.

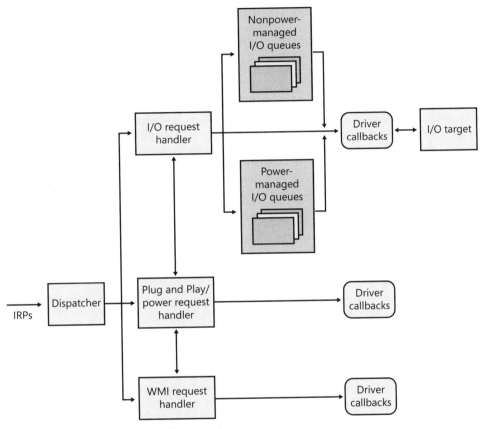

FIGURE 7-31 KMDF I/O flow and IRP processing

These components will then notify the driver of any events it registered for, potentially forward the request to another handler for further processing, and then complete the request based on an internal handler action or as the result of a driver call. If KMDF has finished processing the IRP but the request itself has still not been fully processed, KMDF will take one of the following two actions:

- For bus drivers and function drivers, complete the IRP with STATUS_INVALID_DEVICE_REQUEST

- For filter drivers, forward the request to the next lower driver

I/O processing by KMDF is based on the mechanism of *queues* (WDFQUEUE, not the KQUEUE object discussed in Chapter 3). KMDF queues are highly scalable containers of I/O requests (packaged as WDFREQUEST objects) and provide a rich feature set beyond merely sorting

the pending I/Os for a given device. For example, queues also track currently active requests and support I/O cancellation, I/O concurrency (the ability to perform and complete more than one I/O request at a time), and I/O synchronization (as noted in the list of object attributes in Table 7-6). A typical KMDF driver creates at least one queue (if not more) and associates one or more events with each queue, as well as some of the following options:

- The callbacks registered with the events associated with this queue

- The power management state for the queue. KMDF supports both power-managed and nonpower-managed queues. For the former, the I/O handler will handle waking up the device when required (and when possible), arm the idle timer when the device has no I/Os queued up, and call the driver's I/O cancellation routines when the system is switching away from a working state.

- The dispatch method for the queue. KMDF can deliver I/Os from a queue either in a sequential, parallel, or manual mode. Sequential I/Os are delivered one at a time (KMDF waits for the driver to complete the previous request), while parallel I/Os are delivered to the driver as soon as possible. In manual mode, the driver must manually retrieve I/Os from the queue.

- Whether or not the queue can accept zero-length buffers, such as incoming requests that don't actually contain any data.

 Note The dispatch method affects solely the number of requests that are allowed to be active inside a driver's queue at one time. It does not determine whether the event callbacks themselves will be called concurrently or serially. That behavior is determined through the synchronization scope object attribute described earlier. Therefore, it is possible for a parallel queue to have concurrency disabled but still have multiple incoming requests.

Based on the mechanism of queues, the KMDF I/O handler can perform several possible tasks upon receiving either a create, close, cleanup, write, read, or device control (IOCTL) request:

- For create requests, the driver can request to be immediately notified through *EvtDeviceFileCreate*, or it can create a nonmanual queue to receive create requests. It must then register an *EvtIoDefault* callback to receive the notifications. Finally, if none of these methods are used, KMDF will simply complete the request with a success code, meaning that by default, applications will be able to open handles to KMDF drivers that don't supply their own code.

- For cleanup and close requests, the driver will be immediately notified through *EvtFileCleanup* and *EvtFileClose* callbacks, if registered. Otherwise, the framework will simply complete with a success code.

- Finally, Figure 7-32 illustrates the flow of an I/O request to a KMDF driver for the most common driver operations (read, write, and I/O control codes).

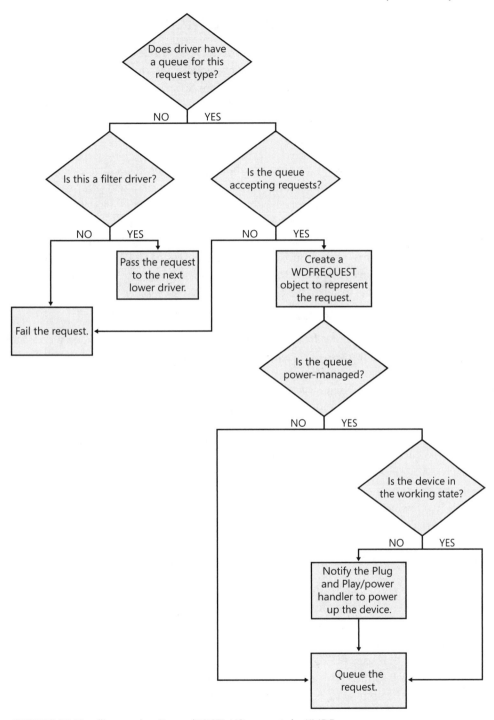

FIGURE 7-32 Handling read, write, and IOCTL I/O requests by KMDF

User-Mode Driver Framework (UMDF)

Although this chapter focuses on kernel-mode drivers, Windows includes a growing number of drivers that actually run in user mode, as previously described, using the User-Mode Driver Framework (UMDF) that is part of the WDF. Before finishing our discussion on drivers, we'll take a quick look at the architecture of UMDF and what it offers. Once again, for a much more complete overview on the subject, please refer to *Developing Drivers with Windows Driver Foundation* by Penny Orwick and Guy Smith.

UMDF is designed specifically to support what are called *protocol device classes*, which refers to devices that all use the same standardized, generic protocol and offer specialized functionality on top of it. These protocols currently include IEEE 1394 (FireWire), USB, Bluetooth, and TCP/IP. Any device running on top of these buses (or connected to a network) is a potential candidate for UMDF—examples include portable music players, PDAs, cell phones, cameras and webcams, and so on. Two other large users of UMDF are SideShow-compatible devices (auxiliary displays) and the Windows Portable Device (WPD) Framework, which supports USB removable storage (USB bulk transfer devices). Finally, as with KMDF, it's possible to implement software-only drivers, such as for a virtual device, in UMDF.

To make porting code easier from kernel mode to user mode, and to keep a consistent architecture, UMDF uses the same conceptual driver programming model as KMDF, but it uses different components, interfaces, and data structures. For example, KMDF includes objects unique to kernel mode, while UMDF includes some objects unique to user mode. Objects and functionality that can't be accessed through UMDF include direct handling of interrupts, DMA, nonpaged pool, and strict timing requirements. Furthermore, a UMDF driver can't be on any kernel driver stack or be a client of another driver or the kernel itself.

Unlike KMDF drivers, which run as driver objects representing a .sys image file, UMDF drivers run in a *driver host process*, similar to a service-hosting process. The host process contains the driver itself (which is implemented as an in-process COM component), the user-mode driver framework (implemented as a DLL containing COM-like components for each UMDF object), and a run-time environment (responsible for I/O dispatching, driver loading, device stack management, communication with the kernel, and a thread pool).

Just like in the kernel, each UMDF driver runs as part of a stack, which can contain multiple drivers that are responsible for managing a device. Naturally, since user-mode code can't access the kernel address space, UMDF also includes some components that allow this access to occur through a specialized interface to the kernel. This is implemented by a kernel-mode side of UMDF that uses ALPC (see Chapter 3 for more information on advanced local procedure call) to talk to the run-time environment in the user-mode driver host processes. Figure 7-33 displays the architecture of the UMDF driver model.

FIGURE 7-33 UMDF architecture

Figure 7-33 shows two different device stacks that manage two different hardware devices, each with a UMDF driver running inside its own driver host process. From the diagram, you can see that the following components take part in the architecture:

- **Applications** Applications are the clients of the drivers. These are standard Windows applications that use the same APIs to perform I/Os as they would with a KMDF-managed or a WDM-managed device. Applications don't know that they're talking to a UMDF-based device, and the calls are still sent to the kernel's I/O manager.

- **Windows kernel (I/O manager)** Based on the application I/O APIs, the I/O manager builds the IRPs for the operations, just like for any other standard device.

- **Reflector** The reflector is what makes UMDF "tick." It is a standard WDM filter driver that sits at the top of the device stack of each device that is being managed by a UMDF driver. The reflector is responsible for managing the communication between the kernel and the user-mode driver host process. IRPs related to power management, Plug and Play, and standard I/O are redirected to the host process through ALPC. This lets the UMDF driver respond to the I/Os and perform work, as well as be involved in the Plug and Play model, by providing enumeration, installation, and management of its devices. The reflector is also responsible for keeping an eye on the driver host processes by making sure that they remain responsive to requests within an adequate time to prevent drivers and applications from hanging.

- **Driver manager** The driver manager is responsible for starting and quitting the driver host processes, based on which UMDF-managed devices are present, and also for managing information on them. It is also responsible for responding to messages coming from the reflector and applying them to the appropriate host process (such as reacting to device installation). The driver manager runs as a standard Windows service and is configured for automatic startup as soon as the first UMDF driver for a device is installed. Only one instance of the driver manager runs for all driver host processes, and it must always be running to allow UMDF drivers to work.

- **Host process** The host process provides the address space and run-time environment for the actual driver. Although it runs in the local service account, it is not actually a Windows service and is not managed by the SCM—only by the driver manager. The host process is also responsible for providing the user-mode device stack for the actual hardware, which is visible to all applications on the system. In the current UMDF release, each device instance has its own device stack, which runs in a separate host process. In the future, multiple instances may share the same host process. Host processes are child processes of the driver manager.

- **Kernel-mode drivers** If specific kernel support for a device that is managed by a UMDF driver is needed, it is also possible to write a companion kernel-mode driver that fills that role. In this way, it is possible for a device to be managed both by a UMDF and a KMDF (or WDM) driver.

You can easily see UMDF in action on your system by inserting any USB flash drive with some content on it. Run Process Explorer, and you should see a WUDFHost.exe process that corresponds to a driver host process. Switch to DLL view and scroll down until you see DLLs similar to the ones shown in Figure 7-34.

FIGURE 7-34 DLL in UMDF host process

You can identify three main components, which match the architectural overview described earlier:

- WUDFx.dll, the framework itself

- WUDFPlatform.dll, the run-time environment

- WpdFs.dll, the COM component representing the WPD driver, exposing contents of USB storage devices to Windows shell and media applications

The Plug and Play (PnP) Manager

The PnP manager is the primary component involved in supporting the ability of Windows to recognize and adapt to changing hardware configurations. A user doesn't need to understand the intricacies of hardware or manual configuration to install and remove devices. For example, it's the PnP manager that enables a running Windows laptop that is placed on a docking station to automatically detect additional devices located in the docking station and make them available to the user.

Plug and Play support requires cooperation at the hardware, device driver, and operating system levels. Industry standards for the enumeration and identification of devices attached to buses are the foundation of Windows Plug and Play support. For example, the USB standard defines the way that devices on a USB bus identify themselves. With this foundation in place, Windows Plug and Play support provides the following capabilities:

- The PnP manager automatically recognizes installed devices, a process that includes enumerating devices attached to the system during a boot and detecting the addition and removal of devices as the system executes.

- Hardware resource allocation is a role the PnP manager fills by gathering the hardware resource requirements (interrupts, I/O memory, I/O registers, or bus-specific resources) of the devices attached to a system and, in a process called *resource arbitration*, optimally assigning resources so that each device meets the requirements necessary for its operation. Because hardware devices can be added to the system after boot-time resource assignment, the PnP manager must also be able to reassign resources to accommodate the needs of dynamically added devices.

- Loading appropriate drivers is another responsibility of the PnP manager. The PnP manager determines, based on the identification of a device, whether a driver capable of managing the device is installed on the system, and if one is, instructs the I/O manager to load it. If a suitable driver isn't installed, the kernel-mode PnP manager communicates with the user-mode PnP manager to install the device, possibly requesting the user's assistance in locating a suitable set of drivers.

■ The PnP manager also implements application and driver mechanisms for the detection of hardware configuration changes. Applications or drivers sometimes require a specific hardware device to function, so Windows includes a means for them to request notification of the presence, addition, or removal of devices.

■ It also provides a place for storage device state, and it participates in system setup, upgrade, migration, and offline image management.

■ In addition, it supports network connected devices, such as network projects and printers, by allowing specialized bus drivers to detect the network as a bus and create device nodes for the devices running on it.

Level of Plug and Play Support

Windows aims to provide full support for Plug and Play, but the level of support possible depends on the attached devices and installed drivers. If a single device or driver doesn't support Plug and Play, the extent of Plug and Play support for the system can be compromised. In addition, a driver that doesn't support Plug and Play might prevent other devices from being usable by the system. Table 7-7 shows the outcome of various combinations of devices and drivers that can and can't support Plug and Play.

TABLE 7-7 **Device and Driver Plug and Play Capability**

	Type of Driver	
Type of Device	**Plug and Play**	**Non–Plug and Play**
Plug and Play	Full Plug and Play	No Plug and Play
Non–Plug and Play	Possible partial Plug and Play	No Plug and Play

A device that isn't Plug and Play–compatible is one that doesn't support automatic detection, such as a legacy ISA sound card. Because the operating system doesn't know where the hardware physically lies, certain operations—such as laptop undocking, sleep, and hibernation—are disallowed. However, if a Plug and Play driver is manually installed for the device, the driver can at least implement PnP manager–directed resource assignment for the device.

Drivers that aren't Plug and Play–compatible include legacy drivers, such as those that ran on Windows NT 4. Although these drivers might continue to function on later versions of Windows, the PnP manager can't reconfigure the resources assigned to such devices in the event that resource reallocation is necessary to accommodate the needs of a dynamically added device. For example, a device might be able to use I/O memory ranges A and B, and during the boot the PnP manager assigns it range A. If a device that can use only A is attached to the system later, the PnP manager can't direct the first device's driver to reconfigure itself to use range B. This prevents the second device from obtaining required resources, which results in the device being unavailable for use by the system. Legacy drivers

also impair a machine's ability to sleep or hibernate. (See the section "The Power Manager" for more details.)

Driver Support for Plug and Play

To support Plug and Play, a driver must implement a Plug and Play dispatch routine, a power management dispatch routine (described in the section "The Power Manager" later in this chapter), and an add-device routine. Bus drivers must support different types of Plug and Play requests than function or filter drivers do, however. For example, when the PnP manager is guiding device enumeration during the system boot (described in detail later in this chapter), it asks bus drivers for a description of the devices that they find on their respective buses. The description includes data that uniquely identifies each device as well as the resource requirements of the devices. The PnP manager takes this information and loads any function or filter drivers that have been installed for the detected devices. It then calls the add-device routine of each driver for every installed device the drivers are responsible for.

Function and filter drivers prepare to begin managing their devices in their add-device routines, but they don't actually communicate with the device hardware. Instead, they wait for the PnP manager to send a *start-device* command for the device to their Plug and Play dispatch routine. Prior to sending the *start-device* command the PnP manager performs resource arbitration to decide what resources to assign the device. The *start-device* command includes the resource assignment that the PnP manager determines during resource arbitration. When a driver receives a *start-device* command, it can configure its device to use the specified resources. If an application tries to open a device that hasn't finished starting, it receives an error indicating that the device does not exist.

After a device has started, the PnP manager can send the driver additional Plug and Play commands, including ones related to a device's removal from the system or to resource reassignment. For example, when the user invokes the remove/eject device utility, shown in Figure 7-35 (accessible by right-clicking on the PC card icon in the taskbar and selecting Safely Remove Hardware), to tell Windows to eject a USB flash drive, the PnP manager sends a *query-remove* notification to any applications that have registered for Plug and Play notifications for the device. Applications typically register for notification on their handles, which they close during a query-remove notification. If no applications veto the query-remove request, the PnP manager sends a *query-remove* command to the driver that owns the device being ejected. At that point, the driver has a chance to deny the removal or to ensure that any pending I/O operations involving the device have completed and to begin rejecting further I/O requests aimed at the device. If the driver agrees to the remove request and no open handles to the device remain, the PnP manager next sends a *remove* command to the driver to request that the driver discontinue accessing the device and release any resources the driver has allocated on behalf of the device.

FIGURE 7-35 Remove/eject utility

When the PnP manager needs to reassign a device's resources, it first asks the driver whether it can temporarily suspend further activity on the device by sending the driver a *query-stop* command. The driver either agrees to the request, if doing so wouldn't cause data loss or corruption, or denies the request. As with a *query-remove* command, if the driver agrees to the request, the driver completes pending I/O operations and won't initiate further I/O requests for the device that can't be aborted and subsequently restarted. The driver typically queues new I/O requests so that the resource reshuffling is transparent to applications currently accessing the device. The PnP manager then sends the driver a *stop* command. At that point, the PnP manager can direct the driver to assign different resources to the device and once again send the driver a *start-device* command for the device.

The various Plug and Play commands essentially guide a device through an assortment of operational states, forming a well-defined state-transition table, which is shown in simplified form in Figure 7-36. (Several possible transitions and Plug and Play commands have been omitted for clarity. Also, the state diagram depicted is that implemented by function drivers. Bus drivers implement a more complex state diagram.) A state shown in the figure that we haven't discussed is the one that results from the PnP manager's *surprise-remove* command. This command results when either a user removes a device without warning, as when the user ejects a PCMCIA card without using the remove/eject utility, or the device fails. The *surprise-remove* command tells the driver to immediately cease all interaction with the device because the device is no longer attached to the system and to cancel any pending I/O requests.

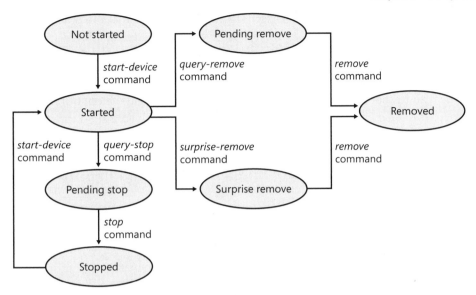

FIGURE 7-36 Device Plug and Play state transitions

Driver Loading, Initialization, and Installation

Driver loading and initialization on Windows consists of two types of loading: explicit load-ing and enumeration-based loading. Explicit loading is guided by the HKLM\SYSTEM\ CurrentControlSet\Services branch of the registry, as described in the section "Service Applications" in Chapter 4. Enumeration-based loading results when the PnP manager dynamically loads drivers for the devices that a bus driver reports during bus enumeration.

The Start Value

In Chapter 4, we explained that every driver and Windows service has a registry key under the Services branch of the current control set. The key includes values that specify the type of the image (for example, Windows service, driver, and file system), the path to the driver or service's image file, and values that control the driver or service's load ordering. There are two main differences between explicit device driver loading and Windows service loading:

- Only device drivers can specify Start values of boot-start (0) or system-start (1).

- Device drivers can use the Group and Tag values to control the order of loading within a phase of the boot, but unlike services, they can't specify DependOnGroup or DependOnService values.

Chapter 13 describes the phases of the boot process and explains that a driver Start value of 0 means that the operating system loader loads the driver. A Start value of 1 means that the I/O manager loads the driver after the executive subsystems have finished initializing.

The I/O manager calls driver initialization routines in the order that the drivers load within a boot phase. Like Windows services, drivers use the Group value in their registry key to specify which group they belong to; the registry value HKLM\SYSTEM\CurrentControlSet\Control\ServiceGroupOrder\List determines the order that groups are loaded within a boot phase.

A driver can further refine its load order by including a Tag value to control its order within a group. The I/O manager sorts the drivers within each group according to the Tag values defined in the drivers' registry keys. Drivers without a tag go to the end of the list in their group. You might assume that the I/O manager initializes drivers with lower-number tags before it initializes drivers with higher-number tags, but such isn't necessarily the case. The registry key HKLM\SYSTEM\CurrentControlSet\Control\GroupOrderList defines tag precedence within a group; with this key, Microsoft and device driver developers can take liberties with redefining the integer number system.

Here are the guidelines by which drivers set their Start value:

- Non–Plug and Play drivers set their Start value to reflect the boot phase they want to load in.

- Drivers, including both Plug and Play and non–Plug and Play drivers, that must be loaded by the boot loader during the system boot specify a Start value of boot-start (0). Examples include system bus drivers and the boot file system driver.

- A driver that isn't required for booting the system and that detects a device that a system bus driver can't enumerate specifies a Start value of system-start (1). An example is the serial port driver, which informs the PnP manager of the presence of standard PC serial ports that were detected by Setup and recorded in the registry.

- A non–Plug and Play driver or file system driver that doesn't have to be present when the system boots specifies a Start value of auto-start (2). An example is the Multiple Universal Naming Convention (UNC) Provider (MUP) driver, which provides support for UNC-based path names to remote resources (for example, \\REMOTECOMPUTERNAME\SHARE).

- Plug and Play drivers that aren't required to boot the system specify a Start value of demand-start (3). Examples include network adapter drivers.

The only purpose that the Start values for Plug and Play drivers and drivers for enumerable devices have is to ensure that the operating system loader loads the driver—if the driver is required for the system to boot successfully. Beyond that, the PnP manager's device enumeration process, described next, determines the load order for Plug and Play drivers.

Device Enumeration

The PnP manager begins device enumeration with a virtual bus driver called Root, which represents the entire computer system and acts as the bus driver for non–Plug and Play drivers

and for the HAL. The HAL acts as a bus driver that enumerates devices directly attached to the motherboard as well as system components such as batteries. Instead of actually enumerating, the HAL relies on the hardware description the Setup process recorded in the registry to detect the primary bus (a PCI bus in most cases) and devices such as batteries and fans.

The primary bus driver enumerates the devices on its bus, possibly finding other buses, for which the PnP manager initializes drivers. Those drivers in turn can detect other devices, including other subsidiary buses. This recursive process of enumeration, driver loading (if the driver isn't already loaded), and further enumeration proceeds until all the devices on the system have been detected and configured.

As the bus drivers report detected devices to the PnP manager, the PnP manager creates an internal tree called the *device tree* that represents the relationships between devices. Nodes in the tree are called *devnodes*, and a devnode contains information about the device objects that represent the device as well as other Plug and Play–related information stored in the devnode by the PnP manager. Figure 7-37 shows an example of a simplified device tree. This system is ACPI-compliant, so an ACPI-compliant HAL serves as the primary bus enumerator. A PCI bus serves as the system's primary bus, which USB, ISA, and SCSI buses are connected to.

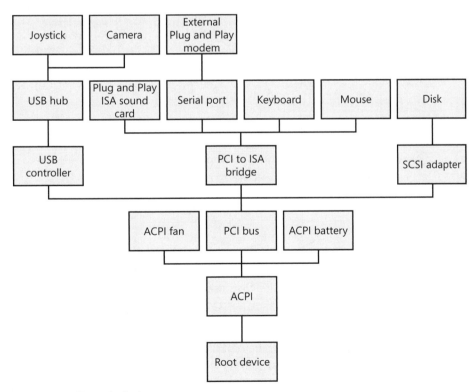

FIGURE 7-37 Example device tree

The Device Manager utility, which is accessible from the Computer Management snap-in in the Programs/Administrative Tools folder of the Start menu (and also from the Hardware tab of the System utility in Control Panel), shows a simple list of devices present on a system in its default configuration. You can also select the Devices By Connection option from the Device Manager's View menu to see the devices as they relate to the device tree. Figure 7-38 shows an example of the Device Manager's Devices By Connection view.

FIGURE 7-38 Device Manager showing the device tree

Taking device enumeration into account, the load and initialization order of drivers is as follows:

1. The I/O manager invokes the driver entry routine of each boot-start driver. If a boot driver has child devices, the I/O manager enumerates those devices, reporting their presence to the PnP manager. The child devices are configured and started if their drivers are boot-start drivers. If a device has a driver that isn't a boot-start driver, the PnP manager creates a devnode for the device but doesn't start it or load its driver.

2. After the boot-start drivers are initialized, the PnP manager walks the device tree, loading the drivers for devnodes that weren't loaded in step 1 and starting their devices. As each device starts, the PnP manager enumerates its child devices, if it has any, starting those devices' drivers and performing enumeration of their children as required. The

PnP manager loads the drivers for detected devices in this step *regardless of the driver's Start value*. (The one exception is if the Start value is set to disabled.) At the end of this step, all Plug and Play devices have their drivers loaded and are started, except devices that aren't enumerable and the children of those devices.

3. The PnP manager loads any drivers with a Start value of system-start that aren't yet loaded. Those drivers detect and report their nonenumerable devices. The PnP manager loads drivers for those devices until all enumerated devices are configured and started.

4. The service control manager loads drivers marked as auto-start.

The device tree serves to guide both the PnP manager and the power manager as they issue Plug and Play and power IRPs to devices. In general, IRPs flow from the top of a devnode to the bottom, and in some cases a driver in one devnode creates new IRPs to send to other devnodes, always moving toward the root. The flow of Plug and Play and power IRPs is further described later in this chapter.

EXPERIMENT: Dumping the Device Tree

A more detailed way to view the device tree than using Device Manager is to use the *!devnode* kernel debugger command. Specifying *0 1* as command options dumps the internal device tree devnode structures, indenting entries to show their hierarchical relationships, as shown here:

```
1kd> !devnode 0 1
Dumping IopRootDeviceNode (= 0x85161a98)
DevNode 0x85161a98 for PDO 0x84d10390
  InstancePath is "HTREE\ROOT\0"
  State = DeviceNodeStarted (0x308)
  Previous State = DeviceNodeEnumerateCompletion (0x30d)
  DevNode 0x8515bea8 for PDO 0x8515b030
  DevNode 0x8515c698 for PDO 0x8515c820
    InstancePath is "Root\ACPI_HAL\0000"
    State = DeviceNodeStarted (0x308)
    Previous State = DeviceNodeEnumerateCompletion (0x30d)
    DevNode 0x84d1c5b0 for PDO 0x84d1c738
      InstancePath is "ACPI_HAL\PNP0C08\0"
      ServiceName is "ACPI"
      State = DeviceNodeStarted (0x308)
      Previous State = DeviceNodeEnumerateCompletion (0x30d)
      DevNode 0x85ebf1b0 for PDO 0x85ec0210
        InstancePath is "ACPI\GenuineIntel_-_x86_Family_6_Model_15\_0"
        ServiceName is "intelppm"
        State = DeviceNodeStarted (0x308)
        Previous State = DeviceNodeEnumerateCompletion (0x30d)
      DevNode 0x85ed6970 for PDO 0x8515e618
        InstancePath is "ACPI\GenuineIntel_-_x86_Family_6_Model_15\_1"
        ServiceName is "intelppm"
        State = DeviceNodeStarted (0x308)
        Previous State = DeviceNodeEnumerateCompletion (0x30d)
```

```
            DevNode 0x85ed75c8 for PDO 0x85ed79e8
               InstancePath is "ACPI\ThermalZone\THM_"
               State = DeviceNodeStarted (0x308)
               Previous State = DeviceNodeEnumerateCompletion (0x30d)
            DevNode 0x85ed6cd8 for PDO 0x85ed6858
               InstancePath is "ACPI\pnp0c14\0"
               ServiceName is "WmiAcpi"
               State = DeviceNodeStarted (0x308)
               Previous State = DeviceNodeEnumerateCompletion (0x30d)
            DevNode 0x85ed7008 for PDO 0x85ed6730
               InstancePath is "ACPI\ACPI0003\2&daba3ff&2"
               ServiceName is "CmBatt"
               State = DeviceNodeStarted (0x308)
               Previous State = DeviceNodeEnumerateCompletion (0x30d)
            DevNode 0x85ed7e60 for PDO 0x84d2e030
               InstancePath is "ACPI\PNP0C0A\1"
               ServiceName is "CmBatt"
```
§

Information shown for each devnode includes the InstancePath, which is the name of the device's enumeration registry key stored under HKLM\SYSTEM\CurrentControlSet\ Enum, and the ServiceName, which corresponds to the device's driver registry key under HKLM\SYSTEM\CurrentControlSet\Services. To see the resources, such as inter-rupts, ports, and memory, assigned to each devnode, specify *0 3* as the command options for the *!devnode* command.

A record of all the devices detected since the system was installed is recorded under the HKLM\SYSTEM\CurrentControlSet\Enum registry key. Subkeys are in the form <Enumerator>\<Device ID>\<Instance ID>, where the enumerator is a bus driver, the device ID is a unique identifier for a type of device, and the instance ID uniquely identifies different instances of the same hardware.

Devnodes

Figure 7-39 shows that a devnode is made up of at least two, and sometimes more, device objects:

- A *physical device object* (PDO) that the PnP manager instructs a bus driver to create when the bus driver reports the presence of a device on its bus during enumeration. The PDO represents the physical interface to the device.

- One or more optional filter device objects (FiDOs) that layer between the PDO and the FDO (described next), and that are created by bus filter drivers.

- One or more optional FiDOs that layer between the PDO and the FDO (and that layer above any FiDOs created by bus filter drivers) that are created by lower-level filter drivers.

- A *functional device object* (FDO) that is created by the driver, which is called a function driver, that the PnP manager loads to manage a detected device. An FDO represents the logical interface to a device. A function driver can also act as a bus driver if devices are attached to the device represented by the FDO. The function driver often creates an interface (described earlier) to the FDO's corresponding PDO so that applications and other drivers can open the device and interact with it. Sometimes function drivers are divided into a separate class/port driver and miniport driver that work together to manage I/O for the FDO.

- One or more optional FiDOs that layer above the FDO and that are created by upper-level filter drivers.

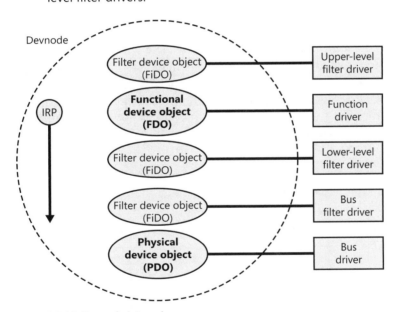

FIGURE 7-39 Devnode internals

Devnodes are built from the bottom up and rely on the I/O manager's layering functionality, so IRPs flow from the top of a devnode toward the bottom. However, any level in the devnode can choose to complete an IRP. For example, the function driver can handle a read request without passing the IRP to the bus driver. Only when the function driver requires the help of a bus driver to perform bus-specific processing does the IRP flow all the way to the bottom and then into the devnode containing the bus driver.

Devnode Driver Loading

So far, we've avoided answering two important questions: "How does the PnP manager determine what function driver to load for a particular device?" and "How do filter drivers register their presence so that they are loaded at appropriate times in the creation of a devnode?"

The answer to both these questions lies in the registry. When a bus driver performs device enumeration, it reports device identifiers for the devices it detects back to the PnP manager. The identifiers are bus-specific; for a USB bus, an identifier consists of a *vendor ID* (VID) for the hardware vendor that made the device and a *product ID* (PID) that the vendor assigned to the device. (See the WDK for more information on device ID formats.) Together these IDs form what Plug and Play calls a *device ID*. The PnP manager also queries the bus driver for an *instance ID* to help it distinguish different instances of the same hardware. The instance ID can describe either a bus-relative location (for example, the USB port) or a globally unique descriptor (for example, a serial number).

The device ID and instance ID are combined to form a *device instance ID* (DIID), which the PnP manager uses to locate the device's key in the enumeration branch of the registry (HKLM\SYSTEM\CurrentControlSet\Enum). Figure 7-40 presents an example of a keyboard's enumeration subkey. The device's key contains descriptive data and includes values named Service and ClassGUID (which are obtained from a driver's INF file) that help the PnP manager locate the device's drivers.

FIGURE 7-40 Keyboard enumeration key

EXPERIMENT: Viewing Detailed Devnode Information in Device Manager

The Device Manager applet that you can access from the Hardware tab of the System Control Panel application can show detailed information about a device node by using a tab called Details. The tab allows you to view an assortment of fields, including the devnode's device instance ID, hardware ID, service name, filters, and power capabilities.

The following screen shows the selection combo box of the Details tab expanded to reveal the types of information you can access:

Using the ClassGUID value, the PnP manager locates the device's class key under HKLM\ SYSTEM\CurrentControlSet\Control\Class. The keyboard class key is shown in Figure 7-41. The enumeration key and class key supply the PnP manager the information it needs to load the drivers necessary for the device's devnode. Drivers are loaded in the following order:

1. Any lower-level filter drivers specified in the LowerFilters value of the device's enumeration key.

2. Any lower-level filter drivers specified in the LowerFilters value of the device's class key.

3. The function driver specified by the Service value in the device's enumeration key. This value is interpreted as the driver's key under HKLM\SYSTEM\CurrentControlSet\ Services.

4. Any upper-level filter drivers specified in the UpperFilters value of the device's enumeration key.

5. Any upper-level filter drivers specified in the UpperFilters value of the device's class key.

In all cases, drivers are referenced by the name of their key under HKLM\SYSTEM\CurrentControlSet\Services.

FIGURE 7-41 Keyboard class key

Note The WDK refers to a device's enumeration key as its *hardware key* and to the class key as the *software key*.

The keyboard device shown in Figure 7-40 and Figure 7-41 has no lower-level filter drivers. The function driver is the i8042prt driver, and there are two upper-level filter drivers specified in the keyboard's class key: kbdclass and vmkbd2.

Driver Installation

If the PnP manager encounters a device for which no driver is installed, it relies on the user-mode PnP manager to guide the installation process. If the device is detected during the system boot, a devnode is defined for the device but the loading process is postponed until the user-mode PnP manager starts. (The user-mode PnP manager is implemented in \%SystemRoot%\System32\Umpnpmgr.dll and runs as a service in the Services.exe process.)

The components involved in a driver's installation are shown in Figure 7-42. Shaded objects in the figure correspond to components generally supplied by the system, whereas objects that aren't shaded are included in a driver's installation files. First, a bus driver informs the PnP manager of a device it enumerates using a DIID (1). The PnP manager checks the registry for the presence of a corresponding function driver, and when it doesn't find one, it informs the user-mode PnP manager (2) of the new device by its DIID. The user-mode PnP manager first tries to perform an automatic install without user intervention. If the installation process involves the posting of dialog boxes that require user interaction and the currently logged-on user has administrator privileges, (3) the user-mode PnP manager launches the Rundll32.exe application (the same application that hosts Control Panel utilities) to execute the Hardware Installation Wizard (\Windows\System32\Newdev.dll). If the currently logged-on user doesn't have administrator privileges (or if no user is logged on) and the installation of the device requires user interaction, the user-mode PnP manager defers the installation until a privileged user logs on. The Hardware Installation Wizard uses Setup and CfgMgr (configuration manager) API functions to locate INF files that correspond to drivers that are compatible with the detected device. This process might involve having the user insert installation media containing a vendor's INF files, or the wizard might locate a suitable INF file in the driver store (\Windows\System32\DriverStore) that contains drivers that ship with Windows. Installation is performed in two steps. In the first, the third-party driver developer imports the driver package into the driver store, and in the second step, the system performs the actual installation, which is always done through the %SystemRoot%\System32\Drvinst.exe process.

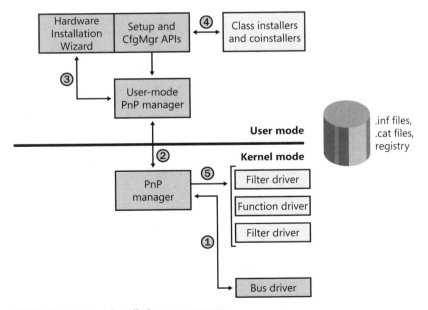

FIGURE 7-42 Driver installation components

To find drivers for the new device, the installation process gets a list of *hardware IDs* and *compatible IDs* from the bus driver. These IDs describe all the various ways the hardware might be identified in a driver installation file (.inf). The lists are ordered so that the most specific description of the hardware is listed first. If matches are found in multiple INFs, more precise matches are preferred over less precise matches, digitally signed INFs are preferred over unsigned ones, and newer signed INFs are preferred over older signed ones. If a match is found based on a compatible ID, the Hardware Installation Wizard can choose to prompt for media in case a more up-to-date driver came with the hardware.

The INF file locates the function driver's files and contains commands that fill in the driver's enumeration and class keys, and the INF file might direct the Hardware Installation Wizard to (4) launch class or device co-installer DLLs that perform class or device-specific installation steps, such as displaying configuration dialog boxes that let the user specify settings for a device.

EXPERIMENT: Looking at a Driver's INF File

When a driver or other software that has an INF file is installed, the system copies its INF file to the \Windows\Inf directory. One file that will always be there is Keyboard.inf because it's the INF file for the keyboard class driver. View its contents by opening it in Notepad and you should see something like this:

```
; Copyright (c) 1993-1996, Microsoft Corporation

[version]
signature="$Windows NT$"
Class=Keyboard
ClassGUID={4D36E96B-E325-11CE-BFC1-08002BE10318}
Provider=%MS%
LayoutFile=layout.inf
DriverVer=07/01/2001,5.1.2600.1106

[ClassInstall32.NT]
AddReg=keyboard_class_addreg
...
```

If you search the file for ".sys", you'll come across the entry that directs the user-mode PnP manager to install the i8042prt.sys and kbdclass.sys drivers:

```
...
[STANDARD_CopyFiles]
i8042prt.sys
kbdclass.sys
...
```

Before actually installing a driver, the user-mode PnP manager checks the system's driver-signing policy. If the settings specify that the system should block or warn of the installation of unsigned drivers, the user-mode PnP manager checks the driver's INF file for an entry

that locates a catalog (a file that ends with the .cat extension) containing the driver's digital signature.

Microsoft's WHQL tests the drivers included with Windows and those submitted by hardware vendors. When a driver passes the WHQL tests, it is "signed" by Microsoft. This means that WHQL obtains a *hash*, or unique value representing the driver's files, including its image file, and then cryptographically signs it with Microsoft's private driver-signing key. The signed hash is stored in a catalog file and included on the Windows installation media or returned to the vendor that submitted the driver for inclusion with its driver.

EXPERIMENT: Viewing Catalog Files

When you install a component such as a driver that includes a catalog file, Windows copies the catalog file to a directory under \Windows\System32\Catroot. Navigate to that directory in Explorer and you find the subdirectory that contains .cat files. Nt5.cat and Nt5inf.cat store the signatures for Windows system files, for example.

If you open one of the catalog files, a dialog box appears with two pages. The page labeled General shows information about the signature on the catalog file, and the Security Catalog page has the hashes of the components that are signed with the catalog file. This screen shot of a catalog file for NVIDIA video drivers shows the hash for the video adapter's kernel miniport driver. Other hashes in the catalog are associated with the various support DLLs that ship with the driver.

As it is installing a driver, the user-mode PnP manager extracts the driver's signature from its catalog file, decrypts the signature using the public half of Microsoft's driver-signing private/public key pair, and compares the resulting hash with a hash of the driver file it's about to install. If the hashes match, the driver is verified as having passed WHQL testing. If a driver fails the signature verification, the user-mode PnP manager acts according to the settings of the system driver-signing policy, either failing the installation attempt, warning the user that the driver is unsigned, or silently installing the driver.

Note Drivers installed using setup programs that manually configure the registry and copy driver files to a system and driver files that are dynamically loaded by applications aren't checked for signatures by the PnP manager's signing policy. Instead, they are checked by the Kernel Mode Code Signing policy described in Chapter 3. Only drivers installed using INF files are validated against the PnP manager's driver-signing policy.

After a driver is installed, the kernel-mode PnP manager (step 5 in Figure 7-42) starts the driver and calls its add-device routine to inform the driver of the presence of the device it was loaded for. The construction of the devnode then continues as described earlier.

Note The user-mode PnP manager also checks to see whether the driver it's about to install is on the *protected driver list* maintained by Windows Update and, if so, blocks the installation with a warning to the user. Drivers that are known to have incompatibilities or bugs are added to the list and blocked from installation.

The Power Manager

Just as Windows Plug and Play features require support from a system's hardware, its power-management capabilities require hardware that complies with the Advanced Configuration and Power Interface (ACPI) specification (available at *www.teleport.com/~acpi/spec.htm*).

The ACPI standard defines various power levels for a system and for devices. The six system power states are described in Table 7-8. They are referred to as S0 (*fully on* or *working*) through S5 (*fully off*). Each state has the following characteristics:

- **Power consumption** The amount of power the computer consumes
- **Software resumption** The software state from which the computer resumes when moving to a "more on" state
- **Hardware latency** The length of time it takes to return the computer to the fully on state

TABLE 7-8 System Power-State Definitions

State	Power Consumption	Software Resumption	Hardware Latency
S0 (fully on)	Maximum	Not applicable	None
S1 (sleeping)	Less than S0, more than S2	System resumes where it left off (returns to S0)	Less than 2 seconds
S2 (sleeping)	Less than S1, more than S3	System resumes where it left off (returns to S0)	2 or more seconds
S3 (sleeping)	Less than S2; processor is off	System resumes where it left off (returns to S0)	Same as S2
S4 (hibernating)	Trickle current to power button and wake circuitry	System restarts from saved hibernate file and resumes where it left off prior to hibernation (returns to S0)	Long and undefined
S5 (fully off)	Trickle current to power button	System boot	Long and undefined

States S1 through S4 are sleeping states, in which the computer appears to be off because of reduced power consumption. However, the computer retains enough information, either in memory or on disk, to move to S0. For states S1 through S3, enough power is required to preserve the contents of the computer's memory so that when the transition is made to S0 (when the user or a device wakes up the computer), the power manager continues executing where it left off before the suspend.

When the system moves to S4, the power manager saves the compressed contents of memory to a hibernation file named Hiberfil.sys, which is large enough to hold the uncompressed contents of memory, in the root directory of the system volume. (Compression is used to minimize disk I/O and to improve hibernation and resume-from-hibernation performance.) After it finishes saving memory, the power manager shuts off the computer. When a user subsequently turns on the computer, a normal boot process occurs, except that Bootmgr checks for and detects a valid memory image stored in the hibernation file. If the hibernation file contains saved system state, Bootmgr launches Winresume, which reads the contents of the file into memory, and then resumes execution at the point in memory that is recorded in the hibernation file.

On systems with hybrid sleep enabled (by default, only desktop computers), a user request to put the computer to sleep will actually be a combination of both the S3 state and the S4 state: while the computer is put to sleep, an emergency hibernation file will also be written to disk. Unlike typical hibernation files, which contain almost all active memory, the emergency hibernation file includes only data that could not be paged in at a later time, making the suspend operation faster than a typical hibernation (because less data is written to disk). Drivers will then be notified that an S4 transition is occurring, allowing them to configure themselves and save state just as if an actual hibernation request had been initiated. After this point, the system is put in the normal sleep state just like during a standard sleep transition. However, if

the power goes out, the system is now essentially in an S4 state—the user can power on the machine, and Windows will resume from the emergency hibernation file.

The computer never directly transitions between states S1 and S4; instead, it must move to state S0 first. As illustrated in Figure 7-43, when the system is moving from any of states S1 through S5 to state S0, it's said to be *waking*, and when it's transitioning from state S0 to any of states S1 through S5, it's said to be *sleeping*.

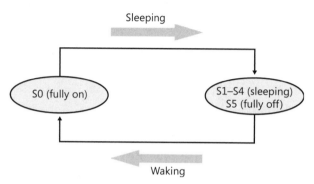

FIGURE 7-43 System power-state transitions

Although the system can be in one of six power states, ACPI defines devices as being in one of four power states, D0 through D3. State D0 is *fully on*, and state D3 is *fully off*. The ACPI standard leaves it to individual drivers and devices to define the meanings of states D1 and D2, except that state D1 must consume an amount of power less than or equal to that consumed in state D0, and when the device is in state D2, it must consume power less than or equal to that consumed in D1. Microsoft, in conjunction with the major hardware OEMs, has defined a series of power management reference specifications that specify the device power states that are required for all devices in a particular class (for the major device classes: display, network, SCSI, and so on). For some devices, there's no intermediate power state between fully on and fully off, which results in these states being undefined.

Power Manager Operation

Power management policy in Windows is split between the power manager and the individual device drivers. The power manager is the owner of the system power policy. This ownership means that the power manager decides which system power state is appropriate at any given point, and when a sleep, hibernation, or shutdown is required, the power manager instructs the power-capable devices in the system to perform appropriate system power-state transitions. The power manager decides when a system power-state transition is necessary by considering a number of factors:

- System activity level
- System battery level

- Shutdown, hibernate, or sleep requests from applications

- User actions, such as pressing the power button

- Control Panel power settings

When the PnP manager performs device enumeration, part of the information it receives about a device is its power-management capabilities. A driver reports whether or not its devices support device states D1 and D2 and, optionally, the latencies, or times required, to move from states D1 through D3 to D0. To help the power manager determine when to make system power-state transitions, bus drivers also return a table that implements a mapping between each of the system power states (S0 through S5) and the device power states that a device supports.

The table lists the lowest possible device power state for each system state and directly reflects the state of various power planes when the machine sleeps or hibernates. For example, a bus that supports all four device power states might return the mapping table shown in Table 7-9. Most device drivers turn their devices completely off (D3) when leaving S0 to minimize power consumption when the machine isn't in use. Some devices, however, such as network adapter cards, support the ability to wake up the system from a sleeping state. This ability, along with the lowest device power state in which the capability is present, is also reported during device enumeration.

TABLE 7-9 Example System-to-Device Power Mappings

System Power State	Device Power State
S0 (fully on)	D0 (fully on)
S1 (sleeping)	D1
S2 (sleeping)	D2
S3 (sleeping)	D2
S4 (hibernating)	D3 (fully off)
S5 (fully off)	D3 (fully off)

Driver Power Operation

When the power manager decides to make a transition between system power states, it sends power commands to a driver's power dispatch routine. More than one driver can be responsible for managing a device, but only one of the drivers is designated as the device power-policy owner. This driver determines, based on the system state, a device's power state. For example, if the system transitions between state S0 and S1, a driver might decide to move a device's power state from D0 to D1.

Instead of directly informing the other drivers that share the management of the device of its decision, the device power-policy owner asks the power manager, via the *PoRequestPowerIrp* function, to tell the other drivers by issuing a device power command to their power dispatch

routines. This behavior allows the power manager to control the number of power commands that are active on a system at any given time. For example, some devices in the system might require a significant amount of current to power up. The power manager ensures that such devices aren't powered up simultaneously.

EXPERIMENT: Viewing a Driver's Power Mappings

You can see a driver's system power state to driver power state mappings with Device Manager. Open the Properties dialog box for a device, and choose the Power Data entry in the drop-down list of the Details tab to see the mappings.

The dialog box also displays the current power state of the device, the device-specific power capabilities that it provides, and the power states from which it is able to wake the system.

Many power commands have corresponding query commands. For example, when the system is moving to a sleep state, the power manager will first ask the devices on the system whether the transition is acceptable. A device that is busy performing time-critical operations or interacting with device hardware might reject the command, which results in the system maintaining its current system power-state setting.

EXPERIMENT: Viewing the System Power Capabilities and Policy

You can view a computer's system power capabilities by using the *!pocaps* kernel debugger command. Here's the output of the command when run on an ACPI-compliant laptop running Windows Vista:

```
lkd> !pocaps
PopCapabilities @ 0x82114d80
  Misc Supported Features:   PwrButton SlpButton Lid S3 S4 S5 HiberFile FullWake
                             VideoDim
  Processor Features:        Thermal
  Disk Features:             SpinDown
  Battery Features:          BatteriesPresent
    Battery 0 - Capacity:        0  Granularity:        0
    Battery 1 - Capacity:        0  Granularity:        0
    Battery 2 - Capacity:        0  Granularity:        0
  Wake Caps
    Ac OnLine Wake:          Sx
    Soft Lid Wake:           Sx
    RTC Wake:                S4
    Min Device Wake:         Sx
    Default Wake:            Sx
```

The Misc Supported Features line reports that, in addition to S0 (fully on), the system supports system power states S1, S3, S4, and S5 (it doesn't implement S2) and has a valid hibernation file to which it can save system memory when it hibernates (state S4).

The Power Options page, shown here (available by selecting Power Options in Control Panel), lets you configure various aspects of the system's power policy. The exact properties you can configure depend on the system's power capabilities, which we just examined.

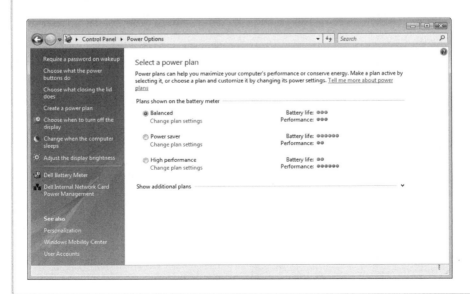

By changing any of the preconfigured plan settings, you can set the idle detection timeouts that control when the system turns off the monitor, spins down hard disks, goes to standby mode (moves to system power state S1), and hibernates (moves the system to power state S4). In addition, selecting the Change Advanced Power Settings option lets you specify the power-related behavior of the system when you press the power or sleep buttons or close a laptop's lid.

The settings you configure in Power Options directly affect values in the system's power policy, which you can display with the *!popolicy* debugger command. Here's the output of the command on the same system:

```
lkd> !popolicy
SYSTEM_POWER_POLICY (R.1) @ 0x82107994
    PowerButton:       Sleep  Flags: 00000000   Event: 00000000
    SleepButton:       Sleep  Flags: 00000000   Event: 00000000
    LidClose:          Sleep  Flags: 00000000   Event: 00000000
    Idle:              Sleep  Flags: 00000000   Event: 00000000
    OverThrottled:     None   Flags: 00000000   Event: 00000000
    IdleTimeout:         384  IdleSensitivity:        90%
    MinSleep:             S3  MaxSleep:                S3
    LidOpenWake:          S0  FastSleep:               S0
    WinLogonFlags:         1  S4Timeout:             fd20
    VideoTimeout:        300  VideoDim:                 0
```

```
SpinTimeout:            258  OptForPower:        0
FanTolerance:            0%  ForcedThrottle:     0%

SpinTimeout:            258  OptForPower:        0
MinThrottle:             0%  DyanmicThrottle:    None
```

The first lines of the display correspond to the button behaviors specified on the Advanced Settings tab of Power Options, and on this system both the power and the sleep buttons put the computer in a sleep state, just as closing the lid does.

The timeout values shown at the end of the output are expressed in seconds and displayed in hexadecimal notation. The values reported here directly correspond to the settings you can see configured on the Power Options page. (The laptop is on battery.) For example, the video timeout is 300, meaning the monitor turns off after 300 seconds, or 5 minutes, and the hard disk spin-down timeout is 0x258, which corresponds to 600 seconds, or 10 minutes.

Driver and Application Control of Device Power

Besides responding to power manager commands related to system power-state transitions, a driver can unilaterally control the device power state of its devices. In some cases, a driver might want to reduce the power consumption of a device it controls when the device is left inactive for a period of time. Examples include monitors that support a dimmed mode and disks that support spin-down. A driver can either detect an idle device itself or use facilities provided by the power manager. If the device uses the power manager, it registers the device with the power manager by calling the *PoRegisterDeviceForIdleDetection* function.

This function informs the power manager of the timeout values to use to detect a device as idle and of the device power state that the power manager should apply when it detects the device as being idle. The driver specifies two timeouts: one to use when the user has configured the computer to conserve energy and the other to use when the user has configured the computer for optimum performance. After calling *PoRegisterDeviceForIdleDetection*, the driver must inform the power manager, by calling the *PoSetDeviceBusy* function, whenever the device is active.

Although a device has control over its own power state, it does not have the ability to manipulate the system power state or to prevent system power transitions from occurring. For example, if a badly designed driver doesn't support any low-power states, it can choose to remain on or turn itself completely off without hindering the system's overall ability to enter a low-power state—this is because the power manager only *notifies* the driver of a transition and doesn't ask for *consent*.

Although drivers and the kernel are chiefly responsible for power management, applications are also allowed to provide their input. User-mode processes can register for a variety of power notifications, such as when the battery is low or critically low, when the laptop has switched from DC (battery) to AC (adapter/charger) power, or when the system is initiating a power transition. Just like drivers, however, applications cannot veto these operations, and they can have up to two seconds to clean up any state necessary before a sleep transition.

Conclusion

The I/O system defines the model of I/O processing on Windows and performs functions that are common to or required by more than one driver. Its chief responsibility is to create IRPs representing I/O requests and to shepherd the packets through various drivers, returning results to the caller when an I/O is complete. The I/O manager locates various drivers and devices by using I/O system objects, including driver and device objects. Internally, the Windows I/O system operates asynchronously to achieve high performance and provides both synchronous and asynchronous I/O capabilities to user-mode applications.

Device drivers include not only traditional hardware device drivers but also file system, network, and layered filter drivers. All drivers have a common structure and communicate with one another and the I/O manager by using common mechanisms. The I/O system interfaces allow drivers to be written in a high-level language to lessen development time and to enhance their portability. Because drivers present a common structure to the operating system, they can be layered one on top of another to achieve modularity and reduce duplication between drivers. Also, all Windows device drivers should be designed to work correctly on multiprocessor systems.

Finally, the role of the PnP manager is to work with device drivers to dynamically detect hardware devices and to build an internal device tree that guides hardware device enumeration and driver installation. The power manager works with device drivers to move devices into low-power states when applicable to conserve energy and prolong battery life.

Four more upcoming chapters in the book will cover additional topics related to the I/O system: storage management, file systems (including details on the NTFS file system), the cache manager, and networking.

Chapter 8
Storage Management

Storage management defines the way that an operating system interfaces with nonvolatile storage devices and media. The term *storage* encompasses many different devices, including tape drives, optical media, USB flash drives, floppy disks, hard disks, network storage such as iSCSI, and storage area networks (SANs). Windows provides specialized support for each of these classes of storage media. Because our focus in this book is on the kernel components of Windows, in this chapter we'll concentrate on just the fundamentals of the hard-disk storage subsystem in Windows, which includes support for external disks and flash drives. Significant portions of the support Windows provides for removable media and remote storage (offline archiving) are implemented in user mode.

In this chapter, we'll examine how kernel-mode device drivers interface file system drivers to disk media, discuss how disks are partitioned, describe the way volume managers abstract and manage volumes, and present the implementation of multipartition disk-management features in Windows, including replicating and dividing file system data across physical disks for reliability and for performance enhancement. We'll also describe how file system drivers mount volumes they are responsible for managing, and we'll conclude by discussing drive encryption technology in Windows and support for automatic backups and recovery.

Storage Terminology

To fully understand the rest of this chapter, you need to be familiar with some basic terminology:

- *Disks* are physical storage devices such as a hard disk, a 3.5-inch floppy disk, or a CD-ROM.

- A disk is divided into *sectors*, which are addressable blocks of fixed size. Sector sizes are determined by hardware. Most hard disk sectors are 512 bytes, and CD-ROM sectors are typically 2048 bytes.

- *Partitions* are collections of contiguous sectors on a disk. A partition table or other disk-management database stores a partition's starting sector, size, and other characteristics and is located on the same disk as the partition.

- *Simple volumes* are objects that represent sectors from a single partition that file system drivers manage as a single unit.

- *Multipartition volumes* are objects that represent sectors from multiple partitions and that file system drivers manage as a single unit. Multipartition volumes offer performance, reliability, and sizing features that simple volumes do not.

Disk Drivers

The device drivers involved in managing a particular storage device are collectively known as a *storage stack*. Figure 8-1 shows each type of driver that might be present in a stack and includes a brief description of its purpose. This chapter describes the behavior of device drivers below the file system layer in the stack. (The file system driver operation is described in Chapter 11.)

FIGURE 8-1 Windows storage stack

Winload

As you saw in Chapter 4, Winload is the Windows operating system file that conducts the first portion of the Windows boot process. Although Winload isn't technically part of the storage stack, it is involved with storage management because it includes support for accessing disk devices before the Windows I/O system is operational. Winload resides on the boot volume; the boot-sector code on the system volume executes Bootmgr. Bootmgr reads the BCD from the system volume or EFI firmware and presents the computer's boot choices to the user. Bootmgr translates the name of the BCD boot entry that a user selects to the appropriate boot partition and then runs Winload to load the Windows system files (starting with the registry, Ntoskrnl.exe and its dependencies, and the boot drivers) into memory to continue the boot process. In all cases, Winload uses the computer firmware to read the disk containing the system volume.

Disk Class, Port, and Miniport Drivers

During initialization, the Windows I/O manager starts the disk storage drivers. Storage drivers in Windows follow a class/port/miniport architecture, in which Microsoft supplies a storage class driver that implements functionality common to all storage devices and a storage port driver that implements functionality common to a particular bus—such as a Small Computer System Interface (SCSI) bus or an Integrated Device Electronics (IDE) system—and OEMs supply miniport drivers that plug into the port driver to interface Windows to a particular controller implementation.

In the disk storage driver architecture, only class drivers conform to the standard Windows device driver interfaces. Miniport drivers use a port driver interface instead of the device driver interface, and the port driver simply implements a collection of device driver support routines that interface miniport drivers to Windows. This approach simplifies the role of miniport driver developers and, because Microsoft supplies operating system–specific port drivers, allows driver developers to focus on hardware-specific driver logic. Windows includes Disk (\Windows\System32\Drivers\Disk.sys), a class driver that implements functionality common to disks. Windows also provides a handful of disk port drivers. For example, Scsiport.sys is the legacy port driver for disks on SCSI buses, and Ataport.sys is a port driver for IDE-based systems. Most newer drivers use the Storport.sys port driver as a replacement for Scsiport.sys. Storport.sys is designed to realize the high performance capabilities of hardware RAID and Fibre Channel adapters. The Storport model is similar to Scsiport, making it easy for vendors to migrate existing Scsiport miniport drivers to Storport. Miniport drivers that developers write to use Storport take advantage of several of Storport's performance enhancing features, including support for the parallel execution of I/O initiation and completion on multiprocessor systems, more controllable I/O request-queue architecture, and execution of more code at lower IRQL to minimize the duration of hardware interrupt masking. Storport also includes support for dynamic redirection of interrupts and DPCs to the best (most local) NUMA node on systems that support it.

Both the Scsiport.sys and Ataport.sys drivers implement a version of the disk scheduling algorithm known as C-LOOK. The drivers place disk I/O requests in lists sorted by the first sector (also known as the *logical block address,* or LBA) at which an I/O request is directed. They use the *KeInsertByKeyDeviceQueue* and *KeRemoveByKeyDeviceQueue* functions (documented in the Windows Driver Kit) representing I/O requests as items and using a request's starting sector as the key required by the functions. When servicing requests, the drivers proceed through the list from lowest sector to highest. When they reach the end of the list the drivers start back at the beginning, since new requests might have been inserted in the meantime. If disk requests are spread throughout a disk this approach results in the disk head continuously moving from near the outermost cylinders of the disk toward the innermost cylinders. Storport.sys does not implement disk scheduling because it is commonly used for managing I/Os directed at storage arrays where there is no clearly defined notion of a disk start and end.

Windows ships with several miniport drivers, including one—Aha154x.sys—for Adaptec's 1540 family of SCSI controllers. On systems that have at least one ATAPI-based IDE device, Atapi.sys, Pciidex.sys, and Pciide.sys together provide miniport functionality. Most Windows installations include one or more of the drivers mentioned.

iSCSI Drivers

The development of iSCSI as a disk transport protocol integrates the SCSI protocol with TCP/IP networking so that computers can communicate with block-storage devices, including disks, over IP networks. Storage area networking (SAN) is usually architected on Fibre Channel networking, but administrators can leverage iSCSI to create relatively inexpensive SANs from networking technology such as Gigabit Ethernet to provide scalability, disaster protection, efficient backup, and data protection. Windows support for iSCSI comes in the form of the Microsoft iSCSI Software Initiator, which can be installed as a feature on Windows Vista Enterprise and Windows Vista Ultimate, as well as on Windows Server 2008.

The Microsoft iSCSI Software Initiator includes several components:

- **Initiator** This optional component, which consists of the Storport port driver and the iSCSI miniport driver (\Windows\System32\Drivers\Msiscsi.sys), uses the TCP/IP driver to implement software iSCSI over standard Ethernet adapters and TCP/IP offloaded network adapters.

- **Initiator service** This service, implemented in \Windows\System32\Iscsiexe.exe, manages the discovery and security of all iSCSI initiators as well as session initiation and termination. iSCSI device discovery functionality is implemented in \Windows\System32\ Iscsium.dll and conforms to the Internet Storage Name Service (iSNS) protocol.

- **Management applications** These include Iscsicli.exe, a command-line tool for managing iSCSI device connections and security, and the corresponding Control Panel application.

Some vendors produce iSCSI adapters that offload the iSCSI protocol to hardware. The Initiator service works with these adapters, which must support iSNS, so that all iSCSI devices, including those discovered by the Initiator service and those discovered by iSCSI hardware, are recognized and managed through standard Windows interfaces.

Multipath I/O (MPIO) Drivers

Most disk devices have one *path*—or series of adapters, cables, and switches—between them and a computer. Servers requiring high levels of availability use *multipathing* solutions, where more than one set of connection hardware exists between the computer and a disk so that if a path fails the system can still access the disk via an alternate path. Without support from the operating system or disk drivers, however, a disk with two paths, for example, appears as two different disks. Windows includes multipath I/O support to manage multipath disks as

a single disk. This support relies on built-in or third-party drivers called *device-specific modules* (DSMs) to manage details of the path management—for example, load balancing policies that choose which path to use for routing requests and error detection mechanisms to inform Windows when a path fails. MPIO support is available for Windows Server 2008 in the form of the Microsoft MPIO Driver Development Kit, which hardware and software vendors can license.

In a Windows MPIO storage stack, shown in Figure 8-2, the disk driver includes functionality for MPIO devices. Disk.sys is responsible for claiming ownership of device objects representing multipath disks—so that it can ensure that only one device object is created to represent those disks—and for locating the appropriate DSM to manage the paths to the device. The Multipath Bus Driver (\Windows\System32\Drivers\Mpio.sys) manages connections between the computer and the device, including power management for the device. Disk.sys informs Mpio.sys of the presence of the devices for it to manage. Finally, the port driver for a multipath disk is also MPIO-aware in order to manage information passed up the device stack. There are therefore a total of three disk device stacks, two representing the physical paths (children of the adapter device stacks) and one representing the disk (child of the MPIO adapter device stack). When the latter receives a request, it uses the DSM to determine which path to forward that request to. The DSM makes the selection based on policy, and the request is sent to the corresponding disk device stack, which in turn forwards it to the device via the corresponding adapter.

EXPERIMENT: Watching Physical Disk I/O

Diskmon from Windows Sysinternals (*www.microsoft.com/technet/sysinternals*) uses the disk class driver's Event Tracing for Windows (or ETW, which is described in Chapter 3) instrumentation to monitor I/O activity to physical disks and display it in a window. Diskmon updates once a second with new data. For each operation, Diskmon shows the time, duration, target disk number, type and offset, and length, as you can see in the screen shown here.

#	Time	Duration (s)	Disk	Request	Sector	Length
21	5.034749	0.00643730	0	Write	222408832	8
22	5.035441	0.00643730	0	Write	27244544	8
23	5.072749	0.00643730	0	Write	27244544	8
24	5.073164	0.00643730	0	Write	258235032	32
25	5.074025	0.00643730	0	Write	222408840	24
26	5.074473	0.00643730	0	Write	258235064	32
27	5.074910	0.00643730	0	Write	256123320	32
28	5.075335	0.00643730	0	Write	256123224	32
29	5.075825	0.00643730	0	Write	31155656	8
30	5.136805	0.00643730	0	Write	31155656	8
31	5.137212	0.00643730	0	Write	222408832	8
32	5.137901	0.00643730	0	Write	27244552	8

Disk Monitor - Sysinternals: www.sysinternals.com
File Edit Options Help

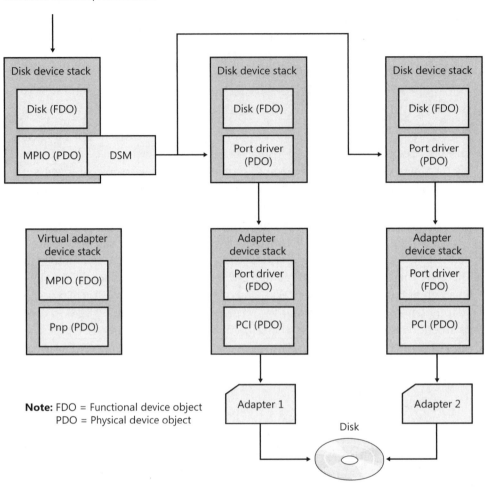

FIGURE 8-2 Windows MPIO storage stack

Disk Device Objects

The Windows disk class driver creates device objects that represent disks. Device objects that represent disks have names of the form \Device\Harddisk*X*\DR*X*; the number that identifies the disk replaces both *X*s. To maintain compatibility with applications that use older naming conventions, the disk class driver creates symbolic links with Windows NT 4–formatted names that refer to the device objects the driver created. For example, the volume manager driver creates the link \Device\Harddisk0\Partition0 to refer to \Device\Harddisk0\DR0, and \Device\Harddisk0\Partition1 to refer to the first partition device object of the first disk. For backward compatibility with applications that expect legacy names, the disk class driver also creates the same symbolic links in Windows that represent physical drives that it would have created on Windows NT 4 systems. Thus, for example, the link \GLOBAL??\PhysicalDrive0 references \Device\Harddisk0\DR0. Figure 8-3 shows the WinObj utility from Sysinternals displaying the

contents of a Harddisk directory for a basic disk. You can see the physical disk and partition device objects in the pane at the right.

FIGURE 8-3 WinObj showing a Harddisk directory of a basic disk

As you saw in Chapter 3, the Windows API is unaware of the Windows object manager namespace. Windows reserves two groups of namespace subdirectories to use, one of which is the \Global?? subdirectory. (The other group is the collection of per-session \BaseNamed-Objects subdirectories, which are covered in Chapter 3.) In this subdirectory, Windows makes available device objects that Windows applications interact with—including COM and parallel ports—as well as disks. Because disk objects actually reside in other subdirectories, Windows uses symbolic links to connect names under \Global?? with objects located elsewhere in the namespace. For each physical disk on a system, the I/O manager creates a \Global??\ PhysicalDrive*X* link that points to \Device\Harddisk*X*\DR*X*. (Numbers, starting from 0, replace *X*.) Windows applications that directly interact with the sectors on a disk open the disk by calling the Windows *CreateFile* function and specifying the name \\.\PhysicalDrive*X* (in which *X* is the disk number) as a parameter. The Windows application layer converts the name to \Global??\PhysicalDrive*X* before handing the name to the Windows object manager.

Partition Manager

The partition manager, \Windows\System32\Drivers\Partmgr.sys, is responsible for dis-covering, creating, deleting, and managing partitions. To become aware of partitions, the partition manager acts as the function driver for disk device objects created by disk class drivers. The partition manager uses the I/O manager's *IoReadPartitionTableEx* function to

identify partitions and create device objects that represent them. As miniport drivers present the disks that they identify early in the boot process to the disk class driver, the disk class driver invokes the *IoReadPartitionTableEx* function for each disk. This function invokes sector-level disk I/O that the class, port, and miniport drivers provide to read a disk's MBR or GPT (described later in this chapter) and construct an internal representation of the disk's partitioning. The partition manager driver creates device objects to represent each primary partition (including logical drives within extended partitions) that the driver obtains from *IoReadPartitionTableEx*. These names have the form \Device\HarddiskVolume*Y*, where *Y* represents the partition number.

When a partition is added, a private IOCTL command is sent to each registered volume manager, asking the volume manager if it owns that partition. If so, the partition manager remembers the specific volume manager that claimed that partition, and from this point on it notifies that driver when the partition is either deleted or modified. Volume manager device drivers receive the notification of partitions for disks that they manage and define volume objects when they account for all the partitions that make up the volumes.

The partition manager is also responsible for ensuring that all disks and partitions have a unique ID (signature for MBR and GUIDs for GPT). If it encounters two disks with the same ID, it tries to determine (by writing to one disk and reading from the other) whether they are two different disks or the same disk being viewed via two different paths (this can happen if the MPIO software isn't present or isn't working correctly). If the two disks are different, the partition manager changes the ID of one of them; if they are two paths to the same disk, the partition manager hides all the partitions on one of the disks from the volume managers to prevent the partitions from being mounted twice.

By managing disk attributes that are persisted in the registry (such as *read-only* and *offline*), the partition manager can perform actions such as hiding partitions from the volume managers, which inhibits the volumes from manifesting on the system. Clustering and Hyper-V use these attributes. The partition manager also redirects write operations that are sent directly to the disk but fall within a partition space to the corresponding volume manager. The volume manager determines whether to allow the write operation based on whether the volume is dismounted or not.

Volume Management

Windows has the concept of *basic* and *dynamic* disks. Windows calls disks that rely exclusively on the MBR-style or GPT partitioning scheme *basic disks*. Dynamic disks implement a more flexible partitioning scheme than that of basic disks. The fundamental difference between basic and dynamic disks is that dynamic disks support the creation of new multipartition volumes. Recall from the list of terms earlier in the chapter that multipartition volumes provide performance, sizing, and reliability features not supported by simple volumes. Windows

manages all disks as basic disks unless you manually create dynamic disks or convert existing basic disks (with enough free space) to dynamic disks. Microsoft recommends that you use basic disks unless you require the multipartition functionality of dynamic disks.

> **Note** Windows does not support multipartition volumes on basic disks. For a number of reasons, including the fact that laptops usually have only one disk and laptop disks typically don't move easily between computers, Windows uses only basic disks on laptops. In addition, only fixed disks can be dynamic, and disks located on IEEE 1394 or USB buses or on shared cluster server disks are always basic disks (or fixed dynamic disks).

Basic Disks

This section describes the two types of partitioning, MBR-style and GPT, that Windows uses to define volumes on basic disks, and the volume manager driver that presents the volumes to file system drivers. Windows silently defaults to defining all disks as basic disks.

MBR-Style Partitioning

The standard BIOS implementations that BIOS-based (non-EFI) x86 hardware uses dictate one requirement of the partitioning format in Windows—that the first sector of the primary disk contains the Master Boot Record (MBR). When a BIOS-based x86 system boots, the computer's BIOS reads the MBR and treats part of the MBR's contents as executable code. The BIOS invokes the MBR code to initiate an operating system boot process after the BIOS performs preliminary configuration of the computer's hardware. In Microsoft operating systems such as Windows, the MBR also contains a *partition table*. A partition table consists of four entries that define the locations of as many as four *primary partitions* on a disk. The partition table also records a partition's type. Numerous predefined partition types exist, and a partition's type specifies which file system the partition includes. For example, partition types exist for FAT32 and NTFS.

A special partition type, an *extended partition*, contains another MBR with its own partition table. The equivalent of a primary partition in an extended partition is called a *logical drive*. By using extended partitions, Microsoft's operating systems overcome the apparent limit of four partitions per disk. In general, the recursion that extended partitions permit can continue indefinitely, which means that no upper limit exists to the number of possible partitions on a disk. The Windows boot process makes evident the distinction between primary and logical drives. The system must mark one primary partition of the primary disk as active. The Windows code in the MBR loads the code stored in the first sector of the active partition (the system volume) into memory and then transfers control to that code. Because of the role in the boot process played by this first sector in the primary partition, Windows designates the first sector of any partition as the boot sector. As you will see in Chapter 13, every partition

formatted with a file system has a boot sector that stores information about the structure of the file system on that partition.

GUID Partition Table Partitioning

As part of an initiative to provide a standardized and extensible firmware platform for operating systems to use during their boot process, Intel has designed the Extensible Firmware Interface (EFI) specification. EFI includes a mini–operating system environment implemented in firmware (typically ROM) that operating systems use early in the system boot process to load system diagnostics and their boot code. EFI defines a partitioning scheme, called the GUID (globally unique identifier) Partition Table (GPT) that addresses some of the shortcomings of MBR-style partitioning. For example, the sector addresses that the GPT structures use are 64 bits wide instead of 32 bits. A 32-bit sector address is sufficient to access only 2 terabytes (TB) of storage, while a GPT allows the addressing of disk sizes into the foreseeable future. Other advantages of the GPT scheme include the fact that it uses cyclic redundancy checksums (CRC) to ensure the integrity of the partition table, and it maintains a backup copy of the partition table. GPT takes its name from the fact that in addition to storing a 36-byte Unicode partition name for each partition, it assigns each partition a GUID.

Figure 8-4 shows a sample GPT partition layout. Like for MBR-style partitioning, the first sector of a GPT disk is an MBR that serves to protect the GPT partitioning in case the disk is accessed from a non-GPT aware operating system. However, the second and last sectors of the disk store the GPT headers with the actual partition table following the second sector and preceding the last sector. With its extensible list of partitions, GPT partitioning doesn't require nested partitions, as MBR partitions do.

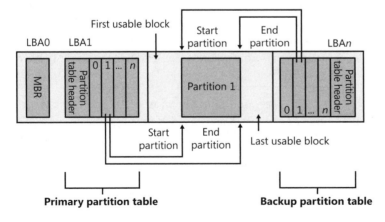

Note: LBA = Logical block address

FIGURE 8-4 Example GPT partition layout

> **Note** Because Windows doesn't support the creation of multipartition volumes on basic disks, a new basic disk partition is the equivalent of a volume. For this reason, the Disk Management MMC snap-in uses the term *partition* when you create a volume on a basic disk.

Basic Disk Volume Manager

The volume manager driver (\Windows\System32\Drivers\Volmgr.sys) creates disk device objects that represent volumes on basic disks and plays an integral role in managing all basic disk volumes, including simple volumes. For each volume, the volume manager creates a device object of the form \Device\HarddiskVolume*X*, in which *X* is a number (starting from 1) that identifies the volume.

The volume manager is actually a bus driver because it's responsible for enumerating basic disks to detect the presence of basic volumes and report them to the Windows Plug and Play (PnP) manager. To implement this enumeration, the volume manager leverages the PnP manager, with the aid of the partition manager (Partmgr.sys) driver to determine what basic disk partitions exist. The partition manager registers with the PnP manager so that Windows can inform the partition manager whenever the disk class driver creates a partition device object. The partition manager informs the volume manager about new partition objects through a private interface and creates filter device objects that the partition manager then attaches to the partition objects. The existence of the filter objects prompts Windows to inform the partition manager whenever a partition device object is deleted so that the partition manager can update the volume manager. The disk class driver deletes a partition device object when a partition in the Disk Management MMC snap-in is deleted. As the volume manager becomes aware of partitions, it uses the basic disk configuration information to determine the correspondence of partitions to volumes and creates a volume device object when it has been informed of the presence of all the partitions in a volume's description.

Windows volume drive-letter assignment, a process described shortly, creates drive-letter symbolic links under the \Global?? object manager directory that point to the volume device objects that the volume manager creates. When the system or an application accesses a volume for the first time, Windows performs a mount operation that gives file system drivers the opportunity to recognize and claim ownership for volumes formatted with a file system type they manage. (Mount operations are described in the section "Volume Mounting" later in this chapter.)

Dynamic Disks

As we've stated, dynamic disks are the disk format in Windows necessary for creating mul-tipartition volumes such as mirrors, striped arrays, and RAID-5 arrays (described later in the chapter). Dynamic disks are partitioned using Logical Disk Manager (LDM) partitioning. LDM is part of the Virtual Disk Service (VDS) subsystem in Windows, which consists of user-mode and device driver components and oversees dynamic disks. A major difference between LDM's partitioning and MBR-style and GPT partitioning is that LDM maintains one unified database that stores partitioning information for all the dynamic disks on a system—includ-ing multipartition-volume configuration.

The LDM Database

The LDM database resides in a 1-MB reserved space at the end of each dynamic disk. The need for this space is the reason Windows requires free space at the end of a basic disk before you can convert it to a dynamic disk. The LDM database consists of four regions, which Figure 8-5 shows: a header sector that LDM calls the Private Header, a table of con-tents area, a database records area, and a transactional log area. (The fifth region shown in Figure 8-5 is simply a copy of the Private Header.) The Private Header sector resides 1 MB before the end of a dynamic disk and anchors the database. As you spend time with Windows, you'll quickly notice that it uses GUIDs to identify just about everything, and disks are no exception. A GUID (globally unique identifier) is a 128-bit value that various compo-nents in Windows use to uniquely identify objects. LDM assigns each dynamic disk a GUID, and the Private Header sector notes the GUID of the dynamic disk on which it resides—hence the Private Header's designation as information that is private to the disk. The Private Header also stores the name of the disk group, which is the name of the computer concatenated with Dg0 (for example, Daryl-Dg0 if the computer's name is Daryl), and a pointer to the beginning of the database table of contents. For reliability, LDM keeps a copy of the Private Header in the disk's last sector.

The database table of contents is 16 sectors in size and contains information regarding the database's layout. LDM begins the database record area immediately following the table of contents with a sector that serves as the database record header. This sector stores informa-tion about the database record area, including the number of records it contains, the name and GUID of the disk group the database relates to, and a sequence number identifier that LDM uses for the next entry it creates in the database. Sectors following the database record header contain 128-byte fixed-size records that store entries that describe the disk group's partitions and volumes.

A database entry can be one of four types: partition, disk, component, and volume. LDM uses the database entry types to identify three levels that describe volumes. LDM connects entries with internal object identifiers. At the lowest level, *partition entries* describe soft partitions, which are contiguous regions on a disk; identifiers stored in a partition entry link the entry

to a component and disk entry. A *disk entry* represents a dynamic disk that is part of the disk group and includes the disk's GUID. A *component entry* serves as a connector between one or more partition entries and the volume entry each partition is associated with. A *volume entry* stores the GUID of the volume, the volume's total size and state, and a drive-letter hint. Disk entries that are larger than a database record span multiple records; partition, component, and volume entries rarely span multiple records.

FIGURE 8-5 LDM database layout

LDM requires three entries to describe a simple volume: a partition, component, and volume entry. The following listing shows the contents of a simple LDM database that defines one 200-MB volume that consists of one partition:

```
Disk Entry       Volume Entry      Component Entry      Partition Entry
Name: Disk1      Name: Volume1     Name: Volume1-01     Name: Disk1-01
GUID: XXX-XX...  ID: 0x408         ID: 0x409            ID: 0x407
Disk ID: 0x404   State: ACTIVE     Parent ID: 0x408     Parent ID: 0x409
                 Size: 200MB                            Disk ID: 0x404
                 GUID: XXX-XX...                        Start: 300MB
                 Drive Hint: H:                         Size: 200MB
```

The partition entry describes the area on a disk that the system assigned to the volume, the component entry connects the partition entry with the volume entry, and the volume entry contains the GUID that Windows uses internally to identify the volume. Multipartition volumes require more than three entries. For example, a striped volume (which is described later in the chapter) consists of at least two partition entries, a component entry, and a volume entry. The only volume type that has more than one component entry is a mirror; mirrors have two component entries, each of which represents one-half of the mirror. LDM uses two component entries for mirrors so that when you break a mirror, LDM can split it at the component level, creating two volumes with one component entry each.

The final area of the LDM database is the transactional log area, which consists of a few sectors for storing backup database information as the information is modified. This setup safeguards the database in case of a crash or power failure because LDM can use the log to return the database to a consistent state.

EXPERIMENT: Using LDMDump to View the LDM Database

You can use LDMDump from Sysinternals to view detailed information about the contents of the LDM database. LDMDump takes a disk number as a command-line argument, and its output is usually more than a few screens in size, so you should pipe its output to a file for viewing in a text editor—for example, *ldmdump /d0 > disk.txt*. The following example shows excerpts of LDMDump output. The LDM database header displays first, followed by the LDM database records that describe a 12-GB disk with three 4-GB dynamic volumes. The volume's database entry is listed as Volume1. At the end of the output, LDMDump lists the soft partitions and definitions of volumes it locates in the database.

```
C:\>ldmdump /d0
Logical Disk Manager Configuration Dump v1.03
Copyright (C) 2000-2002 Mark Russinovich

PRIVATE HEAD:
Signature          : PRIVHEAD
Version            : 2.12
Disk Id            : b5f4a801-758d-11dd-b7f0-000c297f0108
Host Id            : 1b77da20-c717-11d0-a5be-00a0c91db73c
Disk Group Id      : b5f4a7fd-758d-11dd-b7f0-000c297f0108
Disk Group Name    : WIN-SL5V78KD01W-Dg0
Logical disk start : 3F
Logical disk size  : 7FF7C1 (4094 MB)
Configuration start: 7FF800
Configuration size : 800 (1 MB)
Number of TOCs     : 2
TOC size           : 7FD (1022 KB)
Number of Configs  : 1
Config size        : 5C9 (740 KB)
Number of Logs     : 1
Log size           : E0 (112 KB)

TOC 1:
Signature          : TOCBLOCK
Sequence           : 0x1
Config bitmap start: 0x11
Config bitmap size : 0x5C9
Log bitmap start   : 0x5DA
Log bitmap size    : 0xE0
...
VBLK DATABASE:
0x000004: [000001] <DiskGroup>
         Name       : WIN-SL5V78KD01W-Dg0
         Object Id  : 0x0001
         GUID       : b5f4a7fd-758d-11dd-b7f0-000c297f010
0x000006: [000003] <Disk>
         Name       : Disk1
         Object Id  : 0x0002
         Disk Id    : b5f4a7fe-758d-11dd-b7f0-000c297f010
```

```
0x000007: [000005] <Disk>
        Name        : Disk2
        Object Id   : 0x0003
        Disk Id     : b5f4a801-758d-11dd-b7f0-000c297f010

0x000008: [000007] <Disk>
        Name        : Disk3
        Object Id   : 0x0004
        Disk Id     : b5f4a804-758d-11dd-b7f0-000c297f010

0x000009: [000009] <Component>
        Name        : Volume1-01
        Object Id   : 0x0006
        Parent Id   : 0x0005

0x00000A: [00000A] <Partition>
        Name        : Disk1-01
        Object Id   : 0x0007
        Parent Id   : 0x3157
        Disk Id     : 0x0000
        Start       : 0x7C100
        Size        : 0x0 (0 MB)
        Volume Off  : 0x3 (0 MB)

0x00000B: [00000B] <Partition>
        Name        : Disk2-01
        Object Id   : 0x0008
        Parent Id   : 0x3157
        Disk Id     : 0x0000
        Start       : 0x7C100
        Size        : 0x0 (0 MB)
        Volume Off  : 0x7FE80003 (1047808 MB)

0x00000C: [00000C] <Partition>
        Name        : Disk3-01
        Object Id   : 0x0009
        Parent Id   : 0x3157
        Disk Id     : 0x0000
        Start       : 0x7C100
        Size        : 0x0 (0 MB)
        Volume Off  : 0xFFD00003 (2095616 MB)

0x00000D: [00000F] <Volume>
        Name        : Volume1
        Object Id   : 0x0005
        Volume state: ACTIVE
        Size        : 0x017FB800 (12279 MB)
        GUID        : b5f4a806-758d-11dd-b7f0-c297f0108
        Drive Hint  : E:
```

LDM and GPT or MBR-Style Partitioning

When you install Windows on a computer, one of the first things it requires you to do is to create a partition on the system's primary physical disk. Windows defines the system volume on this partition to store the files that it invokes early in the boot process. In addition, Windows Setup requires you to create a partition that serves as the home for the boot volume, onto which the setup program installs the Windows system files and creates the system directory (\Windows). The system and boot volumes can be the same volume, in which case you don't have to create a new partition for the boot volume. The nomenclature that Microsoft defines for system and boot volumes is somewhat confusing. The system volume is where Windows places boot files, including the boot loader (Winload) and Boot Manager (Bootmgr), and the boot volume is where Windows stores operating system files such as Ntoskrnl.exe, the core kernel file.

Although the partitioning data of a dynamic disk resides in the LDM database, LDM implements MBR-style partitioning or GPT partitioning so that the Windows boot code can find the system and boot volumes when the volumes are on dynamic disks. (Winload and the IA64 firmware, for example, know nothing about LDM partitioning.) If a disk contains the system or boot volumes, partitions in the MBR or GPT describe the location of those volumes. Otherwise, one partition encompasses the entire usable area of the disk. LDM marks this partition as type "LDM". The region encompassed by this place-holding MBR-style or GPT partition is where LDM creates partitions that the LDM database organizes. On MBR-partitioned disks the LDM database resides in hidden sectors at the end of the disk, and on GPT-partitioned disks there exists an LDM metadata partition that encompasses the LDM database near the beginning of the disk.

Another reason LDM creates an MBR or a GPT is so that legacy disk-management utilities, including those that run under Windows and under other operating systems in dual-boot environments, don't mistakenly believe a dynamic disk is unpartitioned.

Because LDM partitions aren't described in the MBR or GPT of a disk, they are called *soft partitions*; MBR-style and GPT partitions are called *hard partitions*. Figure 8-6 illustrates this dynamic disk layout on an MBR-style partitioned disk.

FIGURE 8-6 Internal dynamic disk organization

Dynamic Disk Volume Manager

The Disk Management MMC snap-in DLL (DMDiskManager, located in \Windows\System32\ Dmdskmgr.dll), shown in Figure 8-7, is used to create and change the contents of the LDM database. When you launch the Disk Management MMC snap-in, DMDiskManager loads into memory and reads the LDM database from each disk and returns the information it obtains to the user. If it detects a database from another computer's disk group, it notes that the volumes on the disk are foreign and lets you import them into the current computer's database if you want to use them. As you change the configuration of dynamic disks, DMDiskManager updates its in-memory copy of the database. When DMDiskManager commits changes, it passes the updated database to the VolMgrX driver (%SystemRoot%\System32\Drivers\Volmgrx.sys). VolMgrX is a kernel-mode DLL that provides dynamic disk functionality for VolMgr, so it controls access to the on-disk database and creates device objects that represent the volumes on dynamic disks. When you exit Disk Management, DMDiskManager stops.

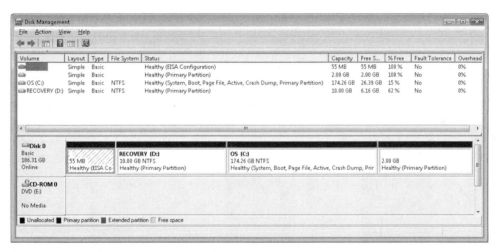

FIGURE 8-7 Disk Management MMC snap-in

Multipartition Volume Management

VolMgr is responsible for presenting volumes that file system drivers manage and for mapping I/O directed at volumes to the underlying partitions that they're part of. For simple volumes, this process is straightforward: the volume manager ensures that volume-relative offsets are translated to disk-relative offsets by adding the volume-relative offset to the volume's starting disk offset.

Multipartition volumes are more complex because the partitions that make up a volume can be located on discontiguous partitions or even on different disks. Some types of multipartition volumes use data redundancy, so they require more involved volume-to-disk–offset translation. Thus, VolMgr uses VolMgrX to process all I/O requests aimed at the multipartition volumes they manage by determining which partitions the I/O ultimately affects.

The following types of multipartition volumes are available in Windows:

- Spanned volumes
- Mirrored volumes
- Striped volumes
- RAID-5 volumes

After describing multipartition-volume partition configuration and logical operation for each of the multipartition-volume types, we'll cover the way that the VolMgr driver handles IRPs that a file system driver sends to multipartition volumes. The term *volume manager* is used to represent VolMgr and the VolMgrX extension DLL throughout the explanation of multipartition volumes.

Spanned Volumes

A *spanned volume* is a single logical volume composed of a maximum of 32 free partitions on one or more disks. The Disk Management MMC snap-in combines the partitions into a spanned volume, which can then be formatted for any of the Windows-supported file systems. Figure 8-8 shows a 100-MB spanned volume identified by drive letter D that has been created from the last third of the first disk and the first third of the second. Spanned volumes were called *volume sets* in Windows NT 4.

FIGURE 8-8 Spanned volume

A spanned volume is useful for consolidating small areas of free disk space into one larger volume or for creating a single large volume out of two or more small disks. If the spanned volume has been formatted for NTFS, it can be extended to include additional free areas or additional disks without affecting the data already stored on the volume. This extensibility is one of the biggest benefits of describing all data on an NTFS volume as a file. NTFS can dynamically increase the size of a logical volume because the bitmap that records the allocation status of the volume is just another file—the bitmap file. The bitmap file can be extended to include any space added to the volume. Dynamically extending a FAT volume, on the other hand, would require the FAT itself to be extended, which would dislocate everything else on the disk.

A volume manager hides the physical configuration of disks from the file systems installed on Windows. NTFS, for example, views volume D: in Figure 8-8 as an ordinary 100-MB volume. NTFS consults its bitmap to determine what space in the volume is free for allocation. It then calls the volume manager to read or write data beginning at a particular byte offset on the volume. The volume manager views the physical sectors in the spanned volume as numbered sequentially from the first free area on the first disk to the last free area on the last disk. It determines which physical sector on which disk corresponds to the supplied byte offset.

Striped Volumes

A *striped volume* is a series of up to 32 partitions, one partition per disk, that gets combined into a single logical volume. Striped volumes are also known as *RAID level 0* (RAID-0) volumes. Figure 8-9 shows a striped volume consisting of three partitions, one on each of three disks. (A partition in a striped volume need not span an entire disk; the only restriction is that the partitions on each disk be the same size.)

FIGURE 8-9 Striped volume

To a file system, this striped volume appears to be a single 450-MB volume, but a volume manager optimizes data storage and retrieval times on the striped volume by distributing the volume's data among the physical disks. The volume manager accesses the physical sectors of the disks as if they were numbered sequentially in stripes across the disks, as illustrated in Figure 8-10.

FIGURE 8-10 Logical numbering of physical sectors on a striped volume

Because each stripe unit is a relatively narrow 64 KB (a value chosen to prevent small individual reads and writes from accessing two disks), the data tends to be distributed evenly among the disks. Striping thus increases the probability that multiple pending read and

write operations will be bound for different disks. And because data on all three disks can be accessed simultaneously, latency time for disk I/O is often reduced, particularly on heavily loaded systems.

Spanned volumes make managing disk volumes more convenient, and striped volumes spread the I/O load over multiple disks. These two volume-management features don't provide the ability to recover data if a disk fails, however. For data recovery, a volume manager implements two redundant storage schemes: mirrored volumes and RAID-5 volumes. These features are created with the Windows Disk Management administrative tool.

Mirrored Volumes

In a *mirrored volume*, the contents of a partition on one disk are duplicated in an equal-sized partition on another disk. Mirrored volumes are sometimes referred to as *RAID level 1* (RAID-1). A mirrored volume is shown in Figure 8-11.

C:

C:
(mirror)

FIGURE 8-11 Mirrored volume

When a program writes to drive C:, the volume manager writes the same data to the same location on the mirror partition. If the first disk or any of the data on its C: partition becomes unreadable because of a hardware or software failure, the volume manager automatically accesses the data from the mirror partition. A mirror volume can be formatted for any of the Windows-supported file systems. The file system drivers remain independent and are not affected by the volume manager's mirroring activity.

Mirrored volumes can aid in read I/O throughput on heavily loaded systems. When I/O activity is high, the volume manager balances its read operations between the primary partition and the mirror partition (accounting for the number of unfinished I/O requests pending from each disk). Two read operations can proceed simultaneously and thus theoretically finish in half the time. When a file is modified, both partitions of the mirror set must be written, but disk writes are performed in parallel, so the performance of user-mode programs is generally not affected by the extra disk update.

Mirrored volumes are the only multipartition volume type supported for system and boot volumes. The reason for this is that the Windows boot code, including the MBR code and Winload, don't have the sophistication required to understand multipartition volumes—mirrored volumes are the exception because the boot code treats them as simple volumes, reading from the half of the mirror marked as the boot or system drive in the MBR-style partition table. Because the boot code doesn't modify the disk, it can safely ignore the other half of the mirror.

EXPERIMENT: Watching Mirrored Volume I/O Operations

Using the Reliability and Performance Monitor, you can verify that write operations directed at mirrored volumes copy to both disks that make up the mirror and that read operations, if relatively infrequent, occur primarily from one half of the volume. This experiment requires three hard disks. If you don't have three disks, you can skip the experiment setup instructions and view the Performance tool screen shot in this experiment that demonstrates the experiment's results.

Use the Disk Management MMC snap-in to create a mirrored volume. To do this, perform the following steps:

1. Run Disk Management by starting Computer Management, expanding the Storage tree, and clicking Disk Management (or by inserting Disk Management as a snap-in in an MMC console).

2. Right-click on an unallocated space of a drive, and then click New Simple Volume.

3. Follow the instructions in the New Simple Volume Wizard to create a simple volume. (Make sure there's enough room on another disk for a volume of the same size as the one you're creating.)

4. Right-click on the new volume, and then click Add Mirror on the context menu.

Once you have a mirrored volume, run the Performance tool and add counters for the PhysicalDisk performance object for both disk instances that contain a partition belonging to the mirror. Select the Disk Writes/sec counters for each instance. Select a large directory from the third disk (the one that isn't part of the mirrored volume), and copy it to the mirrored volume. The Performance tool output window should look something like the one on the following page as the copy operation progresses.

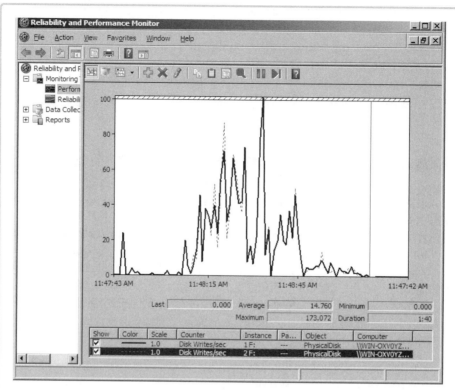

The top two lines, which overlap throughout the timeline, are the Disk Writes/sec counters for each disk. The screen shot reveals that the volume manager (in this case VolMgr) is writing the copied file data to both halves of the volume. This read behavior occurs because the number of outstanding I/O operations during the copy didn't warrant that the volume manager perform more aggressive read-operation load balancing.

RAID-5 Volumes

A *RAID-5 volume* is a fault tolerant variant of a regular striped volume. RAID-5 volumes implement *RAID level 5*. They are also known as *striped volumes with rotated parity* because they are based on the striping approach taken by striped volumes. Fault tolerance is achieved by reserving the equivalent of one disk for storing parity for each stripe. Figure 8-12 is a visual representation of a RAID-5 volume.

In Figure 8-12, the parity for stripe 1 is stored on disk 1. It contains a byte-for-byte logical sum (XOR) of the first stripe units on disks 2 and 3. The parity for stripe 2 is stored on disk 2, and the parity for stripe 3 is stored on disk 3. Rotating the parity across the disks in this way is an I/O optimization technique. Each time data is written to a disk, the parity bytes corresponding to the modified bytes must be recalculated and rewritten. If the parity were always written to the same disk, that disk would be busy continually and could become an I/O bottleneck.

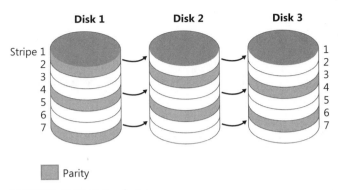

FIGURE 8-12 RAID-5 volume

Recovering a failed disk in a RAID-5 volume relies on a simple arithmetic principle: in an equation with n variables, if you know the value of $n - 1$ of the variables, you can determine the value of the missing variable by subtraction. For example, in the equation $x + y = z$, where z represents the parity stripe unit, the volume manager computes $z - y$ to determine the contents of x; to find y, it computes $z - x$. The volume manager uses similar logic to recover lost data. If a disk in a RAID-5 volume fails or if data on one disk becomes unreadable, the volume manager reconstructs the missing data by using the XOR operation (bitwise logical addition).

If disk 1 in Figure 8-12 fails, the contents of its stripe units 2 and 5 are calculated by XORing the corresponding stripe units of disk 3 with the parity stripe units on disk 2. The contents of stripes 3 and 6 on disk 1 are similarly determined by XORing the corresponding stripe units of disk 2 with the parity stripe units on disk 3. At least three disks (or rather, three same-sized partitions on three disks) are required to create a RAID-5 volume.

The Volume Namespace

The volume namespace mechanism handles the assignment of drive letters to device objects that represent actual volumes, which lets Windows applications access these drives through familiar means, and also provides mount and dismount functionality.

The Mount Manager

The Mount Manager device driver (Mountmgr.sys) assigns drive letters for dynamic disk volumes and basic disk volumes created after Windows is installed, CD-ROMs, floppies, and removable devices. Windows stores all drive-letter assignments under HKLM\SYSTEM\ MountedDevices. If you look in the registry under that key, you'll see values with names such as \??\Volume{X} (where X is a GUID) and values such as \DosDevices\C:. Every volume has a volume name entry, but a volume doesn't necessarily have an assigned drive letter. Figure 8-13 shows the contents of an example Mount Manager registry key. Note that the MountedDevices key, like the Disk key in Windows NT 4, isn't included in a control set and so

isn't protected by the last known good boot option. (See the section "Accepting the Boot and Last Known Good" in Chapter 13 for more information on control sets and the last known good boot option.)

The data that the registry stores in values for basic disk volume drive letters and volume names is the Windows NT 4–style disk signature and the starting offset of the first partition associated with the volume. The data that the registry stores in values for dynamic disk volumes includes the volume's VolMgr-internal GUID. When the Mount Manager initializes during the boot process, it registers with the Windows Plug and Play subsystem so that it receives notification whenever a device identifies itself as a volume. When the Mount Manager receives such a notification, it determines the new volume's GUID or disk signature and uses the GUID or signature as a guide to look in its internal database, which reflects the contents of the MountedDevices registry key. The Mount Manager then determines whether its internal database contains the drive-letter assignment. If the volume has no entry in the database, the Mount Manager asks VolMgr for a suggested drive-letter assignment and stores that in the database. VolMgr doesn't return suggestions for simple volumes, but it looks at the drive-letter hint in the volume's database entry for dynamic volumes.

FIGURE 8-13 Mounted devices listed in the Mount Manager's registry key

If no suggested drive-letter assignment exists for the volume, the Mount Manager uses the first unassigned drive letter (if one exists), defines a new assignment, creates a symbolic link for the assignment (for example, \Global??\D:), and updates the MountedDevices registry key. If there are no available drive letters, no drive-letter assignment is made. At the same time, the Mount Manager creates a volume symbolic link (that is, \Global??\Volume{X}) that defines a new volume GUID if the volume doesn't already have one. This GUID is different from the volume GUIDs that VolMgr uses internally.

Mount Points

Mount points let you link volumes through directories on NTFS volumes, which makes volumes with no drive-letter assignment accessible. For example, an NTFS directory that you've named C:\Projects could mount another volume (NTFS or FAT) that contains your project directories and files. If your project volume had a file you named \CurrentProject\ Description.txt, you could access the file through the path C:\Projects\CurrentProject\ Description.txt. What makes mount points possible is *reparse point* technology. (Reparse points are discussed in more detail in Chapter 11.)

A reparse point is a block of arbitrary data with some fixed header data that Windows associates with an NTFS file or directory. An application or the system defines the format and behavior of a reparse point, including the value of the unique reparse point tag that identifies reparse points belonging to the application or system and specifies the size and meaning of the data portion of a reparse point. (The data portion can be as large as 16 KB.) Reparse points store their unique tag in a fixed segment. Any application that implements a reparse point must supply a file system filter driver to watch for reparse-related return codes for file operations that execute on NTFS volumes, and the driver must take appropriate action when it detects the codes. NTFS returns a reparse status code whenever it processes a file operation and encounters a file or directory with an associated reparse point.

The Windows NTFS file system driver, the I/O manager, and the object manager all partly implement reparse point functionality. The object manager initiates pathname parsing operations by using the I/O manager to interface with file system drivers. Therefore, the object manager must retry operations for which the I/O manager returns a reparse status code. The I/O manager implements pathname modification that mount points and other reparse points might require, and the NTFS file system driver must associate and identify reparse point data with files and directories. You can therefore think of the I/O manager as the reparse point file system filter driver for many Microsoft-defined reparse points.

One common use of reparse points is the symbolic link functionality offered on Windows by NTFS (see Chapter 11 for more information on NTFS symbolic links). If the I/O manager receives a reparse status code from NTFS and the file or directory for which NTFS returned the code isn't associated with one of a handful of built-in Windows reparse points, no filter driver claimed the reparse point. The I/O manager then returns an error to the object manager that propagates as a "file cannot be accessed by the system" error to the application making the file or directory access.

Mount points are reparse points that store a volume name (\Global??\Volume{*X*}) as the reparse data. When you use the Disk Management MMC snap-in to assign or remove path assignments for volumes, you're creating mount points. You can also create and display mount points by using the built-in command-line tool *Mountvol.exe* (\Windows\System32\ Mountvol.exe).

The Mount Manager maintains the Mount Manager remote database on every NTFS volume in which the Mount Manager records any mount points defined for that volume. The database file resides in the directory System Volume Information on the NTFS volume. Mount points move when a disk moves from one system to another and in dual-boot environments—that is, when booting between multiple Windows installations—because of the existence of the Mount Manager remote database. NTFS also keeps track of reparse points in the NTFS metadata file \$Extend\$Reparse. (NTFS doesn't make any of its metadata files available for viewing by applications.) NTFS stores reparse point information in the metadata file so that Windows can, for example, easily enumerate the mount points (which are reparse points) defined for a volume when a Windows application, such as Disk Management, requests mount-point definitions.

Volume Mounting

Because Windows assigns a drive letter to a volume doesn't mean that the volume contains data that has been organized in a file system format that Windows recognizes. The volume-recognition process consists of a file system claiming ownership for a partition; the process takes place the first time the kernel, a device driver, or an application accesses a file or directory on a volume. After a file system driver signals its responsibility for a partition, the I/O manager directs all IRPs aimed at the volume to the owning driver. Mount operations in Windows consist of three components: file system driver registration, volume parameter blocks (VPBs), and mount requests.

Note The partition manager honors the system SAN policy, which can be set with the Windows DiskPart utility, that specifies whether it should surface disks for visibility to the volume manager. The default policy in Windows Server 2008 Enterprise and Datacenter editions is to not make SAN disks visible, which prevents the system from aggressively mounting their volumes.

The I/O manager oversees the mount process and is aware of available file system drivers because all file system drivers register with the I/O manager when they initialize. The I/O manager provides the *IoRegisterFileSystem* function to local disk (rather than network) file system drivers for this registration. When a file system driver registers, the I/O manager stores a reference to the driver in a list that the I/O manager uses during mount operations.

Every device object contains a VPB data structure, but the I/O manager treats VPBs as meaningful only for volume device objects. A VPB serves as the link between a volume device object and the device object that a file system driver creates to represent a mounted file system instance for that volume. If a VPB's file system reference is empty, no file system has mounted the volume. The I/O manager checks a volume device object's VPB whenever an open API that specifies a file name or a directory name on a volume device object executes.

For example, if the Mount Manager assigns drive letter D to the second volume on a system, it creates a \Global??\D: symbolic link that resolves to the device object \Device\ HarddiskVolume2. A Windows application that attempts to open the \Temp\Test.txt file on the D: drive specifies the name D:\Temp\Test.txt, which the Windows subsystem converts to \Global??\D:\Temp\Test.txt before invoking *NtCreateFile*, the kernel's file-open routine. *NtCreateFile* uses the object manager to parse the name, and the object manager encounters the \Device\HarddiskVolume2 device object with the path \Temp\Test.txt still unresolved. At that point, the I/O manager checks to see whether \Device\HarddiskVolume2's VPB references a file system. If it doesn't, the I/O manager asks each registered file system driver via a mount request whether the driver recognizes the format of the volume in question as the driver's own.

EXPERIMENT: Looking at VPBs

You can look at the contents of a VPB by using the *!vpb* kernel debugger command. Because the VPB is pointed to by the device object for a volume, you must first locate a volume device object. To do this, you must dump a volume manager's driver object, locate a device object that represents a volume, and display the device object, which reveals its Vpb field.

```
lkd> !drvobj volmgr
Driver object (84905030) is for:
 \Driver\volmgr
Driver Extension List: (id , addr)

Device Object list:
84a64780   849d5b28   84a64518   84a64030
84905e00
```

The *!drvobj* command lists the addresses of the device objects a driver owns. In this example, there are five device objects. One of them represents the programmatic interface to the device driver, and the rest are volume device objects. Because the objects are listed in reverse order from the way that they were created and the driver creates the device driver interface object first, you know the first device object listed is that of a volume. Now execute the *!devobj* kernel debugger command on the volume device object address:

```
lkd> !devobj 84a64780
Device object (84a64780) is for:
 HarddiskVolume4 \Driver\volmgr DriverObject 84905030
Current Irp 00000000 RefCount 0 Type 00000007 Flags 00001050
Vpb 84a64228 Dacl 8b1a8674 DevExt 84a64838 DevObjExt 84a64930 Dope 849fd838 DevNode
    849d5938
ExtensionFlags (0x00000800)
                            Unknown flags 0x00000800
AttachedDevice (Upper) 84a66020 \Driver\volsnap
Device queue is not busy
```

The *!devobj* command shows the Vpb field for the volume device object. (The device object shown is named HarddiskVolume4.) Now you're ready to execute the *!vpb* command:

```
lkd> !vpb 84a64228
Vpb at 0x84a64228
Flags: 0x1 mounted
DeviceObject: 0x84a6b020
RealDevice:   0x849d5b28
RefCount: 4311
Volume Label:   OS
```

The command reveals that the volume device object is mounted by a file system driver that has assigned the volume the name OS. The RealDevice field in the VPB points back to the volume device object, and the DeviceObject field points to the mounted file system device object. You can use *!devobj* on this address to get more information on the mounted file system, as seen in the output below, which shows that NTFS has mounted the volume:

```
lkd> !devobj 0x84a6b020
Device object (84a6b020) is for:
  \FileSystem\Ntfs DriverObject 84a02ad0
Current Irp 00000000 RefCount 0 Type 00000008 Flags 00040000
DevExt 84a6b0d8 DevObjExt 84a6bc00
ExtensionFlags (0x00000800)
                              Unknown flags 0x00000800
AttachedDevice (Upper) 84a63ac0 \FileSystem\FltMgr
Device queue is not busy
```

The convention followed by file system drivers for recognizing volumes mounted with their format is to examine the volume's boot record, which is stored in the first sector of the volume. Boot records for Microsoft file systems contain a field that stores a file system format type. File system drivers usually examine this field, and if it indicates a format they manage, they look at other information stored in the boot record. This information usually includes a file system name field and enough data for the file system driver to locate critical metadata files on the volume. NTFS, for example, will recognize a volume only if the Type field is NTFS, the Name field is "NTFS," and the critical metadata files described by the boot record are consistent.

If a file system driver signals affirmatively, the I/O manager fills in the VPB and passes the open request with the remaining path (that is, \Temp\Test.txt) to the file system driver. The file system driver completes the request by using its file system format to interpret the data that the volume stores. After a mount fills in a volume device object's VPB, the I/O manager hands subsequent open requests aimed at the volume to the mounted file system driver. If no file system driver claims a volume, Raw—a file system driver built into Ntoskrnl.exe—claims the volume and fails all requests to open files on that partition. Figure 8-14 shows a simplified

example (that is, the figure omits the file system driver's interactions with the Windows cache and memory managers) of the path that I/O directed at a mounted volume follows.

FIGURE 8-14 Mounted volume I/O flow

Instead of having every file system driver loaded, regardless of whether they have any volumes to manage, Windows tries to minimize memory usage by using a surrogate driver named File System Recognizer (\Windows\System32\Drivers\Fs_rec.sys) to perform preliminary file system recognition. File System Recognizer knows enough about each file system format that Windows supports to be able to examine a boot record and determine whether it's associated with a Windows file system driver. When the system boots, File System Recognizer registers as a file system driver, and when the I/O manager calls it during a file system mount operation for a new volume, File System Recognizer loads the appropriate file system driver if the boot record corresponds to one that isn't loaded. After loading a file system driver, File System Recognizer forwards the mount IRP to the driver and lets the file system driver claim ownership of the volume.

Aside from the boot volume, which a driver mounts while the kernel is initializing, file system drivers mount most volumes when the Chkdsk file system consistency-checking application runs during a boot sequence. The boot-time version of Chkdsk is a native application (as opposed to a Windows application) named Autochk.exe (\Windows\System32\Autochk.exe), and the Session Manager (\Windows\System32\Smss.exe) runs it because it is specified as a boot-run program in the HKLM\SYSTEM\CurrentControlSet\Control\Session Manager\BootExecute value. Chkdsk accesses each drive letter to see whether the volume associated with the letter requires a consistency check.

One place in which mounting can occur more than once for the same disk is with removable media. Windows file system drivers respond to media changes by querying the disk's volume identifier. If they see the volume identifier change, the driver dismounts the disk and attempts to remount it.

Volume I/O Operations

File system drivers manage data stored on volumes but rely on volume managers to interact with storage drivers to transfer data to and from the disk or disks on which a volume resides. File system drivers obtain references to a volume manager's volume objects through the mount process and then send the volume manager requests via the volume objects. Applications can also send the volume manager requests, bypassing file system drivers, when they want to directly manipulate a volume's data. File-undelete programs are an example of applications that do this.

Whenever a file system driver or application sends an I/O request to a device object that represents a volume, the Windows I/O manager routes the request (which comes in an IRP—a self-contained package) to the volume manager that created the target device object. Thus, if an application wants to read the boot sector of the second volume on the system (which is a simple volume in this example), it opens the device object \Device\HarddiskVolume2 and then sends the object a request to read 512 bytes starting at offset zero on the device. The I/O manager sends the application's request in the form of an IRP to the volume manager that owns the device object, notifying it that the IRP is directed at the HarddiskVolume2 device.

Because volumes are logical conveniences that Windows uses to represent contiguous areas on one or more physical disks, the volume manager must translate offsets that are relative to a volume to offsets that are relative to the beginning of a disk. If volume 2 consists of one partition that begins 4096 sectors into the disk, the partition manager would adjust the IRP's parameters to designate an offset with that value before passing the request to the disk class driver. The disk class driver uses a miniport driver to carry out physical disk I/O and read requested data into an application buffer designated in the IRP.

Some examples of a volume manager's operations will help clarify its role when it handles requests aimed at multipartition volumes. If a striped volume consists of two partitions, partition 1 and partition 2, the VolMgr device object intercepts file system disk I/O aimed at the device object for the volume, and the VolMgr driver adjusts the request before passing it to the disk class driver. The adjustment that VolMgr makes configures the request to refer to the correct offset of the request's target stripe on either partition 1 or partition 2. If the I/O spans both partitions of the volume, VolMgr must issue two subsidiary I/O requests, one aimed at each disk. This is shown in Figure 8-15.

FIGURE 8-15 VolMgr I/O operations

In the case of writes to a mirrored volume, VolMgr splits each request so that each half of the mirror receives the write operation. For mirrored reads, VolMgr performs a read from half of a mirror, relying on the other half when a read operation fails.

Virtual Disk Service

A company that makes storage products such as RAID adapters, hard disks, or storage arrays has to implement custom applications for installing and managing their devices. The use of different management applications for different storage devices has obvious drawbacks from the perspective of system administration. These drawbacks include learning multiple interfaces and the inability to use standard Windows storage management tools to manage third-party storage devices.

Windows includes the Virtual Disk Service (or VDS, located at \Windows\System32\Vds.exe), which provides a unified high-level storage interface so that administrators can manage storage devices from different vendors using the same user interfaces. VDS is shown in Figure 8-16. VDS exports a COM-based API that allows applications to create and format disks and to view and manage hardware RAID adapters. For example, a utility can use the VDS API to query the list of physical disks that map to a RAID logical unit number (LUN). Windows disk management utilities, including the Disk Management MMC snap-in and the DiskPart and DiskRAID command-line tools, use VDS APIs.

FIGURE 8-16 VDS service architecture

VDS supplies two interfaces, one for software providers and one for hardware providers:

- Software providers implement interfaces to high-level storage abstractions such as disks, disk partitions, and volumes. Examples of operations supported by these interfaces include creating, extending, and deleting volumes; adding or breaking mirrors; and formatting and assigning drive letters. VDS looks for registered software providers in HKLM\SYSTEM\CurrentControlSet\Services\Vds\SoftwareProviders. Windows includes the VDS Dynamic Disk Provider (\Windows\System32\Vdsdyn.dll) for interfacing to dynamic disks and the VDS Basic Provider (\Windows\System32\Vdsbas.dll) for interfacing to basic disks.

- Hardware vendors implement VDS hardware providers as DLLs that register under HKLM\SYSTEM\CurrentControlSet\Services\Vds\HardwareProviders and that translate device-independent VDS commands into commands for their hardware. The hardware provider allows for management of a storage subsystem such as a hardware RAID array or an adapter card, and supported operations include creating, extending, deleting, masking, and unmasking LUNs.

When an application initiates a connection to the VDS API and the VDS service isn't started, the Svchost process hosting the RPC service starts the VDS loader process

(\Windows\System32\Vdsldr.exe), which starts the VDS service process and then exits. When the last connection to the VDS API closes, the VDS service process exits.

BitLocker Drive Encryption

An operating system can enforce its security policies only while it's active, so you have to take additional measures to protect data when the physical security of a system can be compromised and the data accessed from outside the operating system. Hardware-based mechanisms such as BIOS passwords and encryption are two technologies commonly used to prevent unauthorized access, especially on laptops, which are the computers most likely to be lost or stolen.

While Windows supports the Encrypting File System (EFS), you can't use EFS to protect access to sensitive areas of the system, such as the registry hive files. For example, if Group Policy allows you to log on to your laptop even when you're not connected to a domain, then your domain credential verifiers are cached in the registry, so an attacker could use tools to obtain your domain account password hash and use that to try to obtain your password with a password cracker. The password would provide access to your account and EFS files (assuming you didn't store the EFS key on a smart card). To make it easy to encrypt the entire boot volume, including all its system files and data, Windows includes a full-volume encryption feature called Windows BitLocker Drive Encryption.

BitLocker helps prevent unauthorized access to data on lost or stolen computers by combining two major data-protection procedures:

- Encrypting the entire Windows operating system volume on the hard disk.
- Verifying the integrity of early boot components and boot configuration data.

The most secure implementation of BitLocker leverages the enhanced security capabilities of a Trusted Platform Module (TPM) version 1.2. The TPM is a hardware component installed in many newer computers by computer manufacturers. It works with BitLocker to help protect user data and to ensure that a computer running Windows has not been tampered with while the system was offline. On computers that do not have a TPM version 1.2, BitLocker can still encrypt the Windows operating system volume. However, this implementation requires the user to insert a USB startup key to start the computer or resume from hibernation, and it does not provide the full offline and preboot protection that a TPM-enabled system does.

BitLocker Architecture

BitLocker's architecture provides functionality and management mechanisms both in kernel mode and user mode. At a high level, the main components of BitLocker are:

- The Trusted Platform Module driver (%SystemRoot%\System32\Drivers\Tpm.sys), a kernel-mode driver that accesses the TPM chip.

- The TPM Base Services, which include a user-mode service that provides user-mode access to the TPM (%SystemRoot%\System32\tbssvc.dll), a WMI provider, and an MMC snap-in for configuration (%SystemRoot%\System32\Tpm.msc).

- The BitLocker-related code in the Boot Manager (Bootmgr) that authenticates access to the disk, handles boot-related unlocking, and allows recovery.

- The BitLocker filter driver (%SystemRoot%\System32\Drivers\Fvevol.sys), a kernel-mode filter driver that performs on-the-fly encryption and decryption of the volume.

- The BitLocker WMI provider and management script, which allow configuration and scripting of the BitLocker interface.

In the next sections, we'll take a look at these various components and the services they provide. Figure 8-17 provides an overview of the BitLocker architecture.

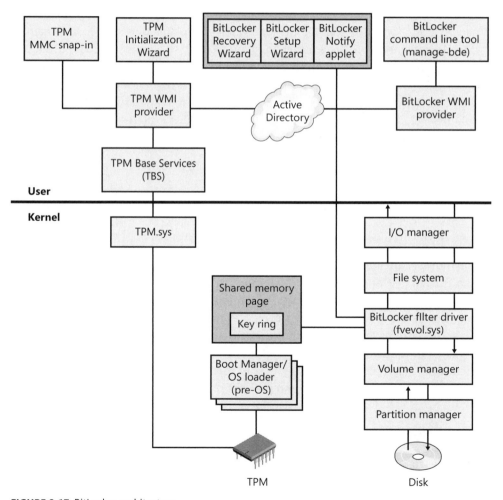

FIGURE 8-17 BitLocker architecture

Encryption Keys

BitLocker encrypts the contents of the volume using a full volume encryption key (FVEK) and cryptography that uses the AES128-CBC (by default) or AES256-CBC algorithm, with a Microsoft-specific extension called a diffuser. In turn, the FVEK is encrypted with a volume master key (VMK) and stored in a special metadata region of the volume. Securing the volume master key is an indirect way of protecting data on the volume: the addition of the volume master key allows the system to be rekeyed easily when keys upstream in the trust chain are lost or compromised. This ability to rekey the system saves the expense of decrypting and encrypting the entire volume again.

When you configure BitLocker, you have a number of options for how the VMK will be protected, depending on the system's hardware capabilities. If the system has a TPM, you can either encrypt the VMK with the TPM, have the system encrypt the VMK using a key stored in the TPM and one stored on a USB flash device, encrypt the VMK using a TPM-stored key and a PIN you enter when the system boots, or a combination of both a PIN and a USB flash device. For systems that don't have a compatible TPM, BitLocker offers the option of encrypting the VMK using a key stored on an external USB flash device.

In any case you'll need an unencrypted 1.5 GB NTFS system volume, the volume where the Boot Manager and BCD are stored, because the MBR and boot-sector code are legacy code, run in 16-bit real mode (as previously discussed), and do not have the ability to perform any on-the-fly decryption of the same volume they're running on. This means that these components must remain on an unencrypted volume so that the BIOS can access them and they can run and locate Bootmgr.

Figure 8-18 and Table 8-1 summarize the various ways in which the VMK can be generated.

TABLE 8-1 VMK Sources

Source	Identifies	Security	User Impact
TPM only	What it is	Protects against software attacks, but vulnerable to hardware attacks.	None
TPM + PIN	What it is + What you know	Adds protection against most hardware attacks as well.	User must enter PIN each boot
TPM + USB key	What it is + What you have	Fully protects against hardware attacks, but vulnerable to stolen USB key.	User must insert USB key each boot
TPM + USB key + PIN	What it is + What you have + What you know	Maximum level of protection.	User must enter PIN and insert USB key each boot
USB key only	What you have	Minimum level of protection for systems without TPM, but vulnerable to stolen key.	User must insert USB key each boot

FIGURE 8-18 BitLocker key generation

Finally, BitLocker also provides a simple encryption-based authentication scheme to ensure the integrity of the drive contents. Although AES encryption is currently considered uncrackable through brute-force attacks and is one of the most widely used algorithms in the industry today, it doesn't provide a way to ensure that modified encrypted data can't in some way

be modified such that it is translated back to plaintext data that an attacker could make use of. For example, by precise manipulation of the encrypted data, a hacker might be able to cause a certain logon function to behave differently and allow all logons.

To protect the system against this type of attack, BitLocker includes a *diffuser* algorithm called Elephant. The job of the diffuser is to make sure that even a single bit change in the ciphertext (encrypted data) will result in a totally random plaintext data output, ensuring that the modified executable code will most likely arbitrarily crash instead of performing a specific malicious function. Additionally, when combined with code integrity (see Chapter 3 for more information on code integrity), the diffuser will also cause core system files to fail their signature checks, rendering the system unbootable.

Trusted Platform Module (TPM)

A TPM is a tamper-resistant processor mounted on a motherboard that provides various cryptographic services such as key and random number generation and sealed storage. Support for TPM in Windows reaches beyond supporting BitLocker, however. Through the TPM Base Services (TBS), other applications on the system can also take advantage of compatible hardware TPM chips and use WMI to administer and script access to the TPM. For example, Windows uses a TPM as an additional seed into random number generation, which enhances the overall security of all applications on the system that depend on strong security or hashing algorithms (including mechanisms such as logons).

Although your computer may have a TPM, that does not necessarily mean that Windows will be able to support it. There are two requirements for Windows TPM support:

- The computer must have a TPM version 1.2 or higher

- The computer must have a Trusted Computing Group (TCG)-compliant BIOS. The BIOS establishes a chain of trust for the preboot environment and must include support for TCG-specific Static Root of Trust Measurement (SRTM).

The easiest way to determine whether your machine contains a compatible TPM is to run the TPM MMC snap-in (%SystemRoot%\System32\Tpm.msc). If Windows detects a compatible TPM, you should see a window similar to the one shown in Figure 8-19. Otherwise, an error message will appear.

As stated earlier, BitLocker can be configured to use the TPM to perform system integrity checks on critical early boot components. At a high level, the TPM collects and stores measurements from multiple early boot components and boot configuration data to create a system identifier (much like a fingerprint) for that computer. It stores each part of this fingerprint as a hash in a *platform configuration register* (PCR). BitLocker uses the hash of these functions

to *seal* the VMK, which is the key that BitLocker uses to protect other keys, including the FVEKs used to encrypt volumes.

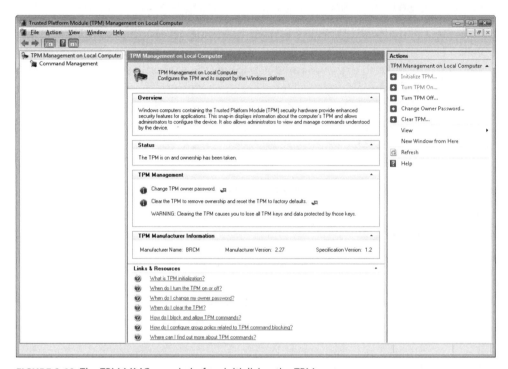

FIGURE 8-19 The TPM MMC snap-in before initializing the TPM.

If the early boot components are changed or tampered with, such as by changing the BIOS or MBR, or moving the hard disk to a different computer, the TPM prevents BitLocker from unsealing the VMK, and Windows enters a key recovery mode (described later in the chapter). If the PCR values match those used to seal the key, however, it unseals the key, and BitLocker can decrypt the keys used to protect volumes. Once the keys are unsealed, Windows starts and system protection becomes the responsibility of the user and the operating system.

A platform validation profile supported by TPMs consists of 24 PCRs that can be extended to contain additional information and only reset after a TPM reset (implying a machine reboot). Each PCR is associated with components that run when an operating system starts, as shown in Table 8-2.

BitLocker uses registers 0, 4, 8, 9, 10, and 11 to seal the VMK. This secures the encryption key against changes to the Core Root of Trust of Measurement (CRTM), BIOS, and platform extensions; Master Boot Record (MBR) code; the NTFS boot sector; the NTFS boot block; the Boot Manager; and the BitLocker Access Control.

TABLE 8-2 Platform Configuration Registers

Index	Meaning
0	Core Root of Trust of Measurement (CRTM), BIOS, and platform extensions
1	Platform and motherboard configuration and data
2	Option ROM code
3	Option ROM configuration and data
4	Master Boot Record (MBR) code
5	Master Boot Record (MBR) partition table
6	State transition and wake events
7	Computer manufacturer-specific
8	NTFS boot sector
9	NTFS boot block
10	Boot Manager
11	BitLocker Access Control
12	Defined for use by the static operating system
13	Defined for use by the static operating system
14	Defined for use by the static operating system
15	Defined for use by the static operating system
16	Used for debugging
17	Dynamic CRTM
18	Platform defined
19	Used by a trusted operating system
20	Used by a trusted operating system
21	Used by a trusted operating system
22	Used by a trusted operating system
23	Application support

BitLocker Boot Process

The actual measurements stored in the TPM PCRs are generated by the TPM itself, the TPM BIOS, and Windows. When the system boots, the TPM does a self-test, following which the CRTM in the BIOS measures its own hashing and PCR loading code and writes the hash to the first PCR of the TPM. It then hashes the BIOS and stores that measurement in the first PCR as well. The BIOS in turn hashes the next component in the boot sequence, the MBR of the boot drive, and this process continues until the operating system loader is measured. Each subsequent piece of code that runs is responsible for measuring the code that it loads and for storing the measurement in the appropriate register in the TPM.

Finally, when the user selects which operating system to boot, the Boot Manager (Bootmgr) reads the encrypted VMK from the volume and asks the TPM to unseal it. As described previously, only if all the measurements are the same as when the VMK was sealed, including the optional PIN, will the TPM successfully decrypt the VMK. This process not only guarantees that the machine and system files are identical to the applications or operating systems that are allowed to read the drive, but also verifies the uniqueness of the operating system installation. For example, even another identical Windows operating system installed on the same machine will not get access to the drive because Bootmgr takes an active role in protecting the VMK from being passed to an operating system to which it doesn't belong (by generating a MAC hash of several system configuration options).

You can think of this scheme as a verification chain, where each component in the boot sequence describes the next component to the TPM. Only if all the descriptions match the original ones given to it will the TPM divulge its secret. BitLocker therefore protects the encrypted data even when the disk is removed and placed in another system, the system is booted using a different operating system, or the unencrypted files on the boot volume are compromised. Figure 8-20 shows the various steps of the preboot process up until Winload begins loading the operating system.

FIGURE 8-20 BitLocker preboot process

BitLocker Key Recovery

For recovery purposes, BitLocker uses a recovery key (stored on a USB device) or a recovery password (numerical password), as shown in Figure 8-18. You create the recovery key or recovery password during BitLocker initialization. A copy of the VMK is encrypted with a

256-bit AES-CCM key that can be computed with the recovery password and a salt stored in the metadata block. The password is a 48-digit number, eight groups of 6 digits, with three properties for checksumming:

- Each group of 6 digits must be divisible by 11. This check can be used to identify groups mistyped by the user.

- Each group of 6 digits must be less than $2**16 * 11$. Each group contains 16 bits of key information. The eight groups, therefore, hold 128 bits of key.

- The sixth digit in each group is a checksum digit.

Inserting the recovery key or typing the recovery password enables an authorized user to regain access to the encrypted volume in the event of an attempted security breach or system failure. Figure 8-21 displays the prompt requesting the user to type the recovery password.

FIGURE 8-21 BitLocker recovery screen

The recovery key or password is also used in cases in which parts of the system have changed, resulting in different measurements. One common example of this is when a user has modified the BCD, such as by adding the *debug* option. Upon reboot, Bootmgr will detect the change and ask the user to validate it by inputting the recovery key. For this reason, it is extremely important not to lose this key, because it isn't only used for recovery but for validating system changes. Another application of the recovery key is for *foreign volumes*. Foreign volumes are operating system volumes that were BitLocker-enabled on another computer and have been transferred to a different Windows computer. An administrator can unlock these volumes by entering the recovery password.

Full Volume Encryption Driver

Unlike EFS, which is implemented by the NTFS file system driver and operates at the file level, BitLocker encrypts at the volume level using the full volume encryption (FVE) driver (%SystemRoot%\System32\Drivers\Fvevol.sys), as shown in Figure 8-22.

FIGURE 8-22 BitLocker filter driver implementation

FVE is a filter driver, so it automatically sees all the I/O requests that NTFS sends to the volume, encrypting blocks as they're written and decrypting them as they're read using the FVEK assigned to the volume when it's initially configured to use BitLocker. Because the encryption and decryption happen beneath NTFS in the I/O system, the volume appears to NTFS as if it's unencrypted, and NTFS does not even need to be aware that BitLocker is enabled. If you attempt to read data from the volume from outside Windows, however, it appears to be random data.

BitLocker also uses an extra measure to make plain-text attacks in which an attacker knows the contents of a sector and uses that information to try and derive the key used to encrypt it more difficult. By combining the FVEK with the sector number to create the key used to encrypt a particular sector, and passing the encrypted data through the Elephant diffuser, BitLocker ensures that every sector is encrypted with a slightly different key, resulting in different encrypted data for different sectors even if their contents are identical.

BitLocker Management

BitLocker provides three different kinds of administrative interfaces, each suited to a particular role or task. It provides a WMI interface (and works with the TBS WMI interface) for programmatic access to the BitLocker functionality, a set of Group Policies that allow administrators to define the behavior across the network or a series of machines, and integration with Active Directory.

Developers and system administrators with scripting familiarity can access the *Win32_Tpm* and *Win32_EncryptableVolume* interfaces to protect keys, define authentication methods, define which PCR registers are used as part of the BitLocker profile, and manually initiate encryption or decryption of an entire volume. The *manage-bde.wsf* script, located in %SystemRoot%\System32, uses these interfaces to allow command-line management of the BitLocker service.

On systems that are joined to a domain, the key for each machine can automatically be backed up as part of a key escrow service, allowing IT administrators to easily recover and gain access to machines that are part of the corporate network. Additionally, various Group Policies related to BitLocker can be configured. You can access these by using the Local Group Policy Editor, under the Computer Configuration, Administrative Templates, Windows Components, BitLocker Drive Encryption entry. For example, Figure 8-23 displays the option for enabling the Active Directory key backup functionality.

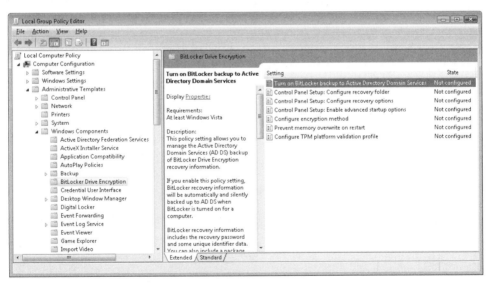

FIGURE 8-23 BitLocker Group Policy settings

If a TPM chip is present on the system, additional options (such as TPM Key Backup) can be accessed from the Trusted Platform Module Services entry under Windows Components.

Volume Shadow Copy Service

The Volume Shadow Copy Service (VSS) is a built-in Windows mechanism that enables the creation of consistent, point-in-time copies of data, known as *shadow copies* or *snapshots*. VSS coordinates with applications, file-system services, backup applications, fast-recovery solutions, and storage hardware to produce consistent shadow copies.

Shadow Copies

Shadow copies are created through one of two mechanisms—*clone* and *copy-on-write*. The VSS provider (described in more detail later) determines the method to use. (Providers can implement the snapshot as they see fit. For example, certain hardware providers will take a hybrid approach: clone first, and then copy-on-write.)

Clone Shadow Copies

A clone shadow copy, also called a *split mirror*, is a full duplicate of the original data on a volume, created either by software or hardware mirroring. Software or hardware keeps a clone synchronized with the master copy until the mirror connection is broken in order to create a shadow copy. At that moment, the live volume (also called the original volume) and the shadow volume become independent. The live volume is writable and still accepts changes, but the shadow volume is read-only and stores contents of the live volume at the time it was created.

Copy-on-Write Shadow Copies

A copy-on-write shadow copy, also called a *differential copy*, is a differential, rather than a full, duplicate of the original data. Similar to a clone copy, differential copies can be created by software or hardware mechanisms. Whenever a change is made to the live data, the block of data being modified is copied to a "differences area" associated with the shadow copy before the change is written to the live data block. Overlaying the modified data on the live data creates a view of the live data at the point in time when the shadow copy was created.

 Note The in-box VSS provider that ships with Windows only supports copy-on-write shadow copies.

VSS Architecture

VSS (%SystemRoot%\System32\Vssvc.exe) coordinates VSS writers, VSS providers, and VSS requestors. A VSS writer is a software component that enables shadow-copy-aware applications, such as Microsoft SQL Server, Microsoft Exchange Server, and Active Directory, to

receive freeze and thaw notifications to ensure that backup copies of their data files are internally consistent. Implementing a VSS provider allows an ISV or IHV with unique storage schemes to integrate with the shadow copy service. For instance, an IHV with mirrored storage devices might define a shadow copy as the frozen half of a split mirrored volume. VSS requestors are the applications that request the creation of volume shadow copies and include backup utilities and the Windows System Restore feature. Figure 8-24 shows the relationship between the VSS shadow copy service, writers, providers, and requestors.

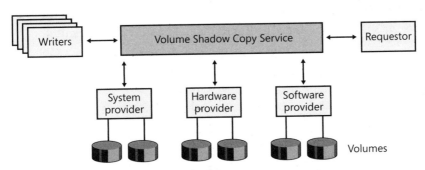

FIGURE 8-24 VSS architecture

VSS Operation

Regardless of the specific purpose for the copy and the application making use of VSS, shadow copy creation follows the same steps, shown in Figure 8-25. First, a requestor sends a command to VSS to enumerate writers, gather metadata, and prepare for the copy (1). VSS asks each writer to return information on its restore capabilities and an XML description of its backup components (2). Next, each writer prepares for the copy in its own appropriate way, which might include completing outstanding transactions and flushing caches. A prepare command is sent to all involved providers as well (3).

At this point, VSS initiates the *commit* phase of the copy (4). VSS instructs each writer to quiesce its data and temporarily freeze all write I/O requests (read requests are still passed through). VSS then flushes volume file system buffers and requests that the volume file system drivers freeze their I/O by sending them the IOCTL_VOLSNAP_FLUSH_AND_HOLD_WRITES device I/O control command, ensuring that all the file system metadata is written out to disk consistently (5). Once the system is in this state, VSS sends a command telling the provider to perform the actual copy creation (6). VSS allows up to 10 seconds for the creation, after which it aborts the operation if it is not already completed in this interval. After the provider has created the shadow copy, VSS asks the file systems to *thaw*, or resume write I/O operations, by sending them the IOCTL_VOLSNAP_RELEASE_WRITES command, and it releases the writers from their temporary freeze. All queued write I/O operations then proceed (7).

VSS next queries the writers to confirm that I/O operations were successfully held during the creation to ensure that the created shadow copy is consistent. If the shadow copy is inconsistent as the result of file system damage, the shadow copy is deleted by VSS. In other cases of writer failure, VSS simply notifies the requestor. At this point, the requestor can retry the procedure from (1), or wait for user action. If the copy was created consistently, VSS tells the requestor the location of the copy.

An optional final step is to make the snapshot device(s) writable, such that interested writers such as TxF can perform additional recovery actions on the snapshot device itself. After this recovery step, the snapshot is sealed read-only and handed out to the requestor.

Note VSS also allows the surfacing of shadow copy devices on a different server—called *transportable* shadow copies.

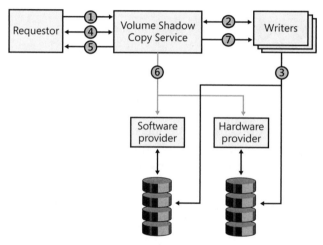

FIGURE 8-25 VSS shadow copy creation

Shadow Copy Provider

The Shadow Copy Provider (\%SystemRoot%\System32\Drivers\Swprov.dll) implements software-based differential copies with the aid of the Volume Shadow Copy Driver (Volsnap—\%SystemRoot\System32\Drivers\Volsnap.sys). Volsnap is a storage filter driver that resides between file system drivers and volume manager drivers (the drivers that present views of the sectors that represent a volume) so that the I/O system forwards it I/O operations directed at a volume.

When asked by VSS to create a shadow copy, Volsnap queues I/O operations directed at the target volume and creates a differential file in the volume's System Volume Information directory to store volume data that subsequently changes. Volsnap also creates a virtual volume through which applications can access the shadow copy. For example, if a volume's

name in the object manager namespace is \Device\HarddiskVolume1, the shadow volume would have a name like \Device\HarddiskVolumeShadowCopy*N*, where *N* is a unique ID.

Whenever Volsnap sees a write operation directed at a live volume, it reads a copy of the sectors that will be overwritten into a paging file—a backed memory section that's associated with the corresponding shadow copy. It services read operations directed at the shadow copy of modified sectors from this memory section, and it services reads to nonmodified areas by reading from the live volume. Because the backup utility won't save the paging file or the contents of the system-managed System Volume Information directory located on every volume (which includes shadow copy differential files), Volsnap uses the defragmentation API to determine the location of these files and directories and does not record changes to them.

Figure 8-26 demonstrates the behavior of applications accessing a volume and a backup application accessing the volume's shadow volume copy. When an application writes to a sector after the snapshot time, the Volsnap driver makes a backup copy, like it has for sectors a, b, and c of volume C: in the figure. Subsequently, when an application reads from sector c, Volsnap directs the read to volume C:, but when a backup application reads from sector c, Volsnap reads the sector from the snapshot. When a read occurs for any unmodified sector, such as d, Volsnap routes the read to volume C:.

 Note Volsnap avoids copy-on-write operations for the paging file, hibernation file, and the difference data stored in the System Volume Information folder. All other files will get copy-on-write protection.

FIGURE 8-26 Volsnap operation

EXPERIMENT: Looking at Microsoft Shadow Copy Provider Filter Device Objects

You can see the Microsoft Shadow Copy Provider driver's device objects attached to each volume device on a Windows system in a kernel debugger. Every system has at least one volume, and the following command displays the device object of the first volume on a system:

```
lkd> !devobj \device\harddiskvolume1
Device object (84a64030) is for:
 HarddiskVolume1 \Driver\volmgr DriverObject 84905030
Current Irp 00000000 RefCount 0 Type 00000007 Flags 00001050
Vpb 84a40818 Dacl 8b1a8674 DevExt 84a640e8 DevObjExt 84a641e0 Dope 84a02be0 DevNode
    84a64390
ExtensionFlags (0x00000800)
                              Unknown flags 0x00000800
AttachedDevice (Upper) 84a656c0 \Driver\volsnap
Device queue is not busy.
```

The AttachedDevice field in the output for the *!devobj* command displays the address of any device object, and the name of the owning driver, attached to (filtering) the device object being examined. For volume device objects, you should see a device object belonging to the Volsnap driver, as in the example output.

Uses in Windows

Several features in Windows make use of VSS, including Backup, System Restore, Previous Versions, and Shadow Copies for Shared Folders. We'll look at some of these uses and describe why VSS is needed and which VSS functionality is applicable to the applications.

Backup

A limitation of many backup utilities relates to open files. If an application has a file open for exclusive access, a backup utility can't gain access to the file's contents. Even if the backup utility can access an open file, the utility runs the risk of creating an inconsistent backup. Consider an application that updates a file at its beginning and then at its end. A backup utility saving the file during this operation might record an image of the file that reflects the start of the file before the application's modification and the end after the modification. If the file is later restored the application might deem the entire file corrupt because it might be prepared to handle the case where the beginning has been modified and not the end, but not vice versa. These two problems illustrate why most backup utilities skip open files altogether.

EXPERIMENT: Viewing Shadow Volume Device Objects

You can see the existence of shadow volume device objects in the object manager namespace by running the Windows backup application (under System Tools in the Accessories folder of the Start menu) and selecting enough backup data to cause the backup process to take long enough for you to run WinObj and see the objects in the \Device subdirectory, as shown here.

Instead of opening files to back up on the live volume, the backup utility opens them on the shadow volume. A shadow volume represents a point-in-time view of a volume, so by relying on the shadow copy facility, the backup utility overcomes both the backup problems related to open files.

Previous Versions and System Restore

The Windows Previous Versions feature also integrates support for automatically creating volume snapshots, typically one per day, that you can access through Explorer (by opening a Properties dialog box) using the same interface used by Shadow Copies for Shared Folders. This enables you to view, restore, or copy old versions of files and directories that you might have accidentally modified or deleted.

Windows also takes advantage of volume snapshots to unify user and system data-protection mechanisms and avoid saving redundant backup data. When an application installation or configuration change causes incorrect or undesirable behaviors, you can use System Restore to restore system files and data to their state as it existed when a restore point was created. When you use the System Restore user interface in Windows Vista to go back to a restore point, you're actually copying earlier versions of modified system files from the snapshot associated with the restore point to the live volume.

EXPERIMENT: Navigating Through Previous Versions

As you saw earlier, each time Windows creates a new system restore point, this results in a shadow copy being taken for that volume. You can navigate through time and see older copies of each drive being shadowed with Windows Explorer. To see a list of all previous versions of an entire volume, right-click on a partition, such as C:, and select Restore Previous Versions. You will see a dialog box similar to the one shown here.

Pick any of the versions shown, and then click the Open button. This opens a new Explorer window displaying that volume at the point in time when the snapshot was taken. The path shown will include \\localhost\C$\@GMT-<date>-<time>, which is how Explorer virtualizes the different shadow copies taken. (C$ is the local hidden default share that Windows networking uses; for more information, see Chapter 12.)

Internally, each volume shadow copy shown isn't a complete copy of the drive, so it doesn't duplicate the entire contents twice, which would double disk space requirements for every single copy. Previous Versions uses the copy-on-write mechanism described earlier to create shadow copies. For example, if the only file that changed between time A and time B, when a volume shadow copy was taken, is New.txt, the shadow copy will contain only New.txt. This allows VSS to be used in client scenarios with minimal visible impact on the user, since entire drive contents are not duplicated and size constraints remain small.

Although shadow copies for previous versions are taken daily (or whenever a Windows Update or software installation is performed, for example), you can manually request a copy to be taken. This can be useful if, for example, you're about to make major changes to the system or have just copied a set of files you want to save immediately for the purpose of creating a previous version. You can access these settings by right-clicking Computer on the Start Menu or desktop, selecting Properties, and then clicking System Protection. You can also open Control Panel, click System And Maintenance, and then click System. The dialog box shown in Figure 8-27 allows you to select the volumes on which to enable System Restore (which also affects previous versions) and to create an immediate restore point and name it.

FIGURE 8-27 System Restore and Previous Versions configuration

EXPERIMENT: Mapping Volume Shadow Device Objects

Although you can browse previous versions by using Explorer, this doesn't give you a permanent interface through which you can access that view of the drive in an application-independent, persistent way. You can use the Vssadmin utility (%System-Root%\System32\Vssadmin.exe) included with Windows to view all the shadow copies taken, and you can then take advantage of symbolic links to map a copy. This experiment will show you how.

1. List all shadow copies available on the system by using the *list shadows* command:

 vssadmin list shadows

 You'll see output that resembles the following. Each entry is either a previous version copy or a shared folder with shadow copies enabled.

   ```
   vssadmin 1.1 - Volume Shadow Copy Service administrative command-line tool
   (C) Copyright 2001-2005 Microsoft Corp.

   Contents of shadow copy set ID: {dfe617b7-ef2b-4280-9f4e-ddf94c2ccfac}
      Contained 1 shadow copies at creation time: 8/27/2008 1:59:58 PM
         Shadow Copy ID: {f455a794-6b0c-49e4-9ae5-e54647fd1f31}
            Original Volume: (C:)\\?\Volume{f5f9d9c3-7466-11dd-9ba5-806e6f6e6963}\
            Shadow Copy Volume: \\?\GLOBALROOT\Device\HarddiskVolumeShadowCopy1
            Originating Machine: WIN-SL5V78KD01W
            Service Machine: WIN-SL5V78KD01W
            Provider: 'Microsoft Software Shadow Copy provider 1.0'
            Type: ClientAccessibleWriters
            Attributes: Persistent, Client-accessible, No auto release,
               Differential, Auto recovered

   Contents of shadow copy set ID: {02dad996-e7b0-4d2d-9fb9-7e692be8fe3c}
      Contained 1 shadow copies at creation time: 8/29/2008 1:51:14 AM
         Shadow Copy ID: {79c9ee14-ca1f-4e46-b3f0-0dc98f8eb0d4}
            Original Volume: (C:)\\?\Volume{f5f9d9c3-7466-11dd-9ba5-806e6f6e6963}\
            Shadow Copy Volume: \\?\GLOBALROOT\Device\HarddiskVolumeShadowCopy2.
   ...
   ```

 Note that each *shadow copy set ID* displayed in this output matches the C$ entries shown by Explorer in the previous experiment, and the tool also displays the *shadow copy volume*, which corresponds to the shadow copy device objects that you can see with WinObj.

2. You can now use the Mklink.exe utility to create a directory symbolic link (for more information on symbolic links, see Chapter 11), which will let you map a shadow copy into an actual location. Use the /d flag to create a directory link, and specify a folder on your drive to map to the given volume device object. Make sure to append the path with a backslash (\) as shown here:

 mklink /d c:\old \\?\GLOBALROOT\Device\HarddiskVolumeShadowCopy2

3. Finally, with the Subst.exe utility, you can map the c:\old directory to a real volume using the command shown here:

 Subst g: c:\old

 You can now access the old contents of your drive from any application by using the c:\old path, or from any command-prompt utility by using the g:\ path—for example, try *dir g:* to list the contents of your drive.

Shadow Copies for Shared Folders

Windows also takes advantage of Volume Shadow Copy to provide a feature that lets standard users access backup versions of volumes on file servers so that they can recover old versions of files and folders that they might have deleted or changed. The feature alleviates the burden on systems administrators who would otherwise have to load backup media and access previous versions on behalf of these users.

The Properties dialog box for a volume includes a tab named Shadow Copies, shown in Figure 8-28. An administrator can enable scheduled snapshots of volumes using this tab, as shown in the following screen. Administrators can also limit the amount of space consumed by snapshots so that the system deletes old snapshots to honor space constraints.

FIGURE 8-28 Shadow Copies for Shared Folders

When a client Windows system (running Windows Vista Business, Enterprise, or Ultimate) maps a share from a folder on a volume for which snapshots exist, the Previous Versions tab appears in the Properties dialog box for folders and files on the share, just like for local folders. The Previous Versions tab shows a list of snapshots that exist on the server, instead of the client, allowing the user to view or copy a file or folder's data as it existed in a previous snapshot.

Conclusion

In this chapter, we've reviewed the on-disk organization, components, and operation of Windows disk storage management. In Chapter 10, we delve into the cache manager, an executive component integral to the operation of file system drivers that mount the volume types presented in this chapter. However, next, we'll take a close look at an integral component of the Windows kernel: the memory manager.

Chapter 9
Memory Management

In this chapter, you'll learn how Windows implements virtual memory and how it manages the subset of virtual memory kept in physical memory. We'll also describe the internal structure and components that make up the memory manager, including key data structures and algorithms. Before examining these mechanisms, we'll review the basic services provided by the memory manager and key concepts such as reserved memory versus committed memory and shared memory.

Introduction to the Memory Manager

By default, the virtual size of a process on 32-bit Windows is 2 GB. If the image is marked specifically as large address space aware, and the system is booted with a special option (described later in this chapter), a 32-bit process can grow to be 3 GB on 32-bit Windows and to 4 GB on 64-bit Windows. The process virtual address space size on 64-bit Windows is 7,152 GB on IA64 systems and 8,192 GB on x64 systems. (This value could be increased in future releases.)

As you saw in Chapter 2 (specifically in Table 2-3), the maximum amount of physical memory currently supported by Windows ranges from 2 GB to 2,048 GB, depending on which version and edition of Windows you are running. Because the virtual address space might be larger or smaller than the physical memory on the machine, the memory manager has two primary tasks:

- Translating, or mapping, a process's virtual address space into physical memory so that when a thread running in the context of that process reads or writes to the virtual address space, the correct physical address is referenced. (The subset of a process's virtual address space that is physically resident is called the *working set*. Working sets are described in more detail later in this chapter.)

- Paging some of the contents of memory to disk when it becomes overcommitted—that is, when running threads or system code try to use more physical memory than is currently available—and bringing the contents back into physical memory when needed.

In addition to providing virtual memory management, the memory manager provides a core set of services on which the various Windows environment subsystems are built. These services include memory mapped files (internally called *section objects*), copy-on-write memory, and support for applications using large, sparse address spaces. In addition, the memory manager provides a way for a process to allocate and use larger amounts of physical

memory than can be mapped into the process virtual address space (for example, on 32-bit systems with more than 4 GB of physical memory). This is explained in the section "Address Windowing Extensions" later in this chapter.

Memory Manager Components

The memory manager is part of the Windows executive and therefore exists in the file Ntoskrnl.exe. No parts of the memory manager exist in the HAL. The memory manager consists of the following components:

- A set of executive system services for allocating, deallocating, and managing virtual memory, most of which are exposed through the Windows API or kernel-mode device driver interfaces

- A translation-not-valid and access fault trap handler for resolving hardware-detected memory management exceptions and making virtual pages resident on behalf of a process

- Several key components that run in the context of six different kernel-mode system threads:

 - The *working set manager* (priority 16), which the balance set manager (a system thread that the kernel creates) calls once per second as well as when free memory falls below a certain threshold, drives the overall memory management policies, such as working set trimming, aging, and modified page writing.

 - The *process/stack swapper* (priority 23) performs both process and kernel thread stack inswapping and outswapping. The balance set manager and the thread-scheduling code in the kernel awaken this thread when an inswap or outswap operation needs to take place.

 - The *modified page writer* (priority 17) writes dirty pages on the modified list back to the appropriate paging files. This thread is awakened when the size of the modified list needs to be reduced.

 - The *mapped page writer* (priority 17) writes dirty pages in mapped files to disk (or remote storage). It is awakened when the size of the modified list needs to be reduced or if pages for mapped files have been on the modified list for more than 5 minutes. This second modified page writer thread is necessary because it can generate page faults that result in requests for free pages. If there were no free pages and there was only one modified page writer thread, the system could deadlock waiting for free pages.

❑ The *dereference segment thread* (priority 18) is responsible for cache reduction as well as for page file growth and shrinkage. (For example, if there is no virtual address space for paged pool growth, this thread trims the page cache so that the paged pool used to anchor it can be freed for reuse.)

❑ The *zero page thread* (priority 0) zeroes out pages on the free list so that a cache of zero pages is available to satisfy future demand-zero page faults. (Memory zeroing in some cases is done by a faster function called *MiZeroInParallel*. See the note in the section "Page List Dynamics.")

Each of these components is covered in more detail later in the chapter.

Internal Synchronization

Like all other components of the Windows executive, the memory manager is fully reentrant and supports simultaneous execution on multiprocessor systems—that is, it allows two threads to acquire resources in such a way that they don't corrupt each other's data. To accomplish the goal of being fully reentrant, the memory manager uses several different internal synchronization mechanisms to control access to its own internal data structures, such as spinlocks. (Synchronization objects are discussed in Chapter 3.)

Systemwide resources to which the memory manager must synchronize access include the page frame number (PFN) database (controlled by a spinlock), section objects and the system working set (controlled by pushlocks), and page file creation (controlled by a guarded mutex). Per-process memory management data structures that require synchronization include the working set lock (held while changes are being made to the working set list) and the address space lock (held whenever the address space is being changed). Both these locks are implemented using pushlocks.

Examining Memory Usage

The Memory and Process performance counter objects provide access to most of the details about system and process memory utilization. Throughout the chapter, we'll include references to specific performance counters that contain information related to the component being described. We've included relevant examples and experiments throughout the chapter. One word of caution, however: different utilities use varying and sometimes inconsistent or confusing names when displaying memory information. The following experiment illustrates this point. (We'll explain the terms used in this example in subsequent sections.)

EXPERIMENT: Viewing System Memory Information

The Performance tab in the Windows Task Manager, shown in the following screen shot, displays basic system memory information. This information is a subset of the detailed memory information available through the performance counters.

The following table shows the meaning of the memory-related values.

Task Manager Value	Definition
Memory bar histogram	Physical memory usable by Windows (not available as a performance counter; represents RAM usable by the operating system, and does not include BIOS shadow pages, device memory, and so on). Measured in available bytes.
Physical Memory (MB): Total	Physical memory usable by Windows
Physical Memory (MB): Cached	Cache bytes + modified page list bytes + standby cache core bytes + standby cache normal priority bytes + standby cache reserve bytes
Physical Memory (MB): Free	Free and zero page list bytes
Kernel Memory (MB): Total	Pool paged bytes + pool nonpaged bytes
Kernel Memory (MB): Paged	Pool paged bytes
Kernel Memory (MB): Nonpaged	Pool nonpaged bytes
System: Page File (two numbers shown)	Committed bytes / commit limit

To see the specific usage of paged and nonpaged pool, use the Poolmon utility, described in the "Monitoring Pool Usage" section.

Finally, the *!vm* command in the kernel debugger shows the basic memory management information available through the memory-related performance counters. This command can be useful if you're looking at a crash dump or hung system. Here's an example of its output from a 512-MB Windows Server 2008 system:

```
lkd> !vm

*** Virtual Memory Usage ***
        Physical Memory:      130772 (      523088 Kb)
        Page File: \??\C:\pagefile.sys
          Current:   1048576 Kb  Free Space:    1039500 Kb
          Minimum:   1048576 Kb  Maximum:       4194304 Kb
        Available Pages:       47079 (      188316 Kb)
        ResAvail Pages:       111511 (      446044 Kb)
        Locked IO Pages:           0 (           0 Kb)
        Free System PTEs:     433746 (     1734984 Kb)
        Modified Pages:         2808 (       11232 Kb)
        Modified PF Pages:      2801 (       11204 Kb)
        NonPagedPool Usage:     5301 (       21204 Kb)
        NonPagedPool Max:      94847 (      379388 Kb)
        PagedPool 0 Usage:      4340 (       17360 Kb)
        PagedPool 1 Usage:      3129 (       12516 Kb)
        PagedPool 2 Usage:       402 (        1608 Kb)
        PagedPool 3 Usage:       349 (        1396 Kb)
        PagedPool 4 Usage:       420 (        1680 Kb)
        PagedPool Usage:        8640 (       34560 Kb)
        PagedPool Maximum:    523264 (     2093056 Kb)
        Shared Commit:          7231 (       28924 Kb)
        Special Pool:              0 (           0 Kb)
        Shared Process:         1767 (        7068 Kb)
        PagedPool Commit:       8635 (       34540 Kb)
        Driver Commit:          2246 (        8984 Kb)
        Committed pages:       73000 (      292000 Kb)
        Commit limit:         386472 (     1545888 Kb)

Total Private:         44889 (      179556 Kb)
        0400 svchost.exe        5436 (       21744 Kb)
        0980 explorer.exe       4123 (       16492 Kb)
        0a7c windbg.exe         3713 (       14852 Kb)
```

Services the Memory Manager Provides

The memory manager provides a set of system services to allocate and free virtual memory, share memory between processes, map files into memory, flush virtual pages to disk, retrieve information about a range of virtual pages, change the protection of virtual pages, and lock the virtual pages into memory.

Like other Windows executive services, the memory management services allow their caller to supply a process handle indicating the particular process whose virtual memory is to be manipulated. The caller can thus manipulate either its own memory or (with the proper permissions) the memory of another process. For example, if a process creates a child process, by default it has the right to manipulate the child process's virtual memory. Thereafter, the parent process can allocate, deallocate, read, and write memory on behalf of the child process by calling virtual memory services and passing a handle to the child process as an argument. This feature is used by subsystems to manage the memory of their client processes, and it is also key for implementing debuggers because debuggers must be able to read and write to the memory of the process being debugged.

Most of these services are exposed through the Windows API. The Windows API has three groups of functions for managing memory in applications: page granularity virtual memory functions (*Virtualxxx*), memory-mapped file functions (*CreateFileMapping, CreateFileMappingNuma, MapViewOfFile, MapViewOfFileEx, and MapViewOfFileExNuma*), and heap functions (*Heapxxx* and the older interfaces *Localxxx* and *Globalxxx,* which internally make use of the *Heapxxx* APIs). (We'll describe the heap manager later in this chapter.)

The memory manager also provides a number of services (such as allocating and deallocating physical memory and locking pages in physical memory for direct memory access [DMA] transfers) to other kernel-mode components inside the executive as well as to device drivers. These functions begin with the prefix *Mm*. In addition, though not strictly part of the memory manager, some executive support routines that begin with *Ex* are used to allocate and deallocate from the system heaps (paged and nonpaged pool) as well as to manipulate look-aside lists. We'll touch on these topics later in this chapter in the section "Kernel-Mode Heaps (System Memory Pools)."

Although we'll be referring to Windows functions and kernel-mode memory management and memory allocation routines provided for device drivers, we won't cover the interface and programming details but rather the internal operations of these functions. Refer to the Windows Software Development Kit (SDK) and Windows Driver Kit (WDK) documentation on MSDN for a complete description of the available functions and their interfaces.

Large and Small Pages

The virtual address space is divided into units called pages. That is because the hardware memory management unit translates virtual to physical addresses at the granularity of a page. Hence, a page is the smallest unit of protection at the hardware level. (The various page protection options are described in the section "Protecting Memory" later in the chapter.) There are two page sizes: small and large. The actual sizes vary based on hardware architecture, and they are listed in Table 9-1.

TABLE 9-1 **Page Sizes**

Architecture	Small Page Size	Large Page Size
x86	4 KB	4 MB (2 MB on PAE systems)
x64	4 KB	2 MB
IA64	8 KB	16 MB

Note IA64 processors support a variety of dynamically configurable page sizes, from 4 KB up to 256 MB. Windows uses 8 KB and 16 MB for small and large pages, respectively, as a result of performance tests that confirmed these values as optimal. Additionally, recent x64 processors support a size of 1 GB for large pages, but Windows does not currently use this feature.

The advantage of large pages is speed of address translation for references to other data within the large page. This advantage exists because the first reference to any byte within a large page will cause the hardware's translation look-aside buffer (or TLB, which is described in the section "Translation Look-Aside Buffer") to have in its cache the information necessary to translate references to any other byte within the large page. If small pages are used, more TLB entries are needed for the same range of virtual addresses, thus increasing recycling of entries as new virtual addresses require translation. This, in turn, means having to go back to the page table structures when references are made to virtual addresses outside the scope of a small page whose translation has been cached. The TLB is a very small cache, and thus large pages make better use of this limited resource.

To take advantage of large pages on systems with more than 255 MB of RAM, Windows maps with large pages the core operating system images (Ntoskrnl.exe and Hal.dll) as well as core operating system data (such as the initial part of nonpaged pool and the data structures that describe the state of each physical memory page). Windows also automatically maps I/O space requests (calls by device drivers to *MmMapIoSpace*) with large pages if the request is of satisfactory large page length and alignment. In addition, Windows allows applications to map their images, private memory, and page-file-backed sections with large pages. (See the MEM_LARGE_PAGE flag on the *VirtualAlloc*, *VirtualAllocEx*, and *VirtualAllocExNuma* functions.) You can also specify other device drivers to be mapped with large pages by adding

a multistring registry value to HKLM\SYSTEM\CurrentControlSet\Control\Session Manager\ Memory Management\LargePageDrivers and specifying the names of the drivers as separately null- terminated strings.

One side-effect of large pages is that because each large page must be mapped with a single protection (because hardware memory protection is on a per-page basis), if a large page contains both read-only code and read/write data, the page must be marked as read/write, which means that the code will be writable. This means device drivers or other kernel-mode code could, as a result of a bug, modify what is supposed to be read-only operating system or driver code without causing a memory access violation. However, if small pages are used to map the kernel, the read-only portions of Ntoskrnl.exe and Hal.dll will be mapped as read-only pages. Although this reduces efficiency of address translation, if a device driver (or other kernel-mode code) attempts to modify a read-only part of the operating system, the system will crash immediately, with the finger pointing at the offending instruction, as opposed to allowing the corruption to occur and the system crashing later (in a harder-to-diagnose way) when some other component trips over that corrupted data. If you suspect you are experiencing kernel code corruptions, enable Driver Verifier (described later in this chapter), which will disable the use of large pages.

Reserving and Committing Pages

Pages in a process virtual address space are free, reserved, or committed. Applications can first *reserve* address space and then *commit* pages in that address space. Or they can reserve and commit in the same function call. These services are exposed through the Windows *VirtualAlloc*, *VirtualAllocEx*, and *VirtualAllocExNuma* functions.

Reserved address space is simply a way for a thread to reserve a range of virtual addresses for future use. Attempting to access reserved memory results in an access violation because the page isn't mapped to any storage that can resolve the reference.

Committed pages are pages that, when accessed, ultimately translate to valid pages in physical memory. Committed pages are either private and not shareable or mapped to a view of a section (which might or might not be mapped by other processes). Sections are described in two upcoming sections, "Shared Memory and Mapped Files" and "Section Objects."

If the pages are private to the process and have never been accessed before, they are created at the time of first access as zero-initialized pages (or *demand zero*). Private committed pages can later be automatically written to the paging file by the operating system if memory demands dictate. Committed pages that are private are inaccessible to any other process unless they're accessed using cross-process memory functions, such as *ReadProcessMemory* or *WriteProcessMemory*. If committed pages are mapped to a portion of a mapped file, they might need to be brought in from disk when accessed unless they've already been read earlier, either by the process accessing the page or by another process that had the same file

mapped and had previously accessed the page, or if they've been prefetched by the system. (See the section "Shared Memory and Mapped Files" later in this chapter.)

Pages are written to disk through normal modified page writing as pages are moved from the process working set to the modified list and ultimately to disk (or remote storage). (Working sets and the modified list are explained later in this chapter.) Mapped file pages can also be written back to disk as a result of an explicit call to *FlushViewOfFile* or by the mapped page writer as memory demands dictate.

You can decommit pages and/or release address space with the *VirtualFree* or *VirtualFreeEx* function. The difference between decommittal and release is similar to the difference between reservation and committal—decommitted memory is still reserved, but released memory is neither committed nor reserved. (It's freed.)

Using the two-step process of reserving and committing memory can reduce memory usage by deferring committing pages until needed but keeping the convenience of virtual contiguity. Reserving memory is a relatively fast and inexpensive operation under Windows because it doesn't consume any committed pages (a precious system resource) or process page file quota (a limit on the number of committed pages a process can consume—not necessarily page file space). All that needs to be updated or constructed is the relatively small internal data structures that represent the state of the process address space. (We'll explain these data structures, called *virtual address descriptors*, or VADs, later in the chapter.)

Reserving and then committing memory is useful for applications that need a potentially large virtually contiguous memory buffer; rather than committing pages for the entire region, the address space can be reserved and then committed later when needed. A use of this technique in the operating system is the user-mode stack for each thread. When a thread is created, a stack is reserved. (1 MB is the default; you can override this size with the *CreateThread* and *CreateRemoteThread* function calls or change it on an imagewide basis by using the /STACK linker flag.) By default, the initial page in the stack is committed and the next page is marked as a guard page (which isn't committed) that traps references beyond the end of the committed portion of the stack and expands it.

Locking Memory

In general, it's better to let the memory manager decide which pages remain in physical memory. However, there might be special circumstances where it might be necessary for an application or device driver to lock pages in physical memory. Pages can be locked in memory in two ways:

- Windows applications can call the *VirtualLock* function to lock pages in their process working set. The number of pages a process can lock can't exceed its minimum working set size minus eight pages. Therefore, if a process needs to lock more pages, it

can increase its working set minimum with the *SetProcessWorkingSetSizeEx* function (referred to in the section "Working Set Management").

■ Device drivers can call the kernel-mode functions *MmProbeAndLockPages*, *MmLockPagableCodeSection*, *MmLockPagableDataSection*, or *MmLockPagableSectionByHandle*. Pages locked using this mechanism remain in memory until explicitly unlocked. No quota is imposed on the number of pages a driver can lock in memory because (for the last three APIs) the resident available page charge is obtained when the driver first loads to ensure that it can never cause a system crash due to overlocking. For the first API, charges must be obtained or the API will return a failure status.

Allocation Granularity

Windows aligns each region of reserved process address space to begin on an integral boundary defined by the value of the system *allocation granularity*, which can be retrieved from the Windows *GetSystemInfo* or *GetNativeSystemInfo* function. This value is 64 KB, a granularity that is used by the memory manager to efficiently allocate metadata (for example, VADs, bitmaps, and so on) to support various process operations. In addition, if support were added for future processors with larger page sizes (for example, up to 64 KB) or virtually indexed caches that require systemwide physical-to-virtual page alignment, the risk of requiring changes to applications that made assumptions about allocation alignment would be reduced.

> **Note** Windows kernel-mode code isn't subject to the same restrictions; it can reserve memory on a single-page granularity (although this is not exposed to device drivers for the reasons detailed earlier). This level of granularity is primarily used to pack TEB allocations more densely, and because this mechanism is internal only, this code can easily be changed if a future platform requires different values. Also, for the purposes of supporting 16-bit and MS-DOS applications on x86 systems only, the memory manager provides the MEM_DOS_LIM flag to the *MapViewOfFileEx* API, which is used to force the use of single-page granularity.

Finally, when a region of address space is reserved, Windows ensures that the size and base of the region is a multiple of the system page size, whatever that might be. For example, because x86 systems use 4-KB pages, if you tried to reserve a region of memory 18 KB in size, the actual amount reserved on an x86 system would be 20 KB. If you specified a base address of 3 KB for an 18-KB region, the actual amount reserved would be 24 KB. Note that the internal memory manager structure describing the allocation (this structure will be described later) would then also be rounded to 64-KB alignment/length, thus making the remainder of it inaccessible.

Shared Memory and Mapped Files

As is true with most modern operating systems, Windows provides a mechanism to share memory among processes and the operating system. *Shared memory* can be defined as memory that is visible to more than one process or that is present in more than one process virtual address space. For example, if two processes use the same DLL, it would make sense to load the referenced code pages for that DLL into physical memory only once and share those pages between all processes that map the DLL, as illustrated in Figure 9-1.

FIGURE 9-1 Sharing memory between processes

Each process would still maintain its private memory areas in which to store private data, but the program instructions and unmodified data pages could be shared without harm. As we'll explain later, this kind of sharing happens automatically because the code pages in executable images are mapped as execute-only and writable pages are mapped as copy-on-write. (See the section "Copy-on-Write" for more information.)

The underlying primitives in the memory manager used to implement shared memory are called *section objects*, which are called *file mapping objects* in the Windows API. The internal structure and implementation of section objects are described in the section "Section Objects" later in this chapter.

This fundamental primitive in the memory manager is used to map virtual addresses, whether in main memory, in the page file, or in some other file that an application wants to access as if it were in memory. A section can be opened by one process or by many; in other words, section objects don't necessarily equate to shared memory.

A section object can be connected to an open file on disk (called a mapped file) or to committed memory (to provide shared memory). Sections mapped to committed memory are called *page-file-backed sections* because the pages are written to the paging file if memory demands dictate. (Because Windows can run with no paging file, page-file-backed sections might in fact be "backed" only by physical memory.) As with any other empty page that is made visible to user mode (such as private committed pages), shared committed pages are always zero-filled when they are first accessed to ensure that no sensitive data is ever leaked.

To create a section object, call the Windows *CreateFileMapping* or *CreateFileMappingNuma* function, specifying the file handle to map it to (or INVALID_HANDLE_VALUE for a page-file-backed section) and optionally a name and security descriptor. If the section has a name, other processes can open it with *OpenFileMapping*. Or you can grant access to section objects through handle inheritance (by specifying that the handle be inheritable when opening or creating the handle) or handle duplication (by using *DuplicateHandle*). Device drivers can also manipulate section objects with the *ZwOpenSection*, *ZwMapViewOfSection*, and *ZwUnmapViewOfSection* functions.

A section object can refer to files that are much larger than can fit in the address space of a process. (If the paging file backs a section object, sufficient space must exist in the paging file and/or RAM to contain it.) To access a very large section object, a process can map only the portion of the section object that it requires (called a *view* of the section) by calling the *MapViewOfFile*, *MapViewOfFileEx*, or *MapViewOfFileExNuma* function and then specifying the range to map. Mapping views permits processes to conserve address space because only the views of the section object needed at the time must be mapped into memory.

Windows applications can use mapped files to conveniently perform I/O to files by simply making them appear in their address space. User applications aren't the only consumers of section objects: the image loader uses section objects to map executable images, DLLs, and device drivers into memory, and the cache manager uses them to access data in cached files. (For information on how the cache manager integrates with the memory manager, see Chapter 10.) How shared memory sections are implemented, both in terms of address translation and the internal data structures, is explained later in this chapter.

EXPERIMENT: Viewing Memory Mapped Files

You can list the memory mapped files in a process by using Process Explorer from Windows Sysinternals (*www.microsoft.com/technet/sysinternals*). To view the memory mapped files by using Process Explorer, configure the lower pane to show the DLL view. (Click on View, Lower Pane View, DLLs.) Note that this is more than just a list of DLLs—it represents all memory mapped files in the process address space. Some of these are DLLs, one is the image file (EXE) being run, and additional entries might represent memory mapped data files. For example, the following display from Process Explorer shows a Microsoft Word process that has memory mapped the Word document being edited into its address space:

You can also search for memory mapped files by clicking on Find, DLL. This can be useful when trying to determine which process(es) are using a DLL that you are trying to replace.

Protecting Memory

As explained in Chapter 1, Windows provides memory protection so that no user process can inadvertently or deliberately corrupt the address space of another process or the operating system itself. Windows provides this protection in four primary ways.

First, all systemwide data structures and memory pools used by kernel-mode system components can be accessed only while in kernel mode—user-mode threads can't access these pages. If they attempt to do so, the hardware generates a fault, which in turn the memory manager reports to the thread as an access violation.

Second, each process has a separate, private address space, protected from being accessed by any thread belonging to another process. The only exceptions are if the process decides to share pages with other processes or if another process has virtual memory read or write access to the process object and thus can use the *ReadProcessMemory* or *WriteProcessMemory* function. Each time a thread references an address, the virtual memory hardware, in concert with the memory manager, intervenes and translates the virtual address into a physical one. By controlling how virtual addresses are translated, Windows can ensure that threads running in one process don't inappropriately access a page belonging to another process.

Third, in addition to the implicit protection virtual-to-physical address translation offers, all processors supported by Windows provide some form of hardware-controlled memory protection (such as read/write, read-only, and so on); the exact details of such protection vary according to the processor. For example, code pages in the address space of a process are marked read-only and are thus protected from modification by user threads.

Table 9-2 lists the memory protection options defined in the Windows API. (See the *VirtualProtect*, *VirtualProtectEx*, *VirtualQuery*, and *VirtualQueryEx* functions.)

TABLE 9-2 Memory Protection Options Defined in the Windows API

Attribute	Description
PAGE_NOACCESS	Any attempt to read from, write to, or execute code in this region causes an access violation.
PAGE_READONLY	Any attempt to write to (and on processors with no execute support, execute code in) memory causes an access violation, but reads are permitted.
PAGE_READWRITE	The page is readable and writable but not executable.
PAGE_EXECUTE	Any attempt to write to code in memory in this region causes an access violation, but execution (and read operations on all existing processors) is permitted.
PAGE_EXECUTE_READ*	Any attempt to write to code in memory in this region causes an access violation, but executes and reads are permitted.
PAGE_EXECUTE_READWRITE*	The page is readable, writable, and executable—no action will cause an access violation.
PAGE_WRITECOPY	Any attempt to write to memory in this region causes the system to give the process a private copy of the page. On processors with no execute support, attempts to execute code in memory in this region cause an access violation.
PAGE_EXECUTE_WRITECOPY	Any attempt to write to memory in this region causes the system to give the process a private copy of the page. Reading and executing code in this region is permitted. (No copy is made in this case.)

Attribute	Description
PAGE_GUARD	Any attempt to read from or write to a guard page raises an EXCEPTION_GUARD_PAGE exception and turns off the guard page status. Guard pages thus act as a one-shot alarm. Note that this flag can be specified with any of the page protections listed in this table except PAGE_NOACCESS.
PAGE_NOCACHE	Use physical memory that is not cached. This is not recommended for general usage. It is useful for device drivers—for example, mapping a video frame buffer with no caching.
PAGE_WRITECOMBINE	Enables write-combined memory accesses. When enabled, the processor does not cache memory writes (this can cause significant memory traffic), but it does try to aggregate write requests to optimize performance. For example, if multiple writes are made to the same address, only the most recent write might occur. This is not typically used for general applications, but it is useful for device drivers—for example, mapping a video frame buffer as write combined.

* No execute protection is supported on processors that have the necessary hardware support (for example, all x64 and IA64 processors) but not in older x86 processors.

And finally, shared memory section objects have standard Windows access control lists (ACLs) that are checked when processes attempt to open them, thus limiting access of shared memory to those processes with the proper rights. Security also comes into play when a thread creates a section to contain a mapped file. To create the section, the thread must have at least read access to the underlying file object or the operation will fail.

Once a thread has successfully opened a handle to a section, its actions are still subject to the memory manager and the hardware-based page protections described earlier. A thread can change the page-level protection on virtual pages in a section if the change doesn't violate the permissions in the ACL for that section object. For example, the memory manager allows a thread to change the pages of a read-only section to have copy-on-write access but not to have read/write access. The copy-on-write access is permitted because it has no effect on other processes sharing the data.

No Execute Page Protection

No execute page protection (also referred to as data execution prevention, or DEP) causes an attempt to transfer control to an instruction in a page marked as "no execute" to generate an access fault. This can prevent certain types of malware from exploiting bugs in the system through the execution of code placed in a data page such as the stack. DEP can also catch poorly written programs that don't correctly set permissions on pages from which they intend to execute code. If an attempt is made in kernel mode to execute code in a page marked as no execute, the system will crash with the ATTEMPTED_EXECUTE_OF_NOEXECUTE_ MEMORY bugcheck code. (See Chapter 14 for an explanation of these codes.) If this occurs in

user mode, a STATUS_ACCESS_VIOLATION (0xc0000005) exception is delivered to the thread attempting the illegal reference. If a process allocates memory that needs to be executable, it must explicitly mark such pages by specifying the PAGE_EXECUTE, PAGE_EXECUTE_READ, PAGE_EXECUTE_READWRITE, or PAGE_EXECUTE_WRITECOPY flags on the page granularity memory allocation functions.

On 32-bit x86 systems, the flag in the page table entry to mark a page as nonexecutable is available only when the processor is running in Physical Address Extension (PAE) mode. (See the section "Physical Address Extension (PAE)" later in this chapter.) Thus, support for hardware DEP on 32-bit systems requires loading the PAE kernel (\%SystemRoot%\System32\ Ntkrnlpa.exe), even if that system does not require extended physical addressing (for example, physical addresses greater than 4 GB). The operating system loader does this automatically unless explicitly configured not to by setting the BCD option *pae* to *ForceDisable*.

On 64-bit versions of Windows, execution protection is always applied to all 64-bit processes and device drivers and can be disabled only by setting the *nx* BCD option to *AlwaysOff*. Execution protection for 32-bit programs depends on system configuration settings, described shortly. On 64-bit Windows, execution protection is applied to thread stacks (both user and kernel mode), user-mode pages not specifically marked as executable, kernel paged pool, and kernel session pool (for a description of kernel memory pools, see the section "Kernel-Mode Heaps (System Memory Pools)." However, on 32-bit Windows, execution protection is applied only to thread stacks and user-mode pages, not to paged pool and session pool.

The application of execution protection for 32-bit processes depends on the value of the BCD *nx* option. The settings can be changed by going to the Data Execution Prevention tab under Computer, Properties, Advanced System Settings, Performance Settings. (See Figure 9-2.) When you configure no execute protection in the Performance Options dialog box, the BCD *nx* option is set to the appropriate value. Table 9-3 lists the variations of the values and how they correspond to the DEP settings tab. Thirty-two-bit applications that are excluded from execution protection are listed as registry values under the key HKLM\SOFTWARE\Microsoft\ Windows NT\CurrentVersion\AppCompatFlags\Layers, with the value name being the full path of the executable and the data set to "DisableNXShowUI".

On Windows Vista (both 64-bit and 32-bit versions) execution protection for 32-bit processes is configured by default to apply only to core Windows operating system executables (the *nx* BCD option is set to *OptIn*) so as not to break 32-bit applications that might rely on being able to execute code in pages not specifically marked as executable, such as self-extracting or packed applications. On Windows Server 2008 systems, execution protection for 32-bit applications is configured by default to apply to all 32-bit programs (the *nx* BCD option is set to *OptOut*).

FIGURE 9-2 Data Execution Prevention tab settings

Note To obtain a complete list of which programs are protected, install the Windows Application Compatibility Toolkit (downloadable from *www.microsoft.com*) and run the Compatibility Administrator Tool. Click System Database, Applications, and then Windows Components. The pane at the right shows the list of protected executables.

TABLE 9-3 BCD *nx* Values

Value	Option on DEP Settings Tab	Meaning
OptIn	Turn on DEP for necessary Windows programs and services only.	Enables DEP for core Windows system images. Enables 32-bit processes to dynamically configure DEP for their lifetime.
OptOut	Turn on DEP for all programs and services except those that I select.	Enables DEP for all executables except those specified. Enables 32-bit processes to dynamically configure DEP for their lifetime. Enables system compatibility fixes for DEP.
AlwaysOn	No dialog box option for this setting	Enables DEP for all components with no ability to exclude certain applications. Disables dynamic configuration for 32-bit processes, and disables system compatibility fixes.
AlwaysOff	No dialog box option for this setting	Disables DEP (not recommended). Disables dynamic configuration for 32-bit processes.

Even if you force DEP to be enabled, there are still other methods through which applications can disable DEP or their own images. For example, regardless of the execution protection options that are enabled, the image loader (see Chapter 3 for more information about the image loader) will verify the signature of the executable against known copy-protection mechanisms (such as SafeDisc and SecuROM) and disable execution protection to provide compatibility with older copy-protected software such as computer games.

Additionally, to provide compatibility with older versions of the Active Template Library (ATL) framework (version 7.1 or earlier), the Windows kernel provides an ATL thunk emulation environment. This environment detects ATL thunk code sequences that have caused the DEP exception and emulates the expected operation. Application developers can request that ATL thunk emulation not be applied by using the latest Microsoft C++ compiler and specifying the /NXCOMPAT flag (which sets the IMAGE_DLLCHARACTERISTICS_NX_COMPAT flag in the PE header), which tells the system that the executable fully supports DEP. Note that ATL thunk emulation is permanently disabled if the *AlwaysOn* value is set.

Finally, if the system is in *OptIn* or *OptOut* mode and executing a 32-bit process, the *SetProcessDEPPolicy* function allows a process to dynamically disable DEP or to permanently enable it. (Once enabled through this API, DEP cannot be disabled programmatically for the lifetime of the process.) This function can also be used to dynamically disable ATL thunk emulation in case the image wasn't compiled with the /NXCOMPAT flag. On 64-bit processes or systems booted with *AlwaysOff* or *AlwaysOn*, the function always returns a failure. The *GetProcessDEPPolicy* function returns the 32-bit per-process DEP policy (it fails on 64-bit systems, where the policy is always the same—enabled), while the *GetSystemDEPPolicy* can be used to return a value corresponding to the policies in Table 9-3.

EXPERIMENT: Looking at DEP Protection on Processes

Process Explorer can show you the current DEP status for all the processes on your system, including whether the process is opted-in or benefiting from permanent protection. To look at the DEP status for processes, right-click any column in the process tree, choose Select Columns, and then select DEP Status on the Process Image tab. Three values are possible:

- **DEP (permanent)** This means that the process has DEP enabled because it is a "necessary Windows program or service."

- **DEP** This means that the process opted-in to DEP, either as part of a system-wide policy to opt-in all 32-bit processes or because of an API call such as SetProcessDEPPolicy.

- **Nothing** If the column displays no information for this process, DEP is disabled, either because of a systemwide policy or an explicit API call or shim.

The following Process Explorer window shows an example of a system on which DEP is enabled for all programs and services.

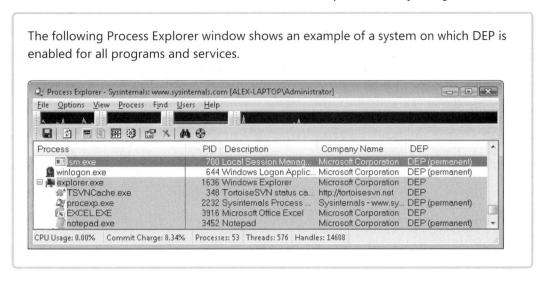

Software Data Execution Prevention

For older processors that do not support hardware no execute protection, Windows supports limited *software data execution prevention* (DEP). One aspect of software DEP reduces exploits of the exception handling mechanism in Windows. (See Chapter 3 for a description of structured exception handling.) If the program's image files are built with safe structured exception handling (a feature in the Microsoft Visual C++ compiler that is enabled with the /SAFESEH flag), before an exception is dispatched, the system verifies that the exception handler is registered in the function table (built by the compiler) located within the image file. If the program's image files are not built with safe structured exception handling, software DEP ensures that before an exception is dispatched, the exception handler is located within a memory region marked as executable.

Two other methods for software DEP that the system implements are *stack cookies* and *pointer encoding*. The first relies on the compiler to insert special code at the beginning and end of each potentially exploitable function. The code saves a special numerical value (the *cookie*) on the stack on entry and validates the cookie's value before returning to the caller saved on the stack (which would have now been corrupted to point to a piece of malicious code). If the cookie value is mismatched, the application is terminated and not allowed to continue executing. The cookie value is computed for each boot when executing the first user-mode thread, and it is saved in the KUSER_SHARED_DATA structure. The image loader reads this value and initializes it when a process starts executing in user mode. (See Chapter 3 for more information on the shared data section and the image loader.)

The cookie value that is calculated is also saved for use with the *EncodeSystemPointer* and *DecodeSystemPointer* APIs, which implement pointer encoding. When an application or a DLL has static pointers that are dynamically called, it runs the risk of having malicious code

overwrite the pointer values with code that the malware controls. By encoding all pointers with the cookie value and then decoding them, when malicious code sets a nonencoded pointer, the application will still attempt to decode the pointer, resulting in a corrupted value and causing the program to crash. The *EncodePointer* and *DecodePointer* APIs provide similar protection but with a per-process cookie (created on demand) instead of a per-system cookie.

Note The system cookie is a combination of the system time at generation, the stack value of the saved system time, the number of page faults, and the current interrupt time.

Copy-on-Write

Copy-on-write page protection is an optimization the memory manager uses to conserve physical memory. When a process maps a copy-on-write view of a section object that contains read/write pages, instead of making a process private copy at the time the view is mapped, the memory manager defers making a copy of the pages until the page is written to. For example, as shown in Figure 9-3, two processes are sharing three pages, each marked copy-on-write, but neither of the two processes has attempted to modify any data on the pages.

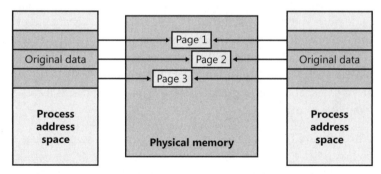

FIGURE 9-3 The "before" of copy-on-write

If a thread in either process writes to a page, a memory management fault is generated. The memory manager sees that the write is to a copy-on-write page, so instead of reporting the fault as an access violation, it allocates a new read/write page in physical memory, copies the contents of the original page to the new page, updates the corresponding page-mapping information (explained later in this chapter) in this process to point to the new location, and dismisses the exception, thus causing the instruction that generated the fault to be reexecuted. This time, the write operation succeeds, but as shown in Figure 9-4, the newly copied page is now private to the process that did the writing and isn't visible to the other process still sharing the copy-on-write page. Each new process that writes to that same shared page will also get its own private copy.

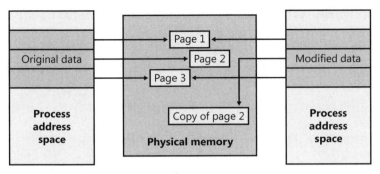

FIGURE 9-4 The "after" of copy-on-write

One application of copy-on-write is to implement breakpoint support in debuggers. For example, by default, code pages start out as execute-only. If a programmer sets a break-point while debugging a program, however, the debugger must add a breakpoint instruction to the code. It does this by first changing the protection on the page to PAGE_EXECUTE_READWRITE and then changing the instruction stream. Because the code page is part of a mapped section, the memory manager creates a private copy for the process with the break-point set, while other processes continue using the unmodified code page.

Copy-on-write is one example of an evaluation technique known as *lazy evaluation* that the memory manager uses as often as possible. Lazy-evaluation algorithms avoid performing an expensive operation until absolutely required—if the operation is never required, no time is wasted on it.

To examine the rate of copy-on-write faults, see the performance counter Memory: Write Copies/sec.

Address Windowing Extensions

Although the 32-bit version of Windows can support up to 128 GB of physical memory (as shown in Table 2-3), each 32-bit user process has by default only a 2-GB virtual address space. (This can be configured up to 3 GB when using the *increaseuserva* BCD option, described in the upcoming section "x86 User Address Space Layouts.") For 32-bit processes that require more fine-grained, high-performance control over their physical pages than *MapViewOfFile* can provide, Windows provides a set of functions called *Address Windowing Extensions* (AWE) that can be used to allocate and access more physical memory than can be represented in a 32-bit process's limited address space. For example, on a 32-bit Windows Server 2008 system with 8 GB of physical memory, a database server application could use AWE to allocate and use perhaps 6 GB of memory as a database cache. An allocation like this can also be done by memory mapping the file and then mapping views as needed, at the expense of 64-KB granularity (instead of 4-KB) and without requiring a special privilege.

Allocating and using memory via the AWE functions is done in three steps:

1. Allocating the physical memory to be used

2. Creating a region of virtual address space to act as a window to map views of the physical memory

3. Mapping views of the physical memory into the window

To allocate physical memory, an application can call the Windows functions *AllocateUser-PhysicalPages* or *AllocateUserPhysicalPagesNuma*. (These functions require the Lock pages in memory user right.) The application then uses the Windows *VirtualAlloc* or *VirtualAllocExNuma* function with the MEM_PHYSICAL flag to create a window in the private portion of the process's address space that can then be mapped to any portion of the physical memory previously allocated. The AWE-allocated memory can then be used with nearly all the Windows APIs. (For example, the Microsoft DirectX functions can't use AWE memory.)

For example, if an application creates a 256-MB window in its address space and allocates 4 GB of physical memory (on a system with more than 4 GB of physical memory), the application can use the *MapUserPhysicalPages* or *MapUserPhysicalPagesScatter* Windows function to access any portion of the physical memory by mapping the memory into the 256-MB window. The size of the application's virtual address space window determines the amount of physical memory that the application can access with a given mapping. Figure 9-5 shows an AWE window in a server application address space mapped to a portion of physical memory previously allocated by *AllocateUserPhysicalPages* or *AllocateUserPhysicalPagesNuma*.

FIGURE 9-5 Using AWE to map physical memory

The AWE functions exist on all editions of Windows and are usable regardless of how much physical memory a system has. However, AWE is most useful on systems with more than 2 GB of physical memory because it provides a way for a 32-bit process to control physical page usage when dealing with more than 2 GB of memory. Another use is for security purposes: because AWE memory is never paged out, the data in AWE memory can never have a copy in the paging file that someone could examine by rebooting into an alternate operating system. (*VirtualLock* provides the same guarantee for pages in general.)

Finally, there are some restrictions on memory allocated and mapped by the AWE functions:

- Pages can't be shared between processes.

- The same physical page can't be mapped to more than one virtual address in the same process.

- Page protection is limited to read/write, read-only, and no access.

For a description of the page table data structures used to map memory on systems with more than 4 GB of physical memory, see the section "Physical Address Extension (PAE)."

Kernel-Mode Heaps (System Memory Pools)

At system initialization, the memory manager creates two types of dynamically sized memory pools that the kernel-mode components use to allocate system memory:

- **Nonpaged pool** Consists of ranges of system virtual addresses that are guaranteed to reside in physical memory at all times and thus can be accessed at any time (from any IRQL level and from any process context) without incurring a page fault. One of the reasons nonpaged pool is required is because of the rule described in Chapter 2: page faults can't be satisfied at DPC/dispatch level or above.

- **Paged pool** A region of virtual memory in system space that can be paged into and out of the system. Device drivers that don't need to access the memory from DPC/dispatch level or above can use paged pool. It is accessible from any process context.

Both memory pools are located in the system part of the address space and are mapped in the virtual address space of every process. The executive provides routines to allocate and deallocate from these pools; for information on these routines, see the functions that start with *ExAllocatePool* in the WDK documentation.

Systems start with four paged pools (combined to make the overall system paged pool) and one nonpaged pool; more are created, up to a maximum of 64, depending on the number of NUMA nodes on the system. Having more than one paged pool reduces the frequency of system code blocking on simultaneous calls to pool routines. Additionally, the different pools created are mapped across different virtual address ranges that correspond to different

NUMA nodes on the system. (The different data structures, such as the large page look-aside lists, to describe pool allocations are also mapped across different NUMA nodes. More information on NUMA optimizations will follow later.)

Nonpaged pool starts at an initial size based on the amount of physical memory on the system and then grows as needed. For nonpaged pool, the initial size is 3 percent of system RAM, if this is less than 40 MB, in which case the system will instead use 40 MB as long as 10 percent of RAM results in more than 40 MB; otherwise 10 percent of RAM is chosen as a minimum.

Pool Sizes

Windows dynamically chooses the maximum size of the pools and allows a given pool to grow from its initial size to the maximums shown in Table 9-4.

TABLE 9-4 Maximum Pool Sizes

Pool Type	Maximum on 32-Bit Systems	Maximum on 64-Bit Systems
Nonpaged	75% of physical memory or 2 GB, whichever is smaller	75% of physical memory or 128 GB, whichever is smaller
Paged	2 GB	128 GB

Four of these computed sizes are stored in kernel variables, three of which are exposed as performance counters, and one is computed only as a performance counter value. These variables and counters are listed in Table 9-5.

TABLE 9-5 System Pool Size Variables and Performance Counters

Kernel Variable	Performance Counter	Description
MmSizeOfNonPagedPoolInBytes	Memory: Pool Nonpaged Bytes	Size of the initial nonpaged pool. This can be reduced automatically by the system if memory demands dictate.
MmMaximumNonPagedPoolInBytes	Not available	Maximum size of nonpaged pool
Not available	Memory: Pool Paged Bytes	Current total virtual size of paged pool
MmPagedPoolPage (number of pages)	Memory: Pool Paged Resident Bytes	Current physical (resident) size of paged pool
MmSizeOfPagedPoolInBytes	Not available	Maximum (virtual) size of paged pool

EXPERIMENT: Determining the Maximum Pool Sizes

You can obtain the pool maximums by using either Process Explorer or live kernel debugging (explained in Chapter 1). To view pool maximums with Process Explorer, click on View, System Information. The pool maximums are displayed in the Kernel Memory section as shown here:

Note that for Process Explorer to retrieve this information, it must have access to the symbols for the kernel running on your system. (For a description of how to configure Process Explorer to use symbols, see the experiment "Viewing Process Details with Process Explorer" in Chapter 1.)

To view the same information by using the kernel debugger, you can use the *!vm* command as shown here:

```
lkd> !vm

*** Virtual Memory Usage ***
    Physical Memory:      851388 (    3405552 Kb)
    Page File: \??\C:\pagefile.sys
      Current:   4194304 Kb  Free Space:    4109736 Kb
      Minimum:   4194304 Kb  Maximum:       4194304 Kb
    Available Pages:       517820 (    2071280 Kb)
    ResAvail Pages:        780018 (    3120072 Kb)
    Locked IO Pages:            0 (          0 Kb)
```

```
Free System PTEs:      279002 (   1116008 Kb)
Modified Pages:         26121 (    104484 Kb)
Modified PF Pages:      26107 (    104428 Kb)
NonPagedPool Usage:     10652 (     42608 Kb)
NonPagedPool Max:      523064 (   2092256 Kb)
PagedPool 0 Usage:       9040 (     36160 Kb)
PagedPool 1 Usage:       4007 (     16028 Kb)
PagedPool 2 Usage:       1255 (      5020 Kb)
PagedPool 3 Usage:        946 (      3784 Kb)
PagedPool 4 Usage:        666 (      2664 Kb)
PagedPool Usage:        15914 (     63656 Kb)
PagedPool Maximum:     523264 (   2093056 Kb)
```

On this 4-GB system, nonpaged and paged pool were far from their maximums. You can also examine the values of the kernel variables listed in Table 9-6:

```
1kd> ? poi(MmMaximumNonPagedPoolInBytes)
Evaluate expression: 2142470144 = 7fb38000

1kd> ? poi(MmSizeOfPagedPoolInBytes)
Evaluate expression: 2143289344 = 7fc00000
```

From this example, you can see that the maximum size of both nonpaged and paged pool is 2 GB, typical values on 32-bit systems with large amounts of RAM. On the system used for this example, current nonpaged pool usage was 40 MB and paged pool usage was 60 MB, so both pools were far from full.

Monitoring Pool Usage

The Memory performance counter object has separate counters for the size of nonpaged pool and paged pool (both virtual and physical). In addition, the Poolmon utility (in the WDK) allows you to monitor the detailed usage of nonpaged and paged pool.

When you run Poolmon, you should see a display like the one shown in Figure 9-6.

The highlighted lines you might see represent changes to the display. (You can disable the highlighting feature by typing a slash (/) while running Poolmon. Type / again to reenable highlighting.) Type ? while Poolmon is running to bring up its help screen. You can configure which pools you want to monitor (paged, nonpaged, or both) and the sort order. Also, the command-line options are shown, which allow you to monitor specific tags (or every tag but one tag). For example, the command *poolmon –iCM* will monitor only CM tags (allocations from the configuration manager, which manages the registry). The columns have the meanings shown in Table 9-6.

```
C:\solsem\poolmon.exe                                              _ □ ×
Memory: 3405552K Avail: 2081680K  PageFlts:      39   InRam Krnl: 6068K P:63312K
Commit:1266636K Limit:7490308K Peak:1411044K           Pool N:42608K P:63648K
System pool information
Tag  Type      Allocs            Frees         Diff    Bytes      Per Alloc
 OPM Paged        9 <   0)        5 <   0)       4      192 <   0)      48
1394 Paged       10 <   0)       10 <   0)       0        0 <   0)       0
1394 Nonp        16 <   0)        3 <   0)      13    17504 <   0)    1346
139c Paged        1 <   0)        1 <   0)       0        0 <   0)       0
8042 Paged       12 <   0)       12 <   0)       0        0 <   0)       0
8042 Nonp        10 <   0)        3 <   0)       7     4016 <   0)     573
ACPI Nonp         4 <   0)        4 <   0)       0        0 <   0)       0
ADAP Nonp         8 <   0)        6 <   0)       2      544 <   0)     272
AFGp Nonp         1 <   0)        1 <   0)       0        0 <   0)       0
AFGr Paged        1 <   0)        0 <   0)       1       32 <   0)      32
ALPC Nonp      7898 <   0)     6984 <   0)     914   257280 <   0)     281
ARFT Paged        5 <   0)        2 <   0)       3       96 <   0)      32
AcdN Nonp         2 <   0)        0 <   0)       2     1072 <   0)     536
AcpA Paged       52 <   0)       52 <   0)       0        0 <   0)       0
AcpA Nonp         5 <   0)        3 <   0)       2       80 <   0)      40
AcpB Paged       33 <   0)       32 <   0)       1       16 <   0)      16
AcpD Nonp       459 <   0)      350 <   0)     109    44872 <   0)     411
AcpF Nonp       664 <   0)      646 <   0)      18      720 <   0)      40
AcpI Paged     1311 <   0)     1251 <   0)      60     7264 <   0)     121
AcpI Nonp       309 <   0)      309 <   0)       0        0 <   0)       0
```

FIGURE 9-6 Poolmon output

TABLE 9-6 Poolmon Columns

Column	Explanation
Tag	Four-byte tag given to the pool allocation
Type	Pool type (paged or nonpaged pool)
Allocs	Count of all allocations (The number in parentheses shows the difference in the Allocs column since the last update.)
Frees	Count of all Frees (The number in parentheses shows the difference in the Frees column since the last update.)
Diff	Count of Allocs minus Frees
Bytes	Total bytes consumed by this tag (The number in parentheses shows the difference in the Bytes column since the last update.)
Per Alloc	Size in bytes of a single instance of this tag

In this example, CM25-tagged allocations are taking up the most space in paged pool, and Cont-tagged allocations (contiguous physical memory allocations) are taking up the most space in nonpaged pool.

For a description of the meaning of the pool tags used by Windows, see the file \Program Files\Debugging Tools for Windows\Triage\Pooltag.txt. (This file is installed as part of the Debugging Tools for Windows, described in Chapter 1.) Because third-party device driver pool tags are not listed in this file, you can use the –c switch on the 32-bit version of Poolmon that comes with the WDK to generate a local pool tag file (Localtag.txt). This file will contain pool tags used by drivers found on your system, including third-party drivers. (Note that if a device driver binary has been deleted after it was loaded, its pool tags will not be recognized.)

Alternatively, you can search the device drivers on your system for a pool tag by using the Strings.exe tool from Sysinternals. For example, the command

```
strings %SYSTEMROOT%\system32\drivers\*.sys | findstr /i "abcd"
```

will display drivers that contain the string "abcd". Note that device drivers do not necessarily have to be located in %SystemRoot%\System32\Drivers—they can be in any folder. To list the full path of all loaded drivers, open the Run dialog box from the Start menu, and then type **Msinfo32**. Click Software Environment, and then click System Drivers. As already noted, if a device driver has been loaded and then deleted from the system, it will not be listed here.

An alternative to view pool usage by device driver is to enable the pool tracking feature of Driver Verifier, explained later in this chapter. While this makes the mapping from pool tag to device driver unnecessary, it does require a reboot (to enable Driver Verifier on the desired drivers). After rebooting with pool tracking enabled, you can either run the graphical Driver Verifier Manager (%SystemRoot%\System32\Verifier.exe) or use the Verifier /Log command to send the pool usage information to a file.

Finally, if you are looking at a crash dump, you can view pool usage with the kernel debugger *!poolused* command. The command *!poolused 2* shows nonpaged pool usage sorted by pool tag using the most amount of pool. The command *!poolused 4* lists paged pool usage, again sorted by pool tag using the most amount of pool. The following example shows the partial output from these two commands:

```
1kd> !poolused 2
   Sorting by   NonPaged Pool Consumed
   Pool Used:
              NonPaged              Paged
   Tag    Allocs      Used    Allocs      Used
   Cont    1669  15801344         0         0    Contiguous physical memory allocations for
                                                 device drivers
   Int2     414   5760072         0         0    UNKNOWN pooltag 'Int2', please update
                                                 pooltag.txt
   LSwi       1   2623568         0         0    initial work context
   EtwB     117   2327832        10    409600    Etw Buffer , Binary: nt!etw
   Pool       5   1171880         0         0    Pool tables, etc.

1kd> !poolused 4
   Sorting by   Paged Pool Consumed
   Pool Used:
              NonPaged              Paged
   Tag    Allocs      Used    Allocs      Used
   CM25       0         0      3921  16777216    Internal Configuration manager allocations ,
                                                 Binary: nt!cm
   MmRe       0         0       720  13508136    UNKNOWN pooltag 'MmRe', please update
                                                 pooltag.txt
   MmSt       0         0      5369  10827440    Mm section object prototype ptes ,
                                                 Binary: nt!mm
   Ntff       9      2232      4210   3738480    FCB_DATA , Binary: ntfs.sys
   AlMs       0         0       212   2450448    ALPC message , Binary: nt!alpc
   ViMm     469    440584       608   1468888    Video memory manager , Binary: dxgkrnl.sys
```

EXPERIMENT: Troubleshooting a Pool Leak

In this experiment, you will fix a real paged pool leak on your system so that you can put to use the techniques described in the previous section to track down the leak. The leak will be generated by the NotMyFault tool from Sysinternals. When you run NotMyFault.exe, it loads the device driver Myfault.sys and presents the following dialog box:

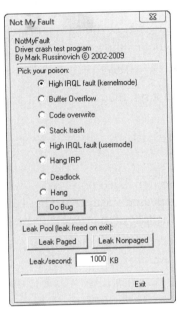

1. Click the Leak Paged button. This causes NotMyFault to begin sending requests to the Myfault device driver to allocate paged pool. (Do not click the Do Bug button or you will experience a system crash; this button is used in Chapter 14 to demonstrate various types of crashes.) NotMyFault will continue sending requests until you click the Stop Paged button. Note that paged pool is not normally released even when you close a program that has caused it to occur (by interacting with a buggy device driver); the pool is permanently leaked until you reboot the system. However, to make testing easier, the Myfault device driver detects that the process was closed and frees its allocations.

2. While the pool is leaking, first open Task Manager and click on the Performance tab. You should notice Kernel Memory (MB): Paged climbing. You can also check this with Process Explorer's System Information display. (Click on View and then System Information.)

3. To determine the pool tag that is leaking, run Poolmon and press the B key to sort by the number of bytes. Press P twice so that Poolmon is showing only paged pool. You should notice the pool tag "Leak" climbing to the top of the list. (Poolmon shows changes to pool allocations by highlighting the lines that change.)

4. Now press the Stop Paged button so that you don't exhaust paged pool on your system.

5. Using the technique described in the previous section, run Strings (from Sysinternals) to look for driver binaries that contain the pool tag "Leak":

```
Strings %SystemRoot%\system32\drivers\*.sys  |  findstr Leak
```

This should display a match on the file Myfault.sys, thus confirming it as the driver using the "Leak" pool tag.

Look-Aside Lists

Windows also provides a fast memory allocation mechanism called *look-aside lists*. The basic difference between pools and look-aside lists is that while general pool allocations can vary in size, a look-aside list contains only fixed-sized blocks. Although the general pools are more flexible in terms of what they can supply, look-aside lists are faster because they don't use any spinlocks.

Executive components and device drivers can create look-aside lists that match the size of frequently allocated data structures by using the *ExInitializeNPagedLookasideList* and *ExInitializePagedLookasideList* functions (documented in the WDK). To minimize the overhead of multiprocessor synchronization, several executive subsystems (such as the I/O manager, cache manager, and object manager) create separate look-aside lists for each processor for their frequently accessed data structures. The executive also creates a general per-processor paged and nonpaged look-aside list for small allocations (256 bytes or less).

If a look-aside list is empty (as it is when it's first created), the system must allocate from paged or nonpaged pool. But if it contains a freed block, the allocation can be satisfied very quickly. (The list grows as blocks are returned to it.) The pool allocation routines automatically tune the number of freed buffers that look-aside lists store according to how often a device driver or executive subsystem allocates from the list—the more frequent the allocations, the more blocks are stored on a list. Look-aside lists are automatically reduced in size if they aren't being allocated from. (This check happens once per second when the balance set manager system thread wakes up and calls the function *ExAdjustLookasideDepth*.)

EXPERIMENT: Viewing the System Look-Aside Lists

You can display the contents and sizes of the various system look-aside lists with the kernel debugger *!lookaside* command. The following excerpt is from the output of this command:

```
lkd> !lookaside

Lookaside "nt!IopSmallIrpLookasideList" @ 81f47c00 "Irps"
    Type        =    0000 NonPagedPool
    Current Depth =       3   Max Depth  =        4
    Size        =     148   Max Alloc  =      592
    AllocateMisses =     930   FreeMisses =      780
    TotalAllocates =   13748   TotalFrees =    13601
    Hit Rate    =     93%   Hit Rate   =      94%

Lookaside "nt!IopLargeIrpLookasideList" @ 81f47c80 "Irpl"
    Type        =    0000 NonPagedPool
    Current Depth =       4   Max Depth  =        4
    Size        =     472   Max Alloc  =     1888
    AllocateMisses =   16555   FreeMisses =    15636
    TotalAllocates =   59287   TotalFrees =    58372
    Hit Rate    =     72%   Hit Rate   =      73%

Lookaside "nt!IopMdlLookasideList" @ 81f47b80 "Mdl "
    Type        =    0000 NonPagedPool
    Current Depth =       4   Max Depth  =        4
    Size        =      96   Max Alloc  =      384
    AllocateMisses =   16287   FreeMisses =    15474
    TotalAllocates =   72835   TotalFrees =    72026
    Hit Rate    =     77%   Hit Rate   =      78%
§

Total NonPaged currently allocated for above lists =        0
Total NonPaged potential for above lists        =     3280
Total Paged currently allocated for above lists  =      744
Total Paged potential for above lists           =     1536
```

Heap Manager

Most applications allocate smaller blocks than the 64-KB minimum allocation granularity possible using page granularity functions such as *VirtualAlloc* and *VirtualAllocExNuma*. Allocating such a large area for relatively small allocations is not optimal from a memory usage and performance standpoint. To address this need, Windows provides a component called the *heap manager*, which manages allocations inside larger memory areas reserved using the page granularity memory allocation functions. The allocation granularity in the heap manager is relatively small: 8 bytes on 32-bit systems, and 16 bytes on 64-bit systems.

The heap manager has been designed to optimize memory usage and performance in the case of these smaller allocations.

The heap manager exists in two places: Ntdll.dll and Ntoskrnl.exe. The subsystem APIs (such as the Windows heap APIs) call the functions in Ntdll, and various executive components and device drivers call the functions in Ntoskrnl. Its native interfaces (prefixed with *Rtl*) are available only for use in internal Windows components or kernel-mode device drivers. The documented Windows API interfaces to the heap (prefixed with *Heap*) are forwarders to the native functions in Ntdll.dll. In addition, legacy APIs (prefixed with either *Local* or *Global*) are provided to support older Windows applications, which also internally call the heap manager, using some of its specialized interfaces to support legacy behavior. The C runtime (CRT) also uses the heap manager when using functions such as *malloc* and *free*. The most common Windows heap functions are:

- *HeapCreate* or *HeapDestroy* Creates or deletes, respectively, a heap. The initial reserved and committed size can be specified at creation.

- *HeapAlloc* Allocates a heap block.

- *HeapFree* Frees a block previously allocated with *HeapAlloc*.

- *HeapReAlloc* Changes the size of an existing allocation (grows or shrinks an existing block).

- *HeapLock* or *HeapUnlock* Controls mutual exclusion to the heap operations.

- *HeapWalk* Enumerates the entries and regions in a heap.

Types of Heaps

Each process has at least one heap: the default process heap. The default heap is created at process startup and is never deleted during the process's lifetime. It defaults to 1 MB in size, but it can be made bigger by specifying a starting size in the image file by using the /HEAP linker flag. This size is just the initial reserve, however—it will expand automatically as needed. (You can also specify the initial committed size in the image file.)

The default heap can be explicitly used by a program or implicitly used by some Windows internal functions. An application can query the default process heap by making a call to the Windows function *GetProcessHeap*. Processes can also create additional private heaps with the *HeapCreate* function. When a process no longer needs a private heap, it can recover the virtual address space by calling *HeapDestroy*. An array with all heaps is maintained in each process, and a thread can query them with the Windows function *GetProcessHeaps*.

A heap can manage allocations either in large memory regions reserved from the memory manager via *VirtualAlloc* or from memory mapped file objects mapped in the process address space. The latter approach is rarely used in practice, but it's suitable for scenarios where the content of the blocks needs to be shared between two processes or between a

kernel-mode and a user-mode component. The Win32 GUI subsystem driver (Win32k.sys) uses such a heap for sharing GDI and User objects with user mode. If a heap is built on top of a memory mapped file region, certain constraints apply with respect to the component that can call heap functions. First, the internal heap structures use pointers, and therefore do not allow relocation to different addresses. Second, the synchronization across multiple processes or between a kernel component and a user process is not supported by the heap functions. Also, in the case of a shared heap between user mode and kernel mode, the user-mode mapping should be read-only to prevent user-mode code from corrupting the heap's internal structures, which would result in a system crash. The kernel-mode driver is also responsible for not putting any sensitive data in a shared heap to avoid leaking it to user mode.

Heap Manager Structure

As shown in Figure 9-7, the heap manager is structured in two layers: an optional front-end layer and the core heap. The core heap handles the basic functionality and is mostly common across the user-mode and kernel-mode heap implementations. The core functionality includes the management of blocks inside segments, the management of the segments, policies for extending the heap, committing and decommitting memory, and management of the large blocks.

For user-mode heaps only, an optional front-end heap layer can exist on top of the existing core functionality. The only front-end supported on Windows is the Low Fragmentation Heap (LFH). Only one front-end layer can be used for one heap at one time.

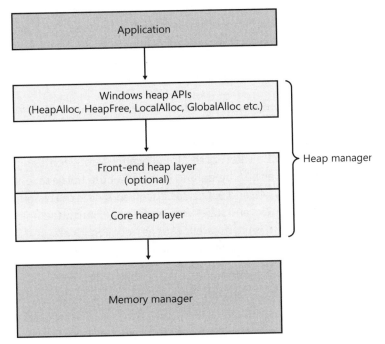

FIGURE 9-7 Heap manager layers

Heap Synchronization

The heap manager supports concurrent access from multiple threads by default. However, if a process is single threaded or uses an external mechanism for synchronization, it can tell the heap manager to avoid the overhead of synchronization by specifying HEAP_NO_SERIALIZE either at heap creation or on a per-allocation basis.

A process can also lock the entire heap and prevent other threads from performing heap operations for operations that would require consistent states across multiple heap calls. For instance, enumerating the heap blocks in a heap with the Windows function *HeapWalk* requires locking the heap if multiple threads can perform heap operations simultaneously.

If heap synchronization is enabled, there is one lock per heap that protects all internal heap structures. In heavily multithreaded applications (especially when running on multiprocessor systems), the heap lock might become a significant contention point. In that case, performance might be improved by enabling the front-end heap, described in an upcoming section.

The Low Fragmentation Heap

Many applications running in Windows have relatively small heap memory usage (usually less than 1 MB). For this class of applications, the heap manager's best-fit policy helps keep a low memory footprint for each process. However, this strategy does not scale for large processes and multiprocessor machines. In these cases, memory available for heap usage might be reduced as a result of heap fragmentation. Performance can suffer in scenarios where only certain sizes are often used concurrently from different threads scheduled to run on different processors. This happens because several processors need to modify the same memory location (for example, the head of the look-aside list for that particular size) at the same time, thus causing significant contention for the corresponding cache line.

The LFH avoids fragmentation by managing allocated blocks in predetermined different block-size ranges called buckets. When a process allocates memory from the heap, the LFH chooses the bucket that maps to the smallest block large enough to hold the required size. (The smallest block is 8 bytes.) The first bucket is used for allocations between 1 and 8 bytes, the second for allocations between 9 and 16 bytes, and so on, until the thirty-second bucket, which is used for allocations between 249 and 256 bytes, followed by the thirty-third bucket, which is used for allocations between 257 and 272 bytes, and so on. Finally, the one hundred twenty-eighth bucket, which is the last, is used for allocations between 15,873 and 16,384 bytes. Table 9-7 summarizes the different buckets, their granularity, and the range of sizes that they map to.

TABLE 9-7 **Buckets**

Buckets	Granularity	Range
1–32	8	1—256
33–48	16	257–512
49–64	32	513–1,024
65–80	64	1,025–2,048
81–96	128	2,049–4,096
97–112	256	4,097–8,194
113–128	512	8,195–16,384

The LFH addresses these issues by using the core heap manager and look-aside lists. The Windows heap manager implements an automatic tuning algorithm that can enable the LFH by default under certain conditions, such as lock contention or the presence of popular size allocations that have shown better performance with the LFH enabled. For large heaps, a significant percentage of allocations is frequently grouped in a relatively small number of buckets of certain sizes. The allocation strategy used by LFH is to optimize the usage for these patterns by efficiently handling same-size blocks.

To address scalability, the LFH expands the frequently accessed internal structures to a number of slots that is two times larger than the current number of processors on the machine. The assignment of threads to these slots is done by an LFH component called the *affinity manager*. Initially, the LFH starts using the first slot for heap allocations; however, if a contention is detected when accessing some internal data, the LFH switches the current thread to use a different slot. Further contentions will spread threads on more slots. These slots are controlled for each size bucket to improve locality and minimize the overall memory consumption.

Even if the LFH is enabled as a front-end heap, the less frequent allocation sizes may still continue to use the core heap functions to allocate memory, while the most popular allocation classes will be performed from the LFH. The LFH can also be disabled by using the *HeapSetInformation* API with the *HeapCompatibilityInformation* class.

Heap Security Features

As the heap manager has evolved, it has taken an increased role in early detection of heap usage errors and in mitigating effects of potential heap-based exploits. These measures exist to lessen the security effect of potential vulnerabilities in applications. The metadata used by the heap for internal management is packed with a high degree of randomization to make it difficult for an attempted exploit to patch the internal structures to prevent crashes or conceal the attack attempt. These blocks are also subject to an integrity check mechanism on the header to detect simple corruptions such as buffer overruns. Finally, the heap also uses a small degree of randomization of the base address (or handle). By using the *HeapSetInformation* API with the *HeapEnableTerminationOnCorruption* class, processes can

opt in for an automatic termination in case of detected inconsistencies to avoid executing unknown code.

As an effect of block metadata randomization, using the debugger to dump a block header is not that useful anymore. For example, the size of the block and whether it is busy or not are not easy to spot from a regular dump. The same applies to LFH blocks that have a different type of metadata stored in the header, partially randomized as well. To dump these details, the *!heap –i* command in the debugger does all the work to retrieve the metadata fields from a block, flagging checksum or free list inconsistencies as well if they exist. The command works for both the LFH and regular heap blocks. The total size of the blocks, the user requested size, the segment owning the block, as well as the header partial checksum are available in the output, as shown in the following sample. Because the randomization algorithm uses the heap granularity, the *!heap –i* command should be used only in the proper context of the heap containing the block. In the example, the heap handle is 0x001a0000. If the current heap context was different, the decoding of the header would be incorrect. To set the proper context, the same *!heap –i* command with the heap handle as an argument needs to be executed first.

```
0:000> !heap -i 001a0000
Heap context set to the heap 0x001a0000
0:000> !heap -i 1e2570          •
Detailed information for block entry 001e2570
Assumed heap        : 0x001a0000 (Use !heap -i NewHeapHandle to change)
Header content      : 0x1570F4EC 0x0C0015BE (decoded : 0x07010006 0x0C00000D)
Owning segment      : 0x001a0000 (offset 0)
Block flags         : 0x1 (busy )
Total block size    : 0x6 units (0x30 bytes)
Requested size      : 0x24 bytes (unused 0xc bytes)
Previous block size: 0xd units (0x68 bytes)
Block CRC           : OK - 0x7
Previous block      : 0x001e2508
Next block          : 0x001e25a0
```

Heap Debugging Features

The heap manager leverages the 8 bytes used to store internal metadata as a consistency checkpoint, which makes potential heap usage errors more obvious, and also includes several features to help detect bugs by using the following heap functions:

- **Enable tail checking** The end of each block carries a signature that is checked when the block is released. If a buffer overrun destroyed the signature entirely or partially, the heap will report this error.

- **Enable free checking** A free block is filled with a pattern that is checked at various points when the heap manager needs to access the block (such as at removal from the free list to allocate the block). If the process continued to write to the block after freeing it, the heap manager will detect changes in the pattern and the error will be reported.

- **Parameter checking** This function consists of extensive checking of the parameters passed to the heap functions.

- **Heap validation** The entire heap is validated at each heap call.

- **Heap tagging and stack traces support** This function supports specifying tags for allocation and/or captures user-mode stack traces for the heap calls to help narrow the possible causes of a heap error.

The first three options are enabled by default if the loader detects that a process is started under the control of a debugger. (A debugger can override this behavior and turn off these features.) The heap debugging features can be specified for an executable image by setting various debugging flags in the image header using the Gflags tool. (See the section "Windows Global Flags" in Chapter 3.) Or, heap debugging options can be enabled using the *!heap* command in the standard Windows debuggers. (See the debugger help for more information.)

Enabling heap debugging options affects all heaps in the process. Also, if any of the heap debugging options are enabled, the LFH will be disabled automatically and the core heap will be used (with the required debugging options enabled). The LFH is also not used for heaps that are not expandable (because of the extra overhead added to the existing heap structures) or for heaps that do not allow serialization.

Pageheap

Because the tail and free checking options described in the preceding sections might be discovering corruptions that occurred well before the problem was detected, an additional heap debugging capability, called *pageheap*, is provided that directs all or part of the heap calls to a different heap manager. Pageheap is enabled using the Gflags tool (which is part of the Debugging Tools for Windows). When enabled, the heap manager places allocations at the end of pages so that if a buffer overrun occurs, it will cause an access violation, making it easier to detect the offending code. Optionally, pageheap allows placing the blocks at the beginning of the pages to detect buffer underrun problems. (This is a rare occurrence.) The pageheap also can protect freed pages against any access to detect references to heap blocks after they have been freed.

Note that using the pageheap can result in running out of address space because of the significant overhead added for small allocations. Also, performance can suffer as a result of the increase of references to demand zero pages, loss of locality, and additional overhead caused by frequent calls to validate heap structures. A process can reduce the impact by specifying that the pageheap be used only for blocks of certain sizes, address ranges, and/or originating DLLs.

For more information on pageheap, see the Debugging Tools for Windows Help file.

Virtual Address Space Layouts

This section describes the components in the user and system address space, followed by the specific layouts on 32-bit and 64-bit systems. This information helps you to understand the limits on process and system virtual memory on both platforms.

Three main types of data are mapped into the virtual address space in Windows: per-process private code and data, sessionwide code and data, and systemwide code and data.

As explained in Chapter 1, each process has a private address space that cannot be accessed by other processes (unless they have permission to open the process for read or write access). Threads within the process can never access virtual addresses outside this private address space, unless they map to shared memory sections and/or use the cross-process memory functions that allow access to another process's address space. The information that describes the process virtual address space, called *page tables*, is described in the section on address translation. Page tables are marked as kernel-mode-only accessible pages so that user threads in a process cannot modify their own address space layout.

Session space contains information global to each session. (For a description of sessions, see Chapter 2.) A *session* consists of the processes and other system objects (such as the window station, desktops, and windows) that represent a single user's logon session. Each session has a session-specific paged pool area used by the kernel-mode portion of the Windows subsystem (Win32k.sys) to allocate session-private GUI data structures. In addition, each session has its own copy of the Windows subsystem process (Csrss.exe) and logon process (Winlogon.exe). The session manager process (Smss.exe) is responsible for creating new sessions, which includes loading a session-private copy of Win32k.sys, creating the session-private object manager namespace, and creating the session-specific instances of the Csrss and Winlogon processes. To virtualize sessions, all sessionwide data structures are mapped into a region of system space called *session space*. When a process is created, this range of addresses is mapped to the pages associated with the session that the process belongs to.

Finally, *system space* contains global operating system code and data structures visible by kernel-mode code regardless of which process is currently executing. System space consists of the following components:

- **System code** Contains the operating system image, HAL, and device drivers used to boot the system.

- **System mapped views** Used to map Win32k.sys, the loadable kernel-mode part of the Windows subsystem, as well as kernel-mode graphics drivers it uses. (See Chapter 2 for more information on Win32k.sys.)

- **Hyperspace** A special region used to map the process working set list, invalidating page table entries in other page tables (such as when a page is removed from the standby list), and process creation to set up a new process's address space.

- **System working set list** The working set list data structures that describe the system working set.

- **System cache** Virtual address space used to map files open in the system cache. (See Chapter 10 for detailed information about the cache manager.)

- **Paged pool** Pageable system memory heap.

- **System page table entries (PTEs)** Pool of system PTEs used to map system pages such as I/O space, kernel stacks, and memory descriptor lists. You can see how many system PTEs are available by examining the value of the Memory: Free System Page Table Entries counter in the Reliability and Performance Monitor.

- **Nonpaged pool** Nonpageable system memory heap.

- **Crash dump information** Reserved to record information about the state of a system crash.

- **HAL usage** System memory reserved for HAL-specific structures.

> **Note** Internally, the system working set is called the *system cache working set*. This term is misleading, however, because the system working set includes not only the system cache but also the paged pool, pageable system code and data, and pageable driver code and data.

Now that we've described the basic components of the virtual address space in Windows, let's examine the specific layout on the x86, IA64, and x64 platforms.

x86 Address Space Layouts

By default, each user process on 32-bit versions of Windows has a 2-GB private address space; the operating system takes the remaining 2 GB. However, the system can be configured with the *increaseuserva* BCD boot option to permit user address spaces up to 3 GB. Two possible address space layouts are shown in Figure 9-8.

The ability for a 32-bit process to grow beyond 2 GB was added to accommodate the need for 32-bit applications to keep more data in memory than could be done with a 2-GB address space. Of course, 64-bit systems provide a much larger address space.

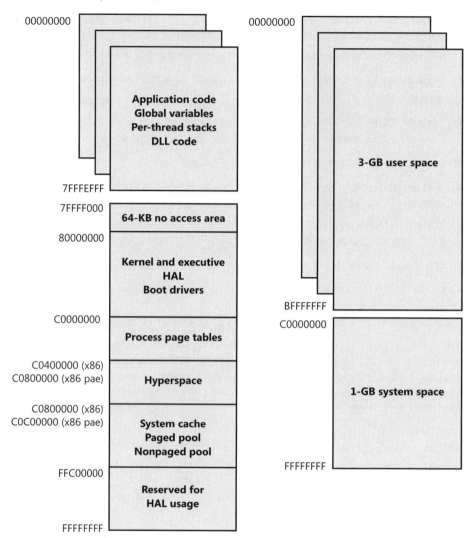

FIGURE 9-8 x86 virtual address space layouts

For a process to grow beyond 2 GB of address space, the image file must have the IMAGE_FILE_LARGE_ADDRESS_AWARE flag set in the image header. Otherwise, Windows reserves the additional address space for that process so that the application won't see virtual addresses greater than 0x7FFFFFFF. Access to the additional virtual memory is opt-in because some applications have assumed that they'd be given at most 2 GB of the address space. Since the high bit of a pointer referencing an address below 2 GB is always zero, these applications would use the high bit in their pointers as a flag for their own data, clearing it, of course, before referencing the data. If they ran with a 3-GB address space, they would inadvertently truncate pointers that have values greater than 2 GB, causing program

errors, including possible data corruption. You set this flag by specifying the linker flag /LARGEADDRESSAWARE when building the executable. This flag has no effect when running the application on a system with a 2-GB user address space.

Several system images are marked as large address space aware so that they can take advantage of systems running with large process address spaces. These include:

- Lsass.exe The Local Security Authority Subsystem
- Inetinfo.exe Internet Information Server
- Chkdsk.exe The Check Disk utility
- Smss.exe The Session Manager
- Dllhst3g.exe A special version of Dllhost.exe (for COM+ applications)
- Dispdiag.exe The display diagnostic dump utility
- Esentutl.exe The Active Directory Database Utility tool

EXPERIMENT: Checking If an Application Is Large Address Aware

You can use the Dumpbin utility from the Windows SDK to check other executables to see if they support large address spaces. Use the /HEADERS flag to display the results. Here's a sample output of Dumpbin on the Session Manager:

```
c:\>dumpbin /headers c:\Windows\system32\smss.exe | more
Microsoft (R) COFF/PE Dumper Version 9.00.21022.08
Copyright (C) Microsoft Corporation.  All rights reserved.

Dump of file c:\Windows\system32\smss.exe
PE signature found

File Type: EXECUTABLE IMAGE

FILE HEADER VALUES
            14C machine (x86)
              4 number of sections
       47918AFD time date stamp Sat Jan 19 00:30:37 2008
              0 file pointer to symbol table
              0 number of symbols
             E0 size of optional header
            122 characteristics
                Executable
                Application can handle large (>2GB) addresses
                32 bit word machine
```

Finally, because memory allocations using *VirtualAlloc*, *VirtualAllocEx*, and *VirtualAllocEx-Numa* start with low virtual addresses and grow higher by default, unless a process allocates a lot of virtual memory or it has a very fragmented virtual address space, it will never get

back very high virtual addresses. Therefore, for testing purposes, you can force memory allocations to start from high addresses by using the MEM_TOP_DOWN flag or by adding a DWORD registry value, HKLM\SYSTEM\CurrentControlSet\Control\Session Manager\Memory Management\AllocationPreference, and setting it to 0x100000.

Figure 9-9 shows two screen shots of the TestLimit utility (shown in previous experiments) leaking memory on a 32-bit Windows machine booted with and without the *increaseuserva* option set to 3 GB. Note that in the second screen shot, TestLimit was able to leak almost 3 GB, as expected.

```
C:\Temp>testlimit -r

Testlimit v5.0 - tests Windows limits
By Mark Russinovich

Reserving private bytes (MB)...
Reserved 2010 MB of private memory. Lasterror: 8
Not enough storage is available to process this command.
```

```
C:\>testlimit -r

Testlimit v5.0 - tests Windows limits
By Mark Russinovich

Reserving private bytes (MB)...
Reserved 2962 MB of private memory. Lasterror: 8
Not enough storage is available to process this command.
```

FIGURE 9-9 TestLimit leaking memory on a 32-bit Windows computer, with and without *increaseuserva* set to 3 GB

x86 System Address Space Layout

Although 32-bit versions of Windows implement a dynamic system address space layout by using a virtual address allocator (we'll describe this functionality later in this section), there are still specifically reserved areas, as shown in Figure 9-8. Figure 9-10 shows the different system structures in memory, but their size is not proportional because it is not fixed.

x86 Session Space

For systems with multiple sessions, the code and data unique to each session is mapped into system address space but shared by the processes in that session. Figure 9-11 shows the general layout of session space.

80000000

NTLDR loads the kernel, HAL, and boot drivers here. The kernel then relocates the drivers to the system PTE area.
Additional system PTEs, system cache, or special pool
System mapped views
Session space
Page tables
Hyperspace and process working set lists
System cache structures
System cache
Start of paged system area
System PTE area
Nonpaged system area
Crash dump driver area
Reserved for HAL usage

FFFFFFFF

FIGURE 9-10 x86 kernel address space layout

Win32k.sys & video drivers
MM_SESSION_SPACE & session WSLs
Mapped views for this session
Paged pool for this session

FIGURE 9-11 x86 session space layout (not proportional)

The sizes of the components of session space, just like the rest of kernel system address space, is dynamically configured and resized by the memory manager on demand.

EXPERIMENT: Viewing Sessions

You can display which processes are members of which sessions by examining the session ID. This can be viewed with Task Manager, Process Explorer, or the kernel debugger. Using the kernel debugger, you can list the active sessions with the !session command as follows:

```
lkd> !session
Sessions on machine: 2
Valid Sessions: 0 1
Current Session 1
```

Then you can set the active session using the !session –s command and display the address of the session data structures and the processes in that session with the !sprocess command:

```
lkd> !session -s 1
Sessions on machine: 2
Implicit process is now 8631dd90
Using session 1
lkd> !sprocess
Dumping Session 1

_MM_SESSION_SPACE 975c6000
_MMSESSION        975c6d00
PROCESS 8631dd90  SessionId: 1  Cid: 0244    Peb: 7ffdf000  ParentCid: 023c
    DirBase: ce2aa0a0  ObjectTable: 97a0c208  HandleCount: 563.
    Image: csrss.exe

PROCESS 8633d4e0  SessionId: 1  Cid: 0288    Peb: 7ffd5000  ParentCid: 023c
    DirBase: ce2aa040  ObjectTable: 97a5f380  HandleCount: 131.
    Image: winlogon.exe
```

To view the details of the session, dump the MM_SESSION_SPACE structure using the dt command, as follows:

```
lkd> dt nt!_MM_SESSION_SPACE 975c6000
    +0x000 ReferenceCount    : 25
    +0x004 u                 : <unnamed-tag>
    +0x008 SessionId         : 1
    +0x00c ProcessReferenceToSession : 30
    +0x010 ProcessList       : _LIST_ENTRY [ 0x8631de5c - 0x86dea0ec ]
    +0x018 LastProcessSwappedOutTime : _LARGE_INTEGER 0x0
    +0x020 SessionPageDirectoryIndex : 0xc1b09
    +0x024 NonPagablePages   : 0x42
    +0x028 CommittedPages    : 0x13fa
    +0x02c PagedPoolStart    : 0x80000000
    +0x030 PagedPoolEnd      : 0xffbfffff
```

```
+0x034 SessionObject    : 0x84adfb80
+0x038 SessionObjectHandle : 0x8000049c
+0x03c ResidentProcessCount : 17
+0x040 ImageLoadingCount : 0
+0x044 SessionPoolAllocationFailures : [4] 0
+0x054 ImageList       : _LIST_ENTRY [ 0x863192e8 - 0x88a763c0 ]
+0x05c LocaleId        : 0x409
+0x060 AttachCount     : 0
+0x064 AttachGate      : _KGATE
+0x074 WsListEntry     : _LIST_ENTRY [ 0x81f49008 - 0x8ca69074 ]
+0x080 Lookaside       : [25] _GENERAL_LOOKASIDE
+0xd00 Session         : _MMSESSION
+0xd38 PagedPoolInfo   : _MM_PAGED_POOL_INFO
+0xd70 Vm              : _MMSUPPORT
+0xdb8 Wsle            : 0x80e30058 _MMWSLE
+0xdbc DriverUnload    : 0x81720c71    void  +ffffffff81720c71
+0xdc0 PagedPool       : _POOL_DESCRIPTOR
+0x1df4 PageTables     : 0x8631a000 _MMPTE
+0x1df8 SpecialPool    : _MI_SPECIAL_POOL
+0x1e20 SessionPteLock : _KGUARDED_MUTEX
+0x1e40 PoolBigEntriesInUse : 639
+0x1e44 PagedPoolPdeCount : 0x10
+0x1e48 SpecialPoolPdeCount : 0
+0x1e4c DynamicSessionPdeCount : 0
+0x1e50 SystemPteInfo   : _MI_SYSTEM_PTE_TYPE
+0x1e7c PoolTrackTableExpansion : (null)
+0x1e80 PoolTrackTableExpansionSize : 0
+0x1e84 PoolTrackBigPages : 0x8a037000
+0x1e88 PoolTrackBigPagesSize : 0x800
+0x1e8c SessionPoolPdes  : _RTL_BITMAP
```

EXPERIMENT: Viewing Session Space Utilization

You can view session space memory utilization with the *!vm 4* command in the kernel debugger. For example, the following output was taken from a 32-bit Windows Vista system with two active sessions:

```
lkd> !vm 4
.
.
Terminal Server Memory Usage By Session:

    Session ID 0 @ 8ca69000:
    Paged Pool Usage:         5316K
    Commit Usage:             7504K

    Session ID 1 @ 975c6000:
    Paged Pool Usage:         19152K
    Commit Usage:             21524K
```

System Page Table Entries

System page table entries (PTEs) are used to dynamically map system pages such as I/O space, kernel stacks, and the mapping for memory descriptor lists. System PTEs aren't an infinite resource. On 32-bit Windows, the number of available system PTEs is such that the system can theoretically describe 2 GB of contiguous system virtual address space. On 64-bit Windows, system PTEs can describe up to 128 GB of contiguous virtual address space.

EXPERIMENT: Viewing System PTE Information

You can see how many system PTEs are available by examining the value of the Memory: Free System Page Table Entries counter in the Reliability and Performance Monitor or by using the *!sysptes* or *!vm* command in the debugger. You can also dump the _MI_SYSTEM_PTE_TYPE structure associated with the *MiSystemPteInfo* global variable. This will also show you how many PTE allocation failures occurred on the system—a high count indicates a problem and possibly a system PTE leak.

```
lkd> !sysptes

System PTE Information
  Total System Ptes 46576
    starting PTE: c0400000

  free blocks: 461    total free: 4196    largest free block: 129

lkd> ? nt!MiSystemPteInfo
Evaluate expression: -2114679136 = 81f48ea0
lkd> dt _MI_SYSTEM_PTE_TYPE 81f48ea0
nt!_MI_SYSTEM_PTE_TYPE
    +0x000 Bitmap           : _RTL_BITMAP
    +0x008 Hint             : 0x31a62
    +0x00c BasePte          : 0xc0400000 _MMPTE
    +0x010 FailureCount     : 0x81f48ec4  -> 3
    +0x014 Vm               : 0x81f4e7e0 _MMSUPPORT
    +0x018 TotalSystemPtes  : 12784
    +0x01c TotalFreeSystemPtes : 4234
    +0x020 CachedPteCount   : 497
    +0x024 PteFailures      : 3
    +0x028 GlobalMutex      : (null)
```

If you are seeing lots of system PTE failures, you can enable system PTE tracking by creating a new DWORD value in the HKLM\SYSTEM\CurrentControlSet\Control\Session Manager\Memory Management key called TrackPtes and setting its value to 1. You can then use *!syspte 4* to show a list of allocators, as shown here:

```
lkd>!sysptes 4
0x1ca2 System PTEs allocated to mapping locked pages

VA       MDL       PageCount  Caller/CallersCaller
ecbfdee8 f0ed0958         2   netbt!DispatchIoctls+0x56a/netbt!NbtDispatchDevCtrl+0xcd
f0a8d050 f0ed0510         1   netbt!DispatchIoctls+0x64e/netbt!NbtDispatchDevCtrl+0xcd
ecef5000        1        20   nt!MiFindContiguousMemory+0x63
ed447000        0         2   Ntfs!NtfsInitializeVcb+0x30e/Ntfs!NtfsInitializeDevice+0x95
ee1ce000        0         2   Ntfs!NtfsInitializeVcb+0x30e/Ntfs!NtfsInitializeDevice+0x95
ed9c4000        1        ca   nt!MiFindContiguousMemory+0x63
eda8e000        1        ca   nt!MiFindContiguousMemory+0x63
efb23d68 f8067888         2   mrxsmb!BowserMapUsersBuffer+0x28
efac5af4 f8b15b98         2   ndisuio!NdisuioRead+0x54/nt!NtReadFile+0x566
f0ac688c f848ff88         1   ndisuio!NdisuioRead+0x54/nt!NtReadFile+0x566
efac7b7c f82fc2a8         2   ndisuio!NdisuioRead+0x54/nt!NtReadFile+0x566
ee4d1000        1        38   nt!MiFindContiguousMemory+0x63
efa4f000        0         2   Ntfs!NtfsInitializeVcb+0x30e/Ntfs!NtfsInitializeDevice+0x95
efa53000        0         2   Ntfs!NtfsInitializeVcb+0x30e/Ntfs!NtfsInitializeDevice+0x95
eea89000        0         1   TDI!DllInitialize+0x4f/nt!MiResolveImageReferences+0x4bc
ee798000        1        20   VIDEOPRT!pVideoPortGetDeviceBase+0x1f1
f0676000        1        10   hal!HalpGrowMapBuffers+0x134/hal!HalpAllocateAdapterEx+0x1ff
f0b75000        1         1   cpqasm2+0x2af67/cpqasm2+0x7847
f0afa000        1         1   cpqasm2+0x2af67/cpqasm2+0x6d82
```

64-Bit Address Space Layouts

The theoretical 64-bit virtual address space is 16 exabytes (18,446,744,073,709,551,616 bytes, or approximately 17.2 billion GB). Unlike on x86 systems, where the default address space is divided in two parts (half for a process and half for the system), the 64-bit address is divided into a number of different size regions whose components match conceptually the portions of user, system, and session space. The various sizes of these regions, listed in Table 9-8, represent current implementation limits that could easily be extended in future releases. Clearly, 64 bits provides a tremendous leap in terms of address space sizes.

TABLE 9-8 64-Bit Address Space Sizes

Region	IA64	x64
Process Address Space	7,152 GB	8,192 GB
System PTE Space	128 GB	128 GB
System Cache	1 TB	1 TB
Paged Pool	128 GB	128 GB
Nonpaged Pool	75% of physical memory	75% of physical memory

Also, on 64-bit Windows, another useful feature of having an image that is large address space aware is that while running on 64-bit Windows (under Wow64), such an image will actually receive all 4 GB of user address space available—after all, if the image can support 3-GB pointers, 4-GB pointers should not be any different, because unlike the switch from 2 GB to 3 GB, there are no additional bits involved. Figure 9-12 shows TestLimit, running as a 32-bit application, reserving address space on a 64-bit Windows machine, followed by the 64-bit version of TestLimit leaking memory on the same machine.

FIGURE 9-12 32-bit and 64-bit TestLimit reserving address space on a 64-bit Windows computer

The detailed IA64 and x64 address space layouts vary slightly. The IA64 address space layout is shown in Figure 9-13, and the x64 address space layout is shown in Figure 9-14.

FIGURE 9-13 IA64 address space layout

0000000000000000 000007FFFFFEFFFF	User mode addresses: 8TB minus 64KB
000007FFFFFF0000 000007FFFFFFFFFF	64KB no access region
	⋮
FFFF080000000000	Start of system space
FFFFF68000000000	512GB four-level page table map
FFFFF70000000000	Hyperspace: working set lists and per process memory management structures mapped in this 512GB region
FFFFF78000000000	Shared system page
FFFFF78000001000	The system cache working set information resides in this 512GB – 4K region
	⋮

Note: The ranges below are sign-extended for >43 bits and therefore can be used with interlocked slists. The system address space above is NOT.

⋮

FFFFF80000000000	Mappings initialized by the loader. This is a 512GB region.
FFFFF88000000000	Start of paged system area. Kernel mode access only. 128GB.
FFFFF90000000000	Win32k.sys. Session data structures. This is a 512GB region.
FFFFF98000000000	MM_SYSTEM_SPACE_START for a length of MI_DYNAMIC_KERNEL_VA_BYTES is managed by the MiSystemVaBitMap. This is typically 1TB and is used for the system cache, system PTEs, and special pool.
FFFFFA8000000000	

Note: A large VA range is deliberately reserved here to support machines with a large number of bits of physical addressing with RAM present at the very top (i.e., a PFN database virtual span of ~6TB is required for 49-bit physical addressing using a 4KB page size with 8 byte PTEs).

⋮

	PFN database
	Initial and expansion nonpaged pool. Kernel mode access only. Up to 128GB.
	⋮
FFFFFFFF00C00000	Minimum 4MB reserved for the HAL. Loader/HAL can consume additional virtual accesss memory by leaving it
FFFFFFFFFFFFFFFF	mapped at kernel bootup.

FIGURE 9-14 x64 address space layout

64-Bit Virtual Addressing Limitations

As discussed previously, 64 bits of virtual address space allow for a possible maximum of 16 exabytes (EB) of virtual memory, a notable improvement over the 4 GB offered by 32-bit addressing. With such a copious amount of memory, it is obvious that today's computers, as well as tomorrow's foreseeable machines (at least in the consumer market), are not even close to requiring support for that much memory.

For these reasons, as well as to simplify current chip architecture, the x64 systems that AMD and Intel support on today's x64 processors support only 48 bits of virtual address space, requiring the other 16 bits to be set to the same value as the "valid," or "implemented," bits, resulting in canonical addresses. The bottom half of the address space starts at 0x0000000000000000, with only 12 of those zeroes being part of an actual address (resulting in an end at 0x00007FFFFFFFFFFF). The top half of the address space starts at 0xFFFF800000000000, ending at 0xFFFFFFFFFFFFFFFF. As newer processors support more of the addressing bits, the lower half of memory will expand upward, toward 0x7FFFFFFFFFFFFFFF, while the upper half of memory will expand downward, toward 0x8000000000000000 (a similar split to today's memory space but with 32 more bits).

In Windows, a number of mechanisms have made, and continue to make, assumptions about usable bits in the address space: pushlocks, fast references, Patchguard DPC contexts, and singly linked lists are common examples of data structures that use bits within a pointer for nonaddressing purposes. Singly linked lists, combined with the lack of a CPU instruction in the original x64 CPUs required to "port" the data structure to 64-bit Windows, have caused an interesting memory addressing limit on 64-bit Windows.

Here is the SLIST_HEADER, the data structure Windows uses to represent an entry inside a list:

```
typedef union _SLIST_HEADER {
    ULONGLONG Alignment;
    struct {
        SLIST_ENTRY Next;
        USHORT Depth;
        USHORT Sequence;
    } DUMMYSTRUCTNAME;
} SLIST_HEADER, *PSLIST_HEADER;
```

Note that this is an 8-byte structure, guaranteed to be aligned as such, composed of three elements: the pointer to the next entry (32 bits, or 4 bytes) and depth and sequence numbers, each 16 bits (or 2 bytes). To create lock-free push and pop operations, the implementation makes use of an instruction present on Pentium processors or higher—CMPXCHG8B (Compare and Exchange 8 bytes), which allows the atomic modification of 8 bytes of data. By using this native CPU instruction, which also supports the LOCK prefix (guaranteeing atomicity on a multiprocessor system), the need for a spinlock to combine two 32-bit accesses is eliminated, and all operations on the list become lock free (increasing speed and scalability).

On 64-bit computers, addresses are 64 bits, so the pointer to the next entry should logically be 64 bits. If the depth and sequence numbers remain within the same parameters, the system must provide a way to modify at minimum 64+32 bits of data—or better yet, 128 bits, in order to increase the entropy of the depth and sequence numbers. However, the first x64 processors did not implement the essential CMPXCHG16B instruction to allow this. The implementation, therefore, was written to pack as much information as possible into only 64 bits, which was the most that could be modified atomically at once. The 64-bit SLIST_HEADER thus looks like this:

```
struct {  // 8-byte header
        ULONGLONG Depth:16;
        ULONGLONG Sequence:9;
        ULONGLONG NextEntry:39;
} Header8;
```

The first change is the reduction of the space for the sequence number to 9 bits instead of 16 bits, reducing the maximum sequence number the list can achieve. This leaves only 39 bits for the pointer, still far from 64 bits. However, by forcing the structure to be 16-byte aligned when allocated, 4 more bits can be used because the bottom bits can now always be assumed to be 0. This gives 43 bits for addresses, but there is one more assumption that can be made. Because the implementation of linked lists is used either in kernel mode or user mode but cannot be used across address spaces, the top bit can be ignored, just as on 32-bit machines. The code will assume the address to be kernel mode if called in kernel mode and vice versa. This allows us to address up to 44 bits of memory in the NextEntry pointer and is the defining constraint of the addressing limit in Windows.

Forty-four bits is a much better number than 32. It allows 16 TB of virtual memory to be described and thus splits Windows into two even chunks of 8 TB for user-mode and kernel-mode memory. Nevertheless, this is still 16 times smaller than the CPU's own limit (48 bits is 256 TB), and even farther still from the maximum that 64 bits can describe. So, with scalability in mind, some other bits do exist in the SLIST_HEADER that define the type of header being dealt with. This means that when the day comes when all x64 CPUs support 128-bit Compare and Exchange, Windows can easily take advantage of it (and to do so before then would mean distributing two different kernel images). Here's a look at the full 8-byte header:

```
  struct {  // 8-byte header
        ULONGLONG Depth:16;
        ULONGLONG Sequence:9;
        ULONGLONG NextEntry:39;
        ULONGLONG HeaderType:1; // 0: 8-byte; 1: 16-byte
        ULONGLONG Init:1;       // 0: uninitialized; 1: initialized
        ULONGLONG Reserved:59;
        ULONGLONG Region:3;
  } Header8;
```

Note how the HeaderType bit is overlaid with the Depth bits and allows the implementation to deal with 16-byte headers whenever support becomes available. For the sake of completeness, here is the definition of the 16-byte header:

```
struct {  // 16-byte header
      ULONGLONG Depth:16;
      ULONGLONG Sequence:48;
      ULONGLONG HeaderType:1; // 0: 8-byte; 1: 16-byte
      ULONGLONG Init:1;       // 0: uninitialized; 1: initialized
      ULONGLONG Reserved:2;
      ULONGLONG NextEntry:60; // last 4 bits are always 0's
} Header16;
```

Notice how the NextEntry pointer has now become 60 bits, and because the structure is still 16-byte aligned, with the 4 free bits, leads to the full 64 bits being addressable.

Dynamic System Virtual Address Space Management

Thirty-two-bit versions of Windows manage the system address space through an internal kernel virtual allocator mechanism that we'll describe in this section. Currently, 64-bit versions of Windows have no need to use the allocator for virtual address space management (and thus bypass the cost), because each region is statically defined as shown in Table 9-8 earlier.

When the system initializes, the *MiInitializeDynamicVa* function sets up the basic dynamic ranges (the ranges currently supported are described in Table 9-9) and sets the available virtual address to all available kernel space. It then initializes the address space ranges for boot loader images, process space (hyperspace), and the HAL through the *MiIntializeSystemVaRange* function, which is used to set hard-coded address ranges. Later, when nonpaged pool is initialized, this function is used again to reserve the virtual address ranges for it. Finally, whenever a driver loads, the address range is relabeled to a driver image range (instead of a boot loaded range).

After this point, the rest of the system virtual address space can be dynamically requested and released through *MiObtainSystemVa* (and its analogous *MiObtainSessionVa*) and *MiReturnSystemVa*. Operations such as expanding the system cache, the system PTEs, nonpaged pool, paged pool, and/or special pool; mapping memory with large pages; creating the PFN database; and creating a new session all result in dynamic virtual address allocations for a specific range.

TABLE 9-9 **System Virtual Address Types**

Region	Description	Limitable
MiVaSessionSpace (0x1)	Addresses for session space	Yes
MiVaProcessSpace (0x2)	Addresses for process address space	No
MiVaBootLoaded (0x3)	Addresses for images loaded by the boot loader	No
MiVaPfnDatabase (0x4)	Addresses for the PFN database	No
MiVaNonPagedPool (0x5)	Addresses for the nonpaged pool	Yes
MiVaPagedPool (0x6)	Addresses for the paged pool	Yes
MiVaSpecialPool (0x7)	Addresses for the special pool	No
MiVaSystemCache (0x8)	Addresses for the system cache	Yes
MiVaSystemPtes (0x9)	Addresses for system PTEs	Yes
MiVaHal (0xA)	Addresses for the HAL	No
MiVaSessionGlobalSpace (0xB)	Addresses for session global space	No
MiVaDriverImages (0xC)	Addresses for loaded driver images	No

Although the ability to dynamically reserve virtual address space on demand allows better management of virtual memory, it would be useless without the ability to free this memory. As such, when paged pool or the system cache can be shrunk, or when special pool and large page mappings are freed, the associated virtual address is freed. (Another case is when the boot registry is released.) This allows dynamic management of memory depending on each component's use. Additionally, components can reclaim memory through *MiReclaimSystemVa*, which requests virtual addresses associated with the system cache to be flushed out (through the dereference segment thread) if available virtual address space has dropped below 128 MB. (Reclaiming can also be satisfied if initial nonpaged pool has been freed.)

EXPERIMENT: Determining the Virtual Address Type for an Address

Each time the kernel virtual address space allocator obtains virtual memory ranges for use by a certain type of virtual address, it updates the *MiSystemVaType* array, which contains the virtual address type for the newly allocated range.

By taking any given kernel address and calculating its PDE index from the beginning of system space, you can dump the appropriate byte field in this array to obtain the virtual address type. For example, the following commands will display the virtual address types for Win32k.sys, the process object for WinDbg, the handle table for WinDbg, the kernel, a file system cache segment, and hyperspace:

```
lkd> ?? nt!_MI_SYSTEM_VA_TYPE (((char*)@@(nt!MiSystemVaType))[@@((win32k -
poi(nt!MmSystemRangeStart))/(1000*1000/@@(sizeof(nt!MMPTE)) ))])
_MI_SYSTEM_VA_TYPE MiVaSessionGlobalSpace (11)
lkd> ?? nt!_MI_SYSTEM_VA_TYPE (((char*)@@(nt!MiSystemVaType))[@@((864753b0    -
poi(nt!MmSystemRangeStart))/(1000*1000/@@(sizeof(nt!MMPTE)) ))])
_MI_SYSTEM_VA_TYPE MiVaNonPagedPool (5)
lkd> ?? nt!_MI_SYSTEM_VA_TYPE (((char*)@@(nt!MiSystemVaType))[@@((8b2001d0  -
poi(nt!MmSystemRangeStart))/(1000*1000/@@(sizeof(nt!MMPTE)) ))])
_MI_SYSTEM_VA_TYPE MiVaPagedPool (6)
lkd> ?? nt!_MI_SYSTEM_VA_TYPE (((char*)@@(nt!MiSystemVaType))[@@((nt -
poi(nt!MmSystemRangeStart))/(1000*1000/@@(sizeof(nt!MMPTE)) ))])
_MI_SYSTEM_VA_TYPE MiVaBootLoaded (3)
lkd> ?? nt!_MI_SYSTEM_VA_TYPE (((char*)@@(nt!MiSystemVaType))[@@((0xb3c80000   -
poi(nt!MmSystemRangeStart))/(1000*1000/@@(sizeof(nt!MMPTE)) ))])
_MI_SYSTEM_VA_TYPE MiVaSystemCache (8)
lkd> ?? nt!_MI_SYSTEM_VA_TYPE (((char*)@@(nt!MiSystemVaType))[@@((c0400000 -
poi(nt!MmSystemRangeStart))/(1000*1000/@@(sizeof(nt!MMPTE)) ))])

_MI_SYSTEM_VA_TYPE MiVaProcessSpace (2)
```

In addition to better proportioning and better management of virtual addresses dedicated to different kernel memory consumers, the dynamic virtual address allocator also has advantages when it comes to memory footprint reduction. Instead of having to manually preallocate static page table entries and page tables, paging-related structures are allocated on demand. On both 32-bit and 64-bit systems, this reduces boot-time memory usage because unused addresses won't have their page tables allocated. It also means that on 64-bit systems, the large address space regions that are reserved don't need to have their page tables mapped in memory, which allows them to have arbitrarily large limits, especially on systems that have little physical RAM to back the resulting paging structures.

EXPERIMENT: Querying System Virtual Address Usage

You can look at the current usage and peak usage of each system virtual address type by using the kernel debugger. For each system virtual address type described in Table 9-9, the *MiSystemVaTypeCount, MiSystemVaTypeCountFailures,* and *MiSystemVaTypeCountPeak* arrays in the kernel contain the sizes, count failures, and peak sizes for each type. Here's how you can dump the usage for the system, followed by the peak usage (you can use a similar technique for the failure counts):

```
lkd> dd /c 1 MiSystemVaTypeCount l c
81f4f880  00000000
81f4f884  00000028
81f4f888  00000008
81f4f88c  0000000c
81f4f890  0000000b
81f4f894  0000001a
81f4f898  0000002f
81f4f89c  00000000
81f4f8a0  000001b6
81f4f8a4  00000030
81f4f8a8  00000002
81f4f8ac  00000006
lkd> dd /c 1 MiSystemVaTypeCountPeak  l c
81f4f840  00000000
81f4f844  00000038
81f4f848  00000000
81f4f84c  00000000
81f4f850  0000003d
81f4f854  0000001e
81f4f858  00000032
81f4f85c  00000000
81f4f860  00000238
81f4f864  00000031
81f4f868  00000000
81f4f86c  00000006
```

Although theoretically, the different virtual address ranges assigned to components can grow arbitrarily in size as long as enough system virtual address space is available, the kernel allocator implements the ability to set limits on each virtual address type for the purposes of both reliability and stability. Although no limits are imposed by default, system administrators can use the registry to modify these limits for the virtual address types that are currently marked as limitable (see Table 9-9).

If the current request during the *MiObtainSystemVa* call exceeds the available limit, a failure is marked (see the previous experiment) and a reclaim operation is requested regardless of available memory. This should help alleviate memory load and might allow the virtual address allocation to work during the next attempt. (Recall, however, that reclaiming affects only system cache and nonpaged pool).

EXPERIMENT: Setting System Virtual Address Limits

The *MiSystemVaTypeCountLimit* array contains limitations for system virtual address usage that can be set for each type. Currently, the memory manager allows only certain virtual address types to be limited, and it provides the ability to use an undocumented system call to set limits for the system dynamically during run time. (These limits can also be set through the registry, as described at *http://msdn.microsoft.com/en-us/library/bb870880(VS.85).aspx*. These limits can be set for those types marked in Table 9-9.

You can use the MemLimit utility from Winsider Seminars & Solutions (*www.winsiderss.com/tools/memlimit.html*) to query and set the different limits for these types, and also to see the current and peak virtual address space usage. Here's how you can query the current limits with the *−q* flag:

```
C:\ >memlimit.exe -q

MemLimit v1.00 - Query and set hard limits on system VA space consumption
Copyright (C) 2008 Alex Ionescu
www.alex-ionescu.com

System Va Consumption:

Type                   Current           Peak              Limit
Non Paged Pool          102400 KB           0 KB             0 KB
Paged Pool               59392 KB       83968 KB             0 KB
System Cache            534528 KB      536576 KB             0 KB
System PTEs              73728 KB       75776 KB             0 KB
Session Space            75776 KB       90112 KB             0 KB
```

As an experiment, use the following command to set a limit of 100 MB for paged pool:

```
memlimit.exe -p 100M
```

And now try running the *testlimit −h* experiment from Chapter 3 again, which attempted to create 16 million handles. Instead of reaching the 16 million handle count, the process will fail, because the system will have run out of address space available for paged pool allocations.

Finally, as of Windows Vista and Windows Server 2008, the system virtual address space limits apply only to 32-bit systems, where 1 to 2 GB of kernel address space can lead to exhaustion. Sixty-four-bit systems have 8 TB of kernel address space, so limiting virtual address space usage is currently not a concern.

System Virtual Address Space Quotas

The system virtual address space limits described in the previous section allow for limiting systemwide virtual address space usage of certain kernel components, but they work only on 32-bit systems when applied to the system as a whole. To address more specific quota requirements that system administrators might have, the memory manager also collaborates with the process manager to enforce either systemwide or user-specific quotas for each process.

The PagedPoolQuota, NonPagedPoolQuota, PagingFileQuota, and WorkingSetPagesQuota values in the HKLM\SYSTEM\CurrentControlSet\Control\Session Manager\Memory Management key can be configured to specify how much memory of each type a given process can use. This information is read at initialization, and the default system quota block is generated and then assigned to all system processes (user processes will get a copy of the default system quota block unless per-user quotas have been configured as explained next).

To enable per-user quotas, subkeys under the registry key HKLM\SYSTEM\CurrentControlSet\Session Manager\Quota System can be created, each one representing a given user SID. The values mentioned previously can then be created under this specific SID subkey, enforcing the limits only for the processes created by that user. Table 9-10 shows how to configure these values, which can be configured at run time or not, and which privileges are required.

TABLE 9-10 Process Quota Types

Value Name	Description	Value Type	Dynamic	Privilege
PagedPoolQuota	Maximum size of paged pool that can be allocated by this process	Size in MB	Only for processes running with the system token	SeIncreaseQuotaPrivilege
NonPagedPoolQuota	Maximum size of nonpaged pool that can be allocated by this process	Size in MB	Only for processes running with the system token	SeIncreaseQuotaPrivilege
PagingFileQuota	Maximum number of pages that a process can have backed by the page file	Pages	Only for processes running with the system token	SeIncreaseQuotaPrivilege
WorkingSetPagesQuota	Maximum number of pages that a process can have in its working set (in physical memory)	Pages	Yes	SeIncreaseBasePriorityPrivilege unless operation is a purge request

User Address Space Layout

Just as address space in the kernel is dynamic, the user address space in Windows Vista and later versions is also built dynamically—the addresses of the thread stacks, process heaps, and loaded images (such as DLLs and an application's executable) are dynamically computed (if the application and its images support it) through a mechanism known as Address Space Layout Randomization, or ASLR.

At the operating system level, user address space is divided into a few well-defined regions of memory, shown in Figure 9-15. The executable and DLLs themselves are present as memory mapped image files, followed by the heap(s) of the process and the stack(s) of its thread(s). Apart from these regions (and some reserved system structures such as the TEBs and PEB), all other memory allocations are run-time dependent and generated. ASLR is involved with the location of all these regions and, combined with DEP, provides a mechanism for making remote exploitation of a system through memory manipulation harder to achieve—by having code and data at dynamic locations, an attacker cannot typically hardcode a meaningful offset.

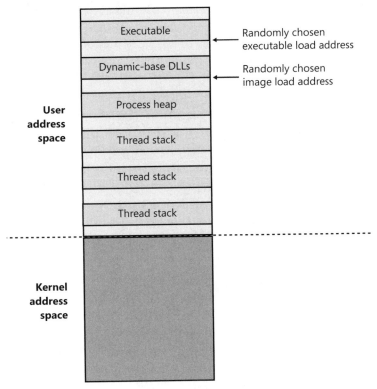

FIGURE 9-15 User address space layout with ASLR enabled

EXPERIMENT: Analyzing User Virtual Address Space

The Vmmap utility from Sysinternals can show you a detailed view of the virtual memory being utilized by any process on your machine, divided into categories for each type of allocation, summarized as follows:

- **Image** Displays memory allocations used to map the process and its dependencies (such as dynamic libraries) and any other memory mapped image files

- **Private** Displays memory allocations marked as private, such as internal data structures, other than the stack and heap

- **Shareable** Displays memory allocations marked as shareable, typically including shared memory (but not memory mapped files, which are either Image or Mapped File)

- **Mapped File** Displays memory allocations for memory mapped data files

- **Heap** Displays memory allocated for the heap(s) that this process owns

- **Stack** Displays memory allocated for the stack of each thread in this process

- **System** Displays kernel memory allocated for the process (such as the process object)

The following screen shot shows a typical view of Explorer as seen through Vmmap.

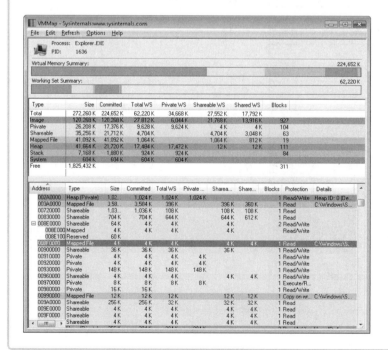

Depending on the type of memory allocation, Vmmap can show additional informa-
tion, such as file names (for mapped files), heap IDs (for heap allocations), and thread
IDs (for stack allocations). Furthermore, each allocation's cost is shown both in commit-
ted memory and working set memory. The size and protection of each allocation is also
displayed.

ASLR begins at the image level, with the executable for the process and its dependent
DLLs. Any image file that has specified ASLR support in its PE header (IMAGE_DLL_
CHARACTERISTICS_DYNAMIC_BASE), typically specified by using the /DYNAMICBASE linker
flag in Microsoft Visual Studio, and contains a relocation section will be processed by ASLR.
When such an image is found, the system selects an image offset valid globally for the cur-
rent boot. This offset is selected from a bucket of 256 values, all of which are 64-KB aligned.

Note You can control ASLR behavior by creating a key called MoveImages under HKLM\
SYSTEM\CurrentControlSet\Session Manager\Memory Management. Setting this value to 0 will
disable ASLR, while a value of 0xFFFFFFFF (–1) will enable ASLR regardless of the IMAGE_DLL_
CHARACTERISTICS_DYNAMIC_BASE flag. (Images must still be relocatable, however.)

Image Randomization

For executables, the load offset is calculated by computing a delta value each time an exe-
cutable is loaded. This value is a pseudo-random 8-bit number from 0x10000 to 0xFE0000,
calculated by taking the current processor's time stamp counter (TSC), shifting it by four
places, and then performing a division modulo 254 and adding 1. This number is then mul-
tiplied by the allocation granularity of 64 KB discussed earlier. By adding 1, the memory
manager ensures that the value can never be 0, so executables will never load at the address
in the PE header if ASLR is being used. This delta is then added to the executable's preferred
load address, creating one of 256 possible locations within 16 MB of the image address in the
PE header.

For DLLs, computing the load offset begins with a per-boot, systemwide value called the
image bias, which is computed by *MiInitializeRelocations* and stored in *MiImageBias*. This
value corresponds to the time stamp counter (TSC) of the current CPU when this function was
called during the boot cycle, shifted and masked into an 8-bit value, which provides 256 pos-
sible values. Unlike executables, this value is computed only once per boot and shared across
the system to allow DLLs to remain shared in physical memory and relocated only once.
Otherwise, if every DLL was loaded at a different location inside different processes, each DLL
would have a private copy loaded in physical memory.

Once the offset is computed, the memory manager initializes a bitmap called the *MiImageBitMap*. This bitmap is used to represent ranges from 0x50000000 to 0x78000000 (stored in *MiImageBitMapHighVa*), and each bit represents one unit of allocation (64 KB, as mentioned earlier). Whenever the memory manager loads a DLL, the appropriate bit is set to mark its location in the system; when the same DLL is loaded again, the memory manager shares its section object with the already relocated information.

As each DLL is loaded, the system scans the bitmap from top to bottom for free bits. The *MiImageBias* value computed earlier is used as a start index from the top to randomize the load across different boots as suggested. Because the bitmap will be entirely empty when the first DLL (which is always Ntdll.dll) is loaded, its load address can easily be calculated: 0x78000000 – *MiImageBias* * 0x10000. Each subsequent DLL will then load in a 64-KB chunk below. Because of this, if the address of Ntdll.dll is known, the addresses of other DLLs could easily be computed. To mitigate this possibility, the order in which known DLLs are mapped by the Session Manager during initialization is also randomized when Smss loads.

Finally, if no free space is available in the bitmap (which would mean that most of the region defined for ASLR is in use, the DLL relocation code defaults back to the executable case, loading the DLL at a 64-KB chunk within 16 MB of its preferred base address.

Stack Randomization

The next step in ASLR is to randomize the location of the initial thread's stack (and, subsequently, of each new thread). This randomization is enabled unless the flag *StackRandomizationDisabled* was enabled for the process and consists of first selecting one of 32 possible stack locations separated by either 64 KB or 256 KB. This base address is selected by finding the first appropriate free memory region and then choosing the *x*th available region, where *x* is once again generated based on the current processor's TSC shifted and masked into a 5-bit value (which allows for 32 possible locations).

Once this base address has been selected, a new TSC-derived value is calculated, this one 9 bits long. The value is then multiplied by 4 to maintain alignment, which means it can be as large as 2,048 bytes (half a page). It is added to the base address to obtain the final stack base.

Heap Randomization

Finally, ASLR randomizes the location of the initial process heap (and subsequent heaps) when created in user mode. The *RtlCreateHeap* function uses another pseudo-random, TSC-derived value to determine the base address of the heap. This value, 5 bits this time, is multiplied by 64 KB to generate the final base address, starting at 0, giving a possible range of 0x00000000 to 0x001F0000 for the initial heap. Additionally, the range before the heap base address is manually deallocated in an attempt to force an access violation if an attack is doing a brute-force sweep of the entire possible heap address range.

EXPERIMENT: Looking at ASLR Protection on Processes

You can use Process Explorer from Sysinternals to look over your processes (and, just as important, the DLLs they load) to see if they support ASLR. To look at the ASLR status for processes, right-click on any column in the process tree, choose Select Columns, and then check ASLR Enabled on the Process Image tab. The following screen shot displays an example of a system on which you can notice that ASLR is enabled for all in-box Windows programs and services but that some third-party applications and services are not yet built with ASLR support.

Address Translation

Now that you've seen how Windows structures the virtual address space, let's look at how it maps these address spaces to real physical pages. User applications and system code reference virtual addresses. This section starts with a detailed description of 32-bit x86 address translation and continues with a brief description of the differences on the 64-bit IA64 and x64 platforms. In the next section, we'll describe what happens when such a translation doesn't resolve to a physical memory address (paging) and explain how Windows manages physical memory via working sets and the page frame database.

x86 Virtual Address Translation

Using data structures the memory manager creates and maintains called *page tables*, the CPU translates virtual addresses into physical addresses. Each virtual address is associated with a system-space structure called a *page table entry* (PTE), which contains the physical address to which the virtual one is mapped. For example, Figure 9-16 shows how three consecutive virtual pages are mapped to three physically discontiguous pages on an x86 system. There may not even be any PTEs for regions that have been marked as reserved or committed but never accessed, because the page table itself might be allocated only when the first page fault occurs.

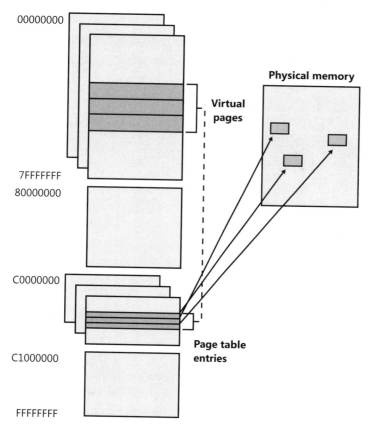

FIGURE 9-16 Mapping virtual addresses to physical memory (x86)

The dashed line connecting the virtual pages to the PTEs in Figure 9-16 represents the indirect relationship between virtual pages and physical memory.

Note Kernel-mode code (such as device drivers) can reference physical memory addresses by mapping them to virtual addresses. For more information, see the memory descriptor list (MDL) support routines described in the WDK documentation.

By default, Windows on an x86 system uses a two-level page table structure to translate virtual to physical addresses. (x86 systems running the PAE kernel use a three-level page table—this section assumes non-PAE systems.) A 32-bit virtual address mapped by a normal 4-KB page is interpreted as three separate components—the page directory index, the page table index, and the byte index—that are used as indexes into the structures that describe page mappings, as illustrated in Figure 9-17. The page size and the PTE width dictate the width of the page directory and page table index fields. For example, on x86 systems, the byte index is 12 bits because pages are 4,096 bytes ($2^{12} = 4,096$).

FIGURE 9-17 Components of a 32-bit virtual address on x86 systems

The *page directory index* is used to locate the page table in which the virtual address's PTE is located. The *page table index* is used to locate the PTE, which, as mentioned earlier, contains the physical address to which a virtual page maps. The *byte index* finds the proper address within that physical page. Figure 9-18 shows the relationship of these three values and how they are used to map a virtual address into a physical address.

FIGURE 9-18 Translating a valid virtual address (x86-specific)

The following basic steps are involved in translating a virtual address:

1. The memory management hardware locates the page directory for the current process. On each process context switch, the hardware is told the address of a new process page directory by the operating system setting a special CPU register (CR3 in Figure 9-18).

2. The page directory index is used as an index into the page directory to locate the page directory entry (PDE) that describes the location of the page table needed to map the virtual address. The PDE contains the page frame number (PFN) of the page table (if it is resident—page tables can be paged out or not yet created). In both of these cases, the page table is first made resident before proceeding. For large pages, the PDE points directly to the PFN of the target page, and the rest of the address is treated as the byte offset within this frame.

3. The page table index is used as an index into the page table to locate the PTE that describes the physical location of the virtual page in question.

4. The PTE is used to locate the page. If the page is valid, it contains the PFN of the page in physical memory that contains the virtual page. If the PTE indicates that the page isn't valid, the memory management fault handler locates the page and tries to make it valid. (See the section on page fault handling.) If the page should not be made valid (for example, because of a protection fault), the fault handler generates an access violation or a bug check.

5. When the PTE is pointed to a valid page, the byte index is used to locate the address of the desired data within the physical page.

Now that you have the overall picture, let's look at the detailed structure of page directories, page tables, and PTEs.

Page Directories

Each process has a single *page directory*, a page the memory manager creates to map the location of all page tables for that process. The physical address of the process page directory is stored in the kernel process (KPROCESS) block, but it is also mapped virtually at address 0xC0300000 on x86 systems (0xC0600000 on systems running the PAE kernel image). Most code running in kernel mode references virtual addresses, not physical ones. (For more detailed information about KPROCESS and other process data structures, refer to Chapter 5.)

The CPU knows the location of the page directory page because a special register (CR3 on x86 systems) inside the CPU that is loaded by the operating system contains the physical address of the page directory. Each time a context switch occurs to a thread that is in a different process than that of the currently executing thread, this register is loaded from the KPROCESS block of the target process being switched to by the context-switch routine in the kernel. Context switches between threads in the same process don't result in reloading the

physical address of the page directory because all threads within the same process share the same process address space.

The page directory is composed of *page directory entries* (PDEs), each of which is 4 bytes long (8 bytes on systems running the PAE kernel image) and describes the state and location of all the possible page tables for that process. (If the page table does not yet exist, the VAD tree is consulted to determine whether an access should materialize it.) (As described later in the chapter, page tables are created on demand, so the page directory for most processes points only to a small set of page tables.) The format of a PDE isn't repeated here because it's mostly the same as a hardware PTE.

On x86 systems running in non-PAE mode, 1,024 page tables are required to describe the full 4-GB virtual address space. The process page directory that maps these page tables contains 1,024 PDEs. Therefore, the page directory index needs to be 10 bits wide (2^{10} = 1,024). On x86 systems running in PAE mode, there are 512 entries in a page table (because the PTE size is 8 bytes and page tables are 4 KB in size). Because there are 4 page directories, the result is a maximum of 2,048 page tables.

EXPERIMENT: Examining the Page Directory and PDEs

You can see the physical address of the currently running process's page directory by examining the DirBase field in the *!process* kernel debugger output:

```
lkd> !process
PROCESS 87248070  SessionId: 1  Cid: 088c    Peb: 7ffdf000  ParentCid: 06d0
    DirBase: ce2a8980  ObjectTable: a72ba408  HandleCount:  95.
    Image: windbg.exe
    VadRoot 86ed30a0 Vads 85 Clone 0 Private 3474. Modified 187. Locked 1.
    DeviceMap 98fd1008
    Token                        affe1c48
    ElapsedTime                  00:18:17.182
    UserTime                     00:00:00.000
    KernelTime                   00:00:00.000
```

You can see the page directory's virtual address by examining the kernel debugger output for the PTE of a particular virtual address, as shown here:

```
lkd> !pte 50001
            VA 00050001
PDE at 00000000C0600000    PTE at 00000000C0000280
contains 0000000056C74867  contains 80000000C0EBD025
pfn 56c74      ---DA--UWEV   pfn c0ebd      ----A--UR-V
```

The PTE part of the kernel debugger output is defined in the section "Page Tables and Page Table Entries."

Because Windows provides a private address space for each process, each process has its own set of process page tables to map that process's private address space. However, the

page tables that describe system space are shared among all processes (and session space is shared only among processes in a session). To avoid having multiple page tables describing the same virtual memory, when a process is created, the page directory entries that describe system space are initialized to point to the existing system page tables. If the process is part of a session, session space page tables are also shared by pointing the session space page directory entries to the existing session page tables.

Page Tables and Page Table Entries

The process page directory entries point to individual page tables. Page tables are composed of an array of PTEs. The virtual address's page table index field (as shown in Figure 9-17) indicates which PTE within the page table maps the data page in question. On x86 systems, the page table index is 10 bits wide (9 on PAE), allowing you to reference up to 1,024 4-byte PTEs (512 8-byte PTEs on PAE systems). However, because 32-bit Windows provides a 4-GB private virtual address space, more than one page table is needed to map the entire address space. To calculate the number of page tables required to map the entire 4-GB process virtual address space, divide 4 GB by the virtual memory mapped by a single page table. Recall that each page table on an x86 system maps 4 MB (2 MB on PAE) of data pages. Thus, 1,024 page tables (4 GB/4 MB)—or 2,048 page tables (4 GB/2 MB) for PAE—are required to map the full 4-GB address space.

You can use the *!pte* command in the kernel debugger to examine PTEs. (See the experiment "Translating Addresses.") We'll discuss valid PTEs here and invalid PTEs in a later section. Valid PTEs have two main fields: the page frame number (PFN) of the physical page containing the data or of the physical address of a page in memory, and some flags that describe the state and protection of the page, as shown in Figure 9-19.

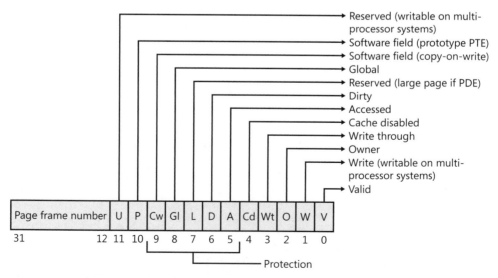

FIGURE 9-19 Valid x86 hardware PTEs

As you'll see later, the bits labeled Reserved in Figure 9-19 are used only when the PTE is valid. (The bits are interpreted by software.) Table 9-11 briefly describes the hardware-defined bits in a valid PTE.

TABLE 9-11 PTE Status and Protection Bits

Name of Bit	Meaning
Accessed	Page has been read.
Cache disabled	Disables caching for that page.
Copy-on-write	Page is using copy-on-write (described earlier).
Dirty	Page has been written to.
Global	Translation applies to all processes. (For example, a translation buffer flush won't affect this PTE.)
Large page	Indicates that the PDE maps a 4-MB page (or 2 MB on PAE systems). See the section "Large and Small Pages" earlier in the chapter.
Owner	Indicates whether user-mode code can access the page or whether the page is limited to kernel-mode access.
Prototype	The PTE is a prototype PTE, which is used as a template to describe shared memory associated with section objects.
Valid	Indicates whether the translation maps to a page in physical memory.
Write through	Disables caching of writes to this page so that changes are immediately flushed to disk.
Write	Indicates whether the page is writable. (The Write bit is stored in a reserved bit in the PTE.)

On x86 systems, a hardware PTE contains a Dirty bit and an Accessed bit. The Accessed bit is clear if a physical page represented by the PTE hasn't been read or written since the last time it was cleared; the processor sets this bit when the page is read or written if and only if the bit is clear at the time of access. The memory manager sets the Dirty bit when a page is first written, compared to the backing store copy. In addition to those two bits, the x86 memory management implementation uses a Write bit to provide page protection. When this bit is clear, the page is read-only; when it is set, the page is read/write. If a thread attempts to write to a page with the Write bit clear, a memory management exception occurs, and the memory manager's access fault handler (described in the next section) must determine whether the thread can write to the page (for example, if the page was really marked copy-on-write) or whether an access violation should be generated.

The additional Write bit implemented in software (as described above) is used to optimize flushing of the PTE cache (called the *translation look-aside buffer*, described in the next section).

Byte Within Page

Once the memory manager has found the physical page in question, it must find the requested data within that page. This is where the byte index field comes in. The byte index field tells the CPU which byte of data in the page you want to reference. On x86 systems, the byte index is 12 bits wide, allowing you to reference up to 4,096 bytes of data (the size of a page). So, adding the byte offset to the physical page number retrieved from the PTE completes the translation of a virtual address to a physical address.

Translation Look-Aside Buffer

As you've learned so far, each hardware address translation requires two lookups: one to find the right page table in the page directory and one to find the right entry *in* the page table. Because doing two additional memory lookups for every reference to a virtual address would result in unacceptable system performance, all CPUs cache address translations so that repeated accesses to the same addresses don't have to be retranslated. The processor provides such a cache in the form of an array of associative memory called the *translation look-aside buffer*, or TLB. Associative memory, such as the TLB, is a vector whose cells can be read simultaneously and compared to a target value. In the case of the TLB, the vector contains the virtual-to-physical page mappings of the most recently used pages, as shown in Figure 9-20, and the type of page protection, size, attributes, and so on applied to each page. Each entry in the TLB is like a cache entry whose tag holds portions of the virtual address and whose data portion holds a physical page number, protection field, valid bit, and usually a dirty bit indicating the condition of the page to which the cached PTE corresponds. If a PTE's global bit is set (used for system space pages that are globally visible to all processes), the TLB entry isn't invalidated on process context switches.

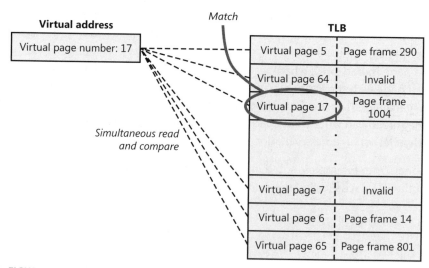

FIGURE 9-20 Accessing the translation look-aside buffer

Virtual addresses that are used frequently are likely to have entries in the TLB, which provides extremely fast virtual-to-physical address translation and, therefore, fast memory access. If a virtual address isn't in the TLB, it might still be in memory, but multiple memory accesses are needed to find it, which makes the access time slightly slower. If a virtual page has been paged out of memory or if the memory manager changes the PTE, the memory manager is required to explicitly invalidate the TLB entry. If a process accesses it again, a page fault occurs, and the memory manager brings the page back into memory (if needed) and re-creates its PTE entry (which then results in an entry for it in the TLB).

Physical Address Extension (PAE)

The Intel x86 Pentium Pro processor introduced a memory-mapping mode called *Physical Address Extension* (PAE). With the proper chipset, the PAE mode allows 32-bit operating systems access to up to 64 GB of physical memory on current Intel x86 processors and up to 1,024 GB of physical memory when running on x64 processors in legacy mode (although Windows currently limits this to 64 GB due to the size of the PFN database required to map so much memory). When the processor executes in PAE mode, the memory management unit (MMU) divides virtual addresses mapped by normal pages into four fields, as shown in Figure 9-21.

FIGURE 9-21 Page mappings with PAE

The MMU still implements page directories and page tables, but a third level, the page directory pointer table, exists above them. PAE mode can address more memory than the standard translation mode not because of the extra level of translation but because PDEs and

PTEs are 64 bits wide rather than 32 bits. A 32-bit system represents physical addresses internally with 24 bits, which gives the ability to support a maximum of 2^{24+12} bytes, or 64 GB, of memory. One way in which 32-bit applications can take advantage of such large memory configurations is described in the earlier section "Address Windowing Extensions." However, even if applications are not using such functions, the memory manager will use all available physical memory for multiple processes' working sets, file cache, and trimmed private data through the use of the system cache, standby, and modified lists (described in the section "Page Frame Number Database").

As explained in Chapter 2, there is a special version of the 32-bit Windows kernel with support for PAE called Ntkrnlpa.exe. This PAE kernel is loaded on 32-bit systems that have hardware support for nonexecutable memory (described earlier in the section "No Execute Page Protection") or on systems that have more than 4 GB of RAM on an edition of Windows that supports more than 4 GB of RAM (for example, Windows Server 2008 Enterprise Edition). To force the loading of this PAE-enabled kernel, you can set the *pae* BCD option to *ForceEnable*.

Note that the PAE kernel is present on all 32-bit Windows systems, even systems with small memory without hardware no-execute support. The reason for this is to facilitate device driver testing. Because the PAE kernel presents 64-bit addresses to device drivers and other system code, booting with *pae* even on a small memory system allows device driver developers to test parts of their drivers with large addresses. The other relevant BCD option is *nolowmem*, which discards memory below 4 GB (assuming you have at least 5 GB of physical memory) and relocates device drivers above this range. This guarantees that drivers will be presented with physical addresses greater than 32 bits, which makes any possible driver sign extension bugs easier to find.

EXPERIMENT: Translating Addresses

To clarify how address translation works, this experiment shows a real example of translating a virtual address on an x86 PAE system (which is typical on today's processors, which support hardware no-execute protection, not because PAE itself is actually in use), using the available tools in the kernel debugger to examine page directories, page tables, and PTEs. In this example, we'll work with a process that has virtual address 0x50001 currently mapped to a valid physical address. In later examples, you'll see how to follow address translation for invalid addresses with the kernel debugger.

First let's convert 0x50001 to binary and break it into the three fields that are used to translate an address. In binary, 0x50001 is 101.0000.0000.0000.0001. Breaking it into the component fields yields the following:

31	22	12	0
0000.0000.00	00.0101.0000	0000.0000.0001	
Page directory index (0)	Page table index (80 or 0x50)	Byte index (1)	

To start the translation process, the CPU needs the physical address of the process page directory, stored in the CR3 register while a thread in that process is running. You can display this address by examining the CR3 register itself or by dumping the KPROCESS block for the process in question with the *!process* command, as shown here:

```
lkd> !process
PROCESS 87248070  SessionId: 1  Cid: 088c    Peb: 7ffdf000  ParentCid: 06d0
    DirBase: ce2a8980  ObjectTable: a72ba408  HandleCount:  95.
    Image: windbg.exe
    VadRoot 86ed30a0 Vads 85 Clone 0 Private 3559. Modified 187. Locked 1.
    DeviceMap 98fd1008
    Token                             affe1c48
```

In this case, the page directory is stored at physical address 0xce2a8980. As shown in the preceding illustration, the page directory index field in this example is 0. Therefore, the PDE is at physical address 0xce2a8980.

The kernel debugger *!pte* command displays the PDE and PTE that describe a virtual address, as shown here:

```
lkd> !pte 50001
               VA 00050001
PDE at 00000000C0600000    PTE at 00000000C0000280
contains 0000000056C74867  contains 80000000C0EBD025
pfn 56c74      ---DA--UWEV  pfn c0ebd      ----A--UR-V
```

In the first column the kernel debugger displays the PDE, and in the second column it displays the PTE. Notice that the PDE address is shown as a virtual address, not a physical address—as noted earlier, the process page directory starts at virtual address 0xC0600000 on x86 systems with PAE (in this case, the PAE kernel is loaded because the CPU supports no-execute protection). Because we're looking at the first PDE in the page directory, the PDE address is the same as the page directory address.

The PTE is at virtual address 0xC0000280. You can compute this address by multiplying the page table index (0x50 in this example) by the size of a PTE: 0x50 multiplied by 8 (on a non-PAE system, this would be 4) equals 0x280. Because the memory manager maps page tables starting at 0xC0000000, adding 280 yields the virtual address shown in the kernel debugger output: 0xC0000280. The page table page is at PFN 0x56c74, and the data page is at PFN 0xc0ebd.

The PTE flags are displayed to the right of the PFN number. For example, the PTE that describes the page being referenced has flags of --A--UR-V. Here, *A* stands for accessed (the page has been read), *U* for user-mode page (as opposed to a kernel-mode page), *R* for read-only page (rather than writable), and *V* for valid. (The PTE represents a valid page in physical memory.)

IA64 Virtual Address Translation

The virtual address space for IA64 is divided into eight regions by the hardware. Each region can have its own set of page tables. Windows uses five of the regions, three of which have page tables. Table 9-12 lists the regions and how they are used.

TABLE 9-12 The IA64 Regions

Region	Use
0	User code and data
1	Session space code and data
2	Unused
3	Unused
4	Kseg3, which is a cached 1-to-1 mapping of physical memory. No page tables are needed for this region because the necessary TLB inserts are done directly by the memory manager.
5	Kseg4, which is a noncached 1-to-1 mapping for physical memory. This is used only in a few places for accessing I/O locations such as the I/O port range. There are no page tables needed for this region.
6	Unused
7	Kernel code and data

Address translation by 64-bit Windows on the IA64 platform uses a three-level page table scheme. Each process has a page directory pointer structure that contains 1,024 pointers to page directories. Each page directory contains 1,024 pointers to page tables, which in turn point to physical pages. Figure 9-22 shows the format of an IA64 hardware PTE.

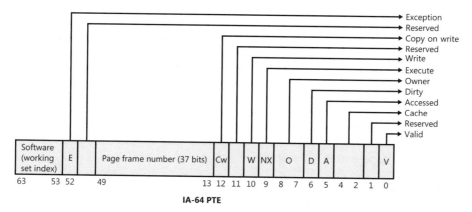

FIGURE 9-22 IA64 page table entry

x64 Virtual Address Translation

64-bit Windows on the x64 architecture uses a four-level page table scheme. Each process has a top-level extended page directory (called the page map level 4) that contains 512 pointers to a third-level structure called a page parent directory. Each page parent directory contains 512 pointers to second-level page directories, each of which contain 512 pointers to the individual page tables. Finally, the page tables (each of which contain 512 page table entries) point to pages in memory. Current implementations of the x64 architecture limit virtual addresses to 48 bits. The components that make up this 48-bit virtual address are shown in Figure 9-23. The connections between these structures are shown in Figure 9-24. Finally, the format of an x64 hardware page table entry is shown in Figure 9-25.

x64 64-bit (48-bit in today's processors)

FIGURE 9-23 x64 virtual address

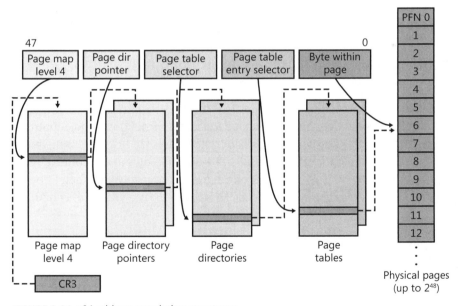

FIGURE 9-24 x64 address translation structures

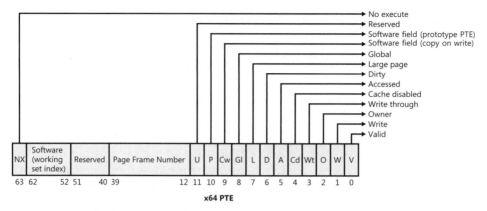

FIGURE 9-25 x64 hardware page table entry

Page Fault Handling

Earlier, you saw how address translations are resolved when the PTE is valid. When the PTE valid bit is clear, this indicates that the desired page is for some reason not (currently) accessible to the process. This section describes the types of invalid PTEs and how references to them are resolved.

 Note Only the 32-bit x86 PTE formats are detailed in this book. PTEs for 64-bit systems contain similar information, but their detailed layout is not presented.

A reference to an invalid page is called a *page fault*. The kernel trap handler (introduced in the section "Trap Dispatching" in Chapter 3) dispatches this kind of fault to the memory manager fault handler (*MmAccessFault*) to resolve. This routine runs in the context of the thread that incurred the fault and is responsible for attempting to resolve the fault (if possible) or raise an appropriate exception. These faults can be caused by a variety of conditions, as listed in Table 9-13.

TABLE 9-13 Reasons for Access Faults

Reason for Fault	Result
Accessing a page that isn't resident in memory but is on disk in a page file or a mapped file	Allocate a physical page, and read the desired page from disk and into the relevant working set
Accessing a page that is on the standby or modified list	Transition the page to the relevant process, session, or system working set
Accessing a page that isn't committed (for example, reserved address space or address space that isn't allocated)	Access violation
Accessing a page from user mode that can be accessed only in kernel mode	Access violation

Reason for Fault	Result
Writing to a page that is read-only	Access violation
Accessing a demand-zero page	Add a zero-filled page to the relevant working set
Writing to a guard page	Guard-page violation (if a reference to a user-mode stack, perform automatic stack expansion)
Writing to a copy-on-write page	Make process-private (or session-private) copy of page, and replace original in process or system working set
Writing to a page that is valid but hasn't been written to the current backing store copy	Set dirty bit in PTE
Executing code in a page that is marked as no execute	Access violation (supported only on hardware platforms that support no execute protection)

The following section describes the four basic kinds of invalid PTEs that are processed by the access fault handler. Following that is an explanation of a special case of invalid PTEs, prototype PTEs, which are used to implement shareable pages.

Invalid PTEs

The following list details the four kinds of invalid PTEs and their structure. Some of the flags are the same as those for a hardware PTE as described in Table 9-11.

- **Page file** The desired page resides within a paging file. An in-page operation is initiated, as illustrated in Figure 9-26.

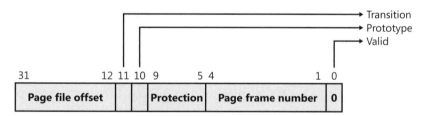

FIGURE 9-26 An in-page operation

- **Demand zero** The desired page must be satisfied with a page of zeros. The pager looks at the zero page list. If the list is empty, the pager takes a page from the free list and zeroes it. If the free list is also empty, it takes a page from one of the standby lists and zeroes it. The PTE format is the same as the page file PTE shown in the previous entry, but the page file number and offset are zeros.

- **Transition** The desired page is in memory on either the standby, modified, or modified-no-write list or not on any list. The page will be removed from the list (if it is on one) and added to the working set as shown in Figure 9-27.

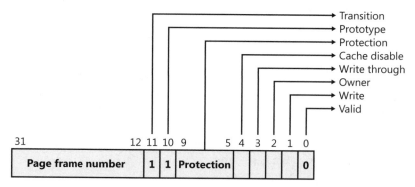

FIGURE 9-27 A transition operation

- **Unknown** The PTE is zero, or the page table doesn't yet exist. In both cases, this flag means that you should examine the virtual address descriptors (VADs) to determine whether this virtual address has been committed. If so, page tables are built to represent the newly committed address space. (See the discussion of VADs later in the chapter.)

Prototype PTEs

If a page can be shared between two processes, the memory manager uses a software structure called *prototype page table entries* (prototype PTEs) to map these potentially shared pages. For page-file-backed sections, an array of prototype PTEs is created when a section object is first created; for mapped files, portions of the array are created on demand as each view is mapped. These prototype PTEs are part of the *segment* structure, described at the end of this chapter.

When a process first references a page mapped to a view of a section object (recall that the VADs are created only when the view is mapped), the memory manager uses the information in the prototype PTE to fill in the real PTE used for address translation in the process page table. When a shared page is made valid, both the process PTE and the prototype PTE point to the physical page containing the data. To track the number of process PTEs that reference a valid shared page, a counter in its PFN database entry is incremented. Thus, the memory manager can determine when a shared page is no longer referenced by any page table and thus can be made invalid and moved to a transition list or written out to disk.

When a shareable page is invalidated, the PTE in the process page table is filled in with a special PTE that points to the prototype PTE entry that describes the page, as shown in Figure 9-28.

FIGURE 9-28 Structure of an invalid PTE that points to the prototype PTE

Thus, when the page is later accessed, the memory manager can locate the prototype PTE using the information encoded in this PTE, which in turn describes the page being referenced. A shared page can be in one of six different states as described by the prototype PTE entry:

- **Active/valid** The page is in physical memory as a result of another process that accessed it.

- **Transition** The desired page is in memory on the standby or modified list (or not on any list).

- **Modified-no-write** The desired page is in memory and on the modified-no-write list. (See Table 9-20.)

- **Demand zero** The desired page should be satisfied with a page of zeros.

- **Page file** The desired page resides within a page file.

- **Mapped file** The desired page resides within a mapped file.

Although the format of these prototype PTE entries is the same as that of the real PTE entries described earlier, these prototype PTEs aren't used for address translation—they are a layer between the page table and the page frame number database and never appear directly in page tables.

By having all the accessors of a potentially shared page point to a prototype PTE to resolve faults, the memory manager can manage shared pages without needing to update the page tables of each process sharing the page. For example, a shared code or data page might be paged out to disk at some point. When the memory manager retrieves the page from disk, it needs only to update the prototype PTE to point to the page's new physical location—the PTEs in each of the processes sharing the page remain the same (with the valid bit clear and still pointing to the prototype PTE). Later, as processes reference the page, the real PTE will get updated.

Figure 9-29 illustrates two virtual pages in a mapped view. One is valid, and the other is invalid. As shown, the first page is valid and is pointed to by the process PTE and the prototype PTE. The second page is in the paging file—the prototype PTE contains its exact location. The process PTE (and any other processes with that page mapped) points to this prototype PTE.

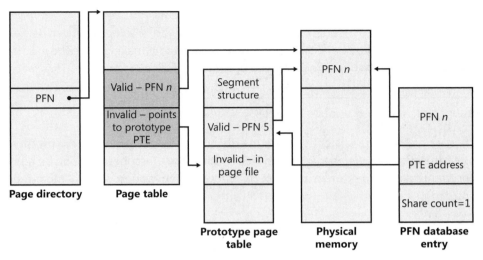

Page directory **Page table** **Prototype page table** **Physical memory** **PFN database entry**

FIGURE 9-29 Prototype page table entries

In-Paging I/O

In-paging I/O occurs when a read operation must be issued to a file (paging or mapped) to satisfy a page fault. Also, because page tables are pageable, the processing of a page fault can incur additional I/O if necessary when the system is loading the page table page that contains the PTE or the prototype PTE that describes the original page being referenced.

The in-page I/O operation is synchronous—that is, the thread waits on an event until the I/O completes—and isn't interruptible by asynchronous procedure call (APC) delivery. The pager uses a special modifier in the I/O request function to indicate paging I/O. Upon completion of paging I/O, the I/O system triggers an event, which wakes up the pager and allows it to continue in-page processing.

While the paging I/O operation is in progress, the faulting thread doesn't own any critical memory management synchronization objects. Other threads within the process are allowed to issue virtual memory functions and handle page faults while the paging I/O takes place. But a number of interesting conditions that the pager must recognize when the I/O completes are exposed:

- Another thread in the same process or a different process could have faulted the same page (called a *collided page fault* and described in the next section).

- The page could have been deleted (and remapped) from the virtual address space.

- The protection on the page could have changed.

- The fault could have been for a prototype PTE, and the page that maps the prototype PTE could be out of the working set.

The pager handles these conditions by saving enough state on the thread's kernel stack before the paging I/O request such that when the request is complete, it can detect these conditions and, if necessary, dismiss the page fault without making the page valid. When and if the faulting instruction is reissued, the pager is again invoked and the PTE is reevaluated in its new state.

Collided Page Faults

The case when another thread in the same process or a different process faults a page that is currently being in-paged is known as a *collided page fault*. The pager detects and handles collided page faults optimally because they are common occurrences in multithreaded systems. If another thread or process faults the same page, the pager detects the collided page fault, noticing that the page is in transition and that a read is in progress. (This information is in the PFN database entry.) In this case, the pager may issue a wait operation on the event specified in the PFN database entry, or it can choose to issue a parallel I/O to protect the file systems from deadlocks (the first I/O to complete "wins," and the others are discarded). This event was initialized by the thread that first issued the I/O needed to resolve the fault.

When the I/O operation completes, all threads waiting on the event have their wait satisfied. The first thread to acquire the PFN database lock is responsible for performing the in-page completion operations. These operations consist of checking I/O status to ensure that the I/O operation completed successfully, clearing the read-in-progress bit in the PFN database, and updating the PTE.

When subsequent threads acquire the PFN database lock to complete the collided page fault, the pager recognizes that the initial updating has been performed because the read-in-progress bit is clear and checks the in-page error flag in the PFN database element to ensure that the in-page I/O completed successfully. If the in-page error flag is set, the PTE isn't updated and an in-page error exception is raised in the faulting thread.

Clustered Page Faults

The memory manager prefetches large clusters of pages to satisfy page faults and populate the system cache. The prefetch operations read data directly into the system's page cache instead of into a working set in virtual memory, so the prefetched data does not consume virtual address space, and the size of the fetch operation is not limited to the amount of virtual address space that is available. (Also, no expensive TLB-flushing Inter-Processor Interrupt is needed if the page will be repurposed.) The prefetched pages are put on the standby list and marked as in transition in the PTE. If a prefetched page is subsequently referenced, the memory manager adds it to the working set. However, if it is never referenced, no system resources are required to release it. If any pages in the prefetched cluster are already in memory, the memory manager does not read them again. Instead, it uses a dummy page to represent them so that an efficient single large I/O can still be issued, as Figure 9-30 shows.

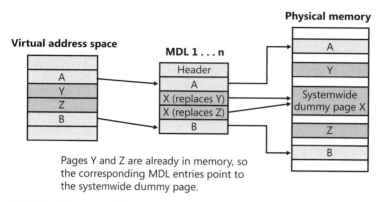

Pages Y and Z are already in memory, so the corresponding MDL entries point to the systemwide dummy page.

FIGURE 9-30 Usage of dummy page during virtual address to physical address mapping in an MDL

In the figure, the file offsets and virtual addresses that correspond to pages A, Y, Z, and B are logically contiguous, although the physical pages themselves are not necessarily contiguous. Pages A and B are nonresident, so the memory manager must read them. Pages Y and Z are already resident in memory, so it is not necessary to read them. (In fact, they might already have been modified since they were last read in from their backing store, in which case it would be a serious error to overwrite their contents.) However, reading pages A and B in a single operation is more efficient than performing one read for page A and a second read for page B. Therefore, the memory manager issues a single read request that comprises all four pages (A, Y, Z, and B) from the backing store. Such a read request includes as many pages as make sense to read, based on the amount of available memory, the current system usage, and so on.

When the memory manager builds the memory descriptor list (MDL) that describes the request, it supplies valid pointers to pages A and B. However, the entries for pages Y and Z point to a single systemwide dummy page X. The memory manager can fill the dummy page X with the potentially stale data from the backing store because it does not make X visible. However, if a component accesses the Y and Z offsets in the MDL, it sees the dummy page X instead of Y and Z.

The memory manager can represent any number of discarded pages as a single dummy page, and that page can be embedded multiple times in the same MDL or even in multiple concurrent MDLs that are being used for different drivers. Consequently, the contents of the locations that represent the discarded pages can change at any time.

Page Files

Page files are used to store modified pages that are still in use by some process but have had to be written to disk (because they were unmapped or memory pressure resulted in a trim). Page file space is reserved when the pages are initially committed, but the actual optimally clustered page file locations cannot be chosen until pages are written out to disk.

The important point is that the system commit limit is charged for private pages as they are created. Thus, the Process: Page File Bytes performance counter is actually the total process private committed memory, of which none, some, or all may be in the paging file. (In fact, it's the same as the Process: Private Bytes performance counter.)

The memory manager keeps track of private committed memory usage on a global basis, termed *commitment*, and on a per-process basis as *page file quota*. (Again, this memory usage doesn't represent page file usage—it represents private committed memory usage.) Commitment and page file quota are charged whenever virtual addresses that require new private physical pages are committed. Once the global commit limit has been reached (physical memory and the page files are full), allocating virtual memory will fail until processes free committed memory (for example, when a process exits or calls *VirtualFree*).

When the system boots, the Session Manager process (described in Chapter 13) reads the list of page files to open by examining the registry value HKLM\SYSTEM\CurrentControlSet\Control\Session Manager\Memory Management\PagingFiles. This multistring registry value contains the name, minimum size, and maximum size of each paging file. Windows supports up to 16 paging files. On x86 systems running the normal kernel, each page file can be a maximum of 4,095 MB. On x86 systems running the PAE kernel and x64 systems, each page file can be 16 terabytes (TB) while the maximum is 32 TB on IA64 systems. Once open, the page files can't be deleted while the system is running because the System process (described in Chapter 2) maintains an open handle to each page file. The fact that the paging files are open explains why the built-in defragmentation tool cannot defragment the paging file while the system is up. To defragment your paging file, use the freeware Pagedefrag tool from Sysinternals. It uses the same approach as other third-party defragmentation tools—it runs its defragmentation process early in the boot process before the page files are opened by the Session Manager.

Because the page file contains parts of process and kernel virtual memory, for security reasons the system can be configured to clear the page file at system shutdown. To enable this, set the registry value HKLM\SYSTEM\CurrentControlSet\Control\Session Manager\Memory Management\ClearPageFileAtShutdown to 1. Otherwise, after shutdown, the page file will contain whatever data happened to have been paged out while the system was up. This data could then be accessed by someone who gained physical access to the machine.

If no paging files are specified, the system virtual memory commit limit is based on available memory. If the minimum and maximum paging file sizes are both zero, this indicates a system managed paging file, which causes the system to choose the page file size as shown in Table 9-14.

TABLE 9-14 Default Page File Sizes

System Memory Size	Minimum Page File Size	Maximum Page File Size
< 1 GB	1.5 * RAM	3 * RAM
>= 1 GB	1 * RAM	3 * RAM

EXPERIMENT: Viewing System Page Files

To view the list of page files, look in the registry at HKLM\SYSTEM\CurrentControlSet\ Control\Session Manager\Memory Management\PagingFiles. This entry contains the paging file configuration settings modified through the System utility in Control Panel. Open the properties window for your computer, click Advanced System Settings, click the Settings button in the Performance area, click the Advanced tab, and finally, click the Change button in the Virtual Memory section.

To add a new page file, Control Panel uses the (internal only) *NtCreatePagingFile* system service defined in Ntdll.dll. Page files are always created as noncompressed files, even if the directory they are in is compressed. To keep new page files from being deleted, a handle is duplicated into the System process so that when the creating process closes the handle to the new page file, another process can still open the page file.

The performance counters listed in Table 9-15 allow you to examine private committed memory usage on a systemwide or per-page-file basis. There's no way to determine how much of a process's private committed memory is resident and how much is paged out to paging files.

TABLE 9-15 Committed Memory and Page File Performance Counters

Performance Counter	Description
Memory: Committed Bytes	Number of bytes of virtual (not reserved) memory that has been committed. This number doesn't necessarily represent page file usage because it includes private committed pages in physical memory that have never been paged out. Rather, it represents the charged amount that must be backed by page file space and/or RAM.
Memory: Commit Limit	Number of bytes of virtual memory that can be committed without having to extend the paging files; if the paging files can be extended, this limit is soft.
Paging File: % Usage	Percentage of the paging file committed.
Paging File: % Usage Peak	Highest percentage of the paging file committed.

Note that these counters can assist you in choosing a page file size. Although most users do it, basing page file size as a function of RAM makes no sense (except for saving a crash dump) because the more memory you have, the less likely you are to need to page data out. To determine how much page file space your system really needs based on the mix of applications that have run since the system booted, examine the peak commit charge in Process Explorer's System Information display. This number represents the peak amount of page file space since the system booted that would have been needed if the system had to page out the majority of private committed virtual memory (which rarely happens).

If the page file on your system is too big, the system will not use it any more or less—in other words, increasing the size of the page file does not change system performance, it simply means the system can have more committed virtual memory. If the page file is too small for the mix of applications you are running, you might get the "system running low on virtual memory" error message. In this case, first check to see whether a process has a memory leak by examining the process private bytes count. If no process appears to have a leak, check the system paged pool size—if a device driver is leaking paged pool, this might also explain the error. (See the "Troubleshooting a Pool Leak" experiment in the "Kernel-Mode Heaps (System Memory Pools)" section for how to troubleshoot a pool leak.)

EXPERIMENT: Viewing Page File Usage with Task Manager

You can also view committed memory usage with Task Manager by clicking its Performance tab. You'll see the following counters related to page files:

Note that the Memory Usage bar is actually the sum of all the process's private working sets and not the system commit total—that number is actually displayed as the Page File number in the System area. The first number represents *potential* page file usage, not actual page file usage. It is how much page file space would be used if the majority of the private committed virtual memory in the system had to be paged out all at once. The second number displayed is the *commit limit*, which displays the maximum virtual memory usage that the system can support before running out of virtual memory (it includes virtual memory backed in physical memory as well as by the paging files).

Process Explorer's System Information display shows an additional piece of information about system commit usage, namely the percentage of the peak as compared to the limit and the current usage as compared to the limit:

Stacks

Whenever a thread runs, it must have access to a temporary storage location in which to store function parameters, local variables, and the return address after a function call. This part of memory is called a *stack*. On Windows, the memory manager provides two stacks for each thread, the *user stack* and the *kernel stack*, as well as per-processor stacks called *DPC stacks*. We have already described how the stack can be used to generate stack traces and how exceptions and interrupts store structures on the stack, and we have also talked about how system calls, traps, and interrupts cause the thread to switch from a user stack to its kernel stack. Now, we'll look at some extra services the memory manager provides to efficiently use stack space.

User Stacks

When a thread is created, the memory manager automatically reserves a predetermined amount of memory, which by default is 1 MB. This amount can be configured in the call to the *CreateThread* or *CreateRemoteThread* function or when compiling the application, by using the /STACKRESERVE switch in the Microsoft C/C++ compiler, which will store the information in the image header. Although 1 MB is reserved, only the first 64 KB (unless the PE header of the image specifies otherwise) of the stack will be committed, along with a guard page. When a thread's stack grows large enough to touch the guard page, an exception will occur, causing an attempt to allocate another guard. Through this mechanism, a user stack doesn't immediately consume all 1 MB of committed memory but instead grows with demand. (However, it will never shrink back.)

EXPERIMENT: Creating the Maximum Number of Threads

With only 2 GB of user address space available to each 32-bit process, the relatively large memory that is reserved for each thread's stack allows for an easy calculation of the maximum number of threads that a process can support: a little less than 2,048, for a total of nearly 2 GB of memory (unless the *increaseuserva* BCD option is used and the image is large address space aware). By forcing each new thread to use the smallest possible stack reservation size, 64 KB, the limit can grow to about 30,400 threads, which you can test for yourself by using the TestLimit utility from Sysinternals. Here is some sample output:

```
C:\>testlimit -t
Testlimit - tests Windows limits
By Mark Russinovich

Creating threads...
Created 30399 threads. Lasterror: 8
```

If you attempt this experiment on a 64-bit Windows installation (with 8 TB of user address space available), you would expect to see potentially hundreds of thousands of threads created (as long as sufficient memory were available). Interestingly, however, TestLimit will actually create fewer threads than on a 32-bit machine, which has to do with the fact that Testlimit.exe is a 32-bit application and thus runs under the Wow64 environment. (See Chapter 3 for more information on Wow64.) Each thread will therefore have not only its 32-bit Wow64 stack but also its 64-bit stack, thus consuming more than twice the memory, while still keeping only 2 GB of address space. To properly test the thread-creation limit on 64-bit Windows, use the Testlimit64.exe binary instead.

Note that you will need to terminate TestLimit with Process Explorer or Task Manager—using Ctrl+C to break the application will not function because this operation itself creates a new thread, which will not be possible once memory is exhausted.

Kernel Stacks

Although user stack sizes are typically 1 MB, the amount of memory dedicated to the kernel stack is significantly smaller: 12 KB, followed by another guard PTE (for a total of 16 KB of virtual address space). Code running in the kernel is expected to have less recursion than user code, as well as contain more efficient variable use and keep stack buffer sizes low. Additionally, because kernel stacks live in system address space, their memory usage has a bigger impact of the system: the 2,048 threads really consumed only 1 GB of pageable virtual memory due to their user stacks. On the other hand, they consumed 360 MB of actual physical memory with their kernel stacks.

Although kernel code is usually not recursive, interactions between graphics system calls handled by Win32k.sys and its subsequent callbacks into user mode can cause recursive re-entries in the kernel on the same kernel stack. As such, Windows provides a mechanism for dynamically expanding and shrinking the kernel stack from its initial size of 16 KB. As each additional graphics call is performed from the same thread, another 16-KB kernel stack is allocated (anywhere in system address space; the memory manager provides the ability to jump stacks when nearing the guard page). Whenever each call returns to the caller (unwinding), the memory manager frees the additional kernel stack that had been allocated, as shown in Figure 9-31.

This mechanism allows reliable support for recursive system calls, as well as efficient use of system address space, and is also provided for use by driver developers when performing recursive callouts through the *KeExpandKernelStackAndCallout* API, as necessary.

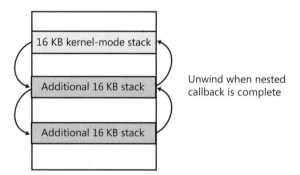

Unwind when nested
callback is complete

FIGURE 9-31 Kernel stack jumping

EXPERIMENT: Viewing Kernel Stack Usage

You can use the MemInfo tool from Winsider Seminars & Solutions to display the physical memory currently being occupied by kernel stacks. The *–u* flag displays physical memory usage for each component, as shown here:

```
C:\>MemInfo.exe -u | findstr /i "Kernel Stack"
        Kernel Stack:    980 (   3920 kb)
```

Note the kernel stack after repeating the previous TestLimit experiment:

```
C:\>MemInfo.exe -u | findstr /i "Kernel Stack"
        Kernel Stack:  92169 ( 368676 kb)
```

Running TestLimit a couple more times would easily exhaust physical memory on a 32-bit system, and this limitation results in one of the primary limits on systemwide 32-bit thread count.

DPC Stack

Finally, Windows keeps a per-processor DPC stack available for use by the system whenever DPCs are executing, an approach that isolates the DPC code from the current thread's kernel stack (which is unrelated to the DPC's actual operation because DPCs run in arbitrary thread context). The DPC stack is also configured as the initial stack for handling the SYSENTER or SYSCALL instruction during a system call. Because the CPU is responsible for switching the stack, it doesn't know how to access the current thread's kernel stack, as this is an internal Windows implementation detail, so Windows configures the per-processor DPC stack as the stack pointer.

Virtual Address Descriptors

The memory manager uses a demand-paging algorithm to know when to load pages into memory, waiting until a thread references an address and incurs a page fault before retrieving the page from disk. Like copy-on-write, demand paging is a form of *lazy evaluation—* waiting to perform a task until it is required.

The memory manager uses lazy evaluation not only to bring pages into memory but also to construct the page tables required to describe new pages. For example, when a thread commits a large region of virtual memory with *VirtualAlloc* or *VirtualAllocExNuma*, the memory manager could immediately construct the page tables required to access the entire range of allocated memory. But what if some of that range is never accessed? Creating page tables for the entire range would be a wasted effort. Instead, the memory manager waits to create a page table until a thread incurs a page fault, and then it creates a page table for that page.

This method significantly improves performance for processes that reserve and/or commit a lot of memory but access it sparsely.

With the lazy-evaluation algorithm, allocating even large blocks of memory is a fast operation. When a thread allocates memory, the memory manager must respond with a range of addresses for the thread to use. To do this, the memory manager maintains another set of data structures to keep track of which virtual addresses have been reserved in the process's address space and which have not. These data structures are known as *virtual address descriptors* (VADs).

Process VADs

For each process, the memory manager maintains a set of VADs that describes the status of the process's address space. VADs are structured as a self-balancing AVL tree algorithm (named after their inventors, Adelson-Velskii and Landis) that better balances the VAD tree, resulting in, on average, fewer comparisons when searching for a VAD corresponding with a virtual address. A diagram of a VAD tree is shown in Figure 9-32.

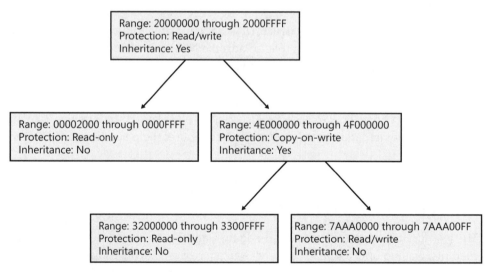

FIGURE 9-32 Virtual address descriptors

When a process reserves address space or maps a view of a section, the memory manager creates a VAD to store any information supplied by the allocation request, such as the range of addresses being reserved, whether the range will be shared or private, whether a child process can inherit the contents of the range, and the page protection applied to pages in the range.

When a thread first accesses an address, the memory manager must create a PTE for the page containing the address. To do so, it finds the VAD whose address range contains the accessed address and uses the information it finds to fill in the PTE. If the address falls outside the range covered by the VAD or in a range of addresses that are reserved but not committed, the memory manager knows that the thread didn't allocate the memory before attempting to use it and therefore generates an access violation.

EXPERIMENT: Viewing Virtual Address Descriptors

You can use the kernel debugger's *!vad* command to view the VADs for a given process. First find the address of the root of the VAD tree with the *!process* command. Then specify that address to the *!vad* command, as shown in the following example of the VAD tree for a process running Notepad.exe:

```
lkd> !process 0 1 notepad.exe
PROCESS 8718ed90  SessionId: 1  Cid: 1ea68    Peb: 7ffdf000  ParentCid: 0680
    DirBase: ce2aa880  ObjectTable: ee6e01b0  HandleCount:  48.
    Image: notepad.exe
    VadRoot 865f10e0 Vads 51 Clone 0 Private 210. Modified 0. Locked 0.

lkd> !vad 865f10e0
VAD      level     start     end     commit
8a05bf88 ( 6)        10      1f          0 Mapped      READWRITE
88390ad8 ( 5)        20      20          1 Private     READWRITE
87333740 ( 6)        30      33          0 Mapped      READONLY
86d09d10 ( 4)        40      41          0 Mapped      READONLY
882b49a0 ( 6)        50      50          1 Private     READWRITE
877bf260 ( 5)        60      61          0 Mapped      READONLY
86c0bb10 ( 6)        70      71          0 Mapped      READONLY
86fd1800 ( 3)        80      81          0 Mapped      READONLY
8a125d00 ( 5)        90      91          0 Mapped      READONLY
8636e878 ( 6)        a0      a0          0 Mapped      READWRITE
871a3998 ( 4)        b0      1af        51 Private     READWRITE
a20235f0 ( 5)       200      20f         1 Private     READWRITE
86e7b308 ( 2)       210      24f        19 Private     READWRITE
877f1618 ( 4)       250      317         0 Mapped      READONLY
87333380 ( 5)       340      37f        26 Private     READWRITE
87350cd8 ( 3)       3a0      3af         3 Private     READWRITE
86c09cc0 ( 5)       3b0      4b2         0 Mapped      READONLY
86e759d8 ( 4)       510      537         4 Mapped   Exe  EXECUTE_WRITECOPY
8688c2e8 ( 1)       540      8bf         0 Mapped      READONLY
867e2a68 ( 4)       8c0      14bf        0 Mapped      READONLY
8690ad20 ( 5)       14c0     156f        0 Mapped      READONLY
873851a8 ( 3)       15e0     15ef        8 Private     READWRITE
86390d20 ( 4)       15f0     196f        0 Mapped      READONLY
86c6b660 ( 5)       1970     19ef        1 Private     READWRITE
87873318 ( 2)       1a00     1bff        0 Mapped   LargePagSec READONLY
88bd9bc0 ( 5)       1c00     1fff        0 Mapped      READONLY
86d9c558 ( 4)       2000     20ff       12 Private     READWRITE
```

```
86c7f318 (  6)      2100      24ff       0 Mapped            READONLY
88394ab0 (  5)      73b40     73b81      4 Mapped       Exe  EXECUTE_WRITECOPY
8690b1b0 (  3)      74da0     74f3d     15 Mapped       Exe  EXECUTE_WRITECOPY
88b917e8 (  5)      75100     7513e      5 Mapped       Exe  EXECUTE_WRITECOPY
86c180a0 (  4)      761f0     762b7      3 Mapped       Exe  EXECUTE_WRITECOPY
86660fd0 (  5)      763f0     764b2      2 Mapped       Exe  EXECUTE_WRITECOPY
865f10e0 (  0)      765a0     76665     16 Mapped       Exe  EXECUTE_WRITECOPY
86c4a058 (  4)      76890     76902      5 Mapped       Exe  EXECUTE_WRITECOPY
b138eb10 (  5)      769a0     769a8      2 Mapped       Exe  EXECUTE_WRITECOPY
877debb8 (  3)      769b0     769fa      3 Mapped       Exe  EXECUTE_WRITECOPY
8718c0c0 (  4)      76a00     76b43      8 Mapped       Exe  EXECUTE_WRITECOPY
88a9ad08 (  2)      76b50     76b6d      2 Mapped       Exe  EXECUTE_WRITECOPY
8a112960 (  5)      76b70     76bec     17 Mapped       Exe  EXECUTE_WRITECOPY
863b6a58 (  4)      76bf0     76c7c      4 Mapped       Exe  EXECUTE_WRITECOPY
863d6400 (  3)      76c80     76d1c      3 Mapped       Exe  EXECUTE_WRITECOPY
86bc1d18 (  5)      76d20     76dfa      4 Mapped       Exe  EXECUTE_WRITECOPY
8717fd20 (  4)      76e00     76e57      3 Mapped       Exe  EXECUTE_WRITECOPY
a2065008 (  5)      76e60     7796e     25 Mapped       Exe  EXECUTE_WRITECOPY
8a0216b0 (  1)      77970     77a96     11 Mapped       Exe  EXECUTE_WRITECOPY
87079410 (  4)      77b20     77bc9      8 Mapped       Exe  EXECUTE_WRITECOPY
87648ba0 (  3)      7f6f0     7f7ef      0 Mapped            READONLY
86c5e858 (  4)      7ffb0     7ffd2      0 Mapped            READONLY
8707fe88 (  2)      7ffde     7ffde      1 Private           READWRITE
86e5e848 (  3)      7ffdf     7ffdf      1 Private           READWRITE

Total VADs:     51  average level:     5  maximum depth: 6
```

Rotate VADs

A video card driver must typically copy data from the user-mode graphics application to various other system memory, including the video card memory and the AGP port's memory, both of which have different caching attributes as well as addresses. In order to quickly allow these different views of memory to be mapped into a process, and to support the different cache attributes, the memory manager implements *rotate VADs*, which allow video drivers to transfer data directly by using the GPU and to rotate unneeded memory in and out of the process view pages on demand. Figure 9-33 shows an example of how the same virtual address can rotate between video RAM and virtual memory.

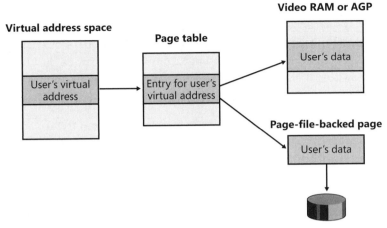

FIGURE 9-33 Rotate virtual address descriptors

NUMA

Each new release of Windows provides new enhancements to the memory manager to better make use of Non Uniform Memory Architecture (NUMA) machines, such as large server systems (but also Intel i7 and AMD Opteron SMP workstations). The NUMA support in the memory manager adds intelligent knowledge of node information such as location, topology, and access costs to allow applications and drivers to take advantage of NUMA capabilities, while abstracting the underlying hardware details.

When the memory manager is initializing, it calls the *MiComputeNumaCosts* function to perform various page and cache operations on different nodes and then computes the time it took for those operations to complete. Based on this information, it builds a node graph of access costs (the distance between a node and any other node on the system). When the system requires pages for a given operation, it consults the graph to choose the most optimal node (that is, the closest). If no memory is available on that node, it chooses the next closest node, and so on.

Although the memory manager ensures that, whenever possible, memory allocations come from the ideal processor's node (the *ideal node*) of the thread making the allocation, it also provides functions that allow applications to choose their own node, such as the *VirtualAllocExNuma*, *CreateFileMappingNuma*, *MapViewOfFileExNuma*, and *AllocateUserPhysicalPagesNuma* APIs.

The ideal node isn't used only when applications allocate memory but also during kernel operation and page faults. For example, when a thread is running on a nonideal processor and takes a page fault, the memory manager won't use the current node but will instead

allocate memory from the thread's ideal node. Although this might result in slower access time while the thread is still running on this CPU, overall memory access will be optimized as the thread migrates back to its ideal node. In any case, if the ideal node is out of resources, the closest node to the ideal node is chosen and not a random other node. Just like user-mode applications, however, drivers can specify their own node when using APIs such as *MmAllocatePagesforMdlEx* or *MmAllocateContiguousMemorySpecifyCacheNode*.

Various memory manager pools and data structures are also optimized to take advantage of NUMA nodes. The memory manager tries to evenly use physical memory from all the nodes on the system to hold the nonpaged pool. When a nonpaged pool allocation is made, the memory manager looks at the ideal node and uses it as an index to choose a virtual memory address range inside nonpaged pool that corresponds to physical memory belonging to this node. In addition, per-NUMA node pool freelists are created to efficiently leverage these types of memory configurations. Apart from nonpaged pool, the system cache and system PTEs are also similarly allocated across all nodes, as well as the memory manager's look-aside lists.

Finally, when the system needs to zero pages, it does so in parallel across different NUMA nodes by creating threads with NUMA affinities that correspond to the nodes in which the physical memory is located. The logical prefetcher and SuperFetch (described later) also use the ideal node of the target process when prefetching, while soft page faults cause pages to migrate to the ideal node of the faulting thread.

Section Objects

As you'll remember from the section on shared memory earlier in the chapter, the *section object*, which the Windows subsystem calls a *file mapping object*, represents a block of memory that two or more processes can share. A section object can be mapped to the paging file or to another file on disk.

The executive uses sections to load executable images into memory, and the cache manager uses them to access data in a cached file. (See Chapter 10 for more information on how the cache manager uses section objects.) You can also use section objects to map a file into a process address space. The file can then be accessed as a large array by mapping different views of the section object and reading or writing to memory rather than to the file (an activity called *mapped file I/O*). When the program accesses an invalid page (one not in physical memory), a page fault occurs and the memory manager automatically brings the page into memory from the mapped file (or page file). If the application modifies the page, the memory manager writes the changes back to the file during its normal paging operations (or the application can flush a view by using the Windows *FlushViewOfFile* function).

Section objects, like other objects, are allocated and deallocated by the object manager. The object manager creates and initializes an object header, which it uses to manage the objects; the memory manager defines the body of the section object. The memory manager also implements services that user-mode threads can call to retrieve and change the attributes stored in the body of section objects. The structure of a section object is shown in Figure 9-34.

FIGURE 9-34 A section object

Table 9-16 summarizes the unique attributes stored in section objects.

TABLE 9-16 **Section Object Body Attributes**

Attribute	Purpose
Maximum size	The largest size to which the section can grow in bytes; if mapping a file, the maximum size is the size of the file.
Page protection	Page-based memory protection assigned to all pages in the section when it is created.
Paging file/Mapped file	Indicates whether the section is created empty (backed by the paging file—as explained earlier, page-file-backed sections use page-file resources only when the pages need to be written out to disk) or loaded with a file (backed by the mapped file).
Based/Not based	Indicates whether a section is a based section, which must appear at the same virtual address for all processes sharing it, or a nonbased section, which can appear at different virtual addresses for different processes.

EXPERIMENT: Viewing Section Objects

With the Object Viewer (Winobj.exe from Sysinternals), you can see the list of sections that have global names. You can list the open handles to section objects with any of the tools described in the "Object Manager" section in Chapter 3 that list the open handle table. (As explained in Chapter 3, these names are stored in the object manager directory \Sessions\x\BaseNamedObjects, where x is the appropriate Session directory.)

You can use Process Explorer from Sysinternals to view mapped files. Select DLLs from the Lower Pane View entry of the View menu. Files marked as "Data" in the Mapping column are mapped files (rather than DLLs and other files the image loader loads as modules). Here's an example:

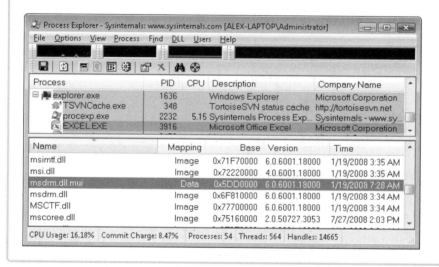

The data structures maintained by the memory manager that describe mapped sections are shown in Figure 9-35. These structures ensure that data read from mapped files is consistent, regardless of the type of access (open file, mapped file, and so on).

For each open file (represented by a file object), there is a single *section object pointers* structure. This structure is the key to maintaining data consistency for all types of file access as well as to providing caching for files. The section object pointers structure points to one or two *control areas*. One control area is used to map the file when it is accessed as a data file, and one is used to map the file when it is run as an executable image.

A control area in turn points to *subsection* structures that describe the mapping information for each section of the file (read-only, read-write, copy-on-write, and so on). The control area also points to a *segment* structure allocated in paged pool, which in turn points to the prototype PTEs used to map to the actual pages mapped by the section object. As described earlier in the chapter, process page tables point to these prototype PTEs, which in turn map the pages being referenced.

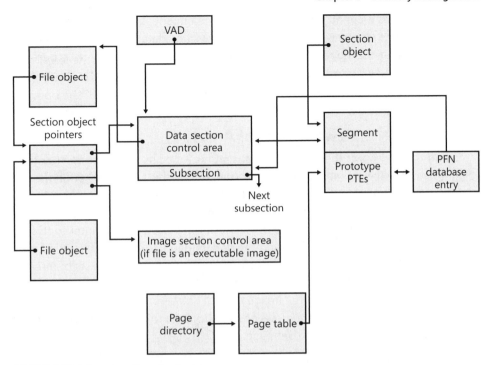

FIGURE 9-35 Internal section structures

Although Windows ensures that any process that accesses (reads or writes) a file will always see the same, consistent data, there is one case in which two copies of pages of a file can reside in physical memory (but even in this case, all accessors get the latest copy and data consistency is maintained). This duplication can happen when an image file has been accessed as a data file (having been read or written) and then run as an executable image (for example, when an image is linked and then run—the linker had the file open for data access, and then when the image was run, the image loader mapped it as an executable). Internally, the following actions occur:

1. If the executable file was created using the file mapping APIs (or the cache manager), a data control area is created to represent the data pages in the image file being read or written.

2. When the image is run and the section object is created to map the image as an executable, the memory manager finds that the section object pointers for the image file point to a data control area and flushes the section. This step is necessary to ensure that any modified pages have been written to disk before accessing the image through the image control area.

3. The memory manager then creates a control area for the image file.

4. As the image begins execution, its (read-only) pages are faulted in from the image file (or copied directly over from the data file if the corresponding data page is resident).

Because the pages mapped by the data control area might still be resident (on the standby list), this is the one case in which two copies of the same data are in two different pages in memory. However, this duplication doesn't result in a data consistency issue because, as mentioned, the data control area has already been flushed to disk, so the pages read from the image are up to date (and these pages are never written back to disk).

EXPERIMENT: Viewing Control Areas

To find the address of the control area structures for a file, you must first get the address of the file object in question. You can obtain this address through the kernel debugger by dumping the process handle table with the *!handle* command and noting the object address of a file object. Although the kernel debugger *!file* command displays the basic information in a file object, it doesn't display the pointer to the section object pointers structure. Then, using the *dt* command, format the file object to get the address of the section object pointers structure. This structure consists of three pointers: a pointer to the data control area, a pointer to the shared cache map (explained in Chapter 10), and a pointer to the image control area. From the section object pointers structure, you can obtain the address of a control area for the file (if one exists) and feed that address into the *!ca* command.

For example, if you open a PowerPoint file and display the handle table for that process using *!handle*, you will find an open handle to the PowerPoint file as shown below. (For information on using *!handle*, see the "Object Manager" section in Chapter 3.)

```
1kd> !handle 1 f 86f57d90 File
.
.
.
0324: Object: 865d2768  GrantedAccess: 00120089 Entry: c848e648
Object: 865d2768  Type: (8475a2c0) File
    ObjectHeader: 865d2750 (old version)
        HandleCount: 1  PointerCount: 1
        Directory Object: 00000000  Name: \Users\Administrator\Documents\Downloads\
SVR-T331_WH07 (1).pptx {HarddiskVolume3}
```

Taking the file object address (865d2768) and formatting it with *dt* results in this:

```
1kd> dt nt!_FILE_OBJECT 865d2768
    +0x000 Type             : 5
    +0x002 Size             : 128
    +0x004 DeviceObject     : 0x84a62320 _DEVICE_OBJECT
    +0x008 Vpb              : 0x84a60590 _VPB
    +0x00c FsContext        : 0x8cee4390
    +0x010 FsContext2       : 0xbf910c80
    +0x014 SectionObjectPointer : 0x86c45584 _SECTION_OBJECT_POINTERS
```

Then taking the address of the section object pointers structure (0x86c45584) and formatting it with *dt* results in this:

```
lkd> dt 0x86c45584 nt!_SECTION_OBJECT_POINTERS
   +0x000 DataSectionObject : 0x863d3b00
   +0x004 SharedCacheMap    : 0x86f10ec0
   +0x008 ImageSectionObject : (null)
```

Finally, use *!ca* to display the control area using the address:

```
lkd> !ca 0x863d3b00

ControlArea  @ 863d3b00
   Segment      b1de9d48  Flink        00000000  Blink         8731f80c
   Section Ref         1  Pfn Ref            48  Mapped Views         2
   User Ref            0  WaitForDel          0  Flush Count          0
   File Object  86cf6188  ModWriteCount       0  System Views         2
   WritableRefs        0
   Flags (c080) File WasPurged Accessed

        No name for file

Segment @ b1de9d48
   ControlArea      863d3b00  ExtendInfo      00000000
   Total Ptes            100
   Segment Size       100000  Committed              0
   Flags (c0000) ProtectionMask

Subsection 1 @ 863d3b48
   ControlArea  863d3b00  Starting Sector      0  Number Of Sectors  100
   Base Pte     bf85e008  Ptes In Subsect    100  Unused Ptes          0
   Flags               d  Sector Offset        0  Protection           6
   Accessed
   Flink        00000000  Blink         8731f87c  MappedViews          2
```

Another technique is to display the list of all control areas with the *!memusage* command. The following excerpt is from the output of this command:

```
lkd> !memusage
 loading PFN database
loading (100% complete)
Compiling memory usage data (99% Complete).
           Zeroed:    2654 ( 10616 kb)
             Free:     584 (  2336 kb)
          Standby:  402938 (1611752 kb)
         Modified:   12732 ( 50928 kb)
   ModifiedNoWrite:      3 (    12 kb)
     Active/Valid:  431478 (1725912 kb)
       Transition:    1186 (  4744 kb)
              Bad:       0 (     0 kb)
          Unknown:       0 (     0 kb)
            TOTAL:  851575 (3406300 kb)
  Building kernel map
  Finished building kernel map
Scanning PFN database - (100% complete)
```

```
    Usage Summary (in Kb):
 Control Valid Standby Dirty Shared Locked PageTables   name
 86d75f18     0     64     0      0      0          0   mapped_file( netcfgx.dll )
 8a124ef8     0      4     0      0      0          0     No Name for File
 8747af80     0     52     0      0      0          0   mapped_file( iebrshim.dll )
 883a2e58    24      8     0      0      0          0   mapped_file( WINWORD.EXE )
 86d6eae0     0     16     0      0      0          0   mapped_file( oem13.CAT )
 84b19af8     8      0     0      0      0          0     No Name for File
 b1672ab0     4      0     0      0      0          0     No Name for File
 88319da8     0     20     0      0      0          0   mapped_file( Microsoft-Windows-
 MediaPlayer-Package~31bf3856ad364e35~x86~en-US~6.0.6001.18000.cat )
 8a04db00     0     48     0      0      0          0   mapped_file( eapahost.dll )
```

The Control column points to the control area structure that describes the mapped file. You can display control areas, segments, and subsections with the kernel debugger *!ca* command. For example, to dump the control area for the mapped file Winword.exe in this example, type the *!ca* command followed by the Control number, as shown here:

```
lkd> !ca 883a2e58

ControlArea  @ 883a2e58
  Segment       ee613998  Flink       00000000  Blink        88a985a4
  Section Ref          1  Pfn Ref            8  Mapped Views        1
  User Ref             2  WaitForDel         0  Flush Count         0
  File Object   88b45180  ModWriteCount      0  System Views     ffff
  WritableRefs  80000006
  Flags (40a0) Image File Accessed

       File: \PROGRA~1\MICROS~1\Office12\WINWORD.EXE

Segment @ ee613998
  ControlArea      883a2e58  BasedAddress   2f510000
  Total Ptes             57
  Segment Size        57000  Committed             0
  Image Commit            1  Image Info     ee613c80
  ProtoPtes        ee6139c8
  Flags (20000) ProtectionMask

Subsection 1 @ 883a2ea0
  ControlArea  883a2e58  Starting Sector        0  Number Of Sectors   2
  Base Pte     ee6139c8  Ptes In Subsect        1  Unused Ptes         0
  Flags               2  Sector Offset          0  Protection          1

Subsection 2 @ 883a2ec0
  ControlArea  883a2e58  Starting Sector        2  Number Of Sectors   a
  Base Pte     ee6139d0  Ptes In Subsect        2  Unused Ptes         0
  Flags               6  Sector Offset          0  Protection          3

Subsection 3 @ 883a2ee0
  ControlArea  883a2e58  Starting Sector        c  Number Of Sectors   1
  Base Pte     ee6139e0  Ptes In Subsect        1  Unused Ptes         0
  Flags               a  Sector Offset          0  Protection          5
```

```
Subsection 4 @ 883a2f00
  ControlArea  883a2e58  Starting Sector     d  Number Of Sectors  28b
  Base Pte     ee6139e8  Ptes In Subsect    52  Unused Ptes          0
  Flags               2  Sector Offset       0  Protection           1

Subsection 5 @ 883a2f20
  ControlArea  883a2e58  Starting Sector   298  Number Of Sectors    1
  Base Pte     ee613c78  Ptes In Subsect     1  Unused Ptes          0
  Flags               2  Sector Offset       0  Protection           1
```

Driver Verifier

As introduced in Chapter 7, Driver Verifier is a mechanism that can be used to help find and isolate commonly found bugs in device driver or other kernel-mode system code. This section describes the memory management–related verification options Driver Verifier provides (the options related to device drivers are described in Chapter 7).

The verification settings are stored in the registry under HKLM\SYSTEM\CurrentControlSet\ Control\Session Manager\Memory Management. The value VerifyDriverLevel contains a bitmask that represents the verification types enabled. The VerifyDrivers value contains the names of the drivers to validate. (These values won't exist in the registry until you select drivers to verify in the Driver Verifier Manager.) If you choose to verify all drivers, VerifyDrivers is set to an asterisk (*) character. Depending on the settings you have made, you might need to reboot the system for the selected verification to occur.

Early in the boot process, the memory manager reads the Driver Verifier registry values to determine which drivers to verify and which Driver Verifier options you enabled. (Note that if you boot in safe mode, any Driver Verifier settings are ignored.) Subsequently, if you've selected at least one driver for verification, the kernel checks the name of every device driver it loads into memory against the list of drivers you've selected for verification. For every device driver that appears in both places, the kernel invokes the *VfLoadDriver* function, which calls other internal *Vf** functions to replace the driver's references to a number of kernel functions with references to Driver Verifier–equivalent versions of those functions. For example, *ExAllocatePool* is replaced with a call to *VerifierAllocatePool*. The windowing system driver (Win32k.sys) also makes similar changes to use Driver Verifier–equivalent functions.

Now that we've reviewed how Driver Verifier is set up, we'll examine the six memory-related verification options that can be applied to device drivers: Special Pool, Pool Tracking, Force IRQL Checking, Low Resources Simulation, Miscellaneous Checks, and Automatic Checks

Special Pool The Special Pool option causes the pool allocation routines to bracket pool allocations with an invalid page so that references before or after the allocation will result in a kernel-mode access violation, thus crashing the system with the finger pointed at the

buggy driver. Special pool also causes some additional validation checks to be performed when a driver allocates or frees memory.

When special pool is enabled, the pool allocation routines allocate a region of kernel memory for Driver Verifier to use. Driver Verifier redirects memory allocation requests that drivers under verification make to the special pool area rather than to the standard kernel-mode memory pools. When a device driver allocates memory from special pool, Driver Verifier rounds up the allocation to an even-page boundary. Because Driver Verifier brackets the allocated page with invalid pages, if a device driver attempts to read or write past the end of the buffer, the driver will access an invalid page, and the memory manager will raise a kernel-mode access violation.

Figure 9-36 shows an example of the special pool buffer that Driver Verifier allocates to a device driver when Driver Verifier checks for overrun errors.

FIGURE 9-36 Layout of special pool allocations

By default, Driver Verifier performs *overrun* detection. It does this by placing the buffer that the device driver uses at the end of the allocated page and fills the beginning of the page with a random pattern. Although the Driver Verifier Manager doesn't let you specify under-run detection, you can set this type of detection manually by adding the DWORD registry value HKLM\SYSTEM\CurrentControlSet\Control\Session Manager\Memory Management\ PoolTagOverruns and setting it to 0 (or by running the Gflags utility and selecting the Verify Start option instead of the default option, Verify End). When Windows enforces underrun detection, Driver Verifier allocates the driver's buffer at the beginning of the page rather than at the end.

The overrun-detection configuration includes some measure of underrun detection as well. When the driver frees its buffer to return the memory to Driver Verifier, Driver Verifier ensures that the pattern preceding the buffer hasn't changed. If the pattern is modified, the device driver has underrun the buffer and written to memory outside the buffer.

Special pool allocations also check to ensure that the processor IRQL at the time of an allocation and deallocation is legal. This check catches an error that some device drivers make: allocating pageable memory from an IRQL at DPC/dispatch level or above.

You can also configure special pool manually by adding the DWORD registry value HKLM\ SYSTEM\CurrentControlSet\Control\Session Manager\Memory Management\PoolTag, which represents the allocation tags the system uses for special pool. Thus, even if Driver Verifier isn't configured to verify a particular device driver, if the tag the driver associates with the memory it allocates matches what is specified in the PoolTag registry value, the pool allocation routines will allocate the memory from special pool. If you set the value of PoolTag to 0x0000002a or to the wildcard (*), all memory that drivers allocate is from special pool, provided there's enough virtual and physical memory. (The drivers will revert to allocating from regular pool if there aren't enough free pages—bounding exists, but each allocation uses two pages.)

Pool Tracking If pool tracking is enabled, the memory manager checks at driver unload time whether the driver freed all the memory allocations it made. If it didn't, it crashes the system, indicating the buggy driver. Driver Verifier also shows general pool statistics on the Driver Verifier Manager's Pool Tracking tab. You can also use the *!verifier* kernel debugger command. This command shows more information than Driver Verifier and is useful to driver writers.

Driver Verifier can also perform locked memory page tracking, which additionally checks for pages that have been left locked after an I/O operation and generates the DRIVER_LEFT_ LOCKED_PAGES_IN_PROCESS instead of the PROCESS_HAS_LOCKED_PAGES crash code—the former indicates the driver responsible for the error as well as the function responsible for the locking of the pages.

Force IRQL Checking One of the most common device driver bugs occurs when a driver accesses pageable data or code when the processor on which the device driver is executing is at an elevated IRQL. As explained in Chapter 3, the memory manager can't service a page fault when the IRQL is DPC/dispatch level or above. The system often doesn't detect instances of a device driver accessing pageable data when the processor is executing at a high IRQL level because the pageable data being accessed happens to be physically resident at the time. At other times, however, the data might be paged out, which results in a system crash with the stop code IRQL_NOT_LESS_OR_EQUAL (that is, the IRQL wasn't less than or equal to the level required for the operation attempted—in this case, accessing pageable memory).

Although testing device drivers for this kind of bug is usually difficult, Driver Verifier makes it easy. If you select the Force IRQL Checking option, Driver Verifier forces all kernel-mode pageable code and data out of the system working set whenever a device driver under verification raises the IRQL. The internal function that does this is *MiTrimAllSystemPagableMemory*. With this setting enabled, whenever a device driver under verification accesses pageable memory when the IRQL is elevated, the system instantly detects the violation, and the resulting system crash identifies the faulty driver.

Another common driver crash that results from incorrect IRQL usage occurs when synchronization objects are part of data structures that are paged and then waited on. Synchronization objects should never be paged because the dispatcher needs to access them at an elevated IRQL, which would cause a crash. Driver Verifier checks whether any of the following structures are present in pageable memory: KTIMER, KMUTEX, KSPIN_LOCK, KEVENT, KSEMAPHORE, ERESOURCE, FAST_MUTEX.

Low Resources Simulation Enabling Low Resources Simulation causes Driver Verifier to randomly fail memory allocations that verified device drivers perform. In the past, developers wrote many device drivers under the assumption that kernel memory would always be available and that if memory ran out, the device driver didn't have to worry about it because the system would crash anyway. However, because low-memory conditions can occur temporarily, it's important that device drivers properly handle allocation failures that indicate kernel memory is exhausted.

The driver calls that will be injected with random failures include the *ExAllocatePool**, *MmProbeAndLockPages, MmMapLockedPagesSpecifyCache, MmMapIoSpace, MmAllocateContiguousMemory, MmAllocatePagesForMdl, IoAllocateIrp, IoAllocateMdl, IoAllocateWorkItem*, and *IoAllocateErrorLogEntry* APIs. Additionally, you can specify the probability that allocation will fail (6 percent by default), which applications should be subject to the simulation (all are by default), which pool tags should be affected (all are by default), and what delay should be used before fault injection starts (the default is 7 minutes after the system boots, which is enough time to get past the critical initialization period in which a low-memory condition might prevent a device driver from loading).

After the delay period, Driver Verifier starts randomly failing allocation calls for device drivers it is verifying. If a driver doesn't correctly handle allocation failures, this will likely show up as a system crash.

Miscellaneous Checks Some of the checks that Driver Verifier calls "miscellaneous" allow Driver Verifier to detect the freeing of certain system structures in the pool that are still active. For example, Driver Verifier will check for:

- Active work items in freed memory (a driver calls *ExFreePool* to free a pool block in which one or more work items queued with *IoQueueWorkItem* are present).

- Active resources in freed memory (a driver calls *ExFreePool* before calling *ExDelete-Resource* to destroy an ERESOURCE object).

- Active look-aside lists in freed memory (a driver calls *ExFreePool* before calling *ExDeleteNPagedLookasideList* or *ExDeletePagedLookasideList* to delete the look-aside list).

Finally, when verification is enabled, Driver Verifier also performs certain automatic checks that cannot be enabled or disabled. These include:

- Calling *MmProbeAndLockPages* or *MmProbeAndLockProcessPages* on a memory descriptor list (MDL) having incorrect flags. For example, it is incorrect to call *MmProbeAndLockPages* for an MDL setup by calling *MmBuildMdlForNonPagedPool*.

- Calling *MmMapLockedPages* on an MDL having incorrect flags. For example, it is incorrect to call *MmMapLockedPages* for an MDL that is already mapped to a system address. Another example of incorrect driver behavior is calling *MmMapLockedPages* for an MDL that was not locked.

- Calling *MmUnlockPages* or *MmUnmapLockedPages* on a partial MDL (created by using *IoBuildPartialMdl*).

- Calling *MmUnmapLockedPages* on an MDL that is not mapped to a system address.

Driver Verifier is a valuable addition to the arsenal of verification and debugging tools available to device driver writers. Many device drivers that first ran with Driver Verifier had bugs that Driver Verifier was able to expose. Thus, Driver Verifier has resulted in an overall improvement in the quality of all kernel-mode code running in Windows

Page Frame Number Database

In several previous sections, we've concentrated on the virtual view of a Windows process—page tables, PTEs, and VADs. In the remainder of this chapter, we'll explain how Windows manages physical memory, starting with how Windows keeps track of physical memory. Whereas working sets describe the resident pages owned by a process or the system, the *page frame number (PFN) database* describes the state of each page in physical memory. The page states are listed in Table 9-17.

TABLE 9-17 **Page States**

Status	Description
Active (also called Valid)	The page is part of a working set (either a process working set or the system working set) or it's not in any working set (for example, nonpaged kernel page) and a valid PTE usually points to it.
Transition	A temporary state for a page that isn't owned by a working set and isn't on any paging list. A page is in this state when an I/O to the page is in progress. The PTE is encoded so that collided page faults can be recognized and handled properly. (Note that this use of the term "transition" differs from the use of the word in the section on Invalid PTEs; an invalid transition PTE refers to a page on the standby or modified list.)
Standby	The page previously belonged to a working set but was removed (or was prefetched/clustered directly into the standby list). The page wasn't modified since it was last written to disk. The PTE still refers to the physical page but is marked invalid and in transition.
Modified	The page previously belonged to a working set but was removed. However, the page was modified while it was in use and its current contents haven't yet been written to disk or remote storage. The PTE still refers to the physical page but is marked invalid and in transition. It must be written to the backing store before the physical page can be reused.
Modified no-write	Same as a modified page, except that the page has been marked so that the memory manager's modified page writer won't write it to disk. The cache manager marks pages as modified no-write at the request of file system drivers. For example, NTFS uses this state for pages containing file system metadata so that it can first ensure that transaction log entries are flushed to disk before the pages they are protecting are written to disk. (NTFS transaction logging is explained in Chapter 11.)
Free	The page is free but has unspecified dirty data in it. (These pages can't be given as a user page to a user process without being initialized with zeros, for security reasons.)
Zeroed	The page is free and has been initialized with zeros by the zero page thread (or was determined to already contain zeros).
Rom	The page represents read-only memory
Bad	The page has generated parity or other hardware errors and can't be used. This is also used internally by the system for pages that may be transitioning from one state to another or are on internal look-aside caches.

The PFN database consists of an array of structures that represent each physical page of memory on the system. The PFN database and its relationship to page tables are shown in Figure 9-37. As this figure shows, valid PTEs usually point to entries in the PFN database, and the PFN database entries (for nonprototype PFNs) point back to the page table that is using them (if it is being used by a page table). For prototype PFNs, they point back to the prototype PTE.

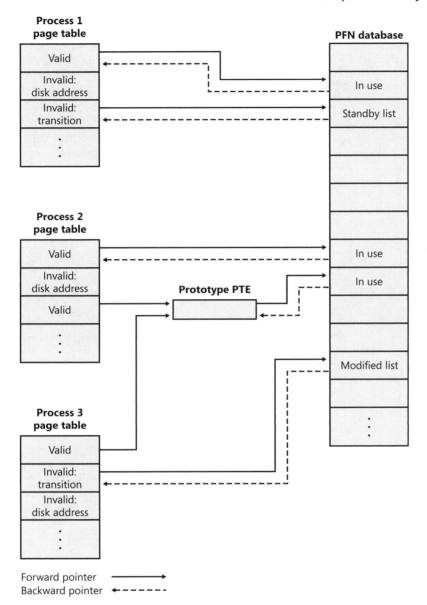

FIGURE 9-37 Page tables and the page frame number database

Of the page states listed in Table 9-17, six are organized into linked lists so that the memory manager can quickly locate pages of a specific type. (Active/valid pages, transition pages, and overloaded "bad" pages aren't in any systemwide page list.) Additionally, the standby state is actually associated with eight different lists ordered by priority (we'll talk about page priority in the next section). Figure 9-38 shows an example of how these entries are linked together.

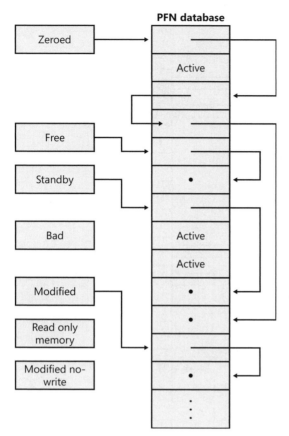

FIGURE 9-38 Page lists in the PFN database

In the next section, you'll find out how these linked lists are used to satisfy page faults and how pages move to and from the various lists.

EXPERIMENT: Viewing the PFN Database

You can use the MemInfo tool from Winsider Seminars & Solutions to dump the size of the various paging lists by using the –s flag. The following is the output from this command:

```
C:\>MemInfo.exe -s

MemInfo v2.00 - Show PFN database information
Copyright (C) 2007-2009 Alex Ionescu
www.alex-ionescu.com

Initializing PFN Database... Done
```

```
PFN Database List Statistics
           Zeroed:    487 (   1948 kb)
             Free:      0 (      0 kb)
          Standby: 379745 (1518980 kb)
         Modified:   1052 (   4208 kb)
   ModifiedNoWrite:      0 (      0 kb)
      Active/Valid: 142703 ( 570812 kb)
       Transition:    184 (    736 kb)
              Bad:      0 (      0 kb)
          Unknown:      2 (      8 kb)
            TOTAL: 524173 (2096692 kb)
```

Using the kernel debugger *!memusage* command, you can obtain similar information, although this will take considerably longer and will require booting into debugging mode.

Page List Dynamics

Figure 9-39 shows a state diagram for page frame transitions. For simplicity, the modified-no-write list isn't shown.

Page frames move between the paging lists in the following ways:

- When the memory manager needs a zero-initialized page to service a demand-zero page fault (a reference to a page that is defined to be all zeros or to a user-mode committed private page that has never been accessed), it first attempts to get one from the zero page list. If the list is empty, it gets one from the free page list and zeroes the page. If the free list is empty, it goes to the standby list and zeroes that page.

 One reason zero-initialized pages are required is to meet C2 security requirements. C2 specifies that user-mode processes must be given initialized page frames to prevent them from reading a previous process's memory contents. Therefore, the memory manager gives user-mode processes zeroed page frames unless the page is being read in from a backing store. If that's the case, the memory manager prefers to use nonzeroed page frames, initializing them with the data off the disk or remote storage.

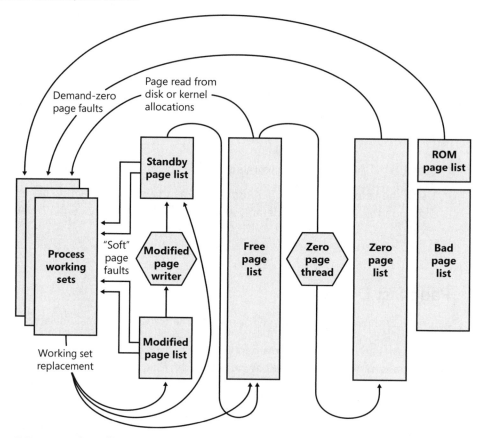

FIGURE 9-39 State diagram for page frames

The zero page list is populated from the free list by a system thread called the *zero page thread* (thread 0 in the System process). The zero page thread waits on a gate object to signal it to go to work. When the free list has eight or more pages, this gate is signaled. However, the zero page thread will run only if no other threads are running, because the zero page thread runs at priority 0 and the lowest priority that a user thread can be set to is 1.

Note When memory needs to be zeroed as a result of a physical page allocation by a driver that calls *MmAllocatePagesForMdl* or *MmAllocatePagesForMdlEx,* by a Windows application that calls *AllocateUserPhysicalPages* or *AllocateUserPhysicalPagesNuma,* or when an application allocates large pages, the memory manager zeroes the memory by using a higher performing function called *MiZeroInParallel* that maps larger regions than the zero page thread, which only zeroes a page at a time. In addition, on multiprocessor systems, the memory manager creates additional system threads to perform the zeroing in parallel (and in a NUMA-optimized fashion on NUMA platforms).

- When the memory manager doesn't require a zero-initialized page, it goes first to the free list. If that's empty, it goes to the zeroed list. If the zeroed list is empty, it goes to the standby lists. Before the memory manager can use a page frame from the standby lists, it must first backtrack and remove the reference from the invalid PTE (or prototype PTE) that still points to the page frame. Because entries in the PFN database contain pointers back to the previous user's page table (or to a prototype PTE for shared pages), the memory manager can quickly find the PTE and make the appropriate change.

- When a process has to give up a page out of its working set (either because it referenced a new page and its working set was full or the memory manager trimmed its working set), the page goes to the standby lists if the page was clean (not modified) or to the modified list if the page was modified while it was resident. When a process exits, all the private pages go to the free list. Also, when the last reference to a page-file-backed section is closed, these pages also go to the free list.

Page Priority

Because every page of memory has a priority in the range 0 to 7, the memory manager divides the standby list into eight lists that each store pages of a particular priority. When the memory manager wants to take a page from the standby list, it takes pages from low-priority lists first, as shown in Figure 9-40. A page's priority usually reflects the priority of the thread that first causes its allocation. (If the page is shared, it reflects the highest memory priority among the sharing threads.) A thread inherits its page-priority value from the process to which it belongs. The memory manager uses low priorities for pages it reads from disk speculatively when anticipating a process's memory accesses.

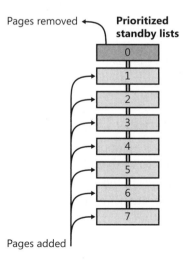

FIGURE 9-40 Prioritized standby lists

By default, processes have a page-priority value of 5, but functions allow applications and the system to change process and thread page-priority values. You can look at the memory priority of a thread with Process Explorer (per-page priority can be displayed by looking at the PFN entries, as you'll see in an experiment later in the chapter). Figure 9-41 shows Process Explorer's Threads tab displaying information about Winlogon's main thread. Although the thread priority itself is high, the memory priority is still the standard 5.

FIGURE 9-41 Process Explorer's Threads tab.

The real power of memory priorities is realized only when the relative priorities of pages are understood at a high level, which is the role of SuperFetch, covered at the end of this chapter.

EXPERIMENT: Viewing the Prioritized Standby Lists

You can use the MemInfo tool from Winsider Seminars & Solutions to dump the size of each standby paging list by using the –c flag. MemInfo will also display the number of repurposed pages for each standby list—this corresponds to the number of pages in each list that had to be reused to satisfy a memory allocation, and thus thrown out of the standby page lists. The following is the relevant output from this command:

```
C:\>MemInfo.exe -s

MemInfo v2.00 - Show PFN database information
Copyright (C) 2007-2009 Alex Ionescu
www.alex-ionescu.com
```

```
Initializing PFN Database... Done

Priority                Standby              Repurposed
0 - Idle         1756 (    7024 KB)    798 (  3192 KB)
1 - Very Low   236518 (  946072 KB)      0 (     0 KB)
2 - Low         37014 (  148056 KB)      0 (     0 KB)
3 - Background  64367 (  257468 KB)      0 (     0 KB)
4 - Background  15576 (   62304 KB)      0 (     0 KB)
5 - Normal      14445 (   57780 KB)      0 (     0 KB)
6 - SuperFetch   3889 (   15556 KB)      0 (     0 KB)
7 - SuperFetch   6641 (   26564 KB)      0 (     0 KB)
TOTAL          380206 (1520824 KB)    798 (  3192 KB)
```

You can add the –*i* flag to MemInfo to display the live state of the standby page lists and repurpose counts, which is useful for tracking memory usage as well as the following experiment. Additionally, the system information panel in Process Explorer (choose View, System Information) can also be used to display the live state of the prioritized standby lists, as shown in this screen shot:

On the system used in this experiment (see the previous MemInfo output), there is about 7 MB of cached data at priority 0, and more than 900 MB at priority 1. Your system probably has some data in those priorities as well. The following shows what happens when we use the TestLimit tool from Sysinternals to commit and touch 1 GB of memory. Here is the command you use (to leak and touch memory in chunks of 50 MB):

```
testlimit -d 50
```

Here is the output of MemInfo during the leak:

```
Priority                 Standby             Repurposed
0 - Idle            0 (        0 KB)    2554 (  10216 KB)
1 - Very Low    92915 (  371660 KB)  141352 ( 565408 KB)
2 - Low         35783 (  143132 KB)       0 (      0 KB)
3 - Background  50666 (  202664 KB)       0 (      0 KB)
4 - Background  15236 (   60944 KB)       0 (      0 KB)
5 - Normal      34197 (  136788 KB)       0 (      0 KB)
6 - SuperFetch   2912 (   11648 KB)       0 (      0 KB)
7 - SuperFetch   5876 (   23504 KB)       0 (      0 KB)
TOTAL          237585 (  950340 KB)  143906 ( 575624 KB)
```

And here is the output after the leak:

```
Priority                 Standby             Repurposed
0 - Idle            0 (        0 KB)    2554 (  10216 KB)
1 - Very Low        5 (       20 KB)  234351 ( 937404 KB)
2 - Low             0 (        0 KB)   35830 ( 143320 KB)
3 - Background   9586 (   38344 KB)   41654 ( 166616 KB)
4 - Background  15371 (   61484 KB)       0 (      0 KB)
5 - Normal      34208 (  136832 KB)       0 (      0 KB)
6 - SuperFetch   2914 (   11656 KB)       0 (      0 KB)
7 - SuperFetch   5881 (   23524 KB)       0 (      0 KB)
TOTAL           67965 (  271860 KB)  314389 (1257556 KB)
```

Note how the lower-priority standby page lists were used first (shown by the repurposed count) and are now depleted, while the higher lists still contain valuable cached data.

Modified Page Writer

The memory manager employs two system threads to write pages back to disk and move those pages back to the standby lists (based on their priority). One system thread writes out modified pages (*MiModifiedPageWriter*) to the paging file, and a second one writes modified pages to mapped files (*MiMappedPageWriter*). Two threads are required to avoid creating a deadlock, which would occur if the writing of mapped file pages caused a page fault that in turn required a free page when no free pages were available (thus requiring the modified page writer to create more free pages). By having the modified page writer perform mapped file paging I/Os from a second system thread, that thread can wait without blocking regular page file I/O.

Both threads run at priority 17, and after initialization they wait for separate objects to trigger their operation. The mapped page writer is woken in the following cases:

- The *MmMappedPageWriterEvent* event was signaled by the memory manager's working set manager (*MmWorkingSetManager*), which runs as part of the kernel's balance

set manager (once every second). The working set manager signals this event if the number of filesystem-destined pages on the modified page list has reached more than 800. This event can also be signaled when a request to flush all pages is being processed or when the system is attempting to obtain free pages (and more than 16 are available on the modified page list).

■ One of the *MiMappedPageListHeadEvent* events associated with the 16 mapped page lists has been signaled. Each time a mapped page is dirtied, it is inserted into one of these 16 mapped page lists based on a bucket number (*MiCurrentMappedPageBucket*). This bucket number is updated by the working set manager whenever the system considers that mapped pages have gotten old enough, which is currently 100 seconds (the *MiWriteGapCounter* variable controls this and is incremented whenever the working set manager runs). The reason for these additional events is to reduce data loss in the case of a system crash or power failure by eventually writing out modified mapped pages even if the modified list hasn't reached its threshold of 800 pages.

The modified page writer waits on a single gate object (*MmModifiedPageWriterGate*), which can be signaled in the following scenarios:

■ The working set manager detects that the size of the zeroed and free page lists has dropped below 20,000 pages.

■ A request to flush all pages has been received.

■ The number of available pages (*MmAvailablePages*) has dropped below 262,144 pages during the working set manager's check, or below 256 pages during a page list operation.

Additionally, the modified page writer also waits on an event (*MiRescanPageFilesEvent*) and an internal event in the paging file header (*MmPagingFileHeader*), which allows the system to manually request flushing out data to the paging file when needed.

When invoked, the mapped page writer attempts to write as many pages as possible to disk with a single I/O request. It accomplishes this by examining the original PTE field of the PFN database elements for pages on the modified page list to locate pages in contiguous locations on the disk. Once a list is created, the pages are removed from the modified list, an I/O request is issued, and, at successful completion of the I/O request, the pages are placed at the tail of the standby list corresponding to their priority.

Pages that are in the process of being written can be referenced by another thread. When this happens, the reference count and the share count in the PFN entry that represents the physical page are incremented to indicate that another process is using the page. When the I/O operation completes, the modified page writer notices that the reference count is no longer 0 and doesn't place the page on any standby list.

PFN Data Structures

Although PFN database entries are of fixed length, they can be in several different states, depending on the state of the page. Thus, individual fields have different meanings depending on the state. The states of a PFN entry are shown in Figure 9-42.

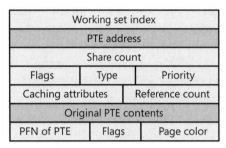

**PFN for a page in a
working set**

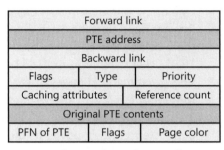

**PFN for a page on the standby
or the modified list**

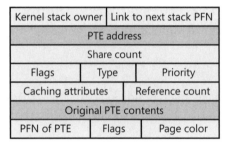

**PFN for a page belonging
to a kernel stack**

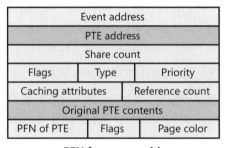

**PFN for a page with
an I/O in progress**

FIGURE 9-42 States of PFN database entries

Several fields are the same for several PFN types, but others are specific to a given type of PFN. The following fields appear in more than one PFN type:

- **PTE address** Virtual address of the PTE that points to this page.

- **Reference count** The number of references to this page. The reference count is incremented when a page is first added to a working set and/or when the page is locked in memory for I/O (for example, by a device driver). The reference count is decremented when the share count becomes 0 or when pages are unlocked from memory. When the share count becomes 0, the page is no longer owned by a working set. Then, if the reference count is also zero, the PFN database entry that describes the page is updated to add the page to the free, standby, or modified list.

- **Type** The type of page represented by this PFN. (Types include active/valid, standby, modified, modified-no-write, free, zeroed, bad, and transition.)

- **Flags** The information contained in the flags field is shown in Table 9-18.

- **Priority** The priority associated with this PFN, which will determine on which standby list it will be placed.

- **Original PTE contents** All PFN database entries contain the original contents of the PTE that pointed to the page (which could be a prototype PTE). Saving the contents of the PTE allows it to be restored when the physical page is no longer resident. PFN entries for AWE allocations are exceptions; they store the AWE reference count in this field instead.

- **PFN of PTE** Physical page number of the page table page containing the PTE that points to this page.

- **Color** Besides being linked together on a list, PFN database entries use an additional field to link physical pages by "color," their location in the processor CPU memory cache. Windows attempts to minimize unnecessary thrashing of CPU memory caches by using different physical pages in the CPU cache. It achieves this optimization by avoiding using the same cache entry for two different pages wherever possible. For systems with direct mapped caches, optimally using the hardware's capabilities can result in a significant performance advantage.

- **Flags** A second flags field is used to encode additional information on the PTE. These flags are described in Table 9-19.

TABLE 9-18 **Flags Within PFN Database Entries**

Flag	Meaning
Write in progress	Indicates that a page write operation is in progress. The first DWORD contains the address of the event object that will be signaled when the I/O is complete.
Modified state	Indicates whether the page was modified. (If the page was modified, its contents must be saved to disk before removing it from memory.)
Read in progress	Indicates that an in-page operation is in progress for the page. The first DWORD contains the address of the event object that will be signaled when the I/O is complete.
Rom	Indicates that this page comes from the computer's firmware or another piece of read-only memory such as a device register.
In-page error	Indicates that an I/O error occurred during the in-page operation on this page. (In this case, the first field in the PFN contains the error code.)
Kernel stack	Indicates that this page is being used to contain a kernel stack. In this case, the PFN entry contains the owner of the stack and the next stack PFN for this thread.
Removal requested	Indicates that the page is the target of a remove (due to ECC/scrubbing or hot memory removal).
Parity error	Indicates that the physical page contains parity or error correction control errors.

TABLE 9-19 Secondary Flags Within PFN Database Entries

Flag	Meaning
PFN image verified	The code signature for this PFN (contained in the cryptographic signature catalog for the image being backed by this PFN) has been verified.
AWE allocation	This PFN backs an AWE allocation.
Prototype PTE	Indicates that the PTE referenced by the PFN entry is a prototype PTE. (For example, this page is shareable.)

The remaining fields are specific to the type of PFN. For example, the first PFN in Figure 9-42 represents a page that is active and part of a working set. The share count field represents the number of PTEs that refer to this page. (Pages marked read-only, copy-on-write, or shared read/write can be shared by multiple processes.) For page table pages, this field is the number of valid and transition PTEs in the page table. As long as the share count is greater than 0, the page isn't eligible for removal from memory.

The working set index field is an index into the process working set list (or the system or session working set list, or zero if not in any working set) where the virtual address that maps this physical page resides. If the page is a private page, the working set index field refers directly to the entry in the working set list because the page is mapped only at a single virtual address. In the case of a shared page, the working set index is a hint that is guaranteed to be correct only for the first process that made the page valid. (Other processes will try to use the same index where possible.) The process that initially sets this field is guaranteed to refer to the proper index and doesn't need to add a working set list hash entry referenced by the virtual address into its working set hash tree. This guarantee reduces the size of the working set hash tree and makes searches faster for these particular direct entries.

The second PFN in Figure 9-42 is for a page on either the standby or the modified list. In this case, the forward and backward link fields link the elements of the list together within the list. This linking allows pages to be easily manipulated to satisfy page faults. When a page is on one of the lists, the share count is by definition 0 (because no working set is using the page) and therefore can be overlaid with the backward link. The reference count is also 0 if the page is on one of the lists. If it is nonzero (because an I/O could be in progress for this page—for example, when the page is being written to disk), it is first removed from the list.

The third PFN in Figure 9-42 is for a page that belongs to a kernel stack. As mentioned earlier, kernel stacks in Windows are dynamically allocated, expanded, and freed whenever a callback to user mode is performed and/or returns, or when a driver performs a callback and requests stack expansion. For these PFNs, the memory manager must keep track of the thread actually associated with the kernel stack, or if it is free it keeps a link to the next free look-aside stack.

The fourth PFN in Figure 9-42 is for a page that has an I/O in progress (for example, a page read). While the I/O is in progress, the first field points to an event object that will be signaled when the I/O completes. If an in-page error occurs, this field contains the Windows error status code representing the I/O error. This PFN type is used to resolve collided page faults.

EXPERIMENT: Viewing PFN Entries

You can examine individual PFN entries with the kernel debugger *!pfn* command. You first need to supply the PFN as an argument. (For example, *!pfn 1* shows the first entry, *!pfn 2* shows the second, and so on.) In the following example, the PTE for virtual address 0x50000 is displayed, followed by the PFN that contains the page directory, and then the actual page:

```
lkd> !pte 50000
                 VA 00050000
PDE at 00000000C0600000    PTE at 00000000C0000280
contains 000000002C9F7867  contains 800000002D6C1867
pfn 2c9f7      ---DA--UWEV  pfn 2d6c1      ---DA--UW-V

lkd> !pfn 2c9f7
    PFN 0002C9F7 at address 834E1704
    flink       00000026  blink / share count 00000091  pteaddress C0600000
    reference count 0001   Cached      color 0    Priority 5
    restore pte 00000080   containing page       02BAA5  Active    M
    Modified

lkd> !pfn 2d6c1
    PFN 0002D6C1 at address 834F7D1C
    flink       00000791  blink / share count 00000001  pteaddress C0000280
    reference count 0001   Cached      color 0    Priority 5
    restore pte 00000080   containing page       02C9F7  Active    M
    Modified
```

You can also use the MemInfo tool to obtain information about a PFN. MemInfo can sometimes give you more information than the debugger's output, and it does not require being booted into debugging mode. Here's MemInfo's output for those same two PFNs:

```
C:\>meminfo -p 2c9f7

PFN: 2c9f7
PFN List: Active and Valid
PFN Type: Page Table
PFN Priority: 5
Page Directory: 0x866168C8
Physical Address: 0x2C9F7000

C:\>meminfo -p 2d6c1

PFN: 2d6c1
PFN List: Active and Valid
PFN Type: Process Private
PFN Priority: 5
EPROCESS: 0x866168C8 [windbg.exe]
Physical Address: 0x2D6C1000
```

MemInfo correctly recognized that the first PFN was a page table and that the second PFN belongs to WinDbg, which was the active process when the *!pte 50000* command was used in the debugger.

In addition to the PFN database, the system variables in Table 9-20 describe the overall state of physical memory.

TABLE 9-20 System Variables That Describe Physical Memory

Variable	Description
MmNumberOfPhysicalPages	Total number of physical pages available on the system
MmAvailablePages	Total number of available pages on the system—the sum of the pages on the zeroed, free, and standby lists
MmResidentAvailablePages	Total number of physical pages that would be available if every process were at its minimum working set size

Physical Memory Limits

Now that you've learned how Windows keeps track of physical memory, we'll describe how much of it Windows can actually support. Because most systems access more code and data than can fit in physical memory as they run, physical memory is in essence a window into the code and data used over time. The amount of memory can therefore affect performance, because when data or code that a process or the operating system needs is not present, the memory manager must bring it in from disk or remote storage.

Besides affecting performance, the amount of physical memory impacts other resource limits. For example, the amount of nonpaged pool, operating system buffers backed by physical memory, is obviously constrained by physical memory. Physical memory also contributes to the system virtual memory limit, which is the sum of roughly the size of physical memory plus the current configured size of any paging files. Physical memory also can indirectly limit the maximum number of processes.

Windows support for physical memory is dictated by hardware limitations, licensing, operating system data structures, and driver compatibility. Table 9-21 lists the currently supported amounts of physical memory across editions of Windows Vista and Windows Server 2008, along with the limiting factors.

Although some 64-bit processors can access up to 2 TB of physical memory (and up to 1 TB even when running 32-bit operating systems through an extended version of PAE), the maximum 32-bit limit supported by Windows Server Datacenter and Enterprise is 64 GB. This restriction comes from the fact that structures the memory manager uses to track physical memory (the PFN database entries seen earlier) would consume too much of the CPU's 32-bit virtual address space on larger systems. Because a PFN entry is 28 bytes, on a 64-GB system this requires about 465 MB for the PFN database, which leaves only 1.5 GB for mapping the kernel, device drivers, system cache, and other system data structures, making the 64-GB restriction a reasonable cutoff. On systems with the *increaseuserva* BCD option set, the kernel might have as little as 1 GB of virtual address space, so allowing the PFN database to consume more than half of available address space would lead to premature exhaustion of other resources.

TABLE 9-21 Physical Memory Support

Version	32-Bit Limit	64-Bit Limit	Limiting Factors
Windows Server 2008 Datacenter and Enterprise	64 GB	2 TB on IA64, 1 TB on x64	Hardware PTE size on 32-bit, PFN database size if running 32-bit Windows on 64-bit hardware, hardware platform support on 64-bit
Windows Server 2008 Standard and Web Server	4 GB	32 GB	Licensing
Windows Server 2008 HPC Edition	N/A	128 GB	Licensing
Windows Vista Ultimate, Enterprise, and Business	4 GB	128 GB	Licensing on 64-bit, licensing, hardware support, and driver compatibility on 32-bit
Windows Vista Home Premium	4 GB	16 GB	Licensing on 64-bit, licensing, hardware support, and driver compatibility on 32-bit
Windows Vista Home Basic	4 GB	8 GB	Licensing on 64-bit, licensing, hardware support, and driver compatibility on 32-bit
Windows Vista Starter	1 GB	N/A	Licensing

The memory manager could accommodate more memory by mapping pieces of the PFN database into the system address as needed, but that would add complexity and reduce performance with the added overhead of mapping, unmapping, and locking operations. It's only recently that systems have become large enough for that to be considered, but because the system address space is not a constraint for mapping the entire PFN database on 64-bit Windows, support for more memory is left to 64-bit Windows.

The maximum 2-TB limit of 64-bit Windows Server 2008 Datacenter for Itanium doesn't come from any implementation or hardware limitation, but because Microsoft will support only configurations it can test. As of the release of Windows Server 2008, the largest Itanium system available was 2 TB, so Windows caps its use of physical memory there. On x64 configurations, the 1-TB limit derives from the maximum amount of memory that current x64 page tables can address.

Windows Client Memory Limits

64-bit Windows client editions support different amounts of memory as a differentiating feature, with the low end being 4 GB for Windows Vista Home Basic, increasing to 128 GB for the Ultimate, Enterprise, and Business editions. All 32-bit Windows client editions, however, support a maximum of 4 GB of physical memory, which is the highest physical address accessible with the standard x86 memory management mode.

Although client SKUs support PAE addressing modes in order to provide hardware no-execute protection (which would also enable access to more than 4 GB of physical memory),

testing revealed that many of the systems would crash, hang, or become unbootable because some device drivers, commonly those for video and audio devices found typically on clients but not servers, were not programmed to expect physical addresses larger than 4 GB. As a result, the drivers truncated such addresses, resulting in memory corruptions and corruption side effects. Server systems commonly have more generic devices, with simpler and more stable drivers, and therefore had not generally revealed these problems. The problematic client driver ecosystem led to the decision for client editions to ignore physical memory that resides above 4 GB, even though they can theoretically address it. Driver developers are encouraged to test their systems with the *nolowmem* BCD option, which will force the kernel to use physical addresses above 4 GB only, if sufficient memory exists on the system to allow it. This will immediately lead to the detection of such issues in faulty drivers.

32-Bit Client Effective Memory Limits

While 4 GB is the licensed limit for 32-bit client editions, the effective limit is actually lower and dependent on the system's chipset and connected devices. The reason is that the physical address map includes not only RAM but device memory, and x86 and x64 systems typically map all device memory below the 4 GB address boundary to remain compatible with 32-bit operating systems that don't know how to handle addresses larger than 4 GB. Newer chipsets do support PAE-based device remapping, but client editions of Windows do not support this feature for the driver compatibility problems explained earlier (otherwise, drivers would receive 64-bit pointers to their device memory).

If a system has 4 GB of RAM and devices such as video, audio, and network adapters that implement windows into their device memory that sum to 500 MB, 500 MB of the 4 GB of RAM will reside above the 4 GB address boundary, as seen in Figure 9-43.

FIGURE 9-43 Physical memory layout on a 4-GB system

The result is that if you have a system with 3 GB or more of memory and you are running a 32-bit Windows client, you may not be getting the benefit of all of the RAM. You can see how much RAM Windows has detected as being installed in the System Properties dialog box, but to see how much memory is actually available to Windows, you need to look at Task Manager's Performance page or the Msinfo32 and Winver utilities. On a 4-GB laptop, when booted with 32-bit Windows Vista, the amount of physical memory available is 3.5 GB, as seen in the Msinfo32 utility:

Installed Physical Memory (RAM) *4.00 GB*
Total Physical Memory *3.50 GB*

You can see the physical memory layout with the MemInfo tool from Winsider Seminars & Solutions. Figure 9-44 shows the output of MemInfo when run on the Windows Vista system, using the *–r* switch to dump physical memory ranges:

```
C:\>MemInfo.exe -r

MemInfo v1.11 - Show PFN database information
Copyright (C) 2007-2008 Alex Ionescu
www.alex-ionescu.com

Physical Memory Range: 00001000 to 0009F000 (158 pages, 632 KB)
Physical Memory Range: 00100000 to DFE6D000 (916845 pages, 3667380 KB)
MmHighestPhysicalPage: 917101
```

FIGURE 9-44 Memory ranges on a 32-bit Windows system

Note the gap in the memory address range from page 9F0000 to page 100000, and another gap from DFE6D000 to FFFFFFFF (4 GB). When the system is booted with 64-bit Windows Vista, on the other hand, all 4 GB show up as available (see Figure 9-45), and you can see how Windows uses the remaining 500 MB of RAM that are above the 4-GB boundary.

```
MemInfo v1.11 - Show PFN database information
Copyright (C) 2007-2008 Alex Ionescu
www.alex-ionescu.com

Physical Memory Range: 0000000000001000 to 000000000009F000 (158 pages, 632 KB)
Physical Memory Range: 0000000000100000 to 00000000DFE6D000 (916845 pages, 3667380 KB)
Physical Memory Range: 0000000100002000 to 0000000120000000 (131070 pages, 524280 KB)
MmHighestPhysicalPage: 1179648
```

FIGURE 9-45 Memory ranges on an x64 Windows system

You can use Device Manager on your machine to see what is occupying the various reserved memory regions that can't be used by Windows (and that will show up as holes in MemInfo's output). To check Device Manager, run devmgmt.msc, select Resources By Connection on the View menu, and then expand the Memory node. On the laptop computer used for the output shown in Figure 9-46, the primary consumer of mapped device memory is, unsurprisingly, the video card, which consumes 256 MB in the range E0000000-EFFFFFFF.

```
 ▷ ┈🖳 [DFF00000 - E06FFFFF] System board
 ▲ ┈🖳 [E0000000 - F7FFFFFF] PCI bus
      ▲ ┈🖳 [E0000000 - EFFFFFFF] Mobile Intel(R) PM965/GM965/GL960 Express PCI Express Root Port - 2A01
              ┈🖳 [E0000000 - EFFFFFFF] NVIDIA GeForce 8400M GS
      ▷ ┈🖳 [F1A00000 - F1AFFFFF] Intel(R) 82801 PCI Bridge - 2448
      ▷ ┈🖳 [F1B00000 - F1BFFFFF] Intel(R) ICH8 Family PCI Express Root Port 6 - 2849
      ▷ ┈🖳 [F1F00000 - F1FFFFFF] Intel(R) ICH8 Family PCI Express Root Port 2 - 2841
      ▷ ┈🖳 [F2000000 - F6EFFFFF] Mobile Intel(R) PM965/GM965/GL960 Express PCI Express Root Port - 2A01
        ┈🖳 [F6FFB700 - F6FFB7FF] Intel(R) ICH8 Family SMBus Controller - 283E
        ┈🖳 [F6FFB800 - F6FFBFFF] Intel(R) 82801HEM/HBM SATA AHCI Controller
        ┈🖳 [F6FFC000 - F6FFFFFF] High Definition Audio Controller
   ┈🖳 [F8000000 - FBFFFFFF] System board
```

FIGURE 9-46 Hardware-reserved memory ranges on a 32-bit Windows system

Other miscellaneous devices account for most of the rest, and the PCI bus reserves additional ranges for devices as part of the conservative estimation the firmware uses during boot.

The consumption of memory addresses below 4 GB can be drastic on high-end gaming systems with large video cards. For example, on a test machine with 8 GB of RAM and two 1-GB video cards, only 2.2 GB of the memory was accessible by 32-bit Windows. A large memory hole from 8FEF0000 to FFFFFFFF is visible in the MemInfo output from the system on which 64-bit Windows is installed, shown in Figure 9-47.

```
C:\>meminfo64.exe -r

MemInfo v1.11 - Show PFN database information
Copyright (C) 2007-2008 Alex Ionescu
www.alex-ionescu.com

Physical Memory Range: 0000000000001000 to 000000000009B000 (154 pages, 616 KB)
Physical Memory Range: 0000000000100000 to 000000008FEF0000 (589296 pages, 2357184 KB)
Physical Memory Range: 0000000100000000 to 0000000270000000 (1507328 pages, 6029312 KB)
MmHighestPhysicalPage: 2555904
```

FIGURE 9-47 Memory ranges on a 64-bit Windows system

Device Manager revealed that 512 MB of the more than 2-GB gap is for the video cards (256 MB each) and that the firmware had reserved more either for dynamic mappings or because it was conservative in its estimate. Finally, even systems with as little as 2 GB can be prevented from having all their memory usable under 32-bit Windows because of chipsets that aggressively reserve memory regions for devices.

Working Sets

Now that we've looked at how Windows keeps track of physical memory, and how much memory it can support, we'll explain how Windows keeps a subset of virtual addresses in physical memory.

As you'll recall, the term used to describe a subset of virtual pages resident in physical memory is called a *working set*. There are three kinds of working sets:

- Process working sets contain the pages referenced by threads within a single process.

- The system working set contains the resident subset of the pageable system code (for example, Ntoskrnl.exe and drivers), paged pool, and the system cache.

- Each session has a working set that contains the resident subset of the kernel-mode session-specific data structures allocated by the kernel-mode part of the Windows subsystem (Win32k.sys), session paged pool, session mapped views, and other session-space device drivers.

Before examining the details of each type of working set, let's look at the overall policy for deciding which pages are brought into physical memory and how long they remain. After that, we'll explore the various types of working sets.

Demand Paging

The Windows memory manager uses a demand-paging algorithm with clustering to load pages into memory. When a thread receives a page fault, the memory manager loads into memory the faulted page plus a small number of pages preceding and/or following it. This strategy attempts to minimize the number of paging I/Os a thread will incur. Because programs, especially large ones, tend to execute in small regions of their address space at any given time, loading clusters of virtual pages reduces the number of disk reads. For page faults that reference data pages in images, the cluster size is 3 pages. For all other page faults, the cluster size is 7 pages.

However, a demand-paging policy can result in a process incurring many page faults when its threads first begin executing or when they resume execution at a later point. To optimize the startup of a process (and the system), Windows has an intelligent prefetch engine called the *logical prefetcher*, described in the next section. Further optimization and prefetching is performed by another component called SuperFetch, that we'll describe later in the chapter.

Logical Prefetcher

During a typical system boot or application startup, the order of faults is such that some pages are brought in from one part of a file, then perhaps from a distant part of the same file, then from a different file, perhaps from a directory, and then again from the first file. This jumping around slows down each access considerably and, thus, analysis shows that disk seek times are a dominant factor in slowing boot and application startup times. By prefetching batches of pages all at once, a more sensible ordering of access, without excessive backtracking, can be achieved, thus improving the overall time for system and application startup. The pages that are needed can be known in advance because of the high correlation in accesses across boots or application starts.

The prefetcher tries to speed the boot process and application startup by monitoring the data and code accessed by boot and application startups and using that information at the

beginning of a subsequent boot or application startup to read in the code and data. When the prefetcher is active, the memory manager notifies the prefetcher code in the kernel of page faults, both those that require that data be read from disk (hard faults) and those that simply require data already in memory be added to a process's working set (soft faults). The prefetcher monitors the first 10 seconds of application startup. For boot, the prefetcher by default traces from system start through the 30 seconds following the start of the user's shell (typically Explorer) or, failing that, up through 60 seconds following Windows service initialization or through 120 seconds, whichever comes first.

The trace assembled in the kernel notes faults taken on the NTFS Master File Table (MFT) metadata file (if the application accesses files or directories on NTFS volumes), on referenced files, and on referenced directories. With the trace assembled, the kernel prefetcher code waits for requests from the prefetcher component of the SuperFetch service (%SystemRoot%\ System32\Sysmain.dll), running in a copy of Svchost. The Supferfetch service is responsible for both the logical prefetching component in the kernel and for the SuperFetch component that we'll talk about later. The prefetcher signals the event \KernelObjects\PrefetchTracesReady to inform the SuperFetch service that it can now query trace data.

> **Note** You can enable or disable prefetching of the boot or application startups by editing the DWORD registry value HKLM\SYSTEM\CurrentControlSet\Control\Session Manager\Memory Management\PrefetchParameters\EnablePrefetcher. Set it to 0 to disable prefetching altogether, 1 to enable prefetching of only applications, 2 for prefetching of boot only, and 3 for both boot and applications.

The SuperFetch service (which hosts the logical prefetcher, although it is a completely separate component from the actual SuperFetch functionality) performs a call to the internal *NtQuerySystemInformation* system call requesting the trace data. The logical prefetcher postprocesses the trace data, combining it with previously collected data, and writes it to a file in the %SystemRoot%\Prefetch folder, which is shown in Figure 9-48. The file's name is the name of the application to which the trace applies followed by a dash and the hexadecimal representation of a hash of the file's path. The file has a .pf extension; an example would be NOTEPAD.EXE-AF43252301.PF.

There are two exceptions to the file name rule. The first is for images that host other components, including the Microsoft Management Console (%SystemRoot%\System32\Mmc.exe), the Service Hosting Process (%SystemRoot%\System32\Svchost.exe), the Run DLL Component (%SystemRoot%\System32\Rundll32.exe), and Dllhost (%SystemRoot%\System32\Dllhost.exe). Because add-on components are specified on the command line for these applications, the prefetcher includes the command line in the generated hash. Thus, invocations of these applications with different components on the command line will result in different traces. The prefetcher reads the list of executables that it should treat this way from the *HostingAppList* value in its parameters registry key, HKLM\SYSTEM\CurrentControlSet\

Control\Session Manager\Memory Management\PrefetchParameters, and then allows the SuperFetch service to query this list through the *NtQuerySystemInformation* API.

The other exception to the file name rule is the file that stores the boot's trace, which is always named NTOSBOOT-B00DFAAD.PF. (If read as a word, "boodfaad" sounds similar to the English words *boot fast*.) Only after the prefetcher has finished the boot trace (the time of which was defined earlier) does it collect page fault information for specific applications.

FIGURE 9-48 Prefetch folder

EXPERIMENT: Looking Inside a Prefetch File

A prefetch file's contents serve as a record of files and directories accessed during the boot or an application startup, and you can use the Strings utility from Sysinternals to see the record. The following command lists all the files and directories referenced during the last boot:

```
C:\Windows\Prefetch>Strings –n 5 ntosboot-boodfaad.pf

Strings v2.4
Copyright (C) 1999-2007 Mark Russinovich
Sysinternals - www.sysinternals.com

NTOSBOOT
\DEVICE\HARDDISKVOLUME1\$MFT
\DEVICE\HARDDISKVOLUME1\WINDOWS\SYSTEM32\DRIVERS\TUNNEL.SYS
```

```
\DEVICE\HARDDISKVOLUME1\WINDOWS\SYSTEM32\DRIVERS\TUNMP.SYS
\DEVICE\HARDDISKVOLUME1\WINDOWS\SYSTEM32\DRIVERS\I8042PRT.SYS
\DEVICE\HARDDISKVOLUME1\WINDOWS\SYSTEM32\DRIVERS\KBDCLASS.SYS
\DEVICE\HARDDISKVOLUME1\WINDOWS\SYSTEM32\DRIVERS\VMMOUSE.SYS
\DEVICE\HARDDISKVOLUME1\WINDOWS\SYSTEM32\DRIVERS\MOUCLASS.SYS
\DEVICE\HARDDISKVOLUME1\WINDOWS\SYSTEM32\DRIVERS\PARPORT.SYS

. . .
```

When the system boots or an application starts, the prefetcher is called to give it an opportunity to perform prefetching. The prefetcher looks in the prefetch directory to see if a trace file exists for the prefetch scenario in question. If it does, the prefetcher calls NTFS to prefetch any MFT metadata file references, reads in the contents of each of the directories referenced, and finally opens each file referenced. It then calls the memory manager function *MmPrefetchPages* to read in any data and code specified in the trace that's not already in memory. The memory manager initiates all the reads asynchronously and then waits for them to complete before letting an application's startup continue.

EXPERIMENT: Watching Prefetch File Reads and Writes

If you capture a trace of application startup with Process Monitor from Sysinternals on a client edition of Windows (Windows Server editions disable prefetching by default), you can see the prefetcher check for and read the application's prefetch file (if it exists), and roughly 10 seconds after the application started, see the prefetcher write out a new copy of the file. Below is a capture of Notepad startup with an Include filter set to "prefetch" so that Process Monitor shows only accesses to the %SystemRoot%\Prefetch directory:

Lines 1 through 4 show the Notepad prefetch file being read in the context of the Notepad process during its startup. Lines 5 through 11, which have time stamps 10 seconds later than the first three lines, show the SuperFetch service, which is running in the context of a Svchost process, write out the updated prefetch file.

To minimize seeking even further, every three days or so, during system idle periods, the SuperFetch service organizes a list of files and directories in the order that they are

referenced during a boot or application start and stores the list in a file named Windows\ Prefetch\Layout.ini, shown in Figure 9-49. This list also includes frequently accessed files tracked by SuperFetch.

FIGURE 9-49 Prefetch defragmentation layout file

Then it launches the system defragmenter with a command-line option that tells the defragmenter to defragment based on the contents of the file instead of performing a full defrag. The defragmenter finds a contiguous area on each volume large enough to hold all the listed files and directories that reside on that volume and then moves them in their entirety into the area so that they are stored one after the other. Thus, future prefetch operations will even be more efficient because all the data read in is now stored physically on the disk in the order it will be read. Because the files defragmented for prefetching usually number only in the hundreds, this defragmentation is much faster than full volume defragmentations. (See Chapter 11 for more information on defragmentation.)

Placement Policy

When a thread receives a page fault, the memory manager must also determine where in physical memory to put the virtual page. The set of rules it uses to determine the best position is called a *placement policy*. Windows considers the size of CPU memory caches when choosing page frames to minimize unnecessary thrashing of the cache.

If physical memory is full when a page fault occurs, a *replacement policy* is used to determine which virtual page must be removed from memory to make room for the new page. Common replacement policies include *least recently used* (LRU) and *first in, first out* (FIFO). The LRU algorithm (also known as the *clock algorithm*, as implemented in most versions of UNIX) requires the virtual memory system to track when a page in memory is used. When a

new page frame is required, the page that hasn't been used for the greatest amount of time is removed from the working set. The FIFO algorithm is somewhat simpler; it removes the page that has been in physical memory for the greatest amount of time, regardless of how often it's been used.

Replacement policies can be further characterized as either global or local. A global replacement policy allows a page fault to be satisfied by any page frame, whether or not that frame is owned by another process. For example, a global replacement policy using the FIFO algorithm would locate the page that has been in memory the longest and would free it to satisfy a page fault; a local replacement policy would limit its search for the oldest page to the set of pages already owned by the process that incurred the page fault. Global replacement policies make processes vulnerable to the behavior of other processes—an ill-behaved application can undermine the entire operating system by inducing excessive paging activity in all processes.

Windows implements a combination of local and global replacement policy. When a working set reaches its limit and/or needs to be trimmed because of demands for physical memory, the memory manager removes pages from working sets until it has determined there are enough free pages.

Working Set Management

Every process starts with a default working set minimum of 50 pages and a working set maximum of 345 pages. Although it has little effect, you can change the process working set limits with the Windows *SetProcessWorkingSetSize* function, though you must have the "increase scheduling priority" user right to do this. However, unless you have configured the process to use hard working set limits, these limits are ignored, in that the memory manager will permit a process to grow beyond its maximum if it is paging heavily and there is ample memory (and conversely, the memory manager will shrink a process below its working set minimum if it is not paging and there is a high demand for physical memory on the system). Hard working set limits can be set using the *SetProcessWorkingSetSizeEx* function along with the QUOTA_LIMITS_HARDWS_ENABLE flag, but it is almost always better to let the system manage your working set instead of setting your own hard working set minimums.

The maximum working set size can't exceed the systemwide maximum calculated at system initialization time and stored in the kernel variable *MiMaximumWorkingSet*, which is a hard upper limit based on the working set maximums listed in Table 9-22.

TABLE 9-22 Upper Limit for Working Set Maximums

Windows Version	Working Set Maximum
x86	2,047.9 MB
x86 versions of Windows booted with *increaseuserva*	2,047.9 MB+ user virtual address increase (MB)
IA64	7,152 GB
x64	8,192 GB

When a page fault occurs, the process's working set limits and the amount of free memory on the system are examined. If conditions permit, the memory manager allows a process to grow to its working set maximum (or beyond if the process does not have a hard working set limit and there are enough free pages available). However, if memory is tight, Windows replaces rather than adds pages in a working set when a fault occurs.

Although Windows attempts to keep memory available by writing modified pages to disk, when modified pages are being generated at a very high rate, more memory is required in order to meet memory demands. Therefore, when physical memory runs low, the *working set manager*, a routine that runs in the context of the balance set manager system thread (described in the next section), initiates automatic working set trimming to increase the amount of free memory available in the system. (With the Windows *SetProcessWorkingSet-SizeEx* function mentioned earlier, you can also initiate working set trimming of your own process—for example, after process initialization.)

The working set manager examines available memory and decides which, if any, working sets need to be trimmed. If there is ample memory, the working set manager calculates how many pages could be removed from working sets if needed. If trimming is needed, it looks at working sets that are above their minimum setting. It also dynamically adjusts the rate at which it examines working sets as well as arranges the list of processes that are candidates to be trimmed into an optimal order. For example, processes with many pages that have not been accessed recently are examined first; larger processes that have been idle longer are considered before smaller processes that are running more often; the process running the foreground application is considered last; and so on.

When it finds processes using more than their minimums, the working set manager looks for pages to remove from their working sets, making the pages available for other uses. If the amount of free memory is still too low, the working set manager continues removing pages from processes' working sets until it achieves a minimum number of free pages on the system.

The working set manager tries to remove pages that haven't been accessed recently. It does this by checking the accessed bit in the hardware PTE to see whether the page has been accessed. If the bit is clear, the page is *aged*, that is, a count is incremented indicating that the page hasn't been referenced since the last working set trim scan. Later, the age of pages is used to locate candidate pages to remove from the working set.

If the hardware PTE accessed bit is set, the working set manager clears it and goes on to examine the next page in the working set. In this way, if the accessed bit is clear the next time the working set manager examines the page, it knows that the page hasn't been accessed since the last time it was examined. This scan for pages to remove continues through the working set list until either the number of desired pages has been removed or the scan has returned to the starting point. (The next time the working set is trimmed, the scan picks up where it left off last.)

EXPERIMENT: Viewing Process Working Set Sizes

You can use the Performance tool to examine process working set sizes by looking at the performance counters shown in the following table.

Counter	Description
Process: Working Set	Current size of the selected process's working set in bytes
Process: Working Set Peak	Peak size of the selected process's working set in bytes
Process: Page Faults/sec	Number of page faults for the process that occur each second

Several other process viewer utilities (such as Task Manager and Process Explorer) also display the process working set size.

You can also get the total of all the process working sets by selecting the _Total process in the instance box in the Performance tool. This process isn't real—it's simply a total of the process-specific counters for all processes currently running on the system. The total you see is misleading, however, because the size of each process working set includes pages being shared by other processes. Thus, if two or more processes share a page, the page is counted in each process's working set.

EXPERIMENT: Viewing the Working Set List

You can view the individual entries in the working set by using the kernel debugger *!wsle* command. The following example shows a partial output of the working set list of WinDbg.

```
lkd> !wsle 7

Working Set @ c0802000
    FirstFree     209c  FirstDynamic         6
    LastEntry     242e  NextSlot             6  LastInitialized    24b9
    NonDirect        0  HashTable            0  HashTableSize        0

Reading the WSLE data ...................................................

Virtual Address       Age  Locked  ReferenceCount
        c0600203        0       1       1
        c0601203        0       1       1
        c0602203        0       1       1
        c0603203        0       1       1
        c0604213        0       1       1
        c0802203        0       1       1
         2865201        0       0       1
         1a6d201        0       0       1
          3f4201        0       0       1
        707ed101        0       0       1
```

2d27201	0	0	1
2d28201	0	0	1
772f5101	0	0	1
2d2a201	0	0	1
2d2b201	0	0	1
2d2c201	0	0	1
779c3101	0	0	1
c0002201	0	0	1
7794f101	0	0	1
7ffd1109	0	0	1
7ffd2109	0	0	1
7ffc0009	0	0	1
7ffb0009	0	0	1
77940101	0	0	1
77944101	0	0	1
112109	0	0	1
320109	0	0	1
322109	0	0	1
77949101	0	0	1
110109	0	0	1
77930101	0	0	1
111109	0	0	1

Notice that some entries in the working set list are page table pages (the ones with addresses greater than 0xC0000000), some are from system DLLs (the ones in the 0x7nnnnnnn range), and some are from the code of Windbg.exe itself.

Balance Set Manager and Swapper

Working set expansion and trimming take place in the context of a system thread called the *balance set manager* (routine *KeBalanceSetManager*). The balance set manager is created during system initialization. Although the balance set manager is technically part of the kernel, it calls the memory manager's working set manager (*MmWorkingSetManager*) to perform working set analysis and adjustment.

The balance set manager waits for two different event objects: an event that is signaled when a periodic timer set to fire once per second expires and an internal working set manager event that the memory manager signals at various points when it determines that working sets need to be adjusted. For example, if the system is experiencing a high page fault rate or the free list is too small, the memory manager wakes up the balance set manager so that it will call the working set manager to begin trimming working sets. When memory is more plentiful, the working set manager will permit faulting processes to gradually increase the size of their working sets by faulting pages back into memory, but the working sets will grow only as needed.

When the balance set manager wakes up as the result of its 1-second timer expiring, it takes the following five steps:

1. It queues a DPC associated to a 1-second timer. The DPC routine is the *KiScanReady-Queues* routine, which looks for threads that might warrant having their priority boosted because they are CPU starved. (See the section "Priority Boosts for CPU Starvation" in Chapter 5.)

2. Every fourth time the balance set manager wakes up because its 1-second timer has expired, it signals an event that wakes up another system thread called the swapper (*KiSwapperThread*) (routine *KeSwapProcessOrStack*).

3. The balance set manager then checks the look-aside lists and adjusts their depths if necessary (to improve access time and to reduce pool usage and pool fragmentation).

4. It adjusts IRP credits to optimize the usage of the per-processor look-aside lists used in IRP completion. This allows better scalability when certain processors are under heavy I/O load.

5. It calls the memory manager's working set manager. (The working set manager has its own internal counters that regulate when to perform working set trimming and how aggressively to trim.)

The swapper is also awakened by the scheduling code in the kernel if a thread that needs to run has its kernel stack swapped out or if the process has been swapped out. The swapper looks for threads that have been in a wait state for 15 seconds (or 3 seconds on a system with less than 12 MB of RAM). If it finds one, it puts the thread's kernel stack in transition (moving the pages to the modified or standby lists) so as to reclaim its physical memory, operating on the principle that if a thread's been waiting that long, it's going to be waiting even longer. When the last thread in a process has its kernel stack removed from memory, the process is marked to be entirely outswapped. That's why, for example, processes that have been idle for a long time (such as Winlogon is after you log on) can have a zero working set size.

System Working Set

Just as processes have working sets, the pageable code and data in the operating system are managed by a single *system working set*. Five different kinds of pages can reside in the system working set:

- System cache pages
- Paged pool
- Pageable code and data in Ntoskrnl.exe
- Pageable code and data in device drivers
- System mapped views

You can examine the size of the system working set or the size of the five components that contribute to it with the performance counters or system variables shown in Table 9-23. Keep in mind that the performance counter values are in bytes whereas the system variables are measured in terms of pages.

You can also examine the paging activity in the system working set by examining the Memory: Cache Faults/sec performance counter, which describes page faults that occur in the system working set (both hard and soft).

TABLE 9-23 System Working Set Performance Counters

Performance Counter (in Bytes)	System Variable (in Pages)	Description
Memory: Cache Bytes*	MmSystemCache-Ws.WorkingSetSize	Total size of system working set (including the cache, paged pool, pageable Ntoskrnl and driver code, and system mapped views); this is *not* the size of the system cache alone, even though the name implies that it is.
Memory: Cache Bytes Peak	MmSystemCacheWs.Peak	Peak system working set size.
Memory: System Cache Resident Bytes	MmSystemCachePage	Physical memory consumed by the system cache.
Memory: System Code Resident Bytes	MmSystemCodePage	Physical memory consumed by pageable code in Ntoskrnl.exe.
Memory: System Driver Resident Bytes	MmSystemDriverPage	Physical memory consumed by pageable device driver code.
Memory: Pool Paged Resident Bytes	MmPagedPoolPage	Physical memory consumed by paged pool.

* Internally, this working set is called the system cache working set, even though the system cache is just one of five different components in it. Thus, several utilities think they are displaying the size of the file cache when they are displaying the total size of the system working set.

MmSystemCacheWs.PageFaultCount is the system variable that contains the value for this counter.

Memory Notification Events

Windows provides a way for user-mode processes and kernel-mode drivers to be notified when physical memory, paged pool, nonpaged pool, and commit charge are low and/or plentiful. This information can be used to determine memory usage as appropriate. For example, if available memory is low, the application can reduce memory consumption. If available paged pool is high, the driver can allocate more memory. Finally, the memory manager also provides an event that permits notification when corrupted pages have been detected.

User-mode processes can be notified only of low or high memory conditions. An application can call the *CreateMemoryResourceNotification* function, specifying whether low or high memory notification is desired. A handle can be provided to any of the wait functions. When memory is low (or high), the wait completes, thus notifying the thread of the condition. Alternatively, the *QueryMemoryResourceNotification* can be used to query the system memory condition at any time.

Drivers, on the other hand, use the specific event name that the memory manager has set up in the \KernelObjects directory, since notification is implemented by the memory manager signaling one of the globally named event objects it defines, shown in Table 9-24.

TABLE 9-24 Memory Manager Notification Events

Event Name	Description
HighCommitCondition	This event is set when the commit charge is near the maximum commit limit. In other words, memory usage is very high, very little space is available in physical memory or paging files, and the operating system cannot increase the size of its paging files.
HighMemoryCondition	This event is set whenever the amount of free physical memory exceeds the defined amount.
HighNonPagedPoolCondition	This event is set whenever the amount of nonpaged pool exceeds the defined amount.
HighPagedPoolCondition	This event is set whenever the amount of paged pool exceeds the defined amount.
LowCommitCondition	This event is set when the commit charge is low, relative to the current commit limit. In other words, memory usage is low and a lot of space is available in physical memory or paging files.
LowMemoryCondition	This event is set whenever the amount of free physical memory falls below the defined amount.
LowNonPagedPoolCondition	This event is set whenever the amount of free nonpaged pool falls below the defined amount.
LowPagedPoolCondition	This event is set whenever the amount of free paged pool falls below the defined amount.
MaximumCommitCondition	This event is set when the commit charge is near the maximum commit limit. In other words, memory usage is very high, very little space is available in physical memory or paging files, and the operating system cannot increase the size or number of paging files.
MemoryErrors	A bad page (non-zeroed zero page) has been detected.

When a given memory condition is detected, the appropriate event is signaled, thus waking up any waiting threads.

Note The high and low memory values can be overridden by adding a DWORD registry value, *LowMemoryThreshold* or *HighMemoryThreshold*, under HKLM\SYSTEM\CurrentControlSet\ Session Manager\Memory Management that specifies the number of megabytes to use as the low or high threshold. The system can also be configured to crash the system when a bad page is detected, instead of signaling a memory error event, by setting the *PageValidationAction* DWORD registry value in the same key.

EXPERIMENT: Viewing the Memory Resource Notification Events

To see the memory resource notification events, run Winobj from Sysinternals and click on the KernelObjects folder. You will see both the low and high memory condition events shown in the right pane:

If you double-click either event, you can see how many handles and/or references have been made to the objects.

To see whether any processes in the system have requested memory resource notification, search the handle table for references to "LowMemoryCondition" or "HighMemoryCondition." You can do this by using Process Explorer's Find menu and choosing the Handle capability or by using WinDbg. (For a description of the handle table, see the section on the "Object Manager" in Chapter 3.)

Proactive Memory Management (SuperFetch)

Traditional memory management in operating systems has focused on the demand-paging model we've shown until now, with some advancements in clustering and prefetching so that disk I/Os can be optimized at the time of the demand-page fault. Client versions of Windows Vista and later releases, however, include a significant improvement in the management of physical memory with the implementation of SuperFetch, a memory management scheme that enhances the least-recently accessed approach with historical information and proactive memory management.

The standby list management of previous Windows versions has had two limitations. First, the prioritization of pages relies only on the recent past behavior of processes and does not anticipate their future memory requirements. Second, the data used for prioritization is limited to the list of pages owned by a process at any given point in time. These shortcomings can result in scenarios in which the computer is left unattended for a brief period of time, during which a memory-intensive system application runs (doing work such as an antivirus scan or a disk defragmentation) and then causes subsequent interactive application use (or launch) to be sluggish. The same situation can happen when a user purposely runs a data and/or memory intensive application and then returns to use other programs, which appear to be significantly less responsive.

This decline in performance occurs because the memory-intensive application forces the code and data that active applications had cached in memory to be overwritten by the memory-intensive activities—applications perform sluggishly as they have to request their data and code from disk. Client versions of Windows Vista and later take a big step toward resolving these limitations with SuperFetch.

Components

SuperFetch is composed of several components in the system that work hand in hand to proactively manage memory and limit the impact on user activity when SuperFetch is performing its work. These components include:

- **Tracer** The tracer mechanisms are part of a kernel component (Pf) that allows SuperFetch to query detailed page usage, session, and process information at any time. SuperFetch also makes use of the FileInfo driver (%SystemRoot%\System32\Drivers\ Fileinfo.sys) to track file usage.

- **Trace Collector and Processor** This collector works with the tracing components to provide a raw log based on the tracing data that has been acquired. This tracing data is kept in memory and handed off to the processor. The processor then hands the

log entries in the trace to the agents, which maintain history files (described below) in memory and persist them to disk when the service stops (such as during a reboot).

- **Agents** SuperFetch keeps file page access information in history files, which keep track of virtual offsets. Agents group pages by attributes, such as:

 - ❏ Page access while the user was active

 - ❏ Page access by a foreground process

 - ❏ Hard fault while the user was active

 - ❏ Page access during an application launch

 - ❏ Page access upon the user returning after a long idle period

- **Scenario manager** This component, also called the context agent, manages the three SuperFetch scenario plans: hibernation, standby, and fast-user switching The kernel-mode part of the scenario manager provides APIs for initiating and terminating scenarios, managing current scenario state, and associating tracing information with these scenarios.

- **Rebalancer** Based on the information provided by the SuperFetch agents, as well as the current state of the system (such as the state of the prioritized page lists), the rebalancer, a specialized agent that is located in the SuperFetch user-mode service, queries the PFN database and reprioritizes it based on the associated score of each page, thus building the prioritized standby lists. The rebalancer can also issue commands to the memory manager that modify the working sets of processes on the system, and it is the only agent that actually takes action on the system—other agents merely filter information for the rebalancer to use in its decisions. Other than reprioritization, the rebalancer also initiates prefetching through the prefetcher thread, which makes use of FileInfo and kernel services to preload memory with useful pages.

Finally, all these components make use of facilities inside the memory manager that allow querying detailed information about the state of each page in the PFN database, the current page counts for each page list and prioritized list, and more. Figure 9-50 displays an architectural diagram of SuperFetch's multiple components. SuperFetch components also make use of prioritized I/O (see Chapter 7 for more information on I/O priority) to minimize user impact.

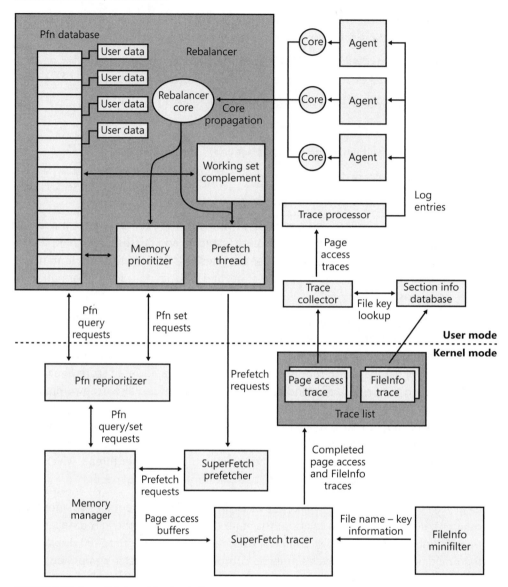

FIGURE 9-50 SuperFetch architectural diagram

Tracing and Logging

SuperFetch makes most of its decisions based on information that has been integrated, parsed, and post-processed from raw traces and logs, making these two components among the most critical. Tracing is similar to ETW in some ways because it makes use of certain triggers in code throughout the system to generate events, but it also works in conjunction with facilities already provided by the system, such as power manager notification, process

callbacks, and file system filtering. The tracer also makes use of traditional page aging mechanisms that exist in the memory manager, as well as newer working set aging and access tracking implemented for SuperFetch.

SuperFetch always keeps a trace running and continuously queries trace data from the system, which tracks page usage and access through the memory manager's access bit tracking and working set aging. To track file-related information, which is as critical as page usage because it allows prioritization of file data in the cache, SuperFetch leverages existing filtering functionality with the addition of the FileInfo driver. (See Chapter 7 for more information on filter drivers.) This driver sits on the file system device stack and monitors access and changes to files at the stream level (for more information on NTFS data streams, see Chapter 11), which provides it with fine-grained understanding of file access. The main job of the FileInfo driver is to associate streams (identified by a unique key, currently implemented as the *FsContext* field of the respective file object) with file names so that the user-mode SuperFetch service can identify the specific file steam and offset with which a page in the standby list belonging to a memory mapped section is associated. It also provides the interface for prefetching file data transparently, without interfering with locked files and other file system state. The rest of the driver ensures that the information stays consistent by tracking deletions, renaming operations, truncations, and the reuse of file keys by implementing sequence numbers.

At any time during tracing, the rebalancer might be invoked to repopulate pages differently. These decisions are made by analyzing information such as the distribution of memory within working sets, the zero page list, the modified page list and the standby page lists, the number of faults, the state of PTE access bits, the per-page usage traces, current virtual address consumption, and working set size.

A given trace can be either a page access trace, in which the tracer keeps track (by using the access bit) of which pages were accessed by the process (both file page and private memory), or a name logging trace, which monitors the file-name-to-file-key-mapping updates (which allow SuperFetch to map a page associated with a file object) to the actual file on disk.

Although a SuperFetch trace only keeps track of page accesses, the SuperFetch service processes this trace in user mode and goes much deeper, adding its own richer information such as where the page was loaded from (such as resident memory or a hard page fault), whether this was the initial access to that page, and what the rate of page access actually is. Additional information, such as the system state, is also kept, as well as information about in which recent scenarios each traced page was last referenced. The generated trace information is kept in memory through a logger into data structures, which identify, in the case of page access traces, a virtual-address-to-working-set pair or, in the case of a name logging trace, a file-to-offset pair. SuperFetch can thus keep track of which range of virtual addresses for a given process have page-related events and which range of offsets for a given file have similar events.

Scenarios

One aspect of SuperFetch that is distinct from its primary page repriorization and prefetching mechanisms (covered in more detail in the next section) is its support for scenarios, which are specific actions on the machine for which SuperFetch strives to improve the user experience. These scenarios are standby and hibernation as well as fast user switching. Each of these scenarios has different goals, but all are centered around the main purpose of minimizing or removing hard faults.

- For hibernation, the goal is to intelligently decide which pages are saved in the hibernation file other than the existing working set pages. The goal is to minimize the amount of time that it takes for the system to become responsive after a resume.

- For standby, the goal is to completely remove hard faults after resume. Because a typical system can resume in less than 2 seconds, but can take 5 seconds to spin-up the hard drive after a long sleep, a single hard fault could cause such a delay in the resume cycle. SuperFetch prioritizes pages needed after a standby to remove this chance.

- For fast user switching, the goal is to keep an accurate priority and understanding of each user's memory, so that switching to another user will cause the user's session to be immediately usable, and not require a large amount of lag time to allow pages to be faulted in.

Scenarios are hardcoded, and SuperFetch manages them through the *NtSetSystem-Information* and *NtQuerySystemInformation* APIs that control system state. For SuperFetch purposes, a special information class, *SystemSuperFetchInformation,* is used to control the kernel-mode components and to generate requests such as starting, ending, and querying a scenario or associating one or more traces with a scenario.

Each scenario is defined by a plan file, which contains, at minimum, a list of pages associated with the scenario. Page priority values are also assigned according to certain rules we'll describe next. When a scenario starts, the scenario manager is responsible for responding to the event by generating the list of pages that should be brought into memory and at which priority.

Page Priority and Rebalancing

We've already seen that the memory manager implements a system of page priorities to define from which standby list pages will be repurposed for a given operation and in which list a given page will be inserted. This mechanism provides benefits when processes and threads can have associated priorities—such that a defragmenter process doesn't pollute the standby page list and/or steal pages from an interactive, foreground process—but its real power is unleashed through SuperFetch's page prioritization schemes and rebalancing, which don't require manual application input or hardcoded knowledge of process importance.

SuperFetch assigns page priority based on an internal score it keeps for each page, part of which is based on frequency-based usage. This usage counts how many times a page was used in given relative time intervals, such as an hour, a day, or a week. Time of use is also kept track of, which records for how long a given page has not been accessed. Finally, data such as where this page comes from (which list) and other access patterns are used to compute this final score, which is then translated into a priority number, which can be anywhere from 1 to 6 (7 is used for another purpose described later). Going down each level, the lower standby page list priorities are repurposed first, as shown in the Experiment "Viewing Prioritized Standby Lists." Priority 5 is typically used for normal applications, while priority 1 is meant for background applications that third-party developers can mark as such. Finally, priority 6 is used to keep a certain number of high-importance pages as far away as possible from repurposing. The other priorities are a result of the score associated with each page.

Because SuperFetch "learns" a user's system, it can start from scratch with no existing historical data and slowly build up an understanding of the different page usage accesses associated with the user. However, this would result in a significant learning curve whenever a new application, user, or service pack was installed. Instead, by using an internal tool, Microsoft has the ability to pretrain SuperFetch to capture SuperFetch data and then turn it into prebuilt traces. Before Windows shipped, the SuperFetch team traced common usages and patterns that all users will probably encounter, such as clicking the Start menu, opening Control Panel, or using the File Open/Save dialog box. This trace data was then saved to history files (which ship as resources in Sysmain.dll) and is used to prepopulate the special priority 7 list, which is where the most critical data is placed and which is very rarely repurposed. Pages at priority 7 are file pages kept in memory even after the process has exited and even across reboots (by being repopulated at the next boot). Finally, pages with priority 7 are static, in that they are never reprioritized, and SuperFetch will never dynamically load pages at priority 7 other than the static pretrained set.

The prioritized list is loaded into memory (or prepopulated) by the rebalancer, but the actual act of rebalancing is actually handled both by SuperFetch and the memory manager. As shown earlier, the prioritized standby page list mechanism is internal to the memory manager, and decisions as to which pages to throw out first and which to protect are innate, based on the priority number. The rebalancer actually does its job not by manually rebalancing memory but by reprioritizing it, which will cause the operation of the memory manager to perform the needed tasks. The rebalancer is also responsible for reading the actual pages from disk, if needed, so that they are present in memory (prefetching). It then assigns the priority that is mapped by each agent to the score for each page, and the memory manager will then ensure that the page is treated according to its importance.

The rebalancer can also take action without relying on other agents; for example, if it notices that the distribution of pages across paging lists is suboptimal or that the number of repurposed pages across different priority levels is detrimental. The rebalancer also has the ability to cause working set trimming if needed, which might be required for creating an

appropriate budget of pages that will be used for SuperFetch prepopulated cache data. The rebalancer will typically take low-utility pages—such as those that are already marked as low priority, pages that are zeroed, and pages with valid contents but not in any working set and have been unused—and build a more useful set of pages in memory, given the budget it has allocated itself.

Once the rebalancer has decided which pages to bring into memory and at which priority level they need to be loaded (as well as which pages can be thrown out), it performs the required disk reads to prefetch them. It also works in conjunction with the I/O manager's prioritization schemes so that the I/Os are performed with very low priority and do not interfere with the user. It is important to note that the actual memory consumption used by prefetching is all backed by standby pages—as described earlier in the discussion of page dynamics, standby memory is available memory because it can be repurposed as free memory for another allocator at any time. In other words, if SuperFetch is prefetching the "wrong data," there is no real impact to the user, because that memory can be reused when needed and doesn't actually consume resources.

Finally, the rebalancer also runs periodically to ensure that pages it has marked as high priority have actually been recently used. Because these pages will rarely (sometimes never) be repurposed, it is important not to waste them on data that is rarely accessed but may have appeared to be frequently accessed during a certain time period. If such a situation is detected, the rebalancer runs again to push those pages down in the priority lists.

In addition to the rebalancer, a special agent called the application launch agent is also involved in a different kind of prefetching mechanism, which attempts to predict application launches and builds a Markov chain model that describes the probability of certain application launches given the existence of other application launches within a time segment. These time segments are divided across four different periods—morning, noon, evening, and night; roughly 6 hours each—and are also kept track of separately as weekdays or weekends. For example, if on Saturday and Sunday evening a user typically launches Outlook (to send e-mail) after having launched Word (to write letters), the application launch agent will probably have prefetched Outlook based on the high probability of it running after Word during weekend evenings.

Because systems today have sufficiently large amounts of memory, on average more than 2 GB (although SuperFetch works well on low-memory systems, too), the actual real amount of memory that frequently used processes on a machine need resident for optimal performance ends up being a manageable subset of their entire memory footprint, and SuperFetch can often fit all the pages required into RAM. When it can't, technologies such as ReadyBoost and ReadyDrive can further avoid disk usage.

Robust Performance

A final performance enhancing functionality of SuperFetch is called *robustness,* or *robust performance.* This component, managed by the user-mode SuperFetch service, but ultimately implemented in the kernel (*Pf* routines), watches for specific file I/O access that might harm system performance by populating the standby lists with unneeded data. For example, if a process were to copy a large file across the file system, the standby list would be populated with the file's contents, even though that file might never be accessed again (or not for a long period of time). This would throw out any other data within that priority (and if this was an interactive and useful program, chances are its priority would've been at least 5).

SuperFetch responds to two specific kinds of I/O access patterns: sequential file access (going through all the data in a file) and sequential directory access (going through every file in a directory). When SuperFetch detects that a certain amount of data (past an internal threshold) has been populated in the standby list as a result of this kind of access, it applies aggressive deprioritization (robustion) to the pages being used to map this file, within the targeted process only (so as not to penalize other applications). These pages, so-called robusted, essentially become reprioritized to priority 2.

Because this component of SuperFetch is reactive and not predictive, it does take some time for the robustion to kick in. SuperFetch will therefore keep track of this process for the next time it runs. Once SuperFetch has determined that it appears that this process always performs this kind of sequential access, SuperFetch remembers it and robusts the file pages as soon as they're mapped, instead of waiting on the reactive behavior. At this point, the entire process is now considered robusted for future file access.

Just by applying this logic, however, SuperFetch could potentially hurt many legitimate applications or user scenarios that perform sequential access in the future. For example, by using the Sysinternals Strings.exe utility, you can look for a string in all executables that are part of a directory. If there are many files, SuperFetch would likely perform robustion. Now, next time you run Strings with a different search parameter, it would run just as slowly as it did the first time, even though you'd expect it to run much faster. To prevent this, SuperFetch keeps a list of processes that it watches into the future, as well as an internal hard-coded list of exceptions. If a process is detected to later re-access robusted files, robustion is disabled on the process in order to restore expected behavior.

The main point to remember when thinking about robustion, and SuperFetch optimizations in general, is that SuperFetch constantly monitors usage patterns and updates its understanding of the system, so that it can avoid fetching useless data. Although changes in a user's daily activities or application startup behavior might cause SuperFetch to incorrectly "pollute" the cache with irrelevant data or to throw out data that SuperFetch might think is useless, it will quickly adapt to any pattern changes. If the user's actions are erratic and random, the worst that can happen is that the system behaves in a similar state as if SuperFetch was not present at all. If SuperFetch is ever in doubt or cannot track data reliably, it quiets

itself and doesn't make changes to a given process or page, keeping the behavior as it would have been on a Windows XP machine, for example.

ReadyBoost

Although RAM today is somewhat easily available and relatively cheap compared to a decade ago, it still doesn't beat the cost of secondary storage such as hard disk drives. Unfortunately, hard disks today contain many moving parts, are fragile, and, more importantly, relatively slow compared to RAM, especially during seeking, so storing active SuperFetch data on the drive would be as bad as paging out a page and hard faulting it inside memory. (Solid state disks offset some of these disadvantages, but they are pricier and still slow compared to RAM.) On the other hand, portable solid state media such as USB keys, CompactFlash cards, and Secure Digital cards provide a useful compromise. They are cheaper than RAM and available in larger sizes, but they also have seek times much shorter than hard drives because of the lack of moving parts.

Random disk I/O is especially expensive because disk head seek times are on the order of 10 milliseconds—an eternity for today's 3-GHz processors. Flash memory, however, can service random reads up to 10 times faster than a typical hard disk. Windows therefore includes a feature called ReadyBoost to take advantage of flash memory storage devices by creating an intermediate caching layer on them that logically sits between memory and disks.

ReadyBoost consists of a service (%SystemRoot%\System32\Emdmgmt.dll) that runs in a Service Host process and a volume filter driver (%SystemRoot%\System32\Drivers\Ecache.sys). (Emd is short for External Memory Device, the working name for ReadyBoost during its development.) When you insert a flash device like a USB key into a system, the ReadyBoost service looks at the device to determine its performance characteristics and stores the results of its test in HKLM\SOFTWARE\Microsoft\Windows NT\CurrentVersion\Emdmgmt, as shown in Figure 9-51.

FIGURE 9-51 ReadyBoost device test results in the registry

If you aren't already using a device for caching and the new device is between 256 MB and 32 GB in size, has a transfer rate of 2.5 MB per second or higher for random 4-KB reads, and has a transfer rate of 1.75 MB per second or higher for random 512-KB writes, then ReadyBoost will ask if you'd like to dedicate up to 4 GB of the storage for disk caching. (Although ReadyBoost can use NTFS, it limits the maximum cache size to 4 GB to accommodate FAT32 limitations.) If you agree, the service creates a caching file named ReadyBoost.sfcache in the root of the device, which it will use to store cached pages (the initial cache is built by querying SuperFetch's cache, but later contents are fully managed by ReadyBoost independently).

After the ReadyBoost service initializes caching, the Ecache.sys device driver intercepts all reads and writes to local hard disk volumes (C:\, for example) and copies any data being read or written into the caching file that the service created, with certain exceptions such as data that hasn't been read in a long while, or data that belongs to Volume Snapshot requests. Ecache.sys compresses data and typically achieves a 2:1 compression ratio, so a 4-GB cache file will usually contain 8 GB of data. The driver encrypts each block it writes using Advanced Encryption Standard (AES) encryption with a randomly generated per-boot session key in order to guarantee the privacy of the data in the cache if the device is removed from the system.

When ReadyBoost sees random reads that can be satisfied from the cache, it services them from there, but because hard disks have better sequential read access than flash memory, it lets reads that are part of sequential access patterns go directly to the disk even if the data is in the cache. Likewise, when reading the cache, if large I/Os have to be done, the on-disk cache will be read insead.

One disadvantage of depending on flash media is that the user can remove it at any time, which means the system can never solely store critical data on the media (as we've seen, writes always go to the secondary storage first). A related technology, ReadyDrive, covered in the next section, offers additional benefits and solves this problem.

ReadyDrive

ReadyDrive is a Windows feature that takes advantage of hybrid hard disk drives called H-HDDs. An H-HDD is a disk with embedded nonvolatile flash memory (also known as NVRAM). Typical H-HDDs include between 50 MB and 512 MB of cache, but the Windows cache limit is 2 TB.

Windows uses ATA-8 commands to define the disk data to be held in the flash memory. For example, Windows will save boot data to the cache when the system shuts down, allowing for

faster restarting. It also stores portions of hibernation file data in the cache when the system hibernates so that the subsequent resume is faster. Because the cache is enabled even when the disk is spun down, Windows can use the flash memory as a disk-write cache, which avoids spinning up the disk when the system is running on battery power. Keeping the disk spindle turned off can save much of the power consumed by the disk drive under normal usage.

Another consumer of ReadyDrive is SuperFetch, since it offers the same advantages as ReadyBoost with some enhanced functionality, such as not requiring an external flash device and having the ability to work persistently. Because the cache is on the actual physical hard drive (which typically a user cannot remove while the computer is running), the hard drive controller typically doesn't have to worry about the data disappearing and can avoid making writes to the actual disk, using solely the cache.

RAM Optimization Software

While SuperFetch provides valuable and realistic optimization of memory usage for the various scenarios it aims to support, many third-party software manufacturers are involved in the distribution of so-called "RAM Optimization" software, which aims to significantly increase available memory on a user's system. These memory optimizers typically present a user interface that shows a graph labeled "Available Memory," and a line typically shows the amount of memory that the optimizer will try to free when it runs. After the optimization job runs, the utility's available memory counter often goes up, sometimes dramatically, implying that the tool is actually freeing up memory for application use. RAM optimizers work by allocating and then freeing large amounts of virtual memory. The following illustration shows the effect a RAM optimizer has on a system:

The Before bar depicts the process and system working sets, the pages in standby lists, and free memory before optimization. The During bar shows that the RAM optimizer creates a high memory demand, which it does by incurring many page faults in a short time. In response, the memory manager increases the RAM optimizer's working set. This working-set expansion occurs at the expense of free memory, followed by standby pages and—when available memory becomes low—at the expense of other process working sets. The After bar illustrates how, after the RAM optimizer frees its memory, the memory manager moves all the pages that were assigned to the RAM optimizer to the free page list (which ultimately get zeroed by the zero page thread and moved to the zeroed page list), thus contributing to the free memory value.

Although gaining more free memory might seem like a good thing, it isn't. As RAM optimizers force the available memory counter up, they force other processes' data and code out of memory. If you're running Microsoft Word, for example, the text of open documents and the program code that was part of Word's working set before the optimization (and was therefore present in physical memory) must be reread from disk as you continue to edit your document. Additionally, by depleting the standby lists, valuable cached data is lost, including much of SuperFetch's cache. The performance degradation can be especially severe on servers, where the trimming of the system working set causes cached file data in physical memory to be thrown out, causing hard faults the next time it is accessed.

Conclusion

In this chapter, we've examined how the Windows memory manager implements virtual memory management. As with most modern operating systems, each process is given access to a private address space, protecting one process's memory from another's but allowing processes to share memory efficiently and securely. Advanced capabilities, such as the inclusion of mapped files and the ability to sparsely allocate memory, are also available. The Windows environment subsystem makes most of the memory manager's capabilities available to applications through the Windows API.

The next chapter covers a component tightly integrated with the memory manager, the cache manager.

Chapter 10
Cache Manager

The cache manager is a set of kernel-mode functions and system threads that cooperate with the memory manager to provide data caching for all Windows file system drivers (both local and network). In this chapter, we'll explain how the cache manager, including its key internal data structures and functions, works; how it is sized at system initialization time; how it interacts with other elements of the operating system; and how you can observe its activity through performance counters. We'll also describe the five flags on the Windows *CreateFile* function that affect file caching.

 Note None of the cache manager's internal functions are outlined in this chapter beyond the depth required to explain how the cache manager works. The programming interfaces to the cache manager are documented in the Windows Driver Kit (WDK). For more information about the WDK, see *www.microsoft.com/whdc/devtools/wdk/default.mspx*.

Key Features of the Cache Manager

The cache manager has several key features:

- Supports all file system types (both local and network), thus removing the need for each file system to implement its own cache management code

- Uses the memory manager to control which parts of which files are in physical memory (trading off demands for physical memory between user processes and the operating system)

- Caches data on a virtual block basis (offsets within a file)—in contrast to many caching systems, which cache on a logical block basis (offsets within a disk volume)—allowing for intelligent read-ahead and high-speed access to the cache without involving file system drivers (This method of caching, called *fast I/O*, is described later in this chapter.)

- Supports "hints" passed by applications at file open time (such as random versus sequential access, temporary file creation, and so on)

- Supports recoverable file systems (for example, those that use transaction logging) to recover data after a system failure

Although we'll talk more throughout this chapter about how these features are used in the cache manager, in this section we'll introduce you to the concepts behind these features.

Single, Centralized System Cache

Some operating systems rely on each individual file system to cache data, a practice that results either in duplicated caching and memory management code in the operating system or in limitations on the kinds of data that can be cached. In contrast, Windows offers a centralized caching facility that caches all externally stored data, whether on local hard disks, floppy disks, network file servers, or CD-ROMs. Any data can be cached, whether it's user data streams (the contents of a file and the ongoing read and write activity to that file) or file system *metadata* (such as directory and file headers). As you'll discover in this chapter, the method Windows uses to access the cache depends on the type of data being cached.

The Memory Manager

One unusual aspect of the cache manager is that it never knows how much cached data is actually in physical memory. This statement might sound strange because the purpose of a cache is to keep a subset of frequently accessed data in physical memory as a way to improve I/O performance. The reason the cache manager doesn't know how much data is in physical memory is that it accesses data by mapping views of files into system virtual address spaces, using standard *section objects* (*file mapping objects* in Windows API terminology). (Section objects are the basic primitive of the memory manager and are explained in detail in Chapter 9.) As addresses in these mapped views are accessed, the memory manager pages in blocks that aren't in physical memory. And when memory demands dictate, the memory manager pages data out of the cache and back to the files that are open in (mapped into) the cache.

By caching on the basis of a virtual address space using mapped files, the cache manager avoids generating read or write I/O request packets (IRPs) to access the data for files it's caching. Instead, it simply copies data to or from the virtual addresses where the portion of the cached file is mapped and relies on the memory manager to fault in (or out) the data into (or out of) memory as needed. This process allows the memory manager to make global trade-offs on how much memory to give to the system cache versus how much to give to user processes. (The cache manager also initiates I/O, such as lazy writing, which is described later in this chapter; however, it calls the memory manager to write the pages.) Also, as you'll learn in the next section, this design makes it possible for processes that open cached files to see the same data as do processes that are mapping the same files into their user address spaces.

Cache Coherency

One important function of a cache manager is to ensure that any process accessing cached data will get the most recent version of that data. A problem can arise when one process opens a file (and hence the file is cached) while another process maps the file into its address space directly (using the Windows *MapViewOfFile* function). This potential problem doesn't occur under Windows because both the cache manager and the user applications that map

files into their address spaces use the same memory management file mapping services. Because the memory manager guarantees that it has only one representation of each unique mapped file (regardless of the number of section objects or mapped views), it maps all views of a file (even if they overlap) to a single set of pages in physical memory, as shown in Figure 10-1. (For more information on how the memory manager works with mapped files, see Chapter 9.)

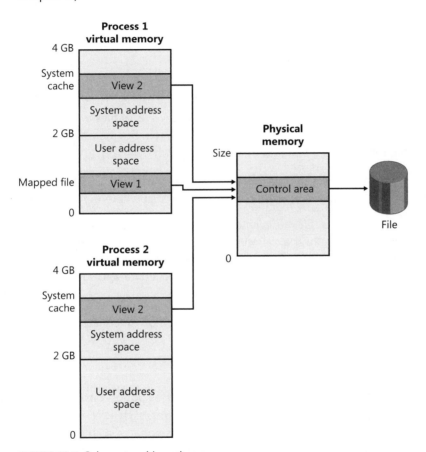

FIGURE 10-1 Coherent caching scheme

So, for example, if Process 1 has a view (View 1) of the file mapped into its user address space, and Process 2 is accessing the same view via the system cache, Process 2 will see any changes that Process 1 makes as they're made, not as they're flushed. The memory manager won't flush *all* user-mapped pages—only those that it knows have been written to (because they have the modified bit set). Therefore, any process accessing a file under Windows always sees the most up-to-date version of that file, even if some processes have the file open through the I/O system and others have the file mapped into their address space using the Windows file mapping functions.

> **Note** Cache coherency in this case refers to coherency between user-mapped data and cached I/O and not between noncached and cached hardware access and I/Os, which are almost guaranteed to be incoherent. Also, cache coherency is somewhat more difficult for network redirectors than for local file systems because network redirectors must implement additional flushing and purge operations to ensure cache coherency when accessing network data. See Chapter 11 for a description of opportunistic locking, the Windows distributed cache coherency mechanism.

Virtual Block Caching

The Windows cache manager uses a method known as *virtual block caching*, in which the cache manager keeps track of which parts of which *files* are in the cache. The cache manager is able to monitor these file portions by mapping 256-KB views of files into system virtual address spaces, using special system cache routines located in the memory manager. This approach has the following key benefits:

- It opens up the possibility of doing intelligent read-ahead; because the cache tracks which parts of which files are in the cache, it can predict where the caller might be going next.

- It allows the I/O system to bypass going to the file system for requests for data that is already in the cache (fast I/O). Because the cache manager knows which parts of which files are in the cache, it can return the address of cached data to satisfy an I/O request without having to call the file system.

Details of how intelligent read-ahead and fast I/O work are provided later in this chapter.

Stream-Based Caching

The cache manager is also designed to do *stream caching*, as opposed to file caching. A *stream* is a sequence of bytes within a file. Some file systems, such as NTFS, allow a file to contain more than one stream; the cache manager accommodates such file systems by caching each stream independently. NTFS can exploit this feature by organizing its master file table (described in Chapter 11) into streams and by caching these streams as well. In fact, although the cache manager might be said to cache files, it actually caches streams (all files have at least one stream of data) identified by both a file name and, if more than one stream exists in the file, a stream name.

> **Note** Internally, the cache manager is not aware of file or stream names, but uses pointers to these objects.

Recoverable File System Support

Recoverable file systems such as NTFS are designed to reconstruct the disk volume structure after a system failure. This capability means that I/O operations in progress at the time of a system failure must be either entirely completed or entirely backed out from the disk when the system is restarted. Half-completed I/O operations can corrupt a disk volume and even render an entire volume inaccessible. To avoid this problem, a recoverable file system maintains a log file in which it records every update it intends to make to the file system structure (the file system's metadata) before it writes the change to the volume. If the system fails, interrupting volume modifications in progress, the recoverable file system uses information stored in the log to reissue the volume updates.

 Note The term *metadata* applies only to changes in the file system structure: file and directory creation, renaming, and deletion.

To guarantee a successful volume recovery, every log file record documenting a volume update must be completely written to disk before the update itself is applied to the volume. Because disk writes are cached, the cache manager and the file system must coordinate metadata updates by ensuring that the log file is flushed ahead of metadata updates. Overall, the following actions occur in sequence:

1. The file system writes a log file record documenting the metadata update it intends to make.

2. The file system calls the cache manager to flush the log file record to disk.

3. The file system writes the volume update to the cache—that is, it modifies its cached metadata.

4. The cache manager flushes the altered metadata to disk, updating the volume structure. (Actually, log file records are batched before being flushed to disk, as are volume modifications.)

When a file system writes data to the cache, it can supply a *logical sequence number* (LSN) that identifies the record in its log file, which corresponds to the cache update. The cache manager keeps track of these numbers, recording the lowest and highest LSNs (representing the oldest and newest log file records) associated with each page in the cache. In addition, data streams that are protected by transaction log records are marked as "no write" by NTFS so that the mapped page writer won't inadvertently write out these pages before the corresponding log records are written. (When the mapped page writer sees a page marked this way, it moves the page to a special list that the cache manager then flushes at the appropriate time, such as when lazy writer activity takes place.)

When it prepares to flush a group of dirty pages to disk, the cache manager determines the highest LSN associated with the pages to be flushed and reports that number to the file system. The file system can then call the cache manager back, directing it to flush log file data up to the point represented by the reported LSN. *After* the cache manager flushes the log file up to that LSN, it flushes the corresponding volume structure updates to disk, thus ensuring that it records what it's going to do before actually doing it. These interactions between the file system and the cache manager guarantee the recoverability of the disk volume after a system failure.

Cache Virtual Memory Management

Because the Windows system cache manager caches data on a virtual basis, it uses up regions of system virtual address space (instead of physical memory) and manages them in structures called *virtual address control blocks*, or VACBs. VACBs define these regions of address space into 256-KB slots called *views*. When the cache manager initializes during the bootup process, it allocates an initial array of VACBs to describe cached memory. As caching requirements grow and more memory is required, the cache manager allocates more VACB arrays, as needed. It can also shrink virtual address space as other demands put pressure on the system.

At a file's first I/O (read or write) operation, the cache manager maps a 256-KB view of the 256-KB-aligned region of the file that contains the requested data into a free slot in the system cache address space. For example, if 10 bytes starting at an offset of 300,000 bytes were read into a file, the view that would be mapped would begin at offset 262144 (the second 256-KB-aligned region of the file) and extend for 256 KB.

The cache manager maps views of files into slots in the cache's address space on a round-robin basis, mapping the first requested view into the first 256-KB slot, the second view into the second 256-KB slot, and so forth, as shown in Figure 10-2. In this example, File B was mapped first, File A second, and File C third, so File B's mapped chunk occupies the first slot in the cache. Notice that only the first 256-KB portion of File B has been mapped, which is due to the fact that only part of the file has been accessed and because although File C is only 100 KB (and thus smaller than one of the views in the system cache), it requires its own 256-KB slot in the cache.

The cache manager guarantees that a view is mapped as long as it's active (although views can remain mapped after they become inactive). A view is marked active, however, only during a read or write operation to or from the file. Unless a process opens a file by specifying the FILE_FLAG_RANDOM_ACCESS flag in the call to *CreateFile*, the cache manager unmaps inactive views of a file as it maps new views for the file if it detects that the file is being accessed sequentially. Pages for unmapped views are sent to the standby or modified lists (depending on whether they have been changed), and because the memory manager

exports a special interface for the cache manager, the cache manager can direct the pages to be placed at the end or front of these lists. Pages that correspond to views of files opened with the FILE_FLAG_SEQUENTIAL_SCAN flag are moved to the front of the lists, whereas all others are moved to the end. This scheme encourages the reuse of pages belonging to sequentially read files and specifically prevents a large file copy operation from affecting more than a small part of physical memory. The flag also affects unmapping: the cache manager will aggressively unmap views when this flag is supplied.

FIGURE 10-2 Files of varying sizes mapped into the system cache

If the cache manager needs to map a view of a file and there are no more free slots in the cache, it will unmap the least recently mapped inactive view and use that slot. If no views are available, an I/O error is returned, indicating that insufficient system resources are available to perform the operation. Given that views are marked active only during a read or write operation, however, this scenario is extremely unlikely because thousands of files would have to be accessed simultaneously for this situation to occur.

Cache Size

In the following sections, we'll explain how Windows computes the size of the system cache, both virtually and physically. As with most calculations related to memory management, the size of the system cache depends on a number of factors.

Cache Virtual Size

On a 32-bit Windows system, the virtual size of the system cache is limited solely by the amount of kernel-mode virtual address space and the SystemCacheLimit registry key that

can be optionally configured. (See Chapter 9 for more information on limiting the size of the kernel virtual address space.) This means that the cache size is capped by the 2-GB system address space, but it is typically significantly smaller because the system address space is shared with other resources, including system paged table entries (PTEs), nonpaged and paged pool, and page tables. The maximum virtual cache size is 1,024 GB (1 TB) on 64-bit Windows.

Cache Working Set Size

As mentioned earlier, one of the key differences in the design of the cache manager from that of other operating systems is the delegation of physical memory management to the global memory manager. Because of this, the existing code that handles working set expansion and trimming, as well as managing the modified and standby lists, is also used to control the size of the system cache, dynamically balancing demands for physical memory between processes and the operating system.

The system cache doesn't have its own working set but rather shares a single system set that includes cache data, paged pool, pageable Ntoskrnl code, and pageable driver code. As explained in the section "System Working Set" in Chapter 9, this single working set is called internally the *system cache working set* even though the system cache is just one of the components that contribute to it. For the purposes of this book, we'll refer to this working set simply as the *system working set*. Also explained in Chapter 9 is the fact that if the LargeSystemCache registry value is 1, the memory manager favors the system working set over that of processes running on the system.

You can examine the physical size of the system cache compared to that of the total system working set as well as page fault information on the system working set by examining the performance counters or system variables listed in Table 10-1.

TABLE 10-1 **System Variables for the Physical Size of the System Cache and Page Fault Information**

Performance Counter	System Variable (in Pages)	Description
Memory: System Cache Resident Bytes	MmSystemCachePage	Physical memory consumed by the system cache.
Memory: Cache Bytes	MmSystemCacheWs.WorkingSetSize	Total size of the system working set (including the cache, paged pool, pageable code, and system mapped views). This is *not* the size of the cache (as the name implies)!
Memory: Cache Bytes Peak	MmSystemCacheWs.PeakWorkingSetSize	Peak system working set size.
Memory: Cache Faults/ sec	MmSystemCacheWs.PageFaultCount	Page faults in the system working set (not just the cache).

EXPERIMENT: Looking at the Cache's Working Set

The *!filecache* debugger command dumps information about the physical memory the cache is using, the current and peak working set sizes, the number of valid pages associated with views, and the names of files mapped into views, where applicable, as you can see in the following output. (File system drivers cache metadata, such as directory structures and volume bitmaps, by using unnamed file streams.)

```
lkd> !filecache
***** Dump file cache******
 Reading and sorting VACBs ...
 Processing 572 active VACBs ...
File Cache Information
 Current size 91372 kb
 Peak size    112580 kb
 572 Control Areas
 Loading file cache database (100% of 523264 PTEs)
 SkippedPageTableReads = 936
 File cache has 14099 valid pages

 Usage Summary (in Kb):
Control Valid Standby/Dirty Shared Locked FsContext Name
84445288  5220      16        0      0 8443dd70 $Mft
84bbcaf8    76       0        0      0 87748b18 $Directory
850b5158     4       0        0      0 9000e528 $Directory
8522b008  1136       0        0      0 900b3d80 INDEX.BTR
84c6b008    60       0        0      0 8d7b5708 $Directory
8443e2a8  3088    6656        0      0 8443e578 $LogFile
84c03ae8    68       0        0      0 93fc4548
Microsoft-Windows-Resource-Exhaustion-Detector%4Operational.evtx
84453368    28       0        0      0 93f79d08 $Directory
84a20398    20       0        0      0 93ea18d8 $Directory
850f4298   288     128        0      0 91dbf0f8
Microsoft-Windows-RestartManager%4Operational.evtx
8520f2e0  5792     120        0      0 93e60a08 ntkrpamp.pdb
850e6bc8     4       0        0      0 85cffd08 $Directory
8505d910     4       0        0      0 92e560f8 $Directory
8443d368     4       0        0      0 8443d760 $MftMirr
84ba59d8   128       0        0      0 8de50d80 NTUSER.DAT
84446820   512       0        0      0 84446a98 $BitMap
84447270    12       0        0      0 844475a0 $Mft
84f36880   128       0        0      0 8de21358 NTUSER.DAT
8444c440    44       0        0      0 8318be60 $Directory
8462a8e0 16656       0        0      0 877560f8 COMPONENTS
84402a00     4       0        0      0 83144d08 $Directory
 ...
```

Cache Physical Size

While the system working set includes the amount of physical memory that is mapped into views in the cache's virtual address space, it does not necessarily reflect the total amount of file data that is cached in physical memory. There can be a discrepancy between the two values because additional file data might be in the memory manager's standby or modified page lists.

Recall from Chapter 9 that during the course of working set trimming or page replacement the memory manager can move dirty pages from a working set to either the standby list or modified page list, depending on whether the page contains data that needs to be written to the paging file or another file before the page can be reused. If the memory manager didn't implement these lists, any time a process accessed data previously removed from its working set, the memory manager would have to hard-fault it in from disk. Instead, if the accessed data is present on either of these lists, the memory manager simply soft-faults the page back into the process's working set. Thus, the lists serve as in-memory caches of data that's stored in the paging file, executable images, or data files. Thus, the total amount of file data cached on a system includes not only the system working set but the combined sizes of the standby and modified page lists as well.

An example illustrates how the cache manager can cause much more file data than that containable in the system working set to be cached in physical memory. Consider a system that acts as a dedicated file server. A client application accesses file data from across the network, while a server, such as the file server driver (\Windows\System32\Drivers\Srv2.sys, described in Chapter 13), uses cache manager interfaces to read and write file data on behalf of the client. If the client reads through several thousand files of 1 MB each, the cache manager will have to start reusing views when it runs out of mapping space (and can't enlarge the VACB mapping area). For each file read thereafter, the cache manager unmaps views and remaps them for new files. When the cache manager unmaps a view, the memory manager doesn't discard the file data in the cache's working set that corresponds to the view, it moves the data to the standby list. In the absence of any other demand for physical memory, the standby list can consume almost all the physical memory that remains outside the system working set. In other words, virtually all the server's physical memory will be used to cache file data, as shown in Figure 10-3.

FIGURE 10-3 Example in which most of physical memory is being used by the file cache

Because the total amount of file data cached includes the system working set, modified page list, and standby list—the sizes of which are all controlled by the memory manager—it is in a sense the real cache manager. The cache manager subsystem simply provides convenient interfaces for accessing file data through the memory manager. It also plays an important role with its read-ahead and write-behind policies in influencing what data the memory manager keeps present in physical memory, as well as with managing system virtual address views of the space.

To try and accurately reflect the total amount of file data that's cached on a system, both Task Manager and Process Explorer show a value named System Cache in their performance view that reflects the combined size of the system working set, standby list, and modified page list. Figure 10-4 shows the system information view in Process Explorer and the System Cache value in the Physical Memory area in the middle of the figure.

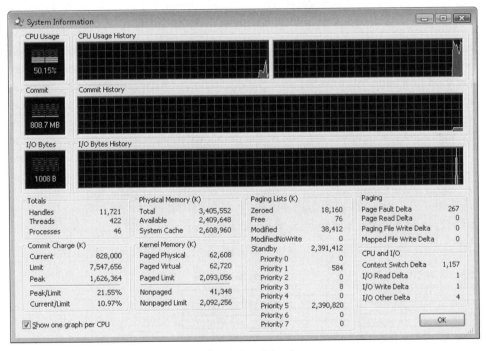

FIGURE 10-4 Process Explorer's System Information dialog box

Cache Data Structures

The cache manager uses the following data structures to keep track of cached files:

- Each 256-KB slot in the system cache is described by a VACB.

- Each separately opened cached file has a private cache map, which contains information used to control read-ahead (discussed later in the chapter).

- Each cached file has a single shared cache map structure, which points to slots in the system cache that contain mapped views of the file.

These structures and their relationships are described in the next sections.

Systemwide Cache Data Structures

As previously described, the cache manager keeps track of the state of the views in the system cache by using an array of data structures called *virtual address control block* (VACB) *arrays* that are stored in nonpaged pool. On a 32-bit system, each VACB is 32 bytes in size and a VACB array is 128 KB, resulting in 4,096 VACBs per array. On a 64-bit system, a VACB is 64 bytes, resulting in 2,048 VACBs per array. The cache manager allocates the initial VACB array during system initialization and links it into the systemwide list of VACB arrays called *CcVacbArrays*. Each VACB represents one 256-KB view in the system cache, as shown in Figure 10-5. The structure of a VACB is shown in Figure 10-6.

Additionally, each VACB array is composed of two kinds of VACB: *low priority mapping* VACBs and *high priority mapping* VACBs. The system allocates 64 initial high priority VACBs for each VACB array. High priority VACBs have the distinction of having their views preallocated from system address space. When the memory manager has no views to give to the cache manager at the time of mapping some data, and if the mapping request is marked as high priority, the cache manager will use one of the preallocated views present in a high priority VACB. It uses these high priority VACBs, for example, for critical file system metadata as well as for purging data from the cache. After high priority VACBs are gone, however, any operation requiring a VACB view will fail with insufficient resources. Typically, the mapping priority is set to the default of low, but by using the PIN_HIGH_PRIORITY flag when pinning (described later) cached data, file systems can request a high priority VACB to be used instead, if one is needed.

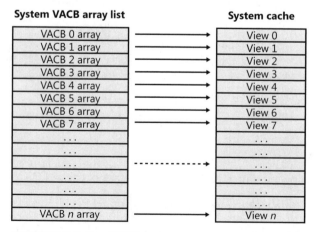

FIGURE 10-5 System VACB array

Virtual address of data in system cache	
Pointer to shared cache map	
File offset	Active count
Link entry to LRU list head	
Pointer to owning VACB array	

FIGURE 10-6 VACB structure

As you can see in Figure 10-6, the first field in a VACB is the virtual address of the data in the system cache. The second field is a pointer to the shared cache map structure, which identifies which file is cached. The third field identifies the offset within the file at which the view begins (always based on 256-KB granularity). Given this granularity, the bottom 16 bits of the file offset will always be zero, so those bits are reused to store the number of references to the view—that is, how many active reads or writes are accessing the view. The fourth field links the VACB into a list of least-recently-used (LRU) VACBs when the cache manager frees the VACB; the cache manager first checks this list when allocating a new VACB. Finally, the fifth field links this VACB to the VACB array header representing the array in which the VACB is stored.

During an I/O operation on a file, the file's VACB reference count is incremented and then it's decremented when the I/O operation is over. When the reference count is nonzero the VACB is *active*. For access to file system metadata, the active count represents how many file system drivers have the pages in that view locked into memory.

EXPERIMENT: Looking at VACBs and VACB Statistics

The cache manager internally keeps track of various values that are useful to developers and support engineers when debugging crash dumps. All these debugging variables start with the *CcDbg* prefix, which makes it easy to see the whole list, thanks to the *x* command:

```
lkd> x nt!*ccdbg*
81d7c09c nt!CcDbgNumberOfFailedMappingsDueToVacbSpace = <no type information>
81d7c0a8 nt!CcDbgNumberOfVacbArraysAllocated = <no type information>
81d7c08c nt!CcDbgNumberOfFailedBitmapAllocations = <no type information>
81d7c098 nt!CcDbgNumberOfFailedHighPriorityMappingsDueToMmResources = <no type
information>
. . .
```

Using these variables and your knowledge of the VACB array header data structures, you can use the kernel debugger to list all the VACB array headers. The *CcVacbArrays* variable stores the list head, which you can print with the *dl* or *!list* command, and then use the debugger's support for list traversal and type referencing to dump the contents of the _VACB_ARRAY_HEADERs on the list:

```
lkd> !list "-t _LIST_ENTRY.Flink -e -x \"dt _VACB_ARRAY_HEADER @$extret\"
poi(CcVacbArrays)"
dt _VACB_ARRAY_HEADER @$extret
nt!_VACB_ARRAY_HEADER
    +0x000 Links              : _LIST_ENTRY [ 0x81d7c0c8 - 0x81d7c0c8 ]
    +0x008 MappingCount       : 0x810
    +0x00c Reserved           : 0
```

The output shows that the system has only one VACB array with 2,064 (0x810) active
VACBs.

Finally, the *CcNumberOfFreeVacbs* variable stores the number of VACBs on the free
VACB list. Dumping this variable on the system used for the experiment results in 2,032
(0x7f1):

```
lkd> dd CcNumberOfFreeVacbs 1 1
81d7c0d8   000007f1
```

As expected, the sum of the free (2,032) and active VACBs (0x7f1—2,064 decimal) on
a 32-bit system with one VACB array equals 4,096, the number of VACBs in one VACB
array. If the system were to run out of free VACBs, the cache manager would try to allo-
cate a new VACB array.

Per-File Cache Data Structures

Each open handle to a file has a corresponding file object. (File objects are explained in detail
in Chapter 7.) If the file is cached, the file object points to a *private cache map* structure that
contains the location of the last two reads so that the cache manager can perform intelligent
read-ahead (described later in the section "Intelligent Read-Ahead"). In addition, all the pri-
vate cache maps for open instances of a file are linked together.

Each cached file (as opposed to file object) has a *shared cache map* structure that describes
the state of the cached file, including its size and its valid data length. (The function of the
valid data length field is explained in the section "Write-Back Caching and Lazy Writing.") The
shared cache map also points to the *section object* (maintained by the memory manager and
which describes the file's mapping into virtual memory), the list of private cache maps associ-
ated with that file, and any VACBs that describe currently mapped views of the file in the sys-
tem cache. (See Chapter 9 for more about section object pointers.) The relationships among
these per-file cache data structures are illustrated in Figure 10-7.

When asked to read from a particular file, the cache manager must determine the answers to
two questions:

1. Is the file in the cache?

2. If so, which VACB, if any, refers to the requested location?

In other words, the cache manager must find out whether a view of the file at the desired address is mapped into the system cache. If no VACB contains the desired file offset, the requested data isn't currently mapped into the system cache.

FIGURE 10-7 Per-file cache data structures

To keep track of which views for a given file are mapped into the system cache, the cache manager maintains an array of pointers to VACBs, which is known as the *VACB index array*. The first entry in the VACB index array refers to the first 256 KB of the file, the second entry to the second 256 KB, and so on. The diagram in Figure 10-8 shows four different sections from three different files that are currently mapped into the system cache.

When a process accesses a particular file in a given location, the cache manager looks in the appropriate entry in the file's VACB index array to see whether the requested data has been mapped into the cache. If the array entry is nonzero (and hence contains a pointer to a VACB), the area of the file being referenced is in the cache. The VACB, in turn, points to the location in the system cache where the view of the file is mapped. If the entry is zero, the cache manager must find a free slot in the system cache (and therefore a free VACB) to map the required view.

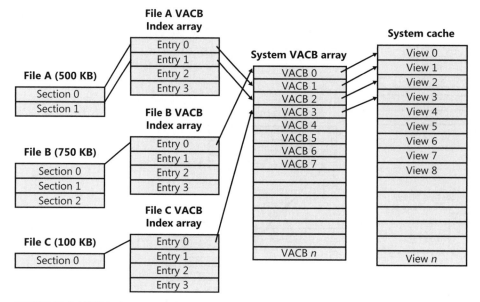

FIGURE 10-8 VACB index arrays

As a size optimization, the shared cache map contains a VACB index array that is four entries in size. Because each VACB describes 256 KB, the entries in this small, fixed-size index array can point to VACB array entries that together describe a file of up to 1 MB. If a file is larger than 1 MB, a separate VACB index array is allocated from nonpaged pool, based on the size of the file divided by 256 KB and rounded up in the case of a remainder. The shared cache map then points to this separate structure.

As a further optimization, the VACB index array allocated from nonpaged pool becomes a sparse multilevel index array if the file is larger than 32 MB, where each index array consists of 128 entries. You can calculate the number of levels required for a file with the following formula:

(Number of bits required to represent file size – 18) / 7

Round the result of the equation up to the next whole number. The value 18 in the equation comes from the fact that a VACB represents 256 KB, and 256 KB is 2^{18}. The value 7 comes from the fact that each level in the array has 128 entries and 2^7 is 128. Thus, a file that has a size that is the maximum that can be described with 63 bits (the largest size the cache manager supports) would require only seven levels. The array is sparse because the only branches that the cache manager allocates are ones for which there are active views at the lowest-level index array. Figure 10-9 shows an example of a multilevel VACB array for a sparse file that is large enough to require three levels.

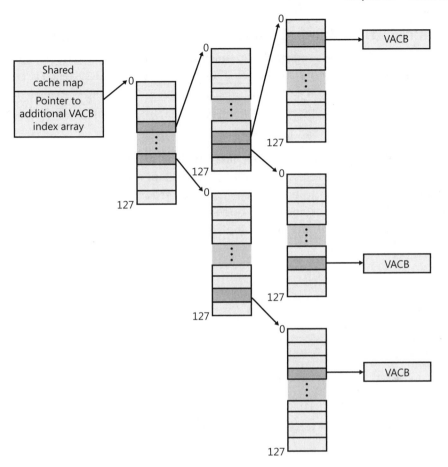

FIGURE 10-9 Multilevel VACB arrays

This scheme is required to efficiently handle sparse files that might have extremely large file sizes with only a small fraction of valid data because only enough of the array is allocated to handle the currently mapped views of a file. For example, a 32-GB sparse file for which only 256 KB is mapped into the cache's virtual address space would require a VACB array with three allocated index arrays because only one branch of the array has a mapping and a 32-GB (2^{35} bytes) file requires a three-level array. If the cache manager didn't use the multilevel VACB index array optimization for this file, it would have to allocate a VACB index array with 128,000 entries, or the equivalent of 1,000 VACB index arrays.

EXPERIMENT: Looking at Shared and Private Cache Maps

You can use the kernel debugger's *dt* command to look at the shared and private cache map data structure definitions and examine the structures on a live system. First, execute the *!filecache* command and locate an entry in the VACB output with a file name you recognize. In this example, the file is the Debugging Tools for Windows Help file:

```
8653c828  120  160   0   0 debugger.chw
```

The first address is that of a control area data structure, which the memory manager uses to keep track of an address range. (See Chapter 9 for more information.) The control area stores the pointer to the file object that corresponds to the view in the cache. A file object identifies an instance of an open file. Execute the following command using the address of the control area of the entry you identified to see the control area structure:

```
lkd> !ca 8653c828

ControlArea @8653c828
  Segment:      e1bce428   Flink             0   Blink              0
  Section Ref          1   Pfn Ref          46   Mapped Views       4
  User Ref             0    WaitForDel        0   Flush Count        0
  File Object 86960228     ModWriteCount     0   System Views       0

  Flags (8008080) File WasPurged Accessed

  File: \Program Files\Debugging Tools for Windows (x86)\debugger.chw
```

Next look at the file object referenced by the control area with this command:

```
lkd> dt nt!_FILE_OBJECT 0x86960228
   +0x000 Type              : 5
   +0x002 Size              : 128
   +0x004 DeviceObject      : 0x84a69a18 _DEVICE_OBJECT
   +0x008 Vpb               : 0x84a63278 _VPB
   +0x00c FsContext         : 0x9ae3e768
   +0x010 FsContext2        : 0xad4a0c78
   +0x014 SectionObjectPointer : 0x86724504 _SECTION_OBJECT_POINTERS
   +0x018 PrivateCacheMap   : 0x86b48460
   +0x01c FinalStatus       : 0
   +0x020 RelatedFileObject : (null)
   +0x024 LockOperation     : 0 ''
...
```

The private cache map is at offset 0x18:

```
lkd> dt nt!_PRIVATE_CACHE_MAP 0x86b48460
   +0x000 NodeTypeCode      : 766
   +0x000 Flags             : _PRIVATE_CACHE_MAP_FLAGS
   +0x000 UlongFlags        : 0x1402fe
   +0x004 ReadAheadMask     : 0xffff
   +0x008 FileObject        : 0x86960228 _FILE_OBJECT
   +0x010 FileOffset1       : _LARGE_INTEGER 0x146
```

```
    +0x018 BeyondLastByte1  : _LARGE_INTEGER 0x14a
    +0x020 FileOffset2      : _LARGE_INTEGER 0x14a
    +0x028 BeyondLastByte2  : _LARGE_INTEGER 0x156
    +0x030 ReadAheadOffset  : [2] _LARGE_INTEGER 0x0
    +0x040 ReadAheadLength  : [2] 0
    +0x048 ReadAheadSpinLock : 0
    +0x04c PrivateLinks     : _LIST_ENTRY [ 0x86b48420 - 0x86b48420 ]
    +0x054 ReadAheadWorkItem : (null)
```

Finally, you can locate the shared cache map in the SectionObjectPointer field of the file object and then view its contents:

```
lkd> dt nt!_SECTION_OBJECT_POINTERS  0x86724504
    +0x000 DataSectionObject : 0x867548f0
    +0x004 SharedCacheMap    : 0x86b48388
    +0x008 ImageSectionObject : (null)

lkd> dt nt!_SHARED_CACHE_MAP 0x86b48388
    +0x000 NodeTypeCode      : 767
    +0x002 NodeByteSize      : 320
    +0x004 OpenCount         : 1
    +0x008 FileSize          : _LARGE_INTEGER 0x125726
    +0x010 BcbList           : _LIST_ENTRY [ 0x86b48398 - 0x86b48398 ]
    +0x018 SectionSize       : _LARGE_INTEGER 0x140000
    +0x020 ValidDataLength   : _LARGE_INTEGER 0x125726
    +0x028 ValidDataGoal     : _LARGE_INTEGER 0x125726
    +0x030 InitialVacbs      : [4] (null)
    +0x040 Vacbs             : 0x867de330  -> 0x84738b30 _VACB
    +0x044 FileObjectFastRef : _EX_FAST_REF
    +0x048 ActiveVacb        : 0x84738b30 _VACB
...
```

Alternatively, you can use the *!fileobj* command to look up and display much of this information automatically. For example, using this command on the same file object referenced earlier results in the following output:

```
lkd> !fileobj 0x86960228

\Program Files\Debugging Tools for Windows (x86)\debugger.chw

Device Object: 0x84a69a18   \Driver\volmgr
Vpb: 0x84a63278
Event signalled
Access: Read SharedRead SharedWrite

Flags:  0xc0042
    Synchronous IO
    Cache Supported
    Handle Created
    Fast IO Read

FsContext: 0x9ae3e768 FsContext2: 0xad4a0c78
Private Cache Map: 0x86b48460
CurrentByteOffset: 156
```

```
Cache Data:
  Section Object Pointers: 86724504
  Shared Cache Map: 86b48388        File Offset: 156 in VACB number 0
  Vacb: 84738b30
  Your data is at: b1e00156
```

File System Interfaces

The first time a file's data is accessed for a read or write operation, the file system driver is responsible for determining whether some part of the file is mapped in the system cache. If it's not, the file system driver must call the *CcInitializeCacheMap* function to set up the per-file data structures described in the preceding section.

Once a file is set up for cached access, the file system driver calls one of several functions to access the data in the file. There are three primary methods for accessing cached data, each intended for a specific situation:

- The copy method copies user data between cache buffers in system space and a process buffer in user space.

- The mapping and pinning method uses virtual addresses to read and write data directly from and to cache buffers.

- The physical memory access method uses physical addresses to read and write data directly from and to cache buffers.

File system drivers must provide two versions of the file read operation—cached and noncached—to prevent an infinite loop when the memory manager processes a page fault. When the memory manager resolves a page fault by calling the file system to retrieve data from the file (via the device driver, of course), it must specify this noncached read operation by setting the "no cache" flag in the IRP.

Figure 10-10 illustrates the typical interactions between the cache manager, the memory manager, and file system drivers in response to user read or write file I/O. The cache manager is invoked by a file system through the copy interfaces (the *CcCopyRead* and *CcCopyWrite* paths). To process a *CcFastCopyRead* or *CcCopyRead* read, for example, the cache manager creates a view in the cache to map a portion of the file being read and reads the file data into the user buffer by copying from the view. The copy operation generates page faults as it accesses each previously invalid page in the view, and in response the memory manager initiates noncached I/O into the file system driver to retrieve the data corresponding to the part of the file mapped to the page that faulted.

The next three sections explain these cache access mechanisms, their purpose, and how they're used.

FIGURE 10-10 File system interaction with cache and memory managers

Copying to and from the Cache

Because the system cache is in system space, it is mapped into the address space of every process. As with all system space pages, however, cache pages aren't accessible from user mode because that would be a potential security hole. (For example, a process might not have the rights to read a file whose data is currently contained in some part of the system cache.) Thus, user application file reads and writes to cached files must be serviced by kernel-mode routines that copy data between the cache's buffers in system space and the application's buffers residing in the process address space. The functions that file system drivers can use to perform this operation are listed in Table 10-2.

TABLE 10-2 Kernel-Mode Functions for Copying to and from the Cache

Function	Description
CcCopyRead	Copies a specified byte range from the system cache to a user buffer
CcFastCopyRead	Faster variation of CcCopyRead, but limited to 32-bit file offsets and synchronous reads
CcCopyWrite	Copies a specified byte range from a user buffer to the system cache
CcFastCopyWrite	Variant of CcCopyWrite, but limited to 32-bit file offsets and synchronous, non-write-through writes; used by redirectors

You can examine read activity from the cache via the performance counters or system per-processor variables stored in the processor's control block (KPRCB) listed in Table 10-3.

TABLE 10-3 KPRCB Fields for Examining Read Activity from the Cache

Performance Counter	KPRCB Field (Count)	Description
Cache: Copy Read Hits %	(CcCopyReadWait + CcCopyReadNoWait) / (CcCopyReadWait + (CcCopyReadWaitMiss + CcCopyReadNoWait) + CcCopyReadNoWaitMiss)	Percentage of copy reads to parts of files that were in the cache (A copy read can still generate paging I/O—the Memory: Cache Faults/sec counter reports page fault activity for the system working set but includes both hard and soft page faults, so the counter still doesn't indicate actual paging I/O caused by cache faults.)
Cache: Copy Reads/sec	CcCopyReadWait + CcCopyReadNoWait	Total copy reads from the cache
Cache: Sync Copy Reads/sec	CcCopyReadWait	Synchronous copy reads from the cache
Cache: Async Copy Reads/sec	CcCopyReadNoWait	Asynchronous copy reads from the cache

Caching with the Mapping and Pinning Interfaces

Just as user applications read and write data in files on a disk, file system drivers need to read and write the data that describes the files themselves (the metadata, or volume structure data). Because the file system drivers run in kernel mode, however, they could, if the cache manager were properly informed, modify data directly in the system cache. To permit this optimization, the cache manager provides the functions shown in Table 10-4. These functions permit the file system drivers to find where in virtual memory the file system metadata resides, thus allowing direct modification without the use of intermediary buffers.

TABLE 10-4 Functions for Finding Metadata Locations

Function	Description
CcMapData	Maps the byte range for read access
CcPinRead	Maps the byte range for read/write access and pins it
CcPreparePinWrite	Maps and pins the byte range for write access (reads are not valid)
CcPinMappedData	Pins a previously mapped buffer
CcSetDirtyPinnedData	Notifies the cache manager that the data has been modified
CcUnpinData	Releases the pages so that they can be removed from memory

If a file system driver needs to read file system metadata in the cache, it calls the cache manager's mapping interface to obtain the virtual address of the desired data. The cache manager touches all the requested pages to bring them into memory and then returns control to the file system driver. The file system driver can then access the data directly.

If the file system driver needs to modify cache pages, it calls the cache manager's pinning services, which keep the pages active in virtual memory so that they cannot be reclaimed.

The pages aren't actually locked into memory (such as when a device driver locks pages for direct memory access transfers). Most of the time, a file system driver will mark its metadata stream "no write", which instructs the memory manager's mapped page writer (explained in Chapter 9) to not write the pages to disk until explicitly told to do so. When the file system driver unpins (releases) them, the cache manager releases its resources so that it can lazily flush any changes to disk and release the cache view that the metadata occupied.

The mapping and pinning interfaces solve one thorny problem of implementing a file system: buffer management. Without directly manipulating cached metadata, a file system must predict the maximum number of buffers it will need when updating a volume's structure. By allowing the file system to access and update its metadata directly in the cache, the cache manager eliminates the need for buffers, simply updating the volume structure in the virtual memory the memory manager provides. The only limitation the file system encounters is the amount of available memory.

You can examine pinning and mapping activity in the cache via the performance counters or per-processor variables stored in the processor's control block (KPRCB) listed in Table 10-5.

TABLE 10-5 KPRCB Fields for Examining Pinning and Mapping Activity

Performance Counter	KPRCB Field (Count)	Description
Cache: Data Map Hits %	(CcMapDataWait + CcMapDataNoWait) / (CcMapDataWait + CcMapDataNoWait) + (CcMapDataWaitMiss + CcMapDataNoWaitMiss)	Percentage of data maps to parts of files that were in the cache (A copy read can still generate paging I/O.)
Cache: Data Maps/sec	CcMapDataWait + CcMapDataNoWait	Total data maps from the cache
Cache: Sync Data Maps/sec	CcMapDataWait	Synchronous data maps from the cache
Cache: Async Data Maps/sec	CcMapDataNoWait	Asynchronous data maps from the cache
Cache: Data Map Pins/sec	CcPinMappedDataCount	Number of requests to pin mapped data
Cache: Pin Read Hits %	(CcPinReadWait + CcPinReadNoWait) / (CcPinReadWait + CcPinReadNoWait) + (CcPinReadWaitMiss + CcPinReadNoWaitMiss)	Percentage of pinned reads to parts of files that were in the cache (A pin read can still generate paging I/O.)
Cache: Pin Reads/sec	CcPinReadWait + CcPinReadNoWait	Total pinned reads from the cache
Cache: Sync Pin Reads/sec	CcPinReadWait	Synchronous pinned reads from the cache
Cache: Async Pin Reads/sec	CcPinReadNoWait	Asynchronous pinned reads from the cache

Caching with the Direct Memory Access Interfaces

In addition to the mapping and pinning interfaces used to access metadata directly in the cache, the cache manager provides a third interface to cached data: *direct memory access* (DMA). The DMA functions are used to read from or write to cache pages without intervening buffers, such as when a network file system is doing a transfer over the network.

The DMA interface returns to the file system the physical addresses of cached user data (rather than the virtual addresses, which the mapping and pinning interfaces return), which can then be used to transfer data directly from physical memory to a network device. Although small amounts of data (1 KB to 2 KB) can use the usual buffer-based copying interfaces, for larger transfers the DMA interface can result in significant performance improvements for a network server processing file requests from remote systems.

To describe these references to physical memory, a *memory descriptor list* (MDL) is used. (MDLs were introduced in Chapter 9.) The four separate functions described in Table 10-6 create the cache manager's DMA interface.

TABLE 10-6 Functions That Create the DMA Interface

Function	Description
CcMdlRead	Returns an MDL describing the specified byte range
CcMdlReadComplete	Frees the MDL
CcMdlWrite	Returns an MDL describing a specified byte range (possibly containing zeros)
CcMdlWriteComplete	Frees the MDL, and marks the range as modified

You can examine MDL activity from the cache via the performance counters or per-processor variables stored in the processor's control block (KPRCB) listed in Table 10-7.

TABLE 10-7 KPRCB Fields for Examining MDL Activity from the Cache

Performance Counter	KPRCB Field (Count)	Description
Cache: MDL Read Hits %	*(CcMdlReadWait + CcMdlReadNoWait) / (CcMdlReadWait + CcMdlReadNoWait) + (CcMdlReadWaitMiss + CcMdlReadNoWaitMiss)*	Percentage of MDL reads to parts of files that were in the cache (References to pages satisfied by an MDL read can still generate paging I/O.)
Cache: MDL Reads/sec	*CcMdlReadWait + CcMdlReadNoWait*	Total MDL reads from the cache
Cache: Sync MDL Reads/sec	*CcMdlReadWait*	Synchronous MDL reads from the cache
Cache: Async MDL Reads/sec	*CcMdlReadNoWait*	Asynchronous MDL reads from the cache

Fast I/O

Whenever possible, reads and writes to cached files are handled by a high-speed mechanism named *fast I/O*. Fast I/O is a means of reading or writing a cached file without going through the work of generating an IRP, as described in Chapter 7. With fast I/O, the I/O manager calls the file system driver's fast I/O routine to see whether I/O can be satisfied directly from the cache manager without generating an IRP.

Because the cache manager is architected on top of the virtual memory subsystem, file system drivers can use the cache manager to access file data simply by copying to or from pages mapped to the actual file being referenced without going through the overhead of generating an IRP.

Fast I/O doesn't always occur. For example, the first read or write to a file requires setting up the file for caching (mapping the file into the cache and setting up the cache data structures, as explained earlier in the section "Cache Data Structures"). Also, if the caller specified an asynchronous read or write, fast I/O isn't used because the caller might be stalled during paging I/O operations required to satisfy the buffer copy to or from the system cache and thus not really providing the requested asynchronous I/O operation. But even on a synchronous I/O, the file system driver might decide that it can't process the I/O operation by using the fast I/O mechanism, say, for example, if the file in question has a locked range of bytes (as a result of calls to the Windows *LockFile* and *UnlockFile* functions). Because the cache manager doesn't know what parts of which files are locked, the file system driver must check the validity of the read or write, which requires generating an IRP. The decision tree for fast I/O is shown in Figure 10-11.

These steps are involved in servicing a read or a write with fast I/O:

1. A thread performs a read or write operation.

2. If the file is cached and the I/O is synchronous, the request passes to the fast I/O entry point of the file system driver stack. If the file isn't cached, the file system driver sets up the file for caching so that the next time, fast I/O can be used to satisfy a read or write request.

3. If the file system driver's fast I/O routine determines that fast I/O is possible, it calls the cache manager's read or write routine to access the file data directly in the cache. (If fast I/O isn't possible, the file system driver returns to the I/O system, which then generates an IRP for the I/O and eventually calls the file system's regular read routine.)

4. The cache manager translates the supplied file offset into a virtual address in the cache.

5. For reads, the cache manager copies the data from the cache into the buffer of the process requesting it; for writes, it copies the data from the buffer to the cache.

6. One of the following actions occurs:

- ❏ For reads where FILE_FLAG_RANDOM_ACCESS wasn't specified when the file was opened, the read-ahead information in the caller's private cache map is updated. Read-ahead may also be queued for files for which the FO_RANDOM_ACCESS flag is not specified.

- ❏ For writes, the dirty bit of any modified page in the cache is set so that the lazy writer will know to flush it to disk.

- ❏ For write-through files, any modifications are flushed to disk.

FIGURE 10-11 Fast I/O decision tree

The performance counters or per-processor variables stored in the processor's control block (KPRCB) listed in Table 10-8 can be used to determine the fast I/O activity on the system.

TABLE 10-8 KPRCB Fields for Determining Fast I/O Activity

Performance Counter	KPRCB Field (Count)	Description
Cache: Sync Fast Reads/sec	*CcFastReadWait*	Synchronous reads that were handled as fast I/O requests
Cache: Async Fast Reads/sec	*CcFastReadNoWait*	Asynchronous reads that were handled as fast I/O requests (These are always zero because asynchronous fast reads aren't done in Windows.)
Cache: Fast Read Resource Misses/sec	*CcFastReadResourceMiss*	Fast I/O operations that couldn't be satisfied because of resource conflicts (This situation can occur with FAT but not with NTFS.)
Cache: Fast Read Not Possibles/sec	*CcFastReadNotPossible*	Fast I/O operations that couldn't be satisfied (The file system driver decides; for example, files with byte range locks can't use fast I/O.)

Read Ahead and Write Behind

In this section, you'll see how the cache manager implements reading and writing file data on behalf of file system drivers. Keep in mind that the cache manager is involved in file I/O only when a file is opened without the FILE_FLAG_NO_BUFFERING flag and then read from or written to using the Windows I/O functions (for example, using the Windows *ReadFile* and *WriteFile* functions). Mapped files don't go through the cache manager, nor do files opened with the FILE_FLAG_NO_BUFFERING flag set.

> **Note** When an application uses the FILE_FLAG_NO_BUFFERING flag to open a file, its file I/O must start at device-aligned offsets and be of sizes that are a multiple of the alignment size; its input and output buffers must also be device-aligned virtual addresses. For file systems, this usually corresponds to the sector size (512 bytes on NTFS, typically, and 2,048 bytes on CDFS). One of the benefits of the cache manager, apart from the actual caching performance, is the fact that it performs intermediate buffering to allow arbitrarily aligned and sized I/O.

Intelligent Read-Ahead

The cache manager uses the principle of spatial locality to perform *intelligent read-ahead* by predicting what data the calling process is likely to read next based on the data that it is reading currently. Because the system cache is based on virtual addresses, which are contiguous for a particular file, it doesn't matter whether they're juxtaposed in physical memory. File read-ahead for logical block caching is more complex and requires tight cooperation between file system drivers and the block cache because that cache system is based on the

relative positions of the accessed data on the disk, and, of course, files aren't necessarily stored contiguously on disk. You can examine read-ahead activity by using the Cache: Read Aheads/sec performance counter or the *CcReadAheadIos* system variable.

Reading the next block of a file that is being accessed sequentially provides an obvious performance improvement, with the disadvantage that it will cause head seeks. To extend read-ahead benefits to cases of strided data accesses (both forward and backward through a file), the cache manager maintains a history of the last two read requests in the private cache map for the file handle being accessed, a method known as *asynchronous read-ahead with history*. If a pattern can be determined from the caller's apparently random reads, the cache manager extrapolates it. For example, if the caller reads page 4000 and then page 3000, the cache manager assumes that the next page the caller will require is page 2000 and prereads it.

Note Although a caller must issue a minimum of three read operations to establish a predictable sequence, only two are stored in the private cache map.

To make read-ahead even more efficient, the Win32 *CreateFile* function provides a flag indicating forward sequential file access: FILE_FLAG_SEQUENTIAL_SCAN. If this flag is set, the cache manager doesn't keep a read history for the caller for prediction but instead performs sequential read-ahead. However, as the file is read into the cache's working set, the cache manager unmaps views of the file that are no longer active and, if they are unmodified, directs the memory manager to place the pages belonging to the unmapped views at the front of the standby list so that they will be quickly reused. It also reads ahead two times as much data (2 MB instead of 1 MB, for example). As the caller continues reading, the cache manager prereads additional blocks of data, always staying about one read (of the size of the current read) ahead of the caller.

The cache manager's read-ahead is asynchronous because it is performed in a thread separate from the caller's thread and proceeds concurrently with the caller's execution. When called to retrieve cached data, the cache manager first accesses the requested virtual page to satisfy the request and then queues an additional I/O request to retrieve additional data to a system worker thread. The worker thread then executes in the background, reading additional data in anticipation of the caller's next read request. The preread pages are faulted into memory while the program continues executing so that when the caller requests the data it's already in memory.

For applications that have no predictable read pattern, the FILE_FLAG_RANDOM_ACCESS flag can be specified when the *CreateFile* function is called. This flag instructs the cache manager not to attempt to predict where the application is reading next and thus disables read-ahead. The flag also stops the cache manager from aggressively unmapping views of the file as the file is accessed so as to minimize the mapping/unmapping activity for the file when the application revisits portions of the file.

Write-Back Caching and Lazy Writing

The cache manager implements a write-back cache with lazy write. This means that data written to files is first stored in memory in cache pages and then written to disk later. Thus, write operations are allowed to accumulate for a short time and are then flushed to disk all at once, reducing the overall number of disk I/O operations.

The cache manager must explicitly call the memory manager to flush cache pages because otherwise the memory manager writes memory contents to disk only when demand for physical memory exceeds supply, as is appropriate for volatile data. Cached file data, how-ever, represents nonvolatile disk data. If a process modifies cached data, the user expects the contents to be reflected on disk in a timely manner.

The decision about how often to flush the cache is an important one. If the cache is flushed too frequently, system performance will be slowed by unnecessary I/O. If the cache is flushed too rarely, you risk losing modified file data in the cases of a system failure (a loss especially irritating to users who know that they asked the application to save the changes) and running out of physical memory (because it's being used by an excess of modified pages).

To balance these concerns, once per second the cache manager's *lazy writer* function exe-cutes on a system worker thread and queues one-eighth of the dirty pages in the system cache to be written to disk. If the rate at which dirty pages are being produced is greater than the amount the lazy writer had determined it should write, the lazy writer writes an additional number of dirty pages that it calculates are necessary to match that rate. System worker threads from the systemwide critical worker thread pool actually perform the I/O operations.

Note The cache manager provides a means for file system drivers to track when and how much data has been written to a file. After the lazy writer flushes dirty pages to the disk, the cache manager notifies the file system, instructing it to update its view of the valid data length for the file. (The cache manager and file systems separately track the valid data length for a file in memory.)

You can examine the activity of the lazy writer by examining the cache performance counters or per-processor variables stored in the processor's control block (KPRCB) listed in Table 10-9.

TABLE 10-9 KPRCB Fields for Examining the Activity of the Lazy Writer

Performance Counter	KPRCB Field (Count)	Description
Cache: Lazy Write Flushes/sec	*CcLazyWritelos*	Number of lazy writer flushes
Cache: Lazy Write Pages/sec	*CcLazyWritePages*	Number of pages written by the lazy writer

EXPERIMENT: Watching the Cache Manager in Action

In this experiment, we'll use Process Monitor to view the underlying file system activity, including cache manager read-ahead and write-behind, when Windows Explorer copies a large file (in this example, a CD-ROM image) from one local directory to another.

First, configure Process Monitor's filter to include the source and destination file paths, the Explorer.exe and System processes, and the ReadFile and WriteFile operations. In this example, the c:\source.iso file was copied to c:\programming\source.iso, so the filter is configured as follows:

You should see a Process Monitor trace like the one shown here after you copy the file:

The first few entries show the initial I/O processing performed by the copy engine and the first cache manager operations. Here are some of the things that you can see:

- The initial 1-MB cached read from Explorer at the first entry. The size of this read depends on an internal matrix calculation based on the file size and can vary from 128 KB to 1 MB. Because this file was large, the copy engine chose 1 MB.

- The 1-MB read is followed by 16 64-KB noncached reads. Noncached reads typically indicate activity due to page faults or cache manager access. A closer look at the stack trace for these events, which you can see by double-clicking an entry and choosing the Stack tab, reveals that indeed the *CcCopyRead* cache manager routine, which is called by the NTFS driver's read routine, causes the memory manager to fault the source data into physical memory:

- After these 64-KB page fault I/Os, the cache manager's read-ahead mechanism starts reading the file, which includes the System process's subsequent non-cached 2-MB read at the 1-MB offset. Because of the file size and Explorer's read I/O sizes, the cache manager chose 2 MB as the optimal read-ahead size. The stack trace for one of the read-ahead operations, shown next, confirms that one of the cache manager's worker threads is performing the read-ahead.

After this point, Explorer's 1-MB reads aren't followed by 64-KB page faults, because the read-ahead thread stays ahead of Explorer, prefetching the file data with its 2-MB noncached reads. Eventually, after reading about 4 MB of the file, Explorer starts performing writes to the destination file. These are sequential, cached 64-KB writes. After about 32 MB of reads, the first WriteFile operation from the System process occurs, shown here:

The write operation's stack trace, shown here, indicates that the memory manager's *mapped page writer* thread was actually responsible for the write:

This occurs because for the first couple of megabytes of data, the cache manager hadn't started performing write-behind, so the memory manager's mapped page writer began flushing the modified destination file data (see Chapter 9 for more information on the mapped page writer).

To get a clearer view of the cache manager operations, remove Explorer from the Process Monitor's filter so that only the System process operations are visible, as shown next.

With this view, it's much easier to see the cache manager's 16-MB write-behind operations (the maximum write sizes are 1 MB on client versions of Windows and 32 MB on server versions; this experiment was performed on a server system). The Time Of Day column shows that these operations occur almost exactly 1 second apart. The stack trace for one of the write-behind operations, shown here, verifies that a cache manager worker thread is performing write-behind:

As an added experiment, try repeating this process with a remote copy instead (from one Windows system to another) and by copying files of varying sizes. You'll notice some different behaviors by the copy engine and the cache manager, both on the receiving and sending sides.

Disabling Lazy Writing for a File

If you create a temporary file by specifying the flag FILE_ATTRIBUTE_TEMPORARY in a call to the Windows *CreateFile* function, the lazy writer won't write dirty pages to the disk unless there is a severe shortage of physical memory or the file is explicitly flushed. This characteristic of the lazy writer improves system performance—the lazy writer doesn't immediately write data to a disk that might ultimately be discarded. Applications usually delete temporary files soon after closing them.

Forcing the Cache to Write Through to Disk

Because some applications can't tolerate even momentary delays between writing a file and seeing the updates on disk, the cache manager also supports write-through caching on a per–file object basis; changes are written to disk as soon as they're made. To turn on write-through caching, set the FILE_FLAG_WRITE_THROUGH flag in the call to the *CreateFile* function. Alternatively, a thread can explicitly flush an open file, by using the Windows *FlushFileBuffers* function, when it reaches a point at which the data needs to be written to disk. You can observe cache flush operations that are the result of write-through I/O requests or explicit calls to *FlushFileBuffers* via the performance counters or per-processor variables stored in the processor's control block (KPRCB) shown in Table 10-10.

TABLE 10-10 KPRCB Fields for Viewing Cache Flush Operations

Performance Counter	KPRCB Field (Count)	Description
Cache: Data Flushes/sec	*CcDataFlushes*	Number of times cache pages were flushed explicitly because of write through or because of the lazy writer
Cache: Data Flush Pages/sec	*CcDataPages*	Number of pages flushed explicitly because of write through or because of the lazy writer

Flushing Mapped Files

If the lazy writer must write data to disk from a view that's also mapped into another process's address space, the situation becomes a little more complicated, because the cache manager will only know about the pages it has modified. (Pages modified by another process are known only to that process because the modified bit in the page table entries for modified pages is kept in the process private page tables.) To address this situation, the memory

manager informs the cache manager when a user maps a file. When such a file is flushed in the cache (for example, as a result of a call to the Windows *FlushFileBuffers* function), the cache manager writes the dirty pages in the cache and then checks to see whether the file is also mapped by another process. When the cache manager sees that the file is, the cache manager then flushes the entire view of the section to write out pages that the second process might have modified. If a user maps a view of a file that is also open in the cache, when the view is unmapped, the modified pages are marked as dirty so that when the lazy writer thread later flushes the view, those dirty pages will be written to disk. This procedure works as long as the sequence occurs in the following order:

1. A user unmaps the view.

2. A process flushes file buffers.

If this sequence isn't followed, you can't predict which pages will be written to disk.

EXPERIMENT: Watching Cache Flushes

You can see the cache manager map views into the system cache and flush pages to disk by running the Reliability and Performance Monitor and adding the Data Maps/ sec and Lazy Write Flushes/sec counters and then copying a large file from one location to another. The generally higher line in the following screen shot shows Data Maps/sec and the other shows Lazy Write Flushes/sec.

Write Throttling

The file system and cache manager must determine whether a cached write request will affect system performance and then schedule any delayed writes. First the file system asks the cache manager whether a certain number of bytes can be written right now without hurting performance by using the *CcCanIWrite* function and blocking that write if necessary. For asynchronous I/O, the file system sets up a callback with the cache manager for automatically writing the bytes when writes are again permitted by calling *CcDeferWrite*. Otherwise, it just blocks and waits on *CcCanIWrite* to continue. Once it's notified of an impending write operation, the cache manager determines how many dirty pages are in the cache and how much physical memory is available. If few physical pages are free, the cache manager momentarily blocks the file system thread that's requesting to write data to the cache. The cache manager's lazy writer flushes some of the dirty pages to disk and then allows the blocked file system thread to continue. This *write throttling* prevents system performance from degrading because of a lack of memory when a file system or network server issues a large write operation.

> **Note** The effects of write throttling are global to the system because the resource it is based on, available physical memory, is global to the system. This means that if heavy write activity to a slow device triggers write throttling, writes to other devices will also be throttled.

The *dirty page threshold* is the number of pages that the system cache will allow to be dirty before throttling cached writers. This value is computed at system initialization time and depends on the product type (client or server). Two other values are also computed—the *top* dirty page threshold and the *bottom* dirty page threshold. Depending on memory consumption and the rate at which dirty pages are being processed, the lazy writer calls the internal function *CcAdjustThrottle,* which, on server systems, performs dynamic adjustment of the current threshold based on the calculated top and bottom values. This adjustment is made to preserve the read cache in cases of a heavy write load that will inevitably overrun the cache and become throttled. Table 10-11 lists the algorithms used to calculate the dirty page thresholds.

TABLE 10-11 Algorithms for Calculating the Dirty Page Thresholds

Product Type	Dirty Page Threshold	Top Dirty Page Threshold	Bottom Dirty Page Threshold
Client	Physical pages / 8	Physical pages / 8	Physical pages / 8
Server	Physical pages / 2	Physical pages / 2	Physical pages / 8

Write throttling is also useful for network redirectors transmitting data over slow communication lines. For example, suppose a local process writes a large amount of data to a remote file system over a 9600-baud line. The data isn't written to the remote disk until the cache manager's lazy writer flushes the cache. If the redirector has accumulated lots of dirty pages

that are flushed to disk at once, the recipient could receive a network timeout before the data transfer completes. By using the *CcSetDirtyPageThreshold* function, the cache manager allows network redirectors to set a limit on the number of dirty cache pages they can tolerate (for each stream), thus preventing this scenario. By limiting the number of dirty pages, the redirector ensures that a cache flush operation won't cause a network timeout.

EXPERIMENT: Viewing the Write-Throttle Parameters

The *!defwrites* kernel debugger command dumps the values of the kernel variables the cache manager uses, including the number of dirty pages in the file cache (*CcTotalDirtyPages*), when determining whether it should throttle write operations:

```
lkd> !defwrites
*** Cache Write Throttle Analysis ***

    CcTotalDirtyPages:                  7 (        28 Kb)
    CcDirtyPageThreshold:          425694 ( 1702776 Kb)
    MmAvailablePages:              572387 ( 2289548 Kb)
    MmThrottleTop:                    450 (      1800 Kb)
    MmThrottleBottom:                  80 (       320 Kb)
    MmModifiedPageListHead.Total:   10477 (     41908 Kb)

Write throttles not engaged
```

This output shows that the number of dirty pages is far from the number that triggers write throttling (*CcDirtyPageThreshold*), so the system has not engaged in any write throttling.

System Threads

As mentioned earlier, the cache manager performs lazy write and read-ahead I/O operations by submitting requests to the common critical system worker thread pool. However, it does limit the use of these threads to one less than the total number of critical system worker threads for small and medium memory systems (two less than the total for large memory systems).

Internally, the cache manager organizes its work requests into four lists (though these are serviced by the same set of executive worker threads):

- The express queue is used for read-ahead operations.

- The regular queue is used for lazy write scans (for dirty data to flush), write-behinds, and lazy closes.

- The fast teardown queue is used when the memory manager is waiting for the data section owned by the cache manager to be freed so that the file can be opened with

an image section instead, which causes *CcWriteBehind* to flush the entire file and tear down the shared cache map.

■ The post tick queue is used for the cache manager to internally register for a notification after each "tick" of the lazy writer thread—in other words, at the end of each pass.

To keep track of the work items the worker threads need to perform, the cache manager creates its own internal *per-processor look-aside list*, a fixed-length list—one for each processor—of worker queue item structures. (Look-aside lists are discussed in Chapter 9.) The number of worker queue items depends on system size: 32 for small-memory systems, 64 for medium-memory systems, 128 for large-memory client systems, and 256 for large-memory server systems. For cross-processor performance, the cache manager also allocates a *global look-aside list* at the same sizes as just described.

Conclusion

The cache manager provides a high-speed, intelligent mechanism for reducing disk I/O and increasing overall system throughput. By caching on the basis of virtual blocks, the cache manager can perform intelligent read-ahead. By relying on the global memory manager's mapped file primitive to access file data, the cache manager can provide the special fast I/O mechanism to reduce the CPU time required for read and write operations and also leave all matters related to physical memory management to the single Windows global memory manager, thus reducing code duplication and increasing efficiency.

Chapter 11
File Systems

In this chapter, we present an overview of the file system formats supported by Windows. We then describe the types of file system drivers and their basic operation, including how they interact with other system components, such as the memory manager and the cache manager. Following that is a description of how to use Process Monitor from Windows Sysinternals (at *www.microsoft.com/technet/sysinternals*) to troubleshoot a wide variety of file system access problems.

In the balance of the chapter, we first describe the Common Log File System (CLFS), a transactional logging virtual file system implemented on the native Windows file system format, NTFS. Then we focus on the on-disk layout of NTFS and its advanced features, such as compression, recoverability, quotas, symbolic links, transactions (which use the services provided by CLFS), and encryption.

To fully understand this chapter, you should be familiar with the terminology introduced in Chapter 8, including the terms *volume* and *partition*. You'll also need to be acquainted with these additional terms:

- *Sectors* are hardware-addressable blocks on a storage medium. Hard disks for x86 systems almost always define a 512-byte sector size; however, Windows also supports large sector disks, which are a new technology that allows access to even larger disks. Thus, if the sector size is the standard 512 bytes and the operating system wants to modify the 632nd byte on a disk, it must write a 512-byte block of data to the second sector on the disk.

- *File system formats* define the way that file data is stored on storage media, and they affect a file system's features. For example, a format that doesn't allow user permissions to be associated with files and directories can't support security. A file system format can also impose limits on the sizes of files and storage devices that the file system supports. Finally, some file system formats efficiently implement support for either large or small files or for large or small disks. NTFS and exFAT are examples of file system formats that offer a different set of features and usage scenarios.

- *Clusters* are the addressable blocks that many file system formats use. Cluster size is always a multiple of the sector size, as shown in Figure 11-1. File system formats use clusters to manage disk space more efficiently; a cluster size that is larger than the sector size divides a disk into more manageable blocks. The potential trade-off of a larger cluster size is wasted disk space, or internal fragmentation, that results when file sizes aren't perfect multiples of cluster sizes.

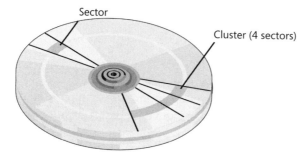

FIGURE 11-1 Sectors and a cluster on a disk

- *Metadata* is data stored on a volume in support of file system format management. It isn't typically made accessible to applications. Metadata includes the data that defines the placement of files and directories on a volume, for example.

Windows File System Formats

Windows includes support for the following file system formats:

- CDFS
- UDF
- FAT12, FAT16, and FAT32
- exFAT
- NTFS

Each of these formats is best suited for certain environments, as you'll see in the following sections.

CDFS

CDFS (\Windows\System32\Drivers\Cdfs.sys), or CD-ROM file system, is a read-only file system driver that supports a superset of the ISO-9660 format as well as a superset of the Joliet disk format. While the ISO-9660 format is relatively simple and has limitations such as ASCII uppercase names with a maximum length of 32 characters, Joliet is more flexible and supports Unicode names of arbitrary length, for example. If structures for both formats are present on a disk (to offer maximum compatibility), CDFS uses the Joliet format. CDFS has a couple of restrictions:

- A maximum file size of 4 GB
- A maximum of 65,535 directories

CDFS is considered a legacy format because the industry has adopted the Universal Disk Format (UDF) as the standard for optical media.

UDF

The Windows UDF file system implementation is OSTA (Optical Storage Technology Association) UDF-compliant. (UDF is a subset of the ISO-13346 format with extensions for formats such as CD-R and DVD-R/RW.) OSTA defined UDF in 1995 as a format to replace the ISO-9660 format for magneto-optical storage media, mainly DVD-ROM. UDF is included in the DVD specification and is more flexible than CDFS. The UDF file system format has the following traits:

- Directory and file names can be 254 ASCII or 127 Unicode characters long.

- Files can be sparse. (Sparse files are defined later in the chapter.)

- File sizes are specified with 64-bits.

- Support for access control lists (ACLs).

- Support for alternate data streams.

The UDF driver supports UDF versions up to 2.60. The UDF format was designed with rewritable media in mind. The Windows UDF driver (\Windows\System32\Drivers\Udfs.sys) provides read-write support for DVD-RAM, CD-R/RW, and DVD+-R/RW drives when using UDF 2.50 and read-only support when using UDF 2.60. However, Windows does not implement support for certain UDF features such as named streams and access control lists.

FAT12, FAT16, and FAT32

Windows supports the FAT file system primarily to enable upgrades from previous versions of Windows, for compatibility with other operating systems in multiboot systems, and as a format for flash drives or memory cards. The Windows FAT file system driver is implemented in \Windows\System32\Drivers\Fastfat.sys.

The name of each FAT format includes a number that indicates the number of bits the format uses to identify clusters on a disk. FAT12's 12-bit cluster identifier limits a partition to storing a maximum of 2^{12} (4,096) clusters. Windows uses cluster sizes from 512 bytes to 8 KB in size, which limits a FAT12 volume size to 32 MB.

 Note All FAT file system types reserve the first two clusters and the last 16 clusters of a volume, so the number of usable clusters for a FAT12 volume, for instance, is slightly less than 4,096.

FAT16, with a 16-bit cluster identifier, can address 2^{16} (65,536) clusters. On Windows, FAT16 cluster sizes range from 512 bytes (the sector size) to 64 KB, which limits FAT16 volume sizes to 4 GB. The cluster size Windows uses depends on the size of a volume. The various sizes are listed in Table 11-1. If you format a volume that is less than 16 MB as FAT by using the *format* command or the Disk Management snap-in, Windows uses the FAT12 format instead of FAT16.

TABLE 11-1 Default FAT16 Cluster Sizes in Windows

Volume Size	Default Cluster Size
0–32 MB	512 bytes
32 MB–64 MB	1 KB
64 MB–128 MB	2 KB
128 MB–256 MB	4 KB
256 MB–512 MB	8 KB
512 MB–1,024 MB	16 KB
1,024 MB–2,048 MB	32 KB
2,048 MB–4,096 MB	64 KB

A FAT volume is divided into several regions, which are shown in Figure 11-2. The file allocation table, which gives the FAT file system format its name, has one entry for each cluster on a volume. Because the file allocation table is critical to the successful interpretation of a volume's contents, the FAT format maintains two copies of the table so that if a file system driver or consistency-checking program (such as Chkdsk) can't access one (because of a bad disk sector, for example), it can read from the other.

Boot sector	File allocation table 1	File allocation table 2 (duplicate)	Root directory	Other directories and all files

FIGURE 11-2 FAT format organization

Entries in the file allocation table define file-allocation chains (shown in Figure 11-3) for files and directories, where the links in the chain are indexes to the next cluster of a file's data. A file's directory entry stores the starting cluster of the file. The last entry of the file's allocation chain is the reserved value of 0xFFFF for FAT16 and 0xFFF for FAT12. The FAT entries for unused clusters have a value of 0. You can see in Figure 11-3 that FILE1 is assigned clusters 2, 3, and 4; FILE2 is fragmented and uses clusters 5, 6, and 8; and FILE3 uses only cluster 7. Reading a file from a FAT volume can involve reading large portions of a file allocation table to traverse the file's allocation chains.

FIGURE 11-3 Sample FAT file-allocation chains

The root directory of FAT12 and FAT16 volumes is preassigned enough space at the start of a volume to store 256 directory entries, which places an upper limit on the number of files and directories that can be stored in the root directory. (There's no preassigned space or size limit on FAT32 root directories.) A FAT directory entry is 32 bytes and stores a file's name, size, starting cluster, and time stamp (last-accessed, created, and so on) information. If a file has a name that is Unicode or that doesn't follow the MS-DOS 8.3 naming convention, additional directory entries are allocated to store the long file name. The supplementary entries precede the file's main entry. Figure 11-4 shows a sample directory entry for a file named "The quick brown fox." The system has created a THEQUI~1.FOX 8.3 representation of the name (that is, you don't see a "." in the directory entry because it is assumed to come after the eighth character) and used two more directory entries to store the Unicode long file name. Each row in the figure is made up of 16 bytes.

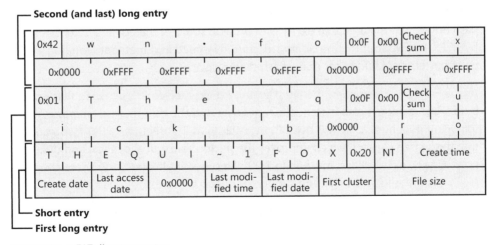

FIGURE 11-4 FAT directory entry

FAT32 uses 32-bit cluster identifiers but reserves the high 4 bits, so in effect it has 28-bit cluster identifiers. Because FAT32 cluster sizes can be as large as 32 KB, FAT32 has a theoretical ability to address 8-terabyte (TB) volumes. Although Windows works with existing FAT32 volumes of larger sizes (created in other operating systems), it limits new FAT32 volumes to a maximum of 32 GB. FAT32's higher potential cluster numbers let it manage disks more efficiently than FAT16; it can handle up to 128-GB volumes with 512-byte clusters. Table 11-2 shows default cluster sizes for FAT32 volumes.

TABLE 11-2 Default Cluster Sizes for FAT32 Volumes

Partition Size	Default Cluster Size
32 MB–8 GB	4 KB
8 GB–16 GB	8 KB
16 GB–32 GB	16 KB
32 GB	32 KB

Besides the higher limit on cluster numbers, other advantages FAT32 has over FAT12 and FAT16 include the fact that the FAT32 root directory isn't stored at a predefined location on the volume, the root directory doesn't have an upper limit on its size, and FAT32 stores a second copy of the boot sector for reliability. A limitation FAT32 shares with FAT16 is that the maximum file size is 4 GB because directories store file sizes as 32-bit values.

exFAT

Designed by Microsoft, the Extended File Allocation Table file system (exFAT, also called FAT64) is an improvement over the traditional FAT file systems and is specifically designed for flash drives. The main goal of exFAT is to provide some of the advanced functionality offered by NTFS, but without the metadata structure overhead and metadata logging that create write patterns not suited for many flash media devices.

As the FAT64 name implies, the file size limit is increased to 2^{64}, allowing files up to 16 exabytes. This change is also matched by an increase in the maximum cluster size, which is currently implemented as 32 MB but can be as large as 2^{255} sectors. exFAT also adds a bitmap that tracks free clusters, which improves the performance of allocation and deletion operations. Finally, exFAT allows more than 1,000 files in a single directory. These characteristics result in increased scalability and support for large disk sizes.

Additionally, exFAT implements certain features previously available only in NTFS, such as support for access control lists (ACLs) and transactions (called Transaction-Safe FAT, or TFAT). While the Windows Embedded CE implementation of exFAT includes these features, the version of exFAT in Windows Vista and Windows Server 2008 does not.

Note ReadyBoost (described in Chapter 9) does not work with exFAT-formatted flash drives.

NTFS

As we said at the beginning of the chapter, the NTFS file system is the native file system format of Windows. NTFS uses 64-bit cluster numbers. This capacity gives NTFS the ability to address volumes of up to 16 exaclusters; however, Windows limits the size of an NTFS volume to that addressable with 32-bit clusters, which is slightly less than 256 TB (using 64-KB clusters). Table 11-3 shows the default cluster sizes for NTFS volumes. (You can override the default when you format an NTFS volume.) NTFS also supports $2^{32}-1$ files per volume. The NTFS format allows for files that are 16 exabytes in size, but the implementation limits the maximum file size to 16 TB.

TABLE 11-3 Default Cluster Sizes for NTFS Volumes

Volume Size	Default Cluster Size
512 MB or less	512 bytes
512 MB–1,024 MB (1 GB)	1 KB
1,024 MB–2,048 MB (2 GB)	2 KB
Greater than 2,048 MB	4 KB

NTFS includes a number of advanced features, such as file and directory security, alternate data streams, disk quotas, sparse files, file compression, symbolic (soft) and hard links, support for transactional semantics, and encryption. One of its most significant features is *recoverability*. If a system is halted unexpectedly, the metadata of a FAT volume can be left in an inconsistent state, leading to the corruption of large amounts of file and directory data. NTFS logs changes to metadata in a transactional manner so that file system structures can be repaired to a consistent state with no loss of file or directory structure information. (File data can be lost, however.) Additionally, the NTFS driver in Windows also implements *self-healing*, a mechanism through which it makes most minor repairs to corruption of file system on-disk structures while Windows is running and without requiring a reboot.

We'll describe NTFS data structures and advanced features in detail later in this chapter.

File System Driver Architecture

File system drivers (FSDs) manage file system formats. Although FSDs run in kernel mode, they differ in a number of ways from standard kernel-mode drivers. Perhaps most significant, they must register as an FSD with the I/O manager and they interact more extensively with the memory manager. For enhanced performance, file system drivers also usually rely on the services of the cache manager. Thus, they use a superset of the exported Ntoskrnl.exe functions that standard drivers use. Just as for standard kernel-mode drivers, you must have the Windows Driver Kit (WDK) to build file system drivers. (See Chapter 1 and *www.microsoft.com/whdc/devtoolswdk* for more information on the WDK.)

Windows has two different types of file system drivers:

- *Local FSDs* manage volumes directly connected to the computer.
- *Network FSDs* allow users to access data volumes connected to remote computers.

Local FSDs

Local FSDs include Ntfs.sys, Fastfat.sys, Exfat.sys, Udfs.sys, Cdfs.sys, and the Raw FSD (integrated in Ntoskrnl.exe). Figure 11-5 shows a simplified view of how local FSDs interact with the I/O manager and storage device drivers. As we described in the section "Volume Mounting" in Chapter 8, a local FSD is responsible for registering with the I/O manager. Once the FSD is registered, the I/O manager can call on it to perform volume recognition when applications or the system initially access the volumes. Volume recognition involves an examination of a volume's boot sector and often, as a consistency check, the file system metadata.

The first sector of every Windows-supported file system format is reserved as the volume's boot sector. A boot sector contains enough information so that a local FSD can both identify the volume on which the sector resides as containing a format that the FSD manages and locate any other metadata necessary to identify where metadata is stored on the volume.

When a local FSD recognizes a volume, it creates a device object that represents the mounted file system format. The I/O manager makes a connection through the volume parameter block (VPB) between the volume's device object (which is created by a storage device driver) and the device object that the FSD created. The VPB's connection results in the I/O manager redirecting I/O requests targeted at the volume device object to the FSD device object. (See Chapter 8 for more information on VPBs.)

FIGURE 11-5 Local FSD

To improve performance, local FSDs usually use the cache manager to cache file system data, including metadata. (For more information on the cache manager, see Chapter 10.) They also integrate with the memory manager so that mapped files are implemented correctly. For example, they must query the memory manager whenever an application attempts to truncate a file in order to verify that no processes have mapped the part of the file beyond the truncation point. (See Chapter 9 for more information on the memory manager.) Windows doesn't permit file data that is mapped by an application to be deleted either through truncation or file deletion.

Local FSDs also support file system dismount operations, which permit the system to disconnect the FSD from the volume object. A dismount occurs whenever an application requires raw access to the on-disk contents of a volume or the media associated with a volume is changed. The first time an application accesses the media after a dismount, the I/O manager reinitiates a volume mount operation for the media.

Remote FSDs

Remote FSDs consist of two components: a client and a server. A client-side remote FSD allows applications to access remote files and directories. The client FSD accepts I/O requests from applications and translates them into network file system protocol commands that the FSD sends across the network to a server-side component, which is typically a remote FSD. A server-side FSD listens for commands coming from a network connection and fulfills them by issuing I/O requests to the local FSD that manages the volume on which the file or directory that the command is intended for resides.

Windows includes a client-side remote FSD named LANMan Redirector (redirector) and a server-side remote FSD named LANMan Server (\%SystemRoot%\System32\Drivers\Srv2.sys). The redirector is implemented as a port/miniport driver combination, where the port driver (\%SystemRoot%\System32\Drivers\Rdbss.sys) is implemented as a driver subroutine library, and the miniport (\%SystemRoot%\System32\Drivers\Mrxsmb.sys) uses services implemented by the port driver. Another redirector miniport driver is WebDAV (\%SystemRoot%\System32\Drivers\Mrxdav.sys), which implements the client side of file access over HTTP. The port/miniport model simplifies redirector development because the port driver, which all remote FSD miniport drivers share, handles many of the mundane details involved with interfacing a client-side remote FSD to the Windows I/O manager. In addition to the FSD components, both LANMan Redirector and LANMan Server include Windows services named Workstation and Server, respectively. Figure 11-6 shows the relationship between a client accessing files remotely from a server through the redirector and server FSDs.

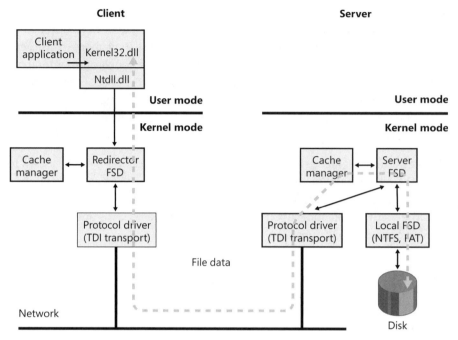

FIGURE 11-6 Common Internet File System file sharing

Windows relies on the Common Internet File System (CIFS) protocol to format messages exchanged between the redirector and the server. CIFS is a version of Microsoft's Server Message Block (SMB) protocol. (For more information on CIFS, go to *www.cifs.com*.)

Like local FSDs, client-side remote FSDs usually use cache manager services to locally cache file data belonging to remote files and directories. However, client-side remote FSDs must implement a distributed cache coherency protocol, called *oplock* (opportunistic locking), so that the data an application sees when it accesses a remote file is the same as the data applications running on other computers that are accessing the same file see. Although server-side remote FSDs participate in maintaining cache coherency across their clients, they don't cache data from the local FSDs because local FSDs cache their own data.

When a client wants to access a server file, it must first request an oplock. The client dictates the kind of caching that the client can perform based on the type of oplock that the server grants.

There are three main types of oplocks:

- A Level I oplock is granted when a client has exclusive access to a file. A client holding this type of oplock for a file can cache both reads and writes on the client system.

- A Level II oplock represents a shared file lock. Clients that hold a Level II oplock can cache reads, but writing to the file invalidates the Level II oplock.

- A Batch oplock is the most permissive kind of oplock. A client with this oplock can cache both reads and writes to the file as well as open and close the file without requesting additional oplocks. Batch oplocks are typically used only to support the execution of batch files, which can open and close a file repeatedly as they execute.

If a client has no oplock, it can cache neither read nor write data locally and instead must retrieve data from the server and send all modifications directly to the server.

An example, shown in Figure 11-7, will help illustrate oplock operation. The server automatically grants a Level I oplock to the first client to open a server file for access. The redirector on the client caches the file data for both reads and writes in the file cache of the client machine. If a second client opens the file, it too requests a Level I oplock. However, because there are now two clients accessing the same file, the server must take steps to present a consistent view of the file's data to both clients. If the first client has written to the file, as is the case in Figure 11-7, the server revokes its oplock and grants neither client an oplock. When the first client's oplock is revoked, or *broken*, the client flushes any data it has cached for the file back to the server.

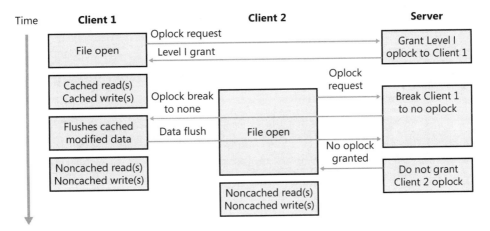

FIGURE 11-7 Oplock example

If the first client hadn't written to the file, the first client's oplock would have been broken to a Level II oplock, which is the same type of oplock the server would grant to the second client. Now both clients can cache reads, but if either writes to the file, the server revokes their oplocks so that noncached operation commences. Once oplocks are broken, they aren't granted again for the same open instance of a file. However, if a client closes a file and then reopens it, the server reassesses what level of oplock to grant the client based on which other clients have the file open and whether or not at least one of them has written to the file.

EXPERIMENT: Viewing the List of Registered File Systems

When the I/O manager loads a device driver into memory, it typically names the driver object it creates to represent the driver so that it's placed in the \Driver object manager directory. The driver objects for any driver the I/O manager loads that have a Type attribute value of SERVICE_FILE_SYSTEM_DRIVER (2) are placed in the \FileSystem directory by the I/O manager. Thus, using a tool such as WinObj (from Sysinternals), you can see the file systems that have registered on a system, as shown in the following screen shot. (Note that some file system drivers also place device objects in the \FileSystem directory.)

Another way to see registered file systems is to run the System Information viewer. Run Msinfo32 from the Start menu's Run dialog box and select System Drivers under Software Environment. Sort the list of drivers by clicking the Type column, and drivers with a Type attribute of SERVICE_FILE_SYSTEM_DRIVER group together.

Note that just because a driver registers as a file system driver type doesn't mean that it is a local or remote FSD. For example, Npfs (Named Pipe File System), which is visible in the list just shown, is a network API driver that supports named pipes but implements a private namespace, and therefore is in some ways like a file system driver. See Chapter 12 for an experiment that reveals the Npfs namespace.

File System Operation

Applications and the system access files in two ways: directly, via file I/O functions (such as *ReadFile* and *WriteFile*), and indirectly, by reading or writing a portion of their address space that represents a mapped file section. (See Chapter 9 for more information on mapped files.) Figure 11-8 is a simplified diagram that shows the components involved in these file system operations and the ways in which they interact. As you can see, an FSD can be invoked through several paths:

- From a user or system thread performing explicit file I/O
- From the memory manager's modified and mapped page writers
- Indirectly from the cache manager's lazy writer
- Indirectly from the cache manager's read-ahead thread
- From the memory manager's page fault handler

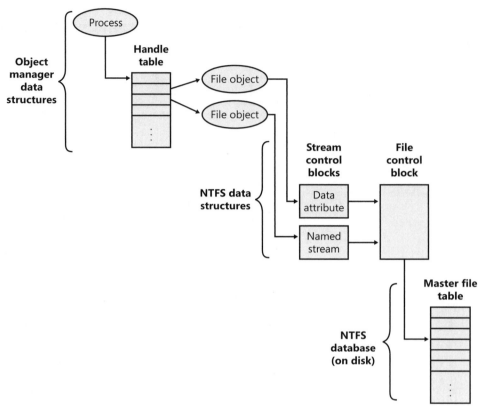

FIGURE 11-8 Components involved in file system I/O

The following sections describe the circumstances surrounding each of these scenarios and the steps FSDs typically take in response to each one. You'll see how much FSDs rely on the memory manager and the cache manager.

Explicit File I/O

The most obvious way an application accesses files is by calling Windows I/O functions such as *CreateFile*, *ReadFile*, and *WriteFile*. An application opens a file with *CreateFile* and then reads, writes, or deletes the file by passing the handle returned from *CreateFile* to other Windows functions. The *CreateFile* function, which is implemented in the Kernel32.dll Windows client-side DLL, invokes the native function *NtCreateFile*, forming a complete root-relative pathname for the path that the application passed to it (processing "." and ".." symbols in the pathname) and prepending the path with "\??" (for example, \??\C:\Daryl\Todo.txt).

The *NtCreateFile* system service uses *ObOpenObjectByName* to open the file, which parses the name starting with the object manager root directory and the first component of the path name ("??"). Chapter 3 includes a thorough description of object manager name resolution and its use of process device maps, but we'll review the steps it follows here with a focus on volume drive letter lookup.

The first step the object manager takes is to translate \?? to the process's per-session namespace directory that the DosDevicesDirectory field of the device map structure in the process object references (which was propagated from the first process in the logon session by using the logon session references field in the logon session's token). Only volume names for network shares and drive letters mapped by the Subst.exe utility are typically stored in the per-session directory, so on those systems when a name (C: in this example) is not present in the per-session directory, the object manager restarts its search in the directory referenced by the GlobalDosDevicesDirectory field of the device map associated with the per-session directory. The GlobalDosDevicesDirectory always points at the \Global?? directory, which is where Windows stores volume drive letters for local volumes. (See the section "Session Namespace" in Chapter 3 for more information.)

The symbolic link for a volume drive letter points to a volume device object under \Device, so when the object manager encounters the volume object, the object manager hands the rest of the pathname to the parse function that the I/O manager has registered for device objects, *IopParseDevice*. (In volumes on dynamic disks, a symbolic link points to an intermediary symbolic link, which points to a volume device object.) Figure 11-9 shows how volume objects are accessed through the object manager namespace. The figure shows how the \GLOBAL??\C: symbolic link points to the \Device\HarddiskVolume3 volume device object.

After locking the caller's security context and obtaining security information from the caller's token, *IopParseDevice* creates an I/O request packet (IRP) of type IRP_MJ_CREATE, creates a file object that stores the name of the file being opened, follows the VPB of the volume device object to find the volume's mounted file system device object, and uses *IoCallDriver* to pass the IRP to the file system driver that owns the file system device object.

When an FSD receives an IRP_MJ_CREATE IRP, it looks up the specified file, performs security validation, and if the file exists and the user has permission to access the file in the way requested, returns a success code. The object manager creates a handle for the file object in the process's handle table, and the handle propagates back through the calling chain, finally reaching the application as a return parameter from *CreateFile*. If the file system fails the create operation, the I/O manager deletes the file object it created for it.

We've skipped over the details of how the FSD locates the file being opened on the volume, but a *ReadFile* function call operation shares many of the FSD's interactions with the cache manager and storage driver. Both *ReadFile* and *CreateFile* are system calls that map to I/O manager functions, but the *NtReadFile* system service doesn't need to perform a name lookup—it calls on the object manager to translate the handle passed from *ReadFile* into a file object pointer. If the handle indicates that the caller obtained permission to read the file when the file was opened, *NtReadFile* proceeds to create an IRP of type IRP_MJ_READ and sends it to the FSD on which the file resides. *NtReadFile* obtains the FSD's device object, which is stored in the file object, and calls *IoCallDriver*, and the I/O manager locates the FSD from the device object and gives the IRP to the FSD.

FIGURE 11-9 Drive-letter name resolution

If the file being read can be cached (that is, the FILE_FLAG_NO_BUFFERING flag wasn't passed to *CreateFile* when the file was opened), the FSD checks to see whether caching has already been initiated for the file object. The PrivateCacheMap field in a file object points to a private cache map data structure (which we described in Chapter 10) if caching is initiated for a file object. If the FSD hasn't initialized caching for the file object (which it does the first time a file object is read from or written to), the PrivateCacheMap field will be null. The FSD calls the cache manager *CcInitializeCacheMap* function to initialize caching, which involves the cache manager creating a private cache map and, if another file object referring to the same file hasn't initiated caching, a shared cache map and a section object.

After it has verified that caching is enabled for the file, the FSD copies the requested file data from the cache manager's virtual memory to the buffer that the thread passed to the *ReadFile* function. The file system performs the copy within a try/except block so that it catches any faults that are the result of an invalid application buffer. The function the file system uses to perform the copy is the cache manager's *CcCopyRead* function. *CcCopyRead* takes as parameters a file object, file offset, and length.

When the cache manager executes *CcCopyRead*, it retrieves a pointer to a shared cache map, which is stored in the file object. Recall from Chapter 10 that a shared cache map stores pointers to virtual address control blocks (VACBs), with one VACB entry for each 256-KB block of the file. If the VACB pointer for a portion of a file being read is null, *CcCopyRead* allocates a VACB, reserving a 256-KB view in the cache manager's virtual address space, and maps (using *MmMapViewInSystemCache*) the specified portion of the file into the view. Then *CcCopyRead* simply copies the file data from the mapped view to the buffer it was passed (the buffer originally passed to *ReadFile*). If the file data isn't in physical memory, the copy operation generates page faults, which are serviced by *MmAccessFault*.

When a page fault occurs, *MmAccessFault* examines the virtual address that caused the fault and locates the virtual address descriptor (VAD) in the VAD tree of the process that caused the fault. (See Chapter 9 for more information on VAD trees.) In this scenario, the VAD describes the cache manager's mapped view of the file being read, so *MmAccessFault* calls *MiDispatchFault* to handle a page fault on a valid virtual memory address. *MiDispatchFault* locates the control area (which the VAD points to) and through the control area finds a file object representing the open file. (If the file has been opened more than once, there might be a list of file objects linked through pointers in their private cache maps.)

With the file object in hand, *MiDispatchFault* calls the I/O manager function *IoPageRead* to build an IRP (of type IRP_MJ_READ) and sends the IRP to the FSD that owns the device object the file object points to. Thus, the file system is reentered to read the data that it requested via *CcCopyRead*, but this time the IRP is marked as noncached and paging I/O. These flags signal the FSD that it should retrieve file data directly from disk, and it does so by determining which clusters on disk contain the requested data and sending IRPs to the volume manager that owns the volume device object on which the file resides. The volume parameter block (VPB) field in the FSD's device object points to the volume device object.

The memory manager waits for the FSD to complete the IRP read and then returns control to the cache manager, which continues the copy operation that was interrupted by a page fault. When *CcCopyRead* completes, the FSD returns control to the thread that called *NtReadFile*, having copied the requested file data—with the aid of the cache manager and the memory manager—to the thread's buffer.

The path for *WriteFile* is similar except that the *NtWriteFile* system service generates an IRP of type IRP_MJ_WRITE and the FSD calls *CcCopyWrite* instead of *CcCopyRead*. *CcCopyWrite*, like *CcCopyRead*, ensures that the portions of the file being written are mapped into the cache and then copies to the cache the buffer passed to *WriteFile*.

If a file's data is already stored in the system's working set, there are several variants on the scenario we've just described. If a file's data is already stored in the cache, *CcCopyRead* doesn't incur page faults. Also, under certain conditions, *NtReadFile* and *NtWriteFile* call an FSD's fast I/O entry point instead of immediately building and sending an IRP to the FSD. Some of these conditions follow: the portion of the file being read must reside in the first

4 GB of the file, the file can have no locks, and the portion of the file being read or written must fall within the file's currently allocated size.

The fast I/O read and write entry points for most FSDs call the cache manager's *CcFastCopy-Read* and *CcFastCopyWrite* functions. These variants on the standard copy routines ensure that the file's data is mapped in the file system cache before performing a copy operation. If this condition isn't met, *CcFastCopyRead* and *CcFastCopyWrite* indicate that fast I/O isn't possible. When fast I/O isn't possible, *NtReadFile* and *NtWriteFile* fall back on creating an IRP. (See the section "Fast I/O" in Chapter 10 for a more complete description of fast I/O.)

Memory Manager's Modified and Mapped Page Writer

The memory manager's modified and mapped page writer threads wake up periodically and when available memory runs low to flush modified pages. The threads call *IoAsynchronousPageWrite* to create IRPs of type IRP_MJ_WRITE and write pages to either a paging file or a file that was modified after being mapped. Like the IRPs that *MiDispatchFault* creates, these IRPs are flagged as noncached and paging I/O. Thus, an FSD bypasses the file system cache and issues IRPs directly to a storage driver to write the memory to disk.

Cache Manager's Lazy Writer

The cache manager's lazy writer thread also plays a role in writing modified pages because it periodically flushes views of file sections mapped in the cache that it knows are dirty. The flush operation, which the cache manager performs by calling *MmFlushSection*, triggers the memory manager to write any modified pages in the portion of the section being flushed to disk. Like the modified and mapped page writers, *MmFlushSection* uses *IoSynchronousPageWrite* to send the data to the FSD.

Cache Manager's Read-Ahead Thread

The cache manager includes a thread that is responsible for attempting to read data from files before an application, a driver, or a system thread explicitly requests it. The read-ahead thread uses the history of read operations that were performed on a file, which are stored in a file object's private cache map, to determine how much data to read. When the thread performs a read-ahead, it simply maps the portion of the file it wants to read into the cache (allocating VACBs as necessary) and touches the mapped data. The page faults caused by the memory accesses invoke the page fault handler, which reads the pages into the system's working set.

Memory Manager's Page Fault Handler

We described how the page fault handler is used in the context of explicit file I/O and cache manager read-ahead, but it is also invoked whenever any application accesses virtual

memory that is a view of a mapped file and encounters pages that represent portions of a file that aren't part of the application's working set. The memory manager's *MmAccessFault* handler follows the same steps it does when the cache manager generates a page fault from *CcCopyRead* or *CcCopyWrite*, sending IRPs via *IoPageRead* to the file system on which the file is stored.

File System Filter Drivers

A filter driver that layers over a file system driver is called a *file system filter driver*. (See Chapter 7 for more information on filter drivers.) The ability to see all file system requests and optionally modify or complete them enables a range of applications, including remote file replication services, file encryption, efficient backup, and licensing. Every commercial on-access virus scanner includes a file system filter driver that intercepts IRPs that deliver IRP_MJ_CREATE commands that issue whenever an application opens a file. Before propagating the IRP to the file system driver to which the command is directed, the virus scanner examines the file being opened to ensure that it's clean of a virus. If the file is clean, the virus scanner passes the IRP on, but if the file is infected the virus scanner communicates with its associated Windows service process to quarantine or clean the file. If the file can't be cleaned, the driver fails the IRP (typically with an access-denied error) so that the virus cannot become active.

Process Monitor

Process Monitor (Procmon), a system activity monitoring utility from Sysinternals that has been used throughout this book, is an example of a passive filter driver, which is one that does not modify the flow of IRPs between applications and file system drivers. Windows includes the Filesystem Filter Manager (%SystemRoot%\System32\Drivers\Fltmgr.sys) as part of a port/miniport model for file system filter drivers. The Filesystem Filter Manager greatly simplifies the development of filter drivers by interfacing a filter miniport driver to the Windows I/O system and providing services for querying file names, attaching to volumes, and interacting with other filters. Process Monitor's file system monitoring is implemented as a *minifilter* driver.

Process Monitor works by extracting a file system filter device driver from its executable image (Procmon.exe) the first time you run it after a boot, installing the driver in memory, and then deleting the driver image from disk. Through the Process Monitor GUI, you can direct the driver to monitor file system activity on local volumes that have assigned drive letters, network shares, named pipes, and mail slots. When the driver receives a command to start monitoring a volume, it registers filtering callbacks with the Filter Manager, which is attached to the device object that represents a mounted file system on the volume. After an attach operation, the I/O manager redirects an IRP targeted at the underlying device object to the driver owning the attached device, in this case the Filter Manager, which sends the event to registered minifilter drivers, in this case Process Monitor.

When the Process Monitor driver intercepts an IRP, it records information about the IRP's command, including target file name and other parameters specific to the command (such as read and write lengths and offsets) to a nonpaged kernel buffer. Twice a second the Process Monitor GUI sends an IRP to Process Monitor's interface device object, which requests a copy of the buffer containing the latest activity and displays the activity in its output window. Process Monitor's use is described further in the next section, "Troubleshooting File System Problems."

Troubleshooting File System Problems

Chapter 4 describes the way that the system and applications store data in the registry. Registry-related problems such as misconfigured security and missing registry values and keys are the source of many system and application failures. The system and applications also use files to store data, and they access executable and DLL image files. Misconfigured NTFS security and missing files or directories are therefore also a common source of system and application failures because the system and applications often make assumptions about what they should be able to access and then misbehave in unexpected ways when the assumptions are violated.

Process Monitor shows all file activity as it occurs, which makes it an ideal tool for trouble-shooting file system–related system and application failures. To run Process Monitor the first time on a system, an account must have the Load Driver and Debug privileges. After loading, the driver remains resident, so subsequent executions require only the Debug privilege.

Process Monitor Basic vs. Advanced Modes

When you run Process Monitor, it starts in basic mode, which shows the file system activity most often useful for troubleshooting. When in basic mode, Process Monitor omits certain file system operations from being displayed, including:

- I/O to NTFS metadata files
- I/O to the paging file
- I/O generated by the System process
- I/O generated by the Process Monitor process

While in basic mode, Process Monitor also reports file I/O operations with friendly names rather than with the IRP types used to represent them. For example, both IRP_MJ_WRITE and FASTIO_WRITE operations display as WriteFile, and IRP_MJ_CREATE operations show as Open if they represent an open operation and as Create for the creation of new files.

EXPERIMENT: Viewing File System Activity on an Idle System

Windows file system drivers implement support for *file change notification*, which enables applications to request notifications of file system changes without polling for them. The Windows functions for doing so include *ReadDirectoryChangesW* and the *FindFirstChangeNotification*, *FindNextChangeNotification* pair. When you run Process Monitor on a system that's idle, you should therefore not see the repeated accesses to files or directories because that activity unnecessarily negatively affects a system's overall performance.

Run Process Monitor, and after several seconds examine the output log to see whether you can spot polling behavior. Right-click on an output line associated with polling, click Properties on the context menu, and then click the Process tab in the Properties dialog box to view details of the process performing the activity.

Process Monitor Troubleshooting Techniques

The two basic Process Monitor troubleshooting techniques for file system problems are identical to those for registry-related problems: looking in a Process Monitor trace at the last thing an application did before it failed, or comparing a Process Monitor trace of a failing application with a trace from a working system. See the section "Process Monitor Troubleshooting Techniques" in Chapter 4 for more information on these techniques.

Entries in a Process Monitor trace that have values of NAME NOT FOUND, NO SUCH FILE, PATH NOT FOUND, SHARING VIOLATION, and ACCESS DENIED in the Result column are ones that you should investigate. The first three are reported when an application or the system attempts to open a nonexistent file or directory. In many cases, these errors do not indicate a serious problem. When you execute a program from the Start menu's Run dialog box without specifying its full path, for instance, Windows Explorer will search the directories listed in the system PATH environment variable for the image file until it locates the file or has searched all the listed directories. Each attempt to find the image in a directory that does not contain it results in a Process Monitor output line similar to this:

```
25314     7:44:27.4180943 PM     Explorer.EXE    1640     CreateFile     C:\Program Files\
Microsoft Windows Performance Toolkit\test.exe     NAME NOT FOUND     Desired Access: Read
Attributes, Disposition: Open, Options: Open Reparse Point, Attributes: n/a, ShareMode:
Read, Write, Delete, AllocationSize: n/a
```

Access-denied errors are a common source of file system–related application failures, and they occur when an application does not have permission to open the file or directory for the access types it desires. Some applications do not check error codes or perform error recovery, and they fail by crashing or terminating; others display misleading error messages that mask the root cause of the error.

Buffer-overflow exploits are a serious security concern, but a code result of BUFFER OVERFLOW is simply a file system driver's way to indicate to an application that the buffer it specified to store result data was too small to hold the data. Application developers use this behavior to determine how large a buffer should be because the file system driver also returns the size of the buffer required to store the data. Operations with a buffer overflow result are usually followed by the same operation with a successful result.

Process Monitor has been used extensively within Microsoft and other organizations to solve difficult or nearly impossible-to-diagnose problems.

Common Log File System

Transactional semantics for a database or a journaled file system often require keeping track of changes made to the data and metadata contained in the files or entries. Typically, these changes are stored in data structures called *log records* through an operation called *logging*. These log records can then be used to undo (roll back), redo, or validate the changes at a later time, even across system reboots.

Windows provides this kind of logging service through the Common Log File System (CLFS) to support the transactional features built into Windows, including transactional NTFS (TxF) and transactional registry (TxR), and to enable third-party developers to take advantage of similar technology. CLFS provides both user-mode and kernel-mode services for creating, reading, and writing CLFS log files. The services are flexible and extensible, which allows the implementation details and structure of the log records stored in a log file to be defined by a caller.

Although CLFS calls itself a file system, it actually provides a virtual abstraction layer on top of NTFS by using *streams* and *containers*, described later. What CLFS exposes as a single virtual log file could actually be a single physical log file, a single log file divided into multiple physical files, or even different log files each divided into multiple physical files. Later, we'll describe how NTFS interacts with CLFS to provide transactional support.

Marshalling

Internally, CLFS encapsulates the functionality of the Algorithm for Recovery and Isolation Exploiting Semantics (ARIES), which allows it to provide reliable recovery and replication of operations by using an industry-approved standard. However, CLFS is not limited to supporting ARIES; it is well suited to a variety of logging scenarios. You can find the full ARIES specification at *www.sai.msu.su/~megera/postgres/gist/papers/concurrency/p94-mohan.pdf*.

The primary job of any high-performance transactional log is to allow log clients to accurately repeat history. CLFS does this by marshalling client log records into memory buffers, forcing them to stable storage, and reading records back on request. After a record makes it

to stable storage and the storage media is intact, CLFS is able to read the record across system failures.

Both user-mode and kernel-mode clients marshal data buffers into log records that are part of a *marshalling area* maintained in the client's address space. When creating a marshalling area, a client must specify the number and size of the log I/O buffers it wants to maintain in its marshaling area. The marshalling runtime implements policy on allocating log I/O buffers, appending them to the log internal queue and flushing them to disk. Clients can override the default marshalling code policy by forcing queue appends and flushes to disk via API calls.

One of the design goals of the CLFS marshalling runtime is to minimize kernel transitions, which it achieves, among other things, through log-space reservation, a requirement for supporting scenarios such as transaction rollbacks. Every time the log marshalling area talks to the CLFS driver (which implies a kernel transition for user-mode clients), the marshalling area tries to negotiate a desired amount of reserved space, usually larger than what is currently required. This means that if the client requires more space in the future, the marshalling area can immediately satisfy the new request without issuing a new kernel transition. Note, however, that if the amount of the reservation cannot be satisfied, the marshalling area will try to get just enough of the reservation to satisfy the user's request (without extra reserved space), which could potentially lead to additional kernel transitions.

Log Types

CLFS supports two types of logs: *dedicated* logs and *multiplexed* logs (also called *common logs*). A dedicated log has a single stream of log records that is used by all the log's clients. A multiplexed log has several streams: each stream has its own clients and its own memory buffers for marshalling log records, but the records from all those buffers are multiplexed into a single queue and written to a single log on stable storage. Multiplexing allows the I/O operations of several streams to be consolidated. When a log is created or opened, CLFS determines whether the log is dedicated or multiplexed depending on whether a dedicated log path or a multiplexed log path is specified.

If the request is for a client on a dedicated log (called a *physical client*), CLFS locates the physical file control block (FCB) object for the file proper and handles the request.

If the request is for a client on a multiplexed log (called a *virtual client*), CLFS locates the corresponding virtual FCB and context control block (CCB) objects to translate the request into an operation on the physical FCB object. CLFS then handles the operation on the CLFS physical FCB object as just described.

In either case, if the request is a cached read, CLFS uses the cache manager's services for accessing cached data. (For more information on the cache manager, see Chapter 10.) Just as it does for requests from other file system drivers, the cache manager maps a view of the file and references the view, which might cause the memory manager to issue noncached reads

to CLFS against the physical log. For flushes and noncached reads, CLFS finds the target container object through the log metadata and issues IRPs to NTFS directly. Figure 11-10 shows the possible CLFS paths for a request coming from user mode or kernel mode.

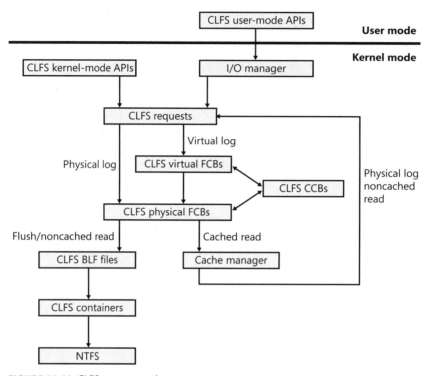

FIGURE 11-10 CLFS request paths

Because each stream of a multiplexed log provides its clients with the illusion that their stream is the entire log, CLFS must include metadata in the physical log that identifies which client each data block belongs to. This data is called the *owner page* and is always exactly one page (4 KB) in size. Each 512 KB of client data results in an owner page to describe it. Since dedicated logs require no tracking of client and data mapping, they don't include owner pages. Figure 11-11 shows two clients writing log records to a multiplexed log and how the writes are kept together in a unified *flush queue* that can then be uniformly flushed to physical storage through a single I/O operation.

Client A
Write three blocks at time t1, t3, and t4

Client B
Write two blocks at time t2 and t5

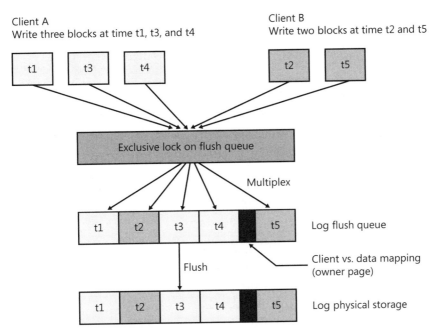

FIGURE 11-11 CLFS multiplexing

The flush queue will be emptied in the following conditions:

- The amount of data in the flush queue exceeds a certain threshold. (The default is 40,000 bytes.)

- The CLFS flush API is called.

- A restart area is being written, and the log needs to be flushed beyond the restart area.

When flushing, CLFS scans the flush queue and determines how many entries need to be flushed. It then issues IRPs to NTFS for the corresponding log files of each of the entries and waits for all the IRPs to complete. If some IRPs fail, CLFS may re-issue IRPs (failures such as low memory condition, lack of quota, and so on are subject to retry) to redo the work and wait again.

Log Layout

A log file is made up of a *base log file* (BLF) that contains metadata and up to 1,023 *containers* that hold the actual data. The base log file is initially 64 KB in size and grows as needed. The log metadata stores information about the log, including the beginning of the log, the container size, the container path, the location from which restart operations should be performed, the log state, the log name, and the log clients. For consistency in case a system failure occurs during a log update, the base log file stores two copies of the log metadata, and

when it makes updates it overwrites the older copy. The BFL stores a value, the *dump count*, that indicates which copy is newer.

A container is the unit of allocation for an active physical log stream. All the containers in a log have the same size, which is a multiple of 512 KB with a 4 GB maximum size. A CLFS client grows or shrinks a log stream by adding or deleting containers from the log file. CLFS implements containers as contiguous files on the volume on which the BLF resides. Figure 11-12 shows the relationship between a base log file and the associated log data stored in containers.

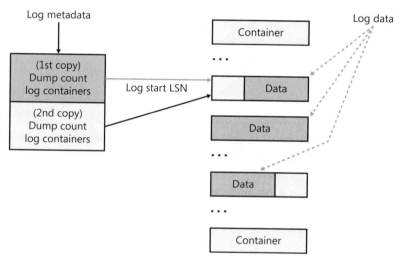

FIGURE 11-12 CLFS base log file and containers

Internally, the CLFS driver places the containers in a container queue to give clients a logical view of a single contiguous physical log stream; in doing so, the CLFS driver maps the *physical container identifier* to a *logical container identifier*. Containers are recycled when the tail of the active log migrates beyond the last sector of the container. Recycling a container involves moving it from the tail to the head of the container queue and appropriately updating its logical container identifier.

Log Sequence Numbers

When a client writes a record to a stream, CLFS returns a *log sequence number* (LSN) that identifies the log record for future reference. The LSNs assigned to the records that are written to a particular stream form an increasing sequence. That is, the LSN assigned to a record that is written to a stream is always greater than the LSN assigned to the previous record written to that same stream. Two critical LSNs that the base log file keeps track of are the *log start LSN* and the *restart LSN*, which, as described earlier, are stored in the BLF metadata.

An LSN is 64 bits wide and consists of three parts, as shown in Figure 11-13:

- A 32-bit container index that identifies the log container where the log record resides
- A 23-bit block offset that identifies an offset within a container
- A 9-bit record offset that identifies a record within a block

32 bits	23 bits	9 bits
Container ID	Block offset	Record offset

FIGURE 11-13 CLFS LSN structure

Log Blocks

Because it is possible that a write to a log might fail, which is called a *torn write,* CLFS uses *log blocks* to track whether log records are fully committed to storage. CLFS stores log records within log blocks, which correspond to 512-byte sectors, and reads and writes data to a log using log blocks. Each log block includes a 2-byte *sector signature* at the end of each sector in the block that stores a sequence number and flags, as well as a copy of the most recently committed signatures in a signature array at the end of the block, as shown in Figure 11-14. Only if all the sector signatures in a log block are valid and match the signatures in the array, does CLFS consider the block valid. If a log block is partially written and a system failure occurs, for example, the signatures won't match, and CLFS considers the log block invalid.

FIGURE 11-14 CLFS log blocks

Owner Pages

As mentioned previously, each 512-KB block of data in a multiplexed log (called a *region*) is correlated with its virtual log through an owner page. Each region consists of 4-KB *pages,* and each page contains one or more sectors, which contain log blocks. The owner page is the last page of a region, as shown in Figure 11-15. Because the owner page is itself a log block, CLFS can detect torn writes on the owner page, just as for a log record, by using the log block signature array.

FIGURE 11-15 CLFS regions and owner pages

An owner page contains two kinds of information:

- For each sector in the region, the virtual log to which the sector belongs as well as the sector's serial number (starting from 0). Because the sector size is 512 bytes, there can be at most 1,024 sectors in a region.

- For each virtual log, the minimum and maximum virtual log LSN for the region. These values give the range of valid virtual LSNs for the region.

CLFS can tell by looking at the owner page of a virtual log LSN whether the record specified by the LSN resides in the current region or not. If the record does not reside in the current region, CLFS can decide whether it should search the previous region or the next region by comparing the virtual log LSN with the virtual log LSN range for the region.

When CLFS inserts log blocks into a multiplexed log's physical FCB flush queue, if it finds that the current log block will overlap the owner page of the current region, it splits the current log block and inserts an owner page log block after the first half of the split log block (as shown in Figure 11-15). In other words, the owner page is only written to disk after the region that it describes becomes full. When a client reopens a multiplexed log file, CLFS scans the regions and rebuilds an in-memory owner page describing the latest region for which it hasn't written an owner page log block.

Note that when reopening the log file, CLFS doesn't know exactly where the log end LSN is, so it must find the LSN to avoid losing data or using corrupted data. For a dedicated log, CLFS reads the log blocks sequentially until an invalid log block is found and then sets the end of the log there. For a multiplexed log, CLFS reads the last owner page (the base log file saves a copy of the last flushed owner page's LSN when the log metadata is last flushed) and verifies it is indeed valid. CLFS then reads the next region's owner page repeatedly until an invalid owner page is found. After that, CLFS scans backward to find the first region with only valid log data blocks. CLFS then assumes the end of the log must fall within the next region. It will scan log block by log block until an invalid log block is found and then set the end of the log there.

Translating Virtual LSNs to Physical LSNs

CLFS relies on physical LSNs to identify log blocks within a physical log. However, CLFS combines several virtual logs in a physical log for multiplexed logs and uses virtual LSNs to locate log blocks in a virtual log. Therefore, for a virtual log client, a log block can be addressed both by a physical LSN and by a virtual LSN.

To translate a virtual log LSN to a physical log LSN, CLFS follows these steps:

1. Reads the owner page for the region indicated by the virtual log LSN.

2. Checks the owner page's virtual LSN region to see whether the virtual LSN is actually in the region or not. Most of the time the log block will be in the region.

3. If the virtual LSN is in the region, CLFS refers to the *sector to client mapping* in the owner page to find the physical LSN's block offset. Given a client's virtual LSN and its size, CLFS can calculate the virtual LSN of the next log block. Applying this rule, CLFS can deterministically calculate the physical LSN of every virtual log block in the region, as shown in Figure 11-16.

4. If the virtual LSN is not in the region, CLFS searches either the previous region or the next region depending on whether the virtual LSN is smaller or larger than the current region's virtual LSN range.

```
Owner page
Sector 0: Client 1 1st sector of block
Sector 1: Client 1 2nd sector of block
Sector 2: Client 2 1st sector of block
Sector 3: Client 2 2nd sector of block
Sector 4: Client 2 3rd sector of block
Sector 5: Client 2 4th sector of block
Sector 6: Client 1 1st sector of block
Sector 7: Client 1 2nd sector of block
Sector 8: Client 1 1st sector of block
Sector 9: Client 1 2nd sector of block
Sector 10: Client 2 1st sector of block
Client 1 virtual LSN range (0.0.0 ~ 0.1400.0)
Client 2 virtual LSN range (0.0.0 ~ 0.1600.0)
```

```
To translate client 1 virtual LSN 0.1000.0:
1.  Search owner page. The first sector
    that belongs to client 1 is physical LSN
    0.0.0. This block's size is 2 sectors. So,
    its next virtual LSN must be 0.400.0.
2.  Search owner page again. The next
    block that belongs to client 1 is physical
    LSN 0.C00.0. This block's size is 2 sectors.
    So, its next virtual LSN must be 0.1000.0.
    Find a match.
3.  Search the owner page again. The next
    block that belongs to client 1 is physical
    LSN 0.1000.0. Done. Return 0.1000.0.
```

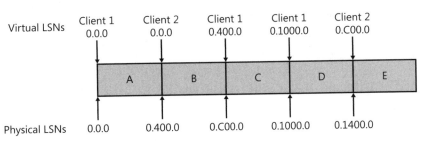

FIGURE 11-16 CLFS virtual to physical LSN translation

Management Policies

Each CLFS log can be defined by a set of management policies that are configurable by the client. Table 11-4 lists these policies and their usage.

TABLE 11-4 CLFS Management Policies

Policy Name	Description
ClfsMgmtPolicyMaximumSize	Specifies the maximum size of a log.
ClfsMgmtPolicyMinimumSize	Specifies the minimum size of a log.
ClfsMgmtPolicyNewContainerSize	Specifies the size of new containers that are created.
ClfsMgmtPolicyGrowthRate	Specifies how many new containers will be added to the log each time the log grows. Can be specified as either a relative percentage or an absolute number.
ClfsMgmtPolicyLogTail	Specifies how much free space will be requested when a client is notified to move its log tail. Can be specified as either a minimum percentage of free space or a minimum number of containers.
ClfsMgmtPolicyAutoShrink	Specifies when the log will shrink based on the percentage of the log that is free.
ClfsMgmtPolicyAutoGrow	Specifies whether the log should grow when fewer than two containers are free.
ClfsMgmtPolicyNewContainerPrefix	Specifies a prefix for the file name of each container, as well as the full path to the directory where the containers are located.

NTFS Design Goals and Features

In the following section, we'll look at the requirements that drove the design of NTFS. Then in the subsequent section, we'll examine the advanced features of NTFS.

High-End File System Requirements

From the start, NTFS was designed to include features required of an enterprise-class file system. To minimize data loss in the face of an unexpected system outage or crash, a file system must ensure that the integrity of its metadata is guaranteed at all times; and to protect sensitive data from unauthorized access, a file system must have an integrated security model. Finally, a file system must allow for software-based data redundancy as a low-cost alternative to hardware-redundant solutions for protecting user data. In this section, you'll find out how NTFS implements each of these capabilities.

Recoverability

To address the requirement for reliable data storage and data access, NTFS provides file system recovery based on the concept of an *atomic transaction*. Atomic transactions are a

technique for handling modifications to a database so that system failures don't affect the correctness or integrity of the database. The basic tenet of atomic transactions is that some database operations, called *transactions*, are all-or-nothing propositions. (A *transaction* is defined as an I/O operation that alters file system data or changes the volume's directory structure.) The separate disk updates that make up the transaction must be executed *atomically*—that is, once the transaction begins to execute, all its disk updates must be completed. If a system failure interrupts the transaction, the part that has been completed must be undone, or *rolled back*. The rollback operation returns the database to a previously known and consistent state, as if the transaction had never occurred.

NTFS uses atomic transactions to implement its file system recovery feature. If a program initiates an I/O operation that alters the structure of an NTFS volume—that is, changes the directory structure, extends a file, allocates space for a new file, and so on—NTFS treats that operation as an atomic transaction. It guarantees that the transaction is either completed or, if the system fails while executing the transaction, rolled back. The details of how NTFS does this are explained in the section "NTFS Recovery Support" later in the chapter. In addition, NTFS uses redundant storage for vital file system information so that if a sector on the disk goes bad, NTFS can still access the volume's critical file system data.

Security

Security in NTFS is derived directly from the Windows object model. Files and directories are protected from being accessed by unauthorized users. (For more information on Windows security, see Chapter 6.) An open file is implemented as a file object with a security descriptor stored on disk as a part of the file. Before a process can open a handle to any object, including a file object, the Windows security system verifies that the process has appropriate authorization to do so. The security descriptor, combined with the requirement that a user log on to the system and provide an identifying password, ensures that no process can access a file unless given specific permission to do so by a system administrator or by the file's owner. (For more information about security descriptors, see the section "Security Descriptors and Access Control" in Chapter 6, and for more details about file objects, see the section "Opening Devices" in Chapter 7.)

Data Redundancy and Fault Tolerance

In addition to recoverability of file system data, some customers require that their own data not be endangered by a power outage or catastrophic disk failure. The NTFS recovery capabilities do ensure that the file system on a volume remains accessible, but they make no guarantees for complete recovery of user files. Protection for applications that can't risk losing file data is provided through data redundancy.

Data redundancy for user files is implemented via the Windows layered driver model (explained in Chapter 7), which provides fault-tolerant disk support. NTFS communicates with a volume manager, which in turn communicates with a hard disk driver to write data to

disk. A volume manager can *mirror*, or duplicate, data from one disk onto another disk so that a redundant copy can always be retrieved. This support is commonly called *RAID level 1*. Volume managers also allow data to be written in *stripes* across three or more disks, using the equivalent of one disk to maintain parity information. If the data on one disk is lost or becomes inaccessible, the driver can reconstruct the disk's contents by means of exclusive-OR operations. This support is called *RAID level 5*. (See Chapter 8 for more information on striped volumes, mirrored volumes, and RAID-5 volumes.)

Advanced Features of NTFS

In addition to NTFS being recoverable, secure, reliable, and efficient for mission-critical systems, it includes the following advanced features that allow it to support a broad range of applications. Some of these features are exposed as APIs for applications to leverage, and others are internal features:

- Multiple data streams
- Unicode-based names
- General indexing facility
- Dynamic bad-cluster remapping
- Hard links
- Symbolic (soft) links and junctions
- Compression and sparse files
- Change logging
- Per-user volume quotas
- Link tracking
- Encryption
- POSIX support
- Defragmentation
- Read-only support and dynamic partitioning

The following sections provide an overview of these features.

Multiple Data Streams

In NTFS, each unit of information associated with a file—including its name, its owner, its time stamps, its contents, and so on—is implemented as a file attribute (NTFS object attribute). Each attribute consists of a single *stream*—that is, a simple sequence of bytes. This generic implementation makes it easy to add more attributes (and therefore more streams)

to a file. Because a file's data is "just another attribute" of the file and because new attributes can be added, NTFS files (and file directories) can contain multiple data streams.

An NTFS file has one default data stream, which has no name. An application can create additional, named data streams and access them by referring to their names. To avoid altering the Windows I/O APIs, which take a string as a file name argument, the name of the data stream is specified by appending a colon (:) to the file name. Because the colon is a reserved character, it can serve as a separator between the file name and the data stream name, as illustrated in this example:

```
myfile.dat:stream2
```

Each stream has a separate allocation size (which defines how much disk space has been reserved for it), actual size (which is how many bytes the caller has used), and valid data length (which is how much of the stream has been initialized). In addition, each stream is given a separate file lock that is used to lock byte ranges and to allow concurrent access.

One component in Windows that uses multiple data streams is the Attachment Execution Service, which is invoked whenever the standard Windows API for saving Internet-based attachments is used by applications such as Internet Explorer or Outlook. Depending on which *zone* the file was downloaded from (such as the My Computer zone, the Intranet zone or the Untrusted zone), Windows Explorer might warn the user that the file came from a possibly untrusted location or even completely block access to the file. For example, Figure 11-17 shows the dialog box that's displayed when executing Process Explorer after it was downloaded from the Sysinternals site.

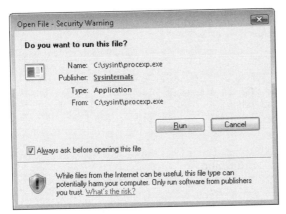

FIGURE 11-17 Security warning for files downloaded from the Internet

Other applications can use the multiple data stream feature as well. A backup utility, for example, might use an extra data stream to store backup-specific time stamps on files. Or an archival utility might implement hierarchical storage in which files that are older than a certain date or that haven't been accessed for a specified period of time are moved to tape.

The utility could copy the file to tape, set the file's default data stream to 0, and add a data stream that specifies the name and location of the tape on which the file is stored.

EXPERIMENT: Looking at Streams

Most Windows applications aren't designed to work with alternate named streams, but both the *echo* and *more* commands are. Thus, a simple way to view streams in action is to create a named stream using *echo* and then display it using *more*. The following command sequence creates a file named test with a stream named stream:

```
C:\>echo hello > test:stream
C:\>more < test:stream
hello
C:\>
```

If you perform a directory listing, test's file size doesn't reflect the data stored in the alternate stream because NTFS returns the size of only the unnamed data stream for file query operations, including directory listings.

```
C:\>dir test
 Volume in drive C is WINDOWS
 Volume Serial Number is 3991-3040

 Directory of C:\

08/01/00  02:37p                        0 test
               1 File(s)                0 bytes
                         112,558,080 bytes free
```

You can determine what files and directories on your system have alternate data streams with the Streams utility from Sysinternals (see the following output) or by using the */r* switch in the *dir* command.

```
C:\>streams test

Streams v1.56 - Enumerate alternate NTFS data streams
Copyright (C) 1999-2007 Mark Russinovich
Sysinternals - www.sysinternals.com

C:\Temp\test:
        :stream:$DATA 8
```

Unicode-Based Names

Like Windows as a whole, NTFS is fully Unicode enabled, using Unicode characters to store names of files, directories, and volumes. Unicode, a 16-bit character-coding scheme, allows each character in each of the world's major languages to be uniquely represented, which aids in moving data easily from one country to another. Unicode is an improvement over the

traditional representation of international characters—using a double-byte coding scheme that stores some characters in 8 bits and others in 16 bits, a technique that requires loading various code pages to establish the available characters. Because Unicode has a unique representation for each character, it doesn't depend on which code page is loaded. Each directory and file name in a path can be as many as 255 characters long and can contain Unicode characters, embedded spaces, and multiple periods.

General Indexing Facility

The NTFS architecture is structured to allow indexing of file attributes on a disk volume. This structure enables the file system to efficiently locate files that match certain criteria— for example, all the files in a particular directory. The FAT file system indexes file names but doesn't sort them, making lookups in large directories slow.

Several NTFS features take advantage of general indexing, including consolidated security descriptors, in which the security descriptors of a volume's files and directories are stored in a single internal stream, have duplicates removed, and are indexed using an internal security identifier that NTFS defines. The use of indexing by these features is described in the section "NTFS On-Disk Structure" later in this chapter.

Dynamic Bad-Cluster Remapping

Ordinarily, if a program tries to read data from a bad disk sector, the read operation fails and the data in the allocated cluster becomes inaccessible. If the disk is formatted as a fault-tolerant NTFS volume, however, the Windows fault-tolerant driver dynamically retrieves a good copy of the data that was stored on the bad sector and then sends NTFS a warning that the sector is bad. NTFS allocates a new cluster, replacing the cluster in which the bad sector resides, and copies the data to the new cluster. It flags the bad cluster and no longer uses it. This data recovery and dynamic bad-cluster remapping is an especially useful feature for file servers and fault-tolerant systems or for any application that can't afford to lose data. If the volume manager isn't loaded when a sector goes bad, NTFS still replaces the cluster and doesn't reuse it, but it can't recover the data that was on the bad sector.

Hard Links

A hard link allows multiple paths to refer to the same file. (Hard links are not supported on directories.) If you create a hard link named C:\Documents\Spec.doc that refers to the existing file C:\Users\Administrator\Documents\Spec.doc, the two paths link to the same on-disk file and you can make changes to the file using either path. Processes can create hard links with the Windows *CreateHardLink* function or the *ln* POSIX function.

NTFS implements hard links by keeping a reference count on the actual data, where each time a hard link is created for the file, an additional file name reference is made to the data. This means that if you have multiple hard links for a file, you can delete the original file name

that referenced the data (C:\Users\Administrator\Documents\Spec.doc in our example), and the other hard links (C:\Documents\Spec.doc) will remain and point to the data. However, because hard links are on-disk local references to data (represented by *file reference records*), they can exist only within the same volume and can't span volumes or computers.

EXPERIMENT: Creating a Hard Link

There are two ways you can create a hard link: the *fsutil hardlink create* command or the *mklink* utility with the */H* option. In this experiment we'll use *mklink* because we'll use this utility later to create a symbolic link as well. First, create a file called test.txt and add some text to it, as shown here.

```
C:\>echo hello > test.txt
```

Now create a hard link called hard.txt as shown here:

```
C:\>mklink hard.txt test.txt /H
Hardlink created for hard.txt <<===>> test.txt
```

If you list the directory's contents, you'll notice that the two files will be identical in every way, with the same creation date, permissions, and file size; only the file names differ.

```
C:\>dir *.txt
 Volume in drive C is OS
 Volume Serial Number is 38D4-EA71
 Directory of C:\
10/18/2008  11:55 PM                     8 hard.txt
10/18/2008  11:55 PM                     8 test.txt
               2 File(s)             16 bytes
               0 Dir(s)   10,646,011,904 bytes free
```

Symbolic (Soft) Links and Junctions

In addition to hard links, NTFS supports another type of file-name aliasing called *symbolic links* or *soft links*. Unlike hard links, symbolic links are strings that are interpreted dynamically and can be relative or absolute paths that refer to locations on any storage device, including ones on a different local volume or even a share on a different system. This means that symbolic links don't actually increase the reference count of the original file, so deleting the original file will result in the loss of the data, and a symbolic link that points to a non-existing file will be left behind. Finally, unlike hard links, symbolic links can point to directories, not just files, which gives them an added advantage.

For example, if the path C:\Drivers is a directory symbolic link that redirects to C:\%SystemRoot%\System32\Drivers, an application reading C:\Drivers\Ntfs.sys actually reads C:\%SystemRoot%\System\Drivers\Ntfs.sys. Directory symbolic links are a useful way to lift

directories that are deep in a directory tree to a more convenient depth without disturbing the original tree's structure or contents. The example just cited lifts the Drivers directory to the volume's root directory, reducing the directory depth of Ntfs.sys from three levels to one when Ntfs.sys is accessed through the directory symbolic link. File symbolic links work much the same way—you can think of them as shortcuts, except they are actually implemented on the file system instead of being .lnk files managed by Windows Explorer. Just like hard links, symbolic links can be created with the *mklink* utility (without the */H* option) or through the *CreateSymbolicLink* API.

Because certain legacy applications might not behave securely in the presence of symbolic links, especially across different machines, the creation of symbolic links requires the SeCreateSymbolicLink privilege, which is typically granted only to administrators. The file system also has a behavior option called *SymLinkEvaluation* that can be configured with the following command:

```
fsutil behavior set SymLinkEvaluation
```

By default, the Windows default symbolic link evaluation policy allows only local-to-local and local-to-remote symbolic links but not the opposite, as shown here:

```
C:\>fsutil behavior query SymLinkEvaluation
Local to local symbolic links are enabled.
Local to remote symbolic links are enabled.
Remote to local symbolic links are disabled.
Remote to Remote symbolic links are disabled.
```

Symbolic links are based on an NTFS mechanism called *reparse points*. (Reparse points are discussed further in the section "Reparse Points" later in this chapter.) A reparse point is a file or directory that has a block of data called *reparse data* associated with it. Reparse data is user-defined data about the file or directory, such as its state or location, that can be read from the reparse point by the application that created the data, a file system filter driver, or the I/O manager. When NTFS encounters a reparse point during a file or directory lookup, it returns a *reparse status code*, which signals file system filter drivers that are attached to the volume and the I/O manager to examine the reparse data. Each reparse point type has a unique *reparse tag*. The reparse tag allows the component responsible for interpreting the reparse point's reparse data to recognize the reparse point without having to check the reparse data. A reparse tag owner, either a file system filter driver or the I/O manager, can choose one of the following options when it recognizes reparse data:

- The reparse tag owner can manipulate the pathname specified in the file I/O operation that crosses the reparse point and let the I/O operation reissue with the altered pathname. Junctions (described shortly) take this approach to redirect a directory lookup, for example.

- The reparse tag owner can remove the reparse point from the file, alter the file in some way, and then reissue the file I/O operation.

There are no Windows functions for creating reparse points. Instead, processes must use the FSCTL_SET_REPARSE_POINT file system control code with the Windows *DeviceIoControl* function. A process can query a reparse point's contents with the FSCTL_GET_REPARSE_POINT file system control code. The FILE_ATTRIBUTE_REPARSE_POINT flag is set in a reparse point's file attributes, so applications can check for reparse points by using the Windows *GetFileAttributes* function.

Another type of reparse point that NTFS supports is the *junction*. Junctions are a legacy NTFS concept and work almost identically to directory symbolic links, except they can only be local to a volume. There is no advantage to using a junction instead of a directory symbolic link, except that junctions are compatible with older versions of Windows, while directory symbolic links are not.

EXPERIMENT: Creating a Symbolic Link

This experiment shows you the main difference between a symbolic link and a hard link, even when dealing with files on the same volume. Create a symbolic link called soft.txt as shown here, pointing to the test.txt file created in the previous experiment:

```
C:\>mklink soft.txt test.txt
symbolic link created for soft.txt <<===>> test.txt
```

If you list the directory's contents, you'll notice that the symbolic link doesn't have a file size and is identified by the <SYMLINK> type. Furthermore, you'll note that the creation time is that of the symbolic link, not of the target file. The symbolic link can also have security permissions that are different from the permissions on the target file.

```
C:\>dir *.txt
 Volume in drive C is OS
 Volume Serial Number is 38D4-EA71

 Directory of C:\

10/18/2008  11:55 PM                     8 hard.txt
10/19/2008  12:28 AM    <SYMLINK>          soft.txt [test.txt]
10/18/2008  11:55 PM                     8 test.txt
               3 File(s)             16 bytes
               0 Dir(s)   10,636,480,512 bytes free
```

Finally, if you delete the original test.txt file, you can verify that both the hard link and symbolic link still exist but that the symbolic link does not point to a valid file anymore, while the hard link references the file data.

Compression and Sparse Files

NTFS supports compression of file data. Because NTFS performs compression and decompression procedures transparently, applications don't have to be modified to take advantage of this feature. Directories can also be compressed, which means that any files subsequently created in the directory are compressed.

Applications compress and decompress files by passing *DeviceIoControl* the FSCTL_SET_COMPRESSION file system control code. They query the compression state of a file or directory with the FSCTL_GET_COMPRESSION file system control code. A file or directory that is compressed has the FILE_ATTRIBUTE_COMPRESSED flag set in its attributes, so applications can also determine a file or directory's compression state with *GetFileAttributes*.

A second type of compression is known as *sparse files*. If a file is marked as sparse, NTFS doesn't allocate space on a volume for portions of the file that an application designates as empty. NTFS returns 0-filled buffers when an application reads from empty areas of a sparse file. This type of compression can be useful for client/server applications that implement circular-buffer logging, in which the server records information to a file and clients asynchronously read the information. Because the information that the server writes isn't needed after a client has read it, there's no need to store the information in the file. By making such a file sparse, the client can specify the portions of the file it reads as empty, freeing up space on the volume. The server can continue to append new information to the file without fear that the file will grow to consume all available space on the volume.

As for compressed files, NTFS manages sparse files transparently. Applications specify a file's sparseness state by passing the FSCTL_SET_SPARSE file system control code to *DeviceIoControl*. To set a range of a file to empty, applications use the FSCTL_SET_ZERO_DATA code, and they can ask NTFS for a description of what parts of a file are sparse by using the control code FSCTL_QUERY_ALLOCATED_RANGES. One application of sparse files is the NTFS *change journal*, described next.

Change Logging

Many types of applications need to monitor volumes for file and directory changes. For example, an automatic backup program might perform an initial full backup and then incremental backups based on file changes. An obvious way for an application to monitor a volume for changes is for it to scan the volume, recording the state of files and directories, and on a subsequent scan detect differences. This process can adversely affect system performance, however, especially on computers with thousands or tens of thousands of files.

An alternate approach is for an application to register a directory notification by using the *FindFirstChangeNotification* or *ReadDirectoryChangesW* Windows function. As an input parameter, the application specifies the name of a directory it wants to monitor, and the function returns whenever the contents of the directory change. Although this approach

is more efficient than volume scanning, it requires the application to be running at all times. Using these functions can also require an application to scan directories because *FindFirstChangeNotification* doesn't indicate what changed—just that something in the directory has changed. An application can pass a buffer to *ReadDirectoryChangesW* that the FSD fills in with change records. If the buffer overflows, however, the application must be prepared to fall back on scanning the directory.

NTFS provides a third approach that overcomes the drawbacks of the first two: an application can configure the NTFS change journal facility by using the *DeviceIoControl* function's FSCTL_CREATE_USN_JOURNAL file system control code to have NTFS record information about file and directory changes to an internal file called the *change journal*. A change journal is usually large enough to virtually guarantee that applications get a chance to process changes without missing any. Applications use the FSCTL_QUERY_USN_JOURNAL file system control code to read records from a change journal, and they can specify that the *DeviceIoControl* function not complete until new records are available.

Per-User Volume Quotas

Systems administrators often need to track or limit user disk space usage on shared storage volumes, so NTFS includes quota-management support. NTFS quota-management support allows for per-user specification of quota enforcement, which is useful for usage tracking and tracking when a user reaches warning and limit thresholds. NTFS can be configured to log an event indicating the occurrence to the System event log if a user surpasses his warning limit. Similarly, if a user attempts to use more volume storage then her quota limit permits, NTFS can log an event to the System event log and fail the application file I/O that would have caused the quota violation with a "disk full" error code.

NTFS tracks a user's volume usage by relying on the fact that it tags files and directories with the security ID (SID) of the user who created them. (See Chapter 6 for a definition of SIDs.) The logical sizes of files and directories a user owns count against the user's administrator-defined quota limit. Thus, a user can't circumvent his or her quota limit by creating an empty sparse file that is larger than the quota would allow and then fill the file with nonzero data. Similarly, whereas a 50-KB file might compress to 10 KB, the full 50 KB is used for quota accounting.

By default, volumes don't have quota tracking enabled. You need to use the Quota tab of a volume's Properties dialog box, shown in Figure 11-18, to enable quotas, to specify default warning and limit thresholds, and to configure the NTFS behavior that occurs when a user hits the warning or limit threshold. The Quota Entries tool, which you can launch from this dialog box, enables an administrator to specify different limits and behavior for each user. Applications that want to interact with NTFS quota management use COM quota interfaces, including *IDiskQuotaControl*, *IDiskQuotaUser*, and *IDiskQuotaEvents*.

FIGURE 11-18 Volume Properties dialog box

Link Tracking

Shell shortcuts allow users to place files in their shell namespace (on their desktop, for example) that link to files located in the file system namespace. The Windows Start menu uses shell shortcuts extensively. Similarly, object linking and embedding (OLE) links allow documents from one application to be transparently embedded in the documents of other applications. The products of the Microsoft Office suite, including PowerPoint, Excel, and Word, use OLE linking.

Although shell and OLE links provide an easy way to connect files with one another and with the shell namespace, they can be difficult to manage if a user moves the source of a shell or OLE link (a link source is the file or directory to which a link points). NTFS in Windows includes support for a service application called distributed link-tracking, which maintains the integrity of shell and OLE links when link targets move. Using the NTFS link-tracking support, if a link target located on an NTFS volume moves to any other NTFS volume within the originating volume's domain, the link-tracking service can transparently follow the movement and update the link to reflect the change.

NTFS link-tracking support is based on an optional file attribute known as an *object ID*. An application can assign an object ID to a file by using the FSCTL_CREATE_OR_GET_OBJECT_ID (which assigns an ID if one isn't already assigned) and FSCTL_SET_OBJECT_ID file system

control codes. Object IDs are queried with the FSCTL_CREATE_OR_GET_OBJECT_ID and FSCTL_GET_OBJECT_ID file system control codes. The FSCTL_DELETE_OBJECT_ID file system control code lets applications delete object IDs from files.

Encryption

Corporate users often store sensitive information on their computers. Although data stored on company servers is usually safely protected with proper network security settings and physical access control, data stored on laptops can be exposed when a laptop is lost or stolen. NTFS file permissions don't offer protection because NTFS volumes can be fully accessed without regard to security by using NTFS file-reading software that doesn't require Windows to be running. Furthermore, NTFS file permissions are rendered useless when an alternate Windows installation is used to access files from an administrator account. Recall from Chapter 6 that the administrator account has the take-ownership and backup privileges, both of which allow it to access any secured object by overriding the object's security settings.

NTFS includes a facility called Encrypting File System (EFS), which users can use to encrypt sensitive data. The operation of EFS, as that of file compression, is completely transparent to applications, which means that file data is automatically decrypted when an application running in the account of a user authorized to view the data reads it and is automatically encrypted when an authorized application changes the data.

Note NTFS doesn't permit the encryption of files located in the system volume's root directory or in the \Windows directory because many files in these locations are required during the boot process and EFS isn't active during the boot process. BitLocker, described in Chapter 6, is a technology much better suited for environments in which this is a requirement because it supports full-volume encryption.

EFS relies on cryptographic services supplied by Windows in user mode, so it consists of both a kernel-mode component that tightly integrates with NTFS as well as user-mode DLLs that communicate with the Local Security Authority Subsystem (Lsass) and cryptographic DLLs.

Files that are encrypted can be accessed only by using the private key of an account's EFS private/public key pair, and private keys are locked using an account's password. Thus, EFS-encrypted files on lost or stolen laptops can't be accessed using any means (other than a brute-force cryptographic attack) without the password of an account that is authorized to view the data.

Applications can use the *EncryptFile* and *DecryptFile* Windows API functions to encrypt and decrypt files, and *FileEncryptionStatus* to retrieve a file or directory's EFS-related attributes, such as whether the file or directory is encrypted. A file or directory that is encrypted has the FILE_ATTRIBUTE_ENCRYPTED flag set in its attributes, so applications can also determine a file or directory's encryption state with *GetFileAttributes*.

POSIX Support

As explained in Chapter 2, one of the mandates for Windows was to fully support the POSIX 1003.1 standard. In the file system area, the POSIX standard requires support for case-sensitive file and directory names, traversal permissions (where security for each directory of a path is used when determining whether a user has access to a file or directory), a "file-change-time" time stamp (which is different from the MS-DOS "time-last-modified" stamp), and hard links. NTFS implements each of these features.

Defragmentation

Even though NTFS makes efforts to keep files contiguous, a volume's files can still become fragmented over time, especially when there is limited free space. A file is fragmented if its data occupies discontiguous clusters. For example, Figure 11-19 shows a fragmented file consisting of five fragments. However, like most file systems (including versions of FAT on Windows), NTFS makes no special efforts to keep files contiguous, other than to reserve a region of disk space known as the *master file table* (MFT) zone for the MFT. (NTFS lets other files allocate from the MFT zone when volume free space runs low.) Keeping an area free for the MFT can help it stay contiguous, but it, too, can become fragmented. (See the section "Master File Table" later in this chapter for more information on MFTs.)

Fragmented file **Contiguous file**

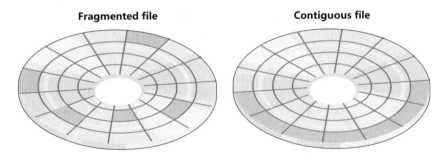

FIGURE 11-19 Fragmented and contiguous files

To facilitate the development of third-party disk defragmentation tools, Windows includes a defragmentation API that such tools can use to move file data so that files occupy contiguous clusters. The API consists of file system controls that let applications obtain a map of a volume's free and in-use clusters (FSCTL_GET_VOLUME_BITMAP), obtain a map of a file's cluster usage (FSCTL_GET_RETRIEVAL_POINTERS), and move a file (FSCTL_MOVE_FILE).

Windows includes a built-in defragmentation tool that is accessible by using the Disk Defragmenter utility (\%SystemRoot%\System32\Dfrgui.exe), shown in Figure 11-20, as well as a command-line interface, \%SystemRoot%\System32\Defrag.exe, that you can run interactively or schedule but that does not produce detailed reports or offer control—such as excluding files or directories—over the defragmentation process.

FIGURE 11-20 Disk Defragmenter

The only limitation imposed by the defragmentation implementation in NTFS is that paging files and NTFS log files cannot be defragmented.

Dynamic Partitioning

The NTFS driver allows users to dynamically resize any partition, including the system partition, either shrinking or expanding it (if enough space is available). Expanding a partition is easy if enough space exists on the disk and is performed through the FSCTL_EXPAND_VOLUME file system control code. Shrinking a partition is a more complicated process, because it requires moving any file system data that is currently in the area to be thrown away to the region that will still remain after the shrinking process (a mechanism similar to defragmentation). Shrinking is implemented by two components: the *shrinking engine* and the file system driver.

The shrinking engine is implemented in user mode. It communicates with NTFS to determine the maximum number of reclaimable bytes—that is, how much data can be moved from the region that will be resized into the region that will remain. The shrinking engine uses the standard defragmentation mechanism shown earlier, which doesn't support relocating page file fragments that are in use or any other files that have been marked as unmovable with the FSCTL_MARK_HANDLE file system control code (like the hibernation file). The master file table backup and other NTFS metadata files (described later), including the change journal, also cannot be moved, which limits the minimum size of the shrunk volume and causes wasted space.

The file system driver shrinking code is responsible for ensuring that the volume remains in a consistent state throughout the shrinking process. To do so, it exposes an interface that

uses three requests that describe the current operation, which are sent through the FSCTL_ SHRINK_VOLUME control code:

- The *ShrinkPrepare* request, which must be issued before any other operation. This request takes the desired size of the new volume in sectors and is used so that the file system can block further allocations outside the new volume boundary. The prepare request doesn't verify whether the volume can actually be shrunk by the specified amount, but it does make sure that the amount is numerically valid and that there aren't any other shrinking operations ongoing. Note that after a prepare operation, the file handle to the volume becomes associated with the shrink request. If the file handle is closed, the operation is assumed to be aborted.

- The *ShrinkCommit* request, which the shrinking engine issues after a ShrinkPrepare request. In this state, the file system attempts the removal of the requested number of clusters in the most recent prepare request. (If multiple prepare requests have been sent with different sizes, the last one is the determining one.) The ShrinkCommit request assumes that the shrinking engine has completed and will fail if any allocated blocks remain in the area to be shrunk.

- The *ShrinkAbort* request, which can be issued by the shrinking engine or caused by events such as the closure of the file handle to the volume. This request undoes the commit operation by returning the partition to its original size and allows new allocations outside the shrunk region to occur again. However, defragmentation changes made by the shrinking engine remain.

If a system is rebooted during a shrinking operation, NTFS restores the file system to a consistent state via its metadata recovery mechanism, explained later in the chapter. Because the actual shrink operation isn't executed until all other operations have been completed, the volume retains its original size and only defragmentation operations that had already been flushed out to disk persist.

Finally, shrinking a volume has several effects on the volume shadow copy mechanism (for more information on VSS, see Chapter 8). Recall that the copy-on-write mechanism allows VSS to simply retain parts of the file that were actually modified while still linking to the original file data. For deleted files, this file data will not be associated with visible files but appear as free space instead—free space that will likely be located in the area that is about to be shrunk. The shrinking engine therefore communicates with VSS to engage it in the shrinking process. In summary, the VSS mechanism's job is to copy deleted file data into its differencing area and to increase the differencing area as required to accommodate additional data. This detail is important because it poses another constraint on the size to which even volumes with ample free space can shrink.

NTFS File System Driver

As described in Chapter 7, in the framework of the Windows I/O system, NTFS and other file systems are loadable device drivers that run in kernel mode. They are invoked indirectly by applications that use Windows or other I/O APIs (such as POSIX). As Figure 11-21 shows, the Windows environment subsystems call Windows system services, which in turn locate the appropriate loaded drivers and call them. (For a description of system service dispatching, see the section "System Service Dispatching" in Chapter 3.)

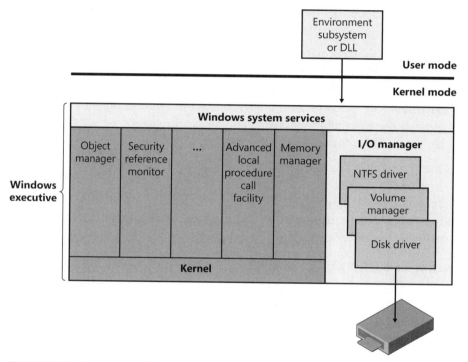

FIGURE 11-21 Components of the Windows I/O system

The layered drivers pass I/O requests to one another by calling the Windows executive's I/O manager. Relying on the I/O manager as an intermediary allows each driver to maintain independence so that it can be loaded or unloaded without affecting other drivers. In addition, the NTFS driver interacts with the three other Windows executive components, shown in the left side of Figure 11-22, that are closely related to file systems.

The log file service (LFS) is the part of NTFS that provides services for maintaining a log of disk writes. The log file that LFS writes is used to recover an NTFS-formatted volume in the case of a system failure. (See the section "Log File Service (LFS)" later in the chapter.)

FIGURE 11-22 NTFS and related components

The cache manager is the component of the Windows executive that provides systemwide caching services for NTFS and other file system drivers, including network file system drivers (servers and redirectors). All file systems implemented for Windows access cached files by mapping them into system address space and then accessing the virtual memory. The cache manager provides a specialized file system interface to the Windows memory manager for this purpose. When a program tries to access a part of a file that isn't loaded into the cache (a *cache miss*), the memory manager calls NTFS to access the disk driver and obtain the file contents from disk. The cache manager optimizes disk I/O by using its lazy writer threads to call the memory manager to flush cache contents to disk as a background activity (asynchronous disk writing). (For a complete description of the cache manager, see Chapter 10.)

NTFS participates in the Windows object model by implementing files as objects. This implementation allows files to be shared and protected by the object manager, the component of Windows that manages all executive-level objects. (The object manager is described in the section "Object Manager" in Chapter 3.)

An application creates and accesses files just as it does other Windows objects: by means of object handles. By the time an I/O request reaches NTFS, the Windows object manager and security system have already verified that the calling process has the authority to access the file object in the way it is attempting to. The security system has compared the caller's access token to the entries in the access control list for the file object. (See Chapter 6 for more information about access control lists.) The I/O manager has also transformed the file handle into a pointer to a file object. NTFS uses the information in the file object to access the file on disk.

Figure 11-23 shows the data structures that link a file handle to the file system's on-disk structure.

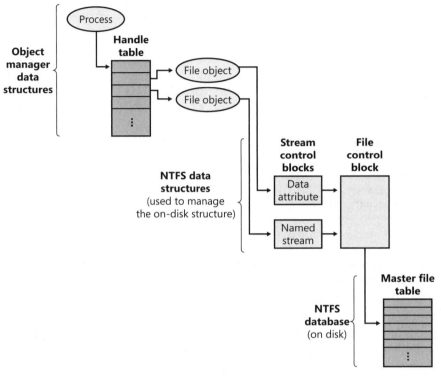

FIGURE 11-23 NTFS data structures

NTFS follows several pointers to get from the file object to the location of the file on disk. As Figure 11-23 shows, a file object, which represents a single call to the open-file system service, points to a *stream control block* (SCB) for the file attribute that the caller is trying to read or write. In Figure 11-23, a process has opened both the unnamed data attribute and a named stream (alternate data attribute) for the file. The SCBs represent individual file attributes and contain information about how to find specific attributes within a file. All the SCBs for a file point to a common data structure called a *file control block* (FCB). The FCB contains a pointer (actually, a file reference, explained in the section "File Reference Numbers" later in this chapter) to the file's record in the disk-based master file table (MFT), which is described in detail in the following section.

NTFS On-Disk Structure

This section describes the on-disk structure of an NTFS volume, including how disk space is divided and organized into clusters, how files are organized into directories, how the actual file data and attribute information is stored on disk, and finally, how NTFS data compression works.

Volumes

The structure of NTFS begins with a volume. A *volume* corresponds to a logical partition on a disk, and it is created when you format a disk or part of a disk for NTFS. You can also create a RAID volume that spans multiple disks by using the Windows Disk Management MMC snap-in or the *diskpart* command available from the Windows command prompt.

A disk can have one volume or several. NTFS handles each volume independently of the others. Three sample disk configurations for a 150-MB hard disk are illustrated in Figure 11-24.

FIGURE 11-24 Sample disk configurations

A volume consists of a series of files plus any additional unallocated space remaining on the disk partition. In the FAT file system, a volume also contains areas specially formatted for use by the file system. An NTFS volume, however, stores all file system data, such as bitmaps and directories, and even the system bootstrap, as ordinary files.

Note The on-disk format of NTFS volumes on Windows Vista and Windows Server 2008 is version 3.1, the same as on Windows XP and Windows Server 2003. The version number of a volume is stored in its $Volume metadata file.

Clusters

The cluster size on an NTFS volume, or the *cluster factor*, is established when a user formats the volume with either the *format* command or the Disk Management MMC snap-in. The default cluster factor varies with the size of the volume, but it is an integral number of physical sectors, always a power of 2 (1 sector, 2 sectors, 4 sectors, 8 sectors, and so on). The cluster factor is expressed as the number of bytes in the cluster, such as 512 bytes, 1 KB, or 2 KB.

Internally, NTFS refers only to clusters. (However, NTFS forms low-level volume I/O operations such that clusters are sector-aligned and have a length that is a multiple of the sector size.) NTFS uses the cluster as its unit of allocation to maintain its independence from physical sector sizes. This independence allows NTFS to efficiently support very large disks by using a larger cluster factor or to support nonstandard disks that have a sector size other than 512 bytes. On a larger volume, use of a larger cluster factor can reduce fragmentation and speed allocation, at a small cost in terms of wasted disk space. Both the *format* command available from the command prompt and the Format menu option under the All Tasks option on the Action menu in the Disk Management MMC snap-in choose a default cluster factor based on the volume size, but you can override this size.

NTFS refers to physical locations on a disk by means of *logical cluster numbers* (LCNs). LCNs are simply the numbering of all clusters from the beginning of the volume to the end. To convert an LCN to a physical disk address, NTFS multiplies the LCN by the cluster factor to get the physical byte offset on the volume, as the disk driver interface requires. NTFS refers to the data within a file by means of *virtual cluster numbers* (VCNs). VCNs number the clusters belonging to a particular file from 0 through m. VCNs aren't necessarily physically contiguous, however; they can be mapped to any number of LCNs on the volume.

Master File Table

In NTFS, all data stored on a volume is contained in files, including the data structures used to locate and retrieve files, the bootstrap data, and the bitmap that records the allocation state of the entire volume (the NTFS metadata). Storing everything in files allows the file system to easily locate and maintain the data, and each separate file can be protected by a security descriptor. In addition, if a particular part of the disk goes bad, NTFS can relocate the metadata files to prevent the disk from becoming inaccessible.

The MFT is the heart of the NTFS volume structure. The MFT is implemented as an array of file records. The size of each file record is fixed at 1 KB, regardless of cluster size. (The structure of a file record is described in the "File Records" section later in this chapter.) Logically, the MFT contains one record for each file on the volume, including a record for the MFT itself. In addition to the MFT, each NTFS volume includes a set of metadata files containing the information that's used to implement the file system structure. Each of these NTFS metadata files has a name that begins with a dollar sign ($), although the signs are hidden. For example, the file name of the MFT is $MFT. The rest of the files on an NTFS volume are normal user files and directories, as shown in Figure 11-25.

Usually, each MFT record corresponds to a different file. If a file has a large number of attributes or becomes highly fragmented, however, more than one record might be needed for a single file. In such cases, the first MFT record, which stores the locations of the others, is called the *base file record*.

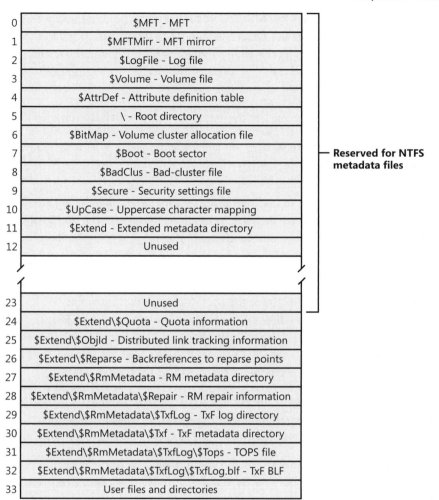

0	$MFT - MFT
1	$MFTMirr - MFT mirror
2	$LogFile - Log file
3	$Volume - Volume file
4	$AttrDef - Attribute definition table
5	\ - Root directory
6	$BitMap - Volume cluster allocation file
7	$Boot - Boot sector
8	$BadClus - Bad-cluster file
9	$Secure - Security settings file
10	$UpCase - Uppercase character mapping
11	$Extend - Extended metadata directory
12	Unused
23	Unused
24	$Extend\$Quota - Quota information
25	$Extend\$ObjId - Distributed link tracking information
26	$Extend\$Reparse - Backreferences to reparse points
27	$Extend\$RmMetadata - RM metadata directory
28	$Extend\$RmMetadata\$Repair - RM repair information
29	$Extend\$RmMetadata\$TxfLog - TxF log directory
30	$Extend\$RmMetadata\$Txf - TxF metadata directory
31	$Extend\$RmMetadata\$TxfLog\$Tops - TOPS file
32	$Extend\$RmMetadata\$TxfLog\$TxfLog.blf - TxF BLF
33	User files and directories

— Reserved for NTFS metadata files

FIGURE 11-25 File records for NTFS metadata files in the MFT

When it first accesses a volume, NTFS must *mount* it—that is, read metadata from the disk and construct internal data structures so that it can process application file system accesses. To mount the volume, NTFS looks in the boot sector to find the physical disk address of the MFT. The MFT's own file record is the first entry in the table; the second file record points to a file located in the middle of the disk called the *MFT mirror* (file name $MFTMirr) that contains a copy of the first few rows of the MFT. This partial copy of the MFT is used to locate metadata files if part of the MFT file can't be read for some reason.

Once NTFS finds the file record for the MFT, it obtains the VCN-to-LCN mapping information in the file record's data attribute and stores it in memory. Each run (runs are explained later in this chapter in the section "Resident and Nonresident Attributes") has a VCN-to-LCN mapping and a run length because that's all the information necessary to locate an LCN for any VCN. This mapping information tells NTFS where the runs composing the MFT are located

on the disk. NTFS then processes the MFT records for several more metadata files and opens the files. Next, NTFS performs its file system recovery operation (described in the section "Recovery"), and finally, it opens its remaining metadata files. The volume is now ready for user access.

> **Note** For the sake of clarity, the text and diagrams in this chapter depict a run as including a VCN, an LCN, and a run length. NTFS actually compresses this information on disk into an LCN/next-VCN pair. Given a starting VCN, NTFS can determine the length of a run by subtracting the starting VCN from the next VCN.

As the system runs, NTFS writes to another important metadata file, the *log file* (file name $LogFile). NTFS uses the log file to record all operations that affect the NTFS volume structure, including file creation or any commands, such as *copy*, that alter the directory structure. The log file is used to recover an NTFS volume after a system failure and is also described in the "Recovery" section later in this chapter.

Another entry in the MFT is reserved for the *root directory* (also known as "\"). Its file record contains an index of the files and directories stored in the root of the NTFS directory structure. When NTFS is first asked to open a file, it begins its search for the file in the root directory's file record. After opening a file, NTFS stores the file's MFT file reference so that it can directly access the file's MFT record when it reads and writes the file later.

NTFS records the allocation state of the volume in the *bitmap file* (file name $BitMap). The data attribute for the bitmap file contains a bitmap, each of whose bits represents a cluster on the volume, identifying whether the cluster is free or has been allocated to a file.

The *security file* (file name $Secure) stores the volume-wide security descriptor database. NTFS files and directories have individually settable security descriptors, but to conserve space, NTFS stores the settings in a common file, which allows files and directories that have the same security settings to reference the same security descriptor. In most environments, entire directory trees have the same security settings, so this optimization provides a significant savings.

Another system file, the *boot file* (file name $Boot), stores the Windows bootstrap code. For the system to boot, the bootstrap code must be located at a specific disk address. During formatting, however, the *format* command defines this area as a file by creating a file record for it. Creating the boot file allows NTFS to adhere to its rule of making everything on the disk a file. The boot file as well as NTFS metadata files can be individually protected by means of the security descriptors that are applied to all Windows objects. Using this "everything on the disk is a file" model also means that the bootstrap can be modified by normal file I/O, although the boot file is protected from editing.

NTFS also maintains a *bad-cluster file* (file name $BadClus) for recording any bad spots on the disk volume and a file known as the *volume file* (file name $Volume), which contains the volume name, the version of NTFS for which the volume is formatted, and a bit that when

set signifies that a disk corruption has occurred and must be repaired by the Chkdsk utility. (The Chkdsk utility is covered in more detail later in the chapter.) The *uppercase file* (file name $UpCase) includes a translation table between lowercase and uppercase characters. NTFS maintains a file containing an *attribute definition table* (file name $AttrDef) that defines the attribute types supported on the volume and indicates whether they can be indexed, recovered during a system recovery operation, and so on.

NTFS stores several metadata files in the *extensions* (directory name $Extend) metadata directory, including the *object identifier file* (file name $ObjId), the *quota file* (file name $Quota), the *change journal file* (file name $UsnJrnl), the *reparse point file* (file name $Reparse), and the *default resource manager directory* (directory name $RmMetadata). These files store information related to optional features of NTFS. The object identifier file stores file object IDs, the quota file stores quota limit and behavior information on volumes that have quotas enabled, the change journal file records file and directory changes, and the reparse point file stores information about which files and directories on the volume include reparse point data.

The default resource manager directory contains directories related to transactional NTFS (TxF) support, including the *transaction log directory* (directory name $TxfLog), the *transaction isolation directory* (directory name $Txf), and the *transaction repair directory* (file name $Repair). The transaction log directory contains the *TxF base log file* (file name $TxfLog.blf) and any number of log container files, depending on the size of the transaction log, but it always contains at least two: one for the Kernel Transaction Manager (KTM) log stream (file name $TxfLogContainer00000000000000000001), and one for the TxF log stream (file name $TxfLogContainer00000000000000000002). The transaction log directory also contains the *TxF old page stream* (file name $Tops), which we'll describe later.

EXPERIMENT: Viewing NTFS Information

You can use the built-in Fsutil.exe command-line program to view information about an NTFS volume, including the placement and size of the MFT and MFT zone:

```
C:\Users\Administrator>fsutil fsinfo ntfsinfo c:
NTFS Volume Serial Number :        0x9a38d50e38d4ea71
Version :                          3.1
Number Sectors :                   0x0000000015c82ff0
Total Clusters :                   0x0000000002b905fe
Free Clusters  :                   0x000000000013c332
Total Reserved :                   0x0000000000000780
Bytes Per Sector  :                512
Bytes Per Cluster :                4096
Bytes Per FileRecord Segment    :  1024
Clusters Per FileRecord Segment :  0
Mft Valid Data Length :            0x0000000023db0000
Mft Start Lcn  :                   0x00000000000c0000
Mft2 Start Lcn :                   0x00000000016082ff
Mft Zone Start :                   0x0000000002751f60
Mft Zone End   :                   0x000000000275cd60
RM Identifier:          CF7234E7-39E3-11DC-BDCE-00188BDD5F49
```

File Reference Numbers

A file on an NTFS volume is identified by a 64-bit value called a *file reference*. The file reference consists of a file number and a sequence number. The file number corresponds to the position of the file's file record in the MFT minus 1 (or to the position of the base file record minus 1 if the file has more than one file record). The sequence number, which is incremented each time an MFT file record position is reused, enables NTFS to perform internal consistency checks. A file reference is illustrated in Figure 11-26.

FIGURE 11-26 File reference

File Records

Instead of viewing a file as just a repository for textual or binary data, NTFS stores files as a collection of attribute/value pairs, one of which is the data it contains (called the *unnamed data attribute*). Other attributes that comprise a file include the file name, time stamp information, and possibly additional named data attributes. Figure 11-27 illustrates an MFT record for a small file.

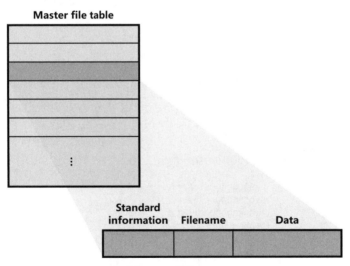

FIGURE 11-27 MFT record for a small file

Each file attribute is stored as a separate stream of bytes within a file. Strictly speaking, NTFS doesn't read and write files—it reads and writes attribute streams. NTFS supplies these attribute operations: create, delete, read (byte range), and write (byte range). The read and write services normally operate on the file's unnamed data attribute. However, a caller can specify a different data attribute by using the named data stream syntax.

Table 11-5 lists the attributes for files on an NTFS volume. (Not all attributes are present for every file.)

TABLE 11-5 Attributes for NTFS Files

Attribute	Attribute Type Name	Description
Volume information	$VOLUME_INFORMATION, $VOLUME_NAME	These attributes are present only in the $Volume metadata file. They store volume version and label information.
Standard information	$STANDARD_INFORMATION	File attributes such as read-only, archive, and so on; time stamps, including when the file was created or last modified; and how many directories point to the file (its *hard link count*).
Filename	$FILE_NAME	The file's name in Unicode characters. A file can have multiple filename attributes, as it does when a hard link to a file exists or when a file with a long name has an automatically generated "short name" for access by MS-DOS and 16-bit Windows applications.
Security descriptor	$SECURITY_DESCRIPTOR	This attribute is present for backward compatibility with previous versions of NTFS. The latest versions of NTFS store all security descriptors in the $Secure metadata file, sharing descriptors among files and directories that have the same settings. Previous versions of NTFS stored private security descriptor information with each file and directory.
Data	$DATA	The contents of the file. In NTFS, a file has one default unnamed data attribute and can have additional named data attributes—that is, a file can have multiple data streams. A directory has no default data attribute but can have optional named data attributes.
Index root, index allocation, and index bitmap	$INDEX_ROOT, $INDEX_ALLOCATION, $BITMAP	Three attributes used to implement file name allocation and bitmap indexes for large directories (directories only).
Attribute list	$ATTRIBUTE_LIST	A list of the attributes that make up the file and the file reference of the MFT file record in which each attribute is located. This seldom-used attribute is present when a file requires more than one MFT file record.

Attribute	Attribute Type Name	Description
Object ID	$OBJECT_ID	A 64-byte identifier for a file or directory, with the lowest 16 bytes (128 bits) unique to the volume. The link-tracking service assigns object IDs to shell shortcut and OLE link source files. NTFS provides APIs so that files and directories can be opened with their object ID rather than their file name.
Reparse information	$REPARSE_POINT	This attribute stores a file's reparse point data. NTFS junctions and mount points include this attribute.
Extended attributes	$EA, $EA_INFORMATION	Extended attributes aren't actively used but are provided for backward compatibility with OS/2 applications.
Logged utility stream	$LOGGED_UTILITY_STREAM	EFS stores data in this attribute ($EFS) that's used to manage a file's encryption, such as the encrypted version of the key needed to decrypt the file and a list of users who are authorized to access the file. When a file or directory becomes part of a transaction, TxF also stores transaction data in the $TXF_DATA attribute, such as the file's unique *transaction ID*.

Table 11-5 shows attribute names; however, attributes actually correspond to numeric type codes, which NTFS uses to order the attributes within a file record. The file attributes in an MFT record are ordered by these type codes (numerically in ascending order), with some attribute types appearing more than once—if a file has multiple data attributes, for example, or multiple file names.

Each attribute in a file record is identified with its attribute type code and has a value and an optional name. An attribute's value is the byte stream composing the attribute. For example, the value of the $FILE_NAME attribute is the file's name; the value of the $DATA attribute is whatever bytes the user stored in the file.

Most attributes never have names, although the index-related attributes and the $DATA attribute often do. Names distinguish between multiple attributes of the same type that a file can include. For example, a file that has a named data stream has two $DATA attributes: an unnamed $DATA attribute storing the default unnamed data stream and a named $DATA attribute having the name of the alternate stream and storing the named stream's data.

File Names

Both NTFS and FAT allow each file name in a path to be as many as 255 characters long. File names can contain Unicode characters as well as multiple periods and embedded spaces. However, the FAT file system supplied with MS-DOS is limited to 8 (non-Unicode) characters for its file names, followed by a period and a 3-character extension. Figure 11-28 provides a visual representation of the different file namespaces Windows supports and shows how they intersect.

FIGURE 11-28 Windows file namespaces

The POSIX subsystem requires the biggest namespace of all the application execution environments that Windows supports, and therefore the NTFS namespace is equivalent to the POSIX namespace. The POSIX subsystem can create names that aren't visible to Windows and MS-DOS applications, including names with trailing periods and trailing spaces. Ordinarily, creating a file using the large POSIX namespace isn't a problem because you would do that only if you intended the POSIX subsystem or POSIX client systems to use that file.

The relationship between 32-bit Windows (Windows) applications and MS-DOS and 16-bit Windows applications is a much closer one, however. The Windows area in Figure 11-28 represents file names that the Windows subsystem can create on an NTFS volume but that MS-DOS and 16-bit Windows applications can't see. This group includes file names longer than the 8.3 format of MS-DOS names, those containing Unicode (international) characters, those with multiple period characters or a beginning period, and those with embedded spaces. When a file is created with such a name, NTFS automatically generates an alternate, MS-DOS-style file name for the file. Windows displays these short names when you use the */x* option with the *dir* command.

The MS-DOS file names are fully functional aliases for the NTFS files and are stored in the same directory as the long file names. The MFT record for a file with an autogenerated MS-DOS file name is shown in Figure 11-29.

FIGURE 11-29 MFT file record with an MS-DOS filename attribute

The NTFS name and the generated MS-DOS name are stored in the same file record and therefore refer to the same file. The MS-DOS name can be used to open, read from, write to, or copy the file. If a user renames the file using either the long file name or the short file name, the new name replaces both the existing names. If the new name isn't a valid MS-DOS name, NTFS generates another MS-DOS name for the file (note that NTFS only generates MS-DOS-style file names for the first file name).

Note Hard links are implemented in a similar way. When a hard link to a file is created, NTFS adds another file name attribute to the file's MFT file record. The two situations differ in one regard, however. When a user deletes a file that has multiple names (hard links), the file record and the file remain in place. The file and its record are deleted only when the last file name (hard link) is deleted. If a file has both an NTFS name and an autogenerated MS-DOS name, however, a user can delete the file using either name.

Here's the algorithm NTFS uses (the algorithm is actually implemented in the kernel function *RtlGenerate8dot3Name* and is also used by other drivers, such as CDFS, FAT, and third-party file systems) to generate an MS-DOS name from a long file name:

1. Remove from the long name any characters that are illegal in MS-DOS names, including spaces and Unicode characters. Remove preceding and trailing periods. Remove all other embedded periods, except the last one.

2. Truncate the string before the period (if present) to six characters (it may already be six or fewer because this algorithm is applied when any character that is illegal in MS-DOS is present in the name); if it is two or fewer characters, generate and concatenate a four-character hex checksum string. Append the string ~n (where n is a number, starting with 1, that is used to distinguish different files that truncate to the same name). Truncate the string after the period (if present) to three characters.

3. Put the result in uppercase letters. MS-DOS is case-insensitive, and this step guarantees that NTFS won't generate a new name that differs from the old only in case.

4. If the generated name duplicates an existing name in the directory, increment the ~*n* string. If *n* is greater than 4, and a checksum was not concatenated already, truncate the string before the period to two characters and generate and concatenate a four-character hex checksum string.

Table 11-6 shows the long Windows file names from Figure 11-28 and their NTFS-generated MS-DOS versions. The current algorithm and the examples in Figure 11-28 should give you an idea of what NTFS-generated MS-DOS-style file names look like.

> **Note** Although not generally recommended because it can cause incompatibilities with applications that rely on them, you can disable short name generation by setting HKLM\SYSTEM\CurrentControlSet\Control\FileSystem\NtfsDisable8dot3NameCreation in the registry to a DWORD value of 1.

TABLE 11-6 NTFS-Generated File Names

Windows Long Name	NTFS-Generated Short Name
LongFileName	LONGFI~1
UnicodeName.ΦΔΠΛ	UNICOD~1
File.Name.With.Dots	FILENA~1.DOT
File.Name2.With.Dots	FILENA~2.DOT
File.Name3.With.Dots	FILENA~3.DOT
File.Name4.With.Dots	FILENA~4.DOT
File.Name5.With.Dots	FIF596~1.DOT
Name With Embedded Spaces	NAMEWI~1
.BeginningDot	BEGINN~1
25¢.two characters	255440~1.TWO
©	6E2D~1

Tunneling

NTFS uses the concept of *tunneling* to allow compatibility with older programs that depend on the file system to cache certain file metadata for a period of time even after the file is gone, such as when it has been deleted or renamed. With tunneling, any new file created with the same name as the original file, and within a certain period of time, will keep some of the same metadata. The idea is to replicate behavior expected by MS-DOS programs when using the *safe save* programming method, in which modified data is copied to a temporary file, the original file is deleted, and then the temporary file is renamed to the original name. The expected behavior in this case is that the renamed temporary file should appear to be the same as the original file, otherwise the creation time would continuously update itself with each modification (which is how the modified time is used).

NTFS uses tunneling so that when a file name is removed from a directory, its long name and short name, as well as its creation time, are saved into a cache. When a new file is added to a directory, the cache is searched to see whether there is any tunneled data to restore. Because these operations apply to directories, each directory instance has its own cache, which is deleted if the directory is removed. NTFS will use tunneling for the following series of operations if the names used result in the deletion and re-creation of the same file name:

- Delete + Create
- Delete + Rename
- Rename + Create
- Rename + Rename

By default, NTFS keeps the tunneling cache for 15 seconds, although you can modify this timeout by modifying the MaximumTunnelEntryAgeInSeconds value in the HKLM\SYSTEM\CurrentControlSet\Control\FileSystem registry key. Tunneling can also be completely disabled by creating a new value called MaximumTunnelEntries and setting it to 0; however, this will cause older applications to break if they rely on the compatibility behavior.

You can see tunneling in action with the following simple experiment in the command prompt:

1. Create a file called file1.
2. Wait for more than 15 seconds (the default tunnel cache timeout).
3. Create a file called file2.
4. Perform a dir /TC. Note the creation times.
5. Rename file1 to file.
6. Rename file2 to file1.
7. Perform a dir /TC. Note that the creation times are identical.

Resident and Nonresident Attributes

If a file is small, all its attributes and their values (its data, for example) fit in the file record. When the value of an attribute is stored directly in the MFT, the attribute is called a *resident attribute*. (In Figure 11-29, for example, all attributes are resident.) Several attributes are defined as always being resident so that NTFS can locate nonresident attributes. The standard information and index root attributes are always resident, for example.

Each attribute begins with a standard header containing information about the attribute, information that NTFS uses to manage the attributes in a generic way. The header, which is always resident, records whether the attribute's value is resident or nonresident. For resident attributes, the header also contains the offset from the header to the attribute's value and the length of the attribute's value, as Figure 11-30 illustrates for the filename attribute.

FIGURE 11-30 Resident attribute header and value

When an attribute's value is stored directly in the MFT, the time it takes NTFS to access the value is greatly reduced. Instead of looking up a file in a table and then reading a succession of allocation units to find the file's data (as the FAT file system does, for example), NTFS accesses the disk once and retrieves the data immediately.

The attributes for a small directory, as well as for a small file, can be resident in the MFT, as Figure 11-31 shows. For a small directory, the index root attribute contains an index of file references for the files and the subdirectories in the directory.

Standard information **Filename** **Index root**

		Index of files	Empty
		file1, file2, file3, ...	

FIGURE 11-31 MFT file record for a small directory

Of course, many files and directories can't be squeezed into a 1-KB, fixed-size MFT record. If a particular attribute, such as a file's data attribute, is too large to be contained in an MFT file record, NTFS allocates clusters for the attribute's data separate from the MFT. This area is called a *run* (or an *extent*). If the attribute's value later grows (if a user appends data to the file, for example), NTFS allocates another run for the additional data. Attributes whose values are stored in runs rather than in the MFT are called *nonresident attributes*. The file system decides whether a particular attribute is resident or nonresident; the location of the data is transparent to the process accessing it.

When an attribute is nonresident, as the data attribute for a large file might be, its header contains the information NTFS needs to locate the attribute's value on the disk. Figure 11-32 shows a nonresident data attribute stored in two runs.

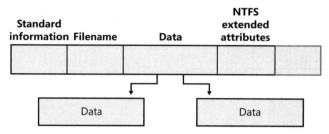

FIGURE 11-32 MFT file record for a large file with two data runs

Among the standard attributes, only those that can grow can be nonresident. For files, the attributes that can grow are the data and the attribute list (not shown in Figure 11-32). The standard information and filename attributes are always resident.

A large directory can also have nonresident attributes (or parts of attributes), as Figure 11-33 shows. In this example, the MFT file record doesn't have enough room to store the index of files that make up this large directory. A part of the index is stored in the index root attribute, and the rest of the index is stored in nonresident runs called *index buffers*. The index root, index allocation, and bitmap attributes are shown here in a simplified form. They are described in more detail in the next section. The standard information and filename attributes are always resident. The header and at least part of the value of the index root attribute are also resident for directories.

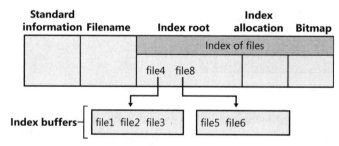

FIGURE 11-33 MFT file record for a large directory with a nonresident file name index

When a file's (or a directory's) attributes can't fit in an MFT file record and separate allocations are needed, NTFS keeps track of the runs by means of VCN-to-LCN mapping pairs. LCNs represent the sequence of clusters on an entire volume from 0 through n. VCNs number the clusters belonging to a particular file from 0 through m. For example, the clusters in the runs of a nonresident data attribute are numbered as shown in Figure 11-34.

FIGURE 11-34 VCNs for a nonresident data attribute

If this file had more than two runs, the numbering of the third run would start with VCN 8. As Figure 11-35 shows, the data attribute header contains VCN-to-LCN mappings for the two runs here, which allows NTFS to easily find the allocations on the disk.

FIGURE 11-35 VCN-to-LCN mappings for a nonresident data attribute

Although Figure 11-34 shows just data runs, other attributes can be stored in runs if there isn't enough room in the MFT file record to contain them. And if a particular file has too many attributes to fit in the MFT record, a second MFT record is used to contain the additional attributes (or attribute headers for nonresident attributes). In this case, an attribute called the *attribute list* is added. The attribute list attribute contains the name and type code of each of the file's attributes and the file reference of the MFT record where the attribute is located. The attribute list attribute is provided for those cases in which a file grows so large or so fragmented that a single MFT record can't contain the multitude of VCN-to-LCN mappings needed to find all its runs. Files with more than 200 runs typically require an attribute list.

Data Compression and Sparse Files

NTFS supports compression on a per-file, per-directory, or per-volume basis. (NTFS compression is performed only on user data, not file system metadata.) You can tell whether a volume is compressed by using the Windows *GetVolumeInformation* function. To retrieve the

actual compressed size of a file, use the Windows *GetCompressedFileSize* function. Finally, to examine or change the compression setting for a file or directory, use the Windows *DeviceIoControl* function. (See the FSCTL_GET_COMPRESSION and FSCTL_SET_COMPRESSION file system control codes.) Keep in mind that although setting a file's compression state compresses (or decompresses) the file right away, setting a directory's or volume's compression state doesn't cause any immediate compression or decompression. Instead, setting a directory's or volume's compression state sets a default compression state that will be given to all newly created files and subdirectories within that directory or volume.

The following section introduces NTFS compression by examining the simple case of compressing sparse data. The subsequent sections extend the discussion to the compression of ordinary files and sparse files.

Compressing Sparse Data

Sparse data is often large but contains only a small amount of nonzero data relative to its size. A sparse matrix is one example of sparse data. As described earlier, NTFS uses VCNs, from 0 through m, to enumerate the clusters of a file. Each VCN maps to a corresponding LCN, which identifies the disk location of the cluster. Figure 11-36 illustrates the runs (disk allocations) of a normal, noncompressed file, including its VCNs and the LCNs they map to.

FIGURE 11-36 Runs of a noncompressed file

This file is stored in 3 runs, each of which is 4 clusters long, for a total of 12 clusters. Figure 11-37 shows the MFT record for this file. As described earlier, to save space the MFT record's data attribute, which contains VCN-to-LCN mappings, records only one mapping for each run, rather than one for each cluster. Notice, however, that each VCN from 0 through 11 has a corresponding LCN associated with it. The first entry starts at VCN 0 and covers 4 clusters, the second entry starts at VCN 4 and covers 4 clusters, and so on. This entry format is typical for a noncompressed file.

Standard information	Filename		Data		
		Starting VCN	Starting LCN	Number of clusters	
		0	1355	4	
		4	1588	4	
		8	2033	4	

FIGURE 11-37 MFT record for a noncompressed file

When a user selects a file on an NTFS volume for compression, one NTFS compression technique is to remove long strings of zeros from the file. If the file's data is sparse, it typically shrinks to occupy a fraction of the disk space it would otherwise require. On subsequent writes to the file, NTFS allocates space only for runs that contain nonzero data.

Figure 11-38 depicts the runs of a compressed file containing sparse data. Notice that certain ranges of the file's VCNs (16–31 and 64–127) have no disk allocations.

FIGURE 11-38 Runs of a compressed file containing sparse data

The MFT record for this compressed file omits blocks of VCNs that contain zeros and therefore have no physical storage allocated to them. The first data entry in Figure 11-39, for example, starts at VCN 0 and covers 16 clusters. The second entry jumps to VCN 32 and covers 16 clusters.

Standard information	Filename	Data		
		Starting VCN	Starting LCN	Number of clusters
		0	133	16
		32	193	16
		48	96	16
		128	324	16

FIGURE 11-39 MFT record for a compressed file containing sparse data

When a program reads data from a compressed file, NTFS checks the MFT record to determine whether a VCN-to-LCN mapping covers the location being read. If the program is

reading from an unallocated "hole" in the file, it means that the data in that part of the file consists of zeros, so NTFS returns zeros without accessing the disk. If a program writes non-zero data to a "hole," NTFS quietly allocates disk space and then writes the data. This technique is very efficient for sparse file data that contains a lot of zero data.

Compressing Nonsparse Data

The preceding example of compressing a sparse file is somewhat contrived. It describes "compression" for a case in which whole sections of a file were filled with zeros but the remaining data in the file wasn't affected by the compression. The data in most files isn't sparse, but it can still be compressed by the application of a compression algorithm.

In NTFS, users can specify compression for individual files or for all the files in a directory. (New files created in a directory marked for compressed are automatically compressed— existing files must be compressed individually.) When it compresses a file, NTFS divides the file's unprocessed data into *compression units* 16 clusters long (equal to 8 KB for a 512-byte cluster, for example). Certain sequences of data in a file might not compress much, if at all; so for each compression unit in the file, NTFS determines whether compressing the unit will save at least 1 cluster of storage. If compressing the unit won't free up at least 1 cluster, NTFS allocates a 16-cluster run and writes the data in that unit to disk without compressing it. If the data in a 16-cluster unit will compress to 15 or fewer clusters, NTFS allocates only the number of clusters needed to contain the compressed data and then writes it to disk. Figure 11-40 illustrates the compression of a file with four runs. The unshaded areas in this figure represent the actual storage locations that the file occupies after compression. The first, second, and fourth runs were compressed; the third run wasn't. Even with one noncompressed run, compressing this file saved 26 clusters of disk space, or 41 percent.

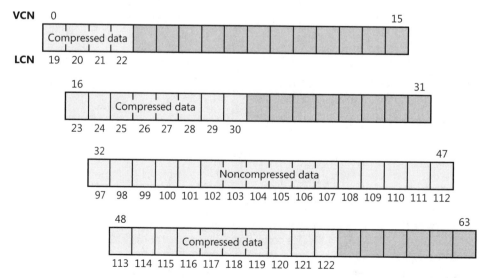

FIGURE 11-40 Data runs of a compressed file

> **Note** Although the diagrams in this chapter show contiguous LCNs, a compression unit need not be stored in physically contiguous clusters. Runs that occupy noncontiguous clusters produce slightly more complicated MFT records than the one shown in Figure 11-40.

When it writes data to a compressed file, NTFS ensures that each run begins on a virtual 16-cluster boundary. Thus the starting VCN of each run is a multiple of 16, and the runs are no longer than 16 clusters. NTFS reads and writes at least one compression unit at a time when it accesses compressed files. When it writes compressed data, however, NTFS tries to store compression units in physically contiguous locations so that it can read them all in a single I/O operation. The 16-cluster size of the NTFS compression unit was chosen to reduce internal fragmentation: the larger the compression unit, the less the overall disk space needed to store the data. This 16-cluster compression unit size represents a trade-off between producing smaller compressed files and slowing read operations for programs that randomly access files. The equivalent of 16 clusters must be decompressed for each cache miss. (A cache miss is more likely to occur during random file access.) Figure 11-41 shows the MFT record for the compressed file shown in Figure 11-40.

Standard information	Filename	Data		
		Starting VCN	Starting LCN	Number of clusters
		0	19	4
		16	23	8
		32	97	16
		48	113	10

FIGURE 11-41 MFT record for a compressed file

One difference between this compressed file and the earlier example of a compressed file containing sparse data is that three of the compressed runs in this file are less than 16 clusters long. Reading this information from a file's MFT file record enables NTFS to know whether data in the file is compressed. Any run shorter than 16 clusters contains compressed data that NTFS must decompress when it first reads the data into the cache. A run that is exactly 16 clusters long doesn't contain compressed data and therefore requires no decompression.

If the data in a run has been compressed, NTFS decompresses the data into a scratch buffer and then copies it to the caller's buffer. NTFS also loads the decompressed data into the cache, which makes subsequent reads from the same run as fast as any other cached read. NTFS writes any updates to the file to the cache, leaving the lazy writer to compress and write the modified data to disk asynchronously. This strategy ensures that writing to a compressed file produces no more significant delay than writing to a noncompressed file would.

NTFS keeps disk allocations for a compressed file contiguous whenever possible. As the LCNs indicate, the first two runs of the compressed file shown in Figure 11-39 are physically contiguous, as are the last two. When two or more runs are contiguous, NTFS performs disk read-ahead, as it does with the data in other files. Because the reading and decompression of contiguous file data take place asynchronously before the program requests the data, subsequent read operations obtain the data directly from the cache, which greatly enhances read performance.

Sparse Files

Sparse files (the NTFS file type, as opposed to files that consist of sparse data, described earlier) are essentially compressed files for which NTFS doesn't apply compression to the file's nonsparse data. However, NTFS manages the run data of a sparse file's MFT record the same way it does for compressed files that consist of sparse and nonsparse data.

The Change Journal File

The change journal file, \$Extend\$UsnJrnl, is a sparse file in which NTFS stores records of changes to files and directories. Applications like the Windows File Replication Service (FRS) and the Windows Search service make use of the journal to respond to file and directory changes as they occur.

The journal stores change entries in the $J data stream and the maximum size of the journal in the $Max data stream. Entries are versioned and include the following information about a file or directory change:

- The time of the change
- The reason for the change (see Table 11-7)
- The file or directory's attributes
- The file or directory's name
- The file or directory's file reference number
- The file reference number of the file's parent directory
- The security ID
- The *update sequence number* (USN) of the record

TABLE 11-7 Change Journal Change Reasons

Identifier	Reason
USN_REASON_DATA_OVERWRITE	The data in the file or directory was overwritten
USN_REASON_DATA_EXTEND	Data was added to the file or directory
USN_REASON_DATA_TRUNCATION	The data in the file or directory was truncated
USN_REASON_NAMED_DATA_OVERWRITE	The data in a file's data stream was overwritten
USN_REASON_NAMED_DATA_EXTEND	The data in a file's data stream was extended
USN_REASON_NAMED_DATA_TRUNCATION	The data in a file's data stream was truncated
USN_REASON_FILE_CREATE	A new file or directory was created
USN_REASON_FILE_DELETE	A file or directory was deleted
USN_REASON_EA_CHANGE	The extended attributes for a file or directory changed
USN_REASON_SECURITY_CHANGE	The security descriptor for a file or directory was changed
USN_REASON_RENAME_OLD_NAME	A file or directory was renamed; this is the old name
USN_REASON_RENAME_NEW_NAME	A file or directory was renamed; this is the new name
USN_REASON_INDEXABLE_CHANGE	The indexing state for the file or directory was changed (whether or not the Indexing service will process this file or directory)
USN_REASON_BASIC_INFO_CHANGE	The file or directory attributes and/or the time stamps were changed
USN_REASON_HARD_LINK_CHANGE	A hard link was added or removed from the file or directory
USN_REASON_COMPRESSION_CHANGE	The compression state for the file or directory was changed
USN_REASON_ENCRYPTION_CHANGE	The encryption state (EFS) was enabled or disabled for this file or directory
USN_REASON_OBJECT_ID_CHANGE	The object ID for this file or directory was changed
USN_REASON_REPARSE_POINT_CHANGE	The reparse point for a file or directory was changed, or a new reparse point (such as a symbolic link) was added or deleted from a file or directory
USN_REASON_STREAM_CHANGE	A new data stream was added to or removed from a file or renamed
USN_REASON_TRANSACTED_CHANGE	This value is added (ORed) to the change reason to indicate that the change was the result of a recent *commit* of a TxF transaction
USN_REASON_CLOSE	The handle to a file or directory was closed, indicating that this is the final modification made to the file in this series of operations

EXPERIMENT: Reading the Change Journal

You can use the Usndump.exe command-line program from Winsider Seminars & Solutions (*www.winsiderss.com/tools/usndump/usndump.htm*) to dump the contents of the change journal if the current volume has one. You can also create, delete, or query journal information with the built-in Fsutil.exe utility, as shown here:

```
C:\>fsutil usn queryjournal c:
Usn Journal ID    : 0x01c89ddaec1b9648
First Usn         : 0x0000000038140000
Next Usn          : 0x000000003a22fa50
Lowest Valid Usn  : 0x0000000000000000
Max Usn           : 0x00000ffffffff0000
Maximum Size      : 0x0000000002000000
Allocation Delta  : 0x0000000000400000
```

The output indicates the maximum size of the change journal on the volume and its current state. As a simple experiment to see how NTFS records changes in the journal, create a file called Usn.txt in the current directory, rename it to UsnNew.txt, and then dump the journal with Usndump, as shown here:

```
C:\>echo hello > Usn.txt
C:\>ren Usn.txt UsnNew.txt
C:\>Usndump.exe
...
File Ref#        : 0x00670000000006BF
ParentFile Ref# : 0x0005000000000005
Usn             : 0x0000000000000000
SecurityId      : 0x00000000
Reason          : 0x00000100 (USN_REASON_FILE_CREATE)
Name (014)      : usn.txt

File Ref#        : 0x00670000000006BF
ParentFile Ref# : 0x0005000000000005
Usn             : 0x0000000000000050
SecurityId      : 0x00000000
Reason          : 0x00000102 (USN_REASON_FILE_CREATE | USN_REASON_DATA_EXTEND)
Name (014)      : usn.txt

File Ref#        : 0x00670000000006BF
ParentFile Ref# : 0x0005000000000005
Usn             : 0x00000000000000A0
SecurityId      : 0x00000000
Reason          : 0x80000102 (USN_REASON_FILE_CREATE | USN_REASON_DATA_EXTEND)
Name (014)      : usn.txt

File Ref#        : 0x00670000000006BF
ParentFile Ref# : 0x0005000000000005
Usn             : 0x0000000000000138
SecurityId      : 0x00000000
Reason          : 0x00001000 (USN_REASON_RENAME_OLD_NAME)
Name (014)      : usn.txt
```

```
File Ref#        : 0x00670000000006BF
ParentFile Ref# : 0x0005000000000005
Usn              : 0x0000000000000188
SecurityId       : 0x00000000
Reason           : 0x00002000 (USN_REASON_RENAME_NEW_NAME)
Name (020)       : UsnNew.txt

File Ref#        : 0x00670000000006BF
ParentFile Ref# : 0x0005000000000005
Usn              : 0x00000000000001D8
SecurityId       : 0x00000000
Reason           : 0x80002000 (USN_REASON_CLOSE | USN_REASON_RENAME_NEW_NAME)
Name (020)       : UsnNew.txt
```

The entries reflect the individual modification operations involved in the operations underlying the command-line operations.

The journal is sparse so that it never overflows; when the journal's on-disk size exceeds the maximum defined for the file, NTFS simply begins zeroing the file data that precedes the window of change information having a size equal to the maximum journal size, as shown in Figure 11-42. To prevent constant resizing when an application is continuously exceeding the journal's size, NTFS shrinks the journal only when its size is twice an application-defined value over the maximum configured size.

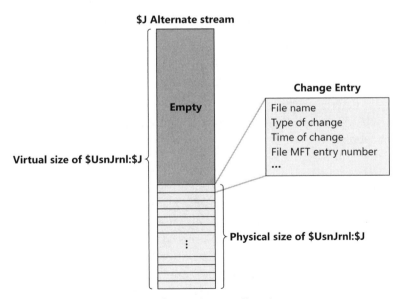

FIGURE 11-42 Change journal ($UsnJrnl) space allocation

Indexing

In NTFS, a file directory is simply an index of file names—that is, a collection of file names (along with their file references) organized in a particular way for quick access. To create a directory, NTFS indexes the filename attributes of the files in the directory. The MFT record for the root directory of a volume is shown in Figure 11-43.

FIGURE 11-43 File name index for a volume's root directory

Conceptually, an MFT entry for a directory contains in its index root attribute a sorted list of the files in the directory. For large directories, however, the file names are actually stored in 4-KB, fixed-size index buffers that contain and organize the file names. Index buffers implement a *b-tree* data structure, which minimizes the number of disk accesses needed to find a particular file, especially for large directories. The index root attribute contains the first level of the b-tree (root subdirectories) and points to index buffers containing the next level (more subdirectories, perhaps, or files).

Figure 11-43 shows only file names in the index root attribute and the index buffers (*file6*, for example), but each entry in an index also contains the file reference in the MFT where the file is described and time stamp and file size information for the file. NTFS duplicates the time stamp and file size information from the file's MFT record. This technique, which is used by FAT and NTFS, requires updated information to be written in two places. Even so, it's a significant speed optimization for directory browsing because it enables the file system to display each file's time stamps and size without opening every file in the directory.

The index allocation attribute maps the VCNs of the index buffer runs to the LCNs that indicate where the index buffers reside on the disk, and the bitmap attribute keeps track of which VCNs in the index buffers are in use and which are free. Figure 11-43 shows one file entry per VCN (that is, per cluster), but file name entries are actually packed into each cluster. Each 4-KB index buffer can contain about 20 to 30 file name entries.

The b-tree data structure is a type of balanced tree that is ideal for organizing sorted data stored on a disk because it minimizes the number of disk accesses needed to find an entry. In the MFT, a directory's index root attribute contains several file names that act as indexes into the second level of the b-tree. Each file name in the index root attribute has an optional pointer associated with it that points to an index buffer. The index buffer it points to contains file names with lexicographic values less than its own. In Figure 11-43, for example, *file4* is a first-level entry in the b-tree. It points to an index buffer containing file names that are (lexicographically) less than itself—the file names *file0*, *file1*, and *file3*. Note that the names *file1*, *file3*, and so on that are used in this example are not literal file names but names intended to show the relative placement of files that are lexicographically ordered according to the displayed sequence.

Storing the file names in b-trees provides several benefits. Directory lookups are fast because the file names are stored in a sorted order. And when higher-level software enumerates the files in a directory, NTFS returns already-sorted names. Finally, because b-trees tend to grow wide rather than deep, NTFS's fast lookup times don't degrade as directories grow.

NTFS also provides general support for indexing data besides file names, and several NTFS features—including object IDs, quota tracking, and consolidated security—use indexing to manage internal data.

Object IDs

In addition to storing the object ID assigned to a file or directory in the $OBJECT_ID attribute of its MFT record, NTFS also keeps the correspondence between object IDs and their file reference numbers in the $O index of the \$Extend\$ObjId metadata file. The index collates entries by object ID, making it easy for NTFS to quickly locate a file based on its ID. This feature allows applications, using undocumented native API functionality, to open a file or directory using its object ID. Figure 11-44 demonstrates the correspondence of the $ObjId metadata file and $OBJECT_ID attributes in MFT records.

ID passed when an application opens a file using its object ID

$ObjId metadata file MFT entry

Standard information	Filename	$O index root	$O index allocation

$O index

| Object ID 0 |
| MFT entry number optional application data |
| Object ID 1 |
| MFT entry number optional application data |
| Object ID 2 |
| MFT entry number optional application data |

MFT

File 3	$OBJECT_ID	
File 1		$OBJECT_ID
File 2	$OBJECT_ID	
⋮		

FIGURE 11-44 $ObjId and $OBJECT_ID relationships

Quota Tracking

NTFS stores quota information in the \$Extend\$Quota metadata file, which consists of the indexes $O and $Q. Figure 11-45 shows the organization of these indexes. Just as NTFS assigns each security descriptor a unique internal security ID, NTFS assigns each user a unique user ID. When an administrator defines quota information for a user, NTFS allocates a user ID that corresponds to the user's SID. In the $O index, NTFS creates an entry that maps an SID to a user ID and sorts the index by user ID; in the $Q index, NTFS creates a quota control entry. A quota control entry contains the value of the user's quota limits, as well as the amount of disk space the user consumes on the volume.

SID taken from application when a file or directory is created

User ID taken from a file's $STANDARD_INFORMATION attribute during a file operation

$O index

| SID 0 |
| User ID 0 |
| SID 1 |
| User ID 1 |
| SID 2 |
| User ID 2 |

$Q index

| User ID 0 |
| Quota entry for user 0 |
| User ID 1 |
| Quota entry for user 1 |
| User ID 2 |
| Quota entry for user 2 |

FIGURE 11-45 $Quota indexing

When an application creates a file or directory, NTFS obtains the application user's SID and looks up the associated user ID in the $O index. NTFS records the user ID in the new file or directory's $STANDARD_INFORMATION attribute, which counts all disk space allocated to the file or directory against that user's quota. Then NTFS looks up the quota entry in the $Q index and determines whether the new allocation causes the user to exceed his or her warning or limit threshold. When a new allocation causes the user to exceed a threshold, NTFS takes appropriate steps, such as logging an event to the System event log or not letting the user create the file or directory. As a file or directory changes size, NTFS updates the quota control entry associated with the user ID stored in the $STANDARD_INFORMATION attribute. NTFS uses general indexing to efficiently correlate user IDs with account SIDs, and, given a user ID, to efficiently look up a user's quota control information.

Consolidated Security

NTFS has always supported security, which lets an administrator specify which users can and can't access individual files and directories. NTFS optimizes disk utilization for security descriptors by using a central metadata file named $Secure to store only one instance of each security descriptor on a volume.

The $Secure file contains two index attributes—$SDH and $SII—and a data-stream attribute named $SDS, as Figure 11-46 shows. NTFS assigns every unique security descriptor on a volume an internal NTFS security ID (not to be confused with an SID, which uniquely identifies computers and user accounts) and hashes the security descriptor according to a simple hash algorithm. A hash is a potentially nonunique shorthand representation of a descriptor. Entries in the $SDH index map the security descriptor hashes to the security descriptor's storage location within the $SDS data attribute, and the $SII index entries map NTFS security IDs to the security descriptor's location in the $SDS data attribute.

When you apply a security descriptor to a file or directory, NTFS obtains a hash of the descriptor and looks through the $SDH index for a match. NTFS sorts the $SDH index entries according to the hash of their corresponding security descriptor and stores the entries in a b-tree. If NTFS finds a match for the descriptor in the $SDH index, NTFS locates the offset of the entry's security descriptor from the entry's offset value and reads the security descriptor from the $SDS attribute. If the hashes match but the security descriptors don't, NTFS looks for another matching entry in the $SDH index. When NTFS finds a precise match, the file or directory to which you're applying the security descriptor can reference the existing security descriptor in the $SDS attribute. NTFS makes the reference by reading the NTFS security identifier from the $SDH entry and storing it in the file or directory's $STANDARD_INFORMATION attribute. The NTFS $STANDARD_INFORMATION attribute, which all files and directories have, stores basic information about a file, including its attributes, time stamp information, and security identifier.

FIGURE 11-46 $Secure indexing

If NTFS doesn't find in the $SDH index an entry that has a security descriptor that matches the descriptor you're applying, the descriptor you're applying is unique to the volume and NTFS assigns the descriptor a new internal security ID. NTFS internal security IDs are 32-bit values, whereas SIDs are typically several times larger, so representing SIDs with NTFS security IDs saves space in the $STANDARD_INFORMATION attribute. NTFS then adds the security descriptor to the $SDS attribute, which is sorted in a b-tree by the NTFS security ID, and it adds to the $SDH and $SII indexes entries that reference the descriptor's offset in the $SDS data.

When an application attempts to open a file or directory, NTFS uses the $SII index to look up the file or directory's security descriptor. NTFS reads the file or directory's internal security ID from the MFT entry's $STANDARD_INFORMATION attribute. It then uses the $Secure file's $SII index to locate the ID's entry in the $SDS attribute. The offset into the $SDS attribute lets NTFS read the security descriptor and complete the security check. NTFS stores the 32 most recently accessed security descriptors with their $SII index entries in a cache so that it will access the $Secure file only when the $SII isn't cached.

NTFS doesn't delete entries in the $Secure file, even if no file or directory on a volume references the entry. Not deleting these entries doesn't significantly decrease disk space because most volumes, even those used for long periods, have relatively few unique security descriptors.

NTFS's use of general indexing lets files and directories that have the same security settings efficiently share security descriptors. The $SII index lets NTFS quickly look up a security descriptor in the $Secure file while performing security checks, and the $SDH index lets NTFS

quickly determine whether a security descriptor being applied to a file or directory is already stored in the $Secure file and can be shared.

Reparse Points

As described earlier in the chapter, a *reparse point* is a block of up to 16 KB of application-defined reparse data and a 32-bit reparse tag that are stored in the $REPARSE_POINT attribute of a file or directory. Whenever an application creates or deletes a reparse point, NTFS updates the \$Extend\$Reparse metadata file, in which NTFS stores entries that identify the file record numbers of files and directories that contain reparse points. Storing the records in a central location enables NTFS to provide interfaces for applications to enumerate all a volume's reparse points or just specific types of reparse points, such as mount points. (See Chapter 8 for more information on mount points.) The \$Extend\$Reparse file uses the general indexing facility of NTFS by collating the file's entries (in an index named $R) by reparse point tags.

Transaction Support

By leveraging the Kernel Transaction Manager (KTM) support in the kernel, as well as the facilities provided by the Common Log File System that were described earlier, NTFS implements a transactional model called *Transactional NTFS* or *TxF*. TxF provides a set of user-mode APIs that applications can use for transacted operations on their files and directories and also a file system control (FSCTL) interface for managing its resource managers.

> **Note** Support for TxF was added to the NTFS driver starting with Windows Vista and Windows Server 2008 without actually changing the format of the NTFS data structures, which is why the NTFS format version number, 3.1, is the same as for Windows XP and Windows Server 2003. TxF achieves backward compatibility by reusing the attribute type that was previously used only for EFS support instead of adding a new one.

The overall architecture for TxF, shown in Figure 11-47, uses several components:

- *Transacted* APIs implemented in the Kernel32.dll library
- A library for reading TxF logs (%SystemRoot%\System32\Txfw32.dll)
- A COM component for TxF logging functionality (%SystemRoot\System32\Txflog.dll)
- The transactional NTFS library inside the NTFS driver
- The CLFS infrastructure for reading and writing log records

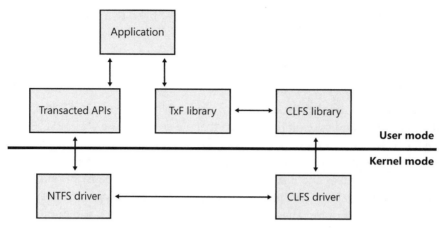

FIGURE 11-47 TxF architecture

Isolation

Although transactional file operations are opt-in, just like the transactional registry (TxR) operations described in Chapter 4, TxF has an impact on regular applications that are not transaction-aware because it ensures that the transactional operations are *isolated*. For example, if an antivirus program is scanning a file that's currently being modified by another application via a transacted operation, TxF must make sure that the scanner reads the pre-transaction data, while applications that access the file within the transaction work with the modified data. This model is called *read-committed isolation*.

Read-committed isolation involves the concept of *transacted writers* and *transacted readers*. The former always view the most up-to-date version of a file, including all changes made by the transaction that is currently associated with the file. At any given time, there can be only one transacted writer for a file, which means that its write access is exclusive. Transacted readers, on the other hand, only have access to the committed version of the file at the time they open the file. They are therefore isolated from changes made by transacted writers. This allows for readers to have a consistent view of a file, even when a transacted writer commits its changes. To see the updated data, the transacted reader must open a new handle to the modified file.

Nontransacted writers, on the other hand, are prevented from opening the file by both transacted writers and transacted readers, so they cannot make changes to the file without being part of the transaction. Nontransacted readers act similarly to transacted readers in that they see only the file contents that were last committed when the file handle was open. Unlike transacted readers, however, they do not receive read-committed isolation, and as such they always receive the updated view of the latest committed version of a transacted file without

having to open a new file handle. This allows non-transaction-aware applications to behave as expected.

To summarize, TxF's read-committed isolation model has the following characteristics:

- Changes are isolated from transacted readers

- Changes are rolled back (undone) if the associated transaction is rolled back, if the machine crashes, or if the volume is forcibly dismounted.

- Changes are flushed to disk if the associated transaction is committed.

EXPERIMENT: Understanding and Managing Transactions

In this experiment we'll use the Transactdemo.exe tool to create a new file, add some data to it as part of a transaction, and see how nontransacted clients interact with the file while the transaction is active. First, open a Command Prompt window and run Transactdemo.exe:

```
C:\>Transactdemo.exe

Transaction Demo v1.0
by Mark Russinovich

Transaction created: {5CD5E900-9DA8-11DD-8379-005056C00008}

Created C:\TransactionDemo.txt.
Pass TransDemo the GUID listed above to see the transacted file.

Rollback or commit transaction? (r/c):
```

Transactdemo creates c:\TransactionDemo.txt within a transaction that it has not committed. Open a second Command Prompt window, and use the *dir* command to look for the presence of the TransactionDemo.txt file:

```
C:\>dir transactiondemo.txt
 Volume in drive C is OS
 Volume Serial Number is 0C30-686E

 Directory of C:\
File Not Found
```

According to this second command prompt, the file doesn't even exist. Now simulate a nontransacted writer by trying to add data to the file via the *echo* command:

```
C:\>echo Hello > TransactionDemo.txt
The function attempted to use a name that is reserved for use by another transaction.
```

As expected, nontransacted writers are blocked from modifying the file.

The Ktmutil and Fsutil built-in applications can be very useful for dealing with transactional operations on the file system. For example, you can get a list of all current transactions on the system with the following command:

```
C:\>ktmutil list transactions
TxGuid                                Description
------------------------------------- -----------------------------------------------
{5cd5e900-9da8-11dd-8379-005056c00008}  Demo Transaction?
```

Note that the GUID matches what Transactdemo returned. With the GUID, you can now use the Fsutil command to query information about the transaction and to commit it or roll it back. For example, here's how to list the files part of the transaction and the owner account:

```
C:\>fsutil transaction query all {5cd5e900-9da8-11dd-8379-005056c00008}
dwOutcome:         1
dwIsolationLevel:  0
dwIsolationFlags:  0
dwTimeout:         -1
Owner:             BUILTIN\Administrators
Number of Files:   1
---- \TransactionDemo.txt
```

Although the Transactdemo tool presents you with the option to roll back or commit the current transaction, the Fsutil utility allows commits or rollbacks to any ongoing transaction your account has access to. Go back to the command prompt where you ran Transactdemo and press C to commit the transaction, after which the file becomes a standard nontransacted file.

Transactional APIs

TxF implements transacted versions of the Windows file I/O APIs, which use the suffix *Transacted*:

- **Create APIs** *CreateDirectoryTransacted, CreateFileTransacted, CreateHardLinkTransacted, CreateSymbolicLinkTransacted*

- **Find APIs** *FindFirstFileNameTransacted, FindFirstFileTransacted, FindFirstStreamTransacted*

- **Query APIs** *GetCompressedFileSizeTransacted, GetFileAttributesTransacted, GetFullPathNameTransacted, GetLongPathNameTransacted*

- **Delete APIs** *DeleteFileTransacted, RemoveDirectoryTransacted*

- **Copy and Move/Rename APIs** *CopyFileTransacted, MoveFileTransacted*

- **Set APIs** *SetFileAttributesTransacted*

In addition, some APIs automatically participate in transacted operations when the file handle they are passed is part of a transaction, like one created by the *CreateFileTransacted* API. Table 11-8 lists Windows APIs that have modified behavior when dealing with a transacted file handle.

TABLE 11-8 API Behavior Changed by TxF

API Name	Change
CloseHandle	Transactions will not be committed until all applications close transacted handles to the file.
CreateFileMapping, MapViewOfFile	Modifications to mapped views of a file part of a transaction will be associated with the transaction themselves.
FindNextFile, ReadDirectoryChanges, GetInformationByHandle, GetFileSize	If the file handle is part of a transaction, read-isolation rules will be applied to these operations.
GetVolumeInformation	Function will return FILE_SUPPORTS_TRANSACTIONS if the volume supports TxF.
ReadFile, WriteFile	Read and write operations to a transacted file handle will be part of the transaction.
SetFileInformationByHandle	Changes to the *FileBasicInfo, FileRenameInfo, FileAllocationInfo, FileEndOfFileInfo*, and *FileDispositionInfo* classes will be transacted if the file handle is part of a transaction.
SetEndOfFile, SetFileShortName, SetFileTime	Changes will be transacted if the file handle is part of a transaction.

Resource Managers

Just like TxR uses a resource manager (RM) to keep track of transactional metadata and log files, TxF uses a *default resource manager*, one for each volume, to keep track of its transactional state. TxF, however, also supports additional resource managers called *secondary resource managers*. These resource managers can be defined by application writers and have their metadata located in any directory of the application's choosing, defining their own transactional work units for undo, backup, restore, and redo operations. TxF uses the default resource manager for transacted APIs, and applications that use transactions with the *Distributed Transaction Coordinator* or the .NET Framework's *System.Transaction* classes create and manage secondary TxF resource managers with TxF resource manager file system control commands. Applications can create and manage secondary RMs by using file system control codes defined for TxF, such as FSCTL_TXFS_CREATE_SECONDARY_RM, FSCTL_TXFS_START_RM, and FSCTL_TXFS_SHUTDOWN_RM. When a secondary RM is created, it must be made consistent by one or more FSCTL_TXFS_ROLLFORWARD_REDO calls followed by FSCTL_TXFS_ROLLFORWARD_UNDO, which redo and/or undo operations that were stored in the log but never committed (such as in the case of a machine crash). We'll cover the recovery

procedure for resource managers shortly. Both the default resource manager and secondary resource managers contain a number of metadata files and directories that describe their current state:

- The $Txf directory, which is where files are linked when they are deleted or overwritten by transactional operations. If a file is deleted in a transaction, read-isolation rules specify that nontransacted readers should still be able to access the file before the delete operation is actually committed. This isolation is achieved by moving the transaction-deleted file into the $Txf directory. The NTFS driver will then keep track of the isolation by inserting a temporary structure in the SCB of the parent directory where the deleted file was originally located. In this way, the file will continue to show up if the parent is enumerated, and it will store the file reference, allowing the file to be opened. When the transaction is committed, NTFS deletes the temporary structure and deletes the file from the $Txf directory. On the other hand, if the transaction is rolled back, NTFS moves the file back to its original directory.

- The $Tops, or TxF Old Page Stream (TOPS) file, which contains a default data stream and an alternate stream called $T. The default stream for the TOPS file contains metadata about the resource manager, such as its GUID, its CLFS log policy, and the LSN at which recovery should start. The $T stream contains file data that is partially overwritten by a transactional writer (as opposed to a full overwrite, which would move the file into the $Txf directory). NTFS keeps a structure in memory that keeps track of which parts of a file are being modified under a transaction so that nontransacted readers can still access the noncommitted data by having their reads forwarded to $Tops:$T. When the transaction is committed or aborted, the pages are either moved from the $T stream into the original file or simply thrown out in the case of an abort.

- The TxF log files, which are CLFS log files storing transaction records. For the default resource manager, these files are part of the $TxfLog directory, but secondary resource managers can store them anywhere. TxF uses a multiplexed base log file called $TxfLog.blf, which contains two streams: the KtmLog stream used for Kernel Transaction Manager metadata records, and the TxfLog stream, which contains the TxF log records. Each stream is stored in CLFS log containers that start with $TxfLogContainer and are followed by a unique, increasing ID, such as 00000000000000000001. As the TxF log grows, more container files are created.

As described earlier, the default resource manager stores its files in the \$Extend\$RmMetadata directory on each NTFS-formatted volume on the machine.

EXPERIMENT: Querying Resource Manager Information

You can use the built-in Fsutil.exe command-line program to query information about the default resource manager, as well as to create, start, and stop secondary resource managers and configure their logging policies and behaviors. The following command queries information about the default resource manager, which is identified by the root directory (\):

```
C:\>fsutil resource info \
RM Identifier:         CF7234E7-39E3-11DC-BDCE-00188BDD5F49
KTM Log Path for RM:   \Device\HarddiskVolume3\$Extend\$RmMetadata\$TxfLog\
                       $TxfLog::KtmLog
Space used by TOPS:    79 Mb
TOPS free space:       100%
RM State:              Active
Running transactions: 0
One phase commits:     0
Two phase commits:     1
System initiated rollbacks: 0
Age of oldest transaction:  00:00:00
Logging Mode:          Simple
Number of containers: 2
Container size:        10 Mb
Total log capacity:    20 Mb
Total free log space: 14 Mb
Minimum containers:    2
Maximum containers:    20
Log growth increment: 2 container(s)
Auto shrink:           Not enabled

RM prefers availability over consistency.
```

As mentioned, the *fsutil resource* command has many options for configuring TxF resource managers, including the ability to create a secondary resource manager in any directory of your choice. For example, you can use the *fsutil resource create c:\rmtest* command to create a secondary resource manager in the Rmtest directory, followed by the *fsutil resource start c:\rmtest* command to initiate it. Note the presence of the $Tops and $TxfLogContainer* files and of the TxfLog and $Txf directories in this folder.

On-Disk Implementation

As shown earlier in Table 11-5, TxF uses the $LOGGED_UTILITY_STREAM attribute type to store additional data for files and directories that are or have been part of a transaction. This attribute is called $TXF_DATA and contains important information that allows TxF to keep active offline data for a file part of a transaction. The attribute is permanently stored in the MFT; that is, even after the file is not part of a transaction anymore, the stream remains, for reasons we'll explain shortly. The major components of the attribute are shown in Figure 11-48.

File reference to RM root
Flags
TxF file ID (TxID)
LSN for NTFS metadata
LSN for user data
LSN for directory index
USN index

FIGURE 11-48 $TXF_DATA attribute

The first field shown is the file reference to the root of the resource manager responsible for the transaction associated with this file. For the default resource manager, the file reference ID is 5, which is the file record for the root directory (\), as shown earlier in Figure 11-25. TxF needs this information when it creates an FCB for the file so that it can link it to the correct resource manager, which in turn needs to create an enlistment for the transaction when a transacted file request is received by NTFS. (For more information on enlistments and transactions, see the KTM section in Chapter 3.)

Another important piece of data stored in the $TXF_DATA attribute is the TxF file ID, or TxID, and this explains why $TXF_DATA attributes are never deleted. Because NTFS writes file names to its records when writing to the transaction log, it needs a way to uniquely identify files in the same directory that may have had the same name. For example, if sample.txt is deleted from a directory in a transaction and later a new file with the same name is created in the same directory (and as part of the same transaction), TxF needs a way to uniquely identify the two instances of sample.txt. This identification is provided by a 64-bit unique number, the TxID, that TxF increments when a new file (or an instance of a file) becomes part of a transaction. Because they can never be reused, TxIDs are permanent, so the $TXF_DATA attribute will never be removed from a file.

Last but not least, three CLFS LSNs are stored for each file part of a transaction. Whenever a transaction is active, such as during create, rename, or write operations, TxF writes a log record to its CLFS log. Each record is assigned an LSN, and that LSN gets written to the appropriate field in the $TXF_DATA attribute. The first LSN is used to store the log record that identifies the changes to NTFS metadata in relation to this file. For example, if the standard attributes of a file are changed as part of a transacted operation, TxF must update the relevant MFT file record, and the LSN for the log record describing the change is stored. TxF uses the second LSN when the file's data is modified. Finally, TxF uses the third LSN when the file name index for the directory requires a change related to a transaction the file took part in, or when a directory was part of a transaction and received a TxID.

The $TXF_DATA attribute also stores internal flags that describe the state information to TxF and the index of the USN record that was applied to the file on commit. A TxF transaction can span multiple USN records that may have been partly updated by NTFS's recovery

mechanism (described shortly), so the index tells TxF how many more USN records must be applied after a recovery.

Logging Implementation

As mentioned earlier, each time a change is made to the disk because of an ongoing transaction, TxF writes a record of the change to its log. TxF uses a variety of log record types to keep track of transactional changes, but regardless of the record type, all TxF log records have a generic header that contains information identifying the type of the record, the action related to the record, the TxID that the record applies to, and the GUID of the KTM transaction that the record is associated with.

A *redo record* specifies how to reapply a change part of a transaction that's already been committed to the volume if the transaction has actually never been flushed from cache to disk. An *undo record*, on the other hand, specifies how to reverse a change part of a transaction that hasn't been committed at the time of a rollback. Some records are redo-only, meaning they don't contain any equivalent undo data, while other records contain both redo and undo information.

Through the TOPS file, TxF maintains two critical pieces of data, the *base LSN* and the *restart LSN*. The base LSN determines the LSN of the first valid record in the log, while the restart LSN indicates at which LSN recovery should begin when starting the resource manager. When TxF writes a *restart record*, it updates these two values, indicating that changes have been made to the volume and flushed out to disk—meaning that the file system is fully consistent up to the new restart LSN.

TxF also writes *compensating log records* or CLRs. These records store the actions that are being performed during transaction rollback (explained next). They're primarily used to store the *undo-next LSN,* which allows the recovery process to avoid repeated undo operations by bypassing undo records that have already been processed, a situation that can happen if the system fails during the recovery phase and has already performed part of the undo pass. Finally, TxF also deals with *prepare records, abort records,* and *commit records,* which describe the state of the KTM transactions related to TxF.

Recovery Implementation

When a resource manager starts because of an FSCTL_TXFS_START_RM call (or, for the default resource manager, as soon as the volume is mounted), TxF runs the recovery process. It reads the TOPS file to determine the restart LSN, where the recovery process should start, and then reads each record forward through the log (called the *redo pass*). As each record is being processed, TxF opens the file referenced by the record and compares the LSN in the $TXF_DATA attribute with the LSN in the record. If the LSN stored in the attribute is greater than or equal to the LSN of the log record, the action is not applied because the on-disk copy of the file is as new or newer than that of the log record action. If the LSN is not greater than or equal

to the LSN in the record, the log contains information about the file that was never written to the file itself. In this case, TxF applies whichever action was recorded in the log record and updates the LSN in the $TXF_DATA attribute with the LSN from the record.

As TxF is processing its redo pass, it builds its *transaction table*, which describes the operations that it has completed; if it encounters an abort or commit record along the way, TxF discards the related transactions. By the end of the redo pass, TxF parses the final transaction table and connects to the KTM to see whether the KTM recorded a commit or an abort for the transactions. (KTM stores this information in the KtmLog stream of the TxF multiplexed log, as explained earlier.)

After TxF has finished communicating with the KTM, it looks at any leftover transactions in the transaction table and begins the *undo pass*. In the undo pass, TxF aborts all the remaining transactions in the transaction table by traversing each transaction's undo LSN chain and applying the undo action for each log record. At the end of the undo pass, the resource manager is consistent and initialized.

This process is very similar to the log file service's recovery procedure, which is described later in more detail. You should refer to this description for a complete picture of the standard transactional recovery mechanisms.

NTFS Recovery Support

NTFS recovery support ensures that if a power failure or a system failure occurs, no file system operations (transactions) will be left incomplete and the structure of the disk volume will remain intact without the need to run a disk repair utility. The NTFS Chkdsk utility is used to repair catastrophic disk corruption caused by I/O errors (bad disk sectors, electrical anomalies, or disk failures, for example) or software bugs. But with the NTFS recovery capabilities in place, Chkdsk is rarely needed.

As mentioned earlier (in the section "Recoverability"), NTFS uses a transaction-processing scheme to implement recoverability. This strategy ensures a full disk recovery that is also extremely fast (on the order of seconds) for even the largest disks. NTFS limits its recovery procedures to file system data to ensure that at the very least the user will never lose a volume because of a corrupted file system; however, unless an application takes specific action (such as flushing cached files to disk), NTFS's recovery support doesn't guarantee user data to be fully updated if a crash occurs. This is the job of Transactional NTFS (TxF).

The following sections detail the transaction-logging scheme NTFS uses to record modifications to file system data structures and explain how NTFS recovers a volume if the system fails.

Design

NTFS implements the design of a *recoverable file system*. These file systems ensure volume consistency by using logging techniques (sometimes called *journaling*) originally developed for transaction processing. If the operating system crashes, the recoverable file system restores consistency by executing a recovery procedure that accesses information that has been stored in a log file. Because the file system has logged its disk writes, the recovery procedure takes only seconds, regardless of the size of the volume. The recovery procedure for a recoverable file system is exact, guaranteeing that the volume will be restored to a consistent state.

A recoverable file system incurs some costs for the safety it provides. Every transaction that alters the volume structure requires that one record be written to the log file for each of the transaction's suboperations. This logging overhead is ameliorated by the file system's *batching* of log records—writing many records to the log file in a single I/O operation. In addition, the recoverable file system can employ the optimization techniques of a lazy write file system. It can even increase the length of the intervals between cache flushes because the file system can be recovered if the system crashes before the cache changes have been flushed to disk. This gain over the caching performance of lazy write file systems makes up for, and often exceeds, the overhead of the recoverable file system's logging activity.

Neither careful write nor lazy write file systems guarantee protection of user file data. If the system crashes while an application is writing a file, the file can be lost or corrupted. Worse, the crash can corrupt a lazy write file system, destroying existing files or even rendering an entire volume inaccessible.

The NTFS recoverable file system implements several strategies that improve its reliability over that of the traditional file systems. First, NTFS recoverability guarantees that the volume structure won't be corrupted, so all files will remain accessible after a system failure. Second, although NTFS doesn't guarantee protection of user data in the event of a system crash—some changes can be lost from the cache—applications can take advantage of the NTFS write-through and cache-flushing capabilities to ensure that file modifications are recorded on disk at appropriate intervals.

Both *cache write-through*—forcing write operations to be immediately recorded on disk—and *cache flushing*—forcing cache contents to be written to disk—are efficient operations. NTFS doesn't have to do extra disk I/O to flush modifications to several different file system data structures because changes to the data structures are recorded—in a single write operation—in the log file; if a failure occurs and cache contents are lost, the file system modifications can be recovered from the log. Furthermore, unlike the FAT file system, NTFS guarantees that user data will be consistent and available immediately after a write-through operation or a cache flush, even if the system subsequently fails.

Metadata Logging

NTFS provides file system recoverability by using the same logging technique used by TxF, which consists of recording all operations that modify file system metadata to a log file. Unlike TxF, however, NTFS's built-in file system recovery support doesn't make use of CLFS but uses an internal logging implementation called the *log file service*. Another difference is that while TxF is used only when callers opt-in for transacted operations, NTFS records all metadata changes so that the file system can be made consistent in the face of a system failure.

Log File Service

The log file service (LFS) is a series of kernel-mode routines inside the NTFS driver that NTFS uses to access the log file. NTFS passes the LFS a pointer to an open file object, which specifies a log file to be accessed. The LFS either initializes a new log file or calls the Windows cache manager to access the existing log file through the cache, as shown in Figure 11-49. Note that although LFS and CLFS have similar sounding names, they are separate logging implementations used for different reasons, although their operation is similar in many ways.

FIGURE 11-49 Log file service (LFS)

The LFS divides the log file into two regions: a *restart area* and an "infinite" *logging area*, as shown in Figure 11-50.

FIGURE 11-50 Log file regions

NTFS calls the LFS to read and write the restart area. NTFS uses the restart area to store context information such as the location in the logging area at which NTFS will begin to read during recovery after a system failure. The LFS maintains a second copy of the restart data in case the first becomes corrupted or otherwise inaccessible. The remainder of the log file is the logging area, which contains transaction records NTFS writes to recover a volume in the event of a system failure. The LFS makes the log file appear infinite by reusing it circularly (while guaranteeing that it doesn't overwrite information it needs). Just like CLFS, the LFS uses LSNs to identify records written to the log file. As the LFS cycles through the file, it increases the values of the LSNs. NTFS uses 64 bits to represent LSNs, so the number of possible LSNs is so large as to be virtually infinite.

NTFS never reads transactions from or writes transactions to the log file directly. The LFS provides services that NTFS calls to open the log file, write log records, read log records in forward or backward order, flush log records up to a particular LSN, or set the beginning of the log file to a higher LSN. During recovery, NTFS calls the LFS to perform the same actions as described in the TxF recovery section: a redo pass for nonflushed committed changes, followed by an undo pass for noncommitted changes.

Here's how the system guarantees that the volume can be recovered:

1. NTFS first calls the LFS to record in the (cached) log file any transactions that will modify the volume structure.

2. NTFS modifies the volume (also in the cache).

3. The cache manager prompts the LFS to flush the log file to disk. (The LFS implements the flush by calling the cache manager back, telling it which pages of memory to flush. Refer back to the calling sequence shown in Figure 11-49.)

4. After the cache manager flushes the log file to disk, it flushes the volume changes (the metadata operations themselves) to disk.

These steps ensure that if the file system modifications are ultimately unsuccessful, the corresponding transactions can be retrieved from the log file and can be either redone or undone as part of the file system recovery procedure.

File system recovery begins automatically the first time the volume is used after the system is rebooted. NTFS checks whether the transactions that were recorded in the log file before the crash were applied to the volume, and if they weren't, it redoes them. NTFS also guarantees that transactions not completely logged before the crash are undone so that they don't appear on the volume.

Log Record Types

The NTFS recovery mechanism uses similar log record types as the TxF recovery mechanism: *update records*, which correspond to the redo and undo records that TxF uses, and *checkpoint records*, which are similar to the restart records used by TxF. Figure 11-51 shows three update records in the log file. Each record represents one suboperation of a transaction, creating a new file. The redo entry in each update record tells NTFS how to reapply the suboperation to the volume, and the undo entry tells NTFS how to roll back (undo) the suboperation.

FIGURE 11-51 Update records in the log file

After logging a transaction (in this example, by calling the LFS to write the three update records to the log file), NTFS performs the suboperations on the volume itself, in the cache. When it has finished updating the cache, NTFS writes another record to the log file, recording the entire transaction as complete—a suboperation known as *committing* a transaction. Once a transaction is committed, NTFS guarantees that the entire transaction will appear on the volume, even if the operating system subsequently fails.

When recovering after a system failure, NTFS reads through the log file and redoes each committed transaction. Although NTFS completed the committed transactions from before the system failure, it doesn't know whether the cache manager flushed the volume modifications to disk in time. The updates might have been lost from the cache when the system failed. Therefore, NTFS executes the committed transactions again just to be sure that the disk is up to date.

After redoing the committed transactions during a file system recovery, NTFS locates all the transactions in the log file that weren't committed at failure and rolls back each suboperation that had been logged. In Figure 11-51, NTFS would first undo the T1*c* suboperation and then follow the backward pointer to T1*b* and undo that suboperation. It would continue to follow

the backward pointers, undoing suboperations, until it reached the first suboperation in the transaction. By following the pointers, NTFS knows how many and which update records it must undo to roll back a transaction.

Redo and undo information can be expressed either physically or logically. As the lowest layer of software maintaining the file system structure, NTFS writes update records with *physical descriptions* that specify volume updates in terms of particular byte ranges on the disk that are to be changed, moved, and so on, unlike TxF, which uses *logical descriptions* that express updates in terms of operations such as "delete file A.dat." NTFS writes update records (usually several) for each of the following transactions:

- Creating a file
- Deleting a file
- Extending a file
- Truncating a file
- Setting file information
- Renaming a file
- Changing the security applied to a file

The redo and undo information in an update record must be carefully designed because although NTFS undoes a transaction, recovers from a system failure, or even operates normally, it might try to redo a transaction that has already been done or, conversely, to undo a transaction that never occurred or that has already been undone. Similarly, NTFS might try to redo or undo a transaction consisting of several update records, only some of which are complete on disk. The format of the update records must ensure that executing redundant redo or undo operations is *idempotent*, that is, has a neutral effect. For example, setting a bit that is already set has no effect, but toggling a bit that has already been toggled does. The file system must also handle intermediate volume states correctly.

In addition to update records, NTFS periodically writes a checkpoint record to the log file, as illustrated in Figure 11-52.

FIGURE 11-52 Checkpoint record in the log file

A checkpoint record helps NTFS determine what processing would be needed to recover a volume if a crash were to occur immediately. Using information stored in the checkpoint record, NTFS knows, for example, how far back in the log file it must go to begin its recovery. After writing a checkpoint record, NTFS stores the LSN of the record in the restart area so that it can quickly find its most recently written checkpoint record when it begins file system recovery after a crash occurs—this is similar to the restart LSN used by TxF for the same reason.

Although the LFS presents the log file to NTFS as if it were infinitely large, it isn't. The generous size of the log file and the frequent writing of checkpoint records (an operation that usually frees up space in the log file) make the possibility of the log file filling up a remote one. Nevertheless, the LFS, just like CLFS, accounts for this possibility by tracking several numbers:

- The available log space
- The amount of space needed to write an incoming log record and to undo the write, should that be necessary
- The amount of space needed to roll back all active (noncommitted) transactions, should that be necessary

If the log file doesn't contain enough available space to accommodate the total of the last two items, the LFS returns a "log file full" error, and NTFS raises an exception. The NTFS exception handler rolls back the current transaction and places it in a queue to be restarted later.

To free up space in the log file, NTFS must momentarily prevent further transactions on files. To do so, NTFS blocks file creation and deletion and then requests exclusive access to all system files and shared access to all user files. Gradually, active transactions either are completed successfully or receive the "log file full" exception. NTFS rolls back and queues the transactions that receive the exception.

Once it has blocked transaction activity on files as just described, NTFS calls the cache manager to flush unwritten data to disk, including unwritten log file data. After everything is safely flushed to disk, NTFS no longer needs the data in the log file. It resets the beginning of the log file to the current position, making the log file "empty." Then it restarts the queued transactions. Beyond the short pause in I/O processing, the "log file full" error has no effect on executing programs.

This scenario is one example of how NTFS uses the log file not only for file system recovery but also for error recovery during normal operation. You'll find out more about error recovery in the following section.

Recovery

NTFS automatically performs a disk recovery the first time a program accesses an NTFS volume after the system has been booted. (If no recovery is needed, the process is trivial.) Recovery depends on two tables NTFS maintains in memory: a transaction table, which behaves just like the one TxF maintains, and a *dirty page table,* which records which pages in the cache contain modifications to the file system structure that haven't yet been written to disk. This data must be flushed to disk during recovery.

NTFS writes a checkpoint record to the log file once every 5 seconds. Just before it does, it calls the LFS to store a current copy of the transaction table and of the dirty page table in the log file. NTFS then records in the checkpoint record the LSNs of the log records containing the copied tables. When recovery begins after a system failure, NTFS calls the LFS to locate the log records containing the most recent checkpoint record and the most recent copies of the transaction and dirty page tables. It then copies the tables to memory.

The log file usually contains more update records following the last checkpoint record. These update records represent volume modifications that occurred after the last checkpoint record was written. NTFS must update the transaction and dirty page tables to include these operations. After updating the tables, NTFS uses the tables and the contents of the log file to update the volume itself.

To effect its volume recovery, NTFS scans the log file three times, loading the file into memory during the first pass to minimize disk I/O. Each pass has a particular purpose:

1. Analysis
2. Redoing transactions
3. Undoing transactions

Analysis Pass

During the *analysis pass*, as shown in Figure 11-53, NTFS scans forward in the log file from the beginning of the last checkpoint operation to find update records and use them to update the transaction and dirty page tables it copied to memory. Notice in the figure that the checkpoint operation stores three records in the log file and that update records might be interspersed among these records. NTFS therefore must start its scan at the beginning of the checkpoint operation.

FIGURE 11-53 Analysis pass

Most update records that appear in the log file after the checkpoint operation begins represent a modification to either the transaction table or the dirty page table. If an update record is a "transaction committed" record, for example, the transaction the record represents must be removed from the transaction table. Similarly, if the update record is a "page update" record that modifies a file system data structure, the dirty page table must be updated to reflect that change.

Once the tables are up to date in memory, NTFS scans the tables to determine the LSN of the oldest update record that logs an operation that hasn't been carried out on disk. The transaction table contains the LSNs of the noncommitted (incomplete) transactions, and the dirty page table contains the LSNs of records in the cache that haven't been flushed to disk. The LSN of the oldest update record that NTFS finds in these two tables determines where the redo pass will begin. If the last checkpoint record is older, however, NTFS will start the redo pass there instead.

> **Note** In the TxF recovery model, there is no distinct analysis pass. Instead, as described in the TxF recovery section, TxF performs the equivalent work in the redo pass.

Redo Pass

During the *redo pass*, as shown in Figure 11-54, NTFS scans forward in the log file from the LSN of the oldest update record, which it found during the analysis pass. It looks for "page update" records, which contain volume modifications that were written before the system failure but that might not have been flushed to disk. NTFS redoes these updates in the cache.

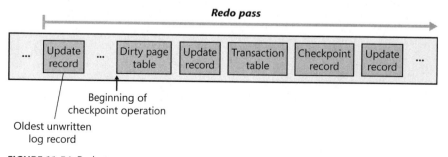

FIGURE 11-54 Redo pass

When NTFS reaches the end of the log file, it has updated the cache with the necessary volume modifications, and the cache manager's lazy writer can begin writing cache contents to disk in the background.

Undo Pass

After it completes the redo pass, NTFS begins its *undo pass*, in which it rolls back any transactions that weren't committed when the system failed. Figure 11-55 shows two transactions in the log file; transaction 1 was committed before the power failure, but transaction 2 wasn't. NTFS must undo transaction 2.

FIGURE 11-55 Undo pass

Suppose that transaction 2 created a file, an operation that comprises three suboperations, each with its own update record. The update records of a transaction are linked by backward pointers in the log file because they are usually not contiguous.

The NTFS transaction table lists the LSN of the last-logged update record for each noncommitted transaction. In this example, the transaction table identifies LSN 4049 as the last update record logged for transaction 2. As shown from right to left in Figure 11-56, NTFS rolls back transaction 2.

FIGURE 11-56 Undoing a transaction

After locating LSN 4049, NTFS finds the undo information and executes it, clearing bits 3 through 9 in its allocation bitmap. NTFS then follows the backward pointer to LSN 4048, which directs it to remove the new file name from the appropriate file name index. Finally, it follows the last backward pointer and deallocates the MFT file record reserved for the file, as the update record with LSN 4046 specifies. Transaction 2 is now rolled back. If there are other noncommitted transactions to undo, NTFS follows the same procedure to roll them back. Because undoing transactions affects the volume's file system structure, NTFS must log the undo operations in the log file. After all, the power might fail again during the recovery, and NTFS would have to redo its undo operations!

When the undo pass of the recovery is finished, the volume has been restored to a consistent state. At this point, NTFS is prepared to flush the cache changes to disk to ensure that the volume is up to date. Before doing so, however, it executes a callback that TxF registers for notifications of LFS flushes. Because TxF and NTFS both use write-ahead logging, TxF must flush its log through CLFS before the NTFS log is flushed to ensure consistency of its own metadata. (And similarly, the TOPS file must be flushed before the CLFS-managed log files.) NTFS then writes an "empty" LFS restart area to indicate that the volume is consistent and that no recovery need be done if the system should fail again immediately. Recovery is complete.

NTFS guarantees that recovery will return the volume to some preexisting consistent state, but not necessarily to the state that existed just before the system crash. NTFS can't make that guarantee because, for performance, it uses a "lazy commit" algorithm, which means that the log file isn't immediately flushed to disk each time a "transaction committed" record is written. Instead, numerous "transaction committed" records are batched and written together, either when the cache manager calls the LFS to flush the log file to disk or when the LFS writes a checkpoint record (once every 5 seconds) to the log file. Another reason the recovered volume might not be completely up to date is that several parallel transactions might be active when the system crashes and some of their "transaction committed" records might make it to disk whereas others might not. The consistent volume that recovery produces includes all the volume updates whose "transaction committed" records made it to disk and none of the updates whose "transaction committed" records didn't make it to disk.

NTFS uses the log file to recover a volume after the system fails, but it also takes advantage of an important "freebie" it gets from logging transactions. File systems necessarily contain a lot of code devoted to recovering from file system errors that occur during the course of normal file I/O. Because NTFS logs each transaction that modifies the volume structure, it can use the log file to recover when a file system error occurs and thus can greatly simplify its error handling code. The "log file full" error described earlier is one example of using the log file for error recovery.

Most I/O errors a program receives aren't file system errors and therefore can't be resolved entirely by NTFS. When called to create a file, for example, NTFS might begin by creating a file record in the MFT and then enter the new file's name in a directory index. When it tries to allocate space for the file in its bitmap, however, it could discover that the disk is full and the create request can't be completed. In such a case, NTFS uses the information in the log file to undo the part of the operation it has already completed and to deallocate the data structures it reserved for the file. Then it returns a "disk full" error to the caller, which in turn must respond appropriately to the error.

NTFS Bad-Cluster Recovery

The volume manager included with Windows (VolMgr) can recover data from a bad sector on a fault-tolerant volume, but if the hard disk doesn't use the SCSI protocol or runs out of spare sectors, a volume manager can't perform sector sparing to replace the bad sector. (See Chapter 8 for more information on the volume manager.) When the file system reads from the sector, the volume manager instead recovers the data and returns the warning to the file system that there is only one copy of the data.

The FAT file system doesn't respond to this volume manager warning. Moreover, neither FAT nor the volume manager keeps track of the bad sectors, so a user must run the Chkdsk or Format utility to prevent the volume manager from repeatedly recovering data for the file system. Both Chkdsk and Format are less than ideal for removing bad sectors from use. Chkdsk can take a long time to find and remove bad sectors, and Format wipes all the data off the partition it's formatting.

In the file system equivalent of a volume manager's sector sparing, NTFS dynamically replaces the cluster containing a bad sector and keeps track of the bad cluster so that it won't be reused. (Recall that NTFS maintains portability by addressing logical clusters rather than physical sectors.) NTFS performs these functions when the volume manager can't perform sector sparing. When a volume manager returns a bad-sector warning or when the hard disk driver returns a bad-sector error, NTFS allocates a new cluster to replace the one containing the bad sector. NTFS copies the data that the volume manager has recovered into the new cluster to reestablish data redundancy.

Figure 11-57 shows an MFT record for a user file with a bad cluster in one of its data runs as it existed before the cluster went bad. When it receives a bad-sector error, NTFS reassigns the cluster containing the sector to its bad-cluster file. This prevents the bad cluster from being allocated to another file. NTFS then allocates a new cluster for the file and changes the file's VCN-to-LCN mappings to point to the new cluster. This bad-cluster remapping (introduced earlier in this chapter) is illustrated in Figure 11-57. Cluster number 1357, which contains the bad sector, must be replaced by a good cluster.

FIGURE 11-57 MFT record for a user file with a bad cluster

Bad-sector errors are undesirable, but when they do occur, the combination of NTFS and the volume manager provides the best possible solution. If the bad sector is on a redundant volume, the volume manager recovers the data and replaces the sector if it can. If it can't replace the sector, it returns a warning to NTFS, and NTFS replaces the cluster containing the bad sector.

If the volume isn't configured as a redundant volume, the data in the bad sector can't be recovered. When the volume is formatted as a FAT volume and the volume manager can't recover the data, reading from the bad sector yields indeterminate results. If some of the file system's control structures reside in the bad sector, an entire file or group of files (or potentially, the whole disk) can be lost. At best, some data in the affected file (often, all the data in the file beyond the bad sector) is lost. Moreover, the FAT file system is likely to reallocate the bad sector to the same or another file on the volume, causing the problem to resurface.

Like the other file systems, NTFS can't recover data from a bad sector without help from a volume manager. However, NTFS greatly contains the damage a bad sector can cause. If NTFS discovers the bad sector during a read operation, it remaps the cluster the sector is in, as shown in Figure 11-58. If the volume isn't configured as a redundant volume, NTFS returns a "data read" error to the calling program. Although the data that was in that cluster is lost, the rest of the file—and the file system—remains intact; the calling program can respond appropriately to the data loss, and the bad cluster won't be reused in future allocations. If NTFS discovers the bad cluster on a write operation rather than a read, NTFS remaps the cluster before writing and thus loses no data and generates no error.

The same recovery procedures are followed if file system data is stored in a sector that goes bad. If the bad sector is on a redundant volume, NTFS replaces the cluster dynamically, using the data recovered by the volume manager. If the volume isn't redundant, the data can't be recovered, and NTFS sets a bit in the volume file that indicates corruption on the volume. The NTFS Chkdsk utility checks this bit when the system is next rebooted, and if the bit is set, Chkdsk executes, fixing the file system corruption by reconstructing the NTFS metadata.

FIGURE 11-58 Bad-cluster remapping

In rare instances, file system corruption can occur even on a fault-tolerant disk configuration. A double error can destroy both file system data and the means to reconstruct it. If the system crashes while NTFS is writing the mirror copy of an MFT file record—of a file name index or of the log file, for example—the mirror copy of such file system data might not be fully updated. If the system were rebooted and a bad-sector error occurred on the primary disk at exactly the same location as the incomplete write on the disk mirror, NTFS would be unable to recover the correct data from the disk mirror. NTFS implements a special scheme for detecting such corruptions in file system data. If it ever finds an inconsistency, it sets the corruption bit in the volume file, which causes Chkdsk to reconstruct the NTFS metadata when the system is next rebooted. Because file system corruption is rare on a fault-tolerant disk configuration, Chkdsk is seldom needed. It is supplied as a safety precaution rather than as a first-line data recovery strategy.

The use of Chkdsk on NTFS is vastly different from its use on the FAT file system. Before writing anything to disk, FAT sets the volume's dirty bit and then resets the bit after the modification is complete. If any I/O operation is in progress when the system crashes, the dirty bit

is left set and Chkdsk runs when the system is rebooted. On NTFS, Chkdsk runs only when unexpected or unreadable file system data is found and NTFS can't recover the data from a redundant volume or from redundant file system structures on a single volume. (The system boot sector is duplicated, as are the parts of the MFT required for booting the system and running the NTFS recovery procedure. This redundancy ensures that NTFS will always be able to boot and recover itself.)

Table 11-9 summarizes what happens when a sector goes bad on a disk volume formatted for one of the Windows-supported file systems according to various conditions we've described in this section.

TABLE 11-9 Summary of NTFS Data Recovery Scenarios

Scenario	With a SCSI Disk That Has Spare Sectors	With a Non-SCSI Disk or a Disk with No Spare Sectors[1]
Fault-tolerant volume[2]	1. Volume manager recovers the data. 2. Volume manager performs sector sparing (replaces the bad sector). 3. File system remains unaware of the error.	1. Volume manager recovers the data. 2. Volume manager sends the data and a bad-sector error to the file system. 3. NTFS performs cluster remapping.
Non-fault-tolerant volume	1. Volume manager can't recover the data. 2. Volume manager sends a bad-sector error to the file system. 3. NTFS performs cluster remapping. Data is lost.[3]	1. Volume manager can't recover the data. 2. Volume manager sends a bad-sector error to the file system. 3. NTFS performs cluster remapping. Data is lost.

[1] In neither of these cases can a volume manager perform sector sparing: (1) hard disks that don't use the SCSI protocol have no standard interface for providing sector sparing; (2) some hard disks don't provide hardware support for sector sparing, and SCSI hard disks that do provide sector sparing can eventually run out of spare sectors if a lot of sectors go bad.

[2] A fault-tolerant volume is one of the following: a mirror set or a RAID-5 set.

[3] In a write operation, no data is lost: NTFS remaps the cluster before the write.

If the volume on which the bad sector appears is a fault-tolerant volume (a mirrored or RAID-5 volume) and if the hard disk is one that supports sector sparing (and that hasn't run out of spare sectors), it doesn't matter which file system you're using (FAT or NTFS). The volume manager replaces the bad sector without the need for user or file system intervention.

If a bad sector is located on a hard disk that doesn't support sector sparing, the file system is responsible for replacing (remapping) the bad sector or—in the case of NTFS—the cluster in which the bad sector resides. The FAT file system doesn't provide sector or cluster remapping. The benefits of NTFS cluster remapping are that bad spots in a file can be fixed without harm to the file (or harm to the file system, as the case may be) and that the bad cluster won't be reallocated to the same or another file.

Self-Healing

With today's multiterabyte storage devices, taking a volume offline for a consistency check can result in a service outage of many hours. Recognizing that many disk corruptions are localized to a single file or portion of metadata, NTFS implements a self-healing feature to repair damage while a volume remains online. When NTFS detects corruption, it prevents access to the damaged file or files and creates a system worker thread that executes Chkdsk-like corrections to the corrupted data structures, allowing access to the repaired files when it has finished. Access to other files continues normally during this operation, minimizing service disruption.

You can use the *fsutil repair set* command to view and set a volume's repair options, which are summarized in Table 11-10. The Fsutil utility uses the FSCTL_SET_REPAIR file system control code to set these settings, which are saved in the VCB for the volume.

TABLE 11-10 NTFS Self-Healing Behaviors

Flag	Behavior
SET_REPAIR_ENABLED	Enable self-healing for the volume.
SET_REPAIR_WARN_ABOUT_DATA_LOSS	If the self-healing process is unable to fully recover a file, specifies whether the user should be visually warned.
SET_REPAIR_DISABLED_AND_BUGCHECK_ON_CORRUPTION	If the NtfsBugCheckOnCorrupt NTFS registry value was set by using *fsutil behavior set NtfsBugCheckOnCorrupt 1* and this flag is set, the system will crash with a STOP error 0x24, indicating file system corruption. This setting is automatically cleared during boot time to avoid repeated reboot cycles.

In all cases, including when the visual warning is disabled (the default), NTFS will log any self-healing operation it undertook in the System event log.

Apart from periodic automatic self-healing, NTFS also supports manually initiated self-healing cycles through the FSCTL_INITIATE_REPAIR and FSCTL_WAIT_FOR_REPAIR control codes, which can be initiated with the *fsutil repair initiate* and *fsutil repair wait* commands. This allows the user to force the repair of a specific file and to wait until repair of that file is complete.

To check the status of the self-healing mechanism, the FSCTL_QUERY_REPAIR control code or the *fsutil repair query* command can be used, as shown here:

```
C:\>fsutil repair query c:
Self healing is enabled for volume c: with flags 0x1.
 flags: 0x01 - enable general repair
        0x08 - warn about potential data loss
        0x10 - disable general repair and bugcheck once on first corruption
```

Encrypting File System Security

EFS security relies on cryptography support. The first time a file is encrypted, EFS assigns the account of the user performing the encryption a private/public key pair for use in file encryption. Users can encrypt files via Windows Explorer by opening a file's Properties dialog box, clicking Advanced, and then selecting the Encrypt Contents To Secure Data option, as shown in Figure 11-59. Users can also encrypt files via a command-line utility named *cipher*. Windows automatically encrypts files that reside in directories that are designated as encrypted directories. When a file is encrypted, EFS generates a random number for the file that EFS calls the file's file encryption key (FEK). EFS uses the FEK to encrypt the file's contents with a stronger variant of the Data Encryption Standard (DES) algorithm—Triple-DES (3DES) or Advanced Encryption Standard (AES). EFS stores the file's FEK with the file but encrypts the FEK with the user's EFS public key by using the RSA public key–based encryption algorithm. After EFS completes these steps, the file is secure: other users can't decrypt the data without the file's decrypted FEK, and they can't decrypt the FEK without the private key.

FIGURE 11-59 Encrypt files by using the Advanced Attributes dialog box

EFS FEK Key Strength

The default FEK encryption algorithm is AES. The Windows AES algorithm uses 256-bit keys. Use of 3DES allows access to larger sized keys, so if you require greater key strength you can enable 3DES encryption in one of two ways: either as the algorithm for all system cryptographic services or just for EFS.

To have 3DES be the encryption algorithm for all system cryptographic services, open the Local Security Policy Editor by entering **secpol.msc** in the Run dialog box from the Start menu and open the Security Options node under Local Policies. View the properties of System Cryptography: Use FIPS Compliant Algorithms For Encryption, Hashing And Signing, and enable it.

To enable 3DES for EFS only, create the DWORD value HKLM\SOFTWARE\Microsoft\Windows NT\CurrentVersion\EFS\AlgorithmID, set it to 0x6603, and reboot.

EFS uses a private/public key algorithm to encrypt FEKs. To encrypt file data, EFS uses AES or 3DES because both are *symmetric encryption algorithms*, which means that they use the same key to encrypt and decrypt data. Symmetric encryption algorithms are typically very fast, which makes them suitable for encrypting large amounts of data, such as file data. However, symmetric encryption algorithms have a weakness: you can bypass their security if you obtain the key. If multiple users want to share one encrypted file protected only by AES or 3DES, each user would require access to the file's FEK. Leaving the FEK unencrypted would obviously be a security problem, but encrypting the FEK once would require all the users to share the same FEK decryption key—another potential security problem.

Keeping the FEK secure is a difficult problem, which EFS addresses with the public key–based half of its encryption architecture. Encrypting a file's FEK for individual users who access the file lets multiple users share an encrypted file. EFS can encrypt a file's FEK with each user's public key and can store each user's encrypted FEK with the file. Anyone can access a user's public key, but no one can use a public key to decrypt the data that the public key encrypted. The only way users can decrypt a file is with their private key, which the operating system must access. A user's private key decrypts the user's encrypted copy of a file's FEK. Public key–based algorithms are usually slow, but EFS uses these algorithms only to encrypt FEKs. Splitting key management between a publicly available key and a private key makes key management a little easier than symmetric encryption algorithms do and solves the dilemma of keeping the FEK secure.

Windows stores a user's private keys in the user's profile directory (typically under \Users) within the AppData\Roaming\Microsoft\Crypto\RSA subdirectory. To protect private keys, Windows encrypts all files within the RSA folder with a random symmetric key called the user's master key. The master key is 64 bytes in length and is generated by a strong random number generator. The master key is also stored in the user's profile under the AppData\Roaming\Microsoft\Protect directory and is 3DES-encrypted with a key that's in part based on the user's password. When a user changes his or her password, master keys are automatically unencrypted and re-encrypted using the new password.

Several components work together to make EFS work, as the diagram of EFS architecture in Figure 11-60 shows. EFS support is merged into the NTFS driver. Whenever NTFS encounters an encrypted file, NTFS executes EFS functions that it contains. The EFS functions encrypt and decrypt file data as applications access encrypted files. Although EFS stores an FEK with a file's data, users' public keys encrypt the FEK. To encrypt or decrypt file data, EFS must decrypt the file's FEK with the aid of cryptography services that reside in user mode.

FIGURE 11-60 EFS architecture

The Local Security Authority Subsystem (Lsass; \%SystemRoot%\System32\Lsass.exe) manages logon sessions but also handles EFS key management chores. For example, when EFS needs to decrypt an FEK to decrypt file data a user wants to access, NTFS sends a request to Lsass. EFS sends the request via an advanced local procedure call (ALPC) message. The KSecDD (\%SystemRoot%\System32\Drivers\Ksecdd.sys) device driver exports functions for other drivers that need to send ALPC messages to Lsass. The Local Security Authority Server (Lsasrv; \%SystemRoot%\System32\Lsasrv.dll) component of Lsass that listens for remote procedure call (RPC) requests passes requests to decrypt an FEK to the appropriate EFS-related decryption function, which also resides in Lsasrv. Lsasrv uses functions in Microsoft CryptoAPI (also referred to as CAPI) to decrypt the FEK, which the NTFS driver sent to Lsass in encrypted form.

CryptoAPI comprises cryptographic service provider (CSP) DLLs that make various cryptography services (such as encryption/decryption and hashing) available to applications. The CSP DLLs manage retrieval of user private and public keys, for example, so that Lsasrv doesn't need to concern itself with the details of how keys are protected or even with the details of the encryption algorithms. EFS uses the RSA encryption algorithms provided by the Microsoft Enhanced Cryptographic provider (\%SystemRoot%\System32\Rsaenh.dll). After Lsasrv decrypts an FEK, Lsasrv returns the FEK to the NTFS driver via an ALPC reply message. After EFS receives the decrypted FEK, EFS can use AES to decrypt the file data for NTFS.

Let's look at the details of how EFS integrates with NTFS and how Lsasrv uses CryptoAPI to manage keys.

Encrypting a File for the First Time

The NTFS driver calls its internal EFS functions when it encounters an encrypted file. A file's attributes record that the file is encrypted in the same way that a file records that it is compressed (discussed earlier in this chapter). NTFS has specific interfaces for converting a file from nonencrypted to encrypted form, but user-mode components primarily drive the process. As described earlier, Windows lets you encrypt a file in two ways: by using the *cipher* command-line utility or by checking the Encrypt Contents To Secure Data check box in the Advanced Attributes dialog box for a file in Windows Explorer. Both Windows Explorer and the *cipher* command rely on the *EncryptFile* Windows API that Advapi32.dll (Advanced Windows APIs DLL) exports. Advapi32 loads another DLL, Feclient.dll (File Encryption Client DLL), to obtain APIs that Advapi32 can use to invoke EFS interfaces in Lsasrv via ALPC.

When Lsasrv receives an RPC message from Feclient to encrypt a file, Lsasrv uses the Windows impersonation facility to impersonate the user that ran the application (either *cipher* or Windows Explorer) that is encrypting the file. (Impersonation is described in Chapter 6.) This procedure lets Windows treat the file operations that Lsasrv performs as if the user who wants to encrypt the file is performing them. Lsasrv usually runs in the System account. (The System account is described in Chapter 6.) In fact, if it doesn't impersonate the user, Lsasrv usually won't have permission to access the file in question.

Lsasrv next creates a log file in the volume's System Volume Information directory into which Lsasrv records the progress of the encryption process. The log file usually has the name Efs0. log, but if other files are undergoing encryption, increasing numbers replace the 0 until a unique log file name for the current encryption is created.

CryptoAPI relies on information that a user's registry profile stores, so if the profile is not already loaded, Lsasrv next uses the *LoadUserProfile* API function of Userenv.dll (User Environment DLL) to load the profile into the registry of the user it is impersonating. Typically, the user profile is already loaded because Winlogon loads a user's profile when a user logs on. However, if a user uses the Windows *RunAs* command to log on to a different account, when the user tries to access encrypted files from that account, the account's profile might not be loaded.

Lsasrv then generates an FEK for the file by using the RSA encryption facilities of the Microsoft Base Cryptographic Provider 1.0 CSP.

Constructing Key Rings

At this point, Lsasrv has an FEK and can construct EFS information to store with the file, including an encrypted version of the FEK. Lsasrv reads the HKEY_ CURRENT_USER\Software\ Microsoft\Windows NT\CurrentVersion\EFS\CurrentKeys\CertificateHash value of the user performing the encryption to obtain the user's public key signature. (Note that this key doesn't appear in the registry until a file or folder is encrypted.) Lsasrv uses the signature to access the user's public key and encrypt FEKs.

Lsasrv can now construct the information that EFS stores with the file. EFS stores only one block of information in an encrypted file, and that block contains an entry for each user sharing the file. These entries are called *key entries*, and EFS stores them in the Data Decryption Field (DDF) portion of the file's EFS data. A collection of multiple key entries is called a *key ring* because, as mentioned earlier, EFS lets multiple users share encrypted files.

Figure 11-61 shows a file's EFS information format and key entry format. EFS stores enough information in the first part of a key entry to precisely describe a user's public key. This data includes the user's security ID (SID) (note that the SID is not guaranteed to be present), the container name in which the key is stored, the cryptographic provider name, and the private/ public key pair certificate hash. Only the private/public key pair certificate hash is used by the decryption process. The second part of the key entry contains an encrypted version of the FEK. Lsasrv uses the CryptoAPI to encrypt the FEK with the RSA algorithm and the user's public key.

FIGURE 11-61 Format of EFS information and key entries

Next, Lsasrv creates another key ring that contains recovery key entries. EFS stores information about recovery key entries in a file's Data Recovery Field (DRF). The format of DRF entries is identical to the format of DDF entries. The DRF's purpose is to let designated accounts, or Recovery Agents, decrypt a user's file when administrative authority must have

access to the user's data. For example, suppose a company employee forgot his or her logon password. An administrator can reset the user's password, but without Recovery Agents, no one can recover the user's encrypted data.

Recovery Agents are defined with the Encrypted Data Recovery Agents security policy of the local computer or domain. This policy is available from the Local Security Policy MMC snap-in, as shown in Figure 11-62. When you use the Add Recovery Agent Wizard (by right-clicking Encrypting File System and then clicking Add Data Recovery Agent), you can add Recovery Agents and specify which private/public key pairs (designated by their certificates) the Recovery Agents use for EFS recovery. Lsasrv interprets the recovery policy when it initializes and when it receives notification that the recovery policy has changed. EFS creates a DRF key entry for each Recovery Agent by using the cryptographic provider registered for EFS recovery.

FIGURE 11-62 Encrypted Data Recovery Agents group policy

In the final step in creating EFS information for a file, Lsasrv calculates a checksum for the DDF and DRF by using the MD5 hash facility of Base Cryptographic Provider 1.0. Lsasrv stores the checksum's result in the EFS information header. EFS references this checksum during decryption to ensure that the contents of a file's EFS information haven't become corrupted or been tampered with.

Encrypting File Data

Figure 11-63 illustrates the flow of the encryption process. After Lsasrv constructs the necessary information for a file a user wants to encrypt, it can begin encrypting the file. Lsasrv creates a backup file, Efs0.tmp, for the file undergoing encryption. (Lsasrv uses higher numbers in the backup file name if other backup files exist.) Lsasrv creates the backup file in the directory that contains the file undergoing encryption. Lsasrv applies a restrictive security descriptor to the backup file so that only the System account can access the file's contents. Lsasrv next initializes the log file that it created in the first phase of the encryption process. Finally, Lsasrv records in the log file that the backup file has been created. Lsasrv encrypts the original file only after the file is completely backed up.

Lsasrv next sends the EFS kernel-mode code inside NTFS a command to add to the original file the EFS information that it just created. The EFS kernel-mode code takes the EFS information that Lsasrv sent and applies the information to the file, which lets EFS add the $EFS attribute to NTFS files. Execution returns to Lsasrv, which copies the contents of the file undergoing encryption to the backup file. When the backup copy is complete, including backups of all alternate data streams, Lsasrv records in the log file that the backup file is up to date. Lsasrv then sends another command to NTFS to tell NTFS to encrypt the contents of the original file.

FIGURE 11-63 Flow of EFS

When NTFS receives the EFS command to encrypt the file, NTFS deletes the contents of the original file and copies the backup data to the file. After NTFS copies each section of the file, NTFS flushes the section's data from the file system cache, which prompts the cache manager to tell NTFS to write the file's data to disk. Because the file is marked as encrypted, at this point in the file-writing process, NTFS calls its EFS routines to encrypt the data before it writes the data to disk. EFS uses the unencrypted FEK that NTFS passes it to perform AES or 3DES encryption of the file as appropriate, one sector (512 bytes) at a time.

After EFS encrypts the file, Lsasrv records in the log file that the encryption was successful and deletes the file's backup copy. Finally, Lsasrv deletes the log file and returns control to the application that requested the file's encryption.

Encryption Process Summary

The following list summarizes the steps EFS performs to encrypt a file:

1. The user profile is loaded if necessary.

2. A log file is created in the System Volume Information directory with the name Efs*x*.log, where *x* is a unique number (for example, Efs0.log). As subsequent steps are performed, records are written to the log so that the file can be recovered in case the system fails during the encryption process.

3. Base Cryptographic Provider 1.0 generates a random 128-bit FEK for the file.

4. A user EFS private/public key pair is generated or obtained. HKEY_CURRENT_USER\ Software\Microsoft\Windows NT\CurrentVersion\EFS\CurrentKeys\CertificateHash identifies the user's key pair.

5. A DDF key ring is created for the file that has an entry for the user. The entry contains a copy of the FEK that has been encrypted with the user's EFS public key.

6. A DRF key ring is created for the file. It has an entry for each Recovery Agent on the system, with each entry containing a copy of the FEK encrypted with the agent's EFS public key.

7. A backup file with a name in the form Efs0.tmp is created in the same directory as the file to be encrypted.

8. The DDF and DRF key rings are added to a header and augment the file as its EFS attribute.

9. The backup file is marked as encrypted, and the original file is copied to the backup.

10. The original file's contents are destroyed, and the backup is copied to the original. This copy operation results in the data in the original file being encrypted because the file is now marked as encrypted.

11. The backup file is deleted.

12. The log file is deleted.

13. The user profile is unloaded (if it was loaded in step 1).

If the system crashes during the encryption process, either the original file remains intact or the backup file contains a consistent copy. When Lsasrv initializes after a system crash, it looks for log files under the System Volume Information subdirectory on each NTFS volume on the system. If Lsasrv finds one or more log files, it examines their contents and determines how recovery should take place. Lsasrv deletes the log file and the corresponding backup file if the original file wasn't modified at the time of the crash; otherwise, Lsasrv copies the

backup file over the original, partially encrypted file and then deletes the log and backup. After Lsasrv processes log files, the file system will be in a consistent state with respect to encryption, with no loss of user data.

The Decryption Process

The decryption process begins when a user opens an encrypted file. NTFS examines the file's attributes when opening the file and reads the $EFS attribute associated with the encrypted file. NTFS completes the necessary steps to open the file and ensures that the user opening the file has access privileges to the file's encrypted data (that is, that an encrypted FEK in either the DDF or DRF key ring corresponds to a private/public key pair associated with the user). As EFS performs this validation, EFS obtains the file's decrypted FEK to use in subsequent data operations the user might perform on the file.

EFS can't decrypt an FEK and relies on Lsasrv (which can use CryptoAPI) to perform FEK decryption. EFS sends an ALPC message by way of the Ksecdd.sys driver to Lsasrv that asks Lsasrv to obtain the decrypted form of the encrypted FEK in the $EFS attribute data (the EFS data) that corresponds to the user who is opening the file.

When Lsasrv receives the ALPC message, Lsasrv executes the Userenv.dll (User Environment DLL) *LoadUserProfile* API function to bring the user's profile into the registry, if the profile isn't already loaded. Lsasrv proceeds through each key field in the EFS data, using the user's private key to try to decrypt each FEK. For each key, Lsasrv attempts to decrypt a DDF or DRF key entry's FEK. If the certificate hash in a key field doesn't refer to a key the user owns, Lsasrv moves on to the next key field. If Lsasrv can't decrypt any DDF or DRF key field's FEK, the user can't obtain the file's FEK. Consequently, EFS denies access to the application opening the file. However, if Lsasrv identifies a hash as corresponding to a key the user owns, it decrypts the FEK with the user's private key using CryptoAPI.

Because Lsasrv processes both DDF and DRF key rings when decrypting an FEK, it automatically performs file recovery operations. If a Recovery Agent that isn't registered to access an encrypted file (that is, it doesn't have a corresponding field in the DDF key ring) tries to access a file, EFS will let the Recovery Agent gain access because the agent has access to a key pair for a key field in the DRF key ring.

Decrypted FEK Caching

Traveling the path from the NTFS driver to Lsasrv and back can take a relatively long time—in the process of decrypting an FEK, CryptoAPI results in more than 2,000 registry API calls and 400 file system accesses on a typical system. The NTFS driver uses a cache to try to avoid this expense.

Decrypting File Data

After an application opens an encrypted file, the application can read from and write to the file. NTFS uses EFS to decrypt file data as NTFS reads the data from the disk and before NTFS places the data in the file system cache. Similarly, when an application writes data to a file, the data remains in unencrypted form in the file system cache until the application or the cache manager uses NTFS to flush the data back to disk. When an encrypted file's data writes back from the cache to the disk, NTFS uses EFS to encrypt the data.

As stated earlier, EFS performs encryption and decryption in 512-byte units. The 512-byte size is the most convenient for the driver because disk reads and writes occur in multiples of the 512-byte sector.

Backing Up Encrypted Files

An important aspect of any file encryption facility's design is that file data is never available in unencrypted form except to applications that access the file via the encryption facility. This restriction particularly affects backup utilities, in which archival media store files. EFS addresses this problem by providing a facility for backup utilities so that the utilities can back up and restore files in their encrypted states. Thus, backup utilities don't have to be able to decrypt file data, nor do they need to encrypt file data in their backup procedures.

Backup utilities use the EFS API functions *OpenEncryptedFileRaw*, *ReadEncryptedFileRaw*, *WriteEncryptedFileRaw*, and *CloseEncryptedFileRaw* in Windows to access a file's encrypted contents. The Advapi32.dll library provides these API functions, which all use ALPC to invoke corresponding functions in Lsasrv. For example, after a backup utility opens a file for raw access during a backup operation, the utility calls *ReadEncryptedFileRaw* to obtain the file data. The Lsasrv function *EfsReadFileRaw* issues control commands (which the EFS session key encrypts with AES or 3DES) to the NTFS driver to read the file's EFS attribute first and then the encrypted contents.

EfsReadFileRaw might have to perform multiple read operations to read a large file. As *EfsReadFileRaw* reads each portion of such a file, Lsasrv sends an RPC message to Advapi32.dll that executes a callback function that the backup program specified when it issued the *ReadEncryptedFileRaw* API function. *EfsReadFileRaw* hands the encrypted data it just read to the callback function, which can write the data to the backup media. Backup utilities restore encrypted files in a similar manner. The utilities call the *WriteEncryptedFileRaw* API function, which invokes a callback function in the backup program to obtain the unencrypted data from the backup media while Lsasrv's *EfsWriteFileRaw* function is restoring the file's contents.

EXPERIMENT: Viewing EFS Information

EFS has a handful of other API functions that applications can use to manipulate encrypted files. For example, applications use the *AddUsersToEncryptedFile* API function to give additional users access to an encrypted file and *RemoveUsersFromEncryptedFile* to revoke users' access to an encrypted file. Applications use the *QueryUsersOn-EncryptedFile* function to obtain information about a file's associated DDF and DRF key fields. *QueryUsersOnEncryptedFile* returns the SID, certificate hash value, and display information that each DDF and DRF key field contains. The following output is from the EFSDump utility, from Sysinternals, when an encrypted file is specified as a command-line argument:

```
C:\>efsdump test.txt
EFS Information Dumper v1.02
Copyright (C) 1999 Mark Russinovich
Systems Internals - http://www.sysinternals.com

test.txt:
DDF Entry:
    DARYL\Mark:
        CN=Mark,L=EFS,OU=EFS File Encryption Certificate
DRF Entry:
    Unknown user:
        EFS Data Recovery
```

You can see that the file test.txt has one DDF entry for user Mark and one DRF entry for the EFS Data Recovery agent, which is the only Recovery Agent currently registered on the system.

Conclusion

Windows supports a wide variety of file system formats accessible to both the local system and remote clients. The file system filter driver architecture provides a clean way to extend and augment file system access, and NTFS provides a reliable, secure, scalable file system format for local file system storage. In the next chapter, we'll look at networking on Windows.

Chapter 12
Networking

Windows was designed with networking in mind, and it includes broad networking support that is integrated with the I/O system and the Windows API. The four basic types of networking software are services, APIs, protocols, and network adapter device drivers, and each is layered on the next to form a network stack. Windows has well-defined interfaces for each layer, so in addition to using the wide variety of APIs, protocols, and adapter device drivers that ship with Windows, third parties can extend the operating system's networking capabilities by developing their own.

In this chapter, we take you from the top of the Windows networking stack to the bottom. First, we present the mapping between the Windows networking software components and the Open Systems Interconnection (OSI) reference model. Then we briefly describe the networking APIs available on Windows and explain how they are implemented. You'll learn how multiple redirector support and name resolution work and how protocol drivers are implemented. After looking at the implementation of network adapter device drivers, we examine *binding*, which is the glue that connects services, protocol stacks, and network adapters.

Windows Networking Architecture

The goal of network software is to take a request (usually an I/O request) from an application on one machine, pass it to another machine, execute the request on the remote machine, and return the results to the first machine. In the course of this process, the request must be transformed several times. A high-level request, such as "read *x* number of bytes from file *y* on machine *z*," requires software that can determine how to get to machine *z* and what communication software that machine understands. Then the request must be altered for transmission across a network—for example, divided into short packets of information. When the request reaches the other side, it must be checked for completeness, decoded, and sent to the correct operating system component for execution. Finally, the reply must be encoded for sending back across the network.

The OSI Reference Model

To help different computer manufacturers standardize and integrate their networking software, in 1984 the International Organization for Standardization (ISO) defined a software model for sending messages between machines. The result was the *Open Systems Interconnection* (OSI) *reference model*. The model defines six layers of software and one physical layer of hardware, as shown in Figure 12-1.

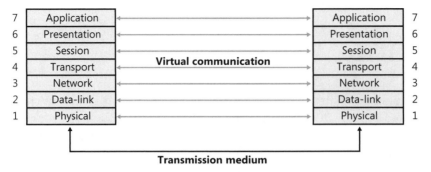

FIGURE 12-1 OSI reference model

The OSI reference model is an idealized scheme that few systems implement precisely, but it's often used to frame discussions of networking principles. Each layer on one machine assumes that it is "talking to" the same layer on the other machine. Both machines "speak" the same language, or protocol, at the same level. In reality, however, a network transmission must pass down each layer on the client machine, be transmitted across the network, and then pass up the layers on the destination machine until it reaches a layer that can understand and implement the request.

The purpose of each layer in the OSI model is to provide services to higher layers and to abstract how the services are implemented at lower layers. Detailing the purpose of each layer is beyond the scope of this book, but here are some brief descriptions of the various layers:

■ **Application layer** Handles information transfer between two network applications, including functions such as security checks, identification of the participating machines, and initiation of the data exchange.

■ **Presentation layer** Handles data formatting, including issues such as whether lines end in a carriage return/line feed (CR/LF) or just a carriage return (CR), whether data is to be compressed or encrypted, and so forth.

■ **Session layer** Manages the connection between cooperating applications, including high-level synchronization and monitoring of which application is "talking" and which is "listening."

■ **Transport layer** On the client, this layer divides messages into packets and assigns them sequence numbers to ensure that they are all received in the proper order. On the destination, it assembles packets that have been received. It also shields the session layer from the effects of changes in hardware.

■ **Network layer** Creates packet headers and handles routing, congestion control, and internetworking. It is the highest layer that understands the network's topology—that is, the physical configuration of the machines in the network, any limitations in bandwidth, and so on.

- **Data-link layer** Transmits low-level data frames, waits for acknowledgment that they were received, and retransmits frames that were lost over unreliable lines as a result of collisions.

- **Physical layer** Passes bits to the network cable or other physical transmission medium.

The gray lines in Figure 12-1 represent protocols used in transmitting a request to a remote machine. As stated earlier, each layer of the hierarchy assumes that it is speaking to the same layer on another machine and uses a common protocol. The collection of protocols through which a request passes on its way down and back up the layers of the network is called a *protocol stack*.

Windows Networking Components

Figure 12-2 provides an overview of the components of Windows networking, showing how each component fits into the OSI reference model and which protocols are used between layers. The mapping between OSI layers and networking components isn't precise, which is the reason that some components cross layers. The various components include the following:

- *Networking APIs* provide a protocol-independent way for applications to communicate across a network. Networking APIs can be implemented in user mode or in both user mode and kernel mode, and in some cases they are wrappers around another networking API that implements a specific programming model or provides additional services. (Note that the term *networking API* also describes any programming interfaces provided by networking-related software.)

- *Transport Driver Interface (TDI) clients* are legacy kernel-mode device drivers that usually implement the kernel-mode portion of a networking API's implementation. TDI clients get their name from the fact that the I/O request packets (IRPs) they send to protocol drivers are formatted according to the Windows Transport Driver Interface standard (documented in the Windows Driver Kit). This standard specifies a common programming interface for kernel-mode device drivers. (See Chapter 7 for more information about IRPs.)

- *TDI transports*, also known as *transports*, *Network Driver Interface Specification (NDIS) protocol drivers*, and *protocol drivers*, are kernel-mode protocol drivers. They accept IRPs from TDI clients and process the requests these IRPs represent. This processing might require network communications with a peer, prompting the TDI transport to add protocol-specific headers (for example, TCP, UDP, and/or IP) to data passed in the IRP and to communicate with adapter drivers using NDIS functions (also documented in

the Windows Driver Kit). TDI transports generally facilitate application network communications by transparently performing message operations such as segmentation and reassembly, sequencing, acknowledgment, and retransmission.

■ *Winsock Kernel (WSK)* is a transport-independent, kernel-mode networking API that replaces the legacy TDI mechanism. WSK provides network communication by using socketlike programming semantics similar to user-mode Winsock, while also providing unique features such as asynchronous I/O operations built on IRPs and event callbacks. WSK also natively supports IP version 6 (IPv6) functionality in the Next Generation TCP/IP network stack in Windows.

■ The *Windows Filtering Platform* (WFP) is a set of APIs and system services that provide the ability to create network filtering applications. The WFP allows applications to interact with packet processing at different levels of the Windows networking stack, much like file system filters. Similarly, network data can be traced, filtered, and also modified before it reaches its destination.

■ *WFP callout drivers* are kernel-mode drivers that implement one or more *callouts*, which extend the capabilities of the WFP by processing TCP/IP-based network data in ways that extend the basic functionality provided by the WFP.

■ The *NDIS library* (Ndis.sys) provides encapsulation for adapter drivers, hiding from them specifics of the Windows kernel-mode environment. The NDIS library exports functions for use by TDI transports as well as support functions for adapter drivers.

■ *NDIS miniport drivers* are kernel-mode drivers that are responsible for interfacing TDI transports to particular network adapters. NDIS miniport drivers are written so that they are wrapped by the Windows NDIS library. NDIS miniport drivers don't process IRPs; rather, they register a call-table interface to the NDIS library that contains pointers to functions corresponding to ones that the NDIS library exports to TDI transports. NDIS miniport drivers communicate with network adapters by using NDIS library functions that resolve to hardware abstraction layer (HAL) functions.

As Figure 12-2 shows, the OSI layers don't correspond to actual software. WSK transport providers, for example, frequently cross several boundaries. In fact, the bottom three layers of software and the hardware layer are often referred to collectively as "the transport." Software components residing in the upper three layers are referred to as "users of the transport."

FIGURE 12-2 OSI model and Windows networking components

In the remainder of this chapter, we'll examine the networking components shown in Figure 12-2 (as well as others not shown in the figure), looking at how they fit together and how they relate to Windows as a whole.

Networking APIs

Windows implements multiple networking APIs to provide support for legacy applications and compatibility with industry standards. In this section, we'll briefly look at the networking APIs and describe how applications use them. It's important to keep in mind that the decision about which API an application uses depends on characteristics of the API, such as which protocols the API can layer over, whether the API supports reliable or bidirectional communication, and the API's portability to other Windows platforms the application might run on. We'll discuss the following networking APIs:

- Windows Sockets (Winsock)
- Winsock Kernel
- Remote procedure call (RPC)
- Web access APIs
- Named pipes and mailslots
- NetBIOS
- Other networking APIs

Windows Sockets

The original Windows Sockets (Winsock) (version 1.0) was Microsoft's implementation of BSD (Berkeley Software Distribution) Sockets, a programming API that became the standard by which UNIX systems have communicated over the Internet since the 1980s. Support for sockets on Windows makes the task of porting UNIX networking applications to Windows relatively straightforward. The modern versions of Winsock include most of the functionality of BSD Sockets but also include Microsoft-specific enhancements, which continue to evolve. Winsock supports reliable-connection-oriented communication as well as unreliable-connectionless communication. Windows provides Winsock 2.2, which adds numerous features beyond the BSD Sockets specification, such as functions that take advantage of Windows asynchronous I/O to offer far better performance and scalability than straight BSD Socket programming.

Winsock includes the following features:

- Support for scatter-gather and asynchronous application I/O.
- Quality of service (QoS) conventions so that applications can negotiate latency and bandwidth requirements when the underlying network supports QoS.
- Extensibility so that Winsock can be used with protocols other than those Windows requires it to support.

- Support for integrated namespaces other than those defined by a protocol that an application is using with Winsock. A server can publish its name in Active Directory, for example, and by using namespace extensions, a client can look up the server's address in Active Directory.

- Support for multipoint messages where messages transmit from a single source to multiple receivers simultaneously.

We'll examine typical Winsock operation and then describe ways that Winsock can be extended.

Winsock Client Operation

The first step a Winsock application takes is to initialize the Winsock API with a call to an initialization function. A Winsock application's next step is to create a *socket* that will represent a communications endpoint. The application obtains the address of the server to which it wants to connect by calling *getaddrinfo* (and later calling *freeaddrinfo* to release the information). The *getaddrinfo* function returns the list of addresses assigned to the server, and the client attempts to connect to each one in turn until it is able to establish a connection with one of them. This ensures that a client that supports both IP version 4 (IPv4) and IPv6 will connect to the appropriate and/or most efficient address on a server that might have both IPv4 and IPv6 addresses assigned to it. Winsock is a protocol-independent API, so an address can be specified for any protocol installed on the system over which Winsock operates (TCP/IP or TCP/IP with IPv6). After obtaining the server address, a connection-oriented client attempts to connect to the server by using *connect* and specifying the server address.

When a connection is established, the client can send and receive data over its socket using *recv* and *send*, for example. A connectionless client specifies the remote address with connectionless APIs, such as the connectionless equivalents of *send* and *recv*, and *sendto* and *recvfrom*. Clients can also use the *select* and *WSAPoll* APIs to wait on or poll multiple sockets for synchronous I/O operations or to check their state.

Winsock Server Operation

The sequence of steps for a server application differs from that of a client. After initializing the Winsock API, the server creates a socket and then binds it to a local address by using *bind*. Again, the address type specified—whether TCP/IP, TCP/IP with IPv6, or some other address type—is up to the server application.

If the server is connection oriented, it performs a *listen* operation on the socket, indicating the *backlog*, or the number of connections the server asks Winsock to hold until the server is able to accept them. Then it performs an *accept* operation to allow a client to connect to the socket. If there is a pending connection request, the *accept* call completes immediately; otherwise, it completes when a connection request arrives. When a connection is made, the

accept function returns a new socket that represents the server's end of the connection. The server can perform receive and send operations by using functions such as *recv* and *send*. Like Winsock clients, servers can use the *select* and *WSAPoll* functions to query the state of one or more sockets; however, the Winsock *WSAEventSelect* function and overlapped I/O extensions are preferable for higher scalability. Figure 12-3 shows connection-oriented communication between a Winsock client and server.

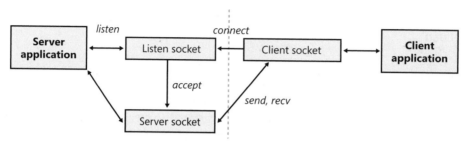

FIGURE 12-3 Connection-oriented Winsock operation

After binding an address, a connectionless server is no different from a connectionless client: it can send and receive data over the socket simply by specifying the remote address with each operation. Most connectionless protocols are unreliable and in general will not know whether the destination actually received the sent data packets, known as *datagrams*. Datagram protocols are ideal for quick message passing, where the overhead of establishing a connection is too much and reliability is not required (although an application can build reliability on top of the protocol).

Winsock Extensions

In addition to supporting functions that correspond directly to those implemented in BSD Sockets, Microsoft has added a handful of functions that aren't part of the Winsock standard. Two of these functions, *AcceptEx* and *TransmitFile*, are worth describing because many Web servers on Windows use them to achieve high performance. *AcceptEx* is a version of the *accept* function that, in the process of establishing a connection with a client, returns the client's address and the client's first message. *AcceptEx* allows the server application to prepost multiple accept operations so that high volumes of incoming connection requests can be handled. With this function, a Web server avoids executing multiple Winsock functions that would otherwise be required.

After establishing a connection with a client, a Web server sometimes sends a file, such as a Web page, to the client. The *TransmitFile* function's implementation is integrated with the Windows cache manager so that a client can send a file directly from the file system cache. Sending data in this way is called *zero-copy* because the server doesn't have to touch the

file data to send it; it simply specifies a handle to a file and the ranges of the file to send. In addition, *TransmitFile* allows a server to prepend or append data to the file's data so that the server can send header information, which might include the name of the Web server and a field that indicates to the client the size of the message the server is sending. Internet Information Services (IIS), which is included with Windows, uses both *AcceptEx* and *TransmitFile*.

Windows also supports a handful of other, multifunction APIs, including *ConnectEx*, *DisconnectEx*, and *TransmitPackets*. *ConnectEx* establishes a connection and sends the first message on the connection. *DisconnectEx* closes a connection and allows the socket handle representing the connection to be reused in a call to *AcceptEx* or *ConnectEx*. Finally, *TransmitPackets* is similar to *TransmitFile*, except that it allows for the sending of in-memory data in addition to or in lieu of file data. Finally, by using the *WSAImpersonateSocketPeer* and *WSARevertImpersonation* functions, Winsock servers can perform impersonation (described in Chapter 6) to perform authorization or to gain access to resources based on the client's security credentials.

Extending Winsock

Winsock is an extensible API on Windows because third parties can add a *transport service provider* that interfaces Winsock with other protocols or layers on top of existing protocols to provide functionality such as proxying. Third parties can also add a *namespace service provider* to augment Winsock's name-resolution facilities. Service providers plug in to Winsock by using the Winsock *service provider interface* (SPI). When a transport service provider is registered with Winsock, Winsock uses the transport service provider to implement socket functions, such as *connect* and *accept*, for the address types that the provider indicates it implements. There are no restrictions on how the transport service provider implements the functions, but the implementation usually involves communicating with a transport driver in kernel mode.

A requirement of any Winsock client/server application is for the server to make its address available to clients so that the clients can connect to the server. Standard services that execute on the TCP/IP protocol use "well-known addresses" to make their addresses available. As long as a browser knows the name of the computer a Web server is running on, it can connect to the Web server by specifying the well-known Web server address (the IP address of the server concatenated with :80, the port number used for HTTP). Namespace service providers make it possible for servers to register their presence in other ways. For example, one namespace service provider might on the server side register the server's address in Active Directory, and on the client side look up the server's address in Active Directory. Namespace service providers supply this functionality to Winsock by implementing standard Winsock name-resolution functions such as *getaddrinfo* and *getnameinfo*.

EXPERIMENT: Looking at Winsock Service Providers

The Net Shell (Netsh.exe) utility included with Windows is able to show the registered Winsock transport and namespace providers by using the *netsh winsock show catalog* command. For example, if there are two TCP/IP transport service providers, the first one listed is the default provider for Winsock applications using the TCP/IP protocol. Here's sample output from Netsh showing the registered transport service providers:

```
C:\Users\Administrator>netsh winsock show catalog

Winsock Catalog Provider Entry
------------------------------------------------------
Entry Type:                    Base Service Provider
Description:                   MSAFD Tcpip [TCP/IP]
Provider ID:                   {E70F1AA0-AB8B-11CF-8CA3-00805F48A192}
Provider Path:                 %SystemRoot%\system32\mswsock.dll
Catalog Entry ID:              1001
Version:                       2
Address Family:                2
Max Address Length:            16
Min Address Length:            16
Socket Type:                   1
Protocol:                      6
Protocol Chain Length:         1

Winsock Catalog Provider Entry
------------------------------------------------------
Entry Type:                    Base Service Provider
Description:                   MSAFD Tcpip [UDP/IP]
Provider ID:                   {E70F1AA0-AB8B-11CF-8CA3-00805F48A192}
Provider Path:                 %SystemRoot%\system32\mswsock.dll
Catalog Entry ID:              1002
Version:                       2
Address Family:                2
Max Address Length:            16
Min Address Length:            16
Socket Type:                   2
Protocol:                      17
Protocol Chain Length:         1

Winsock Catalog Provider Entry
------------------------------------------------------
Entry Type:                    Base Service Provider
Description:                   MSAFD Tcpip [RAW/IP]
Provider ID:                   {E70F1AA0-AB8B-11CF-8CA3-00805F48A192}
Provider Path:                 %SystemRoot%\system32\mswsock.dll
Catalog Entry ID:              1003
Version:                       2
Address Family:                2
Max Address Length:            16
Min Address Length:            16
Socket Type:                   3
Protocol:                      0
Protocol Chain Length:         1
```

You can also use the Autoruns utility from Windows Sysinternals (*www.microsoft.com/ technet/sysinternals*) to view namespace and transport providers, as well as to disable those that might be causing problems or unwanted behavior on the system.

Winsock Implementation

Winsock's implementation is shown in Figure 12-4. Its application interface consists of an API DLL, Ws2_32.dll (\%SystemRoot%\System32\Ws2_32.dll), which provides applications access to Winsock functions. Ws2_32.dll calls on the services of namespace and transport service providers to carry out name and message operations. The Mswsock.dll library acts as a transport service provider for the protocols Microsoft provides support for in Winsock and uses *Winsock Helper* libraries that are protocol specific to communicate with kernel-mode protocol drivers. For example, Wshtcpip.dll is the TCP/IP helper. Mswsock.dll (\%SystemRoot%\ System32\Mswsock.dll) implements the Microsoft Winsock extension functions, such as *TransmitFile*, *AcceptEx*, and *WSARecvEx*.

Windows ships with helper DLLs for TCP/IP, TCP/IP with IPv6, Bluetooth, NetBIOS, IrDA (Infrared Data Association), and PGM (Pragmatic General Multicast). It also includes namespace service providers for DNS (TCP/IP), Active Directory (LDAP), and NLA (Network Location Awareness).

FIGURE 12-4 Winsock implementation

Like the named pipe and mailslot APIs (described later in this chapter), Winsock integrates with the Windows I/O model and uses file handles to represent sockets. This support requires the aid of a kernel-mode file system driver, so Msafd.dll uses the services of the Ancillary Function Driver (AFD—\%SystemRoot%\System32\Drivers\Afd.sys) to implement socket-based functions. AFD is a Transport Layer Network Provider Interface (TLNPI) client and executes network socket operations, such as sending and receiving messages, by sending TDI IRPs to protocol drivers. AFD isn't coded to use particular protocol drivers; instead, Msafd.dll informs AFD of the name of the protocol used for each socket so that AFD can open the device object representing the protocol.

Winsock Kernel (WSK)

To enable kernel-mode drivers and modules to have access to networking API interfaces similar to those available to user-mode applications, Windows implements a socket-based networking programming interface called Winsock Kernel (WSK). WSK replaces the legacy TDI API interface present on older versions of Windows but maintains the TDI SPI interface for transport providers. Compared to TDI, WSK provides better performance and scalability and much easier programming, because it relies less on internal kernel behavior and more on socket-based semantics. Additionally, WSK was written to take full advantage of the latest technologies in the Windows TCP/IP stack, which TDI was not originally anticipated to support. As shown in Figure 12-5, WSK makes use of the Network Module Registrar (NMR) component of Windows to attach to and detach from transport devices, and it can be used, just like Winsock, to support many different kinds of network clients—for example, the Http.sys driver for the HTTP Server API (mentioned later in the chapter) is a WSK client.

FIGURE 12-5 WSK overview

WSK Implementation

WSK's implementation is shown in Figure 12-6. At its core is the WSK subsystem itself, which uses the Next Generation TCP/IP Stack (%SystemRoot%\System32\Drivers\Netio.sys) but is actually implemented in AFD. The subsystem is responsible for the provider side of the WSK

API. The subsystem interfaces with transport providers (shown at the bottom of Figure 12-5) to provide support for various transport protocols. Attached to the WSK subsystem are WSK applications, which are kernel-mode drivers that implement the client-side WSK API in order to perform network operations. The WSK subsystem calls WSK applications to notify them of asynchronous events.

FIGURE 12-6 WSK implementation

WSK applications are bound to the WSK subsystem through the NMR or through the WSK's registration functions, which allow WSK applications to dynamically detect when the WSK subsystem becomes available and then load their own dispatch table to describe the provider and client-side implementations of the WSK API. These implementations provide the standard WSK socket-based functions, such as *WskSocket*, *WskAccept*, *WskBind*, *WskConnect*, *WskReceive*, and *WskSend,* which have similar semantics (but not necessarily similar parameters) as their user-mode Winsock counterparts. However, unlike user-mode Winsock, the WSK subsystem defines four different kinds of *socket categories*, which identify which functions and events are available:

- Basic sockets, which are used only to get and set information on the transport. They cannot be used to send or receive data or be bound to an address.

- Listening sockets, which are used for sockets that accept only incoming connections.

- Datagram sockets, which are used solely for sending and receiving datagrams.

- Connection-oriented sockets, which support all the functionality required to send and receive network traffic over an established connection.

Apart from the socket functions described, WSK also provides events through which applications are notified of network status. Unlike the model for socket functions, in which a client controls the connection, events allow the subsystem to control the connection and merely notify the client. These include the *WskAcceptEvent*, *WskInspectEvent*, *WskAbortEvent*, *WskReceiveFromEvent*, *WskReceiveEvent*, *WskDisconnectEvent*, and *WskSendBacklogEvent* routines.

Finally, like user-mode Winsock, WSK can be extended through *extension interfaces* that applications can associate with sockets. These extensions can enhance the default functionality provided by the WSK subsystem.

Remote Procedure Call

Remote procedure call (RPC) is a network programming standard originally developed in the early 1980s. The Open Software Foundation (now The Open Group) made RPC part of the distributed computing environment (DCE) distributed computing standard. Although there is a second RPC standard, SunRPC, the Microsoft RPC implementation is compatible with the OSF/DCE standard. RPC builds on other networking APIs, such as named pipes or Winsock, to provide an alternate programming model that in some sense hides the details of networking programming from an application developer.

RPC Operation

An RPC facility is one that allows a programmer to create an application consisting of any number of procedures, some that execute locally and others that execute on remote computers via a network. It provides a procedural view of networked operations rather than a transport-centered view, thus simplifying the development of distributed applications.

Networking software is traditionally structured around an I/O model of processing. In Windows, for example, a network operation is initiated when an application issues a remote I/O request. The operating system processes the request accordingly by forwarding it to a *redirector*, which acts as a remote file system by making the client interaction with the remote file system invisible to the client. The redirector passes the operation to the remote file system, and after the remote system fills the request and returns the results, the local network card interrupts. The kernel handles the interrupt, and the original I/O operation completes, returning results to the caller.

RPC takes a different approach altogether. RPC applications are like other structured applications, with a main program that calls procedures or procedure libraries to perform specific tasks. The difference between RPC applications and regular applications is that some of the procedure libraries in an RPC application execute on remote computers, as shown in Figure 12-7, whereas others execute locally.

To the RPC application, all the procedures appear to execute locally. In other words, instead of making a programmer actively write code to transmit computational or I/O-related requests across a network, handle network protocols, deal with network errors, wait for results, and so forth, RPC software handles these tasks automatically. And the Windows RPC facility can operate over any available transports loaded into the system.

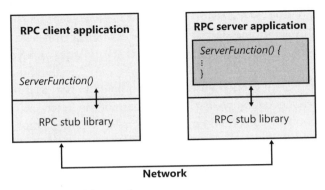

FIGURE 12-7 RPC operation

To write an RPC application, the programmer decides which procedures will execute locally and which will execute remotely. For example, suppose an ordinary workstation has a network connection to a Cray supercomputer or to a machine designed specifically for high-speed vector operations. If the programmer were writing an application that manipulated large matrices, it would make sense from a performance point of view to off-load the mathematical calculations to the remote computer by writing the program as an RPC application.

RPC applications work like this: As an application runs, it calls local procedures as well as procedures that aren't present on the local machine. To handle the latter case, the application is linked to a local static-link library or DLL that contains *stub procedures*, one for each remote procedure. For simple applications, the stub procedures are statically linked with the application, but for bigger components the stubs are included in separate DLLs. In DCOM, covered later in the chapter, the latter method is typically used. The stub procedures have the same name and use the same interface as the remote procedures, but instead of performing the required operations, the stub takes the parameters passed to it and *marshals* them for transmission across the network. Marshaling parameters means ordering and packaging them in a particular way to suit a network link, such as resolving references and picking up a copy of any data structures that a pointer refers to.

The stub then calls RPC run-time procedures that locate the computer where the remote procedure resides, determine which transport mechanisms that computer uses, and send the request to it using local transport software. When the remote server receives the RPC request, it *unmarshals* the parameters (the reverse of marshaling them), reconstructs the original procedure call, and calls the procedure. When the server finishes, it performs the reverse sequence to return results to the caller.

In addition to the synchronous function-call-based interface described here, Windows RPC also supports *asynchronous RPC*. Asynchronous RPC lets an RPC application execute a function but not wait until the function completes to continue processing. Instead, the application can execute other code and later, when a response has arrived from the server, the RPC runtime notifies the client that the operation has completed. The RPC runtime uses

the notification mechanism requested by the client. If the client uses an event synchronization object for notification, it waits for the signaling of the event object by calling the *WaitForSingleObject* or *WaitForMultipleObject* function. If the client provides an asynchronous procedure call (APC), the runtime queues the execution of the APC to the thread that executed the RPC function. If the client program uses an I/O completion port as its notification mechanism, it must call *GetQueuedCompletionStatus* to learn of the function's completion. Alternatively, a client can poll for completion by calling *RpcAsyncGetCallStatus*.

In addition to the RPC runtime, Microsoft's RPC facility includes a compiler, called the *Microsoft Interface Definition Language* (MIDL) compiler. The MIDL compiler simplifies the creation of an RPC application. The programmer writes a series of ordinary function prototypes (assuming a C or C++ application) that describe the remote routines and then places the routines in a file. The programmer then adds some additional information to these prototypes, such as a network-unique identifier for the package of routines and a version number, plus attributes that specify whether the parameters are input, output, or both. The embellished prototypes form the developer's Interface Definition Language (IDL) file.

Once the IDL file is created, the programmer compiles it with the MIDL compiler, which produces both client-side and server-side stub routines, mentioned previously, as well as header files to be included in the application. When the client-side application is linked to the stub routines file, all remote procedure references are resolved. The remote procedures are then installed, using a similar process, on the server machine. A programmer who wants to call an existing RPC application need only write the client side of the software and link the application to the local RPC run-time facility.

The RPC runtime uses a generic RPC *transport provider interface* to talk to a transport protocol. The provider interface acts as a thin layer between the RPC facility and the transport, mapping RPC operations onto the functions provided by the transport. The Windows RPC facility implements transport provider DLLs for named pipes, HTTP, TCP/IP, and UDP. In a similar fashion, the RPC facility is designed to work with different network security facilities.

Most of the Windows networking services are RPC applications, which means that both local processes and processes on remote computers can call them. Thus, a remote client computer can call the server service to list shares, open files, write to print queues, or activate users on your server, all subject to security constraints, of course.

Server name publishing, which is the ability of a server to register its name in a location accessible for client lookup, is in RPC and is integrated with Active Directory. If Active Directory isn't installed, the RPC name locator services fall back on NetBIOS broadcast. This behavior allows RPC to function on stand-alone servers and workstations.

RPC Security

Windows RPC includes integration with security support providers (SSPs) so that RPC clients and servers can use authenticated or encrypted communications. When an RPC server wants secure communication, it tells the RPC runtime what authentication service to add to the list of available *authentication services*. When a client wants to use secure communication, it binds to the server. At that time, it must tell the RPC runtime the authentication service and *authentication level* it wants. Various authentication levels exist to ensure that only authorized clients connect to a server, verify that each message a server receives originates at an authorized client, check the integrity of RPC messages to detect manipulation, and even encrypt RPC message data. Obviously, higher authentication levels require more processing. The client can also optionally specify the server *principal name*. A principal is an entity that the RPC security system recognizes. The server must register its SSP-specific principal name with an SSP.

An SSP handles the details of performing network communication authentication and encryption, not only for RPC but also for Winsock. Windows includes a number of built-in SSPs, including a Kerberos SSP to implement Kerberos version 5 authentication (including AES support) and Secure Channel (SChannel), which implements Secure Sockets Layer (SSL) and the Transport Layer Security (TLS) protocols. SChannel also supports TLS and SSL extensions, which allow you to use the AES cipher as well as elliptic curve cryptographic (ECC) ciphers on top of the protocols. Also, because it supports an *open cryptographic interface* (OCI) and crypto-agile capabilities, SChannel allows government organizations to substitute the existing ciphers with more complex combinations. In the absence of a specified SSP, RPC software uses the built-in security of the underlying transport. Some transports, such as named pipes or local RPC, have built-in security. Others, like TCP, do not, and in this case RPC makes unsecure calls in the absence of a specified SSP.

Another feature of RPC security is the ability of a server to impersonate the security identity of a client with the *RpcImpersonateClient* function. After a server has finished performing impersonated operations on behalf of a client, it returns to its own security identity by calling *RpcRevertToSelf* or *RpcRevertToSelfEx*. (See Chapter 6 for more information on impersonation.)

RPC Implementation

RPC implementation is depicted in Figure 12-8, which shows that an RPC-based application links with the RPC run-time DLL (\%SystemRoot%\System32\Rpcrt4.dll). The RPC run-time DLL provides marshaling and unmarshaling functions for use by an application's RPC function stubs as well as functions for sending and receiving marshaled data. The RPC run-time DLL includes support routines to handle RPC over a network as well as a form of RPC called *local RPC*. Local RPC can be used for communication between two processes located on the same system, and the RPC run-time DLL uses the advanced local procedure call (ALPC) facilities in kernel mode as the local networking API. (See Chapter 3 for more information on ALPCs.)

When RPC is based on nonlocal communication mechanisms, the RPC run-time DLL uses the Winsock or named pipe APIs.

FIGURE 12-8 RPC implementation

The RPC subsystem (RPCSS—\%SystemRoot%\System32\Rpcss.dll) is implemented as a Windows service. RPCSS is itself an RPC application that communicates with instances of itself on other systems to perform name lookup, registration, and dynamic endpoint mapping. (For clarity, Figure 12-8 doesn't show RPCSS linked with the RPC run-time DLL.)

Windows also includes support for RPC in kernel mode through the kernel-mode RPC driver (%SystemRoot%\System32\Drivers\Msrpc.sys). Kernel-mode RPC is for internal use by the system and is implemented on top of ALPC. Winlogon includes an RPC server with a documented set of interfaces that user-mode RPC clients can access, while Win32k.sys includes an RPC client that communicates with Winlogon for internal notifications, such as the secure attention sequence (SAS; see Chapter 6 for more information). The TCP/IP stack in Windows (as well as the WFP) also uses kernel-mode RPC to communicate with the *Network Store Interface (NSI)* service, which handles network routing information.

Web Access APIs

To ease the development of Internet applications, Windows provides both client and server Internet APIs. By using the APIs, applications can provide and use FTP and HTTP services without knowledge of the intricacies of the corresponding protocols. The client APIs include Windows Internet, also known as WinInet, which enables applications to interact with the FTP and HTTP protocols, and WinHTTP, which enables applications to interact with the HTTP protocol and is more suitable than WinInet in certain situations. HTTP Server is a server-side API that enables the development of Web server applications.

WinInet

WinInet supports the FTP and HTTP 1.0 and 1.1 protocols. The APIs break down into sub-API sets specific to each protocol. Using the FTP-related APIs—such as *InternetConnect* to connect to an FTP server, *FtpFindFirstFile* and *FtpFindNextFile* to enumerate the contents of an FTP directory, and *FtpGetFile* and *FtpPutFile* to receive and send files—an application developer avoids the details of establishing a connection and formatting TCP/IP messages to the FTP protocol. The HTTP-related APIs provide similar levels of abstraction, providing cookie persistence, automatic dial-up services, client-side file caching, and automatic credential dialog handling. WinInet is used by core Windows components such as Windows Explorer and Internet Explorer.

WinHTTP

The current version of the WinHTTP API, 6.0, is available on Windows Vista and Windows Server 2008. It provides an abstraction of the HTTP/1.1 protocol for HTTP client applications similar to what the WinInet HTTP-related APIs provide. However, whereas the WinInet HTTP API is intended for user-interactive client-side applications, the WinHTTP API is designed for server applications that communicate with HTTP servers. Server applications are often implemented as Windows services that do not provide a user interface and so do not desire the dialog boxes that WinInet APIs display. In addition, the WinHTTP APIs are more scalable (such as supporting uploads of greater than 4 GB) and offer security functionality, such as thread impersonation, not available from the WinInet API. WinHTTP also provides support for chunked transfer encoding, issuer list retrieval for SSL authentication, client certificate requests, and port range reservations.

HTTP

Using the HTTP Server API, which Windows Vista and Windows Server 2008 implement, server applications can register to receive HTTP requests for particular URLs, receive HTTP requests, and send HTTP responses. The HTTP Server API includes SSL support so that applications can exchange data over secure HTTP connections. The API includes server-side caching capabilities, synchronous and asynchronous I/O models, and both IPv4 and IPv6 addressing. IIS version 7, the version that ships with Windows Server 2008, uses the HTTP Server API.

The HTTP Server API, which applications access through the Httpapi.dll library, relies on the kernel-mode Http.sys driver. Http.sys starts on demand the first time any application on the system calls *HttpInitialize*. Applications then call *HttpCreateServerSession* to initialize a server session for the HTTP Server API. Next they use *HttpCreateRequestQueue* to create a private request queue and *HttpCreateUrlGroup* to create a URL group, specifying the URLs that they want to handle requests for with *HttpAddUrlToUrlGroup*. Using the request queues and their registered URLs (which they associate by using *HttpSetUrlGroupProperty*), Http.sys allows more than one application to service HTTP requests on a given port (port 80 for example),

with each servicing HTTP requests to different parts of the URL namespace, as shown in Figure 12-9.

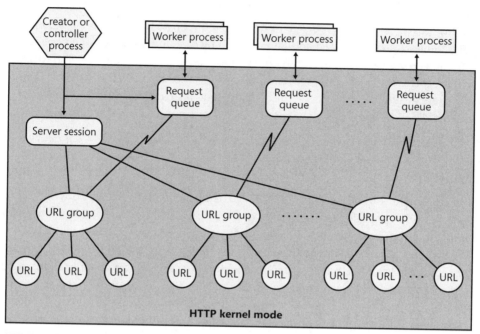

FIGURE 12-9 HTTP request queues and URL groups

HttpReceiveHttpRequest receives incoming requests directed at registered URLs, and *HttpSendHttpResponse* sends HTTP responses. Both functions offer asynchronous operation so that an application can use *GetOverlappedResult* or I/O completion ports to determine when an operation is completed.

Applications can use Http.sys to cache data in nonpaged physical memory by calling *HttpAddFragmentToCache* and associating a *fragment name* (specified as a URL prefix) with the cached data. Http.sys invokes the memory manager function *MmAllocatePagesForMdlEx* to allocate unmapped physical pages (for large requests, Http.sys also attempts to use large pages to optimize access to the buffered data). When Http.sys requires a virtual address mapping for the physical memory described by an entry in the cache—for instance, when it copies data to the cache or sends data from the cache—it uses *MmMapLockedPages-SpecifyCache* and then *MmUnmapLockedPages* after it completes its access. Http.sys maintains cached data until an application invalidates it or an optional application-specified timeout associated with the data expires. Http.sys also trims cached data in a worker thread that wakes up when the low memory notification event is signaled. (See Chapter 9 for information on the low memory notification event.) When an application specifies one or more fragment names in a call to *HttpSendHttpResponse*, Http.sys passes a pointer to the cached data in physical memory to the TCP/IP driver and avoids a copy operation. Http.sys also

contains code for performing server-side authentication, including full SSL support, which removes the need to call back to the user-mode API to perform encryption and decryption of traffic.

Finally, the HTTP Server API contains many configuration options that clients can use to set functionality, such as authentication policies, bandwidth throttling, logging, connection limits, server state, response caching, and SSL certificate binding.

Named Pipes and Mailslots

Named pipes and mailslots are programming APIs for interprocess communication. Named pipes provide for reliable bidirectional communications, whereas mailslots provide unreliable unidirectional data transmission. An advantage of mailslots is that they support broadcast capability. In Windows, both APIs take advantage of Windows security, which allows a server to control precisely which clients can connect to it.

The names that servers assign to named pipes and clients conform to the Windows Universal Naming Convention (UNC), which is a protocol-independent way to identify resources on a Windows network. The implementation of UNC names is described later in the chapter.

Named Pipe Operation

Named pipe communication consists of a named pipe server and a named pipe client. A named pipe server is an application that creates a named pipe to which clients can connect. A named pipe's name has the format \\Server\Pipe\PipeName. The *Server* component of the name specifies the computer on which the named pipe server is executing. (A named pipe server can't create a named pipe on a remote system.) The name can be a DNS name (for example, *mspress.microsoft.com*), a NetBIOS name (*mspress*), or an IP address (131.107.0.1). The *Pipe* component of the name must be the string "Pipe", and *PipeName* is the unique name assigned to a named pipe. The unique portion of the named pipe's name can include subdirectories; an example of a named pipe name with a subdirectory is \\MyComputer\Pipe\ MyServerApp\ConnectionPipe.

A named pipe server uses the *CreateNamedPipe* Windows function to create a named pipe. One of the function's input parameters is a pointer to the named pipe name, in the form \\.\Pipe\PipeName. The "\\.\" is a Windows-defined alias for "this computer." Other parameters the function accepts include an optional security descriptor that protects access to the named pipe, a flag that specifies whether the pipe should be bidirectional or unidirectional, a value indicating the maximum number of simultaneous connections the pipe supports, and a flag specifying whether the pipe should operate in *byte mode* or *message mode*.

Most networking APIs operate only in byte mode, which means that a message sent with one send function might require the receiver to perform multiple receive operations, building up the complete message from fragments. A named pipe operating in message mode simplifies

the implementation of a receiver because there is a one-to-one correspondence between send and receive requests. A receiver therefore obtains an entire message each time it completes a receive operation and doesn't have to concern itself with keeping track of message fragments.

The first call to *CreateNamedPipe* for a particular name creates the first instance of that name and establishes the behavior of all named pipe instances having that name. A server creates additional instances, up to the maximum specified in the first call, with additional calls to *CreateNamedPipe*. After creating at least one named pipe instance, a server executes the *ConnectNamedPipe* Windows function, which enables the named pipe the server created to establish connections with clients. *ConnectNamedPipe* can be executed synchronously or asynchronously, and it doesn't complete until a client establishes a connection with the instance (or an error occurs).

A named pipe client uses the Windows *CreateFile* or *CallNamedPipe* function, specifying the name of the pipe a server has created, to connect to a server. If the server has performed a *ConnectNamedPipe* call, the client's security profile and the access it requests to the pipe (read, write) are validated against the named pipe's security descriptor. (See Chapter 6 for more information on the security-check algorithms Windows uses.) If the client is granted access to a named pipe, it receives a handle representing the client side of a named pipe connection and the server's call to *ConnectNamedPipe* completes.

After a named pipe connection is established, the client and server can use the *ReadFile* and *WriteFile* Windows functions to read from and write to the pipe. Named pipes support both synchronous and asynchronous operations for message transmittal. Figure 12-10 shows a server and client communicating through a named pipe instance.

FIGURE 12-10 Named pipe communications

Another characteristic of the named pipe networking API is that it allows a server to impersonate a client by using the *ImpersonateNamedPipeClient* function. See the "Impersonation" section in Chapter 6 for a discussion of how impersonation is used in client/server applications. A second advanced area of functionality of the named pipe API is that it allows for atomic send and receive operations through the *TransactNamedPipe* API, which behaves according to a simple transactional model in which a message is both sent and received in the same operation.

Mailslot Operation

Mailslots provide an unreliable unidirectional broadcast mechanism. One example of an application that can use this type of communication is a time-synchronization service, which might broadcast a source time across the domain every few seconds. Receiving the source-time message isn't crucial for every computer on the network and is therefore a good candidate for the use of mailslots.

Like named pipes, mailslots are integrated with the Windows API. A mailslot server creates a mailslot by using the *CreateMailslot* function. *CreateMailslot* accepts a name of the form "\\.\Mailslot\MailslotName" as an input parameter. Again like named pipes, a mailslot server can create mailslots only on the machine it's executing on, and the name it assigns to a mailslot can include subdirectories. *CreateMailslot* also takes a security descriptor that controls client access to the mailslot. The handles returned by *CreateMailslot* are *overlapped*, which means that operations performed on the handles, such as sending and receiving messages, are asynchronous.

Because mailslots are unidirectional and unreliable, *CreateMailslot* doesn't take many of the parameters that *CreateNamedPipe* does. After it creates a mailslot, a server simply listens for incoming client messages by executing the *ReadFile* function on the handle representing the mailslot.

Mailslot clients use a naming format similar to that used by named pipe clients but with variations that make it possible to broadcast messages to all the mailslots of a given name within the client's domain or a specified domain. To send a message to a particular instance of a mailslot, the client calls *CreateFile*, specifying the computer-specific name. An example of such a name is "\\Server\Mailslot\MailslotName". (The client can specify "\\.\" to represent the local computer.) If the client wants to obtain a handle representing all the mailslots of a given name on the domain it's a member of, it specifies the name in the format "*\Mailslot\MailslotName", and if the client wants to broadcast to all the mailslots of a given name within a different domain, the format it uses is "\\DomainName\Mailslot\MailslotName".

After obtaining a handle representing the client side of a mailslot, the client sends messages by calling *WriteFile*. Because of the way mailslots are implemented, only messages smaller than 424 bytes can be broadcast. If a message is larger than 424 bytes, the mailslot implementation uses a reliable communications mechanism that requires a one-to-one client/server connection, which precludes broadcast capability. This limitation makes mailslots generally unsuitable for messages larger than 424 bytes. Figure 12-11 shows an example of a client broadcasting to multiple mailslot servers within a domain.

FIGURE 12-11 Mailslot broadcast

Named Pipe and Mailslot Implementation

As evidence of their tight integration with Windows, named pipe and mailslot functions are all implemented in the Kernel32.dll Windows client-side DLL. *ReadFile* and *WriteFile*, which are the functions applications use to send and receive messages using named pipes or mailslots, are the primary Windows I/O routines. The *CreateFile* function, which a client uses to open either a named pipe or a mailslot, is also a standard Windows I/O routine. However, the names specified by named pipe and mailslot applications specify file system namespaces managed by the named pipe file system driver (\%SystemRoot%\System32\Drivers\Npfs.sys) and the mailslot file system driver (\%SystemRoot%\System32\Drivers\Msfs.sys), as shown in Figure 12-12.

The named pipe file system driver creates a device object named \Device\NamedPipe and a symbolic link to that object named \Global??\Pipe. The mailslot file system driver creates a device object named \Device\Mailslot and a symbolic link named \Global??\Mailslot that points to that object. (See Chapter 3 for an explanation of the \Global?? object manager directory.) Names passed to *CreateFile* of the form \\.\Pipe\... and \\.\Mailslot\... have their prefix of \\.\ translated to \Global??\ so that the names resolve through a symbolic link to a device object. The special functions *CreateNamedPipe* and *CreateMailslot* use the corresponding native functions *NtCreateNamedPipeFile* and *NtCreateMailslotFile*.

FIGURE 12-12 Named pipe and mailslot implementation

Later in the chapter, we'll discuss how the redirector file system driver is involved when a name that specifies a remote named pipe or mailslot resolves to a remote system. However, when a named pipe or mailslot is created by a server or opened by a client, the appropriate file system driver (FSD) on the machine where the named pipe or mailslot is located is eventually invoked. There are several reasons why FSDs in kernel mode implement named pipes and mailslots, the main one being that they integrate with the object manager namespace and can use file objects to represent opened named pipes and mailslots. This integration results in several benefits:

- The FSDs use kernel-mode security functions to implement standard Windows security for named pipes and mailslots.

- Applications can use *CreateFile* to open a named pipe or mailslot because FSDs integrate with the object manager namespace.

- Applications can use Windows functions such as *ReadFile* and *WriteFile* to interact with named pipes and mailslots.

- The FSDs rely on the object manager to track handle and reference counts for file objects representing named pipes and mailslots.

- The FSDs can implement their own named pipe and mailslot namespaces, complete with subdirectories.

Because named pipes and mailslots use name resolution that relies on the redirector FSD to communicate across the network, they indirectly rely on the Server Message Block (SMB) protocol. SMB works by using the TCP/IP and TCP/IP with IPv6 protocols, so applications running on systems that have at least one of these in common can use named pipes and mailslots. For more information about SMB, see Chapter 11.

EXPERIMENT: Listing the Named Pipe Namespace and Watching Named Pipe Activity

It's not possible to use the Windows API to open the root of the named pipe FSD and perform a directory listing, but you can do this by using native API services. The PipeList tool from Sysinternals shows you the names of the named pipes defined on a computer as well as the number of instances that have been created for a name and the maximum number of instances as defined by a server's call to *CreateNamedPipe*. Here's an example of PipeList output:

```
C:\>pipelist

PipeList v1.01
by Mark Russinovich
http://www.sysinternals.com
```

Pipe Name	Instances	Max Instances
InitShutdown	3	-1
lsass	6	-1
protected_storage	3	-1
ntsvcs	3	-1
scerpc	3	-1
net\NtControlPipe1	1	1
plugplay	3	-1
net\NtControlPipe2	1	1
Winsock2\CatalogChangeListener-394-0	1	1
epmapper	3	-1
Winsock2\CatalogChangeListener-25c-0	1	1
LSM_API_service	3	-1
net\NtControlPipe3	1	1
eventlog	3	-1
net\NtControlPipe4	1	1
Winsock2\CatalogChangeListener-3f8-0	1	1
net\NtControlPipe5	1	1
net\NtControlPipe6	1	1
net\NtControlPipe0	1	1
atsvc	3	-1
Winsock2\CatalogChangeListener-438-0	1	1
Winsock2\CatalogChangeListener-2c8-0	1	1
net\NtControlPipe7	1	1
net\NtControlPipe8	1	1
net\NtControlPipe9	1	1
net\NtControlPipe10	1	1
net\NtControlPipe11	1	1
net\NtControlPipe12	1	1
142CDF96-10CC-483c-A516-3E9057526912	1	1
net\NtControlPipe13	1	1
net\NtControlPipe14	1	1
TSVNCache-000000000001b017	20	-1
TSVNCacheCommand-000000000001b017	2	-1
Winsock2\CatalogChangeListener-2b0-0	1	1
Winsock2\CatalogChangeListener-468-0	1	1
TermSrv_API_service	3	-1
Ctx_WinStation_API_service	3	-1
PIPE_EVENTROOT\CIMV2SCM EVENT PROVIDER	2	-1
net\NtControlPipe15	1	1
keysvc	3	-1

It's clear from this output that several system components use named pipes as their communications mechanism. For example, the *InitShutdown* pipe is created by Winlogon to accept remote shutdown commands, and the *Atsvc* pipe is created by the Task Scheduler service to enable applications to communicate with it to schedule tasks. You can determine what process has each of these pipes open by using the object search facility in Process Explorer.

Note A Max Instances value of –1 means that there is no upper limit on the number of instances.

NetBIOS

Until the 1990s, the Network Basic Input/Output System (NetBIOS) programming API had been the most widely used network programming API on PCs. NetBIOS allows for both reliable-connection-oriented and unreliable-connectionless communication. Windows supports NetBIOS for its legacy applications. Microsoft discourages application developers from using NetBIOS because other APIs, such as named pipes and Winsock, are much more flexible and portable. NetBIOS is supported by the TCP/IP protocol on Windows.

NetBIOS Names

NetBIOS relies on a naming convention whereby computers and network services are assigned a 16-byte name called a NetBIOS name. The sixteenth byte of a NetBIOS name is treated as a modifier that can specify a name as unique or as part of a group. Only one instance of a unique NetBIOS name can be assigned to a network, but multiple applications can assign the same group name. A client can broadcast messages by sending them to a group name.

To support interoperability with Windows NT 4 systems as well as Windows 9x/Me, Windows automatically defines a NetBIOS name for a domain that includes up to the first 15 bytes of the left-most Domain Name System (DNS) name that an administrator assigns to the domain. For example, if a domain were named *mspress.microsoft.com*, the NetBIOS name of the domain would be *mspress*. Similarly, Windows requires an administrator to assign each computer a NetBIOS name at the time of installation.

Another concept used by NetBIOS is that of LAN adapter (LANA) numbers. A LANA number is assigned to every NetBIOS-compatible protocol that layers above a network adapter. For example, if a computer has two network adapters and TCP/IP and NWLink can use either adapter, there would be four LANA numbers. LANA numbers are important because a NetBIOS application must explicitly assign its service name to each LANA through which it's willing to accept client connections. If the application listens for client connections on a particular name, clients can access the name only via protocols on the network adapters for which the name is registered.

The "Windows Internet Name Service" section later in this chapter describes the resolution of NetBIOS names to TCP/IP addresses.

NetBIOS Operation

A NetBIOS server application uses the NetBIOS API to enumerate the LANAs present on a system and assign a NetBIOS name representing the application's service to each LANA. If the server is connection oriented, it performs a NetBIOS listen command to wait for client connection attempts. After a client is connected, the server executes NetBIOS functions to send and receive data. Connectionless communication is similar, but the server simply reads messages without establishing connections.

A connection-oriented client uses NetBIOS functions to establish a connection with a NetBIOS server and then executes further NetBIOS functions to send and receive data. An established NetBIOS connection is also known as a *session*. If the client wants to send connectionless messages, it simply specifies the NetBIOS name of the server with the send function.

NetBIOS consists of a number of functions, but they all route through the same interface: *Netbios*. This routing scheme is the result of a legacy left over from the time when NetBIOS was implemented on MS-DOS as an MS-DOS interrupt service. A NetBIOS application would execute an MS-DOS interrupt and pass a data structure to the NetBIOS implementation that specified every aspect of the command being executed. As a result, the *Netbios* function in Windows takes a single parameter, which is a data structure that contains the parameters specific to the service the application requests.

EXPERIMENT: Using *Nbtstat* to See NetBIOS Names

You can use the *Nbtstat* command, which is included with Windows, to list the active sessions on a system, the NetBIOS-to-TCP/IP name mappings cached on a computer, and the NetBIOS names defined on a computer. Here's an example of the *Nbtstat* command with the *–n* option, which lists the NetBIOS names defined on the computer:

```
C:\Users\Administrator>nbtstat -n

Local Area Connection:
Node IpAddress: [192.168.0.193] Scope Id: []

              NetBIOS Local Name Table

        Name               Type         Status
    ---------------------------------------------
    WIN-NLRTEOW2ILZ<00>   UNIQUE       Registered
    WORKGROUP      <00>   GROUP        Registered
    WIN-NLRTEOW2ILZ<20>   UNIQUE       Registered
```

NetBIOS API Implementation

The components that implement the NetBIOS API are shown in Figure 12-13. The *Netbios* function is exported to applications by \%SystemRoot%\System32\Netapi32.dll. Netapi32.dll opens a handle to the kernel-mode driver named the *NetBIOS emulator* (\%SystemRoot%\ System32\Drivers\Netbios.sys) and issues Windows *DeviceIoControl* file commands on behalf of an application. The NetBIOS emulator translates NetBIOS commands issued by an application into TDI commands that it sends to protocol drivers.

FIGURE 12-13 NetBIOS API implementation

If an application wants to use NetBIOS over the TCP/IP protocol, the NetBIOS emulator requires the presence of the NetBT driver (\%SystemRoot%\System32\Drivers\Netbt.sys). NetBT is known as the NetBIOS over TCP/IP driver and is responsible for supporting NetBIOS semantics that are inherent to the NetBIOS Extended User Interface (NetBEUI) protocol (included in previous versions of Windows) but not the TCP/IP protocol. For example, NetBIOS relies on NetBEUI's message-mode transmission and NetBIOS name resolution facilities, so the NetBT driver implements them on top of the TCP/IP protocol.

Other Networking APIs

Windows includes other networking APIs that are used less frequently or are layered on the APIs already described (and outside the scope of this book). Five of these, however— Background Intelligent Transfer Service (BITS), Distributed Component Object Model (DCOM), Message Queuing, Peer-to-Peer Infrastructure (P2P), and Universal Plug and Play (UPnP) with Plug and Play Extensions (PnP-X)—are important enough to the operation of a Windows system and many applications to merit brief descriptions.

BITS

The BITS API, currently at version 3.0 on Windows Vista and Windows Server 2008, allows application developers to transfer files between a client and a server asynchronously with *transfer jobs*, which can be either *download, upload,* or *upload-reply.* A download job downloads a file from a client, an upload job uploads a file to a server, and an upload-reply job receives a reply from the server after the data transfer is complete. BITS continues to transfer files even after the requesting application has exited, as long as there is an active network connection (BITS will not force a connection, such as initiating a dial-up connection) and the user who initiated the transfer is still logged on. If the network connection is dropped, the user logs off, or the system is restarted, BITS suspends the transfer, retaining enough information to resume the job when the user logs on again and the connection is restored.

BITS also allows for prioritization of different jobs, based on two priority classes: foreground transfers and background transfers. Background transfers are further divided into three priority levels. BITS uses a scheduling algorithm in which higher-level priorities preempt lower-priority transfers, while equal priorities execute concurrently. Therefore, under the BITS scheduling algorithm, lower-priority jobs remain suspended until no higher-priority jobs are eligible for execution.

Furthermore, BITS only makes use of idle networking bandwidth to perform its transfers, and it fine-tunes the upload and download speeds based on the amount of idle networking bandwidth available. If client network applications start using more bandwidth, BITS decreases its own usage to give priority to the user's network activities.

Finally, BITS supports peer caching, and if a job allows it, BITS will attempt to obtain the content from one or more peers instead of the direct Internet source, especially in LAN environments.

> **Note** Peer caching is disabled by default, and jobs must explicitly permit downloading from peers. BITS implements its own peer-caching protocols and does not make use of the Peer-to-Peer Infrastructure described in the next section.

Peer-to-Peer Infrastructure

Peer-to-Peer Infrastructure is a set of APIs that cover different technologies to enhance the Windows networking stack by providing flexible peer-to-peer (P2P) support for applications and services. The P2P infrastructure covers four major technologies, shown in Figure 12-14.

FIGURE 12-14 Peer-to-peer architecture

- Peer-to-Peer Graphing allows applications to pass data between peers efficiently and reliably by using nodes and events.

- Peer-to-Peer Namespace Provider enables serverless name resolution of peers and their services (described later in the "Name Resolution" section).

- Peer-to-Peer Grouping combines graphing and namespace technologies to group and isolate services and/or peers into a defined group and uniquely identify it.

- Peer-to-Peer Identity Manager enhances the services offered by the namespace provider to securely create, publish, and identify peer names, as well as to identify group members that are part of the grouping API.

The Peer-to-Peer Infrastructure in Windows is also paired with the Peer-to-Peer Collaboration Interface, which adds support for creating collaborative P2P applications, such as online games and group instant messaging, and supersedes the Real-Time Communications (RTC) architecture in earlier versions of Windows. It also provides presence capabilities through the People Near Me (PNM) architecture.

DCOM

Microsoft's COM API lets applications consist of different components, each component being a replaceable self-contained module. A COM object exports an object-oriented

interface to methods for manipulating the data within the object. Because COM objects present well-defined interfaces, developers can implement new objects to extend existing interfaces and dynamically update applications with the new support.

DCOM extends COM by letting an application's components reside on different computers, which means that applications don't need to be concerned that one COM object might be on the local computer and another might be across the LAN. DCOM thus provides location transparency, which simplifies developing distributed applications. DCOM isn't a self-contained API but relies on RPC to carry out its work.

Message Queuing

Message Queuing is a general-purpose platform for developing distributed applications that take advantage of loosely coupled messaging. Message Queuing is therefore an API and a messaging infrastructure. Its flexibility comes from the fact that its queues serve as message repositories in which senders can queue messages for receivers, and receivers can de-queue the messages at their discretion. Senders and receivers do not need to establish connections to use Message Queuing, nor do they even need to be executing at the same time, which allows for disconnected asynchronous message exchange.

A notable feature of Message Queuing is that it is integrated with Microsoft Transaction Server (MTS) and SQL Server, so it can participate in Microsoft Distributed Transaction Coordinator (MS DTC) coordinated transactions. Using MS DTC with Message Queuing allows you to develop reliable transaction functionality for three-tier applications.

UPnP with PnP-X

Universal Plug and Play is an architecture for peer-to-peer network connectivity of intelligent appliances, devices, and *control points*. It is designed to bring easy-to-use, flexible, standards-based connectivity to ad-hoc, managed, or unmanaged networks, whether these networks are in the home, in small businesses, or attached directly to the Internet. Universal Plug and Play is a distributed, open networking architecture that uses existing TCP/IP and Web technologies to enable seamless proximity networking in addition to control and data transfer among networked devices.

Universal Plug and Play supports zero-configuration, invisible networking, and automatic discovery for a range of device categories from a wide range of vendors. This enables a device to dynamically join a network, obtain an IP address, and convey its capabilities upon request. Then other control points can use the Control Point API with UPnP technology to learn about the presence and capabilities of other devices. A device can leave a network smoothly and automatically when it is no longer in use.

Plug and Play Extensions (PnP-X), shown in Figure 12-15, is an additional component of Windows that allows network-attached devices to integrate with the Plug and Play manager

in the kernel. With PnP-X, network-connected devices are shown in the Device Manager like locally attached devices and provide the same installation, management, and behavioral experience as a local device. (For example, installation is performed through the standard Add New Hardware wizard.)

FIGURE 12-15 PnP-X implementation

PnP-X uses a virtual network bus driver that uses an IP bus enumerator (%SystemRoot%\System32\Ipbusenum.dll) to discover PnP-X compatible devices, which include UPnP devices (through the Simple Service Discovery Protocol) and newer Device Profile for Web Services (DPWS) devices (through the WS-Discovery protocol). The IP bus enumerator reports devices it discovers to the Plug and Play manager, which uses user-mode Plug and Play manager services if needed (such as for driver installation). Similar to wireless discovery (like Bluetooth) and unlike wired device discovery (USB), however, PnP-X enumeration and driver installation must be explicitly requested by a user from the Network Explorer.

Note DPWS is a specification created by Microsoft that has goals similar to those of UPnP but is tightly integrated with Web services standards and frameworks and allows greater extensibility than UPnP.

Multiple Redirector Support

Applications can examine or access resources on remote systems in two ways. One way is by using the UNC standard with Windows functions to directly address a remote resource; a second way is by using the Windows Networking (WNet) API to enumerate computers and resources that those computers export for sharing. Both these approaches use the capabilities of a redirector to find their way to the network. As we stated earlier, to access SMB servers from a client, Microsoft supplies an SMB redirector, which has a kernel-mode component called the redirector FSD and a user-mode component called the Workstation service. (SMB is described in Chapter 11.) Microsoft also makes available redirectors that can access WebDAV resources, Terminal Services–shared drives, and resources shared by Novell NetWare servers.

Third parties can add their own redirectors to Windows. In this section, we'll examine the software that decides which redirector to invoke when remote I/O requests are issued. Here are the responsible components:

- *Multiple Provider Router* (MPR) is a DLL (\%SystemRoot%\System32\Mpr.dll) that determines which network to access when an application uses the Windows WNet API for browsing remote file systems.

- *Multiple UNC Provider* (MUP) is a driver (\%SystemRoot%\System32\Drivers\Mup.sys) that determines which network to access when an application uses the Windows I/O API to open remote files.

Multiple Provider Router

The Windows WNet functions allow applications (including the Network and Sharing Center) to connect to network resources, such as file servers and printers, and to browse the different share points. Because the WNet API can be called to work across different networks using different transport protocols, software must be present to send the request correctly over the network and to understand the results that the remote server returns. Figure 12-16 shows the redirector software responsible for these tasks.

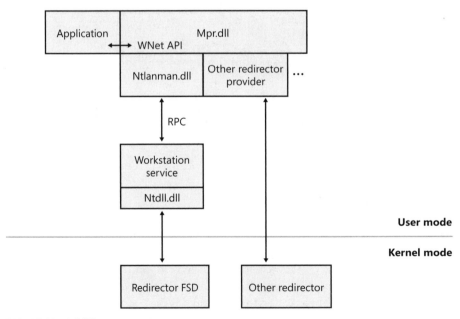

FIGURE 12-16 MPR components

A *provider* is software that establishes Windows as a client of a remote network server. Some of the operations a WNet provider performs include making and breaking network connections as well as supporting network printing. The built-in SMB WNet provider includes a DLL,

the Workstation service, and the redirector. Other network vendors need to supply only a DLL and a redirector.

When an application calls a WNet routine, the call passes directly to the MPR DLL. MPR takes the call and determines which network provider recognizes the resource being accessed. Each provider DLL beneath MPR supplies a set of standard functions collectively called the *network provider interface*. This interface allows MPR to determine which network the application is trying to access and to direct the request to the appropriate WNet provider software. The SMB Workstation service's provider is \%SystemRoot%\System32\Ntlanman.dll, as directed by the ProviderPath value under the HKLM\SYSTEM\CurrentControlSet\Services\ lanmanworkstation\NetworkProvider registry key.

When called by the *WNetAddConnection2* or *WNetAddConnection3* API function to connect to a remote network resource, MPR checks the HKLM\SYSTEM\CurrentControlSet\Control\ NetworkProvider\HwOrder\ProviderOrder registry value to determine which network providers are loaded. It polls them one at a time in the order in which they're listed in the registry until a redirector recognizes the resource or until all available providers have been polled. You can change the ProviderOrder by using the Advanced Settings dialog box shown in Figure 12-17. You can access the dialog box by first opening the Network Connections folder (by right-clicking the Network icon on the desktop or Start menu, selecting Properties from the pop-up menu to display the Network and Sharing Center, and then clicking Manage Network Connections). Open the Advanced menu, choose Advanced Settings, and then click the Provider Order tab.

FIGURE 12-17 The provider order editor

The *WNetAddConnection* function can also assign a drive letter or device name to a remote resource. When called to do so, *WNetAddConnection* routes the call to the appropriate network provider. The provider, in turn, creates a symbolic-link object in the object manager namespace that maps the drive letter being defined to the redirector (that is, the remote FSD) for that network.

Figure 12-18 shows the Session 0 DosDevices directory corresponding to the LUID (Logon ID) of the user that performed the drive letter mapping, which is where connections to remote file shares are stored. The symbolic link created by network providers relies on MUP to serve as the connection between a network path and the corresponding redirector. The figure shows that MUP creates a device object named \Device\LanmanRedirector, which is itself a symbolic link to \Device\MUP (which is not shown in the figure because the symbolic link is in the \Device directory) with additional text included in the symbolic link's value indicating to the MUP redirector which mini-redirector the drive letter corresponds to. The \Global?? directory shows you the drive letters available to the system session—others will be mapped in the session-specific DosDevices directory.

FIGURE 12-18 Resolving a network resource name

Then, when the WNet or other API calls the object manager to open a resource on a different network, the object manager uses the device object as a jumping-off point into the remote file system. It calls an I/O manager parse method associated with the device object to locate the redirector FSD that can handle the request. (See Chapter 11 for more information on file system drivers.)

Multiple UNC Provider

The Multiple UNC Provider is a networking component similar to MPR but which registers itself as a file system with the I/O manager, allowing it to field all remote file system I/O requests. MUP takes such requests and, like MPR, determines which local redirector recognizes the remote resource. Unlike MPR, MUP is a device driver (loaded at system boot time) that issues I/O requests to lower-layer drivers, in this case to redirectors, as shown in Figure 12-19.

When MUP loads during the boot it creates a device object named \Device\Mup. When a network redirector, like SMB, loads the redirector, it creates an unnamed device object and supplies a device name (for example \Device\LanmanRedirector) to register itself with MUP as a UNC provider by calling the function *FsRtlRegisterUncProviderEx*. *FsRtlRegisterUncProviderEx* creates a symbolic link name for the specified device name to point to its own device object, \Device\Mup. Because all network redirectors' namespaces are represented as symbolic links to the MUP device object, filter drivers can attach to \Device\Mup to intercept all remote file I/O operations.

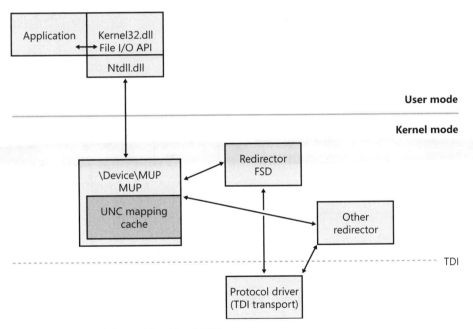

FIGURE 12-19 Multiple UNC Provider (MUP)

The MUP driver is activated when an application first attempts to open a remote file or device by specifying a UNC name (instead of a redirected drive letter, as described earlier). When the Windows client-side DLL Kernel32.dll (which is the DLL that exports file-I/O-related APIs) receives a file I/O request with UNC paths, the subsystem appends the UNC path to the string \Global??\UNC and then calls the *NtCreateFile* system service to open the file.

\global??\UNC resolves to \Device\Mup, and MUP must determine which provider should process the request.

When the MUP driver receives an I/O, MUP uses the HKLM\SYSTEM\CurrentControlSet\ Control\NetworkProvider\Order\ProviderOrder registry value to determine priority order of the network providers that registered with it using *FsRtlRegisterUncProviderEx*. It polls them one at a time in the order in which they're listed in the value until one of them indicates that it recognizes the path or until all available providers have been polled. MUP ignores those redirectors that are listed in the registry key but not registered. When a redirector recognizes a path the redirector indicates how much of the path is unique to it. For example, if the path is \\WIN2K3SERVER\PUBLIC\Windowsinternals\Chap12.doc, the redirector might recognize it and claim the prefix \\WIN2K3SERVER\PUBLIC as its own. The MUP driver caches this information and thereafter sends requests beginning with that prefix directly to the redirector, skipping the polling operation. The MUP driver's cache has a timeout feature, so after a period, a prefix's association with a particular redirector expires.

To simplify development of redirectors, Windows implements a mini-redirector model similar to the miniport driver model used by other device classes (see Chapter 7). The equivalent of the port driver in this case is the Redirected Drive Buffering Subsystem (RDBSS) (%SystemRoot%\System32\Drivers\Rdbss.sys). WebDAV and SMB redirectors are mini-redirectors that register with RDBSS by using *RxRegisterMinirdr* (instead of *FsRtlRegisterUncProviderEx)*. As shown in Figure 12-20, RDBSS is ultimately responsible for communicating with MUP and the I/O manager and for providing mapped-file buffering through the cache manager.

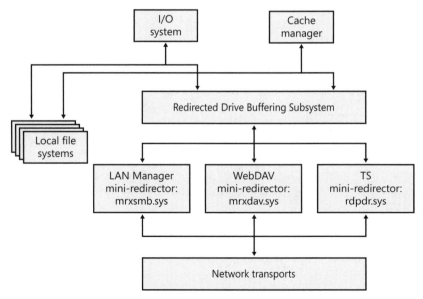

FIGURE 12-20 Mini-redirector architecture

Name Resolution

Name resolution is the process by which a character-based name, such as www.micro-soft.com or Mycomputer, is translated into a numeric address, such as 192.168.1.1, that the protocol stack can recognize. This section describes the three TCP/IP-related name resolution protocols provided by Windows: Domain Name System (DNS), Windows Internet Name Service (WINS), and Peer Name Resolution Protocol (PNRP).

Domain Name System

Domain Name System (DNS) is a standard by which Internet names (such as *www.micro-soft.com*) are translated to their corresponding IP addresses. A network application that wants to resolve a DNS name to an IP address sends a DNS lookup request using the TCP/IP protocol to a DNS server. DNS servers implement a distributed database of name/IP address pairs that are used to perform translations, and each server maintains the translations for a particular *zone*. Describing the details of DNS is outside the scope of this book, but DNS is the foundation of naming in Windows and so it is the primary Windows name resolution protocol.

The Windows DNS server is implemented as a Windows service (\%SystemRoot%\System32\ Dns.exe) that is included in server versions of Windows. Standard DNS server implementation relies on a text file as the translation database, but the Windows DNS server can be configured to store zone information in Active Directory.

Windows Internet Name Service

A networking service called *Windows Internet Name Service (WINS)* maintains the mapping between NetBIOS names and IP addresses used for NetBIOS-based TCP/IP applications. If WINS isn't installed, NetBIOS uses local broadcast messages for name operations on a subnet. Note that NetBIOS names are secondary to DNS names for Windows Sockets applications; computer names are registered and resolved first through DNS, with Windows falling back on NetBIOS names only if DNS name resolution fails. Link-Local Multicast Name Resolution (LLMNR) is a secondary fallback mechanism, used in cases in which IPv4 is not installed on the host machine. LLMNR extends the DNS packet format to allow both IPv4 and IPv6 name resolution to function on the same local link.

Peer Name Resolution Protocol

The *Peer Name Resolution Protocol (PNRP)* is a distributed peer-to-peer protocol that allows for dynamic name resolution and publication exclusively across IPv6 networks. It allows Internet-connected devices to publish *peer names* and their associated IPv6 address, as well as optional information. Other devices will then resolve the peer name, retrieve the IPv6 address, and establish a connection.

PNRP offers significant advantages over DNS, mainly by being distributed, which means that it is essentially serverless (other than for early bootstrapping), can scale to potentially millions of names, and is fault tolerant and bottleneck free. Because it includes secure name publication services, changes to name records can be performed from any system. DNS generally requires contacting a DNS server administrator to perform updates. PNRP name updates also occur in real time, making it appropriate for highly mobile devices, whereas DNS caches results. Finally, PNRP allows for naming more than just computers and services by allowing extended information to be published with name records.

Windows exposes PNRP via a PNRP API for applications and services, as well as by extending the *getaddrinfo* Winsock API described earlier in the chapter to perform resolution of PNRP IDs (described next) when an address includes the reserved *.pnrp.net* domain suffix.

PNRP peer names (also called *P2P IDs*) are made up of two components:

- **Authority** For *secure clients* (which have their name records signed by a certifying authority), the authority is identified by an SHA-1 hash of an associated public key, while for *unsecured clients*, it is zero. If a client is secure, PNRP validates the name record before publishing it.

- **Classifier** The classifier uses a simple string to identify a service provided by a peer, which allows multiple services to be provided by the same device.

To create a PNRP ID, PNRP hashes the P2P ID and combines it with a unique 128-bit ID called the *service location*, as shown in Figure 12-21. The service location identifies different instances of the same P2P ID in the same *cloud*. (PNRP uses two clouds: a *global cloud,* which corresponds to all IPv6 addresses on the Internet, and the *link-local cloud,* which corresponds to IPv6 addresses within a single subnet.)

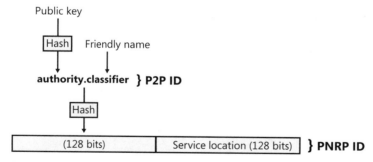

FIGURE 12-21 PNRP ID generation

PNRP Resolution and Publication

PNRP name resolution occurs in two phases:

- **Endpoint determination** In this phase, the requesting peer determines the IPv6 address associated with the peer responsible for publishing the PNRP ID of the desired service.

- **PNRP ID resolution** In this phase, once the requesting peer has located and confirmed the availability of the peer associated with the IPv6 address, it sends a PNRP request message for the PNRP ID of the service being requested. The peer providing the service replies to confirm the PNRP ID and can supply a comment and up to 4 KB of additional data, such as context information related to the service.

During the first phase, PNRP iterates over nodes while locating the publishing node, such that the node performing name resolution will be responsible for contacting nodes that are successively closer to the desired PNRP ID. Each iteration works as follows: Once a peer receives a request message, it performs a lookup in its cache for the requested PNRP ID. If a match is found, the request message is sent directly; otherwise, it is sent to the next closest PNRP ID (by seeing how much of the ID matches).

When a node receives a request message for which it cannot find a PNRP ID, it checks the distance of any other IDs in the cache to the target ID. If it finds a node that is closer, the requested node sends a reply to the requesting node, where the reply contains the IPv6 address of the peer that most closely matches the target PNRP ID. The requesting node can then use the IPv6 address to send another query to that address's node. If no node is closer, the requesting node is notified, and that node sends the request to the next closest node. Assuming PNRP IDs of 200, 350, 450, 500, and 800, Figure 12-22 depicts a possible endpoint determination phase for an example in which peer A is trying to find the endpoint for PNRP 800 (peer E).

To publish its PNRP ID(s), a peer first sends PNRP publication messages to its closest neighbors (entries in its cache that have IDs that are in the lowest levels) to seed their caches. It then randomly chooses nodes in the cloud that are not neighbors and sends them PNRP name resolution requests for its own PNRP ID. Through the mechanism described earlier, the endpoint determination phase will result in the seeding of the PNRP ID across the caches of the random nodes that were chosen in the cloud.

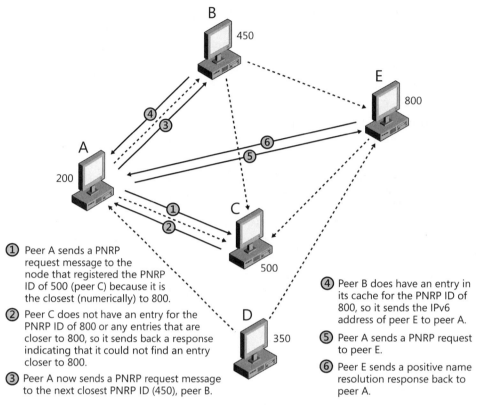

① Peer A sends a PNRP request message to the node that registered the PNRP ID of 500 (peer C) because it is the closest (numerically) to 800.

② Peer C does not have an entry for the PNRP ID of 800 or any entries that are closer to 800, so it sends back a response indicating that it could not find an entry closer to 800.

③ Peer A now sends a PNRP request message to the next closest PNRP ID (450), peer B.

④ Peer B does have an entry in its cache for the PNRP ID of 800, so it sends the IPv6 address of peer E to peer A.

⑤ Peer A sends a PNRP request to peer E.

⑥ Peer E sends a positive name resolution response back to peer A.

FIGURE 12-22 Example of PNRP name resolution.

Location and Topology

Today's networked computers often move between networks that require different configuration settings, for example, a corporate LAN and a home-based wireless network. Additionally, today's networks are complex, often spanning multiple devices across different topologies. Windows includes the Network Location Awareness (NLA) service to enable the dynamic configuration of network applications and settings based on location, and Link-Layer Topology Discovery (LLTD) to enable the intelligent discovery and mapping of networked devices.

Network Location Awareness (NLA)

The NLA service provider is implemented as a Winsock Namespace Provider (NSP) and provides the necessary framework for allowing computers and devices that move across different networks to select the most appropriate configuration settings. For example, an application taking advantage of NLA can detect when the user moves from a high-speed

LAN to a high-latency wireless network and fine-tune its bandwidth use appropriately. NLA can also detect when a home computer on a LAN may also have a secondary VPN connection to the office and select the proper configuration options.

Instead of having developers rely on manual network interface information to figure out the type of network, and the IP addresses or DNS names associated with them, NLA provides a standardized query API for enumerating all the local network attachment information and correlating it with network interface information. The NLA API also includes notifications that enable applications to respond to changes when they occur. NLA provides applications two pieces of location information:

- **Logical network identity** This identity is based on the logical network's DNS domain name. If one does not exist, NLA uses custom static information stored in the registry together with the network's subnet address as the identity.

- **Logical network interfaces** For each network that a device is attached to, NLA creates an *adapter name* that identifies interfaces such as NICs or RAS connections in a unique fashion. Applications use adapter names with the IP Helper API (%SystemRoot%\ System32\Iphlpapi.dll) to query interface information and characteristics.

Each logical network is implemented as a service class with an associated GUID and properties. NLA creates instances of that service class when it returns information about a logical network. Service classes are schemas that describe a namespace; they define the name, identifier, and namespace-specific information that is common to all instances. These classes are then used in combination with the *WSALookupService** API when performing name resolution.

Link-Layer Topology Discovery (LLTD)

The LLTD protocol operates over both wired and wireless networks and enables applications to discover the topology of a network. For example, the *Network Map* functionality in Windows uses LLTD to draw the local network topology for the connected devices that support the LLTD protocol. Additionally, LLTD supports Quality of Service (QoS) extensions, which allow applications to diagnose network problems such as low signal strength on a wireless network and bandwidth constraints on home networks. Because it operates on the OSI Data-link layer (2), LLTD works only on a single subnet, and therefore can't cross routers, but its capabilities make it suitable for most home and small-office networks.

The *LLTD Mapper I/O* and the *LLTD Responder* components implement LLTD. The former is responsible for the discovery process and for generating network maps. Because it uses a protocol different from IP, the LLTD Mapper uses NDIS APIs to directly send commands to the network via the network adapter. The LLTD Responder listens for and responds to discovery commands with information about the computer. As mentioned earlier, only devices that have a responder are shown in the network map.

Protocol Drivers

Networking API drivers must take API requests and translate them into low-level network protocol requests for transmission across the network. The API drivers rely on transport protocol drivers in kernel mode to do the actual translation. Separating APIs from underlying protocols gives the networking architecture the flexibility of letting each API use a number of different protocols. The Internet's explosive growth and reliance on the TCP/IP protocol has made TCP/IP the preeminent protocol in Windows. The Defense Advanced Research Projects Agency (DARPA) developed TCP/IP in 1969 specifically as the foundation for the Internet; therefore, TCP/IP has WAN-friendly characteristics such as routability and good WAN performance. TCP/IP is the preferred Windows protocol and is installed by default, although it can be removed.

However, the 4-byte network addresses used by the IPv4 protocol on the legacy TCP/IP stack limits the number of public IP addresses to roughly 4 billion, which is a limit that will be pressed as more and more devices, such as cell phones and PDAs, acquire an Internet presence. For that reason, the IPv6 protocol, which has 16-byte addresses, is gaining adoption. Windows includes a combined TCP/IP stack, called the *Next Generation TCP/IP Stack,* which supports both IP and IPv6. When operating on IPv6 networks, the stack also supports coexistence with IPv4 networks through the use of tunneling. The Next Generation TCP/IP Stack offers several advanced features to improve network performance, some of which are outlined in the following list:

- Receive Window Auto Tuning. The TCP protocol defines a *receive window size,* which determines how much data a receiver can accept before the server requests an acknowledgment. A higher size favors low-latency networks with high throughput, while lower values work better on networks such as Wi-Fi. The Windows TCP/IP stack is capable of analyzing the conditions of a network and choosing the optimal receive window size, adjusting it as needed if the network conditions change.

- Compound TCP (CTCP). While automatically changing the receive window size allows more data to be received, CTCP aggressively increases the amount of data that can be sent by a machine, while monitoring bandwidth, latency, and packet loss. Using CTCP on a high-bandwidth, low-latency network can significantly improve transfer speeds. CTCP is disabled by default.

- Explicit Congestion Notification (ECN). Whenever a TCP packet is lost, the TCP protocol assumes that the data was dropped because of router congestion and enforces congestion control, dramatically lowering the sender's transmission rate. ECN allows routers to explicitly mark packets as being forwarded during congestion, which is read by the Windows TCP/IP stack as a sign that transmission rates should be lowered. Lowering rates in this manner results in better performance than relying on congestion control. ECN is disabled by default.

- High-loss throughput improvements, including the NewReno Fast Recovery Algorithm, Enhanced Selective Acknowledgment (SACK), Forward RTO-Recovery (F-RTO), and Limited Transit. These algorithms reduce the overall retransmission of acknowledgments or TCP segments during high-loss scenarios while still maintaining the integrity of the TCP stream. This allows for greater bandwidth in these environments and preserves TCP's reliable transport semantics.

The Next Generation TCP/IP Stack (\%SystemRoot%\Drivers\Tcpip.sys), shown in Figure 12-23, implements TCP, UDP, IP, ARP, ICMP, and IGMP. To support legacy protocols such as NetBIOS, which make use of the deprecated TDI interface, the network stack also includes a component called TDX, which creates device objects that represent particular protocols so that clients can obtain a file object representing a protocol and issue network I/O to the protocol using TDI IRPs. The TDX component creates several device objects that represent various TDI client–accessible protocols: \Device\Tcp6, \Device\Tcp, \Device\Udp6, \Device\Udp, \Device\Rawip, and \Device\Tdx.

FIGURE 12-23 Windows Next Generation TCP/IP Stack

EXPERIMENT: Looking at TCP/IP's Device Objects

Using the kernel debugger to look at a live system, you can examine TCP/IP's device objects. After performing the *!drvobj* command to see the addresses of each of the driver's device objects, execute *!devobj* to view the name and other details about the device object.

```
kd> !drvobj tdx
Driver object (861d9478) is for:
 \Driver\tdx
Driver Extension List: (id , addr)
```

```
Device Object list:
861db310  861db440  861d8440  861d03e8
861cd440  861d2318  861d9350
lkd> !devobj 861cd440
Device object (861cd440) is for:
 Tcp6 \Driver\tdx DriverObject 861d9478
Current Irp 00000000 RefCount 7 Type 00000012 Flags 00000050
Dacl 8b1bc54c DevExt 861cd4f8 DevObjExt 861cd500
ExtensionFlags (0x00000800)
                            Unknown flags 0x00000800
Device queue is not busy.
lkd> !devobj 861db440
Device object (861db440) is for:
 RawIp \Driver\tdx DriverObject 861d9478
Current Irp 00000000 RefCount 0 Type 00000012 Flags 00000050
Dacl 8b1bc54c DevExt 861db4f8 DevObjExt 861db500
ExtensionFlags (0x00000800)
                            Unknown flags 0x00000800
Device queue is not busy.
lkd> !devobj 861d8440
Device object (861d8440) is for:
 Udp6 \Driver\tdx DriverObject 861d9478
Current Irp 00000000 RefCount 0 Type 00000012 Flags 00000050
Dacl 8b1bc54c DevExt 861d84f8 DevObjExt 861d8500
ExtensionFlags (0x00000800)
                            Unknown flags 0x00000800
Device queue is not busy.
lkd> !devobj 861d03e8
Device object (861d03e8) is for:
 Udp \Driver\tdx DriverObject 861d9478
Current Irp 00000000 RefCount 6 Type 00000012 Flags 00000050
Dacl 8b1bc54c DevExt 861d04a0 DevObjExt 861d04a8
ExtensionFlags (0x00000800)
                            Unknown flags 0x00000800
Device queue is not busy.
lkd> !devobj 861cd440
Device object (861cd440) is for:
 Tcp6 \Driver\tdx DriverObject 861d9478
Current Irp 00000000 RefCount 7 Type 00000012 Flags 00000050
Dacl 8b1bc54c DevExt 861cd4f8 DevObjExt 861cd500
ExtensionFlags (0x00000800)
                            Unknown flags 0x00000800
Device queue is not busy.
lkd> !devobj 861d2318
Device object (861d2318) is for:
 Tcp \Driver\tdx DriverObject 861d9478
Current Irp 00000000 RefCount 167 Type 00000012 Flags 00000050
Dacl 8b1bc54c DevExt 861d23d0 DevObjExt 861d23d8
ExtensionFlags (0x00000800)
                            Unknown flags 0x00000800
Device queue is not busy.
lkd> !devobj 861d9350
Device object (861d9350) is for:
 Tdx \Driver\tdx DriverObject 861d9478
```

```
Current Irp 00000000 RefCount 0 Type 00000021 Flags 00000050
Dacl 8b0649a8 DevExt 00000000 DevObjExt 861d9408
ExtensionFlags (0x00000800)
                              Unknown flags 0x00000800
Device queue is not busy.
```

Windows Filtering Platform (WFP)

Windows includes a rich and extensible platform for monitoring, intercepting, and processing network traffic at all levels in the network stack. Other Windows networking services extend basic networking features of the TCP/IP protocol driver by relying on the WFP. These include network address translation (NAT), IP filtering, IP inspection, and Internet Protocol Security (IPSec). Figure 12-24 shows how the different components of the WFP are integrated with the TCP/IP stack. These include:

- **Filter engine** The filter engine is implemented in both user mode and kernel mode and performs all the filtering operations on the network. Each filter engine component consists of filtering layers, one for each component of the network stack. The user-mode engine, responsible for RPC and IPSec keying policy, among other things, contains approximately 10 filters, while the kernel-mode engine, which performs the network and transport layer filtering of the TCP/IP stack, contains around 50.

- **Shims** Shims are the kernel-mode components that reside between the network stack and the filter engine. They are responsible for making the decision to allow or block network traffic based on their filtering behavior, which is defined by the filter engine. A shim operates in three steps: it parses the incoming data to match incoming values with entries in the filter engine, calls the filter engine to return an action based on the incoming values, and then interprets the action (drop the packet, for example).

- **Base filtering engine (BFE)** The BFE is a user-mode service (%SystemRoot%\System32\Bfe.dll) that manages all WFP operations. It is responsible for adding and removing filters from the WFP stack, managing the filter configuration, and enforcing security on the filter database.

- **Callout drivers** Callout drivers are kernel-mode components that add custom filtering functionality outside the basic support provided by the WFP. Callout drivers associate callout functions with one or more kernel-mode filtering layers, and the WFP enables callout functions to perform deep packet inspection and modification. Network address translation (described next) and IPSec, are implemented as callout drivers, for example.

FIGURE 12-24 Windows Filtering Platform architecture

Network Address Translation

Network address translation (NAT) is a routing service that allows multiple private IP addresses to map to a single public IP address. Without NAT, each computer of a LAN must be assigned a public IP address to communicate across the Internet. NAT allows one computer of the LAN to be assigned an IP address and the other computers to use private IP addresses and be connected to the Internet through that computer. NAT translates between private IP addresses and the public IP address as necessary, routing packets between LAN computers and the Internet.

NAT components on Windows consist of a NAT device driver, \%SystemRoot%\System32\Drivers\Ipnat.sys, that interfaces with the WFP stack as a callout driver, as well as editors that can perform additional packet processing beyond address and port translation. NAT can be installed as a routing protocol component with the Routing And Remote Access MMC snap-in or by configuring Internet Connection Sharing (ICS), although NAT is much more configurable when installed using the Routing And Remote Access MMC snap-in.

IP Filtering

Windows includes a very basic IP filtering capability with which a user can choose to allow only certain ports or IP protocols into or out of the network. While this capability can serve to protect a computer from unauthorized network accesses, its drawback is that it is static and does not automatically create new filters for traffic initiated by applications running on the computer.

Windows also includes host firewall capability, called Windows Firewall, that goes beyond the basic filtering just described. Windows Firewall uses WFP to provide a *stateful firewall*, which is one that keeps track of traffic flow so that it distinguishes between TCP/IP traffic that originates on the local LAN and unsolicited traffic that originates on the Internet. When Windows Firewall is enabled on an interface, one of three profiles can be applied—public, private, and domain. By default, when the public profile is chosen (or until a profile is selected), all unsolicited incoming and outgoing traffic received and sent by the computer is discarded, other than traffic from network services and other system applications. A user or application can define exceptions so that services running on the computer, such as file and printer sharing or a Web site, can be accessed from other computers.

The Windows Firewall service, which executes in a Svchost process, uses the BFE to pass exception rules defined in the configuration user interface to the IPNat driver. The WFP filter engine executes the callback functions of each registered callout driver as it processes both inbound and outbound IP packets. A callback function can provide NAT functionality by modifying source and destination addresses in a packet, or as a firewall by returning a status code to TCP/IP that requests that TCP/IP drop the packet and cease processing for it. In kernel mode, Windows Firewall uses a driver (%SystemRoot%\System32\Drivers\Mpsdrv.sys) that provides support for PPTP and FTP filtering, since those protocols provide their own

independent control and data channels. The driver must analyze the control channel to figure out which data channel to manipulate. The driver is also used for displaying notification windows when an application starts listening on a socket.

Internet Protocol Security

Internet Protocol Security (IPSec), which is integrated with the Windows TCP/IP stack, helps protect unicast (IPSec itself supports multicast, but the Windows implementation does not) IP data against attacks such as eavesdropping, sniffer attacks, data modification, IP address spoofing, and man-in-the-middle attacks (as long as the identity of the remote machine can be verified, such as a VPN). You can use IPSec to provide defense-in-depth against network-based attacks from untrusted computers; certain attacks that can result in the denial-of-service of applications, services, or the network; data corruption, data theft, and user-credential theft; and the administrative control over servers, other computers, and the network. IPSec helps defend against network-based attacks through cryptography-based security services, security protocols, and dynamic key management.

IPSec provides the following properties for unicast IP packets sent between trusted hosts:

- Data origin authentication, which verifies the origin of an IP packet and ensures that unauthenticated parties cannot access data.

- Data integrity, which protects an IP packet from being modified in transit without being detected.

- Data confidentiality, which encrypts the payload of IP packets before transmission. Data confidentiality ensures that only the IPSec peer with which a computer is communicating can read and interpret the contents of the packets. This property is optional.

- Anti-replay (or replay protection), which ensures that each IP packet is unique and can't be reused. This property prevents an attacker from intercepting IP packets and inserting modified packets into a data stream between a source computer and a destination computer. When anti-replay is used, attackers cannot reply to captured messages to establish a session or gain unauthorized access to data.

You can use IPSec to help defend against network-based attacks by configuring host-based IPSec packet filtering and enforcing trusted communications. When you use IPSec for host-based IPSec packet filtering, IPSec can permit or block specific types of unicast IP traffic based on source and destination address combinations and specific protocols and specific ports.

In an Active Directory environment, Group Policy can be used to configure domains, sites, and organizational units (OUs), and IPSec policies (called *connection security rules*) can then be assigned as required to Group Policy objects (GPOs) through Windows Firewall with Advanced Security configuration settings. Alternatively, you can configure and assign local IPSec policies. Active Directory–based connection security rules are stored in Active

Directory, and a copy of the current policy is maintained in a cache in the local registry. Local connection security rules are stored in the local system registry.

To establish trusted communications, IPSec uses mutual authentication, and it supports the following authentication methods through AuthIP, Microsoft's extension to Internet Key Exchange (IKE):

- Interactive user Kerberos 5 credentials or interactive user NTLMv2 credentials
- User x.509 certificates
- Computer SSL certificates
- NAP health certificates
- Anonymous authentication (optional authentication)
- Preshared key

If AuthIP is not available, plain IKE is also supported by IPSec. The Windows implementation of IPSec is based on IPSec Requests for Comments (RFCs). The Windows IPSec architecture includes Windows Firewall with Advanced Security, the legacy IPSec Policy Agent, the IKE and Authenticated Internet Protocol (AuthIP) protocols, and an IPSec WFP callout driver.

- **Windows Firewall with Advanced Security** In addition to the filtering functionality described earlier, the Windows Firewall service is also responsible for providing the security and policy configuration settings for IPSec, which can be configured through Group Policy either locally or on an Active Directory domain.

- **Legacy IPSec Policy Agent** The legacy IPSec Policy Agent runs as a service. In the Services snap-in in the Microsoft Management Console (MMC), the IPSec Policy Agent appears in the list of computer services under the name IPSEC Policy Agent. The IPSec Policy Agent obtains legacy IPSec policy from an Active Directory domain or the local registry and then passes IP address filters to the IPSec driver and authentication and security settings to IKE. These policies are honored for compatibility with older versions of Windows, which implement IPSec management through Active Directory.

- **IKE and AuthIP** IKE is a protocol that supports the authentication and key negotiation services required by IPSec. For outgoing traffic, IKE waits for requests to negotiate security associations (SAs) from the IPSec driver, negotiates the SAs, and then sends the SA settings back to the IPSec driver. For incoming traffic, IKE receives a negotiation request directly from the remote peer, and all other traffic from the peer is dropped until the SAs have been successfully negotiated. SAs are a combination of mutually agreeable IPSec policy settings and keys that defines the security services, mechanisms, and keys that are used to help secure communications between IPSec peers. Each SA is a one-way or simplex connection that secures the traffic it carries. IKE negotiates main mode SAs and quick mode SAs when requested by the IPSec driver. The IKE main mode (or ISAKMP) SA protects the IKE negotiation. The quick mode (or IPSec) SAs protect

application traffic. AuthIP is an extension to IKE supported by Windows Vista and later versions. It adds a secondary authentication mechanism to increase security and simplify maintenance and configuration of IPSec.

- **IPSec WFP callout driver** The IPSec WFP callout driver is a device driver (\%SystemRoot%\System32\Drivers\Ipsec.sys) that is bound to the WFP and that processes packets that pass through the TCP/IP driver. The IPSec driver monitors and secures outbound unicast IP traffic, and it monitors, decrypts, and validates inbound unicast IP packets. The WFP receives filters from the IPSec Policy Agent and invokes the callout, which then permits, blocks, or secures packets as required. To secure traffic, the IPSec driver uses active SA settings, or it requests that new SAs be created.

You can use the Windows Firewall with Advanced Security (Wf.msc) snap-in that is available in MMC to create and manage connection security rules by using the New Connection Security Rule Wizard, shown in Figure 12-25. This snap-in can be used to create, modify, and store local connection security rules or Active Directory–based connection security rules, and to modify connection security rules on remote computers. Alternatively, you can use the Netsh utility with the *netsh advfirewall consec* command to manage connection security rules. After IPSec-secured communication is established, you can monitor IPSec information for local computers and for remote computers by using the Windows Firewall with Advanced Security snap-in or the Netsh utility with the *netsh advfirewall monitor* command.

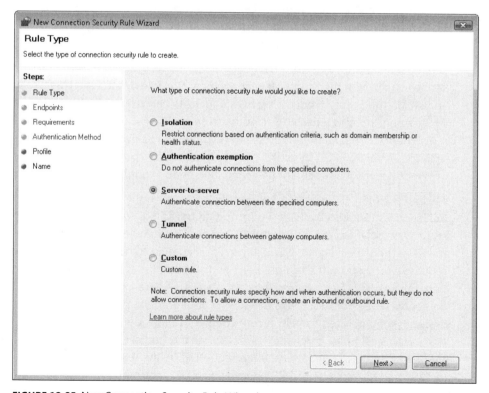

FIGURE 12-25 New Connection Security Rule Wizard

NDIS Drivers

When a protocol driver wants to read or write messages formatted in its protocol's format from or to the network, the driver must do so using a network adapter. Because expecting protocol drivers to understand the nuances of every network adapter on the market (proprietary network adapters number in the thousands) isn't feasible, network adapter vendors provide device drivers that can take network messages and transmit them via the vendors' proprietary hardware. In 1989, Microsoft and 3Com jointly developed the Network Driver Interface Specification (NDIS), which lets protocol drivers communicate with network adapter drivers in a device-independent manner. Network adapter drivers that conform to NDIS are called NDIS drivers or NDIS miniport drivers. The version of NDIS that ships with Windows Vista SP1 and Windows Server 2008 is NDIS 6.1.

The NDIS library (\%SystemRoot%\System32\Drivers\Ndis.sys) implements the NDIS boundary that exists between network transports, such as the TCP/IP driver, and NDIS drivers. The NDIS library is a helper library that NDIS driver clients use to format commands they send to NDIS drivers. NDIS drivers interface with the library to receive requests and send back responses. Figure 12-26 shows the relationship between various NDIS-related components.

FIGURE 12-26 NDIS components

Instead of merely providing the NDIS boundary helper routines, the NDIS library provides NDIS drivers with an entire execution environment. NDIS drivers aren't genuine Windows drivers because they can't function without the encapsulation the NDIS library gives them.

This insulation layer wraps NDIS drivers so thoroughly that NDIS drivers don't accept and process IRPs. Rather, protocol drivers such as TCP/IP call a function in the NDIS library, *NdisAllocateNetBuffer*, and pass the packets to an NDIS miniport by calling an NDIS library function (*NdisSendNetBufferLists*, for example). Additionally, to make development simpler, all components of the Windows Next Generation TCP/IP Stack make use of net buffers, including TCP/IP and WSK, which streamlines communications with NDIS.

NDIS includes the following features:

- NDIS drivers can report whether or not their network medium is active, which allows Windows to display a network connected/disconnected icon on the taskbar. This feature also allows protocols and other applications to be aware of this state and react accordingly. The TCP/IP transport, for example, will use this information to determine when it should reevaluate addressing information it receives from DHCP.

- NDIS drivers can be paused and resumed, which enables run-time reconfiguration, such as during a response to a Plug and Play event. This allows dynamic operations such as binding and unbinding a protocol driver without requiring a reboot.

- TCP/IP offloading, including task and chimney offloading. Task offloading allows a miniport to use advanced features of a network adapter to perform operations such as packet checksums and IPSec. NDIS includes support for IPSec Task Offload Version 2, which includes support for additional cryptography suites used in IPSec, such as AES, as well as IPv6 support. Chimney offloading provides a direct connection (the so-called chimney) between network applications and the network card hardware, enabling greater offloading and connection state management to be implemented by the network card. These offloading operations can improve system performance by relieving the CPU from the tasks.

- Receive scaling enables multiple processors to perform packet receive operations and appropriate scaling to be selected based on the most efficient use of available target processors. NDIS supports the receive-side scaling (RSS) interface at the hardware level and queues DPCs to the appropriate processors.

- Wake-on-LAN allows a wake-on-LAN-capable network adapter to bring Windows out of a suspend power state. Events that can trigger the network adapter to signal the system include media connections (such as plugging a network cable into the adapter), the receipt of protocol-specific patterns registered by a protocol (the TCP/IP transport asks to be woken for Address Resolution Protocol [ARP] requests), and, for Ethernet adapters, the receipt of a *magic* packet (a network packet that contains 16 contiguous copies of the adapter's Ethernet address).

- Header-data split allows compatible network cards to improve network performance by splitting the data and header part of an Ethernet frame into different buffers and subsequently combining the buffers into smaller regions of memory than if the buffers were combined. This allows more efficient memory usage as well as better caching because multiple headers can fit in a single page.

- Connection-oriented NDIS (CoNDIS) allows NDIS drivers to manage connection-oriented media such as PPP devices. (CoNDIS is described in more detail shortly.)

The interfaces that the NDIS library provides for NDIS drivers to interface with network adapter hardware are available via functions that translate directly to corresponding functions in the HAL.

EXPERIMENT: Listing the Loaded NDIS Miniports

The Ndiskd kernel debugger extension library includes the *!miniports* and *!miniport* commands, which let you list the loaded miniports using a kernel debugger and, given the address of a miniport block (a data structure Windows uses to track miniports), see detailed information about the miniport driver. The following example shows the *!miniports* and *!miniport* commands being used to list all the miniports and then specifics about the miniport responsible for interfacing the system to a PCI Ethernet adapter. (Note that WAN miniport drivers work with dial-up connections.)

```
lkd> .load ndiskd
Loaded ndiskd extension DLL

lkd> !miniports
NDIS Driver verifier level: 0
NDIS Failed allocations    : 0
Miniport Driver Block: 86880d78, Version 0.0
  Miniport: 868cf0e8, NetLuidIndex: 1, IfIndex: 9, RAS Async Adapter
Miniport Driver Block: 84c3be60, Version 4.0
  Miniport: 84c3c0e8, NetLuidIndex: 3, IfIndex: 15, VMware Virtual Ethernet Adapter
Miniport Driver Block: 84c29240, Version 0.0
  Miniport: 84c2b438, NetLuidIndex: 0, IfIndex: 2, WAN Miniport (SSTP)

...
lkd> !miniport 84bcc0e8

 Miniport 84bcc0e8 : Broadcom NetXtreme 57xx Gigabit Controller, v6.0

    AdapterContext : 85f6b000
    Flags          : 0c452218
                     BUS_MASTER, 64BIT_DMA, IGNORE_TOKEN_RING_ERRORS
                     DESERIALIZED, RESOURCES_AVAILABLE, SUPPORTS_MEDIA_SENSE
                     DOES_NOT_DO_LOOPBACK, SG_DMA,
                     NOT_MEDIA_CONNECTED,
    PnPFlags       : 00610021
                     PM_SUPPORTED, DEVICE_POWER_ENABLED, RECEIVED_START
                     HARDWARE_DEVICE, NDIS_WDM_DRIVER,
    MiniportState      : STATE_RUNNING
    IfIndex            : 10
    Ndis5MiniportInNdis6Mode : 0
    InternalResetCount : 0000
    MiniportResetCount : 0000
    References         : 5
    UserModeOpenReferences: 0
```

```
    PnPDeviceState          : PNP_DEVICE_STARTED
    CurrentDevicePowerState : PowerDeviceD0
    Bus PM capabilities
    DeviceD1:               0
    DeviceD2:               0
    WakeFromD0:             0
    WakeFromD1:             0
    WakeFromD2:             0
    WakeFromD3:             1

    SystemState             DeviceState
    PowerSystemUnspecified  PowerDeviceUnspecified
    S0                      D0
    S1                      PowerDeviceUnspecified
    S2                      PowerDeviceUnspecified
    S3                      D3
    S4                      D3
    S5                      D3
    SystemWake: S5
    DeviceWake: D3

    WakeupMethods Enabled 2:
    WAKE_UP_PATTERN_MATCH
    WakeUpCapabilities:
     MinMagicPacketWakeUp: 4
     MinPatternWakeUp: 4
     MinLinkChangeWakeUp: 0
    Current PnP and PM Settings:         : 00000030
                    DISABLE_WAKE_UP, DISABLE_WAKE_ON_RECONNECT,
    Translated Allocated Resources:
        Memory: ecef0000, Length: 10000
        Interrupt Level: 9, Vector: a8
    MediaType       : 802.3
    DeviceObject    : 84bcc030, PhysDO : 848fd6b0  Next DO: 848fc7b0
    MapRegisters    : 00000000
    FirstPendingPkt: 00000000
    DriverVerifyFlags : 00000000
    Miniport Interrupt : 85f72000
    Miniport version 6.0
    Miniport Filter List:
    Miniport Open Block Queue:
      8669bad0: Protocol 86699530 = NDISUIO, ProtocolBindingContext 8669be88, v6.0
      86690008: Protocol 86691008 = VMNETBRIDGE, ProtocolBindingContext 866919b8, v5.0
      84f81c50: Protocol 849fb918 = TCPIP6, ProtocolBindingContext 84f7b930, v6.1
      84f7b230: Protocol 849f43c8 = TCPIP, ProtocolBindingContext 84f7b5e8, v6.1
```

The Flags field for the miniport that was examined indicates that the miniport supports 64-bit direct memory access operation (64BIT_DMA), that the media is currently not active (NOT_MEDIA_CONNECTED), and that it can dynamically detect whether the media is connected or disconnected (SUPPORTS_MEDIA_SENSE). Also listed are the adapter's system-to-device power-state mappings and the bus resources that the Plug and Play manager assigned to the adapter. (See the section "The Power Manager" in Chapter 7 for more information on power-state mappings.)

Variations on the NDIS Miniport

The NDIS model also supports hybrid network transport NDIS drivers, called *NDIS intermediate drivers*. These drivers lie between transport drivers and NDIS drivers. To an NDIS driver, an NDIS intermediate driver looks like a transport driver; to a transport driver, an NDIS intermediate driver looks like an NDIS driver. NDIS intermediate drivers can see all network traffic taking place on a system because the drivers lie between protocol drivers and network drivers. Software that provides fault tolerant and load balancing options for network adapters, such as Microsoft's Network Load Balancing Provider, are based on NDIS intermediate drivers.

Finally, the NDIS model also implements *lightweight filter drivers* (LWDs), which are similar to intermediate drivers but specifically designed for filtering network traffic. LWDs support dynamic insertion and removal while the protocol stack is running. Filter drivers have the ability to filter almost all communications to and from the underlying miniport adapter because they're not associated with a particular protocol driver. They also have the ability to select only certain services for filtering and to be bypassed for those that they are not interested in. Just like insertion and removal, these service bindings are also dynamic and can change at run time.

Connection-Oriented NDIS

Support for connection-oriented network hardware (for example, PPP) is native in Windows, which makes connection management and establishment standard in the Windows network architecture. Connection-oriented NDIS drivers use many of the same APIs that standard NDIS drivers use; however, connection-oriented NDIS drivers send packets through established network connections rather than place them on the network medium.

In addition to miniport support for connection-oriented media, NDIS includes definitions for drivers that work to support a connection-oriented miniport driver:

- Call managers are NDIS drivers that provide call setup and teardown services for connection-oriented clients (described shortly). A call manager uses a connection-oriented miniport to exchange signaling messages with other network entities such as network switches or other call managers. A call manager supports one or more signaling protocols.

- An integrated miniport call manager (MCM) is a connection-oriented miniport driver that also provides call manager services to connection-oriented clients. An MCM is essentially an NDIS miniport driver with a built-in call manager.

- A connection-oriented client uses the call setup and teardown services of a call manager or MCM and the send and receive services of a connection-oriented NDIS miniport driver. A connection-oriented client can provide its own protocol services to higher levels in the network stack, or it can implement an emulation layer that interfaces connectionless legacy protocols and connection-oriented media. An example of an emulation layer fulfilled by a connection-oriented client is a LAN emulation (LANE), which hides the connected-oriented characteristics of ATM and presents a connectionless media (such as Ethernet) to protocols above it.

Figure 12-27 shows the relationships between these components.

FIGURE 12-27 Connection-oriented NDIS drivers

EXPERIMENT: Using Network Monitor to Capture Network Packets

Microsoft provides a tool named Network Monitor that lets you capture packets that flow through one or more NDIS miniport drivers on your system by installing an NDIS lightweight filter driver (Netmon). You can obtain the latest version of Network Monitor by going to the Microsoft Support Knowledge Base Article *http://support.micro-soft.com/kb/955998*. When you first start Network Monitor, you'll see a window similar to the one shown here:

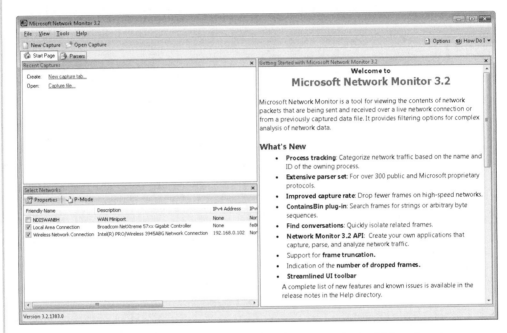

In the Select Networks pane, Network Monitor lets you select which network connection you want to monitor. After selecting one or more, start the capture environment by clicking the New Capture button on the toolbar. You can now initiate monitoring by clicking the Start button on the toolbar. Perform operations that generate network activity on the connection you're monitoring (such as browsing to a Web site), and after you see that Network Monitor has captured packets, stop monitoring by clicking the Stop button. In the Frame Summary pane, you will see all the raw network traffic during the capture period. The Network Conversations pane will display network traffic isolated by process, whenever possible. By clicking on the Iexplore.exe process in this example, Network Monitor shows only the relevant frames in the Frame Summary view, as shown next.

The window shows the HTTP packets that Network Monitor captured as the Microsoft Web site was accessed through Internet Explorer. If you click on a frame, Network Monitor displays a view of the packet that breaks it apart to show various layered application and protocol headers in the Frame Details pane, as shown in the previous screen shot.

Network Monitor also includes a number of other features, such as capture triggers and filters, that make it a powerful tool for troubleshooting network problems. You can also add parsers for other protocols, as well as view and modify their source code. Network Monitor parsers are hosted on CodePlex, the Microsoft open source project site.

Remote NDIS

Prior to the development of Remote NDIS, a vendor that developed a USB network device, for example, had to provide a driver that interfaced with NDIS as a miniport driver as well as interfacing with a USB WDM bus driver, as shown in Figure 12-28. If the vendor's hardware supported other buses, such as IEEE 1394, the vendor was required to implement drivers that interfaced with each specific bus type.

FIGURE 12-28 NDIS miniport driver for a USB network device

Remote NDIS is a specification for network devices on dynamic Plug and Play I/O buses such as USB, IEEE 1394, Bluetooth, and Infiniband. The specification eliminates the need for a hardware vendor to write an NDIS miniport driver at all by defining bus-independent messages and the mechanism by which the messages are transmitted over various buses. Remote NDIS messages mirror the NDIS interface and include messages for initializing and resetting a device, transmitting and receiving packets, setting and querying device parameters, and indicating media link status.

The Remote NDIS architecture, in Figure 12-29, relies on a Microsoft-supplied NDIS miniport driver, \%SystemRoot%\System32\Drivers\Rndismp.sys, that translates NDIS commands and forwards them to a bus transport driver for the bus on which a device is located. The architecture allows for a single NDIS miniport driver to be used for all Remote NDIS drivers and a single bus transport driver for each supported bus.

FIGURE 12-29 Remote NDIS architecture for USB network devices

Currently, Remote NDIS for USB devices is included on Windows. While Remote NDIS on IEEE 1394 is fully specified, Windows does not yet support it, nor does it support it over Infiniband.

QoS

If no special measures are taken, IP traffic is delivered over a network on a first-come, first-serve basis. Applications have no control over the priority of their messages, and they can experience *bursty* network behavior, where they occasionally obtain high throughput and low latencies, but otherwise receive poor network performance. While this level of service is acceptable in most situations, an increasing number of network applications demand more consistent service levels, or *quality of service* (QoS) guarantees. Video conferencing, media streaming, and enterprise resource planning (ERP) are examples of applications that require good network performance. QoS allows an application to specify minimum bandwidth and maximum latencies, which can be satisfied only if every networking software and hardware component between a sender and a receiver supports QoS standards such as IEEE 802.1P, an industry standard that specifies the format of QoS packets and how OSI layer 2 devices (switches and network adapters) respond to them.

Windows supports QoS through a *policy-based QoS* implementation that takes full advantage of the Next Generation TCP/IP network stack, the WFP, and NDIS lightweight filter drivers. The implementation allows for managing or prioritizing bandwidth use based on different conditions, such as the application, the source or destination IP address, the protocol being used, and the source or destination ports. Network administrators typically apply QoS settings to a logon session or a computer with Active Directory–based Group Policy, but they can be applied locally as well.

Policy-based QoS provides two methods through which bandwidth can be managed. The first uses a special field in the IP header called the Differentiated Services Code Point (DSCP). Routers that support DSCP read the value and separate packets into specific queues. The QoS architecture in Windows can mark outgoing packets with the appropriate DSCP field so that network devices can provide differentiated levels of service. The other bandwidth management method is the ability to simply throttle outgoing traffic based on the conditions outlined earlier, where the QoS components limit bandwidth to a specified rate.

The Windows QoS implementation consists of several components, as shown in Figure 12-30. First, the QoS Client Side Extension (%SystemRoot%\System32\Gptext.dll) notifies the Group Policy client and the QoS Inspection Module that QoS settings have changed. Next, the QoS Inspection Module (eQoS), which is a WFP packet-inspection component implemented in the TCP/IP driver that reacts to policy changes, retrieves the updated policy and works with the transport layer and QoS Packet Scheduler to mark traffic that matches the policy. Finally, the QoS Packet Scheduler, or Pacer (%SystemRoot%\System32\Drivers\Pacer.sys), provides

the NDIS lightweight filter functionality, such as throttling and setting the DSCP value, to control packet scheduling based on the QoS policies. Pacer also provides the GQoS (Generic QoS) and TC (Traffic Control) API support for legacy Windows applications that used these mechanisms.

In addition to the systemwide, policy-based QoS support provided by the QoS architecture, Windows enables specific classes of socket-based applications to have individual and specific control of QoS behavior through an API called the Quality Windows Audio/Video Experience, or qWAVE. Network-based multimedia applications, like Voice over IP (VoIP), can use the qWAVE API to query information on real-time network bandwidth and adapt to changing network conditions, as well as to prioritize packets to efficiently use the available bandwidth. qWAVE also takes advantage of the topology protocols described earlier to dynamically determine if the current network devices will support the required bandwidth for a video stream, for example. It can notify applications of diminishing bandwidth, at which point the multimedia application is expected to reduce the stream quality, for example.

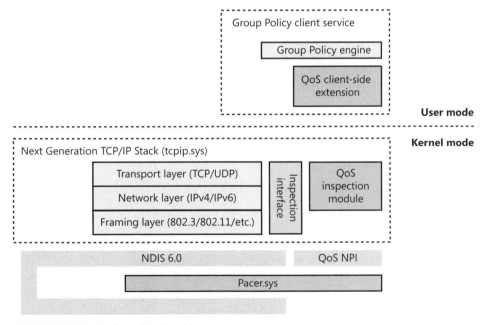

FIGURE 12-30 Policy-based QoS architecture

qWAVE is implemented in the QoS2 (%SystemRoot%\System32\Qwave.dll) API library and provides four main components:

- Admission control, which determines, when a new network multimedia stream is started, if the current network can support the sustained bandwidth requested.

- Caching, which allows the detailed admission control checks to be bypassed if similar usage patterns occurred in the past and the calculation result was already cached.

- Monitoring and probing, which keep track of available bandwidth and notify applications during low-bandwidth or high-latency situations.

- Traffic tagging and shaping, which uses the 802.11p and DSCP technologies mentioned earlier to tag packets with the appropriate priority to ensure timely delivery.

Figure 12-31 shows the general overview of the qWAVE architecture:

FIGURE 12-31 qWAVE architecture

Binding

The final piece in the Windows networking architecture puzzle is the way in which the components at the various layers—networking API layer, transport driver layer, NDIS driver layer—locate one another. The name of the process that connects the layers is *binding*. You've witnessed binding taking place if you've changed your network configuration by adding or removing a component using the Network Connections folder.

When you install a networking component, you must supply an INF file for the component. (INF files are described in Chapter 7.) This file includes directions that setup API routines must follow to install and configure the component, including binding dependencies or binding relationships. A developer can specify binding dependencies for a proprietary component so that the Service Control Manager (the Service Control Manager is described in Chapter 4) will not only load the component in the correct order but will load the component only if other components the proprietary component depends on are present on the system. Binding relationships, which the bind engine determines with the aid of additional information in a

component's INF file, establish connections between components at the various layers. The connections specify which components a network component on one layer can use on the layer beneath it.

For example, the Workstation service (redirector) will automatically bind to the TCP/IP protocol. The order of the binding, which you can examine on the Adapters And Bindings tab in the Advanced Settings dialog box, shown in Figure 12-32, determines the priority of the binding. (See the section "Multiple Redirector Support" earlier in this chapter for instructions on how to launch the Advanced Settings dialog box.) When the redirector receives a request to access a remote file, it submits the request to both protocol drivers simultaneously. When the response comes, the redirector waits until it has also received responses from any higher-priority protocol drivers. Only then will the redirector return the result to the caller. Thus, it can be advantageous to reorder bindings so that bindings of high priority are also the most performance efficient or applicable to most of the computers in your network. You can also manually remove bindings with the Advanced Settings dialog box.

FIGURE 12-32 Editing bindings with the Advanced Settings dialog box

The Bind value, in the Linkage subkey of a network component's registry configuration key, stores binding information for that component. For example, if you examine HKLM\SYSTEM\CurrentControlSet\Services\LanmanWorkstation\Linkage\Bind, you'll see the binding information for the Workstation service.

Layered Network Services

Windows includes network services that build on the APIs and components we've presented in this chapter. Describing the capabilities and detailed internal implementation of these services is outside the scope of this book, but this section provides a brief overview of remote access, Active Directory, Network Load Balancing, and Distributed File System (DFS), including DFS Replication (DFSR).

Remote Access

Remote access, which is available with Windows Server with the Routing and Remote Access service, allows remote access clients to connect to remote access servers and access network resources such as files, printers, and network services as if the client were physically connected to the remote access server's network. Windows provides two types of remote access:

- Dial-up remote access is used by clients that connect to a remote access server via a telephone or other telecommunications infrastructure. The telecommunications medium is used to create a temporary physical or virtual connection between the client and the server.

- Virtual private network (VPN) remote access lets a VPN client establish a virtual point-to-point connection to the server over an IP network such as the Internet. Windows also supports the Secure Socket Transmission Protocol (SSTP), which is a newer tunneling protocol for VPN connections that has the ability to pass through most firewalls and routers that block PPTP or L2TP/IPSec traffic. It does so by packaging PPP data over the SSL channel of the HTTPS protocol. Because the latter operates on port 443 and is usually part of typical Web browsing behavior, it is much more likely to be available than traditional VPN tunneling protocols.

Remote access differs from remote control solutions because remote access acts as a proxy connection to a Windows network, whereas remote control software executes applications on a server, presenting a user interface to the client.

Active Directory

Active Directory is the Windows implementation of Lightweight Directory Access Protocol (LDAP) directory services. Active Directory is based on a database that stores objects representing resources defined by applications in a Windows network. For example, the structure and membership of a Windows domain, including the user account and password information, are stored in Active Directory.

Object classes and the attributes that define properties of objects are specified by a *schema*. The objects in the Active Directory are hierarchically arranged, much like the registry's logical organization, where container objects can store other objects, including other container objects. (See Chapter 6 for more information on container objects.)

Active Directory supports a number of APIs that clients can use to access objects within an Active Directory database:

- The LDAP C API is a C language API that uses the LDAP networking protocol. Applications written in C or C++ can use this API directly, and applications written in other languages can access the APIs through translation layers.

- Active Directory Service Interfaces (ADSI) is a COM interface to Active Directory implemented on top of LDAP that abstracts the details of LDAP programming. ADSI supports multiple languages, including Microsoft Visual Basic, C, and Microsoft Visual C++. ADSI can also be used by Microsoft Windows Script Host (WSH) applications.

- Messaging API (MAPI) is supported for compatibility with Microsoft Exchange client and Outlook Address Book client applications.

- Security Account Manager (SAM) APIs are built on top of Active Directory to provide an interface to logon authentication packages such as MSV1_0 (\%SystemRoot%\ System32\Msv1_0.dll, which is used for legacy NT LAN Manager authentication) and Kerberos (\%SystemRoot%\System32\Kdcsvc.dll).

- Windows NT 4 networking APIs (Net APIs) are used by Windows NT 4 clients to gain access to Active Directory through SAM.

- NTDS API is used to look up SIDs and GUIDs in an Active Directory implementation (via *DsCrackNames* mostly) as well as for its main purposes, Active Directory management and replication. Several third parties have written applications that monitor Active Directory from these APIs.

Active Directory is implemented as a database file that by default is named \%SystemRoot%\ Ntds\Ntds.dit, and that is replicated across the domain controllers in a domain. The Active Directory directory service, which is a Windows service that executes in the Local Security Authority Subsystem (Lsass) process, manages the database, using DLLs that implement the on-disk structure of the database as well as provide transaction-based updates to protect the integrity of the database. The Active Directory database store is based on a version of the Extensible Storage Engine (ESE), also known as JET Blue, database used by Microsoft Exchange Server 2007, Desktop Search, and Windows Mail. The ESE library (%SystemRoot%\ System32\Esent.dll) provides routines for accessing the database, which are open for other applications to use as well. Figure 12-33 shows the Active Directory architecture.

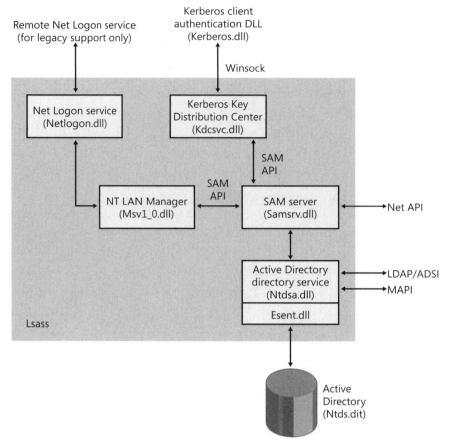

Remote Net Logon service
(for legacy support only)

Kerberos client
authentication DLL
(Kerberos.dll)

Winsock

Net Logon service
(Netlogon.dll)

Kerberos Key
Distribution Center
(Kdcsvc.dll)

SAM
API

SAM
API

NT LAN Manager
(Msv1_0.dll)

SAM server
(Samsrv.dll)

Net API

Active Directory
directory service
(Ntdsa.dll)

LDAP/ADSI

MAPI

Esent.dll

Lsass

Active
Directory
(Ntds.dit)

FIGURE 12-33 Active Directory architecture

Network Load Balancing

As we stated earlier in the chapter, Network Load Balancing, which is included with Windows Server 2008, is based on NDIS lightweight filter technology. Network Load Balancing allows for the creation of a cluster containing up to 32 computers, which are called *cluster hosts* in Network Load Balancing. The cluster can maintain multiple dedicated IP addresses and a single virtual IP address that is published for access by clients. Client requests go to all the computers in the cluster, but only one cluster host responds to the request. The Network Load Balancing NDIS drivers effectively partition the client space among available cluster hosts in a distributed manner. This way, each host handles its portion of incoming client requests and every client request always gets handled by one and only one host. The cluster host that determines it should handle a client request allows the request to propagate up to the TCP/IP protocol driver and eventually a server application; the other cluster hosts don't. If a cluster host fails, the rest of the cluster realizes that the cluster host is no longer a candidate for processing requests and redistributes the incoming client requests to the remaining

cluster hosts. No new client requests are sent to the downed cluster host. Another cluster host can be added to the cluster as a replacement, and it will then seamlessly start handling client requests.

Network Load Balancing isn't a general-purpose clustering solution because the server application that clients communicate with must have certain characteristics: the first is that it must be based on protocols supported by the Windows TCP/IP stack, and the second is that it must be able to handle client requests on any system in a Network Load Balancing cluster. This second requirement typically means that an application that must have access to shared state in order to service client requests must manage the shared state itself—Network Load Balancing doesn't include services for automatically distributing shared state across cluster hosts. Applications that are ideally suited for Network Load Balancing include a Web server that serves static content, Windows Media Server, and Terminal Services. Figure 12-34 shows an example of a Network Load Balancing operation.

FIGURE 12-34 Network Load Balancing operation

Distributed File System and DFS Replication

Distributed File System (DFS) is a service that layers on top of the Workstation service to connect together file shares into a single namespace. The file shares can reside on the same computer or on different computers, and DFS provides client access to the resources in a location-transparent manner. The root of a DFS namespace must be a file share defined on a Windows server.

In addition to delivering a unified network-resource namespace, DFS provides other benefits through DFS replica sets. An administrator can create a DFS replica set from two or more shares and use a replication mechanism such as File Replication Service (FRS) to copy data between the shares of a replica set to keep their contents synchronized. DFS provides several forms of load balancing by ordering and/or selecting members of a replica set to fulfill a client request for data on the replica set. In addition, DFS achieves high availability by routing requests to the working member or members of a replica set when a member becomes unavailable.

The components that make up the DFS architecture are shown in Figure 12-35. The server-side implementation of DFS consists of a Windows service (\%SystemRoot%\System32\ Dfssvc.exe) and a device driver (\%SystemRoot%\System32\Drivers\Dfs.sys). The DFS service is responsible for exporting DFS topology-management interfaces and maintaining the DFS topology in either the registry (on non–Active Directory systems) or Active Directory. The DFS driver performs topology lookups when it receives a client request so that it can direct the client to the system where the file it is requesting resides.

FIGURE 12-35 DFS components

On the client side, DFS support is implemented in another device driver (%SystemRoot%\ System32\Drivers\Dfsc.sys) and uses the SMB redirector for its internal communication with DFS servers. The DFS client provider is implemented in \%SystemRoot%\System32\ Ntlanman.dll. When a client issues a file I/O request that specifies a file in the DFS namespace, the DFS client driver communicates with the target file server by using the appropriate redirector.

DFS also includes DFS Replication (DFSR). Its primary purpose is to replicate the contents of any DFS share, as well as the domain controller's \SYSVOL directory, which is where Windows domain controllers store logon scripts and Group Policy files. (Group Policy permits

administrators to define usage and security policies for the computers that belong to a domain.) DFSR allows for distributed multimaster replication, which enables any server to perform replication activity. When a replicated directory or file is changed, the changes are propagated to the other domain controllers.

The fundamental concept in DFSR is a *replica set*, which consists of two or more systems that replicate between themselves the contents of a directory tree according to an administratively defined schedule and *replication topology,* which is the set of connections that defines the relationship between domain controllers in a forest and the directory partition replicas they share. Only directories on NTFS volumes can be replicated because DFSR relies on the NTFS change journal to detect changes to files in directories in a replica set. Because DFSR is based on multimaster replication, it can theoretically support hundreds or even thousands of systems as part of a replica set, and the computers of a replica set (called a *replica group*) can be connected with arbitrary network topologies (such as ring, star, or mesh). Computers can also be members of multiple replica sets. DFSR uses Remote Differential Compression (RDC) to compress replica sets, which means that only differences between two servers are replicated, reducing bandwidth. DFSR is implemented as a Windows service (\%SystemRoot%\ System32\Dfsr.exe) that uses authenticated RPC with encryption to communicate between instances of itself running on different computers. In addition, because Active Directory contains its own replication capabilities, DFSR uses Active Directory APIs to retrieve FRS configuration information from a domain's Active Directory. DFSR also exposes a WMI interface for tracing, configuration, and management of the service.

Conclusion

The Windows network architecture provides a flexible infrastructure for networking APIs, network protocol drivers, and network adapter drivers. The Windows networking architecture takes advantage of I/O layering to give networking support the extensibility to evolve as computer networking evolves. When new protocols appear, developers can write a TDI transport to implement the protocol on Windows. Similarly, new APIs can interface to existing Windows protocol drivers. Finally, the range of networking APIs implemented on Windows affords network application developers a range of possible implementations, each with different programming models and protocol support.

Chapter 13
Startup and Shutdown

In this chapter, we'll describe the steps required to boot Windows and the options that can affect system startup. Understanding the details of the boot process will help you diagnose problems that can arise during a boot. Then we'll explain the kinds of things that can go wrong during the boot process and how to resolve them. Finally, we'll explain what occurs on an orderly system shutdown.

Boot Process

In describing the Windows boot process, we'll start with the installation of Windows and proceed through the execution of boot support files. Device drivers are a crucial part of the boot process, so we'll explain the way that they control the point in the boot process at which they load and initialize. Then we'll describe how the executive subsystems initialize and how the kernel launches the user-mode portion of Windows by starting the Session Manager process (Smss.exe), which starts the initial two sessions (session 0 and session 1). Along the way, we'll highlight the points at which various text appears on the screen to help you correlate the internal process with what you see when you watch Windows boot.

The early phases of the boot process differ significantly on x86 and x64 systems with a BIOS (basic input output system) versus systems with an EFI (Extensible Firmware Interface). EFI is a newer standard that does away with much of the legacy 16-bit code that BIOS systems use and allows the loading of preboot programs and drivers to support the operating system loading phase. The next sections describe the portions of the boot process specific to BIOS-based systems and are followed with a section describing the EFI-specific portions of the boot process.

To support these different firmware implementations (as well as EFI 2.0, also called Unified EFI, or UEFI), Windows provides a boot architecture that abstracts many of the differences away from users and developers in order to provide a consistent environment and experience regardless of the type of firmware used on the installed system.

BIOS Preboot

The Windows boot process doesn't begin when you power on your computer or press the reset button. It begins when you install Windows on your computer. At some point during the execution of the Windows Setup program, the system's primary hard disk is prepared with code that takes part in the boot process. Before we get into what this code does, let's

look at how and where Windows places the code on a disk. Since the early days of MS-DOS, a standard has existed on x86 systems for the way physical hard disks are divided into volumes.

Microsoft operating systems split hard disks into discrete areas known as *partitions* and use file systems (such as FAT and NTFS) to format each partition into a volume. A hard disk can contain up to four primary partitions. Because this apportioning scheme would limit a disk to four volumes, a special partition type, called an *extended partition*, further allocates up to four additional partitions within each extended partition. Extended partitions can contain extended partitions, which can contain extended partitions, and so on, making the number of volumes an operating system can place on a disk effectively infinite. Figure 13-1 shows an example of a hard disk layout, and Table 13-1 summarizes the files involved in the BIOS boot process. (You can learn more about Windows partitioning in Chapter 8, which covers storage management.)

TABLE 13-1 BIOS Boot Process Components

Component	Processor Execution	Responsibilities	Location
Master Boot Record (MBR)	16-bit real mode	Reads and loads partition boot sectors	Per storage device
Boot sector	16-bit real mode	Reads the root directory to load Bootmgr.	Per partition
Bootmgr	16-bit real mode and 32-bit without paging	Reads the Boot Configuration Database (BCD), presents boot menu, and allows execution of preboot programs such as the Memory Test application (Memtest.exe). If a 64-bit installation is booted, switches to 64-bit long mode before loading Winload.	Per system
Winload.exe	32-bit protected mode with paging, 64-bit protected mode if booting a Win64 installation	Loads Ntoskrnl.exe and its dependencies (Bootvid.dll on 32-bit systems, Hal.dll, Kdcom.dll, Ci.dll, Clfs.sys, Pshed.dll) and boot-start device drivers.	Per Windows installation
Winresume.exe	32-bit protected mode, 64-bit protected mode if resuming a Win64 installation	If resuming after a hibernation state, resumes from the hibernation file (Hiberfil.sys) instead of typical Windows loading.	Per Windows installation

Component	Processor Execution	Responsibilities	Location
Memtest.exe	32-bit protected mode	If selected from the Boot Manager, starts up and provides a graphical interface for scanning memory and detecting damaged RAM.	Per system
Ntoskrnl.exe	Protected mode with paging	Initializes executive subsystems and boot and system-start device drivers, prepares the system for running native applications, and runs Smss.exe.	Per Windows installation
Hal.dll	Protected mode with paging	Kernel-mode DLL that interfaces Ntoskrnl and drivers to the hardware.	Per Windows installation
Smss.exe	Native application	Initial instance starts a copy of itself to initialize each session. The session 0 instance loads the Windows subsystem driver (Win32k.sys) and starts the Windows subsystem process (Csrss.exe) and Windows initialization process (Wininit.exe). All other per-session instances start a Csrss and Winlogon process.	Per Windows installation
Wininit.exe	Windows application	Starts the service control manager (SCM), the Local Security Authority process (LSASS), and the local session manager (LSM). Initializes the rest of the registry and performs user-mode initialization tasks.	Per Windows installation
Winlogon.exe	Windows application	Coordinates logon and user security, launches LogonUI.	Per Windows installation
Logonui.exe	Windows application	Presents interactive logon dialog box.	Per Windows installation
Services.exe	Windows application	Loads and initializes auto-start device drivers and Windows services.	Per Windows installation

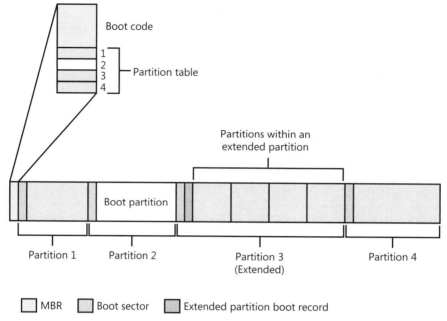

Boot code

1
2 — Partition table
3
4

Partitions within an
extended partition

Boot partition

Partition 1 Partition 2 Partition 3 Partition 4
 (Extended)

☐ MBR ▨ Boot sector ▦ Extended partition boot record

FIGURE 13-1 Sample hard disk layout

Physical disks are addressed in units known as *sectors*. A hard disk sector on a BIOS PC is typically 512 bytes. Utilities that prepare hard disks for the definition of volumes, such as the Windows Setup program, write a sector of data called a Master Boot Record (MBR) to the first sector on a hard disk. (MBR partitioning is described in Chapter 8.) The MBR includes a fixed amount of space that contains executable instructions (called *boot code*) and a table (called a *partition table*) with four entries that define the locations of the primary partitions on the disk. When a BIOS-based computer boots, the first code it executes is called the BIOS, which is encoded into the computer's ROM. The BIOS selects a boot device, reads that device's MBR into memory, and transfers control to the code in the MBR.

The MBRs written by Microsoft partitioning tools, such as the one integrated into Windows Setup and the Disk Management MMC snap-in, go through a similar process of reading and transferring control. First, an MBR's code scans the primary partition table until it locates a partition containing a flag that signals the partition is bootable. When the MBR finds at least one such flag, it reads the first sector from the flagged partition into memory and transfers control to code within the partition. This type of partition is called a *system partition*, and the first sector of such a partition is called a *boot sector*. The volume defined for this partition is called the *system volume*.

Operating systems generally write boot sectors to disk without a user's involvement. For example, when Windows Setup writes the MBR to a hard disk, it also writes the file system boot code (part of the boot sector) to the first bootable partition of the disk.

Before writing to a partition's boot sector, Windows Setup ensures that the boot partition is formatted with NTFS, the only supported file system that Windows can boot from, or formats

the boot partition (and any other partition) with NTFS. Note that the format of the system partition can be any format that Windows supports (such as FAT32). If partitions are already formatted appropriately, you can instruct Setup to skip this step. After Setup formats the system partition, Setup copies the Boot Manager program (Bootmgr) that Windows uses to the system partition (the system volume).

Another of Setup's roles is to prepare the Boot Configuration Database (BCD), which on BIOS systems is stored in the \Boot\BCD file on the root directory of the system volume. This file contains options for starting the version of Windows that Setup installs and any preexisting Windows installations. If the BCD already exists, the Setup program simply adds new entries relevant to the new installation.

The BIOS Boot Sector and Bootmgr

Setup must know the partition format before it writes a boot sector because the contents of the boot sector vary depending on the format. For a partition that is in NTFS format, Windows writes NTFS-capable code. The role of the boot-sector code is to give Windows information about the structure and format of a volume and to read in the Bootmgr file from the root directory of the volume. Thus, the boot-sector code contains just enough read-only file system code to accomplish this task. After the boot-sector code loads Bootmgr into memory, it transfers control to Bootmgr's entry point. If the boot-sector code can't find Bootmgr in the volume's root directory, it displays the error message "BOOTMGR is missing".

Bootmgr begins its existence while a system is executing in an x86 operating mode called *real mode*. In real mode, no virtual-to-physical translation of memory addresses occurs, which means that programs that use the memory addresses interpret them as physical addresses and that only the first 1 MB of the computer's physical memory is accessible. Simple MS-DOS programs execute in a real-mode environment. However, the first action Bootmgr takes is to switch the system to *protected mode*. Still no virtual-to-physical translation occurs at this point in the boot process, but a full 32 bits of memory becomes accessible. After the system is in protected mode, Bootmgr can access all of physical memory. After creating enough page tables to make memory below 16 MB accessible with paging turned on, Bootmgr enables paging. Protected mode with paging enabled is the mode in which Windows executes in normal operation.

After Bootmgr enables protected mode, it is fully operational. However, it still relies on functions supplied by BIOS to access IDE-based system and boot disks as well as the display. Bootmgr's BIOS-interfacing functions briefly switch the processor back to a mode in which services provided by the BIOS can be executed, called *real mode*. Bootmgr next reads the BCD file from the \Boot directory using built-in file system code. Like the boot sector's code, Bootmgr contains read-only NTFS code (Bootmgr also supports other file systems, such as FAT, El Torito CDFS, UDFS, and WIM files); unlike the boot sector's code, however, Bootmgr's file system code can read subdirectories.

> **Note** Bootmgr and other boot applications can still write to preallocated files on NTFS volumes, because only the data needs to be written, instead of performing all the complex allocation work that is typically required on an NTFS volume. This is how these applications can write to bootsect.dat, for example.

Bootmgr next clears the screen. If Windows enabled the BCD setting to inform Bootmgr of a hibernation resume, this shortcuts the boot process by launching Winresume.exe, which will read the contents of the file into memory and transfer control to code in the kernel that resumes a hibernated system. That code is responsible for restarting drivers that were active when the system was shut down. Hiberfil.sys will be valid only if the last time the computer was shut down it was hibernated. (See the section "The Power Manager" in Chapter 7 for information on hibernation.)

If there is more than one boot-selection entry in the BCD, Bootmgr presents the user with the boot-selection menu (if there is only one entry, Bootmgr bypasses the menu and proceeds to launch Winload.exe). Selection entries in the BCD direct Bootmgr to the partition on which the Windows system directory (typically \Windows) of the selected installation resides. This partition might be the same as the system partition, or it might be another primary or extended partition.

Entries in the BCD can include optional arguments that Bootmgr, Winload, and other components involved in the boot process interpret. Table 13-2 contains a list of these options and their effects for Bootmgr, Table 13-3 shows a list of BCD options for boot applications, and Table 13-4 shows BCD options for the Windows boot loader.

The Bcdedit.exe tool provides a convenient interface for setting a number of the switches. Some options that are included in the BCD save to the registry value HKLM\SYSTEM\ CurrentControlSet\Control\SystemStartOptions if they correspond to command-line switches; otherwise, they are kept only in the BCD.

TABLE 13-2 BCD Options for the Windows Boot Manager (Bootmgr)

BCD Element	Values	Meaning
bcdfilepath	Path	Points to the Boot Configuration Database (usually \Boot\BCD) file on the disk.
displaybootmenu	Boolean	Determines whether the Boot Manager shows the boot menu or picks the default entry automatically.
keyringaddress	Physical address	Specifies the physical address where the BitLocker key ring is located.
noerrordisplay	Boolean	Silences the output of errors encountered by the Boot Manager.
resume	Boolean	Whether or not resuming from hibernation should be attempted. This option is automatically set when Windows hibernates.
timeout	Seconds	Number of seconds that the Boot Manager should wait before choosing the default entry.

TABLE 13-3 BCD Options for Boot Applications

BCD Element	Values	Meaning
badmemoryaccess	Boolean	Forces usage of memory pages in the Bad Page List (see Chapter 9 for more information on the page lists).
badmemorylist	Array of page frame numbers (PFNs)	Specifies a list of physical pages on the system that are known to be bad because of faulty RAM.
baudrate	Baud rate in bps	Specifies an override for the default baud rate (19200) at which a remote kernel debugger host will connect through a serial port.
bootdebug	Boolean	Enables remote boot debugging for the boot loader. With this option enabled, you can use Kd.exe or Windbg.exe to connect to the boot loader.
bootems	Boolean	Used to cause Windows to enable Emergency Management Services (EMS) for boot applications, which reports boot information and accepts system management commands through a serial port.
channel	Channel between 0 and 62	Used in conjunction with {debugtype, 1394} to specify the IEEE 1394 channel through which kernel debugging communications will flow.
configaccesspolicy	Default, DisallowMmConfig	Configures whether the system uses memory mapped I/O to access the PCI manufacturer's configuration space or falls back to using the HAL's I/O port access routines. Can sometimes be helpful in solving platform device problems.
debugaddress	Hardware address	Specifies the hardware address of the serial (COM) port used for debugging.
debugport	COM port number	Specifies an override for the default serial port (usually COM2 on systems with at least two serial ports) to which a remote kernel debugger host is connected.
debugstart	Active, AutoEnable, Disable	Specifies settings for the debugger when kernel debugging is enabled. AutoEnable enables the debugger when a breakpoint or kernel exception, including kernel crashes, occurs.
debugtype	Serial, 1394, USB	Specifies whether kernel debugging will be communicated through a serial, FireWire (IEEE 1394), or USB 2.0 port. (The default is serial.)
emsbaudrate	Baud rate in bps	Specifies the baud rate to use for EMS.
emsport	COM port number	Specifies the serial (COM) port to use for EMS.
extendedinput	Boolean	Enables boot applications to leverage BIOS support for extended console input.
firstmegabytepolicy	UseNone, UseAll, UsePrivate	Specifies how the low 1 MB of physical memory is consumed by the HAL to mitigate corruptions by the BIOS during power transitions.

BCD Element	Values	Meaning
graphicsmodedisabled	Boolean	Disables graphics mode for boot applications.
graphicsresolution	Resolution	Sets the graphics resolution for boot applications.
initialconsoleinput	Boolean	Specifies an initial character that the system inserts into the PC/AT keyboard input buffer.
locale	Localization string	Sets the locale for the boot application (such as EN-US).
noumex	Boolean	Disables user-mode exceptions when kernel debugging is enabled. If you experience system hangs (freezes) when booting in debugging mode, try enabling this option.
novesa	Boolean	Disables the usage of VESA display modes.
relocatephysical	Physical address	Relocates an automatically selected NUMA node's physical memory to the specified physical address.
testsigning	Boolean	Enables test-signing mode, which allows driver developers to load locally signed 64-bit drivers. This option results in a watermarked desktop.
truncatememory	Address in bytes	Disregards physical memory above the specified physical address.

TABLE 13-4 BCD Options for the Windows Boot Loader (Winload)

BCD Element	Values	Meaning
advancedoptions	Boolean	If false, executes the default behavior of launching the auto-recovery command boot entry when the boot fails; otherwise, displays the boot error and offers the user the advanced boot option menu associated with the boot entry. This is equivalent to pressing F8.
bootlog	Boolean	Causes Windows to write a log of the boot to the file %SystemRoot%\Ntbtlog.txt.
bootstatuspolicy	DisplayAllFailures, IgnoreAllFailures, IgnoreShutdown-Failures, IgnoreBoot-Failures	Overrides the system's default behavior of offering the user a troubleshooting boot menu if the system did not complete the previous boot or shutdown.
clustermodeaddressing	Number of processors	Defines the maximum number of processors to include in a single Advanced Programmable Interrupt Controller (APIC) cluster.
configflags	Flags	Specifies processor-specific configuration flags.
dbgtransport	Transport image name	Overrides using one of the default kernel debugging transports (Kdcom.dll, Kd1394, Kdusb.dll) and instead uses the given file, permitting specialized debugging transports to be used that are not typically supported by Windows.

BCD Element	Values	Meaning
debug	Boolean	Enables kernel-mode debugging.
detecthal	Boolean	Enables the dynamic detection of the HAL.
driverloadfailurepolicy	Fatal, UseErrorControl	Describes the loader behavior to use when a boot driver has failed to load. Fatal will prevent booting, while UseErrorControl causes the system to honor a driver's default error behavior, specified in its service key.
ems	Boolean	Instructs the kernel to use EMS as well. (If only *bootems* is used, only the boot loader will use EMS.)
exportascd	Boolean	If this option is set, the kernel will treat the ramdisk file specified as an ISO image and not a Windows Installation Media (WIM) or System Deployment Image (SDI) file.
hal	HAL image name	Overrides the default file name for the HAL image (hal.dll). This option can be useful when booting a combination of a checked HAL and checked kernel (requires specifying the *kernel* element as well).
halbreakpoint	Boolean	Causes the HAL to stop at a breakpoint early in HAL initialization. The first thing the Windows kernel does when it initializes is to initialize the HAL, so this breakpoint is the earliest one possible (unless boot debugging is used). If the switch is used without the /DEBUG switch, the system will elicit a blue screen with a STOP code of 0x00000078 (PHASE0_EXCEPTION).
hypervisorbaudrate	Baud rate in bps	If using serial hypervisor debugging, specifies the baud rate to use.
hypervisorchannel	Channel number from 0 to 62	If using FireWire (IEEE 1394) hypervisor debugging, specifies the channel number to use.
hypervisordebug	Boolean	Enables debugging the hypervisor.
hypervisordebugport	COM port number	If using serial hypervisor debugging, specifies the COM port to use.
hypervisordebugtype	Serial, 1394	Specifies which hardware port to use for hypervisor debugging.
hypervisorlaunchtype	Off, Auto	Enables loading of the hypervisor on a Hyper-V system, or forces it to be disabled.
hypervisorpath	Hypervisor binary image name	Specifies the path of the hypervisor binary.
increaseuserva	Size in MB	Increases the size of the user process address space from 2 GB to the specified size, up to 3 GB (and therefore reduces the size of system space). Giving virtual-memory-intensive applications such as database servers a larger address space can improve their performance. (See the section "Address Space Layout" in Chapter 9 for more information.)

BCD Element	Values	Meaning
kernel	Kernel image name	Overrides the default file name for the kernel image (ntoskrnl.exe). This option can be useful when booting a combination of a checked HAL and checked kernel (requires specifying the *hal* element to be used as well).
lastknowngood	Boolean	Boots the last known good configuration, instead of the current control set.
loadoptions	Extra command-line parameters	This option is used to add other command-line parameters that are not defined by BCD elements. These parameters could be used to configure or define the operation of other components on the system that might not be able to use the BCD (such as legacy components).
maxproc	Boolean	Forces the maximum number of supported processors that Windows will report to drivers and applications to accommodate the arrival of additional CPUs via dynamic processor support.
msi	Default, ForceDisable	Allows disabling support for message signaled interrupts.
nocrashautoreboot	Boolean	Disables the automatic reboot after a system crash (blue screen).
nointegritychecks	Boolean	Disables integrity checks performed by Windows when loading drivers. Automatically removed at the next reboot.
nolowmem	Boolean	Requires that PAE be enabled and that the system have more than 4 GB of physical memory. If these conditions are met, the PAE-enabled version of the Windows kernel, Ntkrnlpa.exe, won't use the first 4 GB of physical memory. Instead, it will load all applications and device drivers and allocate all memory pools from above that boundary. This switch is useful only to test device-driver compatibility with large memory systems.
numproc	Number of processors	Specifies the number of CPUs that can be used on a multiprocessor system. Example: /NUMPROC=2 on a four-way system will prevent Windows from using two of the four processors
nx	OptIn, OptOut, AlwaysOff, AlwaysOn	This option is available only on 32-bit versions of Windows when running on processors that support no-execute memory and only when PAE (explained further in the *pae* entry) is also enabled. It enables no-execute protection. No-execute protection is always enabled on 64-bit versions of Windows on x64 processors. See Chapter 9 for a description of this behavior.

BCD Element	Values	Meaning
onecpu	Boolean	Causes Windows to use only one CPU on a multiprocessor system.
optionsedit	Boolean	Enables the options editor in the Boot Manager. With this option, Boot Manager allows the user to interactively set on-demand command-line options and switches for the current boot. This is equivalent to pressing F10.
pae	Default, ForceEnable, ForceDisable	Default allows the boot loader to determine whether the system supports PAE and loads the PAE kernel. ForceEnable forces this behavior, while ForceDisable forces the loader to load the non–PAE version of the Windows kernel, even if the system is detected as supporting x86 PAEs and has more than 4 GB of physical memory.
pciexpress	Default, ForceDisable	Can be used to disable support for PCI Express buses and devices.
perfmem	Size in MB	Size of the buffer to allocate for performance data logging. This option acts similarly to the *removememory* element, since it prevents Windows from seeing the size specified as available memory.
quietboot	Boolean	Instructs Windows not to initialize the VGA video driver responsible for presenting bitmapped graphics during the boot process. The driver is used to display boot progress information, so disabling it will disable the ability of Windows to show this information.
ramdiskimagelength	Length in bytes	Size of the ramdisk specified.
ramdiskimageoffset	Offset in bytes	If the ramdisk contains other data (such as a header) before the virtual file system, instructs the boot loader where to start reading the ramdisk file from.
ramdisksdipath	Image file name	Specifies the name of the SDI ramdisk to load.
ramdisktftpblocksize	Block size	If loading a WIM ramdisk from a network Trivial FTP (TFTP) server, specifies the block size to use.
ramdisktftpclientport	Port number	If loading a WIM ramdisk from a network TFTP server, specifies the port.
ramdisktftpwindowsize	Window size	If loading a WIM ramdisk from a network TFTP server, specifies the window size to use.
removememory	Amount in bytes	Specifies an amount of memory Windows won't use.
restrictapiccluster	Cluster number	Defines the largest APIC cluster number to be used by the system.
resumeobject	Object GUID	Describes which application to use for resuming from hibernation, typically Winresume.exe.

BCD Element	Values	Meaning
safeboot	Minimal, Network, DsRepair	Specifies options for a safe-mode boot. Minimal corresponds to safe mode without networking, Network to safe mode with networking, and DsRepair to safe mode with Directory Services Restore mode. (Safe mode is described later in this chapter.)
safebootalternateshell	Boolean	Tells Windows to use the program specified by the HKLM\SYSTEM\CurrentControlSet\Control\SafeBoot\AlternateShell value as the graphical shell rather than the default, which is Windows Explorer. This option is referred to as Safe Mode With Command Prompt in the alternate boot menu.
sos	Boolean	Causes Windows to list the device drivers marked to load at boot time and then to display the system version number (including the build number), amount of physical memory, and number of processors.
stampdisks	Boolean	Specifies that Winload will write an MBR disk signature to a RAW disk when booting Windows PE (Preinstallation Environment). This can be required in deployment environments in order to create a mapping from operating system–enumerated hard disks to BIOS-enumerated hard disks to know which disk should be the system disk.
targetname	Name	For USB 2.0 debugging, assigns a name to the machine that is being debugged.
usefirmwarepcisettings	Boolean	Stops Windows from dynamically assigning IO/IRQ resources to PCI devices and leaves the devices configured by the BIOS. See Microsoft Knowledge Base article Q148501 for more information.
usephysicaldestination	Boolean	Forces the use of the APIC in physical destination mode.
vga	Boolean	Forces Windows to use of the VGA display driver instead of the third-party high-performance driver.
winpe	Boolean	Used by Windows PE, this option causes the configuration manager to load the registry SYSTEM hive as a volatile hive such that changes made to it in memory are not saved back to the hive image.

If the user doesn't select an entry from the selection menu within the timeout period the BCD specifies, Bootmgr chooses the default selection specified in the BCD (if there is only one entry, it chooses this one). Once the boot selection has been made, Bootmgr loads the boot loader associated with that entry, which will be Winload.exe for Windows installations.

Winload.exe also contains code that queries the system's ACPI BIOS to retrieve basic device and configuration information. This information includes the following:

- The time and date information stored in the system's CMOS (nonvolatile memory)

- The number, size, and type of disk drives on the system

- Legacy device information, such as buses (for example, ISA, PCI, EISA, Micro Channel Architecture [MCA]), mice, parallel ports, and video adapters are not queried and instead faked out

This information is gathered into internal data structures that will be stored under the HKLM\ HARDWARE\DESCRIPTION registry key later in the boot.

Next, Winload begins loading the files from the *boot volume* needed to start the kernel initialization. The boot volume is the volume that corresponds to the partition on which the system directory (usually \Windows) of the installation being booted is located. The steps Winload follows here include:

1. Loads the appropriate kernel and HAL images (Ntoskrnl.exe and Hal.dll by default) as well as any of their dependencies. If Winload fails to load either of these files, it prints the message "Windows could not start because the following file was missing or corrupt", followed by the name of the file.

2. Reads in the VGA font file (by default, vgaoem.fon). If this file fails, the same error message as described in step 1 will be shown.

3. Reads in the NLS (National Language System) files used for internationalization. By default, these are l_intl.nls, c_1252.nls, and c_437.nls.

4. Reads in the SYSTEM registry hive, \Windows\System32\Config\System, so that it can determine which device drivers need to be loaded to accomplish the boot. (A hive is a file that contains a registry subtree. You'll find more details about the registry in Chapter 4.)

5. Scans the in-memory SYSTEM registry hive and locates all the *boot device drivers*. Boot device drivers are drivers necessary to boot the system. These drivers are indicated in the registry by a start value of SERVICE_BOOT_START (0). Every device driver has a registry subkey under HKLM\SYSTEM\CurrentControlSet\Services. For example, Services has a subkey named fvevol for the BitLocker driver, which you can see in Figure 13-2. (For a detailed description of the Services registry entries, see the section "Services" in Chapter 4.)

FIGURE 13-2 BitLocker driver service settings

6. Adds the file system driver that's responsible for implementing the code for the type of partition (NTFS) on which the installation directory resides to the list of boot drivers to load. Winload must load this driver at this time; if it didn't, the kernel would require the drivers to load themselves, a requirement that would introduce a circular dependency.

7. Loads the boot drivers, which should only be drivers that, like the file system driver for the boot volume, would introduce a circular dependency if the kernel was required to load them. To indicate the progress of the loading, Winload updates a progress bar displayed below the text "Starting Windows". If the *sos* option is specified in the BCD, Winload doesn't display the progress bar but instead displays the file names of each boot driver. Keep in mind that the drivers are loaded but not initialized at this time—they initialize later in the boot sequence.

8. Prepares CPU registers for the execution of Ntoskrnl.exe.

This action is the end of Winload's role in the boot process. At this point, Winload calls the main function in Ntoskrnl.exe (*KiSystemStartup*) to perform the rest of the system initialization.

The EFI Boot Process

An EFI-compliant system has firmware that runs boot loader code that's been programmed into the system's nonvolatile RAM (NVRAM) by Windows Setup. The boot code reads the BCD's contents, which are also stored in NVRAM. The Bcdedit.exe tool mentioned earlier also has the ability to abstract the firmware's NVRAM variables in the BCD, allowing for full transparency of this mechanism.

The EFI standard defines the ability to prompt the user with an EFI Boot Manager that can be used to select an operating system or additional applications to load. However, to provide a consistent user interface between BIOS systems and EFI systems, Windows sets a 2-second timeout for selecting the EFI Boot Manager, after which the EFI-version of Bootmgr (Bootmgfw.efi) loads instead.

Hardware detection occurs next, where the boot loader uses EFI interfaces to determine the number and type of the following devices:

- Network adapters
- Video adapters
- Keyboards
- Disk controllers
- Storage devices

On EFI systems, all operations and programs execute in the native CPU mode with paging enabled and no part of the Windows boot process executes in 16-bit mode. Note that although EFI is supported on both 32-bit and 64-bit systems, Windows provides support for EFI only on 64-bit platforms.

Just as Bootmgr does on x86 and x64 systems, the EFI Boot Manager presents a menu of boot selections with an optional timeout. Once a boot selection is made, the loader navigates to the subdirectory on the EFI System partition corresponding to the selection and loads the EFI version of the Windows boot loader (Winload.efi).

The EFI specification requires that the system have a partition designated as the EFI System partition that is formatted with the FAT file system and is between 100 MB and 1 GB in size or up to one percent of the size of the disk, and each Windows installation has a subdirectory on the EFI System partition under EFI\Microsoft.

Note that through the unified boot process and model in Windows Vista, the components in Table 13-1 apply almost identically to EFI systems, except that those ending in *.exe* end in *.efi*, and they use EFI APIs and services instead of BIOS interrupts. Another difference is that to avoid limitations of the MBR partition format (including a maximum of four partitions per disk), EFI systems use the GPT (GUID Partition Table) format, which uses GUIDs to identify different partitions and their roles on the system.

Note Although the EFI standard has been available since early 2001, very few computer manufacturers have started using this technology because of backward compatibility concerns and the difficulty of moving from an entrenched 20-year-old technology to a new one. Two notable exceptions are Itanium machines and Apple's Intel Macintosh computers. The latter, however, require a specialized BIOS emulation module to load Windows, because of implementation incompatibilities.

Initializing the Kernel and Executive Subsystems

When Winload calls Ntoskrnl, it passes a data structure called the loader parameter block that contains the system and boot partition paths, a pointer to the memory tables Winload generated to describe the physical memory on the system, a pointer to the in-memory copy of the HARDWARE and SYSTEM registry hives, a pointer to the list of boot drivers Winload loaded, as well as various other information related to the boot processing performed until this point.

Ntoskrnl then begins the first of its two-phase initialization process, called *phase 0* and *phase 1*. Most executive subsystems have an initialization function that takes a parameter that identifies which phase is executing.

During phase 0, interrupts are disabled. The purpose of this phase is to build the rudimentary structures required to allow the services needed in phase 1 to be invoked. Ntoskrnl's main function calls *KiSystemStartup*, which in turn calls *HalInitializeProcessor* and *KiInitializeKernel* for each CPU. *KiInitializeKernel*, if running on the boot CPU, performs systemwide kernel initialization, such as initializing internal lists and other data structures that all CPUs share. It also checks whether virtualization was specified as a BCD option (*hypervisor-launchtype*), and whether the CPU supports hardware virtualization technology. The first instance of *KiInitializeKernel* then calls the function responsible for orchestrating phase 0, *InitBootProcessor*, while subsequent processors only call *HalInitSystem*.

InitBootProcessor starts by initializing the pool look-aside pointers for the initial CPU and by checking for and honoring the BCD *burnmemory* boot option, where it discards the amount of physical memory the value specifies. It then performs enough initialization of the NLS files that were loaded by Winload (described earlier) to allow Unicode to ANSI and OEM translation to work. Next, it continues by calling the HAL function *HalInitSystem*, which gives the HAL a chance to gain system control before Windows performs significant further initialization. One responsibility of *HalInitSystem* is to prepare the system interrupt controller of each CPU for interrupts and to configure the interval clock timer interrupt, which is used for CPU time accounting. (See the section "Quantum Accounting" in Chapter 5 for more on CPU time accounting.)

When *HalInitSystem* returns control, *InitBootProcessor* proceeds by computing the reciprocal for timer expiration. Reciprocals are used for optimizing divisions on most modern processors. They can perform multiplications faster, and because Windows must divide the current 64-bit time value in order to find out which timers need to expire, this static calculation reduces interrupt latency when the clock interval fires. *InitBootProcessor* then continues by setting up the system root path and searching the kernel image for the location of the crash message strings it displays on blue screens, caching their location to avoid looking up the strings during a crash, which could be dangerous and unreliable. Next, *InitBootProcessor* initializes the quota functionality part of the process manager and reads the *control vector*.

This data structure contains more than 150 kernel-tuning options that are part of the HKLM\
SYSTEM\CurrentControlSet\Control registry key, including information such as the licensing
data and version information for the installation.

InitBootProcessor is now ready to call the phase 0 initialization routines for the executive,
Driver Verifier, and memory manager. These components perform the following initialization
steps:

1. The executive initializes various internal locks, resources, lists, and variables and vali-
 dates that the product suite type in the registry is valid, discouraging casual modifica-
 tion of the registry in order to "upgrade" to a SKU of Windows that was not actually
 purchased. This is only one of the many such checks in the kernel.

2. The Driver Verifier, if enabled, initializes various settings and behaviors based on the
 current state of the system (such as whether safe mode is enabled) and verification
 options. It also picks which drivers to target for tests that target randomly chosen
 drivers.

3. The memory manager constructs page tables and internal data structures that are nec-
 essary to provide basic memory services. It also builds and reserves an area for the sys-
 tem file cache and creates memory areas for the paged and nonpaged pools (described
 in Chapter 9). The other executive subsystems, the kernel, and device drivers use these
 two memory pools for allocating their data structures.

Next, *InitBootProcessor* calls *HalInitializeBios* to set up the BIOS emulation code part of the
HAL. This code is used both on real BIOS systems, as well as on EFI systems, to allow access
(or to emulate access) to 16-bit real mode interrupts and memory, which are used mainly
by Bootvid to display the early VGA boot screen and bugcheck screen. After the function
returns, the kernel initializes the Bootvid library and displays early boot status messages by
calling *InbvEnableBootDriver* and *InbvDriverInitailize*.

At this point, *InitBootProcessor* enumerates the boot-start drivers that were loaded by
Winload and calls *DbgLoadImageSymbols* to inform the kernel debugger (if attached) to load
symbols for each of these drivers. If the host debugger has configured the *break on symbol
load* option, this will be the earliest point for a kernel debugger to gain control of the sys-
tem. *InitBootProcessor* now calls *HvlInitSystem,* which attempts to connect to the hypervisor
in case Windows might be running inside a Hyper-V host system's child partition. When the
function returns, it calls *HeadlessInit* to initialize the serial console if the machine was config-
ured for Emergency Management Services (EMS).

Next, *InitBootProcessor* builds the versioning information that will be used later in the boot
process, such as the build number, service pack version, and beta version status. Then it cop-
ies the NLS tables that Winload previously loaded into paged pool, re-initializes them, and
creates the kernel stack trace database if the global flags specify creating one. (For more
information on the global flags, see Chapter 3.)

Finally, *InitBootProcessor* calls the object manager, security reference monitor, process manager, user-mode debugging framework, and the Plug and Play manager. These components perform the following initialization steps:

1. During the object manager initialization, the objects that are necessary to construct the object manager namespace are defined so that other subsystems can insert objects into it. A handle table is created so that resource tracking can begin.

2. The security reference monitor initializes the token type object and then uses the object to create and prepare the first local system account token for assignment to the initial process. (See Chapter 6 for a description of the local system account.)

3. The process manager performs most of its initialization in phase 0, defining the process and thread object types and setting up lists to track active processes and threads. The process manager also creates a process object for the initial process and names it *Idle*. As its last step, the process manager creates the System process and a system thread to execute the routine *Phase1Initialization*. This thread doesn't start running right away because interrupts are still disabled.

4. The user-mode debugging framework creates the definition of the debug object type that is used for attaching a debugger to a process and receiving debugger events. For more information on user-mode debugging, see Chapter 3.

5. The Plug and Play manager's phase 0 initialization then takes place, which involves simply initializing an executive resource used to synchronize bus resources.

When control returns to *KiInitializeKernel*, the last step is to allocate the DPC stack for the current processor and the I/O privilege map save area (on x86 systems only), after which control proceeds to the *Idle* loop, which then causes the system thread created in step 3 of the previous process description to begin executing phase 1. (Secondary processors wait to begin their initialization until step 8 of phase 1, described in the following list.)

Phase 1 consists of the following steps:

1. *Phase1InitializationDiscard*, which, as the name implies, discards the code that is part of the INIT section of the kernel image in order to preserve memory.

2. The initialization thread sets its priority to 31, the highest possible, in order to prevent preemption.

3. *HalInitSystem* prepares the system to accept interrupts from devices and to enable interrupts.

4. The boot video driver is called, which in turn displays the Windows startup screen, which by default consists of a black screen and a progress bar. If the *quietboot* boot option was used, this step will not occur.

5. The kernel builds various strings and version information, which are displayed on the boot screen through Bootvid if the *sos* boot option was enabled. This includes the

full version information, number of processors supported, and amount of memory supported.

6. The power manager's initialization is called.

7. The system time is initialized (by calling *HalQueryRealTimeClock*) and then stored as the time the system booted.

8. On a multiprocessor system, the remaining processors are initialized by *KeStartAllProcessors* and *HalAllProcessorsStarted*. The number of processors that will be initialized and supported depends on a combination of the actual physical count, the licensing information for the installed SKU of Windows, boot options such as *numproc* and *onecpu*, and whether dynamic partitioning is enabled (Windows Server 2008 systems only). After all the available processors have initialized, the affinity of the system process is updated to include all processors.

9. The object manager creates the namespace root directory (\), \ObjectTypes directory, and the DOS device name mapping directory (\Global??). It then creates the \DosDevices symbolic link that points at the Windows subsystem device name mapping directory.

10. The executive is called to create the executive object types, including semaphore, mutex, event, and timer.

11. The I/O manager is called to create the I/O manager object types, including device, driver, controller, adapter, and file objects.

12. The kernel debugger library finalizes initialization of debugging settings and parameters if the debugger has not been triggered prior to this point.

13. The transaction manager also creates its object types, such as the enlistment, resource manager, and transaction manager types.

14. The kernel initializes scheduler (dispatcher) data structures and the system service dispatch table.

15. If the Driver Verifier is enabled and, depending on verification options, pool verification is enabled, object handle tracing is started for the system process.

16. The security reference monitor creates the \Security directory in the object manager namespace and initializes auditing data structures if auditing is enabled.

17. The memory manager is called to create the section object and the memory manager's system worker threads (which are explained in Chapter 9).

18. NLS tables are mapped into system space so that they can be easily mapped by user-mode processes.

19. Ntdll.dll is mapped into the system address space.

20. The cache manager initializes the file system cache data structures and creates its worker threads.

21. The configuration manager creates the \Registry key object in the object manager namespace and copies the initial registry data passed by Winload into the HARDWARE and SYSTEM hives.

22. The errata manager initializes and scans the registry for errata information, as well as the INF (driver installation file, described in Chapter 7) database containing errata for various drivers.

23. SuperFetch and the prefetcher are initialized.

24. The current time zone information is initialized.

25. Global file system driver data structures are initialized.

26. Phase 1 of debugger-transport-specific information is performed by calling the *KdDebuggerInitialize1* routine in the registered transport, such as Kdcom.dll.

27. The Plug and Play manager calls the Plug and Play BIOS.

28. The advanced local procedure call (ALPC) subsystem initializes the ALPC port type and ALPC waitable port type objects. The older LPC objects are set as aliases.

29. If the system was booted with boot logging (with the BCD *bootlog* option), the boot log file is initialized. If the system was booted in safe mode, a string is displayed on the boot screen with the current safe mode boot type.

30. The executive is called to execute its second initialization phase, where it configures part of the Windows licensing functionality in the kernel, such as validating the registry settings that hold license data. Also, if persistent data from boot applications is present (such as memory diagnostic results or resume from hibernation information), the relevant log files and information are written to disk or to the registry.

31. The MiniNT/WinPE registry keys are created if this is such a boot, and the NLS object directory is created in the namespace, which will be used later to host the section objects for the various memory-mapped NLS files.

32. The I/O manager initialization now takes place. This stage is a complex phase of system startup that accounts for most of the boot time.

 The I/O manager first initializes various internal structures and creates the driver and device object types. It then calls the Plug and Play manager, power manager, and HAL to begin the various stages of dynamic device enumeration and initialization. (Because this process is complex and specific to the I/O system, we cover the details in Chapter 7.) Then the Windows Management Instrumentation (WMI) subsystem is initialized, which provides WMI support for device drivers. (See the section "Windows Management Instrumentation" in Chapter 4 for more information.) This also initializes Event Tracing for Windows (ETW). Next, all the boot-start drivers are called to perform their driver-specific initialization, and then the system-start device drivers are loaded and initialized. (Details on the processing of the driver load control information on the

registry are also covered in Chapter 7.) Finally, the Windows subsystem device names are created as symbolic links in the object manager's namespace.

33. The transaction manager sets up the Windows software trace preprocessor (WPP) and ETW and initializes with WMI. (ETW and WMI are described in Chapter 4.)

34. Now that boot-start and system-start drivers are loaded, the errata manager loads the INF database with the driver errata and begins parsing it, which includes applying registry PCI configuration workarounds.

35. If the computer is booting in safe mode, this fact is recorded in the registry.

36. Unless explicitly disabled in the registry, paging of kernel-mode code (in Ntoskrnl and drivers) is enabled.

37. The configuration manager makes sure that all processors on an SMP system are identical in terms of the features that they support; otherwise, it crashes the system.

38. On 32-bit systems, VDM (Virtual Dos Machine) support is initialized, which includes determining whether the processor supports Virtual Machine Extensions (VME).

39. The process manager is called to set up rate limiting for jobs, initialize the static environment for protected processes, and look up the various system-defined entry points in the user-mode system library (Ntdll.dll).

40. The power manager is called to initialize various power management structures.

41. The rest of the licensing information for the system is initialized, including caching the current policy settings stored in the registry.

42. The security reference monitor is called to create the Command Server Thread that communicates with Lsass. (See the section "Security System Components" in Chapter 6 for more on how security is enforced in Windows.)

43. The Session Manager (Smss) process (introduced in Chapter 2) is started. Smss is responsible for creating the user-mode environment that provides the visible interface to Windows—its initialization steps are covered in the next section.

44. All the memory used up by the loader parameter block and all its references is now freed.

As a final step before considering the executive and kernel initialization complete, the phase 1 initialization thread waits for the handle to the Session Manager process with a timeout value of 5 seconds. If the Session Manager process exits before the 5 seconds elapse, the system crashes with a SESSION5_INITIALIZATION_FAILED stop code.

If the 5-second wait times out (that is, if 5 seconds elapse), the Session Manager is assumed to have started successfully, and the phase 1 initialization function calls the memory manager's zero page thread function (explained in Chapter 9). Thus, this system thread becomes the zero page thread for the remainder of the life of the system.

Smss, Csrss, and Wininit

Smss is like any other user-mode process except for two differences: First, Windows considers Smss a trusted part of the operating system. Second, Smss is a *native* application. Because it's a trusted operating system component, Smss can perform actions few other processes can perform, such as creating security tokens. Because it's a native application, Smss doesn't use Windows APIs—it uses only core executive APIs known collectively as the Windows native API. Smss doesn't use the Win32 APIs because the Windows subsystem isn't executing when Smss launches. In fact, one of Smss's first tasks is to start the Windows subsystem.

Smss then calls the configuration manager executive subsystem to finish initializing the registry, fleshing the registry out to include all its keys. The configuration manager is programmed to know where the core registry hives are stored on disk (excluding hives corresponding to user profiles), and it records the paths to the hives it loads in the HKLM\SYSTEM\CurrentControlSet\Control\hivelist key.

The main thread of Smss performs the following initialization steps:

1. Marks itself as a critical process and its main thread as a critical thread. As discussed earlier, this will cause the kernel to crash the system if Smss quits unexpectedly. Smss also enables the automatic affinity update mode to support dynamic processor addition (see Chapter 5 for more information).

2. Creates *protected prefixes* for the mailslot and named pipe file system drivers, creating privileged paths for administrators and service accounts to communicate through those paths.

3. Calls *SmpInit,* which tunes the maximum concurrency level for Smss, meaning the maximum number of parallel sessions that will be created by spawning copies of Smss into other sessions. This is at minimum four and at most the number of active CPUs.

4. *SmpInit* then creates an ALPC port object (*SmApiPort*) to receive client requests (such as to load a new subsystem or create a session).

5. *SmpInit* calls *SmpLoadDataFromRegistry,* which starts by setting up the default environment variables for the system, and sets the SAFEBOOT variable if the system was booted in safe mode.

6. *SmpLoadDataFromRegistry* calls *SmpInitializeDosDevices* to define the symbolic links for MS-DOS device names (such as COM1 and LPT1).

7. *SmpLoadDataFromRegistry* creates the \Sessions directory in the object manager's namespace (for multiple sessions).

8. *SmpLoadDataFromRegistry* runs any programs defined in HKLM\SYSTEM\CurrentControlSet\Control\Session Manager\BootExecute with *SmpExecuteCommand.* Typically, this value contains one command to run Autochk (the boot-time version of Chkdsk).

9. *SmpLoadDataFromRegistry* calls *SmpProcessFileRenames* to perform delayed file rename and delete operations as directed by HKLM\SYSTEM\CurrentControlSet\

Control\Session Manager\PendingFileRenameOperations and HKLM\SYSTEM\ CurrentControlSet\Control\Session Manager\PendingFileRenameOperations2.

10. *SmpLoadDataFromRegistry* calls *SmpCreatePagingFiles* to create additional paging files. Paging file configuration is stored under HKLM\SYSTEM\CurrentControlSet\Control\ Session Manager\Memory Management\PagingFiles.

11. *SmpLoadDataFromRegistry* initializes the registry by calling the native function *NtInitializeRegistry*. The configuration manager builds the rest of the registry by load- ing the registry hives for the HKLM\SAM, HKLM\SECURITY, and HKLM\SOFTWARE keys. Although HKLM\SYSTEM\CurrentControlSet\Control\hivelist locates the hive files on disk, the configuration manager is coded to look for them in \Windows\System32\ Config.

12. *SmpLoadDataFromRegistry* calls *SmpCreateDynamicEnvironmentVariables* to add system environment variables that are defined in HKLM\SYSTEM\CurrentControlSet\ Session Manager\Environment, as well as processor-specific environment variables such as NUMBER_PROCESSORS, PROCESSOR_ARCHITECTURE, and PROCESSOR_LEVEL.

13. *SmpLoadDataFromRegistry* runs any programs defined in HKLM\SYSTEM\Current- ControlSet\Control\Session Manager\SetupExecute with *SmpExecuteCommand*. Typically, this value is set only if Windows is being booted as part of the second stage of installation and Setupcl.exe is the default value.

14. *SmpLoadDataFromRegistry* calls *SmpConfigureSharedSessionData* to initialize the list of subsystems that will be started in each session (both immediately and deferred) as well as the Session 0 initialization command (which, by default, is to launch the Wininit.exe process). The initialization command can be overridden by creating a string value called S0InitialCommand in HKLM\SYSTEM\CurrentControlSet\Control\Session Manager and setting it as the path to another program.

15. *SmpLoadDataFromRegistry* calls *SmpInitializeKnownDlls* to open known DLLs, and creates section objects for them in the \Knowndlls directory of the object man- ager namespace. The list of DLLs considered known is located in HKLM\SYSTEM\ CurrentControlSet\Control\Session Manager\KnownDLLs, and the path to the directory in which the DLLs are located is stored in the Dlldirectory value of the key.

16. Finally, *SmpLoadDataFromRegistry* calls *SmpTranslateSystemPartitionInformation* to convert the SystemPartition key stored in HKLM\SYSTEM\Setup, which is stored in native NT object manager path format, to a volume drive letter stored in the BootDir value. Among other components, Windows Update uses this registry key to figure out what the system volume is.

17. At this point, *SmpLoadDataFromRegistry* returns to *SmpInit*, which returns to the main thread entry point. Smss then creates the number of initial sessions that were defined (typically, only one, session 0, but you can change this number through the NumberOfInitialSessions registry value in the Smss registry key mentioned earlier) by

calling *SmpCreateInitialSession,* which creates an Smss process for each user session. This function's main job is to call *SmpStartCsr* to start Csrss in each session.

18. As part of Csrss's initialization, it loads the kernel-mode part of the Windows subsystem (Win32k.sys). The initialization code in Win32k.sys uses the video driver to switch the screen to the resolution defined by the default profile, so this is the point at which the screen changes from the VGA mode the boot video driver uses to the default resolution chosen for the system.

19. Meanwhile, each spawned Smss in a different user session starts the other subsystem processes, such as Psxss if the Subsystem for Unix-based Applications feature was installed. (See Chapter 3 for more information on subsystem processes.)

20. The first Smss from session 0 executes the Session 0 initialization command (described in step 14), by default launching the Windows initialization process (Wininit). Other Smss instances start the interactive logon manager process (Winlogon), which, unlike Wininit, is hardcoded. The startup steps of Wininit and Winlogon are described shortly.

Pending File Rename Operations

The fact that executable images and DLLs are memory-mapped when they are used makes it impossible to update core system files after Windows has finished booting (unless hotpatching technology is used, which is only for Microsoft patches to the operating system). The *MoveFileEx* Windows API has an option to specify that a file move be delayed until the next boot. Service packs and hotfixes that must update in-use memory-mapped files install replacement files onto a system in temporary locations and use the *MoveFileEx* API to have them replace otherwise in-use files. When used with that option, *MoveFileEx* simply records commands in the PendingFileRenameOperations and PendingFileRenameOperations2 values under HKLM\SYSTEM\CurrentControlSet\Control\Session Manager. These registry values are of type MULTI_SZ, where each operation is specified in pairs of file names: the first file name is the source location, and the second is the target location. Delete operations use an empty string as their target path. You can use the Pendmoves utility from Windows Sysinternals (*www.microsoft.com/technet/sysinternals*) to view registered delayed rename and delete commands.

After performing these initialization steps, the main thread in Smss waits forever on the process handle of Winlogon, while the other ALPC threads wait for messages to create new sessions or subsystems. If either Wininit or Csrss terminate unexpectedly, the kernel crashes the system because these processes are marked as *critical.* If Winlogon terminates unexpectedly, the session associated with it is logged off.

Wininit then performs its startup steps, such as creating the initial window station and desktop objects. It also configures the Session 0 window hook, which is used by the Interactive Services Detection service (UI0Detect.exe) to provide backward compatibility with interactive services (see Chapter 4 for more information on services). Wininit then creates the service control manager (SCM) process (\Windows\System32\Services.exe), which loads all services and device drivers marked for auto-start, and the Local Security Authority subsystem (Lsass) process (\Windows\System32\Lsass.exe). Finally, it loads the local session manager (\Windows\System32\Lsm.exe). On session 1 and beyond, Winlogon runs instead and loads the registered credential providers for the system (by default, the Microsoft credential provider supports password-based and smartcard-based logons) into a child process called LogonUI (\Windows\System32\Logonui.exe, which is responsible for displaying the logon interface. (For more details on the startup sequence for Wininit, Winlogon, and Lsass, see the section "Winlogon Initialization" in Chapter 6.)

After the SCM initializes the auto-start services and drivers and a user has successfully logged on at the console, the SCM deems the boot successful. The registry's last known good control set (as indicated by HKLM\SYSTEM\Select\LastKnownGood) is updated to match \CurrentControlSet.

> **Note** Because noninteractive servers might never have an interactive logon, they might not get LastKnownGood updated to reflect the control set used for a successful boot. You can override the definition of a successful boot by setting HKLM\SOFTWARE\Microsoft\Windows NT\ CurrentVersion\Winlogon\ReportBootOk to 0, writing a custom boot verification program that calls the *NotifyBootConfigStatus* Windows API when a boot is successful, and entering the path to the verification program in HKLM\SYSTEM\CurrentControlSet\Control\BootVerificationProgram.

After launching the SCM, Winlogon waits for an interactive logon notification from the credential provider. When it receives a logon and validates the logon (a process for which you can find more information in the section "User Logon Steps" in Chapter 6), Winlogon loads the registry hive from the profile of the user logging in and maps it to HKCU. It then sets the user's environment variables that are stored in HKCU\Environment and notifies the Winlogon notification packages registered in HKLM\SOFTWARE\Microsoft\Windows NT\ CurrentVersion\Winlogon\Notify that a logon has occurred.

Winlogon next starts the shell by launching the executable or executables specified in HKLM\ SOFTWARE\Microsoft\Windows NT\CurrentVersion\WinLogon\Userinit (with multiple executables separated by commas) that by default points at \Windows\System32\Userinit.exe. Userinit.exe performs the following steps:

1. Processes the user scripts specified in HKCU\Software\Policies\Microsoft\Windows\ System\Scripts and the machine logon scripts in HKLM\SOFTWARE\Policies\Microsoft\ Windows\System\Scripts. (Because machine scripts run after user scripts, they can override user settings.)

2. If Group Policy specifies a user profile quota, starts \Windows\System32\Proquota.exe to enforce the quota for the current user.

3. Launches the comma-separated shell or shells specified in HKCU\Software\Microsoft\ Windows NT\CurrentVersion\Winlogon\Shell. If that value doesn't exist, Userinit.exe launches the shell or shells specified in HKLM\SOFTWARE\Microsoft\Windows NT\ CurrentVersion\Winlogon\Shell, which is by default Explorer.exe.

Winlogon then notifies registered network providers that a user has logged in. The Microsoft network provider, Multiple Provider Router (\Windows\System32\Mpr.dll), restores the user's persistent drive letter and printer mappings stored in HKCU\Network and HKCU\Printers, respectively. Figure 13-3 shows the process tree as seen in Process Monitor after a logon (using its boot logging capability). Note the Smss processes that are dimmed (meaning that they have since exited). These refer to the spawned copies that initialized each session.

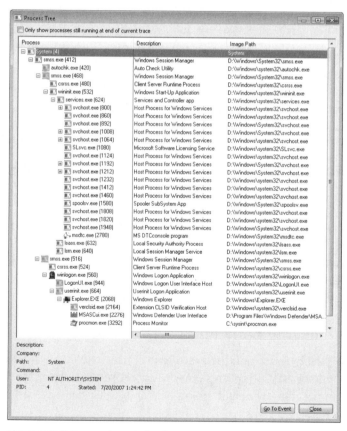

FIGURE 13-3 Process tree during logon

ReadyBoot

Windows uses the standard logical boot-time prefetcher (described in Chapter 9) if the system has less than 512 MB of memory, but if the system has 700 MB or more of RAM, it uses an in-RAM cache to optimize the boot process. The size of the cache depends on the total RAM available, but it is large enough to create a reasonable cache and yet allow the system the memory it needs to boot smoothly.

After every boot, the ReadyBoost service (see Chapter 9 for information on ReadyBoost) uses idle CPU time to calculate a boot-time caching plan for the next boot. It analyzes file trace information from the five previous boots and identifies which files were accessed and where they are located on disk. It stores the processed traces in %SystemRoot%\Prefetch\Readyboot as .fx files and saves the caching plan under HKLM\SYSTEM\CurrentControlSet\Services\ Ecache\Parameters in REG_BINARY values named for internal disk volumes they refer to.

The cache is implemented by the same device driver that implements ReadyBoost caching (Ecache.sys), but the cache's population is guided by the boot plan previously stored in the registry. Although the boot cache is compressed like the ReadyBoost cache, another difference between ReadyBoost and ReadyBoot cache management is that while in ReadyBoot mode, other than the ReadyBoost service's updates, the cache doesn't change to reflect data that's read or written during the boot. The ReadyBoost service deletes the cache 90 seconds after the start of the boot, or if other memory demands warrant it, and records the cache's statistics in HKLM\SYSTEM\CurrentControlSet\Services\Ecache\Parameters\ReadyBootStats, as shown in Figure 13-4.

FIGURE 13-4 ReadyBoot statistics

Images That Start Automatically

In addition to the Userinit and Shell registry values in Winlogon's key, there are many other registry locations and directories that default system components check and process for automatic process startup during the boot and logon processes. The Msconfig utility (Windows\System32\Msconfig.exe) displays the images configured by several of the locations. The Autoruns tool, which you can download from Sysinternals and that is shown in Figure 13-5, examines more locations than Msconfig and displays more information about the images configured to automatically run. By default, Autoruns shows only the locations that are configured to automatically execute at least one image, but selecting the Include Empty Locations entry on the Options menu causes Autoruns to show all the locations it inspects. The Options menu also has selections to direct Autoruns to hide Microsoft entries, but you should always combine this option with Verify Image Signatures; otherwise, you risk hiding malicious programs that include false information about their company name information.

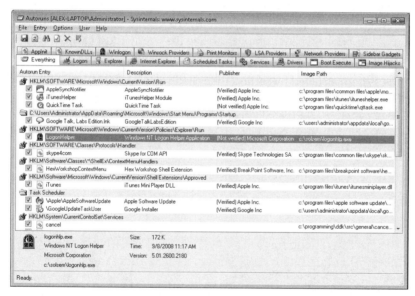

FIGURE 13-5 The Autoruns tool available from Sysinternals

EXPERIMENT: Autoruns

Many users are unaware of how many programs execute as part of their logon. Original equipment manufacturers (OEMs) often configure their systems with add-on utilities that execute in the background using registry values or file system directories processed for automatic execution and so are not normally visible. See what programs are configured to start automatically on your computer by running the Autoruns utility from Sysinternals. Compare the list shown in Autoruns with that shown in Msconfig and identify any differences. Then ensure that you understand the purpose of each program.

Troubleshooting Boot and Startup Problems

This section presents approaches to solving problems that can occur during the Windows startup process as a result of hard disk corruption, file corruption, missing files, and third-party driver bugs. First we describe three Windows boot-problem recovery modes: last known good, safe mode, and Windows Recovery Environment (WinRE). Then we present common boot problems, their causes, and approaches to solving them. The solutions refer to last known good, safe mode, WinRE, and other tools that ship with Windows.

Last Known Good

Last known good (LKG) is a useful mechanism for getting a system that crashes during the boot process back to a bootable state. Because the system's configuration settings are stored in HKLM\SYSTEM\CurrentControlSet\Control and driver and service configuration is stored in HKLM\SYSTEM\CurrentControlSet\Services, changes to these parts of the registry can render a system unbootable. For example, if you install a device driver that has a bug that crashes the system during the boot, you can press the F8 key during the boot and select last known good from the resulting menu. The system marks the control set that it was using to boot the system as failed by setting the Failed value of HKLM\SYSTEM\Select and then changes HKLM\SYSTEM\Select\Current to the value stored in HKLM\SYSTEM\Select\ LastKnownGood. It also updates the symbolic link HKLM\SYSTEM\CurrentControlSet to point at the LastKnownGood control set. Because the new driver's key is not present in the Services subkey of the LastKnownGood control set, the system will boot successfully.

Safe Mode

Perhaps the most common reason Windows systems become unbootable is that a device driver crashes the machine during the boot sequence. Because software or hardware config-urations can change over time, latent bugs can surface in drivers at any time. Windows offers a way for an administrator to attack the problem: booting in *safe mode*. Safe mode is a boot configuration that consists of the minimal set of device drivers and services. By relying on only the drivers and services that are necessary for booting, Windows avoids loading third-party and other nonessential drivers that might crash.

When Windows boots, you press the F8 key to enter a special boot menu that contains the safe-mode boot options. You typically choose from three safe-mode variations: Safe Mode, Safe Mode With Networking, and Safe Mode With Command Prompt. Standard safe mode includes the minimum number of device drivers and services necessary to boot successfully. Networking-enabled safe mode adds network drivers and services to the drivers and services that standard safe mode includes. Finally, safe mode with command prompt is identical to standard safe mode except that Windows runs the command prompt application (Cmd.exe) instead of Windows Explorer as the shell when the system enables GUI mode.

Windows includes a fourth safe mode—Directory Services Restore mode—which is different from the standard and networking-enabled safe modes. You use Directory Services Restore mode to boot the system into a mode where the Active Directory service of a domain controller is offline and unopened. This allows you to perform repair operations on the database or restore it from backup media. All drivers and services, with the exception of the Active Directory service, load during a Directory Services Restore mode boot. In cases where you can't log on to a system because of Active Directory database corruption, this mode enables you to repair the corruption.

Driver Loading in Safe Mode

How does Windows know which device drivers and services are part of standard and networking-enabled safe mode? The answer lies in the HKLM\SYSTEM\CurrentControlSet\Control\SafeBoot registry key. This key contains the Minimal and Network subkeys. Each subkey contains more subkeys that specify the names of device drivers or services or of groups of drivers. For example, the vga.sys subkey identifies the VGA display device driver that the startup configuration includes. The VGA display driver provides basic graphics services for any PC-compatible display adapter. The system uses this driver as the safe-mode display driver in lieu of a driver that might take advantage of an adapter's advanced hardware features but that might also prevent the system from booting. Each subkey under the SafeBoot key has a default value that describes what the subkey identifies; the vga.sys subkey's default value is "Driver".

The Boot file system subkey has as its default value "Driver Group". When developers design a device driver's installation script, they can specify that the device driver belongs to a driver group. The driver groups that a system defines are listed in the List value of the HKLM\SYSTEM\CurrentControlSet\Control\ServiceGroupOrder key. A developer specifies a driver as a member of a group to indicate to Windows at what point during the boot process the driver should start. The ServiceGroupOrder key's primary purpose is to define the order in which driver groups load; some driver types must load either before or after other driver types. The Group value beneath a driver's configuration registry key associates the driver with a group.

Driver and service configuration keys reside beneath HKLM\SYSTEM\CurrentControlSet\Services. If you look under this key, you'll find the VgaSave key for the VGA display device driver, which you can see in the registry is a member of the Video Save group. Any file system drivers that Windows requires for access to the Windows system drive are automatically loaded as if part of the Boot file system group. Other file system drivers are part of the File system group, which the standard and networking-enabled safe-mode configurations also include.

When you boot into a safe-mode configuration, the boot loader (Winload) passes an associated switch to the kernel (Ntoskrnl.exe) as a command-line parameter, along with any switches you've specified in the BCD for the installation you're booting. If you boot into any safe mode, Winload sets the *safeboot* BCD option with a value describing the type of safe mode you select. For standard safe mode, Winload sets *minimal*, and for networking-enabled safe mode, it adds *network*. Winload adds *minimal* and sets *safebootalternateshell* for safe mode with command prompt and *dsrepair* for Directory Services Restore mode.

The Windows kernel scans boot parameters in search of the safe-mode switches early during the boot, during the *InitSafeBoot* function, and sets the internal variable *InitSafeBootMode* to a value that reflects the switches the kernel finds. The kernel writes the *InitSafeBootMode* value to the registry value HKLM\SYSTEM\CurrentControlSet\Control\SafeBoot\Option\ OptionValue so that user-mode components, such as the SCM, can determine what boot mode the system is in. In addition, if the system is booting in safe mode with command prompt, the kernel sets the HKLM\SYSTEM\CurrentControlSet\Control\SafeBoot\Option\ UseAlternateShell value to 1. The kernel records the parameters that Winload passes to it in the value HKLM\SYSTEM\CurrentControlSet\Control\SystemStartOptions.

When the I/O manager kernel subsystem loads device drivers that HKLM\SYSTEM\ CurrentControlSet\Services specifies, the I/O manager executes the function *IopLoadDriver*. When the Plug and Play manager detects a new device and wants to dynamically load the device driver for the detected device, the Plug and Play manager executes the function *PipCallDriverAddDevice*. Both these functions call the function *IopSafebootDriverLoad* before they load the driver in question. *IopSafebootDriverLoad* checks the value of *InitSafeBootMode* and determines whether the driver should load. For example, if the system boots in standard safe mode, *IopSafebootDriverLoad* looks for the driver's group, if the driver has one, under the Minimal subkey. If *IopSafebootDriverLoad* finds the driver's group listed, *IopSafebootDriverLoad* indicates to its caller that the driver can load. Otherwise, *IopSafebootDriverLoad* looks for the driver's name under the Minimal subkey. If the driver's name is listed as a subkey, the driver can load. If *IopSafebootDriverLoad* can't find the driver group or driver name subkeys, the driver can't load. If the system boots in networking-enabled safe mode, *IopSafebootDriverLoad* performs the searches on the Network subkey. If the system doesn't boot in safe mode, *IopSafebootDriverLoad* lets all drivers load.

> **Note** An exception exists regarding the drivers that safe mode excludes from a boot: Winload, rather than the kernel, loads any drivers with a Start value of 0 in their registry key, which specifies loading the drivers at boot time. Winload doesn't check the SafeBoot registry key because it assumes that any driver with a Start value of 0 is required for the system to boot successfully. Because Winload doesn't check the SafeBoot registry key to identify which drivers to load, Winload loads all boot-start drivers (and later Ntoskrnl starts them).

Safe-Mode-Aware User Programs

When the service control manager (SCM) user-mode component (which Services.exe implements) initializes during the boot process, the SCM checks the value of HKLM\SYSTEM\ CurrentControlSet\Control\SafeBoot\Option\OptionValue to determine whether the system is performing a safe-mode boot. If so, the SCM mirrors the actions of *IopSafebootDriverLoad*. Although the SCM processes the services listed under HKLM\SYSTEM\CurrentControlSet\ Services, it loads only services that the appropriate safe-mode subkey specifies by name. You can find more information on the SCM initialization process in the section "Services" in Chapter 4.

Userinit, the component that initializes a user's environment when the user logs on (\Windows\System32\Userinit.exe), is another user-mode component that needs to know whether the system is booting in safe mode. It checks the value of HKLM\SYSTEM\Current-ControlSet\Control\SafeBoot\Option\UseAlternateShell. If this value is set, Userinit runs the program specified as the user's shell in the value HKLM\SYSTEM\CurrentControlSet\Control\ SafeBoot\AlternateShell rather than executing Explorer.exe. Windows writes the program name Cmd.exe to the AlternateShell value during installation, making the Windows command prompt the default shell for safe mode with command prompt. Even though the command prompt is the shell, you can type **Explorer.exe** at the command prompt to start Windows Explorer, and you can run any other GUI program from the command prompt as well.

How does an application determine whether the system is booting in safe mode? By calling the Windows *GetSystemMetrics(SM_CLEANBOOT)* function. Batch scripts that need to perform certain operations when the system boots in safe mode look for the SAFEBOOT_ OPTION environment variable because the system defines this environment variable only when booting in safe mode.

Boot Logging in Safe Mode

When you direct the system to boot into safe mode, Winload hands the string specified by the *bootlog* option to the Windows kernel as a parameter, together with the parameter that requests safe mode. When the kernel initializes, it checks for the presence of the boot log parameter whether or not any safe-mode parameter is present. If the kernel detects a boot log string, the kernel records the action the kernel takes on every device driver it considers for loading. For example, if *IopSafebootDriverLoad* tells the I/O manager not to load a driver, the I/O manager calls *IopBootLog* to record that the driver wasn't loaded. Likewise, after *IopLoadDriver* successfully loads a driver that is part of the safe-mode configuration, *IopLoadDriver* calls *IopBootLog* to record that the driver loaded. You can examine boot logs to see which device drivers are part of a boot configuration.

Because the kernel wants to avoid modifying the disk until Chkdsk executes, late in the boot process, *IopBootLog* can't simply dump messages into a log file. Instead, *IopBootLog* records messages in the HKLM\SYSTEM\CurrentControlSet\BootLog registry value. As the first user-mode component to load during a boot, the Session Manager (\Windows\System32\ Smss.exe) executes Chkdsk to ensure the system drives' consistency and then completes registry initialization by executing the *NtInitializeRegistry* system call. The kernel takes this action as a cue that it can safely open a log file on the disk, which it does, invoking the function *IopCopyBootLogRegistryToFile*. This function creates the file Ntbtlog.txt in the Windows system directory (\Windows by default) and copies the contents of the BootLog registry value to the file. *IopCopyBootLogRegistryToFile* also sets a flag for *IopBootLog* that lets *IopBootLog* know that writing directly to the log file, rather than recording messages in the registry, is now OK. The following output shows the partial contents of a sample boot log:

```
Microsoft (R) Windows (R) Version 6.0 (Build 6000)
10  4 2007 09:04:53.375
Loaded driver \SystemRoot\system32\ntkrnlpa.exe
Loaded driver \SystemRoot\system32\hal.dll
Loaded driver \SystemRoot\system32\kdcom.dll
Loaded driver \SystemRoot\system32\mcupdate_GenuineIntel.dll
Loaded driver \SystemRoot\system32\PSHED.dll
Loaded driver \SystemRoot\system32\BOOTVID.dll
Loaded driver \SystemRoot\system32\CLFS.SYS
Loaded driver \SystemRoot\system32\CI.dll
Loaded driver \SystemRoot\system32\drivers\Wdf01000.sys
Loaded driver \SystemRoot\system32\drivers\WDFLDR.SYS
Loaded driver \SystemRoot\system32\drivers\acpi.sys
Loaded driver \SystemRoot\system32\drivers\WMILIB.SYS
Loaded driver \SystemRoot\system32\drivers\msisadrv.sys
Loaded driver \SystemRoot\system32\drivers\pci.sys
Loaded driver \SystemRoot\system32\drivers\volmgr.sys
Loaded driver \SystemRoot\system32\DRIVERS\compbatt.sys
Loaded driver \SystemRoot\system32\DRIVERS\BATTC.SYS
Loaded driver \SystemRoot\System32\drivers\mountmgr.sys
Loaded driver \SystemRoot\system32\drivers\intelide.sys
Loaded driver \SystemRoot\system32\drivers\PCIIDEX.SYS
Loaded driver \SystemRoot\system32\DRIVERS\pciide.sys
Loaded driver \SystemRoot\System32\drivers\volmgrx.sys
Loaded driver \SystemRoot\system32\drivers\atapi.sys
Loaded driver \SystemRoot\system32\drivers\ataport.SYS
Loaded driver \SystemRoot\system32\drivers\fltmgr.sys
Loaded driver \SystemRoot\system32\drivers\fileinfo.sys
§
Did not load driver @battery.inf,%acpi\acpi0003.devicedesc%;Microsoft AC Adapter
Did not load driver @battery.inf,%acpi\pnp0c0a.devicedesc%;Microsoft ACPI-Compliant Control
Method Battery
Did not load driver @oem46.inf,%nvidia_g71.dev_0297.1%;NVIDIA GeForce Go 7950 GTX
Did not load driver @oem5.inf,%nic_mpciex%;Intel(R) PRO/Wireless 3945ABG Network Connection
Did not load driver @netb57vx.inf,%bcm5750a1clnahkd%;Broadcom NetXtreme 57xx Gigabit
Controller
Did not load driver @sdbus.inf,%pci\cc_080501.devicedesc%;SDA Standard Compliant SD Host
Controller
§
```

Windows Recovery Environment (WinRE)

Safe mode is a satisfactory fallback for systems that become unbootable because a device driver crashes during the boot sequence, but in some situations a safe-mode boot won't help the system boot. For example, if a driver that prevents the system from booting is a member of a Safe group, safe-mode boots will fail. Another example of a situation in which safe mode won't help the system boot is when a third-party driver, such as a virus scanner driver, that loads at the boot prevents the system from booting. (Boot-start drivers load whether or not the system is in safe mode.) Other situations in which safe-mode boots will fail are when a system module or critical device driver file that is part of a safe-mode configuration becomes corrupt or when the system drive's Master Boot Record (MBR) is damaged.

You can get around these problems by using the Windows Recovery Environment. The Windows Recovery Environment provides an assortment of tools and automated repair technologies to automatically fix the most common startup problems. It includes five main tools:

- **Startup Repair** An automated tool that detects the most common Windows startup problems and automatically attempts to repair them.

- **System Restore** Allows restoring to a previous restore point in cases in which you cannot boot the Windows installation to do so, even in safe mode.

- **Complete PC Restore** Called ASR (Automated System Recovery) in previous versions of Windows, this restores a Windows installation from a complete backup, not just a system restore point, which may not contain all damaged files and lost data.

- **Windows Memory Diagnostic Tool** Performs memory diagnostic tests that check for signs of faulty RAM. Faulty RAM can be the reason for random kernel and application crashes and erratic system behavior.

- **Command Prompt** For cases where troubleshooting or repair requires manual intervention (such as copying files from another drive or manipulating the BCD), you can use the command prompt to have a full Windows shell that can launch any Windows program—unlike the Recovery Console on earlier versions of Windows, which only supported a limited set of specialized commands.

When you boot a system from the Windows CD or boot disks, Windows Setup gives you the choice of installing Windows or repairing an existing installation. If you choose to repair an installation, the system displays a dialog box called System Recovery Options, shown in Figure 13-6.

Some OEMs install WinRE to a recovery partition on their systems. On these systems, you can access WinRE by using the F8 option to access advanced boot options during Bootmgr execution. If you see an option Repair Your Computer, your machine has a local hard disk copy. By following the instructions at the Microsoft WinRE blog (*http://blogs.msdn.com/winre*) you can also install WinRE on the hard disk yourself from your Windows installation media and Windows Automated Installation Kit (AIK).

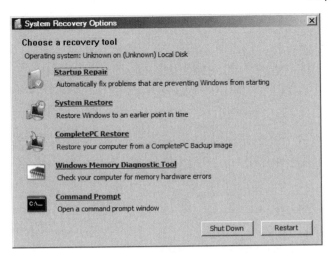

FIGURE 13-6 The System Recovery Options dialog box

Additionally, if your system failed to boot as the result of damaged files or any other reason that Winload can understand, it instructs Bootmgr to automatically start WinRE at the next reboot cycle. Instead of the dialog box shown in Figure 13-6, the recovery environment will automatically launch the Startup Repair tool, shown in Figure 13-7.

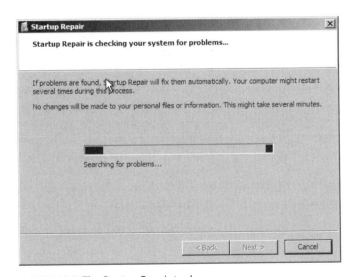

FIGURE 13-7 The Startup Repair tool

At the end of the scan and repair cycle, the tool will automatically attempt to fix any damage found, including replacing system files from the installation media. You can click the details link to see information about the damage that was fixed. For example, in Figure 13-8, the Startup Repair tool fixed a damaged boot sector.

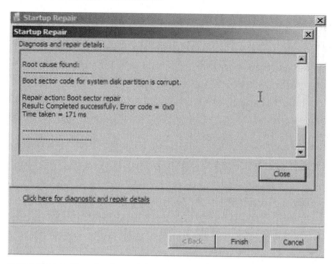

FIGURE 13-8 Details view of the Startup Repair tool

If the Startup Repair tool cannot automatically fix the damage, or if you cancel the operation, you'll get a chance to try other methods and the System Recovery Options dialog box will be displayed.

Boot Status File

Windows uses a *boot status file* (%SystemRoot%\Bootstat.dat) to record the fact that it has progressed through various stages of the system life cycle, including boot and shutdown. This allows the Boot Manager, Windows loader, and the Startup Repair tool to detect abnormal shutdown or a failure to shut down cleanly and offer the user recovery and diagnostic boot options, like Last Known Good and Safe Mode. This binary file contains information through which the system reports the success of the following phases of the system life cycle:

- Boot (the definition of a successful boot is the same as the one used for determining Last Known Good status, which was described earlier)
- Shutdown
- Resume from hibernate or suspend

The boot status file also indicates whether a problem was last detected and the recovery options shown, indicating that the user has been made aware of the problem and taken action. Runtime Library APIs (Rtl) in Ntdll.dll contain the private interfaces that Windows uses to read from and write to the file. Like the BCD, it cannot be edited by users.

Solving Common Boot Problems

This section describes problems that can occur during the boot process, describing their symptoms, causes, and approaches to solving them. To help you locate a problem that you might encounter, they are organized according to the place in the boot at which they occur. Note that for most of these problems, you should be able to simply boot into the Windows Recovery Environment and allow the Startup Repair tool to scan your system and perform any automated repair tasks.

MBR Corruption

- **Symptoms** A system that has Master Boot Record (MBR) corruption will execute the BIOS power-on self test (POST), display BIOS version information or OEM branding, switch to a black screen, and then hang. Depending on the type of corruption the MBR has experienced, you might see one of the following messages: "Invalid partition table," "Error loading operating system," or "Missing operating system."

- **Cause** The MBR can become corrupt because of hard-disk errors, disk corruption as a result of a driver bug while Windows is running, or intentional scrambling as a result of a virus.

- **Resolution** Boot into the Windows Recovery Environment, choose the Command Prompt option, and then execute the *bootrec /fixmbr* command. This command replaces the executable code in the MBR.

Boot Sector Corruption

- **Symptoms** Boot sector corruption can look like MBR corruption, where the system hangs after BIOS POST at a black screen, or you might see the messages "A disk read error occurred," "BOOTMGR is missing," or " BOOTMGR is compressed" displayed on a black screen.

- **Cause** The boot sector can become corrupt because of hard-disk errors, disk corruption as a result of a driver bug while Windows is running, or intentional scrambling as a result of a virus.

- **Resolution** Boot into the Windows Recovery Environment, choose the Command Prompt option, and then execute the *bootrec /fixboot* command. This command rewrites the boot sector of the volume that you specify. You should execute the command on both the system and boot volumes if they are different.

BCD Misconfiguration

- **Symptom** After BIOS POST, you'll see a message that begins "Windows could not start because of a computer disk hardware configuration problem," "Could not read from selected boot disk," or "Check boot path and disk hardware."

- **Cause** The BCD has been deleted, become corrupt, or no longer references the boot volume because the addition of a partition has changed the name of the volume.

- **Resolution** Boot into the Windows Recovery Environment, choose the Command Prompt option, and then execute the *bootrec /scanos* and *bootrec /rebuildbcd* commands. These commands will scan each volume looking for Windows installations. When they discover an installation, they will ask you whether they should add it to the BCD as a boot option and what name should be displayed for the installation in the boot menu. For other kinds of BCD-related damage, you can also use Bcdedit.exe to perform tasks such as building a new BCD from scratch or cloning an existing good copy.

System File Corruption

- **Symptoms** There are several ways the corruption of system files—which include executables, drivers, or DLLs—can manifest. One way is with a message on a black screen after BIOS POST that says, "Windows could not start because the following file is missing or corrupt," followed by the name of a file and a request to reinstall the file. Another way is with a blue screen crash during the boot with the text, "STOP: 0xC0000135 {Unable to Locate Component}."

- **Causes** The volume on which a system file is located is corrupt or one or more system files have been deleted or become corrupt.

- **Resolution** Boot into the Windows Recovery Environment, choose the Command Prompt option, and then execute the *chkdsk* command. Chkdsk will attempt to repair volume corruption. If Chkdsk does not report any problems, obtain a backup copy of the system file in question. One place to check is in the \Windows\winsxs\Backup directory, in which Windows places copies of many system files for access by Windows Resource Protection. (See the "Windows Resource Protection" sidebar.) If you cannot find a copy of the file there, see if you can locate a copy from another system in the network. Note that the backup file must be from the same service pack or hotfix as the file that you are replacing.

In some cases, multiple system files are deleted or become corrupt, so the repair process can involve multiple reboots and boot failures as you repair the files one by one. If you believe the system file corruption to be extensive, you should consider restoring the system from a backup image, such as one generated by Windows Vista CompletePC Backup or from a system restore point.

When you run Windows Backup (located in the System folder under Accessories on the Start menu), you can generate a CompletePC backup image, which includes all the files on the system and boot volumes, plus a floppy disk on which it stores information about the system's disks and volumes. To restore a system from an ASR backup image, back up boot from the Windows setup media and press F2 when prompted.

If you do not have a backup from which to restore, a last resort is to execute a Windows repair install: boot from the Windows setup media, and follow the wizard as if you were going to perform a new installation. The wizard will ask you whether you want to perform a repair or fresh install. When you tell it that you want to repair, Setup reinstalls all system files, leaving your application data and registry settings intact.

Windows Resource Protection

To preserve the integrity of the many components involved in the boot process, as well as other critical Windows files, libraries, and applications, Windows implements a technology called Windows Resource Protection (WRP). WRP is implemented through access control lists (ACLs) that protect critical system files on the machine. It is also exposed through an API (located in \Windows\System32\Sfc.dll and \Windows\System32\Sfc_os.dll) that can be accessed by the Sfc.exe utility to manually check a file for corruption and restore it.

WRP will also protect entire critical folders if required, even locking down the folder so that it is inaccessible by administrators (without modifying the access control list on the folder). The only supported way to modify WRP-protected files is through the Windows Modules Installer service, which can run under the TrustedInstaller account. This service is used for the installation of patches, service packs, hotfixes, and Windows Update. This account has access to the various protected files and is trusted by the system (as its name implies) to modify critical files and replace them. WRP also protects critical registry keys, and it may even lock entire registry trees if all the values and subkeys are considered to be critical.

Unlike the previous incarnation of WRP, called WFP (Windows File Protection), this implementation does not make use of file and directory change notifications to prevent replacement of critical files. Instead, the ACL on protected files, directories, or registry keys is set so that only the TrustedInstaller account is able to modify or delete these files. Application developers can use the *SfcIsFileProtected* or *SfcIsKeyProtected* APIs to check whether a file or registry key is locked down.

For backward compatibility, certain installers are considered *well-known*—an application compatibility shim exists that will suppress the "access denied" error that certain installers would receive while attempting to modify WRP-protected resources. Instead, the installer receives a fake "success" code, but the modification isn't made. This virtualization is similar to the User Access Control (UAC) virtualization technology discussed in Chapter 6, but it applies to write operations as well. It applies if the following are true:

- The application is a *legacy* application, meaning that it does not contain a manifest file compatible with Windows Vista or Windows Server 2008 with the *requestedExecutionLevel* value set.

- The application is trying to modify a WRP-protected resource (the file or registry key contains the TrustedInstaller SID).

- The application is being run under an administrator account (always true on systems with UAC enabled because of automatic installer program detection).

WRP copies files that are needed to restart Windows to the *cache directory* located at \Windows\winsxs\Backup. Critical files that are not needed to restart Windows are not copied to the cache directory. The size of the cache directory and the list of files copied to the cache cannot be modified. To recover a file from the cache directory, you can use the System File Checker (Sfc.exe) tool, which can scan your system for modified protected files and restore them from a good copy.

System Hive Corruption

- **Symptoms** If the System registry hive (which is discussed along with hive files in the section "The Registry" in Chapter 4) is missing or corrupted, Winload will display the message "Windows could not start because the following file is missing or corrupt: \WINDOWS\SYSTEM32\CONFIG\SYSTEM," on a black screen after the BIOS POST.

- **Causes** The System registry hive, which contains configuration information necessary for the system to boot, has become corrupt or has been deleted.

- **Resolution** Boot into the Windows Recovery Environment, choose the Command Prompt option, and then execute the *chkdsk* command. If the problem is not corrected, obtain a backup of the System registry hive. Windows makes copies of the registry hives every 12 hours (keeping the immediately previous copy with a .OLD extension) in a folder called \Windows\System32\Config\RegBack, so copy the file named System to \Windows\System32\Config.

If System Restore is enabled (System Restore is discussed in Chapter 11), you can often obtain a more recent backup of the registry hives, including the System hive, from the most recent restore point. You can choose System Restore from the Windows Recovery Environment to restore your registry from the last restore point.

Post–Splash Screen Crash or Hang

- **Symptoms** Problems that occur after the Windows splash screen displays, the desktop appears, or you log on fall into this category and can appear as a blue screen crash or a hang, where the entire system is frozen or the mouse cursor tracks the mouse but the system is otherwise unresponsive.

- **Causes** These problems are almost always a result of a bug in a device driver, but they can sometimes be the result of corruption of a registry hive other than the System hive.

- **Resolution** You can take several steps to try and correct the problem. The first thing you should try is the last known good configuration. Last known good (LKG), which is described earlier in this chapter and in the "Services" section of Chapter 4, consists of the registry control set that was last used to boot the system successfully. Because a control set includes core system configuration and the device driver and services registration database, using a version that does not reflect changes or newly installed drivers or services might avoid the source of the problem. You access last known good by pressing the F8 key early in the boot process to access the same menu from which you can boot into safe mode.

As stated earlier in the chapter, when you boot into LKG, the system saves the control set that you are avoiding and labels it as the *failed* control set. You can leverage the failed control set in cases where LKG makes a system bootable to determine what was causing the system to fail to boot by exporting the contents of the current control set of the successful boot and the failed control set to .reg files. You do this by using the Regedit's export functionality, which you access under the File menu:

1. Run Regedit, and select HKLM\SYSTEM\CurrentControlSet.

2. Select Export from the File menu, and save to a file named good.reg.

3. Open HKLM\SYSTEM\Select, read the value of Failed, and select the subkey named HKLM\SYSTEM\Control*XXX*, where *XXX* is the value of Failed.

4. Export the contents of the control set to bad.reg.

5. Use WordPad (which is found under Accessories on the Start menu) to globally replace all instances of CurrentControlSet in good.reg with ControlSet.

6. Use WordPad to change all instances of Control*XXX* (replacing *XXX* with the value of the Failed control set) in bad.reg with ControlSet.

7. Run Windiff from the Support Tools, and compare the two files.

The differences between a failed control set and a good one can be numerous, so you should focus your examination on changes beneath the Control subkey as well as under the Parameters subkeys of drivers and services registered in the Services subkey. Ignore changes made to Enum subkeys of driver registry keys in the Services branch of the control set.

If the problem you're experiencing is caused by a driver or service that was present on the system since before the last successful boot, LKG will not make the system bootable. Similarly, if a problematic configuration setting changed outside the control set or was made before the last successful boot, LKG will not help. In those cases, the next option to try is safe mode

(described earlier in this section). If the system boots successfully in safe mode and you know that particular driver was causing the normal boot to fail, you can disable the driver by using the Device Manager (accessible from the Hardware tab of the System Control Panel item). To do so, select the driver in question and choose Disable from the Action menu. If you recently updated the driver, and believe that the update introduced a bug, you can choose to roll back the driver to its previous version instead, also with the Device Manager. To restore a driver to its previous version, double-click on the device to open its Properties dialog box and click Roll Back Driver on the Driver tab.

On systems with System Restore enabled, an option when LKG fails is to roll back all system state (as defined by System Restore) to a previous point in time. Safe mode detects the existence of restore points, and when they are present it will ask you whether you want to log on to the installation to perform a manual diagnosis and repair or launch the System Restore Wizard. Using System Restore to make a system bootable again is attractive when you know the cause of a problem and want the repair to be automatic or when you don't know the cause but do not want to invest time to determine the cause.

If System Restore is not an option or you want to determine the cause of a crash during the normal boot and the system boots successfully in safe mode, attempt to obtain a boot log from the unsuccessful boot by pressing F8 to access the special boot menu and choosing the boot logging option. As described earlier in this chapter, Session Manager (\Windows\System32\Smss.exe) saves a log of the boot that includes a record of device drivers that the system loaded and chose not to load to \Windows\ntbtlog.txt, so you'll obtain a boot log if the crash or hang occurs after Session Manager initializes. When you reboot into safe mode, the system appends new entries to the existing boot log. Extract the portions of the log file that refer to the failed attempt and safe-mode boots into separate files. Strip out lines that contain the text "Did not load driver", and then compare them with a text comparison tool such as Windiff. One by one, disable the drivers that loaded during the normal boot but not in the safe-mode boot until the system boots successfully again. (Then reenable the drivers that were not responsible for the problem.)

If you cannot obtain a boot log from the normal boot (for instance, because the system is crashing before Session Manager initializes), if the system also crashes during the safe-mode boot, or if a comparison of boot logs from the normal and safe-mode boots do not reveal any significant differences (for example, when the driver that's crashing the normal boot starts after Session Manager initializes), the next tool to try is the Driver Verifier combined with crash dump analysis. (See Chapter 14 for more information on both these topics.)

Shutdown

If someone is logged on and a process initiates a shutdown by calling the Windows *Exit-WindowsEx* function, a message is sent to that session's Csrss instructing it to perform the shutdown. Csrss in turn impersonates the caller and sends an RPC message to Winlogon, telling it to perform a system shutdown. Winlogon then impersonates the currently logged-on user (who might or might not have the same security context as the user who initiated the system shutdown) and calls *ExitWindowsEx* with some special internal flags. Again, this call causes a message to be sent to the Csrss process inside that session, requesting a system shutdown.

This time, Csrss sees that the request is from Winlogon and loops through all the processes in the logon session of the interactive user (again, not the user who requested a shutdown) in reverse order of their *shutdown level*. A process can specify a shutdown level, which indicates to the system when they want to exit with respect to other processes, by calling *SetProcessShutdownParameters*. Valid shutdown levels are in the range 0 through 1023, and the default level is 640. Explorer, for example, sets its shutdown level to 2 and Task Manager specifies 1. For each process that owns a top-level window, Csrss sends the WM_QUERYENDSESSION message to each thread in the process that has a Windows message loop. If the thread returns TRUE, the system shutdown can proceed. Csrss then sends the WM_ENDSESSION Windows message to the thread to request it to exit. Csrss waits the number of seconds defined in HKCU\Control Panel\Desktop\HungAppTimeout for the thread to exit. (The default is 5000 milliseconds.)

If the thread doesn't exit before the timeout, Csrss fades out the screen and displays the hung-program screen shown in Figure 13-9. (You can disable this screen by changing the registry value HKCU\Control Panel\Desktop\AutoEndTasks to 1.) This screen indicates which programs are currently running and, if available, their current state. Windows indicates which program isn't shutting down in a timely manner and gives the user a choice of either killing the process or aborting the shutdown. (There is no timeout on this screen, which means that a shutdown request could wait forever at this point.) Additionally, third-party applications can add their own specific information regarding state—for example, a virtualization product could display the number of actively running virtual machines.

If the thread does exit before the timeout, Csrss continues sending the WM_QUERYEND-SESSION/WM_ENDSESSION message pairs to the other threads in the process that own windows. Once all the threads that own windows in the process have exited, Csrss terminates the process and goes on to the next process in the interactive session.

EXPERIMENT: Witnessing the HungAppTimeout

You can see the use of the HungAppTimeout registry value by running Notepad, entering text into its editor, and then logging off. After the amount of time specified by the HungAppTimeout registry value has expired, Csrss.exe presents a prompt that asks you whether or not you want to end the Notepad process, which has not exited because it's waiting for you to tell it whether or not to save the entered text to a file. If you click the Cancel button, Csrss.exe aborts the shutdown.

As a second experiment, if you try shutting down again (with Notepad's query dialog box still open), Notepad will display its own message box to inform you that shutdown cannot cleanly proceed. However, this dialog box is merely an informational message to help users—Csrss.exe will still consider that Notepad is "hung" and display the user interface to terminate unresponsive processes.

If Csrss finds a console application, it invokes the console control handler by sending the CTRL_LOGOFF_EVENT event. (Only service processes receive the CTRL_SHUTDOWN_EVENT event on shutdown.) If the handler returns FALSE, Csrss kills the process. If the handler returns TRUE or doesn't respond by the number of seconds defined by HKCU\Control Panel\Desktop\WaitToKillAppTimeout (the default is 20,000 milliseconds), Csrss displays the hung-program screen shown in Figure 13-9.

Next, Winlogon calls *ExitWindowsEx* to have Csrss terminate any COM processes that are part of the interactive user's session.

At this point, all the processes in the interactive user's session have been terminated. Wininit next calls *ExitWindowsEx*, which this time executes within the system process context. This causes Wininit to send a message to the Csrss part of session 0, where the services live. Csrss then looks at all the processes belonging to the system context and performs and sends the WM_QUERYENDSESSION/WM_ENDSESSION messages to GUI threads (as before). Instead of sending CTRL_LOGOFF_EVENT, however, it sends CTRL_SHUTDOWN_EVENT to console applications that have registered control handlers. Note that the SCM is a console program that does register a control handler. When it receives the shutdown request, it in turn sends

the service shutdown control message to all services that registered for shutdown notification. For more details on service shutdown (such as the shutdown timeout Csrss uses for the SCM), see the "Services" section in Chapter 4.

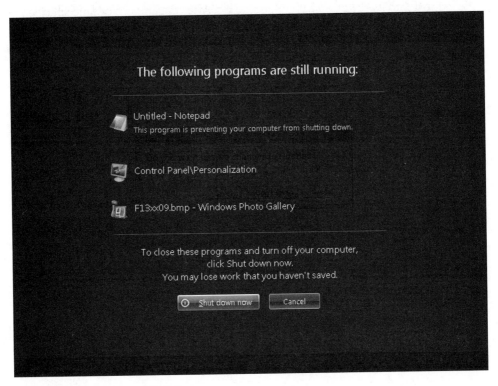

The following programs are still running:

Untitled - Notepad
This program is preventing your computer from shutting down.

Control Panel\Personalization

F13xx09.bmp - Windows Photo Gallery

To close these programs and turn off your computer,
click Shut down now.
You may lose work that you haven't saved.

Shut down now Cancel

FIGURE 13-9 Hung program screen

Although Csrss performs the same timeouts as when it was terminating the user processes, it doesn't display any dialog boxes and doesn't kill any processes. (The registry values for the system process timeouts are taken from the default user profile.) These timeouts simply allow system processes a chance to clean up and exit before the system shuts down. Therefore, many system processes are in fact still running when the system shuts down, such as Smss, Wininit, Services, and Lsass.

Once Csrss has finished its pass notifying system processes that the system is shutting down, Winlogon finishes the shutdown process by calling the executive subsystem function *NtShutdownSystem*. This function calls the function *PoSetSystemPowerState* to orchestrate the shutdown of drivers and the rest of the executive subsystems (Plug and Play manager, power manager, executive, I/O manager, configuration manager, and memory manager).

For example, *PoSetSystemPowerState* calls the I/O manager to send shutdown I/O packets to all device drivers that have requested shutdown notification. This action gives device drivers a chance to perform any special processing their device might require before Windows exits.

The stacks of worker threads are swapped in, the configuration manager flushes any modified registry data to disk, and the memory manager writes all modified pages containing file data back to their respective files. If the option to clear the paging file at shutdown is enabled, the memory manager clears the paging file at this time. The I/O manager is called a second time to inform the file system drivers that the system is shutting down. System shutdown ends in the power manager. The action the power manager takes depends on whether the user specified a shutdown, a reboot, or a power down.

Conclusion

In this chapter, we've examined the detailed steps involved in starting and shutting down Windows (both normally and in error cases). We've examined the overall structure of Windows and the core system mechanisms that get the system going, keep it running, and eventually shut it down. The final chapter of this book explains how to deal with an unusual type of shutdown: system crashes.

Chapter 14
Crash Dump Analysis

Almost every Windows user has heard of, if not experienced, the infamous "blue screen of death." This ominous term refers to the blue screen that is displayed when Windows crashes, or stops executing, because of a catastrophic fault or an internal condition that prevents the system from continuing to run.

In this chapter, we'll cover the basic problems that cause Windows to crash, describe the information presented on the blue screen, and explain the various configuration options available to create a *crash dump*, a record of system memory at the time of a crash that can help you figure out which component caused the crash and why. This section is *not* intended to provide detailed troubleshooting information on how to analyze a Windows system crash. This section will also show you how to analyze a crash dump to identify a faulty driver or component. The effort required to perform basic crash dump analysis is minimal and takes a few minutes. Even if an analysis ascertains the problematic driver for only one out of every five or ten crash dumps, it's still worth doing: one successful analysis can avoid future data loss, system downtime, and frustration.

Why Does Windows Crash?

Windows crashes (stops execution and displays the blue screen) for many possible reasons. A common source is a reference to a memory address that causes an access violation, either a write operation to read-only memory or a read operation on an address that is not mapped. Another common cause is an unexpected exception or trap. Crashes also occur when a kernel subsystem (such as the memory manager and power manager) or a driver (such as a USB or display driver) detect inconsistencies in their operation.

When a kernel-mode device driver or subsystem causes an illegal exception, Windows faces a difficult dilemma. It has detected that a part of the operating system with the ability to access any hardware device and any valid memory has done something it wasn't supposed to do.

But why does that mean Windows has to crash? Couldn't it just ignore the exception and let the device driver or subsystem continue as if nothing had happened? The possibility exists that the error was isolated and that the component will somehow recover. But what's more likely is that the detected exception resulted from deeper problems—for example, from a general corruption of memory or from a hardware device that's not functioning properly. Permitting the system to continue operating would probably result in more exceptions, and data stored on disk or other peripherals could become corrupt—a risk that's too high to take. So Windows adopts a *fail fast* policy in attempting to prevent the corruption in RAM from spreading to disk.

The Blue Screen

Regardless of the reason for a system crash, the function that actually performs the crash is *KeBugCheckEx,* documented in the Windows Driver Kit (WDK). This function takes a *stop code* (sometimes called a *bugcheck code*) and four parameters that are interpreted on a per-stop code basis. After *KeBugCheckEx* masks out all interrupts on all processors of the system, it switches the display into a low-resolution VGA graphics mode (one implemented by all Windows-supported video cards), paints a blue background, and then displays the stop code, followed by some text suggesting what the user can do. Finally, *KeBugCheckEx* calls any registered device driver bugcheck callbacks (registered by calling the *KeRegisterBugCheckCallback* function), allowing drivers an opportunity to stop their devices. It then calls registered reason callbacks (registered with *KeRegisterBugCheckReasonCallback),* which allow drivers to append data to the crash dump or write crash dump information to alternate devices.

(It's possible that system data structures have been so seriously corrupted that the blue screen isn't displayed.) Figure 14-1 shows a sample Windows blue screen.

```
A problem has been detected and windows has been shut down to prevent damage
to your computer.

DRIVER_IRQL_NOT_LESS_OR_EQUAL

If this is the first time you've seen this Stop error screen,
restart your computer. If this screen appears again, follow
these steps:

Check to make sure any new hardware or software is properly installed.
If this is a new installation, ask your hardware or software manufacturer
for any windows updates you might need.

If problems continue, disable or remove any newly installed hardware
or software. Disable BIOS memory options such as caching or shadowing.
If you need to use Safe Mode to remove or disable components, restart
your computer, press F8 to select Advanced Startup Options, and then
select Safe Mode.

Technical information:

*** STOP: 0x000000D1 (0xA35DB800,0x0000001C,0x00000000,0x9879C3DD)

***    myfault.sys - Address 9879C3DD base at 9879C000, DateStamp 453143ee

Collecting data for crash dump ...
Initializing disk for crash dump ...
Beginning dump of physical memory.
Dumping physical memory to disk:  30
```

FIGURE 14-1 Example of a blue screen

KeBugCheckEx displays the textual representation of the stop code near the top of the blue screen and the numeric stop code and four parameters at the bottom of the blue screen.

The first line in the Technical information section lists the stop code and the four additional parameters passed to *KeBugCheckEx.* A text line near the top of the screen provides the text equivalent of the stop code's numeric identifier. According to the example in Figure 14-1, the

stop code 0x000000D1 is a DRIVER_IRQL_NOT_LESS_OR_EQUAL crash. When a parameter contains an address of a piece of operating system or device driver code (as in Figure 14-1), Windows displays the base address of the module the address falls in, the date stamp, and the file name of the device driver. This information alone might help you pinpoint the faulty component.

Although there are more than 300 unique stop codes, most are rarely, if ever, seen on production systems. Instead, just a few common stop codes represent the majority of Windows system crashes. Also, the meaning of the four additional parameters depends on the stop code (and not all stop codes have extended parameter information). Nevertheless, looking up the stop code and the meaning of the parameters (if applicable) might at least assist you in diagnosing the component that is failing (or the hardware device that is causing the crash).

You can find stop code information in the section "Bug Checks (Blue Screens)" in the Debugging Tools for Windows help file. (For information on the Debugging Tools for Windows, see Chapter 1.) You can also search Microsoft's Knowledge Base (*http://support.microsoft.com*) for the stop code and the name of the suspect hardware or application. You might find information about a workaround, an update, or a service pack that fixes the problem you're having. The Bugcodes.h file in the WDK contains a complete list of the 300 or so stop codes, with some additional details on the reasons for some of them.

Based on data collected from the release of Windows Vista through the release of Windows Vista SP1, the top 30 stop codes account for 96 percent of crashes and can be grouped into a dozen categories:

- **Page fault** A page fault on memory backed by data in a paging file or a memory-mapped file occurs at an IRQL of DPC/dispatch level or above, which would require the memory manager to have to wait for an I/O operation to occur. The kernel cannot wait or reschedule threads at an IRQL of DPC/dispatch level or higher. (See Chapter 3 for details on IRQLs.) This category also includes page faults in nonpaged areas. The common stop codes are:

 - 0xA - IRQL_NOT_LESS_OR_EQUAL
 - 0xD1 - DRIVER_IRQL_NOT_LESS_OR_EQUAL

- **Power management** A device driver or an operating system function running in kernel mode is in an inconsistent or invalid power state. Most frequently, some component has failed to complete a power management I/O request operation within 10 minutes. This crash category is new in Windows Vista. In previous versions of the Windows operating system, these failures generally resulted in a system hang with no crash. The stop codes are:

 - 0x9F - DRIVER_POWER_STATE_FAILURE
 - 0xA0 - INTERNAL_POWER_ERROR

- **Exceptions and traps** A device driver or an operating system function running in kernel mode incurs an unexpected exception or trap. The common stop codes are:

 - 0x1E - KMODE_EXCEPTION_NOT_HANDLED

 - 0x3B - SYSTEM_SERVICE_EXCEPTION

 - 0x7E - SYSTEM_THREAD_EXCEPTION_NOT_HANDLED

 - 0x7F - UNEXPECTED_KERNEL_MODE_TRAP

 - 0x8E - KERNEL_MODE_EXCEPTION_NOT_HANDLED with P1 != 0xC0000005 STATUS_ACCESS_VIOLATION

- **Access violations** A device driver or an operating system function running in kernel mode incurs a memory access violation, which is caused either by attempting to write to a read-only page or by attempting to read an address that isn't currently mapped and therefore is not a valid memory location. The common stop codes are:

 - 0x50 - PAGE_FAULT_IN_NONPAGED_AREA

 - 0x8E - KERNEL_MODE_EXCEPTION_NOT_HANDLED with P1 = 0xC0000005 STATUS_ACCESS_VIOLATION

- **Display** The display device driver detects that it can no longer control the graphics processing unit or detects an inconsistency in video memory management. The common stop codes are:

 - 0xEA - THREAD_STUCK_IN_DEVICE_DRIVER

 - 0x10E - VIDEO_MEMORY_MANAGEMENT_INTERNAL

 - 0x116 - VIDEO_TDR_FAILURE

- **Pool** The kernel pool manager detects an improper pool reference. The common stop codes are:

 - 0xC2 - BAD_POOL_CALLER

 - 0xC5 - DRIVER_CORRUPTED_EXPOOL

- **Memory management** The kernel memory manager detects a corruption of memory management data structures or an improper memory management request. The common stop codes are:

 - 0x1A - MEMORY_MANAGEMENT

 - 0x4E - PFN_LIST_CORRUPT

- **Consistency check** This is a catch-all category for various other consistency checks performed by the kernel or device drivers. The common stop codes are:

 - 0x18 - REFERENCE_BY_POINTER

 - 0x35 - NO_MORE_IRP_STACK_LOCATIONS

 - 0x44 - MULTIPLE_IRP_COMPLETE_REQUESTS

❑ 0xCE - DRIVER_UNLOADED_WITHOUT_CANCELLING_PENDING_OPERATIONS

❑ 0x8086 – This is a stop code used by the Intel storage driver iastor.sys

- **Hardware** A hardware error, such as a machine check or a nonmaskable interrupt (NMI), occurs. This category also includes disk failures when the memory manager is attempting to read data to satisfy page faults. The common stop codes are:

 ❑ 0x77 – KERNEL_STACK_INPAGE_ERROR

 ❑ 0x7A - KERNEL_DATA_INPAGE_ERROR

 ❑ 0x124 - WHEA_UNCORRECTABLE_ERROR

 ❑ 0x101 - CLOCK_WATCHDOG_TIMEOUT (Software bugs can cause these errors too, but they are most common on over-clocked hardware systems.)

- **USB** An unrecoverable error occurs in a universal serial bus operation. The common stop code is:

 ❑ 0xFE - BUGCODE_USB_DRIVER

- **Critical object** A fatal error occurs in a critical object without which Windows cannot continue to run. The common stop code is:

 ❑ 0xF4 - CRITICAL_OBJECT_TERMINATION

- **NTFS file system** A fatal error is detected by the NTFS file system. The common stop code is:

 ❑ 0x24 - NTFS_FILE_SYSTEM

Figure 14-2 shows the distribution of these categories for Windows Vista SP1 in September 2008:

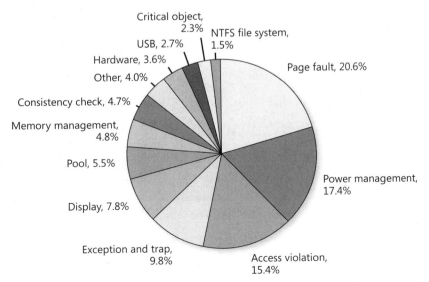

FIGURE 14-2 Distribution of error categories for Windows Vista SP1 as of September 2008.

Troubleshooting Crashes

You often begin seeing blue screens after you install a new software product or piece of hardware. If you've just added a driver, rebooted, and gotten a blue screen early in system initialization, you can reset the machine, press the F8 key when instructed, and then select Last Known Good Configuration. Enabling last known good causes Windows to revert to a copy of the registry's device driver registration key (HKLM\SYSTEM\CurrentControlSet\Services) from the last successful boot (before you installed the driver). From the perspective of last known good, a successful boot is one in which all services and drivers have finished loading and at least one logon has succeeded. (Last known good is further described in Chapter 13.)

During the reboot after a crash, the Boot Manager (Bootmgr) will automatically detect that Windows did not shut down properly and display a Windows Error Recovery message similar to the one shown in Figure 14-3. This screen gives you the option to attempt booting into safe mode so that you can disable or uninstall the software component that might be broken.

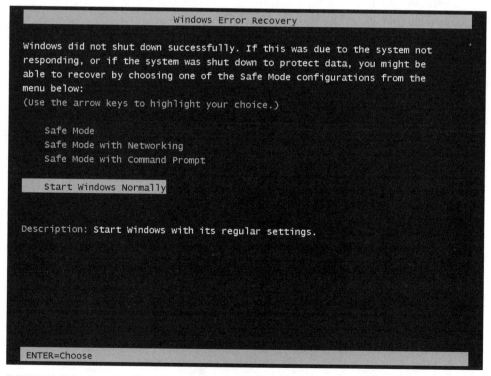

FIGURE 14-3 An example of a Windows Error Recovery message

If you keep getting blue screens, an obvious approach is to uninstall the components you added just before the first blue screen appeared. If some time has passed since you added something new or you added several things at about the same time, you need to note the names of the device drivers referenced in any of the parameters. If you recognize any of the names as being related to something you just added (such as Storport.sys if you put on a new SCSI drive), you've possibly found your culprit.

Many device drivers have cryptic names, but one approach you can take to figure out which application or hardware device is associated with a name is to find out the name of the service in the registry associated with a device driver by searching for the name of the device driver under the HKLM\SYSTEM\CurrentControlSet\Services key. This branch of the registry is where Windows stores registration information for every device driver in the system. If you find a match, look for values named DisplayName and Description. Some drivers fill in these values to describe the device driver's purpose. For example, you might find the string "Virus Scanner" in the DisplayName value, which can implicate the antivirus software you have running. The list of drivers can be displayed in the System Information tool (from the Start menu, select Programs, System Tools, System Information. In System Information, expand Software Environment, and then select System Drivers. Process Explorer also lists the currently loaded drivers, including their version numbers and load addresses, in the DLL view of the System process. Another option is to open the Properties dialog box for the driver file and examine the information on the Details tab, which often contains the description and company information for the driver. Keep in mind that the registry information and file description are provided by the driver manufacturer, and there is nothing to guarantee their accuracy.

More often than not, however, the stop code and the four associated parameters aren't enough information to troubleshoot a system crash. For example, you might need to examine the kernel-mode call stack to pinpoint the driver or system component that triggered the crash. Also, because the default behavior on Windows systems is to automatically reboot after a system crash, it's unlikely that you would have time to record the information displayed on the blue screen. That is why, by default, Windows attempts to record information about the system crash to the disk for later analysis, which takes us to our next topic, crash dump files.

Crash Dump Files

By default, all Windows systems are configured to attempt to record information about the state of the system when the system crashes. You can see these settings by opening the System tool in Control Panel, clicking the Advanced tab in the System Properties dialog box, and then clicking the Settings button under Startup And Recovery. The default settings for a Windows system are shown in Figure 14-4.

FIGURE 14-4 Crash dump settings

Three levels of information can be recorded on a system crash:

■ **Complete memory dump** A complete memory dump contains all of physical memory
at the time of the crash. This type of dump requires that a page file be at least the
size of physical memory plus 1 MB for the header. Device drivers can take advantage
of up to 256 MB for device dump data, but the additional space is not required for a
header. Because it can require an inordinately large page file on large memory sys-
tems, this type of dump file is the least common setting. If the system has more than
2 GB of RAM, this option will be disabled in the UI, but you can manually enable it by
setting the CrashDumpEnabled value to 1 in the HKLM\SYSTEM\CurrentControlSet\
Control\CrashControl registry key. At initialization time, Windows will check whether
the page-file size is large enough for a complete dump and automatically switch to
creating a small memory dump if not. Large server systems might not have space for
a complete dump but may be able to dump useful information, so you can add the
IgnorePagefileSize value to the same registry key to have the system generate a dump
file until it runs out of space.

■ **Kernel memory dump** A kernel memory dump contains only the kernel-mode read/
write pages present in physical memory at the time of the crash. This type of dump
doesn't contain pages belonging to user processes. Because only kernel-mode code
can directly cause Windows to crash, however, it's unlikely that user process pages are
necessary to debug a crash. In addition, all data structures relevant for crash dump
analysis—including the list of running processes, stack of the current thread, and list of
loaded drivers—are stored in nonpaged memory that saves in a *kernel memory dump*.

There is no way to predict the size of a kernel memory dump because its size depends on the amount of kernel-mode memory allocated by the operating system and drivers present on the machine. This is the default setting for both Windows Vista and Windows Server 2008.

- **Small memory dump** A small memory dump, which is typically between 128 KB and 1 MB in size and is also called a *minidump* or *triage dump*, contains the stop code and parameters, the list of loaded device drivers, the data structures that describe the current process and thread (called the EPROCESS and ETHREAD—described in Chapter 5), the kernel stack for the thread that caused the crash, and additional memory considered potentially relevant by crash dump heuristics, such as the pages referenced by processor registers that contain memory addresses and secondary dump data added by drivers.

Note Device drivers can register a secondary dump data callback routine by calling *KeRegister-BugCheckReasonCallback*. The kernel invokes these callbacks after a crash and a callback routine can add additional data to a crash dump file, such as device hardware memory or device information for easier debugging. Up to 256 MB can be added systemwide by all drivers, depending on the space required to store the dump and the size of the file into which the dump is written, and each driver can add at most one-eighth of the available additional space. Once the additional space is consumed, drivers subsequently called are not offered the chance to add data.

The debugger indicates that it has limited information available to it when it loads a minidump, and basic commands like *!process*, which lists active processes, don't have the data they need. Here is an example of *!process* executed on a minidump:

```
Microsoft (R) Windows Debugger Version 6.10.0003.233 X86
Copyright (c) Microsoft Corporation. All rights reserved.

Loading Dump File [C:\Windows\Minidump\Mini100108-01.dmp]
Mini Kernel Dump File: Only registers and stack trace are available
...
0: kd> !process 0 0
**** NT ACTIVE PROCESS DUMP ****
GetPointerFromAddress: unable to read from 81d3a86c
Error in reading nt!_EPROCESS at 00000000
```

A kernel memory dump includes more information, but switching to a different process's address space mappings won't work because required data isn't in the dump file. Here is an example of the debugger loading a kernel memory dump, followed by an attempt to switch process address spaces:

```
Microsoft (R) Windows Debugger Version 6.10.0003.233 X86
Copyright (c) Microsoft Corporation. All rights reserved.
```

```
Loading Dump File [C:\Windows\MEMORY.DMP]
Kernel Summary Dump File: Only kernel address space is available
...
0: kd> !process 0 0 explorer.exe
PROCESS 867250a8 ...

0: kd> .process 867250a8 ...
Process 867250a8 has invalid page directories
```

While a complete memory dump is a superset of the other options, it has the drawback that its size tracks the amount of physical memory on a system and can therefore become unwieldy. It's not unusual for systems today to have several gigabytes of memory, resulting in crash dump files that are too large to be uploaded to an FTP server or burned onto a CD. Because user-mode code and data are not used during the analysis of most crashes (because crashes originate as a result of problems in kernel memory, and system data structures reside in kernel memory) much of the data stored in a complete memory dump is not relevant to analysis and therefore contributes wastefully to the size of a dump file. A final disadvantage is that the paging file on the boot volume (the volume with the \Windows directory) must be at least as large as the amount of physical memory on the system plus up to 365 MB. Because the size of the paging files required, in general, inversely tracks the amount of physical memory present, this requirement can force the paging file to be unnecessarily large. You should therefore consider the advantages offered by the small and kernel memory dump options.

An advantage of a minidump is its small size, which makes it convenient for exchange via e-mail, for example. In addition, each crash generates a file in the directory \Windows\Minidump with a unique file name consisting of the string "Mini" plus the date plus a sequence number that counts the number of minidumps on that day (for example, Mini082608-01.dmp). A disadvantage of minidumps is that to analyze them, you must have access to the exact images used on the system that generated the dump at the time you analyze the dump. (At a minimum, a copy of the matching Ntoskrnl.exe is needed to perform the most basic analysis.) This can be problematic if you want to analyze a dump on a system different from the system that generated the dump. However, the Microsoft symbol server contains images (and symbols) for all recent Windows versions, so you can set the image path in the debugger to point to the symbol server, and the debugger will automatically download the needed images. (Of course, the Microsoft symbol server won't have images for third-party drivers you have installed.)

A more significant disadvantage is that the limited amount of data stored in the dump can hamper effective analysis. You can also get the advantages of minidumps even when you configure a system to generate kernel or complete crash dumps by opening the larger crash with WinDbg and using the *.dump /m* command to extract a minidump. Note that a minidump is automatically created even if the system is set for full or kernel dumps.

> **Note** You can use the *.dump* command from within Livekd to generate a memory image of a live system that you can analyze offline without stopping the system. This approach is useful when a system is exhibiting a problem, but is still delivering services, and you want to troubleshoot the problem without interrupting service. The resultant crash image isn't necessarily fully consistent because the contents of different regions of memory reflect different points in time, but it might contain information useful for an analysis.

The kernel memory dump option offers a practical middle ground. Because it contains all of kernel-mode-owned physical memory, it has the same level of analysis-related data as a complete memory dump, but it omits the usually irrelevant user-mode data and code, and therefore can be significantly smaller. As an example, on a system running Windows Vista with 4 GB of RAM, a kernel memory dump was 160 MB in size.

When you configure kernel memory dumps, the system checks whether the paging file is large enough, as described earlier. Some general recommendations follow in Table 14-1, but these are only estimated sizes because there is no way to predict the size of a kernel memory dump. The reason you can't predict the size of a kernel memory dump is that its size depends on the amount of kernel-mode memory in use by the operating system and drivers present on the machine at the time of the crash.

TABLE 14-1 Default Minimum Paging File Sizes for Kernel Dumps

System Memory Size	Minimum Page File Size for Kernel Dumps
< 128 MB	50 MB
< 4 GB	200 MB
< 8 GB	400 MB
>= 8 GB	800 MB

Therefore, it is possible that at the time of the crash, the paging file is too small to hold a kernel dump. If you want to see the size of a kernel dump on your system, force a manual crash either by configuring the option to allow you to initiate a manual system crash from the console or by using the Notmyfault tool described later in this chapter. (Both these approaches are described later in the chapter.) When you reboot, you can check to make sure that a kernel dump was generated and check its size to gauge how large to make your boot volume paging file. To be conservative, on 32-bit systems you can choose a page file size of 2 GB plus up to 356 MB, because 2 GB is the maximum kernel-mode address space available (unless you are booting with the *3gb* and/or *userva* boot options, in which case this can be up to 3 GB). If you do not have enough space on the boot volume for saving the memory.dmp file, you can choose a location on any other local hard disk through the dialog box shown in Figure 14-4.

Crash Dump Generation

When the system boots, it checks the crash dump options configured by reading the registry value HKLM\SYSTEM\CurrentControlSet\Control\CrashControl. If a dump is configured, it makes a copy of the disk miniport driver used to write to the boot volume in memory and gives it the same name as the miniport with the word "dump_" prefixed. It also checksums the components involved with writing a crash dump—including the copied disk miniport driver, the I/O manager functions that write the dump, and the map of where the boot volume's paging file is on disk—and saves the checksum. When *KeBugCheckEx* executes, it checksums the components again and compares the new checksum with that obtained at the boot. If there's not a match, it does not write a crash dump, because doing so would likely fail or corrupt the disk. Upon a successful checksum match, *KeBugCheckEx* writes the dump information directly to the sectors on disk occupied by the paging file, bypassing the file system driver and storage driver stack (which might be corrupted or even have caused the crash).

> **Note** Because the page file is created early in system startup during memory manager initialization, most crashes the are caused by bugs in system-start driver initialization result in a dump file. Crashes in early Windows boot components such as the HAL or the initialization of boot drivers occur too early for the system to have a page file, so using another computer to debug the startup process is the only way to perform dump analysis in those cases.

When the Session Manager (SMSS) re-initializes the page file during the boot process, it calls the function *SmpCheckForCrashDump*, which looks in the boot volume's current paging file (created by the kernel during the boot process) to see whether a crash dump is present. SMSS then checks whether the target dump file is on a different volume than the paging file. If so, it renames the paging file to a temporary dump file name, Dumpxxx.tmp (where xxx is the current low value of the system's tick count), and truncates the file to the size of the dump data. (This information is stored in the header on top of each dump file.) It also removes both the hidden and system attributes from the file. SMSS then creates the volatile registry key HKLM\SYSTEM\CurrentControlSet\Control\CrashControl\MachineCrash and stores the temporary dump file name in the value "DumpFile". It then writes a REG_DWORD to the "TempDestination" value indicating whether the dump file location is only the temporary destination. If the paging file is on the same volume as the destination dump file, a temporary dump file isn't used, and the paging file is directly renamed to the dump file name. In this case, the DumpFile value will be %SystemRoot%\Memory.dmp and TempDestination will be 0.

Later in the boot, Wininit checks for the presence of the MachineCrash key, and if it exists, Wininit launches WerFault, which reads the TempDestination and DumpFile values and either renames or copies the temporary file to its target location (typically %SystemRoot%\Memory.dmp, unless configured otherwise) depending on whether the target is on the

same volume as the Windows directory. WerFault then writes the final dump file name to the FinalDumpFileLocation value in the MachineCrash key. These steps are shown in Figure 14-5.

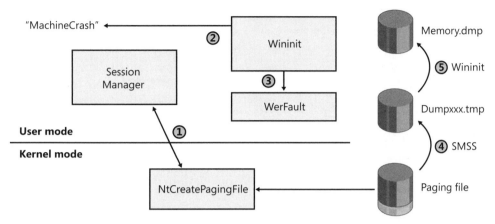

FIGURE 14-5 Crash dump file generation

To support machines that might not have a paging file or no paging file on the boot volume, for example on systems that boot from a SAN or read-only media, Windows also supports the use of a *dedicated dump file* that is configured in the DedicatedDumpFile and DumpFileSize values under the HKLM\SYSTEM\CurrentControlSet\Control\CrashControl registry key. When a dedicated dump file is specified, the crash dump driver (%SystemRoot%\System32\Drivers\Crashdmp.sys) creates the dump file of the required size and writes the crash data there instead of the paging file. If a full or kernel dump is configured but there is not enough space on the target volume to create the dedicated dump file of the required size, the system falls back to writing a minidump.

Windows Error Reporting

As mentioned in Chapter 3, Windows includes a facility called Windows Error Reporting (WER), which facilitates the automatic submission of process and system failures (such as crashes and/or hangs) to Microsoft (or an internal error reporting server) for analysis. This feature is enabled by default, but it can be modified by changing WER's behavior, which takes the additional step of determining whether the system is configured to send a crash dump to Microsoft (or a private server, explained further in the "Online Crash Analysis" section later in the chapter) for analysis on a reboot following a crash. The WER Advanced Settings screen, which you access from the Problem Reports And Solutions screen of the Control Panel's System applet, is shown in Figure 14-6. This dialog box allows you to configure the system's error reporting settings.

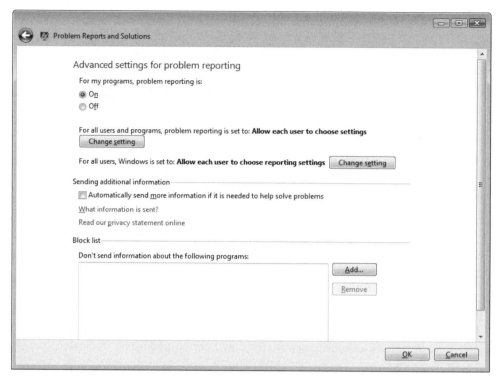

FIGURE 14-6 Error reporting configuration dialog box

As mentioned earlier, if Wininit.exe finds the HKLM\SYSTEM\CurrentControlSet\Control\ CrashControl\MachineCrash key, it executes WerFault.exe with the −k −c flags (the k flag indicates kernel error reporting, and the c flag indicates that the full or kernel dump should be converted to a minidump) to have WerFault.exe check for a kernel crash dump file. WerFault takes the following steps for preparing to send a crash dump report to the Microsoft Online Crash Analysis (OCA) site (or, if configured, an internal error reporting server):

1. If the type of dump it generated was not a minidump, it extracts a minidump from the dump file and stores it in the default location of \Windows\Minidumps, unless otherwise configured through the MinidumpDir value in the HKLM\SYSTEM\ CurrentControlSet\Control\CrashControl\ key.

2. It writes the name of the minidump files to HKLM\SOFTWARE\Microsoft\Windows\ Windows Error Reporting\KernelFaults\Queue.

3. It adds a command to execute WerFault.exe (\Windows\System32\WerFault.exe) to HKLM\SOFTWARE\Microsoft\Windows\CurrentVersion\RunOnce so that WerFault is executed one more time during the first user's logon to the system for purposes of actually sending the error report.

Online Crash Analysis

When the WerFault utility executes during logon, as a result of having configured itself to start, it checks the HKLM\SOFTWARE\Microsoft\Windows\Windows Error Reporting\ KernelFaults\Queue key to look for queued reports that may have been added in the previous dump conversion phase. It also checks whether there are previously unsent crash reports from previous sessions. If there are, it launches WerFault.exe with the *–k –q* flags (the *q* flag specifies the usage of queued reporting mode) to generate an XML-formatted file containing a basic description of the system, including the operating system version, a list of drivers installed on the machine, and the list of Plug and Play drivers loaded on the system at the time of the crash.

If configured to ask for user input (which is not the default), it then presents the dialog box shown in Figure 14-7, which asks the user whether he or she wants to send an error report to Microsoft. If the user chooses to send the error report, and unless overridden by Group Policy, WerFault sends the XML file and minidump to *http://oca.microsoft.com*, which forwards the data to a server farm for automated analysis, described in the next section.

FIGURE 14-7 Crash dump error reporting dialog box

The server farm's automated analysis uses the same analysis engine that the Microsoft kernel debuggers use when you load a crash dump file into them (described shortly). The analysis generates a *bucket ID*, which is a signature that identifies a particular crash type. The server farm queries a database using the bucket ID to see whether a resolution has been found for the crash, and it sends a URL back to WerFault that refers it to the OCA Web site (*http://oca.microsoft.com*). If configured to do so, WerFault launches the Windows Error Reporting Console, or WerCon (%SystemRoot%\System32\Wercon.exe), which is a program that allows users to interface with WER for receiving problem resolution and tracking

information as well as for configuring WER behavior. When browsing for solutions, WerCon contains an Internet browser frame to open the page on the WER Web site that reports the preliminary crash analysis. If a resolution is available, the page instructs the user where to obtain a hotfix, service pack, or third-party driver update.

Basic Crash Dump Analysis

If OCA fails to identify a resolution or you are unable to submit the crash to OCA, an alternative is analyzing crashes yourself. As mentioned earlier, WinDbg and Kd both execute the same analysis engine used by OCA when you load a crash dump file, and the basic analysis can sometimes pinpoint the problem. So you might be fortunate and have the crash dump solved by the automatic analysis. But if not, there are some straightforward techniques to try to solve the crash.

This section explains how to perform basic crash analysis steps, followed by tips on leveraging the Driver Verifier (which is introduced in Chapter 7) to catch buggy drivers when they corrupt the system so that a crash dump analysis pinpoints them.

Note OCA's automated analysis may occasionally identify a highly likely cause of a crash but not be able to inform you of the suspected driver. This happens because it only reports the cause for crashes that have their bucket ID entry populated in the OCA database, and entries are created only when Microsoft crash-analysis engineers have verified the cause. If there's no bucket ID entry, OCA reports that the crash was caused by *"unknown driver."*

Notmyfault

You can use the Notmyfault utility from Windows Sysinternals (*www.microsoft.com/technet/ sysinternals*) to generate the crashes described here. Notmyfault consists of an executable named Notmyfault.exe and a driver named Myfault.sys. When you run the Notmyfault executable, it loads the driver and presents the dialog box shown in Figure 14-8, which allows you to crash the system in various ways or to cause the driver to leak paged pool. The crash types offered represent the ones most commonly seen by Microsoft's product support services. Selecting an option and clicking the Do Bug button causes the executable to tell the driver, by using the *DeviceIoControl* Windows API, which type of bug to trigger.

Note You should execute Notmyfault crashes on a test system or on a virtual machine because there is a small risk that memory it corrupts will be written to disk and result in file or disk corruption.

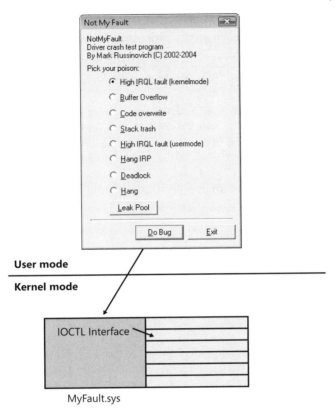

User mode

Kernel mode

MyFault.sys

FIGURE 14-8 Notmyfault

Note The names of the Notmyfault executable and driver highlight the fact that user mode cannot directly cause the system to crash. The Notmyfault executable can cause a crash only by loading a driver to perform an illegal operation for it in kernel mode.

Basic Crash Dump Analysis

The most straightforward Notmyfault crash to debug is the one caused by selecting the High IRQL Fault (Kernelmode) option and clicking the Do Bug button. This causes the driver to allocate a page of paged pool, free the pool, raise the IRQL to above DPC/dispatch level, and then touch the page it has freed. (See Chapter 3 for more information on IRQLs.) If that doesn't cause a crash, the process continues by reading memory past the end of the page until it causes a crash by accessing invalid pages. The driver performs several illegal operations as a result:

1. It references memory that doesn't belong to it.

2. It references paged pool at an IRQL that's DPC/dispatch level or higher, which is illegal because page faults are not permitted when the processor IRQL is DPC/dispatch level or higher.

3. When it goes past the end of the memory that it had allocated, it tries to reference memory that is potentially invalid.

The reason the first page reference might not cause a crash is that it won't generate a page fault if the page that the driver frees remains in the system working set. (See Chapter 9 for information on the system working set.)

When you load a crash generated with this bug into WinDbg, the tool's analysis displays something like this:

```
Microsoft (R) Windows Debugger Version 6.9.0003.113 X86
Copyright (c) Microsoft Corporation. All rights reserved.

Loading Dump File [C:\windows\MEMORY.DMP]
Kernel Summary Dump File: Only kernel address space is available

Symbol search path is: srv*c:\programming\symbols\*http://msdl.microsoft.com/download/
symbols
Executable search path is:
Windows Server 2008 Kernel Version 6001 (Service Pack 1) MP (2 procs) Free x86 compatible
Product: WinNt, suite: TerminalServer SingleUserTS
Built by: 6001.18063.x86fre.vistasp1_gdr.080425-1930
Kernel base = 0x81804000 PsLoadedModuleList = 0x8191bc70
Debug session time: Sun Sep 21 22:58:19.994 2008 (GMT-4)
System Uptime: 2 days 0:11:17.876
Loading Kernel Symbols
............................................................................................
....................................................
Loading User Symbols
Loading unloaded module list
.......
*******************************************************************************
*                                                                             *
*                        Bugcheck Analysis                                    *
*                                                                             *
*******************************************************************************

Use !analyze -v to get detailed debugging information.

BugCheck D1, {a35db800, 1c, 0, 9879c3dd}

*** ERROR: Module load completed but symbols could not be loaded for myfault.sys
Probably caused by : myfault.sys ( myfault+3dd )

Followup: MachineOwner
---------
```

The first thing to note is that WinDbg reports errors trying to load symbols for Myfault.sys and Notmyfault.exe. These are expected because the symbol files for Myfault.sys and Notmyfault.exe are not on the symbol-file path (which is configured to point at the Microsoft symbol server). You'll see similar errors for third-party drivers and executables that do not ship with the operating system.

The analysis text itself is terse, showing the numeric stop code and bug-check parameters followed by a "Probably caused by" line that shows the analysis engine's best guess at the offending driver. In this case it's on the mark and points directly at Myfault.sys, so there's no need for manual analysis.

The "Followup" line is not generally useful except within Microsoft, where the debugger looks for the module name in the Triage.ini file that's located within the Triage directory of the Debugging Tools for Windows installation directory. The Microsoft-internal version of that file lists the developer or group responsible for handling crashes in a specific driver, and the debugger displays the developer's or group's name in the Followup line when appropriate.

Verbose Analysis

Even though the basic analysis of the Notmyfault crash identifies the faulty driver, you should always have the debugger execute a verbose analysis by entering the command:

!analyze –v

The first obvious difference between the verbose and default analysis is the description of the stop code and its parameters. Following is the output of the command when executed on the same dump:

```
DRIVER_IRQL_NOT_LESS_OR_EQUAL (d1)
An attempt was made to access a pageable (or completely invalid) address at an
interrupt request level (IRQL) that is too high.  This is usually
caused by drivers using improper addresses.
If kernel debugger is available get stack backtrace.
Arguments:
Arg1: a35db800, memory referenced
Arg2: 0000001c, IRQL
Arg3: 00000000, value 0 = read operation, 1 = write operation
Arg4: 9879c3dd, address which referenced memory
```

This saves you the trouble of opening the help file to find the same information, and the text sometimes suggests troubleshooting steps, an example of which you'll see in the next section on advanced crash dump analysis.

The other potentially useful information in a verbose analysis is the stack trace of the thread that was executing on the processor that crashed at the time of the crash. Here's what it looks like for the same dump:

```
STACK_TEXT:
80395b78 9879c3dd badb0d00 8312d054 00000003 nt!KiTrap0E+0x2ac
WARNING: Stack unwind information not available. Following frames may be wrong.
80395c44 81a505e5 855802e0 849e26c0 849e2730 myfault+0x3dd
80395c64 81a50d8a 83746238 855802e0 00000000 nt!IopSynchronousServiceTail+0x1d9
80395d00 81a3aa61 83746238 849e26c0 00000000 nt!IopXxxControlFile+0x6b7
80395d34 8185ba7a 0000007c 00000000 00000000 nt!NtDeviceIoControlFile+0x2a
80395d34 770f9a94 0000007c 00000000 00000000 nt!KiFastCallEntry+0x12a
0012f4a0 77e84c9b 0000007c 00000000 00000000 ntdll!ZwDeviceIoControlFile+0xb
0012f504 004017c3 0000007c 83360018 00000000 KERNEL32!DeviceIoControl+0x100
000200ac 00000000 00000000 00000000 00000000 NotMyfault+0x17c3
```

The preceding stack shows that the Notmyfault executable image, shown at the bottom, invoked the *DeviceIoControl* function in Kernel32.dll, which in turn invoked *ZwDeviceIoControlFile* in Ntdll.dll, and so on, until finally the system crashed with the execution of an instruction in the Myfault image. A stack trace like this can be useful because crashes sometimes occur as the result of one driver passing another one that is improperly formatted or corrupt or has illegal parameters. The driver that's passed the invalid data might cause a crash and get the blame in an analysis, when the stack reveals that another driver was involved. In this sample trace, no driver other than Myfault is listed. (The module "nt" is Ntoskrnl.)

If the driver singled out by an analysis is unfamiliar to you, use the *lm* (list modules) command to look at the driver's version information. Add the *k* (kernel modules) and *v* (verbose) options along with the *m* (match) option followed by the name of the driver and a wildcard:

```
lkd> lm kv m myfault*
start    end       module name
a98e1000 a98e1ec0  myfault    (deferred)
    Image path: \??\C:\Windows\system32\drivers\myfault.sys
    Image name: myfault.sys
    Timestamp:         Sat Oct 14 16:09:18 2006 (453143EE)
    CheckSum:          0000295E
    ImageSize:         00000EC0
    File version:      2.0.0.0
    Product version:   2.0.0.0
    File flags:        0 (Mask 3F)
    File OS:           40004 NT Win32
    File type:         3.7 Driver
    File date:         00000000.00000000
    Translations:      0409.04b0
    CompanyName:       Sysinternals
    ProductName:       Sysinternals Myfault
    InternalName:      myfault.sys
    OriginalFilename:  myfault.sys
    ProductVersion:    2.0
    FileVersion:       2.0
    FileDescription:   Crash Test Driver
    LegalCopyright:    Copyright (C) M. Russinovich 2002-2004
```

In addition to using the description to identify the purpose of a driver, you can also use the file and product version numbers to see whether the version installed is the most up-to-date version available. (You can do this by checking the vendor Web site, for instance.) If version information isn't present (because it might have been paged out of physical memory at the time of the crash), look at the driver image file's properties in Windows Explorer on the system that crashed.

Using Crash Troubleshooting Tools

The crash generated in the preceding section with Notmyfault's High IRQL Fault (Kernel-mode) option poses no challenge for the debugger's automated analysis. Unfortunately, most crashes are not so easy and sometimes are impossible to debug. There are several levels of increasing severity in terms of system performance degradation that might help turn system crashes that cannot be analyzed into ones that can be. If the crashes generated after you configure a level and reboot aren't revealing the cause, try the next level.

1. If there are one or more drivers you consider likely sources of the crashes—because they were introduced into the system relatively recently, they were recently updated, or the circumstances of the crash implicate them—enable them for verification using the Driver Verifier and check all the verification options except for low resources simulation. (See Chapter 7 for more information on Driver Verifier.)

2. Enable the same level of verification as in level 1 on all unsigned drivers in the system.

3. Enable the same verification as in level 1 on all drivers in the system. To maintain reasonable performance, you may want to divide the drivers into groups, enabling the Driver Verifier on one group at a time between reboots

Obviously, before you spend time and energy making system configuration changes and analyzing crashes, you should ensure that your system's kernel and drivers are the most recent available by using the services of Windows Update and third-party driver support sites.

 Note If your system becomes unbootable because the Driver Verifier detects a driver error and crashes the system, then start in safe mode (where verification is disabled), run the Driver Verifier, and delete verification settings.

The following sections demonstrate how the Driver Verifier can make impossible-to-debug crashes into ones that you can solve.

Buffer Overrun, Memory Corruptions, and Special Pool

By far the most common source of crashes on Windows is pool corruption. Pool corruption usually occurs when a driver suffers from a buffer overrun or buffer underrun bug that causes it to overwrite data past either the end or start of a buffer it has allocated from paged or nonpaged pool. The Executive's pool-tracking structures reside on either side of a pool buffer and separate buffers from each other. These bugs, therefore, cause corruption to the pool tracking structures, to buffers owned by other drivers, or to both. You can often catch the culprit of a pool overrun by using the *!pool* command to examine the surrounding pool tags. Find the address at which the corruption occurred and use *!pool address_of_corruption*. This command will display all the pool allocations that are on the same page as the corruption. Looking in the left column, find the range of the corrupted address and then look at the allocation just previous to it and find its pool tag. This will likely be the culprit in a buffer overrun. You can use the pooltag.txt file in the Triage folder of the Debugging Tools for Windows installation directory to find the driver that owns the pool tag, or use the Strings utility from Sysinternals.

Pool corruption can also occur when a driver writes to pool it had previously owned but subsequently freed. This is called a *use after free* bug and is usually caused by a race condition in a driver. These bugs are particularly hard to debug because the driver that corrupts memory no longer has any traceable ties to the memory, such as a neighboring pool tag as in a buffer overrun. Another fairly common cause of pool corruption is *direct memory access* (DMA). DMA occurs when hardware writes directly to RAM instead of going through a driver; however, the driver is still responsible for coordinating the whole process by allocating the memory that the hardware will write to and programming the hardware registers of the device with the details of the operation. If a driver has a bug that releases the memory it is using for DMA before the hardware writes to it, the memory can be given to another driver or even to a user-mode application, which will certainly not expect to have hardware writing to it.

The crashes caused by pool corruption are virtually impossible to debug because the system crashes when corrupted data is referenced, not when the corruption occurs. However, sometimes you can take steps to at least obtain a clue about what corrupted the memory. The first step is to try to determine the size of the corruption by looking at the corrupted data. If the corruption is a single bit, it was likely caused by bad RAM. If the corruption is fairly small, it could be caused by hardware or software, and finding a root cause will be nearly impossible. In the case of large corruptions, you can look for patterns in the corruption, like strings (for example, HTTP packet payloads, file contents of text-based files, and so on) or audio/video data (usually patterns of integers less than 1,024). Open an MP3 file in a hex editor to get an idea of what audio data looks like in memory.

 Note To assist in catching pool corruptions, Windows checks the consistency of a buffer's pool-tracking structures, and those of the buffer's immediate neighbors, on every pool allocation and free operation. Thus, buffer overruns are likely to be detected shortly after the corruption and identified with a crash that has the BAD_POOL_HEADER stop code.

You can generate a pool corruption crash by running Notmyfault and selecting the Buffer Overflow bug. This causes Myfault to allocate a buffer and then overwrite the 40 bytes following the buffer. There can be a significant delay between the time you click the Do Bug button and when a crash occurs, and you might even have to generate pool usage by exercising applications before a crash occurs, which highlights the distance between a corruption and its effect on system stability. An analysis of the resultant crash almost always reports Ntoskrnl or another driver as being the likely cause, which demonstrates the usefulness of a verbose analysis with its description of the stop code:

```
DRIVER_CORRUPTED_EXPOOL (c5)
An attempt was made to access a pageable (or completely invalid) address at an
interrupt request level (IRQL) that is too high.  This is
caused by drivers that have corrupted the system pool.  Run the driver
verifier against any new (or suspect) drivers, and if that doesn't turn up
the culprit, then use gflags to enable special pool.
Arguments:
Arg1: 4f4f4f53, memory referenced
Arg2: 00000002, IRQL
Arg3: 00000001, value 0 = read operation, 1 = write operation
Arg4: 81926886, address which referenced memory
```

The advice in the description is to run the Driver Verifier against any new or suspect drivers or to use Gflags to enable special pool. Both accomplish the same thing: to have the system detect a potential corruption when it occurs and crash the system in a way that makes the automated analysis point at the driver causing the corruption.

If the Driver Verifier's special pool option is enabled, verified drivers use special pool, rather than paged or nonpaged pool, for any allocations they make for buffers slightly less than a page in size. A buffer allocated from special pool is sandwiched between two invalid pages and by default is aligned against the top of the page. The special pool routines also fill the unused portions of the page in which the buffer resides with a random pattern. Figure 14-9 depicts a special pool allocation.

The system detects any buffer overruns of under a page in size at the time of the overrun because they cause a page fault on the invalid page following the buffer. The signature serves to catch buffer underruns at the time the driver frees a buffer because the integrity of the pattern placed there at the time of allocation will have been compromised.

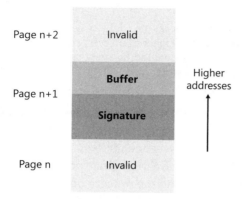

FIGURE 14-9 Special pool buffer allocation

To see how the use of special pool causes a crash that the analysis engine easily diagnoses, run the Driver Verifier Manager. Choose the Create Custom Settings (For Code Developers) option on the first page of the wizard, choose Select Individual Settings From A Full List on the second, and then select Special Pool. Choose the Select Drivers From A List option on the subsequent page, and on the page that lists drivers press the button to add unloaded drivers, and then type **myfault.sys** into the File Find dialog box. (You do not have to find myfault.sys in the File Find dialog box; just enter its name.) Then check the myfault.sys driver, exit the wizard, and reboot.

When you run Notmyfault and cause a buffer overflow, the system will immediately crash and the analysis of the dump reports this:

```
Probably caused by : myfault.sys ( myfault+3f1 )
```

A verbose analysis describes the stop code like this:

```
DRIVER_PAGE_FAULT_BEYOND_END_OF_ALLOCATION (d6)
N bytes of memory was allocated and more than N bytes are being referenced.
This cannot be protected by try-except.
When possible, the guilty driver's name (Unicode string) is printed on
the bugcheck screen and saved in KiBugCheckDriver.
Arguments:
Arg1: beb50000, memory referenced
Arg2: 00000001, value 0 = read operation, 1 = write operation
Arg3: ec3473f1, if non-zero, the address which referenced memory.
Arg4: 00000000, (reserved)
```

Special pool made an elusive bug into one that instantly reveals itself and makes the analysis trivial.

Code Overwrite and System Code Write Protection

A driver with a bug that causes corruption or misinterpretation of its own data structures can reference memory the driver doesn't own when it interprets corrupted data as a memory pointer value. The target of the pointer can be anything in the virtual address space, including data belonging to other drivers, invalid memory, or the code of other drivers or the kernel. As with buffer overruns, by the time that corruption is detected and the system crashes, it's usually impossible to identify the driver that caused the corruption. Enabling special pool increases the chance of catching wild-pointer bugs, but it does not catch code corruption.

When you run Notmyfault and select the Code Overwrite option, the Myfault driver corrupts the entry point to the *NtReadFile* kernel function. One of two things will happen at this point: if your system has 255 MB or less of physical memory, you'll get a crash for which an analysis points at Myfault.sys. The stop code description that a verbose analysis displays tells you that Myfault attempted to write to read-only memory:

```
ATTEMPTED_WRITE_TO_READONLY_MEMORY (be)
An attempt was made to write to readonly memory.  The guilty driver is on the
stack trace (and is typically the current instruction pointer).
When possible, the guilty driver's name (Unicode string) is printed on
the bugcheck screen and saved in KiBugCheckDriver.
Arguments:
Arg1: 804bb7fd, Virtual address for the attempted write.
Arg2: 004bb121, PTE contents.
Arg3: b804db60, (reserved)
Arg4: 0000000b, (reserved)
```

However, if you have more than 255 MB of memory, you'll get a different type of crash because the attempt to corrupt the memory isn't caught. Because *NtReadFile* is a commonly executed system service that is used by the Windows subsystem to read keyboard and mouse input, the system will almost immediately crash as a thread attempts to execute the corrupted code and generates an illegal instruction fault. The analysis of crashes generated with this bug is always wrong, but it might vary, with Win32k.sys and Ntoskrnl.exe commonly being the analyzer's best guess as to what's responsible. The bugcheck description for these crashes is:

```
KMODE_EXCEPTION_NOT_HANDLED (1e)
This is a very common bugcheck.  Usually the exception address pinpoints
the driver/function that caused the problem.  Always note this address
as well as the link date of the driver/image that contains this address.
Arguments:
Arg1: c0000005, The exception code that was not handled
Arg2: 80461885, The address that the exception occurred at
Arg3: 00000000, Parameter 0 of the exception
Arg4: 00000000, Parameter 1 of the exception
```

The reason for the different behaviors on different configurations relates to a mechanism called *system code write protection*. If system code write protection is enabled, the memory

manager maps Ntoskrnl.exe, the HAL, and boot drivers using standard physical pages (4 KB on x86 and x64, and 8 KB on IA64). Because the granularity of protection in an image is the standard page size, the memory manager can write-protect code pages so that an attempt to modify them generates an access fault (as seen in the first crash). However, when system code write protection is disabled on systems with more than 255 MB of RAM, the memory manager uses large pages (4 MB on x86, and 16 MB on IA64 and x86-64) to map Ntoskrnl.exe and the HAL.

If system code write protection is off and crash analysis reports unlikely causes for a crash or you suspect code corruption, you should enable it. Verifying at least one driver with the Driver Verifier is the easiest way to enable it. You can also enable it manually by adding two registry values under HKLM\SYSTEM\CurrentControlSet\Control\Session Manager\Memory Management. First, specify the amount of RAM at which the memory manager uses large pages instead of standard pages to map Ntoskrnl.exe as an effectively infinite value. You do this by creating a DWORD value called LargePageMinimum and setting it to 0xFFFFFFFF. Then add another DWORD value named EnforceWriteProtection and set it to 1. You must reboot for the changes to take effect.

Note When the debugger has access to the image files included in a crash dump, the analysis internally executes the *!chkimg* debugger command to verify that a copy of an image in a crash dump matches the on-disk image and reports any differences. Note that *chkimg* will always report discrepancies in Ntoskrnl.exe if you've enabled the Driver Verifier.

Advanced Crash Dump Analysis

The preceding section leverages the Driver Verifier to create crashes that the debugger's automated analysis engine can resolve. You might still encounter cases where you cannot get a system to produce easily analyzable crashes and, if so, you will need to execute manual analysis to try and determine what the problem is. Here are some examples of basic commands that can provide clues during crash analysis. The Debugging Tools for Windows help file provides complete documentation on these and other commands as well as examples of how to use them during crash analysis:

- Use the *!process 0 0* debugger command to look at the processes running, and make sure that you understand the purpose of each one. Try disabling or uninstalling unnecessary applications and services.

- Use the *lm* command with the *kv* option to list the loaded kernel-mode drivers. Make sure that you understand the purpose of any third-party drivers and that you have the most recent versions.

- Use the *!vm* command to see whether the system has exhausted virtual memory, paged pool, or nonpaged pool. If virtual memory is exhausted, the committed pages will be close to the commit limit, so try to identify a potential memory leak by examining the list of processes to see which one reports high commit usage. If nonpaged pool or paged pool is exhausted (that is, the usage is close to the maximum), see the "Troubleshooting a Pool Leak" experiment in Chapter 9.

There are other debugging commands that can prove useful, but more advanced knowledge is required to apply them. The *!irp* command is one of them. The next section shows the use of this command to identify a suspect driver.

Stack Trashes

Stack overrun or stack trashing typically results from a buffer overrun or underrun or when a driver passes a buffer address located on the stack to a lower driver on the device stack, which then performs the work asynchronously.

In the case of a buffer overrun or underrun, instead of residing in pool, as you saw with Notmyfault's buffer overrun bug, the target buffer is on the stack of the thread that executes the bug. This type of bug is another one that's difficult to debug because the stack is the foundation for any crash dump analysis.

In the case of passing buffers on the stack to lower drivers, if the lower driver returns to the caller immediately because it used a completion routine to perform the work, instead of returning synchronously, when the completion routine is called, it will use the stack address that was passed previously, which could now correspond to a different state on the caller's stack and result in corruption.

When you run Notmyfault and select Stack Trash, the Myfault driver overruns a buffer it allocates on the kernel stack of the thread that executes it. When Myfault tries to return control to the Ntoskrnl function that was invoked, it reads the return address, which is the address at which it should continue executing, from the stack. The address was corrupted by the stack-buffer overrun, so the thread continues execution at some different address in memory—an address that might not even contain code. An illegal exception and crash occur when the thread executes an illegal CPU instruction or it references invalid memory.

The driver that the crash dump analysis of a stack overrun points the blame at will vary from crash to crash, but the stop code will almost always be KMODE_EXCEPTION_NOT_HANDLED. If you execute a verbose analysis, the stack trace looks like this:

```
STACK_TEXT:
881fc744 81c82590 0000008e c0000005 00000000 nt!KeBugCheckEx+0x1e
881fcb14 81ca45da 881fcb30 00000000 881fcb84 nt!KiDispatchException+0x1a9
881fcb7c 81ca458e 881fcc44 00000000 badb0d00 nt!CommonDispatchException+0x4a
881fcc2c 81d07fd3 9762b658 84736e68 84736e68 nt!Kei386EoiHelper+0x186
```

```
881fcc44 81e98615 99321810 84736e68 84736ed8 nt!IofCallDriver+0x63
881fcc64 81e98dba 9762b658 99321810 00000000 nt!IopSynchronousServiceTail+0x1d9
881fcd00 81e82a8d 9762b658 84736e68 00000000 nt!IopXxxControlFile+0x6b7
881fcd34 81ca3a1a 0000007c 00000000 00000000 nt!NtDeviceIoControlFile+0x2a
881fcd34 779e9a94 0000007c 00000000 00000000 nt!KiFastCallEntry+0x12a
WARNING: Frame IP not in any known module. Following frames may be wrong.
0012f9f4 00000000 00000000 00000000 00000000 0x779e9a94
```

Notice how the call to *IofCallDriver* leads immediately to *Kei386EoiHelper* and into an exception, instead of a driver's IRP dispatch routine. This is consistent with the stack having been corrupted and the IRP dispatch routine causing an exception when attempting to return to its caller by referencing a corrupted return address. Unfortunately, mechanisms like special pool and system code write protection can't catch this type of bug. Instead, you must take some manual analysis steps to determine indirectly which driver was operating at the time of the corruption. One way is to examine the IRPs that are in progress for the thread that was executing at the time of the stack trash. When a thread issues an I/O request, the I/O manager stores a pointer to the outstanding IRP on the IRP list of the ETHREAD structure for the thread. The *!thread* debugger command dumps the IRP list of the target thread. (If you don't specify a thread object address, *!thread* dumps the processor's current thread.) Then you can look at the IRP with the *!irp* command:

```
1kd> !thread
THREAD 858d1aa0  Cid 0248.02c0  Teb: 7ffd9000 Win32Thread: ffad4e90 RUNNING on processor 0
IRP List:
    bc5a7f68: (0006,0094) Flags: 00000000  Mdl: 00000000
Not impersonating
Attached Process 84f45d90
...

1kd> !irp bc5a7f68
Irp is active with 1 stacks 1 is current (= 0x837a7ab8)
 No Mdl Thread 858d1aa0:  Irp stack trace.
    cmd  flg cl Device   File     Completion-Context
>[ e, 0]   0  0 856f6378 8504f290 00000000-00000000
        \Driver\MYFAULT Args: 00000000 00000000 83360010 00000000
```

The output shows that the IRP's current and only stack location (designated with the ">" prefix) is owned by the Myfault driver. If this were a real crash, the next steps would be to ensure that the driver version installed is the most recent available, install the new version if it isn't, and if it is, to enable the Driver Verifier on the driver (with all settings except low memory simulation).

Manually analyzing the stack is often the most powerful technique when dealing with crashes such as these. Typically, this involves dumping the current *stack pointer* register (for example, esp and rsp on 32-bit and x64 respectively). However, because the code responsible for crashing the system itself might modify the stack in ways that make analysis difficult, the processor responsible for crashing the system provides a backing store for the current data in the stack, called KiPreBugcheckStackSaveArea, which contains a copy of the stack before

any code in *KeBugCheckEx* executes. By using the *dps* (dump pointer with symbols) command in the debugger, you can dump this area (instead of the CPU's stack pointer register) and resolve symbols in an attempt to discover any potential stack traces. In this crash, here's what dumping the stack area eventually revealed on a 32-bit system.

```
kd> dps KiPreBugcheckStackSaveArea KiPreBugcheckStackSaveArea+3000
81d7dd20  881fcc44
81d7dd24  98fcf406 myfault+0x406
81d7dd28  badb0d00
```

Although this data was located among many other different functions, it is of special interest because it mentions a function in the Myfault driver, which as we've seen was currently executing an IRP, that doesn't show on the stack. For more information on manual stack analysis, see the Debugging Tools for Windows help file and the additional resources referenced later in this chapter.

Hung or Unresponsive Systems

If a system becomes unresponsive (that is, you are receiving no response to keyboard or mouse input), the mouse freezes, or you can move the mouse but the system doesn't respond to clicks, the system is said to have *hung*. A number of things can cause the system to hang:

- A device driver does not return from its interrupt service (ISR) routine or deferred procedure call (DPC) routine

- A high priority real-time thread preempts the windowing system driver's input threads

- A deadlock (when two threads or processors hold resources each other wants and neither will yield what they have) occurs in kernel mode

You can check for deadlocks by using the Driver Verifier option called *deadlock detection*. Deadlock detection monitors the use of spinlocks, fast mutexes, and mutexes, looking for patterns that could result in a deadlock. (For more information on these and other synchronization primitives, see Chapter 3.) If one is found, the Driver Verifier crashes the system with an indication of which driver causes the deadlock. The simplest form of deadlock occurs when two threads hold resources each other thread wants and neither will yield what they have or give up waiting for the one they want. The first step to troubleshooting hung systems is therefore to enable deadlock detection on suspect drivers, then unsigned drivers, and then all drivers, until you get a crash that pinpoints the driver causing the deadlock.

There are two ways to approach a hanging system so that you can apply the manual crash troubleshooting techniques described in this chapter to determine what driver or component is causing the hang: the first is to crash the hung system and hope that you get a dump that you can analyze, and the second is to break into the system with a kernel debugger and analyze the system's activity. Both approaches require prior setup and a reboot. You use the

same exploration of system state with both approaches to try and determine the cause of the hang.

To manually crash a hung system, you must first add the DWORD registry value HKLM\ SYSTEM\CurrentControlSet\Services\i8042prt\Parameters\CrashOnCtrlScroll and set it to 1. After rebooting, the i8042 port driver, which is the port driver for PS2 keyboard input, moni- tors keystrokes in its ISR (discussed further in Chapter 3) looking for two presses of the scroll lock key while the right control key is depressed. When the driver sees that sequence, it calls *KeBugCheckEx* with the MANUALLY_INITIATED_CRASH (0xE2) stop code that indicates a manually initiated crash. When the system reboots, open the crash dump file and apply the techniques mentioned earlier to try and determine why the system was hung (for example, determining what thread was running when the system hung, what the kernel stack indicates was happening, and so on). Note that this works for most hung system scenarios, but it won't work if the i8042 port driver's ISR doesn't execute. (The i8042 port driver's ISR won't execute if all processors are hung as a result of their IRQL being higher than the ISR's IRQL, or if cor- ruption of system data structures extends to interrupt-related code or data.)

 Note Manually crashing a hung system by using the support provided in the i8042 port driver does not work with USB keyboards. It works with PS2 keyboards only.

You can also trigger a crash if your hardware has a built-in "crash" button. (Some high-end servers have this.) In this case, the crash is initiated by signaling the nonmaskable inter- rupt (NMI) pin of the system's motherboard. To enable this, set the registry DWORD value HKLM\SYSTEM\CurrentControlSet\Control\CrashControl\NMICrashDump to 1. Then, when you press the dump switch, an NMI is delivered to the system and the kernel's NMI interrupt handler calls *KeBugCheckEx*. This works in more cases than the i8042 port driver mecha- nism because the NMI IRQL is always higher than that of the i8042 port driver interrupt. See *www.microsoft.com/whdc/system/sysinternals/dmpsw.mspx* for more information.

If you are unable to manually generate a crash dump, you can attempt to break into the hung system by first making the system boot into debugging mode. You do this in one of two ways. You can press the F8 key during the boot and select Debugging Mode, or you can create a debugging-mode boot option in the BCD by copying an existing boot entry and adding the *debug* option. When using the F8 approach, the system will use the default connection (Serial Port COM2 and 19200 Baud), but you can use the F10 key to display the Edit Boot Options screen to edit debug-related boot options. With the *debug* option, you must also configure the connection mechanism to be used between the host system running the kernel debugger and the target system booting in debugging mode and then config- ure the *debugport* and *baudrate* switches appropriately for the connection type. The three connection types are a null modem cable using a serial port, an IEEE 1394 (FireWire) cable using 1394 ports on each system, or a USB 2.0 host-to-host cable using USB ports on each

system. For details on configuring the host and target system for kernel debugging, see the Debugging Tools for Windows help file.

When booting in debugging mode, the system loads the kernel debugger at boot time and makes it ready for a connection from a kernel debugger running on a different computer connected through a serial cable, IEEE 1394 cable, or USB 2.0 host-to-host cable. Note that the kernel debugger's presence does not affect performance. When the system hangs, run the WinDbg or Kd debugger on the connected system, establish a kernel debugging connection, and break into the hung system. This approach will not work if interrupts are disabled or the kernel debugger has become corrupted.

> **Note** Booting a system in debugging mode does not affect performance if it's not connected to another system; however, a system that's configured to automatically reboot after a crash will not do so if it's booted with kernel debugging enabled, because the kernel debugger waits for a connection from another system after a crash.

Instead of leaving the system in its halted state while you perform analysis, you can also use the debugger .*dump* command to create a crash dump file on the host debugger machine. Then you can reboot the hung system and analyze the crash dump offline (or submit it to Microsoft). Note that this can take a long time if you are connected using a serial null modem cable or USB 2.0 connection (versus a higher speed 1394 connection), so you might want to just capture a minidump using the .*dump /m* command. Alternatively, if the target machine is capable of writing a crash dump, you can force it to do so by issuing the .*crash* command from the debugger. This will cause the target machine to create a dump on its local hard drive that you can examine after the system reboots.

You can cause a hang by running Notmyfault and selecting the Hang option. This causes the Myfault driver to queue a DPC on each processor of the system that executes an infinite loop. Because the IRQL of the processor while executing DPC functions is DPC/dispatch level, the keyboard ISR will respond to the special keyboard crashing sequence.

Once you've broken into a hung system or loaded a manually generated dump from a hung system into a debugger, you should execute the !*analyze* command with the –*hang* option. This causes the debugger to examine the locks on the system and try to determine whether there's a deadlock, and if so, what driver or drivers are involved. However, for a hang like the one that Notmyfault's Hang option generates, the !*analyze* analysis command will report nothing useful.

If the !*analyze* command doesn't pinpoint the problem, execute !*thread* and !*process* in each of the dump's CPU contexts to see what each processor is doing. (Switch CPU contexts with the ~ command—for example, use ~*1* to switch to processor 1's context.) If a thread has hung the system by executing in an infinite loop at an IRQL of DPC/dispatch level or higher, you'll see the driver module in which it has become stuck in the stack trace of the !*thread*

command. The stack trace of the crash dump you get when you crash a system experiencing the Notmyfault hang bug looks like this:

```
STACK_TEXT:
f9e66ed8 f9b0d681 000000e2 00000000 00000000 nt!KeBugCheckEx+0x19
f9e66ef4 f9b0cefb 0069b0d8 010000c6 00000000 i8042prt!I8xProcessCrashDump+0x235
f9e66f3c 804ebb04 81797d98 8169b020 00010009 i8042prt!I8042KeyboardInterruptService+0x21c
f9e66f3c fa12e34a 81797d98 8169b020 00010009 nt!KiInterruptDispatch+0x3d
WARNING: Stack unwind information not available. Following frames may be wrong.
ffdff980 8169b288 f9e67000 0000210f 00000004 myfault+0x34a
8054ace4 ffdff980 804ebf58 00000000 0000319c 0x8169b288
8054ace4 ffdff980 804ebf58 00000000 0000319c 0xffdff980
8169ae9c 8054ace4 f9b12b0f 8169ac88 00000000 0xffdff980
...
```

The top few lines of the stack trace reference the routines that execute when you type the i8042 port driver's crash key sequence. The presence of the Myfault driver indicates that it might be responsible for the hang. Another command that might be revealing is *!locks*, which dumps the status of all executive resource locks. By default, the command lists only resources that are under *contention*, which means that they are both owned and have at least one thread waiting to acquire them. Examine the thread stacks of the owners with the *!thread* command to see what driver they might be executing in. Sometimes you will find that the owner of one of the locks is waiting for an IRP to complete (a list of IRPs related to a thread is displayed in the *!thread* output). In these cases it is very hard to tell why an IRP is not making forward progress. (IRPs are usually queued to privately managed driver queues before they are completed). One thing you can do is examine the IRP with the *!irp* command and find the driver that pended the IRP (it will have the word "pending" displayed in its stack location from the *!irp* output). Once you have the driver name, you can use the *!stacks* command to look for other threads that the driver might be running on, which often provides clues about what the lock-owning driver is doing. Much of the time you will find the driver is deadlocked or waiting on some other resource that is blocked waiting for the driver.

When There Is No Crash Dump

In this section, we'll address how to troubleshoot systems that for some reason are not recording a crash dump. One reason why a crash dump might not be recorded is if the paging file on the boot volume is too small to hold the dump. This can easily be remedied by increasing the size of the paging file. A second reason why there might not be a crash dump recorded is because the kernel code and data structures needed to write the crash dump have been corrupted at the time of the crash. As described earlier, this data is checksummed when the system boots, and if the checksum made at the time of the crash does not match, the system does not even attempt to save the crash dump (so as not to risk corrupting data on the disk). So in this case, you need to catch the system as it crashes and then try to determine the reason for the crash.

Another reason occurs when the disk subsystem for the system disk is not able to process disk write requests (a condition that might have triggered the system failure itself). One such condition would be a hardware failure in the disk controller or maybe a cabling issue near the hard disk.

Yet another possibility occurs when the system has drivers that have registered to add secondary dump data to the dump file. When the driver callbacks are called, they might incorrectly access data structures located in paged memory (for example), which will lead to a second crash.

One simple option is to turn off the Automatically Restart option in the Startup And Recovery settings so that if the system crashes, you can examine the blue screen on the console. However, only the most straightforward crashes can be solved from just the blue-screen text.

To perform more in-depth analysis, you need to use the kernel debugger to look at the system at the time of the crash. This can be done by booting the system in debugging mode, which is described in the previous section. When a system is booted in debugging mode and crashes, instead of painting the blue screen and attempting to record the dump, it will wait forever until a host kernel debugger is connected. In this way, you can see the reason for the crash and perhaps perform some basic analysis using the kernel debugger commands described earlier. As mentioned in the previous section, you can use the *.dump* command in the debugger to save a copy of the crashed system's memory space for later debugging, thus allowing you to reboot the crashed system and debug the problem offline.

The operating system code and data structures that handle processor exceptions can become corrupted such that a series of recursive faults occur. One example of this would be if the operating system trap handler got corrupted and caused a page fault. This would invoke the page fault handler, which would fault again, and so on. If such a situation occurred, the system would be hopelessly stuck. To prevent such a situation from occurring, CPUs have a built-in recursive fault protection mechanism, which sets a hard limit on the depth of a recursive fault. On most x86 processors, a fault can nest to two levels deep. When the third recursive fault occurs, the processor resets itself and the machine reboots. This is called a *triple fault*. This can happen when there's a faulty hardware component as well. Even a kernel debugger won't be invoked in a triple fault situation. However, sometimes the mere fact that the kernel debugger doesn't activate can confirm that there's a problem with newly added hardware or drivers.

Note You can use the kernel debugger to trigger a triple fault on a machine by setting a breakpoint on the kernel debugger dispatch routine *KiDispatchException*. This happens because the exception dispatcher now causes a breakpoint exception, which invokes the exception dispatcher, and so on.

EXPERIMENT: The Blue Screen Screen Saver

A great way to remind yourself of what a blue screen looks like or to fool your office workers and friends is to run the Sysinternals Blue Screen screen saver from Sysinternals. The screen saver simulates authentic looking blue screens that reflect the version of Windows on which you run it, generating all blue screen text using actual system information such as the list of loaded drivers. It also mimics an automatic-reboot, complete with the Windows startup splash screen. Note that unlike other screen savers, where a mouse movement dismisses them, the Blue Screen screen saver requires a key press.

Using the following syntax for the Psexec tool from Sysinternals, you can even run the screen saver on another system:

```
psexec \\computername -i -d "c:\sysinternalsbluescreen.scr" -s
```

The command requires that you have administrative privilege on the remote system. (You can use the −u and −p Psexec switches to specify alternate credentials.) Make sure that your coworker has a sense of humor!

Conclusion

Although many crashes can be analyzed with some of the techniques described in this chapter, many require analysis that goes beyond the scope of this book. Here are some additional resources that may be useful if you want to learn more advanced crash analysis techniques and information:

- The Microsoft Platforms Global Escalation Services team blog at *http://blogs.msdn.com/ntdebugging* provides various tips and tricks and real-life scenarios encountered by the team.

- The Web site *www.dumpanalysis.org* provides hundreds of patterns and advanced analysis scenarios and hints.

Glossary

access control list (ACL) The part of a security descriptor that enumerates who has what access to an object. The owner of an object can change the object's ACL to allow or disallow others access to the object. An ACL is made up of an ACL header and zero or more access control entry (ACE) structures. An ACL with zero ACEs is called a null ACL and indicates that no user has access to the object.

access token A data structure that contains the security identification of a process or a thread, which includes its security ID (SID), the list of groups that the user is a member of, User Access Control (UAC) virtualization state, and the list of privileges that are enabled and disabled. Each process has a primary access token that it inherits by default from its creating process.

add-device routine A routine implemented by drivers that supports Plug and Play. The Plug and Play manager sends a driver notification via this routine whenever a device for which the driver is responsible is detected. In this routine, a driver typically allocates a device object to represent the device.

Address Windowing Extensions (AWE) A mechanism in Windows that allows a 32-bit application to allocate up to 64 GB of physical memory and then map views, or windows, into its 2-GB virtual address space. Using AWE puts the burden of managing mappings of virtual-to-physical memory on the programmer but solves the immediate need of being able to directly access more physical memory than can be mapped at any one time in a 32-bit process address space.

advanced local procedure call (ALPC) An interprocess communication facility for high-speed message passing (not available through the Windows API but rather through an internal mechanism available only to Windows operating system components). ALPCs are typically used between a server process and one or more client processes of that server. An ALPC connection can be established between two user-mode processes or between a kernel-mode component and a user-mode process.

affinity mask A bitmask that specifies the processors on which the thread is allowed to run. The initial thread affinity mask is inherited from the process affinity mask.

aging A process performed on a page that increments a count indicating that the page hasn't been referenced since the last working set trim scan. On a single-processor system, the working set manager tries to remove pages that haven't been accessed recently. It does this by first clearing the accessed bit in the hardware page table entry (PTE) and then later checking the bit to see whether the page has been accessed. If the bit remains clear, the page wasn't accessed between scans and is aged. Later, the age of pages is used to locate candidate pages to remove from the working set.

alertable wait state A thread state that the thread enters either by waiting on an object handle and specifying that its wait is alertable (with the Windows *WaitForMultipleObjectsEx* function) or by testing directly whether it has a pending APC (using *SleepEx*). In both cases, if a user-mode APC is pending, the kernel interrupts

(alerts) the thread, transfers control to the APC routine, and resumes the thread's execution when the APC routine completes. User-mode APCs are delivered to a thread only when it's in an alertable wait state.

allocation granularity The granularity with which virtual memory is allocated. Windows aligns each region of reserved process address space to begin on an integral boundary defined by the system allocation granularity value, which can be retrieved from the Windows *GetSystemInfo* or *GetNativeSystemInfo* function. Currently, this value is 64 KB. This size was chosen so that if support were added for future processors with large page sizes (for example, up to 64 KB), the risk of requiring changes to applications that made assumptions about allocation alignment would be reduced. (Windows kernel-mode code isn't subject to the same restrictions; it can reserve memory on a single-page granularity.)

altitudes A way for different vendors to register a "height" on the registry filtering stack so that the order in which the system calls each callback routine can be deterministic and correct. This avoids a scenario in which an antivirus product would be scanning encrypted keys before an encryption product would run its own callback to decrypt them.

APC queue A queue in which asynchronous procedure calls (APCs) waiting to execute reside. The APC queues (one for user mode and one for kernel mode) are thread-specific—each thread has its own APC queues (unlike the DPC queue, which is processor-wide).

asymmetric multiprocessing (ASMP) A system of processing on a multiprocessor system that typically selects one processor to execute operating system code while other processors run only user code.

asynchronous I/O An I/O model that allows an application to issue an I/O request and then continue executing while the request is completed. This type of I/O can improve an application's throughput because it allows the application to continue with other work while an I/O operation is in progress.

asynchronous procedure call (APC) A function that provides a way for user programs and system code to execute code in the context of a particular user thread (and hence a particular process address space). An APC can be either kernel mode or user mode. (Kernel-mode APCs don't require "permission" from a target thread to run in that thread's context, as user-mode APCs do.)

asynchronous read-ahead with history A method in which the cache manager maintains a history of the last two read requests in the private cache map for the file handle being accessed.

atomic transaction A technique for handling modifications to a database so that system failures don't affect the correctness or integrity of the database. The basic tenet of atomic transactions is that some database operations, called transactions, are all-or-nothing propositions. The separate disk updates that make up the transaction must be executed atomically; that is, once the transaction begins to execute, all its disk updates must be completed. If a system failure interrupts the transaction, the part that has been completed must be undone, or rolled back. The rollback operation returns the database to a previously known and consistent state, as if the transaction had never occurred. *See also* transaction.

attribute list A special kind of file attribute in an NTFS file header that contains additional attributes. The attribute list is created if a particular file has too many attributes

to fit in the master file table (MFT) record. The attribute list attribute contains the name and type code of each of the file's attributes and the file reference of the MFT record where the attribute is located.

authentication packages Dynamic-link libraries (DLLs) that run in the context of the LSASS process and that implement Windows authentication policy. An authentication DLL is responsible for checking whether a given user name and password match, and if so, returning to LSASS information detailing the user's security identity. Windows authentication packages include Kerberos and MSV1_0.

automatic working set trimming When physical memory runs low, the working set manager, a routine that runs in the context of the balance set manager system thread, initiates automatic working set trimming to increase the amount of free memory available in the system.

bad-cluster file A system file (file name $Bad-Clus) that records any bad spots on the disk volume.

bad-cluster remapping A process in which NTFS dynamically retrieves good data from a cluster with a bad sector, allocates a new cluster, and copies the data to the new cluster.

balance set manager A system thread that wakes up once per second to check and possibly initiate various scheduling and memory management–related events.

basic disk A disk that relies on the MBR-style or GPT partitioning scheme. *See also* dynamic disk.

BitLocker Drive Encryption A full-volume encryption feature that helps prevent unauthorized access to data on lost or stolen computers by combining two major data-protection procedures: encrypting the entire Windows operating system volume

on the hard disk and verifying the integrity of early boot components and boot configuration data.

bitmap file A system file (file name $BitMap) in which NTFS records the allocation state of the volume. The data attribute for the bitmap file contains a bitmap, each of whose bits represents a cluster on the volume, identifying whether the cluster is free or has been allocated to a file.

boot code Instructions executed when a system is booted.

boot device drivers Device drivers necessary to boot the system.

boot file A system file (file name $Boot) that stores the Windows bootstrap code.

boot sector The first sector of the partition marked as active and from which the MBR boots. The boot sector contains information identifying the partition's file system format and structure.

boot volume The volume that corresponds to the partition on which the system directory (usually \Windows) of the installation being booted is located. The boot volume can be, but does not have to be, the same as the system volume.

bus driver Driver that services a bus controller, adapter, bridge, or any device that has child devices. Bus drivers are required drivers, and Microsoft generally provides them; each type of bus (such as PCI, PCMCIA, and USB) on a system has one bus driver.

cache manager The component of the Windows executive that provides system-wide caching services for NTFS and other file system drivers, including network file system drivers (servers and redirectors).

change journal An internal file where an NTFS file system can record information that allows applications to efficiently monitor file and directory changes. A change

journal is usually large enough to virtually guarantee that applications get a chance to process changes without missing any.

checked build A special debug version of Windows that is available only as part of the MSDN Professional (or Universal) subscription. The checked build is created by compiling the Windows sources with the compile-time flag "DBG" defined.

checkpoint record A record that helps NTFS determine what processing would be needed to recover a volume if a crash were to occur immediately. This record also includes redo and undo information.

class driver A type of kernel-mode device driver that implements the I/O processing for a particular class of devices, such as disk, tape, or CD-ROM.

clock algorithm A working set page replacement policy implemented on uniprocessor systems, similar to a least recently used policy (as implemented in most versions of UNIX).

clock interrupt handler A system routine that updates the system time and then decrements a counter that tracks how long the current thread has run.

cluster factor The cluster size on a volume, which is established when a user formats the volume with either the *format* command or the Disk Management Microsoft Management Console (MMC) snap-in.

clustering A method by which the memory manager resolves a page fault by reading into memory several pages near the page explicitly accessed.

clusters Same-size allocation units into which a volume is divided. Each cluster must be uniquely numbered using 16 bits.

code integrity A mechanism that authenticates the integrity and source of executable images (such as applications, DLLs, or drivers) by validating a digital certificate contained within the image's resources. This mechanism works in conjunction with system policies, defining how signing should be enforced.

collided page fault A fault that occurs when another thread or process faults a page that is currently being in-paged.

commitment The process by which the memory manager keeps track of private committed memory usage on a global basis.

common model A set of classes in the Common Information Model (CIM) that represent objects that are specific to management areas of a system but independent of a particular implementation. These classes are considered an extension of the CIM core model. *See also* core model.

complete memory dump A memory dump that contains all of physical memory at the time of the crash. This type of dump requires that a page file be at least the size of physical memory plus 1 MB for the header. Because it can require an inordinately large page file on large memory systems, this type of dump file is the least common.

completion port A mechanism to deliver I/O completion notification to threads. Once a file is associated with a completion port, any asynchronous I/O operations that complete on the file result in a completion packet being queued to the completion port. A thread can wait for any outstanding I/Os to complete on multiple files simply by waiting for a completion packet to be queued to the completion port. With completion ports, concurrency, or the number of threads that an application has actively servicing client requests, is controlled with the aid of the system.

configuration manager A major component of the executive that's responsible for implementing and managing the system registry.

container object A namespace object that can hold other objects, including other container objects. Examples of containers are directories in the file system namespace and keys in the registry namespace.

context switch The procedure of saving the volatile machine state associated with a running thread, loading another thread's volatile state, and starting the new thread's execution.

control objects A set of kernel objects that establishes semantics for controlling various operating system functions. This set includes the kernel process object, the asynchronous procedure call (APC) object, the deferred procedure call (DPC) object, and several objects the I/O system uses, such as the interrupt object.

core model A set of classes in the Common Information Model (CIM) provided as part of the WBEM standard. These classes are CIM's basic language and represent objects that apply to all areas of management. *See also* common model.

crash dump A record of system memory at the time of a crash that can help you figure out which component caused the crash.

credential provider Credential providers are COM objects located inside DLLs. The default providers are %SystemRoot%\ System32\authui.dll and %Systemroot%\ System32\SmartcardCredentialProvider.dll, which support both password and smartcard PIN authentication. Windows allows other credential providers to be installed, enabling it to use different user-identification mechanisms.

critical sections Sections of code that access a nonshareable resource. To ensure correct code, only one thread at a time can execute in a critical section.

deadlock detection A Driver Verifier option that monitors the use of spinlocks, fast mutexes, and mutexes, looking for patterns that could result in deadlock.

deferred procedure call (DPC) A routine that performs most of the work involved in handling a device interrupt after the interrupt service routine (ISR) executes. The DPC routine executes at an interrupt request level (IRQL) that is lower than that of the ISR to avoid blocking other interrupts unnecessarily. A DPC routine initiates I/O completion and starts the next queued I/O operation on a device.

deferred procedure call (DPC) object A kernel control object that describes a request to defer interrupt processing to DPC/dispatch level. (See interrupt request levels [IRQLS].) This object isn't visible to user-mode programs but is visible to device drivers and other system code. The most important piece of information the DPC object contains is the address of the system function that the kernel will call when it processes the DPC interrupt.

Deferred Ready A state used for threads that have been selected to run on a specific processor but have not yet been scheduled. This state exists so that the kernel can minimize the amount of time the systemwide lock on the scheduling database is held.

demand-paging policies A fetch policy that loads a page into physical memory only when a page fault occurs. In a demand-paging system, a process incurs many page faults when its threads first begin executing because the threads reference the initial set of pages they need to get going. Once this set of pages is loaded into memory, the paging activity of the process decreases.

desired access rights The accesses desired by a process opening an object.

device drivers Loadable kernel-mode modules (typically ending in .sys) that interface between the I/O system and the relevant hardware. Device drivers on Windows don't manipulate hardware devices directly, but rather they call parts of the hardware application layer (HAL) to interface with the hardware.

device ID A device identifier reported to the Plug and Play manager. The identifiers are bus-specific; for a USB bus, an identifier consists of a vendor ID (VID) for the hardware vendor that made the device and a product ID (PID) that the vendor assigned to the device.

device instance ID (DIID) An identifier consisting of a device ID and an instance ID that the Plug and Play manager uses to locate the device's key in the enumeration branch of the registry (HKLM\SYSTEM\CurrentControlSet\Enum).

device object A data structure that represents a physical or logical device on the system and describes its characteristics, such as the alignment it requires for buffers and the location of its device queue to hold incoming I/O request packets.

device-specific module (DSM) Built-in or third-party drivers used to manage details of the path management, such as load balancing policies that choose which path to use for routing requests and error detection mechanisms to inform Windows when a path fails.

device tree An internal tree the Plug and Play manager creates that represents the relationships between devices. Nodes in the tree are called devnodes. *See also* devnode.

devnode A node in a device tree. A devnode contains information about the device

objects that represent the device as well as other Plug and Play–related information the Plug and Play manager stores. *See also* device tree.

direct memory access (DMA) A third interface provided by the cache manager to cached data. The DMA functions are used to read from or write to cache pages without intervening buffers, such as when a network file system is doing a transfer over the network.

dirty page threshold The number of pages that the system cache will allow to be dirty before throttling cached writers. The value is computed at system initialization time and depends on the product type (client or server).

discretionary access control Allows the owner of a resource to determine who can access the resource and what they can do with it. The owner grants rights that permit various kinds of access to a user or to a group.

disk group The name of a computer concatenated with Dg0 (for example, Daryl-Dg0 if the computer's name is Daryl).

dispatch code Instructions of assembly language code stored in an interrupt object when it is initialized. When an interrupt occurs, this code is executed.

dispatch routines The main functions that a device driver provides. Some examples of dispatch routines are open, close, read, and write, and any other capabilities the device, file system, or network supports. When called on to perform an I/O operation, the I/O manager generates an IRP and calls a driver through one of the driver's dispatch routines.

dispatcher A set of routines in the kernel that implement Windows scheduling. Windows doesn't have a single "scheduler" module or routine—the code is spread throughout

the kernel in which scheduling-related events occur.

dispatcher database A set of data structures the kernel maintains to make thread-scheduling decisions. The dispatcher database keeps track of which threads are waiting to execute and which processors are executing which threads. *See also* dispatcher ready queue.

dispatcher header A data structure that contains the object type, the signaled state, and a list of the threads waiting on that object.

dispatcher objects A set of kernel objects that incorporate synchronization capabilities and alter or affect thread scheduling. The dispatcher objects include the kernel thread, mutex (called mutant internally), event, kernel event pair, semaphore, timer, and waitable timer.

dispatcher ready queue The most important structure in the dispatcher database (located at *DispatcherReadyListHead*). The dispatcher ready queue is really a series of queues, one queue for each scheduling priority. The queues contain threads that are in the ready state, waiting to be scheduled for execution.

display driver Driver that translates device-independent graphics requests into device-specific requests. The device-specific requests are then paired with a kernel-mode video miniport driver to complete video display support. A display driver is responsible for implementing drawing operations, either by writing directly to the frame buffer or by communicating with the graphics accelerator chip on the controller.

driver object Data structure that represents an individual driver in the system and records for the I/O manager the address of each of the driver's dispatch routines (entry points).

Driver Verifier A mechanism that can be used to help find and isolate commonly found bugs in device drivers or other kernel-mode system code. Microsoft uses Driver Verifier to check its own device drivers as well as all device drivers that vendors submit for Hardware Compatibility List (HCL) testing.

dynamic disk A disk that supports multipartition volumes, providing a more flexible partitioning scheme than that of a basic disk. *See also* basic disk.

dynamic-link library (DLL) A set of callable subroutines linked as a binary image that can be dynamically loaded by applications that use them.

environment subsystems User processes and DLLs that expose the native operating system services to user applications, thus providing an operating system environment, or personality. Windows Vista Ultimate and Enterprise include support for an enhanced POSIX subsystem called Subsystem for Unix-based Applications.

event An object with a persistent state (signaled or not signaled) that can be used for synchronization; also, a system occurrence that triggers an action.

exception A synchronous condition that results from the execution of a particular instruction. Running a single program with the same data under the same conditions can reproduce exceptions.

exception dispatcher A kernel module that services all exceptions, except those simple enough to be resolved by the trap handler. The exception dispatcher's job is to find an exception handler that can "dispose of" the exception.

executive The upper layer of Ntoskrnl.exe. (The kernel is the lower layer.) The executive contains the base operating system services, such as the process and thread manager, the memory manager, the security reference monitor, the I/O system, and the cache manager. *See also* kernel.

executive objects Objects implemented by various components of the executive (such as the process manager, memory manager, I/O subsystem, and so on). The executive objects and object services are primitives that the environment subsystems use to construct their own versions of objects and other resources. Because executive objects are typically created either by an environment subsystem on behalf of a user application or by various components of the operating system as part of their normal operation, many of them contain (encapsulate) one or more kernel objects. *See also* kernel objects.

executive resources Resources that provide exclusive access (such as a mutex) as well as shared read access (multiple readers sharing read-only access to a structure). Because executive resources are available only to kernel-mode code, they aren't accessible from the Windows API.

extended partition A special partition type that contains a master boot record (MBR) with its own partition table. By using extended partitions, Microsoft's operating systems overcome the apparent limit of four partitions per disk. In general, the recursion that extended partitions permit can continue indefinitely, which means that no upper limit exists to the number of possible partitions on a disk. *See also* partition.

fast I/O A means of reading or writing a cached file without going through the work of generating an I/O request packet (IRP).

fast LPC A special interprocess communication facility used to send messages between threads.

file mapping objects Windows API underlying primitives in the memory manager that are used to implement shared memory (called section objects internally). *See also* section object.

file reference A 64-bit value that identifies a file on an NTFS volume. The file reference consists of a file number and a sequence number. The file number corresponds to the position of the file's file record in the master file table minus 1 (or to the position of the base file record minus 1 if the file has more than one file record).

file system driver (FSD) A type of kernel-mode device driver that accepts I/O requests to files and satisfies the requests by issuing its own, more explicit, requests to physical device drivers. *See also* local file system driver (FSD), network file system driver (FSD).

file system filter driver A type of kernel-mode device driver that intercepts I/O requests, performs additional processing, and passes them on to lower-level drivers.

file system format Defines the way that file data is stored on storage media and impacts a file system's features. For example, a format that doesn't allow user permissions to be associated with files and directories can't support security. A file system format can also impose limits on the sizes of files and storage devices that the file system supports.

filter device object (FiDO) A device object that can be part of a devnode. One or more optional FiDOs can layer either between the physical device object (PDO) and the functional device object (FDO) or above the FDO. *See also* devnode, functional

device object (FDO), physical device object (PDO).

filter driver *See* file system filter driver.

frame-based exception handlers The mechanism that permits each stack frame in a call stack to have its own exception handler declared.

foreground application The process that owns the thread that owns the window that's in focus.

free build The version of the Windows system that can be purchased as a retail product. It is built with full compiler optimizations turned on and has internal symbol table information stripped out from the images. *See also* checked build.

function driver The main device driver that provides the operational interface for its device. It is a required driver unless the device is used raw (an implementation in which I/O is done by the bus driver and any bus filter drivers, such as SCSI PassThru). A function driver is the driver that knows the most about a particular device and is usually the only driver that accesses device-specific registers.

functional device object (FDO) A device object that is a required part of a devnode. The function driver that the Plug and Play manager loads to manage a detected device creates the FDO. An FDO represents the logical interface to a device. *See also* devnode, filter device object (FiDO), physical device object (PDO).

granted access rights The accesses granted to a thread by the security reference monitor as the result of a successful object open.

handle An object identifier. A process receives a handle to an object when it creates or opens an object by name. Referring to an object by its handle is faster than using its name because the object manager can skip the name lookup and find the object directly.

handle table A table that contains pointers to all the objects that the process has opened a handle to. Handle tables are implemented as a three-level scheme, similar to the way that the x86 memory management unit implements virtual-to-physical address translation.

hardware abstraction layer (HAL) A loadable kernel-mode module (Hal.dll) that provides the low-level interface to the hardware platform on which Windows is running. The HAL hides hardware-dependent details such as I/O interfaces, interrupt controllers, and multiprocessor communication mechanisms—any functions that are architecture-specific and machine-dependent.

hardware device drivers Device drivers that manipulate hardware to write output to or retrieve input from a physical device or network. There are many types of hardware device drivers, such as bus drivers, human interface drivers, mass storage drivers, and so on.

hash A statistically unique value that is generated from a block of data (for example, a file) using cryptographic algorithms. Because different data results in different hashes, hashes can be used to detect changes to data from corruption or tampering. The Windows driver signing facility uses hashes.

heap A region of one or more pages that can be subdivided and allocated in smaller chunks by a set of functions provided by the heap manager.

heap manager A component that manages allocations inside larger memory areas reserved using the page granularity memory allocation functions. The

allocation granularity in the heap manager is relatively small: 8 bytes on 32-bit systems and 16 bytes on 64-bit systems. The heap manager has been designed to optimize memory usage and performance in the case of these smaller allocations. The heap manager functions exist in two places: Ntdll.dll and Ntoskrnl.exe. The subsystem APIs (such as the Windows heap APIs) use the copy in Ntdll, and various executive components and device drivers use the copy in Ntoskrnl.

hive One of a number of files stored on disk that contain registry information. Each hive contains a registry tree, which has a key that serves as the root or starting point of the tree.

hyperspace A special region used to map the process working set list, invalidating page table entries in other page tables (such as when a page is removed from the standby list), and on process creation setting up a new process's address space.

hypervisor A thin piece of low-level system software that uses strictly hardware-assisted virtualization support. A hypervisor handles notifications as well as the various configuration steps required for allowing guest operating systems to run concurrently.

I/O completion routine A routine implemented by a layered driver that will notify the driver when a lower-level driver finishes processing an I/O request packet (IRP). For example, the I/O manager calls a file system driver's I/O completion routine after a device driver finishes transferring data to or from a file. The completion routine notifies the file system driver about the operation's success, failure, or cancellation, and it allows the file system driver to perform cleanup operations.

I/O request packet (IRP) A data structure that controls how the I/O operation is processed at each stage. Most I/O requests are represented by an IRP, which travels from one I/O system component to another.

I/O subsystem API The internal executive system services (such as *NtReadFile* and *NtWriteFile*) that subsystem DLLs call to implement a subsystem's documented I/O functions.

I/O system The Windows executive component that accepts I/O requests (from both user-mode and kernel-mode callers) and delivers them, in a different form, to I/O devices.

ideal processor The preferred processor that a particular thread should run on.

idle summary A bitmask (*KiIdleSummary*) in which each set bit represents an idle processor.

image loader A component that performs initialization work for applications outside the kernel, preparing context and the environment. Some of the main tasks of the image loader include initializing the user-mode state for an application, parsing the import table of the application to look for required DLLs, loading and unloading DLLs at run time, allowing for run-time patching, handling manifest files, and reading the application compatibility database for any shims and loading the shim engine DLL if required.

impersonation A mechanism through which a thread can assume a different security context than that of its process. When a thread is impersonating, security validation mechanisms use the thread's security context instead of that of the thread's process.

initialization routine A driver routine that the I/O manager executes when it loads the driver into the operating system. The

initialization routine creates system objects that the I/O manager uses to recognize and access the driver.

in-paging I/O A condition that occurs when a read operation must be issued to a file (paging or mapped) to satisfy a page fault. The in-page I/O operation is synchronous—the thread waits on an event until the I/O completes—and isn't interruptible by asynchronous procedure call (APC) delivery.

instancing The term for making separate copies of the same parts of a namespace. Instancing \DosDevices makes it possible for each user to have different drive letters and Windows objects such as serial ports.

integrity level An element of the integrity mechanism Windows uses to achieve intrauser isolation. The Windows integrity mechanism is used by User Account Control (UAC) elevations, Protected Mode Internet Explorer (PMIE), and User Interface Privilege Isolation (UIPI). To support migrating from previous versions of Windows (whose registry keys and files would not include integrity level information), as well as to make it simpler for application developers, all objects have an implicit integrity level in order to avoid having to manually specify one.

intelligent file read-ahead A technique that predicts what data the calling thread is likely to read next based on the data it's currently reading.

interprocessor interrupt (IPI) An interrupt the kernel issues to request that another processor perform an action, such as dispatching a particular thread for execution or updating its translation look-aside buffer cache.

interrupt An asynchronous event (one that can occur at any time) that is unrelated to what the processor is executing. Interrupts are generated primarily by I/O devices, processor clocks, or timers, and they can be enabled or disabled.

interrupt dispatch table (IDT) A data structure that Windows uses to locate the routine that will handle a particular interrupt. The interrupt request level (IRQL) of the interrupting source serves as a table index, and table entries point to the interrupt-handling routines.

interrupt dispatcher A submodule of the kernel's trap handler that responds to interrupts.

interrupt object A kernel control object that allows device drivers to register interrupt service routines (ISRs) for their devices. An interrupt object contains all the information the kernel needs to associate a device ISR with a particular level of interrupt, including the address of the ISR, the interrupt request level (IRQL) at which the device interrupts, and the entry in the kernel's interrupt dispatch table with which the ISR should be associated.

interrupt request (IRQ) A value identifying an interrupt. On x86 systems, external I/O interrupts come into one of the lines on an interrupt controller. The controller in turn interrupts the processor on a single line. Once the processor is interrupted, it queries the controller to get the interrupt request (IRQ). The interrupt controller translates the IRQ to an interrupt number, uses this number as an index into the interrupt dispatch table (IDT), and transfers control to the appropriate interrupt dispatch routine. At system boot time, Windows fills in the IDT with pointers to the kernel routines that handle each interrupt and exception.

interrupt request levels (IRQLs) An interrupt priority scheme imposed by Windows. The kernel represents IRQLs internally as

a number from 0 through 31 (0 to 15 on 64-bit Windows), with higher numbers representing higher-priority interrupts. Although the kernel defines the standard set of IRQLs for software interrupts, the HAL maps hardware-interrupt numbers to the IRQLs.

interrupt service routine (ISR) A device driver routine that the kernel's interrupt dispatcher transfers control to when a device issues an interrupt. In the Windows I/O model, ISRs run at a high device interrupt request level (IRQL), so they perform as little work as possible to avoid blocking lower-level interrupts unnecessarily. An ISR usually queues a deferred procedure call (DPC), which runs at a lower IRQL, to execute the remainder of interrupt processing. Only drivers for interrupt-driven devices have ISRs; a file system, for example, doesn't have one.

job object A nameable, securable, shareable object in Windows that controls certain attributes of processes associated with the job. A job object's basic function is to allow groups of processes to be managed and manipulated as a unit. The job object also records basic accounting information for all processes associated with the job and for all processes that were associated with the job but have since terminated.

journaling A logging technique originally developed for transaction processing that a recoverable file system such as NTFS uses to ensure volume consistency.

kernel The lowest layer in Ntoskrnl.exe. The kernel, a component of the executive, determines how the operating system uses the processor or processors and ensures that they are used prudently. The kernel provides thread scheduling and dispatching, trap handling and exception dispatching, interrupt handling and dispatching,

and multiprocessor synchronization. *See also* executive.

kernel debugger A tool used to debug drivers, troubleshoot hung systems, and examine crash dumps. It is also a useful tool for investigating Windows internals because it can display internal Windows system information not visible through any standard utility.

kernel handle table A table (referenced internally with the name *ObpKernelHandleTable*) whose handles are accessible only from kernel mode and in any process context. A kernel-mode function can reference the handles in this table in any process context with no performance impact.

kernel memory dump A type of memory dump (the default on Windows Server systems) that contains only the kernel-mode read/write pages present in physical memory at the time of the crash. A kernel memory dump doesn't contain pages belonging to user processes. Because only kernel-mode code can directly cause Windows to crash, however, it's unlikely that user process pages are necessary to debug a crash. There is no way to predict the size of a kernel memory dump because its size depends on the amount of kernel-mode memory allocated by the operating system and drivers present on the machine.

kernel mode A privileged mode of code execution in a processor in which all memory is totally accessible and all CPU instructions can be issued. Operating system code (such as system services and device drivers) runs in kernel mode. *See also* user mode.

kernel objects A primitive set of objects implemented by the Windows kernel. These objects aren't visible to user-mode code but are created and used only within the executive. Kernel objects provide fundamental capabilities, such as synchroniza-

tion, on which executive objects are built. *See also* executive objects.

kernel streaming filter drivers Kernel-mode drivers chained together to perform signal processing on data streams, such as recording or displaying audio and video.

Kernel Transaction Manager (KTM) Provides a common, two-phase commit mechanism to resource managers such as the transactional registry (TxR) and transactional NTFS (TxF).

kernel-mode device driver The only type of driver that can directly control and access hardware devices.

kernel-mode graphics driver A Windows subsystem display or print device driver that translates device-independent graphics (GDI) requests into device-specific requests.

key A mechanism to refer to data in the registry. Although keys appear in the object manager namespace, the registry manages them in a way similar to how it manages file objects. Zero or more key values are associated with a key object; key values contain data about the key. The term *key* also is used for a unique identifier that identifies the instance of the keyed event (an association of the keyed event to a single critical section) when a thread signals a keyed event or performs a wait on it.

key control block A structure that stores the name of a registry key, includes the cell index of the key node that the control block refers to, and contains a flag that notes whether the configuration manager needs to delete the key cell that the key control block refers to when the last handle for the key closes. In Windows, all key control blocks are in an alphabetized binary tree to enable quick searches for existing key control blocks by name. A key object points to its corresponding key control block, so

if two applications open the same registry key, each will receive a key object and both key objects will point to a common key control block.

key object An object type the configuration manager defines to integrate the registry's namespace with the kernel's general namespace.

keyed event A synchronization object that allows a thread to specify a "key" for which it waits, where the thread wakes when another thread of the same process signals the event with the same key. Keyed events were originally implemented to help processes deal with low-memory situations when using critical sections.

last known good control set A copy of the critical boot-time information under the registry key HKLM\SYSTEM\CurrentControlSet, made when a user successfully logs on. The last known good control set can be selected at boot time in case configuration changes made to the registry result in the system not being able to boot successfully.

lazy IRQL A performance optimization that avoids Programmable Interrupt Controller (PIC) accesses. When the interrupt request level (IRQL) is raised, the HAL notes the new IRQL internally instead of changing the interrupt mask. If a lower-priority interrupt subsequently occurs, the HAL sets the interrupt mask to the settings appropriate for the first interrupt and postpones the lower-priority interrupt until the IRQL is lowered. Thus, if no lower-priority interrupts occur while the IRQL is raised, the HAL doesn't need to modify the PIC.

lazy writer A set of system threads that call the memory manager to flush cache contents to disk as a background activity (asynchronous disk writing). The cache manager optimizes disk I/O by using its lazy writer.

legacy drivers Device drivers written for Microsoft Windows NT but that run unchanged on Windows 2000 and later. They are differentiated from other Windows drivers in that they don't support power management or work with the Windows Plug and Play manager.

local file system driver (FSD) A driver that manages volumes directly connected to the computer. *See also* file system driver.

local kernel debugging The ability to connect the kernel debugger to the local running system to view internal state (as opposed to connecting to a target system booted in debugging mode using a null modem or 1394 cable).

local security authority (LSA) server A user-mode process running the image \%SystemRoot%\System32\LSASS.exe that is responsible for the local system security policy (such as which users are allowed to log on to the machine, password policies, privileges granted to users and groups, and the system security auditing settings), user authentication, and sending security audit messages to the Event Log. The LSA service (Lsasrv—\Winnt\System32\Lsasrv.dll), a library that LSASS loads, implements most of this functionality.

local security authority (LSA) server policy database A database (stored in the registry under HKLM\SECURITY) that contains the system security policy settings. This database includes such information as what domains are trusted to authenticate logon attempts, who has permission to access the system and how (interactive, network, and service logons), who is assigned which privileges, and what kind of security auditing is to be performed.

Local Security Authority subsystem (Lsass) The system user-mode process responsible for authentication of accounts accessing a computer.

Local System account A predefined local account that is used to start a service and provide the security context for that service. The name of the account is NT AUTHORITY\System. This account does not have a password, and any password information that you supply is ignored. The Local System account has full access to the system, including the directory service on domain controllers. Because the Local System account acts as a computer on the network, it has access to network resources.

log file A metadata file (file name $LogFile) NTFS uses to record all operations that affect the NTFS volume structure, including file creation or any commands, such as Copy, that alter the directory structure. The log file is used to recover an NTFS volume after a system failure.

log hive A registry hive the configuration manager uses to make sure that a nonvolatile registry hive (one with an on-disk file) is always in a recoverable state. Each nonvolatile hive has an associated log hive, which is a hidden file with the same base name as the hive and a .logN extension. *See also* hive.

logical cluster numbers (LCNs) The numbers of all clusters from the beginning of the volume to the end with which NTFS refers to physical locations on a disk. To convert an LCN to a physical disk address, NTFS multiplies the LCN by the cluster factor to get the physical byte offset on the volume, as the disk driver interface requires.

logical prefetcher The kernel component that monitors boot and application startup file access and that preemptively reads that data to speed up subsequent booting and application startups.

logical sequence numbers (LSNs) The numbers that NTFS uses to identify records written to the log file.

logon process A user-mode process running Winlogon.exe that is responsible for capturing the username and password, sending them to the local security authority server for verification, and creating the initial process in the user's session.

look-aside list A fast memory allocation mechanism that contains only fixed-sized blocks. Look-aside lists can be either pageable or nonpageable, so they are allocated from paged or nonpaged pool.

mapped file I/O The ability to view a file residing on disk as part of a process's virtual memory. A program can access the file as a large array without buffering data or performing disk I/O. The program accesses memory, and the memory manager uses its paging mechanism to load the correct page from the disk file. If the application writes to its virtual address space, the memory manager writes the changes back to the file as part of normal paging.

marshalling area An area maintained in the client's address space. Both user-mode and kernel-mode clients marshal data buffers into log records that are part of a marshalling area. When creating a marshalling area, a client must specify the number and size of the log I/O buffers it wants to maintain in the area. The marshalling runtime implements policy on allocating log I/O buffers, appending them to the log internal queue and flushing them to disk. Clients can override the default marshalling code policy by forcing queue appends and flushes to disk via API calls.

mask The process whereby interrupts wait for an executing thread to lower the IRQL before the interrupt is processed. Interrupts from a source with an IRQL above the current level interrupt the processor, whereas interrupts from sources with IRQLs equal to or below the current level are masked until an executing thread lowers the IRQL.

master file table (MFT) The heart of the NTFS volume structure. The MFT is implemented as an array of file records. The size of each file record is fixed at 1 KB, regardless of cluster size.

memory manager The Windows executive component that implements demand-paged virtual memory, giving each process the illusion that it has a large virtual address space (while mapping a subset of that address space to physical memory).

metadata Data that describes the files on a disk; also called volume structure data.

metadata files A set of files in each NTFS volume that contains the information used to implement the file system structure.

MFT mirror An NTFS metadata file (file name $MFTMirr) located in the middle of the disk called that contains a copy of the first few rows of the master file table.

miniport driver A type of kernel-mode device driver that maps a generic I/O request to a type of port into an adapter type, such as a specific SCSI adapter.

mirrored volume A volume on which the contents of a partition on one disk are duplicated in an equal-sized partition on another disk. Mirrored volumes are sometimes referred to as RAID level 1 (RAID-1).

mirror set A technique by which the contents of a partition on one disk are duplicated in an equal-size partition on another disk.

modified page writer A thread in the virtual memory manager that is responsible for limiting the size of the modified page list by writing pages to their backing store locations when the list becomes too big. The modified page writer consists of two system

threads: one to write out modified pages (*MiModifiedPageWriter*) to the paging file and a second one to write modified pages to mapped files (*MiMappedPageWriter*).

mount A technique NTFS uses when it first accesses a volume; in this context, to mount means to prepare the volume for use. To mount the volume, NTFS looks in the boot file to find the physical disk address of the master file table.

mount points A mechanism that permits the linking of volumes through directories on NTFS volumes, which makes volumes accessible with no drive-letter assignment. Reparse points in NTFS make mount points possible.

MSDN Microsoft Developer Network, Microsoft's support program for developers. For more information, see *msdn.microsoft.com*.

multipartition volumes Objects that represent sectors from multiple partitions and that file system drivers manage as a single unit. Multipartition volumes offer performance, reliability, and sizing features that simple volumes don't.

multipathing Where more than one set of hardware exists between the computer and a disk so that if a path fails, the system can still access the disk via an alternate path.

mutant Internal name for a mutex.

mutex A synchronization mechanism used to serialize access to a resource.

mutual exclusion A means whereby only one thread or processor is allowed access to a resource at any given time.

name retention The first phase of object retention, which the object manager implements. Name retention is controlled by the number of open handles to an object that exist. Every time a process opens a handle to an object, the object manager increments the open handle counter in the object's header. As processes finish using the object and close their handles to it, the object manager decrements the open handle counter. When the counter drops to 0, the object manager deletes the object's name from its global namespace. This deletion prevents new processes from opening a handle to the object.

native application An application that uses only system service APIs provided by Ntdll and that isn't a client of the Windows subsystem. Smss (Session Manager) is an example of a native application.

network file system driver (FSD) A driver that allows users to access data volumes connected to remote computers. *See also* file system driver.

network logon service A Windows service that sets up the secure channel to a domain controller, over which security requests, such as an interactive logon, are sent.

network redirectors and servers File system drivers that transmit remote I/O requests to a machine on the network and receive such requests, respectively.

nonpaged pool Memory pool that consists of ranges of system virtual addresses that are guaranteed to be resident in physical memory at all times and thus can be accessed from any address space without incurring paging I/O. Nonpaged pool is created at system initialization and is used by kernel-mode components to allocate system memory.

Ntdll.dll A special system-support library primarily for the use of subsystem DLLs that contains system service dispatch stubs to Windows executive system services and internal support functions used by subsystems, subsystem DLLs, and other native images.

Ntkrnlmp.exe The executive and kernel for multiprocessor systems.

Ntoskrnl.exe The executive and kernel for uniprocessor systems.

object In the Windows executive, a single, run-time instance of a statically defined object type.

object attribute A field of data in an object that partially defines the object's state.

object directory A container object for other objects. The object directory is used to implement the hierarchical namespace within which other object types are stored.

object handle An index into a process-specific handle table, pointed to by the executive process (EPROCESS) block.

object manager The Windows executive component responsible for creating, deleting, protecting, and tracking objects. The object manager centralizes resource control operations that would otherwise be scattered throughout the operating system.

object methods The means for manipulating objects, usually to read or change the object attributes. For example, the open method for a process would accept a process identifier as input and return a pointer to the object as output.

object reuse protection A means of preventing users from seeing data that another user has deleted or from accessing memory that another user previously used and then released. Object reuse protection prevents potential security holes by initializing all objects, including files and memory, before they are allocated to a user.

object type A system-defined data type, including services that operate on instances of the data type and a set of object attributes; sometimes called an object class.

page directory A page the memory manager creates to map the location of all page tables for that process. Each process has a single page directory.

page directory entries (PDEs) The page directory is composed of PDEs, each of which is 4 bytes long and describes the state and location of all the possible page tables for that process.

page fault A reference to an invalid page. The kernel trap handler dispatches this kind of fault to the memory manager fault handler (*MmAccessFault*) to resolve.

page file backed section A section object that is mapped to committed memory.

page file quota A limit on the number of committed pages a process can consume—not necessarily page file space.

page frame number (PFN) database Describes the state of each page in physical memory.

page table A page of mapping information (made up of an array of page table entries) the operating system constructs that describes the location of the virtual pages in a process address space. Because Windows provides a private address space for each process, each process has its own set of process page tables to map that private address space because the mappings will be different for each process. The page tables that describe system space are shared among all processes.

page table entry (PTE) An entry in a process's page table that contains the address to which the virtual address is mapped. The page can be in physical memory or it can be on disk.

paged pool A region of virtual memory in system space that can be paged in and out of the system process's working set. Paged pool is created at system initialization and

is used by kernel-mode components to allocate system memory. Uniprocessor systems have two paged pools; multiprocessor systems have four. Having more than one paged pool reduces the frequency of system code blocking on simultaneous calls to pool routines.

paging The process of moving memory contents to disk, freeing physical memory so that it can be used for other processes or for the operating system itself. Because most systems have much less physical memory than the total virtual memory in use by the running processes (2 GB or 3 GB for each process), the memory manager transfers, or pages, some of the memory contents to disk.

partition A discrete area of the hard disk in Microsoft operating systems. File systems (such as FAT and NTFS) format each partition into a volume. A hard disk can contain up to four primary partitions. *See also* extended partition.

partition table A part of the master boot record (MBR) that consists of four entries that define the locations of as many as four primary partitions on a disk. The partition table also records a partition's type. Numerous predefined partition types exist, and a partition's type specifies which file system the partition includes.

Peer-to-Peer Infrastructure A set of APIs that cover different technologies to enhance the Windows networking stack by providing flexible peer-to-peer (P2P) support for applications and services. The P2P infrastructure covers four major technologies: Peer-to-Peer Graphing, Peer-to-Peer Namespace Provider, Peer-to-Peer Grouping, and Peer-to-Peer Identity Manager.

Physical Address Extension (PAE) A memory-mapping mode included in all Intel x86 processors since the Pentium Pro. With the proper chipset, the PAE mode allows access to up to 64 GB of physical memory. When the x86 executes in PAE mode, the memory management unit (MMU) divides virtual addresses into four fields.

physical device object (PDO) A device object that's a required part of a devnode. The PDO represents the physical interface to a device. *See also* devnode.

Plug and Play (PnP) manager A major component of the executive that determines which drivers are required to support a particular device and loads those drivers. The PnP manager retrieves the hardware resource requirements for each device during enumeration. Based on the resource requirements of each device, the PnP manager assigns the appropriate hardware resources such as I/O ports, IRQs, DMA channels, and memory locations. It is also responsible for sending proper event notification for device changes (addition or removal of a device) on the system.

port driver A type of kernel-mode device driver that implements the processing of an I/O request specific to a type of I/O port, such as SCSI.

port object A single executive object that an advanced local procedure call (ALPC) exports to maintain the state needed for communication.

power manager A major component of the executive that coordinates power events and generates power management I/O notifications to device drivers. When the system is idle, the power manager can be configured to reduce power consumption by putting the CPU to sleep. Changes in power consumption by individual devices are handled by device drivers but are coordinated by the power manager.

printer driver A driver that translates device-independent graphics requests to printer-specific commands. These commands are

then typically forwarded to a kernel-mode port driver such as the parallel port driver (Parport.sys) or the USB printer port driver (Usbprint.sys).

private cache map A structure that contains the location of the last two reads so that the cache manager can perform intelligent read-ahead.

process The virtual address space and control information necessary for the execution of a set of thread objects.

process and thread manager The services in the executive that export the process and thread object. These services use primitive functions in the kernel to create processes and threads.

process ID A unique identifier for a process (internally called a client ID).

process working set The subset of a process's virtual address space that is resident and owned by the running process. *See also* system working set.

processor affinity The set of processors a thread is permitted to run on.

processor control region (PCR) A data structure that along with its extension, the processor control block (PRCB), contains information about the state of each processor in the system, such as the current interrupt request level (IRQL), a pointer to the hardware interrupt dispatch table (IDT), the currently running thread, and the next thread selected to run. The kernel and the HAL use this information to perform architecture-specific and machine-specific actions. Portions of the PCR and PRCB structures are defined publicly in the Windows Device Driver Kit (DDK) header file Ntddk.h.

program A static sequence of instructions.

protected mode A state during the boot process in which no virtual-to-physical translation occurs but a full 32 bits of memory becomes accessible. After the system is in protected mode, BootMgr can access all of physical memory.

protected processes Processes that exist alongside normal Windows processes; they add significant constraints to the access rights that other processes on the system (even when running with administrative privileges) can request.

protocol driver A driver that implements a networking protocol such as TCP/IP, NetBEUI, or IPX/SPX.

prototype page table entries (prototype PTEs) A software structure the memory manager uses to map potentially shared pages when a page can be shared between two processes. An array of prototype PTEs is created when a section object is first created.

quality of service (QoS) A networking technology that ensures that critical network applications receive highest priority.

quantum The length of time a thread is allowed to run before Windows interrupts the thread to find out whether another thread at the same priority level is waiting to run or whether the thread's priority needs to be reduced.

quantum target An estimate of what the number of CPU clock cycles a thread has consumed should be when its turn would be given up. This target should be equal to an equivalent number of clock interval timer ticks because the calculation of clock cycles per quantum is based on the clock interval timer frequency.

quantum unit A value that represents how long a thread can run until its quantum expires. This value represents one-third of a clock interval.

queue A method for threads to enqueue and dequeue notifications of the completion of I/O operations (called an I/O completion port in the Windows API).

queued spinlock A special type of spinlock that is used only by the kernel and not exported for executive components or device drivers. A queued spinlock scales better on multiprocessor systems than a standard spinlock does. *See also* spinlock.

quota charges In the Windows object manager, the record of how much the object manager subtracts from a process's allotted paged and/or nonpaged pool quota when a thread in the process opens a handle to the object.

RAID-5 volume A fault tolerant variant of a regular stripe volume. Fault tolerance is achieved by reserving the equivalent of one disk for storing parity for each stripe. Also called stripe volume with parity.

ready summary A bit mask (*ReadySummary*) that Windows maintains to speed up the selection of which thread to run or preempt.

real mode An operating mode in which no virtual-to-physical translation of memory addresses occurs, which means that programs that use the memory addresses interpret them as physical addresses and that only the first 1 MB of the computer's physical memory is accessible. Simple MS-DOS programs execute in a real-mode environment.

recoverability An advanced feature of NTFS that allows a system to recover from an unexpected system halt. If a system is halted unexpectedly, the metadata of a FAT volume can be left in an inconsistent state, leading to the corruption of large amounts of file and directory data. NTFS implements recoverability by logging changes to metadata in a transactional manner so that file system structures can be repaired to a consistent state with no loss of file or directory structure information. (File data can be lost, however.)

reference count The object manager's record of how many object pointers it has dispensed to operating system processes. The object manager increments a reference count for an object each time it gives out a pointer to the object; when kernel-mode components finish using the pointer, they call the object manager to decrement the object's reference count.

reparse data User-defined data about the file or directory, such as its state or location, that can be read from the reparse point by the application that created the data, a file system filter driver, or the I/O manager.

reparse point An NTFS file or directory that has a block of data called reparse data associated with it.

reparse tag The reparse tag allows the component responsible for interpreting the reparse point's reparse data to recognize the reparse point without having to check the reparse data.

resident attribute An attribute that is stored directly in the master file table. (If a file is small, all its attributes and their values [its data, for example] fit in the file record.)

resource arbitration A process by which the Plug and Play (PnP) manager optimally assigns hardware resources so that each device meets the requirements necessary for its operation. Because hardware devices can be added to the system after boot-time resource assignment, the PnP manager must also be able to reassign resources to accommodate the needs of dynamically added devices.

restricted token A token created from a primary or impersonation token using the *CreateRestrictedToken* function. The

restricted token is a copy of the token it's derived from, with some possible modifications: Privileges can be removed from the token's privilege array. SIDs in the token can be marked as deny-only. SIDS in the token can be marked as restricted.

ring A privilege level defined in the x86 and x64 processor architectures to protect system code and data from being overwritten either inadvertently or maliciously by code of lesser privilege. Windows on the x86 and x64 platforms use privilege level 0 (or ring 0) for kernel mode and privilege level 3 (or ring 3) for user mode.

safe mode A boot configuration that consists of the minimal set of device drivers and services. By relying on only the drivers and services that are necessary for booting, Windows avoids loading third-party and other nonessential drivers that might crash.

SAM database A database (stored in the registry under HKLM\SAM) that contains the defined users and groups, along with their passwords and other attributes.

scatter/gather I/O A kind of high-performance I/O Windows supports, available via the Windows *ReadFileScatter* and *WriteFileGather* functions. These functions allow an application to issue a single read or write from more than one buffer in virtual memory to a contiguous area of a file on disk. To use scatter/gather I/O, the file must be opened for noncached I/O, the user buffers being used have to be page-aligned, and the I/Os must be asynchronous (overlapped).

section object An object that represents a block of memory that two or more processes can share. A section object can be mapped to the paging file or to another file on disk. The executive uses section objects to load executable images into memory, and the cache manager uses them to access

data in a cached file. In the Windows subsystem, a section object is called a file-mapping object.

section object pointers Structure for each open file (represented by a file object) that is the key to maintaining data consistency for all types of file access as well as to providing caching for files. The section object pointers structure points to one or two control areas. One control area is used to map the file when accessed as a data file, and one is used to map the file when it is run as an executable image.

sector A hardware-addressable portion of a physical disk. A hard disk sector on a BIOS PC is typically 512 bytes. Utilities that prepare hard disks for the definition of volumes, such as the Windows Setup program, write a sector of data called a master boot record (MBR) to the first sector on a hard disk. The MBR includes a fixed amount of space that contains executable instructions (called boot code) and a partition table with four entries that define the locations of the primary partitions on the disk. *See also* boot code, partition table.

secure attention sequence (SAS) A keystroke combination that when entered notifies Winlogon of a user logon request.

secure logon facility Requires that users can be uniquely identified and that they must be granted access to the computer only after they have been authenticated in some way.

Security Accounts Manager (SAM) service A set of subroutines responsible for managing the database that contains the user names and groups defined on the local machine or for a domain (if the system is a domain controller). The SAM runs in the context of the LSASS process.

security auditing A way in which Windows detects and records important security-

related events or any attempts to create, access, or delete system resources. Logon identifiers record the identities of all users, making it easier to trace anyone who performs an unauthorized action.

security descriptor The data structure that specifies who can perform what actions on an object. A security descriptor consists of attributes.

security identifier (SID) A means of uniquely identifying entities that perform actions in a system. A SID is a variable-length numeric value that consists of a SID structure revision number, a 48-bit identifier authority value, and a variable number of 32-bit subauthority or relative identifier (RID) values.

security quality of service (SQOS) The indicator specified by a client opening a server resource that specifies the maximum level of client impersonation the server is allowed.

security reference monitor (SRM) A component in the Windows executive (Ntoskrnl.exe) that enforces security policies on the local computer. It guards operating system resources, performing run-time object protection and auditing.

semaphore A counter that provides a resource gate by allowing some maximum number of threads to access the resources protected by the semaphore.

server processes User processes that are Windows services, such as the Event Log and Schedule services. Many add-on server applications, such as Microsoft SQL Server and Microsoft Exchange Server, also include components that run as Windows services.

session Consists of the processes and other system objects (such as the window station, desktops, and windows) that represent a single user's workstation logon session.

Each session has a session-specific paged pool area used by the kernel-mode portion of the Windows subsystem (Win32k.sys) to allocate session-private GUI data structures. In addition, each session has its own copy of the Windows subsystem process (Csrss.exe) and logon process (Winlogon.exe).

session space A component that contains information global to each session. All sessionwide data structures are mapped into this region of system space. When a process is created, this range of addresses is mapped to the pages appropriate to the session that the process belongs to.

shared cache map A structure that describes the state of a cached file, including its size and its valid data length.

shared memory Memory visible to more than one process or that is present in more than one virtual address space.

shrinking engine In the file system, a mechanism that communicates with NTFS to determine the maximum number of reclaimable bytes—how much data can be moved from a region that will be resized into a region that will remain.

shadow copies The Volume Shadow Copy Service (VSS) is a built-in Windows mechanism that enables the creation of consistent, point-in-time copies of data. These are known as shadow copies or snapshots. VSS coordinates with applications, file-system services, backup applications, fast-recovery solutions, and storage hardware to produce consistent shadow copies.

signaled state One state of a synchronization object. At any given moment, a synchronization object is in either the signaled state or the nonsignaled state.

simple volume A set of objects that represent sectors from a single partition that file system drivers manage as a single unit.

single sign-on The ability for logon information to be simultaneously authenticated on more than one system. For example, a user logging on to a Windows system might simultaneously be authenticated on a UNIX server. That user would then be able to access resources of the UNIX server from the machine running Windows without requiring additional authentication.

small memory dump A small memory dump (typically between 128 KB and 1 MB in size) containing the stop code and parameters, the list of loaded device drivers, the data structures that describe the current process and thread (called the EPROCESS and ETHREAD), and the kernel stack for the thread that caused the crash.

spanned volume A single logical volume composed of a maximum of 32 free partitions on one or more disks. The Disk Management Microsoft Management Console (MMC) snap-in combines the partitions into a spanned volume, which can then be formatted for any of the file systems that Windows supports.

sparse files Files, often large, that contain only a small amount of nonzero data relative to their size.

spinlock The locking mechanism the kernel uses to achieve multiprocessor mutual exclusion. The spinlock gets its name from the fact that the kernel (and thus, the processor) is held in limbo, "spinning," until it gets the lock. Spinlocks, like the data structures they protect, reside in global memory. *See also* queued spinlock.

stack frame Information, representing the activation of a procedure, that is pushed onto the stack when a procedure is invoked. A stack frame can have one or more exception handlers associated with it, each of which protects a particular block of code in the source program.

stream A sequence of bytes within a file.

striped volume Series of up to 32 partitions, one partition per disk, that combines into a single logical volume. Striped volumes are also known as RAID level 0 (RAID-0) volumes. A partition in a striped volume need not span an entire disk; the only restriction is that the partitions on each disk be the same size.

stop code An error code that classifies the type of error detected by a component that crashes the system.

structured exception handling A type of exception handling that allows applications to gain control when exceptions occur. The application can then fix the condition and return to the place the exception occurred, unwind the stack (thus terminating execution of the subroutine that raised the exception), or declare back to the system that the exception isn't recognized, and continue searching for an exception handler that might process the exception.

subsection A structure that describes the mapping information for each section of the file (read-only, read-write, copy-on-write, and so on).

subsystem dynamic-link libraries (DLLs) DLLs that translate a documented function into the appropriate undocumented Windows system service calls. This translation might or might not involve sending a message to the environment subsystem process that is serving the user application.

Subsystem for Unix-based Applications (SUA) An enhanced POSIX subsystem that provides nearly 2,000 UNIX functions and 300 UNIX-like tools and utilities. SUA can be enabled on any Windows Server 2008 machine, as well as for Windows Vista Ultimate and Enterprise editions.

SuperFetch A memory management scheme that enhances the least-recently

accessed approach with historical information and proactive memory management. SuperFetch is composed of several components in the system that work hand in hand to proactively manage memory and limit the impact on user activity when SuperFetch is performing its work.

symbolic link A mechanism for referring to an object name indirectly.

symmetric encryption algorithm An algorithm that uses the same key to encrypt and decrypt data. Symmetric encryption algorithms are typically very fast, which makes them suitable for encrypting large amounts of data, such as file data. They do have a weakness, however; their security can be bypassed if their key is obtained.

symmetric multiprocessing (SMP) A multiprocessing operating system in which there is no master processor—the operating system as well as user threads can be scheduled to run on any processor. All the processors share just one memory space.

synchronization A thread's ability to synchronize its execution by waiting for an object to change from one state to another. A thread can synchronize with executive process, thread, file, event, semaphore, mutex, and timer objects. Section, port, access token, object directory, symbolic-link, profile, and key objects don't support synchronization.

synchronous I/O A model for I/O in which a device performs a data transfer and returns a status code when the I/O is complete. The program can then access the transferred data immediately. When used in their simplest form, the Windows *ReadFile* and *WriteFile* functions are executed synchronously. They complete an I/O operation before returning control to the caller.

system access control list (SACL) Specifies which operations by which users should be logged in the security audit log.

system code write protection The setting of the read-only parts of the kernel as read-only pages.

system audit ACE An access-control entry (ACE) contained by a system access-control list (SACL) that, along with the system audit-object ACE, specifies which operations performed on the object by specific users or groups should be audited. System audit-object ACEs specify a GUID indicating the types of objects or subobjects that the ACE applies to and an optional GUID that controls propagation of the ACE to particular child object types. If an SACL is null, no auditing takes place on the object.

system cache Pages used to map files open in the system cache.

system page table entries (PTEs) Pool of system PTEs used to map system pages such as I/O space, kernel stacks, and memory descriptor lists.

system partition The partition that contains core operating system files. The boot partition is identified by the system at startup. The code in a master boot record (MBR) scans the primary partition table until it locates a partition containing a flag that signals the partition is bootable. When the MBR finds at least one such flag, it reads the first sector from the flagged partition into memory and transfers control to code within the partition.

system service dispatch table Table in which each entry contains a pointer to a system service rather than to an interrupt handling routine.

system services (or executive system services) Native functions in the Windows operating system that are callable from user mode. For example, *NtCreateProcess*

is the internal system service the Windows *CreateProcess* function calls to create a new process.

system support processes User processes, such as the logon process and the Session Manager, that are not Windows services (that is, not started by the service controller).

system thread A kind of thread that runs only in kernel mode. System threads always reside in the system process. These threads have all the attributes and contexts of regular user-mode threads (such as a hardware context, priority, and so on) but run only in kernel-mode executing code loaded in system-space code, whether that be in Ntoskrnl.exe or in any other loaded device driver. System threads don't have a user process address space and hence must allocate any dynamic storage from operating system memory heaps, such as paged or nonpaged pool.

system worker threads Threads created in the system process during system initialization that exist solely to perform work on behalf of other threads.

system working set The physical memory being used by the system cache, paged pool, pageable code in Ntoskrnl.exe, and pageable code in device drivers. *See also* process working set.

thread An entity within a process that Windows schedules for execution. A thread includes the contents of a set of volatile registers representing the state of the processor; two stacks, one for the thread to use while executing in kernel mode and one for executing in user mode; a private storage area for use by subsystems, run-time libraries, and DLLs; and a unique identifier called a thread ID (also internally called a client ID).

thread context A thread's volatile registers, the stacks, and the private storage area. Because this information is different for each machine architecture that Windows runs on, this structure is architecture-specific. In fact, the CONTEXT structure returned by the Windows *GetThreadContext* function is the only public data structure in the Windows API that is machine-dependent.

timer A mechanism that notifies a thread when a fixed period of time elapses.

transaction An I/O operation that alters file system data or changes the volume's directory structure. The separate disk updates that make up the transaction must be executed atomically; that is, once the transaction begins to execute, all its disk updates must be completed. If a system failure interrupts the transaction, the part that has been completed must be undone, or rolled back. The rollback operation returns the database to a previously known and consistent state, as if the transaction had never occurred.

transaction table A table that keeps track of transactions that have been started but that aren't yet committed. The suboperations of these active transactions must be removed from the disk during recovery.

Transactional NTFS (TxF) A transactional model that NTFS implements by leveraging the Kernel Transaction Manger (KTM) support in the kernel as well as facilities provided by the Common Log File System. TxF provides a set of user-mode APIs that applications can use for transacted operations on their files and directories and also a file system control (FSCTL) interface for managing its resource managers. *See also* Kernel Transaction Manager (KTM).

Transactional Registry (TxR) An API that developers can use to implement robust error-recovery capabilities when performing registry operatations. TxR is supported

by the Kernel Transaction Manager (KTM). *See also* Kernel Transaction Manager (KTM).

transition A kind of invalid page table entry (PTE) in which the desired page is in memory on either the standby, modified, or modified-no-write list. The page is removed from the list and added to the working set.

translation look-aside buffer (TLB) A CPU cache of recently translated virtual page numbers.

trap A processor's mechanism for capturing an executing thread when an exception or an interrupt occurs, switching it from user mode into kernel mode, and transferring control to a fixed location in the operating system. In Windows, the processor transfers control to the kernel's trap handler.

trap frame A data structure in which the execution state of the interrupted thread is stored. This information allows the kernel to resume execution of the thread after handling the interrupt or the exception. The trap frame is usually a subset of a thread's complete context.

trap handler A module in the kernel that acts as a switchboard, fielding exceptions and interrupts detected by the processor and transferring control to code that handles the condition.

trusted facility management Requires support for separate account roles for administrative functions. For example, separate accounts are provided for administration (Administrators), user accounts charged with backing up the computer, and standard users.

trusted path functionality Prevents Trojan horse programs from being able to intercept users' names and passwords as they try to log in. The trusted path functionality in Windows comes in the form of its

Ctrl+Alt+Delete logon-attention sequence, which cannot be intercepted by nonprivileged applications. This sequence of keystrokes, which is also known as the secure attention sequence (SAS), always pops up a logon dialog box, so would-be Trojan horses can easily be recognized. A Trojan horse presenting a fake logon dialog box will be bypassed when the SAS is entered.

type object An internal system object that contains information common to each instance of the object.

Unicode An international character set standard that defines unique 16-bit values for most of the world's known character sets.

update records Update records correspond to the redo and undo records that Transactional NTFS (TxF) uses.

User Account Control UAC is a mechanism meant to enable users to run more easily with standard user rights, as opposed to administrative rights. Without administrative rights, users cannot accidentally (or deliberately) modify system settings, malware can't normally alter system security settings or disable antivirus software, and users can't compromise the sensitive information of other users on shared computers.

user mode The nonprivileged processor mode that applications run in. A limited set of interfaces is available in this mode, and the access to system data is limited. *See also* kernel mode.

user-mode debugging A framework responsible for sending events to the user-mode debugging API—allowing breakpoints and stepping through code to work—as well as for changing contexts of running threads.

VACB index array An array of pointers maintained by the cache manager to keep track of which views for a given file are mapped to the system cache.

view The portion of the section object required by a process. A section object can refer to files that are much larger than can fit in the address space of a process. (If the paging file backs a section object, sufficient space must exist in the paging file to contain it.) To access a very large section object, a process can map only a view of the section by calling the *MapViewOfFile*, *MapViewOfFileEx*, or *MapViewOfFileExNuma* function and then specifying the range to map. Mapping views permits processes to conserve address space because only the views of the section object needed at the time must be mapped into memory. *See also* section object.

virtual address control blocks (VACBs) The data structures that the cache manager uses to manage the system address space into which it maps files. When the cache manager initializes during the bootup process, it allocates an initial array of VACBs to describe cached memory. As caching requirements grow and more memory is required, the cache manager allocates more VACB arrays, as needed.

virtual address descriptors (VADs) Data structures the memory manager maintains that keep track of which virtual addresses have been reserved in the process's address space. VADs are structured as a self-balancing AVL tree algorithm (named after its inventors, Adelson-Velskii and Landis) that better balances the VAD tree, resulting in, on average, fewer comparisons when searching for a VAD corresponding with a virtual address.

virtual address space A set of virtual memory addresses that a process can use.

virtual block caching A method the Windows cache manager uses to keep track of which parts of which files are in the cache.

virtual cluster numbers (VCNs) VCNs number the clusters belonging to a particular file from 0 through m. VCNs aren't necessarily physically contiguous, but they can be mapped to any number of logical cluster numbers (LCNs) on a volume.

virtual device drivers (VDDs) Drivers used to emulate 16-bit MS-DOS applications. They trap what an MS-DOS application thinks are references to I/O ports and translate them into native Windows I/O functions. Because Windows is a fully protected operating system, user-mode MS-DOS applications can't access hardware directly and thus must go through a real kernel-mode device driver. Because 64-bit editions of Windows do not support 16-bit applications anymore, these types of drivers are not present on that architecture.

virtualization One of the key technologies in the software industry, used by system administrators, developers, and testers alike. Virtualization refers to the ability to run multiple operating systems simultaneously. One operating system, in which the virtualization software is executing, is called the host, while the other operating systems are running as guests inside the virtualization software. The usage scenarios for virtualization cover everything from testing an application on different platforms to having fully virtual servers all actually running as part of the same machine and managed through one central point.

volume One or more logical disk partitions that are treated as a single unit.

volume file A system file (file name $Volume) that contains the volume name, the version of NTFS for which the volume is formatted, and a bit that when set signifies that a disk corruption has occurred and must be repaired by the Chkdsk utility.

volume set A single logical volume composed of a maximum of 32 areas of free

space on one or more disks. Spanned volumes were called volume sets in Windows NT 4.

wait block A data structure that represents a thread waiting on an object. Each thread that is in a wait state has a list of the wait blocks that represent the objects the thread is waiting on. Each dispatcher object has a list of the wait blocks that represent which threads are waiting on the object.

wait hint A value indicating how long a service should wait before informing the system a shutdown is complete.

WDM drivers Device drivers that adhere to the Windows Driver Model (WDM). WDM includes support for Windows power management, Plug and Play, and Windows Management Instrumentation (WMI). There are three types of WDM drivers: bus drivers, function drivers, and filter drivers.

WDM Windows Management Instrumentation routines Enable device drivers to publish performance and configuration information and receive commands from the user-mode WMI service. Consumers of WMI information can be on the local machine or remote across the network.

WFP callout drivers Kernel-mode drivers that implement one or more callouts, which extend the capabilities of the Windows Filtering Platform (WFP) by processing TCP/IP-based network data in ways that extend the basic functionality provided by the WFP. *See also* Windows Filtering Platform (WFP).

Windows API The system programming interface to the Windows operating system family. In this book, the term Windows API refers to both the 32-bit and 64-bit programming interfaces to Windows Vista and Windows Server 2008.

Windows Diagnostic Infrastructure (WDI) A mechanism that helps to detect, diagnose,

and resolve common problem scenarios with minimal user intervention. Windows components implement triggers that cause WDI to launch scenario-specific troubleshooting modules to detect the occurrence of a problem scenario. A trigger can indicate that the system is approaching or has reached a problematic state.

Windows Driver Foundation A model intended to simplify driver development by providing two frameworks, the Kernel-Mode Driver Framework (KMDF) and the User-Mode Driver Framework (UMDF).

Windows services A mechanism to start processes at system startup time that provide services not tied to an interactive user. Services are similar to UNIX daemon processes and often implement the server side of client/server applications.

window station A window station contains desktops, and desktops contain windows. Only one window station can be visible on a console and receive user mouse and keyboard input. In a Terminal Services environment, one window station per session is visible, but services all run as part of the console session.

Windows drivers Device drivers that integrate with the Windows power manager and Plug and Play manager, when required. They include drivers for mass storage devices, protocol stacks, and network adapters.

Windows Filtering Platform (WFP) A set of APIs and system services that provide the ability to create network filtering applications. The WFP allows applications to interact with packet processing at different levels of the Windows networking stack, much like file system filters. Similarly, network data can be traced, filtered, and also modified before it reaches its destination.

work item A unit of work placed on a queue dispatcher object when an executive component requests a system worker thread's services by calling the executive functions *ExQueueWorkItem* or *IoQueueWorkItem*. (Device drivers should use only the latter because this associates the work item with a Device object, allowing for greater accountability and the handling of scenarios in which a driver unloads while its work item is active.) These functions place a work item on a queue dispatcher object where the threads look for work.

working set A subset of virtual pages resident in physical memory. There are two kinds of working sets—process working sets and the system working set. On systems with Terminal Services enabled, each session also has a working set.

working set manager A routine that runs in the context of the balance set manager system thread to initiate automatic working set trimming to increase the amount of free memory available in the system. Although Windows attempts to keep memory available by writing modified pages to disk, when modified pages are being generated at a very high rate, more memory is required to meet memory demands. The working set manager is called when physical memory runs low (when *MmAvailablePages* is less than *MmMinimumFreePages*).

write throttling Prevents system performance from degrading because of a lack of memory when a file system or network server issues a large write operation.

zero page thread A kernel-mode system thread (thread 0 in the system process). A zero page thread zeroes out pages on the free list so that a cache of zero pages is available to satisfy future demand-zero page faults.

Index

Symbols and Numbers

L

Mark Russinovich

Mark Russinovich is a technical fellow in the Windows Core Operating System Division. He is a member of the core team that provides architectural direction and oversight across Windows, with a focus on security and virtualization. Mark is currently working on the technical direction and architectural plan for Windows 8. He also continues developing tools for the Windows Sysinternals Web site, the most popular TechNet subsite, with 2 million downloads per month. Mark consistently delivers the top-rated sessions at major IT and developer conferences, including Microsoft TechEd, TechReady, and WinHEC.

Mark has written dozens of magazine articles and serves as contributing editor for both *Microsoft TechNet* and *Windows IT Pro* magazines. Mark joined Microsoft in 2006 when the 85-person company he cofounded 10 years earlier, Winternals Software, was acquired along with Sysinternals. At Winternals he was chief software architect, defining the business and technical direction for the company.

David Solomon

David Solomon, president of David Solomon Expert Seminars (*www.solsem.com*), has focused on explaining the internals of the Microsoft Windows NT operating system line since 1992. He has taught his world-renowned Windows internals classes to thousands of developers and IT professionals worldwide. His clients include all the major software and hardware companies, including Microsoft. He was nominated a Microsoft Most Valuable Professional in 1993 and from 2005–2008.

Prior to starting his own company, David worked for nine years as a project leader and developer in the VMS operating system development group at Digital Equipment Corporation. His first book was entitled *Windows NT for Open VMS Professionals* (Digital Press/Butterworth Heinemann, 1996). It explained Windows NT to VMS-knowledgeable programmers and system administrators. His second book, *Inside Windows NT*, Second Edition (Microsoft Press, 1998), covered the internals of Windows NT 4.0. Since the third edition (*Inside Windows 2000*) David has coauthored this book series with Mark Russinovich.

In addition to organizing and teaching seminars, David is a regular speaker at technical conferences such as Microsoft TechEd and Microsoft PDCs. He has also served as technical chair for several past Windows NT conferences. When he's not researching Windows, David enjoys sailing, reading, and watching *Star Trek*.

Alex Ionescu

Alex Ionescu is the founder of Winsider Seminars & Solutions Inc., specializing in low-level system software for administrators and developers. He also teaches Windows internals courses for David Solomon Expert Seminars, including at Microsoft. Alex was the lead kernel developer for ReactOS, an open source clone of Windows XP/Windows Server 2003 written from scratch, for which he wrote most of the Windows NT–based kernel.

Alex is also very active in the security research community, discovering and reporting several vulnerabilities related to the Windows kernel and presenting talks at conferences such as Blackhat and Recon. Alex's experience in operating system design and kernel coding dates back to his early adolescence, when he first played with John Fine's educational operating system and kernel and boot loader code. Since then he has been active in the area of NT kernel development, offering help and advice for driver developers, as well as in the NT reverse engineering and security fields, where he has published a number of articles and source code, such as documentation for the Linux NTFS project, extensive papers on the Visual Basic metadata and pseudo-code format and NTFS structures and data streams. In the last three years, he has contributed to patches and development in two major commercially used operating system kernels.

SIT DOWN WITH THE EXPERTS
who literally wrote the book on Windows internals!

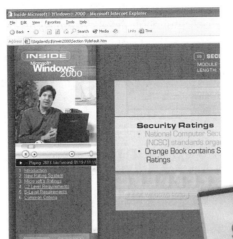

If you liked their book, you'll love hearing them in person. Get one of their video tutorials or come to a live class.

LIVE, INSTRUCTOR LED CLASSES

If you're an IT professional deploying and supporting Windows servers and workstations, you need to be able to dig beneath the surface when things go wrong. In our classes, you'll gain a deep understanding of the internals of the operating system and how to leverage advanced troubleshooting tools to solve system and application problems and understand performance issues more effectively. Attend a public class or schedule a private on site seminar at your location. For dates, course details, pricing, and registration information, see www.solsem.com.

INTERACTIVE DVD TUTORIAL

Sit down with the experts who literally wrote the book on Windows internals. Windows Internals COMPLETE consists of 12 hours of interactive training taking you under the hood of the operating system to learn how the kernel components work. As the ultimate compliment, Microsoft Corporation licensed these videos for their corporate training worldwide.

The Sysinternals Video Library (also 12 hours) covers essential Windows troubleshooting topics such as crash dump analysis and memory troubleshooting as well as how to leverage key Sysinternals tools.

To view video samples or for a detailed outline, visit www.solsem.com or email videos@solsem.com

Windows Internals, Fifth Edition and MCTS Exam 70-660

This book delivers in-depth, kernel-level insights into the Windows OS. You may also find it helpful when preparing for the following topics in Microsoft Certification Exam 70-660:

Exam Objectives/Skills	See Topic-Related Coverage Here
Identifying Architectural Components	
Identify memory types and mechanisms	Chapter 9
Identify I/O mechanisms	Chapter 7, see "I/O Processing"; Chapter 3
Identify subsystems	Chapter 2, see "Key System Components"
Identify processor functions and architecture	Chapter 3, see "System Service Dispatching"; Chapter 5, see "Overview of Windows Scheduling"
Identify processes and threads	Chapter 5, see "Process Internals," "Thread Internals," and "Thread Scheduling"
Designing Solutions	
Optimize a system for its drivers	Chapter 7, see "Device Drivers" and "The Plug and Play (PnP) Manager"; Chapter 3, see "Interrupt Dispatching" and "System Worker Threads"; Chapter 9, see "Driver Verifier"
Design applications	Chapter 3, see "Windows Global Flags," "Exception Dispatching," and "Synchronization"; Chapter 5, see "Thread Internals"; Chapter 9; Chapter 6
Deploy compatible applications	Chapter 3, see "Windows Global Flags" (limited coverage)
Identify optimal I/O models for applications	Chapter 7, see "I/O Processing" and "I/O Completion Ports"
Monitoring Windows	
Monitor I/O latency	Chapters 1, 7, and 8
Monitor I/O throughput	Chapters 3, 7, 8, and 11
Monitor memory usage	Chapter 9
Monitor CPU utilization	Chapters 5 and 14
Monitor handled and unhandled exceptions	Chapter 3, see "Exception Dispatching"; Chapter 14, see "Windows Error Reporting"
Analyzing User Mode	
Analyze heap leaks	Chapter 9, see "Heap Manager"
Analyze heap corruption	Chapter 9, see "Heap Manager"
Handle leaks	Chapter 3, see "Object Handles and the Process Handle Table"
Resolve image load issues	Chapter 3, see "Image Loader"
Analyze services and host processes	Chapter 4, see "Services"
Analyze cross-process application calls	Not covered
Analyze the modification of executables at run time	Not covered
Analyze GUI performance issues	Not covered

Exam Objectives/Skills	See Topic-Related Coverage Here
Analyzing Kernel Mode	
Find and identify objects in object manager namespaces and identify the objects' attributes	Chapter 3, see "Object Manager"
Analyze Plug and Play (PnP) device failure	Chapter 7, see "The Plug and Play (PnP) Manager"; Chapter 13
Analyze pool corruption	Chapters 1 and 3
Analyze pool leaks	Chapters 1, 3, 9, and 14
Isolate the root cause of S state failure	Chapter 7, see "Power Manager"
Analyze kernel mode CPU utilization	Chapter 14, see "Hung or Unresponsive Systems"; Chapter 3
Debugging Windows	
Debug memory	Chapters 9 and 14
Identify a pending I/O	Chapter 7
Identify a blocking thread	Chapter 3, see "Synchronization"; Chapter 5, see "Thread Scheduling"
Identify a runaway thread	Chapter 5, see "Thread Scheduling"; Chapter 14
Debug kernel crash dumps	Chapters 14, 3, and 5
Debug user crash dumps	Not covered
Set up the debugger	Chapters 14, 13, and 1

For complete information on MCTS Exam 70-660, go to *www.microsoft.com/learning/en/us/Exams/70-660.aspx*. And for more information on Microsoft certifications, visit *www.microsoft.com/learning*.

What do you think of this book?

We want to hear from you!

To participate in a brief online survey, please visit:

microsoft.com/learning/booksurvey

...and enter this book's ISBN number (appears above barcode on back cover).

Tell us how well this book meets your needs—what works effectively, and what we can do better. Your feedback will help us continually improve our books and learning resources for you.

Thank you in advance for your input!

Where to find the ISBN on back cover

Example only. Each book has unique ISBN.

Stay in touch!

To subscribe to the *Microsoft Press® Book Connection Newsletter*—for news on upcoming books, events, and special offers—please visit:

microsoft.com/learning/books/newsletter